THE *Cleveland* INDIANS ENCYCLOPEDIA

In the series

Baseball Encyclopedias of North America

edited by Richard Westcott

Also in the series:

The New Phillies Encyclopedia, by Richard Westcott
and Frank Bilovsky, 1993

The Braves Encyclopedia, by Gary Caruso,
1995

The White Sox Encyclopedia, by Richard Lindberg,
in press

The Red Sox Encyclopedia, by George Sullivan,
forthcoming

Russell Schneider

THE *Cleveland* INDIANS ENCYCLOPEDIA

Temple University Press | Philadelphia

Temple University Press, Philadelphia, PA 19122
Copyright © 1996 by Temple University
Published 1996

☾ The paper used in this publication meets the minimum
requirements of the American National Standard for Information
Sciences—Permanence of Paper for Printed Library Materials,
ANSI Z39.48–1984

Printed in the United States of America

Library of Congress Cataloging-in-Publication Data

Schneider, Russell J.
    The Cleveland Indians Encyclopedia / Russell Schneider.
       p.   cm.
    ISBN 1–56639–405–8 (cloth)
    1. Cleveland Indians (Baseball team)—History.   I. Title
GV875.C7S35   1996
796.357′64771′32—dc20   95–23205

Contents

Foreword

Dear Indians Fans:

I have read a lot of books about the Indians, and I've even been the author of two of them, but *The Cleveland Indians Encyclopedia* is without a doubt the most inclusive and best researched history of the franchise ever written. There's no doubt in my mind that all baseball fans—especially fans of the Indians—will enjoy reading this book and using it for reference.

Having been associated with the Indians in one capacity or another for nearly 60 years, beginning in 1936 as a player, I have a thousand memories of the good (and, yes, some not so good) days with the Tribe, and the book has brought so many of them back to mind.

Naturally, I particularly enjoyed reading about and reliving my days with the Indians, from the time I was signed for a bonus of $1 (that's one dollar!) and pitched in my first major league game, an exhibition against the "Gashouse Gang," the St. Louis Cardinals, through the pennant-winning seasons of 1948 and 1954.

The book also brought to mind again so many of my teammates through the years with the Indians, and the managers I pitched for—Steve O'Neill, Oscar Vitt, Lou Boudreau, and Al Lopez.

Since becoming a charter member of the American League, the Indians have had twenty-six of us make it to the Hall of Fame, beginning with the great Cy Young, and I'm sure that a couple more who are still wearing Cleveland uniforms—Eddie Murray and Dave Winfield—will be joining us in Cooperstown eventually.

Russ Schneider and Joe Simenic have done a fine job of researching and writing this book. No doubt it was a labor of love, just as, again, there is no doubt that baseball fans will enjoy it.

Bob Feller

Bob Feller
Elected to the
Hall of Fame
1962

Introduction

The Indians and their predecessors—the Bluebirds, Blues, Bronchos, and Naps—have given Cleveland baseball fans quite a roller-coaster ride over the years.

It all began shortly after Byron Bancroft "Ban" Johnson visited the city in 1900 and convinced two young businessmen, Charles W. Somers and John F. Kilfoyl, to buy a franchise in the newly formed American League that would begin play the following year.

As one of eight charter members of Johnson's league, which owed much of its early existence to Somers' financial support of three other clubs, Cleveland's teams have soared to the heights and plummeted to the depths in the years since Somers and Kilfoyl said yes to Johnson.

They became a contender early on, losing the 1908 pennant by .004 of a percentage point, partly because the champion Detroit Tigers played one less game—a rain postponement that in those days wasn't required to be made up.

The Indians came close again in 1918 and 1919, but didn't win their first pennant until 1920, when they also defeated Brooklyn in the World Series.

It was a victory that some claimed was "tainted" because seven players on the defending champion Chicago White Sox were suspended in the final week of the season, helping the Indians capture the pennant.

They were dethroned by the New York Yankees in a close race in 1921, and except for 1926, when they failed in the final two weeks, didn't come close to winning again until 1940.

That was a season that would have been—perhaps *should have been*—one of the highlights in the history of the Indians.

Instead, it is remembered—and lamented—as the year of the "Cleveland Crybabies," when the players rebelled against Manager Oscar Vitt and lost the pennant to the Tigers in the final series of the season.

Eight years later, under the astute ownership of Bill Veeck and the brilliant on field direction of manager-shortstop Lou Boudreau, the Indians prevailed in what was then, and undoubtedly still is, the biggest game in the history of the franchise.

They beat the Boston Red Sox, 8–3, in a playoff for the pennant after the two teams had finished the regular season in a tie. The playoff-game victory vaulted the Indians into the World Series, where they beat the other Boston team, the National League champion Braves, in six games, and Cleveland fans were ecstatic.

But not for long. The Tribe dropped into third place in 1949, and then to fourth in 1950, and Boudreau, who'd been a favorite of Cleveland fans from the time he joined the team as a fuzzy-cheeked rookie in 1938, was fired.

The change of managers launched the Al Lopez era, a.k.a. the "Golden Years" of baseball in Cleveland when the Indians battled the Yankees tooth and nail, with some very good teams, though they couldn't overtake them until 1954.

That was the year the Indians set an American League record with 111 victories, losing just 43 games, only to fail miserably in the World Series. They were swept in four games by the New York Giants, and some contend the Series loss was the beginning of the Tribe's decline that didn't end until four decades later.

Oh, the Indians challenged the Yankees again in 1955 and 1956, but couldn't prevail, after which the highly respected Lopez quit in frustration.

His departure began a series of 20 managerial changes over the next 30 years. The team passed through eight different ownerships before a degree of stability was restored in 1986 and it finally regained its long-lost stature among major league baseball's elite in 1994.

Only once until then, when Indians fans were thrilled with the probability of their team's reaching postseason playoffs for the first time in 40 seasons, only to be disappointed by the 1994 players' strike, did pennant fever rage in Cleveland.

Albert Belle watches as the ball sails toward the left field bleachers at Jacobs Field. It is September 30, 1995, and Belle has just hit his fiftieth home run in the Indians' pennant-winning season.

That was in 1959, when the Indians and White Sox battled on even terms most of the season, until August 28–30 when Cleveland lost four straight to Chicago. Those losses dropped the Indians into second place by 5½ lengths with 24 games left. They went 14–10 the rest of the way, but it wasn't good enough, and Chicago won the pennant by five games.

And it got worse immediately thereafter.

The downward spiral was accelerated with the arrival of Frank Lane in November 1957. As general manager whose well-deserved nicknames were "Frantic Frank" and "Trader Lane," he completed 59 deals involving 120 players through a period of 39 months, before he was fired in January 1961.

One of those deals involved Rocky Colavito, arguably the most popular player in franchise history.

On April 17, 1960, two days before the season opener against Detroit in Cleveland, Lane sent Colavito to the Tigers for defending American League batting champion Harvey Kuenn.

Fans were outraged, and subsequently attendance sagged steadily to an 18-year low of 562,507 in 1963. The trend wasn't completely reversed until 24 years later.

In fact, one author, Terry Pluto, wrote a book entitled *The Curse of Rocky Colavito,* in which the Tribe's troubles were attributed to the deal that sent the popular outfielder away.

According to a legend that has never really been completely refuted, Bobby Bragan allegedly employed a witch to put a curse on the Indians when he was fired by Lane in June 1958.

When asked in later years if the story was true, Bragan scoffed and said, "If people want to believe that, let 'em."

However, if there is any validity to the belief that the Indians have been afflicted by a "curse," one would have to go all the way back to the 10th season of their existence for the initial indication.

On April 14, 1911, Addie Joss died suddenly of tubercular meningitis. The best pitcher in the major leagues at that time, Joss had pitched two no-hitters, including only the second perfect game in baseball's modern era, and compiled a nine-year career earned run average of 1.89, still second best in baseball history.

But that was only the beginning of the Indians' inordinate share of misfortune over the years. Consider the following:

- On August 16, 1920, nine years after Joss's death, shortstop Ray Chapman was hit in the head by a pitch from the New York Yankees' Carl Mays and died the next day. Chapman is still the only player in major league history to be killed in a game.

- Outfielder Bruce Campbell was stricken with spinal meningitis in 1935, and later suffered two recurrences of the disease that cut short his career.

- Pitcher Don Black's career was ended and he almost died after suffering a brain aneurysm while batting in a game in 1948.

- Walter Bond, a promising young outfielder, was diagnosed with leukemia when he played for the Indians from 1960 to 1962. He died in 1967 at age 29.

- Herb Score was nearly blinded in one eye—and almost killed—when he was hit by a line drive off the bat of the Yankees' Gil McDougald on May 7, 1957, and was never an effective pitcher again.

- Manager Birdie Tebbetts suffered a massive, nearly fatal heart attack during spring training in 1964.

- Later in the 1964 season third baseman Max Alvis, the Indians' 1963 Man of the Year, was hospitalized with spinal meningitis.

- Shortstop Larry Brown almost died when his skull was fractured and he suffered other head and facial injuries in a frightful collision with left fielder Leon Wagner during a game in Yankee Stadium in 1966.

- Slugging first baseman Tony Horton suffered a nervous breakdown, attempted suicide during the 1970 season, and never played again.

- A tragic accident in 1993 took the lives of relief pitchers Steve Olin and Tim Crews and seriously injured pitcher Bob Ojeda when their fishing boat crashed into a dock during an off-day in spring training on March 22.

- And seven and a half months later, on November 4, another relief pitcher, Cliff Young, died in an automobile accident at his home in Willis, Texas.

Despite their roller-coaster performances over the years, the Indians, one of only four charter members—along with Detroit, Boston, and Chicago—of the American League still playing in the city in which the franchise started, own an all-time won-lost record on the plus side: 7,336–7,151, for a winning percentage of .506 (from 1901 to 1994).

Against Boston the Indians' record is 949–876, .520; against Chicago, 856–893, .489; against Detroit, 873–941, .481; against New York, 794–983, .447; against the Athletics, 929–812, .534 (642–529 versus Philadelphia, 151–106 versus Kansas City, and 136–177 versus Oakland); against the Senators-Twins, 931–814, .534 (710–594 versus Washington, 221–220 versus Minnesota); and against the Browns-Orioles, 1,014–780, .565 (680–446 versus St. Louis, 334–334 versus Baltimore).

The Indians' records against expansion franchises: California, 209–234, .472; Senators-Rangers, 229–233, .496 (106–91 versus Washington, 123–142 versus Texas); Pilots-Brewers, 170–180, .486 (7–5 versus Seattle, 163–125 versus Milwaukee); Seattle Mariners, 116–88, .569); Kansas City Royals, 136–162, .456; and Toronto, 100–126, .442.

And against two teams that started in 1901 but didn't remain in the American League for long: Baltimore, 19–20, .487 (1901–02); and Milwaukee, 11–9, .550 (1901).

Cleveland won three pennants since 1901, fewer than seven franchises: New York, 34; Philadelphia–Kansas City–Oakland Athletics, 13; Detroit, 9; Boston, 9; St. Louis Browns–Baltimore Orioles, 7; Washington Senators–Minnesota Twins, 6; and Chicago, 4.

The only clubs that won fewer pennants than Cleveland are the Kansas City Royals, 2; Toronto Blue Jays, 2; Seattle Pilots–Milwaukee Brewers, 1; Texas Rangers, 0; and Seattle Mariners, 0. All these are expansion teams.

Which is not to say the Indians, even during their many losing seasons, were dull.

Certainly not when they put together a 13-game winning streak in 1942 and did it again in 1951, or in 1966 when they won the first 10 games of the season and 14 of their first 15, and not even in 1931 when they lost 12 in a row.

The only unassisted triple play in World Series history was accomplished by Indians second baseman Bill Wambsganss in an 8–1 victory on October 10, 1920, in the fifth game against the Brooklyn Dodgers at League Park.

In that same World Series game Jim Bagby, Sr., became the first pitcher to hit a home run, and outfielder Elmer Smith clubbed the first grand slam.

The Indians also are a team whose pitchers—Len Barker in 1981 as well as Joss in 1908—are credited with having hurled two of the 12 perfect games in the major leagues in the modern era (since 1901). They are among 15 no-hitters by Indians pitchers, including a second one by Joss in 1910.

The Indians also have had 11 no-hitters thrown against them.

Three of the no-hitters by Cleveland pitchers were authored by Bob Feller, one on opening day in 1940, the only time that feat has been accomplished.

Feller's major league career began in 1936, when he was only 17. He made 14 regular-season appearances on the mound, once striking out 15 St. Louis Browns, and later that season tied the then major league strikeout record of 17 against the Philadelphia Athletics.

In 1938, when he was 19, Feller set an American League one-game strikeout record of 18 (since broken).

And when he was 23, with a brilliant pitching career ahead of him, Feller was one of the first major league players to enlist in the service for World War II. He joined the navy two days after Pearl Harbor was bombed by the Japanese on December 7, 1941, and spent 44 months aboard a battleship, not returning to the Indians until August 24, 1945.

It was on November 25, 1941, that owner Alva Bradley hired Lou Boudreau to be player-manager of the Indians. It made Boudreau the youngest—at 24 years, 4 months, and 10 days old—man to manage a major league baseball team.

Boudreau's first four seasons at the helm were difficult because of the manpower shortage caused by World War II. One of his players was Paul O'Dea, a first baseman–outfielder who was blind in one eye, but batted .318 in 76 games in 1944 and .235 in 87 games in 1945.

In 1947, Larry Doby became the American League's first black player (and second to Jackie Robinson in major league baseball).

It also was the Indians who hired the major leagues' first black manager, Frank Robinson, in 1975.

Robinson provided what many fans consider the "most memorable moment" in franchise history when he smashed a home run in his first at bat as the Indians' manager and designated hitter. The blow was struck off the Yankees' Doc Medich on opening day at the Stadium, April 8, 1975.

After the Indians signed Doby, owner Bill Veeck rejected an offer to buy the contract of another black player who became a major league star, Monte Irvin.

And when Hank Greenberg became farm director of the Indians in 1949, Doby recommended that he scout and sign three players he'd played against in the Negro Leagues.

They were Hank Aaron, Ernie Banks, and Willie Mays.

When Doby asked Greenberg the following spring what the Indians scouts thought of the three players, Greenberg replied, "Our guys checked 'em out and their reports were not good. They said that Aaron has a hitch in his swing and will never hit good pitching, Banks is too slow and didn't have enough range [at shortstop], and Mays can't hit a curveball."

It also was during Greenberg's stewardship in the late 1950s that he advocated moving the Indians to Minneapolis. His proposal was squelched by ownership, and Greenberg wound up losing his position.

There also was a threat of the Indians moving out of Cleveland in the winter of 1964–65 when three cities were bidding for the franchise—Seattle, Oakland, and Dallas–Ft. Worth, but this time a civic drive kept the team in town.

The Stadium, which the Indians vacated when their new ball park, Jacobs Field, was completed in 1994, was the place where Joe DiMaggio's consecutive-game hitting streak was ended at 56. He was stopped by Indians pitchers Al Smith and Jim Bagby—and by a couple of fielding gems by third baseman Ken Keltner—on July 17, 1941, in front of 67,486 fans.

Seven years later, on October 10, 1948, a crowd of 86,288, the largest ever to see a baseball game, jammed into the Stadium to see the Indians lose the fifth game of the World Series to the Boston Braves, 11–5.

It also was at the Stadium on July 31, 1963, that four Indians hit consecutive home runs off California Angels right-hander Paul Foytack. Woodie Held started it, followed by Pedro Ramos, Tito Francona, and Larry Brown.

The Stadium, which opened for baseball on July 31, 1932, was the home of the Indians on a part-time basis with League Park for 32 games that season, 77 in 1933, none in 1934 and 1935, one in 1936, 15 in 1937, 18 in 1938, 30 in 1939, 49 in 1940, 32 in 1941, 46 in 1942, 48 in 1943, 44 in 1944, 46 in 1945, and 41 in 1946.

After League Park was abandoned in 1947, the Stadium became the full-time home of the club through 1993.

The Stadium also was the site of one of baseball's ugliest scenes on June 4, 1974.

That night, for a game against the Texas Rangers during which a special promotion featured 10-cent beer, fans from among a crowd of 25,136 swarmed onto the field in the ninth inning causing the Indians to lose by forfeit.

Despite their problems, the Indians have had their lighter moments, and charming characters.

Among them was Gomer Hodge, who came up from the minor leagues as a 27-year-old rookie utility player in 1971 when the overall talent level of the club was particularly thin.

On opening day, against the Red Sox, Hodge delivered an eighth-inning pinch single, then stayed in the lineup and stroked a game-winning hit in the last of the ninth as the Indians prevailed, 3–2.

A couple of games later, Gomer got his third straight single as a pinch hitter, and the next day did it again, giving him 4-for-4, after which he told a group of reporters: "Gollee, gee, fellas, I'm hittin' 4.000."

Hodge's given name was Harold, but he was called Gomer because his speech resembled the character in the popular television series, "Gomer Pyle, U.S.M.C."

But Hodge's nickname wasn't the most colorful of the many given Tribe players over the years.

For example, the Indians had the "Immortal Cuban," Joe Azcue (1963–69), "Jittery Joe" Berry (1946), "Tomato Face" Nick Cullop (1927), "Highpockets" Dave Gregg (1913), Odell "Bad News" Hale (1931, '33–40), Charlie "Piano Legs" Hickman (1902–04, '08), "Baby Doll" Bill Jacobson (1927), and "Twitchy Dick" Porter (1929–34).

And, over the years, members of the Indians won the Player of the Year award four times, the Most Valuable Player award three times, the Rookie of the Year award four times, and the Cy Young award once; captured eight batting championships, six home run titles, and two triple crowns; led the American League in RBIs eight times; won 20 games 55 times; and led the league in victories 16 times, in ERA 14 times, and strikeouts 20 times. Fourteen players have won nine Gold Glove awards, eight have snagged stolen base titles, and two front office chiefs have won the Executive of the Year award.

What's more, the busts of 20 players who once wore Cleveland uniforms are in the Hall of Fame, along with two former managers, one who owned the club, two general managers, and four coaches.

So, all in all, it has not been so bad, even though Frank Robinson once cracked, "Pennant fever in Cleveland usually is a 24-hour virus."

Okay, sometimes it was. But certainly not always.

Down Through the Seasons

The Cleveland franchise that became the Indians began operations in 1901, though the city was first represented by a professional baseball team 32 years earlier, on June 2, 1869, to be exact, when the "Forest Citys" played the famous Cincinnati Red Stockings.

The Indians, originally called the Bluebirds, then simply the Blues, had their inception as part of the newly formed "outlaw" American League organized by Byron "Ban" Johnson.

Johnson, who'd been president of the minor Western Baseball League, founded what he determined would be baseball's second major league to compete with the National League, which had been established in 1876.

Johnson visited Cleveland on February 21, 1900, and outlined his grand plan to a man named Davis Hawley, according to a series of stories in the *Cleveland Plain Dealer* that began December 25, 1943.

Hawley was president of what was then the Cuyahoga Savings and Loan Association, one of the city's leading financial institutions.

But it wasn't only Hawley's prestigious position with the bank that motivated Johnson to call on him.

Johnson's interest also was piqued by the fact that Hawley had been secretary and treasurer of the National League club that played in Cleveland with limited success for 11 seasons, beginning in 1889.

Known as the Cleveland Spiders, they won only 20 games and lost 134 in 1899, still the worst record ever compiled in a 154-game baseball schedule. Little wonder they were dropped, along with franchises in Baltimore, Louisville, and Washington, when the National League cut back to eight teams in 1900.

The *Plain Dealer* reported that Johnson was introduced to Hawley as "the president of the Western Baseball League," but immediately pointed out that a mistake in identification had been made.

"It used to be the Western League, but it is the American League now. We are going to put a club in Cleveland, and we want you to be president," Johnson said to Hawley.

Johnson went on to explain his plans for the new league which, in actuality, amounted to little more than a revision of the Western League.

"We are dropping [moving out of] St. Paul and Grand Rapids," Johnson told Hawley. "Charley Comiskey is going to move his St. Paul club to Chicago, and we plan on transferring the Grand Rapids team to Cleveland.

"As it stands now, we will have Kansas City, Minneapolis, Milwaukee, and Chicago in the west, [and] Detroit, Indianapolis, Cleveland, and Buffalo in the east.

"But we will not stand pat on that circuit. Next year, we will expand even more, and, eventually, we will have the greatest baseball league in the country."

Hawley wasn't particularly interested in returning to professional baseball.

"I have been sizing you up, Mr. Johnson," he reportedly responded. "I can see that instead of being a stand-patter you are a fighter. I imagine that you plan on bucking the National League, and that may mean a long fight. If such is the case you need younger blood to carry on such a battle."

Johnson agreed and asked, "Whom would you recommend?"

Hawley named two young men, Charles W. Somers and John F. Kilfoyl, both native Clevelanders in their early thirties. Somers was in the coal business with his father. Kilfoyl owned a men's clothing store, and his family was in real estate.

Hawley also told Johnson, "Somers is a baseball enthusiast and would be willing, I believe, to go a long way with you. Kilfoyl is more conservative, but the two should make a great team."

Pitchers Wes Ferrell (left) and Willis Hudlin, who combined for 38 victories for the Indians in 1930. Ferrell's record was 25–13. Hudlin's was 13–16.

Johnson met with the two men the next day, and they agreed to finance the new club. The organization was established with Kilfoyl as president and treasurer, and Somers as vice president.

The next step for the two young baseball entrepreneurs was to find a field for their team to play its games. Their search led them to a meeting with Frank DeHaas Robison and his brother M. Stanley Robison.

The Robisons had owned the Spiders, the third of four baseball teams to represent Cleveland dating back to that inglorious "opener" on June 2, 1869, when the Forest Citys were soundly beaten, 25–6, by Cincinnati.

The truth be told, the Forest Citys were what is best described as "neophyte professionals." That is, they were a group of amateur players who decided, for the first time, to play for pay (a practice which was not acceptable in the better social circles at that time).

In reality, they weren't even 100 percent professional. Four of the players on that 1869 Cleveland team declined to accept money for their efforts, according to the late Franklin Lewis's 1949 history of the Indians (*The Cleveland Indians,* published by G. P. Putnam's Sons).

That first game took place on a field then called Case Commons, located at Putnam Avenue (now East 38th Street) between Scovill and Central (now Community College) avenues in Cleveland's inner city.

Many of the reported 2,000 fans in attendance were ladies in hoop skirts and gentlemen wearing high starched collars. They'd paid 25 cents to sit in the makeshift grandstands, and 50 cents to watch the game from their horse-drawn carriages ringing the field.

Unavailable (or perhaps charitably unrecorded and forgotten) are most of the details of the season that followed, though it was reported that the Forest Citys lost again to the Red Stockings, this time 43–20, and also were beaten by Brooklyn, 41–27.

They continued to play a "freelance" schedule in 1870. It was on May 17 that year that the Atlantic Club of Brooklyn dropped into Cleveland for a game.

As Lewis described it in his book, the Atlantics' only excuse for losing must have been that they'd had a rough overland journey.

"At the close of the fifth inning, the Forest Citys were leading, 132 to 1. In the first inning, Cleveland scored 52 runs and beat that total with 54 in the third. The Forest Citys' total of 101 safe hits good for 180 bases never has been equaled. Whether that game went the scheduled nine innings has not been established. It is presumed the scorekeeper swooned from exhaustion in the sixth inning, because there is no record of play thereafter."

The following season the Forest Citys joined a league, the National Association of Professional Base Ball Players (NAPBBP). It also included teams representing Boston, Brooklyn, New York, Philadelphia, Washington, Troy (New York), Chicago, Fort Wayne (Indiana), and Rockford (Illinois).

The 1871 season's home opener against Chicago on May 11, according to Lewis, had been heralded as "the most important day in the history of Cleveland baseball," though it ended in an eighth-inning riot.

The Forest Citys, after falling behind, 11–6, stalked off the field in protest of what they considered a sixth bad call by the umpire, a fellow named James L. Haynie.

Haynie just happened to be a Chicago sportswriter there to cover the game.

It also was in 1871 that, for the first time, season tickets for reserved seats were sold for baseball games.

Purchasers were advised of two plans, according to promotional material. Store clerks informed an eager populace, "If only for yourself, the cost is six dollars for the season. But if you wish to bring a lady, there is a special deal available, only ten dollars for you, your lady, and your carriage.

"The carriage or rig could be pulled up to a specified location behind first or third base and there would be no necessity for stepping down to the turf at any time."

With a poor 10–19 record in 1871, followed by an even worse 6–15 mark in 1872, the Forest City team disbanded, leaving Cleveland unrepresented in national competition by either a professional or amateur team from 1873 through 1878.

In 1879 a young businessman named William Hollinger organized a team and petitioned to join the National League, which was then only three years old. Cleveland became its eighth franchise, joining Providence (Rhode Island), Boston, Buffalo, Chicago, Cincinnati, Syracuse, and Troy.

The Cleveland team, again calling itself the Forest Citys, got another new ballpark to play in, this one on Kennard Avenue (now East 46th Street) at Cedar Avenue.

But neither the new league nor the new ballpark made a difference in the fortunes of the Forest Citys, and they finished in sixth place with a 27–55 record.

They climbed into third place (with a 47–37 record) in 1880, but never did any better through the next four seasons, finishing seventh (36–48) in 1881, fifth (42–40) in 1882, fourth (55–42) in 1883, and seventh again (35–77) in 1884.

It was during the 1880 season that Cleveland had the dubious distinction of participating—on the wrong end—in the first of 14 perfect games in major league history. On June 12 they were beaten, 1–0, by J. Lee Richmond, a left-hander pitching for Worcester, Massachusetts, which had joined the league that year.

That also was the season that a tragedy, the first of several in Cleveland's baseball history, struck the team.

In a game at Cincinnati on May 13, outfielders Al Hall and Pete Hotaling collided, with Hall suffering a broken leg that forced him out of baseball permanently.

Hall's continuous brooding over his forced retirement resulted in intense melancholia and finally in insanity. He died in an asylum in Warren, Pennsylvania, in 1885.

After the Forest Citys' disastrous 1884 season, they dropped out of the National League, again leaving Cleveland without a professional baseball team, until Frank DeHaas Robison came along.

Robison not only reorganized the Forest Citys in 1887 and entered them in the eight-team American Association, then considered to be a second major league, but he also built the team another new ballpark, this one on Payne Avenue at East 39th Street.

Cleveland's debut in the American Association was not a successful one, however, and its second- and last season in the league was only slightly better. The Forest Citys were last with a 39–92 record in 1887, and sixth at 50–82 in 1888.

In 1889 they were invited to rejoin the National League, replacing Detroit in the eight-team circuit, and that's when, as legend has it, the team's nickname was changed to "Spiders."

It allegedly occurred when one of the team's stockholders, George W. Howe, observed the players in practice and exclaimed, "They look awful . . . all skinny and spindly. They're nothing more than spiders."

And, thus, the Forest Citys became the Cleveland Spiders, though the change in identification didn't help on the field. They were still very bad, winding up in sixth place (with a 61–72 record) in 1889, and got even worse in 1890, finishing seventh (44–88).

For a brief period in 1890, Cleveland had two teams—both of them also very bad—one in the National League, the other in the new Players League.

The Players League was formed by the Brotherhood of Professional Base Ball Players, a union that was organized after National League and American Association owners imposed a salary cap of $2,000 per player.

Cleveland's team in the Players League finished seventh (with a 55–75 record). But the new league folded after that one financially disastrous year, and the Spiders again became the city's only professional baseball representative.

It also was during the 1890 season that a thunderstorm struck the Spiders' field. Despite considerable damage, the team played the rest of its schedule there, and that fall the Robisons constructed League Park.

They had a very good reason for building it at the corner of Lexington Avenue and East 66th Street.

In addition to the Spiders, they also owned two streetcar lines—and League Park became a focal point for both.

In fact, the Robisons, being good businessmen, sold streetcar "excursion" tickets to Spiders games. The price included seats both on the trolley and in League Park.

When the Spiders played their first game on May 1, 1891 at League Park, the *Plain Dealer* reported that it was "a magical opening . . . there never was one like it and there never may be another."

There was something else that also had great significance in 1890.

That's when a big and burly farmer, who'd been an infielder for his Tuscarawas County (Ohio) team, was acquired—as a pitcher—by the Spiders.

His name was Denton T. Young, a.k.a. "Cy" because, they said, his fast ball was "like a cyclone."

Young was pitching for the Canton, Ohio, team in the minor Ohio-Pennsylvania League early in the 1890 season when reports of his ability reached none other than Davis Hawley, secretary and treasurer of the Spiders.

The same Davis Hawley would be sought by Ban Johnson to establish a Cleveland franchise in the formation of the American League 10 years hence.

Hawley, proving himself to be an excellent judge of player talent as well as an astute businessman, in July 1890 purchased Young's contract from the Canton club for $250 and agreed to pay the former infielder $75 a month to pitch for the Spiders.

And pitch he did.

Though Young didn't start for the Spiders until August, after having pitched 36 games for Canton, he promptly won nine games and lost seven for a team whose record that season was only 44–88, finishing seventh, 43½ games behind pennant-winning Brooklyn.

And he kept getting better and better, winning 241 games for the Spiders in nine seasons (through 1898)—including 36 in 1892, 35 in 1895, and 34 in 1893—while losing only 135.

It was in 1892 that the Spiders won their only "championship," though it wasn't a clear title.

That was the year the National League, which then included 12 teams for the first time, played a split-season schedule called the Spring and Fall series. The Spiders finished fifth behind Boston with a 40–33 record in the first half, but went 53–23 to win the second half.

But in the first "World Series," as the newspapers of that day called the best-of-nine playoff between Boston and Cleveland, the Spiders were completely outclassed. After the teams battled to a scoreless tie in the first game, Boston won the next five for the league title.

The Spiders finished second in 1895, with an 84–46 record, and again in 1896, when they were 80–48, qualifying both times to play the percentage champion Baltimore Orioles in the Temple Cup Series, a best-of-seven playoff.

With the great Young winning three games, the Spiders captured the Temple Cup in five games in 1895, but were swept by the Orioles in 1896.

Those were the only seasons the Spiders earned any distinction; they were third (73–55) in 1893, sixth (68–61) in 1894, fifth (69–62) in 1897, and fifth (81–68) in 1898.

It was in 1897 that an outfielder named Louis Sockalexis, a full-blooded Penobscot Indian, joined the team. He was one of the Spiders' best hitters, though he played only 94 games in 2½ seasons, batting .313.

According to reports, "Sockalexis . . . was strong and fast, and there was fire in every movement."

But there was fire in his throat, too, and it needed extinguishing. Between remedies for this and the discovery by enemy pitchers that left-handers who threw curves could baffle him, Sockalexis suffered a rapid demise as a big leaguer, and was out of baseball after playing only seven games in 1899.

(Sixteen years later, in 1915, because Sockalexis was believed to be the first American Indian to play in the major leagues, the Cleveland franchise was renamed the Indians in his honor. It was the choice of local sportswriters who were invited by team president Charles Somers to make the selection.)

Frank DeHaas Robison recognized an opportunity to make more money in 1899. Prior to the start of the 1899 season, on April 3, Robison purchased the St. Louis franchise, giving him ownership of two clubs in the same league, which, at that time, the National League permitted.

It was called syndicate baseball, and seven of the 12 teams in the National League were involved in similar arrangements.

Four men owned both the Baltimore and Brooklyn franchises, and they did the same thing with better success than Robison did with his Cleveland and St. Louis teams. The best Baltimore players were transferred to the Brooklyn franchise, which then won the 1899 National League pennant.

It was Robison's intention, after buying the St. Louis franchise, to sell the Spiders.

However, the only prospective purchaser who would pay the asking price wanted to move the team to Detroit. The National League would not approve the sale and relocation of the franchise because, at that time, Detroit was a smaller city than Cleveland.

Thus Robison, deciding that St. Louis was a better place than Cleveland to make money in professional baseball, transferred the best of his Spiders players—including Young and another future Hall of Famer, outfielder Jess Burkett—to St. Louis.

These moves emasculated the Cleveland team, embittering its fans, and the Spiders went on to register the aforementioned worst record in the history of major league baseball.

They finished 12th and last, while St. Louis wound up fifth with an 84–67 record. Young won 26 and lost 16, and Burkett, the National League batting champion with a .409 average in 1895 and .410 in 1896 while playing for Cleveland, batted .396 for St. Louis in 1899.

Again, it was little wonder that baseball died in Cleveland after the 1899 season.

Robison himself was quoted as telling Spider manager Lave Cross, "I'm not interested in winning games here [in Cleveland]. Play out the schedule, that's your job."

It was played out—mainly on the road. Cleveland fans, angered because their favorite players had been sent to St. Louis, stayed away in such large numbers that, after only 27 games at League Park, the team became a road troupe exclusively.

It came as no surprise—or shouldn't have—that the National League decided to drop Cleveland, along with Baltimore, Louisville, and Washington, going to an eight-team format in 1900. The league paid almost $150,000 to buy out the four franchises, with Robison receiving $25,000.

Neither was it a surprise that Robison, who still owned the National League's St. Louis franchise, balked when Somers and Kilfoyl wanted to rent League Park for the new American League team in 1901. Comiskey also had trouble renting the park in Chicago for his relocated St. Paul franchise.

But both problems were solved shortly after Johnson declared war on the established league. He threatened to invade four National League cities—Boston, Philadelphia, Washington, and Baltimore—and claimed he'd been assured that "two-thirds of the players in the National League are ready to jump to us."

Consequently, a meeting of the National League was hastily convened in Cleveland on March 3, 1900, and the conflict was averted, at least temporarily.

The National League agreed for Somers and Kilfoyl to assume the territorial rights to a team in Cleveland and rent League Park from the Robisons for $12,000 annually, and to let Comiskey proceed with his plans to field a team on Chicago's south side.

In exchange for those concessions, Johnson and his new colleagues consented to remain a minor league in 1900 (though the name change from Western League to American League remained in effect), and to be subject to a player draft by the National League.

Initially called the Bluebirds and then simply the Blues because of their all-blue uniforms, the Cleveland team finished sixth, 19½ games behind Chicago with a 63–73 record in the "minor" American League in 1900.

But peace between the two leagues did not last long—only until a few weeks after the American League's first season ended.

On October 11, 1900, Johnson proclaimed that the American League would place franchises in Baltimore and Washington, with or without the approval of the National League.

And two days later he boldly announced that several major changes in the standard player contracts would be made, raising salaries and alleviating other inequities, all of which made playing in the American League much more attractive.

Soon thereafter, more than 100 National League players—including some of the brightest stars—jumped to the American League, among them Cy Young, Napoleon Lajoie, Jimmy Collins, and Clark Griffith.

The National League reacted swiftly—and predictably—declaring on November 14, 1900, that the American League was an "outlaw league."

Two years of all-out war began in 1901, the year that also marked the official beginning of Cleveland's professional baseball legacy.

Note: Parentheses around items in the statistical tables indicate the player led the league in that category for the year.

1901

Record: 55–82
Finish: Seventh
Games Behind: 28½
Manager: James R. McAleer

The date was April 24, in Chicago's White Sox park (a.k.a. South Side Park), when Ollie Pickering stepped to the plate for the Cleveland Blues.

Pickering, an outfielder, hit the second pitch from Chicago White Sox right-hander Roy Patterson to center field.

William Hoy, a deaf-mute who was cruelly nicknamed Dummy, caught the routine fly, and with that the American League officially was under way. It came to life in front of an "enormous crowd, variously estimated at from 10,000 to 15,000," as reported by the *Cleveland Plain Dealer*.

The game was won by Chicago, 8–2, as the White Sox took advantage of the wildness of Blues pitcher Bill "Wizard" Hoffer, about whose performance the *Cleveland Press* reported:

"Wizard Hoffer slipped up yesterday in his effort to mystify umpire Connolly.

"For two innings Hoffer aimed the ball at the tin gutters on the roof of the grand stand. After each pitch he would appeal with his eyes to the umpire, as if to say, 'See that strike?'

"But Connolly only shook his head and sent White Stockings to first on gifts. Beginning with the third inning, Hoffer was as puzzling as of old [when he'd pitched with some success in the National League], but the damage had already been done."

That first game between the Blues and White Sox (who went on to win the first American League pennant) was the only one played in the American League on that inaugural day. The other charter members of Ban Johnson's new league were rained out: Detroit at Milwaukee, Philadelphia at Washington, and Baltimore at Boston.

Pickering and Hoffer were two of the six players the Blues retained from their team in 1900, when the AL was a minor league. Four others—pitcher Ed Scott, third baseman Bill Bradley, outfielder Jack McCarthy, and catcher Bob Wood—jumped from their National League teams to sign with the Blues.

The Blues lost two of their next three in Chicago, but won their home opener at League Park, 4–3, over Milwaukee, rallying for three runs in the eighth inning, giving Hoffer his first victory.

But there was little to cheer about thereafter in that first season, not even a nine-inning no-hitter by Blues rookie Earl Moore against Chicago on May 9. The White Sox scored two unearned runs in the fourth on a walk and two errors, and won the game, 4–2, in the 10th on two singles and two fielder's choices.

The Blues went on to lose 18 of their first 25 games before achieving a franchise highlight. On May 23 they rallied for nine runs with two out in the last of the ninth inning to beat Washington, 14–13.

On June 18 the Blues beat Philadelphia, 9–5, to climb within 10 games of .500 (16–26) but got no better and never made it higher than sixth place. They lost 19 of 29 games in September.

Their lack of success on the field was reflected at the box office as the Blues season attendance of 345,178 (131,380 at home) was the worst in the league.

The team batting average of .271 was sixth in the league, and the Blues' only regulars to hit .300 were McCarthy (.321), Pickering (.309), and first baseman Candy LaChance (.303).

Moore was their best pitcher with a 16–14 won-lost record and 2.90 earned run average, while the staff combined for a 4.12 ERA.

	W	L	G	GS	CG	IP	H	BB	K	ERA
Bock Baker	0	1	1	1	1	8	23	6	0	5.63
Jack Bracken	4	8	12	12	12	100	137	31	18	6.21
Bill Bradley	0	0	1	0	0	1	4	0	0	0.00
Dick Braggins	1	2	4	3	2	32	44	15	1	4.78
Bill Cristall	1	5	6	6	5	48⅓	54	30	12	4.84
Tom Donovan	0	0	1	0	0	7	16	3	0	5.14
Pete Dowling	11	(22)*	33	30	28	256⅓	269	104	99	3.86
Bill Hart	7	11	20	19	16	157⅔	180	57	48	3.77
Bill Hoffer	3	8	16	10	10	99	113	35	19	4.55
Jimmy McAleer	0	0	1	0	0	⅓	2	3	0	0.00
Harry McNeal	5	5	12	10	9	85⅓	120	30	15	4.43
Earl Moore	16	14	31	30	28	251⅓	234	107	99	2.90
Ed Scott	6	6	17	16	11	124⅔	149	38	23	4.40
Gus Weyhing	0	0	2	1	0	11⅓	20	5	0	7.94
	54	82		138	122	1,182⅓	1,365	(464)	334	4.12

*League leader in losses with 26 (4 with Milwaukee)
Shutouts: Moore (4), Dowling (2), Cristall
Saves: Hoffer (3), Scott

	G	AB	R	H	2B	3B	HR	RBI	SB	AVG
Erve Beck (2B)	135	539	78	156	26	8	6	79	7	.289
Bill Bradley (3B)	133	516	95	151	28	13	1	55	15	.293
Ed Cermak	1	4	0	0	0	0	0	0	0	.000
Joe Connor	37	121	13	17	3	1	0	6	2	.140
Frank Cross	1	5	0	3	0	0	0	0	0	.600
Tom Donovan	18	71	9	18	3	1	0	5	1	.254
Truck Eagan	5	18	2	3	0	1	0	2	0	.167
Shorty Gallagher	2	4	0	0	0	0	0	0	0	.000
Frank Genins	26	101	15	23	5	0	0	9	3	.228
Russ Hall	1	4	2	2	0	0	0	0	0	.500
Bill Hallman	5	19	2	4	0	0	0	3	0	.211
Ervin Harvey	45	170	21	60	5	5	1	24	15	.353
Harry Hogan	1	4	0	0	0	0	0	0	0	.000
Candy LaChance (1B)	133	548	81	166	22	9	1	75	11	.303
Paddy Livingston	1	2	0	0	0	0	0	0	0	.000
Jimmy McAleer	3	7	0	1	0	0	0	0	0	.143
Jack McCarthy (LF)	86	343	60	110	14	7	0	32	9	.321
Jim McGuire	18	69	4	16	2	0	0	3	0	.232
Jack O'Brien (RF)	92	375	54	106	14	5	0	39	13	.283
Ollie Pickering (CF)	137	547	102	169	25	6	0	40	36	.309
Frank Scheibeck (SS)	93	329	33	70	11	3	0	38	3	.213
Danny Shay	19	75	4	17	2	2	0	10	0	.227
Bob Wood (C)	98	346	45	101	23	3	1	49	6	.292
George Yeager	39	139	13	31	5	0	0	14	2	.223
	4,833	667	1,311	197	68	12		523	125	.271

1902

Record: 69–67
Finish: Fifth
Games Behind: 14
Manager: William R. Armour

The name was changed from "Blues" to "Bronchos," and William Armour replaced James McAleer as manager. But the team floundered through the first 35 games, losing 24, until June 4 when second baseman Napoleon Lajoie arrived in Cleveland.

Baseball's most famous player at that time, Lajoie came to the Bronchos from the Philadelphia Athletics, for whom he batted .422 in 1901, becoming the first modern major leaguer to hit .400 for an entire season.

Lajoie and pitcher Bill Bernhard were virtually given to the Bronchos by Athletics owner Connie Mack. It was repayment for the financial assistance Mack received from Charles

Somers, co-owner of the Cleveland franchise, when the American League was formed in 1900.

Lajoie and Bernhard were available because of pending litigation against Mack by the Athletics' crosstown rival in Philadelphia, the National League Phillies.

After batting .337 for the Phillies in 1900, Lajoie jumped to the Athletics in 1901 when Mack offered him a $2,400 contract. Bernhard also was a Phillies defector after a contract dispute and joined the Athletics with Lajoie. Mack sent them to Cleveland after the Phillies obtained a court injunction preventing the two from playing with any other team in Pennsylvania.

Lajoie and Bernhard absolutely refused to rejoin the Phillies, and they risked damage suits if they played with the Athletics, so they did neither for a month.

Somers approached Mack and asked for Lajoie and Bernhard. Mack considered their cases, recalled the many favors Somers had done, and said the Bronchos could have both players if satisfactory salary arrangements could be worked out.

One published report said Lajoie was paid $25,000 for three years. Another said he would receive $30,000 for four years.

The Phillies' lawsuit to prevent Lajoie and Bernhard from defecting was thrown out of court, though the restraining order against their appearing with any team other than the Phillies in Pennsylvania was upheld. Thus, for two seasons, through 1903, the Bronchos played games in Philadelphia without Lajoie and Bernhard.

In Lajoie's first game with the Bronchos, who were then languishing in last place with an 11–24 record, he got a double and turned two double plays in a 4–3 victory over Boston.

By July 11 the Bronchos raised their record to 30–39, climbing out of last place, and reached .500 (57–57) and fifth place on September 1. Their record from the time Lajoie and Bernhard came to them was 58–43, better than every team in the AL except the pennant-winning Athletics and the second-place St. Louis Browns, but the early season deficit was too great to make up.

Lajoie was the leading hitter with a .379 average, seven homers, and 64 runs batted in. First baseman Charlie "Piano Legs" Hickman, another early-season acquisition (in a trade with Boston), hit .378 and led the team with 94 RBIs.

Addie Joss, who was one of three pitchers to win 17 games, hurled a one-hitter against St. Louis in his major league debut on April 26.

	G	AB	R	H	2B	3B	HR	RBI	SB	AVG
Harry Bay (CF)	108	455	71	132	10	5	0	23	22	.290
Harry Bemis (C)	93	317	42	99	12	7	1	29	3	.312
Frank Bonner	34	132	14	37	6	0	0	14	1	.280
Bill Bradley (3B)	137	550	104	187	39	12	11	77	11	.340
Elmer Flick (RF)	110	424	70	126	19	11	2	61	20	.297
John Gochnaur (SS)	127	459	45	85	16	4	0	37	7	.185
Peaches Graham	2	6	0	2	0	0	0	1	0	.333
Ervin Harvey	12	46	5	16	2	0	0	5	1	.348
Charlie Hemphill	25	94	14	25	2	0	0	11	4	.266
Charlie Hickman (1B)	102	426	61	(161)*	31	11	8	94	8	.378
Nap Lajoie (2B)	86	348	81	132	35	5	7	64	19	.379
Jack McCarthy (LF)	95	359	45	102	31	5	0	41	12	.284
Hal O'Hagen	3	13	2	5	2	0	0	1	2	.385
Ollie Pickering	69	293	46	75	5	2	3	26	22	.256
Ossee Schreckengost	18	74	5	25	0	0	0	9	2	.338
George Starnagle	1	3	0	0	0	0	0	0	0	.000
Jack Thoney	28	105	14	30	7	1	0	11	4	.286
Bob Wood	81	258	23	16	18	2	0	40	1	.295
	4,840	686	(1,401)	248	68	33	582	140	(.289)	

*League leader in hits with 193 (32 with Boston)

1903

Record: 77–63
Finish: Third
Games Behind: 15
Manager: William R. Armour

Napoleon Lajoie continued to dominate the American League, winning the batting championship with a .344 average. His popularity in Cleveland was so great that the nickname of the team was changed to "Naps" in his honor, the result of balloting by the fans in a contest conducted by the *Cleveland Press*.

The voting totals were: Naps 365, Buckeyes 281, Emperors 276, Metropolitans 239, Giants 223, and Cyclops 214. Other names that drew some votes included Terrors, Pashas, Dachshunds, Majestics, Mastodons, Midgets, Tip Tops, Crackerjacks, and Prospectors.

It also was in 1903 that the American and National leagues signed a peace treaty in the form of an all-embracing national agreement. It led to the playing of the first World Series between the two pennant winners, Boston in the AL and Pittsburgh in the NL.

The Naps got off to a poor start, losing their first three games and seven of nine, but recovered to reach .500 (11–11) on May 19, and continued to play well, climbing into second place, 14 games over .500 (70–56), on September 11.

But then, without their three best pitchers because of injuries—Earl Moore, Addie Joss, and Bill Bernhard—they won only seven of their final 14 games and lost second place by half a game to Philadelphia.

Bernhard suffered a broken finger on July 24 and didn't pitch again (though he still won 14 games); Joss was injured in a train wreck and pitched his final game on August 30, beating St. Louis for an 18–13 record; and Moore, who lost to St. Louis, 8–3, on August 31, missed the final month with a sore arm and finished at 19–9.

With the establishment of the national agreement between the two leagues, the AL adopted the NL's foul strike rule, which decreed that foul balls henceforth would be considered strikes. That had not been the case in the first two years of the AL's existence, undoubtedly benefiting the batters in 1901 and 1902.

	W	L	G	GS	CG	IP	H	BB	K	ERA
Bill Bernhard	17	5	27	24	22	217	169	34	57	2.20
Ginger Clark	1	0	1	0	0	6	10	3	1	6.00
Gus Dorner	3	1	4	4	4	36	33	13	5	1.25
Otto Hess	2	4	7	4	4	43⅔	67	23	13	5.98
Charlie Hickman	0	1	1	1	1	8	11	5	1	7.88
Addie Joss	17	13	32	29	28	269⅓	225	75	106	2.77
Dummy Leitner	0	0	1	1	0	8	11	1	0	4.50
Jack Lundbom	1	1	8	3	1	34	48	16	7	6.62
Earl Moore	17	17	36	34	29	293	304	(101)	84	2.95
Lou Polchow	0	1	1	1	1	8	9	4	2	5.63
Charlie Smith	2	1	3	3	2	20	23	5	5	4.05
Oscar Streit	0	7	8	7	4	51⅓	72	25	10	5.23
Dummy Taylor	1	3	4	4	4	34	37	8	8	1.59
Dike Varney	1	1	3	3	0	14⅔	14	12	7	6.14
Moses Vasbinder	0	0	2	0	0	5	5	8	2	9.00
Ed Walker	0	1	1	1	1	8	11	3	1	3.38
Clarence Wright	7	11	21	18	15	148	150	75	52	3.95
	69	67		137	116	1,204⅓	1,199	(411)	361	3.28

Shutouts: Joss (5), Moore (4), Bernhard (3), Dorner, Smith, Taylor, Wright
Saves: Bernhard, Moore, Wright

	W	L	G	GS	CG	IP	H	BB	K	ERA
Bill Bernhard	14	6	20	19	18	165⅔	151	21	60	2.12
Red Donahue	7	9	16	15	14	136⅔	142	12	45	2.44
Gus Dorner	4	5	12	8	4	73⅔	83	24	28	4.52
Martin Glendon	1	2	3	3	3	27⅔	20	7	9	0.98
Addie Joss	18	13	32	31	31	283⅔	232	37	120	2.19
Ed Killian	3	4	9	8	7	61⅓	61	13	18	2.48
Earl Moore	19	9	29	27	27	247⅔	196	62	148	(1.74)
Alex Pearson	1	2	4	3	2	30⅓	34	3	12	3.56
Bill Pounds	0	0	1	0	0	5	8	0	2	10.80
Bob Rhoads	2	3	5	5	5	41	55	3	21	5.27
Jesse Stovall	5	1	6	6	6	57	44	21	12	2.05
Ed Walker	0	0	3	3	0	12	13	10	4	5.25
Clarence Wright	3	9	15	12	8	101⅓	122	58	42	5.75
	77	63		140	(125)	1,243⅔	1,161	271	521	2.73

Shutouts: Donahue (4), Bernhard (3), Joss(3), Killian (3), Moore (3), Dorner (2), Stovall (2)
Save: Moore

	G	AB	R	H	2B	3B	HR	RBI	SB	AVG
Fred Abbott	77	255	25	60	11	3	1	25	8	.235
Harry Bay (CF)	140	579	94	169	15	12	1	35	(45)	.292
Harry Bemis (C)	92	314	31	82	20	3	1	41	5	.261
Bill Bradley (3B)	136	536	101	168	36	22	6	68	21	.313
Billy Clingman	21	64	10	18	1	1	0	7	2	.281
Elmer Flick (RF)	140	523	81	155	23	16	2	51	24	.296
John Gochnaur (SS)	134	438	48	81	16	4	0	48	10	.185
Jack Hardy	5	19	1	3	1	0	0	1	1	.158
Charlie Hickman (1B)	131	522	64	154	31	11	12	97	14	.295
Hugh Hill	1	1	0	0	0	0	0	0	0	.000
Happy Iott	3	10	1	2	0	0	0	0	1	.200
Nap Lajoie (2B)	125	485	90	167	41	11	7	93	21	(.344)
Jack McCarthy (LF)	108	415	47	110	20	8	0	43	15	.265
Jack Slattery	4	11	1	0	0	0	0	0	0	.000
Jack Thoney	32	122	10	25	3	0	1	9	7	.205
		4,773	639	1,265	(231)	95	31	550	175	.265

1904

Record: 86–65
Finish: Fourth
Games Behind: 7½
Managers: William R. Armour, Napoleon Lajoie

The Naps were one of five teams that fought for the 1904 American League pennant. Until July they were in the thick of the race before it narrowed down to New York and Boston, with the latter prevailing for the second straight season.

Napoleon Lajoie repeated as the AL's batting champion, hitting .376 with 102 runs batted in. He led the Naps to 13 victories in 22 games against Boston, the only team to beat the champions in a season series.

Beset by injuries to several key players, as well as the illness of shortstop Terry Turner, who was sidelined for 40 games with typhoid fever, the Naps were frequently disorganized. The disorganization led to discouragement and dissension and resulted in the resignation of manager William Armour.

Though Armour told Naps owners Charles Somers and Jack Kilfoyl on September 9 that he was relinquishing control of the team, he continued to be listed as manager though Lajoie, as team captain, was in charge on the field. When the season ended, Lajoie was officially named manager.

Cleveland's team batting average of .260 was the best in the AL and three of the Naps were among the league's eight .300 hitters. They were outfielder Elmer Flick (.306) and third baseman Bill Bradley (.300), in addition to Lajoie.

	W	L	G	GS	CG	IP	H	BB	K	ERA
Bill Bernhard	23	13	38	37	35	320⅔	323	55	137	2.13
Red Donahue	19	14	35	32	30	277	281	49	127	2.40
Otto Hess	8	7	21	16	15	151⅓	134	31	64	1.67
John Hickey	0	1	2	2	1	12⅓	14	11	5	7.30
Addie Joss	14	10	25	24	20	192⅓	160	30	83	(1.59)
Earl Moore	12	11	26	24	22	227⅔	186	61	139	2.25
Bob Rhoads	10	9	22	19	18	175⅓	175	48	72	2.87
	86	65		154	141	1,356⅔	1,273	285	627	2.22

Shutouts: Donahue (6), Joss (5), Bernhard (4), Hess (4), Moore
Saves: None

	G	AB	R	H	2B	3B	HR	RBI	SB	AVG
Fred Abbott	41	130	14	22	4	2	0	12	2	.169
Harry Bay (CF)	132	506	69	122	12	9	3	36	(38)	.241
Harry Bemis (C)	97	336	35	76	11	6	0	25	6	.226
Bill Bradley (3B)	154	609	94	183	32	8	5	83	23	.300
Fritz Buelow	42	119	11	21	4	1	0	5	2	.176
Charlie Carr	32	120	9	27	5	1	0	7	0	.225
Mike Donovan	2	2	0	0	0	0	0	0	0	.000
Elmer Flick (RF)	150	579	97	177	31	17	6	56	(38)	.306
Charlie Hickman (1B)	86	337	34	97	22	10	4	45	9	.288
Nap Lajoie (2B)	140	553	92	(208)	(49)	15	6	(102)	29	(.376)
Billy Lush (LF)	138	477	76	123	13	8	1	50	12	.258
Harry Ostdiek	7	18	1	3	0	1	0	3	1	.167
Claude Rossman	18	62	5	13	5	0	0	6	0	.210
Bill Schwartz	24	86	5	13	2	0	0	4	4	.151
George Stovall	52	181	18	54	10	1	1	31	3	.298
Terry Turner (SS)	111	404	41	95	9	6	1	45	5	.235
Rube Vinson	15	49	12	15	1	0	0	2	2	.306
		5,152	(647)	1,340	(225)	90	27	(553)	178	(.260)

1905

Record: 76–78
Finish: Fifth
Games Behind: 19
Manager: Napoleon Lajoie

Misfortune dogged rookie manager Napoleon Lajoie, and the Naps fell to fifth place with their first sub-.500 record in four seasons, since entering the American League in 1901.

Some speculated that taking on the managerial duties hampered the play of Lajoie, whose batting average declined to .329, considerably lower than when he led American League hitters in three of the previous four years. However, it probably was more a matter of a severe injury that caused Lajoie to miss nearly three months of the season.

In July, after the Naps had gotten off to a fast start and held first place for a brief time, Lajoie was spiked in a play at second base, but remained in the game. The next day Lajoie could barely walk because as the wound had become infected and blood poisoning had set in. It idled Lajoie until August 28 when he returned to play in five games at first base.

However, a foul tip that hit his injured ankle caused him to become a bench manager for the rest of the season.

The Naps were further disorganized by injuries to third baseman Bill Bradley and outfielders Harry Bay and Elmer Flick, though the latter was able to play 132 games and win the batting championship with a .308 average. Because of the many injuries late in the season it was necessary for battery men—pitchers and catchers—to play infield and outfield positions.

Despite all their problems, the Naps tied Philadelphia for the highest team batting average, .255, in the AL Lajoie and Flick were two of only six players to hit .300, and Addie Joss, the Naps' best pitcher, was one of nine AL hurlers to win 20 games.

	W	L	G	GS	CG	IP	H	BB	K	ERA
Bill Bernhard	7	13	22	19	17	174⅓	185	34	56	3.36
Red Donahue	6	12	20	18	14	137⅔	132	25	45	3.40
Cy Ferry	0	0	1	1	0	2	3	0	2	13.50
John Halla	0	0	3	0	0	12⅔	12	0	4	2.84
Otto Hess	10	15	26	25	22	213¾	179	72	109	3.16
Addie Joss	20	12	33	32	31	286	246	46	132	2.01
Earl Moore	15	15	31	30	28	269	232	92	131	2.64
Bob Rhoads	16	9	28	26	24	235	219	55	61	2.83
Hi West	2	2	6	4	4	33	43	10	15	4.09
	76	78	155	(140)		1,363⅓	(1,251)	334	555	2.85

Shutouts: Hess (4), Rhoads (4), Joss (3), Moore (3), Donahue, West
Saves: None

	G	AB	R	H	2B	3B	HR	RBI	SB	AVG
Jap Barbeau	11	37	1	10	1	1	0	2	1	.270
Harry Bay (CF)	144	552	90	166	18	10	0	22	36	.301
Harry Bemis	70	226	27	66	13	3	0	28	3	.292
Bill Bradley (3B)	146	541	63	145	34	6	0	51	22	.268
Fritz Buelow (C)	75	239	11	41	4	1	1	18	7	.172
Charlie Carr (1B)	89	306	29	72	12	4	1	31	12	.235
Nig Clarke	42	123	11	24	6	1	0	9	0	.195
Bunk Congalton	12	47	4	17	0	0	0	5	3	.362
Elmer Flick (RF)	132	500	72	154	29	(18)	4	64	35	(.308)
Eddie Grant	2	8	1	3	0	0	0	0	0	.375
Jim Jackson (LF)	109	426	59	109	12	4	2	31	15	.256
Nick Kahl	40	135	16	29	4	1	0	21	1	.215
Nap Lajoie (2B)	65	249	29	82	12	2	2	41	11	.329
Emil Leber	2	6	1	0	0	0	0	0	0	.000
George Stovall	112	423	41	115	31	1	1	47	13	.272
Terry Turner (SS)	155	586	49	155	16	14	4	72	17	.265
Rube Vinson	39	134	12	26	3	1	0	9	4	.194
Howard Wakefield	10	26	3	4	0	0	0	1	0	.154
		5,166	567	(1,318)	211	(72)	18	482	188	(.255)

1906

Record: 89–64
Finish: Third
Games Behind: 5
Manager: Napoleon Lajoie

Again the Naps were considered one of the American League's premier teams and rated a favorite to win the franchise's first pennant.

But after the team again got off to a fast start, the season turned into a virtual repeat of 1905.

The Naps were in or near first place until August, but then were hit hard by injuries again to third baseman Bill Bradley and outfielder Harry Bay, both key players and two of the best hitters on the team. Both were sidelined the latter part of the season, and Bay wound up playing only 68 games and Bradley 82, both batting an identical .275.

Addie Joss, the team's best pitcher, also missed a month of action because of illness, though he still finished as one of the Naps' three 20-game winners, along with Bob Rhoads and Otto Hess.

Despite the loss of Bradley and Bay each for half the season, the Naps' team batting average of .279 was the best in the AL for the second straight year. Lajoie, playing all but one game, rebounded to hit .355, though George Stone of St. Louis beat him out by three percentage points to win the batting championship.

In a close race with New York down the stretch, the pennant was won by Chicago, which came to be called "the hitless wonders" because their team batting average of .228 was the lowest in the league.

	W	L	G	GS	CG	IP	H	BB	K	ERA
Bill Bernhard	16	15	31	30	23	255⅓	235	47	85	2.54
Harry Eells	4	5	14	8	6	86½	77	48	35	2.61
Otto Hess	20	17	43	36	33	333⅔	274	85	167	1.83
Addie Joss	21	9	34	31	28	282	220	43	106	1.72
Glenn Liebhardt	2	0	2	2	2	18	13	1	9	1.50
Earl Moore	1	1	5	4	2	29⅓	27	18	8	3.94
Bob Rhoads	22	10	38	34	31	315	259	92	89	1.80
Jack Townsend	3	7	17	12	8	92⅔	92	31	31	2.91
	89	64		(157)	(133)	(1,412⅔)	1,197	365	530	(2.09)

Shutouts: Joss (9), Hess (7), Rhoads (7), Bernhard (2), Eells, Townsend
Saves: Hess (3), Joss

	G	AB	R	H	2B	3B	HR	RBI	SB	AVG
Jap Barbeau	42	129	8	25	5	3	0	12	5	.194
Harry Bay	68	280	47	77	8	3	0	14	17	.275
Harry Bemis (C)	93	297	28	82	13	5	2	30	8	.276
Joe Birmingham	10	41	5	13	2	1	0	6	2	.317
Bill Bradley (3B)	82	302	32	83	16	2	2	25	13	.275
Fritz Buelow	34	86	7	14	2	0	0	7	0	.163
Ben Caffyn	30	103	16	20	4	0	0	3	2	.194
Nig Clarke	57	179	22	64	12	4	1	21	3	.358
Bunk Congalton (RF)	117	419	51	134	13	5	3	50	12	.320
Elmer Flick (CF)	(157)	(624)	(98)	194	34	(22)	1	62	(39)	.311
Jim Jackson (LF)	105	374	44	80	13	2	0	38	25	.214
Malachi Kittridge	5	10	0	1	0	0	0	0	0	.100
Nap Lajoie (2B)	152	602	88	(214)	(48)	9	0	91	20	.355
Claude Rossman (1B)	118	396	49	122	13	2	1	53	11	.308
Bill Shipke	2	6	0	0	0	0	0	0	0	.000
George Stovall	116	443	54	121	19	5	0	37	15	.273
Terry Turner (SS)	147	584	85	170	27	7	2	62	27	.291
		(5,426)	(663)	(1,516)	(240)	73	12	(548)	203	(.279)

1907

Record: 85–67
Finish: Fourth
Games Behind: 8
Manager: Napoleon Lajoie

It was another good year for the Naps, though they failed again in the latter stages of the season for the third time in a row. They weren't knocked out of contention until the final 10 days when they were locked into fourth place on September 27 after losing a series to Chicago.

Everything considered, it was surprising the Naps did even that well.

Napoleon Lajoie suffered a recurrence of the blood poisoning that idled him in 1905, causing him to miss 15 games. It also affected Lajoie's hitting as his average dipped to .299, the first of only five of his 21 years in the major leagues that he failed to bat .300.

But Lajoie wasn't the only Naps player who had an off year at the plate as the team batting average fell to .241, sixth in the American League.

With the exception of outfielder Elmer Flick, who hit .302, the rest of the team slumped offensively, especially third baseman George Stovall (.236).

But it wasn't only the lack of offense that prevented the Naps from doing better. Addie Joss was their only 20-game winner, tying Chicago's Guy "Doc" White with 27 victories, the most in the American League.

Joss lost 11 games, compared to White's 13, and his earned run average also was better, 1.83 to 2.26. However, it was pennant-winning Detroit's "Wild Bill" Donovan (25–4) whose pitching percentage was best in the AL, and the Tigers' Ty Cobb also won his first of 12 batting championships with a .350 average.

	W	L	G	GS	CG	IP	H	BB	K	ERA
Heinie Berger	3	3	14	7	5	87⅓	74	20	50	2.99
Bill Bernhard	0	4	8	4	3	42	58	11	19	3.21
Walter Clarkson	4	6	17	10	9	90⅔	77	29	32	1.99
Otto Hess	6	6	17	14	7	93⅓	84	37	36	2.89
Addie Joss	(27)	11	42	38	34	338⅔	279	54	127	1.83
Glenn Liebhardt	18	14	38	34	27	280⅓	254	85	110	2.05
Earl Moore	1	1	3	2	1	19¼	18	8	7	4.66
Bob Rhoads	15	14	35	31	23	275	258	84	76	2.29
Jake Thielman	11	8	20	18	18	166	151	34	56	2.33
	85	67		(158)	127	1,392⅔	1,253	362	513	2.26

Shutouts: Joss (6), Rhoads (5), Liebhardt (4), Thielman (3), Clarkson, Berger
Saves: Joss (2), Hess, Liebhardt, Rhoads

	G	AB	R	H	2B	3B	HR	RBI	SB	AVG
Harry Bay	34	95	14	17	1	1	0	7	7	.179
Harry Bemis	65	172	12	43	7	0	0	19	5	.250
Joe Birmingham (CF)	136	476	55	112	10	9	1	33	23	.235
Bill Bradley (3B)	139	498	48	111	20	1	0	34	20	.223
Nig Clarke (C)	120	390	44	105	19	6	3	33	3	.269
Bunk Congalton	9	22	2	4	0	0	0	2	0	.182
Frank Delahanty	15	52	3	9	0	1	0	4	2	.173
Elmer Flick (RF)	147	549	78	166	15	(18)	3	58	41	.302
Bill Hinchman (LF)	152	514	62	117	19	9	1	50	15	.228
Harry Hinchman	15	51	3	11	3	1	0	9	2	.216
Nap Lajoie (2B)	137	509	53	152	30	6	2	63	24	.299
Pete Lister	22	65	5	18	2	0	0	4	2	.277
Rabbit Nill	12	43	5	12	1	0	0	2	2	.279
Pete O'Brien	43	145	9	33	5	2	0	6	1	.228
George Stovall (1B)	124	466	38	110	17	6	1	36	13	.236
Terry Turner (SS)	140	524	57	127	20	7	0	46	27	.242
Howard Wakefield	26	37	4	5	2	0	0	3	0	.135
	5,068	530	1,221	182	68	11	433	193		.241

1908

Record: 90–64
Finish: Second
Games Behind: ½
Manager: Napoleon Lajoie

There were some notable accomplishments by the Naps in 1908, though the season wound up in bitter disappointment and frustration for Napoleon Lajoie and his players.

However, even before the season started, during spring training in Macon, Georgia, Naps' owner Charley Somers made a decision that would have a profound effect on the team, not only that year, but long into the future.

While meeting with a group of sportswriters prior to practice one day in March, Somers received a phone call from Hughie Jennings, manager of the Detroit Tigers.

Jennings called to propose a trade: Ty Cobb for Elmer Flick. Cobb had led the American League with a .350 average and had stolen 49 bases in 1907, while Flick had hit .302 with 41 stolen bases that season, though he'd won the batting championship in 1905.

Somers pondered Jennings' offer and asked why the Tigers wanted to trade Cobb.

Jennings assured Somers there was nothing physically wrong with Cobb, but repeatedly said, "[Cobb] can't get along with our players, and we want to get him away. He's had two fights already this spring. We want harmony on this team, not scrapping."

Somers made his decision immediately. "We'll keep Flick," he said. "Maybe he isn't as good a batter as Cobb, but he's much nicer to have on the team."

Cobb went on to hit .324 that season, winning the second of his 12 AL batting titles, and would play for the Tigers through 1926, compiling a lifetime average of .367, best in

the history of baseball. Flick was a regular for the Naps only through 1907, and would not play beyond 1910.

With Cobb in Cleveland instead of Detroit, the Naps probably would have won the pennant in 1908 as Addie Joss pitched the fourth perfect game in major league history (only the second since the so-called modern era began in 1901) beating Chicago, 1–0, on October 2; Robert "Dusty" Rhoads pitched a no-hitter to beat Boston, 2–1, on September 18; and on June 9 the team set a major league record when every player in the lineup hit safely and scored a run in the fifth inning to wipe out a 2–1 deficit and overwhelm Boston, 15–6.

But those achievements were no consolation to the Naps, who lost what would have been Cleveland's first pennant by the narrowest of margins, .004 of a percentage point and half a game.

Detroit, with Cobb leading the way, repeated as the American League champion with a 90–63 record, the difference being one loss—perhaps a game the Tigers didn't play. They were rained out on August 25 in Washington, giving the Tigers the margin of victory.

In those days baseball did not require that postponed games be made up if they had a bearing on the pennant race. In the season series between Detroit and Washington, the Tigers won 16 and the Senators five.

The Naps, along with Chicago and St. Louis, as well as Detroit, were still in contention to win the pennant with two weeks remaining, though the Browns were eliminated with one week left.

Then, as it turned out, the Naps' chances were destroyed when, in their third-to-last game on October 5, they lost the opener of a doubleheader in St. Louis, 3–1.

The Browns won it with two runs in the fifth inning off Glenn Liebhardt, breaking a 1–1 tie, after Lajoie committed an error on a grounder by leadoff batter Danny Hoffman. Dode Criss followed with a double that scored Hoffman, and Jimmy Williams singled for the Browns' second run of the inning and third of the game.

It proved to be enough as the St. Louis right-hander completed a four-hitter for his 14th victory.

The Naps protested, claiming that the Tigers should be required to make up the rained-out game against Washington, but to no avail. Detroit went to the World Series against Chicago, losing to the Cubs in five games.

A repercussion of the strenuous race and its disappointing conclusion was the resignation of Naps president John Kilfoyl who, along with Charles Somers, had owned the franchise since its inception and the founding of the American League by Ban Johnson in 1900.

Kilfoyl's health failed, and at the end of the season, he stepped down from his position. Somers, who had been the dominant partner, assumed the presidency and promoted Ernest Sargent "Barney" Barnard to vice president.

The former sports editor of the *Columbus Dispatch*, Barnard had been hired in 1904 as the Naps'—and perhaps baseball's—first full-time traveling secretary.

Barnard also was part of another innovation as he, with Somers' approval, built the game's first farm system, enabling the Naps to control minor league franchises in Toledo and Ironton, Ohio; Waterbury, Connecticut; Portland, Oregon; and New Orleans.

Joss posted a 24–11 won-lost record with a remarkable 1.16

earned run average in 325 innings (the AL record by a right-hander in 300 or more innings is 1.14, set by Walter Johnson in 1913). Not one of the Naps regulars batted .300 as Lajoie's average fell to .289.

	W	L	G	GS	CG	IP	H	BB	K	ERA
Heinie Berger	13	8	29	24	16	199⅓	152	66	101	2.12
Charlie Chech	11	7	27	20	14	165⅔	136	34	51	1.74
Walter Clarkson	0	0	2	1	0	3⅓	6	2	1	10.80
Cy Falkenberg	2	4	8	7	2	46⅓	52	10	17	3.88
Slim Foster	1	0	6	1	1	21	16	12	11	2.14
Jack Graney	0	0	2	0	0	3⅓	6	1	0	5.40
Otto Hess	0	0	4	0	0	7	11	1	2	5.14
Addie Joss	24	11	42	35	29	325	232	30	130	(1.16)
Bill Lattimore	1	2	4	4	1	24	24	7	5	4.50
Glenn Liebhardt	15	16	38	26	19	262	222	81	146	2.20
Bob Rhoads	18	12	37	30	20	270	229	73	62	1.77
Jack Ryan	1	1	8	1	1	35⅔	27	2	7	2.27
Jake Thielman	4	3	11	8	5	61⅔	59	9	15	3.65
	(90)	64		(157)	108	(1,424⅓)	1,172	328	548	(2.02)

Shutouts: Joss (9), Chech (4), Liebhardt (3), Lattimore, Rhoads
Saves: Foster (2), Joss (2), Ryan

	G	AB	R	H	2B	3B	HR	RBI	SB	AVG
Dave Altizer	29	89	11	19	1	2	0	5	7	.213
Harry Bay	2	0	0	0	0	0	0	0	0	—
Harry Bemis	91	277	23	62	9	1	0	33	14	.224
Joe Birmingham (CF)	122	413	32	88	10	1	2	38	15	.213
Bill Bradley (3B)	148	548	70	133	24	7	1	46	18	.243
Josh Clarke (LF)	131	492	70	119	8	4	1	21	37	.242
Nig Clarke (C)	97	290	34	70	8	6	1	27	6	.241
Homer Davidson	9	4	2	0	0	0	0	0	1	.000
Elmer Flick	9	35	4	8	1	1	0	2	0	.229
Wilbur Good	46	154	23	43	1	3	1	14	7	.279
Charlie Hickman	65	197	16	46	6	1	2	16	2	.234
Bill Hinchman (RF)	137	464	55	107	23	8	6	59	9	.231
Nap Lajoie (2B)	(157)	581	77	168	32	6	2	74	15	.289
Grover Land	8	16	1	3	0	0	0	2	0	.188
Deacon McGuire	1	4	0	1	1	0	0	2	0	.250
Rabbit Nill	11	23	3	5	0	0	0	1	0	.217
George Perring (SS)	89	310	23	67	8	5	0	19	8	.216
George Stovall (1B)	138	534	71	156	29	6	2	45	14	.292
Denny Sullivan	4	6	0	0	0	0	0	0	0	.000
Terry Turner	60	201	21	48	11	1	0	19	18	.239
		5,108	568	1,221	188	58	18	458	177	.239

1909

Record: 71–82
Finish: Sixth
Games Behind: 27½
Managers: Napoleon Lajoie, James McGuire

The previous season, when Cleveland lost an opportunity to tie for the pennant because the champion Detroit Tigers played and lost one less game, was difficult enough for the Naps, but it proved to be only a portent of the immediate future.

The 1909 Naps struggled from the onset of the season, and on August 17, with the team hopelessly out of contention, Napoleon Lajoie offered to resign as manager. He also volunteered to take a reduction in his $10,000 salary, which was the highest in the American League at the time.

Five days later Naps owner Charles Somers announced he was accepting Lajoie's resignation and that Jim McGuire, one of the team's coaches, would take over as manager.

Lajoie continued as the Naps' second baseman—he was still the greatest in the game at that position—and spent the next five seasons in Cleveland under three different managers.

Great things had been predicted for the Naps, who were favored again to win Cleveland's first pennant, based on the

team's strong showing the previous season, and also the return of Cy Young on February 18.

Young, whose major league career began in Cleveland in 1890 with the National League Spiders, was reacquired from Boston. He had won 241 games while losing only 121 through 1898 when he was sent to St. Louis by Frank DeHaas Robison, the owner of both franchises.

The Naps gave up pitchers Charlie Chech and Jack Ryan and $13,500 to get Young, whose 1908 record was 21–11 with a 1.26 earned run average.

For the Naps, Young, then 42, posted a 19–15 record, only the seventh time in 22 seasons he failed to win 20.

But Young wasn't the only problem for Lajoie and his successor McGuire.

It got so bad that the Cleveland newspapers, reacting to early-season losses, sarcastically reported that the Naps "should be known as the Napkins, the way they fold up."

The Naps started poorly, recovered briefly at midseason, then fell into a deep and prolonged slump. They were never in contention as injuries and illnesses to key players struck again. The pitching staff also failed, including Addie Joss who, at 29, was thought to be in the prime of his career.

Shortstop Terry Turner was disabled for 100 games; outfielder Elmer Flick, who'd won the batting championship with a .306 average four years earlier, was unable to play regularly and missed 87 games; third baseman Bill Bradley was sidelined for 58 games; and even the great Lajoie, whose .324 average was third best in the league, had to sit out 31 games because of injuries.

One of the Naps' few highlights of the disappointing season occurred on July 19. Shortstop Neal Ball, who'd been purchased from the New York Yankees to replace the injured Turner, pulled off the first unassisted triple play in major league baseball history.

He did it in the second inning of the first game of a doubleheader against Boston at League Park. With Heinie Wagner on second and Jake Stahl on first, both runners were off on Cy Young's 3-and-2 pitch to Ambrose McConnell, who sent a line drive up the middle. Ball raced to his left and speared the ball, stepped on second doubling Wagner, and tagged Stahl coming from first.

The Naps' team batting average was .241, fifth in the American League, but only Young pitched consistently well (though not to his previous levels). Joss (14–13) and Cy Falkenberg (10–9) barely won more games than they lost, and Bob Rhoads' record fell to 5–9 from 18–12 in 1908.

	W	L	G	GS	CG	IP	H	BB	K	ERA
Harry Ables	1	1	5	3	3	29⅔	26	10	24	2.12
Heinie Berger	13	14	34	29	19	247	221	58	162	2.73
Red Booles	0	1	4	1	0	22⅔	20	8	6	1.99
Walt Doane	0	1	1	1	0	5	10	1	2	5.40
Cy Falkenberg	10	9	24	18	13	165	135	50	82	2.40
Addie Joss	14	13	33	28	24	242⅔	198	31	67	1.71
Glenn Liebhardt	1	5	12	4	1	52⅓	54	16	15	2.92
Willie Mitchell	1	2	3	3	3	23	18	10	8	1.57
Harry Otis	2	2	5	3	0	26⅓	26	18	6	1.37
Bob Rhoads	5	9	20	15	9	133⅓	124	50	46	2.90
Carl Sitton	3	2	14	5	3	50	50	16	16	2.88
Jerry Upp	2	1	7	4	2	26⅔	26	12	13	1.69
Fred Winchell	0	3	4	3	0	14⅓	16	2	7	6.28
Lucky Wright	0	4	5	4	3	28	21	7	5	3.21
Cy Young	19	15	35	34	30	295	267	59	109	2.26
	71	82		155	110	1,361	1,212	348	568	2.40

Shutouts: Berger (4), Joss (4), Young (3), Falkenberg (2), Rhoads (2)
Saves: Berger, Liebhardt, Winchell

	G	AB	R	H	2B	3B	HR	RBI	SB	AVG
Neal Ball (SS)	96	324	29	83	13	2	1	25	17	.256
Harry Bemis	42	123	4	23	2	3	0	13	2	.187
Joe Birmingham (CF)	100	343	29	99	10	5	1	38	12	.289
Bill Bradley (3B)	95	334	30	62	6	3	0	22	8	.186
Josh Clarke	4	12	1	0	0	0	0	0	0	.000
Nig Clarke	55	164	15	45	4	2	0	14	1	.274
Ted Easterly (C)	98	287	32	75	14	10	1	27	8	.261
Elmer Flick	66	235	28	60	10	2	0	15	9	.255
Wilbur Good (RF)	94	318	33	68	6	5	0	17	13	.214
Bob Higgins	8	23	0	2	0	0	0	0	0	.087
Bill Hinchman (LF)	139	457	57	118	20	13	2	53	22	.258
Nap Lajoie (2B)	128	469	56	152	33	7	1	47	13	.324
Grover Land	1	4	0	2	0	0	0	1	0	.500
Bris Lord	69	249	26	67	7	3	1	25	10	.269
Milo Netzel	10	37	2	7	1	0	0	3	1	.189
George Perring	88	283	26	63	10	9	0	20	6	.223
Tom Raftery	8	32	6	7	2	1	0	0	1	.219
Duke Reilley	20	62	10	13	0	0	0	0	5	.210
Dolly Stark	19	60	4	12	0	0	0	1	4	.200
George Stovall (1B)	145	565	60	139	17	10	2	49	25	.246
Denny Sullivan	3	2	0	1	0	0	0	0	0	.500
Terry Turner	53	208	25	52	7	4	0	16	14	.250
		5,048	493	1,216	173	81	10	407	174	.241

1910

Record: 71–81
Finish: Fifth
Games Behind: 32
Manager: James McGuire

The season started with great promise and fanfare, but soon disintegrated in failure as the Naps dropped out of contention in late May, and Jim McGuire's team soon became ridiculed as the "Molly McGuires."

The Naps got off to a good start and even occupied first place through the first week of May, but faltered and swiftly fell into the second division and out of the race.

By early July, with Addie Joss sidelined with a sore arm, Cy Young, at 43, no longer a dominating pitcher, and two aging veterans, third baseman Bill Bradley and outfielder Elmer Flick, also apparently at the end of their careers, a rebuilding program was launched by Charles Somers and Ernest S. Barnard.

Forty-four players spent time on the Naps' roster in 1910, which began with the gala dedication ceremonies for newly renovated League Park. Its wooden grandstand and pavilion were replaced by steel and concrete stands, increasing the capacity by about 9,000 to 21,000.

Young, who had pitched (and beat Cincinnati, 12–3) in the first game at League Park on May 1, 1891, did not fare as well 19 years later. On April 21, 1910, Young and the Naps lost to Detroit, 5–0, as a crowd of 18,832 fans "initiated into service the world's best ball plant," as reported by the *Cleveland Plain Dealer*.

The day before the rededication of League park, on April 20, Joss pitched his second no-hitter, beating the White Sox, 1–0, in Chicago, but was able to win only four more games (losing five) that season.

The Naps were involved in two more no-hitters in 1910. They lost to Philadelphia's Charles "Chief" Bender, 4–0, on May 12.

Then, on August 20, in the second game of a doubleheader, they were held hitless for nine innings by New York's Thomas Hughes. They got two singles in the 10th and five more in the 11th when they scored all their runs in a 5–0 victory credited to rookie George Kahler.

"Shoeless Joe" Jackson was another rookie who joined the Naps in 1910, acquired from the Philadelphia Athletics in a trade for outfielder Bris Lord.

Jackson had played five games for the Athletics in 1908 and five in 1909, but spent most of those seasons and all of 1910 in the minor leagues, until joining the Naps. Though the trade was made on July 25, Jackson didn't report to the Naps until mid-September, and then he batted .387 in 20 games.

Also featured in 1910 was a season-ending controversy involving Napoleon Lajoie and the Tigers' Ty Cobb.

The Chalmers Motor Car Company offered to award a new automobile to the American or National League player with the highest batting average. Lajoie and Cobb battled neck and neck through most of the season for the top spot.

On the final day, prior to the Naps' doubleheader against the St. Louis Browns, Lajoie trailed Cobb by a few percentage points.

According to published accounts of their race, the Browns detested Cobb and tried their best to help Lajoie, who was credited with eight hits in eight times at bat in the Naps' final two games.

Several of Lajoie's hits were bunts to third baseman Roy Hartzell, who played far back on the grass. The intent was so apparent that President Ban Johnson investigated and reportedly fined Hartzell and another unidentified St. Louis player for their actions.

Despite the Browns' efforts, Cobb still managed to win the championship by a margin of .000974—his final average was .3850687 to Lajoie's .3840947. The Chalmers Company resolved the issue by awarding new cars to both players.

Young, sidelined by illness part of the season, wound up with a 7–10 record, and Cy Falkenberg was the Naps' winningest pitcher at 14–13. Bradley, who'd been one of the Naps' most dependable players since becoming a charter member of the team in 1901, slumped to .196 and was released before the season ended.

	W	L	G	GS	CG	IP	H	BB	K	ERA
Heinie Berger	3	4	13	8	2	65⅓	57	32	24	3.03
Fred Blanding	2	2	6	5	4	45⅓	43	12	25	2.78
Ben DeMott	0	3	6	4	1	28⅓	45	8	13	5.40
Walt Doane	0	0	6	0	0	17⅔	31	8	7	5.60
Cy Falkenberg	14	13	37	29	18	256⅔	246	75	107	2.95
Harry Fanwell	2	9	17	11	5	92	87	38	30	3.62
Specs Harkness	10	7	26	16	6	136⅓	132	55	60	3.04
Addie Joss	5	5	13	12	9	107⅓	96	18	49	2.26
George Kahler	6	4	12	12	8	95⅓	80	46	38	1.60
Harry Kirsch	0	0	2	0	0	3	5	1	5	6.00
Elmer Koestner	5	10	27	13	8	145	145	63	44	3.04
Fred Link	5	6	22	13	6	127⅔	121	50	55	3.17
Willie Mitchell	12	8	35	18	11	183⅔	155	55	102	2.60
Cy Young	7	10	21	20	14	163⅓	149	27	58	2.53
	71	81	(161)	92	(1,467)	(1,392)	488	617	2.88

Shutouts: Falkenberg (3), Kahler (2), Blanding, Fanwell, Harkness, Joss, Koestner, Link, Mitchell, Young
Saves: Koestner (2), Falkenberg, Harkness, Link

	G	AB	R	H	2B	3B	HR	RBI	SB	AVG
Bert Adams	5	13	1	3	0	0	0	0	0	.231
Neal Ball	53	119	13	25	3	1	0	12	4	.210
Harry Bemis	61	167	12	36	5	1	1	16	3	.216
Joe Birmingham (CF)	104	367	41	84	11	2	0	35	18	.229
Bill Bradley (3B)	61	214	12	42	3	0	0	12	6	.196
Herman Bronkie	5	9	1	2	0	0	0	0	1	.222
Dave Callahan	13	44	6	8	1	0	0	2	5	.182
Nig Clarke	21	58	4	9	2	0	0	2	0	.155
Pat Donahue	2	6	0	1	0	0	0	0	0	.167
Ted Easterly (C)	110	363	34	111	16	6	0	55	10	.306
Elmer Flick	24	68	5	18	2	1	1	7	1	.265
Jack Graney (RF)	116	454	62	107	13	9	1	31	18	.236
Eddie Hohnhorst	18	63	8	20	3	1	0	6	3	.317
Joe Jackson	20	75	15	29	2	5	1	11	4	.387
Cotton Knaupp	18	59	3	14	3	1	0	11	1	.237
Art Kruger (LF)	62	223	19	38	6	3	0	14	12	.170
Nap Lajoie (2B)	(159)	(591)	94	(227)	(51)	7	4	76	26	(.384)
Grover Land	34	111	4	23	0	0	0	7	1	.207
Bris Lord	58	210	23	46	8	7	0	17	4	.219
Deacon McGuire	1	3	0	1	0	0	0	0	0	.333
Simon Nicholls	3	0	0	0	0	0	0	0	0	—
Harry Niles	70	240	25	51	6	4	1	18	9	.213
Roger Peckinpaugh	15	45	1	9	0	0	0	6	3	.200
George Perring	39	122	14	27	6	3	0	8	3	.221
Morrie Rath	24	67	5	13	3	0	0	0	2	.194
Jim Rutherford	1	2	0	1	0	0	0	0	0	.500
Syd Smith	9	27	1	9	1	0	0	3	0	.333
George Stovall (1B)	142	521	49	136	19	4	0	52	16	.261
Art Thomason	20	70	4	12	0	1	0	2	3	.171
Terry Turner (SS)	150	574	71	132	14	6	0	33	31	.230
	(5,385)	548	1,316	188	64	9	460	189	.244	

1911

Record: 80–73
Finish: Third
Games Behind: 22
Managers: James McGuire, George Stovall

Everything considered, the Naps did well to finish as high as third in 1911.

Addie Joss died two days before the season opened, Cy Young was released after pitching seven games (winning three and losing four), and Napoleon Lajoie missed 63 games.

They also survived a managerial change when James McGuire resigned on May 3 after the Naps lost 11 of their first 17 games, falling into seventh place.

First baseman George Stovall took over for McGuire and not only played well but also proved to be an excellent leader. Under his direction the Naps won 74 and lost 62 for a winning percentage of .544, which was bettered during that period only by the pennant-winning Philadelphia Athletics.

Joss, who won 160 games (losing 97) from 1901 through 1910, including two no-hitters and six one-hitters, seemed destined to become one of the game's greatest pitchers.

In late March, during a spring training exhibition game in Chattanooga, Tennessee, Joss fainted on the bench. He returned to his home in Toledo, Ohio, and his illness was diagnosed as tubercular meningitis. Within a week, on April 14, Joss died at the age of 31.

Young, then 44, was released by the Naps in August. He pitched 11 games for the Boston Braves in the National League the final month of the season (winning four, losing five), then retired to his farm in Tuscarawas County, Ohio.

Of his 511 career victories, 270 were registered for Cleveland teams (the Spiders 1890–98 and the Naps 1909–11), as were 164 of his 316 losses.

Two rookies—outfielder "Shoeless Joe" Jackson and pitcher Vean Gregg—deserve much of the credit, along with Stovall, for the Naps' doing as well as they did.

Jackson hit .408 and also led the team with seven homers and 83 runs batted in, though he lost the batting championship to Detroit's Ty Cobb (.420). Gregg, whom Cobb called "the best left-hander in the league" that season, won 23 games and lost seven.

Cobb and Jackson were two of 23 American League players in 1911 to compile .300 averages, including three more members of the Naps—Lajoie, .365; catcher Ted Easterly, .324; and outfielder Joe Birmingham, .304.

	W	L	G	GS	CG	IP	H	BB	K	ERA
Jim Baskette	1	2	4	2	2	21⅓	21	9	8	3.38
Fred Blanding	7	11	29	16	11	176	190	60	80	3.68
Ben DeMott	0	1	1	1	0	3⅔	10	2	2	12.27
Cy Falkenberg	8	5	15	13	7	106⅔	117	24	46	3.29
Vean Gregg	23	7	34	26	22	244⅔	172	86	125	(1.80)
Specs Harkness	2	2	12	6	3	53⅔	62	21	25	4.22
Bill James	2	4	8	6	4	51⅓	58	32	21	4.88
George Kahler	9	8	30	17	10	154⅓	153	66	97	3.27
Gene Krapp	13	9	35	26	14	222	188	(138)	132	3.41
Willie Mitchell	7	14	30	22	9	177⅓	190	60	78	3.76
Pat Paige	1	0	2	1	1	16	21	7	6	4.50
Bugs Reisigl	0	1	2	1	1	13	13	3	6	6.23
Josh Swindell	0	1	4	1	1	17⅓	19	4	6	2.08
Hi West	3	4	13	8	3	64⅔	84	18	17	3.76
Earl Yingling	1	0	4	3	1	22⅓	30	9	6	4.43
Cy Young	3	4	7	7	4	46⅓	54	13	20	3.88
	80	73	(156)	93	(1,390⅔)	1,382	(552)	675	3.36	

Shutouts: Gregg (5), Krapp
Saves: Blanding (2), Falkenberg, Kahler, Krapp, West

	G	AB	R	H	2B	3B	HR	RBI	SB	AVG
Bert Adams	2	5	0	1	0	0	0	0	0	.200
Neal Ball (2B)	116	412	45	122	14	9	3	45	21	.296
Joe Birmingham (CF)	125	447	55	136	18	5	2	51	16	.304
Herman Bronkie	2	6	0	1	0	0	0	0	0	.167
Hank Butcher	38	133	21	32	7	3	1	11	9	.241
Dave Callahan	6	16	1	4	0	1	0	0	0	.250
Ted Easterly	99	287	34	93	19	5	1	37	6	.324
Gus Fisher (C)	70	203	20	53	6	3	0	12	6	.261
Jack Graney (LF)	146	527	84	142	25	5	1	45	21	.269
Art Griggs	27	68	7	17	3	2	1	7	1	.250
Tim Hendryx	4	7	0	2	0	0	0	0	0	.286
Joe Jackson (RF)	147	571	126	233	45	19	7	83	41	.408
Cotton Knaupp	13	39	2	4	1	0	0	0	3	.103
Nap Lajoie	90	315	36	115	20	1	2	60	13	.365
Grover Land	35	107	5	15	1	2	0	10	2	.140
Bill Lindsay	19	66	6	16	2	0	0	5	2	.242
Jack Mills	13	17	5	5	0	0	0	1	1	.294
Ivy Olson (SS)	140	545	89	142	20	8	1	50	20	.261
Steve O'Neill	9	27	1	4	1	0	0	1	2	.148
Syd Smith	58	154	8	46	8	1	1	21	0	.299
George Stovall (1B)	126	458	48	124	17	7	0	79	11	.271
Terry Turner (3B)	117	417	59	105	16	9	0	28	29	.252
	(5,321)	691	1,501	(238)	81	20	579	209	.282	

1912

Record: 75–78
Finish: Fifth
Games Behind: 30½
Managers: Harry Davis, Joe Birmingham

Another managerial change by Naps president Charles Somers marked the 1912 season. But it did nothing to help the team—especially the morale of the players—as the Naps fell two places in the standings with the franchise's fifth sub-.500 record in 12 seasons.

Prior to his promotion of George Stovall to replace the

resigned James McGuire in 1911, Somers had made a secret deal with Philadelphia Athletics owner Connie Mack. It was to hire Harry Davis, the Athletics' veteran first baseman, to manage the Naps in 1912.

Somers signed Davis on October 27, 1911, and traded Stovall to the St. Louis Browns for pitcher Thomas "Lefty" George on February 17, 1912.

The Naps players, who had great respect and admiration for Stovall, howled in protest when the trade was announced, but to no immediate avail.

Matters got worse when Davis assumed command and implemented a series of strict rules, among them the banning of handshakes and conversations with opposing players before and during games.

Consequently, the demoralized Naps started poorly again, part of the problem being another injury to Napoleon Lajoie, this one a sprained back that occurred on May 3, causing him to miss 37 games. Outfielder Jack Graney also was sidelined for half the season.

Finally, with the Naps mired in sixth place with a 54–71 record, Davis resigned as manager on September 2.

He was replaced by outfielder Joe Birmingham who made several roster and lineup changes, and the Naps responded by winning 21 of their final 28 games. It was too late, however, to get back in the race, though they climbed one notch in the standings to finish fifth.

"Shoeless Joe" Jackson, who played every game for the Naps, again led them at the plate, hitting .395, but again was beaten out for the batting championship by Detroit's Ty Cobb, who won the title with a .409 average.

Lajoie, in 117 games, equaled Jackson's RBI total of 90 while batting .368, and Ray Chapman, called up from the minors late in the season to play shortstop, broke in with a .312 mark in 31 games. Fred Blanding, fresh out of the University of Michigan, and Vean Gregg were the Naps' only consistent winners on the mound. Gregg was 20–13 and Blanding 18–14.

And Lefty George, the pitcher the Naps received from St. Louis in the trade for Stovall, went 0–5 with a 4.87 ERA in his only season in Cleveland.

	G	AB	R	H	2B	3B	HR	RBI	SB	AVG
Bert Adams	20	54	5	11	2	1	0	6	0	.204
Howard Baker	11	30	1	5	0	0	0	2	0	.167
Neal Ball	40	132	12	30	4	1	0	14	7	.227
Joe Birmingham (CF)	107	369	49	94	19	3	1	45	15	.255
Herman Bronkie	6	16	1	0	0	0	0	0	0	.000
Hank Butcher	26	82	9	16	4	1	1	10	1	.195
Fred Carisch	24	69	4	19	3	1	0	5	3	.275
Ray Chapman	31	109	29	34	6	3	0	19	10	.312
Harry Davis	2	5	0	0	0	0	0	0	0	.000
Ted Easterly	65	186	17	55	4	0	2	21	3	.296
Hack Eibel	1	3	0	0	0	0	0	0	0	.000
Jack Graney	78	264	44	64	13	2	0	20	9	.242
Art Griggs (1B)	89	273	29	83	16	7	0	39	10	.304
Harvey Grubb	1	0	0	0	0	0	0	0	0	—
Art Hauger	15	18	0	1	0	0	0	0	0	.056
Tim Hendryx	23	70	9	17	2	4	1	14	3	.243
Eddie Hohnhorst	15	54	5	11	1	0	0	2	5	.204
Bill Hunter	21	55	6	9	2	0	0	2	0	.164
Joe Jackson (RF)	154	572	121	(226)	44	(26)	3	90	35	.395
Doc Johnston	43	164	22	46	7	4	1	11	8	.280
Jack Kibble	5	8	1	0	0	0	0	0	0	.000
Nap Lajoie (2B)	117	448	66	165	34	4	0	90	18	.368
Paddy Livingston	20	47	5	11	2	1	0	3	0	.234
Moxie Meixell	3	2	0	1	0	0	0	0	0	.500
Lou Nagelsen	2	3	0	0	0	0	0	0	0	.000
Ken Nash*	11	23	2	4	0	0	0	0	0	.174
Ivy Olson	125	467	68	118	13	1	0	33	16	.253
Steve O'Neill (C)	69	215	17	49	4	0	0	14	2	.228
Roger Peckinpaugh (SS)	70	236	18	50	4	1	1	22	11	.212
Bud Ryan (LF)	93	328	53	89	12	9	1	31	12	.271
Terry Turner (3B)	103	370	54	114	14	4	0	33	19	.308
	5,133	677	1,403	219	77	12	561	194	.273

*Played one game under name of Costello

	W	L	G	GS	CG	IP	H	BB	K	ERA
Jim Baskette	8	4	29	11	7	116	109	46	51	3.18
Fred Blanding	18	14	39	31	23	262	259	79	75	2.92
Bert Brenner	1	0	2	1	1	13	14	4	3	2.77
Lefty George	0	5	11	5	2	44⅓	69	18	18	4.87
Vean Gregg	20	13	37	34	26	271⅓	242	90	184	2.59
Bill James	0	0	3	0	0	13⅔	15	9	5	4.61
Lefty James	0	1	3	1	0	6	8	4	2	7.50
George Kahler	12	19	41	32	17	246⅓	263	(121)	104	3.69
Gene Krapp	2	5	9	7	4	58⅔	57	42	22	4.60
Harry Krause	0	1	2	2	0	4⅔	11	2	1	11.57
Willie Mitchell	5	8	29	15	8	163⅔	149	56	94	2.80
Jim Neher	0	0	1	0	0	1	0	0	0	0.00
Bill Steen	9	8	26	16	6	143⅓	163	45	61	3.77
Mysterious Walker	0	0	1	0	0	1	0	1	0	0.00
Roy Walker	0	0	1	0	0	2	0	2	1	0.00
Ernie Wolf	0	0	1	0	0	5⅔	8	4	1	6.35
	75	78		155	94	1,352⅔	1,367	523	622	3:30

Shutouts: Kahler (3), Baskette, Blanding, Gregg, Steen
Saves: Gregg (2), Baskette, Blanding, Lefty James, Kahler, Mitchell

1913

Record: 86–66
Finish: Third
Games Behind: 9½
Manager: Joe Birmingham

Charles Somers was determined not to make the same mistake in 1913 that he'd made a year earlier and retained the 28-year-old Joe Birmingham as manager, much to the displeasure of Napoleon Lajoie.

Birmingham and Lajoie did not get along and openly clashed several times. One confrontation was particularly severe, when Lajoie, in the throes of a batting slump in mid-June, was benched by Birmingham. Lajoie responded by cursing Birmingham to his face, and in the newspapers.

Despite the animosity between the two men, the Naps played well from the start of the season until the final month. Though they never were able to climb into the lead, they clung to second place through August, when they embarked upon what turned out to be a disastrous trip to Washington, Philadelphia, New York, and Boston.

Much of the trouble was their own making, especially by their two winningest pitchers, Cy Falkenberg (23–10), who earlier had won 10 straight games, and Vean Gregg (20–13). The two men engaged in a friendly wrestling match on the train en route to Washington and fell, both suffering injuries to their pitching arms.

Gregg tried to pitch but was beaten in the first and third games of the series against the Senators, Fred Blanding was knocked out of the box in the second game, and Bill Steen and Blanding lost the next two for five consecutive defeats for the Naps.

Joe Jackson (left), then a member of the Cleveland Naps, in a 1913 photo with Ty Cobb (center) and Napoleon Lajoie.

Falkenberg, who had been sent back to Cleveland for treatment on his arm, rejoined the team for its next series in Philadelphia and won the first game. But the Naps lost the next two and were out of the race, which the Athletics ultimately won.

The Naps, who played well through the first half of the season, also were thwarted by injuries to Birmingham, who played the outfield until he was sidelined with a broken leg in late May, catcher Grover Land, shortstop Ray Chapman, Lajoie, and Steen, who suffered a broken wrist in spring training and couldn't pitch until late in the season.

An otherwise-obscure record was set by the Naps on June 11 when two of their players, third baseman Ivy Olson and left fielder Jack Graney, successively stole home in the 15th inning of a game in Boston.

Olson's broke a tie, and Graney's provided the Naps an insurance run. It was the first time in the major leagues that teammates had stolen home in extra innings of the same game.

The 1913 season also was notable in that the Federal League, organized on March 8, placed a team in Cleveland. Others were located in Chicago, Pittsburgh, Indianapolis, St. Louis, and Covington, Kentucky (transferred in late June to Kansas City).

The president of the Cleveland franchise was a local businessman named M. F. Bramley, who owned a chain of motordromes and amusement parks, including Luna Park, where the team played its home games. Bramley induced Cy Young to leave his farm in Tuscarawas County in southern Ohio and return to the game as manager of the Cleveland club.

In its only season in the Federal League in 1913, Cleveland finished second with a 63–54 record, 10½ games behind Indianapolis. Though the Cleveland franchise ceased operations after that first season, the league continued for two more years before it folded.

"Shoeless Joe" Jackson made one of the longest hits ever seen in the Polo Grounds in New York on June 4 when he batted a ball over the right-field wing of the grandstand. Jackson compiled a .373 average, but for the second year in a row was beaten out by Detroit's Ty Cobb (.390), who won his seventh consecutive batting championship.

Lajoie, despite his injury and ongoing problems with Birmingham, hit .335 in what would be his last productive season with the Naps.

	W	L	G	GS	CG	IP	H	BB	K	ERA
Jim Baskette	0	0	2	1	0	4⅔	8	2	0	5.79
Fred Blanding	15	10	41	22	14	215	234	72	63	2.55
Lynn Brenton	0	0	1	0	0	2	4	0	2	9.00
Nick Cullop	3	7	23	8	4	97⅔	105	35	30	4.42
Lee Dashner	0	0	1	0	0	1⅔	0	0	2	5.40
Cy Falkenberg	23	10	39	36	23	276	238	88	166	2.22
Luke Glavenich	0	0	1	0	0	1	3	3	1	9.00
Dave Gregg	0	0	1	0	0	1	2	0	0	18.00
Vean Gregg	20	13	44	34	23	285⅔	258	(124)	166	2.24
Lefty James	2	2	11	4	3	39	42	9	18	3.00
George Kahler	5	11	24	15	5	117⅔	118	32	43	3.14
Willie Mitchell	14	8	35	22	14	217	153	88	141	1.91
Bill Steen	4	5	22	13	7	128½	113	49	57	2.45
	86	66		(155)	93	1,386⅔	1,278	502	689	2.54

Shutouts: Falkenberg (6), Mitchell(4), Blanding (3), Vean Gregg (3), Steen (2)
Saves: Gregg (3), Steen (2)

	G	AB	R	H	2B	3B	HR	RBI	SB	AVG
Johnny Bassler	1	2	0	0	0	0	0	0	0	.000
Ray Bates	27	30	4	5	0	2	0	4	3	.167
Johnny Beall	6	6	0	1	0	0	0	1	0	.167
Josh Billings	1	3	0	0	0	0	0	0	0	.000
Joe Birmingham	47	131	16	37	9	1	0	15	7	.282
Fred Carisch (C)	82	222	11	48	4	2	0	26	6	.216
Ray Chapman (SS)	141	508	78	131	19	7	3	39	29	.258
George Dunlop	7	17	3	4	1	0	0	0	0	.235
Eddie Edmonson	2	5	0	0	0	0	0	0	0	.000
Jack Graney (LF)	148	517	56	138	18	12	3	68	27	.267
Joe Jackson (RF)	148	528	109	(197)	(39)	17	7	71	26	.373
Doc Johnston (1B)	133	530	74	135	19	12	2	39	19	.255
Larry Kopf*	6	10	2	3	1	0	0	1	0	.300
Ernie Krueger	5	6	0	0	0	0	0	0	0	.000
Nap Lajoie (2B)	137	465	66	156	25	2	1	68	17	.335
Grover Land	17	47	3	11	1	0	0	9	1	.234
Nemo Leibold (CF)	93	286	37	74	11	6	0	12	16	.259
Jack Lelivelt	23	23	0	9	2	0	0	7	1	.391
Ivy Olson (3B)	104	370	47	92	13	3	0	32	7	.249
Steve O'Neill	80	234	19	69	13	3	0	29	5	.295
Roger Peckinpaugh	1	0	1	0	0	0	0	0	0	—
Bud Ryan	73	243	26	72	6	1	0	32	9	.296
Billy Southworth	1	0	0	0	0	0	0	0	0	—
Josh Swindell	1	0	0	0	0	0	0	0	0	—
Terry Turner	120	388	60	96	13	4	0	44	13	.247
George Young	2	2	0	0	0	0	0	0	0	.000
		5,031	633	1,349	206	74	16	527	191	.268

*Played under name of Fred Brady

1914

Record: 51–102
Finish: Eighth (last)
Games Behind: 48½
Manager: Joe Birmingham

The Napoleon Lajoie era in Cleveland came to an end in 1914 when the team that was nicknamed Naps in his honor plummeted to the basement of the American League with the franchise's first 100-loss season. They languished in last place from beginning to end, with the exception of two days, June 30 and July 1.

One of the Naps' 102 defeats occurred on July 11 when a rookie for the Boston Red Sox, pitching his first major league game, beat them, 4–3.

His name was Babe Ruth.

It also was in 1914 that Naps owner Charles Somers first ran into financial trouble in his business affairs, and, to complicate his situation, attendance at Naps' games declined to 185,997, lowest since 1901, the first year of the American League.

Some of Somers' problems were attributable to his decision to place a second professional baseball team in Cleveland. He transferred the minor league, Toledo, Ohio, franchise, which he owned in the American Association, to Cleveland.

He did it to keep the newly organized Federal League from operating a club in Cleveland, and he often shifted players between the minor league team and the Naps.

But the shuttle system benefited neither team, and, in addition to the Naps finishing in last place, Somers' minor league club wound up fifth in the American Association. (It continued to operate in Cleveland in 1915, and was moved back to Toledo for the 1916 season.)

Lajoie, who was regularly at odds with manager Joe Birmingham, slumped to .258 and, at his request, was returned to the Philadelphia Athletics for the waiver price.

Before Lajoie left Cleveland, he became the third player in major league history to make 3,000 hits. He reached that prestigious plateau on September 27 with a double against Marty McHale of the New York Yankees in the first game of a doubleheader won by the Naps, 5–3.

(There is some debate, however, as to the actual date of Lajoie's 3,000th hit. One historian has claimed that Lajoie was not credited with nine hits in 1901, his first season with the Athletics. In that case Lajoie's 3,000th hit was made on September 17 in a game against Boston's Rube Foster.)

It was bad enough that the Naps' record was so poor that they finished 48½ games behind pennant-winning Philadelphia. But they also trailed seventh-place New York by 18½ lengths, and on May 31 they were the victims of a no-hitter by Joe Benz in a 6–1 loss to Chicago.

"Shoeless Joe" Jackson hit .338 and was fourth in the American League batting race (as Detroit's Ty Cobb won his eighth consecutive championship with a .368 average), but no other Cleveland regular reached .300.

The loss of Cy Falkenberg to the Federal League and the ineffectiveness of Vean Gregg (9–3) also were key factors in the Naps' decline, as Willie Mitchell (12–17) was their only pitcher to win in double figures.

	W	L	G	GS	CG	IP	H	BB	K	ERA
George Beck	0	0	1	0	0	1	1	0	0	0.00
Henry Benn	0	0	1	0	0	1	0	0	1	0.00
Lloyd Bishop	0	1	3	1	0	8	14	3	1	5.63
Fred Blanding	3	9	29	12	5	116	133	54	35	3.96
Abe Bowman	2	7	22	10	2	72⅔	74	45	27	4.46
Paul Carter	1	3	5	4	1	24⅔	35	5	9	2.92
Allan Collamore	3	7	27	8	3	105⅓	100	49	32	3.25
Fritz Coumbe	1	5	14	5	2	55⅓	59	16	22	3.25
Nick Cullop	0	1	1	0	0	3⅓	4	1	3	2.70
Harley Dillinger	0	1	11	2	1	33⅔	41	25	11	4.54
Vean Gregg	9	3	17	12	6	96⅔	88	48	56	3.07
Rip Hagerman	9	15	37	26	12	198	189	118	112	3.09
Lefty James	0	3	17	6	1	50⅔	44	32	16	3.20
Sad Sam Jones	0	0	1	0	0	3⅓	2	2	0	2.70
George Kahler	0	1	2	1	1	14	17	7	3	3.86
Willie Mitchell	12	17	39	32	16	257	228	124	179	3.19
Guy Morton	1	13	25	13	5	128	116	55	80	3.02
Bill Steen	9	14	30	22	13	200⅔	201	68	97	2.60
Al Tedrow	1	2	4	3	1	22⅓	19	14	4	1.21
	51	(102)		157	69	1,391	(1,365)	(666)	688	3.21

Shutouts: Hagerman (3), Mitchell (3), Bowman, Gregg, Steen
Saves: Blanding, Mitchell, Morton

	G	AB	R	H	2B	3B	HR	RBI	SB	AVG
Walter Barbare	15	52	6	16	2	2	0	5	1	.308
Johnny Bassler	43	77	5	14	1	1	0	6	3	.182
Josh Billings	11	8	2	2	1	0	0	0	1	.250
Joe Birmingham	19	47	2	6	0	0	0	4	0	.128
Rivington Bisland	18	57	9	6	1	0	0	2	2	.105
Fred Carisch	40	102	8	22	3	2	0	5	2	.216
Ray Chapman (SS)	106	375	59	103	16	10	2	42	24	.275
Al Cypert	1	1	0	0	0	0	0	0	0	.000
George Dunlop	1	3	0	0	0	0	0	0	0	.000
Ben Egan	29	88	7	20	2	1	0	11	0	.227
Tinsley Ginn	2	1	0	0	0	0	0	0	0	.000
Jack Graney (LF)	130	460	63	122	17	10	1	39	20	.265
Bruce Hartford	8	22	5	4	1	0	0	0	0	.182
Joe Jackson (RF)	122	453	61	153	22	13	3	53	22	.338
Doc Johnston (1B)	103	340	43	83	15	1	0	23	14	.244
Jay Kirke	67	242	18	66	10	2	1	25	5	.273
Nap Lajoie (2B)	121	419	37	108	14	3	0	50	14	.258
Nemo Leibold (CF)	115	402	46	106	13	3	0	32	12	.264
Jack Lelivelt	34	64	6	21	5	1	0	13	2	.328
Frank Mills	4	8	0	1	0	0	0	0	0	.125
Ivy Olson	89	310	22	75	6	2	1	20	15	.242
Steve O'Neill (C)	87	269	28	68	12	2	0	20	1	.253
Larry Pezold	23	71	4	16	0	1	0	5	2	.225
Tom Reilly	1	1	0	0	0	0	0	0	0	.000
Elmer Smith	13	53	5	17	3	0	0	8	1	.321
Terry Turner (3B)	121	428	43	105	14	9	1	33	17	.245
Bill Wambsganss	43	143	12	31	6	2	0	12	2	.217
Roy Wood	72	220	24	52	6	3	1	15	6	.236
		(5,157)	538	1,262	178	70	10	438	167	.245

1915

Record: 57–95
Finish: Seventh
Games Behind: 44½
Managers: Joe Birmingham, Lee Fohl

With Napoleon Lajoie no longer on the team its nickname had to be changed again.

President Charles Somers invited Cleveland baseball writers to pick a new name and they chose "Indians," reportedly in honor of a Penobscot Indian named Louis Sockalexis. He was the first great player to perform in Cleveland, and was believed to be the first native Indian to play major league baseball.

Sockalexis was an outfielder for the Spiders in the National League from 1897 to 1899, batting .313 in two and a half seasons before he drank himself out of baseball.

The name "Indians," however, was not necessarily permanent, according to the January 16, 1915, edition of the *Cleveland Plain Dealer*, which reported:

"The nickname is but temporarily bestowed, as the club may so conduct itself during the present season as to earn some other cognomen which may be more appropriate. The choice of a name that would be significant just now was rather difficult with the club itself anchored in last place."

Despite its new name, the team's fortunes remained virtually the same. That is, the 1915 season was another bad one for the Cleveland club, which finished in seventh place. Manager Joe Birmingham lost his job after only 28 games with the team's record 12–16.

Somers said he fired Birmingham "because I felt the Cleveland fans demanded a change." Named as Birmingham's successor was Lee Fohl, an ex-catcher who had joined the team as a coach the previous season.

But again, the change—this time in managers—had no great effect on the team.

While the Indians were having more than their share of trouble on the field—they were on the losing end of five one-hitters and compiled the league's third-lowest team batting average (.240)—Somers' financial problems were worsening.

Not only had his coal business fallen off, but he also lost money in several real estate ventures. As a result of these losses, combined with the Indians' failing attendance—they played before only 159,285 fans in 1915—Somers found himself nearly $2 million in debt.

A committee of bankers was appointed to take over the management and direction of Somers' financial affairs, and by season's end it was clear that he would have to sell the Indians or face financial ruin.

But first, with the Indians falling deeply into the second division by midseason, Somers sent the team's best hitter, "Shoeless Joe" Jackson, to the Chicago White Sox for three players and, most importantly, $31,500.

The deal was made on August 21. The Indians received outfielders Bobby "Braggo" Roth and Larry Chappell and pitcher Ed Klepfer.

Jackson, who was hitting .327 in 83 games with the Indians, went on to bat .265 in 46 games in Chicago and finished with a .308 average, the lowest of his career until then.

The following winter, on February 21, 1916, with the help of American League president Byron "Ban" Johnson, Somers sold the Cleveland franchise to a syndicate headed by James C. "Sunny Jim" Dunn.

Dunn was a retired railroad contractor who also was a close friend of Johnson and whose offices had been in Chicago across the street from the AL's headquarters.

With the departure of Jackson, the only member of the Indians to bat .300 was part time outfielder–first baseman Jay Kirke, who compiled a .310 average in 87 games, though Roth hit .299 in 39 games after coming to Cleveland from Chicago.

Even less impressive were the Indians' pitching records. Only Guy Morton (16–15) and Willie Mitchell (11–14) won in double figures, and only one other pitcher, Rip Hagerman, won as many as six games.

	W	L	G	GS	CG	IP	H	BB	K	ERA
Abe Bowman	0	1	2	1	0	1⅓	1	3	0	20.25
Lynn Brenton	2	3	11	5	1	51	60	20	18	3.35
Paul Carter	1	1	11	2	2	42	44	18	14	3.21
Allan Collamore	2	5	11	6	5	64⅓	52	22	15	2.38
Fritz Coumbe	4	7	30	12	4	114	123	37	37	3.47
Clarence Garrett	2	2	4	4	2	23½	19	6	5	2.31
Rip Hagerman	6	14	29	22	7	151	156	77	69	3.52
Oscar Harstad	3	5	32	7	4	82	81	35	35	3.40
Herbert Hill	0	0	1	0	0	2	1	2	0	0.00
Sad Sam Jones	4	9	48	9	2	145⅔	131	63	42	3.65
Ed Klepfer	1	6	8	7	2	43	47	11	13	2.09
Willie Mitchell	11	14	36	30	12	236	210	84	149	2.82
Guy Morton	16	15	34	27	15	240	189	60	134	2.14
Bill Steen	1	4	10	7	2	45⅓	51	15	22	4.96
Roy Walker	4	9	25	15	4	131	122	65	57	3.98
	57	95		154	62	1,372	1,287	518	610	3.13

Shutouts: Morton (6), Collamore (2), Brenton, Coumbe, Mitchell
Saves: Jones (4), Coumbe (2), Harstad, Mitchell, Morton, Walker

	G	AB	R	H	2B	3B	HR	RBI	SB	AVG
Walter Barbare (3B)	77	246	15	47	3	1	0	11	6	.191
Josh Billings	8	21	2	4	1	0	0	0	1	.190
Ray Chapman (SS)	154	570	101	154	14	17	3	67	36	.270
Ben Egan	42	120	4	13	3	0	0	6	0	.108
Jim Eschen	15	42	11	10	1	0	0	2	0	.238
Joe Evans	42	109	17	28	4	2	0	11	6	.257
Lee Gooch	2	2	0	1	0	0	0	0	0	.500
Jack Graney (LF)	116	404	42	105	20	7	1	56	12	.260
Jack Hammond	35	84	9	18	2	1	0	4	0	.214
Howie Haworth	7	7	0	1	0	0	0	1	0	.143
Tex Hoffman	9	13	1	2	0	0	0	2	0	.154
Joe Jackson	83	303	42	99	16	9	3	45	10	.327
Jay Kirke (1B)	87	339	35	105	19	2	2	40	5	.310
Nemo Leibold (CF)	57	207	28	53	5	4	0	4	5	.256
Steve O'Neill (C)	121	386	32	91	14	2	2	34	2	.236
Ben Paschal	9	9	0	1	0	0	0	0	0	.111
Bill Rodgers	16	45	8	14	2	0	0	7	3	.311
Braggo Roth	39	144	23	43	4	7	(4)*	20	14	.299
Pete Shields	23	72	4	15	6	0	0	6	3	.208
Elmer Smith (RF)	144	476	37	118	23	12	3	67	10	.248
Billy Southworth	60	177	25	39	2	5	0	8	2	.220
Terry Turner	75	262	35	66	14	1	0	14	12	.252
Bill Wambsganss (2B)	121	375	30	73	4	4	0	21	8	.195
Denney Wilie	45	131	14	33	4	1	2	10	2	.252
Roy Wood	33	78	5	15	2	1	0	3	1	.192
		5,034	539	1,210	169	79	20	456	138	.240

*League leader in home runs with 7 (3 with Chicago)

1916

Record: 77–77
Finish: Sixth
Games Behind: 14
Manager: Lee Fohl

James C. "Sunny Jim" Dunn took over as the Indians president after a syndicate he headed purchased the franchise from Charles W. Somers on February 21, 1916. One of the first things the new owners did was change the name of League Park to "Dunn Field."

More important, however, was the arrival in Cleveland of Tris "The Gray Eagle" Speaker.

Speaker had been the regular center fielder for the Boston Red Sox for seven seasons, hitting .300 in each of them, including .383 in 1912, and led them to the pennant and world's championship in 1915.

Despite Speaker's contributions to the success of the Red Sox, owner Joseph Lannin wanted to cut Speaker's salary from the $11,000 he was paid in 1915 to $9,000. Speaker, on the other hand, demanded a contract calling for $15,000 and, though unsigned, eventually reported for spring training at Hot Springs, Arkansas.

But Lannin held firm, and the dispute raged on.

Finally on April 8, four days before the season opener, Lannin agreed to trade Speaker to the Indians for pitcher Sad Sam Jones, rookie infielder Fred Thomas, and $55,000.

Before he would agree to report to Cleveland, however, Speaker insisted upon being paid $10,000 out of the $55,000 the Red Sox were to receive from Dunn. His demand created another impasse—but only temporarily, until AL president Byron "Ban" Johnson interceded and convinced Lannin it would be the right thing to do.

And so Tris Speaker, the one-time semipro pitcher from Hubbard, Texas, became a member of the Indians.

It was the biggest deal in baseball up to that time, and represented an impressive beginning for the "Sunny Jim Era" in Cleveland.

Though Speaker went on to capture the American League batting championship, hitting .386 to dethrone Ty Cobb, who'd won the title nine consecutive seasons, the fortunes of the Indians did not improve by much.

They were respectable through the first half of the season, even leading the league from June 1 to 27, chiefly because of Speaker's hitting and field leadership.

But they faltered in July and had fallen out of the race by August 26 when they lost a no-hitter to Philadelphia's "Bullet Joe" Bush, 5–0. Only a first inning walk to Jack Graney prevented it from being a perfect game.

Injuries to shortstop Ray Chapman and pitchers Guy Morton and Ed Klepfer damaged the Indians' chances. While their won-lost record improved to .500, they were able to climb only one place in the standings, to sixth, as Boston, even without Speaker, won the pennant again.

Other than Speaker, the Indians' only consistent batters were right fielder Bobby "Braggo" Roth, who hit .286, and Terry Turner, .262, who played third and second bases.

An obscure Indians utility player named Marty Kavanagh, who also doubled as a coach on the bases, claimed a share of fame in 1916. He delivered the first major league pinch-hit grand slam home run in the fifth inning of what became a 5–3 victory over Boston on September 24 at Dunn Field.

Two rookie pitchers, Jim Bagby and Stan Coveleski, were the hardest workers and biggest winners as Morton and Klepfer were limited because of injuries. Bagby pitched 272⅔ innings with a record of 16–16, and Coveleski was 15–13 in 232 innings.

	W	L	G	GS	CG	IP	H	BB	K	ERA
Jim Bagby	16	16	48	27	14	272⅔	253	67	88	2.61
Fred Beebe	5	3	20	12	5	100⅔	92	37	32	2.41
Joe Boehling	2	4	12	9	3	60⅔	63	23	18	2.67
Fritz Coumbe	7	5	29	13	7	120⅓	121	27	39	2.02
Stan Coveleski	15	13	45	27	11	232	247	58	76	3.41
Paul DesJardien	0	0	1	0	0	1	1	1	0	18.00
Al Gould	5	7	30	9	6	106⅔	101	40	41	2.53
Red Gunkel	0	0	1	0	0	1	0	1	1	0.00
Rip Hagerman	0	0	2	0	0	3⅔	5	2	1	12.27
Ed Klepfer	6	6	31	13	4	143	136	46	62	2.52
Otis Lambeth	4	3	15	9	3	74	69	38	28	2.92
Grover Lowdermilk	1	5	10	9	2	51⅓	52	45	28	3.16
Marty McHale	0	0	5	0	0	11⅓	10	6	2	5.56
Willie Mitchell	2	5	12	6	1	43¾	55	19	24	5.15
Guy Morton	12	8	27	18	9	149⅔	139	42	88	2.89
Ken Penner	1	0	4	2	0	12⅔	14	4	5	4.26
Pop Boy Smith	1	2	5	3	0	25⅔	25	11	4	3.86
	77	77		157	65	1,410	(1,383)	467	537	2.90

Shutouts: Bagby (3), Coumbe (2), Beebe, Coveleski, Gould, Klepfer
Saves: Bagby (5), Coveleski (3), Beebe (2), Klepfer (2), Gould, Lambeth, Mitchell, Smith

	G	AB	R	H	2B	3B	HR	RBI	SB	AVG
Milo Allison	14	18	10	5	0	0	0	0	0	.278
Walter Barbare	13	48	3	11	1	0	0	3	0	.229
Al Bergman	8	14	2	3	0	1	0	0	0	.214
Josh Billings	22	31	2	5	0	0	0	1	0	.161
Jack Bradley	2	3	0	0	0	0	0	0	0	.000
Ray Chapman	109	346	50	80	10	5	0	27	21	.231
Larry Chappell	3	2	0	0	0	0	0	0	1	.000
Bob Coleman	19	28	3	6	2	0	0	4	0	.214
Tom Daly	31	73	3	16	1	1	0	8	0	.219
Hank DeBerry	15	33	7	9	4	0	0	4	0	.273
Clyde Engle	11	26	1	4	0	0	0	1	0	.154
Joe Evans	33	82	4	12	1	0	0	1	4	.146
Chick Gandil (1B)	146	533	51	138	26	9	0	72	13	.259
Jack Graney (LF)	155	589	106	142	(41)	14	5	54	10	.241
Lou Guisto	6	19	2	3	0	0	0	2	1	.158
Ivon Howard (2B)	81	246	20	46	11	5	0	23	9	.187
Marty Kavanagh	19	44	4	11	2	1	1	10	0	.250
Joe Leonard	3	2	1	0	0	0	0	0	0	.000
Howard Lohr	3	7	0	1	0	0	0	1	1	.143
Danny Moeller	25	30	5	2	0	0	0	1	2	.067
Steve O'Neill (C)	130	378	30	89	23	0	0	29	2	.235
Braggo Roth (RF)	125	409	50	117	19	7	4	72	29	.286
Elmer Smith	79	213	25	59	15	3	3	40	3	.277
Tris Speaker (CF)	151	546	102	(211)	(41)	8	2	79	35	(.386)
Terry Turner (3B)	124	428	52	112	15	3	0	38	15	.262
Bill Wambsganss (SS)	136	475	57	117	14	4	0	45	13	.246
Ollie Welf	1	0	0	0	0	0	0	0	0	—
		5,064	630	1,264	(233)	66	16	533	160	.250

1917

Record: 88–66
Finish: Third
Games Behind: 12
Manager: Lee Fohl

The Indians were one of three American League teams— along with Boston and Philadelphia—hardest hit by the military draft as the United States entered World War I a few days prior to the opening of the 1917 season.

Nine Tribe players were called into service with the army at one time or another during the season—pitchers Guy Morton, Ed Klepfer, George Dickerson, and Red Torkelson, catcher Hank DeBerry, infielders Lou Guisto, Joe Harris, and Joe Evans, and outfielder Elmer Smith.

Those who weren't drafted were ordered by the American and National league presidents to undergo daily military training. Drill instructors were assigned to each team, and bats were used instead of rifles.

Then, near the end of the season, army officers inspected the players during their drills, and prizes were awarded to the most efficient.

The Indians finished third in that competition, behind the winning St. Louis Browns and Washington Senators.

On the playing field, with Tris Speaker having another good year and Ray Chapman blossoming into an offensive threat (as well as a slick-fielding shortstop), the Indians were in the thick of a five-team pennant race through most of the season.

Involved were Chicago, Boston, Detroit, and New York, in addition to the Indians. By August the field was narrowed to Chicago and Boston, which finished in that order, as the third-place Indians trailed the Red Sox by three games and led the Tigers by 9½ lengths.

One of the Indians' 66 losses in 1917 was a forfeiture to the White Sox in a game in Chicago on September 9. The two teams were locked in a 3–3 tie in the 10th inning when Indians catcher Steve O'Neill became angered by several decisions by umpire Clarence "Brick" Owens. After catching the last pitch of the 10th inning, O'Neill angrily heaved the ball into left field, whereupon Owens declared the game forfeited to the White Sox.

Jim Bagby (23–13) again was the Indians winningest pitcher, and three others hurled one-hitters in 1917—Al Gould against Philadelphia on May 20, Morton against Boston on June 1 (before he was called to active duty with the army), and Stan Coveleski against New York on September 19.

The only hit off Morton was a single to right field in the eighth inning by the opposing pitcher, Babe Ruth.

Speaker hit .352 and wound up third in the race for the AL batting championship, regained by Detroit's Ty Cobb (.383), with St Louis's George Sisler (.353) second.

	W	L	G	GS	CG	IP	H	BB	K	ERA
Jim Bagby	23	13	49	37	26	320⅔	(277)	73	83	1.96
Joe Boehling	1	6	12	7	1	46⅓	50	16	11	4.66
Fritz Coumbe	8	6	34	10	4	134⅓	119	35	30	2.14
Stan Coveleski	19	14	45	36	24	298⅓	202	94	133	1.81
George Dickerson	0	0	1	0	0	1	0	0	0	0.00
Al Gould	4	4	27	7	1	94	95	52	24	3.64
Ed Klepfer	14	4	41	27	9	213	208	55	66	2.37
Otis Lambeth	7	6	26	10	2	97⅓	97	30	27	3.14
Guy Morton	10	10	35	18	6	161	158	59	62	2.74
Pop Boy Smith	0	1	6	0	0	8⅔	14	4	3	8.31
Red Torkelson	2	1	4	3	0	22⅓	33	13	10	7.66
Smoky Joe Wood	0	1	5	1	0	15⅔	17	7	2	3.45
	88	66		156	73	1,412⅔	1,270	438	451	2.52

Shutouts: Coveleski (9), Bagby (8), Coumbe, Morton
Saves: Bagby (7), Coumbe (5), Coveleski (4), Lambeth (2), Morton (2), Klepfer, Wood

	G	AB	R	H	2B	3B	HR	RBI	SB	AVG
Milo Allison	32	35	4	5	0	0	0	0	3	.143
Josh Billings	66	129	8	23	3	2	0	9	2	.178
Ray Chapman (SS)	156	563	98	170	28	13	2	36	52	.302
Hank DeBerry	25	33	3	9	2	0	0	1	0	.273
Ferd Eunick	1	2	0	0	0	0	0	0	0	.000
Joe Evans (3B)	132	385	36	73	4	5	2	33	12	.190
Jack Graney (LF)	146	535	87	122	29	7	3	35	16	.228
Lou Guisto	73	200	9	37	4	2	0	29	3	.185
Joe Harris (1B)	112	369	40	112	22	4	0	65	11	.304
Ivon Howard	27	39	7	4	0	0	0	0	1	.103
Marty Kavanagh	14	14	1	0	0	0	0	0	0	.000
Ray Miller	19	21	1	4	1	0	0	2	0	.190
Steve O'Neill (C)	129	370	21	68	10	2	0	29	2	.184
Braggo Roth (RF)	145	495	69	141	30	9	1	72	51	.285
Elmer Smith	64	161	21	42	5	1	3	22	6	.261
Tris Speaker (CF)	142	523	90	184	42	11	2	60	30	.352
Terry Turner	69	180	16	37	7	0	0	15	4	.206
Bill Wambsganss (2B)	141	499	52	127	17	6	0	43	16	.255
		4,994	584	1,224	(218)	64	13	475	210	.245

1918

Record: 73–54
Finish: Second
Games Behind: 2½
Manager: Lee Fohl

Most baseball historians believe the Indians would have won their first-ever pennant in 1918 if it had not been for World War 1.

On July 19, Secretary of War Newton D. Baker ruled that baseball was not an essential occupation and that all players of draft age were subject to the "work-or-fight" rule. It caused many to leave their teams for jobs in shipyards and other defense industries.

Before or during the year the Indians lost, to either the service or the defense industry for all or part of the season, second baseman Bill Wambsganss, pitchers Guy Morton, Ed Klepfer, and Otis Lambeth, catcher Jack Billings, and first basemen Lou Guisto and Joe Harris.

What's more—and probably of greater importance—the Indians also were hurt by the decision to cut the season short because of the war.

Initially the plan was to cease operations on July 21. But when Baker amended his decree and announced that players would be exempt from the draft until September 1, it was decided to play through Labor Day, which fell on September 2.

The Indians, a preseason favorite to win their first pennant, were in contention with Boston, New York, and Washington, and took over first place in early July. The Red Sox regained the lead on July 6 and held it the rest of the way, though the Indians stayed close, while the Yankees and Senators fell back.

But disaster struck the Indians in late August of the abbreviated season when they were within four games of first place.

Tris Speaker, their inspirational leader and best hitter, got into a violent argument with umpire Tommy Connolly on August 27. When Speaker made physical contact with Connolly—inadvertently, as he claimed, or otherwise—he was suspended the next day for the remainder of the season.

The Red Sox played the final week on the road where they'd had trouble winning all year, and the Indians managed to gain some ground, but time ran out for them. Boston clinched the pennant on August 31 by winning the first game of a doubleheader in Philadelphia, 6–1.

The Indians played the next day and won. But then, mathematically eliminated, angered because of Speaker's suspension, and discouraged because the shortening of the season left them no chance to catch the Red Sox, they disbanded, failing to appear for a doubleheader in St. Louis on September 2.

AL President Ban Johnson ruled that the Browns would not be credited with the two games forfeited by the Indians. He said that no club could be held for a penalty under the circumstances that existed because of the work-or-fight order.

Despite their frustration, it still was the Indians' best finish since 1908, when Detroit was rained out of a game (which wasn't made up) and beat Cleveland for the pennant by a margin of .004 in winning percentage.

Speaker figured in another incident earlier in the season—an incident that would take on added significance a few years later.

On May 20 in Boston, Speaker was hit in the head by a fastball thrown by Carl Mays, a submarine-style pitcher who had been accused previously of intentionally beaning batters.

Though Speaker was not injured, he was furious with Mays. He reportedly shouted at the pitcher, "I was on the same team [Boston] with you long enough to know what you do. If you throw at anyone else on this ball club, you might not even walk out of this park."

With Morton missing part of the season, Stan Coveleski (22–13) again was the Indians' winningest pitcher. Speaker slumped to .318 as Detroit's Ty Cobb (.382) won his second straight batting championship and 11th in 12 seasons.

	W	L	G	GS	CG	IP	H	BB	K	ERA
Jim Bagby	17	16	(45)	31	23	271⅓	274	78	57	2.69
Ad Brennan	0	0	1	0	0	3	3	3	0	3.00
Fritz Coumbe	13	7	30	17	9	150	164	52	41	3.06
Stan Coveleski	22	13	38	33	25	311	261	76	87	1.82
Johnny Enzmann	5	7	30	14	8	136⅔	130	29	38	2.37
Bob Groom	2	2	14	5	0	43⅓	70	18	8	7.06
Otis Lambeth	0	0	2	0	0	7	10	6	3	6.43
George McQuillan	0	1	5	1	0	23	25	4	7	2.35
Guy Morton	14	8	30	28	13	214⅔	189	77	123	2.64
Roy Wilkinson	0	0	1	0	0	1	0	0	0	0.00
	73	54		129	78	1,161	1,126	343	364	2.64

Shutouts: Bagby (2), Coveleski (2), Morton
Saves: Bagby (6), Coumbe (3), Enzmann (2), Coveleski, McQuillan

	G	AB	R	H	2B	3B	HR	RBI	SB	AVG
Bob Bescher	25	60	12	20	2	1	0	6	3	.333
Josh Billings	2	3	0	1	0	0	0	0	0	.333
Ray Chapman (SS)	128	446	(84)	119	19	8	1	32	30	.267
Joe Evans (3B)	79	243	38	64	6	7	1	22	7	.263
Jack Farmer	7	9	1	2	0	0	0	1	2	.222
Gus Getz	6	15	2	2	1	0	0	0	0	.133
Jack Graney	70	177	27	42	7	4	0	9	3	.237
Al Halt	26	69	9	12	2	0	0	1	4	.174
Doc Johnston (1B)	74	273	30	62	12	2	0	25	12	.227
Marty Kavanagh	13	38	4	8	2	0	0	6	1	.211
Ed Miller	32	96	9	22	4	3	0	3	2	.229
Steve O'Neill (C)	114	359	34	87	8	7	1	35	5	.242
Eddie Onslow	2	6	0	1	0	0	0	0	0	.167
John Peters	1	1	0	0	0	0	0	0	0	.000
Braggo Roth (RF)	106	375	53	106	21	12	1	59	35	.283
Germany Schaefer	1	5	2	0	0	0	0	0	1	.000
Tris Speaker (CF)	127	471	73	150	(33)	11	0	61	27	.318
Pinch Thomas	32	73	2	18	0	1	0	5	0	.247
Terry Turner	74	233	24	58	7	2	0	23	6	.249
Bill Wambsganss (2B)	87	315	34	93	15	2	0	40	16	.295
Rip Williams	28	71	5	17	2	2	0	7	2	.239
Smoky Joe Wood (LF)	119	422	41	125	22	4	5	66	8	.296
		4,166	(504)	1,084	(176)	(67)	9	(423)	(165)	(.260)

1919

Record: 84–55
Finish: Second
Games Behind: 3½
Managers: Lee Fohl, Tris Speaker

The season (in which only 140 games were scheduled as a matter of economy) began with Tris Speaker serving as both captain of the Indians and Lee Fohl's trusted confidant. It ended with Fohl out of a job and Speaker the team's new manager.

And for the second consecutive year the Indians lost the American League pennant in the final week.

Babe Ruth, then a Boston Red Sox pitcher who played the outfield when he was not on the mound, generally is credited—or blamed—for Fohl's resignation (or owner James Dunn's decision to fire him).

It happened on July 18 when the Indians were in third place with a 44–34 record, 5½ games behind Chicago and one behind New York.

That day at Dunn Field the Indians lost to Boston, 8–7, when Ruth hit a ninth-inning grand slam home run off southpaw reliever Fritz Coumbe.

Until that game the Indians had beaten Boston nine straight times and entered the ninth inning with a 7–3 lead. The Red Sox scored a run and loaded the bases with two out when Ruth came to the plate against Elmer Myers, working in relief of starter Hi Jasper.

Fohl, as he usually did because of his deep-rooted faith in Speaker, looked out to the center fielder for advice. Speaker signaled for Fohl to put in one of the two right-handers warming up in the bull pen. But this time Fohl ignored Speaker's suggestion and replaced Myers with Coumbe.

Two pitches later, both slow curves, Ruth drove the ball over the 290-foot right field wall and trotted around the bases behind three of his teammates. It was one of a record 29 home runs Ruth hit that season (when he also won nine games and lost five as a pitcher).

The Indians were devastated. So was Fohl, according to Dunn, who summoned Speaker to his office after the game.

Dunn said that Fohl had resigned and asked Speaker to take over as player-manager of the Indians. Speaker resisted, saying he would accept the job only if Fohl would ask him to do so.

Fohl, who blamed himself for Ruth's game-winning homer, encouraged Speaker to take the job, and the change was made.

But it made no difference in the end. The White Sox were too good.

Speaker, probably recognizing the futility of the chase, turned his efforts to 1920. Among the young players he broke in was right-handed pitcher George Uhle, a Cleveland sandlot graduate who did not make his first major league start until August 20, but won 10 games.

Another was Ray "Slim" Caldwell, also a right-handed pitcher whose drinking problem caused him to be traded from the Yankees to Boston, and then released by the Red Sox late in the season.

Speaker had always liked Caldwell and signed him to a very unusual contract.

It reportedly stipulated that Caldwell was to get drunk after each game he pitched, not show up the next day, go to the park the second day and do as much running as the manager ordered, throw batting practice the third day, and pitch a game the fourth day.

Caldwell, apparently following Speaker's orders, won five games and lost only one after joining the Indians.

One of his victories was a 3–0 no-hitter on September 10 against the Yankees in New York—the team that had traded Caldwell because of his drinking problem.

Another of Caldwell's victories came under extreme duress.

He was hit by lightning and knocked out—literally—when an electric storm suddenly struck League Park on August 24 during a game against Philadelphia. It was the last of the ninth with two out and one strike on the batter when Caldwell was hit.

Unconscious for five minutes, Caldwell was revived and assured Speaker he could continue. Then he fired two more strikes past the batter to end the game.

Under Speaker in the final two and a half months of the season the Indians went 40–21. They took over second place, but were unable to climb any higher.

It also was in the final week of the season, on September 25, that Speaker allegedly was involved in a conspiracy to fix a game between the Indians and Detroit—though the charge wasn't leveled until seven years later, after which he was exonerated.

Others incriminated with Speaker were Indians outfielder and former pitcher "Smoky Joe" Wood, Detroit manager Ty Cobb, and Tigers pitcher Hubert "Dutch" Leonard.

Leonard, apparently resentful of the way he'd been treated by Cobb, alleged that the Indians, with second place locked up, deliberately lost to the Tigers. Leonard said all four men had planned to place large bets on the outcome of the game, which was won by Detroit, 9–5.

It was claimed by Leonard (in 1926) that Cobb had agreed to put up $2,000, Leonard himself $1,500, and Speaker and Wood $1,000 each. However, according to Leonard, both Cobb and Speaker were unable to get their money down on time, while he (Leonard) and Wood each won $130.

Leonard produced letters from Cobb and Wood which he said substantiated his allegation. The matter was investigated first by American League president Byron "Ban" Johnson and then by Judge Kenesaw Mountain Landis, who had been appointed commissioner of Baseball in 1920.

Johnson initially indicated that he believed Leonard's allegations, but Landis, after considering his decision for two months, on January 27, 1927, exonerated everybody.

Whatever the reason, perhaps because of his additional duties as manager, Speaker's average fell to a career-low .296, as first baseman Doc Johnston, shortstop Ray Chapman, and third baseman Larry Gardner were the only regulars to hit .300.

	W	L	G	GS	CG	IP	H	BB	K	ERA
Jim Bagby	17	11	35	32	21	241⅓	258	44	61	2.80
Ray Caldwell	5	1	6	6	4	52⅔	33	19	24	1.71
Fritz Coumbe	1	1	8	2	0	23⅔	32	9	7	5.32
Stan Coveleski	24	12	43	34	24	286	(286)	60	118	2.61
Joe Engel	0	0	1	0	0	0	0	3	0	—
Johnny Enzmann	3	2	14	4	2	55⅓	67	8	13	2.28
Tony Faeth	0	0	6	0	0	18⅓	13	10	7	0.49
Charlie Jamieson	0	0	4	1	0	13	12	8	0	5.54
Hi Jasper	4	5	12	10	5	82⅔	83	28	25	3.59
Ed Klepfer	0	0	5	0	0	7⅓	12	6	7	7.36
Guy Morton	9	9	26	20	9	147⅓	128	47	64	2.81
Elmer Myers	8	7	23	15	6	134⅔	134	43	38	3.74
Tom Phillips	3	2	22	3	2	55	55	34	18	2.95
George Uhle	10	5	26	12	7	127	129	43	50	2.91
Smoky Joe Wood	0	0	1	0	0	⅔	0	0	0	0.00
	84	55		139	80	1,245	1,242	362	432	2.94

Shutouts: Coveleski (4), Morton (3), Caldwell, Myers, Uhle
Saves: Coveleski (4), Bagby (3), Coumbe, Myers, Wood

	G	AB	R	H	2B	3B	HR	RBI	SB	AVG
Ray Chapman (SS)	115	433	75	130	23	10	3	53	18	.300
Joe Evans	21	14	9	1	0	0	0	0	1	.071
Larry Gardner (3B)	139	524	67	157	29	7	2	79	7	.300
Jack Graney (LF)	128	461	79	108	22	8	1	30	7	.234
Joe Harris	62	184	30	69	16	1	1	46	2	.375
Charlie Jamieson	26	17	3	6	2	1	0	2	2	.353
Doc Johnston (1B)	102	331	42	101	17	3	1	33	21	.305
Harry Lunte	26	77	2	15	2	0	0	2	0	.195
Les Nunamaker	26	56	6	14	1	1	0	7	0	.250
Steve O'Neill (C)	125	398	46	115	35	7	2	47	4	.289
Elmer Smith (RF)	114	395	60	110	24	6	9	54	15	.278
Tris Speaker (CF)	134	494	83	146	38	12	2	63	15	.296
Pinch Thomas	34	46	2	5	0	0	0	2	0	.109
Bill Wambsganss (2B)	139	526	60	146	17	6	2	60	18	.278
Smoky Joe Wood	72	192	30	49	10	6	0	27	3	.255
		4,565	636	1,268	(254)	72	24	547	113	.278

1920

Record: 98–56
Finish: First
Games Ahead: 2
Manager: Tris Speaker

It was the best of times, but also the worst of times, in the 20-year existence of the Indians.

They won their first pennant, battling virtually from beginning to end with the defending champion Chicago White Sox and the Babe Ruth–led New York Yankees, and played in front of a franchise-record 912,849 fans at Dunn Field.

But their jubilation was tempered by the tragic death of shortstop Ray Chapman, who was hit in the head by a pitch from the Yankees' Carl Mays in the Polo Grounds on August 16. Chapman, whose skull was fractured, was carried from the field unconscious and died the next morning at the age of 29.

The injury occurred as Chapman led off the fifth inning of a rain-dampened game that the Indians eventually won, 4–3, giving them a 71–40 record and preserving their first place, two-game lead over the White Sox, with the Yankees 2½ lengths back.

It was the same Carl Mays, a submarine-style pitcher, who had hit Tris Speaker with a pitch in 1918 and was then accused by Speaker, his former teammate, of throwing at batters.

The day after Chapman died, players on the Detroit and Boston teams held a meeting and told reporters that Mays should be barred from organized baseball.

This time, however, Speaker exonerated the pitcher and even criticized the Tigers and Red Sox for their indictment of Mays.

Speaker said, "I do not hold Mays responsible in any way. I have been active in discouraging my players from holding Mays responsible, and in respect to Chapman's memory, as well as for the good of baseball, I hope all this kind of talk will stop.

"I realize that Mays feels this thing as deeply as any man could, and I do not want to add anything to his burden. I do not know what prompted the action of the Boston and Detroit players. For my part, I think it was deplorable."

Chapman, the only player in major league history to be killed in a game, was initially replaced by Harry Lunte. But Lunte, who was hitting only .197, got hurt on September 6, and the Indians purchased Joey Sewell from their New Orleans farm club to take over at shortstop.

With Sewell playing well, the Indians managed to put aside their grief and continued their drive to the pennant, leading the American League in runs scored, doubles, triples, runs batted in, and walks. Their team batting average was .303.

Speaker rebounded from his worst season in 1919 and hit a then-career-high .388 and drove in over 100 runs, as did outfielder Elmer Smith and third baseman Larry Gardner; Jim Bagby led the league with 31 victories—still a club record—as well as winning percentage, appearances, complete games, and innings pitched; Stan Coveleski struck out more batters than any other American League pitcher; and rookie left-hander Walter "Duster" Mails was a perfect 7–0 after being purchased from the minor leagues on August 21, though he didn't make his first start until September 1.

The Indians started their drive to the 1920 pennant by winning six of their first seven games and 10 of 13, and moved into first place on May 9. They stayed in the lead most of the way, except for brief periods in late July, mid-August, and early September when they were displaced by either Chicago or New York.

On September 12, after beating Philadelphia, 5–2, the Indians were in first place with a percentage of .61940 to the Yankees' .61871, and a week later, upon winning 17 of 21 games, were ahead of Chicago by 1½ games and New York by three.

At that point the White Sox took three straight from the Yankees, dropping them out of the race, then came to Cleveland and cut their first-place deficit to a half game on September 25 after winning two of three from the Indians.

Three days later, with the Indians ahead by one game with five left to play, a Cook County, Illinois, grand jury announced the indictment of seven players then on the White Sox roster—including four regulars and two starting pitchers—and one former player on charges of conspiring to fix the 1919 World Series.

The players were suspended and, with a makeshift lineup, the White Sox lost two of their final three games to St. Louis. The Indians, who won three of their last five, captured the pennant by two lengths. The clincher came in game number 153 as Bagby beat Detroit, 10–1, for his 31st victory on October 2.

Some called it a tainted championship because of the suspensions that decimated the White Sox. But the Indians justified their place in the World Series by beating Brooklyn, the National League champion, five games to two in what then was a best-of-nine tournament.

The World Series, in which the NL champs won only the second and third games, both played in Brooklyn, was highlighted by several outstanding individual performances by the Indians.

Especially in Game 5 on October 10 at Dunn Field, won by the Tribe, 8–1.

Second baseman Bill Wambsganss made the only unassisted triple play in World Series history, Smith hit the first grand slam homer in a World Series game, and winning pitcher Bagby became the first hurler to hit a home run in the World Series.

Coveleski started and won three games, prevailing 3–1 in the opener, 5–1 in the fourth game, and 3–0 in Game 7, clinching the world's championship for the Indians on October 12. Their other victory was posted by Mails, 1–0, in

Game 6, while Bagby was a 3–0 loser to Burleigh Crimes in the second game, and Ray Caldwell was charged with the 2–1 loss in the third game.

The importance of Sewell's contributions upon taking over for Lunte, who had replaced Chapman, are evident in the final batting statistics: .329 in 22 games. Speaker's .388 average was 92 points better than he compiled in 1919 but placed him only second to AL champion George Sisler, who hit .407. Six points behind Speaker was the suspended former Indian, "Shoeless Joe" Jackson.

	W	L	G	GS	CG	IP	H	BB	K	ERA
Jim Bagby	(31)	12	(48)	38	(30)	(339⅔)	(338)	79	73	2.89
Joe Boehling	0	1	3	2	0	13	16	10	4	4.85
Ray Caldwell	20	10	34	33	20	237⅔	286	63	80	3.86
Bob Clark	1	2	11	2	2	42	59	13	8	3.43
Stan Coveleski	24	14	41	38	26	315	284	65	(133)	2.49
George Ellison	0	0	1	0	0	1	0	2	1	0.00
Tony Faeth	0	0	13	0	0	25	31	20	14	4.32
Duster Mails	7	0	9	8	6	63⅓	54	18	25	1.85
Guy Morton	8	6	29	17	6	137	140	57	72	4.47
Tim Murchison	0	0	2	0	0	5	3	4	0	0.00
Elmer Myers	2	4	16	7	2	71⅓	93	23	16	4.77
Dick Niehaus	1	2	19	3	0	40	42	16	12	3.60
George Uhle	4	5	27	6	2	84⅔	98	29	27	5.21
Smoky Joe Wood	0	0	1	0	0	2	4	2	1	22.50
	(98)	56		154	94	1,377	1,448	401	466	3.41

Shutouts: Bagby (3), Coveleski (3), Mails (2), Caldwell, Clark, Morton
Saves: Coveleski (2), Niehaus (2), Morton, Myers, Uhle

	G	AB	R	H	2B	3B	HR	RBI	SB	AVG
George Burns	44	56	7	15	4	1	0	13	1	.268
Ray Chapman (SS)	111	435	97	132	27	8	3	49	13	.303
Joe Evans	56	172	32	60	9	9	0	23	6	.349
Larry Gardner (3B)	(154)	597	72	185	31	11	3	118	3	.310
Jack Graney	62	152	31	45	11	1	0	13	4	.296
Charlie Jamieson (LF)	108	370	69	118	17	7	1	40	2	.319
Doc Johnston (1B)	147	535	68	156	24	10	2	71	13	.292
Harry Lunte	23	71	6	14	0	0	0	7	0	.197
Les Nunamaker	34	54	10	18	3	3	0	14	1	.333
Steve O'Neill (C)	149	489	63	157	39	5	3	55	3	.321
Joe Sewell	22	70	14	23	4	1	0	12	1	.329
Elmer Smith (RF)	129	456	82	144	37	10	12	103	5	.316
Tris Speaker (CF)	150	552	137	214	(50)	11	8	107	10	.388
Pinch Thomas	9	9	2	3	1	0	0	0	0	.333
Bill Wambsganss (2B)	153	565	83	138	16	11	1	55	9	.244
Smoky Joe Wood	61	137	25	37	11	2	1	30	1	.270
		5,196	(857)	1,574	(300)	95	35	(758)	73	.303

1921

Record: 94–60
Finish: Second
Games Behind: 4½
Manager: Tris Speaker

Just as many things went right in 1920 (with the exception, of course, of the tragic death of Ray Chapman), many things went wrong for the Indians in 1921.

Second baseman Bill Wambsganss broke an arm in spring training. A week later utility infielder Harry Lunte was sidelined with a sprained ankle. Then, still prior to the start of the season, catcher Steve O'Neill suffered a broken finger that kept him out of action until July 15. And, less than a month after O'Neill returned to duty, backup catcher Les Nunamaker went out with a broken leg.

Despite those injuries, the Indians either led the American League or were a close second to New York through the first five months.

On September 11, however, Tris Speaker tore the ligaments in his right knee and was finished for the year. It was the final—and cruelest—blow to the Indians' chances of repeating because Speaker was the one player they absolutely could not afford to lose.

Their flickering hopes faded for good when they lost three games of a four-game series to the Yankees in the Polo Grounds, September 23–26. The losing scores were 4–2, 21–7, and 8–7, and Babe Ruth, who had become a full-time outfielder the year before, hit two of his then-American-League-record 59 homers in that series.

In addition to the injuries, the Indians also were hurt by the failure of two key pitchers to deliver as expected. Jim Bagby, who led the AL with 31 victories in 1920, won 14 and lost 12 in 1920, and Ray Caldwell went from 20–10 to 6–6. Stan Coveleski, who was one of nine AL pitchers allowed to continue using the spitball when it was outlawed (and the rule "grandfathered") the previous winter, won 23 games despite being hampered with a sore arm late in the season.

	W	L	G	GS	CG	IP	H	BB	K	ERA
Jim Bagby	14	12	40	26	13	191⅔	238	44	37	4.70
Ray Caldwell	6	6	37	12	4	147	159	49	76	4.90
Bob Clark	0	0	5	0	0	9⅓	23	6	2	14.46
Stan Coveleski	23	13	43	(40)	28	315	341	84	99	3.37
Bernie Henderson	0	1	2	1	0	3	5	0	1	9.00
Duster Mails	14	8	34	24	10	194⅓	210	89	87	3.94
Guy Morton	8	3	30	7	3	107⅔	98	32	45	2.76
Ted Odenwald	1	0	10	0	0	17⅓	16	6	4	1.56
Jesse Petty	0	0	4	0	0	9	10	0	0	2.00
Allen Sothoron	12	4	22	16	10	144⅔	146	58	61	3.24
George Uhle	16	13	41	28	13	238	288	63	63	4.01
	94	60		154	81	1,377	1,534	431	475	3.90

Shutouts: Coveleski (2), Mails (2), Morton (2), Sothoron (2), Uhle (2), Caldwell
Saves: Bagby (4), Caldwell (4), Coveleski (2), Mails (2), Uhle (2)

	G	AB	R	H	2B	3B	HR	RBI	SB	AVG
George Burns	84	244	52	88	21	4	0	49	3	.361
Joe Evans	57	153	36	51	11	0	0	21	4	.333
Larry Gardner (3B)	153	586	101	187	32	14	3	120	3	.319
Jack Graney	68	107	19	32	3	0	2	18	1	.299
Lou Guisto	2	2	0	1	0	0	0	1	0	.500
Charlie Jamieson (LF)	140	536	94	166	33	10	1	46	8	.310
Tex Jeanes	5	3	2	2	1	0	0	4	0	.667
Doc Johnston (1B)	118	384	53	114	20	7	2	46	2	.297
Les Nunamaker	46	131	16	47	7	2	0	25	1	.359
Steve O'Neill (C)	106	335	39	108	22	1	1	50	0	.322
Joe Sewell (SS)	154	572	101	182	36	12	4	93	7	.318
Luke Sewell	3	6	0	0	0	0	0	1	0	.000
Ginger Shinault	22	29	5	11	1	0	0	4	1	.379
Elmer Smith (RF)	129	431	98	125	28	9	16	85	0	.290
Tris Speaker (CF)	132	506	107	183	(52)	14	3	75	2	.362
Riggs Stephenson	65	206	45	68	17	2	2	34	4	.330
Pinch Thomas	21	35	1	9	3	0	0	4	0	.257
Bill Wambsganss (2B)	107	410	80	117	28	5	2	47	13	.285
Art Wilson	2	1	0	0	0	0	0	0	0	.000
Smoky Joe Wood	66	194	32	71	16	5	4	60	2	.366
		5,383	925	1,656	(355)	90	42	845	51	.308

1922

Record: 78–76
Finish: Fourth
Games Behind: 16
Manager: Tris Speaker

The pennant race lasted almost two weeks for the Indians as they held first place or were tied at the top of the American League from April 12 to 21. Thereafter, a steady decline

set in and they finished fourth only by virtue of a victory over Detroit on the final day of the season, while Chicago was losing to St. Louis.

The season's outcome was a great disappointment because management of the Indians thought the team had been strengthened with the off-season acquisition of first baseman Stuffy McInnis. He was acquired from the Boston Red Sox for three players—first baseman George Burns and outfielders Elmer Smith and Joe Harris.

Once again injuries hampered the team, but a bigger reason for the Indians' lack of success was the failure of several veteran pitchers—namely Jim Bagby, Walter "Duster" Mails, and even Stan Coveleski—to win as expected.

Bagby and Mails each won but four games, while Coveleski went from 23 victories (and 10 over .500) in 1921, to a 17–14 record.

The Indians also were distracted by the long illness of owner James C. "Sunny Jim" Dunn, who died on June 9 at the age of 55. Dunn left the franchise to his widow and specified that vice president Ernest S. "Barney" Barnard be elevated to the presidency of the club and placed in charge of operations.

AL president Ban Johnson said that the death of Dunn "has taken from baseball one of its most noble characters [who] was one of the most popular club owners in the game because he played fair and square with everyone."

No fewer than 46 players were on the Tribe roster at one time or another in 1922. Player-manager Tris Speaker had another good season at the plate, hitting .378, but was only third in the race for the batting championship. Two players hit .400—St. Louis's George Sisler (.420) and Detroit's Ty Cobb (.401).

	W	L	G	GS	CG	IP	H	BB	K	ERA
Jim Bagby	4	5	25	10	4	98⅓	134	39	25	6.32
Phil Bedgood	1	0	1	1	1	9	7	4	5	4.00
Danny Boone	4	6	11	10	4	75⅓	87	19	9	4.06
Stan Coveleski	17	14	35	33	21	276⅔	292	64	98	3.32
Logan Drake	0	0	1	0	0	3	4	2	1	3.00
George Edmondson	0	0	2	0	0	2	4	0	0	9.00
Jim Joe Edwards	3	8	25	7	0	92⅔	113	40	44	4.47
Doc Hamann	0	0	1	0	0	0	3	3	0	—
Charlie Jamieson	0	0	2	0	0	5⅔	7	4	2	3.18
Tex Jeanes	0	0	1	0	0	0	0	1	0	—
Dave Keefe	0	0	18	1	0	36⅓	47	12	11	6.19
Jim Lindsey	4	5	29	5	0	83⅔	105	24	29	6.02
Duster Mails	4	7	26	13	4	104	122	40	54	5.28
Dewey Metivier	2	0	2	2	2	18	18	3	1	4.50
John Middleton	0	1	2	1	0	7⅓	8	6	2	7.36
Guy Morton	14	9	38	23	13	202⅔	218	85	102	4.00
Ted Odenwald	0	0	1	0	0	1⅓	6	2	2	40.50
Nellie Pott	0	0	2	0	0	2	7	2	0	31.50
Joe Shaute	0	0	2	0	0	3⅔	7	3	3	19.64
Sherry Smith	1	0	2	2	1	15⅔	18	3	4	3.45
Allen Sothoron	1	3	6	4	2	25⅓	26	14	8	6.39
George Uhle	22	16	50	(40)	23	287⅓	328	89	82	4.07
George Winn	1	2	8	3	1	33⅔	44	5	7	4.54
	78	76		(155)	76	1,383⅔	(1,605)	464	489	4.59

Shutouts: Uhle (5), Coveleski (3), Morton (3), Boone (2), Mails
Saves: Uhle (3), Coveleski (2), Bagby, Lindsey

	G	AB	R	H	2B	3B	HR	RBI	SB	AVG
Uke Clanton	1	1	0	0	0	0	0	0	0	.000
Joe Connolly	12	45	6	11	2	1	0	6	1	.244
Bill Doran	3	2	0	1	0	0	0	0	0	.500
Joe Evans	75	145	35	39	6	2	0	22	11	.269
Larry Gardner (3B)	137	470	74	134	31	3	2	68	9	.285
Jack Graney	37	58	6	9	0	0	0	2	0	.155
Lou Guisto	35	84	7	21	10	1	0	9	0	.250
Jack Hammond	1	4	1	1	0	0	0	0	0	.250
Charlie Jamieson (LF)	145	567	87	183	29	11	3	57	15	.323
Tex Jeanes	1	1	0	0	0	0	0	0	0	.000
Ike Kahdot	4	2	0	0	0	0	0	0	0	.000
Stuffy McInnis (1B)	142	537	58	164	28	7	1	78	1	.305
Pat McNulty	22	59	10	16	2	1	0	5	4	.271
Les Nunamaker	25	43	8	13	2	0	0	7	0	.302
Steve O'Neill (C)	133	392	33	122	27	4	2	65	2	.311
Joe Rabbitt	2	3	1	1	0	0	0	0	0	.333
Joe Sewell (SS)	153	558	80	167	28	7	2	83	10	.299
Luke Sewell	41	87	14	23	5	0	0	10	1	.264
Ginger Shinault	13	15	1	2	1	0	0	0	0	.133
Chick Sorrells	2	1	0	0	0	0	0	0	0	.000
Tris Speaker (CF)	131	426	85	161	(48)	8	11	71	8	.378
Riggs Stephenson	86	233	47	79	24	5	2	32	3	.339
Homer Summa	12	46	9	16	3	3	1	6	1	.348
Bill Wambsganss (2B)	142	538	89	141	22	6	0	47	17	.262
Smoky Joe Wood (RF)	142	505	74	150	33	8	8	92	5	.297
		5,293	768	1,544	(320)	73	32	698	90	.292

1923

Record: 82–71
Finish: Third
Games Behind: 16½
Manager: Tris Speaker

The Indians improved their won-lost record and gained a place in the standings, but never were seriously in pennant contention despite holding second place through most of July, August, and September. They regained the runner-up position in early October, losing it to Detroit with two games remaining.

Four regulars batted over .300—Tris Speaker, Joey Sewell, Charlie Jamieson, and Homer Summa—as the Indians led the American League in hitting. But they were seventh in fielding, and their pitching weakness carried over from 1922.

George Uhle was their only consistent winner, and Stan Coveleski, whose record slipped below .500 for the first time in his major league career, was sent home because of illness a month before the season ended.

Speaker hit 59 doubles, breaking his own American League record of 53 that he set in 1912. Speaker's .380 average placed him third again in the American League batting race behind Detroit's Harry Heilmann (.403) and New York's Babe Ruth (.393).

	W	L	G	GS	CG	IP	H	BB	K	ERA
Phil Bedgood	0	2	9	2	0	18⅔	16	14	7	5.30
Danny Boone	4	6	27	4	2	70⅓	93	31	15	6.01
Stan Coveleski	13	14	33	31	17	228	251	42	54	(2.76)
Logan Drake	0	0	4	0	0	4⅓	2	4	2	4.15
George Edmondson	0	0	1	0	0	4	8	3	0	11.25
Jim Joe Edwards	10	10	38	21	8	179⅓	200	75	68	3.71
Jay Fry	0	0	1	0	0	3⅔	6	4	0	12.27
Dutch Levsen	0	0	3	0	0	4⅓	4	0	1	0.00
Dewey Metivier	4	2	26	5	1	73⅓	111	38	9	6.50
Guy Morton	6	6	33	14	3	129⅓	133	56	54	4.24
Joe Shaute	10	8	33	16	7	172	176	53	61	3.51
Sherry Smith	9	6	30	16	10	124	129	37	23	3.27
Jim Sullivan	0	1	3	0	0	5	10	5	4	14.40
George Uhle	(26)	16	54	(44)	(29)	(357⅔)	(378)	102	109	3.77
George Winn	0	0	1	0	0	2	0	1	0	0.00
	82	71		153	77	1,376	1,517	465	407	3.91

Shutouts: Coveleski (5), Morton (2), Edwards, Smith, Uhle
Saves: Uhle (5), Coveleski (2), Edwards, Metivier, Morton, Smith

	G	AB	R	H	2B	3B	HR	RBI	SB	AVG
Frank Brower (1B)	126	397	77	113	25	8	16	66	6	.285
Sumpter Clarke	1	3	0	0	0	0	0	0	0	.000
Joe Connolly	52	109	25	33	10	1	3	25	1	.303
Jackie Gallagher	1	1	0	1	0	0	0	1	0	1.000
Larry Gardner	52	79	4	20	5	1	0	12	0	.253
Lou Guisto	40	144	17	26	5	0	0	18	1	.181
Tom Gulley	2	3	1	1	1	0	0	0	0	.333
Ken Hogan	1	0	0	0	0	0	0	0	0	—
Charlie Jamieson (LF)	152	(644)	130	(222)	36	12	2	51	18	.345
Ray Knode	22	38	7	11	0	0	2	4	1	.289
Rube Lutzke (3B)	143	511	71	131	20	6	3	65	9	.256
Glenn Myatt	92	220	36	63	7	6	3	40	0	.286
Steve O'Neill (C)	113	330	31	82	12	0	0	50	0	.248
Joe Sewell (SS)	153	553	98	195	41	10	3	109	9	.353
Luke Sewell	10	10	2	2	0	1	0	1	0	.200
Wally Shaner	3	4	1	1	0	0	0	0	0	.250
Tris Speaker (CF)	150	574	133	218	(59)	11	17	130	8	.380
Riggs Stephenson	91	301	48	96	20	6	5	65	5	.319
Homer Summa (RF)	137	525	92	172	27	6	3	69	9	.328
Bill Wambsganss (2B)	101	345	59	100	20	4	1	59	10	.290
		5,290	(888)	(1,594)	(301)	75	59	(807)	72	(.301)

1924

Record: 67–86
Finish: Sixth
Games Behind: 24½
Manager: Tris Speaker

Illness and injuries again plagued the Indians, who were never in contention—not spending even one day in first place—as their fortunes went from bad to worse.

The Indians never climbed higher than fifth in the race, and late in the season lost 10 of 11 games to the four eastern teams (New York, Philadelphia, Washington, and Boston). They finished in sixth place, a half-game ahead of Boston and a full game above cellar-dwelling Chicago.

First baseman George Burns, who had been dealt to Boston prior to the 1922 season, was reacquired in a January 1924 trade that also brought Chick Fewster and Roxy Walters to Cleveland for Steve O'Neill, Bill Wambsganss, Danny Boone, and Joe Connolly. Burns played well, hitting .310, but his presence wasn't enough to make a great difference.

The Indians had a team batting average of .296 (Detroit led the league with .298), but again their pitching was ineffective. Only Joe Shaute among the starters won more games than he lost.

The Indians were hurt early in the season when player-manager Tris Speaker and pitcher George Uhle both were out for more than two weeks with influenza, and third baseman Rube Lutzke also missed time because of illness. Second baseman Riggs Stephenson was sidelined for three weeks with a wrenched knee, and then a broken leg kept him out of action the final two weeks, when the team also was without the services of Shaute and catcher Glenn Myatt because of injuries.

Stan Coveleski, losing more games than he won for the second straight season (and only the second time in his career), was traded in December to Washington for pitcher Byron Speece, who pitched in only 30 games for the Indians the next two seasons, and outfielder Carr Smith, who never appeared in a game for Cleveland.

	W	L	G	GS	CG	IP	H	BB	K	ERA
Frank Brower	0	0	4	0	0	9⅔	7	4	0	0.93
Virgil Cheeves	0	0	8	1	0	17⅓	26	17	2	7.79
Watty Clark	1	3	12	1	0	25⅔	38	14	6	7.01
Stan Coveleski	15	16	37	33	18	240⅓	286	73	58	4.04
Joe Dawson	1	2	4	4	0	20⅓	24	21	7	6.64
Logan Drake	0	1	5	1	0	11⅓	18	10	8	10.32
George Edmondson	0	0	5	1	0	8	10	5	3	9.00
Jim Joe Edwards	4	3	10	7	5	57	64	34	15	2.84
Paul Fitzke	0	0	1	0	0	4	5	3	1	4.50
Bub Kuhn	0	1	1	0	0	1	4	0	0	27.00
Dutch Levsen	1	1	4	1	1	16⅓	22	4	3	4.41
Jim Lindsey	0	0	3	0	0	3	8	3	0	21.00
Bud Messenger	2	0	5	2	1	25	28	14	4	4.32
Dewey Metivier	1	5	26	6	1	76⅓	110	34	14	5.31
Jake Miller	0	1	2	2	1	12	13	5	4	3.00
Guy Morton	0	1	10	0	0	12⅓	12	13	6	6.57
Luther Roy	0	5	16	5	2	48⅔	62	31	14	7.77
Joe Shaute	20	(17)	46	34	21	283	317	83	68	3.75
Sherry Smith	12	14	39	27	20	247⅔	267	42	34	3.02
George Uhle	9	15	28	25	15	196⅓	238	75	57	4.77
Frank Wayenberg	0	0	2	1	0	6⅔	7	5	3	5.40
Carl Yowell	1	1	4	2	2	27	37	13	8	6.67
	67	86		153	(87)	1,349	1,603	503	315	4.40

Shutouts: Coveleski (2), Shaute (2), Smith (2), Edwards
Saves: Metivier (3), Shaute (2), Smith, Uhle

	G	AB	R	H	2B	3B	HR	RBI	SB	AVG
Frank Brower	66	107	16	30	10	1	3	20	1	.280
George Burns (1B)	129	462	64	143	37	5	4	68	14	.310
Sumpter Clarke	35	104	17	24	6	1	0	11	0	.231
Frank Ellerbe	46	120	7	31	1	3	1	14	0	.258
Chick Fewster (2B)	101	322	36	86	12	2	0	36	12	.267
Larry Gardner	38	50	3	10	0	0	0	4	0	.200
Tom Gulley	8	20	4	3	0	1	0	1	0	.150
Ken Hogan	2	1	0	0	0	0	0	0	0	.000
Charlie Jamieson (LF)	143	594	98	213	34	8	3	54	21	.359
Ray Knode	11	37	6	9	1	0	0	4	2	.243
Rube Lutzke (3B)	106	341	37	83	18	3	0	42	4	.243
Pat McNulty	101	291	46	78	13	5	0	26	10	.268
Glenn Myatt (C)	105	342	55	117	22	7	8	73	6	.342
Joe Sewell (SS)	153	594	99	188	(45)	5	4	106	3	.316
Luke Sewell	63	165	27	48	9	1	0	17	1	.291
Tris Speaker (CF)	135	486	94	167	36	9	9	65	5	.344
Freddy Spurgeon	3	7	0	1	1	0	0	0	0	.143
Riggs Stephenson	71	240	33	89	20	0	4	44	1	.371
Homer Summa (RF)	111	390	55	113	21	6	2	38	4	.290
Roxy Walters	32	74	10	19	2	0	0	5	0	.257
Joe Wyatt	4	12	1	2	0	0	0	1	0	.167
Elmer Yoter	19	66	3	18	1	1	0	7	0	.273
		5,332	755	1,580	306	59	41	676	85	.296

1925

Record: 70–84
Finish: Sixth
Games Behind: 27½
Manager: Tris Speaker

Player-manager Tris Speaker hit a home run in the Indians' opening-day game, and went on to compile a .389 average, the best of his 22-year major league career.

In that first game of 1925 the Indians beat St. Louis, 21–14, setting an American League record for the most runs in an opener.

But it wasn't a good season for his team despite that good start.

The Indians were either in first place or tied with Washington or Philadelphia for the top position from the April 14 opener through May 7, but then faded rapidly. By mid-July they were battling for sixth place, which is where they finished, one game ahead of New York.

Washington, which won the pennant, defeated the Indians 18 times in their 22-game season series. The team's performance was so bad by late July that Cleveland baseball fans and the media called for Speaker to be replaced as manager. President Ernest "Barney" Barnard responded by signing him to a new contract through 1926.

But Barnard's vote of confidence in Speaker did nothing to pull the Indians out of their dive. Nor did a series of personnel changes, none of which made a significant difference.

In the absence of the traded Stan Coveleski, who was the best pitcher in the American League in 1925 (when he won 20 and lost only five for the pennant-winning Senators), the Indians' most effective pitcher was a 27-year-old, 240-pound left-hander named Garland Buckeye.

Buckeye had pitched one game in the major leagues, for Washington in 1918, and in the seven years since then had played semipro baseball while working as a bank teller in Chicago.

But he didn't look like a banker—or a semipro pitcher—in 1925 when he won 13 and lost eight for the Indians, though he never did much for them after that year.

Despite his career-best batting average, Speaker failed to win his second American League batting championship. He was beaten by Detroit's Harry Heilmann, who hit four points higher, while Philadelphia's Al Simmons finished three points below Speaker.

	W	L	G	GS	CG	IP	H	BB	K	ERA
Ray Benge	1	0	2	2	1	11⅔	9	3	3	1.54
Garland Buckeye	13	8	30	18	11	153	161	58	49	3.65
Bert Cole	1	1	13	2	0	44	55	25	9	6.14
Jim Joe Edwards	0	3	13	3	1	36	60	23	12	8.25
Benn Karr	11	12	32	24	12	197⅔	248	80	41	4.78
Dutch Levsen	1	2	4	3	2	24⅓	30	16	9	5.55
Jake Miller	10	13	32	22	13	190⅓	207	62	51	3.31
Luther Roy	0	0	6	1	0	10	14	11	1	3.60
Joe Shaute	4	12	26	17	10	131	160	44	34	5.43
Sherry Smith	11	14	31	30	(22)	237	(296)	48	30	4.86
Byron Speece	3	5	28	3	3	90⅓	106	28	26	4.28
George Uhle	13	11	29	26	17	210⅔	218	78	68	4.10
Carl Yowell	2	3	12	4	1	36⅓	40	17	12	4.46
	70	84		155	(93)	1,372⅓	1,604	493	345	4.49

Shutouts: Benge, Buckeye, Karr, Shaute, Smith, Uhle
Saves: Shaute (4), Miller (2), Cole, Smith, Speece

	G	AB	R	H	2B	3B	HR	RBI	SB	AVG
Gene Bedford	2	3	1	0	0	0	0	0	0	.000
George Burns (1B)	127	488	69	164	41	4	6	79	16	.336
Fred Eichrodt	15	52	4	12	3	1	0	4	0	.231
Chick Fewster (2B)	93	294	39	73	16	1	1	38	6	.248
Harvey Hendrick	25	28	2	8	1	2	0	9	0	.286
Johnny Hodapp	37	130	12	31	5	1	0	14	2	.238
Charlie Jamieson (LF)	138	557	109	165	24	5	4	42	14	.296
Joe Klugmann	38	85	12	28	9	2	0	12	3	.329
Ray Knode	45	108	13	27	5	0	0	11	3	.250
Cliff Lee	77	230	43	74	15	6	4	42	2	.322
Rube Lutzke (3B)	81	238	31	52	9	0	1	16	2	.218
Frank McCrea	1	5	1	1	0	0	0	0	0	.200
Pat McNulty (RF)	118	373	70	117	18	2	6	43	7	.314
Glenn Myatt (C)	106	358	51	97	15	9	11	54	3	.271
Joe Sewell (SS)	155	608	78	204	37	7	1	98	7	.336
Luke Sewell	74	220	30	51	10	2	0	18	6	.232
Tris Speaker (CF)	117	429	79	167	35	5	12	87	5	.389
Freddy Spurgeon	107	376	50	108	9	3	0	32	8	.287
Riggs Stephenson	19	54	8	16	3	1	1	9	1	.296
Homer Summa	75	224	28	74	10	1	0	25	3	.330
Chick Tolson	3	12	0	3	0	0	0	0	0	.250
Dutch Ussat	1	1	0	0	0	0	0	0	0	.000
Roxy Walters	5	20	0	4	0	0	0	0	0	.200
		5,436	782	1,613	285	58	52	697	90	.297

1926

Record: 88–66
Finish: Second
Games Behind: 3
Manager: Tris Speaker

It didn't take long for the Indians and Tris Speaker to quiet their critics—though Speaker's contributions were greater as a manager than as a player in 1926.

Through the first three weeks of the season the Indians were in first place three times and were tied for the top seven times, then faltered and played erratically the next three months, falling into fifth place.

By the time July turned into August, however, they had recovered, making a remarkable comeback that almost won the franchise's second pennant.

They failed to do so in the final 10 days of the season when New York came to Cleveland for a crucial six-game series.

The first-place Yankees had a five-game lead on the Tribe and won the rain-interrupted opener, 6–4, beating George Uhle on September 15.

The Indians came back to sweep a doubleheader the next day: 2–1, on a two-hitter by Emil "Dutch" Levsen, and 5–0, as Garland Buckeye also limited the Yankees to two hits, though he walked 10 batters, including Babe Ruth four times, and hit another.

Then the Indians cut their deficit to two by winning the next two days, 5–1, behind Joe Shaute, and 3–1, on a four-hitter by Uhle, setting the stage for the series finale.

This time, however, the Yankees—six of whom subsequently were elected to the Hall of Fame—prevailed, 8–3, in front of 29,726 fans at Dunn Field, as Dutch Reuther beat Levsen. The win gave the Yankees a three-game lead, which they maintained through the final week.

It was the same Levsen, a 28-year-old right-hander, who three weeks earlier became the last pitcher in major league history to pitch and win two complete nine-inning games in a doubleheader. It happened on August 28, in Boston, as Levsen limited the Red Sox to four hits in each game, beating them 6–1 and 5–1.

Losing the pennant was a bitter disappointment for the 38-year-old Speaker who, two months later, on December 2, stunned the baseball world by announcing his resignation as manager of the Indians and also his retirement as a player. Speaker said he planned to go into private business.

The announcement came exactly one month to the day after Ty Cobb also quit as player-manager of Detroit. The retirement of the two stars lent credence to speculation that both were forced out of baseball because of charges that they and two other players had conspired to fix a game between the Indians and Tigers in 1919.

Nineteen days after Speaker's resignation, on December 21, Commissioner Kenesaw Mountain Landis publicly acknowledged the charges, though he did nothing for a month while Speaker and Cobb protested their innocence.

As outlined in the report on the 1919 incident, the accusation was made by former Tigers pitcher Hubert "Dutch" Leonard, who was involved in the alleged conspiracy, along with former Indians pitcher-outfielder "Smoky Joe" Wood.

Leonard, apparently resentful of his treatment by Cobb, alleged that the Indians, with second place locked up, deliberately lost to the Tigers because all four men had planned to place large bets on the outcome of the game, won by Detroit, 9–5.

In 1926, Leonard claimed that Cobb had agreed to put up $2,000, Leonard himself $1,500, and Speaker and Wood $1,000 each. However, Leonard said, neither Cobb nor Speaker got his money down on time, while he and Wood each won $130.

Leonard produced letters from Cobb and Wood that supposedly substantiated his allegation. The matter was investigated first by American League president Byron "Ban" Johnson, and then by Judge Kenesaw Mountain Landis, the commissioner of baseball.

Although Johnson initially indicated that he believed Leonard's allegations, Landis, after considering his decision for almost two months, exonerated Speaker and Cobb, as well as Wood and their accuser Leonard, on January 27, 1927.

Landis said, "These players have not been, nor are they now found guilty of fixing a ball game. By no decent system of justice could such a finding be made."

As a footnote to the case, Speaker and Cobb both returned to active status as players the following season; Speaker joining Washington, and Cobb with the Philadelphia Athletics.

With Speaker's average falling 85 points, George Burns became the Indians' offensive leader, and he was elected the AL's Most Valuable Player by a committee of eight "expert" baseball writers (though the official MVP balloting by the Baseball Writers Association of American did not begin until 1931). Burns' 64 doubles broke the major league record of 59 set by Speaker in 1923. Shortstop Joey Sewell also distinguished himself by striking out only six times in 578 plate appearances in 154 games while batting .324.

	W	L	G	GS	CG	IP	H	BB	K	ERA
Ray Benge	1	0	8	0	0	11⅔	15	4	3	3.86
Garland Buckeye	6	9	32	18	5	165⅔	160	69	36	3.10
Willis Hudlin	1	3	8	2	1	32⅓	25	13	6	2.78
Benn Karr	5	6	30	7	4	113⅓	137	41	23	5.00
Norm Lehr	0	0	4	0	0	14⅔	11	4	4	3.07
Dutch Levsen	16	13	33	31	18	237⅓	235	85	53	3.41
Jake Miller	7	4	18	11	5	82⅔	99	18	24	3.27
Joe Shaute	14	10	34	25	15	206⅔	215	65	47	3.53
Sherry Smith	11	10	27	24	16	188⅓	214	31	25	3.73
Byron Speece	0	0	2	0	0	3	1	2	1	0.00
George Uhle	(27)	11	39	(36)	(32)	(318⅓)	(300)	(118)	159	2.83
	88	66		154	(96)	1,374	1,412	450	381	3.40

Shutouts: Miller (3), Uhle (3), Levsen (2), Buckeye, Shaute, Smith
Saves: Karr, Miller, Shaute, Uhle

	G	AB	R	H	2B	3B	HR	RBI	SB	AVG
Martin Autry	3	7	1	1	0	0	0	0	0	.143
George Burns (1B)	151	603	97	(216)	(64)	3	4	114	13	.358
Fred Eichrodt	37	80	14	25	7	1	0	7	1	.313
Johnny Hodapp	3	5	0	1	0	0	0	0	0	.200
Charlie Jamieson (LF)	143	555	89	166	33	7	2	45	9	.299
Ray Knode	31	24	6	8	1	1	0	4	0	.333
Guy Lacy	13	24	2	4	0	0	1	2	0	.167
Cliff Lee	21	40	4	7	1	0	1	2	0	.175
Rube Lutzke (3B)	142	475	42	124	28	6	0	59	6	.261
Pat McNulty	48	56	3	14	2	1	0	6	0	.250
Glenn Myatt	56	117	14	29	5	2	0	13	1	.248
Ernie Padgett	36	62	7	13	0	1	0	6	1	.210
Joe Sewell (SS)	154	578	91	187	41	5	4	85	17	.324
Luke Sewell (C)	126	433	41	103	16	4	0	46	9	.238
Tris Speaker (CF)	150	539	96	164	52	8	7	86	6	.304
Freddy Spurgeon (2B)	149	614	101	181	31	3	0	49	7	.295
Homer Summa (RF)	154	581	74	179	31	6	4	76	15	.308
		5,293	738	1,529	(333)	49	27	643	88	.289

1927

Record: 66–87
Finish: Sixth
Games Behind: 43½
Manager: Jack McCallister

It was early in 1927 that American League president Byron "Ban" Johnson's health began to fail, and his illness—along with a disastrous season on the field under new manager Jack McCallister—led to the sale of the Indians and sweeping changes within the organization.

Without Speaker there was little leadership and not much offense. Emil "Dutch" Levsen, the "iron man" of 1926, couldn't win more than three games (and would be out of the major leagues a year later). Ace pitcher George Uhle slumped from 27 victories to eight. And the Indians' only consistent winner was rookie Willis Hudlin, whose record was 18–12.

With New York running away with the pennant—the Yankees won a then record 110 games and were never out of first place—the Indians plummeted into seventh place in late July. They went 14–11 in August, their only winning month of the season, to climb into sixth place.

McCallister, 48, who'd neither played nor managed in the major leagues previously, was not rehired at the end of the season (and never managed again).

With Johnson's health failing, the AL looked for a new president and decided that Ernest S. "Barney" Barnard was the best candidate.

But Barnard was president of the Indians, a position to which he was promoted in 1922 upon the death of James C. "Sunny Jim" Dunn. Barnard had promised Dunn that he would continue as the chief operating officer of the franchise as long as it was owned by Mrs. Dunn.

Thus, when a Cleveland millionaire real estate executive named Alva Bradley and a group of his friends showed an interest in owning the Indians, Barnard was happy to negotiate a deal. He wanted to move on to the AL presidency.

The sale was finalized on November 17, reportedly for the then outrageous sum of $1 million. Bradley's syndicate included his brother Charles, John Sherwin, Sr., George Martin, Percy Morgan, A. C. Ernst, Frank Hobson, former U.S. secretary of war Newton D. Baker, Joseph C. Hostetler, O. P. Van Sweringen, and his brother M. J., all native Clevelanders.

Alva Bradley became the president of the Indians and named William "Billy" Evans to run the team as general manager. Then McCallister was replaced by Roger Peckinpaugh as field manager.

Evans was another former sportswriter who had been an American League umpire the previous 20 years. Peckinpaugh played shortstop for the Indians briefly in 1910 and 1912 before he was traded to the New York Yankees, whom he served as player-manager for 20 games in the final month of the 1914 season.

Another change after the Bradley syndicate took over the Indians was that Dunn Field reverted back to its orginal name, League Park, which it had been called prior to the purchase of the franchise by Dunn in 1915.

	W	L	G	GS	CG	IP	H	BB	K	ERA
Jumbo Brown	0	2	8	0	0	18⅔	19	26	8	6.27
Garland Buckeye	10	17	35	25	13	204⅔	231	74	38	3.96
Hap Collard	0	0	4	0	0	5⅓	8	3	2	5.06
Nick Cullop	0	0	1	0	0	1	3	0	0	9.00
Wes Ferrell	0	0	1	0	0	1	3	2	0	27.00
George Grant	4	6	25	3	2	74⅔	85	40	19	4.46
Willis Hudlin	18	12	43	30	18	264⅔	(291)	83	65	4.01
Benn Karr	3	3	22	5	1	76⅔	92	32	17	5.05
Dutch Levsen	3	7	25	13	2	80⅓	96	37	15	5.49
Hal McKain	0	1	2	1	0	11	18	4	5	4.09
Jake Miller	10	8	34	23	11	185⅔	189	48	53	3.21
Joe Shaute	9	16	45	28	14	230⅓	255	75	63	4.22
Sherry Smith	1	4	11	2	1	38	53	14	8	5.45
George Uhle	8	9	25	22	10	153⅓	187	59	69	4.34
Willie Underhill	0	2	4	1	0	8⅓	12	11	4	9.72
	66	87		153	72	1,353⅓	1,542	508	366	4.27

Shutouts: Buckeye (2), Hudlin, Levsen, Uhle
Saves: Karr (2), Shaute (2), Buckeye, Grant, Smith, Uhle

	G	AB	R	H	2B	3B	HR	RBI	SB	AVG
Martin Autry	16	43	5	11	4	1	0	7	0	.256
Johnny Burnett	17	8	5	0	0	0	0	0	1	.000
George Burns (1B)	140	549	84	175	51	2	3	78	13	.319
Nick Cullop	32	68	9	16	2	3	1	8	0	.235
Fred Eichrodt (CF)	85	267	24	59	19	2	0	25	2	.221
Lew Fonseca (2B)	112	428	60	133	20	7	2	40	12	.311
George Gerken	6	14	1	3	0	0	0	2	0	.214
Johnny Gill	21	60	8	13	3	0	1	4	1	.217
Johnny Hodapp	79	240	25	73	15	3	5	40	2	.304
Baby Doll Jacobson	32	103	13	26	5	0	0	13	0	.252
Charlie Jamieson (LF)	127	489	73	151	23	6	0	36	7	.309
Sam Langford	20	67	10	18	5	0	1	7	0	.269
Carl Lind	12	37	2	5	0	0	0	1	1	.135
Rube Lutzke (3B)	100	311	35	78	12	3	0	41	2	.251
Pat McNulty	19	41	3	13	1	0	0	4	1	.317
Glenn Myatt	55	94	15	23	6	0	2	8	1	.245
Bernie Neis	32	96	17	29	9	0	4	18	0	.302
Ernie Padgett	7	7	1	2	0	0	0	0	0	.286
Joe Sewell (SS)	153	569	83	180	48	5	1	92	3	.316
Luke Sewell (C)	128	470	52	138	27	6	0	53	4	.294
Freddy Spurgeon	57	179	30	45	6	1	1	19	8	.251
Homer Summa (RF)	145	574	73	164	41	7	4	74	6	.286
Dutch Ussat	4	16	4	3	0	1	0	2	0	.188
		5,202	668	1,471	(321)	52	26	616	65	.283

1928

Record: 62–92
Finish: Seventh
Games Behind: 39
Manager: Roger Peckinpaugh

The Indians fared even worse under the new Alva Bradley–Billy Evans–Roger Peckinpaugh regime, though not for a lack of trying.

Roger Peckinpaugh and his wife read the *Cleveland News* account of his being hired to manage the Indians in 1928.

Especially bold was an effort by Bradley—undoubtedly at the urging of Evans and Peckinpaugh—to purchase from the New York Yankees the contract of young first baseman Lou Gehrig who, that winter, was holding out for a pay raise. He hit .373 in 1927, his third full season in the major leagues.

Prior to the start of spring training Bradley wrote the following letter to Ed Barrow, owner of the Yankees:

"Dear Mr. Barrow:

"From time to time during the last week there have been articles in the Cleveland newspapers referring to your inability to sign Lou Gehrig.

"The thought has occurred to me that if you are having real trouble with him that you might want to sell him. I am authorized to make an offer [for Gehrig] of $150,000."

It was rejected, but Bradley, an affable though somewhat introverted man who admittedly knew little about baseball or the business of the game, was persistent.

Bradley made another offer, this one $175,000 plus first baseman George Burns, the Indians' best hitter the previous two seasons who was then nearing the end of a fine career. Rebuffed again, Bradley tried $250,000, but still Barrow said no and finally signed Gehrig.

With the deal definitely off, Bradley wrote another letter to Barrow in which he said: "I was selfish enough to hope you would have more trouble [signing Gehrig]. My sole effort is to build up an organization that will put Cleveland back on the baseball map."

But such success definitely didn't happen in 1928, despite the good intentions of Bradley, Evans, and Peckinpaugh.

It also didn't happen despite a flying start by the Indians. Their record in April was 12–6, only a half game behind New York, which had a 10–3 record the first month and went on to win a third straight pennant.

Everything that followed was downhill, especially in September when the Tribe won only four games while losing 20, and landed in seventh place, its lowest level in 13 years.

Burns slumped 70 points in his batting average and played

The 1928 Cleveland Indians.

only 82 games before he was released, and while George Uhle improved his record, it still was five games under .500 and he, too, was gone at the end of the season.

Before the year ended a bond issue for $2.5 million to finance construction of a downtown stadium was approved by Cleveland voters on November 6. The site was filled-in land on the lakefront at the northern end of West 3rd Street.

It was a project initially proposed in 1927 by Ernest S. Barnard while he was still president of the Indians, prior to the sale of the franchise to the Bradley syndicate. Aware that the club was on the market, Barnard figured—and rightly so—that a new and larger ballpark would enhance its value, and that it also would strengthen the entire American League, which he knew he would soon be heading.

Former sportswriter and umpire Billy Evans (left), who was general manager of the Indians from 1927 to 1935, visits with American League umpire Bil McGowan prior to a game at League Park in 1928.

	W	L	G	GS	CG	IP	H	BB	K	ERA
Les Barnhart	0	1	2	1	0	9	13	4	1	7.00
Bill Bayne	2	5	37	6	3	108⅔	128	43	39	5.13
Clint Brown	0	1	2	1	1	11	14	2	2	4.91
Jumbo Brown	0	1	5	0	0	14⅔	19	15	12	6.75
Garland Buckeye	1	5	9	6	0	35	58	5	6	6.69
Hap Collard	0	0	1	0	0	4	4	4	1	2.25
Wes Ferrell	0	2	2	2	1	16	15	5	4	2.25
George Grant	10	8	28	18	6	155⅓	196	76	39	5.04
Mel Harder	0	2	23	1	0	49	64	32	15	6.61
Willis Hudlin	14	14	42	26	10	220⅓	231	90	62	4.04
Dutch Levsen	0	3	11	3	0	41⅓	39	31	7	5.44
Johnny Miljus	1	4	11	4	1	50⅔	46	20	19	2.66
Jake Miller	8	9	25	24	8	158	203	43	37	4.44
Jim Moore	0	1	1	1	1	9	5	5	1	2.00
Joe Shaute	13	17	36	31	21	253⅔	295	68	81	4.04
George Uhle	12	17	31	28	18	214⅓	252	48	74	4.07
Willie Underhill	1	2	11	3	1	28	33	20	16	4.50
	62	92		(155)	71	1,378	(1,615)	511	416	4.47

Shutouts: Uhle (2), Grant, Shaute
Saves: Hudlin (7), Bayne (3), Shaute (2), Harder, Miljus, Uhle

	G	AB	R	H	2B	3B	HR	RBI	SB	AVG
Martin Autry	22	60	6	18	6	1	1	9	0	.300
Cecil Bolton	4	13	1	2	0	2	0	0	0	.154
Johnny Burnett	3	10	3	5	0	0	0	1	0	.500
George Burns	82	209	29	52	12	1	5	30	2	.249
Bruce Caldwell	18	27	2	6	1	1	0	3	1	.222
Red Dorman	25	77	12	28	6	0	0	11	1	.364
Lew Fonseca (1B)	75	263	38	86	19	4	3	36	4	.327
George Gerken	38	115	16	26	7	2	0	9	3	.226
Johnny Gill	2	2	0	0	0	0	0	0	0	.000
Jonah Goldman	7	21	1	5	1	0	0	2	0	.238
Luther Harvel	40	136	12	30	6	1	0	12	1	.221
Johnny Hodapp (3B)	116	449	51	145	31	6	2	73	2	.323
Charlie Jamieson (LF)	112	433	63	133	18	4	1	37	3	.307
Sam Langford (CF)	110	427	50	118	17	8	4	50	3	.276
Carl Lind (2B)	154	(650)	102	191	42	4	1	54	8	.294
Ed Montague	32	51	12	12	0	1	0	3	0	.235
Ed Morgan	76	265	42	83	24	6	4	54	5	.313
Glenn Myatt	58	125	9	36	7	2	1	15	0	.288
Art Reinholz	2	3	0	1	0	0	0	0	0	.333
Joe Sewell (SS)	(155)	588	79	190	40	2	4	70	7	.323
Luke Sewell (C)	122	411	52	111	16	9	3	52	3	.270
Homer Summa (RF)	134	504	60	143	26	3	3	57	4	.284
Ollie Tucker	14	47	5	6	0	0	1	2	0	.128
Al Van Camp	5	17	0	4	1	0	0	2	1	.235
Aaron Ward	6	9	0	1	0	0	0	0	0	.111
Frank Wilson	2	1	0	0	0	0	0	0	0	.000
		(5,386)	674	1,535	299	61	34	611	50	.285

1929

Record: 81–71
Finish: Third
Games Behind: 24
Manager: Roger Peckinpaugh

Billy Evans and Roger Peckinpaugh had seen enough and, armed with Alva Bradley's checkbook, went shopping in the winter of 1928–29.

Their prime purchase was an outfielder named Earl Averill. They paid San Francisco of the Pacific Coast League $40,000 plus two minor leaguers for Averill—although, in the final analysis, the outfielder actually cost them $45,000 cash.

Before Averill would report for spring training he told the Indians, "If I'm worth $40,000, I'm worth some money to myself." He demanded a bonus of $5,000 and got it.

Evans also acquired two more outfielders, paying $30,000 to Baltimore of the International League for "Twitchy Dick" Porter, and trading with the Chicago White Sox for Bibb Falk.

Right-hander Wes Ferrell was brought up from the minors and, with his blazing fastball, became the Indians' best pitcher, winning 21 games as a rookie.

And though Lew Fonseca was not a newcomer—he was purchased from Newark of the International League in 1927 prior to the Alva Bradley regime in Cleveland—it was under Peckinpaugh that the 30-year-old first baseman blossomed. He won the batting championship with a .369 average.

Fonseca, who'd played five different positions in five seasons for Cincinnati and Philadelphia in the National League from 1921 to 1925, was sent back to the minors in 1926 and hit .381 for Newark.

Primarily a second baseman in 1927, Fonseca batted .311 in 112 games, and in 1928 in 75 games at shortstop and third, second, and first base, he hit .327.

Then, after replacing George Burns at first base, Fonseca was the AL's most proficient batter in 1929, a tribute to his perseverance—and Peckinpaugh's astuteness.

The moves paid off. The Indians were the most improved team in the AL and climbed four places in the standings,

though their deficit behind pennant-winning Philadelphia was huge.

They started poorly, didn't reach the .500 mark until mid-July and finished fast, winning 16 of 25 games in September.

Averill made an auspicious debut with the Indians; in his first at bat in a major league game he hammered a pitch from Detroit southpaw Earl Whitehill over the right-field wall at League Park. He went on to hit 18 homers while batting .332. Another home run at League Park, this one by New York's Babe Ruth, also was memorable. It was hit on August 11 off Willis Hudlin and was the 500th of Ruth's career.

Though construction on the new stadium was to have begun in 1929, it was delayed by a taxpayer's suit and other obstacles that weren't cleared until well into the following year.

It also was in 1929, in a game on May 13 at League Park, that the Indians and Yankees became the first teams in professional baseball to wear numbers on the backs of their uniforms.

	W	L	G	GS	CG	IP	H	BB	K	ERA
Clint Brown	0	2	3	1	1	16⅓	18	6	1	3.31
Wes Ferrell	21	10	43	25	18	242⅔	256	109	100	3.60
George Grant	0	2	12	0	0	24	41	23	5	10.50
Mel Harder	1	0	11	0	0	17⅔	24	5	4	5.60
Ken Holloway	6	5	25	11	6	119	118	37	32	3.03
Willis Hudlin	17	15	40	33	22	280⅓	299	73	60	3.34
Johnny Miljus	8	8	34	15	4	128⅓	174	64	42	5.19
Jake Miller	14	12	29	29	14	206	227	60	58	3.58
Jim Moore	0	0	2	0	0	5⅔	6	4	0	9.53
Joe Shaute	8	8	26	24	8	162	211	52	43	4.28
Milt Shoffner	2	3	11	3	1	44⅔	46	22	15	5.04
Jimmy Zinn	4	6	18	11	6	105⅔	150	33	29	5.04
	81	71		152	80	1,352	1,570	488	389	4.05

Shutouts: Holloway (2), Hudlin (2), Miller (2), Ferrell, Zinn
Saves: Ferrell (5), Miljus (2), Zinn (2), Hudlin

	G	AB	R	H	2B	3B	HR	RBI	SB	AVG
Earl Averill (CF)	151	597	110	198	43	13	18	96	13	.332
Johnny Burnett	19	33	2	5	1	0	0	2	0	.152
Bibb Falk (RF)	125	426	65	133	30	7	13	93	4	.312
Lew Fonseca (1B)	148	566	97	209	44	15	6	103	19	(.369)
Ray Gardner	82	256	28	67	3	2	1	24	10	.262
Grover Hartley	24	33	2	9	0	1	0	8	0	.273
Joe Hauser	37	48	8	12	1	1	3	9	0	.250
Johnny Hodapp (2B)	90	294	30	96	12	7	4	51	3	.327
Charlie Jamieson (LF)	102	364	56	106	22	1	0	26	2	.291
Dan Jessee	1	0	0	0	0	0	0	0	0	—
Carl Lind	66	225	19	54	8	1	0	13	0	.240
Ed Morgan	93	318	60	101	19	10	3	37	4	.318
Glenn Myatt	59	129	14	30	4	1	1	17	0	.233
Dick Porter	71	192	26	63	16	5	1	24	3	.328
Joe Sewell (3B)	152	578	90	182	38	3	7	73	6	.315
Luke Sewell (C)	124	406	41	96	16	3	1	39	6	.236
Jackie Tavener (SS)	92	250	25	53	9	4	2	27	1	.212
		5,187	717	1,525	294	79	62	684	75	.294

1930

Record: 81–73
Finish: Fourth
Games Behind: 21
Manager: Roger Peckinpaugh

Though the Indians' resurgence in 1929 provided great hope for continued improvement in 1930, such was not the case.

In fact, the Indians reversed the old saying, "Good field, no hit," to read, "Good hit, no field." No fewer than five regulars batted .300, topped by second baseman Johnny Hodapp's .354, sixth in the American League race. The trouble was, they were one of the worst defensive teams in the major leagues.

The Tribe committed 237 errors, most in the AL, and

The Indians starting outfield in 1930 (left to right): center fielder Earl Averill, right fielder "Twitchy Dick" Porter, and left fielder Bibb Falk.

	G	AB	R	H	2B	3B	HR	RBI	SB	AVG
Earl Averill (CF)	139	534	102	181	33	8	19	119	10	.339
Johnny Burnett	54	170	28	53	13	0	0	20	2	.312
George Detore	3	12	0	2	1	0	0	2	0	.167
Bibb Falk	82	191	34	62	12	1	4	36	2	.325
Lew Fonseca	40	129	20	36	9	2	0	17	1	.279
Ray Gardner	33	13	7	1	0	0	0	1	0	.077
Jonah Goldman (SS)	111	306	32	74	18	0	1	44	3	.242
Grover Hartley	1	4	0	3	0	0	0	1	0	.750
Johnny Hodapp (2B)	(154)	635	111	(225)	(51)	8	9	121	6	.354
Charlie Jamieson (LF)	103	366	64	110	22	1	1	52	5	.301
Carl Lind	24	69	8	17	3	0	0	6	0	.246
Ed Montague	58	179	37	47	5	2	1	16	1	.263
Ed Morgan (1B)	150	584	122	204	47	11	26	136	8	.349
Glenn Myatt	86	265	30	78	23	2	2	37	2	.294
Dick Porter (RF)	119	480	100	168	43	8	4	57	3	.350
Bob Seeds	85	277	37	79	11	3	3	32	1	.285
Joe Sewell (3B)	109	353	44	102	17	6	0	48	1	.289
Luke Sewell (C)	76	292	40	75	21	2	1	43	5	.257
Joe Sprinz	17	45	5	8	1	0	0	2	0	.178
Joe Vosmik	9	26	1	6	2	0	0	4	0	.231
Ralph Winegarner	5	22	5	10	1	0	0	2	0	.455
		5,439	890	1,654	(358)	59	72	830	51	.304

1931

Record: 78–76
Finish: Fourth
Games Behind: 30
Manager: Roger Peckinpaugh

The Indians continued to hit well, but also—again—fielded poorly. They repeated their fourth-place finish with a won-lost record that wasn't even as good as the previous season.

Several new faces were in the lineup, including third baseman Willie Kamm, who was acquired on May 17 from the Chicago White Sox for Lew Fonseca. Another was rookie outfielder Joe Vosmik, a graduate of the Cleveland sandlots, who was brought up from the minor leagues and established himself as a rising star, hitting .320 and driving in 117 runs.

Another fast start—nine victories in the first 13 games—propelled the Tribe into first place as Wes Ferrell pitched a no-hitter on April 29, beating St. Louis, 9–0, at League Park. Ferrell walked three batters, and three Browns reached on errors.

Ironically, the only ball that came close to being a hit was struck by Ferrell's older brother Rick, the St. Louis catcher, with two out in the eighth. He shot a grounder past third baseman Johnny Burnett, fielded deep in the hole by shortstop Bill Hunnefield. Hunnefield's throw was in time to retire Ferrell at first base, but it was wide and pulled Fonseca off the bag. The official scorer called it an error.

A week later the Indians embarked on a 12-game losing streak that continued from May 7 to 21, longest in their history. It dropped them deep in the standings, and they never completely recovered, though they battled back to reclaim fourth place with a 17–10 record in August.

Eddie Morgan, who replaced the traded Fonseca at first base, finished third in the American League batting race behind Philadelphia's Al Simmons (.390) and New York's Babe Ruth (.373). Earl Averill's 32 home runs, then a club record, also were third behind Ruth and his Yankee teammate, Lou Gehrig, each of whom hit 46. His feat earned for Averill a place on the first official major league all-star team chosen by 229 members of the Baseball Writers Association of America for *The Sporting News.*

The year also was memorable because of the deaths of AL president Ernest S. Barnard and his predecessor, Byron

wound up with a .962 fielding average, tied with Chicago for last place. Pennant-winning Philadelphia led the league with a .975 mark.

The Indians started fast again and maintained their pace the first two months, even taking over first place on June 13 from the Athletics. But after losing 19 of 22 games in July, they fell all the way into the basement briefly in August.

A late spurt, in which they won seven in a row in late August and again in early September, boosted the Indians into fourth place. But they could get no higher and finished five games behind third-place New York.

Earl Averill put on a sensational batting exhibition on September 17 when he smashed four home runs in a doubleheader against Washington. Three of the homers (including a grand slam) were hit consecutively in the opener, won by the Indians, 13–7, and one in his first at bat in the nightcap, a 6–4 loss to the Senators.

Construction on the Stadium finally got under way in late autumn in the hope that it would be completed by late 1931.

	W	L	G	GS	CG	IP	H	BB	K	ERA
Les Barnhart	1	0	1	1	0	8⅓	12	4	1	6.48
Belve Bean	3	3	23	3	1	74½	99	32	19	5.45
Clint Brown	11	13	35	31	16	213⅔	271	51	54	4.97
Wes Ferrell	25	13	43	35	25	296⅔	299	106	143	3.31
Sal Gliatto	0	0	8	0	0	15	21	9	7	6.60
Mel Harder	11	10	36	19	7	175⅓	205	68	44	4.21
Ken Holloway	1	1	12	2	0	30	49	14	8	8.40
Willis Hudlin	13	16	37	33	13	216⅔	255	76	60	4.57
Pete Jablonowski	8	7	39	7	2	118⅔	122	53	45	4.02
Roxie Lawson	1	2	7	4	2	33⅔	46	23	10	6.15
Jake Miller	4	4	24	9	1	88⅓	147	38	31	7.13
Joe Shaute	0	0	4	0	0	4⅔	8	4	2	15.43
Milt Shoffner	3	4	24	10	1	84⅔	129	50	17	7.97
	81	73		(154)	68	1,360	(1,663)	528	441	4.88

Shutouts: Brown (3), Ferrell, Hudlin
Saves: Ferrell (3), Bean (2), Gliatto (2), Harder (2), Holloway (2), Brown, Hudlin, Jablonowski

"Ban" Johnson, the founder of the AL, within 24 hours of each other. Barnard, a longtime front office executive of the Indians and club president from 1922 to 1927, died March 27; Johnson passed away the next day.

Though the Stadium was not far enough along in its construction to house any Indians games, a world heavyweight championship fight between Max Schmeling and W. L. "Young" Stribling was held on July 3. A crowd of 36,936 saw Schmeling retain his title with a 15th-round technical knockout.

	W	L	G	GS	CG	IP	H	BB	K	ERA
Belve Bean	0	1	4	0	0	7	11	4	3	6.43
Clint Brown	11	15	39	33	12	233⅓	284	55	50	4.71
Sarge Connally	5	5	17	9	5	85⅔	87	50	37	4.20
Howard Craghead	0	0	4	0	0	5⅔	8	2	2	6.35
Pete Donohue	0	0	2	0	0	5⅓	9	5	4	8.44
Wes Ferrell	22	12	40	35	(27)	276⅓	276	(130)	123	3.75
Mel Harder	13	14	40	24	9	194	229	72	63	4.36
Oral Hildebrand	2	1	5	2	2	26⅔	25	13	6	4.39
Willis Hudlin	15	14	44	34	15	254⅓	313	88	83	4.60
Pete Jablonowski	4	4	29	4	3	79⅔	100	29	25	4.63
Roxie Lawson	0	2	17	3	0	55⅔	72	36	20	7.60
Jake Miller	2	1	10	5	1	41⅓	45	19	17	4.35
Milt Shoffner	2	3	12	4	1	41	55	26	12	7.24
Fay Thomas	2	4	16	2	1	48⅔	63	32	25	5.18
	78	76		155	76	1,354⅔	1,577	561	470	4.63

Shutouts: Brown (2), Ferrell (2), Hudlin, Miller
Saves: Hudlin (4), Ferrell (3), Connally, Harder

	G	AB	R	H	2B	3B	HR	RBI	SB	AVG
Earl Averill (CF)	155	(627)	140	209	36	10	32	143	9	.333
Moe Berg	10	13	1	1	1	0	0	0	0	.077
Johnny Burnett	111	427	85	128	25	5	1	52	5	.300
Bruce Connatser	12	49	5	14	3	0	0	4	0	.286
George Detore	30	56	3	15	6	0	0	7	0	.268
Bibb Falk	79	161	30	49	13	1	2	28	1	.304
Lew Fonseca	26	108	21	40	9	1	1	14	3	.370
Jonah Goldman	30	62	0	8	1	0	0	3	1	.129
Odell Hale	25	92	14	26	2	4	1	5	2	.283
Johnny Hodapp (2B)	122	468	71	138	19	4	2	56	1	.295
Bill Hunnefield	21	71	13	17	4	1	0	4	3	.239
Charlie Jamieson	28	43	7	13	2	1	0	4	1	.302
Willie Kamm (3B)	114	410	68	121	31	4	0	66	13	.295
Ed Montague (SS)	64	193	27	55	8	3	1	26	3	.285
Ed Morgan (1B)	131	462	87	162	33	4	11	86	4	.351
Glenn Myatt	65	195	21	48	14	2	1	29	2	.246
Dick Porter (RF)	114	414	82	129	24	3	1	38	6	.312
Bob Seeds	48	134	26	41	4	1	1	10	1	.306
Luke Sewell (C)	108	375	45	103	30	4	1	53	1	.275
Joe Sprinz	1	3	0	0	0	0	0	0	0	.000
Joe Vosmik (LF)	149	591	80	189	36	14	7	117	7	.320
		5,445	885	1,612	(321)	69	71	812	63	.296

1932

Record: 87–65
Finish: Fourth
Games Behind: 19
Manager: Roger Peckinpaugh

The highlight of the season was the first game played in the Stadium on July 31 against the defending American League champion Philadelphia Athletics. It turned out to be a loss for the Indians, whose record improved, though they finished fourth for the third straight year.

The largest crowd in baseball history at that time—80,184 fans of whom 76,979 were paid—attended the inaugural as Philadelphia's Lefty Grove won a 1–0 duel against the Tribe's Mel Harder.

The only run of the game was scored in the eighth inning

after Athletics second baseman Max "Camera Eye" Bishop led off with a walk. He was sacrifice bunted to second by Max Bishop, and went home on a single by Mickey Cochrane.

Harder allowed five hits and reliever Oral Hildebrand one (in one inning), while the Indians got only four singles off Grove.

The *Cleveland Plain Dealer* called the Stadium "the ultimate athletic facility in the country," and the Indians played their 32 remaining home games (in 27 dates) at the new facility, completed at a cost of $2.64 million.

So pleased with the Stadium was owner Alva Bradley that he said, "We'll fill the place often, every Sunday," though his prediction did not come close to being accurate.

Other memorable events of the season: Johnny Burnett, then playing shortstop, set a major league record with nine hits—seven singles and two doubles—in 11 at bats in an 18-inning game that the Indians lost, 18–17, to Philadelphia on July 10; Wes Ferrell pitched a one-hitter to beat Boston, 3–0, on August 6, as Dale Alexander got the only safety, a scratch single in the fourth inning; and Burnett cracked the first home run at the Stadium into the lower right-field stands in the sixth inning off Washington's Tommy Thomas in a 7–4 victory over the Senators on August 7.

Otherwise there was little to celebrate in Cleveland except for a brief period in mid-July when the Indians completed a successful trip through the east. It boosted them, if only for a week, into second place with a 55–39 record, though they still trailed New York by 10 games.

It influenced management to move the Indians into the Stadium immediately, rather than to wait (as had been the plan) until 1933. They rescheduled the remainder of home games to the new facility with its larger capacity, hoping for a great surge in attendance.

But it didn't happen. The season total of 468,953 wasn't even as large as it had been in 1931 (483,027) when the Indians played all their home games at League Park.

Though four regulars managed to hit .300, many players—though not pitchers—complained about the large dimensions of the playing field at the Stadium. Then bereft of inner fences, the playing field had distances of 320 feet down the left- and right-field foul lines and 470 feet to dead center. Apparently unfazed, however, was Earl Averill, who tied his own club record by hitting 32 homers for the second year in a row.

	W	L	G	GS	CG	IP	H	BB	K	ERA
Clint Brown	15	12	37	32	21	262⅓	298	50	59	4.08
Sarge Connally	8	6	35	7	4	112⅓	119	42	32	4.33
Wes Ferrell	23	13	38	34	26	287⅔	299	104	105	3.66
Mel Harder	15	13	39	32	17	254⅔	277	68	90	3.75
Oral Hildebrand	8	6	27	15	7	129⅓	124	62	49	3.69
Willis Hudlin	12	8	33	21	12	181⅓	204	59	65	4.71
Pete Jablonowski	0	0	4	0	0	5	11	3	1	16.20
Leo Moon	0	0	1	0	0	5⅔	11	7	1	11.12
Monte Pearson	0	0	8	0	0	8	10	11	5	10.13
Jack Russell	5	7	18	11	6	113	146	27	27	4.70
Ralph Winegarner	1	0	5	1	1	17⅓	7	13	5	1.04
	87	65		153	94	1,377⅓	1,506	446	439	4.12

Shutouts: Ferrell (3), Brown, Connally, Harder
Saves: Connally (3), Hudlin (2), Brown, Ferrell, Russell

	G	AB	R	H	2B	3B	HR	RBI	SB	AVG
Earl Averill (CF)	153	631	116	198	37	14	32	124	5	.314
Boze Berger	1	1	0	0	0	0	0	0	0	.000
Joe Boley	1	4	0	1	0	0	0	0	0	.250
Johnny Burnett (SS)	129	512	81	152	23	5	4	53	2	.297
Bill Cissell (2B)	131	541	78	173	35	6	6	93	18	.320
Bruce Connatser	23	60	8	14	3	1	0	4	1	.233
Johnny Hodapp	7	16	2	2	1	0	0	0	0	.125
Charlie Jamieson	16	16	0	1	1	0	0	0	0	.063
Willie Kamm (3B)	148	524	76	150	34	9	3	83	6	.286
Ed Montague	66	192	29	47	5	1	0	24	3	.245
Ed Morgan (1B)	144	532	96	156	32	7	4	68	7	.293
Glenn Myatt	82	252	45	62	12	1	8	46	2	.246
Dick Porter (RF)	146	621	106	191	42	8	4	60	2	.308
Mike Powers	14	33	4	6	4	0	0	5	0	.182
Frankie Pytlak	12	29	5	7	1	1	0	4	0	.241
Bob Seeds	2	4	0	0	0	0	0	0	0	.000
Luke Sewell (C)	87	300	36	76	20	2	2	52	4	.253
Joe Vosmik (LF)	153	621	106	194	39	12	10	97	2	.312
	5,412	845	1,544	(310)	74	78	778	52	.285

1933

Record: 75–76
Finish: Fourth
Games Behind: 23½
Managers: Roger Peckinpaugh, Bibb Falk, Walter Johnson

The fourth-place habit of the Indians continued for the fourth consecutive year, during the height of the Great Depression. The team's poor start cost Roger Peckinpaugh his job on June 9, in the wake of a 1–7 eastern trip.

Though the Indians' record was 26–25 at the time, they were lodged in fifth place, and owner Alva Bradley had expected better results. Peckinpaugh was replaced by former Washington pitching star Walter Johnson (though Bibb Falk managed the team for one game on June 10, a 5–2 victory over St. Louis).

Firing Peckinpaugh was not a popular move. He was well liked by the media, while Johnson had developed a reputation for impatience while managing the Senators from 1929 to 1932.

Bradley said his decision was based on the fact that the Indians "lacked pep" and "played loosely." He claimed, "We only hire the manager; the public fires him."

The change did not have a positive effect on the Indians. They won 48 and lost 51 under Johnson, though they managed to climb one place in the standings by season's end.

Not all the blame was attributed to Johnson, however, as many of the hitters—again, not the pitchers—lamented the decision to play all home games at the Stadium.

The spacious playing field turned long drives that would be home runs at League Park and elsewhere in the American League into fly-ball outs.

For whatever reason, Earl Averill, who played despite an injury early in the season, was the only regular to bat .300 (which he barely did), though his wasn't the only average to decline. Joe Vosmik also was hurt and sidelined much of the first two months and hit 49 points lower than in 1933. Catcher Frankie Pytlak hit .310 in 80 games after being called up from the minors.

The pitchers slumped, too. Wes Ferrell, complaining of a sore arm, won 12 fewer games. And while Oral Hildebrand was the winningest member of the starting rotation, he clashed several times with Johnson, who didn't understand why everyone couldn't perform as he had.

Indians center fielder Earl Averill (left) and New York Yankees great Babe Ruth with a couple of admirers prior to a game at Cleveland Stadium in 1933.

It also was an unsuccessful season for the Indians at the box office as attendance fell even lower in the giant Stadium to 387,936.

Even before the season started, Bradley ordered a tightening of the purse strings. One of his decisions was to ban radio broadcasting of the games in the belief that play-by-play accounts hurt attendance.

Because the club suffered large financial losses in 1933, Bradley asked General Manager Billy Evans to take a pay cut, reportedly from $30,000 to $12,500. Evans resisted, but finally agreed to accept the $12,500 as a base salary when Bradley consented to pay him a $5,000 bonus if the team made a profit of $100,000.

	W	L	G	GS	CG	IP	H	BB	K	ERA
Belve Bean	1	2	27	2	0	70⅓	80	20	41	5.25
Clint Brown	11	12	33	23	10	185	202	34	47	3.41
Sarge Connally	5	3	41	3	1	103	112	49	30	4.89
Howard Craghead	0	0	11	0	0	17⅓	19	10	2	6.23
Wes Ferrell	11	12	28	26	16	201	225	70	41	4.21
Mel Harder	15	17	43	31	14	253	254	67	81	(2.95)
Oral Hildebrand	16	11	36	31	15	220⅓	205	88	90	3.76
Willis Hudlin	5	13	34	17	6	147⅓	161	61	44	3.97
Thornton Lee	1	1	3	2	2	17⅓	13	11	7	4.15
Monte Pearson	10	5	19	16	10	135⅓	111	55	54	2.33
	75	76		151	(74)	1,350	1,382	465	437	(3.71)

Shutouts: Hildebrand (6), Brown (2), Harder (2), Ferrell
Saves: Harder (4), Brown, Connally, Hudlin

	G	AB	R	H	2B	3B	HR	RBI	SB	AVG
Earl Averill (CF)	151	599	83	180	39	16	11	92	3	.301
Harley Boss (1B)	112	438	54	118	17	7	1	53	2	.269
Johnny Burnett	83	261	39	71	11	2	1	29	3	.272
Bill Cissell	112	409	53	94	21	3	6	33	6	.230
Milt Galatzer	57	160	19	38	2	1	1	17	2	.238
Odell Hale (2B)	98	351	49	97	19	8	10	64	2	.276
Willie Kamm (3B)	133	447	59	126	17	2	1	47	6	.282
Bill Knickerbocker (SS)	80	279	20	63	16	3	2	32	1	.226
Ed Morgan	39	121	10	32	3	3	1	13	1	.264
Glenn Myatt	40	77	10	18	4	0	0	7	0	.234
Johnny Oulliber	22	75	9	20	1	0	0	3	0	.267
Dick Porter (RF)	132	499	73	133	19	6	0	41	4	.267
Mike Powers	24	47	6	13	2	1	0	2	2	.277
Frankie Pytlak	80	248	36	77	10	6	2	33	3	.310
Roy Spencer (C)	75	227	26	46	5	2	0	23	0	.203
Hal Trosky	11	44	6	13	1	2	1	8	0	.295
Joe Vosmik (LF)	119	438	53	115	20	10	4	56	0	.263
	5,240	654	1,366	218	77	50	610	36	.261	

1934

Record: 85–69
Finish: Third
Games Behind: 16
Manager: Walter Johnson

The Indians moved back to League Park for all their home games in 1934, and though their record improved, it was a season of travail.

Manager Walter Johnson continued to have conflicts with pitcher Oral Hildebrand and several other players, which led to severe criticism by the media. He was charged with poor handling of the pitching staff.

Johnson also was blamed—unfairly—for the May 25 trade of Wes Ferrell to Boston, where he won 14 games while losing only five. For Ferrell and outfielder "Twitchy Dick" Porter the Indians received pitcher Bob Weiland and outfielder Bob Seeds, as well as—perhaps most importantly because of the cash crunch they were experiencing—$25,000 cash. Neither of the newcomers did anything to distinguish himself with the Tribe.

Ed Bang, then sports editor of the *Cleveland News*, wrote in his "Between You and Me" column on July 17:

"Johnson showed anything but mental alertness and managerial ability. Truth be told, he fell so far short of what a wide-awake manager should do that the fans who were wont to cheer him in the days gone by as a great pitcher, groaned in despair and booed him."

By the end of July, Johnson and beat reporters covering the team quit speaking except when it was absolutely necessary.

After one distressing series of failure in August when the Indians lost 17 of 27 games, the *Cleveland Press* ran a story topped by an eight-column headline that screamed: "The Indians, Without Leadership, Have Flopped; What Are the Owners Going to Do About It?"

The unstated answer: Nothing. At least not in 1934.

Johnson was re-signed for 1935 after the Indians won 21 games while losing only 10 in September to take over third place, though it was too late to climb any higher.

Local newspapers also were critical of owner Alva Bradley's decision to move the Indians back to League Park full-time. The Stadium was called a white elephant because of its limited use.

One of the few highlights of the season took place on May 30 when rookie first baseman Hal Trosky smashed three home runs in a 5–4 victory over Chicago at League Park. He went on to hit 35 homers, breaking Earl Averill's club record of 32.

Another highlight for Cleveland fans occurred in the second annual All-Star Game at the Polo Grounds in New York, won by the American League, 9–7, on July 10. The victory was credited to Mel Harder, a 20-game winner for the first time in his long career with the Indians. He held the National League to one hit in five innings, and Averill drove in three runs with a triple and double.

Averill also had a memorable day in Philadelphia on August 18. He reached base in nine consecutive at bats in a doubleheader. He walked four times in the opener, won by the Athletics, 2–1, and got five consecutive hits in the nightcap as the Indians won, 10–0.

	W	L	G	GS	CG	IP	H	BB	K	ERA
Belve Bean	5	1	21	1	0	51⅓	53	21	20	3.86
Clint Brown	4	3	17	2	0	50⅓	83	14	15	5.90
Lloyd Brown	5	10	38	15	5	117	116	51	39	3.85
Sarge Connally	0	0	5	0	0	5⅓	4	5	1	5.06
Denny Galehouse	0	0	1	0	0	1	2	1	0	18.00
Mel Harder	20	12	44	29	17	255⅓	246	81	91	2.61
Oral Hildebrand	11	9	33	28	10	198	225	99	72	4.50
Willis Hudlin	15	10	36	26	15	195	210	65	58	4.75
Thornton Lee	1	1	24	6	0	85⅔	105	44	41	5.04
Monte Pearson	18	13	39	33	19	254⅔	257	130	140	4.52
Bill Perrin	0	1	1	1	0	5	13	2	3	14.40
Bob Weiland	1	5	16	7	2	70	71	30	42	4.11
Ralph Winegarner	5	4	22	6	4	78⅓	91	39	32	5.51
	85	69		154	72	1,367	1,476	582	554	4.28

Shutouts: Harder (6), Hildebrand, Hudlin
Saves: Lloyd Brown (6), Harder (4), Hudlin (4), Pearson (2), Clint Brown, Connally, Hildebrand

	G	AB	R	H	2B	3B	HR	RBI	SB	AVG
Earl Averill (CF)	(154)	598	128	187	48	6	31	113	5	.313
Moe Berg	29	97	4	25	3	1	0	9	0	.258
Bill Brenzel	15	51	4	11	3	0	0	3	0	.216
Johnny Burnett	72	208	28	61	11	2	3	30	1	.293
Kit Carson	5	18	4	5	2	1	0	1	0	.278
Milt Galatzer	49	196	29	53	10	2	0	15	3	.270
Bob Garbark	5	11	1	0	0	0	0	0	0	.000
Odell Hale (2B)	143	563	82	170	44	6	13	101	8	.302
Dutch Holland	50	128	19	32	12	1	2	13	0	.250
Willie Kamm (3B)	121	386	52	104	23	3	0	42	7	.269
Bill Knickerbocker (SS)	146	593	82	188	32	5	4	67	6	.317
Eddie Moore	27	65	4	10	2	0	0	8	0	.154
Glenn Myatt	36	107	18	34	6	1	0	12	1	.318
Dick Porter	13	44	9	10	2	1	1	6	0	.227
Frankie Pytlak (C)	91	289	46	75	12	4	0	35	11	.260
Sam Rice (RF)	97	335	48	98	19	1	1	33	5	.293
Bob Seeds	61	186	28	46	8	1	0	18	2	.247
Roy Spencer	5	7	0	1	1	0	0	2	0	.143
Hal Trosky (1B)	(154)	625	117	206	45	9	35	142	2	.330
Joe Vosmik (LF)	104	405	71	138	33	2	6	78	1	.341
		5,396	814	1,550	340	46	100	763	52	.287

1935

Record: 82–71
Finish: Third
Games Behind: 12
Managers: Walter Johnson, Steve O'Neill

All appeared to be harmonious when the Indians reported to New Orleans for spring training in 1935, probably because they'd finished 1934 so well and hopes were high they could be a contender.

But it wasn't long before discontent and dissension set in again as the players were upset by manager Walter Johnson during an eastern trip.

While the team was in Philadelphia, the manager told the media that he had discovered an "anti-Johnson" bloc among the Indians. He said it was headed by catcher Glenn Myatt and third baseman Willie Kamm.

Johnson promptly released Myatt and sent Kamm back to Cleveland under indefinite suspension, taking the action "for the good of the team."

But it created a maelstrom of anger instead, virtually all of it directed at Johnson.

Kamm demanded a chance to clear his name and, with the help of owner Alva Bradley, received a hearing before Commissioner Kenesaw Mountain Landis.

The "trial," as it was called in the newspapers, was held a few days later. "The commissioner ruled, in effect, that, 'They [Johnson and Kamm] are both nice boys of excellent character and reputation, but they just can't get along together. It's too bad, but I can't do anything about it,'" the *Cleveland News* reported.

While Landis couldn't do anything about it, Bradley could—though he didn't do so immediately.

In the wake of Landis's announcement, Kamm was appointed a scout for the Indians. Myatt signed with the New York Giants after turning down offers from the Chicago White Sox and Philadelphia Athletics.

The pot came to a boil on June 6 when an ad appeared in all three Cleveland newspapers, the *Plain Dealer, Press,* and *News.*

It was headed, "Some Inside Stuff Direct from the Camp of the Indians."

The ad stated in part, "We, the members of the Cleveland Baseball Club, want the fans to know that we are not a team split wide open by dissension, arrayed against our manager."

It continued for 12 inches of space and at the bottom was signed by 21 players: Oral Hildebrand, Hal Trosky, Monte Pearson, Mel Harder, Willis Hudlin, Roy Hughes, Thornton Lee, Clint Brown, Ab Wright, Ralph Winegarner, Bill Brenzel, Bosey Berger, Sammy Hale, Billy Knickerbocker, Mike Galatzer, Walter Stewart, Frank Pytlak, Joe Vosmik, Earl Averill, Lloyd Brown, and Bruce Campbell.

The only player on the roster at that time whose name did not appear in the ad was Eddie Phillips, a substitute catcher who appeared in 70 games (and hit .273). It was the only season he was on the team.

A month later, at the height of the anti-Johnson strife, the third annual All-Star Game took place in Cleveland in front of a crowd of 69,831 at the Stadium, though the Indians continued to play all their home games at League Park. Mel Harder earned a save, working in relief of winner Lefty Gomez as Jimmy Foxx homered to give the American League a 4–1 victory.

Bradley tried to weather the storm on behalf of Johnson, whom he genuinely liked. But when attendance suffered because of the hostility of the fans toward the embattled manager, Bradley was compelled to take action.

As the Indians were floundering in fifth place with a 46–48 record on August 4, Bradley stated, as he had two years earlier in his dismissal of Roger Peckinpaugh, "We only hire the manager; the public fires him."

Two of the pitchers in the 1935 All-Star Game—Mel Harder (left) of the Indians, and Bill Walker of the St. Louis Cardinals.

And with that, Johnson was replaced by coach Steve O'Neill, who had been a catcher for the Indians from 1911 to 1923.

Though they were victims of a 6–0 no-hitter by Chicago's Vernon Kennedy on August 31, the Indians improved dramatically under O'Neill. They won 36 and lost 23 in the final two months to ascend two places in the standings to third, although by then it was too late to climb any higher.

Even before Johnson was replaced as manager the Indians made off-the-field headline news.

On August 3 outfielder Bruce Campbell was stricken with a form of spinal meningitis. A 25-year-old left-handed batter who had been acquired the previous winter from the St. Louis Browns in a trade for shortstop Johnny Burnett, pitcher Bob Weiland, and cash, Campbell played no more that season.

Ironically, it also was 1935, the year of his overthrow as manager of the Indians, that Johnson was among the initial class of former players elected to the Hall of Fame, along with Ty Cobb, Babe Ruth, Honus Wagner, and Christy Mathewson.

Joe Vosmik, the former Cleveland sandlotter, lost the American League batting championship to Washington's Buddy Myer by less than a full percentage point. Vosmik's average was .348387, while Myer finished with .349025, after overtaking Vosmik on the final day of the season, September 29.

The morning of that final day Vosmik had a three-point margin as the Indians went into a doubleheader against the St. Louis Browns while the Senators were playing Philadelphia. To protect what he thought was a safe lead, Vosmik sat out the first game, though he made an out as a ninth-inning pinch hitter.

After receiving word that Myer had gone 4-for-5, which put him ahead of the Cleveland outfielder, Vosmik played the second game. He singled in his first three at bats, but the game was called after six innings because of darkness, and Vosmik's bid fell short.

	W	L	G	GS	CG	IP	H	BB	K	ERA
Belve Bean	0	0	1	0	0	1	2	0	0	9.00
Clint Brown	4	3	23	5	1	49	61	14	20	5.14
Lloyd Brown	8	7	42	8	4	122	123	37	45	3.61
Denny Galehouse	1	0	5	1	1	13	16	9	8	9.00
Mel Harder	22	11	42	35	17	287⅓	313	53	95	3.29
Oral Hildebrand	9	8	34	20	8	171⅓	171	63	49	3.94
Willis Hudlin	15	11	36	29	14	231⅔	252	61	45	3.69
Thornton Lee	7	10	32	20	8	180⅔	179	71	81	4.04
Monte Pearson	8	13	30	24	10	181¼	199	103	90	4.90
Lefty Stewart	6	6	24	10	2	91	122	17	24	5.44
Ralph Winegarner	2	2	25	4	2	67⅓	89	29	41	5.75
	82	71		(156)	67	(1,396)	1,527	457	498	4.15

Shutouts: Harder (4), Hudlin (3), Lloyd Brown (2), Lee, Pearson, Stewart
Saves: Hildebrand (5), Hudlin (5), Lloyd Brown (4), Clint Brown (2), Harder (2), Stewart (2), Lee

	G	AB	R	H	2B	3B	HR	RBI	SB	AVG
Earl Averill (CF)	140	563	109	162	34	13	19	79	8	.288
Boze Berger (2B)	124	461	62	119	27	5	5	43	7	.258
Bill Brenzel	52	142	12	31	5	1	0	14	2	.218
Bruce Campbell (RF)	80	308	56	100	26	3	7	54	2	.325
Kit Carson	16	22	1	5	2	0	0	1	0	.227
Milt Galatzer	93	259	45	78	9	3	0	19	4	.301
Bob Garbark	6	18	4	6	1	0	0	4	0	.333
Greek George	2	0	0	0	0	0	0	0	0	—
Odell Hale (3B)	150	589	80	179	37	11	16	101	15	.304
Roy Hughes	82	266	40	78	15	3	0	14	13	.293
Willie Kamm	6	18	2	6	0	0	0	1	0	.333
Bill Knickerbocker (SS)	132	540	77	161	34	5	0	55	2	.298
Glenn Myatt	10	36	1	3	1	0	0	2	0	.083
Eddie Phillips (C)	70	220	18	60	16	1	1	41	0	.273
Frankie Pytlak	55	149	14	44	6	1	1	12	3	.295
Hal Trosky (1B)	(154)	632	84	171	33	7	26	113	1	.271
Joe Vosmik (LF)	152	620	93	(216)	(47)	(20)	10	110	2	.348
Ab Wright	67	160	17	38	11	1	2	18	2	.238
		5,534	776	1,573	(324)	77	93	737	63	.284

1936

Record: 80–74
Finish: Fifth
Games Behind: 22½
Manager: Steve O'Neill

Cyril C. "Cy" Slapnicka took over at the helm of the Indians in 1936, and it was only appropriate that his most famous discovery, Bob Feller, also came to Cleveland that year.

Slapnicka had been a scout for the Tribe for 13 years and signed more than 30 players who eventually made it to the major leagues. He replaced Billy Evans, though given a different title. The position of "general manager" was abolished by owner Alva Bradley, and Slapnicka was named "assistant to the president."

Evans had resigned (though he subsequently claimed he was fired) in November 1935. He'd been asked to take another pay cut as the Indians announced their profits had declined to $70,000. Evans' salary had been slashed the previous year from $30,000 to $12,500 with the stipulation he'd receive a $5,000 bonus if the club's profits exceeded $100,000.

Slapnicka's career with the Indians began 1910. As a minor league pitcher for Rockford, Illinois, he was drafted by the Tribe, though he never got any closer to Cleveland as a player than Toledo, Ohio.

It was in the summer of 1935 that Slapnicka discovered Feller, then 16, pitching for a sandlot team on a dusty diamond in Des Moines, Iowa.

As Slapnicka was quoted in the *Cleveland News* prior to his death in 1979, "Living close by [in Cedar Rapids, Iowa], I'd heard a lot about this kid pitcher who was striking everybody out.

"I went to see him, watched a couple of pitches from the first base line and got the funny feeling that [Feller] was something extra. I moved behind the backstop and sat down on an automobile bumper. I stayed there for six innings. It must have been uncomfortable, but I never noticed.

"All I knew was that this was a kid pitcher I had to get. His fastball was fast and fuzzy; it didn't go on a straight line; it wiggled and shot around.

"I didn't know then that he was smart and that he had the heart of a lion, but I knew I was looking at an arm the likes of which you see only once in a lifetime."

It was on July 22, 1935, that Slapnicka signed Feller to a minor league contract. Feller was "paid" one dollar and given an autographed ball. The young pitcher also received a written promise that he could go home to visit his folks whenever he got lonely.

When Slapnicka met with the directors of the Indians, he raved about Feller, telling them, "Gentlemen, I've found the greatest young pitcher I ever saw. I suppose this sounds like the same old stuff, but this boy will be one of the greatest pitchers the world has ever known."

A problem developed, however, because Slapnicka—either intentionally or inadvertently—violated the major-minor league agreement then in effect. They nearly lost Feller because of it.

They didn't because—to the great relief of Slapnicka—Feller himself, along with his father, made amends for the Indians' transgression.

What Slapnicka did was sign Feller to a contract with Fargo-Moorhead (North Dakota) of the Class D Northern League. Then he had that club assign Feller to New Orleans of the Class A Southern Association. Both Fargo-Moorhead and New Orleans were farm clubs of the Indians.

Instead of going to Fargo-Moorhead or New Orleans, Feller remained at his home in Van Meter, Iowa. He attended high school until late May, after which he reported directly to Cleveland. For nearly a month Feller worked out with the Indians and pitched for a local amateur team.

Thus Feller got to Cleveland without ever wearing a minor league uniform for even one day, though he had been listed in the office of Commissioner Kenesaw Mountain Landis as having been the property of both Fargo-Moorhead and New Orleans.

The rule (since changed) prohibited the signing of a sandlotter to a major league contract. What Slapnicka did, as Judge Landis charged, was an obvious "cover-up."

Then, with the Tribe scheduled to play an exhibition game against the St. Louis Cardinals on July 6, the baseball world saw what Slapnicka already had seen in Feller.

Because manager Steve O'Neill didn't want to use a regular pitcher in the meaningless game, Feller entered the exhibition in the fourth inning and proceeded to strike out eight batters in three innings. He allowed two hits and walked one. Among his strikeout victims were Leo Durocher (twice), Pepper Martin, and Rip Collins.

It was a sensational professional baseball debut by the 17-year-old Iowa farm boy and was duly noted by many. Among them was Judge Landis, whose attention was called to Feller's performance by Lee Keyser, owner of the Des Moines, Iowa, club in the Class A Western League.

Keyser claimed that he had attempted to sign Feller, but that Slapnicka beat him to the punch, which was a violation of the rules.

On August 20, three weeks after Keyser's complaint, and before Feller made another appearance for the Indians, Landis wired Bradley requesting information about the young phenom.

Landis's telegram read: "In view of a suggestion in connection with an inquiry here respecting a club's activities in connection with a club's acquisition of ballplayers, please let me have statement of the Cleveland club's interest in, or contract with, player Feller prior to the assignment of his contract by New Orleans to Cleveland, if any."

Landis conducted an investigation that continued through the end of the season. It was during the hearing early in the case that Feller told Landis, "I don't want to play anyplace else. I want to play for Cleveland."

According to Feller, his father also was adamant. "My dad told Landis, 'My word is as good as my bond, and so is my son's. If you don't let him play for Cleveland, we'll take you to civil court and see what prevails, the laws of the land or baseball's rules.'"

In the meantime, as Landis continued to deliberate, Feller made 14 appearances for the Indians, including eight as a starting pitcher. His first performance was even more sensational than in the exhibition game against the Cardinals.

On August 23, when Feller became the youngest person to play in a major league game up to that time, he pitched a six-hitter to beat the St. Louis Browns, 4–1. Feller struck out 15 batters, only one fewer than Rube Waddell's 1908 American League mark, and two fewer than the then major league record set in 1933 by Dizzy Dean.

And in his fifth start on September 13, Feller tied Dean's record, striking out 17 in a 5–2, two-hit victory over Philadelphia in the first game of a doubleheader.

Landis didn't announce his decision in the Feller case until December 10, during baseball's annual winter meetings.

He found that the Indians were, indeed, guilty of breaking the rule. Feller could have become a free agent. It would have been a financial bonanza for the young pitcher and his family as Feller could have signed with another club for much more money than the Indians were paying him.

However, based on Feller's preference to stay with the Indians—and, probably, Feller's father's threatened lawsuit—Landis allowed them to keep him. But he also ruled that the Tribe had to pay the Des Moines club $7,500 in damages, which Bradley and Slapnicka were more than happy to do.

Feller's arrival and subsequent performances should have been the exclamation point on the Indians' best season in 10 years, since they finished second in 1926.

Through the first two and a half months they were at or close to the top of the American League. Their early success probably was a big reason for the decision to have Feller re-port directly to Cleveland rather than start his professional career at Fargo-Moorhead, or even New Orleans.

It was another Iowan, first baseman Hal Trosky, along with outfielders Earl Averill, Joe Vosmik, and rookie Roy Weatherly, whose offense powered the Indians. Along with new pitcher Johnny Allen, acquired in trade from the New York Yankees, they were the mainstays of the team in 1936.

The Indians were particularly successful at League Park (they played only one game in the Stadium), going 49–30. On the road, however, their record was something else. They won only 31 while losing 44 away from home, ruining whatever hopes they had to win the franchise's second pennant.

In that only game in the Stadium, on August 2, the Indians and New York played to a 4–4 tie. The game was called after 15 innings because of darkness and resumed later at League Park.

Trosky was the AL's premier slugger, leading the league with 162 runs batted in while hitting .343 with a club record 42 homers. Averill's .378 average was second in the batting race only to Luke Appling's .388 in Chicago.

Allen, the hot-tempered right-hander who came in a trade for pitchers Monte Pearson and Steve Sundra, won 20 games, the last 11 of them after undergoing an emergency appendectomy in June.

While Allen had a good inaugural season with the Tribe, and Feller made a significant impact, three other pitchers of whom much was expected—Mel Harder, Oral Hildebrand, and Willis Hudlin—struggled through subpar seasons. Harder came down with arm trouble, Hildebrand's record slipped below .500 for the first time in his career, and Hudlin, who developed bone chips in his elbow but tried to pitch through the pain, went from 15 victories in 1935 to only one in 27 games in 1936.

Bruce Campbell, the outfielder stricken with spinal meningitis the previous season, returned to the Indians on July 2. In his first game, against the St. Louis Browns, Campbell got five singles and a double in six at bats, driving in five runs in a 14–6 victory.

The starting pitchers for the 1936 opening day game at League Park: Mel Harder (left) of the Indians and Schoolboy Rowe of the Detroit Tigers.

	W	L	G	GS	CG	IP	H	BB	K	ERA
Johnny Allen	20	10	36	31	19	243	234	97	165	3.44
George Blaeholder	8	4	35	16	6	134⅓	158	47	30	5.09
Lloyd Brown	8	10	24	16	12	140⅓	166	45	34	4.17
Bob Feller	5	3	14	8	5	62	52	47	76	3.34
Milt Galatzer	0	0	1	0	0	6	7	5	3	4.50
Denny Galehouse	8	7	36	15	5	148⅓	161	68	71	4.85
Mel Harder	15	15	36	30	13	224⅔	294	71	84	5.17
Oral Hildebrand	10	11	36	21	9	174⅔	197	83	65	4.90
Willis Hudlin	1	5	27	7	1	64	112	31	20	9.00
Paul Kardow	0	0	2	0	0	2	1	2	0	4.50
Thornton Lee	3	5	43	8	2	127	138	67	49	4.89
Al Milnar	1	2	4	3	1	22	26	18	9	7.36
George Uhle	0	1	7	0	0	12⅔	26	5	5	8.53
Ralph Winegarner	0	0	9	0	0	14⅔	18	6	3	4.91
Bill Zuber	1	1	2	2	1	13⅓	14	15	5	6.59
	80	74		(157)	74	1,389⅓	1,604	607	619	4.83

Shutouts: Allen (4), Blaeholder, Brown
Saves: Hildebrand (4), Lee (3), Allen, Brown, Feller, Galehouse, Harder

	G	AB	R	H	2B	3B	HR	RBI	SB	AVG
Earl Averill (CF)	152	614	136	(232)	39	(15)	28	126	3	.378
Joe Becker	22	50	5	9	3	1	1	11	0	.180
Boze Berger	28	52	1	9	2	0	0	3	0	.173
Bruce Campbell	76	172	35	64	15	2	6	30	2	.372
Milt Galatzer	49	97	12	23	4	1	0	6	1	.237
Greek George	23	77	3	15	3	0	0	5	0	.195
Jim Gleeson	41	139	26	36	9	2	4	12	2	.259
Odell Hale (3B)	153	620	126	196	50	13	14	87	8	.316
Jeff Heath	12	41	6	14	3	3	1	8	1	.341
Roy Hughes (2B)	152	638	112	188	35	9	0	63	20	.295
Bill Knickerbocker (SS)	(155)	618	81	182	35	3	8	73	5	.294
Frankie Pytlak	75	224	35	72	15	4	0	31	5	.321
Billy Sullivan (C)	93	319	39	112	32	6	2	48	5	.351
Hal Trosky (1B)	151	629	124	216	45	9	42	(162)	6	.343
Joe Vosmik (LF)	138	506	76	145	29	7	7	94	5	.287
Roy Weatherly (RF)	84	349	64	117	28	6	8	53	3	.335
		(5,646)	921	(1,715)	(357)	82	123	852	66	(.304)

1937

Record: 83–71
Finish: Fourth
Games Behind: 19
Manager: Steve O'Neill

Again, as had happened so often in the past, the Indians' high hopes for the new season collapsed in a heap.

In anticipation of fighting for their second pennant in 37 years—and also yielding to pressure from civic officials—the Indians scheduled 15 of their games at the Stadium.

The move also led to an application by Alva Bradley to the American League to play seven night games in the Stadium. Lights would have been installed if permission had been granted. However, the application was rejected by the AL, and night baseball in the major leagues was only played in Cincinnati.

Though the Indians improved their won-lost record by three victories, climbed one place in the standings, and cut 3½ games off their first-place deficit, 1937 was another disappointment. When the season ended, Steve O'Neill was fired.

Before it started the Indians figured in a big deal that was expected to help their infield defense with the acquisition of shortstop Lyn Lary. He came to Cleveland with outfielder Julius Solters and pitcher Ivy Andrews from the St. Louis Browns for outfielder Joe Vosmik, shortstop Bill Knickerbocker, and pitcher Oral Hildebrand.

Solters led the Tribe with a .323 average, and Lary played well, hitting .290, though Andrews was a disappointment and was sold for $7,500 to New York in August.

The Indians waged a spirited battle for second place until June. But they lost 11 of 13 games on an eastern trip, falling into fifth, where they stayed with a few brief exceptions until late September when they overtook Boston and finished fourth.

Bob Feller, of whom so much was expected, developed a sore arm in spring training that prevented him from pitching regularly until midseason. Still, he struck out 16 in an 8–1 victory over the Red Sox at League Park on August 25.

Earl Averill's average slumped 79 points to .299, and Roy Weatherly, who'd had such a splendid season as a rookie in 1936, batted only .201.

The one bright spot was Johnny Allen with 15 consecutive victories and only one defeat, though he pitched only 173 innings, fewer than three other starters. Hal Trosky, whose average slipped below .300, led the Indians again in homers after hitting three in succession in a 14–4 victory over the Browns in St. Louis on July 5.

It was on the final day of the season, in a 1–0 loss to Detroit, that Allen's winning streak was stopped. It fell four short of Rube Marquard's major league record and one shy of the AL mark held jointly by Walter Johnson, Lefty Grove, Joe Wood, and Schoolboy Rowe.

After that game in Detroit, in which Tigers pitcher Jake Wade held the Indians to only a seventh-inning single by Trosky, an irate Allen erupted in anger against teammate Sammy "Bad News" Hale. Allen thought Hale, the Tribe's third baseman, should have fielded a first-inning hit by Hank Greenberg that drove in the Tigers' only run.

Another loss suffered by the Indians in 1937, though it wasn't recorded in the standings, was a ruling by Commissioner Kenesaw Mountain Landis that cost them the services of minor league outfielder Tommy Henrich.

Perhaps because he let the Indians keep Feller despite

Indians outfielders Jeff Heath (left) and Roy Weatherly with batboy Joe Maxse in the dugout at League Park prior to a game in 1937.

Johnny Allen (left), who won 15 consecutive games in 1937, and Bob Feller, then in his second season with the Indians. Allen finished the season with a 15–1 record, while Feller went 9–7.

their violation of rules the previous year, Landis made a free agent of Henrich, who'd batted .346 at New Orleans in 1936. Henrich had complained that the Indians mishandled him by keeping him in the minors. He subsequently signed with the New York Yankees for a bonus of $25,000.

	W	L	G	GS	CG	IP	H	BB	K	ERA
Johnny Allen	15	1	24	20	14	173	157	60	87	2.55
Ivy Andrews	3	4	20	4	1	59⅔	76	9	16	4.37
Lloyd Brown	2	6	31	5	2	77	107	27	32	6.55
Bob Feller	9	7	26	19	9	148⅓	116	106	150	3.39
Carl Fischer	0	1	2	0	0	⅔	2	1	1	27.00
Denny Galehouse	9	14	36	29	7	200⅔	238	83	78	4.57
Mel Harder	15	12	38	30	13	233⅔	269	86	95	4.28
Joe Heving	8	4	40	0	0	72⅔	92	30	35	4.83
Willis Hudlin	12	11	35	23	10	175¾	213	43	31	4.10
Ken Jungels	0	0	2	0	0	3	3	1	0	0.00
Earl Whitehill	8	8	33	22	6	147	189	80	53	6.49
Whit Wyatt	2	3	29	4	2	73	67	40	52	4.44
	83	71		156	64	1,364⅔	1,529	566	630	4.39

Shutouts: Hudlin (2), Andrews, Whitehill
Saves: Heving (5), Galehouse (3), Harder (2), Hudlin (2), Whitehill (2), Feller

	G	AB	R	H	2B	3B	HR	RBI	SB	AVG
Hugh Alexander	7	11	0	1	0	0	0	0	1	.091
Earl Averill (CF)	156	609	121	182	33	11	21	92	5	.299
Joe Becker	18	33	3	11	2	1	0	2	0	.333
Bruce Campbell (RF)	134	448	82	135	42	11	4	61	4	.301
Odell Hale (3B)	154	561	74	150	32	4	6	82	9	.267
Jeff Heath	20	61	8	14	1	4	0	8	0	.230
Roy Hughes	104	346	57	96	12	6	1	40	11	.277
Ken Keltner	1	1	0	0	0	0	0	1	0	.000
John Kroner (2B)	86	283	29	67	14	1	2	26	1	.237
Lyn Lary (SS)	156	644	110	187	46	7	8	77	18	.290
Blas Monaco	5	7	0	2	0	1	0	2	0	.286
Frankie Pytlak (C)	125	397	60	125	15	6	1	44	16	.315
Bill Sodd	1	1	0	0	0	0	0	0	0	.000
Moose Solters (LF)	152	589	90	190	42	11	20	109	6	.323
Billy Sullivan	72	168	26	48	12	3	3	22	1	.286
Hal Trosky (1B)	153	601	104	179	36	9	32	128	3	.298
Roy Weatherly	53	134	19	27	4	0	5	13	1	.201
		5,353	817	1,499	304	76	103	754	78	.280

1938

Record: 86–66
Finish: Third
Games Behind: 13
Manager: Oscar Vitt

The Oscar Vitt era in Cleveland began with high hopes that better things were ahead for the Indians, and for a while it appeared there was justification for their confidence.

"I have every reason to believe we will have a fighting, peppy ball club in 1938," said owner Alva Bradley in announcing that Vitt would take over as the Tribe manager. Vitt replaced Steve O'Neill, who was considered too laid-back, too easygoing to be successful.

"Our team should reflect the personality, the desire to win, the animation of our new manager," Bradley stated.

Vitt, a former infielder for the Detroit Tigers who had managed teams to minor league pennants in the Pacific Coast League and the International League, underscored Bradley's remarks when it was his turn to talk.

"I don't know much about this team, but I can tell you one thing. We'll have the damnedest fighting team you ever had here. There'll be no loafing, Ol' Oz will see to that," Vitt said. It was an obvious reference to O'Neill's laid-back style.

For a while—with rookie outfielder Jeff Heath challenging for the batting championship (he finished second by six percentage points), and Mel Harder, Bob Feller, and Johnny Allen all pitching well—Bradley and Vitt seemed to be prophetic.

Feller pitched a one-hitter on April 20 in a 9–0 victory over St. Louis at League Park. Ironically, the Browns' only hit was a sixth inning bunt single by Billy Sullivan, the catcher the Indians had traded for Rollie Hemsley the previous winter.

Feller's near no-hitter helped the Indians get off to a fast start. They took over first place in early May, lost it briefly, but on May 19 regained the top rung and held it for nearly two months. They were overtaken by New York on July 13, and the Yankees never relinquished the lead, coasting to a third straight pennant.

Another former teammate, Monte Pearson, who had been

Oscar Vitt (left), who managed the Indians from 1938 to 1940, with Detroit manager Mickey Cochrane on opening day in 1938.

traded to the Yankees for Allen two years earlier, pitched a no-hitter against the Indians on August 27, beating them, 13–0, at Yankee Stadium.

The Indians and Boston fought it out for second place the rest of the way, with the Red Sox prevailing by 3½ lengths.

On the final day of the season, October 2, Feller struck out 18 batters to set a new major league record, though he lost the game to Detroit, 4–1.

It was the opener of a doubleheader that had been rescheduled in the spacious Stadium, and 27,000 fans turned out on a cold and drizzly afternoon. They wanted to see if Tiger slugger Hank Greenberg could hit two home runs and tie Babe Ruth's record of 60 in one season.

Greenberg didn't and, instead, was a strikeout victim of Feller twice. Chet Laabs fanned five times, winning pitcher Harry Eisenstat and Mark Christman three times each, Pete Fox and Benny McCoy also twice each, and Tony Piet once. The only Detroit batters Feller didn't strike out were Birdie Tebbetts and Roy Cullenbine.

That doubleheader represented two of the 18 games the Indians played in the Stadium in 1938.

The decline of the Indians that season began about the time that Allen came down with a sore arm during another personal winning streak of 12. By September 13 he was forced to the sidelines for the remainder of the season with bone chips in his elbow.

Earlier, on June 7, the hot-tempered Allen was involved in a controversy with umpire Bill McGowan in a game in Boston.

Allen was wearing an undershirt whose right sleeve was torn and flapped every time he delivered a pitch. McGowan ordered Allen to either change the undershirt or cut off the piece of the sleeve that dangled, thereby—in the umpire's opinion—distracting the batter.

Allen refused, stalked off the field, and sat down in the dugout. Despite the pleading of Vitt and team captain Lyn Lary, Allen refused to comply with McGowan's order.

Finally Vitt fined Allen $250, and the incident became a cause célèbre.

Allen complained to Bradley, who wouldn't rescind the fine but placated the pitcher by "purchasing" the torn undershirt for $250.

Then Bradley sold the undershirt, along with a complete Indians uniform—the total cost of which also was $250—to a large department store in downtown Cleveland. A mannequin was dressed in the uniform and undershirt and displayed in the main window of the store where it attracted much attention and, presumably, many customers.

Not coincidentally, the president of the department store was a man named Chuck Bradley, Alva's brother. (The torn undershirt is now on display in the Hall of Fame.)

Before the season ended, on August 30, two Tribe catchers—Frankie Pytlak and third stringer Hank Helf—set "altitude" records by catching baseballs thrown from the top of the 708-foot-tall Terminal Tower on Cleveland's Public Square. Mathematicians estimated that the balls, dropped from the top of the building by third baseman Ken Keltner, were traveling 138 miles an hour when they were caught.

By doing so, Pytlak and Helf broke the existing record held by Gabby Street who, in 1908, caught a ball dropped from the top of the 550-foot Washington Monument in Washington, D.C.

After the season ended, Bradley again applied to the AL for permission to play seven night games in the Stadium. This time the request was granted, along with approval for Philadelphia and Chicago also to play seven games under the lights.

Bob Feller in the Indians dugout at Cleveland Stadium between innings of the game on October 2, 1938, in which he struck out 18 Detroit batters to set a major league record. The Tigers won the game, 4–1.

Indians third baseman Ken Keltner leaps for a throw from the outfield as Lou Gehrig of the New York Yankees slides safely into third base during a game at League Park in 1938. The short right-field fence is seen in the background.

	W	L	G	GS	CG	IP	H	BB	K	ERA
Johnny Allen	14	8	30	27	13	200	189	81	112	4.18
Bob Feller	17	11	39	36	20	277⅔	225	(208)	(240)	4.08
Denny Galehouse	7	8	36	12	5	114	119	65	66	4.34
Mel Harder	17	10	38	29	15	240	257	62	102	3.83
Joe Heving	1	1	3	0	0	6	10	5	0	9.00
Willis Hudlin	8	8	29	15	8	127	158	45	27	4.89
John Humphries	9	8	(45)	6	1	103⅓	105	63	56	5.23
Ken Jungels	1	0	9	0	0	15⅓	21	18	7	8.80
Al Milnar	3	1	23	5	2	68⅓	90	26	29	5.00
Clay Smith	0	0	4	0	0	11	18	2	3	6.55
Charley Suche	0	0	1	0	0	1⅓	4	3	1	27.00
Earl Whitehill	9	8	26	23	4	160½	187	83	60	5.56
Bill Zuber	0	3	15	0	0	28⅔	33	20	14	5.02
	86	66		153	68	1,353	1,416	681	(717)	4.60

Shutouts: Feller (2), Harder (2), Galehouse
Saves: Humphries (6), Harder (4), Galehouse (3), Feller, Hudlin, Milnar, Zuber

	G	AB	R	H	2B	3B	HR	RBI	SB	AVG
Earl Averill (CF)	134	482	101	159	27	15	14	93	5	.330
Lou Boudreau	1	1	0	0	0	0	0	0	0	.000
Bruce Campbell (RF)	133	511	90	148	27	12	12	72	11	.290
Oscar Grimes	4	10	2	2	0	1	0	2	0	.200
Odell Hale (2B)	130	496	69	138	32	2	8	69	8	.278
Jeff Heath (LF)	126	502	104	172	31	(18)	21	112	3	.343
Hank Helf	6	13	1	1	0	0	0	1	0	.077
Rollie Hemsley	66	203	27	60	11	3	2	28	1	.296
Tommy Irwin	3	9	1	1	0	0	0	0	0	.111
Ken Keltner (3B)	149	576	86	159	31	9	26	113	4	.276
John Kroner	51	117	13	29	16	0	1	17	0	.248
Lyn Lary (SS)	141	568	94	152	36	4	3	51	23	.268
Ray Mack	2	6	2	2	0	1	0	2	0	.333
Frankie Pytlak (C)	113	364	46	112	14	7	1	43	9	.308
Lloyd Russell	2	0	0	0	0	0	0	0	0	—
Moose Solters	67	199	30	40	6	3	2	22	4	.201
Hal Trosky (1B)	150	554	106	185	40	9	19	110	5	.334
Roy Weatherly	83	210	32	55	14	3	2	18	8	.262
Skeeter Webb	20	58	11	16	2	0	0	2	1	.276
Chuck Workman	2	5	1	2	0	0	0	0	0	.400
	5,356	847	1,506	(300)	(89)	113	797	83	.281

1939

Record: 87–67
Finish: Third
Games Behind: 20½
Manager: Oscar Vitt

Bob Feller blossomed into stardom at the tender age of 20, hurling two one-hitters, leading the American League with 24 victories, and pitching 296⅔ innings, helping the Indians recover in September from a dreadful beginning.

They were rained out of their first three games, won four of their next five, then lost three straight and tumbled into seventh place, from which they didn't extricate themselves until the end of April.

The rest of the season was a roller-coaster ride. In fourth place on September 1, the Indians proceeded to lose three straight, then recovered to win 10 of 12, and finished third, a distant 20½ games behind New York, which won its fourth consecutive pennant.

Through it all there were growing rumblings of discord among the players, complaints about manager Oscar Vitt, who had a penchant for airing in the newspapers the team's problems—of which there were many.

Vitt and Johnny Allen were at odds most of the season as the one-time ace of the pitching staff continued to struggle.

Even C. C. Slapnicka, the Indians' front office chief, became disenchanted with Vitt and his style. The two men had words in public on several occasions, including one instance

in which Vitt told the assistant to the president, "You run the front office, and I'll run the ball club."

Slapnicka did. But he, too, fell from favor with the fans by trading popular Earl Averill, who had begun to slip and had gotten into a disagreement about a bonus he thought was due him. Averill was sent to Detroit on June 14 for pitcher Harry Eisenstat and cash.

Feller's one-hitters were the second and third of his burgeoning career.

On May 25 in Boston he allowed only a second-inning single by Bobby Doerr in an 11–0 victory, as third baseman Ken Keltner became the 11th batter in AL history to hit three consecutive homers in one game.

Then, on June 27, Feller beat Detroit, 5–0, in front of 55,305 fans in the first night game played at the Stadium. The only hit he yielded was a sixth-inning single by Averill, his former teammate.

That game was one of 30 the Indians played at the Stadium in 1939, seven of which were under the lights.

Earlier, on May 16, in the AL's first-ever night game, the Indians beat the Athletics, 8–3, in 10 innings in Philadelphia. Rookie Al Milnar, a Cleveland sandlot graduate, started for the Tribe, though the victory was credited to reliever Johnny Humphries, who took over in the eighth inning.

The season also was marked by the arrival of the Indians' heralded shortstop–second base combination of Lou Boudreau and Ray Mack. They were promoted from Class AA Buffalo on August 7 and, that night, helped the Tribe beat St. Louis, 6–5, in front of 16,467 fans in the Stadium. Boudreau broke in with a triple and single in five at bats. Mack went hitless in four trips, but was credited with driving in the winning run.

The Indians rookie double-play combination of shortstop Lou Boudreau (left) and second baseman Ray Mack upon joining the team from Class AAA Buffalo on August 7, 1939.

Indians manager Oscar Vitt (right) with Philadelphia Athletics owner and manager Connie Mack during a spring training meeting in the lobby of the Roosevelt Hotel in New Orleans in 1939.

	W	L	G	GS	CG	IP	H	BB	K	ERA
Johnny Allen	9	7	28	26	9	175	199	56	79	4.58
Johnny Broaca	4	2	22	2	0	46	53	28	13	4.70
Joe Dobson	2	3	35	3	0	78	87	51	27	5.88
Tom Drake	0	1	8	1	0	15	23	19	1	9.00
Harry Eisenstat	6	7	26	11	4	103⅔	109	23	38	3.30
Bob Feller	(24)	9	39	35	(24)	(296⅔)	227	(142)	(246)	2.85
Mel Harder	15	9	29	26	12	208	213	64	67	3.50
Willis Hudlin	9	10	27	20	7	143	175	42	28	4.91
John Humphries	2	4	15	1	0	28⅓	30	32	12	8.26
Al Milnar	14	12	37	26	12	209	212	99	76	3.79
Mike Naymick	0	1	2	1	1	4⅔	3	5	3	1.93
Floyd Stromme	0	1	5	0	0	13	13	13	4	4.85
Lefty Sullivan	0	1	7	1	0	12⅔	9	9	4	4.26
Bill Zuber	2	0	16	1	0	31⅔	41	19	16	5.97
	87	67		154	69	1,364⅔	1,394	602	614	4.08

Shutouts: Feller (4), Allen (2), Milnar (2), Eisenstat, Harder
Saves: Hudlin (3), Milnar (3), Eisenstat (2), Humphries (2), Dobson, Feller, Harder

	G	AB	R	H	2B	3B	HR	RBI	SB	AVG
Earl Averill	24	55	8	15	8	0	1	7	0	.273
Lou Boudreau	53	225	42	58	15	4	0	19	2	.258
Bruce Campbell (RF)	130	450	84	129	23	13	8	72	7	.287
Ben Chapman (CF)	149	545	101	158	31	9	6	82	18	.290
Oscar Grimes	119	364	51	98	20	5	4	56	8	.269
Odell Hale (2B)	108	253	36	79	16	2	4	48	4	.312
Jeff Heath (LF)	121	431	64	126	31	7	14	69	8	.292
Rollie Hemsley (C)	107	395	58	104	17	4	2	36	2	.263
Ken Keltner (3B)	(154)	587	84	191	35	11	13	97	6	.325
Lyn Lary	3	2	0	0	0	0	0	0	0	.000
Ray Mack	36	112	12	17	4	1	1	6	0	.152
Frankie Pytlak	63	183	20	49	2	5	0	14	4	.268
Luke Sewell	16	20	1	3	1	0	0	1	0	.150
Jim Shilling	31	98	8	27	7	2	0	12	1	.276
Moose Solters	41	102	19	28	7	2	2	19	2	.275
Hal Trosky (1B)	122	448	89	150	31	4	25	104	2	.335
Roy Weatherly	95	323	43	100	16	6	1	32	7	.310
Skeeter Webb (SS)	81	269	28	71	14	1	2	26	1	.264
		5,316	797	1,490	(291)	(79)	85	730	72	.280

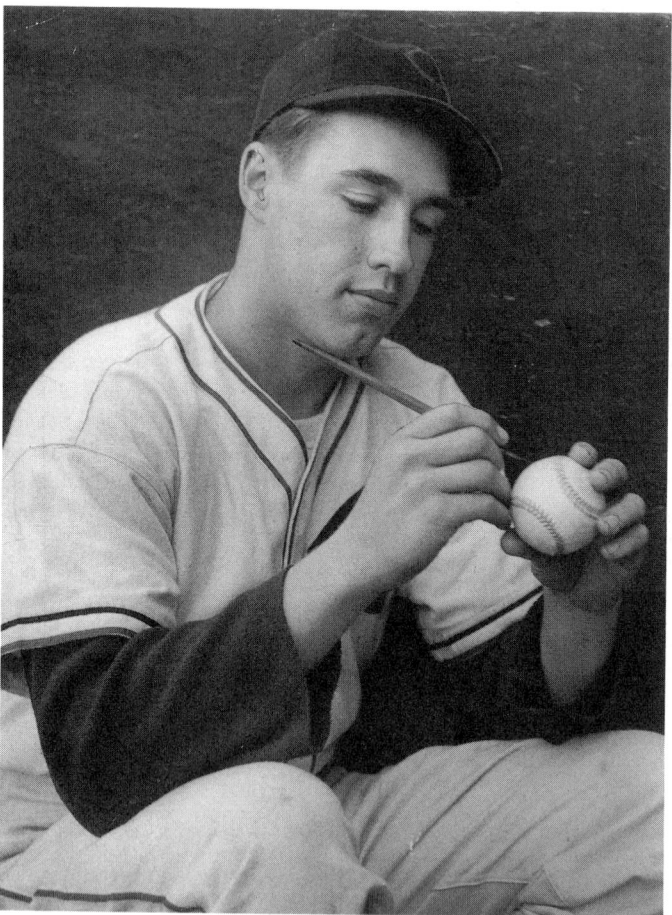

Bob Feller was a 20-year-old rising star pitcher for the Indians in 1939.

1940

Record: 89–65
Finish: Second
Games Behind: 1
Manager: Oscar Vitt

The season started spectacularly, with Bob Feller pitching the first opening day no-hitter in baseball history. But it soon disintegrated into a morass of dissension that cost the Indians what would have been the franchise's second pennant.

In the closest and most interesting battle in the 40-year history of the American League, the Indians occupied first place 74 days, dropping as low as third only seven days, and weren't eliminated until the third-to-last day of the season.

Then it was an obscure rookie named Floyd Giebell who outpitched Feller as Detroit beat the Tribe, 2–0, on September 27, in front of 45,553 fans in the Stadium, one of the 49 games played in the facility that year.

The Detroit victory, in which Rudy York hit a fourth inning, two-run homer that ticked off the glove of left fielder Ben Chapman at the 320-foot foul line, gave the Tigers a three-game lead with two left to play (both of which the Indians won).

It was only the second game Giebell won that season, and the third—and final—of his major league career.

Still, the Indians probably lost the pennant much earlier as the players' animosity toward manager Oscar Vitt reached

Indians owner Alva Bradley (right) discusses the coming season with manager Oscar Vitt in 1940, which came to be known as the year of the "Cleveland Crybabies" because of the palyers' rebellion against Vitt.

a peak in June, earning them the loathsome nickname "Cleveland Crybabies." The trouble between Vitt and the players simmered the rest of the season.

The handwriting might have been on the wall in spring training.

First, promising rookie outfielder Paul O'Dea, a popular graduate of the Cleveland sandlots, was blinded in his right eye when he was hit by a ball during batting practice.

Then Lou Boudreau, beginning his first full season in the major leagues, suffered a broken ankle, though he was able to play by the time the season started.

Despite the travail, it was a great year for Feller, who—with the help of a sensational fielding play by second baseman Ray Mack—pitched his first no-hitter, beating the White Sox, 1–0, in Chicago on April 16. He also hurled a fourth one-hitter, a 1–0 victory over Philadelphia on July 12, and finished the season as the American League pitching leader in six departments.

Feller won the most games (27), and he also led in strikeouts (261), games (43), games started (37), innings pitched (320⅓), and complete games (31).

In the opener, with the temperature in the mid-30s, Jeff Heath's single and Rollie Hemsley's two-out triple in the fourth inning off Bill Dietrich provided the only run Feller needed, though he couldn't have prevailed if not for Mack's spectacular play.

With two out in the ninth and White Sox fans clamoring for a rally, Feller walked Luke Appling. Taft Wright, a left-handed batter, followed with a sharp grounder toward right field. Mack, the Indians' rookie second baseman, raced to his left, scooped up the ball as he fell to his knees and tossed it to first baseman Hal Trosky. It retired Wright by half a step.

Two months later, after the Indians had fallen into third place on June 13 in the wake of a distressing 9–5 defeat in Boston, a contingent of 12 players called on Bradley in the owner's office in Cleveland. They wanted Bradley to fire Vitt.

Veteran pitcher Mel Harder, the spokesman for the players, said to Bradley, "We think we've got a good chance to win the pennant, but we'll never win it with Vitt as manager. If we can get rid of him, we can win. We all feel sure of that."

The players' primary complaints against Vitt were that he constantly criticized them behind their backs, ridiculed

The 1940 Indians, who were nicknamed the "Cleveland Crybabies" because of their attempt to get manager Oscar Vitt fired.

them in the newspapers, held grudges against them, and undermined their confidence.

Apparently the crowning blow occurred during that loss to the Red Sox, charged to Feller, when Vitt sneered in the dugout, "Look at him! He's supposed to be my ace. I'm supposed to win a pennant with that kind of pitching?"

Then, after Harder, the "dean" of the team, took over in relief but failed to stop the Red Sox, he was admonished by Vitt, "It's about time you won one, the money you're making."

All Bradley said to the players was that he'd "look into the matter, investigate it thoroughly and determine if any action should be taken."

None was. At least not immediately.

Bradley also told the players, "If this story ever gets out, you'll be ridiculed the rest of your lives."

It did, in the *Cleveland Plain Dealer* the very next morning—sharing page one with the news that the Nazis had captured Paris in World War II.

And the Indians were, indeed, ridiculed the remainder of that season.

Four days later, because of Bradley's reluctance to chastise Vitt, the players agreed—or were ordered—to sign a statement published on June 17 in the three Cleveland newspapers.

It said: "We the undersigned publicly declare to withdraw all statements referring to the resignation of Oscar Vitt. We feel this action is for the betterment of the Cleveland Baseball Club."

It was signed by 21 of the players then on the roster. Missing were the signatures of outfielders Roy Weatherly and Jeff Heath, third-string catcher Hank Helf (who had been recalled from the minors a few days earlier), and injured infielder Oscar Grimes.

Though the Indians stayed in the race the rest of the way, the atmosphere in the clubhouse and dugout was strained, and they were subjected to constant verbal abuse throughout the league, especially by the fans in Detroit.

In early August, after Heath struck out as a pinch hitter in a game against the Tigers, he was criticized by Vitt. The two men got into a shouting match, and Vitt suspended Heath. The next day C. C. Slapnicka interceded, and got Heath to apologize, and the suspension was lifted.

But the animosity remained; the Indians lost nine of their next 13 games, the last three in a row against Detroit; and morale continued to plummet.

By the time the Tigers arrived in Cleveland for the final series of the season, the Indians were at a low ebb. They went peacefully against Giebell, who pitched the game of his life, allowing only six scattered hits.

On October 28, exactly a month and a day after the Tigers beat the Indians to win the pennant, Bradley finally determined the action that should be taken. He came out of a meeting of directors of the ball club and made this simple announcement: "We have decided not to renew Oscar Vitt's contract."

While Weatherly was the only Indian to hit .300, he failed to join six teammates selected on the AL All-Star team: Feller, Al Milnar, Boudreau, Mack, Ken Keltner, and Hemsley.

	W	L	G	GS	CG	IP	H	BB	K	ERA
Johnny Allen	9	8	32	17	5	138⅔	126	48	62	3.44
Nate Andrews	0	1	6	0	0	12	16	6	3	6.00
Joe Dobson	3	7	40	7	2	100	101	48	57	4.95
Cal Dorsett	0	0	1	0	0	1	1	0	0	9.00
Harry Eisenstat	1	4	27	3	0	71⅓	78	12	27	3.14
Bob Feller	(27)	11	(43)	(37)	(31)	(320½)	245	118	(261)	2.61
Mel Harder	12	11	31	25	5	186⅓	200	59	76	4.06
Dixie Howell	0	0	3	0	0	5	2	4	2	1.80
Willis Hudlin	2	1	4	4	2	23¾	31	2	8	4.94
John Humphries	0	2	19	1	1	33¾	35	29	17	8.29
Ken Jungels	0	0	2	0	0	3⅓	3	1	1	2.70
Al Milnar	18	10	37	33	15	242⅓	242	99	99	3.27
Mike Naymick	1	2	13	4	0	30	36	17	15	5.10
Al Smith	15	7	31	24	11	183	187	55	46	3.44
Bill Zuber	1	1	17	0	0	24	25	14	12	5.63
	89	65		155	72	1,375	1,328	512	686	(3.63)

Shutouts: Feller (4), Milnar (4), Allen (3), Dobson, Smith
Saves: Allen (5), Eisenstat (4), Feller (4), Dobson (3), Milnar (3), Smith (2), Humphries

	G	AB	R	H	2B	3B	HR	RBI	SB	AVG
Beau Bell (RF)	120	444	55	124	22	2	4	58	2	.279
Lou Boudreau (SS)	155	627	97	185	46	10	9	101	6	.295
Soup Campbell	35	62	8	14	1	0	0	2	0	.226
Ben Chapman (LF)	143	548	82	157	40	6	4	50	13	.286
Oscar Grimes	11	13	3	0	0	0	0	0	0	.000
Odell Hale	48	50	3	11	3	1	0	6	0	.220
Jeff Heath	100	356	55	78	16	3	14	50	5	.219
Hank Helf	1	1	0	0	0	0	0	0	0	.000
Rollie Hemsley (C)	119	416	46	111	20	5	4	42	1	.267
Ken Keltner (3B)	149	543	67	138	24	10	15	77	10	.254
Ray Mack (2B)	146	530	60	150	21	5	12	69	4	.283
Rusty Peters	30	71	5	17	3	2	0	7	1	.239
Frankie Pytlak	62	149	16	21	2	1	0	16	0	.141
Hal Trosky (1B)	140	522	85	154	39	4	25	93	1	.295
Roy Weatherly (CF)	135	578	90	175	35	11	12	59	9	.303
		5,361	710	1,422	287	61	101	660	53	.265

1941

Record: 75–79
Finish: Fourth (tied with Detroit)
Games Behind: 26
Manager: Roger Peckinpaugh

Roger Peckinpaugh, who managed the Indians from 1928, when he replaced Jack McCallister, through June 9, 1933, when he was fired—"by the public," as Alva Bradley always said—was given another chance in 1941.

Peckinpaugh replaced Oscar Vitt, and the Indians, with front office chief C. C. "Cy" Slapnicka calling the shots, embarked upon a "strengthening" program, as Bradley was unwilling to say they were "rebuilding" after their near-miss in 1940.

Acquired in a preseason trade with Boston were pitcher Jim Bagby, Jr., whose father won 122 games for the Tribe from 1916 to 1922 (including an American League–leading 31 in 1920), catcher Gene Desautels, and outfielder Gerry "Gee" Walker, in exchange for pitcher Joe Dobson, catcher Frankie Pytlak, and infielder Sammy "Bad News" Hale.

A number of promising rookies also joined the Indians in spring training, including third baseman Bob Lemon and catcher Jim Hegan, though neither remained on the 1941 squad for long.

Optimism reigned supreme again as Peckinpaugh pronounced, "We should win the race . . . we've got the best team in the league."

As it turned out, Peckinpaugh was partly right—at least through late June.

The Indians started fast again, winning 11 of their first 15 games, and took over first place on April 29. They stayed there for 60 days, until June 27, and then collapsed.

Bob Feller pitched well again, but Al Milnar and Al Smith, two southpaws who combined to win 33 games in 1940, were inconsistent, and Mel Harder experienced elbow trouble that required surgery at the end of the season.

Hal Trosky, who hammered 25 homers in 1940, was able to play in only 89 games because of migraine headaches (which eventually forced him into early retirement), and opposing pitchers quickly discovered a weakness in heralded second baseman Ray Mack, who hit .283 as a rookie the previous season.

After falling into second place, the Tribe stayed close to New York for about three weeks, but then turned cold just as the Yankees got hot.

On August 12 the Indians' deficit was 12 games, but they never got any closer and finished in a fourth-place tie with Detroit, which also collapsed after winning the 1940 pennant. The race was all over on September 4 when the Yankees clinched the pennant.

Despite the Indians' failure to live up to Peckinpaugh's optimism, they gained national prominence by stopping Joe DiMaggio's 56-consecutive-game hitting streak. The streak came to an end in front of 67,468 fans on July 17 in one of the 32 games the Tribe played at the Stadium that season.

The crowd was the largest for a night game in the history of baseball and saw the Yankees prevail, 4–3.

DiMaggio went to bat four times that night, the first three against Smith, the fourth against Bagby. He was robbed of hits on spectacular fielding plays by third baseman Ken Keltner in the first and seventh innings and walked in the fourth. In the eighth, against Bagby, DiMaggio grounded into a double play started by shortstop Lou Boudreau (who was celebrating his 24th birthday).

Feller pitched the fifth one-hitter of his career on September 26, beating the Browns, 3–2, in St. Louis. Rick Ferrell's bunt single in the fifth inning of the second game of a doubleheader spoiled the no-hit bid by Feller, who was the AL's most dominant pitcher again. He led the league in victories, games started, innings pitched, strikeouts, and shutouts (6).

Outfielder Jeff Heath was the Indians' best offensive player, but finished fourth in the AL batting race, behind Ted Williams (.406), who became the 13th batter since 1901 to hit .400. Cecil Travis (.359) was second and DiMaggio (.357) third.

Two months after the season ended, Slapnicka resigned, citing health problems. Bradley promoted Peckinpaugh to vice president, taking over Slapnicka's duties, although it was widely speculated that the owner was eager for the opportunity to hire a new field manager.

Surprisingly, on November 25, the job was given to Boudreau, despite his youthful age and limited experience, which consisted of less than three full seasons in the major leagues.

	W	L	G	GS	CG	IP	H	BB	K	ERA
Nate Andrews	0	0	2	0	0	2⅓	3	2	1	11.57
Jim Bagby	9	15	33	27	12	200⅔	214	76	53	4.04
Clint Brown	3	3	41	0	0	74⅓	77	28	22	3.27
Chubby Dean	1	4	8	8	2	53⅓	57	24	14	4.39
Cal Dorsett	0	1	5	2	0	11⅓	21	10	5	10.32
Harry Eisenstat	1	1	21	0	0	34	43	16	11	4.24
Red Embree	0	1	1	1	0	4	7	3	4	6.75
Bob Feller	(25)	13	(44)	(40)	28	(343)	(284)	(194)	(260)	3.15
Steve Gromek	1	1	9	2	1	23⅓	25	11	19	4.24
Mel Harder	5	4	15	10	1	68⅔	76	37	21	5.24
Joe Heving	5	2	27	3	2	70⅔	63	31	18	2.29
Ken Jungels	0	0	6	0	0	13⅔	17	8	6	7.24
Joe Krakauskas	1	2	12	5	0	41⅓	39	29	25	4.10
Al Milnar	12	19	35	30	9	229⅓	236	116	82	4.36
Al Smith	12	13	29	27	13	206⅔	204	75	76	3.83
	75	79		155	68	1,377	1,366	(660)	617	3.90

Shutouts: Feller (6), Smith (2), Heving, Milnar
Saves: Brown (5), Heving (5), Bagby (2), Eisenstat (2), Feller (2), Gromek (2), Harder

	G	AB	R	H	2B	3B	HR	RBI	SB	AVG
Beau Bell	48	104	12	20	4	3	0	9	1	.192
Lou Boudreau (SS)	148	579	95	149	(45)	8	10	56	9	.257
Soup Campbell	104	328	36	82	10	4	3	35	1	.250
Jack Conway	2	2	0	1	0	0	0	1	0	.500
Gene Desautels	66	189	20	38	5	1	1	17	1	.201
Hank Edwards	16	68	10	15	1	1	1	6	0	.221
Les Fleming	2	8	0	2	1	0	0	2	0	.250
Vern Freiburger	2	8	0	1	0	0	0	1	0	.125
Buck Frierson	5	11	2	3	1	0	0	2	0	.273
Fabian Gaffke	4	4	0	1	0	0	0	0	0	.250
Oscar Grimes	77	244	28	58	9	3	4	24	4	.238
Jeff Heath (RF)	151	585	89	199	32	(20)	24	123	18	.340
Jim Hegan	16	47	4	15	2	0	1	5	0	.319
Rollie Hemsley (C)	98	288	29	69	10	5	2	24	2	.240
Oris Hockett	2	6	0	2	0	0	0	1	0	.333
Red Howell	11	7	0	2	0	0	0	2	0	.286
Ken Keltner (3B)	149	581	83	156	31	13	23	84	2	.269
Bob Lemon	5	4	0	1	0	0	0	0	0	.250
Ray Mack (2B)	145	500	54	114	22	4	9	44	8	.228
Rusty Peters	29	63	6	13	2	0	0	2	0	.206
Larry Rosenthal	45	75	10	14	3	1	1	8	1	.187
George Susce	1	0	0	0	0	0	0	0	0	—
Hal Trosky (1B)	89	310	43	91	17	0	11	51	1	.294
Gee Walker (LF)	121	445	56	126	26	11	6	48	12	.283
Roy Weatherly (CF)	102	363	59	105	21	5	3	37	2	.289
Chuck Workman	9	4	2	0	0	0	0	0	0	.000
	5,283	677	1,350	249	(84)	103	618	63	.256

1942

Record: 75–79
Finish: Fourth
Games Behind: 28
Manager: Lou Boudreau

No sooner did 24-year-old Lou Boudreau take command of the Indians at the time the national media was calling Cleveland "the graveyard of managers" than the team lost its best pitcher and one of the greatest of all time, Bob Feller.

Feller enlisted in the navy on December 9, 1941, two days after the start of World War II, forsaking a baseball career that had produced 107 victories and only 54 losses, a no-hitter, and five one-hitters in less than six full seasons in the major leagues.

Also lost that season was Hal Trosky, who retired because of migraine headaches (though he made a brief comeback with the Chicago White Sox in 1944).

Nicknamed the "Boy Manager," Boudreau got the Indians off to a flying start. They beat Detroit, 5–2, in the opener, with Boudreau getting two hits, and though the Indians lost their next three, they followed with 13 consecutive victories, a franchise record. The winning streak ended in an 8–4 loss to Boston on May 3.

Indians manager Lou Boudreau (left) with pitcher Bob Feller prior to a 1942 exhibition game for the benefit of the Army-Navy Relief Fund. The game was played at Cleveland Stadium between a major league all-star team and a team composed of major league players then in the service during World War II.

The streak boosted the Indians into first place, though they didn't stay there for long. In what turned out to be a roller-coaster ride thereafter, by the end of May they were lodged in fourth place, which is where they finished, with the same record the Indians registered the previous season under Roger Peckinpaugh.

Forty-six of the Indians' 77 home games were played at the Stadium, plus the second of two All-Star games on July 7 between the American League and a team of former major leaguers. The AL won, 5–0, in front of 62,094 fans, with the proceeds going to the Army-Navy Relief Fund.

Feller, pitching for the servicemen, was routed in the second inning, while the Tribe's Ken Keltner got two of the AL's 10 hits. Boudreau and Jim Bagby also played for the AL, which on the previous day beat the National League All-Stars, 3–1, at the Polo Grounds in New York.

	W	L	G	GS	CG	IP	H	BB	K	ERA
Jim Bagby	17	9	38	35	16	270⅔	267	64	54	2.96
Clint Brown	1	1	7	0	0	9	16	2	4	6.00
Paul Calvert	0	0	1	0	0	2	0	2	2	0.00
Pete Center	0	0	1	0	0	3⅓	7	4	0	16.20
Chubby Dean	8	11	27	22	8	172⅔	170	66	46	3.81
Harry Eisenstat	2	1	29	1	0	47⅔	58	6	19	2.45
Red Embree	3	4	19	6	2	63	58	31	44	3.86
Tom Ferrick	3	2	31	2	2	81⅓	56	32	28	1.99
Steve Gromek	2	0	14	0	0	44⅓	46	23	14	3.65
Mel Harder	13	14	29	29	13	198⅔	179	82	74	3.44
Joe Heving	5	3	27	2	0	46⅓	52	25	13	4.86
Vern Kennedy	4	8	28	12	4	108	99	50	37	4.08
Joe Krakauskas	0	0	3	0	0	7	7	4	2	3.86
Al Milnar	6	8	28	19	8	157	146	85	35	4.13
Ray Poat	1	3	4	4	1	18⅓	24	9	8	5.40
Allie Reynolds	0	0	2	0	0	5	5	4	2	0.00
Al Smith	10	15	30	24	7	168⅓	163	71	66	3.96
	75	79		(156)	61	(1,402⅔)	1,353	560	448	3.59

Shutouts: Bagby (4), Harder (4), Milnar (2), Poat, Smith
Saves: Ferrick (3), Heving (3), Eisenstat (2), Bagby, Dean, Kennedy

The 1942 Cleveland Indians.

	G	AB	R	H	2B	3B	HR	RBI	SB	AVG
Lou Boudreau (SS)	147	506	57	143	18	10	2	58	7	.283
Otto Denning (C)	92	214	15	45	14	0	1	19	0	.210
Gene Desautels	62	162	14	40	5	0	0	9	1	.247
Hank Edwards	13	48	6	12	2	1	0	7	2	.250
Les Fleming (1B)	(156)	548	71	160	27	4	14	82	6	.292
Fabian Gaffke	40	67	4	11	2	0	0	3	1	.164
Oscar Grimes	51	84	10	15	2	0	0	2	3	.179
Jeff Heath (LF)	147	568	82	158	37	13	10	76	9	.278
Jim Hegan	68	170	10	33	5	0	0	11	1	.194
Oris Hockett (RF)	148	601	85	150	22	7	7	48	12	.250
Ken Keltner (3B)	152	624	72	179	34	4	6	78	4	.287
Bob Lemon	5	5	0	0	0	0	0	0	0	.000
Ray Mack (2B)	143	481	43	108	14	6	2	45	9	.225
Buster Mills	80	195	19	54	4	2	1	26	5	.277
Rusty Peters	34	58	6	13	5	1	0	2	0	.224
Eddie Robinson	8	8	1	1	0	0	0	2	0	.125
Ted Sepkowski	5	10	0	1	0	0	0	0	0	.100
George Susce	2	1	1	1	0	0	0	0	0	1.000
Roy Weatherly (CF)	128	473	61	122	23	7	5	39	8	.258
		5,317	590	1,344	223	58	50	541	69	.253

	W	L	G	GS	CG	IP	H	BB	K	ERA
Jim Bagby	17	14	36	(33)	16	(273)	248	80	70	3.10
Paul Calvert	0	0	5	0	0	8⅓	6	6	2	4.32
Pete Center	1	2	24	1	0	42½	29	18	10	2.76
Chubby Dean	5	5	17	9	3	76	83	34	29	4.50
Steve Gromek	0	0	3	0	0	4	6	0	4	9.00
Mel Harder	8	7	19	18	6	135⅓	126	61	40	3.06
Joe Heving	1	1	30	1	0	72	58	34	34	2.75
Vern Kennedy	10	7	28	17	8	146⅔	130	59	63	2.45
Eddie Klieman	0	1	1	1	0	9	8	5	2	1.00
Al Milnar	1	3	16	6	0	39	51	35	12	8.08
Mike Naymick	4	4	29	4	0	62⅔	32	47	41	2.30
Ray Poat	2	5	17	4	1	45	44	20	31	4.40
Allie Reynolds	11	12	34	21	11	198⅔	140	109	(151)	2.99
Jack Salveson	5	3	23	11	4	86	87	26	24	3.35
Al Smith	17	7	29	27	14	208⅓	186	72	72	2.55
	82	71		153	64	1,406⅓	1,234	606	585	3.15

Shutouts: Bagby (3), Reynolds (3), Salveson (3), Smith (3), Harder, Kennedy
Saves: Heving (9), Reynolds (3), Salveson (3), Naymick (2), Bagby, Center, Smith

1943

Record: 82–71
Finish: Third
Games Behind: 15½
Manager: Lou Boudreau

Wartime baseball and its manpower shortage dictated some drastic, often unorthodox moves by all major league managers, including Lou Boudreau. He designated Jim Bagby, one of the Indians best pitchers, as the team's backup second baseman.

Three other pitchers—Al Smith, Al Milnar, and Allie Reynolds—also practiced in the outfield during spring training, which the Indians held on the campus of Purdue University at West Lafayette, Indiana.

Because of World War II, travel restrictions imposed by Commissioner Kenesaw Mountain Landis decreed that all teams had to train north of the Mason-Dixon Line.

Bagby pitched a three-hitter and drove in the game's only run as he beat Detroit in the opener, 1–0, one of 48 games played at the Stadium. It got the Indians off to another fast start under Boudreau. They took over first place in late May, but couldn't hold it and, by mid-June, had skidded all the way to seventh.

They rallied in August, vaulting into second place, but by then New York was running away with its third straight pennant and seventh in eight years. The Indians were beaten out of second place by Washington in the final two weeks.

Two of the Tribe's three leading hitters were Roy Cullenbine and Buddy Rosar, acquired from the New York Yankees in a preseason trade for Roy Weatherly and Oscar Grimes. Les Fleming, the Indians' best hitter in 1942, no longer was on the team. He temporarily retired from baseball to work in a shipyard, which provided him a deferment from the Selective Service military draft.

	G	AB	R	H	2B	3B	HR	RBI	SB	AVG
Lou Boudreau (SS)	152	539	69	154	32	7	3	67	4	.286
Roy Cullenbine (RF)	138	488	66	141	24	4	8	56	3	.289
Otto Denning	37	129	8	31	6	0	0	13	3	.240
Gene Desautels	68	185	14	38	6	1	0	19	2	.205
Frank Doljack	3	7	0	0	0	0	0	0	0	.000
Hank Edwards	92	297	38	82	18	6	3	28	4	.276
Jimmy Grant	15	22	3	3	2	0	0	1	0	.136
Jeff Heath (LF)	118	424	58	116	22	6	18	79	5	.274
Oris Hockett (CF)	141	601	70	166	33	4	2	51	13	.276
Ken Keltner (3B)	110	427	47	111	31	3	4	39	2	.260
Ray Mack (2B)	153	545	56	120	25	2	7	62	8	.220
Jim McDonnell	2	1	1	0	0	0	0	0	0	.000
Rusty Peters	79	215	22	47	6	2	1	19	1	.219
Mickey Rocco (1B)	108	405	43	97	14	4	5	46	1	.240
Buddy Rosar (C)	115	382	53	108	17	1	1	41	0	.283
Pat Seerey	26	72	8	16	3	0	1	5	0	.222
George Susce	3	1	0	0	0	0	0	0	0	.000
Eddie Turchin	11	13	4	3	0	0	0	1	0	.231
Gene Woodling	8	25	5	8	2	1	1	5	0	.320
		5,269	600	1,344	(246)	45	55	564	47	.255

1944

Record: 72–82
Finish: Fifth (tied with Philadelphia)
Games Behind: 17
Manager: Lou Boudreau

Though they never were higher than fourth in the standings—and then for only two weeks in late July—the Indians were in the pennant race until they collapsed in September when Detroit and then St. Louis, the eventual winner, took charge.

The Indians trained again at Purdue University in West Lafayette, Indiana, because of the wartime travel restrictions.

While it was not a good season for Lou Boudreau the manager, it was an excellent one for Lou Boudreau the shortstop.

He won the American League batting championship in a close race with five other players—Snuffy Stirnweiss of New York, Bobby Doerr, Bob Johnson, and Pete Fox of Boston, and Stan Spence of Washington.

Boudreau got a hit in his final at bat to beat out Doerr by two points and Johnson by three. Stirnweiss, who was the leader with a .331 mark at the end of August, finished eight points behind Boudreau, who batted .371 from September 1 through October 2.

The Indians player-manager also set a new record with a

Indians pitcher Mel Harder is congratulated by manager Lou Boudreau and teammates after winning his 200th major league game in a victory over the Red Sox in Boston on May 10, 1944.

.978 fielding percentage and participated in 134 double plays, the most ever by a shortstop until then.

In addition to Boudreau, two other players, both part-timers, batted over .300. Jeff Heath was one; the other was Paul O'Dea, the Cleveland sandlot graduate signed by the Indians in 1938 who was blinded in his right eye when hit by a batted ball in spring training in 1940. O'Dea made a comeback on the sandlots in 1942, earning another opportunity in the minor leagues in 1943, and winning a place on the Tribe's roster in 1944.

	W	L	G	GS	CG	IP	H	BB	K	ERA
Jim Bagby	4	5	13	10	2	79	101	34	12	4.33
Bill Bonness	0	1	2	1	0	7	11	5	1	7.71
Paul Calvert	1	3	35	4	0	77	89	38	31	4.56
Red Embree	0	1	3	1	0	3⅓	2	5	4	13.50
Steve Gromek	10	9	35	21	12	203⅔	160	70	115	2.56
Mel Harder	12	10	30	27	12	196⅓	211	69	64	3.71
Earl Henry	1	1	2	2	1	17⅔	18	3	5	4.58
Joe Heving	8	3	(63)	1	0	119⅔	106	41	46	1.96
Vern Kennedy	2	5	12	10	2	59	66	37	17	5.03
Hal Kleine	1	2	11	6	1	40⅔	38	36	13	5.75
Eddie Klieman	11	13	47	19	5	178⅓	185	70	44	3.38
Mike Naymick	0	0	7	0	0	13	16	10	4	9.69
Paul O'Dea	0	0	3	0	0	4⅓	5	6	0	2.08
Ray Poat	4	8	36	6	1	80⅔	82	37	40	5.13
Allie Reynolds	11	8	28	21	5	158	141	91	84	3.30
Al Smith	7	13	28	26	7	181⅔	197	69	44	3.42
	72	82		155	48	(1,419½)	(1,428)	(621)	524	3.65

Shutouts: Gromek (2), Harder (2), Klieman, Reynolds, Smith
Saves: Heving (10), Klieman (5), Gromek, Poat, Reynolds

	G	AB	R	H	2B	3B	HR	RBI	SB	AVG
Steve Biras	2	2	0	2	0	0	0	2	0	1.000
Lou Boudreau (SS)	150	584	91	191	(45)	5	3	67	11	(.327)
Roy Cullenbine (RF)	154	571	98	162	34	5	16	80	4	.284
Jim Devlin	1	1	0	0	0	0	0	0	0	.000
Jimmy Grant	61	99	12	27	4	3	1	12	1	.273
Jeff Heath	60	151	20	50	5	2	5	33	0	.331
Myril Hoag	67	277	33	79	9	3	1	27	6	.285
Oris Hockett (CF)	124	457	47	132	29	5	1	50	8	.289
Ken Keltner (3B)	149	573	74	169	41	9	13	91	4	.295
Russ Lyon	7	11	1	2	0	0	0	0	0	.182
Ray Mack (2B)	83	284	24	66	15	3	0	29	4	.232
Jim McDonnell	20	43	5	10	0	0	0	4	0	.233
Paul O'Dea	76	173	25	55	9	0	0	13	2	.318
Rusty Peters	88	282	23	63	13	3	1	24	2	.223
Mickey Rocco (1B)	(155)	(653)	87	174	29	7	13	70	4	.266
Buddy Rosar (C)	99	331	29	87	9	3	0	30	1	.263
Hank Ruszkowski	3	8	1	3	0	0	0	1	0	.375
Norm Schlueter	49	122	2	15	4	0	0	11	0	.123
Pat Seerey (LF)	101	342	39	80	16	0	15	39	0	.234
George Susce	29	61	3	14	1	0	0	4	0	.230
		(5,481)	643	(1,458)	270	50	70	611	48	.266

1945

Record: 73–72
Finish: Fifth
Games Behind: 11
Manager: Lou Boudreau

The Indians' personnel were expected to be better than any of the three previous teams managed by Lou Boudreau, and optimism was high again as the team reported for spring training a third straight year at Purdue University in West Lafayette, Indiana.

But Ken Keltner went into the navy, and the Tribe opened the season with Roy Cullenbine, an outfielder, playing third base; Ray Mack was drafted into the army; Jeff Heath and Buddy Rosar held out for more money until early June; and

Mel Harder, who was working in a war plant, was unavailable until July 1.

Consequently, the Indians floundered at the start—and got worse before they improved. From April 30 to May 21 they were lodged in last place.

A factor in the overall problem was that players were never quite sure where they'd be playing. As Boudreau said, "It was like we were on the road even when we were at home." That's because the Indians went from League Park to the Stadium and back again, depending upon the attraction. They wound up playing 46 games in the Stadium.

Another even greater part of the problem was that Boudreau, the American League's defending batting champion, suffered a broken ankle on August 13 and was finished for the season. The injury happened as Boudreau was covering second on a double play and was hit hard in a slide by Dolph Camilli of Boston.

That was the day before the Japanese surrendered, ending World War II, and Bob Feller was able to return to the Indians after spending 44 months in the navy aboard the USS *Alabama,* earning eight battle stars.

On August 24, 10 days after he rejoined the Tribe, Feller made his first start in a major league game since 1941. He beat archrival Hal Newhouser and the Detroit Tigers, 4–2, striking out 12 in front of a roaring crowd of 46,477 in the Stadium.

Appropriately, Feller struck out Jimmy Outlaw, the first batter he faced that night, on a 3-and-2 pitch, setting off a cascade of cheers.

It was the same Jimmy Outlaw who later, on September 19, spoiled Feller's bid for a second no-hitter as the Indians beat the Tigers, 2–0, at League Park. Outlaw singled in the fifth inning, and Feller wound up with his sixth career one-hitter, leaving no doubt he was as good as ever.

Another highlight of an otherwise disappointing season occurred on July 13 in Yankee Stadium. Pat Seerey clubbed three home runs, one of them a grand slam, in a 16–4 Tribe victory.

Les Fleming returned in August from his shipyard job, and Jeff Heath came back from an injury year to hit .305. But none of them—not even Feller—could salvage the season for the Indians. They were never better than fourth, and were only that high for a week, from August 15 to 21.

Paul O'Dea continued his courageous comeback despite being blind in one eye, hitting .235 in 87 games. But with the servicemen returning from the war, along with those who left baseball to work in war plants, O'Dea never played another major league game after 1945.

	W	L	G	GS	CG	IP	H	BB	K	ERA
Jim Bagby	8	11	25	19	11	159⅓	171	59	38	3.73
Paul Calvert	0	0	1	0	0	1⅓	3	1	1	13.50
Eddie Carnett	0	0	2	0	0	2	0	0	1	0.00
Pete Center	6	3	31	8	2	85⅔	89	28	34	3.99
Red Embree	4	4	8	8	5	70	56	26	42	1.93
Bob Feller	5	3	9	9	7	72	50	35	59	2.50
Steve Gromek	19	9	33	30	21	251	229	66	101	2.55
Mel Harder	3	7	11	11	2	76	93	23	16	3.67
Earl Henry	0	3	15	1	0	21⅔	20	20	10	5.40
Myril Hoag	0	0	2	0	0	3	3	1	0	0.00
Hal Kleine	0	0	3	0	0	7	8	7	5	3.86
Eddie Klieman	5	8	38	12	4	126⅓	123	49	33	3.85
Paul O'Dea	0	0	1	0	0	2	4	2	0	13.50
Allie Reynolds	18	12	44	30	16	247⅓	227	(130)	112	3.20
Jack Salveson	0	0	19	0	0	44	52	6	11	3.68
Al Smith	5	12	21	19	8	133⅔	141	48	34	3.84
	73	72		147	76	1,302⅓	1,269	501	497	3.31

Shutouts: Bagby (3), Gromek (3), Smith (3), Reynolds (2), Embree, Feller, Klieman
Saves: Klieman (4), Reynolds (4), Bagby, Center, Gromek, Smith

The 1945 Cleveland Indians

	G	AB	R	H	2B	3B	HR	RBI	SB	AVG
Stan Benjamin	14	21	1	7	2	0	0	3	0	.333
Lou Boudreau (SS)	97	345	50	106	24	1	3	48	0	.307
Eddie Carnett	30	73	5	16	7	0	0	7	0	.219
Al Cihocki	92	283	21	60	9	3	0	24	2	.212
Roy Cullenbine	8	13	3	1	1	0	0	0	0	.077
Gene Desautels	10	9	1	1	0	0	0	0	0	.111
Les Fleming	42	140	18	46	10	2	3	22	0	.329
Frankie Haves (C)	119	385	39	91	15	6	6	43	1	.236
Jeff Heath (LF)	102	370	60	113	16	7	15	61	3	.305
Myril Hoag	40	128	10	27	5	3	0	3	1	.211
Felix Mackiewicz (CF)	120	359	42	98	14	7	2	37	5	.273
Jim McDonnell	28	51	3	10	2	0	0	8	0	.196
Dutch Meyer (2B)	130	524	71	153	29	8	7	48	2	.292
Paul O'Dea	87	221	21	52	2	2	1	21	3	.235
Mickey Rocco (1B)	143	565	81	149	28	6	10	56	0	.264
Don Ross (3B)	106	363	26	95	15	1	2	43	0	.262
Bob Rothel	4	10	0	2	0	0	0	0	0	.200
Hank Ruszkowski	14	49	2	10	0	0	0	5	0	.204
Pat Seerey (RF)	126	414	56	98	22	2	14	56	1	.237
Red Steiner	12	20	0	3	0	0	0	2	0	.150
Elmer Weingartner	20	39	5	9	1	0	0	1	0	.231
Ed Wheeler	46	72	12	14	2	0	0	1	1	.194
Pap Williams	16	19	0	4	0	0	0	0	0	.211
		4,898	557	1,249	216	48	65	519	19	.255

1946

Record: 68–86
Finish: Sixth
Games Behind: 36
Manager: Lou Boudreau

Along with the players returning from World War II was a 32-year-old, wounded ex-marine named Bill Veeck, who became instantly famous in Cleveland when he purchased the Indians from Alva Bradley for a reported $1.1 million on June 22.

Veeck blew in like a whirlwind and never slowed down. As Boudreau said, "We always had three teams—one on the field, another coming, and one going." Players arrived and were dispatched in the wink of an eye.

Dispatched, too, was Roger Peckinpaugh as Veeck made clear his intention to assume the general manager's duties himself.

Though the Indians continued to struggle on the field, attendance soared over a million (to 1,057,289) for the first time in franchise history. Veeck staged a constant stream of promotions, including fireworks displays, vaudeville acts, and one giveaway after another.

But even before Veeck took over, the Indians were in a state of flux.

More than 60 players reported for spring training in Clearwater, Florida, as travel restrictions were lifted when World War II ended. Among those returning from the service were catcher Jim Hegan, outfielder Gene Woodling, and third baseman Bob Lemon, all of them still rookies though they'd had previous trials with the Tribe.

Manager Lou Boudreau, granted a new two-year contract through 1947 by Bradley the previous winter, was determined to make sweeping changes.

Traded away were veterans Jim Bagby and Jeff Heath, neither of whom was liked by Boudreau. Another nonfavorite of the manager, catcher Frank Hayes, was sent packing in June.

It didn't take long for Bob Feller to reestablish himself as the American League's premier pitcher. He won the opener against Chicago, 1–0. Three starts later Feller fired his sec-

ond career no-hitter, beating the Yankees, 1–0, in New York on April 30 with the help of three critical defensive plays.

Two were made by Boudreau to retire Snuffy Stirnweiss in the first inning and Phil Rizzuto in the eighth, the other by second baseman Ray Mack with the game hanging in the balance in the bottom of the ninth.

The Yankees had the potential tying run on third with two out when Mack went to the edge of the outfield grass to field a sharp grounder by Charlie Keller. In his anxiety to make the play, Mack stumbled and fell to his knees, but recovered in time to throw out Keller by an eyelash.

Feller also hurled his seventh and eighth one-hitters in 1946, on July 31, in a 4–1 victory over Boston at League Park, spoiled by Bobby Doerr, who singled in the second inning, and on August 8 when he beat the White Sox, 5–0, in Chicago, with Hayes, his former catcher, getting a seventh-inning single in the first game of a doubleheader.

Feller prevailed in the opener thanks to the aforementioned rookie third baseman named Lemon, who made a game-saving catch in center field.

Lemon, who had been a good hitter in the minor leagues before going into the navy, was switched to the outfield. Boudreau made the switch because, he said, "We were desperate for a center fielder, and we had a good third baseman in Ken Keltner."

Lemon's diving catch came on a sinking liner by White Sox first baseman Jake Jones with one out and Bob Kennedy on second in the last of the ninth. Kennedy, thinking it was a hit, took off for third and was easily doubled as Lemon scrambled to his feet and tossed the ball to Boudreau at second base, ending the game.

It was the beginning of another magnificent season for Feller, who went on to lead the AL in 10 categories, including winning 26 games and striking out 348 batters. The latter either broke or fell one short of the 1904 record set by Rube Waddell of Philadelphia.

The uncertainty regarding Waddell's number of strikeouts was based on the fact that records were poorly kept in 1904. Some statisticians credited him with 343; others said he struck out 349 batters.

Whatever, Feller's total was remarkable, achieved in 371⅓ innings, which also led the league, as did his 48 appearances, 42 starts, 36 complete games, and 10 shutouts.

Unfortunately, Allie Reynolds was the only other pitcher on the Tribe staff to win in double figures (11), though he also lost 15 games. Steve Gromek, one of the team's big winners in 1945, went from 10 victories over .500 to 10 below (5–15) in 1946.

Even worse was the Indians' offense. Their team batting average was lowest in the AL. Hank Edwards was the only regular to hit .300, and he did it by only one point, while Boudreau's average dropped to .293.

The Indians won their opener, but never again were at the top of the league. They lost five of their first nine and after the first week of May were lodged in seventh place.

By the time Veeck closed his deal with Bradley to become the fourth owner of the franchise, the Indians with a 26–33 record had crept into a fifth-place tie with the St. Louis Browns, but were never able to climb any higher.

From June 22 on, with no fewer than 48 players wearing a Cleveland uniform at one time or another, the Tribe went 42–53, which did not endear Boudreau to Veeck—at least not as a manager, though the new owner had great respect for Boudreau the player.

Boudreau did one thing that Veeck truly appreciated because it produced national publicity for the Indians: He devised an unorthodox shift in an attempt to lessen the productivity of Ted Williams.

Because, as Boudreau said, "Williams is always beating our brains out," he unveiled what came to be known as the "Williams shift."

It happened on July 14, after Williams went 4-for-5 with three homers, all to right field, driving in eight runs as Boston beat the Tribe, 11–10, in the first game of a doubleheader at Fenway Park.

Boudreau positioned first baseman Jimmy Wasdell and right fielder Hank Edwards virtually on the right-field foul line, second baseman Jack Conway close to first base and back on the grass, himself to the right of second base, third baseman Ken Keltner directly behind second on the edge of the outfield grass, center fielder Pat Seerey in right center, and left fielder George Case about 30 feet closer to the infield than normal, so that he was practically playing a deep shortstop.

Williams couldn't believe his eyes when he stepped into the batter's box. He even complained to umpire Jim Boyer, who told Williams, "As long as they have nine guys on the field and eight of them are inside the foul lines, they can play anywhere they please."

The Indians used the shift against Williams every time he batted with the bases empty, and it worked more times than not.

As Boudreau explained, "My plan was predicated on the belief that Williams, who made no secret of the fact that he wanted to be known as the greatest hitter of all time—which I think he was—would be too proud to adjust his style to counteract my strategy, that it would be beneath his dignity to change."

One notable occasion when the shift backfired on the Tribe was in the first inning of a game at League Park on September 13.

Red Embree was on the mound for the Indians and pitched Williams on the outside corner of the plate. Williams poked a routine fly to left field. Because Seerey, then the left fielder, was playing almost where the shortstop would normally be stationed, the ball sailed over his head. Williams legged it out for an inside-the-park homer, the only one of his career.

It also was one of only two hits allowed by Embree, but turned out to be the only run of the game, and the 1–0 victory clinched the 1946 pennant for the Red Sox.

Boudreau, with input from veteran pitcher Mel Harder, also made another "shift" that season, this one involving Lemon.

The erstwhile third baseman–center fielder made his first appearance as a pitcher in the Indians' 21st game of 1946, launching a new career that carried him into the Hall of Fame.

Two factors led to the decision to try Lemon as a pitcher. First, he failed to hit consistently as the Tribe's center fielder, and, second, he was recognized for having a strong arm and had done some pitching while in the navy.

Boudreau, looking for more offensive punch than Lemon provided, replaced him in center field with Seerey.

After the Tribe was blown out in a couple of games in early May because the bull pen was ineffective, Boudreau and Harder asked New York Yankees catcher Bill Dickey about Lemon.

Dickey, who had played with Lemon when they were in the service during the war, told Boudreau that, if he were manager of the Indians, he'd give Lemon a chance to pitch.

Boudreau took Dickey's advice.

On May 12, in the seventh inning of the nightcap of a doubleheader against St. Louis at the Stadium, where the Indians played 41 games that season, Lemon trudged in from the bull pen.

Lemon pitched three innings in his debut, yielding a run on two hits and a walk, and struck out three as the Browns won, 9–3. The Tribe loser was Reynolds.

Lemon made his first start on June 3 when he also was charged with his first decision, a 3–2 loss in the second game of a doubleheader in Philadelphia. He gave up all of the Athletics' runs on four hits and four walks in 3⅔ innings.

Six days later, on June 9—ironically, against the Yankees after Dickey had taken over as their interim manager two weeks earlier—Lemon earned his first victory. He relieved starter Don Black in the sixth inning and the Indians rallied to win, 9–5, in the first game of a doubleheader in New York.

Lemon finished the season with a 4–5 record in 32 appearances, five as a starter.

Eight days before the curtain fell on the 1946 season, on September 21 with the Indians solidly embedded in sixth place with a 66–82 record, they lost to Detroit, 5–3, in front of 2,772 indifferent spectators at League Park.

It was the last time two major league baseball teams played on the field that was the first home of the Cleveland Blues in the brand new American League in 1901, as Veeck earlier had announced that henceforth all home games would be at the Stadium.

Veeck made an issue of Boudreau's being left off the AL All-Star team in favor of Chicago's Luke Appling, St. Louis's Vern Stephens, and Boston's Johnny Pesky, and promised an "investigation" of the managers who then made the selections. When nothing came of it, Veeck staged a big promotion to present Boudreau with a trophy that was engraved, "To the Best Shortstop Not Picked on the All-Star Team."

	W	L	G	GS	CG	IP	H	BB	K	ERA
Joe Berry	3	6	21	0	0	37⅓	32	21	16	3.38
Don Black	1	2	18	4	0	43⅔	45	21	15	4.53
Pete Center	0	2	21	0	0	29	29	20	6	4.97
Red Embree	8	12	28	26	8	200	170	79	87	3.47
Bob Feller	(26)	15	(48)	(42)	(36)	(371⅓)	(277)	(153)	(348)	2.18
Tom Ferrick	0	0	9	0	0	18	25	4	9	5.00
Ray Flanigan	0	1	3	1	0	9	11	8	2	11.00
Charlie Gassaway	1	1	13	6	0	50⅔	54	26	23	3.91
Steve Gromek	5	15	29	21	5	153⅔	159	47	75	4.33
Mel Harder	5	4	13	12	4	92⅓	85	31	21	3.41
Vic Johnson	0	1	9	1	0	13⅔	20	8	3	9.22
Eddie Klieman	0	0	9	0	0	15	18	10	2	6.60
Joe Krakauskas	2	5	29	5	0	47⅓	60	25	20	5.51
Bob Kuzava	1	0	2	2	0	12	9	11	4	3.00
Bob Lemon	4	5	32	5	1	94	77	68	39	2.49
Ralph McCabe	0	1	1	1	0	4	5	2	3	11.25
Johnny Podgajny	0	0	6	0	0	9	13	2	4	5.00
Allie Reynolds	11	15	31	28	9	183⅓	180	108	107	3.88
Les Webber	1	1	4	2	0	5⅓	13	5	5	23.63
	68	86	(156)	63	1,388⅓	1,282	(649)	789	3.62

Shutouts: Feller (10), Reynolds (3), Gromek (2), Harder
Saves: Feller (4), Gromek (4), Berry, Center, Ferrick, Krakauskas, Lemon

	G	AB	R	H	2B	3B	HR	RBI	SB	AVG
Heinz Becker	50	147	15	44	10	1	0	17	1	.299
Lou Boudreau (SS)	140	515	51	151	30	6	6	62	6	.293
Charlie Brewster	3	2	0	0	0	0	0	0	0	.000
George Case (LF)	118	484	46	109	23	4	1	22	(28)	.225
Jack Conway	68	258	24	58	6	2	0	18	2	.225
Hank Edwards (RF)	124	458	62	138	33	(16)	10	54	1	.301
Les Fleming (1B)	99	306	40	85	17	5	8	42	1	.278
Frankie Hayes	51	156	11	40	12	0	3	18	1	.256
Jim Hegan (C)	88	271	29	64	11	5	0	17	1	.236
Tom Jordan	14	35	2	7	1	0	1	3	1	.200
Ken Keltner (3B)	116	398	47	96	17	1	13	45	0	.241
Sherm Lollar	28	62	7	15	6	0	1	9	0	.242
Ray Mack	61	171	13	35	6	2	1	9	2	.205
Felix Mackiewicz	78	258	35	67	15	4	0	16	5	.260
Dutch Meyer (2B)	72	207	13	48	5	3	0	16	0	.232
Buster Mills	9	22	1	6	0	0	0	3	0	.273
Dale Mitchell	11	44	7	19	3	0	0	5	1	.432
Blas Monaco	12	6	2	0	0	0	0	0	0	.000
Howie Moss	8	32	2	2	0	0	0	0	0	.063
Rusty Peters	9	21	0	6	0	0	0	2	0	.286
Jackie Price	7	13	1	3	0	0	0	0	0	.231
Eddie Robinson	8	30	6	12	1	0	3	4	0	.400
Mickey Rocco	34	98	8	24	2	0	2	14	1	.245
Don Ross	55	153	12	41	7	0	3	14	0	.268
Pat Seerey (CF)	117	404	57	91	17	2	26	62	2	.225
Ted Sepkowski	2	8	2	4	1	0	0	1	0	.500
Jimmy Wasdell	32	41	1	11	0	0	0	4	1	.268
Ralph Weigel	6	12	0	2	0	0	0	0	1	.167
Gene Woodling	61	133	8	25	1	4	0	9	1	.188
		5,242	537	1,285	233	56	79	496	57	.245

1947

Record: 80–74
Finish: Fourth
Games Behind: 17
Manager: Lou Boudreau

Bill Veeck began his first full season as owner of the Indians by promising to bring a pennant winner to Cleveland, all the while dismissing speculation that he would soon replace Lou Boudreau as manager of the team.

The season didn't start well as the Tribe and Bob Feller lost the opener, 2–0, to Chicago, but Veeck was thrilled by a turnout of 55,014 fans at the Stadium, the largest opening day crowd in major league history until then.

Two weeks later, on April 28, when the Detroit Tigers visited Cleveland, they were surprised to find a five-foot-high temporary fence installed at the Stadium. It stretched from foul line to foul line, considerably shrinking the spacious outfield dimensions.

No longer would it be necessary for batters to hit a ball 420 feet to left-center and right-center for a home run, nor would a 435-foot drive to dead center be only a long out.

The fence was so temporary, in fact, that Veeck had it installed in pipe-sleeves in the outfield so that it could be—and was—moved in and out depending upon the batting prowess of the team then in town to play the Indians. (The portability of the fence was outlawed by American League president William Harridge the following year when it was decreed that the fence had to remain wherever it was located on opening day.)

Meanwhile, players continued to come and go at a dizzying pace as Veeck did his best to deliver a winner.

The most prominent of the arrivals was Larry Doby, the American League's first black player, whose debut followed by 11 weeks that of Jackie Robinson with the Brooklyn Dodgers.

Hall of Famers Tris Speaker (left) and Rogers Hornsby, who were spring training coaches for the Indians in 1947.

Doby, then a 22-year-old second baseman–shortstop who had played for the Newark Eagles of the Negro National League, signed with the Indians on July 3 and joined them in Chicago on July 5.

That day Doby made his first major league appearance in the seventh inning, striking out against Earl Harrist as a pinch hitter for pitcher Bryan Stephens. The Indians lost, 6–5.

The following day, in the second game of a doubleheader, Doby played first base—his only game at that position in his major league career—and beat out an infield single, driving in a run in the fourth inning, in four at bats, in the Tribe's 5–1 victory over Chicago. He went on to hit .156 in 29 games, all but six as a pinch hitter.

Another newcomer who made a significant contribution was second baseman Joe Gordon, who came from the New York Yankees along with third baseman Eddie Bockman in a trade for pitcher Allie Reynolds.

Important, too, to the fortunes of the Indians was the development of four young players—outfielder Dale Mitchell, first baseman Eddie Robinson, catcher Jim Hegan, and outfielder-turned-pitcher Bob Lemon.

Another who gained prominence, if only briefly, was Don Black, a pitcher who was purchased on waivers from the Philadelphia Athletics the previous year, but was little used until he joined Alcoholics Anonymous.

On July 10, in the first game of a twi-night doubleheader against his former teammates at the Stadium, Black hurled the Indians' ninth no-hitter, beating the Athletics, 3–0.

Bob Feller pitched two more one-hitters, his ninth on April 22, when he beat St. Louis, 5–0, spoiled by Al Zarilla's seventh-inning single, and his 10th on May 2, a 2–0 victory over Boston, as Johnny Pesky singled in the first inning. Both were at the Stadium.

The Indians commuted between second and third place through the first two months of the season, but their early success was too good to last. By late June they had sunk into fifth place, 12 games off the pace, and were never in the race again.

Still, the Indians' season attendance peaked again, this time at 1,521,978, and even though they improved their won-lost record to six games over .500, which boosted them two places in the standings, it didn't help Boudreau's status.

Veeck continued to express dissatisfaction with Lou Boudreau the manager, if not Lou Boudreau the shortstop, whose batting average climbed over .300 for the third time in four years.

It was during the World Series between the Yankees and Brooklyn Dodgers that Veeck confided "off the record" to a couple of reporters that he was thinking about trading Boudreau to the St. Louis Browns for shortstop Vernon "Junior" Stephens.

Veeck's primary objective, however, was that he wanted to bring back Al Lopez to manage the Indians. Lopez, at that time, was managing Indianapolis of the Class AAA American Association.

When the story leaked out and appeared in the Cleveland papers on October 5, Indians fans reacted violently. The *Cleveland News* published a "Boudreau Ballot" on its front page for several days and invited fans to vote to keep or trade the player-manager.

The result was overwhelmingly in favor of retaining Boudreau, as were petitions signed on his behalf.

Finally Veeck relented, said he canceled negotiations with the Browns and, on November 24, signed Boudreau to a new two-year contract through 1949.

There was speculation, however, that the deal was called off by the Browns who, a week earlier, traded Stephens and pitcher Jack Kramer to Boston for six players and $310,000.

Postseason honors were reaped by Boudreau, Gordon, and Feller, as all three were selected on the AL All-Star team, and also received votes in the balloting for the Most Valuable Player award. Boudreau's 168 points were third behind Joe DiMaggio (202) and Ted Williams (201), while Gordon was seventh (59), and Feller, the league's only 20-game winner, was eighth (58).

	W	L	G	GS	CG	IP	H	BB	K	ERA
Gene Bearden	0	0	1	0	0	⅓	2	1	0	81.00
Don Black	10	12	30	28	8	190⅔	177	85	72	3.92
Cal Dorsett	0	0	2	0	0	1⅓	3	3	1	27.00
Red Embree	8	10	27	21	6	162⅔	137	67	56	3.15
Bob Feller	(20)	11	42	(37)	20	(299)	230	127	(196)	2.68
Al Gettel	11	10	31	21	9	149	122	62	64	3.20
Steve Gromek	3	5	29	7	0	84⅓	77	36	39	3.74
Ernie Groth	0	0	2	0	0	1⅓	0	1	1	0.00
Mel Harder	6	4	15	15	4	80	91	27	17	4.50
Eddie Klieman	5	4	(58)	0	0	92	78	39	21	3.03
Bob Kuzava	1	1	4	4	1	21⅔	22	9	9	4.15
Bob Lemon	11	5	37	15	6	167⅓	150	97	65	3.44
Lymie Linde	0	0	1	0	0	⅔	3	1	0	27.00
Bryan Stephens	5	10	31	5	1	92	79	39	34	4.01
Les Willis	0	2	22	2	0	44	58	24	10	3.48
Roger Wolff	0	0	7	2	0	16	15	10	5	3.94
	80	74		157	55	(1,402½)	1,244	(628)	590	3.44

Shutouts: Feller (5), Black (3), Gettel (2), Harder, Kuzava, Lemon
Saves: Klieman (17), Gromek (4), Feller (3), Lemon (3), Stephens, Willis

	G	AB	R	H	2B	3B	HR	RBI	SB	AVG
Heinz Becker	2	2	0	0	0	0	0	0	0	.000
Eddie Bockman	46	66	8	17	2	2	1	14	0	.258
Lou Boudreau (SS)	150	538	79	165	(45)	3	4	67	1	.307
Jack Conway	34	50	3	9	2	0	0	5	0	.180
Larry Doby	29	32	3	5	1	0	0	2	0	.156
Hank Edwards (RF)	108	393	54	102	12	3	15	59	1	.260
Les Fleming	103	281	39	68	14	2	4	43	0	.242
Joe Frazier	9	14	1	1	1	0	0	0	0	.071
Joe Gordon (2B)	155	562	89	153	27	6	29	93	7	.272
Jim Hegan (C)	135	378	38	94	14	5	4	42	3	.249
Ken Keltner (3B)	151	541	49	139	29	3	11	76	5	.257
Al Lopez	61	126	9	33	1	0	0	14	1	.262
Felix Mackiewicz	2	5	0	0	0	0	0	0	0	.000
Catfish Metkovich (CF)	126	473	68	120	22	7	5	40	5	.254
Dale Mitchell (LF)	123	493	69	156	16	10	1	34	2	.316
Hal Peck	114	392	58	115	18	2	8	44	3	.293
Eddie Robinson (1B)	95	318	52	78	10	1	14	52	1	.245
Al Rosen	7	9	1	1	0	0	0	0	0	.111
Hank Ruszkowski	23	27	5	7	2	0	3	4	0	.259
Pat Seerey	82	216	24	37	4	1	11	29	0	.171
Ted Sepkowski	10	8	0	1	1	0	0	0	0	.125
Jimmy Wasdell	1	1	0	0	0	0	0	0	0	.000
		(5,367)	687	1,392	(234)	51	112	646	29	.259

Former Indians outfielder and broadcaster Jack Graney (left) makes a presentation to Hall of Fame pitcher Cy Young during a pre-game ceremony at Cleveland Stadium in 1947.

1948

Record: 97–58
Finish: First
Games Ahead: 1
Manager: Lou Boudreau

Bill Veeck made good on his promise to bring a pennant to Cleveland, but it was Lou Boudreau who delivered it.

After a four-team battle down the stretch with Boston, Philadelphia, and New York, the Indians finished in a tie with the Red Sox, won a one-game playoff, 8–3, at Fenway Park for the pennant, and beat the Boston Braves in six games in the World Series.

Boudreau was a great manager primarily because he had a great shortstop and clutch hitter named Boudreau in the lineup. It was Boudreau who led the Indians to their victory in the pennant playoff with a perfect 4-for-4, including two homers, under the most challenging of conditions.

More than justifying the outpouring of support by his fans who convinced Veeck to re-sign him, Boudreau won the American League's Most Valuable Player award, receiving 22 of the 24 votes cast by a panel of baseball writers. His .355 average was second only to Ted Williams, who batted .369 for his fourth batting championship.

A myriad of promotional stunts—including a special night for "Mr. Average Fan," Joe Earley—coupled with the exciting play of the team, attracted 2,620,627 fans through the turnstiles, then a major league record, and Veeck and Boudreau owned the city.

Even before the season began, one of baseball's biggest names, slugger Hank Greenberg, joined the organization, though not as a player. He purchased stock in the club and assumed the position of vice president and farm director.

Four major player transactions were significant in propelling the Indians to their second pennant since the AL was formed in 1901—the purchase of relief pitcher Russ Christopher from the Philadelphia Athletics on April 3, the acquisition of outfielder Bob Kennedy from the Chicago White Sox (for Al Gettel and Pat Seerey) on June 2, getting pitcher Sam Zoldak from the St. Louis Browns in a trade for

Bill Kennedy and $100,000 on June 15, and the purchase of Leroy "Satchel" Paige from the Kansas City Monarchs of the Negro League on July 7.

But the success of the Indians—in addition to Boudreau's inspirational leadership—revolved around the development of two outstanding pitchers, Gene Bearden and Bob Lemon.

Actually, it was one of those seasons in which every regular had a good year, especially outfielders Dale Mitchell and Larry Doby, both of whom blossomed into stardom.

Bearden, a knuckleballer acquired in a trade with the Yankees in 1947 (though he spent that season in the minors), won 20 games, including the pennant playoff against the Red Sox, and led the AL with a 2.43 earned run average.

Lemon, who was converted in 1946 from a light-hitting third baseman–outfielder, also won 20 and pitched a no-hitter, 10th in Tribe history, beating the Tigers, 2–0, on June 30 in Detroit.

Bob Feller, a 20-game winner in five previous seasons (he missed only in 1945 when he spent the first four months in the navy), slumped to a 19–15 record, but won two games in front of record crowds.

The first was the April 20 opener at the Stadium when 73,163 fans cheered Feller's two-hit, 4–0, victory over St. Louis.

Two months later, on June 20, 82,781 fans jammed the Stadium and saw Feller and Lemon beat Philadelphia in a doubleheader, 4–3 and 10–0.

Paige made his major league debut on July 9 in a relief role in a 5–3 loss to St. Louis at the Stadium. Three weeks later, on August 3, in his first starting assignment, Paige thrilled a record night-game crowd of 72,434 at the Stadium with a 5–3 victory over Washington.

Paige also was the feature attraction on August 20 when another record night-game crowd of 78,382 rocked the Stadium as he hurled a three-hitter to beat Chicago, 1–0.

Still, the highlight of the season because it probably was the turning point for the Indians occurred on August 8, and again it was Boudreau in the spotlight.

Only two percentage points separated the Indians, Philadelphia, and New York as the top three teams in the AL at the start of a doubleheader against the Yankees in front of

The Indians' 1948 pennant, one of only four won by the franchise since its inception in 1901.

Indians manager Lou Boudreau (second from left) with Hall of Famers Tris Speaker (far left) and Hank Greenberg (third from left) and comedian Bob Hope in 1948. Hope was a minority owner of the team, Speaker was a part time batting instructor, and Greenberg was the Indians vice president.

another massive crowd of 73,484 fans in the Stadium. The Indians record was 58–39, New York's was 59–40, and Philadelphia's was 61–42.

Boudreau was not in the lineup after suffering injuries to his right shoulder, right thumb, right knee, and left ankle three days earlier in a collision at second base with Washington's Gil Coan.

With New York leading, 6–4, in the seventh inning, the Indians loaded the bases with two out, and Joe Page, the Yankees ace reliever, was called into the game to replace Spec Shea.

Boudreau, who'd been soaking his sore ankle in a bucket of ice water, put on his sock and shoe, grabbed a bat and limped to the plate as a pinch hitter for Thurman Tucker. With the count 2-and-2, the player-manager lashed a line drive to the right of second base. It normally would have been a double, but Boudreau, hardly able to run, had to stop at first. It scored two runs, tying the game.

Veeck called it "the most courageous thing I've ever seen in baseball," and the Indians went on to win, not only the opener, 8–6, but also the nightcap, 2–1.

But the season also produced a near tragedy, which would have been similar to the one that occurred in 1920 when Ray Chapman was hit by a pitched ball on August 16 and died the next day.

Don Black, the reformed alcoholic who pitched a no-hitter in 1947, suffered a cerebral hemorrhage while at bat in the second inning of a game against St. Louis at the Stadium on September 13. For nearly a week Black's life hung in the balance, and he was hospitalized for a month. He survived but never pitched again.

Though they shared or were in first place all alone most of the season and never fell below third, the Indians' flight to the pennant was not an easy one. On September 7, the day after Labor Day, they were third, 4½ games off the pace with 23 to play. They finished 18–5, while New York went 13–10 and Boston 14–10.

The tie between the Indians and Red Sox was fashioned on the last day of the season, October 3, when Detroit and Hal Newhouser beat Feller and Cleveland, 7–1, and Boston defeated New York, 10–5.

Boudreau's selection of Bearden (over Lemon and Steve Gromek) to pitch the playoff game on October 3 was even more surprising than manager Joe McCarthy's choice of Denny Galehouse to start for the Red Sox.

Boudreau cracked his first homer with the bases bare and two out in the first inning. The Red Sox got the run back in their half of the inning on Johnny Pesky's double and Vernon Stephens' two-out single. The score remained tied until the fourth when Boudreau and Joe Gordon led with singles and Ken Keltner followed with a home run for a 4–1 lead. It went to 5–1 in the fourth on Doby's double, a sacrifice, and an infield grounder by Jim Hegan, and Boudreau homered in the fifth for a 6–1 lead. An error by Gordon and Bobby Doerr's two-out homer in the sixth cut the Red Sox deficit to 6–3. But Bearden would not let them get any closer, and the Indians added single runs in eighth and ninth.

When it was over, Veeck told the media, "We didn't win the pennant in 1948. We won it on November 25, 1947, the day I rehired Lou Boudreau."

The Indians' wondrous year continued through the World Series, though they stumbled in the October 6 opener. Feller lost a two-hitter, 1–0, to the Braves' Johnny Sain because of a controversial decision by National League umpire Bill Stewart. It led to the game's only run in the eighth inning.

The Indians prevailed in the next three, 4–1, as Lemon bested Warren Spahn; 2–0, as Bearden won over Vern Bickford; and 2–1, as Gromek defeated Sain on a third-inning homer by Doby.

Feller was knocked out of the box in Game 5 as Spahn and the Braves won, 11–5; in front of an all-time-record crowd of 86,288 in the Stadium on October 10.

But the next day in Boston the Indians bounced back behind Lemon, with relief help from Bearden, and captured the sixth game, 4–3, and their second world's championship.

The 1948 American League and World Series champion Cleveland Indians.

It earned for each of the Indians $6,772—largest in baseball until then—as their share of the World Series pool.

Not only did Boudreau win the American League Most Valuable Player award, but he also was named the major leagues' outstanding player by *The Sporting News*, and elected, along with Gordon and Lemon, to the AL-NL All-Star team. Veeck also was honored as the major leagues' Executive of the Year.

	W	L	G	GS	CG	IP	H	BB	K	ERA
Gene Bearden	20	7	37	29	15	229⅔	187	106	80	(2.43)
Don Black	2	2	18	10	1	52	57	40	16	5.37
Russ Christopher	3	2	45	0	0	59	55	27	14	2.90
Bob Feller	19	15	44	(38)	18	280⅓	(255)	116	(164)	3.56
Mike Garcia	0	0	1	0	0	2	3	0	1	0.00
Al Gettel	0	1	5	2	0	7⅔	15	10	4	17.61
Steve Gromek	9	3	38	9	4	130	109	51	50	2.84
Ernie Groth	0	0	1	0	0	1	1	2	0	9.00
Bill Kennedy	1	0	6	3	0	11⅓	16	13	12	11.12
Eddie Klieman	3	2	44	0	0	79⅔	62	46	18	2.60
Bob Lemon	20	14	43	37	(20)	(293⅔)	231	129	147	2.82
Lymie Linde	0	0	3	0	0	10	9	4	0	5.40
Bob Muncrief	5	4	21	9	1	72⅓	76	31	24	3.98
Satchel Paige	6	1	21	7	3	72⅔	61	25	45	2.48
Les Webber	0	0	1	0	0	⅔	3	1	1	40.50
Butch Wensloff	0	1	1	0	0	1⅔	2	3	2	10.80
Sam Zoldak	9	6	23	12	4	105⅔	104	24	17	2.81
	(97)	58		(156)	66	(1,409⅓)	1,246	628	595	(3.22)

Shutouts: Lemon (10), Bearden (6), Feller (2), Paige (2), Gromek, Muncrief, Zoldak
Saves: Christopher (17), Klieman (4), Feller (3), Gromek (2), Lemon (2), Bearden, Paige

	G	AB	R	H	2B	3B	HR	RBI	SB	AVG
Johnny Berardino	66	147	19	28	5	1	2	10	0	.190
Ray Boone	6	5	0	2	1	0	0	1	0	.400
Lou Boudreau (SS)	152	560	116	199	34	6	18	106	3	.355
Allie Clark	81	271	43	84	5	2	9	38	0	.310
Larry Doby (RF)	121	439	83	132	23	9	14	66	9	.301
Hank Edwards	55	160	27	43	9	2	3	18	1	.269
Joe Gordon (2B)	144	550	96	154	21	4	32	124	5	.280
Jim Hegan (C)	144	472	60	117	21	6	14	61	6	.248
Walt Judnich	79	218	36	56	13	3	2	29	2	.257
Ken Keltner (3B)	153	558	91	166	24	4	31	119	2	.297
Bob Kennedy	66	73	10	22	3	2	0	5	0	.301
Dale Mitchell (LF)	141	608	82	204	30	8	4	56	13	.336
Ray Murray	4	4	0	0	0	0	0	0	0	.000
Hal Peck	45	63	12	18	3	0	0	8	1	.286
Eddie Robinson (1B)	134	493	53	125	18	5	16	83	1	.254
Al Rosen	5	5	0	1	0	0	0	0	0	.200
Pat Seerey	10	23	7	6	0	0	1	6	0	.261
Joe Tipton	47	90	11	26	3	0	1	13	0	.289
Thurman Tucker (CF)	83	242	52	63	13	2	1	19	11	.260
	(5,446)	840	(1,534)	242	54	(155)	802	54	(.282)

1949

Record: 89–65
Finish: Third
Games Behind: 8
Manager: Lou Boudreau

The accolades didn't last long, though they continued through the winter of 1948–49, which might have been a factor in the Indians' fall from grace.

To capitalize on their winning of the pennant and World Series, the Indians were the subjects of a Bill Veeck–inspired movie, *The Kid from Cleveland*. It featured Rusty Tamblyn, then a teenage star, Lynn Bari, and George Brent. Advance publicity generated by Republic Pictures called it "the story of a kid, a city, and 30 godfathers."

It required the players to be available almost every morning they were home for filming at League Park. The movie debuted September 2 and, to state it kindly, did not win any awards.

It proved to be a major distraction for all of the Indians, and, despite a couple of key player acquisitions, they never came close to repeating their remarkable flight to the 1948 pennant.

First, Veeck traded catcher Joe Tipton to the Chicago White Sox for Joe Haynes. It wasn't that he coveted Haynes, a journeyman pitcher who was the son-in-law of Washington owner Clark Griffith.

What Veeck really wanted was pitcher Early Wynn from the Senators.

But Griffith wouldn't give up Wynn unless he got his son-in-law in exchange, which he did, exactly 22 days after Veeck acquired Haynes. The Indians also received first baseman Mickey Vernon from the Senators, giving up first baseman Eddie Robinson and reliever Ed Klieman in addition to Haynes.

Something else Veeck did prior to the season was to extend Manager Lou Boudreau's contract another year, through 1950. The extension was arranged over the objections of vice president Hank Greenberg, who was never an admirer of Boudreau's managerial ability.

As the Indians struggled through most of the season, never getting back to first place for even a day, Veeck became more and more disenchanted.

With Bearden slumping from 13 victories over .500 to an 8–8 record, Bob Feller apparently on the downside of his brilliant career, Wynn falling short of expectations after starting the season with a sore arm, Joe Gordon slumping and on the way out, and Ken Keltner also on his last legs and able to play only 80 games because of injuries, the Indians got off to a horrible start.

They lost 17 of their first 29 games, falling into seventh place for three weeks in late May and early June. After the team was shut out in both games of a doubleheader in Chicago, White Sox general manager Frank Lane added insult to injury.

He dug up home plate at Comiskey Park and sent it to Veeck with a note that said, "We thought you might like to know what this looks like."

It was so bad that Veeck staged a "second opening day" on May 27, complete with ceremonies and the mayor throwing out the first ball.

On May 31 a local shopkeeper named Charles Lupica—a die-hard Tribe fan—climbed a 65-foot-high pole atop his store and vowed not to come down until the team was back in first place.

Boudreau rallied the Indians in late June, and they climbed back to respectability, though not the top of the league. They reached second place on July 11 and held it for five weeks, then dropped back to third, where they finished.

The closest the Indians got to first place was 2½ games behind the Yankees in August. Lupica gave up on September 25 after living for 117 days atop a 4-by-6-foot platform. While Lupica was aloft, his wife gave birth to their fourth child, a son, on August 7.

The celebrated descent of Lupica, who was transported by truck—still atop his flagpole—approximately 15 miles to the Stadium from his east-side store, attracted a crowd of 33,977 fans to the Stadium that afternoon.

It followed by two days Veeck's official surrender.

He held a mock funeral at the Stadium and, with front office executives wearing top hats and tails, a coffin bearing the 1948 pennant was buried behind the center field fence. Attendance that night was 29,646, and the Indians wound up with a total of 2,233,771 for the season, a decrease of nearly 400,000, which was something else that disappointed Veeck.

On November 22, 41 months to the day after he limped into Cleveland and bought the Indians from Alva Bradley on June 21, 1946, Veeck sold the franchise for a reported $2.2 million.

The buyer was a group headed by Cleveland insurance executive Ellis W. Ryan, who promptly signed Greenberg to a three-year contract as vice president and general manager.

Boudreau managed the American League team to an 11–7 victory in the All-Star Game, which included three Indians—Dale Mitchell, Larry Doby, and Joe Gordon. The shortstops on the team were Vernon Stephens of Boston and Eddie Joost of Philadelphia. Boudreau, who played 88 games at shortstop, 38 at third base, one at second, and even six at first, wasn't picked as a player.

	W	L	G	GS	CG	IP	H	BB	K	ERA
Gene Bearden	8	8	32	19	5	127	140	92	41	5.10
Al Benton	9	6	40	11	4	135⅔	116	51	41	2.12
Bob Feller	15	14	36	28	15	211	198	84	108	3.75
Mike Garcia	14	5	41	20	8	175⅔	154	60	94	(2.36)
Steve Gromek	4	6	27	12	3	92	86	40	22	3.33
Bob Lemon	22	10	37	33	22	279⅔	211	137	138	2.99
Satchel Paige	4	7	31	5	1	83	70	33	54	3.04
Frank Papish	1	0	25	3	1	62	54	39	23	3.19
Early Wynn	11	7	26	23	6	164⅔	186	57	62	4.15
Sam Zoldak	1	2	27	0	0	53	60	18	11	4.25
	89	65		154	65	1,383⅔	1,275	611	594	(3.36)

Shutouts: Garcia (5), Benton (2), Lemon (2)
Saves: Benton (10), Paige (5), Garcia (2), Lemon, Papish

	G	AB	R	H	2B	3B	HR	RBI	SB	AVG
Bobby Avila	31	14	3	3	0	0	0	3	0	.214
Johnny Berardino	50	116	11	23	6	1	0	13	0	.198
Ray Boone	86	258	39	65	4	4	4	26	0	.252
Lou Boudreau (SS)	134	475	53	135	20	3	4	60	0	.284
Allie Clark	35	74	8	13	4	0	1	9	0	.176
Larry Doby (CF)	147	547	106	153	25	3	24	85	10	.280
Luke Easter	21	45	6	10	3	0	0	2	0	.222
Hank Edwards	5	15	3	4	0	0	1	1	0	.267
Joe Gordon (2B)	148	541	74	136	18	3	20	84	5	.251
Jim Hegan (C)	152	468	54	105	19	5	8	55	1	.224
Ken Keltner (3B)	80	246	35	57	9	2	8	30	0	.232
Bob Kennedy (RF)	121	424	49	117	23	5	9	57	5	.276
Freddie Marsh	1	0	0	0	0	0	0	0	0	—
Minnie Minoso	9	16	2	3	0	0	1	1	0	.188
Dale Mitchell (LF)	149	(640)	81	(203)	16	(23)	3	56	10	.317
Milt Nielsen	3	9	1	1	0	0	0	0	0	.111
Hal Peck	33	29	1	9	1	0	0	9	0	.310
Herm Reich	1	2	0	1	0	0	0	0	0	.500
Al Rosen	23	44	3	7	2	0	0	5	0	.159
Mike Tresh	38	37	4	8	0	0	0	1	0	.216
Thurman Tucker	80	197	28	48	5	2	0	14	4	.244
Mickey Vernon (1B)	153	584	72	170	27	4	18	83	9	.291
		5,221	675	1,358	194	58	112	640	44	.260

1950

Record: 92–62
Finish: Fourth
Games Behind: 6
Manager: Lou Boudreau

Hank Greenberg wasted no time making over the Indians, who got back into pennant contention and, until mid-

September, were in the American League race with New York, Detroit, and Boston.

But after the Indians dropped into fourth place when they lost four straight to St. Louis, Greenberg publicly criticized the manager and his players, saying, "We may lose the flag again in 1951, but not with this team."

Perhaps motivated by Greenberg's condemnation, the Indians assumed the role of spoilers, helping the Yankees win their third consecutive championship and 17th in 30 years.

Eight games out of first place on September 20, the Yankees embarked on an eight-game winning streak that included two victories over Boston and four over Detroit. It enabled New York to stretch its lead and, subsequently, coast home in front of the Tigers by three lengths and ahead of the Red Sox by four.

The Indians would have fared better with a good start; instead, they played only .500 ball through June 8 before Early Wynn, Bob Lemon, and Bob Feller got untracked.

Among the changes by Greenberg were the installation of Al Rosen at third base and the release of Ken Keltner, and the promotion from the minors of right fielder–first baseman Luke Easter, who'd been called "the Negro Babe Ruth" in 1949 when he hit 25 homers in 80 games in the Pacific Coast League; shortstop Ray Boone, as player-manager Lou Boudreau became a utility infielder; second baseman Bobby Avila, who replaced Joe Gordon before the season was over; and the release of Gene Bearden, the hero of the 1948 drive to the pennant.

Rosen broke in big as a regular, walloping 37 homers and driving in 116 runs.

Easter started the season in right field, but when he had trouble running because of knee trouble and first baseman Mickey Vernon struggled at the plate, another major change resulted. Easter was moved to first and Vernon, one of the Indians' most consistent hitters the previous season, was traded to Washington for pitcher Dick Weik.

After replacing Vernon, Easter hit what was considered to be the longest home run at the Stadium, a 477-foot shot into the upper right-field stands against Joe Haynes in a 14–3 victory over Washington on June 23.

Doby also had a big day against the Senators on August 2. He hammered three consecutive homers as the Tribe won, 11–0.

And Feller became the 53rd player in major league history to win 200 games when he beat the Tigers, 2–1, in the second game of a doubleheader at the Stadium on July 2.

But it was another disappointing season for the Tribe, and attendance fell again, this time to 1,727,464. Greenberg, never a Boudreau fan, fired him on November 10 and named Al Lopez the Indians' new manager.

Lemon was the AL's winningest pitcher, Wynn wound up with the best earned run average, and Lemon and Doby were picked on the major league All-Star team as the best players at their positions.

	W	L	G	GS	CG	IP	H	BB	K	ERA
Al Aber	1	0	1	1	1	9	5	4	4	2.00
Gene Bearden	1	3	14	3	0	45⅓	57	32	10	6.15
Al Benton	4	2	36	0	0	63	57	30	26	3.57
Bob Feller	16	11	35	34	16	247	230	84	119	3.43
Jesse Flores	3	3	28	2	1	53	53	25	27	3.74
Mike Garcia	11	11	33	29	11	184	191	74	76	3.86
Steve Gromek	10	7	31	13	4	113⅓	94	36	43	3.65
Bob Lemon	(23)	11	44	(37)	(22)	(288)	(281)	146	(170)	3.84
Marino Pieretti	0	1	29	1	0	47⅓	45	30	11	4.18
Dick Rozek	0	0	12	2	0	25⅓	28	19	14	4.97
Dick Weik	1	3	11	2	0	26	18	26	16	3.81
Early Wynn	18	8	32	28	14	213⅔	166	101	143	(3.20)
Sam Zoldak	4	2	33	3	0	63⅔	64	21	15	3.96
	92	62		155	69	1,378⅔	1,289	647	674	(3.75)

Shutouts: Feller (3), Lemon (3), Wynn (2), Flores, Gromek
Saves: Benton (4), Flores (4), Zoldak (4), Lemon (3), Pieretti

	G	AB	R	H	2B	3B	HR	RBI	SB	AVG
Bobby Avila	80	201	39	60	10	2	1	21	5	.299
Johnny Berardino	4	5	1	2	0	0	0	3	0	.400
Ray Boone (SS)	109	365	53	110	14	6	7	58	4	.301
Lou Boudreau	81	260	23	70	13	2	1	29	1	.269
Allie Clark	59	163	19	35	6	1	6	21	0	.215
Herb Conyers	7	9	2	3	0	0	1	1	1	.333
Larry Doby (CF)	142	503	110	164	25	5	25	102	8	.326
Luke Easter (1B)	141	540	96	151	20	4	28	107	0	.280
Joe Gordon (2B)	119	368	59	87	12	1	19	57	4	.236
Jim Hegan (C)	131	415	53	91	16	5	14	58	1	.219
Bob Kennedy (RF)	146	540	79	157	27	5	9	54	3	.291
Jim Lemon	12	34	4	6	1	0	1	1	0	.176
Dale Mitchell (LF)	130	506	81	156	27	5	3	49	3	.308
Ray Murray	55	139	16	38	8	2	1	13	1	.273
Al Rosen (3B)	155	554	100	159	23	4	(37)	116	5	.287
Thurman Tucker	57	101	13	18	2	0	1	7	1	.178
Mickey Vernon	28	90	8	17	0	0	0	10	2	.189
		5,263	806	1,417	222	46	(164)	758	40	.269

1951

Record: 93–61
Finish: Second
Games Behind: 5
Manager: Al Lopez

The Indians started fast under new manager Al Lopez but slumped after two weeks and fell all the way to sixth place in late May then recovered and fought back, regaining the lead on August 13.

They equaled a club record by winning 13 games in a row from August 2 to 15, and on August 23, after four more consecutive victories over Washington and New York, the Indians appeared to be in the driver's seat.

They were 78–43 with a first-place bulge of three lengths over the Yankees.

Then trouble developed.

The hitters slumped and the Indians went 12–11 in their next 23 games. Though they still clung to first place by one game on September 15, the season suddenly turned around for them—in the wrong direction—in Yankee Stadium.

Bob Feller lost the opener of a two-game series, 5–1, to former teammate Allie Reynolds on September 16. Their victory boosted the Yankees into a tie for the lead. Then Bob Lemon was beaten, 2–1, by Eddie Lopat the next day.

The latter loss dropped the Indians a game behind, and they never regained first place, dropping eight of their final 11 games while the Yankees were winning nine of 12, to capture their third straight pennant and 18th in 31 years.

It was a major disappointment for Lopez and Hank Greenberg. The Tribe's pitching staff was the best in the league with the first trio of 20 game winners—Bob Feller, Early Wynn, and Mike Garcia—since the 1931 Philadelphia Athletics.

Though several young position players blossomed, the Indians' offense was anemic, finishing with a .256 team batting average, second lowest in the league.

Luke Easter continued to have trouble with his aching knees and was able to play only 128 games, hitting 27 homers, and Al Rosen and Larry Doby failed to match their 1950 production.

Something else that hurt the Tribe was one of Greenberg's first major trades. It was a three-team deal on April 30 involving the Chicago White Sox and Philadelphia Athletics. The Indians gave up rookie outfielder Orestes "Minnie" Minoso to Chicago and pitcher Sam Zoldak and catcher Ray Murray to Philadelphia, and they received relief pitcher Lou Brissie from the Athletics and outfielder Paul Lehner from the White Sox.

With the White Sox, Minoso went on to hit .326—better than any Tribe regular and second best in the American League—while Brissie's contributions in Cleveland were minimal, and Lehner provided even less.

Second baseman Bobby Avila, one of a crop of good young players coming into their own with the Indians, blasted three home runs in a 14–8 victory over the Red Sox in Boston on June 20.

Then Feller, disproving the skeptics who thought he was on the decline, pitched a record-tying third no-hitter, beating Detroit, 2–1, in the first game of a doubleheader on July 1 at the Stadium, equaling the achievements of Cy Young and Larry Corcoran.

Twelve days later Feller himself was the victim of a no-hitter, this one thrown by former teammate Allie Reynolds, as the Yankees beat the Indians, 1–0, at the Stadium on July 12.

Despite their mid- and late-season decline in the standings, the Indians continued to draw well at the gate, 1,704,984.

Feller, the AL's biggest winner, was named the league's Pitcher of the Year by *The Sporting News*. He also received 118 points, finishing fifth (one place behind Minoso) in the balloting for Most Valuable Player, won by Yogi Berra.

	W	L	G	GS	CG	IP	H	BB	K	ERA
Lou Brissie	4	3	54	4	1	112⅓	90	61	50	3.20
Bob Chakales	3	4	17	10	2	68⅓	80	43	32	4.74
Red Fahr	0	0	5	0	0	5⅔	11	2	0	4.76
Bob Feller	(22)	8	33	32	16	249⅔	239	95	111	3.50
Mike Garcia	20	13	47	30	15	254	239	82	118	3.15
Steve Gromek	7	4	27	8	4	107⅓	98	29	40	2.77
Charlie Harris	0	0	2	0	0	4	5	4	1	4.50
Sam Jones	0	1	2	1	0	8⅔	4	5	4	2.08
Bob Lemon	17	(14)	42	(34)	17	263⅓	(244)	124	132	3.52
Dick Rozek	0	0	7	1	0	15⅓	18	11	5	2.93
Johnny Vander Meer	0	1	1	1	0	3	8	1	2	18.00
Early Wynn	20	13	37	(34)	21	(274⅓)	227	107	133	3.02
George Zuverink	0	0	16	0	0	25⅓	24	13	14	5.33
	93	61		(155)	(76)	1,391⅓	1,287	577	642	(3.38)

Shutouts: Feller (4), Wynn (3), Chakales, Garcia, Lemon
Saves: Brissie (9), Garcia (6), Lemon (2), Gromek, Wynn

	G	AB	R	H	2B	3B	HR	RBI	SB	AVG
Bobby Avila (2B)	141	542	76	165	21	3	10	58	14	.304
Ray Boone (SS)	151	544	65	127	14	1	12	51	5	.233
Sam Chapman	94	246	24	56	9	1	6	36	3	.228
Allie Clark	3	10	3	3	2	0	1	3	0	.300
Merrill Combs	19	28	2	5	2	0	0	2	0	.179
Larry Doby (CF)	134	447	84	132	27	5	20	69	4	.295
Luke Easter (1B)	128	486	65	131	12	5	27	103	0	.270
Doug Hansen	3	0	2	0	0	0	0	0	0	—
Jim Hegan (C)	133	416	60	99	17	5	6	43	0	.238
Bob Kennedy (RF)	108	321	30	79	15	4	7	29	4	.246
Lou Klein	2	2	0	0	0	0	0	0	0	.000
Paul Lehner	12	13	2	3	0	0	0	1	0	.231
Clarence Maddern	11	12	0	2	0	0	0	0	0	.167
Barney McCosky	31	61	8	13	3	0	0	2	1	.213
Minnie Minoso	8	14	3	6	2	0	0	2	0	.429
Dale Mitchell (LF)	134	510	83	148	21	7	11	62	7	.290
Ray Murray	1	1	0	1	0	0	0	1	0	1.000
Hal Naragon	3	8	0	2	0	0	0	0	0	.250
Milt Nielsen	16	6	1	0	0	0	0	0	0	.000
Al Rosen (3B)	(154)	573	82	152	30	1	24	102	7	.265
Harry Simpson	122	332	51	76	7	0	7	24	6	.229
Snuffy Stirnweiss	50	88	10	19	1	0	1	4	1	.216
Birdie Tebbetts	55	137	8	36	6	0	2	18	0	.263
Thurman Tucker	1	1	0	0	0	0	0	0	0	.000
	5,250	696	1,346	208	35	(140)	658	52	.256

1952

Record: 93–61
Finish: Second
Games Behind: 2
Manager: Al Lopez

Once again Indians' pitchers dominated the American League but—also, once again—whatever they did wasn't good enough. The New York Yankees prevailed in one of the American League's closest and most exciting races.

This time the Tribe started sensationally, opening the season with seven straight victories before losing to St. Louis on April 22.

The following night in St. Louis, Bob Feller and the Browns' Bob Cain were involved in an epic pitching duel, a double one-hitter, the 11th of Feller's career. It was the lowest-hit game in the 51-year history of the American League, and it tied the National League record set in 1906.

The Browns won it. Bobby Young led off the bottom of the first inning with a triple to left field and scored as Marty Marion reached on an error by Al Rosen.

Luke Easter ruined Cain's bid for a no-hitter with a single in the fifth inning.

The victory boosted the Browns into first place with Boston, and dropped the Tribe into third, a half-game behind.

Then began a roller-coaster ride that continued through the end of the season.

The first month also featured a three-homer barrage by Al Rosen, and six consecutive hits by rookie Jim Fridley on April 29 when the Tribe routed the Athletics, 21–9, in Philadelphia.

The Indians regained the lead on May 9 and held it for three weeks before giving way to Boston on June 2. A week later the Yankees took over the top spot and either led or were in a virtual tie for first place through the end of the season.

At the All-Star break only 6½ games separated the top five clubs—New York, Chicago, Cleveland, Washington, and Boston—and by the final week of August it was still a four-team race with only the Senators dropping out.

The Yankees swept the Tribe in a doubleheader at the Stadium on July 22, beating Feller and Steve Gromek, 7–3 and 8–1. The sweep shoved the Indians into fourth place by 7½ games, their largest deficit of the season.

But the Tribe fought back to beat the Yankees the next two games, 7–3 and 4–2, behind Bob Lemon and Mike Garcia, and the Yankees went on to lose three more in a row in Detroit.

The Indians' hopes soared as they won 18 of 25 games and overtook New York by a margin of .001 August 22 when Garcia, with relief help from Lemon, beat the Yankees, 6–4.

But the next day Vic Raschi beat Early Wynn, 1–0, and despite going 24–9 down the stretch, including winning streaks of nine, six, and their last three games of the season, the best the Indians could do was climb into a tie with the Yankees on September 11.

But only for a day. The Tribe lost to Boston and on September 14 went head to head one final time with the Yankees. The game attracted the major leagues' largest crowd of the season to the Stadium, 73,609 frenzied fans.

New York prevailed, 7–1, as Eddie Lopat—renowned as an "Indian killer"—bested Garcia, giving the Yankees a two-game lead, and they clung to first place the rest of the way.

Lopat's victory in that crucial game raised his nine-year record against the Tribe to 35–9.

Feller slumped to the worst season of his career, but Wynn, Lemon, and Garcia were outstanding. Rosen rebounded to lead the AL in RBIs and total bases (with 297), and Larry Doby was the home run champ and No. 1 with a .541 slugging percentage.

Luke Easter, a disappointment the first half of the season, was demoted to Class AAA Indianapolis on June 30 when his average fell to .208. He was recalled on July 15 and the rest of the way hit .319 with 20 homers and 64 RBI.

The Indians' erratic defense was a major problem. They tied the Browns with the most errors in the AL, 155, and completed the fewest double plays, 141, which also contributed to the frustration of the fans, as attendance declined again, this time to 1,444,607.

Internal differences in the hierarchy resulted in another change in ownership of the Indians on December 18. A rift that developed between President Ellis Ryan and several directors broke into the open and led to an emergency meeting. Ryan was voted out of office.

Five directors who were loyal to Ryan—B. F. Bernet, Joseph Broderick, Jack Johns, Guy Waters, and David R. Jones—sold their stock in the club. Their shares were purchased by Donald Hornbeck, Harry Small, Nate Dolin, George Medinger, and Charles M. Baxter, all of whom were members of the board.

Myron H. "Mike" Wilson, Jr., a 65-year-old insurance executive who also was a director at the time, was elected to succeed Ryan as president and, according to the announcement, "to restore unity and management" to the club.

In addition to restoring unity, the change in leadership also strengthened the position of vice president and general manager Hank Greenberg.

	W	L	G	GS	CG	IP	H	BB	K	ERA
Bill Abernathie	0	0	1	0	0	2	4	1	0	13.50
Lou Brissie	3	2	42	1	0	82⅓	68	34	28	3.48
Bob Chakales	1	2	5	1	0	12	19	8	7	9.75
Bob Feller	9	13	30	30	11	191⅓	219	83	81	4.74
Mike Garcia	22	11	46	(36)	19	292⅓	(284)	87	143	2.37
Steve Gromek	7	7	29	13	3	122⅔	109	28	65	3.67
Mickey Harris	3	0	29	0	0	46⅔	42	21	23	4.63
Sam Jones	2	3	14	4	0	36	38	37	28	7.25
Bob Lemon	22	11	42	(36)	(28)	(309⅔)	236	105	131	2.50
Dick Rozek	1	0	10	1	0	12⅔	11	13	5	4.97
Ted Wilks	0	0	7	0	0	11⅓	8	7	6	3.86
Early Wynn	23	12	42	33	19	285⅔	239	132	153	2.90
George Zuverink	0	0	1	0	0	1⅓	1	0	1	0.00
	93	61		155	(80)	1,407	1,278	556	671	3.32

Shutouts: Garcia (6), Lemon (5), Wynn (4), Gromek
Saves: Garcia (4), Lemon (4), Wynn (3), Brissie (2), Abernathie, Gromek, Harris, Jones, Wilks

	G	AB	R	H	2B	3B	HR	RBI	SB	AVG
Bobby Avila (2B)	150	597	102	179	26	(11)	7	45	12	.300
Johnny Berardino	35	32	5	3	0	0	0	2	0	.094
Ray Boone (SS)	103	316	57	83	8	2	7	45	0	.263
Merrill Combs	52	139	11	23	1	1	1	10	0	.165
Larry Doby (CF)	140	519	(104)	143	26	8	(32)	104	5	.276
Luke Easter (1B)	127	437	63	115	10	3	31	97	1	.263
Jim Fridley	62	175	23	44	2	0	4	16	3	.251
Bill Glynn	44	92	15	25	5	0	2	7	1	.272
Jim Hegan (C)	112	333	39	75	17	2	4	41	0	.225
Bob Kennedy	22	40	6	12	3	1	0	12	1	.300
Hank Majeski	36	54	7	16	2	0	0	9	0	.296
Barney McCosky	54	80	14	17	4	1	1	6	1	.213
Dale Mitchell (LF)	134	511	61	165	26	3	5	58	6	.323
Dave Pope	12	34	9	10	1	1	1	4	0	.294
Pete Reiser	34	44	7	6	1	0	3	7	1	.136
Al Rosen (3B)	148	567	101	171	32	5	28	(105)	8	.302
Harry Simpson (RF)	146	545	66	145	21	10	10	65	5	.266
Snuffy Stirnweiss	1	0	0	0	0	0	0	0	0	—
George Strickland	31	88	8	19	4	0	1	8	0	.216
Birdie Tebbetts	42	101	4	25	4	0	1	8	0	.248
Joe Tipton	43	105	15	26	2	0	6	22	1	.248
Quincy Trouppe	6	10	1	1	0	0	0	0	0	.100
Wally Westlake	29	69	11	16	4	1	1	9	1	.232
	5,330	(763)	1,399	211	49	(148)	(721)	46	.262

1953

Record: 92–62
Finish: Second
Games Behind: 8½
Manager: Al Lopez

The Indians came close again, but the experience only served to heighten their frustration—and the frustration of the fans, which was reflected in a drastic decline in attendance of nearly 400,000 to 1,069,176.

Casey Stengel's New York Yankees became the first major league club to win five consecutive pennants, breezing home in the race, and the Indians finished second for the third year in a row.

Except for the first week of the season the Yankees led virtually all the way, occupying first place 158 of the 167 days, despite having a couple of losing streaks en route to the pennant.

The Indians got off to a fast start, raising hopes that 1953, finally, would be the season they'd catch the Yankees and win their third pennant since 1920 and their second in five years.

When they swept a three-game series in St. Louis, May 8–10, for a 13–6 record, they took over the top rung of the American League.

But all these wins did was mark the last time the Yankees were out of first place all season as the Tribe dropped its next game to Chicago, 2–1.

By the time New York completed an 18-game winning streak from May 27 to June 14—the last four of which were in Cleveland, the finale part of a doubleheader witnessed by 74,708 fans—the Yankees' lead over the second-place Tribe was 10½ games.

But the season became a race again on July 1, after the Yankees lost nine in a row, including three to the Indians behind Bob Lemon, Mike Garcia, and Early Wynn from June 26 to 28, shrinking New York's lead to six.

A month later, July 21–23, Lemon, Garcia, and Wynn did it again to the Yankees, and pennant hopes in Cleveland soared once more.

But again, only briefly.

By August 19 the Indians were mired in third place, 15 games out, when they embarked upon another spurt as Garcia, Wynn, and Lemon again beat the Yankees three times, August 27–29. They went on to win 20 of 23 games, but to no avail.

The Yankees clinched the pennant on September 14, and the best the Indians could do was to fight off Chicago to finish second—again.

The Indians' downfall was an inability to win on the road. Their home record was a gaudy 53–24, but away from the Stadium it was only 39–38.

They also were hurt by an injury suffered by Luke Easter. His left foot was fractured in the fourth game of the season when he was hit by a pitch from Lou Kretlow of Chicago. Easter was out of action until June 22, and played just 68 games, hitting only seven homers.

Despite the frustration of finishing behind New York again, it was a great season for Al Rosen. He almost captured the Triple Crown and became only the second unanimous winner of the AL Most Valuable Player award. The only other man to garner every vote was Ty Cobb in 1911, when the award was first presented.

Rosen led the league with a club-record 43 homers, one more than Hal Trosky hit in 1936, and 145 RBIs. His batting average was one point less than Mickey Vernon's .337, and he was selected by *The Sporting News* as the major league Player of the Year.

On September 28, Al Lopez was granted a new two-year contract through 1955, dispelling speculation that he was considering quitting as manager of the Indians because of differences with club officials.

	W	L	G	GS	CG	IP	H	BB	K	ERA
Al Aber	1	1	6	0	0	6	6	9	4	7.50
Lou Brissie	0	0	16	0	0	13	21	13	5	7.62
Bob Chakales	0	2	7	3	1	27	28	10	6	2.67
Bob Feller	10	7	25	25	10	175⅓	163	60	60	3.59
Mike Garcia	18	9	38	35	21	271⅓	260	81	134	3.25
Steve Gromek	1	1	5	1	0	11	11	3	8	3.27
Bob Hooper	5	4	43	0	0	69⅓	50	38	16	4.02
Dave Hoskins	9	3	26	7	3	112⅔	102	38	55	3.99
Art Houtteman	7	7	22	13	6	109	113	25	40	3.80
Bob Lemon	21	15	41	36	23	(286⅔)	(283)	110	98	3.36
Dick Tomanek	1	0	1	1	1	9	6	6	6	2.00
Bill Wight	2	1	20	0	0	26⅔	29	16	14	3.71
Ted Wilks	0	0	4	0	0	3⅔	5	3	2	7.36
Early Wynn	17	12	36	34	16	251⅓	234	107	138	3.93
	92	62	155		(81)	1,373	1,311	519	586	3.64

Shutouts: Lemon (5), Garcia (3), Feller, Houtteman, Wynn
Saves: Hooper (7), Houtteman (3), Brissie (2), Hoskins, Lemon, Wight

	G	AB	R	H	2B	3B	HR	RBI	SB	AVG
Bobby Avila (2B)	141	559	85	160	22	3	8	55	10	.286
Dick Aylward	4	3	0	0	0	0	0	0	0	.000
Ray Boone	34	112	21	27	1	2	4	21	1	.241
Larry Doby (CF)	149	513	92	135	18	5	29	102	3	.263
Luke Easter	68	211	26	64	9	0	7	31	0	.303
Hank Foiles	7	7	2	1	0	0	0	0	0	.143
Owen Friend	34	68	7	16	2	0	2	13	0	.235
Joe Ginsberg	46	109	10	31	4	0	0	10	0	.284
Bill Glynn (1B)	147	411	60	100	14	2	3	30	1	.243
Jim Hegan (C)	112	299	37	65	10	1	9	37	1	.217
Bob Kennedy	100	161	22	38	5	0	3	22	0	.236
Jim Lemon	16	46	5	8	1	0	1	5	0	.174
Hank Majeski	50	50	6	15	1	0	2	12	0	.300
Barney McCosky	22	21	3	4	3	0	0	3	0	.190
Dale Mitchell (LF)	134	500	76	150	26	4	13	60	3	.300
Al Rosen (3B)	155	599	(115)	201	27	5	(43)	(145)	8	.336
Harry Simpson	82	242	25	55	3	1	7	22	0	.227
Al Smith	47	150	28	36	9	0	3	14	2	.240
George Strickland (SS)	123	419	43	119	17	4	5	47	0	.284
Joe Tipton	47	109	17	25	2	0	6	13	0	.229
Dick Weik	1	0	1	0	0	0	0	0	0	—
Wally Westlake (RF)	82	218	42	72	7	1	9	46	2	.330
	5,285	770	1,426	201	29	(160)	729	33	.270

1954

Record: 111–43
Finish: First
Games Ahead: 8
Manager: Al Lopez

Al Lopez called the Indians 1954 pitching staff "the greatest ever assembled," and not many would disagree.

It comprised starters Early Wynn, Bob Lemon, Mike Garcia, Art Houtteman, and Bob Feller; the relievers were Hal Newhouser and rookies Ray Narleski and Don Mossi.

The starting pitchers had a cumulative record of 93 victories and only 36 defeats, while the relievers were 18–7, with a league-leading earned run average of 2.78.

Wynn and Lemon were the American League's biggest winners, each with 23 victories. Lemon, who won 11 straight from July 22 to August 29, lost only seven.

What's more, in Bobby Avila and Larry Doby the Indians also had the AL's best hitters. Avila won the batting championship with a .341 average, and Doby led the league with 32 homers and 126 runs batted in.

The Tribe's 111 victories were one more than won by the 1927 New York Yankees, long regarded as the best team in major league history.

The Indians lost six of their first nine games the first two weeks of the season and tumbled into the basement, then got hot and climbed back to the top. They reached fourth place on May 1, and 16 days later were in first place. Thereafter, except for four days, June 8–11 when Chicago took over the top rung, the Tribe was never headed en route to its third pennant.

The Indians record was 56–27 and their lead was only a half game over New York at the All-Star break, July 11–14, but again they regained their momentum to win nine of 10 and 15 of 18 to stay in front. From August 6 to 19 they went 13–1, including nine consecutive victories.

The 1954 campaign ended the five-year championship reign of the Yankees, who finished second with a 103–51 record, making them only the fourth club in major league history to reach the century mark in victories without winning the pennant. It wasn't until September 18 that the Yankees were mathematically eliminated.

The 1954 American League champion Cleveland Indians.

The Tribe won 11 straight from September 8 to 20, with two of the victories coming against New York, 4–1 and 3–2, behind Lemon and Wynn on September 12. The games were witnessed by a doubleheader record crowd of 84,587 at the Stadium.

Unlike the 1927 Yankees who swept the World Series from Pittsburgh, however, the 1954 Indians lost four straight to the National League champion New York Giants.

The Indians won the pennant with essentially the same team that had finished second to the Yankees for a third straight season in 1953. The principal additions were Newhouser, signed on April 12 after he'd been released by Detroit, and the acquisition of outfielder Vic Wertz in a trade with Baltimore for pitcher Bob Chakales on June 1. Wertz was switched to first base and replaced Luke Easter, who was hobbled by knee problems.

A crowd of 68,751 fans attended the second All-Star Game played at the Stadium, won by the American League, 11–9, on July 13, and 1954 also was a season of significant individual performances by the Indians:

- Feller registered his 250th career victory, beating Baltimore, 14–3, at the Stadium on May 23.

- Feller recorded his 2,500th major league strikeout in a 4–3 victory over the Red Sox in Boston on June 12.

- Garcia, Narleski, and Wynn collaborated on a one-hitter, beating Chicago, 2–1, at the Stadium as Minnie Minoso singled with two out in the ninth inning on July 4.

- Bill Glynn whacked three consecutive home runs in a 13–6 victory over the Tigers in Detroit on July 5.

- Al Rosen went 3-for-5 as the Indians beat Philadelphia, 5–4, in 11 innings to become the first team in franchise history and the 20th in the AL since 1901 to win 100 games, the victory being credited to Newhouser, at the Stadium on September 9.

- Dale Mitchell and Jim Hegan clouted homers to beat the Tigers, 3–2, giving the Indians their 107th victory and clinching the AL pennant in Detroit on September 18.

- Wynn pitched a two-hitter to beat Detroit, 11–1, at the Stadium and give the Indians a major-league-record 111th victory on September 25.

There also were some lowlights—four, to be exact—in the World Series. The Indians were swept by the Giants, 5–2 in 10 innings and 3–1 at the Polo Grounds in New York on September 29 and 30, and 6–2 and 7–4, at the Stadium on October 1 and 2.

Lopez was convinced the Indians would have fared better—at least they would not have lost Games 1 and 2—if the Series had opened in Cleveland instead of New York.

The Giants won the opener when, first, Willie Mays made a spectacular catch of a 460-foot drive by Wertz to dead center field in the eighth inning, and then, in the 10th, New York's Dusty Rhodes hit a 260-foot, three-run pinch homer down the right-field line off Lemon.

Rhodes hit another homer into the close right-field stands off Wynn in Game 2.

It was Lopez's contention that both of Rhodes' homers would have been routine fly-ball outs in Cleveland, and Wertz's drive caught by Mays would have cleared the center-field fence at the Stadium.

Aside from that, Lopez said, "We were due for a slump. We didn't have a slump all year, and no team goes through a season without one."

Avila was outhit by Ted Williams, whose .345 average topped the AL. But Williams didn't qualify for the title because he fell 14 short of the required 400 at bats after missing 39 games with injuries and illness, and also walked 136 times.

In the balloting for the Most Valuable Player award, Doby was second, Avila third, Lemon fifth, and Wynn sixth behind New York's Yogi Berra, and Avila, Rosen, and Lemon were named on the major league All-Star team.

The Indians' rallying cry during the second half of the season was "Win plenty with Sam Dente." Dente was the utility infielder who played well after replacing shortstop George Strickland, who suffered a broken jaw when he was hit by a thrown ball and was out of the lineup from July 23 to September 6.

	W	L	G	GS	CG	IP	H	BB	K	ERA
Bob Chakales	2	0	3	0	0	10⅓	4	12	3	0.87
Bob Feller	13	3	19	19	9	140	127	39	59	3.09
Mike Garcia	19	8	45	34	13	258⅔	220	71	129	(2.64)
Bob Hooper	0	0	17	0	0	34⅔	39	16	12	4.93
Dave Hoskins	0	1	14	1	0	26⅔	29	10	9	3.04
Art Houtteman	15	7	32	25	11	188	198	59	68	3.35
Bob Lemon	(23)	7	36	33	(21)	258⅓	228	92	110	2.72
Don Mossi	6	1	40	5	2	93	56	39	55	1.94
Ray Narleski	3	3	42	2	1	89	59	44	52	2.22
Hal Newhouser	7	2	26	1	0	46⅔	34	18	25	2.51
Jose Santiago	0	0	1	0	0	1⅓	0	2	1	0.00
Dick Tomanek	0	0	1	0	0	1⅔	1	1	0	5.40
Early Wynn	(23)	11	40	(36)	20	(270⅔)	225	83	155	2.73
	(111)	43		(156)	(77)	(1,419½)	1,220	486	678	(2.78)

Shutouts: Garcia (5), Wynn (3), Lemon (2), Feller, Houtteman
Saves: Narleski (13), Mossi (7), Newhouser (7), Garcia (5), Hooper (2), Wynn (2)

	G	AB	R	H	2B	3B	HR	RBI	SB	AVG
Bobby Avila (2B)	143	555	112	189	27	2	15	67	9	(.341)
Sam Dente	68	169	18	45	7	1	1	19	0	.266
Larry Doby (CF)	153	577	94	157	18	4	(32)	(126)	3	.272
Jim Dyck	2	1	0	1	0	0	0	1	0	1.000
Luke Easter	6	6	0	1	0	0	0	0	0	.167
Joe Ginsberg	3	2	0	1	0	1	0	1	0	.500
Bill Glynn	111	171	19	43	3	2	5	18	3	.251
Mickey Grasso	4	6	1	2	0	0	1	1	0	.333
Jim Hegan (C)	139	423	56	99	12	7	11	40	0	.234
Bob Kennedy	1	0	0	0	0	0	0	0	0	—
Hank Majeski	57	121	10	34	4	0	3	17	0	.281
Dale Mitchell	53	60	6	17	1	0	1	6	0	.283
Hal Naragon	46	101	10	24	2	2	0	12	0	.238
Rocky Nelson	4	4	0	0	0	0	0	0	0	.000
Dave Philley (RF)	133	452	48	102	13	3	12	60	2	.226
Dave Pope	60	102	21	30	2	1	4	13	2	.294
Rudy Regalado	65	180	21	45	5	0	2	24	0	.250
Al Rosen (3B)	137	466	76	140	20	2	24	102	6	.300
Al Smith (LF)	131	481	101	135	29	6	11	50	2	.281
George Strickland (SS)	112	361	42	77	13	3	6	37	2	.213
Vic Wertz (1B)	94	295	33	81	14	2	14	48	0	.275
Wally Westlake	85	240	36	63	9	2	11	42	0	.262
		5,222	746	1,368	188	39	(156)	714	30	.262

1955

Record: 93–61
Finish: Second
Games Behind: 3
Manager: Al Lopez

The Indians made two major additions in 1955, purchasing slugging outfielder Ralph Kiner from the Chicago Cubs and promoting pitcher Herb Score from the minors, but they weren't enough, and the New York Yankees regained the American League pennant.

The Indians started fast, holding first place the first three weeks in May. But they floundered in June and July, and were in and out of the lead in August and September before faltering again in the final 11 days. They lost six of their last nine games while the Yankees were in the midst of a 15–4 streak.

On September 16 they had dropped into second place, beating out Chicago, which also had been in the race, along with Boston, through most of the second half. As late as September 8 only three games had separated the top four clubs.

While Score burst into stardom, winning 16 games and the Rookie of the Year award, and Ray Narleski and Don Mossi repeated as the AL's top relievers, the Tribe's "Big Three" of Bob Lemon, Early Wynn, and Mike Garcia combined for only 46 victories, 19 fewer than in 1954.

Among Wynn's 17 victories was his 200th in the major leagues, 6–0, over the Orioles in Baltimore on September 7.

Bob Feller and Mike Garcia also faltered badly after being part of the 1954 pitching staff that manager Al Lopez called "the greatest ever assembled."

Still, Feller came up with one final hurrah, nearly achieving a record fourth no-hitter.

Instead, Feller had to settle for his 12th career one-hitter, beating Boston, 2–0, at the Stadium in the first game of a May 1 doubleheader, after which Score struck out 16 to top the Red Sox, 2–1, boosting the Indians into first place.

Feller's bid for another no-hitter was broken up by Sammy White, who singled in the seventh inning, and the one-time "Strikeout King" won only three more games in 1955—and his star-studded career.

Feller beat Baltimore, 9–2, on June 23, and again, 5–1, on July 24, and what turned out to be his final—and 266th—victory came on August 27 over the Yankees, 7–6, in front of 34,382 fans at the Stadium.

But it wasn't just the Tribe pitching that fell off; so did the offense.

Defending AL batting champion Bobby Avila slumped 69 points to .272; Al Rosen, playing most of the season despite a broken index finger on his right hand, dropped 56 points to .244; Larry Doby went from 126 RBI and 32 homers in 1954 to 75 and 26 in 1955; and Vic Wertz, another star the previous season, was stricken with polio on August 26 when he was batting .253 and didn't play again that year.

Kiner delivered 18 homers and drove in 54 runs, but his average was only .243 in 113 games.

Al Smith was the only regular to hit .300, and he finished third in the balloting for the Most Valuable Player award behind winner Yogi Berra and runner-up Al Kaline.

Lopez met with general manager Hank Greenberg after the season ended and said he planned to resign, citing "stomach problems" brought on partly by the frustration of finishing second to the Yankees in four of the five previous seasons. But Greenberg talked Lopez into continuing as the Tribe manager in 1956.

	W	L	G	GS	CG	IP	H	BB	K	ERA
Hank Aguirre	2	0	4	1	1	12⅔	6	12	6	1.42
Bud Daley	0	1	2	1	0	7	10	1	2	6.43
Bob Feller	4	4	25	11	2	83	71	31	25	3.47
Mike Garcia	11	13	38	31	6	210⅓	230	56	120	4.02
Ted Gray	0	0	2	0	0	2	5	2	1	18.00
Art Houtteman	10	6	35	12	3	124⅓	126	44	53	3.98
Bob Lemon	(18)	10	35	31	5	211⅓	218	74	100	3.88
Sal Maglie	0	2	10	2	0	25⅔	26	7	11	3.86
Don Mossi	4	3	57	1	0	81⅓	81	18	69	2.42
Ray Narleski	9	1	(60)	1	1	111⅓	91	52	94	3.71
Hal Newhouser	0	0	2	0	0	2⅓	1	4	1	0.00
Jose Santiago	2	0	17	0	0	32⅔	31	14	19	2.48
Herb Score	16	10	33	32	11	227⅓	158	154	(245)	2.85
Bill Wight	0	0	17	0	0	24	24	9	9	2.63
Early Wynn	17	11	32	31	16	230	207	80	122	2.82
	93	61		154	45	1,386⅓	1,285	558	(877)	3.39

Shutouts: Wynn (6), Garcia (2), Score (2), Aguirre, Feller, Houtteman
Saves: Narleski (19), Mossi (9), Garcia (3), Lemon (2), Maglie (2), Wight

	G	AB	R	H	2B	3B	HR	RBI	SB	AVG
Joe Altobelli	42	75	8	15	3	0	2	5	0	.200
Bobby Avila (2B)	141	537	83	146	22	4	13	61	1	.272
Rocky Colavito	5	9	3	4	2	0	0	0	0	.444
Sam Dente	73	105	10	27	4	0	0	10	0	.257
Larry Doby (CF)	131	491	91	143	17	5	26	75	2	.291
Hoot Evers	39	66	10	19	7	1	2	9	0	.288
Ferris Fain	56	118	9	30	3	0	0	8	3	.254
Hank Foiles	62	111	13	29	9	0	1	7	0	.261
Billy Harrell	13	19	2	8	0	0	0	1	1	.421
Jim Hegan (C)	116	304	30	67	5	2	9	40	0	.220
Ralph Kiner (LF)	113	321	56	78	13	0	18	54	0	.243
Kenny Kuhn	4	6	0	2	0	0	0	0	1	.333
Stu Locklin	16	18	4	3	1	0	0	0	0	.167
Hank Majeski	36	48	3	9	2	0	2	6	0	.188
Dale Mitchell	61	58	4	15	2	1	0	10	0	.259
Hal Naragon	57	127	12	41	9	2	1	14	1	.323
Stan Pawloski	2	8	0	1	0	0	0	0	0	.125
Dave Philley	43	104	15	31	4	2	2	9	0	.298
Dave Pope	35	104	17	31	5	0	6	22	0	.298
Rudy Regalado	10	26	2	7	2	0	0	5	0	.269
Al Rosen (3B)	139	492	61	120	13	1	21	81	4	.244
Harry Simpson	3	1	1	0	0	0	0	0	0	.000
Al Smith (RF)	(154)	607	(123)	186	27	4	22	77	11	.306
George Strickland (SS)	130	388	34	81	9	5	2	34	1	.209
Vic Wertz (1B)	74	257	30	65	11	2	14	55	1	.253
Wally Westlake	16	20	2	5	1	0	0	1	0	.250
Gene Woodling	79	259	33	72	15	1	5	35	2	.278
Bobby Young	18	45	7	14	1	1	0	6	0	.311
		5,146	698	1,325	195	31	148	657	28	.257

1956

Record: 88–66
Finish: Second
Games Behind: 9
Manager: Al Lopez

It was another runaway pennant dash by the New York Yankees, leaving the Indians in the dust, this time with their lowest victory total in nine years and their largest second-place deficit in seven.

There was considerable activity even before the season got under way as the Indians went through another change in ownership.

On February 29 a group headed by Cleveland industrialist William R. Daley purchased the franchise for $3,961,800, the highest price ever paid for a major league team.

Daley's two major partners were Indians general manager Hank Greenberg, whose stock amounted to 19 percent of the total, and Ignatius A. O'Shaughnessy, a St. Paul, Minnesota, businessman. Daley took over as chairman of the board, but all the club's officials retained their positions, including My-

ron H. Wilson, Jr., who kept his stock and remained as president.

The Indians were in and out of first place the first five weeks of 1956 as they went 15–9. But when they lost to New York, 4–1, on May 16, they relinquished the lead to the Yankees, who were never headed thereafter.

The Yankees clinched their seventh pennant in eight years on September 18. Twelve days later, on the morning of the final game, Al Lopez announced his intention to resign as the Indians' manager after six years, in five of which the club finished second to the Yankees.

It also was a disappointing season at the gate for the Indians, as attendance declined to 865,467, the first time in 11 years it fell below one million.

Among the few highlights was Bob Lemon's 200th major league victory, 3–1, over Baltimore at the Stadium on September 11. He, along with Herb Score and Early Wynn, were 20-game winners in 1956.

But the season was still the most frustrating one for Lopez as the Indians, with a 45–35 record on July 15, trailed the Yankees by 10½ games, a deficit that never got smaller than seven.

Once again the Indians' offense suffered a power failure as rookie Rocky Colavito posted the best average, .276. He smashed 21 homers and drove in 65 runs despite spending six weeks in the minors at midseason at San Diego of the Pacific Coast League (whose ranking was then "open" classification).

Colavito's home-run production was second only to Vic Wertz, who made a comeback from the attack of polio he suffered the previous season, hitting .264 with 32 homers and 106 RBI.

But Bobby Avila and Al Rosen were major disappointments, and the Indians' team batting average was .244, last in the league.

The 1956 season also marked the end of Bob Feller's brilliant pitching career. He appeared in 19 games, only four as a starter, and most of the other 15 in a mop-up relief role, and was 0–4 with a 4.97 earned run average, highest in his 18 years with the Indians. Feller struck out only 18 batters in 58 innings—the same number he struck out in a nine-inning game against Detroit on October 2, 1938, when he set a major league record.

The Indians designated September 9 as "Bob Feller Night" at the Stadium, during which he was honored for his long years of service, and three weeks later, in the final game of the season on September 30 at the Stadium, he pitched his last game.

It was an 8–4 loss to Detroit in front of 5,918 fans. Feller went all the way, giving up 14 hits, including a home run by Wayne Belardi, and three walks, but didn't record even one strikeout. The victory was credited to Billy Hoeft, his 20th, as he pitched four innings in relief of Detroit starter Ned Garver.

In his search for a new manager, Greenberg initially offered the job to Leo Durocher, who was then working for NBC-TV. But Durocher's price was too high, and on November 28, Greenberg hired Kerby Farrell, who had managed the Tribe's Class AAA farm club, Indianapolis, to the 1956 American Association pennant and Junior World Series title.

Colavito was tied with Baltimore's Tito Francona behind Chicago's Luis Aparicio for Rookie of the Year honors, while Wertz and Lemon were ninth and 10th in balloting for the

Most Valuable Player award, won by the Yankees' Mickey Mantle.

	W	L	G	GS	CG	IP	H	BB	K	ERA
Hank Aguirre	3	5	16	9	2	65⅓	63	27	31	3.72
Bud Daley	1	0	14	0	0	20⅓	21	14	13	6.20
Bob Feller	0	4	19	4	2	58	63	23	18	4.97
Mike Garcia	11	12	35	30	8	197⅔	213	74	119	3.78
Art Houtteman	2	2	22	4	0	46⅔	60	31	19	6.56
Bob Lemon	20	14	39	35	(21)	255½	230	89	94	3.03
Sal Maglie	0	0	2	0	0	5	6	2	2	3.60
Cal McLish	2	4	37	2	0	61⅓	67	32	27	4.96
Don Mossi	6	5	48	3	0	87⅔	79	33	59	3.59
Ray Narleski	3	2	32	0	0	59⅓	36	19	42	1.52
Herb Score	20	9	35	33	16	249½	162	129	(263)	2.53
Early Wynn	20	9	38	35	18	277⅔	233	91	158	2.72
	88	66		(155)	(67)	1,384	1,233	564	(845)	(3.32)

Shutouts: Score (5), Garcia (4), Wynn (4), Lemon (2), Aguirre
Saves: Mossi (11), Narleski (4), Lemon (3), Wynn (2), Aguirre, Feller, Houtteman, McLish

	G	AB	R	H	2B	3B	HR	RBI	SB	AVG
Earl Averill	42	93	12	22	6	0	3	14	0	.237
Bobby Avila (2B)	138	513	74	115	14	2	10	54	17	.224
Jim Busby (CF)	135	494	72	116	17	3	12	50	8	.235
Joe Caffie	12	38	7	13	0	0	0	1	3	.342
Chico Carrasquel (SS)	141	474	60	115	15	1	7	48	0	.243
Rocky Colavito (RF)	101	322	55	89	11	4	21	65	0	.276
Hoot Evers	3	0	1	0	0	0	0	0	0	—
Hank Foiles	1	0	0	0	0	0	0	0	0	—
Jim Hegan (C)	122	315	42	70	15	2	6	34	1	.222
Kenny Kuhn	27	22	7	6	1	0	0	2	0	.273
Stu Locklin	9	6	0	1	0	0	0	0	0	.167
Sam Mele	57	114	17	29	7	0	4	20	0	.254
Dale Mitchell	38	30	2	4	0	0	0	6	0	.133
Hal Naragon	53	122	11	35	3	1	3	18	0	.287
Dave Pope	25	70	6	17	3	1	0	3	0	.243
Rudy Regalado	16	47	4	11	1	0	0	2	0	.234
Al Rosen (3B)	121	416	64	111	18	2	15	61	1	.267
Al Smith (LF)	141	526	87	144	26	5	16	71	6	.274
George Strickland	85	171	22	36	1	2	3	17	0	.211
Preston Ward	87	150	18	38	10	0	6	21	0	.253
Vic Wertz (1B)	136	481	65	127	22	0	32	106	0	.264
Gene Woodling	100	317	56	83	17	0	8	38	2	.262
Bobby Young	1	0	0	0	0	0	0	0	0	—
		5,148	712	1,256	199	23	153	675	40	.244

1957

Record: 76–77
Finish: Sixth
Games Behind: 21½
Manager: Kerby Farrell

It was a season of travail, near tragedy, and upheaval for the Indians, who regressed under Kerby Farrell and in 1957 fell to their worst record and lowest place in the standings in 11 years.

Herb Score, the best young pitcher in baseball, was nearly blinded—even almost killed—when he was hit in the right eye by a line drive off the bat of New York's Gil McDougald on May 7, in front of 18,386 horrified fans at the Stadium.

It happened in the first inning, as McDougald was the Yankees' second batter, and Score spent the next three weeks in the hospital. He recovered and returned to uniform in 1957, but didn't pitch again that season.

The Indians won the game, 2–1, after Bob Lemon replaced Score, who was making his fifth start.

A few hours after the final game on September 29, Farrell was fired by general manager Hank Greenberg. Farrell was replaced by Bobby Bragan, who had managed the Pittsburgh Pirates until he was dismissed on August 3.

And 17 days later, on October 16, Greenberg himself was fired.

It was a surprising decision by Indians directors, who voted 10–2 to terminate Greenberg, himself a director (who abstained in the voting). Greenberg was the second-largest stockholder to William R. Daley, owning 19 percent of the club. His dismissal was effective December 31.

William O. DeWitt, a longtime baseball official, initially was interviewed for the general manager's job.

But then, also surprisingly, on November 9 an application was submitted by Frank Lane, who had just been named the major leagues' Executive of the Year for 1957 by *The Sporting News*.

Lane was hired on November 12 and given a three-year contract through 1960. It called for a raise over the $50,000 base pay Lane was paid by the Cardinals, plus—a provision which angered many Tribe fans—a bonus of five cents for each admission over 800,000 in each of the next three seasons.

The skids had been greased under Farrell and Greenberg when the Tribe started the season poorly despite the presence of two of baseball's best young sluggers, Rocky Colavito and Roger Maris, and the reemergence of Gene Woodling and Vic Wertz.

The Indians fell into last place on April 21, and, though they rallied briefly to climb eight games over .500 (18–10) and into second place on May 21, they never were in the race thereafter.

The losing was reflected in a shocking decline in attendance to a 12-year low of 722,256. It was the second lowest in the American League that year.

It fueled speculation that the Indians were considering moving to Minneapolis–St. Paul, as rumors persisted most of the season that Greenberg was negotiating a transfer of the franchise.

Woodling was the Tribe's only .300 hitter, while Wertz was

A remorseful Gil McDougald reads the *Cleveland News* on May 8, 1957, the morning after a line drive off his bat struck pitcher Herb Score in the eye during a game at Cleveland Stadium between the Indians and New York Yankees.

most productive with 28 homers and 105 runs batted in. Colavito clouted 25 homers, giving him a two-year total of 46, and Maris showed promise of big things to come with 14 homers in 116 games.

The pitching, however, was a disaster.

Early Wynn led the staff with 14 victories but lost 17. Lemon, after gaining credit for winning the game in which Score was hurt, tore a muscle in his thigh in late May and was disabled for three weeks. A month after returning to action, Lemon was sidelined again, this time with bone chips in his elbow, and won only four more games. He made his final appearance on August 11, a 9–8 loss to Kansas City at the Stadium.

Ray Narleski and Don Mossi, the Tribe's ace relievers the previous three years, combined for 22 victories after Farrell pressed them into starting duty, considerably weakening the bull pen.

Lane's first trade for the Indians, which turned out to be one of his worst, was made on December 4, during the winter meetings in Colorado Springs, Colorado. He sent pitcher Early Wynn and outfielder Al Smith to the Chicago White Sox for outfielder Minnie Minoso and infielder Freddie Hatfield.

	W	L	G	GS	CG	IP	H	BB	K	ERA
Hank Aguirre	1	1	10	1	0	20⅓	26	13	9	5.75
Bob Alexander	0	1	5	0	0	7	10	5	1	9.00
Bud Daley	2	8	34	10	1	87⅓	99	40	54	4.43
Mike Garcia	12	8	38	27	9	211⅓	221	73	110	3.75
John Gray	1	3	7	3	1	20	21	13	3	5.85
Art Houtteman	0	0	3	0	0	4	6	3	3	6.75
Bob Lemon	6	11	21	17	2	117⅓	129	64	45	4.60
Cal McLish	9	7	42	7	2	144⅓	118	67	88	2.74
Don Mossi	11	10	36	22	6	159	165	57	97	4.13
Ray Narleski	11	5	46	15	7	154⅓	136	70	93	3.09
Stan Pitula	2	2	23	5	1	59⅔	67	32	17	4.98
Herb Score	2	1	5	5	3	36	18	26	39	2.00
Dick Tomanek	2	1	34	2	0	69⅔	67	37	55	5.68
Vito Valentinetti	2	2	11	2	1	23⅔	26	13	9	4.94
Hoyt Wilhelm	1	0	2	0	0	3⅔	2	1	0	2.45
Early Wynn	14	17	40	(37)	13	263	(270)	104	(184)	4.31
	76	77		153	46	1,380⅔	1,381	(618)	807	4.06

Shutouts: Garcia, Gray, Mossi, Narleski, Score, Wynn
Saves: Narleski (16), Daley (2), Mossi (2), McLish, Wilhelm, Wynn

	G	AB	R	H	2B	3B	HR	RBI	SB	AVG
Joe Altobelli	83	87	9	18	3	2	0	9	3	.207
Bobby Avila (2B)	129	463	60	124	19	3	5	48	2	.268
Dick Brown	34	114	10	30	4	0	4	22	1	.263
Jim Busby	30	74	9	14	2	1	2	4	0	.189
Joe Caffie	32	89	14	24	2	1	3	10	0	.270
Chico Carrasquel (SS)	125	392	37	108	14	1	8	57	0	.276
Rocky Colavito (RF)	134	461	66	116	26	0	25	84	1	.252
Billy Harrell	22	57	6	15	1	1	1	5	3	.263
Jim Hegan (C)	58	148	14	32	7	0	4	15	0	.216
Kenny Kuhn	40	53	5	9	0	0	0	5	0	.170
Roger Maris (CF)	116	358	61	84	9	5	14	51	8	.235
Hal Naragon	57	121	12	31	1	1	0	8	0	.256
Russ Nixon	62	185	15	52	7	1	2	18	0	.281
Larry Raines	96	244	39	64	14	0	2	16	5	.262
Eddie Robinson	19	27	1	6	1	0	1	3	0	.222
Al Smith (3B)	135	507	78	125	23	5	11	49	12	.247
George Strickland	89	201	21	47	8	2	1	19	0	.234
Bob Usher	10	8	1	1	0	0	0	0	0	.125
Preston Ward	10	11	2	2	1	0	0	0	0	.182
Vic Wertz (1B)	144	515	84	145	21	0	28	105	2	.282
Dick Williams	67	205	33	58	7	0	6	17	3	.283
Gene Woodling (LF)	133	430	74	138	25	2	19	78	0	.321
		5,171	682	1,304	199	26	140	649	40	.252

1958

Record: 77–76
Finish: Fourth
Games Behind: 14½
Managers: Bobby Bragan, Joe Gordon

The Frank Lane era began with a whirlwind of activity, similar to the arrival of Bill Veeck 12 years earlier, but without the same positive results.

Following his deal that sent Early Wynn and Al Smith to the Chicago White Sox for Minnie Minoso and Freddie Hatfield the previous December, Lane made no fewer than 19 transactions—trades, sales, purchases—in 1958.

Lane's acquisitions included Mickey Vernon from Boston, Larry Doby and Don Ferrarese from Baltimore, Billy Hunter, Vic Power, and Woodie Held from Kansas City, and, after the season ended, Billy Martin and Al Cicotte from Detroit, and Jimmy Piersall from Boston.

Sent packing by Lane were Jim Hegan and Hank Aguirre to the Tigers, Gene Woodling, Dick Williams, and Bud Daley to the Orioles, Roger Maris and Chico Carrasquel to the Athletics, and, at the end of the season, Ray Narleski and Don Mossi to the Tigers, Bobby Avila to the Orioles, and Vic Wertz and Gary Geiger to the Red Sox.

But Lane's frantic wheeling and dealing did little to help the Tribe, except for an improvement of one game in the won-lost record and two places in the standings, as New York led the race from wire to wire.

Nor did the trades help at the gate, as attendance continued to decline, this time to 663,805, lowest since 1945, though the low turnout obviously didn't affect Lane's status. Late in the season he was given the additional title of executive vice president.

In fairness it should be pointed out that injuries to four key players were major factors in the inability of the Indians to make a race of it.

Wertz fractured his right ankle on March 30 in spring training and played only 25 games; Herb Score, trying to make a comeback from an eye injury in 1957, suffered an inflamed ligament in his left elbow and failed to win a game after April 30; Mike Garcia pitched only six games because of a slipped disc in his back and was released June 3; and Bob Lemon didn't recover from off-season elbow surgery and was released July 9.

The Indians started the season in the second division after losing their first two games and five of 10. They were lodged in sixth place with a 31–36 record, 12 games behind New York, when Lane lost his patience and fired Bragan on June 26.

Bragan was replaced by Joe Gordon, who had retired from baseball after managing San Francisco to the 1957 championship of the Pacific Coast League ("open" classification).

The change of managers made little difference, however, although the Indians spurted briefly under Gordon.

They went 20–16 in the next five and a half weeks, climbing into second place on August 3 with a 51–52 record. The standings presented the unusual situation in which every team but the front-running Yankees (17 lengths ahead of the Tribe) was playing sub-.500 baseball.

The Indians reached .500 (54–54) on August 9, but by

then they had dropped back to fourth place and never got any higher.

Still, it wasn't a completely negative season for the Tribe.

Rocky Colavito emerged as one of baseball's top stars as he hit .303 and smashed 41 homers, one short of Hal Trosky's 1936 club record. His performance placed him second in the AL in home runs and runs batted in (113), while his .620 slugging percentage led the league.

Colavito also was third in the balloting for the Most Valuable Player award, garnering 181 points. He finished behind Boston's Jackie Jensen, who had 233 points, and New York's Bob Turley with 191.

Famous for his strong throwing arm, Colavito also made a surprise appearance as a relief pitcher on August 13 in the second game of a doubleheader against Detroit at the Stadium. He replaced starter Hoyt Wilhelm in the seventh inning with runners on second and third and nobody out.

A sacrifice fly scored the run, charged to Wilhelm, but Colavito blanked the Tigers and didn't give up a hit in three innings, though he walked three while striking out one. Detroit won, 3–2, with the loss charged to Wilhelm.

Cal McLish was the Tribe's winningest pitcher with a 16–8 record, while two rookies, Gary Bell and Jim "Mudcat" Grant, made impressive debuts.

Bell, who won 12 and lost 10, pitched a two-hitter to beat Washington, 5–1, at the Stadium on September 16. He placed third in the voting for AL Rookie of the Year, won by Washington's Albie Pearson with New York's Ryne Duren second.

Power also made his presence known as he hit .317 in 93 games after joining the Tribe, and he tied a major league record by stealing home twice in the same game, against Detroit on August 14 at the Stadium.

The first theft came in the eighth inning against Bill Fischer, the second against Frank Lary in the 10th inning, giving the Indians a 10–9 victory.

Power became the 11th player to steal home twice in the same game.

With attendance continuing to dwindle during the season, Indians chairman William R. Daley admitted that moving the franchise was a possibility. He acknowledged receiving offers from out-of-town interests, including one from the Houston Sports Association, which made a bid to buy the Indians for $6 million.

Finally, on October 15, Daley ended all speculation by announcing that the club's directors had rejected all offers and that the Indians would remain in Cleveland.

"In spite of some very attractive offers, we think the [Indians] baseball club is a good thing for Cleveland, and we think we can restore Cleveland to where it is again a leading baseball city," Daley said.

Hank Greenberg, who still was a director and owned 19 percent of the Indians despite having been fired as general manager in 1957, also had sought a transfer of the franchise to Minneapolis–St. Paul. He was allied with two other dissident directors, Andrew and Charles Baxter, who together also owned 19 percent of the club. In a stormy, showdown meeting on November 18, Greenberg and the Baxters were voted down and bought out.

	W	L	G	GS	CG	IP	H	BB	K	ERA
Gary Bell	12	10	33	23	10	182	141	73	110	3.21
Dick Brodowski	1	0	5	0	0	10	3	6	12	0.00
Chuck Churn	0	0	6	0	0	8⅔	12	5	4	6.23
Rocky Colavito	0	0	1	0	0	3	0	3	1	0.00
Jim Constable	0	1	6	2	0	9⅓	17	4	3	11.57
Don Ferrarese	3	4	28	10	2	94⅔	91	46	62	3.71
Mike Garcia	1	0	6	1	0	8	15	7	2	9.00
Gary Geiger	0	0	1	0	0	2	2	1	2	9.00
Mudcat Grant	10	11	44	28	11	204	173	104	111	3.84
Bob Kelly	0	2	13	3	0	27⅔	29	13	12	5.20
Bob Lemon	0	1	11	1	0	25⅓	41	16	8	5.33
Morrie Martin	2	0	14	0	0	18⅔	20	8	5	2.41
Cal McLish	16	8	39	30	13	225⅔	214	70	97	2.99
Don Mossi	7	8	43	5	0	101⅔	106	30	55	3.90
Ray Narleski	13	10	44	24	7	183⅓	179	91	102	4.07
Steve Ridzik	0	2	6	0	0	8⅔	9	5	6	2.08
Herb Score	2	3	12	5	2	41	29	34	48	3.95
Dick Tomanek	2	3	18	6	2	57⅔	61	28	42	5.62
Hoyt Wilhelm	2	7	30	6	1	90⅓	70	35	57	2.49
Hal Woodeshick	6	6	14	9	3	71⅔	71	25	27	3.64
	77	76		153	51	1,373⅓	1,283	(604)	766	3.73

Shutouts: Grant, Score

Saves: Wilhelm (5), Grant (4), Mossi (3), Score (3), Bell, Ferrarese, Martin, McLish, Narleski

	G	AB	R	H	2B	3B	HR	RBI	SB	AVG
Earl Averill	17	55	2	10	1	0	2	7	1	.182
Bobby Avila (2B)	113	375	54	95	21	3	5	30	5	.253
Dick Brown	68	173	20	41	5	0	7	20	1	.237
Chico Carrasquel	49	156	14	40	6	0	2	21	0	.256
Rocky Colavito (RF)	143	489	80	148	26	3	41	113	0	.303
Larry Doby (CF)	89	247	41	70	10	1	13	45	0	.283
Gary Geiger	91	195	28	45	3	1	1	6	2	.231
Rod Graber	4	8	0	1	0	0	0	0	0	.125
Carroll Hardy	27	49	10	10	3	0	1	6	1	.204
Billy Harrell (3B)	101	229	36	50	4	0	7	19	12	.218
Fred Hatfield	3	8	0	1	0	0	0	1	0	.125
Woodie Held	67	144	12	28	4	1	3	17	1	.194
Billy Hunter (SS)	76	190	21	37	10	2	0	9	4	.195
Randy Jackson	29	91	7	22	3	1	4	13	0	.242
Roger Maris	51	182	26	41	5	1	9	27	4	.225
Minnie Minoso (LF)	149	556	94	168	25	2	24	80	14	.302
Billy Moran	115	257	26	58	11	0	1	18	3	.226
Hal Naragon	9	9	2	3	0	1	0	0	0	.333
Russ Nixon (C)	113	376	42	113	17	4	9	46	0	.301
Jay Porter	40	85	13	17	1	0	4	19	0	.200
Vic Power	93	385	63	122	24	(6)*	12	53	2	.317
Larry Raines	7	9	1	0	0	0	0	0	0	.000
Mickey Vernon (1B)	119	355	49	104	22	3	8	55	0	.293
Preston Ward	48	148	22	50	3	1	4	21	0	.338
Vic Wertz	25	43	5	12	1	0	3	12	0	.279
		5,201	694	1,340	210	30	160	653	50	.258

*League leader in triples with 10 (4 with Kansas City)

1959

Record: 89–65
Finish: Second
Games Behind: 5
Manager: Joe Gordon

Frank Lane, who came to be called "Frantic Frank" and "Trader Lane," continued his wheeling and dealing, making 14 transactions involving 33 players in 1959. To his credit—at least this time—one proved to be a major acquisition.

It was Tito Francona, whom Lane got from Detroit for an almost finished Larry Doby on March 21.

Francona nearly won the American League batting championship, hitting over .400 until August 10. Francona and Cal McLish, who won 19 games, were the team leaders as the Indians came close to winning the franchise's fourth pennant.

But again, as had happened previously, the Indians collapsed at the end, after a sensational start, and were beaten out by the Chicago White Sox, who were then owned by Bill Veeck and managed by Al Lopez.

The Tribe won its first six games and 10 of 11, taking over and holding first place for all but 12 days until July 16, as Francona tore the cover off the ball and McLish won 11 of 14 decisions.

But then, late in May after they had constructed a 3½ game lead over the White Sox, the Indians went 2–11, including seven straight losses, and the race tightened up.

The slump was broken by Rocky Colavito on June 10, when he became only the sixth player in major league history since 1901 to smash four home runs in one game—and only the second, along with Lou Gehrig, to hit them consecutively. Colavito's achievement came in an 11–8 victory over the Orioles in Baltimore.

The first homer was a two-run shot off Jerry Walker in the third inning. The second was a solo blow off Arnold Portocarrero in the fifth. Portocarrero also was the victim of Colavito's third homer, which came in the sixth with one aboard. The fourth also was a solo shot, off Ernie Johnson in the ninth.

Colavito went on to tie Washington's Harmon Killebrew for the AL home run championship, as well as Hal Trosky's 1936 club record of 42, while driving in 111 runs and batting .257. His four-homer performance launched the Indians on a seven-game winning streak.

With their 44–32 record, the Indians led the league by two lengths at the All-Star break. They lost a doubleheader in New York and were caught by the White Sox on July 16. The two teams went back and forth for 11 days, after which the Tribe lost three of four to Boston, and Chicago took over first place to stay on July 27.

Still, the Tribe had a chance to regain the lead when the White Sox came to Cleveland for a crucial four-game series, August 28–30.

When it started, the Indians were behind by only a few percentage points. But they proceeded to lose four straight to Veeck and Lopez's team, then known as the "Go-Go White Sox."

The AL's largest crowd of the season, 70,398 at the Stadium, saw the Tribe, behind Jim "Mudcat" Grant, drop the opener to Bob Shaw, 7–3. Dick Donovan beat Jim Perry, 2–0, the next day, and in the series-ending doubleheader Early Wynn outdueled McLish, 5–4, and Barry Latman was a 9–4 winner over Gary Bell in front of 66,586 fans.

By the time the White Sox left town, the Indians were four behind and never caught up, despite winning two of three in Chicago in a series that started two days later.

The Tribe cut its deficit to two on September 20, winning three straight from Kansas City, but the end officially came two days later, again at the hands of the White Sox.

With the help of reliever Gerry Staley, Wynn and the White Sox prevailed, 4–2. After the Indians had loaded the bases with one out in the ninth, Staley took over and, to the dismay of a Stadium crowd of 54,293, induced Vic Power to rap the first pitch into a game-ending double play.

Not only did it clinch the pennant for the White Sox, but Wynn's victory also was his sixth in seven decisions against his former teammates in 1959.

It also resulted in the firing of Manager Joe Gordon—if only for a day.

The weird chain of events had started several weeks earlier when Gordon made public his resentment of Lane's criticism. (He had been feuding all season with two of Lane's favorites, Jim Piersall and Billy Martin.)

On the morning of September 18, Gordon told reporters he would resign when the season was over, regardless of whether the Tribe won the pennant or not.

Lane, upon reading the manager's comments, announced that Gordon would be relieved of his duties the moment the Indians were mathematically eliminated.

The 1959 Cleveland Indians, who finished second in the American League pennant race to the Chicago White Sox. The Indians would not be in contention for the pennant again until 1994.

Then Lane went to Pittsburgh to meet with Leo Durocher, who earlier had disclosed that he was giving up his executive position with NBC-TV to return to baseball.

After the White Sox clinched the pennant by beating the Indians, Lane and Gordon huddled, then issued a joint announcement. It was that Gordon was out "as of now," and that coach Mel Harder would manage the team in the final four games.

However, the next day Lane, reportedly angered by Durocher's demand for a better contract, did a flip-flop. He called reporters to the Stadium and told them, "Gentlemen, I want you to meet the man who will manage the Indians next year."

With that—to everybody's surprise— Gordon walked into the room.

Not only was Gordon rehired, but Lane also gave him a two-year contract and a raise in pay. "I made a mistake," Lane said, "and I decided I didn't have to live with it, so I tried to correct it."

The 1959 season was a memorable one for Colavito and Francona, who finished fourth and fifth in the balloting for the Most Valuable Player award, and for Minnie Minoso, who was picked on the major league All-Star team, as well as Jim Perry and Jim Baxes, who were named to the All-Rookie team.

On the other hand, it was a particularly frustrating year for Billy Martin. The one-time star of the New York Yankees, who had been acquired from Detroit the previous winter, suffered a shoulder injury on June 23 that sidelined him for more than three weeks.

Then, on August 5, Martin's jaw and cheekbone were broken when he was hit by a pitch by Washington's Truman Clevenger, and he was finished for the season.

It also was a difficult year for Herb Score. He won seven of 10 decisions by mid-June, but failed to register a victory after July 3.

Because of the tightness of the pennant race, the Indians' attendance rebounded significantly as nearly 1.5 million fans spun the turnstiles, providing Lane with a bonus—computed at five cents per head over 800,000—of nearly $35,000.

Lane didn't wait long to swing into action again after the season ended. On December 6 he acquired Norm Cash, John Romano, and Bubba Phillips from the White Sox for Minnie Minoso, Don Ferrarese, Jake Striker, and Dick Brown. Nine days later, on December 15, he sent McLish, Gordon Coleman, and Martin to Cincinnati for Johnny Temple.

	W	L	G	GS	CG	IP	H	BB	K	ERA
Gary Bell	16	11	44	28	12	234	208	105	136	4.04
Johnny Briggs	0	1	4	1	0	12⅔	12	3	5	2.13
Dick Brodowski	2	2	18	0	0	30	19	21	9	1.80
Al Cicotte	3	1	26	1	0	44	46	25	23	5.32
Don Ferrarese	5	3	15	10	4	76	58	51	45	3.20
Mike Garcia	3	6	29	8	1	72	72	31	49	4.00
Mudcat Grant	10	7	38	19	6	165¼	140	81	85	4.14
Jack Harshman	5	1	13	6	5	66	46	13	35	2.59
Bobby Locke	3	2	24	7	0	77⅔	66	41	40	3.13
Cal McLish	19	8	35	32	13	235⅓	(253)	72	113	3.63
Jim Perry	12	10	44	13	8	153	122	55	79	2.65
Bud Podbielan	0	1	6	0	0	12⅓	17	2	5	5.84
Humberto Robinson	1	0	5	0	0	8⅔	9	4	6	4.15
Herb Score	9	11	30	25	9	160⅔	123	115	147	4.71
Riverboat Smith	0	1	12	3	0	29⅓	31	12	17	5.22
Jake Striker	1	0	1	1	0	6⅔	8	4	5	2.70
	89	65		154	(58)	1,383⅔	1,230	(635)	799	3.75

Shutouts: Perry (2), Bell, Grant, Harshman, Score
Saves: Bell (5), Brodowski (5), Perry (4), Grant (3), Locke (2), Cicotte, Garcia, Harshman

	G	AB	R	H	2B	3B	HR	RBI	SB	AVG
Jim Baxes	77	247	35	59	11	0	15	34	0	.239
Jim Bolger	8	7	0	0	0	0	0	0	0	.000
Dick Brown	48	141	15	31	7	0	5	16	0	.220
Rocky Colavito (RF)	154	588	90	151	24	0	(42)	111	3	.257
Gordy Coleman	6	15	5	8	0	1	0	2	0	.533
Don Dillard	10	10	0	4	0	0	0	1	0	.400
Ed FitzGerald	49	129	12	35	6	1	1	4	0	.271
Tito Francona	122	399	68	145	17	2	20	79	2	.363
Granny Hamner	27	67	4	11	1	1	1	3	0	.164
Carroll Hardy	32	53	12	11	1	0	0	2	1	.208
Woodie Held (SS)	143	525	82	132	19	3	29	71	1	.251
Randy Jackson	3	7	0	1	0	0	0	0	0	.143
Willie Jones	11	18	1	4	1	0	0	1	0	.222
Gene Leek	13	36	7	8	3	0	1	5	0	.222
Billy Martin (2B)	73	242	37	63	7	0	9	24	0	.260
Minnie Minoso (LF)	148	570	92	172	32	0	21	92	8	.302
Billy Moran	11	17	1	5	0	0	0	2	0	.294
Hal Naragon	14	36	6	10	4	1	0	5	0	.278
Russ Nixon (C)	82	258	23	62	10	3	1	29	0	.240
Jimmy Piersall (CF)	100	317	42	78	13	2	4	30	6	.246
Vic Power (1B)	147	595	102	172	31	6	10	60	9	.289
George Strickland (3B)	132	441	55	105	15	2	3	48	1	.238
Chuck Tanner	14	48	6	12	2	0	1	5	0	.250
Elmer Valo	34	24	3	7	0	0	0	5	0	.292
Ray Webster	40	74	10	15	2	1	2	10	1	.203
	5,288	(745)	1,390	216	25	(167)	(682)	33		(.263)

1960

Record: 76–78
Finish: Fourth
Games Behind: 21
Managers: Joe Gordon, Jo-Jo White, Jimmy Dykes

Frustrated after coming so close to winning the pennant in 1959, and obviously unsatisfied after a two-year total of 31 trades, Frank Lane pulled off a deal on April 17 for which he always will be remembered—and hated by most Indians fans.

It happened two days before the season opened. The Indians were playing an exhibition game against the Chicago White Sox in Memphis, Tennessee, on their trip back to Cleveland from spring training in Tucson, Arizona.

Lane traded Rocky Colavito, one of the most popular players in franchise history—if not *the* most popular player—to Detroit for Harvey Kuenn.

Fans in Cleveland were outraged. It wasn't that they didn't like Kuenn, or that he lacked ability. Kuenn had won the American League batting championship with a .353 average in 1959, and he was a very good defensive center fielder.

But the boyishly handsome Colavito was an idol in Cleveland, especially in the wake of the 42 home runs he clouted in 1959 that tied for the league lead. They also gave him 129 in the four years he played for the Tribe.

Like the fans, Colavito also was crushed.

Lane, who did not have great affection for Colavito, justified the deal by saying that Rocky was interested only in hitting home runs, and that Kuenn would be a better team player for the Indians.

Manager Joe Gordon shared Lane's sentiments—in fact, it was speculated that he prompted the deal—in the belief that Kuenn would make the Indians a more complete team.

Two days after Colavito and Kuenn switched uniforms, the Tigers opened the season in Cleveland. Many of the 52,756 fans, angry at Lane, showed up with signs and placards blasting the general manager and cheered their lungs out for Colavito.

Lane even was hanged in effigy from a rafter in the grandstand.

Colavito went hitless in six at bats in his debut with the Tigers, striking out four times and grounding into a double play. He even lost a fly ball in the sun, letting it fall for a single.

Kuenn singled and doubled and was flawless in center field as the Tigers won, 4–2, in 15 innings.

The Colavito-for-Kuenn deal was the zenith of a very busy spring for Lane, but it wasn't the only trade he made in 1960.

Five days earlier, Lane had traded Norman Cash to Detroit for Steve Demeter.

And the day after he brought Kuenn to Cleveland, Lane dealt Colavito's best friend and another popular Tribesman, Herb Score, to the Chicago White Sox for Barry Latman.

An even greater shock, this time to all of baseball, followed four and a half months later.

On August 3, in the wake of 13 Tribe losses in 17 games, Lane swapped Gordon to the Tigers for their manager, Jimmy Dykes. It was the first time in baseball history that two managers were traded for each other.

Tribe coach Joyner "Jo-Jo" White managed the Indians for one game, after the Gordon-Dykes trade.

Then, five days after the managers exchanged uniforms, White was released by Lane and rejoined Gordon in Detroit, and coach Luke Appling was let go by the Tigers and hired by Dykes in Cleveland.

Lane justified sending Gordon to Detroit by insisting that the Indians were still in the pennant race—though they were in fourth place with a 49–46 record, seven games behind New York—and claiming that Dykes could make a difference in the final 58 games.

"If I thought the change wouldn't be an improvement, I wouldn't have made it," said Lane. "We have a good ball club, but it needs a shot in the arm. Dykes is a solid guy. He has the ability to snap teams out of troubles. I'm hoping he'll do it here."

At the time of the trade of managers, the Tigers under Dykes were sixth with a 44–52 record, 12½ games behind the Yankees. They also trailed the Indians by 5½.

Another reason, though unstated, that led to the Gordon-Dykes deal was the common knowledge that Gordon had an intense dislike for two of Lane's favorites, Billy Martin and Jim Piersall.

Their difficulties had arisen during the 1959 season. Martin was traded during the winter, but Piersall was still a member of the Indians in 1960, though he didn't play much under Gordon.

The unprecedented trade provided one more bit of irony. With Gordon going to the Tigers, he would again be united with Colavito, whom he didn't want on the team when they were together in Cleveland.

The managerial change turned out to make little difference in the fortunes of both clubs.

The Indians under Dykes went 26–32 (White managed the team to a victory before Dykes reported) and finished fourth, one place higher, though their first-place deficit was greater by 14 games.

The Tigers under Gordon went 26–31 (coach Billy Hitchcock also managed them to one victory before Gordon reported) and finished sixth, exactly where they'd been under Dykes, though at season end they trailed the Yankees by 26 lengths.

Kuenn led the Indians with a .308 average that included

nine homers and 54 runs batted in, while Colavito hit .249 with 35 homers and 87 RBIs for the Tigers.

Latman was 7–7 with a 4.03 earned run average compared to Score's 5–10 and 3.72 for Chicago.

But whatever satisfaction Lane might have felt—if any—in trading Colavito and Score, there could be absolutely no satisfaction in the Cash-Demeter deal.

Demeter played in but four games for the Indians in 1960, his only season in the major leagues, going hitless in five at bats.

Cash went on to hit .286 with 18 homers and 63 RBIs for the Tigers. (He won the AL batting championship in 1961 and played in the major leagues through 1974.)

Still, the Indians' fall from contention also could be blamed on a couple of key injuries. The first idled shortstop Woodie Held for six weeks with a broken finger incurred on July 18. The second was an inflamed tendon in Gary Bell's pitching shoulder that prevented him from winning a game after July 20.

The Indians were 45–33 and second by only 1½ games two days before the injury to Held, who was leading the team in homers and RBIs.

Before the year ended Lane went on to complete 20 trades, for a total of 51, involving 118 players in his three seasons at the helm of the team.

The Indians also lost seven players in the AL expansion draft in December when new franchises in California (then Los Angeles) and Washington were stocked.

The Angels claimed Red Wilson, Gene Leek, and Ken Aspromonte, and the Senators took Carl Mathias, Johnny Klippstein, Marty Keough, and Jim King. Leek and King played in the Tribe's minor league system in 1960.

And on December 3, during baseball's annual winter meetings, Lane traded Kuenn to the San Francisco Giants for Johnny Antonelli and Willie Kirkland. It was a deal that only compounded the first one that cost the Indians the services of Colavito.

Gone, too, when the year ended, was Lane, whose contract with the Indians had expired. He was hired as executive vice president and general manager of the Kansas City Athletics by new owner Charles O. Finley.

	W	L	G	GS	CG	IP	H	BB	K	ERA
Gary Bell	9	10	28	23	6	154⅔	139	82	109	4.13
Ted Bowsfield	3	4	11	6	1	40⅓	47	20	14	5.09
Johnny Briggs	4	2	21	2	0	36⅓	32	15	19	4.46
Frank Funk	4	2	9	0	0	31⅓	27	9	18	1.99
Mudcat Grant	9	8	33	19	5	159⅔	147	78	75	4.40
Bob Grim	0	1	3	0	0	2⅓	6	1	2	11.57
Jack Harshman	2	4	15	8	0	54⅓	50	30	25	3.98
Wynn Hawkins	4	4	15	9	1	66	68	39	39	4.23
Johnny Klippstein	5	5	49	0	0	74⅓	53	35	46	2.91
Barry Latman	7	7	31	20	4	147⅓	146	72	94	4.03
Mike Lee	0	0	7	0	0	9	6	11	6	2.00
Bobby Locke	3	5	32	11	2	123	121	37	53	3.37
Carl Mathias	0	1	7	0	0	15⅓	14	8	13	3.52
Don Newcombe	2	3	20	2	0	54	61	8	27	4.33
Jim Perry	(18)	10	41	(36)	10	261⅓	257	91	120	3.62
Dick Stigman	5	11	41	18	3	133⅔	118	87	104	4.51
Carl Thomas	1	0	4	0	0	9⅔	8	10	5	7.45
Bobby Tiefenauer	0	1	6	0	0	9	8	3	2	2.00
	76	78	154	32		1,382⅓	1,308	(636)	771	3.95

Shutouts: Perry (4), Bell (2), Locke (2), Bowsfield
Saves: Klippstein (14), Stigman (9), Locke (2), Bell, Briggs, Funk, Newcombe, Perry

	G	AB	R	H	2B	3B	HR	RBI	SB	AVG
Ken Aspromonte (2B)	117	459	65	133	20	1	10	48	4	.290
Walt Bond	40	131	19	29	2	1	5	18	4	.221
Rocky Bridges	10	27	1	9	0	0	0	3	0	.333
Ty Cline	7	26	2	8	1	1	0	2	0	.308
Mike de la Hoz	49	160	20	41	6	2	6	23	0	.256
Steve Demeter	4	5	0	0	0	0	0	0	0	.000
Don Dillard	6	7	0	1	0	0	0	0	0	.143
Hank Foiles	24	68	9	19	1	0	1	6	0	.279
Tito Francona (LF)	147	544	84	159	(36)	2	17	79	4	.292
Bob Hale	70	70	2	21	7	0	0	12	0	.300
Carroll Hardy	29	18	7	2	1	0	0	1	0	.111
Woodie Held (SS)	109	376	45	97	15	1	21	67	0	.258
Marty Keough	65	149	19	37	5	0	3	11	2	.248
Harvey Kuenn (RF)	126	474	65	146	24	0	9	54	3	.308
Joe Morgan	22	47	6	14	2	0	2	4	0	.298
Russ Nixon	25	82	6	20	5	0	1	6	0	.244
Bubba Phillips (3B)	113	304	34	63	14	1	4	33	1	.207
Jimmy Piersall (CF)	138	486	70	137	12	4	18	66	18	.282
Vic Power (1B)	147	580	69	167	26	3	10	84	9	.288
Johnny Powers	8	12	2	2	1	1	0	4	0	.167
Johnny Romano (C)	108	316	40	86	12	2	16	52	0	.272
George Strickland	32	42	4	7	0	0	1	3	0	.167
Chuck Tanner	21	25	2	7	1	0	0	4	1	.280
Johnny Temple	98	381	50	102	13	1	2	19	11	.268
Pete Whisenant	7	6	0	1	0	0	0	0	0	.167
Red Wilson	32	88	5	19	3	0	1	10	0	.216
	(5,296)	667	(1,415)	218	20	127	632	58	.267	

1961

Record: 78–83

Finish: Fifth

Games Behind: 30½

Managers: Jimmy Dykes, Mel Harder

The American League had a new look, with the addition of the Washington Senators and the Los Angeles (California) Angels, and so did the Indians, with the departure of Frank Lane to Kansas City.

But major league baseball regressed again in Cleveland in 1961.

Jimmy Dykes was signed to a one-year contract before Lane left, and the vacancy in the front office was filled on an interim basis by farm director Walter "Hoot" Evers and his assistant, Bob Kennedy, both former Tribe players.

But Evers and Kennedy stood pat with the roster they inherited, and Gabe Paul arrived on April 27 to take over as general manager.

A new series of changes, albeit minor transactions, began, including the acquisition of Chuck Essegian and Bob Nieman, and the reacquisition of Ken Aspromonte, who had been taken by the Angels in the expansion draft.

Paul had been general manager of the Cincinnati Reds for nine years until he resigned on October 25, 1960, to sign a three-year contract with the Houston Colt 45s, one of the two (with the New York Mets) National League expansion franchises.

Paul later said that taking the Houston job was one of the biggest mistakes he ever made after a falling out with the owner, Judge Roy Hofheinz, and he quit to join the Indians.

Under Dykes the Indians fell into fifth place with a 12–13 record through May 13, then created a brief flurry of pennant excitement by winning 22 of their next 26 games to vault into contention.

On May 14 in the first game of a doubleheader at the Stadium the Tribe beat Baltimore, 1–0, in 15 innings, setting the team record for winning the longest extra-inning 1–0 game.

The Indians seized the lead from Detroit on June 6 in the midst of a 10-game winning streak, and clung to the top of the league for nine days.

But New York's Ralph Terry knocked the Tribe out of first place on June 15 with a 3–2, 11-inning victory, and everything that followed was downhill.

The Indians went from a 38–22 record to go 40–61 the rest of the way, including losing streaks of seven (June 18–25) and six (September 6–10). They finished in fifth place, only 2½ games ahead of Boston and 30½ behind the Yankees, their largest deficit in 15 years.

Attendance slumped accordingly, to 725,547, and Dykes was fired the morning of the final game, which the Indians won, 8–5, over the Los Angeles Angels, under the direction of pitching coach Mel Harder.

After the season ended, Mel McGaha, who'd been the Tribe's first base coach, was hired as the team's new manager. Prior to joining the coaching staff McGaha had been a successful minor league manager from 1954 to 1960.

Jimmy Piersall, one of only two regulars to hit .300, was traded on October 5 to Washington for Dick Donovan, Gene Green, and Jim Mahoney. Barry Latman, who'd been used exclusively in relief by Dykes until the end of June, won nine games before sustaining his first defeat on July 23.

And Willie Kirkland, the last player acquired in the 51st of Frank Lane's trades the previous December, drilled three homers in a 9–8 victory over Chicago at the Stadium on July 9. He led the Indians with 27 home runs.

	W	L	G	GS	CG	IP	H	BB	K	ERA
Bob Allen	3	2	48	0	0	81⅓	96	40	42	3.75
Johnny Antonelli	0	4	11	7	0	48	68	18	23	6.56
Gary Bell	12	16	34	34	11	228⅓	214	100	163	4.10
Bill Dailey	1	0	12	0	0	19	16	6	7	0.95
Frank Funk	11	11	56	0	0	92⅓	79	31	64	3.31
Mudcat Grant	15	9	35	35	11	244⅔	207	109	146	3.86
Steve Hamilton	0	0	2	0	0	3	2	3	4	3.00
Wynn Hawkins	7	9	30	21	3	133	139	59	51	4.06
Russ Heman	0	0	6	0	0	10	8	8	4	3.60
Barry Latman	13	5	45	18	4	176⅔	163	54	108	4.02
Bobby Locke	4	4	37	4	0	95⅓	112	40	37	4.53
Sam McDowell	0	0	1	1	0	6⅓	3	5	5	0.00
Jim Perry	10	17	35	35	6	223⅔	238	87	90	4.71
Joe Schaffernoth	0	1	15	0	0	17	16	14	9	4.76
Dick Stigman	2	5	22	6	0	64⅓	65	25	48	4.62
	78	83		161	35	1,443⅓	1,426	599	801	4.15

Shutouts: Grant (3), Bell (2), Latman (2), Hawkins, Perry

Saves: Funk (11), Latman (5), Allen (3), Locke (2), Hawkins, Heman

	G	AB	R	H	2B	3B	HR	RBI	SB	AVG
Ken Aspromonte	22	70	5	16	6	1	0	5	0	.229
Walt Bond	38	52	7	9	1	1	2	7	1	.173
Ty Cline	12	43	9	9	2	1	0	1	1	.209
Mike de la Hoz	61	173	20	45	10	0	3	23	0	.260
Don Dillard	74	147	27	40	5	0	7	17	0	.272
Chuck Essegian	60	166	25	48	7	1	12	35	0	.289
Tito Francona (LF)	155	592	87	178	30	8	16	85	2	.301
Bob Hale	42	36	0	6	0	0	0	6	0	.167
Woodie Held (SS)	146	509	67	136	23	5	23	78	0	.267
Hal Jones	12	35	2	6	0	0	2	4	0	.171
Willie Kirkland (RF)	146	525	84	136	22	5	27	95	7	.259
Jack Kubiszyn	25	42	4	9	0	0	0	0	0	.214
Al Luplow	5	18	0	1	0	0	0	0	0	.056
Joe Morgan	4	10	0	2	0	0	0	0	0	.200
Bob Nieman	39	65	2	23	6	0	2	10	1	.354
Bubba Phillips (3B)	143	546	64	144	23	1	18	72	1	.264
Jimmy Piersall (CF)	121	484	81	156	26	7	6	40	8	.322
Vic Power (1B)	147	563	64	151	34	4	5	63	4	.268
Johnny Romano (C)	142	509	76	152	29	1	21	80	0	.299
Johnny Temple (2B)	129	518	73	143	22	3	3	30	9	.276
Valmy Thomas	27	86	7	18	3	0	2	6	0	.209
	(5,609)	737	(1,493)	(257)	39	150	682	34	(.266)	

1962

Record: 80–82
Finish: Sixth
Games Behind: 16
Managers: Mel McGaha, Mel Harder

The Indians' record improved, but not their place in the standings; attendance continued to dwindle giving rise to speculation that the club might be moved out of Cleveland; and Mel McGaha, like his predecessor, didn't last the season.

The rookie manager was fired September 29, and pitching coach Mel Harder again was put in charge of the team for its last two games, a doubleheader the Tribe swept from the Los Angeles Angels, 4–3 and 6–1. The first-game victory was credited to rookie Sam McDowell, for whom stardom long had been predicted.

On October 5, a day after the season ended, Gabe Paul hired Birdie Tebbetts to manage the Indians. The two men promised a new era for baseball in Cleveland—one that was sorely needed.

Tebbetts was the Tribe's fifth manager in six years, since Al Lopez had resigned after the 1956 season to take over the Chicago White Sox.

And before the year ended, ownership of the Indians changed hands again, with Paul gaining control.

It was a $6 million deal that was completed November 20. Selling their holdings in the corporation that had owned the Indians were Ignatius A. O'Shaughnessy of St. Paul, a leading stockholder, vice presidents Nate Dolin and George Medinger, both holdovers from the 1946–49 Bill Veeck regime, and treasurer Harry Small.

The old corporation was then liquidated and a new one set up by Paul and William R. Daley, who also had been a major stockholder in the former group. Daley, chairman of the board since he bought into the club in 1956, was elected president in September, following the death of Myron H. Wilson Jr.

Paul owned 20 percent of the club, making him the largest stockholder in the new corporation. Two associates, both former minor league club owners, Grayle Howlett and A. Ray Smith, shared approximately 10 percent interest in the Indians. The remaining 70 percent, and control, was held by Daley and a group of Clevelanders with strong ties to the city.

In setting up the new organization, Paul was elected president and treasurer, in addition to general manager, Daley continued as chairman, and a board of 19 directors was named. It included Paul, Daley, Howlett, Smith, and Thomas A. Burke, former mayor of Cleveland and a U.S. senator.

Before the reorganization took place, the 1962 season began so well that hopes were high the Tribe was already coming out of the doldrums, its losing image polished.

The pitching staff had been bolstered by the addition of Pedro Ramos, who came in a trade with Minnesota for Vic Power and Dick Stigman. After the first 16 games the Tribe and New York were in and out of first place until mid-July.

The Indians so captivated their fans while sweeping four games from the Yankees, June 15–17, climbing into the lead, that a crowd of 70,918—the largest turnout since 1954—jammed the Stadium for the doubleheader that concluded the series.

Dick Donovan, another pitcher who had been acquired

the previous winter in a deal with Washington, won the opener, 6–1, raising his record to 10–2. Ramos completed the sweep with a 6–3 victory.

But the Tribe lost twice to Chicago, 6–3 and 8–4, on July 8, and the Yankees took over the top spot, never relinquishing it thereafter.

The Indians collapsed after the All-Star break, losing nine straight (from July 13 to 21), and 19 of 24, falling into eighth place by August 24, before rebounding. They won only 33 of their last 79 games, and McGaha was finished.

Donovan was the Indians' first 20-game winner since Herb Score in 1956. He pitched five shutouts, tying Minnesota's Camilo Pascual and Jim Kaat for the AL lead. His record earned for Donovan 64 points and fifth place in the balloting for the Most Valuable Player award, won by New York's Mickey Mantle.

On the other hand, not one Tribesman batted .300, as Willie Kirkland slumped to .200, while John Romano led with 25 homers and 81 runs batted in.

	W	L	G	GS	CG	IP	H	BB	K	ERA
Bob Allen	1	1	30	0	0	30⅔	29	25	23	5.87
Gary Bell	10	9	57	6	1	107⅔	104	52	80	4.26
Jackie Collum	0	0	1	0	0	1⅓	4	0	1	13.50
Bill Dailey	2	2	27	0	0	42⅔	43	17	24	3.59
Dick Donovan	20	10	34	34	16	250⅔	255	47	94	3.59
Frank Funk	2	1	47	0	0	80⅔	62	32	49	3.24
Ruben Gomez	1	2	15	4	0	45⅓	50	25	21	4.37
Mudcat Grant	7	10	26	23	6	149⅓	128	81	90	4.27
Bob Hartman	0	1	8	2	0	17⅓	14	8	11	3.12
Wynn Hawkins	1	0	3	0	0	3⅔	9	1	0	7.36
Barry Latman	8	13	45	21	7	179⅓	179	72	117	4.17
Sam McDowell	3	7	25	13	0	87⅔	81	70	70	6.06
Jim Perry	12	12	35	27	7	193⅔	213	59	74	4.14
Pedro Ramos	10	12	37	27	7	201⅓	189	85	96	3.71
Don Rudolph	0	0	1	0	0	⅓	1	0	0	0.00
Ron Taylor	2	2	8	4	1	33⅓	36	13	15	5.94
Dave Tyriver	0	0	4	0	0	10⅔	10	7	7	4.22
Floyd Weaver	1	0	1	1	0	5	3	0	8	1.80
	80	82		162	45	1,441	1,410	594	780	4.14

Shutouts: Donovan (5), Perry (3), Ramos (2), Grant, Latman
Saves: Bell (12), Funk (6), Latman (5), Allen (4), Dailey, Gomez, McDowell, Ramos

	G	AB	R	H	2B	3B	HR	RBI	SB	AVG
Tommie Agee	5	14	0	3	0	0	0	2	0	.214
Max Alvis	12	51	1	11	2	0	0	3	3	.216
Ken Aspromonte	20	28	4	4	2	0	0	1	0	.143
Walt Bond	12	50	10	19	3	0	6	17	1	.380
Ty Cline (CF)	118	375	53	93	15	5	2	28	5	.248
Marlan Coughtry	3	2	1	1	0	0	0	1	0	.500
Mike de la Hoz	12	12	0	1	0	0	0	0	0	.083
Don Dillard	95	174	22	40	5	1	5	14	0	.230
Doc Edwards	53	143	13	39	6	0	3	9	0	.273
Chuck Essegian (LF)	106	336	59	92	12	0	21	50	0	.274
Tito Francona (1B)	158	621	82	169	28	5	14	70	3	.272
Gene Green	66	143	16	40	4	1	11	28	0	.280
Woodie Held (SS)	139	466	55	116	12	2	19	58	5	.249
Hal Jones	5	16	2	5	1	0	0	1	0	.313
Jerry Kindall (2B)	154	530	51	123	21	1	13	55	4	.232
Willie Kirkland (RF)	137	419	56	84	9	1	21	72	9	.200
Jack Kubiszyn	25	59	3	10	2	0	1	2	0	.169
Al Luplow	97	318	54	88	15	3	14	45	1	.277
Jim Mahoney	41	74	12	18	4	0	3	5	0	.243
Bob Nieman	2	1	0	0	0	0	0	1	0	.000
Bubba Phillips (3B)	148	562	53	145	26	0	10	54	4	.258
Johnny Romano (C)	135	459	71	120	19	3	25	81	0	.261
Willie Tasby	75	199	25	48	7	0	4	17	0	.241
		5,484	682	1,341	202	22	180	644	35	.245

The Indians offensive leaders in 1963 (left to right): outfielder Tito Francona, catcher John Romano, shortstop Woodie Held, and first baseman Joe Adcock.

1963

Record: 79–83
Finish: Fifth (tied with Detroit)
Games Behind: 25½
Manager: Birdie Tebbetts

Gabe Paul and new manager Birdie Tebbetts pledged that the Indians would turn the corner in 1963 with a team built around three players whose minor league credentials were outstanding—center fielder Vic Davalillo, shortstop Tony Martinez, and third baseman Max Alvis.

The Tribe already had one of the American League's potentially strongest pitching staffs with established starters Dick Donovan, Gary Bell, Jim "Mudcat" Grant, Jim Perry, Barry Latman, and Pedro Ramos.

Great things were also expected from rookie Tommy

Pitchers Sam McDowell (left) and rookie Tommy John, who in 1963 were expected to become stars for the Indians.

Johns and from young Sam McDowell, who had won three games in 1962.

The previous winter Paul also had acquired veteran slugger Joe Adcock, who played for Tebbetts at Cincinnati and Milwaukee, and management's optimism seemed to be justified.

Then Paul swung a trade for veteran Jack Kralick, who'd pitched a no-hitter for Minnesota in 1962. Kralick "completed the picture by giving us an established left-handed starter," said Tebbetts. Perry was dealt to the Twins to get Kralick on May 2 after a 6–9 start had left the Tribe in eighth place in the expanded (to 10 teams) American League.

But the roster changes didn't work. Very little did again that season, as Martinez failed badly, hitting only .156. He was benched in mid-May and never approached the potential predicted for him.

Davalillo delivered as advertised, but only until June 12. He was batting .304 that morning—but that night suffered a fracture of his right forearm when hit by a pitch from Detroit's Hank Aguirre. It kept Davalillo out of action until August 10, after which his average slipped to .292. Thereafter he was never the same against left-handed pitchers.

Alvis wound up as the Indians' second-best hitter at .274 and led the team with 22 homers and 67 runs batted in. He was elected Man of the Year for 1963.

Adcock also failed to fill the role expected of him, hitting just .251 with 13 homers in 97 games. When the season ended, he was traded to the Los Angeles Angels with Latman for Leon Wagner.

Dick Howser represented another disappointment after being acquired from the Kansas City Athletics on May 25, when it became apparent that Martinez was not the solution at shortstop.

Hampered by a torn hamstring muscle, Howser hit a mere .247 in 49 games, leading to the midseason promotion of Larry Brown from the minor leagues.

Brown proved to be a pleasant surprise, as did catcher Joe Azcue, who was included in the Howser deal, in exchange for catcher Doc Edwards and $100,000 for the financially strapped Indians.

Azcue, quickly nicknamed the Immortal Cuban, was

pressed into duty almost immediately as John Romano, who'd been the Tribe's most productive offensive player in 1962, suffered a broken finger on May 26.

Azcue hit .284 with 14 homers and 46 RBIs in 94 games, and continued as the number-one catcher even after Romano returned.

Overall the Indians' offense was weak. Willie Kirkland and Tito Francona failed to hit with consistency. The team's .239 average was second lowest in the AL.

Particularly disappointing was the pitching staff, which was expected to be a strength. Kralick started well, and the Indians spurted to 18 victories in 21 games from June 2 to 20, boosting them into fourth place, their highest level all season, though nobody finished strong.

Kralick, Grant, and Donovan won in double figures, but totaled only 37 victories among them while losing 36. Latman lost five more than he won.

The team's performance was so bad at midseason—as was the attendance—that Paul signed 43-year-old Early Wynn, a free agent who'd been released with a career total of 299 victories the previous winter by the Chicago White Sox.

Paul wanted the veteran pitcher as much for a gate attraction as anything. Wynn started five games, taking the loss in two of them, before he finally became the 14th pitcher in major league history to win 300 games.

Wynn did it on July 13 in Kansas City, leaving the game after five innings with a 5–4 lead that was protected by reliever Jerry Walker. The Indians won, 7–4. Wynn did not pitch again and was signed as a coach for 1964.

Another of the few highlights of 1963 occurred July 31 in the sixth inning of the second game of a doubleheader when four consecutive home runs were hit by Woodie Held, Ramos, Francona, and Brown in a 9–5 victory over the Los Angeles Angels at the Stadium.

The season also was another financial disaster for the Indians as attendance fell to 562,507, down 153,569 from 1962, and lowest since 1945.

Various reports stated that the club lost between $500,000 and $1.2 million. Presumably as a means of covering some of the deficit, the Indians sold a stock issue of $300,000 to the men who were then the club's owners, all of which led to more speculation that the franchise would be moved.

Fan apathy also was evident for the All-Star Game, played for the third time at the Stadium in front of a turnout of only 44,160—and approximately 30,000 empty seats—on July 9. It was won by the National League, 5–3.

	G	AB	R	H	2B	3B	HR	RBI	SB	AVG
Joe Adcock	97	283	28	71	7	1	13	49	1	.251
Tommie Agee	13	27	3	4	1	0	1	3	0	.148
Max Alvis (3B)	158	602	81	165	32	7	22	67	9	.274
Joe Azcue (C)	94	320	26	91	16	0	14	46	1	.284
Larry Brown (SS)	74	247	28	63	6	0	5	18	4	.255
Ellis Burton	26	31	6	6	3	0	1	1	0	.194
Bob Chance	16	52	5	15	4	0	2	7	0	.288
Vic Davalillo (CF)	90	370	44	108	18	5	7	36	3	.292
Mike de la Hoz	67	150	15	40	10	0	5	25	0	.267
Doc Edwards	10	31	6	8	2	0	0	0	0	.258
Tito Francona (LF)	142	500	57	114	29	0	10	41	9	.228
Gene Green	43	78	4	16	3	0	2	7	0	.205
Woodie Held (2B)	133	416	61	103	19	4	17	61	2	.248
Dick Howser	49	162	25	40	5	0	1	10	9	.247
Jerry Kindall	86	234	27	48	4	1	5	20	3	.205
Willie Kirkland (RF)	127	427	51	98	13	2	15	47	8	.230
Jim Lawrence	2	0	0	0	0	0	0	0	0	—
Bob Lipski	2	1	0	0	0	0	0	0	0	.000
Al Luplow	100	295	34	69	6	2	7	27	4	.234
Tony Martinez	43	141	10	22	4	0	0	8	1	.156
Cal Neeman	9	9	0	0	0	0	0	0	0	.000
Johnny Romano	89	255	28	55	5	2	10	34	4	.216
Willie Tasby	52	116	11	26	3	1	4	5	0	.224
Sammy Taylor	4	10	1	3	0	0	0	1	0	.300
Fred Whitfield (1B)	109	346	44	87	17	3	21	54	0	.251
	5,496	635	1,314	214	29	169	592	59	.239	

1964

Record: 79–83
Finish: Sixth (tied with Minnesota)
Games Behind: 20
Managers: Birdie Tebbetts, George Strickland

The season began on an ominous note as Manager Birdie Tebbetts suffered a heart attack on April 1, during the final days of spring training in Tucson, Arizona. Coach George Strickland was put in charge of the team.

Tebbetts recovered and returned on July 3, though he didn't resume his full managerial duties until August 14. Even before then the Indians, still financially strapped, had fallen into eighth place, where they remained for five weeks.

Another casualty was Max Alvis, the Indians' best player in 1963, who was felled by spinal meningitis on June 26. Alvis returned on August 5, but during his absence the Indians lost 27 of 43 games.

One positive development came out of Alvis's illness. When he was hospitalized the Indians recalled Chico Salmon from Class AAA Portland, and the little Panamanian went on to hit .307, the only position player to top .300.

Leon "Daddy Wags" Wagner, acquired from the Los Angeles Angels in the deal for Joe Adcock and Barry Latman the previous winter, was the Tribe's most productive hitter with 31 homers and 100 runs batted in, with a .253 average.

Two other players promoted from Portland also played prominent roles in what little success the Indians experienced.

Sam McDowell was recalled on May 30 after going 8–0 at Class AAA Portland. He promptly won three games for the Tribe, finishing the season with an 11–6 record and 177 strikeouts in 173⅓ innings. His 2.70 earned run average was best among the starting pitchers on the staff.

Luis Tiant, 15–1 at Portland, was summoned on July 17 and also was an immediate sensation. In his debut July 19 in Yankee Stadium, Tiant pitched a four-hitter to beat New York, 3–0, for the first of his 10 victories—which was one of only three the Indians would register in 18 games with the Yankees that season.

	W	L	G	GS	CG	IP	H	BB	K	ERA
Ted Abernathy	7	2	43	0	0	59⅓	54	29	47	2.88
Bob Allen	1	2	43	0	0	56	58	29	51	4.66
Gary Bell	8	5	58	7	0	119	91	52	98	2.95
Jack Curtis	0	0	4	0	0	5	8	5	3	18.00
Dick Donovan	11	13	30	30	7	206	211	28	84	4.24
Mudcat Grant	13	14	38	32	10	229⅓	213	87	157	3.69
Tommy John	0	2	6	3	0	20⅓	23	6	9	2.21
Jack Kralick	13	9	28	27	10	197⅓	187	41	116	2.92
Barry Latman	7	12	38	21	4	149⅓	146	52	133	4.94
Sam McDowell	3	5	14	12	3	65	63	44	63	4.85
Ron Nischwitz	0	2	14	0	0	16⅔	17	8	10	6.48
Jim Perry	0	0	5	0	0	10⅓	12	2	7	5.23
Pedro Ramos	9	8	36	22	5	184⅔	156	41	169	3.12
Gordon Seyfried	0	1	3	1	0	7⅓	9	3	1	1.23
Jerry Walker	6	6	39	2	0	88	92	36	41	4.91
Early Wynn	1	2	20	5	1	55⅓	50	15	29	2.28
	79	83	(162)	40	(1,469)	1,390	478	(1,018)	3.79	

Shutouts: Donovan (3), Kralick (3), Grant (2), Latman (2), McDowell
Saves: Abernathy (12), Bell (5), Allen (2), Latman (2), Grant, Nischwitz, Walker, Wynn

Though playing without Tebbetts at the helm, the Indians set the AL pace early, winning 11 of their first 16 games, grabbing first place and holding it until May 8.

Shortly thereafter Jim "Mudcat" Grant was traded to Minnesota on June 15 for Lee Stange and George Banks. The Indians also received an undisclosed amount of cash, reportedly to enable them to meet the payroll.

Grant won 11 games for the Twins, while Stange went 4–8, and Banks played only nine games for the Indians.

Gabe Paul was forced to make another deal on September 5 that also was motivated by a need for money to meet the payroll. Pedro Ramos was sent to the Yankees for $75,000 and two players to be named after the season (who turned out to be Ralph Terry and Bud Daley).

And without Ramos's seven saves and one victory in 13 relief appearances down the stretch, the Yankees would not have been able to overtake Baltimore and Chicago to win the pennant.

Attendance improved slightly, to 653,293, but not enough to turn a profit and Paul disclosed that the club's losses would approximate the $1.2 million suffered in 1963. In order to have an operating fund, he further revealed that each stockholder had been called upon to contribute cash over and above his original investment. In his case, Paul said, it amounted to $60,000.

Reports that Seattle was wooing the Indians finally were confirmed on September 17 by that city's mayor. Paul also admitted that an Oakland syndicate had sought to buy the club, offering $6.5 million, but that the bid was turned down.

On October 5, Tribe directors voted to send Paul and William R. Daley, chairman of the board, on a three-day "fact-finding" tour of Seattle, Oakland, and Dallas, all of which were seeking to lure the Tribe away from Cleveland.

Paul and Daley reported back to the directors on October 16 and they voted to keep the team in Cleveland and to sign a new 10-year lease for the Stadium. They insisted upon an escape clause, however, that would enable either party to cancel the contract at the end of any calendar year, upon 90 days notice.

The picture was further brightened when the Greater Cleveland Growth Board sold more than 4,500 season tickets for 1965, representing a dollar amount of more than $900,000.

	W	L	G	GS	CG	IP	H	BB	K	ERA
Ted Abernathy	2	6	53	0	0	72⅔	66	46	57	4.33
Gary Bell	8	6	56	2	0	106	106	53	89	4.33
Dick Donovan	7	9	30	23	5	158⅓	181	29	83	4.55
Mudcat Grant	3	4	13	9	1	62	82	25	43	5.95
Tommy John	2	9	25	14	2	94⅓	97	35	65	3.91
Tom Kelley	0	0	6	0	0	9¾	9	9	7	5.59
Jack Kralick	12	7	30	29	8	190⅔	196	51	119	3.21
Sam McDowell	11	6	31	24	6	173⅓	148	100	177	2.70
Don McMahon	6	4	70	0	0	101	67	52	92	2.41
Pedro Ramos	7	10	36	19	3	133	144	26	98	5.14
Gordon Seyfried	0	0	2	0	0	2⅓	4	0	0	0.00
Sonny Siebert	7	9	41	14	3	156	142	57	144	3.23
Lee Stange	4	8	23	14	0	91¾	98	31	78	4.12
Luis Tiant	10	4	19	16	9	127	94	47	105	2.83
Jerry Walker	0	1	6	0	0	9¾	9	4	5	4.66
	79	83	(164)	37	1,487⅔	1,443	565	(1,162)	3.75

Shutouts: Kralick (3), Tiant (3), McDowell (2), John, Ramos, Siebert
Saves: McMahon (16), Abernathy (11), Bell (4), Siebert (3), Donovan, McDowell, Tiant

	G	AB	R	H	2B	3B	HR	RBI	SB	AVG
Tommie Agee	13	12	0	2	0	0	0	0	0	.167
Max Alvis (3B)	107	381	51	96	14	3	18	53	3	.252
Joe Azcue	83	271	20	74	9	1	4	34	0	.273
George Banks	9	17	6	5	1	0	2	3	0	.294
Larry Brown (2B)	115	335	33	77	12	1	12	40	1	.230
Bob Chance (1B)	120	390	45	109	16	1	14	75	3	.279
Vic Davalillo (CF)	150	577	64	156	26	2	6	51	21	.270
Paul Dicken	11	11	0	0	0	0	0	0	0	.000
Tito Francona (RF)	111	270	35	67	13	2	8	24	1	.248
Vern Fuller	2	1	0	0	0	0	0	0	0	.000
Woodie Held	118	364	50	86	13	0	18	49	1	.236
Dick Howser (SS)	162	637	101	163	23	4	3	52	20	.256
Jerry Kindall	23	25	5	9	1	0	2	2	0	.360
Al Luplow	19	18	1	2	0	0	0	1	0	.111
Tony Martinez	9	14	1	3	1	0	0	2	0	.214
Billy Moran	69	151	14	31	6	0	1	10	0	.205
Wally Post	5	8	1	0	0	0	0	0	0	.000
Johnny Romano (C)	106	352	46	85	18	1	19	47	2	.241
Chico Salmon	86	283	43	87	17	2	4	25	10	.307
Duke Sims	2	6	0	0	0	0	0	0	0	.000
Al Smith	61	136	15	22	1	1	4	9	0	.162
Leon Wagner (LF)	(163)	641	94	162	19	2	31	100	14	.253
Fred Whitfield	101	293	29	79	13	1	10	29	0	.270
		5,603	689	1,386	208	22	164	640	(79)	.247

1965

Record: 87–75
Finish: Fifth
Games Behind: 15
Manager: Birdie Tebbetts

In a bold attempt to undo the 1960 trade of Rocky Colavito that incensed so many fans, Gabe Paul, who was determined to make a success of the Indians on the field and at the gate, reacquired the popular outfielder on January 20.

In so doing, however, Paul compounded the mistake made five years earlier by Frank Lane. Paul gave up two of the Tribe's best young players, Tommy John and Tommie Agee, as well as veteran catcher John Romano, to return Colavito to Cleveland.

Colavito made an immediate impact, hitting .287 with 26 homers and leading the American League with 108 runs batted in. He finished fifth in the voting for the Most Valuable Player award, won by Minnesota's Zoilo Versalles.

But Colavito's contributions weren't enough to cure the Tribe's ills, while John and Agee went on to play well for their new teams.

Colavito, along with Leon Wagner and Fred Whitfield, and the rapid development of Sam McDowell and Sonny Siebert (who won 17 and 16 games, respectively) propelled the Tribe into first place for a week, June 28–July 5.

Wagner clouted 28 homers while batting .294, and Whitfield contributed 26, including a pinch-hit grand slam in the second game of a doubleheader on May 16 as the Indians beat the Senators in Washington, 7–3.

McDowell led the American League with 325 strikeouts in 273 innings, and also compiled the best earned run average, 2.18.

Though they played only .500 ball their first 40 games, after splitting a doubleheader with Chicago on May 31 the Indians spurted to 23 victories in 29 games, including 10 straight from June 13 to 22.

They were second with a 48–34 record at the All-Star break, but fell apart thereafter, going 39–41. Minnesota rolled to the pennant with former Tribesmen Jim "Mudcat" Grant winning 21 games and Jim Perry 12.

Still, the Indians' 87 victories were the most since 1959, and they were the only American League team to win the season series against the Twins, 11–7.

One of the 75 losses was a no-hitter by Dave Morehead of the Red Sox, who beat the Tribe, 2–0, on September 16 in Boston.

Colavito's return together with the Indians' midseason resurgence, brought about a healthy increase in attendance, which climbed to 934,786, further quieting rumors that Cleveland was in jeopardy of losing the franchise.

Gabe Paul was among the final 10 candidates to replace the retiring Ford C. Frick as commissioner of baseball, though the position eventually went to William D. Eckert, a retired Air Force lieutenant general.

The 1965 season also marked the beginning of baseball's amateur draft, and the Indians' first selection was Ray Fosse, an 18-year-old catcher from Marion, Illinois, who was the seventh player picked overall.

	W	L	G	GS	CG	IP	H	BB	K	ERA
Gary Bell	6	5	60	0	0	103⅔	86	50	86	3.04
Dick Donovan	1	3	12	3	0	22⅔	32	6	12	5.96
Steve Hargan	4	3	17	8	1	60⅓	55	28	37	3.43
Mike Hedlund	0	0	6	0	0	5⅓	6	5	4	5.06
Tom Kelley	2	1	4	4	1	30	19	13	31	2.40
Jack Kralick	5	11	30	16	1	86	106	21	34	4.92
Sam McDowell	17	11	42	35	14	273	178	(132)	(325)	(2.18)
Don McMahon	3	3	58	0	0	85	79	37	60	3.28
Sonny Siebert	16	8	39	27	4	188⅔	139	46	191	2.43
Jack Spring	1	2	14	0	0	21⅔	21	10	9	3.74
Lee Stange	8	4	41	12	4	132	122	26	80	3.34
Ralph Terry	11	6	30	26	6	165⅔	154	23	84	3.69
Luis Tiant	11	11	41	30	10	196⅓	166	66	152	3.53
Bobby Tiefenauer	0	5	15	0	0	22⅓	24	10	13	4.84
Floyd Weaver	2	2	32	1	0	61⅓	61	24	37	5.43
Stan Williams	0	0	3	0	0	4⅓	6	3	1	6.23
	87	75	(162)	41		1,458⅓	1,254	500	(1,156)	3.30

Shutouts: McDowell (3), Stange (2), Terry (2), Tiant (2), Siebert
Saves: Bell (17), McMahon (11), McDowell (4), Tiefenauer (4), Hargan (2), Siebert, Tiant, Weaver

	G	AB	R	H	2B	3B	HR	RBI	SB	AVG
Max Alvis (3B)	159	604	88	149	24	2	21	61	12	.247
Joe Azcue (C)	111	335	16	77	7	0	2	35	2	.230
George Banks	4	5	0	1	1	0	0	0	0	.200
Ray Barker	11	6	0	0	0	0	0	0	0	.000
Larry Brown (SS)	124	438	52	111	22	2	8	40	5	.253
Camilo Carreon	19	52	6	12	2	1	1	7	1	.231
Lu Clinton	12	34	2	6	1	0	1	2	0	.176
Rocky Colavito (RF)	(162)	592	92	170	25	2	26	(108)	1	.287
Vic Davalillo (CF)	142	505	67	152	19	1	5	40	26	.301
Bill Davis	10	10	0	3	1	0	0	0	0	.300
Ralph Gagliano	1	0	0	0	0	0	0	0	0	—
Pedro Gonzalez (2B)	116	400	38	101	14	3	5	39	7	.253
Chuck Hinton	133	431	59	110	17	6	18	54	17	.255
Dick Howser	107	307	47	72	8	2	1	6	17	.235
Al Luplow	53	45	3	6	2	0	1	4	0	.133
Tony Martinez	4	3	0	0	0	0	0	0	0	.000
Billy Moran	22	24	1	3	0	0	0	0	0	.125
Phil Roof	43	52	3	9	1	0	0	3	0	.173
Chico Salmon	79	120	20	29	8	0	3	12	7	.242
Richie Scheinblum	4	1	1	0	0	0	0	0	0	.000
Duke Sims	48	118	9	21	0	0	6	15	0	.178
Leon Wagner (LF)	144	517	91	152	18	1	28	79	12	.294
Fred Whitfield (1B)	132	468	49	137	23	1	26	90	2	.293
		5,469	663	1,367	198	21	156	615	109	.250

1966

Record: 81–81
Finish: Fifth
Games Behind: 17
Managers: Birdie Tebbetts, George Strickland

An early case of pennant fever struck Cleveland as the Indians opened the season with 10 consecutive victories, beginning on April 11 as Sam McDowell beat the Senators in Washington, 5–2. They led the American League for most of the first nine weeks.

The winning streak at the beginning of the season broke the AL record of nine set by the St. Louis Browns in 1944 and tied the major league mark held by the 1955 Brooklyn Dodgers and 1962 Pittsburgh Pirates.

After the opening-day victory, the Tribe went on to win over Boston, 8–7, 3–2, and 6–0; New York, 3–1 and 4–2; the Red Sox, 5–4, in Boston; Kansas City, 2–0 and 4–0; and California, 2–1; before losing to Chicago, 4–1, on a six-hitter by Gary Peters.

McDowell, who hurled a one-hitter over the Athletics on April 24, pitched another one in his next start to beat the White Sox, 1–0, on May 1.

Kansas City's only hit was a single by Jose Tartabull in the sixth inning, and Chicago's Don Buford spoiled McDowell's bid for a no-hitter with a bloop double with two out in the third inning.

The Indians raised their record to 12–1, beating New York, 2–1, in Yankee Stadium. It proved to be a costly victory—though, fortunately, it wasn't worse—as shortstop Larry Brown and left fielder Leon Wagner collided while chasing a short fly by Roger Maris that fell for a double.

Brown suffered fractures of the skull, cheekbone, and nose that kept him out of action for six weeks. Wagner escaped with a concussion and broken nose, and was able to play two days later.

After an 8–2 loss in the first game of a May 8 doubleheader in Baltimore dropping the Tribe's record to 15–3, Luis Tiant pitched the second game, putting his 27-consecutive-scoreless-innings streak on the line. It ended in a hurry, however, as Frank Robinson blasted the first home run ever hit completely out of Memorial Stadium in the first inning of an Orioles 8–3 victory.

But the Indians didn't blink and continued winning through May 28 when they led the AL by 4½ lengths, in the wake of five straight victories, for a 27–10 mark.

However, more misfortune struck during the surge as McDowell suffered a strained deltoid muscle in his left shoulder on May 25 that idled him for nearly three weeks.

McDowell was seldom the same thereafter, although on September 18 he appeared to have the major strikeout record in sight in a game in Detroit.

Leading the Tigers, 5–1, McDowell had fanned 14 through the first six innings, but was unable to continue because of a recurrence of his shoulder injury. John O'Donoghue and Luis Tiant finished, and the Indians prevailed, 6–5.

McDowell finished the season with nine victories and eight losses, while striking out 225 batters in 194⅓ innings.

Sonny Siebert pitched the 12th no-hitter in Indians history on June 10, beating Washington, 2–0, at the Stadium. He was the Tribe's biggest winner with 16 victories, while missing the final three weeks of the season also with a sore shoulder.

Despite their fast start and the excellent early pitching of McDowell, Siebert, and Steve Hargan, the Indians went from the best team in the AL to one of the worst in the short space of three months.

Rocky Colavito hammered 30 homers but drove in only 72 runs while slumping to .238. Leon Wagner batted .279, but his home run and RBI production fell off to 23 and 66.

The plunge out of contention began on May 29 when the Indians were beaten in a doubleheader by Minnesota and went on to lose six of seven games.

It was at that point, on June 2, that Dick Radatz was acquired from Boston in an attempt to strengthen the shaky relief corps. It didn't work.

Radatz, the AL's premier fireman from 1962 to 1964, appeared in 39 games in 1966 and was charged with three losses without a victory. He had a bloated 4.61 earned run average.

The Indians fell out of first place on June 14, lost four of their next six, and dropped into third place on June 20. They trailed the league-leading Orioles by 10 games at the All-Star break, and Tebbetts resigned on August 19 with the Indians' record 66–57.

George Strickland again took over on an interim basis, but the change made no difference as the Indians lost 24 of their last 39 games, concluding what had promised to be one of the best seasons in franchise history as one of the most distressing.

The Indians suffered another major setback during 1966, though they didn't realize the extent of it at the time, losing a three-way drawing for the right to sign an amateur pitcher named Tom Seaver. They were in competition with the Philadelphia Phillies and New York Mets for Seaver, and the issue was settled with a lottery conducted by Commissioner William D. Eckert.

Controlling interest in the Indians again changed hands on August 13 as Vernon Stouffer purchased most of the stock held by Gabe Paul, William R. Daley, and their associates, for a reported $8 million. It was the franchise's fifth major change of ownership since 1946 when Bill Veeck bought the club for $1.1 million.

Stouffer, who had been a minor stockholder and member of the board of directors since 1962, took over as chairman. He announced plans to revamp the board to include only Clevelanders "to make sure the club stays here." Paul remained a stockholder and signed a 10-year contract to continue as president and general manager.

	G	AB	R	H	2B	3B	HR	RBI	SB	AVG
Max Alvis (3B)	157	596	67	146	22	3	17	55	4	.245
Joe Azcue (C)	98	302	22	83	10	1	9	37	0	.275
George Banks	4	4	0	1	0	0	0	1	0	.250
Buddy Booker	18	28	6	6	1	0	2	5	0	.214
Larry Brown (SS)	105	340	29	78	12	0	3	17	0	.229
Rocky Colavito (RF)	151	533	68	127	13	0	30	72	2	.238
Del Crandall	50	108	10	25	2	0	4	8	0	.231
Tony Curry	19	16	4	2	0	0	0	3	0	.125
Vic Davalillo (CF)	121	344	42	86	6	4	3	19	8	.250
Bill Davis	23	38	2	6	1	0	1	4	0	.158
Paul Dicken	2	2	0	0	0	0	0	0	0	.000
Vern Fuller	16	47	7	11	2	1	2	2	0	.234
Jim Gentile	33	47	2	6	1	0	2	4	0	.128
Pedro Gonzalez (2B)	110	352	21	82	9	2	2	17	8	.233
Chuck Hinton	123	348	46	89	9	3	12	50	10	.256
Dick Howser	67	140	18	32	9	1	2	4	2	.229
Jim Landis	85	158	23	35	5	1	3	14	2	.222
Tony Martinez	17	17	2	5	0	0	0	0	1	.294
Chico Salmon	126	422	46	108	13	2	7	40	10	.256
Duke Sims	52	133	12	35	2	2	6	19	0	.263
Jose Vidal	17	32	4	6	1	1	0	3	0	.188
Leon Wagner (LF)	150	549	70	153	20	0	23	66	5	.279
Fred Whitfield (1B)	137	502	59	121	15	2	27	78	1	.241
	5,474	574	1,300	156	25	155	536	53	.237	

1967

Record: 75–87
Finish: Eighth
Games Behind: 17
Manager: Joe Adcock

Gabe Paul said that not hiring Bob Lemon in 1967 was his biggest mistake in baseball.

Instead, he gave Joe Adcock a two-year contract to manage the Indians through 1968.

Paul's stated objective in turning the team over to Adcock was to improve both discipline among the players and their execution of fundamentals, though much more was needed—especially a stronger offense and better pitching.

The Indians never progressed under Adcock. Their record never climbed more than two games over .500. It fell below the break-even point on July 9, to 40–41, and never got any better. They wound up in eighth place, their lowest finish since 1914.

The Tribe's 87 losses also were the most since 1928, and the 75 victories the fewest since 1946.

One of the defeats was a no-hitter by Minnesota's Dean Chance, 2–1, in the second game of a doubleheader on August 25 at the Stadium. The Indians' run scored in the first inning on two walks, an error, and a wild pitch.

The day the season ended Paul fired Adcock, eating the last year of the manager's contract. Hired to replace Adcock was Alvin Dark, who had been let out as manager of the Kansas City Athletics by Charlie Finley in late August.

It had been another season of travail as both Rocky Colavito and Leon Wagner resented being platooned by Adcock. Colavito played against left-handers and Wagner against right-handers, and both demanded to be traded.

Colavito, hitting .241 with five homers and 21 runs batted in, was accommodated on July 29. He was sent to the Chicago White Sox for outfielder Jim King, infielder Marvin Staehle, and cash. Neither player did anything worth mentioning for the Tribe.

Wagner then took over as the regular left fielder, but batted only .242 with 15 homers and 54 RBIs.

	W	L	G	GS	CG	IP	H	BB	K	ERA
Bob Allen	2	2	36	0	0	51⅓	56	13	33	4.21
Gary Bell	14	15	40	37	12	254⅓	211	79	194	3.22
George Culver	0	2	5	1	0	9⅔	15	7	6	8.38
Steve Hargan	13	10	38	21	7	192	173	45	132	2.48
Bob Heffner	0	1	5	1	0	13	12	3	7	3.46
Tom Kelley	4	8	31	7	1	95⅓	97	42	64	4.34
Jack Kralick	3	4	27	4	0	68⅓	69	20	31	3.82
Sam McDowell	9	8	35	28	8	194⅓	130	102	(225)	2.87
Don McMahon	1	1	12	0	0	12⅓	8	6	5	2.92
John O'Donoghue	6	8	32	13	2	108	109	23	49	3.83
Dick Radatz	0	3	39	0	0	56⅔	49	34	49	4.61
Sonny Siebert	16	8	34	32	11	241	193	62	163	2.80
Lee Stange	1	0	8	2	1	16	17	3	8	2.81
Luis Tiant	12	11	46	16	7	155	121	50	145	2.79
	81	81		162	49	1,467⅓	1,260	489	(1,111)	3.23

Shutouts: McDowell (5), Tiant (5), Hargan (3), Siebert
Saves: Radatz (10), Tiant (8), Allen (5), McDowell (3), McMahon, Siebert

The Indians big guns of 1967 (left to right): outfielder Chuck Hinton, first baseman Fred Whitfield, outfielders Leon Wagner and Rocky Colavito, and third baseman Max Alvis.

Even before Colavito was traded, Paul dealt Gary Bell, who was only 1–5 in his first nine games, to Boston for Tony Horton and Don Demeter. While Bell couldn't win for Adcock, he was a key factor in the Red Sox drive to the pennant.

The only noteworthy contributions were by Max Alvis, who was elected for the second time the Indians' Man of the Year, and Horton, who played well after coming to Cleveland, resulting in the trading of Fred Whitfield when the season ended.

Pitching, which was supposed to be the Indians' strong point, wasn't. Their "big four"—Sam McDowell, Sonny Siebert, Luis Tiant, and Steve Hargan—accounted for only 49 victories, and they lost the same number.

The Indians' sorry performance on the field resulted in another decline in attendance. Only 667,623 fans came through the turnstiles, a drop of more than 235,000. It was the lowest in the major leagues.

	W	L	G	GS	CG	IP	H	BB	K	ERA
Bob Allen	0	5	47	0	0	54⅓	49	25	50	2.98
Steve Bailey	2	5	32	1	0	64⅔	62	42	46	3.90
Gary Bell	1	5	9	9	1	60⅔	50	24	39	3.71
Ed Connolly	2	1	15	4	0	49⅓	63	34	45	7.48
George Culver	7	3	53	1	0	75	71	31	41	3.96
Steve Hargan	14	13	30	29	15	223	180	72	141	2.62
Tom Kelley	0	0	1	0	0	1	0	2	0	0.00
Jack Kralick	0	2	2	0	0	2	4	1	1	9.00
Sam McDowell	13	15	37	37	10	236⅓	201	(123)	236	3.85
John O'Donoghue	8	9	33	17	5	130⅔	120	33	81	3.24
Orlando Pena	0	3	48	1	0	88⅓	67	22	72	3.36
Dick Radatz	0	0	3	0	0	3	5	2	1	6.00
Sonny Siebert	10	12	34	26	7	185⅓	136	54	136	2.38
Luis Tiant	12	9	33	29	9	213⅔	177	67	219	2.74
Bobby Tiefenauer	0	1	5	0	0	11⅓	9	3	6	0.79
Stan Williams	6	4	16	8	2	79	64	24	75	2.62
	75	87		162	49	1,477⅔	1,258	559	(1,189)	3.25

Shutouts: Hargan (6), O'Donoghue (2), McDowell, Siebert, Tiant, Williams
Saves: Pena (8), Allen (5), Siebert (4), Culver (3), Bailey (2), O'Donoghue (2), Tiant (2), Williams

	G	AB	R	H	2B	3B	HR	RBI	SB	AVG
Max Alvis (3B)	161	637	66	163	23	4	21	70	3	.256
Joe Azcue (C)	86	295	33	74	12	5	11	34	0	.251
Larry Brown (SS)	152	485	38	110	16	2	7	37	4	.227
Rocky Colavito	63	191	10	46	9	0	5	21	2	.241
Vic Davalillo (CF)	139	359	47	103	17	5	2	22	6	.287
Don Demeter	51	121	15	25	4	0	5	12	0	.207
Ray Fosse	7	16	0	1	0	0	0	0	0	.063
Vern Fuller (2B)	73	206	18	46	10	0	7	21	2	.223
Gus Gil	51	96	11	11	4	0	0	5	0	.115
Pedro Gonzalez	80	189	19	43	6	0	1	8	4	.228
Chuck Hinton (RF)	147	498	55	122	19	3	10	37	6	.245
Tony Horton (1B)	106	363	35	102	13	4	10	44	3	.281
Jim King	19	21	2	3	0	0	0	0	0	.143
Gordon Lund	3	8	1	2	1	0	0	0	0	.250
Lee Maye	115	297	43	77	20	4	9	27	3	.259
Chico Salmon	90	203	19	46	13	1	2	19	10	.227
Richie Scheinblum	18	66	8	21	4	2	0	6	0	.318
Duke Sims	88	272	25	55	8	2	12	37	3	.202
Willie Smith	21	32	0	7	2	0	0	2	0	.219
Jose Vidal	16	34	4	4	0	0	0	0	0	.118
Leon Wagner (LF)	135	433	56	105	15	1	15	54	3	.242
Fred Whitfield	100	257	24	56	10	0	9	31	3	.218
		5,461	559	1,282	213	35	131	514	53	.235

1968

Record: 86–75
Finish: Third
Games Behind: 16½
Manager: Alvin Dark

Alvin Dark, the Indians' 25th manager and fourth in three years, led them to their best finish since 1959. As he said, they were "just one player away from winning the pennant."

That one player, according to Dark, was "a consistent, long-ball hitter," as the team batting average was .234. Only two players homered in double figures—Tony Horton with 14 and a team-high 59 RBIs, and Duke Sims with 11 homers.

Indians Manager Alvin Dark (right) gives hitting instructions to first baseman Tony Horton.

The Indians' pitching was something else, led by Luis Tiant, whose 1.60 earned run average was the best in the AL. With his 21–9 won-lost record, Tiant became the first Tribe pitcher to win 20 games since Dick Donovan in 1962.

Sam McDowell was almost as effective, posting a 1.81 ERA while winning 15 games.

The Indians were in or near second place from mid-May to early July. They were still in the thick of the pennant race until they opened a make-or-break series in Detroit on August 6.

At that point, on the eve of the first of seven games in nine days against the American League–leading Tigers, the Tribe was third, 8½ games off the pace.

In the first game of that head-to-head confrontation, the Indians were leading, 1–0, behind Tiant, until Tigers third baseman Don Wert clouted a solo homer in the eighth inning. The game remained tied until the 17th inning when Detroit's Dick Tracewski singled home the winning run off Mike Paul.

The Indians lost six of those seven games against the Tigers, falling 13½ lengths behind. They bounced back in mid-September, winning 10 of their last 14, but it was too late.

The pennant-winning Tigers were tough on the Tribe all season, winning 12 of the 18 games between them. Included was a 14–3 decision on June 24 at the Stadium when Jim Northrup smashed back-to-back grand slam homers in the fifth and sixth innings off Eddie Fisher and Billy Rohr, tying a major league record.

Four promising minor leaguers and two veteran players were lost by the Indians in the expansion draft, as Kansas City and Seattle came into the American League. Seattle selected Lou Piniella (and later traded him to Kansas City), Chico Salmon, and Tommy Harper from the Tribe, while Kansas City took Fran Healy, Mike Hedlund, and Billy Harris.

It also was during the 1968 season that the Indians were

the victims of the eighth unassisted triple play in major league history. It was accomplished by Washington shortstop Ron Hansen in the first inning of a game at the Stadium on July 30. It came on a line drive by Joe Azcue, after Dave Nelson had singled and Russ Snyder walked. The Indians still won the game, 10–1.

	W	L	G	GS	CG	IP	H	BB	K	ERA
Steve Bailey	0	1	2	1	0	5	4	2	1	3.60
Eddie Fisher	4	2	54	0	0	94⅔	87	17	42	2.85
Rob Gardner	0	0	5	0	0	2⅔	5	2	6	6.75
Tommy Gramly	0	1	3	0	0	3⅓	3	2	1	2.70
Steve Hargan	8	15	32	27	4	158⅓	139	81	78	4.15
Mike Hedlund	0	0	3	0	0	1⅔	6	2	0	10.80
Hal Kurtz	1	0	28	0	0	38	37	15	16	5.21
Sam McDowell	15	14	38	37	11	269	181	(110)	(283)	1.81
Mike Paul	5	8	36	7	0	91⅓	72	35	87	3.93
Horacio Pina	1	1	12	3	0	31⅓	24	15	24	1.72
Billy Rohr	1	0	17	0	0	18⅓	18	10	5	6.87
Vicente Romo	5	3	40	1	0	83⅓	43	32	54	1.62
Sonny Siebert	12	10	31	30	8	206	145	88	146	2.97
Willie Smith	0	0	2	0	0	5	2	1	1	0.00
Darrell Sutherland	0	0	3	0	0	3⅓	6	4	2	8.10
Luis Tiant	21	9	34	32	19	258⅓	152	73	264	(1.60)
Stan Williams	13	11	44	24	6	194⅓	163	51	147	2.50
	86	75		162	48	1,464⅓	1,087	(540)	(1,157)	(2.66)

Shutouts: Tiant (9), Siebert (4), McDowell (3), Hargan (2), Williams (2)
Saves: Romo (12), Williams (9), Fisher (4), Paul (3), Pina (2), Kurtz, Rohr

	G	AB	R	H	2B	3B	HR	RBI	SB	AVG
Max Alvis (3B)	131	452	38	101	17	3	8	37	5	.223
Joe Azcue (C)	115	357	23	100	10	0	4	42	1	.280
Larry Brown (SS)	154	495	43	116	18	3	6	35	1	.234
Jose Cardenal (CF)	157	583	78	150	21	7	7	44	40	.257
Vic Davalillo	51	180	15	43	2	3	2	13	8	.239
Ray Fosse	1	0	0	0	0	0	0	0	0	—
Vern Fuller (2B)	97	244	14	59	8	2	0	18	2	.242
Jimmie Hall	53	111	4	22	4	0	1	8	1	.198
Tommy Harper (RF)	130	235	26	51	15	2	6	26	11	.217
Billy Harris	38	94	10	20	5	1	0	3	2	.213
Tony Horton (1B)	133	477	57	119	29	3	14	59	3	.249
Lou Johnson	65	202	25	52	11	1	5	23	6	.257
Lou Klimchock	11	15	0	2	0	0	0	3	0	.133
Eddie Leon	6	1	0	0	0	0	0	0	0	.000
Lee Maye (LF)	109	299	20	84	13	2	4	26	0	.281
Russ Nagelson	5	3	0	1	0	0	0	0	0	.333
Dave Nelson	88	189	26	44	4	5	0	19	23	.233
Lou Piniella	6	5	1	0	0	0	0	1	0	.000
Chico Salmon	103	276	24	59	8	1	3	12	7	.214
Richie Scheinblum	19	55	3	12	5	0	0	5	0	.218
Duke Sims	122	361	48	90	21	0	11	44	1	.249
Willie Smith	33	42	1	6	2	0	0	3	0	.143
Russ Snyder	68	217	30	61	8	2	2	23	1	.281
Ken Suarez	17	10	1	1	0	0	0	0	0	.100
Jose Vidal	37	54	5	9	0	0	2	5	3	.167
Leon Wagner	38	49	5	9	4	0	0	6	0	.184
		5,416	516	1,266	210	36	75	476	115	.234

1969

Record: 62–99
Finish: Sixth
Games Behind: 46½
Manager: Alvin Dark

I t was supposed to be a return to glory for the Indians, based on their strong performance in 1968.

Instead, 1969 turned out to be another disastrous season—not only in the won-lost column, but also in the front office as a nasty power struggle erupted between general manager Gabe Paul and manager Alvin Dark.

On the field the Indians lost 99 games, second-most in the

history of the team. They might have suffered 100 defeats if they had not been rained out in the final game of the season in New York.

And in the front office, climaxing a struggle for control that had been brewing since the winter, principal owner Vernon Stouffer put Dark in charge of all player personnel matters, making him, in essence, the general manager without title.

Paul, relegated to handling the club's financial, marketing, and promotional duties, declined any public criticism of Dark, the man he hired to manage the Indians.

Paul's standard comment: "I am a happy warrior. I have no complaints."

Still, there was no doubt that much animosity existed between the two men.

Though it wasn't until July 8 that Stouffer, in effect, demoted Paul without ever publicly announcing it, the Indians made a major trade 12 days after the season began that should have alerted observers that Dark was calling most of the shots.

On April 19 the Tribe traded Sonny Siebert, Vicente Romo, and Joe Azcue to Boston for one of Dark's longtime favorites, Ken "The Hawk" Harrelson, the American League's Player of the Year in 1968. Dick Ellsworth and Juan Pizarro were included with Harrelson in the deal.

Paul did not like the trade because the Indians already had Tony Horton to play first base, and neither Horton nor Harrelson could play another position to major league standards.

Then, to make the deal even more controversial, Harrelson refused to report unless his contract was renegotiated.

After a week of haggling, Harrelson prevailed, and he joined the Indians, though his presence had little effect on the struggling team. The Tribe lost its first five games, 15 of 16, and resided in sixth (and last) place in the newly formed American League East from wire to wire.

Horton and Harrelson each hit 27 homers, though Horton's RBI total was better, 93–84. So was his batting average, .278–.222.

Sam McDowell was the only starting pitcher to win more than he lost, compiling an 18–14 record, while neither Ellsworth (6–9) nor Pizarro (3–3) made an impact, further damning the trade for Harrelson.

Luis Tiant (9–20) didn't come close to his sensational performance in 1968. During the winter meetings he was traded with Stan Williams to Minnesota for Graig Nettles, Ted Uhlaender, Dean Chance, and Bob Miller.

"It was a horrible season," was Dark's assessment of 1969. Few disagreed, especially not Indians fans, of whom only 619,970 paid their way through the gates.

The Indians were 11 games out of first place on May 1, and never got any closer. They finished with their largest deficit since 1914, when they were last by 48½ lengths.

McDowell led AL pitchers in strikeouts, with 279, for the second straight year and fourth in the last five, and was elected the Indians' Man of the Year for 1969.

	W	L	G	GS	CG	IP	H	BB	K	ERA
Gary Boyd	0	2	8	3	0	11	8	14	9	9.00
Larry Burchart	0	2	29	0	0	42⅓	42	24	26	4.25
Dick Ellsworth	6	9	34	22	3	135	162	40	48	4.13
Jack Hamilton	0	2	20	0	0	30⅔	37	23	13	4.40
Steve Hargan	5	14	32	23	1	143⅔	145	81	76	5.70
Phil Hennigan	2	1	9	0	0	16⅓	14	4	10	3.31
Gary Kroll	0	0	19	0	0	24	16	22	28	4.13
Ron Law	3	4	35	1	0	52⅓	68	34	29	4.99
Sam McDowell	18	14	39	38	18	285	222	102	(279)	2.94
Mike Paul	5	10	47	12	0	117⅓	104	54	98	3.61
Horacio Pina	4	2	31	4	0	46⅔	44	27	32	5.21
Juan Pizarro	3	3	48	4	1	82⅔	67	49	44	3.16
Vicente Romo	1	1	3	0	0	8	7	3	7	2.25
Sonny Siebert	0	1	2	2	0	14	10	8	6	3.21
Luis Tiant	9	(20)	38	37	9	249⅔	229	(129)	156	3.71
Stan Williams	6	14	61	15	3	178¼	155	67	139	3.94
	62	(99)		161	35	1,437	1,330	681	1,000	3.94

Shutouts: McDowell (4), Ellsworth, Hargan, Tiant
Saves: Williams (12), Pizarro (4), Paul (2), Hamilton, Law, McDowell, Pina

	G	AB	R	H	2B	3B	HR	RBI	SB	AVG
Max Alvis (3B)	66	191	13	43	6	0	1	15	1	.225
Joe Azcue	7	24	1	7	0	0	1	1	0	.292
Frank Baker	52	172	21	44	5	3	3	15	2	.256
Larry Brown (SS)	132	469	48	112	10	2	4	24	5	.239
Lou Camilli	13	14	0	0	0	0	0	0	0	.000
Jose Cardenal (CF)	146	557	75	143	26	3	11	45	36	.257
Ray Fosse	37	116	11	20	3	0	2	9	1	.172
Vern Fuller (2B)	108	254	25	60	11	1	4	22	2	.236
Jimmie Hall	4	10	1	0	0	0	0	0	1	.000
Ken Harrelson (RF)	149	519	83	115	13	4	27	84	17	.222
Jack Heidemann	3	3	0	0	0	0	0	0	0	.000
Chuck Hinton	94	121	18	31	3	2	3	19	2	.256
Tony Horton (1B)	159	625	77	174	25	4	27	93	3	.278
Lou Klimchock	90	258	26	74	13	2	6	26	0	.287
Eddie Leon	64	213	20	51	6	0	3	19	2	.239
Lee Maye	43	108	9	27	5	0	1	15	1	.250
Russ Nagelson	12	17	1	6	0	0	0	0	0	.353
Dave Nelson	52	123	11	25	0	0	0	6	4	.203
Cap Peterson	76	110	8	25	3	0	1	14	0	.227
Richie Scheinblum	102	199	13	37	5	1	1	13	0	.186
Duke Sims (C)	114	326	40	77	8	0	18	45	1	.236
Russ Snyder (LF)	122	266	26	66	10	0	2	24	3	.248
Ken Suarez	36	85	7	25	5	0	1	9	1	.294
Zoilo Versalles	72	217	21	49	11	1	1	13	3	.226
		5,365	573	1,272	173	24	119	534	85	.237

1970

Record: 76–86
Finish: Fifth
Games Behind: 32
Manager: Alvin Dark

There was much to appreciate about 1970—but also much to lament—as the Indians improved, though not enough to make a significant difference.

Still, they provided hope for a better immediate future with the infusion of several young players who were, according to manager Alvin Dark, being "force-fed."

Included were Ray Fosse, Jack Heidemann, Eddie Leon, Graig Nettles, Roy Foster, Buddy Bradford, Rich Hand, Mike Paul, Phil Hennigan, Rick Austin, Steve Mingori, and Steve Dunning—all of whom otherwise would have been assigned to the minors for more seasoning.

Especially Dunning, the first player picked in the amateur draft, who, 11 days later, began his professional pitching career in the major leagues. He beat Milwaukee, 9–2, with sixth-inning relief help from Bob Miller, on June 14 at the Stadium.

Dunning's debut helped attract a crowd of 25,380—which might have been the primary objective in giving him the assignment.

Even before the season started, however, dark clouds were forming overhead as Alvin Dark, in his role as general manager without title, negotiated player contracts.

Dark had problems with several players, Tony Horton in particular, and the muscular first baseman was a holdout until mid-March.

Because of the presence of Ken "The Hawk" Harrelson, who also was a first baseman, Horton's bargaining position was not good. He finally capitulated and agreed to terms on March 18.

The very next day, in an exhibition game against Oakland in Mesa, Arizona, Harrelson suffered a broken right ankle that kept him out of action most of the season. It also led to his premature retirement from baseball.

Horton went on to hit .269 with 17 homers and 59 runs batted in while playing 115 games. Three of his homers came in the second game of a doubleheader at the Stadium on May 24 in an 8–7 loss to New York.

On August 28, in a doubleheader against California at the Stadium, Horton—a very intense player even under normal circumstances—snapped after grounding out to the second baseman in the third inning against Tom Murphy. He had to leave the game, suffered a breakdown, and never played another inning of baseball.

At the time the Indians were fighting to reach .500 for the first time all season. The closest they got was 55–57 and 56–58. They collapsed in September, losing nine of their last 12 games.

It also was a bummer of a season for Fosse, who was voted the American League's All-Star catcher upon hitting .312 with 16 homers at the break.

In the All-Star Game at Riverfront Stadium in Cincinnati on July 14, Fosse was hurt in a 12th-inning collision with Pete Rose, as Rose scored the winning run in the National League's 5–4 victory. Fosse suffered injuries to his left shoulder and arm and missed several games.

After returning to action Fosse hit only two more homers the rest of the season, finishing with a .307 average—and never was that good thereafter.

Sam McDowell had another winning season with 20 victories for the first time (while losing 12) and led the AL in strikeouts for the third straight season with 304 in 305 innings.

McDowell and Fosse were the Indians' only representatives on the AL all-star team, and the two of them also were cowinners of the Indians Man of the Year award for 1970.

Pete Rose crashes into Indians catcher Ray Fosse in the 12th inning of the All-Star Game in Cincinnati on July 14, 1970, scoring the winning run in the National League's 5–4 victory. Fosse was seriously injured on the play, which many believe cut short his playing career.

	W	L	G	GS	CG	IP	H	BB	K	ERA
Rick Austin	2	5	31	8	1	67⅔	74	26	53	4.79
Dean Chance	9	8	45	19	1	155	172	59	109	4.24
Vince Colbert	1	1	23	0	0	31	37	16	17	7.26
Steve Dunning	4	9	19	17	0	94⅓	93	54	77	4.96
Dick Ellsworth	3	3	29	1	0	43⅔	49	14	13	4.53
Rich Hand	6	13	35	25	3	159⅔	132	69	110	3.83
Steve Hargan	11	3	23	19	8	142⅔	101	53	72	2.90
Phil Hennigan	6	3	42	1	0	71⅓	69	44	43	4.02
Dennis Higgins	4	6	58	0	0	90⅓	82	54	82	3.99
Fred Lasher	1	7	43	1	0	57⅔	57	30	44	4.06
Sam McDowell	20	12	39	39	19	(305)	236	(131)	(304)	2.92
Bob Miller	2	2	15	2	0	28	35	15	15	4.18
Steve Mingori	1	0	21	0	0	20⅓	17	12	16	2.66
Barry Moore	3	5	13	12	0	70⅓	70	46	35	4.22
Mike Paul	2	8	30	15	1	88	91	45	70	4.81
Jim Rittwage	1	1	8	3	1	26	18	21	16	4.15
	76	86		162	34	1,451⅓	1,333	(689)	(1,076)	3.91

Shutouts: Austin, Chance, Hand, Hargan, McDowell
Saves: Higgins (11), Lasher (5), Chance (4), Austin (3), Hand (3), Hennigan (3), Colbert (2), Ellsworth (2), Miller, Mingori

	G	AB	R	H	2B	3B	HR	RBI	SB	AVG
Buddy Bradford	75	163	25	32	6	1	7	23	0	.196
Larry Brown	72	155	17	40	5	2	0	15	1	.258
Lou Camilli	16	15	0	0	0	0	0	0	0	.000
Ted Ford	26	46	5	8	1	0	1	1	0	.174
Ray Fosse (C)	120	450	62	138	17	1	18	61	1	.307
Roy Foster (LF)	139	477	66	128	26	0	23	60	3	.268
Vern Fuller	29	33	3	6	2	0	1	2	0	.182
Ken Harrelson	17	39	3	11	1	0	1	1	0	.282
Jack Heidemann (SS)	133	445	44	94	14	2	6	37	2	.211
Chuck Hinton	107	195	24	62	4	0	9	29	0	.318
Tony Horton (1B)	115	413	48	111	19	3	17	59	3	.269
Lou Klimchock	41	56	5	9	0	0	1	2	0	.161
Eddie Leon (2B)	152	549	58	136	20	4	10	56	1	.248
John Lowenstein	17	43	5	11	3	1	1	6	1	.256
Russ Nagelson	17	24	3	3	1	0	1	2	0	.125
Graig Nettles (3B)	157	549	81	129	13	1	26	62	3	.235
Vada Pinson (RF)	148	574	74	164	28	6	24	82	7	.286
Rich Rollins	42	43	6	10	0	0	2	4	0	.233
Duke Sims	110	345	46	91	12	0	23	56	0	.264
Ted Uhlaender (CF)	141	473	56	127	21	2	11	46	3	.268
		5,463	649	1,358	197	23	183	617	25	.249

1971

Record: 60–102
Finish: Sixth
Games Behind: 43
Managers: Alvin Dark, Johnny Lipon

Alvin Dark was back for his fourth season as the Indians manager, but he didn't last long after another poor start and the return to power of Gabe Paul.

Actually the Indians lost two managers in 1971 as they equaled a 57-year-old franchise record for futility with 102 defeats.

Dark was fired on July 30, when the Tribe was languishing in sixth place with a 42–61 record, 22 games out of first place.

Johnny Lipon took over as interim manager, and, when the Indians lost 41 of their remaining 59 games, he, too, was dismissed two weeks after the season ended.

Others also departed the Wigwam.

Vice president Hank Peters, who'd been in charge of the Tribe farm system for four years, resigned to become president of the National Association (minor leagues), and Ken "The Hawk" Harrelson, unable to make a full recovery from the broken ankle he suffered on March 19, 1970, retired June 21.

The Indians also lost a decision that cost them $5,000 and considerable embarrassment. Commissioner Bowie Kuhn ruled that they—in this case Dark, acting as general manager—had signed four of their players to illegal performance bonus contracts.

They were Sam McDowell, Ken Harrelson, Vada Pinson, and Graig Nettles.

Their bonus deals were negated by Kuhn, which so angered McDowell that he staged a 10-day walkout from the Indians in mid-August.

Two other players, Ted Uhlaender and Ted Ford, also quit the team for brief periods because of their discontent with management. It also was a factor in the decision by principal owner Vernon Stouffer to restore Paul to command, and to let him get rid of Dark.

Through the first six weeks of the season the Indians managed to hold their own. They got within one game of .500, at 28–29, on June 13.

But then they lost four straight and the bottom dropped out as injuries sidelined Steve Hargan, Roy Foster, and Ray Fosse, and the Indians went on to lose 23 of their next 34 games. Sam McDowell also was hampered by shoulder problems, and his record went from eight over .500 (20–12) to four under (13–17).

Attendance also fell to an eight-year low of 591,361.

Chris Chambliss, who was recalled from Class AAA Wichita in late May, took over at first base, precipitating Harrelson's retirement, and was voted American League Rookie of the Year. Graig Nettles, who led in most offensive departments, was elected the Indians' Man of the Year.

It was appropriate that in 1971, one of the longest seasons the Indians ever suffered through, they also played the longest game in the history of the franchise at that time. It lasted 20 innings, the first 16 at the Stadium on September 14, and the last four at RFK Stadium in Washington. The Senators won, 8–6.

	W	L	G	GS	CG	IP	H	BB	K	ERA
Rick Austin	0	0	23	0	0	23	25	20	20	5.09
Mark Ballinger	1	2	18	0	0	34⅔	30	13	25	4.67
Vince Colbert	7	6	50	10	2	142⅔	140	71	74	3.97
Steve Dunning	8	14	31	29	3	184	173	109	132	4.50
Ed Farmer	5	4	43	4	0	78⅔	77	41	48	4.35
Alan Foster	8	12	36	26	3	181⅓	158	82	97	4.16
Rich Hand	2	6	15	12	0	60⅔	74	38	26	5.79
Steve Hargan	1	13	37	16	1	113⅓	138	56	52	6.19
Phil Hennigan	4	3	57	0	0	82	80	51	69	4.94
Bob Kaiser	0	0	5	0	0	6	8	3	4	4.50
Ray Lamb	6	12	43	21	3	158⅓	147	69	91	3.35
Chuck Machemehl	0	2	14	0	0	18⅓	16	15	9	6.38
Sam McDowell	13	17	35	31	8	214⅔	160	(153)	192	3.40
Steve Mingori	1	2	54	0	0	56⅔	31	24	45	1.43
Camilo Pascual	2	2	9	1	0	23⅓	17	11	20	3.09
Mike Paul	2	7	17	12	1	62	78	14	33	5.95
	60	(102)		(162)	21	1,440	1,352	(770)	937	4.28

Shutouts: McDowell (2), Dunning, Lamb
Saves: Hennigan (14), Farmer (4), Mingori (4), Machemehl (3), Colbert (2), Austin, Dunning, Hargan, Lamb, McDowell

	G	AB	R	H	2B	3B	HR	RBI	SB	AVG
Frank Baker	73	181	18	38	12	1	1	23	1	.210
Kurt Bevacqua	55	137	9	28	3	1	3	13	0	.204
Buddy Bradford	20	38	4	6	2	1	0	3	0	.158
Larry Brown	13	50	4	11	1	0	0	5	0	.220
Lou Camilli	39	81	5	16	2	0	0	0	0	.198
Chris Chambliss (1B)	111	415	49	114	20	4	9	48	2	.275
Jim Clark	13	18	2	3	0	1	0	0	0	.167
Ted Ford	74	196	15	38	6	0	2	14	2	.194
Ray Fosse (C)	133	486	53	134	21	1	12	62	4	.276
Roy Foster (RF)	125	396	51	97	21	1	18	45	6	245
Ken Harrelson	52	161	20	32	2	0	5	14	1	.199
Jack Heidemann (SS)	81	240	16	50	7	0	0	9	1	.208
Chuck Hinton	88	147	13	33	7	0	5	14	0	.224
Gomer Hodge	80	83	3	17	3	0	1	9	0	.205
Eddie Leon (2B)	131	429	35	112	12	2	4	35	3	.261
John Lowenstein	58	140	15	26	5	0	4	9	1	.186
Graig Nettles (3B)	158	598	78	156	18	1	28	86	7	.261
Vada Pinson (CF)	146	566	60	149	23	4	11	35	25	.263
Fred Stanley	60	129	14	29	4	0	2	12	1	.225
Ken Suarez	50	123	10	25	7	0	1	9	0	.203
Ted Uhlaender (LF)	141	500	52	144	20	3	2	47	3	.288
		5,467	543	1,303	200	20	109	507	57	.238

1972

Record: 72–84
Finish: Fifth
Games Behind: 14
Manager: Ken Aspromonte

Even before Ken Aspromonte was hired to manage the Indians in 1972, Gabe Paul, back in command, acquired Alex Johnson, the 1970 American League batting champion, in a trade with the California Angels.

And shortly after Aspromonte came aboard, he and Paul sent Sam McDowell to San Francisco in one of the Indians' best-ever deals, getting Gaylord Perry and Frank Duffy in return.

It also was during 1972, on March 22, that the ownership of the Indians changed hands again, for the ninth time since Charles Somers and Jack Kilfoyl purchased a franchise for Cleveland in Ban Johnson's fledgling AL in 1901.

A group headed by Cleveland businessman Nick Mileti purchased the club from Vernon Stouffer for a reported $8.8 million. Paul was retained as general manager.

Perry won 24 games, which represented 33 percent of the Indians' total victories, five by shutouts, and compiled a 1.92 earned run average, second best in the league.

His performance earned the AL Cy Young Award for

Flamboyant Indians owner Nick Mileti throws out the first ball on opening day, 1972.

Perry, who pitched 342⅔ innings, the most since Bob Feller's 371⅓ in 1946. Eight of Perry's 16 losses were by one run, and the Tribe was shut out four times in games that he started.

Duffy's contributions also were significant as he became one of the league's best defensive shortstops.

The opening of the season was delayed by a 13-day strike by the players (April 1–13), which eliminated six games from the Indians' schedule.

After getting off to a fast start, which landed them in first place in the AL East on May 23 with an 18–10 record, the Indians lost seven straight and 12 of 14. By the All-Star break they'd tumbled all the way to fifth with only 36 victories and 51 losses, one game out of the basement.

They bounced back to finish respectably, going 36–33 in the second half, but still wound up fifth, 7½ games behind fourth-place New York and seven ahead of Milwaukee.

Six weeks after the season ended Paul swung another major trade with the Yankees, sending All-Star third baseman Graig Nettles and Gerry Moses to New York on November 27 for John Ellis, Jerry Kenney, Charlie Spikes, and Rusty Torres.

And then, five and a half weeks later, Paul and F. J. "Steve" O'Neill, both of whom had owned stock in the Indians during Stouffer's regime, left to become part of George Steinbrenner's syndicate that bought the Yankees.

Paul was named president of the Yankees on January 10, 1973.

Prior to leaving the Indians, Paul made a tentative agreement with the operators of the Louisiana Superdome to play upwards of 30 games in New Orleans in 1973. It was a hotly discussed topic in Cleveland, since most fans and the media feared it would lead to the franchise's being moved to New Orleans.

After several weeks of debate, Mileti called off the deal.

The trading of Nettles opened up third base for rookie Buddy Bell, who had been switched to right field and played well, batting .255 in 132 games. Another newcomer, Dick Tidrow, went 14–15 with a 2.77 ERA and was voted the AL's Rookie Pitcher of the Year.

While Chris Chambliss was the Indians' offensive leader again, Johnson was a major disappointment. His average fell to .239 with only 37 RBIs, and he was benched during most of the final month, creating an adversarial relationship between him and Aspromonte.

	W	L	G	GS	CG	IP	H	BB	K	ERA
Bill Butler	0	0	6	2	0	11⅔	9	10	6	1.54
Vince Colbert	1	7	22	11	1	74⅔	74	38	36	4.58
Steve Dunning	6	4	16	16	1	105	98	43	52	3.26
Ed Farmer	2	5	46	1	0	61⅓	51	27	33	4.40
Steve Hargan	0	3	12	1	0	20	23	15	10	5.85
Phil Hennigan	5	3	38	1	0	67⅓	54	18	44	2.67
Tom Hilgendorf	3	1	19	5	1	47	51	21	25	2.68
Mike Kilkenny	4	1	22	7	1	58	51	39	44	3.41
Ray Lamb	5	6	34	9	0	107⅔	101	29	64	3.09
Marcelino Lopez	0	0	4	2	0	8⅓	8	10	1	5.40
Steve Mingori	0	6	41	0	0	57	67	36	47	3.95
Lowell Palmer	0	0	1	0	0	2	2	2	3	4.50
Gaylord Perry	(24)	16	41	40	(29)	342⅔	253	82	234	1.92
Denny Riddleberger	1	3	38	0	0	54	45	22	34	2.50
Dick Tidrow	14	15	39	34	10	237⅓	200	70	123	2.77
Milt Wilcox	7	14	32	27	4	156	145	72	90	3.40
	72	84	(156)	47	1,410	1,232	534	846	2.92

Shutouts: Perry (5), Tidrow (3), Wilcox (2), Colbert
Saves: Mingori (10), Farmer (7), Hennigan (5), Kilkenny, Perry

	G	AB	R	H	2B	3B	HR	RBI	SB	AVG
Buddy Bell (RF)	132	466	49	119	21	1	9	36	5	.255
Kurt Bevacqua	19	35	2	4	0	0	1	1	0	.114
Jack Brohamer (2B)	136	527	49	123	13	2	5	35	3	.233
Lou Camilli	39	41	2	6	2	0	0	3	0	.146
Chris Chambliss (1B)	121	466	51	136	27	2	6	44	3	.292
Frank Duffy (SS)	130	385	23	92	16	4	3	27	6	.239
Ray Fosse (C)	134	457	42	110	20	1	10	41	5	.241
Roy Foster	73	143	19	32	4	0	4	13	0	.224
Jack Heidemann	10	20	0	3	0	0	0	0	0	.150
Alex Johnson (LF)	108	356	31	85	10	1	8	37	6	.239
Larry Johnson	1	2	0	1	0	0	0	0	0	.500
Eddie Leon	89	225	14	45	2	1	4	16	0	.200
Ron Lolich	24	80	4	15	1	0	2	8	0	.188
John Lowenstein	68	151	16	32	8	1	6	21	2	.212
Tom McCraw	129	391	43	101	13	5	7	33	12	.258
Gerry Moses	52	141	9	31	3	0	4	14	0	.220
Graig Nettles (3B)	150	557	65	141	28	0	17	70	2	.253
Adolfo Phillips	12	7	2	0	0	0	0	0	0	.000
Fred Stanley	6	12	1	2	1	0	0	0	0	.167
Del Unser (CF)	132	383	29	91	12	0	1	17	5	.238
	5,207	472	1,220	187	18	91	440	49	.234

1973

Record: 71–91
Finish: Sixth
Games Behind: 26
Manager: Ken Aspromonte

With Gabe Paul gone, Phil Seghi became general manager of the Indians, but that change and others that followed had little bearing on the team's fortunes.

Neither did the signing of Ken Aspromonte to a new two-year contract to manage the team through 1974.

Gaylord Perry's record dropped to 19–19—and he finished that well only by winning 11 of his 15 final decisions—as the Tribe fell into the basement of the American League East.

Inconsistent pitching was the major problem. The Indians' 4.58 earned run average was 11th in the AL. Their pitchers gave up 1,532 hits, most in the league, and 826 runs, for 11th place; seven of their nine shutouts were hurled by Perry.

Alex Johnson, who couldn't get along with Manager Ken Aspromote (or the media), was traded on March 8 to Texas for a couple of pitchers, neither of whom survived the final cut in spring training.

Another change, this one at the top, took place late in the season when attendance was lagging and it became evident the Indians were going nowhere in the AL race.

On August 29, Mileti turned the leadership of the franchise over to Alva T. "Ted" Bonda, a limited partner in the syndicate that owned the Indians. While Mileti continued as general partner and president, Bonda, with the title of executive vice president, took charge of all operations.

Once again the Indians broke from the gate in a rush and, by May 9, were only a half game out of first place. But they went on to lose 38 of their next 53 games and, by the time they reached the halfway mark, were in the cellar with a 28–53 record.

They recovered to go 43–38 in the second half. From the All-Star Game through the end of the season, the Indians tied Boston with the second-best record in the division, behind Baltimore.

The Indians' season attendance reflected the team's nosedive in the standings, although the opening day crowd of 74,420 in the Stadium set a major league record. Thereafter, however, only 530,653 fans paid their way through the gates in the remaining 67 home dates, and the Tribe's total attendance of 605,073, the smallest in the AL, was down nearly 155,000 from 1972.

	W	L	G	GS	CG	IP	H	BB	K	ERA
Dick Bosman	1	8	22	17	2	97	130	29	41	6.22
Steve Dunning	0	2	4	3	0	18	17	13	10	6.50
Ed Farmer	0	2	16	0	0	17⅓	25	5	10	4.67
Tom Hilgendorf	5	3	48	1	1	94⅔	87	36	58	3.14
Mike Jackson	0	0	1	0	0	⅔	1	0	1	0.00
Jerry Johnson	5	6	39	1	0	59⅔	70	39	45	6.18
Mike Kekich	1	4	16	6	0	50	73	35	26	7.02
Mike Kilkenny	0	0	5	0	0	2	5	5	3	22.50
Ray Lamb	3	3	32	1	0	86	98	42	60	4.60
Steve Mingori	0	0	5	0	0	11⅔	10	10	4	6.17
Gaylord Perry	19	19	41	41	(29)	344	315	115	238	3.38
Ken Sanders	5	1	15	0	0	27⅓	18	9	14	1.65
Brent Strom	2	10	27	18	2	123	134	47	91	4.61
Dick Tidrow	14	16	42	40	13	274⅔	289	95	138	4.42
Tom Timmerman	8	7	29	15	4	124⅓	117	54	62	4.92
Milt Wilcox	8	10	26	19	4	134¼	143	68	82	5.83
	71	91	(162)	55	(1,464⅔)	(1,532)	602	883	4.58

Shutouts: Perry (7), Tidrow (2)
Saves: Hilgendorf (6), Johnson (5), Sanders (5), Lamb (2), Timmerman (2), Farmer

	G	AB	R	H	2B	3B	HR	RBI	SB	AVG
Alan Ashby	11	29	4	5	1	0	1	3	0	.172
Buddy Bell (3B)	156	631	86	169	23	7	14	59	7	.268
Jack Brohamer (2B)	102	300	29	66	12	1	4	29	0	.220
Leo Cardenas	72	195	9	42	4	0	0	12	1	.215
Chris Chambliss (1B)	155	572	70	156	30	2	11	53	4	.273
Frank Duffy (SS)	116	361	34	95	16	4	8	50	6	.263
Dave Duncan (C)	95	344	43	80	11	1	17	43	3	.233
John Ellis	127	437	59	118	12	2	14	68	0	.270
Ted Ford	11	40	3	9	0	1	0	3	1	.225
Oscar Gamble (DH)	113	390	56	104	11	3	20	44	3	.267
George Hendrick (CF)	113	440	64	118	18	0	21	61	7	.268
Jerry Kenney	5	16	0	4	0	1	0	2	0	.250
Ron Lolich	61	140	16	32	7	0	2	15	0	.229
John Lowenstein	98	305	42	89	16	1	6	40	5	.292
Tom Ragland	67	183	16	47	7	1	0	12	2	.257
Tommy Smith	14	41	6	10	2	0	2	3	1	.244
Charlie Spikes (LF)	140	506	68	120	12	3	23	73	5	.237
Rusty Torres (RF)	122	312	31	64	8	1	7	28	6	.205
Walt Williams	104	350	43	101	15	1	8	38	9	.289
	5,592	680	1,429	205	29	(158)	636	60	.256

1974

Record: 77–85
Finish: Fourth
Games Behind: 14
Manager: Ken Aspromonte

Despite speculation that he'd be fired, Ken Aspromonte was retained to fulfill the final year of his contract as manager of the Indians, but coaches Rocky Colavito, Joe Lutz, and Warren Spahn were fired and replaced by Larry Doby, Clay Bryant, and Tony Pacheco.

Another major change took place April 27 when general manager Phil Seghi, eager to improve the Indians' starting pitching, swung a deal with his former boss, Gabe Paul, who was then president of the New York Yankees.

The Indians got starters Fritz Peterson and Steve Kline, along with relievers Tom Buskey and Fred Beene, for Chris Chambliss, Dick Tidrow, and Cecil Upshaw.

Though the deal did little to help the Indians, it did reunite Peterson with Mike Kekich, his former Yankee teammate who had been dealt to Cleveland the preceding season. The two pitchers had gained notoriety during spring training of 1973 when they traded families—wives, children, and homes.

The season itself was another roller-coaster trip for the Indians, who alternately hit the depths and then the heights—and then the depths again—en route to their sixth consecutive sub-.500 record.

They lost their first five games and 11 of 16, primarily because of faulty pitching, before Seghi acquired Peterson, Kline, Buskey, and Beene.

After the trade the Indians went on to win 40 while losing only 24 games. They took over first place in the American League East for a week in early July behind the leadership of Gaylord Perry, who recorded 15 consecutive victories after an opening-day, 6–1, loss to the Yankees.

Gaylord's streak was stopped by the Athletics in Oakland on July 8 when he was beaten, 4–3, by Vida Blue as rookie outfielder Claudell Washington drove in the winning run with a 10th-inning single.

Thereafter it was all downhill for the Indians, though they were lifted briefly on July 19 when Dick Bosman pitched the franchise's 13th no-hitter to beat Oakland, 4–0, at the Stadium.

The Indians were only 2½ games out of first place on August 1, but a month later they'd plummeted to fourth, 6½ games off the pace.

It was shortly thereafter that Seghi swung one more deal that he and Bonda hoped would reinvigorate the Indians. Their won-lost record at the time was 71–70. and they trailed the first-place New York Yankees by five games.

The contract of Frank Robinson was purchased on waivers from the California Angels. It was done by Bonda and Seghi without the knowledge of Aspromonte, giving rise to speculation that Robinson would become the new manager of the Indians.

Seghi's only comment was simply, "We need another right-handed bat, and Robinson gives us a good one."

However, not only did Robinson's presence fail to get the Indians back on the winning track—they promptly lost four straight and six of eight games—but his arrival also created dissension in the clubhouse.

The day Robinson joined the Indians he became embroiled in an argument with Gaylord Perry. They had been longtime adversaries in the National League when Robinson played for Cincinnati and Perry for San Francisco, and they almost came to blows before being separated by other members of the team.

The conflict was precipitated by the announcement that Robinson had been signed to a 1975 contract that would pay him $180,000.

It irritated Perry, who was making about $150,000. He was quoted as saying that he also expected to get a new contract and to be paid "one dollar more than Robinson." It reignited the feud that had smoldered within the two men for several years.

As it turned out, the Indians lost 15 of their final 21 games, as Robinson hit .200 on 10-for-50 with two homers and five runs batted in, and their last chance to get back in the race ended in a four-game series in New York, September 20–22.

They lost all four to the Yankees, 5–4, 3–0, 14–7 and 2–1, dropping their record to 73–79 and all but ending whatever slim hope had remained.

The fourth-place finish also cost Aspromonte his job.

As had been speculated, Robinson became major league baseball's first black manager—and the 28th manager in the 75-year history of the Indians, as well as their sixth player-manager—on October 3.

The Indians' second most effective pitcher, and the only one other than Gaylord Perry to win in double figures, was his brother Jim, who was acquired on March 19 in a trade with Detroit. Jim Perry, whose record was 17–12, began his major league career in Cleveland in 1959, was traded to Minnesota in 1963, then to the Tigers in 1973.

The brothers were elected cowinners of the Indians' Man of the Year award for 1974.

While the attendance rebounded dramatically to 1,114,262, climbing over the million mark for the first time in 15 years, one of the largest crowds, 25,134 for a game against Texas on June 4, proved to be a major embarrassment.

It was a "Beer Night" promotion at the Stadium in which unlimited cups of beer were sold for 10 cents. By the sixth inning, fans were becoming unruly, several times delaying the game by running onto the playing field.

The situation got out of hand in the ninth as the Indians rallied for two runs and a 5–5 tie, and had the potential winning run on third with two out.

It was then that several hundred fans swarmed out of the stands again. After about 15 minutes, during which the players had to fight their way off the field, umpire Nestor Chylak declared the game forfeited to the Rangers.

	W	L	G	GS	CG	IP	H	BB	K	ERA
Steve Arlin	2	5	11	10	1	43⅔	59	22	20	6.60
Fred Beene	4	4	32	0	0	73	68	26	35	4.93
Dick Bosman	7	5	25	18	2	127⅓	126	29	56	4.10
Tom Buskey	2	6	51	0	0	93	93	33	40	3.19
Bruce Ellingsen	1	1	16	2	0	42	45	17	16	3.21
Bill Gogolewski	0	0	5	0	0	13⅔	15	2	3	4.61
Tom Hilgendorf	4	3	35	0	0	48⅓	58	17	23	4.84
Bob Johnson	3	4	14	10	0	72	75	37	36	4.38
Jim Kern	0	1	4	3	1	15⅓	16	14	11	4.70
Steve Kline	3	8	16	11	1	71	70	31	17	5.07
Gaylord Perry	21	13	37	37	28	322⅓	230	99	216	2.51
Jim Perry	17	12	36	36	8	252	242	64	71	2.96
Fritz Peterson	9	14	29	29	3	152⅔	187	37	52	4.36
Ken Sanders	0	1	9	0	0	11	21	5	4	9.82
Dick Tidrow	1	3	4	4	0	19	21	13	8	7.11
Tom Timmerman	1	1	4	0	0	10	9	5	2	5.40
Cecil Upshaw	0	1	7	0	0	8	10	4	7	3.38
Milt Wilcox	2	2	41	2	1	71⅓	74	24	33	4.67
	77	85		162	45	1,445⅔	1,419	479	650	3.80

Shutouts: G. Perry (4), J. Perry (3), Bosman
Saves: Buskey (17), Wilcox (4), Hilgendorf (3), Beene (2), Sanders

	G	AB	R	H	2B	3B	HR	RBI	SB	AVG
Luis Alvarado	61	114	12	25	2	0	0	12	1	.219
Dwain Anderson	2	3	0	1	0	0	0	0	0	.333
Alan Ashby	10	7	1	1	0	0	0	0	0	.143
Buddy Bell (3B)	116	423	51	111	15	1	7	46	1	.262
Ossie Blanco	18	36	1	7	0	0	0	2	0	.194
Jack Brohamer (2B)	101	315	33	85	11	1	2	30	2	.270
Rico Carty	33	91	6	33	5	0	1	16	0	.363
Chris Chambliss	17	67	8	22	4	0	0	7	0	.328
Ed Crosby	37	86	11	18	3	0	0	6	0	.209
Frank Duffy (SS)	158	549	62	128	18	0	8	48	7	.233
Dave Duncan (C)	136	425	45	85	10	1	16	46	0	.200
John Ellis (1B)	128	477	58	136	23	6	10	64	1	.285
Oscar Gamble (DH)	135	454	74	132	16	4	19	59	5	.291
Jack Heidemann	12	11	2	1	0	0	0	0	0	.091
George Hendrick (CF)	139	495	65	138	23	1	19	67	6	.279
Angel Hermoso	48	122	15	27	3	1	0	5	2	.221
John Jeter	6	17	3	6	1	0	0	1	1	.353
Larry Johnson	1	0	1	0	0	0	0	0	0	—
Duane Kuiper	10	22	7	11	2	0	0	4	1	.500
Leron Lee	79	232	18	54	13	0	5	25	3	.233
Joe Lis	57	109	15	22	3	0	6	16	1	.202
John Lowenstein (LF)	140	508	65	123	14	2	8	48	36	.242
Tom McCraw	45	112	17	34	8	0	3	17	0	.304
Frank Robinson	15	50	6	10	1	1	2	5	0	.200
Tommy Smith	23	31	4	3	1	0	0	0	0	.097
Charlie Spikes (RF)	155	568	63	154	23	1	22	80	10	.271
Rusty Torres	108	150	19	28	2	0	3	12	2	.187
		5,474	662	1,395	201	19	131	616	79	.255

1975

Record: 79–80
Finish: Fourth
Games Behind: 15½
Manager: Frank Robinson

Major league baseball's first black manager sat behind a bank of microphones, facing more than 100 newsmen and wiped the sweat from his ebony brow.

"If I had one wish I was sure would be granted, it would be that Jackie Robinson could be here, seated alongside me, today," said Frank Robinson on October 3, 1974, as he was introduced as the 28th manager of the Indians, succeeding Ken Aspromonte.

Robinson also was the franchise's sixth player-manager, following Napoleon Lajoie, 1905–09; George Stovall, 1911; Joe Birmingham, 1912–15; Tris Speaker, 1919–26; and Lou Boudreau, 1942–50.

Commissioner Bowie Kuhn and American League president Lee MacPhail were in the audience as general manager

Phil Seghi insisted the Indians wanted Robinson for his motivational ability.

Seghi vehemently denied that the color of Robinson's skin had anything to do with his being hired to manage the team that had suffered so long on the field and at the box office.

"I am not, and never was interested in making history *that* way," said Seghi, referring to speculation that he was eager to be credited with hiring baseball's first black manager. "I wanted Frank Robinson because I wanted the very best man available.

"I feel Robby has an uplifting quality about him. It's the same quality that made him such a great player. He had to overcome so much to reach the top, to become a leader. Because of all the things he's had to go through himself, he knows what it takes and how to impart this to others."

Indians chief executive officer and executive vice president Alva T. "Ted" Bonda was more candid.

"We needed somebody to wake up the city," said Bonda. "We sold no tickets in advance here. We waited for people to come to the ballpark. We felt we had to generate excitement.

"It wasn't a question of suddenly getting rid of Ken Aspromonte. The whole organization had failed. I thought, last year, I'm not a baseball man, I'm a baseball fan.

"And when we got Frank Robinson four weeks ago, he was in my mind as our next manager. But we were still in contention then. If we won the pennant, we wouldn't have changed managers. But we didn't win."

The Indians didn't win in 1975 under Robinson, either.

But the season—and Robinson's career as the Tribe's player-manager—certainly got off to an auspicious start in front of an opening day crowd of 56,715 at the Stadium on April 8.

In his first plate appearance in the first inning against the New York Yankees' George "Doc" Medich, Robinson smashed a home run into the lower left-field stands. It led to a 5–3 victory.

In the postgame celebration Robinson quipped, "Phil [Seghi] said to me this morning, 'Why don't you hit a homer the first time you go to the plate.' I told him, 'You've got to be kidding.'"

Obviously, he wasn't.

In the wake of the victory Robinson also said, "Right now I feel better than I have after anything I've done in baseball. Take all the pennants, the personal awards, the World Series, the All-Star games, and this moment is the greatest."

The opening-day homer was one of nine, along with 24 runs batted in by Robinson, whose average was .237 as a pinch and designated hitter. He was hampered most of the season by a shoulder injury that required off-season surgery.

There also was much to cheer in his first season as a manager, although he was embroiled in several highly publicized controversies.

One took place in spring training involving Gaylord Perry. It probably led to the pitcher's being traded.

On June 13, with a 6–9 record and 3.55 ERA, Gaylord was dealt to Texas for Jim Bibby, Jackie Brown, Rick Waits, and $100,000. Perry went on to win 12 and lose eight for the Rangers that season.

Earlier, on May 20, Gaylord's brother Jim Perry was traded to Oakland.

Robinson also was involved in an argument with umpire Jerry Neudecker, on May 17, and was suspended for three days and fined $250 for pushing the arbiter.

The penalty assessed by MacPhail so angered the Indians that they drew up a statement and signed it, volunteering to sit out the suspension with Robinson and, of course, forfeit the three games. Robinson wouldn't let them do it.

He also was ejected from a game for a third time on July 7 by Larry Barnett, after which Robinson accused all the AL umpires of discriminating against him and his team. The story, including Robinson's volatile quotes, was headlined across the country.

Robinson and catcher John Ellis, a longtime friend of Gaylord Perry, almost came to blows in the dugout on July 18. It was another story carried in newspapers coast to coast.

Ellis subsequently was traded to Texas after the season ended.

Under Robinson's direction, the Indians were the only team in the league to win its season series against the champion Boston Red Sox, doing so with 11 victories in their 18 meetings.

However, despite Robinson's storybook beginning, the Indians struggled through the first two and a half months, never playing better than .500 ball after winning 10 of their first 20 games through May 4.

The Indians hit bottom on June 21 after a fifth straight loss, 11–9, to Milwaukee. It sank their record to 24–39, a season-low 15 games under .500, and dropped them into last place, 13 lengths behind the division-leading Red Sox.

Robinson called the defeat by the Brewers "the turning point of the season" as he held a postgame, closed-clubhouse meeting with the players. It obviously inspired them.

The Indians went from there to win 46 of their next 77 games. They pulled even at 70–70 and into fourth place on September 10, though they were never able to climb over .500. They won the last two games of the season in Boston, and might have had a winning record except that three games against Minnesota were rained out and not made up.

Robinson's assessment of the season: "Anytime you don't finish first, you've got to be disappointed. But the way we played the last couple of months, I'm happy.

"I also was happy the way the kids played after we gave them the opportunity to show what they could do. They're the ones who turned it around for us."

The "kids" included pitchers Dennis Eckersley and Eric Raich, second baseman Duane Kuiper, and center fielder Rick Manning.

One who wasn't a kid anymore but got a second chance was former National Leaguer Rico Carty. He was purchased by Seghi from the Mexican League and proceeded to lead the Indians with a .308 average that included 18 homers and 64 RBIs.

Robinson's former Baltimore teammate, Boog Powell, who came to Cleveland in a trade on February 25, also renewed his career, clouting 27 homers and driving in 86 runs while hitting .297 for the Indians.

Reliever Dave LaRoche, acquired in a February 28 trade with the Chicago Cubs, was elected the Indians' Man of the Year for 1975. Eckersley was the winner of the *Sporting News* Rookie Pitcher of the Year award for the AL. And Robinson, who'd been signed to a one-year contract, was rehired to manage the Indians in 1976.

	W	L	G	GS	CG	IP	H	BB	K	ERA
Larry Andersen	0	0	3	0	0	5⅔	4	2	4	4.76
Fred Beene	1	0	19	1	0	46⅔	63	25	20	6.94
Jim Bibby	5	9	24	12	2	112⅔	99	50	62	3.20
Dick Bosman	0	2	6	3	0	28⅔	33	8	11	4.08
Jackie Brown	1	2	25	3	1	69⅓	72	29	41	4.28
Tom Buskey	5	3	50	0	0	77	69	29	29	2.57
Dennis Eckersley	13	7	34	24	6	186⅔	147	90	152	2.60
Roric Harrison	7	7	19	19	4	126	137	46	52	4.79
Don Hood	6	10	29	19	2	135⅓	136	57	51	4.39
Jim Kern	1	2	13	7	0	71⅔	60	45	55	3.77
Dave LaRoche	5	3	61	0	0	82⅓	61	57	94	2.19
Blue Moon Odom	1	0	3	1	1	10⅓	4	8	10	2.61
Gaylord Perry	6	9	15	15	10	121⅔	120	34	85	3.55
Jim Perry	1	6	8	6	0	37⅔	46	18	11	6.69
Fritz Peterson	14	8	25	25	6	146⅓	154	40	47	3.94
Eric Raich	7	8	18	17	2	92⅔	118	31	34	5.54
Bob Reynolds	0	2	5	0	0	9⅔	11	3	5	4.66
Jim Strickland	0	0	4	0	0	4⅔	4	2	3	1.93
Rick Waits	6	2	16	7	3	70⅓	57	25	34	2.94
	79	80		159	37	1,435⅓	1,395	599	800	3.84

Shutouts: Eckersley (2), Peterson (2), Odom, G. Perry
Saves: LaRoche (17), Buskey (7), Eckersley (2), Reynolds (2), Beene, Bibby, Brown, Strickland, Waits

	G	AB	R	H	2B	3B	HR	RBI	SB	AVG
Alan Ashby (C)	90	254	32	57	10	1	5	32	3	.224
Buddy Bell (3B)	153	553	66	150	20	4	10	59	6	.271
Ken Berry	25	40	6	8	1	0	0	1	0	.200
Jack Brohamer	69	217	15	53	5	0	6	16	2	.244
Rico Carty (DH)	118	383	57	118	19	1	18	64	2	.308
Rick Cerone	7	12	1	3	1	0	0	0	0	.250
Ed Crosby	61	128	12	30	3	0	0	7	0	.234
Frank Duffy (SS)	146	482	44	117	22	2	1	47	10	.243
John Ellis	92	296	22	68	11	1	7	32	0	.230
Oscar Gamble	121	348	60	91	16	3	15	45	11	.261
George Hendrick (LF)	145	561	82	145	21	2	24	86	6	.258
Duane Kuiper (2B)	90	346	42	101	11	1	0	25	19	.292
Leron Lee	13	23	3	3	1	0	0	0	1	.130
Joe Lis	9	13	4	4	2	0	2	8	0	.308
John Lowenstein	91	265	37	64	5	1	12	33	15	.242
Rick Manning (CF)	120	480	69	137	16	5	3	35	19	.285
Tom McCraw	23	51	7	14	1	1	2	5	4	.275
Boog Powell (1B)	134	435	64	129	18	0	27	86	1	.297
Frank Robinson	49	118	19	28	5	0	9	24	0	.237
Tommy Smith	8	8	0	1	0	0	0	2	0	.125
Charlie Spikes (RF)	111	345	41	79	13	3	11	33	7	.229
Bill Sudakis	20	46	4	9	0	0	1	3	0	.196
		5,404	688	1,409	201	25	(153)	643	106	.261

1976

Record: 81–78
Finish: Fourth
Games Behind: 16
Manager: Frank Robinson

For the first time since 1968 the Indians won more games than they lost.

But what would have been their best finish—third place—in nine years slipped out of their grasp on the final day of the season in 6–5 and 4–3 losses in a doubleheader to the pennant-winning Yankees in New York.

It could be rationalized that inclement weather earlier in the summer was responsible for the Indians' being beaten out of third place by Boston by a half game.

The aforementioned doubleheader had been rescheduled for Yankee Stadium to make up for two rained-out games between the two teams in Cleveland. Three other

Frank Robinson, major league baseball's first black manager, reads the *Cleveland Plain Dealer* prior to the Indians 1976 opener.

Tribe games also were postponed because of bad weather, but were not made up.

As it was, the Red Sox, playing a full 162-game schedule, lost one more game than the Indians, but also won two more to claim third place by a margin of .003.

Frank Robinson got the Indians off to a fast start, and as late as July 1 they were in contention with a 36–33 record. They were in second place, seven lengths behind New York, with the Yankees coming to the Stadium for a crucial four-game series.

Pat Dobson, acquired from the Yankees the previous winter, won the opener, 3–2, for the Indians, and pennant fever engulfed Cleveland. More than 200,000 fans attended the series.

But their hopes were cruelly crushed as the Yankees won the next three games, 7–1, 7–3, and 4–3. The losses increased the Indians' deficit to nine, and they never got back in the race, losing five of their next six on a West Coast trip. At the All-Star break the Tribe was fourth, 11 games out with a 38–41 record.

Robinson played only sporadically, batting .224 (15-for-67) with three homers and driving in 10 runs in 36 games. He announced his retirement as a player when the season ended.

In his final plate appearance Robinson got an eighth-inning, run-scoring pinch single to center field off Baltimore's Rudy May in a 2–1 loss to the Orioles on September 18 at the Stadium.

It ended Robinson's Hall of Fame career with 2,943 hits, 586 homers, and a .294 lifetime average for 21 seasons in the major leagues.

The record will show that Robinson played in 2,808 games, eighth most in major league history, and that on August 14 he became only the 11th batter to get 10,000 at bats (he finished with 10,006).

Though Robinson was through as a player, he was granted another one-year contract to manage the Indians in 1977.

Rico Carty, who was rescued from the Mexican League in 1975, continued his renaissance in a major league career that had begun in 1963. He was the Indians' most consistent hitter with a .310 average and a team-leading 83 RBIs, and he was elected the Indians' Man of the Year for 1976.

But then, in the November 5 expansion draft to stock new franchises in Toronto and Seattle, Carty was left unprotected by the Indians. He was claimed by the Blue Jays, while the Mariners took Stan Thomas, Joe Lis, Tom McMillan, and Tommy Smith from the Tribe.

A month later general manager Phil Seghi traded Rick Cerone and John Lowenstein to the Blue Jays to return Carty to the Indians.

For the second straight season and the 19th in 21 years, Indians' attendance (948,776) failed to reach a million. It fell far short of the 1.3 million break-even point, and it was reported that the club's two-year financial losses amounted to more than $1 million.

	W	L	G	GS	CG	IP	H	BB	K	ERA
Jim Bibby	13	7	34	21	4	163⅓	162	56	84	3.20
Jackie Brown	9	11	32	27	5	180	193	55	104	4.25
Tom Buskey	5	4	39	0	0	94⅓	88	34	32	3.63
Pat Dobson	16	12	35	35	6	217⅓	226	65	117	3.48
Dennis Eckersley	13	12	36	30	9	199¼	155	78	200	3.43
Don Hood	3	5	33	6	0	77⅔	89	41	32	4.87
Jim Kern	10	7	50	2	0	117⅔	91	50	111	2.37
Dave LaRoche	1	4	61	0	0	96⅓	57	49	104	2.24
Harry Parker	0	0	3	0	0	7	3	0	5	0.00
Fritz Peterson	0	3	9	9	0	47	59	10	19	5.55
Eric Raich	0	0	1	0	0	2⅔	7	0	1	16.88
Stan Thomas	4	4	37	7	2	105⅓	88	41	54	2.30
Rick Waits	7	9	26	22	4	123⅔	143	54	65	4.00
	81	78		159	30	1,432	1,361	533	928	3.47

Shutouts: Bibby (3), Eckersley (3), Brown (2), Waits (2)
Saves: LaRoche (21), Kern (15), Thomas (6), Bibby, Buskey, Eckersley, Hood

	G	AB	R	H	2B	3B	HR	RBI	SB	AVG
Alan Ashby (C)	89	247	26	59	5	1	4	32	0	.239
Buddy Bell (3B)	159	604	75	170	26	2	7	60	3	.281
Larvell Blanks	104	328	45	92	8	7	5	41	1	.280
Rico Carty (DH)	152	552	67	171	34	0	13	83	1	.310
Rick Cerone	7	16	1	2	0	0	0	1	0	.125
Ed Crosby	2	2	0	1	0	0	0	0	0	.500
Frank Duffy (SS)	133	392	38	83	11	2	2	30	10	.212
Ray Fosse	90	276	26	83	9	1	2	30	1	.301
Orlando Gonzalez	28	68	5	17	2	0	0	4	1	.250
Alfredo Griffin	12	4	0	1	0	0	0	0	0	.250
George Hendrick (LF)	149	551	72	146	20	3	25	81	4	.265
Doug Howard	39	90	7	19	4	0	0	13	1	.211
Duane Kuiper (2B)	135	506	47	133	13	6	0	37	10	.263
Joe Lis	20	51	4	16	1	0	2	7	0	.314
John Lowenstein	93	229	33	47	8	2	2	14	11	.205
Rick Manning (CF)	138	552	73	161	24	7	6	43	16	.292
Boog Powell (1B)	95	293	29	63	9	0	9	33	1	.215
Ron Pruitt	47	86	7	23	1	1	0	5	2	.267
Frank Robinson	36	67	5	15	0	0	3	10	0	.224
Tommy Smith	55	164	17	42	3	1	2	12	8	.256
Charlie Spikes (RF)	101	334	34	79	11	5	3	31	5	.237
		5,412	615	1,423	189	38	85	567	75	.263

1977

Record: 71–90
Finish: Fifth
Games Behind: 28½
Managers: Frank Robinson, Jeff Torborg

The free agent era of baseball began during the winter of 1976–77, and the Indians wasted no time swinging into action.

Despite major financial losses since Nick Mileti's group purchased the Indians in 1972, executive vice president Alva T. "Ted" Bonda and general manager Phil Seghi outbid several other clubs to sign pitcher Wayne Garland.

Garland, who won 20 games and lost seven for Baltimore in 1976, was granted a contract that called for him to be paid $2.3 million, including a $300,000 signing bonus, over 10 years.

It was the longest contract in baseball, and one of the largest in dollar value at the time.

It also turned out to be one of the worst deals.

Garland suffered a shoulder injury that was later diagnosed as a torn rotator cuff. He tried to pitch through it and won only 13 games while losing 19. It was a major factor in the Indians' inability to live up to Bonda's spring training "promise" that they'd win the pennant.

And because they failed so badly, Robinson, major league baseball's first black manager, became major league baseball's first black ex-manager.

He was fired on June 19 with the Indians languishing in fifth place, eight games out, with a 26–31 record.

Robinson was replaced by coach Jeff Torborg, under whom the Indians immediately embarked upon a winning streak of seven, climbing two games over .500.

But it didn't continue and, by the All-Star Game on July 19, they were 41–47, in fourth place, and 10 games behind; and they never got any closer.

Though the Indians' record was only 45–59 under Torborg, he was signed to manage the club through 1978.

Perhaps as a portent of what was to come, Robinson was publicly blasted by Rico Carty in an early-season luncheon attended by 600 fans on April 25.

As he was presented the Man of the Year award he won for 1976—and with Robinson seated at the head table—Carty indicted the manager in no uncertain terms for "a lack of leadership."

Carty subsequently was suspended for 15 days and fined $1,000 for "insubordination."

One of the few highlights of the season occurred on May 30 when Dennis Eckersley pitched the franchise's 14th no-hitter, beating California, 1–0, at the Stadium.

Another was the season-long performance of Andre Thornton, who'd been acquired in a deal with Montreal the previous winter. Thornton led the Indians with 28 homers while hitting .263.

The regression by the Indians on the field also hurt them at the gate. Attendance declined to slightly more than 900,000, and another loss of nearly $1 million was reported.

	W	L	G	GS	CG	IP	H	BB	K	ERA
Larry Andersen	0	1	11	0	0	14⅓	10	9	8	3.14
Jim Bibby	12	13	37	30	9	206⅔	197	73	141	3.57
Tom Buskey	0	0	21	0	0	34	45	8	15	5.29
Card Camper	1	0	3	1	0	9⅓	7	4	9	3.86
Pat Dobson	3	12	33	17	0	133⅓	155	65	81	6.14
Dennis Eckersley	14	13	33	33	12	247⅓	214	54	191	3.53
Al Fitzmorris	6	10	29	21	1	133	164	53	54	5.41
Wayne Garland	13	(19)	38	38	21	282⅔	281	88	118	3.60
Don Hood	2	1	41	5	1	105	87	49	62	3.00
Jim Kern	8	10	60	0	0	92	85	47	91	3.42
Dave LaRoche	2	2	13	0	0	18⅔	15	7	18	5.30
Bill Laxton	0	0	2	0	0	1⅔	2	2	1	5.40
Sid Monge	1	2	33	0	0	39	47	27	25	6.23
Rick Waits	9	7	37	16	1	135⅓	132	64	62	3.99
	71	90		161	45	1,452⅓	1,441	550	876	4.10

Shutouts: Eckersley (3), Bibby (2), Garland
Saves: Kern (18), LaRoche (4), Monge (3), Bibby (2), Waits (2), Dobson

	G	AB	R	H	2B	3B	HR	RBI	SB	AVG
Buddy Bell (3B)	129	479	64	140	23	4	11	64	1	.292
Larvell Blanks	105	322	43	92	10	4	6	38	3	.286
Bruce Bochte (LF)	112	392	52	119	19	1	5	43	3	.304
Rico Carty (DH)	127	461	50	129	23	1	15	80	1	.280
Paul Dade	134	461	65	134	15	3	3	45	16	.291
Frank Duffy (SS)	122	334	30	67	13	2	4	31	8	.201
Ray Fosse	78	238	25	63	7	1	6	27	0	.265
Alfredo Griffin	14	41	5	6	1	0	0	3	2	.146
Johnny Grubb	34	93	8	28	3	3	2	14	0	.301
Fred Kendall (C)	103	317	18	79	13	1	3	39	0	.249
Duane Kuiper (2B)	148	610	62	169	15	8	1	50	11	.277
John Lowenstein	81	149	24	36	6	1	4	12	1	.242
Rick Manning (CF)	68	252	33	57	7	3	5	18	9	.226
Bill Melton	50	133	17	32	11	0	0	14	1	.241
Jim Norris (RF)	133	440	59	119	23	6	2	37	26	.270
Dave Oliver	7	22	2	7	0	1	0	3	0	.318
Ron Pruitt	78	219	29	63	10	2	2	32	2	.288
Charlie Spikes	32	95	13	22	2	0	3	11	0	.232
Andre Thornton (1B)	131	433	77	114	20	5	28	70	3	.263
		5,491	676	1,476	221	46	100	631	87	.269

1978

Record: 69–90
Finish: Sixth
Games Behind: 29
Manager: Jeff Torborg

Change at the top came again to the Indians in 1978 as Gabe Paul and F. J. "Steve" O'Neill left the New York Yankees and returned to Cleveland.

O'Neill purchased controlling interest in the Indians for a reported $11 million (which included the assumption of $5 million in debts) on February 3, and reinstalled Paul as president and chief executive officer. Phil Seghi remained as general manager.

They were determined to restore the Indians' past glory. Paul called Cleveland a sleeping giant, meaning that, given a winning team, the fans would flock to the Stadium in record numbers again.

Jeff Torborg was retained as manager, and a few personnel changes were made, including the trading of Rico Carty back to Toronto on March 15. But the sleeping giant continued to slumber as the Indians fell into sixth place on May 25 and never left it.

One of the early losses—though not on the field—was a front office blunder that cost the pitching services of Jim Bibby. He had earned a $10,000 bonus for starting 30 games (while winning 12) in 1977, but he wasn't paid on time.

Bibby appealed on March 6 to an arbitrator, who ruled that the Indians had breached Bibby's contract and declared him a free agent. Nine days later Bibby signed a million-dollar deal with Pittsburgh.

Another setback was an ill-advised trade that sent Dennis Eckersley and Fred Kendall to Boston on March 30 for Rick Wise, Mike Paxton, Bo Diaz, and Ted Cox.

But the biggest loss probably was Wayne Garland, who underwent surgery on May 5 to repair his torn rotator cuff. He made only six starts, going 2–3 with a 7.89 earned run average, before submitting to surgery that finished him for the season.

The Indians lost 35 games by one run and did not have a .300 hitter, though Andre Thornton was their most productive offensive player. He drove in 105 runs and smashed 33 homers while batting .262, and was elected Man of the Year for 1978.

Jeff Torborg's contract to manage the Indians was extended on July 4 through 1979, though attendance declined even further, to 800,584, and a loss of $1.9 million was reported.

	W	L	G	GS	CG	IP	H	BB	K	ERA
David Clyde	8	11	28	25	5	153⅓	166	60	83	4.28
Al Fitzmorris	0	1	7	0	0	14⅓	19	7	5	6.28
Dave Freisleben	1	4	12	10	0	44⅓	52	31	19	7.11
Wayne Garland	2	3	6	6	0	29⅔	43	16	13	7.89
Don Hood	5	6	36	19	1	154⅔	166	77	73	4.48
Jim Kern	10	10	58	0	0	99⅓	77	58	95	3.08
Dennis Kinney	0	2	18	0	0	38⅔	37	14	19	4.42
Rick Kreuger	0	0	6	0	0	9⅓	6	3	7	3.86
Sid Monge	4	3	48	2	0	84⅔	71	51	54	2.76
Mike Paxton	12	11	33	27	5	191	179	63	96	3.86
Paul Reuschel	2	4	18	6	1	89⅔	95	22	24	3.11
Dan Spillner	3	1	36	0	0	56⅓	54	21	48	3.67
Rick Waits	13	15	34	33	15	230⅓	206	86	97	3.20
Rick Wise	9	(19)	33	31	9	211⅓	226	59	106	4.34
	69	90		159	36	1,407⅓	1,397	568	739	3.97

Shutouts: Paxton (2), Waits (2), Wise
Saves: Kern (13), Monge (6), Kinney (5), Spillner (3), Paxton

	G	AB	R	H	2B	3B	HR	RBI	SB	AVG
Gary Alexander (C)	90	324	39	76	14	3	17	62	0	.235
Buddy Bell (3B)	142	556	71	157	27	8	6	62	1	.282
Larvell Blanks	70	193	19	49	10	0	2	20	0	.254
Dan Briggs	15	49	4	8	0	1	1	1	0	.163
Wayne Cage	36	98	11	24	6	1	4	13	1	.245
Bernie Carbo (DH)	60	174	21	50	8	0	4	16	1	.287
Ted Cox	82	227	14	53	7	0	1	19	0	.233
Paul Dade (RF)	93	307	37	78	12	1	3	20	12	.254
Bo Diaz	44	127	12	30	4	0	2	11	0	.236
Alfredo Griffin	5	4	1	2	1	0	0	0	0	.500
Johnny Grubb (LF)	113	378	54	100	16	6	14	61	5	.265
Ron Hassey	25	74	5	15	0	0	2	9	2	.203
Willie Horton	50	169	15	42	7	0	5	22	3	.249
Duane Kuiper (2B)	149	547	52	155	18	6	0	43	4	.283
Larry Lintz	3	0	1	0	0	0	0	0	1	—
Rick Manning (CF)	148	566	65	149	27	3	3	50	12	.263
Jim Norris	113	315	41	89	14	5	2	27	12	.283
Ron Pruitt	71	187	17	44	6	1	6	17	2	.235
Horace Speed	70	106	13	24	4	1	0	4	2	.226
Andre Thornton (1B)	145	508	97	133	22	4	33	105	4	.262
Mike Vail	14	34	2	8	2	1	0	2	1	.235
Tom Veryzer (SS)	130	421	48	114	18	4	1	32	1	.271
		5,365	639	1,400	223	45	106	596	64	.261

1979

Record: 81–80
Finish: Sixth
Games Behind: 22
Managers: Jeff Torborg, Dave Garcia

Gabe Paul and Phil Seghi continued to shuffle players, most of them of only marginal ability, and though the Indians climbed one game over .500, they couldn't get out of sixth place.

The 1979 season also ushered in the Tribe's 30th manager, Dave Garcia, and on a positive note, more than a million fans (1,011,644) were lured back to the Stadium for the first time in five years.

The season started promisingly as Rick Waits hurled a one-hitter in the home opener to beat Boston, 3–0, on April 7 at the Stadium. Jerry Remy singled in the sixth inning off Waits, who went on to win nine of his first 13 decisions.

But it didn't continue well for the Indians.

Garcia, a coach under Jeff Torborg, was promoted to manager on July 22 in a strange chain of events.

Only 20 days earlier Torborg, depressed after a 42nd loss in the Tribe's 76th game—and aware that Paul had tried to hire Bob Lemon to take over as manager—had told reporters he would resign at the end of the season.

When the Indians lost 10 of their next 18 games, Paul decided not to wait for Torborg to leave voluntarily and appointed Garcia to take charge.

Garcia's strong, quiet approach brought order out of chaos and resulted in an immediate improvement. The Indians won their first 10 games under the new manager and 38 of 66.

When the season ended with the team above .500 for the first time in eight years, Garcia was rewarded with a contract extension through 1980.

Three newcomers were primarily responsible for whatever success the Indians enjoyed—Mike Hargrove, acquired from San Diego for Paul Dade; Toby Harrah, who came from Texas in exchange for Buddy Bell; and Cliff Johnson, obtained from the New York Yankees for Don Hood.

Hargrove, hitting in the leadoff position, batted .355 after the All-Star break for a team-leading .325, with an on-base percentage of .438. Harrah delivered 20 homers and drove in 77 runs while batting .279. Johnson had 18 homers and 61 RBIs, and he hit .271 in only 72 games for the Indians, after coming to Cleveland on June 15.

Wayne Garland continued to struggle in his attempt to make a comeback from rotator cuff surgery and won only four games while losing 10 with a 5.23 earned run average.

	W	L	G	GS	CG	IP	H	BB	K	ERA
Larry Andersen	0	0	8	0	0	16⅔	25	4	7	7.56
Len Barker	6	6	29	19	2	137⅓	146	70	93	4.92
David Clyde	3	4	9	8	1	45⅔	50	13	17	5.91
Victor Cruz	3	9	61	0	0	78⅔	70	44	63	4.23
Wayne Garland	4	10	18	14	2	94⅔	120	34	40	5.23
Don Hood	1	0	13	0	0	22	13	14	7	3.68
Sid Monge	12	10	76	0	0	131	96	64	108	2.40
Mike Paxton	8	8	33	24	3	159⅔	210	52	70	5.92
Paul Reuschel	2	1	17	1	0	45⅓	73	11	22	7.94
Dan Spillner	9	5	49	13	3	157⅔	153	64	97	4.62
Rick Waits	16	13	34	34	8	231	230	91	91	4.44
Sandy Wihtol	0	0	5	0	0	10⅔	10	3	6	3.38
Eric Wilkins	2	4	16	14	0	69⅔	77	38	52	4.39
Rick Wise	15	10	34	34	9	231⅓	229	68	108	3.73
	81	80		161	28	1,431⅔	1,502	570	781	4.57

Shutouts: Waits (3), Wise (2)
Saves: Monge (19), Cruz (10), Hood, Reuschel, Spillner

	G	AB	R	H	2B	3B	HR	RBI	SB	AVG
Gary Alexander (C)	110	358	54	82	9	2	15	54	4	.229
Dell Alston	54	62	10	18	0	2	1	12	4	.290
Bobby Bonds (RF)	146	538	93	148	24	1	25	85	34	.275
Wayne Cage	29	56	6	13	2	0	1	6	0	.232
Ted Cox	78	189	17	40	6	0	4	22	3	.212
Paul Dade	44	170	22	48	4	1	3	18	12	.282
Bo Diaz	15	32	0	5	2	0	0	1	0	.156
Mike Hargrove	100	338	60	110	21	4	10	56	2	.325
Toby Harrah (3B)	149	527	99	147	25	1	20	77	20	.279
Ron Hassey	76	223	20	64	14	0	4	32	1	.287
Cliff Johnson (DH)	72	240	37	65	10	0	18	61	2	.271
Duane Kuiper (2B)	140	479	46	122	9	5	0	39	4	.255
Rick Manning (CF)	144	560	67	145	12	2	3	51	30	.259
Jim Norris (LF)	124	353	50	87	15	6	3	30	15	.246
Ron Pruitt	64	166	23	47	7	0	2	21	2	.283
Dave Rosello	59	107	20	26	6	1	3	14	1	.243
Horace Speed	26	14	6	2	0	0	0	1	2	.143
Andre Thornton (1B)	143	515	89	120	31	1	26	93	5	.233
Tom Veryzer (SS)	149	449	41	99	9	3	0	34	2	.220
		5,376	760	1,388	206	29	138	707	143	.258

1980

Record: 79–81
Finish: Sixth
Games Behind: 23
Manager: Dave Garcia

The magic that Dave Garcia brought to the Indians in 1979 didn't work in 1980, as players continued to be shuttled in and out of Cleveland.

The way the season started probably was a harbinger of things to come.

John Denny, expected to be the ace of the pitching staff, got sick and missed the opener, and his replacements were battered for 10 runs and 15 hits.

And Joe Charboneau, playing in his first major league game, clouted a home run in his second time at bat.

Denny recovered from his illness and, by July 15, had registered eight victories, including six of his previous seven decisions. But then he suffered an injury to his heel that disabled him the rest of the season.

It was a dreadful loss for the Indians' already weak pitching staff, which wound up with a woeful 4.68 earned run average, worst in the major leagues.

Charboneau, acquired from the Philadelphia Phillies in a minor league deal the winter of 1978–79, went on to lead the team with 23 homers and 87 runs batted in, while hitting .289.

He became the third Tribe player to win the American League Rookie of the Year award, following Herb Score in 1955 and Chris Chambliss in 1971.

But otherwise, there was precious little to cheer as, even before the Indians were bombed into submission, 10–2, in that prophetic opener, they lost the services of their leading power hitter, Andre Thornton.

Thornton, who hit 26 homers and drove in 93 runs in 1979, went down with torn ligaments and cartilage damage in his right knee in spring training and didn't play all season.

Second baseman Duane Kuiper also suffered an injury to his right knee on June 1 and missed the rest of the season after undergoing surgery.

And shortstop Tom Veryzer was sidelined for two months with tendinitis in his shoulder.

Denny's incapacitation forced Garcia to rely more heavily on Len Barker and Dan Spillner, and both of them came through as the Indians' biggest winners.

A victory by Barker in the final game of the season would have given the Indians a .500 record and made him their first 20-game winner since Gaylord Perry in 1974.

Instead, the Red Sox prevailed, 7–1, and Barker finished 19–12.

Spillner, primarily a reliever until 1980, went 16–11 in 30 starts.

An early-season injury to Rick Manning also led to the acquisition of Miguel Dilone, who went on to set a club record with 61 stolen bases while leading the Indians with a .341 average, third best in the AL behind George Brett (.390) and Cecil Cooper (.352).

After losing eight of their first 10 games the Indians didn't reach .500 until early June when they leveled at 25–25. After climbing to 30–27, they dropped under the break-even point again. By the end of June they had fallen into sixth place where they remained for all but 15 days the rest of the season.

Despite the disappointing season, Garcia was rehired to manage the Indians in 1981.

Wayne Garland continued to struggle in his attempt to come back from rotator cuff surgery. Though he won only six games while losing nine, one of his victories was a two-hitter against the New York Yankees, beating them, 7–0, in front of 73,096 fans—the major leagues' largest crowd of the season—on July 3 at the Stadium.

	W	L	G	GS	CG	IP	H	BB	K	ERA
Len Barker	19	12	36	36	8	246⅓	237	92	(187)	4.17
Don Collins	0	0	4	0	0	6	9	7	0	7.50
Victor Cruz	6	7	55	0	0	86	71	27	88	3.45
John Denny	8	6	16	16	4	108⅔	116	47	59	4.39
Wayne Garland	6	9	25	20	4	150⅓	163	48	55	4.61
Ross Grimsley	4	5	14	11	2	74⅔	103	24	18	6.75
Sid Monge	3	5	67	0	0	94⅓	80	40	61	3.53
Bob Owchinko	2	9	29	14	1	114⅓	138	47	66	5.27
Mike Paxton	0	0	4	0	0	7⅓	13	6	6	12.91
Dan Spillner	16	11	34	30	7	194⅓	225	74	100	5.28
Mike Stanton	1	3	51	0	0	85⅔	98	44	74	5.46
Rick Waits	13	14	33	33	9	224⅓	231	82	109	4.45
Sandy Wihtol	1	0	17	0	0	35⅓	35	14	20	3.57
	79	81		160	35	1,428	1,519	552	843	4.68

Shutouts: Waits (2), Barker, Denny, Garland, Owchinko, Spillner
Saves: Monge (14), Cruz (12), Stanton (5), Wihtol

	G	AB	R	H	2B	3B	HR	RBI	SB	AVG
Gary Alexander	76	178	22	40	7	1	5	31	0	.225
Dell Alston	52	54	11	12	1	2	0	9	2	.222
Alan Bannister	81	262	41	86	17	4	1	32	9	.328
Jack Brohamer (2B)	53	142	13	32	5	1	1	15	0	.225
Joe Charboneau (DH)	131	453	76	131	17	2	23	87	2	.289
Bo Diaz	76	207	15	47	11	2	3	32	1	.227
Miguel Dilone (LF)	132	528	82	180	30	9	0	40	61	.341
Jerry Dybzinski	114	248	32	57	11	1	1	23	4	.230
Gary Gray	28	54	4	8	1	0	2	4	0	.148
Mike Hargrove (1B)	160	589	86	179	22	2	11	85	4	.304
Toby Harrah (3B)	160	561	100	150	22	4	11	72	17	.267
Ron Hassey (C)	130	390	43	124	18	4	8	65	0	.318
Cliff Johnson	54	174	25	40	3	1	6	28	0	.230
Duane Kuiper	42	149	10	42	5	0	0	9	0	.282
Rick Manning (CF)	140	471	55	110	17	4	3	52	12	.234
Andres Mora	9	18	0	2	0	0	0	0	0	.111
Jorge Orta (RF)	129	481	78	140	18	3	10	64	6	.291
Ron Pruitt	23	36	1	11	1	0	0	4	0	.306
Dave Rosello	71	117	16	29	3	0	2	12	0	.248
Tom Veryzer (SS)	109	358	28	97	12	0	2	28	0	.271
		5,470	738	1,517	221	40	89	692	118	.277

1981

Record: 52–51
Finish: Sixth
Games Behind: 7
Manager: Dave Garcia

With the acquisition of Bert Blyleven, the return of Andre Thornton from the knee injury and surgery that idled him all of 1980, and the presence of Joe Charboneau, the American League's reigning Rookie of the Year, the Indians began the 1981 season with great expectations.

Five weeks after it started, Lenny Barker pitched the 12th perfect game in major league history—only the 10th in the "modern" era that began in 1901—beating the Toronto Blue Jays, 3–0, on May 15, in front of 7,290 fans in the Stadium.

But then, instead of 1981 being a season to cherish and remember with fondness, it turned into one the Tribe (and major league baseball) preferred to forget. It was marred by the first midseason player strike in the annals of professional sports in the United States and Canada.

The players walked off their jobs on June 12 and remained on strike for 50 days, wiping out 371 AL games, 54 by the Indians.

The players returned to their teams on July 31, played the rescheduled 56th All-Star Game on August 9, and resumed the regular season the next day.

The All-Star Game was played for the fourth time at the Stadium, and 72,086 fans, comprising the largest crowd in the history of the midsummer classic that began in 1933, witnessed the National League's 5–4 victory.

Because of the strike, the season was split into two segments with New York winning the AL East and Oakland the AL West in the first half, and Milwaukee and Kansas City prevailing in the second half. The Yankees beat the Brewers and the Athletics defeated the Royals in the division playoffs, and then New York swept Oakland in the best-of-five League Championship Series for the pennant.

The season began with the Indians getting off to another good start. Two days after Barker's perfect game they led the AL East with an 18–9 record.

But once again the Indians couldn't stand prosperity and proceeded to lose 15 of their next 23 games to finish the first half of the season in sixth place. Their 26 victories and 24 losses left them five lengths behind the Yankees.

The second half was no better. The Indians lost seven of their first nine games and wound up fifth, at 26–27, five games behind the Brewers.

Their overall record of 52–51 left the Indians in sixth place for the fourth consecutive season.

Blyleven led a respectable starting staff with 11 victories, but the Indians lacked effective relief pitching. The bull pen was credited with only 13 saves, seven by Dan Spillner and four by Sid Monge, who was hammered for nine homers in 58 innings.

Offensively, while their team batting average of .263 was fifth in the AL, the Indians hit only 39 homers, fewest in the league.

Thornton's comeback was painfully unproductive as he suffered two more injuries that kept him out of 34 games. His hand was broken in a spring training exhibition game, and after returning to the lineup in May, he went out again with a badly sprained right thumb.

Charboneau also failed to deliver as expected, slumping to .210 while experiencing back problems and playing in fewer than half of the Indians' games.

The season also was a major disappointment for Wayne Garland in his efforts to return from the rotator cuff surgery he underwent in 1978. Garland won only three of his 10 starts and retired when the season ended.

One who enjoyed the season was Mike Hargrove, whose .317 batting average led the Indians and was fifth best in the AL.

	W	L	G	GS	CG	IP	H	BB	K	ERA
Len Barker	8	7	22	22	9	154⅓	150	46	(127)	3.91
Bert Blyleven	11	7	20	20	9	159⅓	145	40	107	2.88
Tom Brennan	2	2	7	6	1	48⅓	49	14	15	3.17
John Denny	10	6	19	19	6	145⅔	139	66	94	3.15
Wayne Garland	3	7	12	10	2	56	89	14	15	5.79
Ed Glynn	0	0	4	0	0	7⅔	5	4	4	1.17
Bob Lacey	0	0	14	0	0	21⅓	36	3	11	7.59
Dennis Lewallyn	0	0	7	0	0	13⅓	16	2	11	5.40
Sid Monge	3	5	31	0	0	58	58	21	41	4.34
Dan Spillner	4	4	32	5	1	97⅓	86	39	59	3.14
Mike Stanton	3	3	24	0	0	43⅓	43	18	34	4.36
Rick Waits	8	10	22	21	5	126⅔	173	44	51	4.92
	52	51		103	33	931	989	311	569	3.88

Shutouts: Barker (3), Denny (3), Blyleven, Garland, Waits
Saves: Spillner (7), Monge (4), Stanton (2)

	G	AB	R	H	2B	3B	HR	RBI	SB	AVG
Chris Bando	21	47	3	10	3	0	0	6	0	.213
Alan Bannister	68	232	36	61	11	1	1	17	16	.263
Joe Charboneau	48	138	14	29	7	1	4	18	1	.210
Bo Diaz	63	182	25	57	19	0	7	38	2	.313
Miguel Dilone (LF)	72	269	33	78	5	5	0	19	29	.290
Jerry Dybzinski	48	57	10	17	0	0	0	6	7	.298
Mike Fischlin	22	43	3	10	1	0	0	5	3	.233
Mike Hargrove (1B)	94	322	43	102	21	0	2	49	5	.317
Toby Harrah (3B)	103	361	64	105	12	4	5	44	12	.291
Ron Hassey (C)	61	190	8	44	4	0	1	25	0	.232
Von Hayes	43	109	21	28	8	2	1	17	8	.257
Pat Kelly	48	75	8	16	4	0	1	16	2	.213
Duane Kuiper (2B)	72	206	15	53	6	0	0	14	1	.257
Larry Littleton	26	23	2	0	0	0	0	1	0	.000
Rick Manning (CF)	103	360	47	88	15	3	4	33	25	.244
Jorge Orta (RF)	88	338	50	92	14	3	5	34	4	.272
Karl Pagel	14	15	3	4	0	2	1	4	0	.267
Ron Pruitt	5	9	0	0	0	0	0	0	0	.000
Dave Rosello	43	84	11	20	4	0	1	7	0	.238
Andre Thornton (DH)	69	226	22	54	12	0	6	30	3	.239
Tom Veryzer (SS)	75	221	13	54	4	0	0	14	1	.244
		3,507	431	922	150	21	39	397	(119)	.263

1982

Record: 78–84
Finish: Sixth (tied with Toronto)
Games Behind: 17
Manager: Dave Garcia

Toby Harrah and Andre Thornton had the best seasons of their careers, and rookie Von Hayes made an impressive impact, but the Indians finished in sixth place again, for the fifth year in a row, and Dave Garcia resigned as manager.

Much of Garcia's frustration was based on the organization's high hopes for 1982, in the wake of president Gabe Paul's preseason "assurance" that the Indians were "not just another .500 team."

They weren't—they fell six games under the break-even point—though that wasn't what Paul meant.

Injuries to key players were factors in the lack of success.

Bert Blyleven, the Tribe's best pitcher in 1981, suffered a major elbow injury and missed most of the season after starting only four games.

Bake McBride, who was counted upon to be the Tribe's right fielder after being acquired in a deal with Philadelphia, did not play after May 21 because of an eye infection.

Rick Waits was bothered by a knee injury and won only two games (while losing 13) before undergoing surgery in late September.

And John Denny, who had been re-signed from the free-agent pool for $2 million over three years, developed shoulder trouble and, after going 6–11 in 21 starts, was traded to Philadelphia for three minor leaguers.

Harrah batted .304 with 25 homers, Thornton rebounded from an injury-plagued 1981 to deliver 32 homers and 116 RBIs, and Hayes drove in 82 runs and clouted 14 homers, but the production of Mike Hargrove and Miguel Dilone fell off drastically.

Hargrove, a .300 hitter his first three years in Cleveland, slipped to .271, and Dilone's average slumped 55 points.

Speculation that Garcia would be fired began in late May when the Indians fell into the basement of the American League East with a 15–23 record. The rumors persisted most of the remainder of the season, even after the Indians rallied and climbed two games over .500 (at 54–52) on August 7.

Three weeks later they slipped under .500 again (61–62), and Garcia, who'd managed the Indians since replacing Jeff Torborg in mid-1979, announced that he would resign at the end of the season.

Despite speculation that the 1981 strike would hurt all teams at the gate in 1982, the Indians were one of the 25 major league teams to draw more than one million fans. Their season attendance was 1,044,021. (Minnesota was the only team that did not play before a million customers.) Still, the Indians lost a reported $5 million, and there were rumors that multimillionaire Youngstown developer Edward J. DeBartolo was interested in buying the franchise from F. J. "Steve" O'Neill.

	W	L	G	GS	CG	IP	H	BB	K	ERA
Bud Anderson	3	4	25	5	1	80⅔	84	30	44	3.35
Len Barker	15	11	33	33	10	244⅔	211	88	187	3.90
Bert Blyleven	2	2	4	4	0	20⅓	16	11	19	4.87
John Bohnet	0	0	3	3	0	11⅔	11	7	4	6.94
Tom Brennan	4	2	30	4	0	92⅔	112	10	46	4.27
John Denny	6	11	21	21	5	138⅓	126	73	94	5.01
Ed Glynn	5	2	47	0	0	49⅔	43	30	54	4.17
Neal Heaton	0	2	8	4	0	31	32	16	14	5.23
Dennis Lewallyn	0	1	4	0	0	10⅓	13	1	3	6.97
Jerry Reed	1	1	6	1	0	15⅔	15	3	10	3.45
Lary Sorensen	10	15	32	30	6	189⅔	251	55	62	5.61
Dan Spillner	12	10	65	0	0	133⅔	117	45	90	2.49
Rick Sutcliffe	14	8	34	27	6	216	174	98	142	(2.96)
Rick Waits	2	13	25	21	2	115	128	57	44	5.40
Ed Whitson	4	2	40	9	1	107⅔	91	58	61	3.26
Sandy Wihtol	0	0	6	0	0	11⅔	9	7	8	4.63
	78	84		162	31	1,468⅓	1,433	589	882	4.11

Shutouts: Barker, Sorensen, Sutcliffe, Whitson
Saves: Spillner (21), Glynn (4), Brennan (2), Whitson (2), Sutcliffe

	G	AB	R	H	2B	3B	HR	RBI	SB	AVG
Chris Bando	66	184	13	39	6	1	3	16	0	.212
Alan Bannister	101	348	40	93	16	1	4	41	18	.267
Carmen Castillo	47	120	11	25	4	0	2	11	0	.208
Joe Charboneau	22	56	7	12	2	1	2	9	0	.214
Rodney Craig	49	65	7	15	2	0	0	1	3	.231
Miguel Dilone (LF)	104	379	50	89	12	3	3	25	33	.235
Jerry Dybzinski	80	212	19	49	6	2	0	22	3	.231
Mike Fischlin (SS)	112	276	34	74	12	1	0	21	9	.268
Mike Hargrove (1B)	160	591	67	160	26	1	4	65	2	.271
Toby Harrah (3B)	(162)	602	100	183	29	4	25	78	17	.304
Ron Hassey (C)	113	323	33	81	18	0	5	34	3	.251
Von Hayes (RF)	150	527	65	132	25	3	14	82	32	.250
Rick Manning (CF)	152	562	71	152	18	2	8	44	12	.270
Bake McBride	27	85	8	31	3	3	0	13	2	.365
Larry Milbourne	82	291	29	80	11	4	2	25	2	.275
Bill Nahorodny	39	94	6	21	5	1	4	18	0	.223
Karl Pagel	23	18	3	3	0	0	0	2	0	.167
Jack Perconte (2B)	93	219	27	52	4	4	0	15	9	.237
Kevin Rhomberg	16	18	3	6	0	0	1	1	0	.333
Andre Thornton (DH)	161	589	90	161	26	1	32	116	6	.273
		5,559	683	1,458	225	32	109	639	151	.262

	W	L	G	GS	CG	IP	H	BB	K	ERA
Bud Anderson	1	6	39	1	0	68⅓	64	32	32	4.08
Len Barker	8	13	24	24	4	149⅔	150	52	105	5.11
Rich Barnes	1	1	4	2	0	11⅔	18	10	2	6.94
Rick Behenna	0	2	5	4	0	26	22	14	9	4.15
Bert Blyleven	7	10	24	24	5	156⅓	160	44	123	3.91
Tom Brennan	2	2	11	5	1	39⅔	45	8	21	3.86
Ernie Camacho	0	1	4	0	0	5⅓	5	2	2	5.06
Jamie Easterly	4	2	41	0	0	57	69	22	39	3.63
Juan Eichelberger	4	11	28	15	2	134	132	59	56	4.90
Ed Glynn	0	2	11	0	0	12⅓	22	6	13	5.84
Neal Heaton	11	7	39	16	4	149⅓	157	44	75	4.16
Mike Jeffcoat	1	3	11	2	0	32⅔	32	13	9	3.31
Jerry Reed	0	0	7	0	0	21⅓	26	9	11	7.17
Lary Sorensen	12	11	36	34	8	222⅔	238	65	76	4.24
Dan Spillner	2	9	60	0	0	92⅓	117	38	48	5.07
Rick Sutcliffe	17	11	36	35	10	243⅓	251	102	160	4.29
Rick Waits	0	1	8	0	0	19¾	23	9	13	4.58
	70	92		162	34	1,441⅓	1,531	529	794	4.43

Shutouts: Heaton (3), Sutcliffe (2), Barker, Brennan, Sorensen
Saves: Spillner (8), Anderson (7), Heaton (7), Easterly (3)

1983

Record: 70–92

Finish: Seventh

Games Behind: 28

Managers: Mike Ferraro, Pat Corrales

Mike Ferraro became the Indians 31st manager, but even before he donned a uniform for spring training he had to undergo surgery for the removal of a cancerous kidney. Once the season started, Ferraro had problems of a different kind.

With Bert Blyleven unable to regain his 1981 form, Miguel Dilone slumping to below .200 and unhappy because he wasn't playing regularly, and the slumping team mired in last place with a 40–60 record on July 1, Ferraro was dismissed.

He was replaced by Pat Corrales, who had been fired two weeks earlier by Philadelphia.

The Indians rallied under Corrales and won 30 of their remaining 62 games, but of course it was too late to climb into contention, or even out of last place. They remained in the basement, the position they occupied without respite for even one day from June 24 through the end of the season.

The only positive elements were provided by Rick Sutcliffe, whose two-year record with the Tribe climbed to 31–19; rookie Neal Heaton, who showed promise with an 11–7 mark; and newcomer shortstop Julio Franco, who batted .273, drove in 80 runs, and stole 32 bases.

But Lenny Barker was unable to win consistently and was traded in late August to Atlanta for three players (Brett Butler, Brook Jacoby, and Rick Behenna) in one of the Indians' all-time best deals, and Toby Harrah was disabled for a month with a broken bone in his left hand.

The fans responded to the losing ways of the Indians by staying home. Only 768,941 customers—the major leagues' lowest attendance for 1983—paid their way through the turnstiles.

The Indians also suffered a major loss in 1983 when owner F. J. "Steve" O'Neill died at age 84 on August 29. Ownership of the franchise reverted to his estate, and O'Neill's nephew Patrick J. O'Neill became chairman of the board on September 10.

Though Sutcliffe, Heaton, and Lary Sorenson won 40 games among them, the Indians cumulative earned run average of 4.43 was the second worst in the American League, and while Pat Tabler hit .291 and Mike Hargrove .286, the team's batting average of .265 was eighth in the league.

	G	AB	R	H	2B	3B	HR	RBI	SB	AVG
Chris Bando	48	121	15	31	3	0	4	15	0	.256
Alan Bannister	117	377	51	100	25	4	5	45	6	.265
Carmen Castillo	23	36	9	10	2	1	1	3	1	.278
Wil Culmer	7	19	0	2	0	0	0	1	0	.105
Miguel Dilone	32	68	15	13	3	1	0	7	5	.191
Jim Essian	48	93	11	19	4	0	2	11	0	.204
Mike Fischlin	95	225	31	47	5	2	2	23	9	.209
Julio Franco (SS)	149	560	68	153	24	8	8	80	32	.273
Mike Hargrove (1B)	134	469	57	134	21	4	3	57	0	.286
Toby Harrah (3B)	138	526	81	140	23	1	9	53	16	.266
Ron Hassey (C)	117	341	48	92	21	0	6	42	2	.270
Rick Manning	50	194	20	54	6	0	1	10	7	.278
Bake McBride	70	230	21	67	8	1	1	18	8	.291
Karl Pagel	8	20	1	6	0	0	0	1	0	.300
Jack Perconte	14	26	1	7	1	0	0	0	3	.269
Broderick Perkins	79	184	23	50	10	0	0	24	1	.272
Kevin Rhomberg	12	21	2	10	0	0	0	2	1	.476
Pat Tabler (LF)	124	430	56	125	23	5	6	65	2	.291
Gorman Thomas (CF)	106	371	51	82	17	0	17	51	8	.221
Andre Thornton (DH)	141	508	78	143	27	1	17	77	4	.281
Manny Trillo (2B)	88	320	33	87	13	1	1	29	1	.272
Otto Velez	10	25	1	2	0	0	0	1	0	.080
George Vukovich (RF)	124	312	31	77	13	2	3	44	3	.247
		5,476	704	1,451	249	31	86	659	109	.265

1984

Record: 75–87

Finish: Sixth

Games Behind: 29

Manager: Pat Corrales

The Indians' 1984 season was divided into two parts. Unfortunately only the bottom line—the total of those two segments—counted, and they finished sixth in the American League East again, for the sixth time in seven years.

The Indians recorded only 17 victories in their first 50 games, through June 4, leaving them in last place, 21½ games behind Detroit.

Eight days later Gabe Paul and Phil Seghi, who continued to handle personnel matters following the August 29, 1983, death of owner F. J. "Steve" O'Neill, swung what would turn out to be their last big deal for the Indians.

They acquired Joe Carter and Mel Hall and two lesser players from the Chicago Cubs for Rick Sutcliffe, Ron Hassey, and George Frazier—and the deal obviously breathed new life into the Indians.

The Tribe's two new outfielders made an immediate impact, and the team went on to win 53 games while losing 52 the rest of the season. Still, the resurgence only enabled the Indians to climb out of the basement—which they did on August 17—but no higher.

They finished the year as the third-best run producer in the AL. Over the final 112 games they hit 102 homers, compared to only 21 in the first 50 games.

A healthy-again Andre Thornton put together another splendid season, leading the Indians with 33 homers and 99 runs batted in. Thornton tied an AL record by drawing six bases on balls in a 16-inning game in Baltimore, won by the Indians, 9–7.

Julio Franco followed his excellent rookie year with a .286 average, 79 RBIs, and 19 stolen bases, though he had trouble in the field. Franco committed 36 errors, the most by an Indians player in 1984.

Impressive, too, was Brett Butler, who was among the AL leaders in stolen bases (52), walks (86), runs (108), and triples (9), while batting .269. And Ernie Camacho blossomed into stardom as a reliever, setting a club record of 23 saves with a 5–9 won-lost record and 2.43 earned run average.

Because they had such a poor start and were out of contention practically from the beginning of the season, the Indians' attendance declined again, this time to 734,269, and another cash loss of more than $2 million was reported.

	W	L	G	GS	CG	IP	H	BB	K	ERA
Luis Aponte	1	0	25	0	0	50⅓	53	15	25	4.11
Jeff Barkley	0	0	3	0	0	4	6	1	4	6.75
Rick Behenna	0	3	3	3	0	9⅔	17	8	6	13.97
Bert Blyleven	19	7	33	32	12	245	204	74	170	2.87
Ernie Camacho	5	9	69	0	0	100	83	37	48	2.43
Steve Comer	4	8	22	20	1	117⅓	146	39	39	5.68
Jamie Easterly	3	1	26	1	0	69⅓	74	23	42	3.38
Steve Farr	3	11	31	16	0	116	106	46	83	4.58
George Frazier	3	2	22	0	0	44⅓	45	14	24	3.65
Neal Heaton	12	15	38	34	4	198⅔	231	75	75	5.21
Mike Jeffcoat	5	2	63	1	0	75⅓	82	24	41	2.99
Jose Roman	0	2	3	2	0	6	9	11	3	18.00
Ramon Romero	0	0	1	0	0	3	0	0	3	0.00
Don Schulze	3	6	19	14	2	85⅔	105	27	39	4.83
Roy Smith	5	5	22	14	0	86⅓	91	40	55	4.59
Dan Spillner	0	5	14	8	0	51	70	22	23	5.65
Rick Sutcliffe	4	5	15	15	2	94⅓	111	46	58	5.15
Jerry Ujdur	1	2	4	3	0	14⅓	22	6	6	6.91
Tom Waddell	7	4	58	0	0	97	68	37	59	3.06
	75	87		(163)	21	(1,467⅔)	1,523	545	803	4.26

Shutouts: Blyleven (4), Heaton
Saves: Camacho (23), Waddell (6), Easterly (2), Farr, Frazier, Jeffcoat, Spillner

	G	AB	R	H	2B	3B	HR	RBI	SB	AVG
Chris Bando	75	220	38	64	11	0	12	41	1	.291
Tony Bernazard (2B)	140	439	44	97	15	4	2	38	20	.221
Brett Butler (CF)	159	602	108	162	25	9	3	49	52	.269
Joe Carter	66	244	32	67	6	1	13	41	2	.275
Carmen Castillo	87	211	36	55	9	2	10	36	1	.261
Mike Fischlin	85	133	17	30	4	2	1	14	2	.226
Julio Franco (SS)	160	(658)	82	188	22	5	3	79	19	.286
Mel Hall (LF)	83	257	43	66	13	1	7	30	1	.257
Mike Hargrove (1B)	133	352	44	94	14	2	2	44	0	.267
Ron Hassey	48	149	11	38	5	1	0	19	1	.255
Brook Jacoby (3B)	126	439	64	116	19	3	7	40	3	.264
Jeff Moronko	7	19	1	3	1	0	0	3	0	.158
Otis Nixon	49	91	16	14	0	0	0	1	12	.154
Junior Noboa	23	11	3	4	0	0	0	0	1	.364
Broderick Perkins	58	66	5	13	1	0	0	4	0	.197
Jamie Quirk	1	1	1	1	0	0	1	1	0	1.000
Kevin Rhomberg	13	8	0	2	0	0	0	0	0	.250
Pat Tabler	144	473	66	137	21	3	10	68	3	.290
Andre Thornton (DH)	155	587	91	159	26	0	33	99	6	.271
George Vukovich (RF)	134	437	38	133	22	5	9	60	1	.304
Jerry Willard (C)	87	246	21	55	8	1	10	37	1	.224
		5,643	761	1,498	222	39	123	704	126	.265

1985

Record: 60–102
Finish: Seventh
Games Behind: 39½
Manager: Pat Corrales

Three veteran baseball executives were hired to run the Indians for the estate of the late F. J. "Steve" O'Neill, and in the wake of the team's strong finish in 1984 there appeared to be light at the end of the tunnel.

Instead, matters worsened for the Indians, and they suffered their third 102-loss season in franchise history under the new direction of president and chief executive officer Peter Bavasi, senior vice president Dan O'Brien, and vice president Joe Klein.

Gabe Paul remained a director of the club, but he was soon ushered into retirement, while general manager Phil Seghi was given the new title "senior player personnel adviser."

Very little went right for the beleaguered team under manager Pat Corrales. The Indians lost their first five games, were never higher than fourth (the day after the opener), and spent all but 15 days of the season in the basement of the American League East.

Their 39½-game deficit behind Toronto was the largest in 14 years, and their pitching staff's cumulative earned run average of 4.91 was the worst in the AL.

And the lack of success was reflected at the box office as attendance fell to 655,181, worst in the major leagues and lowest in Cleveland in 12 years.

Despite a potent offense triggered by Brett Butler, who led the team with a .311 average (fifth best in the AL), not one starting pitcher won in double figures, as Bert Blyleven went 9–11 and Neal Heaton 9–17.

Injuries also played a role in the Indians' demise as Andre Thornton was idled for more than six weeks after another knee operation during spring training, and six pitchers spent significant time on the disabled list.

Ernie Camacho, who had set a club record with 23 saves in 1984, underwent elbow surgery in mid-April and was sidelined the rest of the season; Vern Ruhle spent five weeks on the DL; Rick Behenna, trying to come back from May 1984 surgery on his shoulder, was inactive virtually the entire season; Dave Von Ohlen missed three and a half months with injuries; Roy Smith was hit in the ear with a line drive and was unable to pitch for a month; and an elbow operation ended Tom Waddell's season in early September.

The Indians also lost Mel Hall after 23 games when he received multiple injuries, including a broken pelvis, in an automobile accident in Texas on May 9.

Butler was by far the Indians' best offensive player. His on-base percentage (.377), runs (106), stolen bases (47), and triples (14) all were among the league leaders. He also was excellent in the field, making several sensational catches and committing only one error.

Julio Franco also was an offensive leader—but he also led the team in errors again with 36, 35 of them as a shortstop, most in the AL at that position, and one as a second baseman.

	W	L	G	GS	CG	IP	H	BB	K	ERA
Jeff Barkley	0	3	21	0	0	41	37	15	30	5.27
Rick Behenna	0	2	4	4	0	19⅔	29	8	4	7.78
Bert Blyleven*	9	11	23	(23)	(15)	(179⅔)	163	40	(129)	3.26
Ernie Camacho	0	1	2	0	0	3⅓	4	1	2	8.10
Bryan Clark	3	4	31	3	0	62⅔	78	34	24	6.32
Keith Creel	2	5	15	8	0	62	73	23	31	4.79
Jamie Easterly	4	1	50	7	0	98⅔	96	53	58	3.92
Neal Heaton	9	17	36	33	5	207⅔	244	80	82	4.90
Mike Jeffcoat	0	0	9	0	0	9⅔	8	6	4	2.79
Jerry Reed	3	5	33	5	0	72⅓	67	19	37	4.11
Jose Roman	0	4	5	3	0	16⅓	13	14	12	6.61
Ramon Romero	2	3	19	10	0	64⅓	69	38	38	6.58
Vern Ruhle	2	10	42	16	1	125	139	30	54	4.32
Don Schulze	4	10	19	18	1	94⅓	128	19	37	6.01
Roy Smith	1	4	12	11	1	62⅓	84	17	28	5.34
Rich Thompson	3	8	57	0	0	80	95	48	30	6.30
Dave Von Ohlen	3	2	26	0	0	43⅓	47	20	12	2.91
Tom Waddell	8	6	49	9	1	112⅔	104	39	53	4.87
Curt Wardle	7	6	15	12	0	66	78	34	37	6.68
	60	(102)		162	24	1,421	(1,556)	547	702	4.91

*League leader in games started with 37 (14 with Minnesota), complete games with 24 (9 with Minnesota), innings pitched with 293⅔ (114 with Minnesota), strikeouts with 206 (77 with Minnesota).
Shutouts: Blyleven (4), Heaton
Saves: Waddell (9), Reed (8), Thompson (5), Ruhle (3), Clark (2), Barkley

	G	AB	R	H	2B	3B	HR	RBI	SB	AVG
Benny Ayala	46	76	10	19	7	0	2	15	0	.250
Chris Bando	73	173	11	24	4	1	0	13	0	.139
Butch Benton	31	67	5	12	4	0	0	7	0	.179
Tony Bernazard (2B)	153	500	73	137	26	3	11	59	17	.274
Brett Butler (CF)	152	591	106	184	28	14	5	50	47	.311
Joe Carter (LF)	143	489	64	128	27	0	15	59	24	.262
Carmen Castillo	67	184	27	45	5	1	11	25	3	.245
Mike Fischlin	73	60	12	12	4	1	0	2	0	.200
Julio Franco (SS)	160	636	97	183	33	4	6	90	13	.288
Mel Hall	23	66	7	21	6	0	0	12	0	.318
Mike Hargrove	107	284	31	81	14	1	1	27	1	.285
Brook Jacoby (3B)	161	606	72	166	26	3	20	87	2	.274
Johnnie LeMaster	11	20	0	3	0	0	0	2	0	.150
Otis Nixon	104	162	34	38	4	0	3	9	20	.235
Pat Tabler (1B)	117	404	47	111	18	3	5	59	0	.275
Andre Thornton (DH)	124	461	49	109	13	0	22	88	3	.236
George Vukovich (RF)	149	434	43	106	22	0	8	45	2	.244
Jerry Willard (C)	104	300	39	81	13	0	7	36	0	.270
Jim Wilson	4	14	2	5	0	0	0	4	0	.357
		5,527	729	1,465	254	31	116	689	132	.265

1986

Record: 84–78
Finish: Fifth
Games Behind: 11½
Manager: Pat Corrales

For the first time in more than two decades the Indians did more than serve as doormats for the rest of the American League East, though they still fell short of being a contender in 1986.

With the AL's most potent offense featuring four regulars who hit .300, the Indians made a 24 game-improvement over their 1985 record of 60–102, best in the team's history. They led the league with a .284 batting average, 831 runs, and 141 stolen bases.

After a 7–8 start the Indians recovered to win 10 straight, climbing into first place (if only for four days). Though they never made it back to the top, they were third with a 46–39 record at the All-Star break, and on July 23 were within five games of division-leading Boston.

The improvement on the field resulted in a corresponding improvement at the box office as attendance climbed to 1,471,977, highest in 27 years.

The 1986 season also saw the purchase of the Indians by Richard E. and David H. Jacobs from the estate of the late F. J. "Steve" O'Neill.

Announcement of the impending sale for a reported $35 million was made on July 2, though it wasn't approved until November 13 by the O'Neill estate, which owned 59.5 percent of the franchise, and other stockholders. The AL formally sanctioned the sale on December 9.

The Tribe's four .300 hitters were Pat Tabler (.326), who finished fourth in the race for the AL batting championship, Julio Franco (.306), Joe Carter (.302), and Tony Bernazard (.301).

Carter, who led the AL with 121 RBI, smashed 29 homers, including three in a game in Boston on August 29 when the Indians beat the Red Sox, 7–3.

Rookie Cory Snyder, a member of the 1984 U.S. Olympic team and the Tribe's number-one selection (fourth overall) in the amateur draft that year, made a significant impact on the team when he was promoted from Class AAA Maine of the International League on June 12. Snyder cracked 24 homers and drove in 69 runs while batting .272 in 103 games.

Knuckleballer Tom Candiotti also came from virtually nowhere to be the Indians best pitcher. After being given a spring training tryout upon his release by Milwaukee, Candiotti won 16 games and lost 12, and he led the AL with 17 complete games.

Another knuckleballer, 47-year old Phil Niekro, who had been rejected by the New York Yankees, also was signed and responded with an 11–11 record.

Greg Swindell, who three months earlier had pitched for the University of Texas and then became the Indians' number-one pick in the 1986 amateur draft, was promoted to Cleveland on August 21 and proceeded to post a 5–2 record in nine starts.

	W	L	G	GS	CG	IP	H	BB	K	ERA
Scott Bailes	10	10	62	10	0.	112⅔	123	43	60	4.95
John Butcher	1	5	13	8	1	50⅔	86	13	16	6.93
Ernie Camacho	2	4	51	0	0	57⅓	60	31	36	4.08
Tom Candiotti	16	12	36	34	(17)	252⅓	234	106	167	3.57
Jamie Easterly	0	2	13	0	0	17⅔	27	12	9	7.64
Neal Heaton	3	6	12	12	2	74⅓	73	34	24	4.24
Doug Jones	1	0	11	0	0	18	18	6	12	2.50
Jim Kern	1	1	16	0	0	27⅓	34	23	11	7.90
Phil Niekro	11	11	34	32	5	210⅓	241	95	81	4.32
Dickie Noles	3	2	32	0	0	54⅔	56	30	32	5.10
Bryan Oelkers	3	3	35	4	0	69	70	40	33	4.70
Reggie Ritter	0	0	5	0	0	10	14	4	6	6.30
Jose Roman	1	2	6	5	0	22	23	17	9	6.55
Ken Schrom	14	7	34	33	3	206	217	49	87	4.54
Don Schulze	4	4	19	13	1	84⅔	88	34	33	5.00
Greg Swindell	5	2	9	9	1	61⅔	57	15	46	4.23
Frank Wills	4	4	26	0	0	40⅓	43	16	32	4.91
Rich Yett	5	3	39	3	1	78⅔	84	37	50	5.15
	84	78		(163)	31	1,447⅔	1,548	605	744	4.58

Shutouts: Candiotti (3), Butcher, Schrom, Yett
Saves: Camacho (20), Bailes (7), Wills (4), Jones, Oelkers, Yett

	G	AB	R	H	2B	3B	HR	RBI	SB	AVG
Andy Allanson (C)	101	293	30	66	7	3	1	29	10	.225
Chris Bando	92	254	28	68	9	0	2	26	0	.268
Jay Bell	5	14	3	5	2	0	1	4	0	.357
Tony Bernazard (2B)	146	562	88	169	28	4	17	73	17	.301
Brett Butler (CF)	161	587	92	163	17	(14)	4	51	32	.278
Joe Carter (RF)	162	663	108	200	36	9	29	(121)	29	.302
Carmen Castillo	85	205	34	57	9	0	8	32	2	.278
Dave Clark	18	58	10	16	1	0	3	9	1	.276
Julio Franco (SS)	149	599	80	183	30	5	10	74	10	.306
Mel Hall (LF)	140	442	68	131	29	2	18	77	6	.296
Brook Jacoby (3B)	158	583	83	168	30	4	17	80	2	.288
Fran Mullins	28	40	3	7	4	0	0	5	0	.175
Otis Nixon	105	95	33	25	4	1	0	8	23	.263
Dan Rohn	6	10	1	2	0	0	0	2	0	.200
Cory Snyder	103	416	58	113	21	1	24	69	2	.272
Pat Tabler (1B)	130	473	61	154	29	2	6	48	3	.326
Andre Thornton (DH)	120	401	49	92	14	0	17	66	4	.229
Eddie Williams	5	7	2	1	0	0	0	1	0	.143
		5,702	(831)	(1,620)	270	(45)	157	(775)	(141)	(.284)

1987

Record: 61–101
Finish: Seventh
Games Behind: 37
Managers: Pat Corrales, Doc Edwards

The Indians were everybody's favorite to win their first championship of any kind in 33 years, based on their performance in 1986; they appeared on the cover of *Sports Illustrated* and were the subject of a story in the May 1987 issue of *Sport* magazine entitled, "The Erie Sensation."

But instead of running off with the American League pennant, the Indians suffered through the franchise's fourth 100-loss season, the second in three years.

A month after the season ended, Henry J. "Hank" Peters was lured out of retirement to take over as president of the Indians. He replaced Peter Bavasi, who had resigned a month after the purchase of the Cleveland franchise by Richard E. and David H. Jacobs was approved by the AL.

It was a homecoming of sorts for Peters, who had served as vice president and director of player personnel for the Indians from 1966 until he resigned in December 1971 to become president of the National Association (minor leagues).

The failure of the Indians to live up to expectations in 1987 cost Pat Corrales his job. He was fired July 16, with the Tribe languishing in the basement of the AL East with a 31–56 record, 23 games out of first place.

Corrales was replaced by coach Doc Edwards, but the Indians didn't fare much better under their new manager. They won 30 and lost 45 under Edwards as pitching continued to be the primary problem.

Nobody on the staff won more than seven games, and the Tribe's 5.28 earned run average was the highest in the AL since 1956 when the Washington Senators compiled a 5.33 mark.

The pitching was so bad the Tribe signed 42-year old Steve Carlton after he'd been released by the Chicago White Sox. Carlton went 5–9 in 23 appearances (14 as a starter) before he was traded to Minnesota on July 31 for a minor league player.

The bull pen was just as frustrating, first to Corrales and then to Edwards, ranking 13th in the league with 25 saves. Ernie Camacho, who had saved 20 games in 1986 and a club-record 23 in 1984, was demoted to the minors on May 30 with one save, an 0–1 record, and a 9.22 ERA in 15 games.

Defense also was a problem for the Indians, who committed an AL-high 153 errors.

The Indians lost 12 of their first 13 games and then remained in seventh place all season.

Despite the pitching problems, the Indians' offense was respectable with a .263 team average, seventh in the AL, led by Julio Franco's .319, eighth best in the league.

Three Tribesmen—Cory Snyder, Joe Carter, and Brook Jacoby—hit more than 30 home runs, tying an AL record. Snyder's 33 gave him 57 in less than two full major league seasons, but he also set a club record with 166 strikeouts, and his average fell 36 points to .236.

Snyder, Carter, and Jacoby each hit three homers in one game in 1987: Snyder on May 21 against Minnesota in a 6–3 victory at the Stadium; Carter on May 28 against the Red Sox in a 12–8 loss at Boston; and Jacoby on July 3 against Chicago in a 14–9 loss at the Stadium.

Phil Niekro, who went 7–11 before he was traded to Toronto for a minor league player on August 9, beat Detroit, 9–6, at the Stadium on June 1, making him and brother Joe the winningest brother combination in baseball history. It gave the Niekros a total of 530 victories (314 for Phil, 216 for Joe), better than Gaylord and Jim Perry, who won 529 games between them. (The Niekros wound up their careers with 539 victories, 318 by Phil and 221 by Joe.)

Andre Thornton, hobbled by numerous knee injuries, batted only 85 times, hitting for a .118 average without a home run, and retired when the season ended.

In 1987 the Indians also lost longtime front office executive Phil Seghi, who died at age 68 on January 8. He was the organization's "senior player personnel director" at the time of his death in Thousand Oaks, California.

Indians pitcher Phil Niekro (right) gets a champagne shower from center fielder Brett Butler after beating the Detroit Tigers, 9–6, on June 1, 1987. The victory was the 314th of Niekro's career and gave him and brother Joe, then of the New York Yankees, a combined total of 530 victories, the most in major league history.

	W	L	G	GS	CG	IP	H	BB	K	ERA
Darrel Akerfelds	2	6	16	13	1	74⅔	84	38	42	6.75
Mike Armstrong	1	0	14	0	0	18⅔	27	10	9	8.68
Scott Bailes	7	8	39	17	0	120⅓	145	47	65	4.64
Ernie Camacho	0	1	15	0	0	13⅔	21	5	9	9.22
Tom Candiotti	7	18	32	32	7	201⅔	193	93	111	4.78
Steve Carlton	5	9	23	14	3	109	111	63	71	5.37
Jamie Easterly	1	1	16	0	0	31⅔	26	13	22	4.55
John Farrell	5	1	10	9	1	69	68	22	28	3.39
Don Gordon	0	3	21	0	0	39⅔	49	12	20	4.08
Mark Huismann	2	3	20	0	0	35⅓	38	8	23	5.09
Doug Jones	6	5	49	0	0	91⅓	101	24	87	3.15
Jeff Kaiser	0	0	2	0	0	3⅓	4	3	2	16.20
Phil Niekro	7	11	22	22	2	123⅔	142	53	57	5.89
Reggie Ritter	1	1	14	0	0	26⅔	33	16	11	6.08
Ken Schrom	6	13	32	29	4	153⅔	185	57	61	6.50
Sammy Stewart	4	2	25	0	0	27	25	21	25	5.67
Greg Swindell	3	8	16	15	4	102⅓	112	37	97	5.10
Ed Vande Berg	1	0	55	0	0	72⅓	96	21	40	5.10
Tom Waddell	0	1	6	0	0	5⅔	7	7	6	14.29
Frank Wills	0	1	6	0	0	5⅓	3	7	4	5.06
Rich Yett	3	9	37	11	2	97⅔	96	49	59	5.25
	61	(101)		(162)	24	1,422⅔	1,566	606	849	5.28

Shutouts: Candiotti (2), Schrom, Swindell
Saves: Jones (8), Bailes (6), Stewart (3), Huismann (2), Armstrong, Camacho, Carlton, Gordon, Wills, Yett

	G	AB	R	H	2B	3B	HR	RBI	SB	AVG
Andy Allanson	50	154	17	41	6	0	3	16	1	.266
Chris Bando (C)	89	211	20	46	9	0	5	16	0	.218
Jay Bell	38	125	14	27	9	1	2	13	2	.216
Tony Bernazard (2B)	79	293	39	70	12	1	11	30	7	.239
Brett Butler (CF)	137	522	91	154	25	8	9	41	33	.295
Joe Carter (1B)	149	588	83	155	27	2	32	106	31	.264
Carmen Castillo	89	220	27	55	17	0	11	31	1	.250
Dave Clark	29	87	11	18	5	0	3	12	1	.207
Rick Dempsey	60	141	16	25	10	0	1	9	0	.177
Brian Dorsett	5	11	2	3	0	0	1	3	0	.273
Julio Franco (SS)	128	495	86	158	24	3	8	52	32	.319
Doug Frobel	29	40	5	4	0	0	2	5	0	.100
Dave Gallagher	15	36	2	4	1	1	0	1	2	.111
Mel Hall (LF)	142	485	57	136	21	1	18	76	5	.280
Tommy Hinzo	67	257	31	68	9	3	3	21	9	.265
Brook Jacoby (3B)	155	540	73	162	26	4	32	69	2	.300
Otis Nixon	19	17	2	1	0	0	0	1	2	.059
Junior Noboa	39	80	7	18	2	1	0	7	1	.225
Casey Parsons	18	25	2	4	0	0	1	5	0	.160
Cory Snyder (RF)	157	577	74	136	24	2	33	82	5	.236
Pat Tabler (DH)	151	553	66	170	34	3	11	86	5	.307
Andre Thornton	36	85	8	10	2	0	0	5	1	.118
Eddie Williams	22	64	9	11	4	0	1	4	0	.172
		5,606	742	1,476	267	30	187	691	140	.263

1988

Record: 78–84
Finish: Sixth
Games Behind: 11
Manager: Doc Edwards

The Indians solved most of their pitching problems, thanks primarily to the presence of Greg Swindell and Doug Jones, and started the 1988 season with a rush, climbing to the top of the American League East with a club-record 16 victories in April.

As late as June 10 they were still near the top, only a game out of first place with a 36–23 record, and high hopes were building in Cleveland.

But then a decline set in as the offense slumped at midseason. By July 30, after 29 losses in 45 games, the Indians were fourth at 52–52, and never again climbed over .500. On August 2 they dropped into sixth place and stayed there.

Still, they wound up only 11 games behind Boston, which won the AL East. It was the closest the Indians finished to the top since 1959 when their deficit was seven games from the top.

Swindell, who sat out the second half of the 1987 season with an elbow injury, bounced back with an 18–14 record and 3.20 earned run average. Tom Candiotti and John Farrell each won 14 games. The last time the Indians had had three pitchers with at least 14 victories was in 1956, when Early Wynn, Bob Lemon, and Herb Score each won 20.

Jones, 30, who had spent most of the 10 previous seasons in the minors and earned a place on the staff as a spring training invitee, saved a club-record 37 games, third most in the AL. He also set a major league record by recording a save in 15 consecutive opportunities.

But this time it was the offense that failed and dragged the Indians down. Prominently absent was center fielder and leadoff batter Brett Butler, who became a free agent and signed with San Francisco.

Julio Franco, switched from shortstop to second base, came through with his third straight .300 season, but nobody else hit that high.

The fast start by the Indians sparked an early surge in attendance, and though it fell off in the last six weeks, 1,411,610 fans spun the turnstiles.

	W	L	G	GS	CG	IP	H	BB	K	ERA
Scott Bailes	9	14	37	21	5	145	149	46	53	4.90
Bud Black	2	3	16	7	0	59	59	23	44	5.03
Tom Candiotti	14	8	31	31	11	216⅔	225	53	137	3.28
Chris Codiroli	0	4	14	2	0	19⅓	32	10	12	9.31
Jeff Dedmon	1	0	21	0	0	33⅔	35	21	17	4.54
John Farrell	14	10	31	30	4	210⅓	216	67	92	4.24
Don Gordon	3	4	38	0	0	59⅓	65	19	20	4.40
Brad Havens	2	3	28	0	0	57⅓	62	17	30	3.14
Doug Jones	3	4	51	0	0	83⅓	69	16	72	2.27
Jeff Kaiser	0	0	3	0	0	2⅔	2	1	0	0.00
Bill Laskey	1	0	17	0	0	24⅓	32	6	17	5.18
Rod Nichols	1	7	11	10	3	69⅓	73	23	31	5.06
Jon Perlman	0	2	10	0	0	19⅔	25	11	10	5.49
Rick Rodriguez	1	2	10	5	0	33	43	17	9	7.09
Dan Schatzeder	0	2	15	0	0	16	26	2	10	9.56
Greg Swindell	18	14	33	33	12	242	234	45	180	3.20
Mike Walker	0	1	3	1	0	8⅔	8	10	7	7.27
Rich Yett	9	6	23	22	0	134⅓	146	55	71	4.62
	78	84		(162)	35	1,434	1,501	442	812	4.16

Shutouts: Swindell (4), Bailes (2), Candiotti
Saves: Jones (37), Schatzeder (3), Black, Codiroli, Dedmon, Gordon, Havens, Laskey

	G	AB	R	H	2B	3B	HR	RBI	SB	AVG
Andy Allanson (C)	133	434	44	114	11	0	5	50	5	.263
Rod Allen	5	11	1	1	1	0	0	0	0	.091
Chris Bando	32	72	6	9	1	0	1	8	0	.125
Jay Bell (SS)	73	211	23	46	5	1	2	21	4	.218
Joe Carter (CF)	157	621	85	168	36	6	27	98	27	.271
Carmen Castillo	66	176	12	48	8	0	4	14	6	.273
Dave Clark	63	156	11	41	4	1	3	18	0	.263
Don Firova	1	0	0	0	0	0	0	0	0	—
Julio Franco (2B)	152	613	88	186	23	6	10	54	25	.303
Terry Francona	62	212	24	66	8	0	1	12	0	.311
Mel Hall (LF)	150	515	69	144	32	4	6	71	7	.280
Brook Jacoby (3B)	152	552	59	133	25	0	9	49	2	.241
Houston Jimenez	9	21	1	1	0	0	0	1	0	.048
Scott Jordan	7	9	0	1	0	0	0	0	0	.111
Ron Kittle (DH)	75	225	31	58	8	0	18	43	0	.258
Tom Lampkin	4	4	0	0	0	0	0	0	0	.000
Luis Medina	16	51	10	13	0	0	6	8	0	.255
Domingo Ramos	22	46	7	12	1	0	0	5	0	.261
Cory Snyder (RF)	142	511	71	139	24	3	26	75	5	.272
Pat Tabler	41	143	16	32	5	1	1	17	1	.224
Ron Tingley	9	24	1	4	0	0	1	2	0	.167
Willie Upshaw (1B)	149	493	58	121	22	3	11	50	12	.245
Ron Washington	69	223	30	57	14	2	2	21	3	.256
Eddie Williams	10	21	3	4	0	0	0	1	0	.190
Reggie Williams	11	31	7	7	2	0	1	3	0	.226
Paul Zuvella	51	130	9	30	5	1	0	7	0	.231
		5,505	666	1,435	235	28	134	629	97	.261

1989

Record: 73–89
Finish: Sixth
Games Behind: 16
Managers: Doc Edwards, John Hart

Despite a couple of outstanding individual accomplishments by Joe Carter, the Indians' offense slumbered too often again, neutralizing the team's best pitching performance since 1976, and the result was another sixth-place finish.

It was the 11th time in 12 years that the Tribe wound up sixth or seventh in the American·League East standings.

Though their won-lost record was nothing to rave about, the Indians actually had a chance to overtake front-running Toronto as late as August 4. At that juncture the Indians were in second place, only 1½ games behind the Blue Jays with a 54–54 mark, but they folded down the stretch.

They won only 19 and lost 35 in the final two months, and along the way Doc Edwards lost his job. He was fired on September 12 after dropping three out of four to Toronto, leaving the Tribe with a 65–78 record, in sixth place, 14½ games off the pace.

Edwards was replaced on an interim basis by John Hart, then a special assignment scout for the Indians, but his guidance of the team had no great effect. The Tribe went 8–11 under Hart, and John McNamara was hired as the team's 35th manager on November 3.

Among the 20 pitchers employed by the Indians in 1989, reliever Doug Jones sparkled again, and so did starters Greg Swindell, Tom Candiotti, and Bud Black. Jones recorded 32 saves in 59 appearances, while Swindell and Candiotti each won 13 games, and Black 12.

Carter smashed three home runs in each of two games— on June 24 in a 7–3 victory over the Rangers in Arlington, Texas, and again on July 19 as the Tribe beat the Twins, 10–1, in Minneapolis.

But it was the overall failure of the offense that hurt the Indians most.

Jerry Browne, acquired in a preseason deal with Texas that sent Julio Franco to the Rangers, was the Tribe's most consistent batter with a .299 average.

Carter hit only .243, though his 35 homers were a career high, and Cory Snyder, hampered by a sore back in June and July, slumped to .215 with 18 homers. He was benched in August, creating a rift between him and Edwards, which didn't help the manager keep his job.

In addition to the preseason trade that brought Browne, Pete O'Brien, and Oddibe McDowell from Texas in exchange for Franco, the Indians also sent shortstop Jay Bell to Pittsburgh for Felix Fermin. The Franco deal was "to improve team chemistry," according to Tribe officials, and the acquisition of Fermin was to bolster the defense, they said.

	W	L	G	GS	CG	IP	H	BB	K	ERA
Neil Allen	0	1	3	0	0	3	8	0	0	15.00
Keith Atherton	0	3	32	0	0	39	48	13	13	4.15
Scott Bailes	5	9	34	11	0	113⅔	116	29	47	4.28
Bud Black	12	11	33	32	6	222⅓	213	52	88	3.36
Tom Candiotti	13	10	31	31	4	206	188	55	124	3.10
Steve Davis	1	1	12	2	0	25⅔	34	14	12	8.06
John Farrell	9	14	31	31	7	208	196	71	132	3.63
Brad Havens	0	0	7	0	0	13⅓	18	7	6	4.05
Doug Jones	7	10	59	0	0	80⅔	76	13	65	2.34
Jeff Kaiser	0	1	6	0	0	3⅔	5	5	4	7.36
Rod Nichols	4	6	15	11	0	71⅓	81	24	42	4.40
Steve Olin	1	4	25	0	0	36	35	14	24	3.75
Jesse Orosco	3	4	69	0	0	78	54	26	79	2.08
Rudy Seanez	0	0	5	0	0	5	1	4	7	3.60
Joe Skalski	0	2	2	1	0	6⅔	7	4	3	6.75
Tim Stoddard	0	0	14	0	0	21⅓	25	7	12	2.95
Greg Swindell	13	6	28	28	5	184⅓	170	51	129	3.37
Kevin Wickander	0	0	2	0	0	2⅔	6	2	0	3.38
Ed Wojna	0	1	9	3	0	33	31	14	10	4.09
Rich Yett	5	6	32	12	1	99	111	47	47	5.00
	73	89	(162)		23	1,453	1,423	452	844	3.65

Shutouts: Black (3), Farrell (2), Swindell (2)
Saves: Jones (32), Orosco (3), Atherton (2), Olin

	G	AB	R	H	2B	3B	HR	RBI	SB	AVG
Luis Aguayo	47	97	7	17	4	1	1	8	0	.175
Andy Allanson (C)	111	323	30	75	9	1	3	17	4	.232
Beau Allred	13	24	0	6	3	0	0	1	0	.250
Albert Belle	62	218	22	49	8	4	7	37	2	.225
Jerry Browne (2B)	153	598	83	179	31	4	5	45	14	.299
Joe Carter (CF)	(162)	(651)	84	158	32	4	35	105	13	.243
Dave Clark (DH)	102	253	21	60	12	0	8	29	0	.237
Pete Dalena	5	7	0	1	1	0	0	0	0	.143
Felix Fermin (SS)	156	484	50	115	9	1	0	21	6	.238
Denny Gonzalez	8	17	3	5	1	0	0	1	0	.294
Dave Hengel	12	25	2	3	1	0	0	1	0	.120
Mark Higgins	6	10	1	1	0	0	0	0	0	.100
Tommy Hinzo	18	17	4	0	0	0	0	0	1	.000
Brook Jacoby (3B)	147	519	49	141	26	5	13	64	2	.272
Dion James	71	245	26	75	11	0	4	29	1	.306
Pat Keedy	9	14	3	3	2	0	0	1	0	.214
Brad Komminsk	71	198	27	47	8	2	8	33	8	.237
Tom Magrann	9	10	0	0	0	0	0	0	0	.000
Oddibe McDowell (LF)	69	239	33	53	5	2	3	22	12	.222
Luis Medina	30	83	8	17	1	0	4	8	0	.205
Pete O'Brien (1B)	155	554	75	144	24	1	12	55	3	.260
Mark Salas	30	77	4	17	4	1	2	7	0	.221
Danny Sheaffer	7	16	1	1	0	0	0	0	0	.063
Joel Skinner	79	178	10	41	10	0	1	13	1	.230
Cory Snyder (RF)	132	489	49	105	17	0	18	59	6	.215
Mike Young	32	59	2	11	0	0	1	5	1	.186
Paul Zuvella	24	58	10	16	2	0	2	6	0	.276
	5,463	604	1,340	221	26	127	567	74	.245

1990

Record: 77–85
Finish: Fourth
Games Behind: 11
Manager: John McNamara

A flurry of activity, some of which proved beneficial, preceded the 1990 season for the Indians, and while they reversed their usual pattern, the result was pretty much the same.

That is, despite a slow start and an untypical fast finish, they failed again to contend for the pennant and wound up with a sub-.500 record for the eighth time in nine years.

Before the season started—a week late because of a four-week spring training lockout by the owners—the Indians traded their most productive hitter, Joe Carter. They also jumped into the free-agent market by signing Keith Hernandez to a two-year, $3.5 million guaranteed contract.

In two other significant deals made during the season, Alex Cole was acquired and Bud Black dispatched.

The Carter trade was a good one because it brought Sandy Alomar, Jr., and Carlos Baerga, as well as Chris James, from San Diego. Alomar caught 132 games, hit .290, and was the unanimous winner of the American League Rookie of the Year award, the fourth Tribe player to be so honored.

The signing of Hernandez was a disaster. The veteran first baseman was supposed to provide maturity and leadership to the young Indians, according to team officials.

But Hernandez did neither. Because of a series of nagging injuries, he was on the disabled list several times and played in only 43 games, batting .200 on 26-for-130.

Cole, picked up in a minor league transaction on July 11, hit .300 (with an on-base percentage of .379) in 63 games, and stole 40 bases, fourth most in the AL. Five of Cole's thefts—a club record—came in one game, a 4–1 victory over Kansas City at the Stadium on August 1.

The Black deal was necessitated by the fact that he would become a free agent at the end of the season and was seeking a multiyear contract that the Indians were unwilling to consider.

One of the mainstays of the Indians' pitching staff, Black was 11–10 when he was traded on September 16 to Toronto for three minor league pitchers. The trade did not turn out well for the Tribe.

Despite Black's absence, the Indians came on strong in the final month, posting an 18–13 record to climb out of sixth place and into fourth. It was their highest finish since 1976 (excluding the strike-shortened 1981 season).

Doug Jones again anchored the bull pen, erasing his own club record for saves by registering 43 with a team-best 2.56 earned run average. Tom Candiotti and Greg Swindell (along with Black) were the most consistent starters, but an elbow injury suffered by John Farrell was a factor in the Indians' midseason slump when the Tribe lost 15 of 20 games.

Disappointing, too, for the second straight season was Cory Snyder, who hit .233 with 14 homers and struck out an average of once every 3.71 trips to the plate. He batted just once in the Tribe's final 25 games. Two months after the season ended, Snyder was traded to the Chicago White Sox for pitchers Eric King and Shawn Hillegas.

Toronto's Dave Stieb pitched the 10th no-hitter against the Indians on September 2, beating them, 3–0, at the Stadium.

	W	L	G	GS	CG	IP	H	BB	K	ERA
Kevin Bearse	0	2	3	3	0	7⅓	16	5	2	12.91
Bud Black	11	10	29	29	5	191	171	58	103	3.53
Tom Candiotti	15	11	31	29	3	202	207	55	128	3.65
John Farrell	4	5	17	17	1	96⅔	108	33	44	4.28
Mauro Gozzo	0	0	2	0	0	3	2	2	2	0.00
Cecilio Guante	2	3	26	1	0	46⅔	38	18	30	5.01
Doug Jones	5	5	66	0	0	84⅓	66	22	55	2.56
Jeff Kaiser	0	0	5	0	0	12⅔	16	7	9	3.55
Charles Nagy	2	4	9	8	0	45⅔	58	21	26	5.91
Rod Nichols	0	3	4	2	0	16	24	6	3	7.88
Al Nipper	2	3	9	5	0	24	35	19	12	6.75
Steve Olin	4	4	50	1	0	92⅓	96	26	64	3.41
Jesse Orosco	5	4	55	0	0	64⅔	58	38	55	3.90
Rudy Seanez	2	1	24	0	0	27⅓	22	25	24	5.60
Jeff Shaw	3	4	12	9	0	48⅔	73	20	25	6.66
Greg Swindell	12	9	34	34	3	214⅔	245	47	135	4.40
Efrain Valdez	1	1	13	0	0	23⅔	20	14	13	3.04
Sergio Valdez	6	6	24	13	0	102⅔	109	35	63	4.75
Mike Walker	2	6	18	11	0	75⅔	82	42	34	4.88
Colby Ward	1	3	22	0	0	36	31	21	23	4.25
Kevin Wickander	0	1	10	0	0	12⅓	14	4	10	3.65
	77	85		(162)	12	1,427⅓	1,491	518	860	4.26

Shutouts: Black (2), Candiotti
Saves: Jones (43), Orosco (2), Olin, Ward

	G	AB	R	H	2B	3B	HR	RBI	SB	AVG
Beau Allred	4	16	2	3	1	0	1	2	0	.188
Sandy Alomar (C)	132	445	60	129	26	2	9	66	4	.290
Carlos Baerga	108	312	46	81	17	2	7	47	0	.260
Albert Belle	9	23	1	4	0	0	1	3	0	.174
Tom Brookens	64	154	18	41	7	2	1	20	0	.266
Jerry Browne (2B)	140	513	92	137	26	5	6	50	12	.267
Alex Cole	63	227	43	68	5	4	0	13	40	.300
Felix Fermin (SS)	148	414	47	106	13	2	1	40	3	.256
Keith Hernandez (1B)	43	130	7	26	2	0	1	8	0	.200
Brook Jacoby (3B)	155	553	77	162	24	4	14	75	1	.293
Chris James (DH)	140	528	62	158	32	4	12	70	4	.299
Dion James	87	248	28	68	15	2	1	22	5	.274
Stan Jefferson	49	98	21	27	8	0	2	10	8	.276
Candy Maldonado (LF)	155	590	76	161	32	2	22	95	3	.273
Jeff Manto	30	76	12	17	5	1	2	14	0	.224
Mark McLemore	8	12	2	2	0	0	0	0	0	.167
Ken Phelps	24	61	4	7	0	0	0	0	1	.115
Rafael Santana	7	13	3	3	0	0	1	3	0	.231
Joel Skinner	49	139	16	35	4	1	2	16	0	.252
Cory Snyder (RF)	123	438	46	102	27	3	14	55	1	.233
Steve Springer	4	12	1	2	0	0	0	1	0	.167
Turner Ward	14	46	10	16	2	1	1	10	3	.348
Mitch Webster (CF)	128	437	58	110	20	6	12	55	22	.252
		5,485	732	1,465	266	41	110	675	107	.267

1991

Record: 57–105
Finish: Seventh
Games Behind: 34
Managers: John McNamara, Mike Hargrove

It was supposed to be a renaissance season for the Indians, based on their strong finish in 1990, the belief that they had strengthened their pitching staff, and the presence of several promising young players.

Instead, 1991 became the worst in franchise history—the 105 losses exceeding by three the previous club record for futility set in 1914 and equaled in 1971 and 1985.

And because it was so bad, John McNamara was fired on July 6, with the Indians floundering in the basement with a 25–52 record, 20 games out of first place.

First base coach Mike Hargrove took over as the franchise's 36th manager. A former Tribe player (1979–85), Hargrove worked his way up through the managerial ranks after remaining out of baseball in 1986.

Hargrove managed Kinston, North Carolina, in the Class A Carolina League in 1987, Williamsport, Pennsylvania, of the Class AA Eastern League in 1988, and Colorado Springs, Colorado, of the Class AAA Pacific Coast League in 1989. He joined the Tribe as a coach under McNamara in 1990.

The managerial change had little noticeable effect on the Indians, however, as they went 32–53 under Hargrove, and their games-behind deficit had increased by 14 at season's end.

A club-record 53 players were employed during the season, including 24 pitchers, the winningest of whom was rookie Charles Nagy with 10 victories.

Tom Candiotti and Greg Swindell were expected to be the aces of the staff, but Candiotti was dealt to Toronto on June 27, and Swindell won only nine of his 33 starts (while losing 16) and also was traded in November.

Both were scheduled to become free agents at the end of the season, and the Indians, still smarting from the $3.5 million signing of Keith Hernandez, were unwilling to get into a bidding war for either Candiotti or Swindell.

Hernandez was gone, too, despite his two-year contract that extended through the end of 1991. An off-season back injury that necessitated surgery kept Hernandez on the disabled list the entire year, and he never played again.

Doug Jones, who had pitched so well while saving 112 victories over the previous three seasons, struggled in 1991. He recorded just seven saves, lost seven of eight decisions in 32 relief appearances, and was demoted to Class AAA Colorado Springs.

Recalled in September, Jones went 3–1 as a starter, but also became a free agent at the end of the season and signed with Houston.

The Indians did not attempt to keep Jones because of the development of reliever Steve Olin, who spent two months of the season at Colorado Springs. He rejoined the Indians on July 15 and became the primary closer with 17 saves in 22 opportunities.

Albert Belle was another of the few players who did well—leading the Indians with 28 homers and 95 RBIs while hitting .282—though he was the focal point of an ugly incident at the Stadium on May 11. Belle threw a ball at a taunting fan in the stands, hitting him in the chest, and was suspended for seven days.

As a testament to their futility, the Indians' record was above .500 only once the entire season—when it was 4–3 after they beat the Red Sox, 1–0, in Boston on April 15.

Two high-level front office appointments were announced by the Indians on September 18. Former Ohio State athletic director Rick Bay was named executive vice president, and John Hart, who had been director of baseball operations since 1990, was promoted to general manager. They assumed duties that had been filled by president Hank Peters, who planned to retire on January 1, 1992.

It also was in the wake of the 1991 season that construction began in downtown Cleveland on a new ballpark for the Indians, which would be named Jacobs Field upon its opening in 1994.

	G	AB	R	H	2B	3B	HR	RBI	SB	AVG
Mike Aldrete	85	183	22	48	6	1	1	19	1	.262
Beau Allred	48	125	17	29	3	0	3	12	2	.232
Sandy Alomar	51	184	10	40	9	0	0	7	0	.217
Carlos Baerga (3B)	158	593	80	171	28	2	11	69	3	.288
Albert Belle (LF)	123	461	60	130	31	2	28	95	3	.282
Jerry Browne	107	290	28	66	5	2	1	29	2	.228
Alex Cole (CF)	122	387	58	114	17	3	0	21	27	.295
Jose Escobar	10	15	0	3	0	0	0	1	0	.200
Felix Fermin (SS)	129	424	30	111	13	2	0	31	5	.262
Jose Gonzalez	33	69	10	11	2	1	1	4	8	.159
Glenallen Hill	37	122	15	32	3	0	5	14	4	.262
Mike Huff	51	146	28	35	6	1	2	10	11	.240
Brook Jacoby (1B)	66	231	14	54	9	1	4	24	0	.234
Chris James (DH)	115	437	31	104	16	2	5	41	3	.238
Reggie Jefferson	26	101	10	20	3	0	2	12	0	.198
Wayne Kirby	21	43	4	9	2	0	0	5	1	.209
Mark Lewis (2B)	84	314	29	83	15	1	0	30	2	.264
Luis Lopez	35	82	7	18	4	1	0	7	0	.220
Ever Magallanes	3	2	0	0	0	0	0	0	0	.000
Jeff Manto	47	128	15	27	7	0	2	13	2	.211
Carlos Martinez	72	257	22	73	14	0	5	30	3	.284
Luis Medina	5	16	0	1	0	0	0	0	0	.063
Tony Perezchica	17	22	4	8	2	0	0	0	0	.364
Joel Skinner (C)	99	284	23	69	14	0	1	24	0	.243
Eddie Taubensee	26	66	5	16	2	1	0	8	0	.242
Jim Thome	27	98	7	25	4	2	1	9	1	.255
Turner Ward	40	100	11	23	7	0	0	5	0	.230
Mitch Webster	13	32	2	4	0	0	0	0	2	.125
Mark Whiten (RF)	70	258	34	66	14	4	7	26	4	.256
		5,470	576	1,390	236	26	79	546	84	.254

1992

Record: 76–86
Finish: Fourth (tied with New York)
Games Behind: 20
Manager: Mike Hargrove

With Rick Bay taking over as president, and John Hart becoming vice president and general manager upon the January 1 retirement of Hank Peters, the Indians embarked upon a plan they hoped would ensure against the franchise losing its best players to free agency.

They signed Charles Nagy, Carlos Baerga, Albert Belle, Kenny Lofton, Paul Sorrento, and others to multiyear contracts, launching another rebuilding program that would coincide with the construction of Jacobs Field, the team's new ballpark.

The ambitious program did not start well as the Indians lost 30 of their first 44 games and spent most of the first seven weeks in seventh place, falling 13 lengths behind Toronto.

But then the Indians turned the season around, going 62–56 the rest of the way. From August 1 to September 23 they won 28 of 48 games, and though it was too late to climb into contention, they finished in a tie for fourth place with New York.

The key to the resurgence was the pitching of Nagy, a 17-game winner, the relief work of Steve Olin, who was credited with 29 saves in 36 opportunities and an 8–5 won-lost record while appearing in 72 games, and the offensive contributions of Baerga, Belle, Lofton, and Sorrento.

Nagy hurled a one-hitter in a 6–0 victory over the Orioles in Baltimore on August 8. Glenn Davis's infield single in the seventh inning deprived the Tribe ace of a no-hitter.

Baerga became only the second second baseman in history —Hall of Famer Rogers Hornsby was the first—to bat .300 (.312), hit 20 homers, drive in 100 runs (105), and collect 200 hits (205) in one season.

	W	L	G	GS	CG	IP	H	BB	K	ERA
Eric Bell	4	0	10	0	0	18	5	5	7	0.50
Willie Blair	2	3	11	5	0	36	58	10	13	6.75
Denis Boucher	1	4	5	5	0	22⅔	35	8	13	8.34
Tom Candiotti	7	6	15	15	3	108⅓	88	28	86	2.24
Bruce Egloff	0	0	6	0	0	5⅔	8	4	8	4.76
Mauro Gozzo	0	0	2	2	0	4⅔	9	7	3	19.29
Shawn Hillegas	3	4	51	3	0	83	67	46	66	4.34
Doug Jones	4	8	36	4	0	63⅓	87	17	48	5.54
Eric King	6	11	25	24	2	150⅔	166	44	59	4.60
Garland Kiser	0	0	7	0	0	4⅔	7	4	3	9.64
Tom Kramer	0	0	4	0	0	4⅔	10	6	4	17.36
Jeff Mutis	0	3	3	3	0	12⅓	23	7	6	11.68
Charles Nagy	10	15	33	33	6	211⅓	228	66	109	4.13
Rod Nichols	2	11	31	16	3	137⅓	145	30	76	3.54
Steve Olin	3	6	48	0	0	56⅓	61	23	38	3.36
Jesse Orosco	2	0	47	0	0	45¾	52	15	36	3.74
Dave Otto	2	8	18	14	1	100	108	27	47	4.23
Rudy Seanez	0	0	5	0	0	5	10	7	7	16.20
Jeff Shaw	0	5	29	1	0	72⅓	72	27	31	3.36
Greg Swindell	9	16	33	33	7	238	241	31	169	3.48
Efrain Valdez	0	0	7	0	0	6	5	3	1	1.50
Sergio Valdez	1	0	6	0	0	16⅓	15	5	11	5.51
Mike Walker	0	1	5	0	0	4⅓	6	2	2	2.08
Mike York	1	4	14	4	0	34⅔	45	19	19	6.75
	57	(105)		(162)	22	1,441⅓	1,551	441	862	4.23

Shutouts: King, Nagy, Nichols
Saves: Olin (17), Hillegas (7), Jones (7), Nichols, Shaw

Belle, who served a three-game suspension August 4–7 for charging the mound against Kansas City's Neal Heaton on May 4, smashed 34 homers and drove in 112 runs, each of which was fourth best in the American League.

Belle's biggest day at the plate was September 6 when he blasted three home runs in a 12–9, 12-inning victory over Seattle at the Stadium.

Lofton and Sorrento proved to be steals by the Indians, the former coming from Houston in a minor league deal, and the latter acquired late in March from Minnesota in a trade for two farmhands.

Lofton, a college basketball player at the University of Arizona (where he didn't play on the baseball team), became the catalyst of the Tribe's offense. He stole a club-record 66 bases (in 78 attempts) and beat out 31 bunt hits to bat .285. Lofton was narrowly beaten out by Milwaukee's Pat Listach for the AL Rookie of the Year award.

The emergence of Lofton led to the trading of Alex Cole, who, before he left, tied his own club record by stealing five bases in the Tribe's 6–3 loss to California at the Stadium on May 3. Two months later Cole was dealt to Pittsburgh for two minor leaguers.

Sorrento's acquisition was necessitated by a spring-training injury to Reggie Jefferson, who was scheduled to play first base for the Tribe. Sorrento took over and hit .269 with 18 homers and 60 RBIs, and Jefferson never got the job back.

Indians co-owner David H. Jacobs died September 17 at age 71. He and his brother Richard E. Jacobs had bought the franchise from the estate of the late F. J. "Steve" O'Neill in 1986.

Rick Bay, who had taken over as president and chief operating officer on January 1, resigned that position on November 20. He was not replaced, though Richard Jacobs assumed a more active role in the club's operations, and John Hart was given the additional title of executive vice president.

	W	L	G	GS	CG	IP	H	BB	K	ERA
Jack Armstrong	6	15	35	23	1	166⅔	176	67	114	4.64
Brad Arnsberg	0	0	8	0	0	10⅔	13	11	5	11.81
Eric Bell	0	2	7	1	0	15⅓	22	9	10	7.63
Denis Boucher	2	2	8	7	0	41	48	20	17	6.37
Mike Christopher	0	0	10	0	0	18	17	10	13	3.00
Dennis Cook	5	7	32	25	1	158	156	50	96	3.82
Alan Embree	0	2	4	4	0	18	19	8	12	7.00
Derek Lilliquist	5	3	71	0	0	61⅔	39	18	47	1.75
Jose Mesa	4	4	15	15	1	93	92	43	40	4.16
Dave Mlicki	0	2	4	4	0	21⅔	23	16	16	4.98
Jeff Mutis	0	2	3	2	0	11⅓	24	6	8	9.53
Charles Nagy	17	10	33	33	10	252	245	57	169	2.96
Rod Nichols	4	3	30	9	0	105⅓	114	31	56	4.53
Steve Olin	8	5	72	0	0	88⅓	80	27	47	2.34
Dave Otto	5	9	18	16	0	80⅓	110	33	32	7.06
Eric Plunk	9	6	58	0	0	71⅔	61	38	50	3.64
Ted Power	3	3	64	0	0	99⅓	88	35	51	2.54
Scott Scudder	6	10	23	22	0	109	134	55	66	5.28
Jeff Shaw	0	1	2	1	0	7⅔	7	4	3	8.22
Kevin Wickander	2	0	44	0	0	41	39	28	38	3.07
	76	86	(162)	13	(1,470)	1,507	566	890	4.11

Shutouts: Nagy (3), Mesa
Saves: Olin (29), Lilliquist (6), Power (6), Plunk (4), Wickander

	G	AB	R	H	2B	3B	HR	RBI	SB	AVG
Sandy Alomar (C)	89	299	22	75	16	0	2	26	3	.251
Carlos Baerga (2B)	161	657	92	205	32	1	20	105	10	.312
Albert Belle (DH)	153	585	81	152	23	1	34	112	8	.260
Alex Cole	41	97	11	20	1	0	0	5	9	.206
Felix Fermin	79	215	27	58	7	2	0	13	0	.270
Jose Hernandez	3	4	0	0	0	0	0	0	0	.000
Glenallen Hill	102	369	38	89	16	1	18	49	9	.241
Thomas Howard (LF)	117	358	36	99	15	2	2	32	15	.277
Brook Jacoby (3B)	120	291	30	76	7	0	4	36	0	.261
Reggie Jefferson	24	89	8	30	6	2	1	6	0	.337
Wayne Kirby	21	18	9	3	1	0	1	1	0	.167
Jesse Levis	28	43	2	12	4	0	1	3	0	.279
Mark Lewis (SS)	122	413	44	109	21	0	5	30	4	.264
Kenny Lofton (CF)	148	576	96	164	15	8	5	42	(66)	.285
Carlos Martinez	69	228	23	60	9	1	5	35	1	.263
Junior Ortiz	86	244	20	61	7	0	0	24	1	.250
Tony Perezchica	18	20	2	2	1	0	0	1	0	.100
Dave Rohde	5	7	0	0	0	0	0	0	0	.000
Paul Sorrento (1B)	140	458	52	123	24	1	18	60	0	.269
Jim Thome	40	117	8	24	3	1	2	12	2	.205
Mark Whiten (RF)	148	508	73	129	19	4	9	43	16	.254
Craig Worthington	9	24	0	4	0	0	0	2	0	.167
	(5,620)	674	1,495	227	24	127	637	144	.266

1993

Record: 76–86
Finish: Sixth
Games Behind: 19
Manager: Mike Hargrove

March 22, 1993, is a day that will live in infamy in the annals of the Indians.

It was the day pitchers Steve Olin, Tim Crews, and Bob Ojeda, riding in a bass-fishing boat, smashed into a dock on Little Lake Nellie in Clermont, Florida, during a day off from spring training.

The accident killed Olin instantly, and Crews died of massive head injuries the next day. Ojeda survived, but suffered severe damage to his head and scalp that required intensive surgery and subsequent therapy. He did not pitch again until August 6 and appeared in nine games, seven as a starter, with a 2–1 record.

The tragedy devastated the Indians, sent them into mourning from which they did not soon emerge. It was comparable to the anguish an earlier Cleveland team experienced on August 16, 1920, when shortstop Ray Chapman died after being hit by a pitched baseball in a game against the New York Yankees.

It was to the credit of the Indians—and especially to the credit of manager Mike Hargrove—that, under the grievous circumstances, they were able to play as well as they did, just as the 1920 Indians showed remarkable character by going on to win the pennant and World Series after Chapman's death.

There was even more that followed to further test the mettle of the Indians in 1993, which was to be the last season major league baseball would be played in the venerable Cleveland Stadium, prior to moving into Jacobs Field.

Seven and a half months after the crash on Little Lake Nellie, a second tragedy struck down another teammate, Cliff Young, also a relief pitcher who had been signed as a minor league free agent the previous winter. Young was killed in an automobile accident in Willis, Texas, on November 4.

Misfortune, albeit of a lesser nature and degree, also befell the Indians once the season started. They lost their best pitcher, Charles Nagy, and starting catcher Sandy Alomar, Jr.

Nagy, who'd won 27 games the previous two seasons, left spring training with a sore shoulder. He was able to start only nine games (winning two and losing six), went on the disabled list May 17, and underwent surgery on June 29.

Alomar was placed on the DL on May 2 and underwent back surgery to repair a ruptured disc on May 15.

Though there were several noteworthy individual performances, the Indians spent most of the season in sixth and seventh place after starting poorly. Only once—after the first three games, two of which they won against New York—was their record over .500.

The Indians fell to 14 games under the break-even point (27–41) on June 20, and though they played well thereafter, going 49–45, weren't able to catch fifth-place Boston.

One of those late-season losses, 4–0, was a no-hitter thrown at the Indians by New York's Jim Abbott on September 4 at Yankee Stadium.

From strictly a personal record standpoint, 1993 was a good season for Kenny Lofton, Carlos Baerga, and Albert Belle.

Lofton broke his own club record and led the American League with 70 stolen bases (giving him a two year total of 136). His .325 batting average was best on the team and fourth in the league.

Baerga set a major league record by hitting two home runs from each side of the plate in the same inning, the seventh, on April 8 at the Stadium in a 15–5 victory over the Yankees. Batting right-handed against Steve Howe, Baerga drove a two-run shot over the left-center field fence, and then, batting left-handed against Steve Farr, drilled a solo shot into the right field stands.

The year before, Baerga had become only the second second baseman in history to bat .300, hit 20 homers, drive in 100 runs, and collect 200 hits. (Again, Rogers Hornsby had been the first.) In 1993 he repeated the feat, batting .321 with 21 home runs, 114 RBI, and exactly 200 hits.

Belle, who hit .290, was the AL RBI champion with 129, the most by an Indians player since 1953 when Al Rosen drove in 145. Belle's 38 homers also were the most by a Tribesman since 1959 when Rocky Colavito led the league with 42.

In commemoration of the Indians' final season in the Stadium, a total of 2,177,908 fans—third largest in franchise history—spun the turnstiles, including 73,290 for the opener and 216,904 for the final three games against Chicago.

	W	L	G	GS	CG	IP	H	BB	K	ERA
Paul Abbott	0	1	5	5	0	18⅓	19	11	7	6.38
Mike Bielecki	4	5	13	13	0	68⅔	90	23	38	5.90
Mike Christopher	0	0	9	0	0	11¾	14	2	8	3.86
Mark Clark	7	5	26	15	1	109⅓	119	25	57	4.28
Dennis Cook	5	5	25	6	0	54	62	16	34	5.67
Jerry DiPoto	4	4	46	0	0	56⅓	57	30	41	2.40
Jason Grimsley	3	4	10	6	0	42½	52	20	27	5.31
Jeremy Hernandez	6	5	49	0	0	77⅓	75	27	44	3.14
Tom Kramer	7	3	39	16	1	121	126	59	71	4.02
Derek Lilliquist	4	4	56	2	0	64	64	19	40	2.25
Albie Lopez	3	1	9	9	0	49¾	49	32	25	5.98
Jose Mesa	10	12	34	33	3	208⅔	232	62	118	4.92
Bob Milacki	1	1	5	2	0	16	19	11	7	3.38
Dave Mlicki	0	0	3	3	0	13⅓	11	6	7	3.38
Jeff Mutis	3	6	17	13	1	81	93	33	29	5.78
Charles Nagy	2	6	9	9	1	48⅔	66	13	30	6.29
Bob Ojeda	2	1	9	7	0	43	48	21	27	4.40
Eric Plunk	4	5	70	0	0	71	61	30	77	2.79
Ted Power	0	2	20	0	0	20	30	8	11	7.20
Scott Scudder	0	1	2	1	0	4	5	4	1	9.00
Heathcliff Slocumb	3	1	20	0	0	27⅓	28	16	18	4.28
Julian Tavarez	2	2	8	7	0	37	53	13	19	6.57
Bill Wertz	2	3	34	0	0	59⅔	54	32	53	3.62
Kevin Wickander	0	0	11	0	0	8⅔	15	3	3	4.15
Cliff Young	3	3	21	7	0	60⅓	74	18	31	4.62
Matt Young	1	6	22	8	0	74⅓	75	57	65	5.21
	76	86	(162)		7	1,445⅔	(1,591)	591	888	4.58

Shutouts: Mutis
Saves: Plunk (15), DiPoto (11), Lilliquist (10), Hernandez (8), C. Young

	G	AB	R	H	2B	3B	HR	RBI	SB	AVG
Sandy Alomar	64	215	24	58	7	1	6	32	3	.270
Carlos Baerga (2B)	154	624	105	200	28	6	21	114	15	.321
Albert Belle (LF)	159	594	93	172	36	3	38	(129)	23	.290
Alvaro Espinoza (3B)	129	263	34	73	15	0	4	27	2	.278
Felix Fermin (SS)	140	480	48	126	16	2	2	45	4	.263
Glenallen Hill	66	174	19	39	7	2	5	25	7	.224
Sam Horn	12	33	8	15	1	0	4	8	0	.455
Thomas Howard	74	178	26	42	7	0	3	23	5	.236
Reggie Jefferson (DH)	113	366	35	91	11	2	10	34	1	.249
Wayne Kirby (RF)	131	458	71	123	19	5	6	60	17	.269
Jesse Levis	31	63	7	11	2	0	0	4	0	.175
Mark Lewis	14	52	6	13	2	0	1	5	3	.250
Kenny Lofton (CF)	148	569	116	185	28	8	1	42	(70)	.325
Candy Maldonado	28	81	11	20	2	0	5	20	0	.247
Carlos Martinez	80	262	26	64	10	0	5	31	1	.244
Randy Milligan	19	47	7	20	7	0	0	7	0	.426
Junior Ortiz (C)	95	249	19	55	13	0	0	20	1	.221
Lance Parrish	10	20	2	4	1	0	1	2	1	.200
Manny Ramirez	22	53	5	9	1	0	2	5	0	.170
Paul Sorrento (1B)	148	463	75	119	26	1	18	65	3	.257
Jim Thome	47	154	28	41	11	0	7	22	2	.266
Jeff Treadway	97	221	25	67	14	1	2	27	1	.303
		5,619	790	1,547	264	31	141	747	159	.275

1994

Record: 68–47
Finish: Second
Games Behind: 1
Manager: Mike Hargrove

It was a bad year for any major league team to have a good year, and nobody knew it better than the Indians. They should have enjoyed their best season since 1959, but didn't because of a strike by the Players Association that began on August 12.

At the time of the work stoppage the Indians were hot on the trail of the Chicago White Sox in the newly formed American League Central division that also included Kansas City, Minnesota, and Milwaukee.

After an opening-day, 11-inning, 4–3, victory over Seattle to inaugurate their new ballpark, Jacobs Field, in front of President Bill Clinton and a sellout crowd of 41,459 fans, the Indians won three straight and six of seven games before cooling off.

By May 10 they were ice-cold, and after a 5–3 loss in New York, their record slipped below .500, to 14–15, for the first time in the new season.

The Indians went on to lose two more for five straight, falling into fourth place with a 14–17 record, their lowest ebb of the season.

Then, as suddenly as their bats and pitching had become frigid, they heated up again, climbing back to .500 (17–17) on May 15, and never again slipping below the break-even point.

By June 12 the recovery was complete. The Tribe climbed into a tie with the White Sox for first place after winning 16 of 24. Cleveland fans now had more reason to express optimism than they had had in more than three decades.

From that point until the players walked off their jobs in rejecting the owners' plans to institute a salary cap, the Indians were in the thick of the Central division race. They spent the next 29 days (through July 10) either in undisputed possession of first place or tied with Chicago for the top rung.

Through what proved to be their final game on August 10, the Indians were never lower than second, and only once did they fall as much as three lengths behind the White Sox. Of the 129 days that comprised the shortened season, the Indians were in or tied for first place 63 days.

When play was halted by the strike, the Indians, winners of six of their last nine games, were only one step behind the White Sox.

Two games stand out above all others, along with an unpleasant incident involving Albert Belle, the Indians' left fielder and best hitter in 1994.

Mark Clark, the pitcher obtained in a 1993 trade with the St. Louis Cardinals for outfielder Mark Whiten, hurled a six-hitter to beat Detroit, 2–0, on May 13. It halted the Indians' aforementioned slump that saw them lose five straight and seven of eight, and it launched their 18-game home winning streak.

A month later, on June 16, the Indians beat Boston, 7–6, in their most emotion-packed game of the season in front of 41,631 fans at Jacobs Field, boosting their first-place margin to 1½ lengths over the White Sox.

The Indians scored three times in the bottom of the ninth to come back against Red Sox reliever—and soon-to-be teammate—Jeff Russell. Belle climaxed the uprising with a single to center that brought home pinch runner Ruben Amaro with the tying run and Carlos Baerga with the winner.

But the cheering for Belle would not continue for long. On July 16, during a 2–0 victory in Chicago that broke a tie with the White Sox and put the Tribe in first place by a game, Belle was caught using an illegal corked bat.

He was suspended for 10 games by AL President Dr. Bobby Brown, though the penalty was later reduced to six days.

At Jacobs Field, where the Indians' 35–16 mark was the best home record in the major leagues in 1994, they put together an 18-game winning streak from May 13 through June 24.

Unfortunately, the season was never resumed, and Chicago finished first with a 67–46 record, one victory more and one loss less than the Indians.

If the postseason playoffs had not also been canceled, the Indians would have qualified for a "wild card" berth and competed for the pennant against the other division winners—New York of the AL East and Texas of the AL West, in addition to the White Sox.

In that respect the season was an artistic disappointment, although the Indians' winning percentage of .584 was their best in 39 years, since 1955, when it was .604 (93–61).

Their won-lost record of 19 games over .500 also was the best by a Cleveland team since 1959, when the Indians won 24 games more than they lost (89–65), and also finished second to the White Sox.

Financially, however, it was a banner year at the box office as 1,995,165 fans paid their way into 51 games at Jacobs Field, an average of 39,121.

It was the ninth consecutive year the Indians surpassed the one million mark in attendance. Had the season been played to an 81-home-date conclusion, they most certainly would have broken the franchise attendance record of 2,620,627 set in 1948.

Cleveland tied the Yankees for the AL's highest team batting average, .290, which was the Indians' highest since 1936 (when they hit a collective .304). Their 167 home runs also were the most in the major leagues.

On the mound, the Indians and White Sox were the only teams in the major leagues to have four pitchers with 10 or more victories. The Tribe's biggest winners were Clark, 11–3; Dennis Martinez, 11–6; Jack Morris, 10–6; and Charles Nagy, 10–8.

Morris, who'd been signed as a free agent and was released on August 9, recorded his 250th major league victory, 6–5, over Boston on June 19 at Jacobs Field.

Another significant level of achievement was reached by first baseman–designated hitter Eddie Murray when he blasted his 450th career home run against Miguel Jiminez as the Tribe beat the Athletics, 8–2, in Oakland on June 4. Murray was another who had signed as a free agent before the season started.

It also was a good season for Belle and center fielder Kenny Lofton, both of whom were named to the AL All-Star team, as well as for second baseman Carlos Baerga, shortstop Omar Vizquel, and catcher Sandy Alomar, Jr.

Belle, a contender for the Triple Crown, batted .357 with 36 homers and 101 RBIs. Lofton hit .349 and led the league for the third straight year with 60 stolen bases (in 72 attempts). Baerga compiled a .314 average and drove in 80 runs, second only to Belle. Vizquel, another who had been signed as a free agent before the season, solidified the Indians' infield and batted .273. Alomar, despite a couple of injuries, hit .288.

Mike Hargrove's contract as manager of the Indians was extended on July 25 for two more years, through 1996, with a club option for 1997.

	W	L	G	GS	CG	IP	H	BB	K	ERA
Brian Barnes	0	1	6	0	0	13⅓	12	15	5	5.40
Larry Casian	0	2	7	0	0	8⅓	16	4	2	8.64
Mark Clark	11	3	20	20	4	127⅓	133	40	60	3.82
Jerry DiPoto	0	0	7	0	0	15⅔	26	10	9	8.04
Steve Farr	1	1	19	0	0	15¼	17	15	12	5.28
Jason Grimsley	5	2	14	13	1	82⅔	91	34	59	4.57
Derek Lilliquist	1	3	36	0	0	29⅓	34	8	15	4.91
Albie Lopez	1	2	4	4	1	17	20	6	18	4.24
Dennis Martinez	11	6	24	24	7	176⅔	166	44	92	3.52
Jose Mesa	7	5	51	0	0	73	71	26	63	3.82
Jack Morris	10	6	23	23	1	141⅓	163	67	100	5.60
Chris Nabholz	0	1	6	4	0	11	23	9	5	11.45
Charles Nagy	10	8	23	23	3	169⅓	175	48	108	3.45
Chad Ogea	0	1	4	1	0	16⅓	21	10	11	6.06
Eric Plunk	7	2	41	0	0	71	61	37	73	2.54
Jeff Russell	1	1	13	0	0	12⅔	13	3	10	4.97
Paul Shuey	0	1	14	0	0	11⅔	14	12	16	8.49
Russ Swan	0	1	12	0	0	8	13	7	2	11.25
Julian Tavarez	0	1	1	1	0	1⅔	6	1	0	21.60
Matt Turner	1	0	9	0	0	12⅔	13	7	5	2.13
Bill Wertz	0	0	1	0	0	4⅓	9	1	1	10.38
	66	47		113	(17)	1,018⅔	1,097	404	666	4.36

Shutouts: Martinez (3), Clark, Lopez
Saves: Russell (5), Shuey (5), Farr (4), Plunk (3), Mesa (2), Lilliquist, Turner

	G	AB	R	H	2B	3B	HR	RBI	SB	AVG
Sandy Alomar (C)	80	292	44	84	15	1	14	43	8	.288
Ruben Amaro	26	23	5	5	1	0	2	5	2	.217
Carlos Baerga (2B)	103	442	81	139	32	2	19	80	8	.314
Albert Belle (LF)	106	412	90	147	35	2	36	101	9	.357
Alvaro Espinoza	90	231	27	55	13	0	1	19	1	.238
Rene Gonzales	22	23	6	8	1	1	1	5	2	.348
Wayne Kirby	78	191	33	56	6	0	5	23	11	.293
Jesse Levis	1	1	0	1	0	0	0	0	0	1.000
Mark Lewis	20	73	6	15	5	0	1	8	1	.205
Kenny Lofton (CF)	112	459	105	(160)	32	9	12	57	(60)	.349
Candy Maldonado	42	92	14	18	5	1	5	12	1	.196
Matt Merullo	4	10	1	1	0	0	0	0	0	.100
Eddie Murray (DH)	108	433	57	110	21	1	17	76	8	.254
Tony Pena	40	112	18	33	8	1	2	10	0	.295
Herb Perry	4	9	1	1	0	0	0	1	0	.111
Manny Ramirez (RF)	91	290	51	78	22	0	17	60	4	.269
Paul Sorrento (1B)	95	322	43	90	14	0	14	62	0	.280
Jim Thome (3B)	98	321	58	86	20	1	20	52	3	.268
Omar Vizquel (SS)	69	286	39	78	10	1	1	33	13	.273
	(4,022)	(679)	(1,165)	(240)	20	(167)	(647)	131	.290

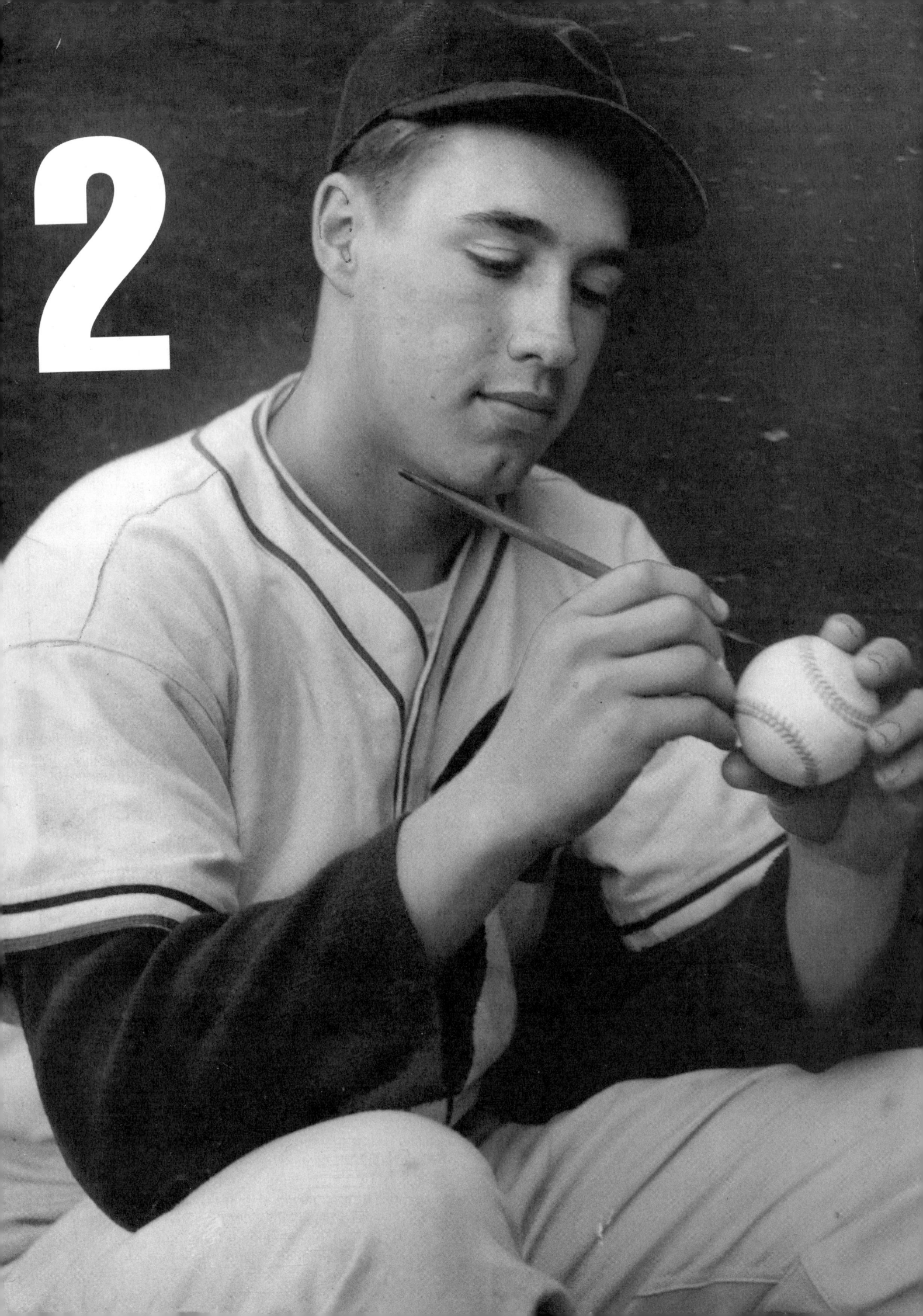

Player Profiles

Since 1901, when Cleveland became a charter member of the American League, more than 1,400 players have come and gone, some for only the proverbial "cup of coffee," others for extended periods, and a few who established themselves as superstars.

Which is not to say that the 200 men profiled in this chapter are considered to have been the elite, the best of the best, if you will, though most of them were.

They are included here because of their ability, their performances, their accomplishments, and, in some cases, simply their intrinsic popularity that established them as being special, the most memorable of all the men who represented Cleveland on the baseball fields of the American League.

Allen, John Thomas

Indians: 1936–40
Pitcher
Nickname: Johnny
Birthplace: Lenoir, North Carolina

B: September 30, 1905
D: March 29, 1959
Batted right, threw right
Ht. 6–0; **Wt.** 180

It's safe to say that Johnny Allen was his own worst enemy, though there is no doubt about his ability and competitiveness.

A prime example of Allen's hot temper occurred on June 7, 1938, at Fenway Park in Boston. In the second inning the Red Sox batters complained that the right sleeve of the torn and tattered undershirt Allen was wearing distracted them.

Umpire Bill McGowan ordered Allen to either change the shirt or cut off the sleeve, but the tempestuous pitcher refused. McGowan was adamant, but so was Allen, who finally angrily stalked off the mound and into the clubhouse.

Indians Manager Oscar Vitt commanded Allen to comply with McGowan's orders, but the pitcher refused—and also refused to return to the field. When Vitt fined Allen $250 for insubordination, Allen vowed he'd never pitch for the Indians again.

Of course he did, but not until after Indians owner Alva Bradley stepped into the controversy.

Bradley made a deal with a department store in downtown Cleveland to buy Allen's uniform, including the torn undershirt, for $250. The store then dressed a mannequin in the uniform and displayed it in its main window.

Then Bradley took the $250 from the store and gave it to Allen, which angered Vitt, but at least the controversy was settled. Allen went on to pitch two more seasons for the Indians, until he was sold to the St. Louis Browns for $20,000 on December 24, 1940.

Unfortunately, Allen often is best remembered for his hot temper, though there were many highlights in his 13-year major league career. He was signed by the New York Yankees in 1927 and spent five years in the minor leagues. He made it to the Yankees in 1932.

Allen, who was traded to the Indians on December 11, 1935, for Monte Pearson and Steve Sundra, won 15 consecutive games in 1937. He didn't lose for the first time that season until the last day, 1–0, in Detroit.

The Tigers' Jake Wade pitched a one-hitter to beat the Tribe and prevent Allen from tying the American League record of 16 straight victories in one season. It was held by Walter Johnson, Smoky Joe Wood, Lefty Grove, and Schoolboy Rowe.

The Tigers' only run was scored in the first inning on a double by Pete Fox and Hank Greenberg's two-out single to left field that precipitated a postgame argument between Allen and Indians third baseman Odell Hale. Allen thought Greenberg's grounder should have been fielded and made his feelings known to Hale.

Johnny Allen

Those 15 straight victories in 1937 also gave Allen 17 in a row over two seasons, an AL record that was tied by Baltimore's Dave McNally in 1968–69.

Allen's victory streak in 1937 is all the more remarkable when it is considered that, on June 20, when his record was 4–0, he underwent an emergency appendectomy. He returned to the mound three weeks later.

As a result of that 15–1 record that gave him a .938 winning percentage in 1937—best in American League history—Allen signed a $20,000 contract in 1938 making him the second-highest-paid pitcher in baseball that year.

Remarkable, too, is that, after losing the opening game of the 1938 season, 6–2 to the St. Louis Browns, Allen went on to win 12 consecutive games from April 23 through July 3.

Thus, as of July 3, 1938, Allen's two-year record was an amazing 27–2.

Late in 1938, however, Allen underwent arm surgery and was never again a big winner. His final season was with the New York Giants in 1944, when he was 4–7 in 18 games. He also pitched for the Brooklyn Dodgers, and later became, of all things, a minor league umpire.

Allen got his start in professional baseball with the Yankees when, at the age of 22, he was working as a desk clerk in a hotel in Sanford, North Carolina.

The late Paul Krichell, a scout for the Yankees, was staying in the hotel and complained to Allen that his room was too hot for comfort. Allen took care of the problem and, in the process, talked Krichell into giving him a tryout. Krichell was impressed and signed Allen to a minor league contract.

Five years later, as a rookie for the Yankees in 1932, Allen won 17 and lost only four, and was on his way to a 142–75 career record that undoubtedly would have been better if he'd had better control of his emotions.

Max Alvis

playing in 107 games and batting .252. He even made the American League All-Star team in 1965, but never again experienced the success he enjoyed as a rookie, though he again was elected the Tribe's Man of the Year for 1967.

Later in his career with the Indians, which ended when he was traded to Milwaukee on April 4, 1970, Alvis admitted that his illness had a negative effect on his playing ability.

"I didn't feel badly, but I was never as strong after I got sick, and I could never totally regain my strength, the strength that I felt my first year [1963] with the Indians," he said.

Alvis played only one season with the Brewers, hitting .163 with three homers in 62 games in 1970, and retired with a .247 career average.

Allen, Johnny

Indians	W	L	Pct	ERA	G	CG	IP	H	BB	SO	ShO
1936	20	10	.667	3.44	36	19	243	234	97	165	4
1937	15	1	.938	2.55	24	14	173	157	60	87	0
1938	14	8	.636	4.18	30	13	200	189	81	112	0
1939	9	7	.563	4.58	28	9	175	199	56	79	2
1940	9	8	.529	3.44	32	5	138⅔	126	48	62	3
Career	142	75	.654	3.75	352	109	1,950⅓	1,849	738	1,070	17

Alvis, Roy Maxwell

Indians: 1962–69
Third baseman
Nickname: Max
Birthplace: Jasper, Texas

B: February 2, 1938
Bats right, throws right
Ht. 5–11; **Wt.** 185

When he was installed as the regular third baseman in 1963, Max Alvis was expected to be part of the cornerstone that would return the Indians to the glory they hadn't known since 1954.

Alvis more than lived up to his advance notices that season, hitting .274 with 22 homers, becoming only the second rookie to be elected the Indians' Man of the Year.

His fine season led to the expectation of even better things by Alvis—and then disaster struck.

On June 26, 1964, he was stricken with spinal meningitis and hospitalized in Boston for six weeks.

Alvis returned and finished the season with the Indians,

Alvis, Max

Indians	G	AB	H	BA	RBI	R	2B	3B	HR	SA	SB
1962	12	51	11	.216	3	1	2	0	0	.255	3
1963	158	602	165	.274	67	81	32	7	22	.460	9
1964	107	381	96	.252	53	51	14	3	18	.446	5
1965	159	604	149	.247	61	88	24	2	21	.397	12
1966	157	596	146	.245	55	67	22	3	17	.378	4
1967	161	637	163	.256	70	66	23	4	21	.403	3
1968	131	452	101	.223	37	38	17	3	8	.327	5
1969	66	191	43	.225	15	13	6	0	1	.272	1
Career	1,013	3,629	895	.247	373	421	142	22	111	.390	43

Ashby, Alan Dean

Indians: 1973–76
Catcher
Birthplace: Long Beach, California

B: July 8, 1951
Bats both, throws right
Ht. 6–2; Wt. 185

I n an effort to improve the Indians' pitching staff, general manager Phil Seghi traded Alan Ashby (with utility infielder-outfielder Doug Howard) to the expansion Toronto Blue Jays for Al Fitzmorris on November 5, 1976.

It was a deal that failed to help the Indians, though it proved to be beneficial to Ashby, who went on to play 17 years in the major leagues, including two seasons with the Blue Jays and 11 with Houston, compiling a career average of .245 with 90 home runs in 1,370 games.

A third-round selection in the 1969 amateur draft, Ashby was deemed expendable by the Indians after their reacquisition of veteran catcher Ray Fosse in December 1975. Ashby shared the Tribe catching duties with John Ellis in 1975, after spending most of the 1973 and 1974 seasons in the minor leagues.

After the Blue Jays traded Ashby to Houston on November 27, 1978, he went on to tie a National League record for the most no-hitters caught, three, by Ken Forsch, April 7, 1979; Nolan Ryan, September 26, 1981; and Mike Scott, September 25, 1986.

On the disabled list five times because of a back injury and broken fingers, Ashby was traded by the Astros to Pittsburgh after the 1989 season. When he refused to report to the Pirates, he was released and didn't play again.

Ashby, Alan Indians	G	AB	H	BA	RBI	R	2B	3B	HR	SA	SB
1973	11	29	5	.172	3	4	1	0	1	.310	0
1974	10	7	1	.143	0	1	0	0	0	.143	0
1975	90	254	57	.224	32	32	10	1	5	.331	3
1976	89	247	59	.239	32	26	5	1	4	.316	0
Career	1,370	4,123	1,010	.245	513	397	183	13	90	.361	7

Averill, Howard Earl

Indians: 1929–39
Center fielder
Nickname: Rock, Rock of Snohomish
Birthplace: Snohomish, Washington

B: May 21, 1902
D: August 16, 1983
Batted left, threw right
Ht. 5–9½; **Wt.** 172

I n his first at bat in the major leagues in 1929, Earl Averill socked a home run, one of a team-record 226 he hit for the Indians until he was traded in a very controversial deal to Detroit on June 14, 1939.

Tribe fans—and most of the Cleveland media—were outraged when Averill was sent to the Tigers for pitcher Harry Eisenstat and cash. As the *Cleveland Press* reported, "Averill was as popular with the fans as he was unpopular with the front office."

Averill, who was elected to the Hall of Fame by the Veterans Committee in 1975, and whose uniform number 3 is one of five retired by the Indians, was the center of controversy from the time he joined the Indians.

Alan Ashby

Earl Averill

They purchased his contract from the then San Francisco Seals of the Pacific Coast League after Averill batted .300 three years in a row, including .354 with 36 homers and 173 RBIs in 1928.

The Indians bought Averill for $50,000 and two players, but he refused to play in Cleveland until he was given a $5,000 bonus. "If I am worth $40,000 [to the Seals], I'm worth $5,000 for myself," Averill was quoted as saying at the time.

And when Alva Bradley, then the Indians' owner, first saw Averill, he reportedly asked general manager Billy Evans, "You mean we paid all that money for a midget?" His query was a reference to the rookie's physical stature.

In addition to being a very good hitter—his major league career batting average was .318 for 13 seasons—Averill also was a great center fielder, probably second-best only to Tris Speaker in Tribe history.

Averill really fell from favor with Bradley when he held out after the 1936 season. That was the year Averill challenged for the American League batting championship with a .378 average (finishing second to Luke Appling's .388), led the AL in hits with 232, and tied for the lead in triples with 15.

Averill wanted a $2,000 raise over the $14,000 he was paid in 1936, and Bradley was outraged.

Finally they agreed on a contract that would pay Averill $15,000, plus a $2,000 bonus if he had a good year in 1937. He didn't, as decreed by Bradley, and the rift between the two men worsened. Averill's average fell to .299 in 1937, though it was only the second season until then that he failed to hit .300.

Averill was named to the American League All-Star team six times (1933 through 1938). It was in the 1937 All-Star Game that his line drive hit Dizzy Dean and broke his toe, an injury that indirectly ended the pitcher's Hall of Fame career.

Averill was showered with gifts, including a new Cadillac, during a "day" in his honor in 1938, when his average rebounded to .330, though it obviously did not make an impact on Bradley.

Bradley said after the deal sending Averill to the Tigers, "Earl was dissatisfied . . . he went on record early in the season that he would like to be traded."

Averill's career declined in Detroit, where he played only part-time in 1940, hitting .280 in 64 games, and was released. He signed with the Boston Braves in 1941, but played only eight games and retired.

In addition to his 226 home runs, Averill also still leads the Indians in six other offensive categories: RBIs, 1,084; runs scored, 1,154; total bases, 3,200; extra-base hits, 724; triples, 121; and bases on balls, 725.

Averill, Earl

Indians	G	AB	H	BA	RBI	R	2B	3B	HR	SA	SB
1929	151	597	198	.332	96	110	43	13	18	.538	13
1930	139	534	181	.339	119	102	33	8	19	.537	10
1931	155	627	209	.333	143	140	36	10	32	.576	9
1932	153	631	198	.314	124	116	37	14	32	.569	5
1933	151	599	180	.301	92	83	39	16	11	.474	3
1934	154	598	187	.313	113	128	48	6	31	.569	5
1935	140	563	162	.288	79	109	34	13	19	.496	8
1936	152	614	232	.378	126	136	39	15	28	.627	3
1937	156	609	182	.299	92	121	33	11	21	.493	5
1938	134	482	159	.330	93	101	27	15	14	.535	5
1939	24	55	15	.273	7	8	8	0	1	.473	0
Career	1,668	6,353	2,019	.318	1,164	1,224	401	128	238	.534	70

Avila, Roberto Francisco

Indians: 1949–58
Second baseman
Nicknames: Bobby, Beto
Birthplace: Veracruz, Mexico

B: April 2, 1924
Bats right, throws right
Ht. 5–10; **Wt.** 175

The first Mexican player to gain stardom in the major leagues, Bobby Avila became a national hero in his country after winning the American League batting championship with a .341 average in 1954, despite playing half the season with a broken thumb.

That was the season Avila was named Player of the Year in the American League by *The Sporting News*, which also chose him as the second baseman on its All-Star major league team.

He was a member of the AL All-Star team in 1952, 1954, and 1955.

Avila starred in the Mexican League before he was signed by the Indians for $17,500 in 1948. He was promoted to Cleveland after one season in the Class AAA International League with Baltimore and was the Tribe's regular second baseman from 1951 through 1958, when he was traded to the Orioles for pitcher Russ Heman and $30,000.

Though not noted as a power hitter, Avila smashed three home runs and also doubled and singled in a game in Boston on June 20, 1951, won by the Indians, 14–8. He led the AL in

Bobby Avila

triples with 11 in 1952, and he was elected the Tribe's Man of the Year in 1954.

An adept bunter, daring base runner, and scrappy player throughout his career, Avila often was criticized by opponents for his penchant for kicking the ball out of a fielder's glove while sliding into a base.

Steve O'Neill, who managed the Red Sox in 1951, once said of Avila, "From all I hear around the league, he's asking for it. He'll be lucky if he doesn't have his legs cut from under him before the season is over. I hear everybody is out to get him."

Avila played for three teams in 1959 after he was traded by the Tribe to Baltimore. He appeared in 20 games for the Orioles, who sold him to Boston on May 21. Exactly two months later, after playing 22 games for the Red Sox, he was sold to the Milwaukee Braves, for whom he played 51 games.

Avila wound up with a .227 average for the 1959 season, retired, and entered politics in Mexico. He later became president of the Mexican League.

Joe Azcue

Avila, Bobby

Indians	G	AB	H	BA	RBI	R	2B	3B	HR	SA	SB
1949	31	14	3	.214	3	3	0	0	0	.214	0
1950	80	201	60	.299	21	39	10	2	1	.383	5
1951	141	542	165	.304	58	76	21	3	10	.410	14
1952	150	597	179	.300	45	102	26	11	7	.415	12
1953	141	559	160	.286	55	85	22	3	8	.379	10
1954	143	555	189	.341	67	112	27	2	15	.477	9
1955	141	537	146	.272	61	83	22	4	13	.400	1
1956	138	513	115	.224	54	74	14	2	10	.318	17
1957	129	463	124	.268	48	60	19	3	5	.354	2
1958	113	375	95	.253	30	54	21	3	5	.365	5
Career	1,300	4,620	1,296	.281	467	725	185	35	80	.388	78

Azcue, Jose Joaquin

Indians: 1963–69
Catcher
Nicknames: Joe, The Immortal Cuban
Birthplace: Cienfuegos, Cuba

B: August 18, 1939
Bats right, throws right
Ht. 6–0; **Wt.** 190

Joe Azcue's nickname, "The Immortal Cuban," was well earned—at least at the time it was penned by some overzealous teammates.

It came about as a result of Azcue's arrival in Cleveland on May 25, 1963, after he'd been acquired (with shortstop Dick Howser) in a trade with the Kansas City Athletics for catcher Doc Edwards and $100,000.

The day he joined the Indians after spending most of the previous night in airports and on an airplane flying to Cleveland, Azcue fell asleep in the bull pen during a game against Washington.

While Azcue snoozed, Tribe catcher John Romano was hit with a foul tip and suffered two broken bones in his right hand.

That quickly Azcue was rushed into action, and a few innings later he delivered a game-winning hit.

He came through in the clutch many times that season while batting .284 with 14 homers and 46 RBIs in 94 games, earning—at least for the time being—"immortality," and in 1968 he was named to the American League All-Star team.

Eventually, of course, Azcue proved to be only human,

and on April 19, 1969, he was traded, along with pitchers Sonny Siebert and Vicente Romo to Boston for outfielder/first baseman Ken Harrelson and pitchers Dick Ellsworth and Juan Pizarro.

Azcue's career went downhill after the deal as the Red Sox sent him to the California Angels later that season. He became embroiled in a contract dispute with the Angels and didn't play in 1971, selling insurance at home in Overland Park, Kansas.

He returned to the Angels in 1972, but was traded to the Milwaukee Brewers in July and retired at the end of the season.

Azcue, born and raised in Cuba, originally was signed in 1956 by the Cincinnati Reds along with four other future major leaguers—Cookie Rojas, Leo Cardenas, Orlando Pena, and Tony Gonzalez.

Azcue played five seasons in the minors and was promoted to the Reds in September 1960. That winter he was claimed by the Milwaukee Braves in the minor league draft, and in December 1961 he was traded to Kansas City, where he hit .229 in 72 games in 1962.

Azcue, Joe

Indians	G	AB	H	BA	RBI	R	2B	3B	HR	SA	SB
1963	94	320	91	.284	46	26	16	0	14	.466	1
1964	83	271	74	.273	34	20	9	1	4	.358	0
1965	111	335	77	.230	35	16	7	0	2	.269	2
1966	98	302	83	.275	37	22	10	1	9	.404	0
1967	86	295	74	.251	34	33	12	5	11	.437	0
1968	115	357	100	.280	42	23	10	0	4	.342	1
1969	7	24	7	.292	1	1	0	0	1	.417	0
Career	909	2,828	712	.252	304	201	94	9	50	.344	5

Bagby, James Charles Jacob, Sr.

Indians: 1916–22
Pitcher
Nicknames: Jim, Sarge
Birthplace: Barnett, Georgia

B: October 5, 1889
D: July 28, 1954
Batted both, threw right
Ht. 6–0; **Wt.** 170

Jim Bagby, Sr., master of the "fadeaway" pitch (now called a screwball), was the ace of the Indians' staff in 1920 when they won their first pennant and world championship, though he never had another year like it before or after.

Bagby's 31 victories in 1920—still a Cleveland record—were the most in the major leagues since Grover Cleveland Alexander's 33 in 1916. Only four pitchers have won 30 since: Alexander, who won 30 in 1917; Lefty Grove, 31 in 1931; Dizzy Dean, 30 in 1934; and Denny McLain, 31 in 1968.

Bagby also led American League pitchers in winning percentage (.721), pitched the most innings (339⅔), and also won the most games in relief (6).

The strong-armed Bagby also became the first pitcher to hit a home run in the World Series when he beat the Brooklyn Dodgers, 8–1, in Game 5, in 1920, after losing the second game, 3–0, to spitballer Burleigh Grimes.

It was in that historic fifth game that two other Indians gained notoriety: Bill Wambsganss, for making the only unassisted triple play in the World Series, and Elmer Smith, for hitting the first grand slam home run in a World Series game.

Except for a brief trial with Cincinnati in 1912 when his record was 2–0 in five games, Bagby was in the minors from 1910 to 1915. After he went 19–16 for New Orleans of the Southern Association in 1915, Bagby was purchased by the Indians. He won 16 games (and lost 16) in 1916, the first of six straight seasons in which he won in double figures.

Bagby's record slumped to 14–12 in 1921, which was a fac-

tor in the Indians' inability to repeat as AL pennant winners. When he won only four games (while losing five), mainly as a reliever, in 1922, Bagby was sold to Pittsburgh. His major league career ended after posting a 3–2 record in 21 games in 1923, and he returned to his farm near Atlanta.

Bagby, Jim, Sr.

Indians	W	L	Pct	ERA	G	CG	IP	H	BB	SO	ShO
1916	16	16	.500	2.61	48	14	272⅔	253	67	88	3
1917	23	13	.639	1.96	49	26	320⅔	277	73	83	8
1918	17	16	.515	2.69	45	23	271⅓	274	78	57	2
1919	17	11	.607	2.80	35	21	241⅓	258	44	61	0
1920	31	12	.721	2.89	48	30	339⅔	338	79	73	3
1921	14	12	.538	4.70	40	13	191⅓	238	44	37	0
1922	4	5	.444	6.32	25	4	98⅓	134	39	25	0
Career	127	88	.591	3.11	316	133	1,821⅔	1,884	458	450	16

Bagby, James Charles Jacob, Jr.

Indians: 1941–45
Pitcher
Nickname: Jim
Birthplace: Cleveland, Ohio

B: September 8,1916
D: September 2,1988
Batted right, threw right
Ht. 6–2; **Wt.** 170

One of the few major leaguers to play more than one position, Jim Bagby, Jr., came to Cleveland in what was then a very unpopular six-player deal with the Boston Red Sox on December 12, 1940.

To get Bagby, along with catcher Gene Desautels and outfielder Gee Walker, the Indians gave up catcher Frankie Pytlak, infielder Odell (Bad News) Hale, and pitcher Joe Dobson. Tribe fans didn't like the trade because Pytlak and Hale were two of their favorites, though Bagby soon won them over.

Bagby started his professional career with the Red Sox at their Charlotte, North Carolina, farm club in 1935, and made it to Boston in 1938 when he went 15–11 as a rookie. His 5–5 and 10–16 records the next two seasons led to his being traded to Cleveland.

In 1941, while winning nine of 24 decisions, Bagby was one of two Tribe pitchers credited with stopping Joe DiMaggio's consecutive-game hitting streak at 56 on July 17. Southpaw Al Smith started the game and was the loser as New York prevailed, 4–3. Bagby took over in the eighth inning and retired DiMaggio in his final at bat, inducing the Yankee star to ground into a bases-loaded double play.

Bagby's best seasons were 1942 and 1943, in each of which he won 17 games, and both years he was named to the American League All-Star team. On one occasion in 1943 he filled in at shortstop, and it also was during that season that Bagby tied a major league record held by Stan Coveleski and Walter Johnson by defeating one club (Detroit) by a 1–0 score three times.

Despite his success, Bagby didn't get along with manager Lou Boudreau and, during the winter of 1943–44, asked to be traded.

He missed the first half of the 1944 season while serving in the U.S. Merchant Marine, but rejoined the Tribe in July after failing a preinduction physical and being classified 4-F in the draft.

But he was never a big winner again, and the Indians traded Bagby back to Boston on December 12, 1945, for

Jim Bagby Sr.

Jim Bagby Jr.

Len Barker

pitcher Vic Johnson and cash. He pitched one season for the Red Sox, going 7–6 in 1946, and as his father had done 24 years earlier, Bagby ended his career with Pittsburgh in 1947.

Bagby, Jim, Jr.

Indians	W	L	Pct	ERA	G	CG	IP	H	BB	SO	ShO
1941	9	15	.375	4.04	33	12	200⅔	214	76	53	0
1942	17	9	.654	2.96	38	16	270⅔	267	64	54	4
1943	17	14	.548	3.10	36	16	273	248	80	70	3
1944	4	5	.444	4.33	13	2	79	101	34	12	0
1945	8	11	.421	3.73	25	11	159⅓	171	59	38	3
Career	97	96	.503	3.96	303	84	1,666⅔	1,815	608	431	13

Barker, Leonard Harold

Indians 1979–83
Pitcher
Nicknames: Len, Large Lenny
Birthplace: Fort Knox, Kentucky

B: July 27, 1955
Bats right, throws right
Ht. 6–5; **Wt.** 225

It's impossible to improve upon perfection, which might have been Len Barker's biggest problem after pitching the ninth perfect game in modern major league history on May 15, 1981, beating Toronto, 3–0, at the Stadium.

Thereafter, though he won 15 games the following season, Barker never again came close to recapturing the rapture of that glorious game against the Blue Jays. In it he made 103 pitches, 74 of them in the strike zone, on 41 fastballs, 60 curves, and two change-ups, striking out 11 batters, all of them swinging.

Only two batted balls were close to being hits, but second

baseman Duane Kuiper fielded both, throwing out Rick Bosetti in the sixth inning and Alfredo Griffin in the seventh.

Kuiper made a backhanded grab of Bosetti's shot toward center field and raced four strides to his left to reach and field Griffin's grounder, catching each runner at first by half a step.

Third baseman Toby Harrah also made a spectacular catch of a foul to retire Willie Upshaw in the fifth inning, and Rick Manning ran a long way to left-center to haul down Damaso Garcia's liner in the second.

Indians manager Dave Garcia, whose professional baseball career began in 1939, spared no accolades in his praise of Barker's performance. "I've never seen a better pitched game," Garcia said after pinch hitter Ernie Whitt routinely flied to Manning to end the game.

The victory for Barker, whose fastball was clocked at 96-plus mph, gave him a 3–1 record and earned him a place on the American League All-Star team. He won two and lost two prior to the June 11 strike interruption of the 1981 season. When play resumed Barker struggled, going 3–4 to finish with a disappointing 8–7 won-lost record and 3.91 earned run average.

It was only Barker's third season as a starter; he was used strictly as a reliever by Texas from 1976 to 1978, prior to his acquisition by the Indians on October 3, 1978. He came to Cleveland in the trade that also brought outfielder Bobby Bonds for pitcher Jim Kern and infielder Larvell Blanks.

Barker rebounded in 1982, winning 15 games while losing 11, but developed arm trouble that later was diagnosed as a bone spur in his elbow. He was in and out of the rotation most of 1983, and on August 28, with an 8–13 record in 24 starts—and because he could become a free agent at the end of the season—Barker was traded to Atlanta.

It proved to be one of the Indians' best deals as they received outfielder Brett Butler, third baseman Brook Jacoby, and pitcher Rick Behenna for the once-perfect pitcher—though not for the Braves.

They signed Barker to a five-year, $5 million contract, but he never had another big season. Barker was 1–3 in six games for Atlanta the rest of 1983, and his won-lost records in 1984 and 1985 were 7–8 and 2–9.

Barker was out of baseball in 1986. He attempted a comeback with Milwaukee in 1987, but after winning just two of three decisions in 11 starts, retired with a 74–76 lifetime record.

Barker, Len

Indians	W	L	Pct	ERA	G	CG	IP	H	BB	SO	ShO
1979	6	6	.500	4.92	29	2	137⅓	146	70	93	0
1980	19	12	.613	4.17	36	8	246⅓	237	92	187	1
1981	8	7	.533	3.91	22	9	154⅓	150	46	127	3
1982	15	11	.577	3.90	33	10	244⅔	211	88	187	1
1983	8	13	.381	5.11	24	4	149¾	150	52	105	1
Career	74	76	.493	4.34	248	35	1,323⅔	1,289	513	975	7

Bay, Harry Elbert

Indians: 1902–08
Outfielder
Nickname: Deerfoot
Birthplace: Pontiac, Illinois

B: January 17, 1878
D: March 20, 1952
Batted left, threw left
Ht. 5–8; **Wt.** 138

Though he hit a career-high .301 in 1905, Harry Bay's primary claim to fame was as a base stealer, which earned for him the nickname "Deerfoot."

Picked up by the Indians—when they were the Bronchos—in 1902 after he'd been released by Cincinnati, Bay went on to lead the American League with 45 stolen bases in 1903 and tie for the lead with 38 in 1904. In his eight-year major league career, Bay stole 169 bases, and he remains among the franchise leaders.

Bay also set a since-tied major league record with 12 outfield putouts in a 12-inning game against Boston on July 19, 1904.

Not only was Bay proficient on the diamond, he was an accomplished musician as well. Throughout his baseball career he carried his cornet with him and appeared in many concerts and vaudeville skits while with the Naps. He also played the piano and a number of string instruments.

Bay, Harry

Indians	G	AB	H	BA	RBI	R	2B	3B	HR	SA	SB
1902	108	455	132	.290	23	71	10	5	0	.334	22
1903	140	579	169	.292	35	94	15	12	1	.364	45
1904	132	506	122	.241	36	69	12	9	3	.318	38
1905	144	552	166	.301	22	90	18	10	0	.370	36
1906	68	280	77	.275	14	47	8	3	0	.325	17
1907	34	95	17	.179	7	14	1	1	0	.211	7
1908	2	0	0	—	0	0	0	0	0	—	0
Career	675	2,640	722	.273	141	413	65	42	5	.336	169

Bearden, Henry Eugene

Indians: 1947–50
Pitcher
Nickname: Gene
Birthplace: Lexa, Arkansas

B: September 5, 1920
Bats left, throws left
Ht. 6–4; **Wt.** 198

His career was brief, but knuckleballer Gene Bearden had one of the most sensational rookie seasons in major league history, and pitched one of the most important games—perhaps the most important game—in Indians history.

After winning 19 while losing seven, Bearden was the surprise choice of manager Lou Boudreau to start the pennant playoff game against Boston on October 4, 1948.

Bearden pitched a five-hitter and struck out six in beating the Red Sox, 8–3, vaulting the Indians into the World Series—in which he beat the Boston Braves, 2–0, in Game 3. Bearden also saved for Bob Lemon the 4–3, sixth-game victory that gave the Indians their second world championship.

Bearden's 2.43 earned run average led all American League pitchers, and six of his 20 victories that season were shutouts. He was voted the Indians' Man of the Year for 1948, the first rookie to win the award.

But Bearden faded into obscurity almost as quickly as he burst into stardom, winning only 25 games and losing 31 in five seasons following his heroics of 1948.

Acquired in a deal with the New York Yankees on December 20, 1946, Bearden was back in the minors by 1954. He was sold to Washington in 1950, then to Detroit in 1951, traded to the St. Louis Browns in 1952, and sold to the Chicago White Sox in 1953. He was out of baseball by 1957 with a career won-lost record of 45–38.

Ironically, Bearden was the second choice of the Indians when he was obtained by the Indians. Owner Bill Veeck initially wanted Spec Shea in the deal that sent catcher Sherman Lollar and second baseman Ray Mack to New York.

The Yankees wouldn't give up Shea and instead sent Bearden to the Tribe in the package that also included outfielder Hal Peck and pitcher Al Gettel.

Gene Bearden

A factor in the Yankees' willingness to give up Bearden probably was their concern for his physical condition. Bearden, a navy veteran, had suffered a fractured skull and a severe knee injury during World War II when his ship, the USS *Helena,* was sunk in the South Pacific near the Solomon Islands on August 9, 1942. He was in the engine room when the ship was struck by a torpedo fired by a Japanese destroyer.

Bearden came home with an aluminum plate in his head and a screw in his knee, and the resumption of his professional baseball career was very much in doubt.

But those problems were not evident in 1948. He beat Washington, 6–1, on May 8 for his first major league victory, and he won seven straight games in the stretch run in August and September, enabling the Indians to force the pennant playoff against Boston.

Bearden was shaky at the start of that game, yielding a run on two hits in the first inning. But thereafter he was masterful, allowing only three more hits in winning one of the most significant games in the history of the franchise.

Bearden, Gene

Indians	W	L	Pct	ERA	G	CG	IP	H	BB	SO	ShO
1947	0	0	—	81.00	1	0	⅓	2	1	0	0
1948	20	7	.741	2.43	37	15	229⅔	187	106	80	6
1949	8	8	.500	5.10	32	5	127	140	92	41	0
1950	1	3	.250	6.15	14	0	45⅓	57	32	10	0
Career	45	38	.542	3.96	193	29	788⅓	791	435	259	7

Bell, David Gus

Indians: 1972–78
Third baseman, outfielder
Nickname: Buddy
Birthplace: Pittsburgh, Pennsylvania

B: August 27, 1951
Bats right, throws right
Ht. 6–1; Wt. 180

Buddy Bell

His major league career began in 1972 as an outfielder because of the presence of Graig Nettles, but after one season Buddy Bell took over as the Indians' third baseman and soon became recognized as one of the best in the American League.

Bell led AL third basemen in putouts and double plays in 1973 when he was voted the Indians' Man of the Year, and he quickly became a fan favorite in his seven seasons with the Tribe, during which he collected 1,016 of his career 2,514 hits.

Buddy and his father Gus, who played for four teams in a 15-year National League career (1950–64), hold the all-time father-son record for hits (4,337), and also combined for 407 home runs (as did Yogi and Dale Berra), second most in major league history.

Buddy was a 16th-round selection in the 1969 amateur draft after starring in baseball and basketball in high school in Cincinnati. It was during a charity basketball exhibition in January 1974 that Bell suffered an injury to his right knee that put him on the disabled list twice that season and led to seven operations before his career was concluded in 1989.

It was as a second baseman that Bell started his pro career, but he was switched to third in the minor leagues in 1970. Because of Nettles, Bell was the opening-day right fielder for the Indians as a rookie in 1972. He made the American League All-Star team in 1973.

Bell was traded to Texas for Toby Harrah during the winter of 1978–79 in a deal the Indians came to regret. Upon joining the Rangers, Bell won his first of six consecutive Gold Glove awards, and again he was picked for the AL All-Star team in 1980, 1981, 1982, and 1984.

It also was with Texas in 1980 that Bell compiled his best batting average, .329 in 129 games. The Rangers traded him to Cincinnati on July 19, 1985, and he led NL third basemen in fielding in 1987. The Reds traded Bell to Houston in June 1988. He returned to the Rangers as a free agent in 1989, but retired on June 23 after 34 games.

Bell rejoined the Indians as a coach in 1994 after serving as director of minor league instruction for the Chicago White Sox from 1991 to 1993.

Bell, Buddy

Indians	G	AB	H	BA	RBI	R	2B	3B	HR	SA	SB
1972	132	466	119	.255	36	49	21	1	9	.363	5
1973	156	631	169	.268	59	86	23	7	14	.393	7
1974	116	423	111	.262	46	51	15	1	7	.352	1
1975	153	553	150	.271	59	66	20	4	10	.376	6
1976	159	604	170	.281	60	75	26	2	7	.366	3
1977	129	479	140	.292	64	64	23	4	11	.426	1
1978	142	556	157	.282	62	71	27	8	6	.392	1
Career	2,405	8,995	2,514	.279	1,106	1,151	425	56	201	.406	55

Bell, Gary

Indians: 1958–67
Pitcher
Nickname: Ding-Dong
Birthplace: San Antonio, Texas

B: November 17, 1936
Bats right, throws right
Ht. 6–1; Wt. 196

Gary Bell showed great promise as both a starter and reliever in his first two seasons with the Indians, winning 12 games as a rookie in 1958 and 16 the following year, when the Tribe was in pennant contention most of the season. Bell started 28 games and relieved in 16 others in 1959.

But his career never got any better until he was traded to Boston early in 1967, when he won 12 games during the Red Sox' pennant drive. The Indians received first baseman Tony Horton and outfielder Don Demeter for Bell.

Though he hated working out of the bull pen, Bell led the American League with nine relief victories in 1962 and again was one of the leading firemen in 1965 when he saved 17 games for the Indians. Of his 519 appearances on the mound, 286 were in relief.

Bell, a member of the AL All-Star team in 1960, 1966, and 1968, compiled a 12-year major league career won-lost record of 121–117.

He was picked by Seattle in the 1969 expansion draft and won the Pilots' home opener. Two months later Bell was traded to the Chicago White Sox. He retired at the end of the season and operates a sporting goods business in San Antonio.

Gary Bell

Bell, Gary

Indians	W	L	Pct	ERA	G	CG	IP	H	BB	SO	ShO
1958	12	10	.545	3.31	33	10	182	141	73	110	0
1959	16	11	.593	4.04	44	12	234	208	105	136	1
1960	9	10	.474	4.13	28	6	154⅓	139	82	109	2
1961	12	16	.429	4.10	34	11	228½	214	100	163	2
1962	10	9	.526	4.26	57	1	107⅔	104	52	80	0
1963	8	5	.615	2.95	58	0	119	91	52	98	0
1964	8	6	.571	4.33	56	0	106	106	53	89	0
1965	6	5	.545	3.04	60	0	103⅔	86	50	86	0
1966	14	15	.483	3.22	40	12	254½	211	79	194	0
1967	1	5	.167	3.71	9	1	60⅔	50	24	39	0
Career	121	117	.508	3.68	519	71	2,015	1,794	842	1,378	9

Bernazard, Antonio

Indians: 1984–87
Second baseman
Nickname: Tony
Birthplace: Caguas, Puerto Rico

B: August 24, 1956
Bats both, throws right
Ht. 5–9; Wt. 150

A potent bat kept Tony Bernazard in the big leagues, but limited range at second base cut short his tenure with the Indians less than four full seasons after he was acquired in what initially appeared to be an excellent trade with the Seattle Mariners.

Bernazard, whose professional career began in the Montreal farm system in 1974, made it to the Expos late in 1979. He was dealt to the Chicago White Sox in December 1980 and was sent to the Mariners in June 1983. Six months later the Indians got him in exchange for outfielder Gorman Thomas and infielder Jack Perconte.

Though Bernazard's debut with the Tribe in 1984 was inauspicious at best—at one time that season he went hitless in 44 consecutive plate appearances, and he batted .221—his average improved in 1985 and peaked at .301 in 1986, when he was picked as the American League All-Star second baseman.

It was during the 1986 season that Bernazard set a club record for home runs by a switch-hitter (17) and also became the first Tribe player to homer from both sides of the plate in the same game, a 9–0 victory in Oakland on July 1. Both records have since been broken.

When Bernazard slumped to .239 in 79 games in 1987, he was traded on July 15 to the Athletics for two minor leaguers. The following season he played in Japan.

Bernazard, Tony

Indians	G	AB	H	BA	RBI	R	2B	3B	HR	SA	SB
1984	140	439	97	.221	38	44	15	4	2	.287	20
1985	153	500	137	.274	59	73	26	3	11	.404	17
1986	146	562	169	.301	73	88	28	4	17	.456	17
1987	79	293	70	.239	30	39	12	1	11	.399	7
Career	1,071	3,700	970	.262	391	523	177	30	75	.387	113

Bernhard, William Henry

Indians: 1902–07
Pitcher
Nicknames: Strawberry Bill, Bernie
Birthplace: Clarence, New York

B: March 16, 1871
D: March 30, 1949
Batted both, threw right
Ht. 6–1; **Wt.** 205

Because he was one of the first players to jump from the National League to the newly founded American League in 1901, Bill Bernhard wound up as a member of the Indians (then the Bronchos) in 1902. He became the first Cleveland pitcher to lead the AL in winning percentage with a .783 mark (18–5 won-lost record—one of his victories was registered for Philadelphia before he joined the Bronchos).

The Bronchos got Bernhard, along with Napoleon Lajoie, from the Philadelphia Athletics, the team to which both of them jumped after they refused to play for the Philadelphia Phillies of the NL.

Bernhard won 17 games and lost 10 for the Athletics in 1901, but was barred by a court order from playing in Philadelphia because of his contract dispute with the Phillies.

Connie Mack, the owner of the Athletics, sent Bernhard and Lajoie to Cleveland in appreciation of the financial assistance given him by Bronchos owner Charles Somers when the AL was formed by Ban Johnson.

A broken finger hampered Bernhard in 1903, though he still compiled a 14–6 record, and he again led the Cleveland staff in 1904, going 23–13, though it was his last good season.

After 16 victories and 15 losses in 1906, Bernhard failed to win a game while losing four in 1907. The poor season ended his career, though he went on to manage in the Southern Association for several more years.

Bernhard, Bill

Indians	W	L	Pct	ERA	G	CG	IP	H	BB	SO	ShO
1902	17	5	.773	2.20	27	22	217	169	34	57	3
1903	14	6	.700	2.12	20	18	165⅔	151	21	60	3
1904	23	13	.639	2.13	38	35	320⅔	323	55	137	4
1905	7	13	.350	3.36	22	17	174⅓	185	34	56	0
1906	16	15	.516	2.54	31	23	255⅓	235	47	85	2
1907	0	4	.000	3.21	8	3	42	58	11	19	0
Career	116	82	.586	3.04	231	175	1,792	1,860	365	545	14

Birmingham, Joseph Leo

Indians: 1906–14
Outfielder
Nickname: Dode
Birthplace: Elmira, New York

B: August 6, 1884
D: April 24, 1946
Batted right, threw right
Ht. 5–10; **Wt.** 185

An outstanding defensive center fielder, Joe Birmingham led American League outfielders with 33 assists in 1907, and became the Indians' (then called the Naps) second player-manager in 1912 when he replaced the fired Harry Davis on September 2.

When Birmingham took over the team, it was mired in sixth place with a 54–71 record, and morale was low because of a series of strict rules implemented by Davis. The Naps rallied under Birmingham, winning 21 of their final 28 games, though it was too late to climb higher than fifth place.

Birmingham, however, did not get along with Napoleon Lajoie, the team's aging star second baseman and former manager (1904–09). Their animosity toward each other reached a climax in mid-June 1913 when Birmingham benched Lajoie, causing a furor among the fans.

Despite the trouble between the manager and Lajoie that divided the team, the Naps under Birmingham were in contention most of 1913 but collapsed in the final month and fell into third place.

Birmingham also was forced to the sidelines after 47 games in 1913 when he suffered a broken leg. He retired as a player after hitting .128 in 19 games in 1914, when the Naps fell into the basement with a 51–102 record. It was the first time the Cleveland baseball franchise lost 100 games.

That also was Lajoie's final season in Cleveland, and his departure back to the Philadelphia Athletics led to renaming the team the Indians.

And when the Indians started the 1915 season with 16 losses in their first 28 games, Birmingham was fired as manager and replaced by Lee Fohl.

Birmingham returned to the minor leagues and managed teams in the International and Eastern leagues, and in 1929 he umpired in the International League.

Birmingham, Joe

Indians	G	AB	H	BA	RBI	R	2B	3B	HR	SA	SB
1906	10	41	13	.317	6	5	2	1	0	.415	2
1907	136	476	112	.235	33	55	10	9	1	.300	23
1908	122	413	88	.213	38	32	10	1	2	.257	15
1909	100	343	99	.289	38	29	10	5	1	.356	12
1910	104	367	84	.229	35	41	11	2	0	.270	18
1911	125	447	136	.304	51	55	18	5	2	.380	16
1912	107	369	94	.255	45	49	19	3	1	.331	15
1913	47	131	37	.282	15	16	9	1	0	.366	7
1914	19	47	6	.128	4	2	0	0	0	.128	0
Career	770	2,634	669	.254	265	284	89	27	7	.316	108

Black, Donald Paul

Indians: 1946–48
Pitcher
Birthplace: Salix, Iowa
B: July 20, 1916

D: April 21, 1959
Batted right, threw right
Ht. 6–0; **Wt.** 185

A drinking problem drove Don Black out of Philadelphia, where he had pitched with varying degrees of success for the Athletics for three seasons until he was suspended and then sold to the Indians on October 2, 1945.

Black barely hung on with the Tribe in 1946 when his record was 1–2 in 18 games and when he finally was convinced—upon orders from owner Bill Veeck—to join Alcoholics Anonymous.

It turned Black's career around, but only briefly because he suffered a near-fatal brain hemorrhage during a game on September 13, 1948.

Fourteen months earlier, on July 10, 1947, in the first game of a twi-night doubleheader, Black reached the heights as a pitcher, hurling the first no-hitter in the Cleveland Stadium, and only the ninth in the history of the Indians franchise. Making the triumph especially sweet, Black pitched it

Don Black

Black, Don											
Indians	W	L	Pct	ERA	G	CG	IP	H	BB	SO	ShO
1946	1	2	.333	4.53	18	0	43⅔	45	21	15	0
1947	10	12	.455	3.92	30	8	190⅔	177	85	72	3
1948	2	2	.500	5.37	18	1	52	57	40	16	0
Career	34	55	.382	4.35	154	37	797	803	400	293	4

Blyleven, Rik Aalbert

Indians: 1981–85　　　　　**B:** April 6, 1951
Pitcher　　　　　**Bats right, throws right**
Nickname: Bert　　　　　**Ht.** 6–3; **Wt.** 200
Birthplace: Zeist, Netherlands

One of the best curveball pitchers of his era, Bert Blyleven joined the Indians near the end of his career and, after three injury-plagued and mediocre seasons, fashioned a staff-leading 19–7 record and 2.87 earned run average in 1984.

It earned for Blyleven the Man of the Year award and third place in the balloting for the American League Cy Young Award, though he was the top vote getter among starting pitchers. Relievers Willie Hernandez and Dan Quisenberry finished first and second.

A model of consistency in 1984, Blyleven pitched at least seven innings in 26 of his 32 starts, and allowed three or fewer runs 22 times. Four of his victories were shutouts, and he walked only 74 batters in 245 innings.

Blyleven's performance that season was all the more impressive when it is considered that he suffered a fractured bone in his right foot that put him on the disabled list from May 23 to June 9. It caused Blyleven to miss five starts.

against his former team, the Athletics, beating them 3–0, striking out five and walking six. It was one of 10 victories Black recorded that year.

It was witnessed by 47,871 fans who turned out expecting to see Larry Doby, the American League's first black player, make his first appearance in a Tribe uniform in Cleveland (though he didn't play that game).

The day he almost died during the game, Black was pitching against the St. Louis Browns at the Stadium, trying to keep the Tribe in contention with Boston, New York, and Philadelphia for the AL pennant.

Batting in the second inning, Black swung viciously and fouled off a pitch from the Browns' Bill Kennedy.

Black staggered slightly as he finished his swing, then walked away from the plate and turned in a small circle in back of umpire Bill Summers.

"My God, Bill, what happened?" Black muttered to Summers. Then he sagged to the ground and lapsed into unconsciousness as blood flooded his brain and spinal cord.

He was rushed to the hospital, where surgery was considered but dismissed because Black's condition was too serious. Doctors gave him only a 50–50 chance to live.

Black survived but never pitched again.

Nine days after he was stricken, while he was still in critical condition, the Indians held a "night" in his honor and raised $40,000 for him.

Bert Blyleven

He also was sidelined with an elbow injury much of 1982 when he pitched only four games, winning two and losing two. He went 7–10 the following season.

Blyleven's desire to pitch for a contender led to his being traded to Minnesota on August 1, 1985, for shortstop Jay Bell, outfielder Jim Weaver, and pitchers Curt Wardle and Rich Yett. Minnesota was the team with which Blyleven began his major league career in 1970 when he was voted the AL's Rookie Pitcher of the Year.

He was named to the AL All-Star team in 1973 and 1985.

The Twins, who selected Blyleven in the third round of the 1969 amateur draft, traded him to Texas in 1976. A year later the Rangers sent him to Pittsburgh, and on December 9, 1980, the Indians got him, along with catcher Manny Sanguillen (who subsequently retired), in exchange for catcher Gary Alexander and pitchers Victor Cruz, Bob Owchinko, and Rafael Vasquez.

Blyleven pitched for the Twins from 1986 to 1988 and was traded again, this time to California, and he ended a 21-year major league career with an 8–12 record in 1992. Among his notable statistics are 3,701 strikeouts in 4,970 innings, the third highest all-time record behind Nolan Ryan (5,714) and Steve Carlton (4,136).

Blyleven pitched a no-hitter for the Rangers on September 22, 1977, beating California, 6–0; was the winner in relief for the Pirates in Game 5 of the 1979 World Series when they defeated Baltimore; and was 1–1 in two starts for the Twins in the 1987 World Series when they beat St. Louis.

Blyleven, Bert

Indians	W	L	Pct	ERA	G	CG	IP	H	BB	SO	ShO
1981	11	7	.611	2.88	20	9	159⅓	145	40	107	1
1982	2	2	.500	4.87	4	0	20⅓	16	11	19	0
1983	7	10	.412	3.91	24	5	156⅓	160	44	123	0
1984	19	7	.731	2.87	33	12	245	204	74	170	4
1985	9	11	.450	3.26	23	15	179⅔	163	49	129	4
Career	287	250	.534	3.31	692	242	4,970	4,632	1,322	3,701	60

Boone, Raymond Otis

Indians: 1948–53
Shortstop
Nickname: Ike
Birthplace: San Diego, California

B: July 27, 1923
Bats right, throws right
Ht. 6–0; **Wt.** 172

A former catcher whose minor league career began in 1942 and was interrupted by military service (1943–45) in World War II, Ray Boone was converted to shortstop while playing for Oklahoma City of the Class AA Texas League in 1947.

Late in the 1948 season Boone was called up by the Indians to replace injured shortstop-manager Lou Boudreau, earning a World Series share. Thus was launched a 13-year major league career that included tours of duty with Detroit, the Chicago White Sox, the Kansas City Athletics, the Milwaukee Braves, and Boston.

Boone shared the shortstop position with Boudreau in 1949 but took it over on a regular basis in 1950 when he batted .301 in 109 games, with the manager moving into a utility infielder's role.

Though he often was erratic in the field, committing 33 errors, which tied him with Detroit's Johnny Lipon for the

Ray Boone

most by an American League shortstop in 1951, Boone continued as the Tribe's shortstop until he was sent to the Tigers on June 15, 1953, in an eight-player deal.

The trade proved to be a good one for Boone, who was switched to third base the following season, a position for which he was much better suited, and he responded by hitting .312, .295, .284, .308, and .273 with 99 homers from 1953 to 1957. He led the AL with 116 RBIs in 1955. He was a member of the AL All-Star team in 1954 and 1956.

After his retirement as a player in 1960, Boone became a major league scout, a position he held with the Boston Red Sox through 1992.

Following Ray Boone to the major leagues were his son Bob, a catcher from 1972 to 1990 for the Philadelphia Phillies, California Angels, and Kansas City Royals, then a coach for Cincinnati and manager of the Royals in 1995, and grandson Bret, a second baseman with Seattle in 1992 and 1993 and then with the Reds.

Boone, Ray

Indians	G	AB	H	BA	RBI	R	2B	3B	HR	SA	SB
1948	6	5	2	.400	1	0	1	0	0	.600	0
1949	86	258	65	.252	26	39	4	4	4	.345	0
1950	109	365	110	.301	58	53	14	6	7	.430	4
1951	151	544	127	.233	51	65	14	1	12	.329	5
1952	103	316	83	.263	45	57	8	2	7	.367	0
1953	34	112	27	.241	21	21	1	2	4	.393	1
Career	1,373	4,589	1,260	.275	737	645	162	46	151	.429	21

Bosman, Richard Allen

Indians: 1973–75
Pitcher
Nickname: Dick
Birthplace: Kenosha, Wisconsin

B: February 17, 1944
Bats right, throws right
Ht. 6–2; **Wt.** 195

His tenure with the Indians was brief—one full season and part of two others—but Dick Bosman pitched one of the best games in Cleveland baseball history on July 19, 1974, when he came within one simple throw of a perfect game.

Instead, because of his own error, Bosman had to settle for a no-hitter, the 13th in the history of the Indians franchise, in a 4–0 victory over the Oakland Athletics at the Stadium.

As Bosman said of his errant throw to first base in the fourth inning of that game, "I've made that play hundreds of times. It's an easy play. You take a couple of steps to your right, pick up the ball and just sort of flip it sidearm to first base."

But that time it sailed . . . it sailed right over first baseman Tom McCraw's head, and Sal Bando became the only A's player to reach base.

Most important to Bosman at the time, he also said later, was that the Indians won the game, keeping them only a game out of first place, though they finished the 1974 season well out of contention.

That victory by Bosman was one of only eight, with 15 losses, he posted for the Indians after they acquired him from Texas on May 10, 1973, and before they traded him to Oakland on May 20, 1975.

He was much more successful for one of the worst teams in major league history, the Washington Senators from 1966 to 1971 (before they became the Texas Rangers in 1972). Bosman had a 14–5 record and an American League–best 2.19 earned run average in 1969, and he went on to win 49 games while losing 49 for the Senators through 1971.

After going to Oakland in 1975, Bosman won 11 games to help the Athletics win the AL West. Bosman's record fell to 4–2 in 1976, and the Athletics released him in spring training the next year, ending his pitching career with an 11-year career mark of 82–85.

Bosman has remained in the game as a minor league instructor and was the pitching coach for the Baltimore Orioles from 1992 to 1994.

Bosman, Dick

Indians	W	L	Pct	ERA	G	CG	IP	H	BB	SO	ShO
1973	1	8	.111	6.22	22	2	97	130	29	41	0
1974	7	5	.583	4.10	25	2	127⅓	126	29	56	1
1975	0	2	.000	4.08	6	0	28⅔	33	8	11	0
Career	82	85	.491	3.67	306	29	1,591	1,594	412	757	10

Boudreau, Louis

Indians: 1938–50
Shortstop
Nickname: Lou
Birthplace: Harvey, Illinois

B: July 17, 1917
Bats right, throws right
Ht. 5–11; **Wt.** 185

When Lou Boudreau was inducted into the Baseball Hall of Fame on July 27, 1970, Commissioner Bowie Kuhn said of him, "The most remarkable thing about this remarkable man was the way he stretched the wonderful skills he had into superlative skills.

"As a shortstop, he was a human computer, he knew all the hitters' habits, he knew all the moves of the base runners, he knew when the pitcher was going to pitch, he had instincts for where the ball would be hit, and from all of this he fashioned the wonderful ballplayer that we knew as Lou Boudreau."

Boudreau was indeed a wonderful ballplayer most of his 15-year major league career, especially in 1948 when he, as the player-manager of the Indians, led them—physically and inspirationally—to the second pennant and world championship in franchise history.

Boudreau won the American League Most Valuable Player award practically by acclamation that season when he hit a career-high .355 with 18 home runs and drove in 106 runs.

Boudreau's heroics carried over into the unprecedented one-game playoff for the pennant, going 4-for-4 with two homers to lead the Indians to an 8–3 victory over the Boston Red Sox. Then he sparked the Tribe against the National League champion Boston Braves, winning the World Series in six games.

The former captain of the baseball and basketball teams at the University of Illinois, Boudreau began his professional career as a third baseman for Cedar Rapids, Iowa, of the Class B Three-I League in 1938.

He started the 1939 season at Buffalo of the Class AA International League where he was switched to shortstop and teamed up with second baseman Ray Mack, though neither stayed in the minors long.

Dick Bosman

Lou Boudreau

Boudreau and Mack, who had gained fame as a slick double-play combination, were promoted on August 7, 1939, to Cleveland—and Boudreau stayed there for 12 years.

In his first full season with the Indians in 1940, Boudreau was named to the American League All-Star team and hit .295 with 101 RBIs. He appeared in six more All-Star games, in 1941, 1942, 1943, 1944, 1947, and 1948; managed the AL to an 11–7 victory over the National League in 1949; tied a record by leading AL shortstops in fielding percentage eight years, won the AL batting championship with a .327 average in 1944, and ended his 13-year playing career with a .295 lifetime average in 1,646 games.

He was the Indians' Man of the Year for 1947.

After the Indians painfully endured their infamous "Crybaby" season in 1940, when they rebelled in June against manager Oscar Vitt, and then failed to contend for the pennant under Roger Peckinpaugh in 1941, Boudreau wrote to owner Alva Bradley.

As Peckinpaugh had been named general manager of the team, Boudreau applied for the vacant manager's job. Despite his age—he was then only 24—Boudreau said he was confident he could handle the position because he'd captained his college baseball and basketball teams.

After Bradley met with the club's directors and they interviewed Boudreau, the owner agreed with the young shortstop. On November 25, 1941, Bradley hired Boudreau to be the franchise's 15th manager and its fifth player-manager.

Boudreau immediately was dubbed the "Boy Manager" by the media because he was the youngest manager in the history of baseball. (Roger Peckinpaugh was only 23 when he took over on a temporary basis as manager of the New York Yankees in mid-September 1914 to replace Frank Chance, but he did not manage the team in 1915.)

Boudreau remained at the helm of the Indians through 1950, though Bill Veeck, who purchased the franchise in 1946, tried to replace him with Jimmy Dykes during the winter of 1947–48.

Veeck didn't because Cleveland fans reacted angrily to reports that he was planning to trade Boudreau to the St. Louis Browns. Instead, Veeck re-signed Boudreau to a new two-year contract.

And when the Indians prevailed the following season, Veeck said, "We didn't win the pennant in 1948; we won it on November 24, 1947, the day I rehired Lou Boudreau."

Under Boudreau the Indians finished well out of the pennant races from 1942 to 1947, but were in contention in 1949 and 1950, before he was fired by general manager Hank Greenberg on November 10, 1950, and replaced by Al Lopez.

It was under Boudreau that Bob Lemon was transformed from a light-hitting third baseman/outfielder to a future Hall of Fame pitcher, and the one-time "Boy Manager" also created the famous "Williams shift" and other innovative defensive tactics that subsequently were employed by other teams.

After leaving the Indians, Boudreau managed Boston from 1952 to 1954, the Kansas City Athletics from 1955 to 1957, and the Chicago Cubs in 1960, but he never again enjoyed the success he had in Cleveland in 1948.

He also served as a radio voice of the Chicago Cubs for nearly 30 years before retiring in 1988.

Boudreau, Lou

Indians	G	AB	H	BA	RBI	R	2B	3B	HR	SA	SB
1938	1	1	0	.000	0	0	0	0	0	.000	0
1939	53	225	58	.258	19	42	15	4	0	.360	2
1940	155	627	185	.295	101	97	46	10	9	.443	6
1941	148	579	149	.257	56	95	45	8	10	.415	9
1942	147	506	143	.283	58	57	18	10	2	.370	7
1943	152	539	154	.286	67	69	32	7	3	.388	4
1944	150	584	191	.327	67	91	45	5	3	.437	11
1945	97	345	106	.307	48	50	24	1	3	.409	0
1946	140	515	151	.293	62	51	30	6	6	.410	6
1947	150	538	165	.307	67	79	45	3	4	.424	1
1948	152	560	199	.355	106	116	34	6	18	.534	3
1949	134	475	135	.284	60	53	20	3	4	.364	0
1950	81	260	70	.269	29	23	13	2	1	.346	1
Career	1,646	6,029	1,779	.295	789	861	385	66	68	.415	51

Bradley, William Joseph

Indians: 1901–10
Third baseman
Nickname: Bill
Birthplace: Cleveland

B: February 13, 1878
D: March 11, 1954
Batted right, threw right
Ht. 6–0; **Wt.** 185

Because he wanted to play in his hometown, Bill Bradley jumped from the National League Chicago Cubs, for whom he'd been their third baseman for two seasons, to the

Cleveland Blues (later called the Indians) when the American League was founded in 1901.

Bradley immediately established himself as the greatest player of his era at that demanding position, until he suffered a serious injury that cut short his 1906 season. His .955 fielding average in 1904 set a record that stood for 10 years.

Bradley's career totals topped all AL third basemen in games, putouts, assists, double plays, total chances, and errors until Frank "Home Run" Baker broke them upon his retirement in 1922.

Bradley was particularly renowned at guarding against bunts and is credited with originating the bare-handed pickup and throw to first with the same motion, now the commonly accepted manner of making the play.

But it was more than his defensive play that established Bradley as one of the all-time great third basemen. He was consistently among the league's leading hitters his first four seasons in Cleveland, compiling a career-best .340 average that was fifth highest in the AL in 1902.

That was the season Bradley's 104 runs were fourth in the AL, 11 home runs tied for second, and 39 doubles tied for third, and he put together a 29-game hitting streak that was a league record until Ty Cobb broke it in 1911.

In 1903, Bradley tied a still-standing AL record (set originally by Cleveland's Elmer Flick in 1902) with three triples in one game, and it was his sensational backhanded grab of John Anderson's sharp grounder over third base that resulted in the final out of Addie Joss's perfect game on October 2, 1908.

Bradley's career suffered in 1909 when he was stricken with a serious attack of typhoid fever that limited him to 95 games and caused his average to drop to .186. He was unconditionally released in August 1910 after playing in only 61 games (and batting .196) and then spent the next three seasons with Toronto in the Eastern and International leagues.

In 1914, Bradley managed the Brooklyn Tip Tops of the newly formed Federal League (and appeared in six games as a pinch hitter), and in 1915 he played third base for the Kansas City Packers of the Federal League.

Bradley retired with a lifetime batting average of .271 for 12 major league seasons.

Later Bradley became a scout for the Indians, serving in that capacity for 25 years through the winter of 1953–54.

Bradley, Bill

Indians	G	AB	H	BA	RBI	R	2B	3B	HR	SA	SB
1901	133	516	151	.293	55	95	28	13	1	.403	15
1902	137	550	187	.340	77	104	39	12	11	.515	11
1903	136	536	168	.313	68	101	36	22	6	.496	21
1904	154	609	183	.300	83	94	32	8	5	.404	23
1905	146	541	145	.268	51	63	34	6	0	.353	22
1906	82	302	83	.275	25	32	16	2	2	.361	13
1907	139	498	111	.223	34	48	20	1	0	.267	20
1908	148	548	133	.243	46	70	24	7	1	.318	18
1909	95	334	62	.186	22	30	6	3	0	.222	8
1910	61	214	42	.196	12	12	3	0	0	.210	6
Career	1,461	5,430	1,471	.271	552	754	275	84	33	.371	181

Brohamer, John Anthony

Indians: 1972–75, 1980
Second baseman
Nickname: Scrappy Jack
Birthplace: Maywood, California

B: February 26, 1950
Bats left, throws right
Ht. 5–10; Wt. 165

He was small, bowlegged, and gutsy—which is the reason Jack Brohamer was called Scrappy Jack during a nine-year major league career in which he made the most of limited ability.

A shortstop when he started his professional career as a 34th-round selection in the 1967 amateur draft, Brohamer was switched to second base in 1972, when he was named to the American League All-Star rookie team.

After suffering a hip injury on May 25, 1975, and losing his starting job to rookie Duane Kuiper, Brohamer publicly criticized general manager Phil Seghi and was traded that winter to the Chicago White Sox for infielder Larvell Blanks.

Brohamer was a regular for the White Sox in 1976 but a part-timer in 1977. After becoming a free agent, he signed with Boston in 1978. The Indians brought Brohamer back to Cleveland in a cash purchase on June 20, 1980, but he didn't make the team the following spring and retired.

Brohamer, Jack

Indians	G	AB	H	BA	RBI	R	2B	3B	HR	SA	SB
1972	136	527	123	.233	35	49	13	2	5	.294	3
1973	102	300	66	.220	29	29	12	1	4	.307	0
1974	101	315	85	.270	30	33	11	1	2	.330	2
1975	69	217	53	.244	16	15	5	0	6	.350	2
1980	53	142	32	.225	15	13	5	1	1	.296	0
Career	805	2,500	613	.245	227	262	91	12	30	.327	9

Jack Brohamer

Brown, Clinton Harold

Indians: 1928–35, 1941–42
Pitcher
Birthplace: Blackash, Pennsylvania
B: July 8, 1903

D: December 31, 1955
Batted left, threw right
Ht. 6–1; **Wt.** 190

Though he was a starter the first five years of his career with the Indians, Clint Brown became one of the first relief aces and, in 1939, four seasons after he was sold to the Chicago White Sox, set a (since broken) major league record by appearing in 61 games.

Clint Brown

A finesse pitcher who threw underhand, sidearm, and with a three-quarters motion depending upon the situation, Brown won in double figures as a starter for the Tribe from 1930 to 1933, compiling a career best 15–12 mark in 1932.

Brown was switched to the bull pen in 1934 when the Indians starters were Mel Harder, Monte Pearson, Willis Hudlin, and Oral Hildebrand. He continued strictly as a reliever with the White Sox from 1936 to 1940, appearing in 197 games, leading the AL in saves with 18 in 1937 and relief victories with 11 in 1939.

The Indians traded another reliever, Johnny Humphries, on February 7, 1941, to reacquire Brown. He pitched in 41 games that season, but was used sparingly in 1942 and retired.

Brown, Clint

Indians	W	L	Pct	ERA	G	CG	IP	H	BB	SO	ShO
1928	0	1	.000	4.91	2	1	11	14	2	2	0
1929	0	2	.000	3.31	3	1	16⅓	18	6	1	0
1930	11	13	.458	4.97	35	16	213⅔	271	51	54	3
1931	11	15	.423	4.71	39	12	233⅓	284	55	50	2
1932	15	12	.556	4.08	37	21	262⅔	298	50	59	1
1933	11	12	.478	3.41	33	10	185	202	34	47	2
1934	4	3	.571	5.90	17	0	50⅓	83	14	15	0
1935	4	3	.571	5.14	23	1	49	61	14	20	0
1941	3	3	.500	3.27	41	0	74⅓	77	28	22	0
1942	1	1	.500	6.00	7	0	9	16	2	4	0
Career	89	93	.489	4.26	434	62	1,485⅔	1,740	368	410	8

Brown, Larry Leslie

Indians: 1963–71
Shortstop, second baseman
Birthplace: Shinnston, West Virginia

B: March 1, 1940
Bats right, throws right
Ht. 5–10; **Wt.** 160

Larry Brown once said that he was most famous for a violent, horrifying collision with an Indians teammate in 1966 in which he was almost killed.

That claim was only partly accurate.

Brown was a dependable hitter and versatile middle infielder for the Indians for eight seasons, from the time he joined them as a shortstop in 1963. He switched to second base in 1964, went back to shortstop from 1965 to 1968, and played both positions, as well as third base, in 1969 and 1970.

After being sold to Oakland on April 24, 1971, Brown served as a utility infielder for the Athletics through 1972, for Baltimore in 1973, and for Texas in 1974 before retiring with a 12-year career batting average of .233 in 1,129 games.

Brown's near-fatal collision with Tribe outfielder Leon Wagner occurred on May 4, 1966, in Yankee Stadium, as they chased Roger Maris's pop fly to short left field in the fourth inning of a game won by the Indians, 2–1.

Brown incurred multiple fractures of the skull, above and below the eye sockets, and a broken nose. After being rushed to the hospital he lapsed into a coma for three days and remained in intensive care for a week.

Only a year earlier Brown's brother Dick, a catcher for the Indians from 1957 to 1959 (he also played for the Chicago White Sox in 1960, Detroit in 1961–62, and Baltimore from 1963 to 1965) died of a brain tumor on April 12, 1970.

Larry Brown survived the collision with Wagner, but was unable to play again for six weeks. When he did return to action, Brown's average dropped from .262, which he was hitting at the time of the collision, to a season-ending .229.

Larry Brown

Wagner suffered only bruises of the head and shoulders and was able to play a few days later.

After leaving the Rangers, Brown became a manufacturer's representative in West Palm Beach, Florida.

Brown, Larry											
Indians	G	AB	H	BA	RBI	R	2B	3B	HR	SA	SB
1963	74	247	63	.255	18	28	6	0	5	.340	4
1964	115	335	77	.230	40	33	12	1	12	.379	1
1965	124	438	111	.253	40	52	22	2	8	.368	5
1966	105	340	78	.229	17	29	12	0	3	.291	0
1967	152	485	110	.227	37	38	16	2	7	.311	4
1968	154	495	116	.234	35	43	18	3	6	.319	1
1969	132	469	112	.239	24	48	10	2	4	.294	5
1970	72	155	40	.258	15	17	5	2	0	.316	1
1971	13	50	11	.220	5	4	1	0	0	.240	0
Career	1,129	3,449	803	.233	254	331	108	13	47	.313	22

Browne, Jerome Austin

Indians: 1989–91
Second baseman, outfielder, third baseman
Nickname: Guv'nor

Birthplace: Christiansted, Virgin Islands
B: February 3, 1966
Bats both, throws right
Ht. 5–10; **Wt.** 170

Jerry Browne was a principal in one of the Indians' worst trades, though he had one outstanding season in Cleveland when he batted a career-high .299 with 179 hits and 14 stolen bases in 1989.

That performance won for Browne the Tribe's Man of the Year award, though he never played that well again and was released March 31, 1992.

The Indians gave up shortstop–second baseman Julio Franco to acquire Browne, first baseman Pete O'Brien, and outfielder Oddibe McDowell in a trade with the Texas Rangers on December 6, 1988.

A good contact hitter but with limited range in the field, Browne started his professional career in 1983 with the Rangers' organization and was their rookie of the year in 1987 when he played his first full season in the major leagues.

Upon leaving the Indians, Browne played for Oakland in 1992 and 1993, after which he became a free agent again and signed with the Florida Marlins.

Browne, Jerry											
Indians	G	AB	H	BA	RBI	R	2B	3B	HR	SA	SB
1989	153	598	179	.299	45	83	31	4	5	.390	14
1990	140	513	137	.267	50	92	26	5	6	.372	12
1991	107	290	66	.228	29	28	5	2	1	.269	2
Career	982	3,190	866	.271	288	431	135	25	23	.351	73

Burnett, John Henderson

Indians: 1927–34
Shortstop, third baseman, second baseman
Birthplace: Bartow, Florida

B: November 1, 1904
D: August 13, 1959
Batted left, threw right
Ht. 5–11; **Wt.** 175

Though he never batted less than .272 as an Indian—and hit as much as .312 and .300 in two seasons—while compiling a nine-year major league career average of .284, Johnny Burnett probably is best remembered for two games he played in 1932.

The first was on July 10, at League Park, against the Philadelphia Athletics when Burnett etched his name in the

Johnny Burnett

record book for getting nine hits in one game in the Tribe's 18–17, 18-inning loss. It is still a major league record.

The previous day, also against the Athletics, Burnett got two hits, giving him 11 in two consecutive games, which also remains a record.

Burnett's other game of distinction occurred on August 7, when he socked the first home run ever hit at the newly constructed Cleveland Stadium, which had been opened only a week earlier. It was the Indians' biggest blow in a 7–4 victory over Washington.

In the marathon against the Athletics, which has been called the "daffiest" baseball game ever played, Burnett, in 11 trips to the plate, lashed two doubles and seven singles. Eight of the hits were off Eddie Rommel, who relieved starter Lew Krausse in the second inning.

Burnett, who joined the Indians in 1927, didn't play much until 1930 when, on July 19, he suffered a fractured right wrist and was sidelined the rest of the season.

Replaced as the Tribe's shortstop by Bill Knickerbocker in 1933, Burnett became a utility infielder. On November 20, 1934, he was traded with pitcher Bob Weiland and cash to the St. Louis Browns for outfielder Bruce Campbell. He ended his career in the spring of 1936 after being dealt to Cincinnati.

Burnett, Johnny

Indians	G	AB	H	BA	RBI	R	2B	3B	HR	SA	SB
1927	17	8	0	.000	0	5	0	0	0	.000	1
1928	3	10	5	.500	1	3	0	0	0	.500	0
1929	19	33	5	.152	2	2	1	0	0	.182	0
1930	54	170	53	.312	20	28	13	0	0	.388	2
1931	111	427	128	.300	52	85	25	5	1	.389	5
1932	129	512	152	.297	53	81	23	5	4	.385	2
1933	83	261	71	.272	29	39	11	2	1	.341	3
1934	72	208	61	.293	30	28	11	2	3	.409	1
Career	558	1,835	521	.284	213	288	94	15	9	.366	15

Burns, George Henry

Indians: 1920–21, 1924–28	**B:** January 31, 1893
First baseman	**D:** January 7, 1978
Nickname: Tioga George	**Batted right, threw right**
Birthplace: Niles, Ohio	**Ht.** 6–1½; **Wt.** 180

It was opening day in New York, April 18, 1923, the first game played in Yankee Stadium, a.k.a. the "House That Ruth Built."

But it wasn't the legendary Yankee slugger who got the first hit in the new ballpark.

That distinction was claimed by a former Tribesman—George Burns—who would return to Cleveland the following season.

Burns, a member of the Indians in 1920, when they won the franchise's first pennant and World Series, would play for them again from 1924 to 1928. But this day, he was the first baseman for the Boston Red Sox—the visiting team when Yankee Stadium was opened.

In his first time at bat in the second inning, Burns lined a single to left field, though Ruth would hit the first homer in Yankee Stadium later in that game.

But that first hit by Burns wasn't his only claim to fame in a 16-year major league career.

It also was during Burns' term with the Red Sox, on Sep-

George Burns

tember 14, 1923, that he pulled off an unassisted triple play against the Indians. The game was in Boston and, in the second inning with Riggs Stephenson on second base and Rube Lutzke on first, Burns caught Frank Brower's line drive. He tagged Lutzke off first and then ran to second and reached the bag before Stephenson could return from third.

And after rejoining the Indians in 1924, Burns went 6-for-6 (a triple, three doubles, and two singles) in the first game of a doubleheader on June 19 in Detroit.

Burns broke in with the Tigers in 1914; went to the Philadelphia Athletics in 1918; was sold to the Indians on May 29, 1920; was traded (with outfielders Joe Harris and Elmer Smith to Boston for first baseman Stuffy McInnis) on December 24, 1921; was dealt back to Cleveland (with catcher Roxy Walters and second baseman Chick Fewster for catcher Steve O'Neill, second baseman Bill Wambsganss, pitcher Danny Boone, and outfielder Joe Connolly) on January 7, 1924; was released by the Tribe and signed by the Yankees in September 1928; and finally was sold back to the Athletics on June 19, 1929.

Burns retired at the end of that season after appearing in 1,866 games with a 16-year career .307 batting average. He hit .300 or better eight times, including a career-high .361 in 84 games for the Indians in 1921, and .358 (with 216 hits in 603 at bats) in 1926.

Though he was a right-handed batter, Burns owned the close right-field wall at League Park, especially in 1926 when he hit 64 doubles, the second-highest total in one season in baseball history.

That also was the season Burns batted .358, tied for the American League with 216 hits, and drove in 114 runs. It won for him the AL's Most Valuable Player award. Right behind Burns in the voting was Ruth, who hit .372 with 47 homers and 146 RBIs that year.

When the Indians beat Brooklyn in the 1920 World Series, Burns batted .300 (3-for-10) and doubled home player-manager Tris Speaker with the game's only run in the sixth game. Burns also played for the Athletics in the 1929 World Series when they defeated the Chicago Cubs.

After his playing career, Burns managed in the minor leagues for nine years, and then became a deputy sheriff in Seattle from 1939 to 1968.

Burns, George

Indians	G	AB	H	BA	RBI	R	2B	3B	HR	SA	SB
1920	44	56	15	.268	13	7	4	1	0	.375	1
1921	84	244	88	.361	49	52	21	4	0	.480	3
1924	129	462	143	.310	68	64	37	5	4	.437	14
1925	127	488	164	.336	79	69	41	4	6	.473	16
1926	151	603	216	.358	114	97	64	3	4	.494	13
1927	140	549	175	.319	78	84	51	2	3	.435	13
1928	82	209	52	.249	30	29	12	1	5	.388	2
Career	1,866	6,573	2,018	.307	951	901	444	72	72	.429	154

Butler, Brett Morgan

Indians: 1984–87
Center fielder
Birthplace: Los Angeles

B: June 15, 1957
Bats left, throws left
Ht. 5–10; **Wt.** 160

The acquisition of Brett Butler on August 28, 1983, was one of the Indians' best-ever deals, though its value was diminished four years later when the pint-sized and feisty center fielder walked away via free agency to sign with San Francisco.

Butler came to the Tribe from Atlanta with third baseman Brook Jacoby and pitcher Rick Behenna for pitcher Len Barker, then proceeded to be one of the most exciting players in the American League.

From 1984 to 1987, Butler was the Indians' leadoff batter and triggered the offense, averaging 99 runs and 41 stolen bases a season. He led the AL with 29 bunt hits in 1984 when his 108 runs were the most by an Indians player since Al Smith led the league with 123 in 1955.

Butler was the Indians' Man of the Year in 1985, when he hit a career-high .311 and also led AL outfielders with a .998 fielding percentage. His 14 triples in 1986 also were tops in the league.

Butler began his professional career as the Braves' 23rd-round selection in the 1979 amateur draft, and he spent parts of the 1981 and 1982 seasons with the Braves before taking over as Atlanta's regular center fielder in 1983, when he hit .281.

He played for the Giants from 1988 to 1990, then again opted for free agency and signed with the Los Angeles Dodgers. He was a member of the National League All-Star team in 1991.

Butler, Brett

Indians	G	AB	H	BA	RBI	R	2B	3B	HR	SA	SB
1984	159	602	162	.269	49	108	25	9	3	.355	52
1985	152	591	184	.311	50	106	28	14	5	.431	47
1986	161	587	163	.278	51	92	17	14	4	.375	32
1987	137	522	154	.295	41	91	25	8	9	.425	33
Career	2,074	7,706	2,243	.291	552	1,285	268	127	54	.380	535

Caldwell, Raymond Benjamin

Indians: 1919–21
Pitcher
Nickname: Slim
Birthplace: Croydon, Pennsylvania

B: April 26, 1888
D: August 17, 1967
Batted left, threw right
Ht. 6–2; **Wt.** 190

Ray Caldwell's first game for the Indians, on August 24, 1919, very nearly was his last.

Instead, he pitched for them in 1920, and without his 20–10 won-lost record, they would not have won the pennant.

Caldwell also hurled a no-hitter on September 10, 1919, the fifth in Tribe history, beating the New York Yankees, 3–0, in the Polo Grounds.

But it was that game two and a half weeks earlier that better established Caldwell's reputation as a battler, a pitcher who would not succumb to adversity.

It was his Cleveland debut, and Caldwell was beating the Philadelphia Athletics, 2–1, with two out in the ninth inning, when a violent thunderstorm hit League Park.

Caldwell was struck by a bolt of lightning and knocked to the ground. After a few minutes he was revived, regained his feet and composure, and shook off the effects of the blow. The storm cleared up as quickly as it arrived, and Caldwell pitched to the next batter. He retired Joe Dugan on a ground-out, ending the game for a victory.

Caldwell pitched for the New York Yankees from 1910 to 1918, compiling a 95–99 record, and was traded in 1919 to Boston, where he was Babe Ruth's roommate. But the Red Sox became disenchanted with Caldwell and released him despite his winning seven games and losing four in the first half of the season.

Tris Speaker, then the Indians' player-manager, jumped

Ray Caldwell

at the chance to sign Caldwell, who went 5–1 the rest of the season.

Caldwell started the third game of the 1920 World Series but was knocked out in the first inning after retiring only one batter, to be replaced by Walter Mails. The Indians lost to Brooklyn, 2–1.

After his record slumped to 6–6 in 1921, Caldwell was released by the Indians, but he continued to pitch in the minor leagues for 10 more years until retiring at the age of 43.

Caldwell, Ray

Indians	W	L	Pct	ERA	G	CG	IP	H	BB	SO	ShO
1919	5	1	.833	1.71	6	4	52⅔	33	19	24	1
1920	20	10	.667	3.86	34	20	237⅔	286	63	80	1
1921	6	6	.500	4.90	37	4	147	159	49	76	1
Career	133	120	.526	3.22	343	184	2,242	2,089	738	1,006	21

Camacho, Ernest Carlos

Indians: 1983–87
Pitcher
Nickname: Ernie
Birthplace: Salinas, California

B: February 1, 1955
Bats right, throws right
Ht. 6–1; **Wt.** 180

Ernie Camacho was a favorite of Indians manager Pat Corrales, but only when he threw his 94-plus-mph fastball—which, for some reason, the pitcher didn't always want to do often enough, an apparent reluctance that caused problems between the two men.

Both came to the Tribe in 1983—Camacho in a June 6 trade with Milwaukee, along with outfielder Gorman Thomas and pitcher Jamie Easterly, for pitcher Rick Waits and outfielder Rick Manning; and Corrales on July 31, replacing fired manager Mike Ferraro.

Camacho previously had pitched, without distinction, in the minors from 1976 to 1979, for Oakland in 1980, and for Pittsburgh in 1981. He was traded to the Chicago White Sox and, after a falling-out with manager Tony LaRussa, went to the Mexican League at the start of 1982. He was granted free agency at the end of that season and signed with the Brewers, who dealt him to the Tribe.

In that first year in Cleveland, Camacho again did nothing to distinguish himself, though he blossomed into stardom in 1984, setting what was then an Indians season save record of 23 in 69 games.

Often, however, Corrales would visit the mound and order Camacho—usually with anger for emphasis—to throw his fast ball instead of trying to finesse the batters. Sometimes it worked, at least in 1984.

Camacho suffered an elbow injury in his second appearance in 1985 and underwent surgery on April 13 for the removal of bone chips. It prevented Camacho from pitching again that season, and when problems persisted, a second operation was performed on October 31.

Camacho came back strong in 1986, recording 20 saves in 51 games, but quickly lost his effectiveness and was never successful again. He pitched so poorly at the start of 1987 that he was booed while warming up in the bull pen.

It was during 1987 that Corrales was fired and replaced by Doc Edwards on July 16. Camacho was granted free agency when the 101-loss season ended.

In an attempt to make a comeback in 1988, Camacho signed with Houston and went 0–3 with one save in 13 games, and again was granted free agency when the season ended. He signed with Phoenix of the Class AAA Pacific Coast League and spent part of 1989 with San Francisco, going 3–0 in 13 relief roles, before being released on June 23, 1990.

Finally, Camacho gave it one more try, joining Louisville of the Class AAA American Association on July 2, 1990, but was cut at the end of the season and retired.

Camacho, Ernie

Indians	W	L	Pct	ERA	G	CG	IP	H	BB	SO	ShO
1983	0	1	.000	5.06	4	0	5⅓	5	2	2	0
1984	5	9	.357	2.43	69	0	100	83	37	48	0
1985	0	1	.000	8.10	2	0	3⅓	4	1	2	0
1986	2	4	.333	4.08	51	0	57⅓	60	31	36	0
1987	0	1	.000	9.22	15	0	13¾	21	5	9	0
Career	10	20	.333	4.21	193	0	262⅔	268	128	159	0

Campbell, Bruce Douglas

Indians: 1935–39
Outfielder
Birthplace: Chicago
B: October 20, 1909

D: June 17, 1995
Batted left, threw right
Ht. 6–1; **Wt.** 185

On August 3, 1935, in the first game of a doubleheader in Detroit, Indians right fielder Bruce Campbell cracked three hits in a 5–4, 12-inning loss to the Tigers.

Midway through the 10th inning, however, Campbell walked in from his position in right field and slumped down on the bench in the Indians dugout. He told manager Walter Johnson he was too sick to continue playing, that he could hardly see the ball.

Campbell was removed from the game and returned to the team hotel.

When Campbell awoke the next day in a delirium, his roommate, Lloyd Brown, frantically called Johnson and trainer Lefty Weisman. Campbell was rushed to Harper Hospital, where he was diagnosed as having a form of spinal meningitis. When Campbell's condition worsened in the days that followed, he was given only a 50–50 chance to survive.

But Campbell beat the odds. Not only did he recover, he played again—seven more seasons—despite two recurrences of the disease that, in those days, was difficult for medical science to treat.

He began his major league career with the Chicago White Sox in 1930, was traded to the St. Louis Browns in 1932, and was acquired by the Indians on November 20, 1934, in a deal for infielder Johnny Burnett, pitcher Bob Weiland, and cash.

Campbell was hospitalized again with meningitis in October 1935 and, after recovering and returning to the Tribe, was struck down a third time on May 1, 1936.

After that last attack Steve O'Neill, then the Indians manager, vowed, "[Campbell] will never play for me again. I have no doubt that his exertion this year restored to activity the germ than had lain dormant since last winter. If he gets better, I intend to insist that he get into some business where there is less chance of the great physical fatigue that follows every hard-fought ball game."

But Campbell wouldn't quit. He returned to the Indians six weeks into the season, and, in his first game back, on

Bruce Campbell

"Bruce Campbell Day" at League Park on June 16, he got three hits. On July 2, in the first game of a doubleheader, a 14–6 victory over the St. Louis Browns, Campbell went 6-for-6, and remarkably went on to post a .372 average in 76 games.

After that season Campbell was honored as the Most Courageous Athlete of the Year.

His health restored, Campbell played three more years for the Indians and was traded on January 20, 1940, to the Tigers, for whom he batted .283 and .275, then was dealt to Washington and hit .278 in 1942.

Campbell spent the next three years in the Air Force during World War II and attempted another comeback in 1946 with minor league teams in Buffalo and Minneapolis, but he was unsuccessful and retired with a 13-year major league batting average of .290.

Campbell, Bruce

Indians	G	AB	H	BA	RBI	R	2B	3B	HR	SA	SB
1935	80	308	100	.325	54	56	26	3	7	.497	2
1936	76	172	64	.372	30	35	15	2	6	.587	2
1937	134	448	135	.301	61	82	42	11	4	.471	4
1938	133	511	148	.290	72	90	27	12	12	.460	11
1939	130	450	129	.287	72	84	23	13	8	.449	7
Career	1,360	4,762	1,382	.290	766	759	295	87	106	.455	53

Candiotti, Thomas Caesar

Indians: 1986–91
Pitcher
Birthplace: Walnut Creek, California

B: August 31, 1957
Bats right, throws right
Ht. 6–3; **Wt.** 205

Success did not come quickly or easily for Tom Candiotti, who labored six years in the minor leagues and was re-

leased by two major league organizations before the Indians signed him as a free agent on December 12, 1985.

Candiotti, who had missed the entire 1982 season after undergoing elbow surgery the previous October 14, earned a 1986 trial with the Tribe after learning to throw a knuckleball at Vancouver of the Class AAA Pacific Coast League in 1985.

He proceeded to become the Indians' ace with a 16–12 record in 1986, leading American League pitchers with 17 complete games, and also was among the AL's top ten pitchers in five other categories.

As the Indians fell (with 101 losses) in 1987, so did Candiotti. Though he pitched a one-hitter against New York, Candiotti struggled, and his record dropped to 7–18. He rebounded with three consecutive winning seasons, and in 1991, when he would be eligible for free agency at the end of the year, Candiotti was traded on June 27 (with outfielder Turner Ward) to Toronto for pitcher Denis Boucher, outfielders Mark Whiten and Glenallen Hill, and cash.

Candiotti fashioned a career-best 2.65 earned run average (second in the AL only to Roger Clemens' 2.62) in 1991 when his record was 13–13 with the Indians and Blue Jays. When the season ended, Candiotti signed a free-agent contract with Los Angeles.

Candiotti, Tom

Indians	W	L	Pct	ERA	G	CG	IP	H	BB	SO	ShO
1986	16	12	.571	3.57	36	17	252⅓	234	106	167	3
1987	7	18	.280	4.78	32	7	201⅔	193	93	111	2
1988	14	8	.636	3.28	31	11	216⅔	225	53	137	1
1989	13	10	.565	3.10	31	4	206	188	55	124	0
1990	15	11	.577	3.65	31	3	202	207	55	128	1
1991	7	6	.538	2.24	15	3	108⅓	88	28	86	0
Career	117	124	.485	3.47	331	64	2,165⅓	2,054	707	1,428	11

Carter, Joseph Chris

Indians: 1984–89
Outfielder, first baseman
Birthplace: Oklahoma City, Oklahoma

B: March 7, 1960
Bats right, throws right
Ht. 6–3; **Wt.** 210

The Indians got lucky when they acquired Joe Carter in a seven-player deal with the Chicago Cubs on June 13, 1984. They were equally fortunate on December 6, 1989, when they traded him to San Diego for catcher Sandy Alomar, Jr., second baseman Carlos Baerga, and outfielder Chris James.

The Indians actually preferred two other outfielders then playing for the Cubs at their Iowa club of the Class AAA American Association, in exchange for pitchers Rick Sutcliffe and George Frazier and catcher Ron Hassey.

But the Cubs insisted on sending Carter and another outfielder, Mel Hall, to the Indians, who—at least initially—reluctantly agreed. In that deal the Indians also received pitchers Don Schulze and Darryl Banks.

Carter, the Cubs' number-one selection (second overall) in the amateur draft in 1981 after he'd been named the college Player of the Year at Wichita State, played briefly for Chicago in 1983, hitting .176 in 23 games.

Initially a disappointment in Cleveland, Carter blossomed in 1986 when he led the American League with 121 runs batted in, hitting .302 with 29 homers, and won the Indians Man of the Year award.

Joe Carter

In 1987, Carter became the first Tribe player to hit 30 home runs and steal 30 bases in the same season—and only the fourth player in American League history to do so. Carter also holds the American League record for the most times hitting three home runs in one game. He did it five times—four while with Cleveland (August 29, 1986, in Boston; May 28, 1987, also in Boston; June 24, 1989, in Texas; and July 19, 1989, in Minnesota) and once for the Blue Jays (August 23, 1993, in Toronto).

Because Carter was to become a free agent after the 1989 season, when his average fell to .243, the Indians, unwilling to enter a bidding war to keep him, made the deal with the Padres that brought Alomar, Baerga, and James to Cleveland.

Carter batted only .232 but drove in 115 runs and hit 24 homers for San Diego, then was traded to Toronto on December 5, 1990. He was a member of the AL All-Star team in 1991, 1992, and 1993.

Carter, Joe

Indians	G	AB	H	BA	RBI	R	2B	3B	HR	SA	SB
1984	66	244	67	.275	41	32	6	1	13	.467	2
1985	143	489	128	.262	59	64	27	0	15	.409	24
1986	162	663	200	.302	121	108	36	9	29	.514	29
1987	149	588	155	.264	106	83	27	2	32	.480	31
1988	157	621	168	.271	98	85	36	6	27	.478	27
1989	162	651	158	.243	105	84	32	4	35	.465	13
Career	1,749	6,797	1,782	.262	1,173	959	345	41	327	.469	212

Carty, Ricardo Adolfo

Indians: 1974–77
Outfielder, first baseman,
  designated hitter
Nicknames: Rico, Big Mon
Birthplace: San Pedro de Macorís,
  Dominican Republic

B: September 1, 1939
Bats right, throws right
Ht. 6–3; **Wt.** 200

Rico Carty won the National League batting championship with a .366 mark for Atlanta in 1970, and when his average dropped to .229 at age 34 in 1973 when he played for Texas, the Chicago Cubs, and Oakland, everybody figured he was washed up.

But not Carty. And obviously not Phil Seghi, then general manager of the Indians.

Seghi rescued Carty from Córdoba of the Mexican League in August 1974, and the big ex-outfielder became the Tribe's designated hitter and sometime first baseman, stringing together three more good seasons (1975–77).

Never one to let protocol or rules stand in his way, Carty, when he entered professional baseball in 1960, signed contracts with no fewer than 10 clubs. When that mess finally was straightened out, he was awarded to the Milwaukee Braves, who switched him from catcher to outfielder.

In his first season in the major leagues in 1964, Carty hit .330 but lost the batting championship to Roberto Clemente (who batted .339) and the Rookie of the Year award to Richie Allen.

Carty contracted tuberculosis in 1968 and spent that season on the inactive-disabled list. The following year—despite no fewer than seven shoulder dislocations—he hit .342. A broken knee suffered in winter baseball sidelined Carty the entire 1971 season, and on October 27, 1972, he was traded by the Braves to Texas, then sold to the Cubs on August 13, 1973, and then sold to the Athletics on September 11, 1973.

He won the Indians' Man of the Year award in 1976 when

Rico Carty

he hit .310, and at the banquet honoring him the following spring, Carty ripped into manager Frank Robinson for his "lack of leadership," while Robinson was seated at the head table.

The Indians lost Carty to Toronto in the expansion draft on November 5, 1976, but a month later, on December 6, reacquired him in a trade that sent outfielder John Lowenstein and catcher Rick Cerone to the Blue Jays.

Carty had another good year for the Tribe in 1977, hitting .280 and driving in 80 runs, then was traded back to the Blue Jays for pitcher Denny DeBarr on March 15, 1978. He again became the property of Oakland in August, and in October was sold back to the Blue Jays, for whom he batted .256 in 1979, after which he retired with a 15-year major league career average of .299.

Carty returned to his native Dominican Republic and entered politics. In May 1994 he ran for mayor of his home town, San Pedro de Macorís, but lost in a close race.

Carty, Rico

Indians	G	AB	H	BA	RBI	R	2B	3B	HR	SA	SB
1974	33	91	33	.363	16	6	5	0	1	.451	0
1975	118	383	118	.308	64	57	19	1	18	.504	2
1976	152	552	171	.310	83	67	34	0	13	.442	1
1977	127	461	129	.280	80	50	23	1	15	.432	1
Career	1,651	5,606	1,677	.299	890	712	278	17	204	.464	21

Chambliss, Carroll Christopher

Indians: 1971–74
First baseman
Nickname: Chris
Birthplace: Dayton, Ohio

B: December 26, 1948
Bats left, throws right
Ht. 6–1; Wt. 195

A first-round draft choice of the Indians in 1970, Chris Chambliss made it to the majors in 1971 when he batted .275 and won the American League's Rookie of the Year award.

He also was a star for the Tribe in 1972 and 1973, but it was with the New York Yankees that Chambliss gained most of his fame, after being traded to them in a controversial seven-player deal on April 26, 1974.

The Indians, desperate for starting pitchers, sent Chambliss and pitchers Cecil Upshaw and Dick Tidrow to the Yankees for starters Fritz Peterson and Steve Kline and relievers Tom Buskey and Fred Beene.

Chris Chambliss

Chambliss, who twice previously had been selected in the amateur draft by Cincinnati (in 1967 and 1968), won the Class AAA American Association batting championship at Wichita with a .342 average in 1970, when he also was that league's Rookie of the Year award winner.

It was in the AL Championship Series in 1976 that Chambliss emerged as the toast of New York. He hit one of baseball's most dramatic home runs, a ninth-inning shot off Kansas City's Mark Littell that won the deciding fifth game and the pennant for the Yankees. Chambliss batted .524 and tied or broke four LCS records in that series.

Chambliss was traded to Toronto in a six-player deal on November 1, 1979, but never played a game for the Blue Jays. Five weeks later he was dealt to Atlanta and served seven seasons with the Braves (1980–86). He is now the hitting coach for St. Louis.

Chambliss, Chris

Indians	G	AB	H	BA	RBI	R	2B	3B	HR	SA	SB
1971	111	415	114	.275	48	49	20	4	9	.407	2
1972	121	466	136	.292	44	51	27	2	6	.397	3
1973	155	572	156	.273	53	70	30	2	11	.390	4
1974	17	67	22	.328	7	8	4	0	0	.388	0
Career	2,175	7,571	2,109	.279	972	912	392	42	185	.415	40

Chapman, Raymond Johnson

Indians: 1912–20
Shortstop
Nickname: Chappy
Birthplace: Beaver Dam, Kentucky

B: January 15, 1891
D: August 17, 1920
Batted right, threw right
Ht. 5–10; Wt. 170

The date was August 16, 1920, the darkest day in Cleveland baseball history.

In the fifth inning of a game against the Yankees at the Polo Grounds in New York, Indians shortstop Ray Chapman, the leadoff batter, crowded the plate, as he always did. Carl Mays wound up and delivered a submarine-style pitch, also as he always did.

It came up and in on Chapman, who instinctively ducked his head—but not enough. The ball struck Chapman on the left temple and bounced back toward Mays.

Eyewitnesses said they thought the pitch had hit Chapman's bat because of the resounding crack, but quickly realized it hadn't when Chapman sagged to the ground.

The late Jack Graney, an Indians outfielder and roommate of Chapman, said, "I helped carry [Chapman] to the clubhouse in center field, and I stayed with him until the ambulance came. He was conscious. He looked at me and tried to speak, but the words wouldn't come out.

"I knew by the look in his eyes that he wanted desperately to tell me something, so I got some paper and put a pencil in his hand. He made a motion to write but the pencil dropped to the floor. Paralysis was setting in. We found out later his skull had been fractured on one side, there was a concussion on the other side, and his neck was broken."

Chapman never regained consciousness and died at 4:40 A.M. the next day, August 17, 1920, the only player in modern major league history to be killed in a baseball game.

Until his death, Chapman was a key—and very popular—player for the Indians from the time he joined the team in

Ray Chapman

A colorful and often eccentric player, Charboneau was given the nickname "Super Joe," and both a book and a song were written extolling his deeds for the Indians when he hit .289 with 23 home runs that first year.

One of his homers was said to be among the three longest ever hit in Yankee Stadium. It flew into the third deck of the left-field stands, an area previously reached only by Hall of Famer Jimmie Foxx and Frank Howard.

Cleveland fans, desperately seeking a hero, fell in love with Charboneau and his well-publicized idiosyncrasies, which included drinking beer through a straw in his nose and eating cigarettes, as well as his claim to having pulled one of his own teeth.

Charboneau reveled in the attention, saying, "I never wanted to be just an ordinary major leaguer. When I was a kid and I dreamed about playing in the majors, I always saw myself as a star."

Charboneau's performance—at least in that first year—made him appear to be one of the Indians' all-time best acquisitions, as he was obtained in a minor league deal with the Philadelphia Phillies for pitcher Cardell Camper on December 6, 1978.

But opposing pitchers quickly caught up with Charboneau, and in midseason 1981 he was demoted to the minors with a .210 average.

After two back operations, Charboneau was given another chance by the Indians in 1982, but it didn't last long. He was assigned to Buffalo of the Class AA Eastern League in 1983, and two months into the season was released.

1912. He played 1,051 games with a lifetime batting average of .278. He led the Indians in stolen bases four times and was tied for the lead another year, setting a franchise record with 52 in 1917 that stood until 1980.

Most baseball historians believe Chapman would have made it to the Hall of Fame had he continued his career. The player who took over at shortstop, Joey Sewell, called up from the minor leagues after the death of Chapman, was elected to the Hall of Fame in 1977.

Mays steadfastly maintained that he hit Chapman accidentally, though Graney—and most of his teammates, as well as members of several other teams—accused the New York pitcher of often trying to hit batters.

Before he died in 1978, Graney, the radio voice of the Indians from 1932 to 1953, said, "People ask me if I still feel that Mays threw at Chappy. My answer has always been the same—yes, definitely."

Some players on other teams in the league even circulated a petition demanding that Mays be barred from baseball, though it was later dropped.

Chapman, Ray

Indians	G	AB	H	BA	RBI	R	2B	3B	HR	SA	SB
1912	31	109	34	.312	19	29	6	3	0	.422	10
1913	141	508	131	.258	39	78	19	7	3	.341	29
1914	106	375	103	.275	42	59	16	10	2	.387	24
1915	154	570	154	.270	67	101	14	17	3	.370	36
1916	109	346	80	.231	27	50	10	5	0	.289	21
1917	156	563	170	.302	36	98	28	13	2	.409	52
1918	128	446	119	.267	32	84	19	8	1	.352	30
1919	115	433	130	.300	53	75	23	10	3	.420	18
1920	111	435	132	.303	49	97	27	8	3	.423	13
Career	1,051	3,785	1,053	.278	364	671	162	81	17	.377	233

Charboneau, Joseph

Indians: 1980–82
Outfielder
Birthplace: Belvidere, Illinois

B: June 17, 1955
Bats right, throws right
Ht. 6–2; **Wt.** 205

Joe Charboneau burst upon the major league scene like a blazing comet in 1980 when he won the American League's Rookie of the Year award, but three seasons later, after a series of injuries, he was playing semipro baseball in Buffalo.

Joe Charboneau

Charboneau, Joe

Indians	G	AB	H	BA	RBI	R	2B	3B	HR	SA	SB
1980	131	453	131	.289	87	76	17	2	23	.488	2
1981	48	138	29	.210	18	14	7	1	4	.362	1
1982	22	56	12	.214	9	7	2	1	2	.393	0
Career	201	647	172	.266	114	97	26	4	29	.453	3

Christopher, Russell Ormand

Indians: 1948
Pitcher
Birthplace: Richmond, California
B: September 12, 1917

D: December 5, 1954
Batted right, threw right
Ht. 6–3½; **Wt.** 170

The Indians had many heroes in 1948, but one of the least heralded—without whose contributions they probably would not have won the pennant and World Series—was relief pitcher Russ Christopher.

Though he was known to have a congenital heart problem (which ultimately was the cause of his death in 1954), Christopher pitched in the major leagues seven years, six with the Philadelphia Athletics for whom he was a starter and won in double figures in 1944 (14–14), 1945 (13–13), and 1947 (10–7).

The Indians purchased Christopher on April 3, 1948, and, because of his devastating sinker, he frequently made no

more than a couple of pitches to get out of a jam. Christopher appeared in 45 games that season, leading the American League with 17 saves. He also compiled a 3–2 won-lost record and 2.90 earned run average that season, before health problems forced him out of baseball in 1949.

Christopher, Russ

Indians	W	L	Pct	ERA	G	CG	IP	H	BB	SO	ShO
1948	3	2	.600	2.90	45	0	59	55	27	14	0
Career	54	64	.458	3.37	241	46	999⅔	931	399	424	3

Colavito, Rocco Domenico

Indians: 1955–59, 1965–67
Outfielder
Nickname: Rocky
Birthplace: New York City

B: August 10, 1933
Bats right, throws right
Ht. 6–3; **Wt.** 190

One of the all-time most popular players to wear a Cleveland uniform, Rocky Colavito, who came up through the Indians' farm system, hit 300 major league home runs faster than all but four players in the history of baseball.

As a rookie in 1956, Colavito began a string of 11 consecutive seasons with more than 20 homers, averaging 32 a year. He tied Harmon Killebrew for the American League lead with 42 homers in 1959 and with 108 RBIs in 1965, and he

Russ Christopher

Rocky Colavito

was a member of the All-Star team six times, in 1959, 1961, 1962, and 1964–66.

Colavito was voted the Indians Man of the Year in 1958 and again in 1965.

It was on June 10, 1959, that Colavito joined one of baseball's most exclusive groups. In a game at Baltimore, Colavito blasted four consecutive homers, becoming only the eighth player to achieve that feat, and the third at that time to do so in consecutive at bats.

Previously, only Hall of Famer Lou Gehrig in 1932 and old-timer Bobby Lowe in 1894 hit four in a row. Since Colavito did it, four other players have hit four homers in one game: Willie Mays in 1961, Mike Schmidt in 1976, Bob Horner in 1986, and Mark Whiten in 1993, though only Schmidt's were consecutive.

Tribe fans were enraged when Colavito was traded to Detroit for defending American League batting champion Harvey Kuenn by general manager Frank Lane the day before the 1960 season began.

Many still harbor resentment—and also the opinion that the deal, on April 17, 1960—started a 34-year streak in which the Indians failed to even resemble a pennant contender.

Colavito went on to hammer 173 homers in the next five seasons for Detroit (1960–63) and Kansas City (1964), while Kuenn, sneeringly called "only a singles hitter," played only one season for the Tribe and was traded away.

Colavito was reacquired by the Indians on January 20, 1965, but the price they paid to get him back (along with catcher Camilo Carreon)—giving up pitcher Tommy John, outfielder Tommie Agee, and catcher John Romano—proved to be even more costly.

Unhappy because he was platooned by manager Joe Adcock, Colavito wanted to be traded and was sent to the Chicago White Sox for outfielder Jim King and second baseman Marv Staehle on July 29, 1967. Colavito finished his career the following season when he played for Los Angeles and the New York Yankees.

Colavito also is in the baseball record books as having appeared in two games as a relief pitcher with a career earned run average of 0.00 and one victory.

He pitched three innings for the Indians in 1958 against Detroit in which he worked three scoreless and hitless innings, walking three and striking out one. Colavito's victory came in a 2⅔-inning relief role for the Yankees in 1968, also against the Tigers, giving up one hit and two walks while striking out one.

After retiring as a player, Colavito rejoined the Indians as a coach in 1973 and again from 1976 to 1978, and he also coached for Kansas City in 1982 and 1983.

Colavito, Rocky

Indians	G	AB	H	BA	RBI	R	2B	3B	HR	SA	SB
1955	5	9	4	.444	0	3	2	0	0	.667	0
1956	101	322	89	.276	65	55	11	4	21	.531	0
1957	134	461	116	.252	84	66	26	0	25	.471	1
1958	143	489	148	.303	113	80	26	3	41	.620	0
1959	154	588	151	.257	111	90	24	0	42	.512	3
1965	162	592	170	.287	108	92	25	2	26	.468	1
1966	151	533	127	.238	72	68	13	0	30	.432	2
1967	63	191	46	.241	21	10	9	0	5	.366	2
Career	1,841	6,503	1,730	.266	1,159	971	283	21	374	.489	19

Coveleski, Stanley Anthony

Indians: 1916–24	**B:** July 13, 1889
Pitcher	**D:** March 20, 1984
Nickname: Covey	**Batted right, threw right**
Birthplace: Shamokin, Pennsylvania	**Ht.** 5–11; **Wt.** 166

Another of the Indians' heroes of their first pennant-winning season of 1920—especially in the World Series—was Stan Coveleski (whose name was spelled Coveleskie during his playing career, and who was born Stanislaus Kowalewski).

Not only did he win 24 games while losing 14, a record second on the staff only to Jim Bagby, Sr.'s 31–12, but Coveleski also beat the Brooklyn Dodgers three times in the best-of-nine World Series in 1920.

He won the first, fourth, and deciding seventh games, yielding a total of only two runs in 27 innings. Only 11 other pitchers in baseball history have won three games in a single World Series.

Coveleski's best pitch was the spitball, which was outlawed in 1920. However, the rule was "grandfathered" to allow 17 pitchers—among them Coveleski—who had been using the pitch to continue to do so until their retirement.

Coveleski learned the spitter during a three-year stint in the minors after making his first major league appearance in 1912 with the Philadelphia Athletics.

After the Indians purchased him from Portland of the Pacific Coast League, Coveleski in 1916 began a string of 11

Stan Coveleski

consecutive seasons in which he won in double figures, including 20 or more five times. He pitched a total of 38 shutouts and had a career earned run average of 2.89.

Coveleski pitched a one-hitter against New York on September 19, 1917. His bid for a no-hitter was spoiled by Fritz Maisel, who singled in the seventh inning.

Elected to the Hall of Fame in 1969, Coveleski was known as a fierce competitor but a very quiet person. "He loved the outdoors and loved to pitch, but he sure hated to talk," is the way Coveleski was described by the late Bill Wambsganss, a teammate from 1916 to 1923.

After two losing seasons in 1923 and 1924, Coveleski was traded to Washington on December 12, 1924, for pitcher Byron Speece and outfielder Carr Smith, and he proceeded to pitch the Senators to the 1925 pennant with a 20–5 won-lost record.

Coveleski, whose brother Harry also was a major league pitcher (1907–10, 1914–18), played three seasons in Washington and one for the New York Yankees before retiring at the end of 1928.

Vic Davalillo

Coveleski, Stan

Indians	W	L	Pct	ERA	G	CG	IP	H	BB	SO	ShO
1916	15	13	.536	3.41	45	11	232	247	58	76	1
1917	19	14	.576	1.81	45	24	298⅓	202	94	133	9
1918	22	13	.629	1.82	38	25	311	261	76	87	2
1919	24	12	.667	2.61	43	24	286	286	60	118	4
1920	24	14	.632	2.49	41	26	315	284	65	133	3
1921	23	13	.639	3.37	43	28	315	341	84	99	2
1922	17	14	.548	3.32	35	21	276⅔	292	64	98	3
1923	13	14	.481	2.76	33	17	228	251	42	54	5
1924	15	16	.484	4.04	37	18	240⅓	286	73	58	2
Career	215	142	.602	2.89	450	224	3,082	3,055	802	981	38

Davalillo, Victor Jose

Indians: 1963–68
Center fielder
Birthplace: Cabimas, Venezuela

B: July 31, 1936
Bats left, throws left
Ht. 5–7; **Wt.** 150

Until he suffered a broken right arm when he was hit by a pitch from Hank Aguirre in 1963, Vic Davalillo showed promise of being a great hitter and center fielder for the Indians for a long time.

And with good reason. Davalillo was certified as a "can't-miss" prospect everywhere he'd played in the minors since signing with the Indians in 1958.

He was, in fact, advertised by general manager Gabe Paul as a potential batting champion, even possibly "another Willie Mays," and part of the cornerstone (along with third baseman Max Alvis and shortstop Tony Martinez) of a team that would return the Tribe to past glory.

It didn't happen, however, as only Alvis lived up to expectations. Martinez found major league pitchers too tough, and so did Davalillo—especially left-handers—after he was hit by Aguirre and sidelined the second half of 1963.

When Davalillo, the "can't-miss" prospect, was injured on June 12, his .304 average was the best on the team, and he was the leading candidate for the American League Rookie of the Year award.

After returning to the lineup in late July, Davalillo was a different hitter, and he never was the same the rest of his career, which continued for 16 seasons, including five and a half in Cleveland. He was traded June 15, 1968, to California for outfielder Jimmie Hall.

Davalillo won a Gold Glove in 1964, made the AL All-Star team in 1965 when he batted .301 for the Tribe, hit .311 for St. Louis in 1970, and batted .318 for Pittsburgh in 1972, but he seldom faced southpaws.

The Angels sent him to the Cardinals in 1969; he went to the Pirates in 1971 and to Oakland in 1973.

In 1974, after he was released by the Athletics, Davalillo went to the Mexican League, remaining there until August 1977 when he was picked up by Los Angeles. He was with the Dodgers through 1980 when he retired with a career batting average of .279 and 95 career pinch hits, sixth most on the all-time list.

Davalillo became the first major leaguer to play for three different teams in the League Championship Series—for the Pirates in 1971 and 1972, Athletics in 1973, and Dodgers in 1977. He went 4-for-20 in 14 games in the World Series in 1971, 1973, 1977, and 1978.

Davalillo, Vic

Indians	G	AB	H	BA	RBI	R	2B	3B	HR	SA	SB
1963	90	370	108	.292	36	44	18	5	7	.424	3
1964	150	577	156	.270	51	64	26	2	6	.354	21
1965	142	505	152	.301	40	67	19	1	5	.372	26
1966	121	344	86	.250	19	42	6	4	3	.317	8
1967	139	359	103	.287	22	47	17	5	2	.379	6
1968	51	180	43	.239	13	15	2	3	2	.317	8
Career	1,458	4,017	1,122	.279	329	509	160	37	36	.364	125

Denny, John Allen

Indians: 1980–82
Pitcher
Birthplace: Prescott, Arizona

B: November 8, 1952
Bats right, throws right
Ht. 6–3; **Wt.** 185

John Denny was expected to be the pitcher the Indians needed in 1980 to become a pennant contender after they acquired him (and outfielder Jerry Mumphrey) from St. Louis in a trade for Bobby Bonds on December 7, 1979.

The deal paid early dividends as Denny, by July 15, won eight games, including six of his last eight decisions. But then he suffered an injury to his right heel and didn't pitch the rest of the season.

He returned in 1981 and, after the season resumed in August following the 50-day strike by the Players Association, Denny won six straight games and seven of nine starts for a 10–6 record.

A hot-and-cold, temperamental, and injury-prone pitcher with an excellent curve and change-up but only a mediocre fastball, Denny struggled again in 1982 and was traded to Philadelphia for three minor leaguers on September 11.

It was with the Phillies in 1983 that Denny finally lived up to expectations, winning the National League Cy Young Award after leading the Phillies to the pennant with 19 victories (while losing six games) and a 2.37 earned run average.

But that was Denny's only big year. He went 7–7 and 11–14 the next two seasons and was traded to Cincinnati where he won 11 and lost 10 in 1986. He ended his career with a 123–108 record.

Denny, John

Indians	W	L	Pct	ERA	G	CG	IP	H	BB	SO	ShO
1980	8	6	.571	4.39	16	4	108⅔	116	47	59	1
1981	10	6	.625	3.15	19	6	145⅔	139	66	94	3
1982	6	11	.353	5.01	21	5	138⅓	126	73	94	0
Career	123	108	.532	3.59	325	62	2,148⅔	2,093	778	1,146	18

Dente, Samuel Joseph

Indians: 1954–55
Shortstop, second baseman, third baseman
Nickname: Blackie

Birthplace: Harrison, New Jersey
B: April 26, 1922
Bats right, throws right
Ht. 5–11; **Wt.** 175

The rallying cry of the 1954 Indians became "Win plenty with Sam Dente," and with good reason.

When George Strickland was injured and missed 42 games, Dente replaced him at shortstop and played well. He also filled in at second base for Bobby Avila with no great loss for the Indians, who won an American League–record 111 games and their third pennant that season.

Dente also appeared in three World Series games that year, taking over for Strickland when he was replaced by a pinch hitter in the first two games and appearing as a starter at shortstop in Game 4.

A nomad player of sorts, Dente began his major league career with the Boston Red Sox in 1947. He played for the St.

John Denny

Sam Dente

Louis Browns in 1948 when he hit .270, batted a career-high .273 in 1949 when he was with the Washington Senators through 1951, and played briefly for the Chicago White Sox the next two years before being sold in May 1953 to Indianapolis (then a farm club of the Indians) in the Class AAA American Association.

In October 1953, the Tribe purchased Dente from Indianapolis, and it proved to be an excellent acquisition. For the next two years in his role as a utility infielder, Dente played in 113 games at shortstop, 13 at third base, and 11 at second base, compiling a .263 batting average. In October 1955 the Indians sold him back to Indianapolis.

Dente, Sam

Indians	G	AB	H	BA	RBI	R	2B	3B	HR	SA	SB
1954	68	169	45	.266	19	18	7	1	1	.337	0
1955	73	105	27	.257	10	10	4	0	0	.295	0
Career	745	2,320	585	.252	214	205	78	16	4	.305	9

Dilone, Miguel Angel

Indians: 1980–83
Center fielder
Birthplace: Santiago, Dominican Republic

B: November 1, 1954
Bats both, throws right
Ht. 6–0; **Wt.** 160

Miguel Dilone was the Indians' center fielder for three seasons, hitting a career-high .341—third best in the American League—and stealing a then-club-record 61 bases in 132

Miguel Dilone

games in 1980 to provide hope for greater deeds in the future.

Those numbers proved to be an illusion, as Dilone never came close to them again.

He batted .290 with 29 stolen bases in the strike-shortened 1981 season, and after his average fell to .235 in 1982, and then to .191 in 32 games in 1983, he was traded to the Chicago White Sox on August 25 for pitcher Rich Barnes.

Dilone began his professional career with Pittsburgh in 1972 and made it to the Pirates for parts of the seasons from 1974 to 1977, was traded to Oakland in April 1978, and was sold to the Chicago Cubs on July 4, 1979.

The Indians purchased Dilone from the Cubs farm club at Wichita of the Class AAA American Association on May 7, 1980.

Dilone, Miguel

Indians	G	AB	H	BA	RBI	R	2B	3B	HR	SA	SB
1980	132	528	180	.341	40	82	30	9	0	.432	61
1981	72	269	78	.290	19	33	5	5	0	.346	29
1982	104	379	89	.235	25	50	12	3	3	.306	33
1983	32	68	13	.191	7	15	3	1	0	.265	5
Career	800	2,000	530	.265	129	314	67	25	6	.333	267

Doby, Lawrence Eugene

Indians: 1947–55, 1958
Outfielder
Nickname: Larry
Birthplace: Camden, South Carolina

B: December 13, 1924
Bats left, throws right
Ht. 6–1; **Wt.** 180

Larry Doby wasn't the first black player in the major leagues—that honor, with all its tribulations, went to Jackie Robinson.

But Doby followed Robinson by four months, enduring the same racial taunts and insults, and prevailed mightily in a 13-year major league career that included two tours of duty with the Indians. He served them first from 1947, when he was the second player to break the "color line," through 1955, and again in 1958.

Though Doby was a shortstop/second baseman when he was purchased on July 3, 1947, by Bill Veeck for $10,000 from the Newark Eagles of the Negro League, he was switched to center field and became the American League's premier player at that position.

In a night game against Washington in Cleveland on August 2, 1950, Doby homered in the first, third, and fifth innings. He had two more opportunities to hit four homers in one game, but walked in the seventh and struck out in the eighth.

Doby was a key contributor in the Indians' drive to the AL pennant in 1948 when he batted .301. He delivered a game-winning home run against the Boston Braves in the fourth game of the World Series, giving Steve Gromek a 2–1 victory.

After that game a photograph of Doby and Gromek embracing was transmitted to newspapers around the country, providing Doby with what he called his favorite memory.

"I will always cherish it because it showed that emotions can be put into a form that's something other than skin color," he said. "We—Steve [Gromek] and I—were both so happy to have won the game, we just grabbed each other and hugged. It was a wonderful moment."

Larry Doby

| Doby, Larry | | | | | | | | | | | |
Indians	G	AB	H	BA	RBI	R	2B	3B	HR	SA	SB
1947	29	32	5	.156	2	3	1	0	0	.188	0
1948	121	439	132	.301	66	83	23	9	14	.490	9
1949	147	547	153	.280	85	106	25	3	24	.468	10
1950	142	503	164	.326	102	110	25	5	25	.545	8
1951	134	447	132	.295	69	84	27	5	20	.512	4
1952	140	519	143	.276	104	104	26	8	32	.541	5
1953	149	513	135	.263	102	92	18	5	29	.487	3
1954	153	577	157	.272	126	94	18	4	32	.484	3
1955	131	491	143	.291	75	91	17	5	26	.505	2
1958	89	247	70	.283	45	41	10	1	13	.490	0
Career	1,533	5,348	1,515	.283	970	960	243	52	253	.490	47

Donovan, Richard Edward

Indians: 1962–65   **B:** December 7, 1927
Pitcher   **Bats left, throws right**
Nickname: Dick   **Ht.** 6–3; **Wt.** 190
Birthplace: Boston, Massachusetts

It took Dick Donovan a while to become a winning pitcher—four season trials in the major leagues, to be exact—and even longer for the Indians to get him.

But once Donovan had mastered the slider, he paid dividends to the Chicago White Sox and later became the ace of the Tribe's pitching staff, if only briefly.

Donovan started in professional baseball in 1947 with the Boston Braves and started three consecutive seasons with them from 1950 to 1952, pitching 25 games without a victory, while losing four. By midseason each year he was sent back to the minor leagues.

The Braves finally gave up on Donovan in 1953, leaving him on the Atlanta (then Class AA Southern Association)

Doby, whose uniform number 14 is one of five retired by the Indians (the others are Earl Averill's 3, Lou Boudreau's 5, Mel Harder's 18, and Bob Feller's 19), hit a career-high .326 in 1950 when he was elected the Indians' Man of the Year, led the AL in homers in 1952 and 1954 and in RBIs (with 126) in 1954, drove in 100 runs a year five times, and played in every All-Star Game from 1949 to 1954.

Doby was traded to the Chicago White Sox on October 25, 1955, for outfielder Jim Busby and shortstop Chico Carrasquel, was sent to Baltimore on December 3, 1957, and was reacquired by the Indians (with pitcher Don Ferrarese) on April 1, 1958, for pitcher Bud Daley, infielder Dick Williams, and outfielder Gene Woodling.

Two years later, on March 21, 1959, the Indians traded Doby again, this time to Detroit for outfielder Tito Francona, and on May 13, 1959, the Tigers sold Doby back to the White Sox for $30,000.

After the 1959 season, Doby played in Japan for two years. Later he worked for the Montreal Expos as a scout, was their batting instructor from 1971 to 1973, was the Indians' first base coach in 1974 and 1975, managed the White Sox in 1977 and 1978, and currently works in the commissioner's office.

Dick Donovan

roster, from which he was claimed by Detroit in the minor league draft that winter.

But his fortunes didn't improve with the Tigers either, and in 1954 they returned him to Atlanta, from which he was drafted again, this time by the Chicago White Sox.

By then, Donovan obviously had mastered the art of pitching, going 15–9 for the White Sox in 1955 and winning a total of 73 games (while losing 50) through 1960, when he was claimed by the new Washington Senators in the American League expansion draft.

Three times Donovan came close to pitching no-hitters: on May 25, 1957, when Eddie Robinson of the Indians doubled in the second inning; on July 20, 1957, when Ted Williams of Boston singled in the fourth inning; and on September 24, 1961, when Joe Altobelli of Minnesota homered in the seventh inning.

Donovan posted a 10–10 won-lost record and the AL's best earned run average, 2.40, with the inept Senators in 1961, and on October 5 he was acquired by the Indians in one of their best trades, if only for a couple of years. They also received outfielder/catcher Gene Green and utility infielder Jim Mahoney for outfielder Jim Piersall, who was then well past his prime.

Donovan went 20–10 for the Indians in 1962, won their Man of the Year award, and was named to the AL All-Star team for the third time (he also was selected in 1955 and 1961).

But 1962 was his last season as a big winner. His record fell to 11–13 in 1963, to 7–9 in 1964, and to 1–3 in 12 games in 1965, and he was released on June 21, ending his baseball career. Donovan returned to Boston where he owns a real estate business.

Frank Duffy

Donovan, Dick

Indians	W	L	Pct	ERA	G	CG	IP	H	BB	SO	ShO
1962	20	10	.667	3.59	34	16	250⅔	255	47	94	5
1963	11	13	.458	4.24	30	7	206	211	28	84	3
1964	7	9	.438	4.55	30	5	158⅓	181	29	83	0
1965	1	3	.250	5.96	12	0	22⅔	32	6	12	0
Career	122	99	.552	3.67	345	101	2,017⅓	1,988	495	880	25

Duffy, Frank Thomas

Indians: 1972–77
Shortstop
Birthplace: Oakland, California

B: October 14, 1946
Bats right, throws right
Ht. 6–1; **Wt.** 180

He was considered only a "throw-in" when the Indians acquired Gaylord Perry for Sam McDowell in a trade with the San Francisco Giants, but Frank Duffy made the November 29, 1971, deal even more outstanding for the Indians.

It was manager Ken Aspromonte who convinced general manager Gabe Paul to insist upon the inclusion of Duffy. Aspromonte had seen Duffy play in the American Association the previous season.

Duffy took over as the Tribe's shortstop from 1972 and held the job through 1977. While he did not hit for a high average, he was good in the clutch and excellent on defense. Duffy led American League shortstops in fielding percentage in both 1973 (when he broke Lou Boudreau's club record) and 1976.

Duffy's batting average fell to a career-low .201 in 1977, and, because he had six years in the major leagues, he was eligible for free agency. The Indians re-signed Duffy to a one-

year contract, but then traded him to Boston on March 23, 1978, for pitcher Rick Kreuger.

Duffy was a utility infielder for the Red Sox that season, and in late May 1979, after appearing in only six games and batting three times, he was released.

Originally a first-round selection of Atlanta in the 1966 amateur draft, Duffy declined to sign and returned to Stanford University, where he earned a degree in psychology and played on the team that finished third in the College World Series in 1967.

Duffy also played that summer for the team that won the National Baseball Congress semipro championship, and he was drafted again, this time by Cincinnati.

He signed with the Reds but, after three good seasons in the minor leagues, quit and went home after a dispute with management. It led to Duffy's being traded to San Francisco in 1971 in the deal that sent George Foster to Cincinnati.

After leaving the Red Sox, Duffy relocated in Tucson, Arizona, where he is in the real estate business.

Duffy, Frank

Indians	G	AB	H	BA	RBI	R	2B	3B	HR	SA	SB
1972	130	385	92	.239	27	23	16	4	3	.325	6
1973	116	361	95	.263	50	34	16	4	8	.396	6
1974	158	549	128	.233	48	62	18	0	8	.310	7
1975	146	482	117	.243	47	44	22	2	1	.303	10
1976	133	392	83	.212	30	38	11	2	2	.265	10
1977	122	334	67	.201	31	30	13	2	4	.287	8
Career	915	2,665	619	.232	240	248	104	14	26	.311	49

Duncan, David Edwin

Indians: 1973–74
Catcher
Birthplace: Dallas, Texas

B: September 26, 1945
Bats right, throws right
Ht. 6–2; **Wt.** 190

Dave Duncan never hit for a high average, but he always was regarded as a key member of every team for which he played, including the Indians in 1973 and 1974.

Dave Duncan

credited with a 9–2 victory over the Milwaukee Brewers in front of 25,380 fans in the Cleveland Stadium on June 14, 1970.

Then only 11 days out of Stanford University, Dunning said that pitching in the major leagues and beating the Brewers in his first professional game was "a dream come true."

On April 18, 1971, Dunning hurled a one-hitter to beat the Washington Senators, 1–0, with Tom McCraw spoiling the bid for a no-hitter with a second-inning single. After the game Ted Williams, then manager of the Senators, said of Dunning, "He is going to be some pitcher some day."

Unfortunately for Dunning and the Indians, his stunning debut and the one-hitter against the Senators a year later proved to be the high points of his seven-year major league career.

Dunning won 18 games and lost 29 for the Indians from 1970 until he was traded May 10, 1973, to Texas for pitcher Dick Bosman and outfielder Ted Ford. Dunning pitched for California and Montreal in 1976 and for Oakland in 1977, after which he was released by the Athletics.

Dunning pitched briefly in 1978 for Hawaii, San Diego's farm club in the Class AAA Pacific Coast League, but retired on July 1 and enrolled in law school, then became an attorney in Irvine, California.

It was his expert handling of pitchers that made Duncan an excellent catcher, a reputation he continues to hold as a major league pitching coach (now with St. Louis) since his retirement as a player at the end of the 1976 season.

Duncan, who received a $65,000 bonus to sign with the Kansas City Athletics in 1963, prior to the 1965 implementation of the amateur draft, caught four pitchers who won the Cy Young Award—Vida Blue and Jim (Catfish) Hunter for the Athletics, Gaylord Perry for the Indians, and Jim Palmer for Baltimore.

He was a member of the American League All-Star team in 1971 and appeared in three World Series games for the Athletics in 1972. That was the season Duncan hit a career-high 19 home runs, after which he was traded to the Tribe on March 24, 1973, with outfielder George Hendrick, for catcher Ray Fosse and shortstop Jack Heidemann.

Duncan was dealt to the Orioles on February 25, 1975, with minor league outfielder Alvin McGrew, for first baseman Boog Powell and pitcher Don Hood. He was traded again on November 18, 1976, to the Chicago White Sox for outfielder Pat Kelly, but was released the next year during spring training.

Dunning, Steve

Indians	W	L	Pct	ERA	G	CG	IP	H	BB	SO	ShO
1970	4	9	.308	4.96	19	0	94⅓	93	54	77	0
1971	8	14	.364	4.50	31	3	184	173	109	132	1
1972	6	4	.600	3.26	16	1	105	98	43	52	0
1973	0	2	.000	6.50	4	0	18	17	13	10	0
Career	23	41	.359	4.56	136	7	613⅔	604	323	390	1

Duncan, Dave

Indians	G	AB	H	BA	RBI	R	2B	3B	HR	SA	SB
1973	95	344	80	.233	43	43	11	1	17	.419	3
1974	136	425	85	.200	46	45	10	1	16	.341	0
Career	929	2,885	617	.214	341	274	79	4	109	.357	5

Dunning, Steven John

Indians: 1970–73
Pitcher
Birthplace: Denver, Colorado

B: May 15, 1949
Bats right, throws right
Ht. 6–2; **Wt.** 205

When he joined the Indians immediately upon being the first player selected in the 1970 amateur draft, Steve Dunning was promptly nicknamed Stunning Steve, which seemed entirely appropriate at the time.

Dunning, after signing for a $50,000 bonus, pitched his first professional game at the major league level and was

Steve Dunning

Easter, Luscious Luke

Indians: 1949–54
First baseman, outfielder
Birthplace: Johnstown, Mississippi
B: August 4, 1915

D: March 29, 1979
Batted left, threw right
Ht. 6–4½; **Wt.** 240

When he was blasting prodigious home runs for the St. Louis Giants, Cincinnati Crescents and Homestead Grays in the Negro League from 1946 to 1948, Luke Easter was called the "Black Babe Ruth."

His reputation led to his purchase from the Grays by the Indians for $5,000 in 1949 and, in 80 games at San Diego of the Class AAA Pacific Coast League, Easter batted .363 with 25 homers and drove in 92 runs. He was promoted to Cleveland in late August and appeared in 21 games for the Tribe the remainder of the season.

The Indians thought so highly of Easter they made room for him at first base by trading Mickey Vernon, a once and future American League batting champion, back to Washington on June 14, 1950. However, it proved to be one of the worst deals the club ever made.

As a rookie in 1950, Easter batted .280 and blasted 28 homers, including one on June 23 that is considered the longest ever hit at the Cleveland Stadium. It was against Washington's Joe Haynes and was measured at 477 feet into the upper right-field stands.

Luke Easter

Another time in 1950, Easter came close to walloping a ball into the Stadium's center-field bleachers, which nobody ever did.

Eyewitnesses claim that Easter's drive would have gone into the bleachers but didn't because Tribe relief pitcher Dick Weik leaped up and caught the ball. At that time the bull pens were behind the fence and in front of the bleachers in right-center and left-center fields.

Bob Feller once remarked, "The only man I ever saw with more power than Luke was the Babe [Ruth]."

In 1952, Easter hit 31 homers, his major league high, and led the AL with a 7.1 percentage (number of home runs per 100 at bats). The following year Easter batted a career high .303 but delivered only seven home runs in 68 games, missing more than half the season with a broken bone in his foot.

Easter also suffered knee problems that plagued him throughout his career despite several operations, and he played only six games in 1954 when the Indians released him.

But Easter refused to quit. He went back to the minor leagues and played for 10 more years, and was still smashing tape-measure home runs—though not running very well—as a player-coach for Rochester of the Class AAA International League in 1964.

After returning to Cleveland, Easter took a factory job and soon became a union steward. It was in that capacity that he lost his life. He was murdered on March 29, 1979, by two thieves after he'd gone to a bank to cash $40,000 worth of paychecks for his fellow workers.

A park on Cleveland's east side was later renamed Luke Easter Park in his memory.

Easter, Luke

Indians	G	AB	H	BA	RBI	R	2B	3B	HR	SA	SB
1949	21	45	10	.222	2	6	3	0	0	.289	0
1950	141	540	151	.280	107	96	20	4	28	.487	0
1951	128	486	131	.270	103	65	12	5	27	.481	0
1952	127	437	115	.263	97	63	10	3	31	.513	1
1953	68	211	64	.303	31	26	9	0	7	.445	0
1954	6	6	1	.167	0	0	0	0	0	.167	0
Career	491	1,725	472	.274	340	256	54	12	93	.481	1

Eckersley, Dennis Lee

Indians: 1975–77
Pitcher
Birthplace: Oakland, California

B: October 3, 1954
Bats right, throws right
Ht. 6–2; **Wt.** 190

When Dennis Eckersley was a rookie with the Indians in 1975, after being their number-three selection in the 1972 amateur draft, there was concern on the part of some that he would not last long because his style of pitching put too much strain on his arm.

But Eckersley proved them wrong, while establishing himself as one of the all-time great relief pitchers in baseball.

Though his career began as a mediocre starter, Eckersley was reborn in Oakland, nine years after he was traded by the Indians on March 30, 1978.

First Eckersley went to the Red Sox with catcher Fred Kendall for catcher Bo Diaz, third baseman Ted Cox, and pitchers Rick Wise and Mike Paxton. Then the Red Sox sent

Dennis Eckersley

Edwards, Henry Albert

Indians: 1941–43, 1946–49   **B:** January 29, 1919
Outfielder   **D:** June 22, 1988
Nickname: Hank   **Batted left, threw left**
Birthplace: Elmwood Place, Ohio **Ht.** 6–0; **Wt.** 190

Hank Edwards was expected to have a bright future with the Indians upon his return from the service in 1946. He was the team's right fielder and best hitter with a .301 average, and led the American League with 16 triples in 124 games.

Even before Uncle Sam called him for duty in World War II, Edwards showed great promise, and his competitive zeal was particularly impressive. In 1939, Edwards hit .395 to lead the Class D Ohio State League, and in 1941 he hit .364 to win the batting championship of the Class B Three-I League.

Unfortunately, it was that very competitiveness that hurt his career, even shortened it, as Edwards incurred a series of injuries in 1947, when he was sidelined for 46 games, and 1948.

It was in the first game of a doubleheader on August 1, 1948, that Edwards suffered a severely dislocated right shoulder making a spectacular leaping catch against the right-field fence at the Stadium. It finished him for the season after only 55 games and, of course, put him out of the World Series that year.

Edwards returned in 1949 but played only five games and was sold to the Chicago Cubs on May 7. This sale began a major league odyssey for the hard-luck outfielder as he was dealt to Brooklyn on October 10, 1950, then to Cincinnati on July 21, 1951, to the Chicago White Sox on September 1, 1952, and to the St. Louis Browns on October 16, 1952.

He retired after hitting .198 in 65 games with the Browns in 1953.

him on May 25, 1984, to the Chicago Cubs, and they passed him along to the Athletics on April 3, 1987.

It was Oakland manager Tony LaRussa who recognized Eckersley's latent ability as a closer. Eckersley holds the American League record for most career saves with 275, and led major league pitchers with 45 saves in 1988 and 51 in 1992. He won both the AL Cy Young and Most Valuable Player awards in 1992.

All of which is not to say that Eckersley was not successful as a starter. In 1990 he became only the sixth major league pitcher to have at least 100 saves and 100 victories.

Eckersley's three-season won-lost record with the Indians was 40–32, including a no-hit, 1–0 victory over California on May 30, 1977, at the Stadium. That was part of a 22⅓ hitless-inning streak by Eckersley, which was the second longest in baseball history. Cy Young pitched 25⅓ hitless innings in 1904.

In his first season with the Indians, Eckersley was named Rookie Pitcher of the Year and finished with the third-lowest earned run average in the AL, and in 1977 he was named to the All-Star team for the first of six times. He also holds the AL career record for the most consecutive errorless games by a pitcher—466 (May 1, 1987, through August 9, 1994).

Hank Edwards

Eckersley, Dennis

Indians	W	L	Pct	ERA	G	CG	IP	H	BB	SO	ShO
1975	13	7	.650	2.60	34	6	186⅔	147	90	152	2
1976	13	12	.520	3.43	36	9	199⅓	155	78	200	3
1977	14	13	.519	3.53	33	12	247⅓	214	54	191	3
Career	192	159	.547	3.48	901	100	3,133	2,916	716	2,285	20

Edwards, Hank

Indians	G	AB	H	BA	RBI	R	2B	3B	HR	SA	SB
1941	16	68	15	.221	6	10	1	1	1	.309	0
1942	13	48	12	.250	7	6	2	1	0	.333	2
1943	92	297	82	.276	28	38	18	6	3	.407	4
1946	124	458	138	.301	54	62	33	16	10	.509	1
1947	108	393	102	.260	59	54	12	3	15	.420	1
1948	55	160	43	.269	18	27	9	2	3	.406	1
1949	5	15	4	.267	1	3	0	0	1	.467	0
Career	735	2,191	613	.280	276	285	116	41	51	.440	9

Falkenberg, Frederick Peter

Indians: 1908–11, 1913
Pitcher
Nickname: Cy
Birthplace: Chicago

B: December 17, 1880
D: April 14, 1961
Batted right, threw right
Ht. 6–5; **Wt.** 180

Cy Falkenberg was acquired by the Cleveland club, then called the Naps, in August 1908 when they purchased him and utility player Dave Altizer from the financially strapped Washington Senators.

The Naps were fighting Detroit for the pennant—they lost it by one-half game—and manager Napoleon Lajoie hoped Falkenberg could make a difference. He didn't, winning only two of six decisions, but he posted a winning record in his next four seasons, reaching a peak of 23–10 with a 2.22 earned run average in 1913. (After going 8–5 in 1911, he was sent to the minors, where he compiled a 25–8 record for Toledo of the American Association, earning a return to Cleveland in 1913.)

But the following year Falkenberg was among the first major leaguers to accept a lucrative contract offer to jump to the Indianapolis club of the outlaw Federal League. He pitched Indianapolis to the pennant with a 25–16 record and another 2.22 ERA. He led the Federals in innings (377⅓), strikeouts (236), and shutouts (9) and tied for the most games pitched (49).

The Indianapolis franchise was transferred to Newark in 1915, and Falkenberg was traded to Brooklyn during the season, but was much less successful, finishing with a 12–14 mark.

In 1916 he pitched for Indianapolis of the Class AA American Association and had a 10–14 record. He signed with the Philadelphia Athletics and was 2–6 for them in 1917, then was let go.

Falkenberg, Cy

Indians	W	L	Pct	ERA	G	CG	IP	H	BB	SO	ShO
1908	2	4	.333	3.88	8	2	46⅓	52	10	17	0
1909	10	9	.526	2.40	24	13	165	135	50	82	2
1910	14	13	.519	2.95	37	18	256⅔	246	75	107	3
1911	8	5	.615	3.29	15	7	106⅔	117	24	46	0
1913	23	10	.697	2.22	39	23	276	238	88	166	6
Career	130	123	.514	2.68	330	180	2,275	2,090	690	1,164	27

Feller, Robert William Andrew

Indians: 1936–41, 1945–56
Pitcher
Nickname: Rapid Robert
Birthplace: Van Meter, Iowa

B: November 3, 1918
Bats right, throws right
Ht. 6–0; **Wt.** 185

The greatest pitcher in Indians history—and one of baseball's all-time best—Bob Feller, was elected to the Hall of Fame in 1962, his first year of eligibility, after winning 266 games in a major league career that spanned 18 seasons.

Feller's victory total would have been much higher, almost certainly well over 300, if he had not spent 44 months in the navy during World War II, serving aboard the battleship U.S.S. *Alabama* as a chief gunnery mate, earning eight battle stars.

He enlisted two days after Pearl Harbor was attacked on December 7, 1941, and was discharged August 14, 1945.

Signed for a "bonus" of one dollar on July 25, 1935, by scout C. C. Slapnicka, who saw the young pitcher in a game on the sandlots of Des Moines, Iowa, Feller went on to pitch a then record three no-hitters and 12 one-hitters, striking out 2,581 batters in 3,827 innings.

But because of a rule in effect then, the Indians almost lost Feller after his sensational debut in 1936, when he won five and lost three of the 14 games he pitched.

After a hearing conducted by Commissioner Kenesaw Mountain Landis, Feller was given the opportunity to become a free agent and sell himself to the highest bidder because he'd been improperly signed by the Indians.

After Feller had agreed to a contract with Fargo-Moorhead, North Dakota, of the Class D Northern League, Slapnicka had that team assign Feller to New Orleans of the Class A Southern Association. Both were farm clubs of the Indians.

Feller never pitched for either team—never even donned one of their uniforms—reporting directly to Cleveland in 1936, though he had been listed as having been the property of both Fargo-Moorhead and New Orleans.

Bob Feller signing his first Cleveland Indians contract on July 25, 1935, under the watchful eyes of his father, William Feller (right rear) and Indians scout C. C. Slapnicka.

The rule then in effect prohibited the signing of a sand-lotter to a major league contract, and Landis called what Slapnicka did a "cover-up."

But Feller told Landis that he didn't want to pitch for any team except the Indians, and his father threatened to sue Landis if Bob were not allowed to do so.

With that, on December 10, 1936, Landis reluctantly approved Feller's contract, though he ordered the Indians to pay what amounted to a $7,500 fine. They were more than willing to comply.

By the time Landis ruled the Indians could keep Feller, he already had established himself as an exceptional young pitcher.

In his first start on August 23, 1936, Feller, then the youngest person to play in a major league game, beat the St. Louis Browns, 4–1. He struck out 15 batters, only one fewer than Rube Waddell's 1904 American League mark, and two fewer than the then-major league record set in 1933 by Dizzy Dean.

Then, in his fifth start on September 13, Feller tied Dean's mark, striking out 17 in a 5–2, two-hit victory over Philadelphia.

Feller broke the record on the final day of the 1938 season, October 2, in the first game of a doubleheader against Detroit at the Stadium. He struck out 18 batters, including Chet Laabs five times, though he lost to the Tigers, 4–1.

Feller pitched his first no-hitter—the only opening day no-hitter in baseball history—on April 16, 1940, beating the White Sox, 1–0, in Chicago. He fired his other two no-hitters against the Yankees, 1–0, in New York, April 30, 1946, and against Detroit, 2–1, in the first game of a doubleheader at the Stadium, July 1, 1951.

His 12 one-hitters were pitched on April 20, 1938, versus St. Louis, at League Park in Cleveland, as Billy Sullivan got a bunt single in the sixth inning; May 25, 1939, versus Boston, in Boston, Bobby Doerr, single, second inning; June 27, 1939, vs. Detroit, in the first night game played in Cleveland Stadium, Earl Averill, single, sixth inning; July 12, 1940, versus Philadelphia, in Philadelphia, Dick Siebert, single, eighth inning; September 26, 1941 (second game), versus St. Louis, in St. Louis, Rick Ferrell, single, fifth inning; September 19, 1945, versus Detroit, at League Park in Cleveland, Jimmy Outlaw, single fifth inning; July 31, 1946, versus Boston, at League Park in Cleveland, Doerr, single, second inning; August 8, 1946, versus Chicago, in Chicago, Frank Hayes, single, seventh inning; April 22, 1947, versus St. Louis, in Cleveland Stadium, Al Zarilla, single, seventh inning; May 2, 1947, versus Boston, in Cleveland Stadium, Johnny Pesky, single, first inning; April 23, 1952, versus St. Louis, in St. Louis, Bobby Young, triple, first inning; and May 1, 1955, versus Boston, in Cleveland Stadium, Sammy White, single, seventh inning.

Feller was a 20-game winner six seasons, each time leading American League pitchers in victories (though he was tied with Detroit's Hal Newhouser in 1946). He also led the AL in strikeouts seven times, including 1946 when he fanned a then-major-league-record 348 batters.

In 1957 his uniform number 19 was the first to be retired by the Indians, and in 1969 he was voted by fans across the country as baseball's greatest living right-handed pitcher in ceremonies for the game's centennial celebration.

Despite all his accomplishments, Feller failed to achieve one of his biggest goals, to win a World Series game, though he came close—and probably should have won it—against the Boston Braves on October 6, 1948.

It was the opening game, and the Braves prevailed, 1–0, the only run being scored by pinch runner Phil Masi in the eighth inning on a two-out single by Tommy Holmes. It came a few minutes after Feller picked off Masi at second base, though umpire Bill Stewart—who later admitted he "blew" the call—ruled that the runner was safe.

Feller also was the loser of the fifth game of that World Series, and he didn't get to pitch in 1954 when the Indians were swept by the New York Giants.

Two years later, after he went 0–4, appearing in 19 games, 15 as a reliever, Feller retired, though he still works for the Indians in a public relations capacity.

Feller, Bob

Indians	W	L	Pct	ERA	G	CG	IP	H	BB	SO	ShO
1936	5	3	.625	3.34	14	5	62	52	47	76	0
1937	9	7	.563	3.39	26	9	148⅔	116	106	150	0
1938	17	11	.607	4.08	39	20	277⅔	225	208	240	2
1939	24	9	.727	2.85	39	24	296⅔	227	142	246	4
1940	27	11	.711	2.61	43	31	320⅓	245	118	261	4
1941	25	13	.658	3.15	44	28	343	284	194	260	6
1945	5	3	.625	2.50	9	7	72	50	35	59	1
1946	26	15	.634	2.18	48	36	371⅓	277	153	348	10
1947	20	11	.645	2.68	42	20	299	230	127	196	5
1948	19	15	.559	3.56	44	18	280⅓	255	116	164	2
1949	15	14	.517	3.75	36	15	211	198	84	108	0
1950	16	11	.593	3.43	35	16	247	230	103	119	3
1951	22	8	.733	3.50	33	16	249⅔	239	95	111	4
1952	9	13	.409	4.74	30	11	191⅓	219	83	81	0
1953	10	7	.588	3.59	25	10	175⅔	163	60	60	1
1954	13	3	.813	3.09	19	9	140	127	39	59	1
1955	4	4	.500	3.47	25	2	83	71	31	25	1
1956	0	4	.000	4.97	19	2	58	63	23	18	0
Career	266	162	.621	3.25	570	279	3,827	3,271	1,764	2,581	44

Ferrell, Wesley Cheek

Indians: 1927–33
Pitcher
Birthplace: Greensboro, North Carolina

B: February 2, 1908
D: December 9, 1976
Batted right, threw right
Ht. 6–2; **Wt.** 195

A fierce competitor who hated to lose in anything, Wes Ferrell set a major league record by winning 20 games in each of his first four full seasons with the Indians, including 13 consecutive victories in 1930.

He also pitched a no-hitter to beat the St. Louis Browns, 9–0, at League Park on April 29, 1931. Ferrell nearly pitched a second no-hitter a year later. On August 6, 1932, he threw a one-hit game at the Boston Red Sox. Dale Alexander's single in the fourth inning was Boston's only hit.

Ferrell also was one of the best hitting pitchers in baseball, setting a record for the most home runs in one season (nine in 1931) and for a career (38) and averaging .280 in 15 major league seasons with six teams. He led the American League with 25 victories with the Boston Red Sox in 1935.

An interesting trivia fact: Wes Ferrell outhomered his brother Rick, 38–28, during their major league careers, though Rick had over 4,800 more at bats.

Ferrell won more games, 193 (while losing 128) than six pitchers in the Hall of Fame—Addie Joss, Dizzy Dean, Lefty Gomez, Dazzy Vance, Sandy Koufax, and Rube Waddell. Fer-

Wes Ferrell

Ferrell, Wes											
Indians	W	L	Pct	ERA	G	CG	IP	H	BB	SO	ShO
1927	0	0	—	27.00	1	0	1	3	2	0	0
1928	0	2	.000	2.25	2	1	16	15	5	4	0
1929	21	10	.677	3.60	43	18	242⅔	256	109	100	1
1930	25	13	.658	3.31	43	25	296⅔	299	106	143	1
1931	22	12	.647	3.75	40	27	276⅓	276	130	123	2
1932	23	13	.639	3.66	38	26	287⅔	299	104	105	3
1933	11	12	.478	4.21	28	16	201	225	70	41	1
Career	193	128	.601	4.04	374	227	2,623	2,845	1,040	985	17

Fleming, Leslie Harvey

Indians: 1941–42, 1945–47   **D:** March 5, 1980
First baseman   **Batted left, threw left**
Nickname: Moe   **Ht.** 5–10; **Wt.** 185
Birthplace: Singleton, Texas
B: August 7, 1915

Called "the greatest power hitter I ever have seen in the minor leagues" by Larry Gilbert, his manager at Nashville of the Class A1 Southern Association after he batted .414 in 1941, Les Fleming was expected to be a star for the Indians for a long time.

He was handed the first base position in 1942 when Hal Trosky was forced into retirement by migraine headaches, and Fleming lived up to his notices, hitting .292 with 14 homers and driving in 82 runs.

But then, after the death of his infant child and because of the lingering illness of his wife, Fleming chose to remain home in Beaumont, Texas, where he worked as a pipe fitter in a shipyard, a job that kept him out of the military service during World War II.

Fleming began in professional baseball in the Detroit organization in 1933. He had several good minor league seasons but couldn't make it with the Tigers because they had Hank Greenberg and Rudy York to play first base.

On September 6, 1941, after Fleming had burned up the

rell also was one of three Indians (Earl Averill and Oral Hildebrand were the others) to be named to the first AL All-Star team in 1933.

In addition to the Indians and Red Sox, Ferrell also pitched for the Washington Senators, New York Yankees, Brooklyn Dodgers, and Boston Braves.

It was during one of his holdouts that the Tribe traded him with outfielder Dick Porter to the Red Sox for pitcher Bob Weiland, outfielder Bob Seeds, and $25,000 on May 25, 1934.

Ferrell's hot temper often got him into trouble. He was fined $1,500 and suspended for 10 days by Indians manager Roger Peckinpaugh for refusing to leave a game in 1932 when he was replaced by a reliever. Four years later he was fined $1,000 by Joe Cronin, his manager in Boston, for walking off the mound without being replaced by another pitcher.

One of Ferrell's idiosyncrasies was that he reportedly walked around golf courses looking for bees because he had a firm belief that getting stung on his arm made him a better pitcher.

After his final season in the major leagues, with the Braves in 1941, Ferrell became a minor league manager and was suspended for hitting an umpire and taking his team off the field in protest of a ruling.

He also staged long contract holdouts three times in his pitching career, including one that lasted six weeks into the 1931 season.

Ferrell's older brother Rick was a catcher who played in the major leagues for 18 seasons from 1929 to 1947 with three teams. They were battery mates in Boston from 1934 to 1937. On June 10, 1937, both Rick and Wes, along with outfielder Mel Almada, were traded by the Red Sox to Washington for pitcher Buck Newsom and outfielder Ben Chapman. They remained teammates with the Senators until Wes was released, August 12, 1938. Another brother, George, had a 20-year career as a minor league pitcher.

Les Fleming

Southern League, the Indians purchased his contract. In addition to his lofty batting average at Nashville, Fleming also cracked 29 home runs and drove in 103 runs in 106 games after recovering from a broken wrist he suffered early in the season.

Fleming returned to the Indians in August 1945 and hit .329 in 42 games, though his power stroke was not the same.

When Fleming's average fell to .278 in 1946, and then to .242 the following season, he was sold to Pittsburgh on December 4, 1947.

He didn't stick with the Pirates in 1948 and was optioned to Indianapolis, where he batted .323, led the league with 143 RBIs, and won the Class AAA American Association's Most Valuable Player award.

It earned him another chance with the Pirates in 1949, but he played only 24 games, hitting .258 without a home run, and never played in the major leagues again.

Fleming, Les

Indians	G	AB	H	BA	RBI	R	2B	3B	HR	SA	SB
1941	2	8	2	.250	2	0	1	0	0	.375	0
1942	156	548	160	.292	82	71	27	4	14	.432	6
1945	42	140	46	.329	22	18	10	2	3	.493	0
1946	99	306	85	.278	42	40	17	5	8	.444	1
1947	103	281	68	.242	43	39	14	2	4	.349	0
Career	434	1,330	369	.277	199	168	69	15	29	.417	7

Flick, Elmer Harrison

Indians: 1902–10
Outfielder
Birthplace: Bedford, Ohio
B: January 11, 1876

D: January 9, 1971
Batted left, threw right
Ht. 5–9; **Wt.** 168

Elmer Flick was the central figure in a trade proposal that wasn't accepted by the Cleveland franchise in 1908—but would have been one of the best deals in baseball history if owner Charles W. Somers had said yes to the Detroit Tigers.

The offer was made by Tigers manager Hughie Jennings in a phone call to Somers during spring training.

After the two men exchanged pleasantries, Jennings said to Somers, "I'd like to make a deal . . . I'll give you Ty Cobb for Elmer Flick, even-up."

Somers was taken aback because Cobb had won the American League batting championship with a .350 average as a rookie in 1907, when Flick had batted .302 in his 10th season in the major leagues.

Somers pondered the proposal, then asked Jennings, "Why are you so anxious to trade Cobb? Is there anything wrong with him physically?"

Jennings replied that Cobb was in perfect health, then gave the reason the Tigers wanted to trade him.

"[Cobb] can't get along with our players, and we want to get him away. He's had two fights already this spring," said Jennings. "We want harmony on this team, not scrapping."

Obviously, Somers also wanted harmony, not scrapping on his Cleveland team, then called the Naps, and declined the Tigers' offer.

"We'll keep Flick," he told Jennings. "Maybe he isn't quite as good a batter as Cobb, but he's much nicer to have on the team. We don't want any troublemakers either."

Elmer Flick

Cobb went on to win the AL batting championship the next eight seasons, giving him nine titles in a row, and 12 in 13 years.

Flick, who'd won the batting championship in 1905 with a .308 average (the lowest in the AL until 1968), got sick early in 1908 and played only nine games that year, and 66 and 24 in the two subsequent seasons, then retired.

Flick began his professional career with the Philadelphia Phillies in 1898. He quickly established himself as one of the

National League's best hitters, averaging .302, .342, .367, and .333 through 1901, and he led the league with 110 RBIs in 1900.

Then, following two of his Phillies teammates, second baseman Napoleon Lajoie and pitcher Bill Bernhard, Flick jumped in 1902 to the American League Philadelphia Athletics, who promptly sold him to Cleveland to avoid legal entanglements.

On July 6, 1902, Flick became the first AL player to hit three triples in one game, set another record (since tied) by leading the AL in triples three consecutive seasons (1905–07), tied for the AL lead in stolen bases with 38 in 1904 and 39 in 1906, and scored the most runs, 98, in 1906.

Flick was elected to the Hall of Fame by the Veterans Committee in 1963.

Flick, Elmer

Indians	G	AB	H	BA	RBI	R	2B	3B	HR	SA	SB
1902	110	424	126	.297	61	70	19	11	2	.408	20
1903	140	523	155	.296	51	81	23	16	2	.413	24
1904	150	579	177	.306	56	97	31	17	6	.449	38
1905	132	500	154	.308	64	72	29	18	4	.462	35
1906	157	624	194	.311	62	98	34	22	1	.441	39
1907	147	549	166	.302	58	78	15	18	3	.412	41
1908	9	35	8	.229	2	4	1	1	0	.314	0
1909	66	235	60	.255	15	28	10	2	0	.315	9
1910	24	68	18	.265	7	5	2	1	1	.368	1
Career	1,483	5,597	1,752	.313	756	948	268	164	48	.445	330

Fonseca, Lewis Albert

Indians: 1927–31
First baseman, second baseman,
third baseman
Birthplace: Oakland, California

B: January 21, 1899
D: November 26, 1989
Batted right, threw right
Ht. 5–10½; **Wt.** 180

Though Lew Fonseca hit .319 in 126 games for the Philadelphia Phillies in 1925, they sent him to the minor leagues where he batted .381 for Newark of the Class AA International League.

The Indians purchased the versatile, sure-handed infielder on September 4, 1926 in what proved to be an excellent deal. Fonseca, playing first base, won the American League batting championship in 1929 with a .369 mark and drove in 103 runs. He also was named Most Valuable Player in the American League in 1929.

However, Fonseca's playing time often was curtailed by injury and illness, and only in four of his 12 seasons in the major leagues (1921–25, 1927–31), did he play 100 games. He was sidelined by broken shoulders (four times), a fractured wrist, a chipped bone in an ankle, a dislocated hip, a concussion, a broken nose and a severed artery in a leg.

After winning the batting championship, Fonseca almost died the following off-season after contracting scarlet fever, and was able to play only 40 games in 1930 when he hit .279.

The Indians traded Fonseca on May 17, 1931, to the Chicago White Sox for third baseman Willie Kamm.

Fonseca was a player-manager for the White Sox the following season, a position he held through the first 15 games of 1934. They finished seventh (49–102) in 1932 and sixth

(67–83) in 1933 under Fonseca, and he was replaced by Jimmy Dykes.

Though he retired with a .316 lifetime average, Fonseca probably was better known for pioneering the use of motion pictures in baseball. After leaving the playing field, Fonseca produced instructional films and World Series highlights movies for more than 20 years before retiring in 1965.

Fonseca, Lew

Indians	G	AB	H	BA	RBI	R	2B	3B	HR	SA	SB
1927	112	428	133	.311	40	60	20	7	2	.404	12
1928	75	263	86	.327	36	38	19	4	3	.464	4
1929	148	566	209	.369	103	97	44	15	6	.532	19
1930	40	129	36	.279	17	20	9	2	0	.380	1
1931	26	108	40	.370	14	21	9	1	1	.500	3
Career	937	3,404	1,075	.316	485	518	203	50	31	.432	64

Fosse, Raymond Earl

Indians: 1967–72, 1976–77
Catcher
Nickname: Mule
Birthplace: Marion, Illinois

B: April 4, 1947
Bats right, throws right
Ht. 6–2; **Wt.** 215

Ray Fosse probably is best known to most baseball fans for being involved in one of the most celebrated plays in All-Star Game history.

But Fosse deserves to be better remembered as one of the best catchers the Indians ever had after being selected in the first round, seventh overall of the first-ever amateur draft—ahead of even Johnny Bench—in 1965.

It was in the All-Star Game in 1970, Fosse's first season as a regular for the Tribe, that he blocked the plate against Pete Rose in the 12th inning with the score tied, 4–4.

Rose, choosing not to slide, crashed into Fosse, jarring the ball loose and scoring the run that gave the National League its victory.

The collision injured Fosse's left shoulder. He was sidelined for a couple of games, but was soon back in the lineup, though he was never the same thereafter.

Going into the All-Star break, Fosse was hitting .325 with 16 homers. He finished the season with a .307 average and 18 homers, and never approached those numbers again in his career, which continued through 1979.

Fosse was traded with shortstop Jack Heidemann to Oakland on March 24, 1973, for outfielder George Hendrick and catcher Dave Duncan. He helped the Athletics win the American League pennant in 1973, 1974, and 1975 and the World Series in 1973 and 1974, then was sold back to the Indians on December 9, 1975.

Besides being a member of the AL All-Star team in 1971, Fosse was a Gold Glove winner in 1970 and 1971 and was the cowinner (with Sam McDowell) of the Indians' Man of the Year award in 1970.

Fosse was traded again by the Indians on September 9, 1977, to Seattle for pitcher Bill Laxton and cash. He retired after the 1979 season with a major league career average of .256.

"I can't say how much better I would have been [if not for the injury he suffered in the collision with Rose], but I can say that, before I got hurt, I had everything together.

Ray Fosse

Franco, Julio Cesar

Indians: 1983–88
**Shortstop, third baseman,
    second baseman,
    designated hitter**
Birthplace: Hato Mayor,
    Dominican Republic

B: August 23, 1958
Bats right, throws right
Ht. 6–0; **Wt.** 160

One of five players the Indians obtained from Philadelphia for outfielder Von Hayes on December 8, 1982, Julio Franco was a key man in one of the franchise's best-ever trades, and then, six years later, was part of one of the club's worst-ever deals.

One of the best hitting shortstops in franchise history, but erratic in the field, Franco was acquired along with second baseman Manny Trillo, outfielder George Vukovich, pitcher Jay Baller, and catcher Jerry Willard.

Franco was sent to Texas on December 6, 1988, for second baseman Jerry Browne, first baseman Pete O'Brien, and outfielder Oddibe McDowell. He won the American League batting championship with a .341 average for the Rangers in 1991.

Flamboyant and often moody and temperamental, Franco led AL shortstops in errors with 36 in 1984 and 35 in 1985, and tied for most errors by second basemen with 19 in 1990. On April 20, 1985, with the Indians in New York, Franco disappeared for two days, later saying that he had been sick at the Bronx home of a friend who had no telephone. He also

"Afterwards, I was never able to swing the bat properly. I never found my stroke again. I never got it back."

Fosse rejoined the Athletics in their speakers' bureau in 1984, became director of sales in 1985, then director of public relations in 1986. He also broadcasts Oakland games on radio and television.

Fosse, Ray

Indians	G	AB	H	BA	RBI	R	2B	3B	HR	SA	SB
1967	7	16	1	.063	0	0	0	0	0	.063	0
1968	1	0	0	—	0	0	0	0	0	—	0
1969	37	116	20	.172	9	11	3	0	2	.250	1
1970	120	450	138	.307	61	62	17	1	18	.469	1
1971	133	486	134	.276	62	53	21	1	12	.397	4
1972	134	457	110	.241	41	42	20	1	10	.354	5
1976	90	276	83	.301	30	26	9	1	2	.362	1
1977	78	238	63	.265	27	25	7	1	6	.378	0
Career	924	2,957	758	.256	324	299	117	13	61	.367	15

Julio Franco

walked out of the Cleveland Stadium before a game on June 8, 1986, saying he was upset because of a fight he'd had with his wife.

When the Indians acquired veteran shortstop Johnnie LeMaster from San Francisco on May 7, 1985, Franco was asked to switch to second base to take over for Tony Bernazard, but balked at replacing his friend. Three weeks later LeMaster was traded to Pittsburgh, allowing Franco to continue to play shortstop.

He finally agreed to move to second base in 1988 and became a star at that position after being traded to the Rangers. He was a member of the AL All-Star team in 1989, 1990, and 1991, and he was named Most Valuable Player in the 1990 game. Franco played five seasons in Texas, became a free agent, and signed with the Chicago White Sox on December 15, 1993.

Franco, Julio

Indians	G	AB	H	BA	RBI	R	2B	3B	HR	SA	SB
1983	149	560	153	.273	80	68	24	8	8	.387	32
1984	160	658	188	.286	79	82	22	5	3	.348	19
1985	160	636	183	.288	90	97	33	4	6	.381	13
1986	149	599	183	.306	74	80	30	5	10	.422	10
1987	128	495	158	.319	52	86	24	3	8	.428	32
1988	152	613	186	.303	54	88	23	6	10	.409	25
Career	1,658	6,381	1,922	.301	861	964	299	45	120	.419	237

Francona, John Patsy

Indians: 1959–64
Outfielder, first baseman
Nickname: Tito
Birthplace: Aliquippa, Pennsylvania

B: November 4, 1933
Bats left, throws left
Ht. 5–11; **Wt.** 190

When Tito Francona was acquired by the Indians from Detroit on March 21, 1959, for veteran outfielder Larry Doby, it did not appear to be a big deal. Francona had been a part-time player for Baltimore, the Chicago White Sox, and Detroit, and Doby was nearing the end of his career.

But, after sitting on the bench most of the first two months of that season, Francona got a chance to play and caught fire. He flirted with a .400 average as late as August and, while platooned with Jim Piersall in center field and Vic Power at first base, almost won the American League batting championship.

He hit .363 in 122 games, but didn't have enough plate appearances (399) to qualify, and the title went to the Tigers' Harvey Kuenn (.353, 561 at bats), though his accomplishments won the Indians' Man of the Year award for Francona in 1959.

"Everything went right . . . nobody could throw a fastball past me," he said of that season. "I'd go 1-for-3 and my average would drop. I don't think I ever went two games without a hit. It was amazing."

It was different, however, in 1960. Francona led the AL with 36 doubles, though his average fell to .292 after he became a regular in the outfield. He hit .301 in 1961, the only other year he batted over .300, and was the Tribe's regular first baseman in 1962.

Francona was sold to St. Louis on December 15, 1964, and played six more years, mainly as a supersub, for Philadelphia, Atlanta, Oakland, and the Milwaukee Brewers through 1970, when he led the AL with 15 pinch hits. Francona's son Terry also played for the Indians in 1988.

Francona, Tito

Indians	G	AB	H	BA	RBI	R	2B	3B	HR	SA	SB
1959	122	399	145	.363	79	68	17	2	20	.566	2
1960	147	544	159	.292	79	84	36	2	17	.460	4
1961	155	592	178	.301	85	87	30	8	16	.459	2
1962	158	621	169	.272	70	82	28	5	14	.401	3
1963	142	500	114	.228	41	57	29	0	10	.346	9
1964	111	270	67	.248	24	35	13	2	8	.400	1
Career	1,719	5,121	1,395	.272	656	650	224	34	125	.403	46

Fuller, Vernon Gordon

Indians: 1964, 1966–70
Second baseman
Birthplace: Menomonie, Wisconsin

B: March 1, 1944
Bats right, throws right
Ht. 6–1; **Wt.** 170

A steady fielder who did not hit for a high average, Vern Fuller was kept by the Indians the entire 1964 season, only his second year in professional baseball, because of the major league bonus rule then in effect.

He also spent much of the year on the disabled list with a fractured shoulder blade, playing in only two games, batting but once.

Fuller went back to the minor leagues in 1965 and remained there most of the next two seasons before being recalled by the Tribe in 1967. He was the Indians' regular second baseman in 1969, but played only 29 games, hitting .182, in 1970, his final season in professional baseball.

Tito Francona

Vern Fuller

Fuller, Vern

Indians	G	AB	H	BA	RBI	R	2B	3B	HR	SA	SB
1964	2	1	0	.000	0	0	0	0	0	.000	0
1966	16	47	11	.234	2	7	2	1	2	.447	0
1967	73	206	46	.223	21	18	10	0	7	.374	2
1968	97	244	59	.242	18	14	8	2	0	.291	2
1969	108	254	60	.236	22	25	11	1	4	.335	2
1970	29	33	6	.182	2	3	2	0	1	.333	0
Career	325	785	182	.232	65	67	33	4	14	.338	6

Galehouse, Dennis Ward

Indians: 1934–38
Pitcher
Nickname: Denny
Birthplace: Marshallville, Ohio

B: December 7, 1911
Bats right, throws right
Ht. 6–1; **Wt.** 195

Many Cleveland fans remember Denny Galehouse as the Boston Red Sox pitcher who lost to the Indians in the historic one-game playoff for the American League pennant on October 4, 1948.

Galehouse was Red Sox manager Joe McCarthy's surprise choice to pitch against Gene Bearden in the game, which was won by the Tribe, 8–3.

Galehouse started his professional baseball career as one of the Indians' most promising young pitchers of the 1930s, though he never fully lived up to the bright future predicted for him.

Traded to the Red Sox on December 15, 1938, with short-stop Tommy Irwin for outfielder Ben Chapman, Galehouse went on to enjoy a 15-year major league career that included

two starts—and a victory—for the St. Louis Browns in the 1944 World Series.

Raised in Doylestown, Ohio, near Akron, Galehouse was signed by the Indians in 1931. Promoted to the Tribe in 1935, Galehouse was described in a newspaper article as a pitcher "who has tremendous speed and a powerful body to keep producing it."

After leaving Cleveland, Galehouse didn't stay in Boston long either, though he was destined to end his career with the Red Sox. He was sold to St. Louis on December 3, 1940, and it was with the Browns that he was most successful.

In the final week of the 1944 season, Galehouse pitched and won a key game against Detroit as the Browns finished one game ahead of the Tigers for the AL pennant. Galehouse beat Mort Cooper and the St. Louis Cardinals, 2–1, in the opener of the World Series, and lost the fifth game, 2–0, which he also pitched against Cooper.

Galehouse was in the Navy in 1945, during World War II. He returned in 1946 to the Browns, who sold him to Boston on June 20, 1947. Galehouse was released by the Red Sox on May 1, 1949, and two years later rejoined them as a scout, working for them from 1951 to 1966. He scouted for Detroit for nine years, the Cardinals in 1977 and 1978, the New York Mets in 1979 and 1980, and the San Diego Padres since 1981.

Galehouse, Denny

Indians	W	L	Pct	ERA	G	CG	IP	H	BB	SO	ShO
1934	0	0	—	18.00	1	0	1	2	1	0	0
1935	1	0	1.000	9.00	5	1	13	16	9	8	0
1936	8	7	.533	4.85	36	5	148⅓	161	68	71	0
1937	9	14	.391	4.57	36	7	200⅔	238	83	78	0
1938	7	8	.467	4.34	36	5	114	119	65	66	1
Career	109	118	.480	3.97	375	100	2,004	2,148	735	851	17

Denny Galehouse

Garcia, Edward Miguel

Indians: 1948–59
Pitcher
Nicknames: Mike, Big Bear
Birthplace: San Gabriel, California

B: November 17, 1923
D: January 13, 1986
Batted right, threw right
Ht. 6–1; **Wt.** 195

Mike Garcia led the Indians' 1954 pitching staff that many experts consider one of the greatest—if not *the* greatest—in baseball history, with an American League–best 2.64 earned run average. He pitched five shutouts while posting a 19–8 won-lost mark.

Four other pitchers on that pennant-winning team that set an AL record with 111 victories—Early Wynn, Bob Lemon, Bob Feller, and Hal Newhouser—are enshrined in the Hall of Fame.

It was Garcia's humility and team spirit that probably prevented him from also winning 20 games in 1954. In the final two weeks of the season he was used strictly in relief, at the request of manager Al Lopez.

"Lopez said he wanted to go for the record and asked if I'd be willing to pitch out of the bull pen," Garcia explained prior to his death from kidney failure in 1986.

"I'd already won 19 and I wanted to go for 20. As I told Lopez, 'The difference between winning 19 and 20 is like the difference between a Ford and a Cadillac.'

"But I also told him I'd do it [pitch relief] if that's what he wanted. Lopez said, 'I'll see to it that you pick up another victory, don't worry.'

"When we got down to the final game, I still hadn't won one more, so Lopez started me against Detroit. But he also put all the scrubbinies in the lineup."

The tenacious Garcia battled the Tigers for 12 innings, before leaving with a 6–6 tie, and Detroit won, 8–7, in the 13th. The loss was charged to reliever Ray Narleski.

Earlier that season, in the second game of a doubleheader in Cleveland on May 16, Garcia threw a one-hitter to beat Philadelphia, 6–0. The Athletics' only hit was a fourth-inning single by Joe DeMaestri.

In the three seasons preceding 1954, Garcia won 60 games, losing only 33, and in 1952, after posting a 22–11 record with a 2.37 ERA, he was the cowinner with Lemon and Wynn of the Indians' Man of the Year award. That was the season he and Lemon tied for the most starts in the AL, 36, and Garcia also tied New York's Allie Reynolds for the most shutouts, six.

He was a member of the AL All-Star team in 1952, 1953, and 1954.

It was after the 1954 season that Garcia ran into physical problems, and his career went downhill.

He slipped on a wet mound early in 1958, suffering a slipped disc in his back that prevented him from pitching after only six starts. Because the major league rules were different then—teams were permitted to have only two players on the disabled list at the same time—Garcia was released.

After undergoing back surgery, Garcia re-signed with the Indians and attempted a comeback in 1959, but he couldn't recapture the success he'd previously enjoyed and was cut loose again.

Garcia still wouldn't quit. He signed with the Chicago White Sox and again attempted to resurrect his career. However, that winter Garcia suffered another setback. In a freak accident while working on a racing car that he operated as a hobby, Garcia lost the tip of his right index finger.

Garcia recovered in time to pitch 15 games as a reliever for the White Sox in 1960, without a decision. He was released, signed with Washington, and, in 16 games in 1961, also all in relief, was 0–1; then he retired, ending the career of the man who was said to "walk like a bear and pitch like a lion."

Mike Garcia

Garcia, Mike

Indians	W	L	Pct	ERA	G	CG	IP	H	BB	SO	ShO
1948	0	0	—	0.00	1	0	2	3	0	1	0
1949	14	5	.737	2.36	41	8	175⅔	154	60	94	5
1950	11	11	.500	3.86	33	11	184	191	74	76	0
1951	20	13	.606	3.15	47	15	254	239	82	118	1
1952	22	11	.667	2.37	46	19	292⅓	284	87	143	6
1953	18	9	.667	3.25	38	21	271⅓	260	81	134	3
1954	19	8	.704	2.64	45	13	258⅔	220	71	129	5
1955	11	13	.458	4.02	38	6	210⅔	230	56	120	2
1956	11	12	.478	3.78	35	8	197⅔	213	74	119	4
1957	12	8	.600	3.75	38	9	211⅓	221	73	110	1
1958	1	0	1.000	9.00	6	0	8	15	7	2	0
1959	3	6	.333	4.00	29	1	72	72	31	49	0
Career	142	97	.594	3.27	428	111	2,174⅔	2,148	719	1,117	27

Gardner, William Lawrence

Indians: 1919–24
Third baseman
Nickname: Larry
Birthplace: Enosburg Falls, Vermont

B: May 13, 1886
D: March 11, 1976
Batted left, threw right
Ht. 5–8; **Wt.** 165

Larry Gardner's best years were with the Boston Red Sox, helping them win three pennants (1912, 1915, 1916) and three world championships, but he still had plenty left when he was acquired by the Indians on March 1, 1919.

A steady fielder who joined the Red Sox out of the University of Vermont in 1908, Gardner was their regular third baseman from 1910 to 1917, after which he was traded to the Philadelphia Athletics and batted .285 in 1918.

Though Tris Speaker was not yet the Tribe manager, it was his recommendation to owner James Dunn that played a prominent role in the deal for Gardner. They'd been teammates in Boston before Speaker was dealt to Cleveland in 1916.

The Indians got Gardner, along with outfielder Charlie Jamieson and pitcher Elmer Myers, in exchange for outfielder Braggo Roth.

Gardner batted .300 his first season in Cleveland, more than justifying the faith of Speaker, who became manager of the Indians on July 18, 1919.

Gardner was even better in 1920, leading the team with 118 runs batted in while hitting .310 as the Indians won their first pennant. His average climbed to a career-high .319 in 1921. His last season as a regular was 1922, when he batted .285, and he retired after the 1924 season with a 17-year major league average of .289.

He appeared in 25 World Series games, 18 with the Red Sox in 1912, 1915, and 1916 and seven with the Indians in 1920, with a .198 average.

After leaving baseball Gardner returned to the University of Vermont as baseball coach and held that position for 25 years. He also was athletic director for eight years, retiring in 1952.

Gardner, Larry

Indians	G	AB	H	BA	RBI	R	2B	3B	HR	SA	SB
1919	139	524	157	.300	79	67	29	7	2	.393	7
1920	154	597	185	.310	118	72	31	11	3	.414	3
1921	153	586	187	.319	120	101	32	14	3	.437	3
1922	137	470	134	.285	68	74	31	3	2	.377	9
1923	52	79	20	.253	12	4	5	1	0	.342	0
1924	38	50	10	.200	4	3	0	0	0	.200	0
Career	1,923	6,688	1,931	.289	934	866	301	129	27	.384	165

Garland, Marcus Wayne

Indians: 1977–81
Pitcher
Nickname: Wayne
Birthplace: Nashville, Tennessee

B: October 26, 1950
Bats right, throws right
Ht. 6–0; **Wt.** 195

One of the first players to benefit from an arbitrator's ruling allowing free agency in baseball, Wayne Garland signed a $2.3 million, 10-year contract with the Indians on November 19, 1976, and was expected to be their ace pitcher for a long time to come.

However, instead of a success story, it was a disaster for Garland and the Tribe.

Near the end of his first season with the Indians, Garland hurt his arm—the injury was subsequently diagnosed as a torn rotator cuff—and he never came close to duplicating the 20–7 won-lost record he posted in 1976 for the Baltimore Orioles.

"I wasn't worth the money; nobody is," Garland candidly admitted after he'd signed with the Indians. "But if they were willing to offer it, who could blame me for taking it?"

Until 1976, Garland had produced only seven victories while losing 11 games for the Orioles in one full season and parts of two others.

In 1977 with the Indians, Garland won 13 games and lost an American League–high 19, and he was just 2–3 in six appearances in 1978 before undergoing shoulder surgery.

He tried to make a comeback, but to no avail. Garland's record fell to 4–10 in 1979, 6–9 in 1980, and 3–7 in 1981, and then it was over.

To his credit, Garland didn't take the money and run; he attempted to resurrect his career in the minors, but couldn't. The fastball was gone, and his curveball, which had been one of the best in baseball in 1976, had lost its snap.

"The big contract and the rotator cuff surgery, they're always there behind my name, in every story that's written about me," he said.

"When Cleveland released me [in spring training 1982] I tried to catch on with other teams, but they all said, 'For what you're getting paid, if you could still pitch you'd be pitching for Gabe Paul in Cleveland.' Nobody wanted me."

Garland, Wayne

Indians	W	L	Pct	ERA	G	CG	IP	H	BB	SO	ShO
1977	13	19	.406	3.60	38	21	282⅔	281	88	118	1
1978	2	3	.400	7.89	6	0	29⅔	43	16	13	0
1979	4	10	.286	5.23	18	2	94⅔	120	34	40	0
1980	6	9	.400	4.61	25	4	150⅓	163	48	55	1
1981	3	7	.300	5.79	12	2	56	89	14	15	1
Career	55	66	.455	3.89	190	43	1,040	1,082	328	450	7

Gordon, Joseph Lowell

Indians: 1947–50
Second baseman
Nickname: Flash
Birthplace: Los Angeles

B: February 18, 1915
D: April 14, 1978
Batted right, threw right
Ht. 5–10; **Wt.** 180

Fortunately for the Indians, it took Joe Gordon a full season to regain his batting eye after spending two years in the army during World War II.

Joe Gordon

Upon returning to the New York Yankees in 1946, Gordon hit a career-low .210, which led to his being traded to Cleveland, and it was with the Indians that he duplicated some of the great seasons he had enjoyed before Uncle Sam beckoned.

Gordon replaced Tony Lazzeri as the Yankees' second baseman in 1938 and became a star with his glove and bat, helping New York win the American League pennant in 1938 and 1939 and for three years running from 1941 to '43.

In the 1941 World Series, Gordon went 7-for-14 with a .929 slugging percentage; he won the AL Most Valuable Player award in 1942 when he hit .322 with 103 runs batted in; and he was on the AL All-Star team for the Yankees from 1939 to '43 and in 1946, despite his subpar batting average.

Gordon also was named to the AL All-Star team three times, 1947–49, while with the Indians.

Interestingly, when the 1946 season—Gordon's last one in New York—ended, he had collected exactly 1,000 hits in exactly 1,000 games for the Yankees.

Bill Veeck, then the new owner of the Indians, saw a chance to trade for Gordon and offered pitcher Red Embree. The Yankees countered with a demand for Allie Reynolds. Veeck reluctantly agreed, so eager was he to acquire Gordon, and the Tribe also received utility infielder Eddie Bockman in the October 19, 1946, deal.

Though he only played four seasons for the Indians, Gordon was a major component in their drive to the 1948 pennant. He teamed with shortstop-manager Lou Boudreau to give them solid defense up the middle and a potent offense—as well as inspirational leadership.

Gordon hit .280 with career highs of 32 homers and 124 RBIs in 1948, the year the Indians beat the Boston Braves in the World Series. His final season as a player was 1950. Gordon finished with the most career home runs, 246, by a second baseman, and also holds the AL record for the most homers by a second baseman in one season, 32 in 1948.

Eight years after retiring as a player, Gordon began another career with the Tribe.

On June 26, 1958, Gordon was hired by general manager Frank Lane to replace Bobby Bragan as manager of the Indians. They went 46–40 under Gordon the remainder of that season, and they were in contention for the pennant in 1959 until the final three weeks, finishing with an 89–65 record, five games behind Chicago.

But it was a season of travail for Gordon, who feuded in the clubhouse with Billy Martin and Jim Piersall, and in the front office with Lane, who supported the two players. Finally, Gordon had enough, and on September 18, with only seven games left, announced his intention to resign at the end of the season. Lane immediately began to court Leo Durocher as Gordon's successor.

Durocher, however, priced himself out of the job, and Lane, given time to reconsider the team's performance under Gordon, asked him to return for the 1960 season.

Gordon, who'd also had time to reflect, agreed and was "introduced" as the Indians' "new" manager at a press conference attended by members of the media who were expecting to greet Durocher.

But the reconciliation didn't last long. Only 95 games into the 1960 season.

On the morning of August 3, with the Indians in fourth place with a 49–46 record, seven games behind the Yankees, Lane traded Gordon to Detroit for Tigers manager Jimmy Dykes. It was the only time in baseball history that managers were traded.

The Indians won 26 and lost 32 under Dykes, and still finished fourth, 21 games out of first place.

The Tigers finished the season with a 26–31 record under Gordon, and he was not rehired. He surfaced again the following year to manage the Kansas City Athletics the final 60 games, winning 26 and losing 33 (with one tie). Gordon also managed the Kansas City Royals in 1969 to a fourth-place, 69–93 record.

Gordon, Joe

Indians	G	AB	H	BA	RBI	R	2B	3B	HR	SA	SB
1947	155	562	153	.272	93	89	27	6	29	.496	7
1948	144	550	154	.280	124	96	21	4	32	.507	5
1949	148	541	136	.251	84	74	18	3	20	.407	5
1950	119	368	87	.236	57	59	12	1	19	.429	4
Career	1,566	5,707	1,530	.268	975	914	264	52	253	.466	89

Graney, John Gladstone

Indians: 1908, 1910–22
Outfielder
Nickname: Jack
Birthplace: St. Thomas, Ontario, Canada

B: June 10, 1886
D: April 20, 1978
Batted left, threw left
Ht. 5–9; **Wt.** 180

Jack Graney began his professional baseball career in 1906 as a left-handed pitcher. A very wild left-handed pitcher. And because Graney was so wild, he became a very good outfielder for the Indians (then called the Naps) from 1910 to 1922.

Jack Graney

It's also possible that his wildness enabled Graney to become the first ex–major league player to become a major league play-by-play broadcaster.

The transformation of Graney began in 1908. Then a rookie up from the minor leagues, Graney was pitching batting practice and wanted to make a good impression.

As Graney told the story before he died in 1978, "I wasn't content to just lob the ball up to the plate. I wanted to put something on it, show the boys what I had.

"The result was that each hitter was up there about 15 minutes before he got four or five pitches he could reach with a fishing rod, I was that wild.

"The fourth batter was the manager, [Napoleon] Lajoie, who also played second base. I knew all about him . . . every kid in America did.

"I was pretty cocky and had a crazy idea I could strike Lajoie out. I wound up, reared back and cut loose with a fastball that was supposed to get past him before he ever saw it.

"But it didn't. Though Lajoie tried to duck, the ball hit him above the left ear and he went down like a load of bricks. Instead of striking him out, I *knocked* him out.

"That evening I was told Lajoie wanted to see me. I went to his room and found him with an ice bag to his head. I started to tell him I was sorry, but he stopped me.

"He said, 'They tell me the place for wild men is out west. So, you're going west, kid, so far west that if you went any farther your hat would float. Here's your railroad ticket.' "

It was a ticket to Portland. There, Graney was switched to the outfield "for humanity's sake," he quipped.

Thus ended Graney's pitching career. The record shows that he appeared in two games for the Naps in 1908, pitching 3⅓ innings. Though he walked only one batter, he was tagged for six hits and charged with a 5.40 earned run average.

By 1910, Graney was called back to the Naps and became their left fielder, a position he held as a regular through most of the next 10 seasons. Though he never hit .300, Graney was a good leadoff batter, smart base runner, and excellent outfielder.

Graney had the distinction of being the first batter to face Babe Ruth, then a rookie pitcher for Boston, in 1914. Graney singled. He also was the first major leaguer to wear a number on his uniform on June 26, 1916. He led the American League in doubles (41) in 1916, and in walks in 1917 (94) and 1919 (105).

Graney retired after the 1922 season and nine years later became the radio voice of the Indians. Billy Evans, then the Indians' general manager, offered Graney the job.

"He asked me if I wanted to try announcing," said Graney. "I said I'd try it, and he took me into the radio booth, introduced me on the air, and then I was on the air."

Graney stayed on the air for 22 baseball seasons, through 1953—but might never have done so if he had not been such a wild left-handed pitcher.

Graney, Jack

Indians	G	AB	H	BA	RBI	R	2B	3B	HR	SA	SB
1908	2	0	0	—	0	0	0	0	0	—	0
1910	116	454	107	.236	31	62	13	9	1	.311	18
1911	146	527	142	.269	45	84	25	5	1	.342	21
1912	78	264	64	.242	20	44	13	2	0	.307	9
1913	148	517	138	.267	68	56	18	12	3	.366	27
1914	130	460	122	.265	39	63	17	10	1	.352	20
1915	116	404	105	.260	56	42	20	7	1	.351	12
1916	155	589	142	.241	54	106	41	14	5	.384	10
1917	146	535	122	.228	35	87	29	7	3	.325	16
1918	70	177	42	.237	9	27	7	4	0	.322	3
1919	128	461	108	.234	30	79	22	8	1	.323	7
1920	62	152	45	.296	13	31	11	1	0	.382	4
1921	68	107	32	.299	18	19	3	0	2	.383	1
1922	37	58	9	.155	2	6	0	0	0	.155	0
Career	1,402	4,705	1,178	.250	420	706	219	79	18	.342	148

Grant, James Timothy

Indians: 1958–64
Pitcher
Nickname: Mudcat
Birthplace: Lacoochee, Florida

B: August 13, 1935
Bats right, throws right
Ht. 6–1; **Wt.** 186

It wasn't until after he was traded by the Indians to Minnesota on June 15, 1964, that Mudcat Grant reached the pinnacle of success.

Grant became the first African-American pitcher to win

"Mudcat" Grant

20 games in the American League in one season when he led the Twins to the pennant with a 21–7 record in 1965, went 2–1 against Los Angeles in the World Series, was a member of the AL All-Star team, and was named AL Pitcher of the Year.

A colorful and popular athlete who also was a talented singer-entertainer, Grant came up through the Indians' farm system, but was sacrificed in 1964 when the franchise was financially strapped. He was traded to the Twins for pitcher Lee Stange, third baseman George Banks, and cash.

It was a deal that saddened Grant, who said he always wanted to pitch his entire career in Cleveland. "It's where I started, where I got my first chance, and the only place I liked almost as much as Lacoochee," he said.

Lacoochee was Grant's hometown in Florida.

Still, as Grant admitted, being traded to Minnesota made him a big winner after being tutored by pitching coach Johnny Sain. It was Sain who refined Grant's curveball, which previously "did little more than spin," he said.

But even without a great curveball, Grant was one of the Indians' most consistent pitchers from the time he started in their farm system in 1954. Mudcat won 70 games and lost only 28 in four minor league seasons.

Despite Sain's influence, Grant's career took a downturn after 1965. His record fell to 13–13, then to 5–6. He was traded November 28, 1967, to the Los Angeles Dodgers, and then on October 14, 1968, was selected by Montreal in the expansion draft.

Grant was a member of the AL All-Star team in 1963 and 1965, and he pitched a one-hitter against the Washington Senators on September 25, 1965, beating them, 5–0. Washington's only hit was a third-inning double by Don Blasingame.

After failing a comeback attempt with the Indians in 1972, Mudcat joined their telecasting team, a job he held into the early 1980s. He also was employed in the Tribe's front office in community relations, and after relocating in Los Angeles, Grant did some television work for the Dodgers and the Athletics.

Still in the entertainment business, Grant founded and is the president of the Black Professional Golfers Association. He is also active in civic and community affairs in Los Angeles.

Grant, Mudcat

Indians	W	L	Pct	ERA	G	CG	IP	H	BB	SO	ShO
1958	10	11	.476	3.84	44	11	204	173	104	111	1
1959	10	7	.588	4.14	38	6	165⅓	140	81	85	1
1960	9	8	.529	4.40	33	5	159⅔	147	78	75	0
1961	15	9	.625	3.86	35	11	244⅔	207	109	146	3
1962	7	10	.412	4.27	26	6	149⅔	128	81	90	1
1963	13	14	.481	3.69	38	10	229⅓	213	87	157	2
1964	3	4	.429	5.95	13	1	62	82	25	43	0
Career	145	119	.549	3.63	571	89	2,441⅓	2,292	849	1,267	18

Gregg, Sylveanus Augustus

Indians: 1911–14   **B:** April 13, 1885
Pitcher   **D:** July 29, 1964
Nickname: Vean   **Batted right, threw left**
Birthplace: Chehalis, Washington   **Ht.** 6–1; **Wt.** 185

Vean Gregg had three of the best seasons any pitcher could hope to achieve, which established him in the minds of some as the best left-handed pitcher in Cleveland baseball history.

Unfortunately, a sore arm robbed Gregg of much of his ability, and his effectiveness was short-lived.

A remarkable 1910 season with Portland of the Pacific Coast League, where he had a record of 32–18, 376 strikeouts, and 14 shutouts, led to Gregg's purchase by the Cleveland club, then called the Naps.

As a rookie in 1910, Gregg won 23 games while losing only seven and led American League pitchers with a 1.80 earned run average.

It was a sensational start for Gregg, and he followed with 20–13 records in each of the next two seasons.

However, Gregg hurt his shoulder and struggled in 1914, winning nine (and losing three) of 17 starts. He was traded to the Boston Red Sox on August 20 for three players—catcher Ben Egan and pitchers Adam Johnson and Fritz Coumbe—none of whom distinguished himself after joining the Naps.

Gregg's fortunes didn't improve in Boston. He went 3–4 for the Red Sox for an overall 12–7 mark in 1914, but was never a big winner again.

He went back to the minors in 1917, was 9–14 with the Philadelphia Athletics in 1918, then remained out of baseball the next three seasons.

Gregg returned in 1922 to pitch three years for Seattle of the Pacific Coast League, winning 25 games in 1924, which led to his being purchased by the Washington Senators.

At the age of 40 in 1925 he posted a 2–2 record in 26 games, and in late August was sent to New Orleans of the Southern Association as partial payment for shortstop Buddy Myer.

Gregg, Vean

Indians	W	L	Pct	ERA	G	CG	IP	H	BB	SO	ShO
1911	23	7	.767	1.80	34	22	244⅔	172	86	125	5
1912	20	13	.606	2.59	37	26	271⅓	242	90	184	1
1913	20	13	.606	2.24	44	23	285⅔	258	124	166	3
1914	9	3	.750	3.07	17	6	96⅔	88	48	56	1
Career	92	63	.594	2.70	239	105	1,393	1,240	552	720	14

Gromek, Stephen Joseph

Indians: 1941–53   **B:** January 15, 1920
Pitcher   **Bats both, throws right**
Birthplace: Hamtramck, Michigan   **Ht.** 6–2; **Wt.** 180

Though he was a 19-game winner in 1945, the highlight of Steve Gromek's career with the Indians came on October 9, 1948, when he won the pivotal fourth game of the World Series, a 2–1 victory over the Boston Braves and their ace, Johnny Sain.

Steve Gromek

Gromek was Detroit's best pitcher with an 18–16 record in 1954, and he won 45 while losing 41 for the Tigers before retiring in 1957.

Gromek, Steve

Indians	W	L	Pct	ERA	G	CG	IP	H	BB	SO	ShO
1941	1	1	.500	4.24	9	1	23⅓	25	11	19	0
1942	2	0	1.000	3.65	14	0	44⅓	46	23	14	0
1943	0	0	—	9.00	3	0	4	6	0	4	0
1944	10	9	.526	2.56	35	12	203⅔	160	70	115	2
1945	19	9	.679	2.55	33	21	251	229	66	101	3
1946	5	15	.250	4.33	29	5	153⅔	159	47	75	2
1947	3	5	.375	3.74	29	0	84⅓	77	36	39	0
1948	9	3	.750	2.84	38	4	130	109	51	50	1
1949	4	6	.400	3.33	27	3	92	86	40	22	0
1950	10	7	.588	3.65	31	4	113⅓	94	36	43	1
1951	7	4	.636	2.77	27	4	107½	98	29	40	0
1952	7	7	.500	3.67	29	3	122⅔	109	28	65	1
1953	1	1	.500	3.27	5	0	11	11	3	8	0
Career	123	108	.532	3.41	447	92	2,064⅔	1,940	630	904	17

Gromek called it the biggest thrill of his 17-year major league career.

It gave the Indians a 3–1 lead in the Series, which they captured in six games, and came on the wings of Larry Doby's 410-foot home run, after which the two men were photographed in a happy embrace.

It was a picture that appeared in major newspapers around the country, and it was considered a landmark in what was then only the second year of the integration of baseball.

Doby, who had been the American League's first black player in 1947, said he would "always cherish that photograph and the memory of Gromek hugging me and me hugging him, because it proved that emotions can be put into a form not based on skin color."

Gromek, who started in professional baseball as a shortstop in 1939, switched to pitching in 1940 after suffering an injury to his left shoulder that hampered his hitting the rest of his career. When he threw overhand, his fastball was ordinary. But when he sidearmed the ball, it either dipped, hopped, or sailed.

Gromek also threw what he called a knuckle-curve, while insisting it was "neither a knuckleball nor a curve, just a pitch that did tricks" en route to the plate.

After brief trials with the Tribe in 1941, 1942, and 1943, Gromek made the team as a regular starter in 1944. He was the Indians' most consistent pitcher with his 19–9 record in 1945, but won in double figures for them only once more, in 1950.

A native of Hamtramck, Michigan, a suburb of Detroit, Gromek was traded on June 15, 1953, to the Tigers, the team he rooted for as a kid.

It was an eight-player deal in which the Indians sent shortstop–third baseman Ray Boone and pitchers Al Aber and Dick Weik with Gromek to Detroit for pitchers Art Houtteman and Bill Wight, catcher Joe Ginsberg, and utility infielder Owen Friend.

Hale, Arvel Odell

Indians: 1931, 1933–40
Third baseman, second baseman
Nicknames: Bad News, Sammy
Birthplace: Hosston, Louisiana

B: August 10, 1908
D: June 9, 1980
Batted right, threw right
Ht. 5–10; **Wt.** 175

Opposing pitchers called him Bad News because Sammy Hale was such a tough hitter in the clutch. Twice in his 10-year major league career Hale drove in more than 100 runs, while batting .300 or better four times.

Hale led American League second basemen with 41 errors in 1934, and after being switched to third base in 1935 he made 31 errors, most by any AL player at that position. But he also led third basemen with 312 assists in 1935 and 323 in 1936.

One assist credited to Hale in 1935 was particularly memorable. It occurred in the ninth inning of the opener of a doubleheader on September 7, against the Red Sox in Boston, and enabled the Indians to win, 5–3.

The Red Sox had scored two runs to knock Mel Harder out of the box. Then, with Dusty Cooke on third, Bill Werber on second, and Mel Almada on first with nobody out, Joe Cronin stepped to the plate against relief pitcher Oral Hildebrand.

Cronin slashed a line drive toward left field. Hale threw up his arms and leaped, but the ball tore through his glove. It struck Hale squarely on the forehead and bounced high and to his left. The Boston runners, off with the crack of the bat, stopped, then started again when they saw the ball carom off Hale's head.

Shortstop Bill Knickerbocker was there to grab the ball before it touched the ground, retiring Cronin, then whirled and threw to Roy Hughes at second, doubling Werber off that base. Hughes' relay to Hal Trosky arrived before Almada could return to first, thus completing a triple play, ending the game, and giving the Indians a victory.

Hale was credited later for "using his head" to start what might have been the strangest triple play in baseball history.

Hale, Odell

Indians	G	AB	H	BA	RBI	R	2B	3B	HR	SA	SB
1931	25	92	26	.283	5	14	2	4	1	.424	2
1933	98	351	97	.276	64	49	19	8	10	.462	2
1934	143	563	170	.302	101	82	44	6	13	.471	8
1935	150	589	179	.304	101	80	37	11	16	.486	15
1936	153	620	196	.316	87	126	50	13	14	.506	8
1937	154	561	150	.267	82	74	32	4	6	.371	9
1938	130	496	138	.278	69	69	32	2	8	.399	8
1939	108	253	79	.312	48	36	16	2	4	.439	4
1940	48	50	11	.220	6	3	3	1	0	.320	0
Career	1,062	3,701	1,071	.289	573	551	240	51	73	.441	57

Hall, Melvin, Jr.

Indians: 1984–88	**B:** September 16, 1960
Outfielder	**Bats left, throws left**
Birthplace: Lyons, New York	**Ht.** 6–0; **Wt.** 185

Much was expected of Mel Hall after he came to the Indians in a June 13, 1984, trade with the Chicago Cubs, though he spent most of the 1985 season on the disabled list after suffering multiple injuries in an automobile accident.

Hall recovered and played well in 1986 and 1987, but his production declined drastically thereafter, and his career in Cleveland ended when he was sent to the New York Yankees on March 19, 1989.

Acquired with outfielder Joe Carter and pitchers Don Schulze and Darryl Banks in exchange for pitchers Rick Sutcliffe and George Frazier and catcher Ron Hassey, Hall delivered 18 homers in 1986 and again in 1987, when he hit .296 and .280, respectively.

But his home run production fell off to six in 1988, and when he was benched against left-handed pitchers, Hall became a disruptive influence on the team. As a result, he was

Mel Hall

sent to the Yankees in a deal that brought catcher Joel Skinner and outfielder Turner Ward to Cleveland.

After four seasons in New York, Hall became a free agent and in 1993 went to Japan to play.

Hall, Mel

Indians	G	AB	H	BA	RBI	R	2B	3B	HR	SA	SB
1984	83	257	66	.257	30	43	13	1	7	.397	1
1985	23	66	21	.318	12	7	6	0	0	.409	0
1986	140	442	131	.296	77	68	29	2	18	.493	6
1987	142	485	136	.280	76	57	21	1	18	.439	5
1988	150	515	144	.280	71	69	32	4	6	.392	7
Career	1,251	4,212	1,168	.277	615	565	229	25	134	.439	31

Harder, Melvin LeRoy

Indians: 1928–47	**B:** October 15, 1909
Pitcher	**Bats right, throws right**
Nicknames: Chief, Wimpy	**Ht.** 6–1; **Wt.** 195
Birthplace: Beemer, Nebraska	

With the possible exception of Bob Feller, it would be difficult to pick any player who has meant more to the Indians than Mel Harder. He wore a Cleveland uniform for 36 years, his entire 20 seasons as one of the American League's best pitchers, and 16 more as a Tribe coach.

Only Feller won more games for the Indians than Harder (266–223), and only Walter Johnson of Washington and Ted Lyons of the Chicago White Sox pitched more years with one club—and all three are in the Hall of Fame, where many believe Harder also belongs.

Among them probably would be two other Hall of Famers, Joe DiMaggio and Ted Williams, both of whom called Harder, a curveball specialist, the toughest pitcher they faced in their long and illustrious careers.

DiMaggio's lifetime average was .325, but he batted only .180 against Harder, and Williams admitted in his autobiography, *My Turn at Bat,* that he found Harder more difficult to hit than any other pitcher he faced.

About DiMaggio, Harder said, "I always seemed to have good luck against him because he usually was looking for the wrong pitch. I threw him a lot of sinkers, in and out."

Nor was Babe Ruth a big problem for Harder, he said, "because Babe tried to pull everything and I always kept the ball away from him, never gave him anything good to hit."

Unlike Ruth, however, Lou Gehrig was tougher for Harder "because he'd go with the pitch, hit my sinker to left field when I'd throw it down and away, and pull me when I pitched him tight."

Harder, whose uniform number 18 is one of five retired by the Indians, also appeared in more games than any other Cleveland pitcher, 582 (to Feller's 570), and always will be remembered for having started the first game in the Cleveland Municipal Stadium.

It was on July 31, 1932, and Harder lost to Lefty Grove and the Philadelphia Athletics, 1–0, in front of a throng of more than 80,000 fans. Harder called it "the biggest thrill of my career."

Harder also appeared in four consecutive All-Star Games, from 1934 to 1937, working 13 scoreless innings. He owns the distinction of being the only man to pitch 10 or more All-Star innings without yielding an earned run. And, based on to-

Mel Harder

early 1950s, and in 1961 he was elected the Indians' Man of the Year, the only coach to be so honored.

Upon leaving the Indians coaching staff, Harder worked for the New York Mets in 1964, the Chicago Cubs in 1965, Cincinnati from 1966 to 1968, and the Kansas City Royals in 1969.

Harder, Mel

Indians	W	L	Pct	ERA	G	CG	IP	H	BB	SO	ShO
1928	0	2	.000	6.61	23	0	49	64	32	15	0
1929	1	0	1.000	5.60	11	0	17⅔	24	5	4	0
1930	11	10	.524	4.21	36	7	175⅓	205	68	44	0
1931	13	14	.481	4.36	40	9	194	229	72	63	0
1932	15	13	.536	3.75	39	17	254⅔	277	68	90	1
1933	15	17	.469	2.95	43	14	253	254	67	81	2
1934	20	12	.625	2.61	44	17	255⅓	246	81	91	6
1935	22	11	.667	3.29	42	17	287⅓	313	53	95	4
1936	15	15	.500	5.17	36	13	224⅔	294	71	84	0
1937	15	12	.556	4.28	38	13	233⅔	269	86	95	0
1938	17	10	.630	3.83	38	15	240	257	62	102	2
1939	15	9	.625	3.50	29	12	208	213	64	67	1
1940	12	11	.522	4.06	31	5	186⅓	200	59	76	0
1941	5	4	.556	5.24	15	1	68⅔	76	37	21	0
1942	13	14	.481	3.44	29	13	198⅔	179	82	74	4
1943	8	7	.533	3.06	19	6	135⅓	126	61	40	1
1944	12	10	.545	3.71	30	12	196⅓	211	69	64	2
1945	3	7	.300	3.67	11	2	76	93	23	16	0
1946	5	4	.556	3.41	13	4	92⅓	85	31	21	1
1947	6	4	.600	4.50	15	4	80	91	27	17	1
Career	223	186	.545	3.80	582	181	3,426⅓	3,706	1,118	1,160	25

Hargan, Steven Lowell

Indians: 1965–72
Pitcher
Birthplace: Fort Wayne, Indiana

B: September 8, 1942
Bats right, throws right
Ht. 6–3; **Wt.** 170

day's standards, Harder would have been credited with saves in the AL's victories in 1935 and 1937.

Though he pitched for Tribe teams that seldom were contenders (which probably is the reason his Hall of Fame credentials have been overlooked), Harder won in double figures 13 times and posted back-to-back 20-victory seasons in 1934 and 1935.

In the history of baseball only 23 pitchers won 15 or more games a season for eight or more consecutive years. Harder did it between 1932 and 1939.

Harder's professional baseball career began in 1927 when his combined won-lost record was 17–13 with Omaha, then in the Class A Western League, and Dubuque of the Class D Mississippi Valley League.

It earned Harder a promotion to Cleveland in 1928, though he spent part of the 1929 season at New Orleans of the Class A Southern Association, where his record was 7–2.

Harder returned to the Indians in 1930 and remained with them until he was released with a sore arm late in the 1941 season. He underwent surgery for bone chips in his elbow that winter, but returned in 1942 and stayed with the Indians through the end of his active career in 1947.

He came close to pitching a no-hitter on June 16, 1935, beating Boston, 4–0, in the first game of a doubleheader at League Park. It was spoiled by Bing Miller, who singled in the second inning.

Harder became the Tribe pitching coach in 1948, a job he held through 1963, serving eight different Cleveland managers. It was under Harder that seven different pitchers were 20-game winners for a total of 17 times.

Harder is given credit for having transformed Bob Lemon from a light-hitting third baseman–outfielder and refining the pitching of Early Wynn, both of whom are in the Hall of Fame. He also was instrumental in the development of Herb Score as one of the best young pitchers in baseball in the

By his own admission, Steve Hargan's career "was like the stock market—up and down—I was never able to put two good seasons together," he said in 1968 after undergoing arm surgery to reposition the ulnar nerve in his right elbow.

Until Hargan injured his arm, he was one of the Indians' best young pitchers.

After five seasons in the minors, Hargan made it to Cleveland in August 1965 and compiled a 4–3 record in eight starts. In his first full season in 1966, he won 13 and lost 10 and had the third-best earned run average (2.48) in the American League. He went 14–13 the following season, tied for the AL lead in shutouts (six), and had a 2.62 ERA, all of which earned him a place on the AL All-Star team.

Hargan started 1968 with losses in his first two starts, then hurled a one-hitter to beat Detroit, 2–0, on April 24. Jim Northrup singled in the third inning to spoil Hargan's bid for a no-hitter.

But then Hargan suffered arm trouble and, after slumping to 8–15 in 1968, underwent surgery on November 21 to remove calcium chips and relocate the ulnar nerve in his right elbow. He failed to respond to the operation until mid-1970, after he returned from a brief stint at Wichita of the Class AAA American Association.

From July 18 until the end of the 1970 season Hargan won 10 games and lost only one for the Indians, but his arm trou-

Steve Hargan

ble returned in 1971. He opened the season as the Tribe's leading pitcher, but wound up winning only one game while losing 13.

Hargan's career hit rock bottom in 1972 when the Indians in midseason demoted him to Portland of the Class AAA Pacific Coast League. He was recalled in September, but then on November 20 the Tribe assigned him outright to Oklahoma City of the American Association.

There, he compiled a disappointing 7–8 record in 1973, and on December 5 the Indians sold him conditionally to the Texas Rangers' Spokane farm team in the Pacific Coast League. On March 23, 1974, the Rangers sent pitcher Bill Gogolewski to the Indians to complete the deal.

On November 5, 1976, after three seasons with the Rangers during which he won 29 games and lost 27, Hargan was selected by Toronto in the expansion draft. He went 1–3 in only six games with the Blue Jays in 1977 and was traded back to Texas.

After another six games and a 1–0 record with the Rangers, Hargan was traded to Atlanta and was winless while losing three decisions the rest of 1977. On December 13, Hargan was released by the Braves, ending his "stock market" career.

Hargrove, Dudley Michael

Indians: 1979–85	**Birthplace:** Perryton, Texas
First baseman	**B:** October 26, 1949
Nicknames: Mike, Grover,	**Bats left, throws left**
Human Rain Delay	**Ht.** 6–0; **Wt.** 195

It was one of the Indians best-ever trades: Paul Dade, a utility player, for Mike Hargrove, who was the American League Rookie of the Year in 1974 when he played for the Texas Rangers after making the jump from Gastonia of the Class A Western Carolinas League.

The deal was made on June 14, 1979, eight months after Hargrove had been traded by the Rangers to San Diego.

Nicknamed the Human Rain Delay because of the deliberate, time-consuming routine he went through at the plate before every pitch, Hargrove batted .325 for the Indians the remainder of 1979 and over .300 twice in the next six seasons.

Hargrove ranks 40th in career on-base percentage in major league history, was a member of the AL All-Star team in 1975, twice led the league in walks (1976 and 1978), and was the league leader among first basemen in putouts once, assists twice, and errors twice (while tying for the most errors another time).

One of the all-time most popular member of the Indians, Hargrove won the team's Man of the Year award in consecutive seasons, in 1980 and 1981, and also twice was voted the Good Guy award.

After being cut by the Tribe in spring training 1986, Hargrove tried out briefly with Oakland and, before the season began, retired as a player—but not from baseball.

Hargrove started a new career at the bottom of the ranks, as the batting instructor at Batavia of the Class A New York–Penn League in the summer of 1986.

Hargan, Steve

Indians	W	L	Pct	ERA	G	CG	IP	H	BB	SO	ShO
1965	4	3	.571	3.43	17	1	60⅓	55	28	37	0
1966	13	10	.565	2.48	38	7	192	173	45	132	3
1967	14	13	.519	2.62	30	15	223	180	72	141	6
1968	8	15	.348	4.15	32	4	158⅓	139	81	78	2
1969	5	14	.263	5.70	32	1	143⅔	145	81	76	1
1970	11	3	.786	2.90	23	8	142⅔	101	53	72	1
1971	1	13	.071	6.19	37	1	113⅓	138	56	52	0
1972	0	3	.000	5.85	12	0	20	23	15	10	0
Career	87	107	.448	3.92	354	56	1,632	1,593	614	891	17

Mike Hargrove

Hargrove managed Kinston of the Class A Carolina League the following season, Williamsport of the Class AA Eastern League in 1988, and Colorado Springs of the Class AAA Pacific Coast League in 1989.

He won the Manager of the Year award at Kinston and Colorado Springs, and was named first base coach of the Indians for 1990. It was a position Hargrove held until July 6, 1991, when he replaced John McNamara as manager of the Indians.

Hargrove, Mike

Indians	G	AB	H	BA	RBI	R	2B	3B	HR	SA	SB
1979	100	338	110	.325	56	60	21	4	10	.500	2
1980	160	589	179	.304	85	86	22	2	11	.404	4
1981	94	322	102	.317	49	43	21	0	2	.401	5
1982	160	591	160	.271	65	67	26	1	4	.338	2
1983	134	469	134	.286	57	57	21	4	3	.367	0
1984	133	352	94	.267	44	44	14	2	2	.335	0
1985	107	284	81	.285	27	31	14	1	1	.352	1
Career	1,666	5,564	1,614	.290	686	783	266	28	80	.391	24

Harrah, Colbert Dale

Indians: 1979–83
Third baseman, shortstop, second baseman, designated hitter
Nickname: Toby

Birthplace: Sissonville, West Virginia
B: October 26, 1948
Bats right, throws right
Ht. 6–0; **Wt.** 175

Toby Harrah

Toby Harrah came to the Indians from Texas late in his career, in a deal for the popular Buddy Bell on December 8, 1978, and was a spark plug and on-field leader his five seasons in Cleveland.

When the trade was made, Harrah said, "Neither team needed a change, but we both [Harrah and Bell] needed a change."

Eleven of Harrah's 17 major league seasons were spent with losing-record teams. He played for the Washington Senators in 1969 and 1971 (before that franchise became the Texas Rangers in 1972), and then with Texas from 1972 to 1978, the Indians 1979–83, the New York Yankees in 1984, and the Rangers again in 1985 and 1986.

He led AL shortstops in putouts in 1974, tied for the lead in 1976, and also established the first of his two odd fielding records, accepting no chances at shortstop in a June 25, 1976, doubleheader, and playing 17 innings at third base without recording an assist on September 17, 1977.

Harrah hit a career-high 27 homers and led the AL with 109 walks in 1977, and he was a member of the American League All-Star team four times, in 1972, 1975, 1976, and 1982.

With the Indians, Harrah played 476 consecutive games until April 16, 1983, when he was hit by a pitch from Baltimore's Dennis Martinez and suffered a broken left hand that caused him to miss 24 games.

It was in June 1983 that Harrah had a disagreement with manager Mike Ferraro and publicly stated, "I don't like the manager and he doesn't like me [though] that doesn't mean I can't be a positive influence and do all I can to help the Indians win."

Six weeks later, on July 30, Ferraro was fired.

Harrah's best year with the Indians was 1982 when he hit

.304 (the only time he batted .300 in his career) with 25 homers and was cowinner with Andre Thornton of the Man of the Year award. He led AL third basemen in fielding in 1983.

The Indians traded Harrah and a minor leaguer to the Yankees on February 5, 1984, receiving pitcher George Frazier, outfielder Otis Nixon, and a minor league player in exchange. A year later Harrah was sent back to the Rangers, whom he served in 1985 and 1986.

When he retired in 1987, Harrah vowed, "I'll never quit this game; they'll have to tear the uniform off my back," and became a minor league coach for Texas.

Harrah rejoined the Rangers as a coach in 1989 and, on July 9, 1992, replaced Bobby Valentine as manager. They finished the season with a 32–44 record under Harrah, after which he returned to the Rangers' farm system as a batting instructor.

Harrah, Toby

Indians	G	AB	H	BA	RBI	R	2B	3B	HR	SA	SB
1979	149	527	147	.279	77	99	25	1	20	.444	20
1980	160	561	150	.267	72	100	22	4	11	.380	17
1981	103	361	105	.291	44	64	12	4	5	.388	12
1982	162	602	183	.304	78	100	29	4	25	.490	17
1983	138	526	140	.266	53	81	23	1	9	.365	16
Career	2,155	7,402	1,954	.264	918	1,115	307	40	195	.395	238

Harrelson, Kenneth Smith

Indians: 1969–71
Outfielder, first baseman
Nickname: Hawk
Birthplace: Woodruff, South Carolina

B: September 4, 1941
Bats right, throws right
Ht. 6–2; **Wt.** 190

His career with the Indians was brief and stormy—make that *very stormy*—but Ken Harrelson will long be remembered primarily for his unwillingness to play in Cleveland.

Acquired in an obvious attempt to bolster attendance, Harrelson refused to join the Indians until his $50,000 salary was doubled, which it finally was three days after the April 19, 1969, six-player trade that got him from Boston.

It turned out to be one of the Indians' worst-ever deals; they gave up pitchers Sonny Siebert and Vicente Romo and catcher Joe Azcue in exchange for Harrelson and pitchers Dick Ellsworth and Juan Pizarro.

Harrelson was a cult hero in Boston with his eccentric personality and dress—love beads, Nehru jackets, and Beatles hairstyle—and Fenway Park was picketed by his fans after he was traded to Cleveland.

Harrelson was the *Sporting News* Comeback Player of the Year and Player of the Year in 1968 when he hit 35 homers and led the American League with 109 RBIs with a career-high .275 average for the Red Sox.

When he finally—though still grudgingly—agreed to come to Cleveland, Harrelson made an entrance befitting a movie star.

Greeted by a throng of teenagers, Harrelson—nicknamed Hawk because of his large nose—led the kids through the airport like a pied piper to his waiting limousine.

He quickly got a television show called "The Hawk's Nest," and his apartment on Cleveland's fashionable "Gold Coast" resembled something out of *Playboy* magazine.

Ken Harrelson

Harrelson's professional baseball career started with the Athletics organization in 1959. He spent parts of the 1963 and 1964 seasons and all of 1965 in Kansas City, then was traded to Washington on June 23, 1966. But he and Senators manager Gil Hodges had what Harrelson called "an instant personality clash," and a year later he went back to the Athletics in a straight cash deal.

Harrelson's "champion" in Cleveland was Alvin Dark, then manager of the Indians. Dark had been manager of the Kansas City Athletics in 1967, and when he was fired, Harrelson called team owner Charles O. Finley "a menace to baseball." Finley promptly released Harrelson, who then was courted by seven teams.

He signed with the Red Sox on August 28 for a $73,000 bonus and helped them win the 1967 AL pennant. Harrelson hit three home runs in a game on June 14, 1968, and that year was named to the American League All-Star team.

After getting a $100,000 contract with the Indians in 1969, Harrelson was employed primarily as a right fielder, though his best position was first base. He hit 27 of his 30 homers and drove in 84 of his 92 runs for the Tribe, though he batted only .222 for the season.

But his presence with the Indians created a problem because they had Tony Horton, another former Red Sox player, whose natural position also was first base.

It became a moot point, however, as Harrelson suffered a badly broken right ankle in a spring training exhibition game on March 19, 1970, and was sidelined most of the season. He returned in September and played 17 games, but hit only one homer and drove in but one run.

On June 21, 1971, as the Indians made their first trip to Boston that season, Harrelson—still hampered by the injury he'd suffered, and batting only .199 in 52 games—announced his retirement.

An accomplished golfer, Harrelson went on the professional tour for a few years, then returned to baseball as a broadcaster for the Chicago White Sox, a job that led to his hiring as their general manager in 1986. But that position lasted only a year, and Harrelson returned to broadcasting. He is still behind a microphone for White Sox games.

Harrelson, Ken											
Indians	G	AB	H	BA	RBI	R	2B	3B	HR	SA	SB
1969	149	519	115	.222	84	83	13	4	27	.418	17
1970	17	39	11	.282	1	3	1	0	1	.385	0
1971	52	161	32	.199	14	20	2	0	5	.304	1
Career	900	2,941	703	.239	421	374	94	14	131	.414	53

Hassey, Ronald William

Indians: 1978–84
Catcher, first baseman
Birthplace: Tucson, Arizona

B: February 27, 1953
Bats left, throws right
Ht. 6–2; **Wt.** 200

It's unlikely that Ron Hassey will ever be elected to the Hall of Fame, but he has an unmatched claim to fame—having caught two of baseball's all-time best-pitched games, one for the Indians, the other for the Montreal Expos.

Hassey was behind the plate in Len Barker's perfect game against the Toronto Blue Jays, a 3–0 Tribe victory on May 15, 1981, and also was the catcher when Dennis Martinez, then

Ron Hassey

| Hassey, Ron | | | | | | | | | | | |
Indians	G	AB	H	BA	RBI	R	2B	3B	HR	SA	SB
1978	25	74	15	.203	9	5	0	0	2	.284	2
1979	75	223	64	.287	32	20	14	0	4	.404	1
1980	130	390	124	.318	65	43	18	4	8	.446	0
1981	61	190	44	.232	25	8	4	0	1	.268	0
1982	113	323	81	.251	34	33	18	0	5	.353	3
1983	117	341	92	.270	42	48	21	0	6	.384	2
1984	48	149	38	.255	19	11	5	1	0	.302	1
Career	1,192	3,440	914	.266	438	348	172	7	71	.382	14

Hayes, Frank Whitman

Indians: 1945–46   **B:** October 13, 1914
Catcher   **D:** June 22, 1955
Nickname: Blimp   **Batted right, threw right**
Birthplace: Jamesburg, New Jersey   **Ht.** 6–0; **Wt.** 185

Frankie Hayes played only 170 games for the Indians over parts of two seasons and is best remembered for a home run he hit against New York in Yankee Stadium on April 30, 1946.

A ninth-inning solo shot into the left-field stands, only the seventh hit allowed by Floyd Bevens, Hayes' home run gave

pitching for Montreal, retired all 27 batters he faced in beating Los Angeles, 2–0, on July 28, 1991.

Barker's was the 10th perfect game since 1900, and Martinez's was the 13th.

Hassey's father was a minor league outfielder from 1949 to 1952, and Ron was an All-American catcher for the 1976 NCAA champion University of Arizona baseball team.

The Indians selected Hassey in the 18th round of the 1976 amateur draft, and he signed with them after rejecting offers from Cincinnati, which picked him in 1972, and Kansas City in 1975, opting to play college baseball instead.

After brief trials with the Indians in 1978 and 1979, Hassey became their regular catcher in 1980 when he hit .318. But injuries to his knee and elbow in separate incidents sidelined him most of 1981, and he was often platooned the rest of his career.

The Tribe traded Hassey, with pitchers Rick Sutcliffe and George Frazier, to the Chicago Cubs for outfielders Joe Carter and Mel Hall and pitchers Don Schulze and Darryl Banks on June 13, 1984.

Thereafter, Hassey's career stops read like a Greyhound Bus schedule: he was traded to the New York Yankees on December 4, 1984, to the Chicago White Sox on December 12, 1985, back to the Yankees on February 13, 1986, and back again to the White Sox on July 30, 1986. He became a free agent on November 30, 1987, and signed with Oakland, then joined Montreal as a free agent on February 15, 1991, and retired at the end of that year.

After retiring as a player, Hassey scouted for several teams and joined the Colorado Rockies in 1993 as their third base coach.

Frank Hayes

Bob Feller a 1–0 victory in his second (of three) no-hitters. It was especially gratifying for Feller because he'd lost two of his first three starts and rumors circulated that he had lost his fastball.

Although Hayes was instrumental in helping Feller beat the Yankees in that no-hitter, three months later he spoiled Feller's bid for another one.

It happened after Hayes was sold to the Chicago White Sox on July 15. In the seventh inning of the first game of a doubleheader against the Indians in Chicago on August 8, Hayes blooped a single to left field for the only hit off Feller.

When Hayes was acquired by the Indians on May 29, 1945, from Philadelphia in a deal for catcher Buddy Rosar, he was in the midst of a then-record streak of catching 312 consecutive games. The streak started in the second game of a doubleheader on October 2, 1943, when Hayes was playing for the St. Louis Browns, and continued until April 24, 1946, when Sherman Lollar replaced him.

A power hitter who produced 119 homers in his 14-year major league career, Hayes tied a major league record by hitting four doubles in one game on July 25, 1936. He was a member of the AL All-Star team in 1940, 1941, 1944, and 1946.

Hayes, Frankie

Indians	G	AB	H	BA	RBI	R	2B	3B	HR	SA	SB
1945	119	385	91	.236	43	39	15	6	6	.353	1
1946	51	156	40	.256	18	11	12	0	3	.391	1
Career	1,364	4,493	1,164	.259	628	545	213	32	119	.400	30

Heath, John Geoffrey

Indians: 1936–45
Outfielder
Nickname: Jeff
Birthplace: Fort William, Ontario, Canada

B: April 1, 1915
D: December 9, 1975
Batted left, threw right
Ht. 5–11½; **Wt.** 200

When Oscar Vitt saw Jeff Heath in spring training 1938, the manager of the Indians called him "the best natural hitter I've seen since Joe Jackson."

Three years later, after Roger Peckinpaugh became manager of the Indians, he had even greater praise for the muscular outfielder.

"If every man on this ball club showed the determination and hustle that Jeff Heath has shown me, we'd be so far ahead you'd think we were in another league," said Peckinpaugh.

It turned out that both tributes were great exaggerations—though Heath went on to have a solid, 14-year major league career, with the Indians from 1936 until he was traded December 14, 1945, to Washington for outfielder George Case, and then to the St. Louis Browns and Boston Braves.

It was with the Braves in the final week of the 1948 season that Heath suffered a severely broken ankle sliding into the plate. Not only did it keep him out of the World Series against his former team, but the injury cut short his career as well.

Though Heath hit a career-high .343 with 21 home runs and drove in 112 runs in 1938, he was an even better all-around player in 1941 when he had 24 homers with 123 RBIs while batting .340.

Jeff Heath

It also was in 1941 that Heath became the first American Leaguer to hit 20 doubles, 20 triples, and 20 homers in one season, a feat duplicated only by George Brett in 1979.

He led the AL in triples in 1938 and 1941, was a member of the All-Star team in 1941 and 1943, and is still among the Tribe's top ten in triples, extra-base hits, and slugging percentage.

On May 25, 1941, Heath led off the fourth inning with a home run to right field off former teammate Johnny Allen of the St. Louis Browns. It was the first upper-deck homer at the Cleveland Stadium.

When Heath's average declined to .219 with 14 homers and 50 RBIs in 1940, he was accused of loafing and was given much of the blame for the Indians' losing the pennant by one game to Detroit.

He responded by threatening several of his critics. The threats caused owner Alva Bradley to warn the hot-tempered outfielder that he would see to it that Heath never played another game in organized baseball if he "touches one hair on anybody's head."

Later, Bradley said that "Jeff Heath's biggest enemy is Jeff Heath."

After suffering the broken ankle in 1948, Heath played in 36 games for the Braves in 1949, and retired after 57 games with Seattle of the Pacific Coast League in 1950.

Heath, Jeff

Indians	G	AB	H	BA	RBI	R	2B	3B	HR	SA	SB
1936	12	41	14	.341	8	6	3	3	1	.634	1
1937	20	61	14	.230	8	8	1	4	0	.377	0
1938	126	502	172	.343	112	104	31	18	21	.602	3
1939	121	431	126	.292	69	64	31	7	14	.494	8
1940	100	356	78	.219	50	55	16	3	14	.399	5
1941	151	585	199	.340	123	89	32	20	24	.586	18
1942	147	568	158	.278	76	82	37	13	10	.442	9
1943	118	424	116	.274	79	58	22	6	18	.481	5
1944	60	151	50	.331	33	20	5	2	5	.490	0
1945	102	370	113	.305	61	60	16	7	15	.508	3
Career	1,383	4,937	1,447	.293	887	777	279	102	194	.509	56

Hegan, James Edward

Indians: 1941–42, 1946–57
Catcher
Nickname: Shanty
Birthplace: Lynn, Massachusetts

B: August 3, 1920
D: June 17, 1984
Batted right, threw right
Ht. 6–2; **Wt.** 195

Though Jim Hegan never hit higher in the major leagues than .249—which he did in his first season as a regular in 1947—his value to the Indians was never lessened by his low average.

Hegan was an excellent catcher and handler of pitchers, as proven by the fact that, in Hegan's 17-year major league career, he caught 20-game winners Bob Feller, Bob Lemon, Early Wynn, Mike Garcia, Herb Score, and Gene Bearden, and no-hitters by Feller, Lemon, and Don Black.

As Hall of Famer Bill Dickey once said about the Tribe receiver, "When you can catch like Hegan, you don't have to hit."

Teammate Joe Tipton, also a catcher, said, "When hitters strike out against the Indians, they cuss out Hegan."

Jim Hegan

And Birdie Tebbetts, another former catcher who became a major league manager and a scout, said, "You start and end any discussion of catchers with Jim Hegan. Of all the things a catcher has to do—catch, throw, call a game—Hegan was the best I ever saw."

Despite his lifetime .228 average, Hegan was a member of the American League All-Star team in 1947 and from 1949 to 1952, and though he hit 14 homers in 1948 and in 1950, and 11 in 1954, one of his "near homers" often is best remembered by old-timers.

It happened in the eighth inning of the opener of the 1954 World Series in the Polo Grounds in New York, a few minutes after Willie Mays had made a remarkable catch to deprive Vic Wertz of what would have been a home run in Cleveland.

The score was tied, 2–2, and the next three Indians reached, loading the bases with two out. That brought up Hegan, who hit a long fly to left field. It, too, would have been a homer—a *grand slam*—if the game had been played at the Stadium.

Instead, Monte Irvin backed against the fence and caught the ball, ending the inning. The Indians lost, 5–2, when the Giants scored three runs in the 10th on Dusty Rhodes' pinch-hit homer.

But who knows what might have happened in that Series—which the Giants swept from the Indians—if Hegan's long fly had been a game-winning homer?

His Cleveland career ended on February 18, 1958, when he was traded to Detroit with pitcher Hank Aguirre for pitcher Hal Woodeshick and catcher J. W. Porter. Hegan was with the Tigers and Philadelphia Phillies in 1958, the Phillies and Giants in 1959, and the Chicago Cubs for 24 games in 1960.

Hegan, whose son Mike was a major league first baseman for 12 seasons, was a coach with the New York Yankees from 1960 to 1973, the Tigers from 1974 to 1978, and the Yankees again in 1979 and 1980.

Hegan, Jim

Indians	G	AB	H	BA	RBI	R	2B	3B	HR	SA	SB
1941	16	47	15	.319	5	4	2	0	1	.426	0
1942	68	170	33	.194	11	10	5	0	0	.224	1
1946	88	271	64	.236	17	29	11	5	0	.314	1
1947	135	378	94	.249	42	38	14	5	4	.344	3
1948	144	472	117	.248	61	60	21	6	14	.407	6
1949	152	468	105	.224	55	54	19	5	8	.338	1
1950	131	415	91	.219	58	53	16	5	14	.383	1
1951	133	416	99	.238	43	60	17	5	6	.346	0
1952	112	333	75	.225	41	39	17	2	4	.324	0
1953	112	299	65	.217	37	37	10	1	9	.348	1
1954	139	423	99	.234	40	56	12	7	11	.374	0
1955	116	304	67	.220	40	30	5	2	9	.339	0
1956	122	315	70	.222	34	42	15	2	6	.340	1
1957	58	148	32	.216	15	14	7	0	4	.345	0
Career	1,666	4,772	1,087	.228	525	550	187	46	92	.344	15

Held, Woodson George

Indians: 1958–64
Shortstop, third baseman,
   second baseman,
   outfielder
Nickname: Woodie

Birthplace: Sacramento,
California
B: March 25, 1932
Bats right, throws right
Ht. 5–10½; **Wt.** 167

An outfielder in the New York Yankees farm system at the onset of his professional career and with the Kansas City Athletics in 1958, Woodie Held was switched to shortstop by Indians manager Joe Gordon over the objection of general manager Frank Lane.

"Go ahead and play Held at short, if you want . . . if he makes good, you'll get the credit, but if he doesn't, it's your neck," Lane told Gordon when the experiment began.

Held, who possessed a very strong arm and quick hands, succeeded at his new position and provided the Indians with great power from a surprise source. He hammered 29 homers his first full season in Cleveland, after being acquired on June 15, 1958, in a trade that included a player who gained great prominence three years later.

To get Held and first baseman Vic Power from Kansas City, the Indians gave up Roger Maris, who in 1961 broke Babe Ruth's single-season home run record with 61. The Athletics also got pitcher Tick Tomanek and first baseman Preston Ward in the deal.

Though easygoing off the field, Held was notorious for tantrums after striking out, which he did often—944 times in 4,019 official at bats, approximately once every 4.25 plate appearances.

Once, in a 1959 game in Baltimore, Held struck out and angrily threw his helmet in the dugout. It bounced off a wall and struck Gordon on the leg. Gordon chastised Held. When

Held responded by cursing the manager, Gordon fined him $200 and later demanded a public apology.

Held hit a career high .267 in 1961. The previous season he had batted .258 after missing the first 45 games because of an operation to remove a malignant tumor on his back.

The Indians traded Held on December 1, 1964, to Washington with first baseman Bob Chance for outfielder Chuck Hinton. A year later Held was dealt to Baltimore, in 1967 to California, and in 1968 to the Chicago White Sox, and he ended his playing career the following season.

Held, Woodie

Indians	G	AB	H	BA	RBI	R	2B	3B	HR	SA	SB
1958	67	144	28	.194	17	12	4	1	3	.299	1
1959	143	525	132	.251	71	82	19	3	29	.465	1
1960	109	376	97	.258	67	45	15	1	21	.471	0
1961	146	509	136	.267	78	67	23	5	23	.468	0
1962	139	466	116	.249	58	55	12	2	19	.406	5
1963	133	416	103	.248	61	61	19	4	17	.435	2
1964	118	364	86	.236	49	50	13	0	18	.420	1
Career	1,390	4,019	963	.240	559	524	150	22	179	.421	14

Woodie Held

Hemsley, Ralston Burdett

Indians: 1938–41
Catcher
Nickname: Rollie
Birthplace: Syracuse, Ohio

B: June 24, 1907
D: July 31, 1972
Batted right, threw right
Ht. 5–10; **Wt.** 170

He was called Rollicking Rollie, a nickname that was all too appropriate until Rollie Hemsley joined Alcoholics Anonymous.

It was during spring training of 1939 that Indians manager Oscar Vitt sent Hemsley home for being drunk. He returned to play that season, hitting .263 in 107 games, and in 1940 Hemsley met with sportswriters covering the Indians.

He told them, "It has been a year now since the most wonderful thing in the world happened to me, so I feel safe in telling you boys about it.

"I didn't have a drink all last season. Alcoholics Anonymous did that for me. I'd like to give credit to this great organization, and you'll do me a favor by writing a story about AA."

A few weeks later, on April 16 at Comiskey Park in Chicago, Hemsley drove in the only run with a triple in Bob Feller's opening-day no-hitter against the White Sox.

From then on Hemsley was Feller's personal catcher until he was sold to Cincinnati on December 4, 1941.

Though the suspicion was never corroborated, Hemsley was thought by many to be the ringleader in the Indians' 1940 "Crybaby rebellion" against manager Oscar Vitt.

To get Hemsley on February 10, 1938, the Indians traded three players—catcher Billy Sullivan, second baseman Roy Hughes, and pitcher Ed Cole—to the St. Louis Browns. He previously had played for Pittsburgh, the Chicago Cubs, and Cincinnati, and later with the Reds again and the New York Yankees, winding up his career in 1947 with the Philadelphia Phillies. He was a member of the American League All-Star team five times, in 1935, 1936, 1939, 1940, and 1944.

After his playing career was ended, Hemsley was a minor league manager through 1952, coached for the Philadelphia Athletics and Washington, and also scouted for several clubs.

Rollie Hemsley

George Hendrick

Hemsley, Rollie

Indians	G	AB	H	BA	RBI	R	2B	3B	HR	SA	SB
1938	66	203	60	.296	28	27	11	3	2	.409	1
1939	107	395	104	.263	36	58	17	4	2	.342	2
1940	119	416	111	.267	42	46	20	5	4	.368	1
1941	98	288	69	.240	24	29	10	5	2	.330	2
Career	1,593	5,047	1,321	.262	555	562	257	72	31	.360	29

Hendrick, George Andrew

Indians: 1973–76
Outfielder
Nickname: Silent George
Birthplace: Los Angeles

B: October 18, 1949
Bats right, throws right
Ht. 6–3; **Wt.** 195

He was called Silent George, and never was a ballplayer's nickname more appropriate.

But George Hendrick's bat seldom was silent—or even quiet—during his 18-year major league career, including four seasons (1973–76) with the Indians, after he was acquired March 24, 1973, with catcher Dave Duncan from the Athletics in a trade for catcher Ray Fosse and shortstop Jack Heidemann.

Interestingly, three of those four players had been number-one selections in previous amateur drafts—Hendrick by Oakland in 1968 and Fosse and Heidemann by the Indians in 1965 and 1967, respectively.

While refusing to be interviewed by the media from the time he joined the Athletics as a rookie in 1971 through the rest of his career, which continued with San Diego, St. Louis, Pittsburgh, and California, until his retirement at the end of the 1988 season, Hendrick always was popular with his teammates.

He also hit for power and average, and could run, catch, and throw with the best of them. With the Indians, Hendrick averaged 22 homers and 74 RBIs a season. He hit three home runs in a game against Detroit at the Stadium on June 19, 1973.

Hendrick's aloofness often caused problems between him and manager Ken Aspromonte in 1973 and 1974, but he served as the Indians' cocaptain (with shortstop Frank Duffy) under manager Frank Robinson in 1975.

The Tribe traded Hendrick to the Padres on December 8, 1976, for outfielder Johnny Grubb, catcher Fred Kendall, and shortstop Hector Torres. He was a member of the American League All-Star team in 1974 and 1975, and he also was a National League All-Star in 1980 and 1983.

After he retired, Hendrick returned to Cleveland for an old-timers' game and explained his reluctance to be interviewed, saying that "a big part of the problem was that I was very young and didn't know how to handle the attention and all that stuff."

Hendrick, George

Indians	G	AB	H	BA	RBI	R	2B	3B	HR	SA	SB
1973	113	440	118	.268	61	64	18	0	21	.452	7
1974	139	495	138	.279	67	65	23	1	19	.444	6
1975	145	561	145	.258	86	82	21	2	24	.431	6
1976	149	551	146	.265	81	72	20	3	25	.448	4
Career	2,048	7,129	1,980	.278	1,111	941	343	27	267	.446	59

Hess, Otto C.

Indians: 1902, 1904–08
Pitcher, outfielder
Birthplace: Berne, Switzerland
B: November 13, 1878

D: February 24, 1926
Batted left, threw left
Ht. 6–1; **Wt.** 170

Otto Hess was one of the best pitchers in baseball in 1906 when Cleveland's team, then called the Naps, finished third in the American League, only five games behind the pennant-winning Chicago White Sox.

Hess pitched briefly for the Cleveland franchise in 1902, after serving with the U.S. Army in the Philippines, but was sent back to the minor leagues in 1903. The Naps brought Hess back to the AL in 1904, and two years later he reached his peak, posting a 1.83 earned run average while winning 20 and losing 17 games.

Though he was said to be nearly unhittable at times, Hess also had a reputation for being erratic from one inning to the next, and 1906 was his only good season on the mound for the Naps.

During his six seasons in Cleveland, Hess also played 50 games as an outfielder, including 27 in 1905 when he batted .254, going 44-for-173 with two homers.

Hess was sent back to the minors after pitching only four games in 1908, and didn't return to the major leagues until 1912 with the Boston Braves, for whom he went 12–17. His record fell to 7–17 in 1913, to 5–6 in 1914, and to 0–1 in four games in 1915, his final season in the major leagues.

Hess, Otto

Indians	W	L	Pct	ERA	G	CG	IP	H	BB	SO	ShO
1902	2	4	.333	5.98	7	4	43⅔	67	23	13	0
1904	8	7	.533	1.67	21	15	151⅓	134	31	64	4
1905	10	15	.400	3.16	26	22	213⅔	179	72	109	4
1906	20	17	.541	1.83	43	33	333⅔	274	85	167	7
1907	6	6	.500	2.89	17	7	93⅓	84	37	36	0
1908	0	0	—	5.14	4	0	7	11	1	2	0
Career	70	90	.438	2.98	198	129	1,418	1,355	448	580	18

Heving, Joseph William

Indians: 1937–38, 1941–44
Pitcher
Birthplace: Covington, Kentucky
B: September 2, 1900

D: April 11, 1970
Batted right, threw right
Ht. 6–1; **Wt.** 185

One of the first relief specialists in professional baseball, Joe Heving appeared in 430 games during his 13-year major league career, 390 of them out of the bull pen. He pitched for the New York Giants, Chicago White Sox, Boston Red Sox, and Boston Braves, in addition to two tours of duty in Cleveland.

The Indians purchased Heving after he'd spent 1935 and 1936 in the minor leagues, sold him to the Red Sox in August 1938, and bought him back on February 3, 1941.

"In those days," Heving said in 1970, a few months before his death, "relievers were guys who weren't good enough to start. Nobody liked being a reliever, but I did. I just wish the times would've been different and I would've been appreciated more."

Who could blame Heving? He didn't get to the major leagues until 1930, with the Giants, when he was 30.

Though he pitched three games in the minor leagues in 1923, he was primarily an outfielder that season and in 1924 and 1925. He did both—pitch and play outfield—in 1926, and the following year took the mound full-time.

A year after joining the Indians, Heving was demoted to Milwaukee of the American Association in May 1938 following a clubhouse altercation with Earl Averill, then the Indians' center fielder and one of their best hitters.

According to a published account at the time: "Heving grumbled something about high-salaried stars who take third strikes with their bats on their shoulders. Averill's reply was a well-placed right hand punch to Heving's mouth. The next day manager Oscar Vitt, never a great admirer of Heving, sent the relief pitcher to the minors."

Three months later he was sold to the Red Sox, who employed Heving the rest of the 1938 season as a starter, going 8–1 with seven complete games in 16 appearances. It was the only time Heving started regularly in the major leagues, and the following year he was back in the bull pen.

The brother of catcher Johnnie Heving, who was in and out of the major leagues with three teams off and on from 1920 to 1932, Joe Heving led the American League with a then record 63 appearances in 1944 when he posted a career-best 1.96 earned run average. That was Heving's last season with the Indians (when he also was the only grandfather playing major league baseball).

Heving also was a league leader three times (though not for the Indians) in relief victories, and he led twice in relief losses.

Heving, Joe

Indians	W	L	Pct	ERA	G	CG	IP	H	BB	SO	ShO
1937	8	4	.667	4.83	40	0	72⅔	92	30	35	0
1938	1	1	.500	9.00	3	0	6	10	5	0	0
1941	5	2	.714	2.29	27	2	70⅔	63	31	18	1
1942	5	3	.625	4.86	27	0	46⅓	52	25	13	0
1943	1	1	.500	2.75	30	0	72	58	34	34	0
1944	8	3	.727	1.96	63	0	119⅔	106	41	46	0
Career	76	48	.613	3.90	430	17	1,038⅔	1,136	380	429	3

Hickman, Charles Taylor

Indians: 1902–04, 1908
First baseman, second baseman, outfielder
Nickname: Piano Legs
Birthplace: Taylortown, Pennsylvania

B: March 4, 1876
D: April 19, 1934
Batted right, threw right
Ht. 5–11½; **Wt.** 215

One of major league baseball's first sluggers, Piano Legs Hickman—so nicknamed because of his massively proportioned legs—also was one of the early jumpers to the American League after playing five seasons (1897–1901) for Boston and New York in the National League.

Hickman initially joined the Boston Pilgrims in the AL in 1902, but after only 28 games was released and signed by the Cleveland franchise, then called the Bronchos.

In the sixth inning of the first game of a doubleheader in St. Louis on June 30, 1902, Hickman, along with Napoleon Lajoie and Bill Bradley, became the first trio to hit consecutive home runs in the modern era of baseball.

Also that year Hickman went on to hit .361, second highest in the AL, and nearly won the Triple Crown. He also led the league with 193 hits, was second in RBIs with 110, and was tied for second in home runs with 11.

While Hickman had 12 homers and 97 RBIs in 1903, his batting average dropped to .295 and, after 86 games in 1904, Hickman was traded on August 7 to Detroit for first baseman Charlie Carr and catcher Fritz Buelow.

After the Tigers sold him to Washington, and then the Senators sold him to the Chicago White Sox in 1907, the Indians reacquired Hickman in a cash purchase in November 1907.

By then Hickman's piano legs were tired, and he retired after batting .234 in 65 games for Cleveland in 1908.

Hickman, Charlie

Indians	G	AB	H	BA	RBI	R	2B	3B	HR	SA	SB
1902	102	426	161	.378	94	61	31	11	8	.559	8
1903	131	522	154	.295	97	64	31	11	12	.466	14
1904	86	337	97	.288	45	34	22	10	4	.448	9
1908	65	197	46	.234	16	16	6	1	2	.305	2
Career	1,081	3,982	1,176	.295	614	478	217	92	59	.440	72

Hildebrand, Oral Clyde

Indians: 1931–36
Pitcher
Birthplace: Indianapolis, Indiana
B: April 7, 1907

D: September 8, 1977
Batted right, threw right
Ht. 6–3; **Wt.** 175

Oral Hildebrand was in the first group of Indians players—Earl Averill and Wes Ferrell were the others—selected to the American League All-Star team, though he did not make an appearance in that inaugural game played July 6, 1933, at Comiskey Park in Chicago.

An outstanding college basketball player at Butler University prior to becoming a pitcher in professional baseball, Hildebrand broke in with the Indians late in 1931.

Hildebrand reached his peak in 1933 when his record was 16–11 and he led AL pitchers in shutouts with six. That season in a game at the Stadium on April 26, Hildebrand pitched a one-hitter to beat the St. Louis Browns, 2–0. Art Scharein's single in the third inning was the Browns' only hit.

He never again won more than 11 games and was traded by the Tribe on January 17, 1937, along with outfielder Joe Vosmik and second baseman Bill Knickerbocker to the St. Louis Browns for pitcher Ivy Andrews, shortstop Lyn Lary, and outfielder Moose Solters. It was then one of baseball's biggest deals.

Hildebrand was traded to the New York Yankees prior to the 1939 season and helped them win the pennant with a 10–4 record, but he was finished after 13 games (with a 1–1 record) in 1941.

Hildebrand, Oral

Indians	W	L	Pct	ERA	G	CG	IP	H	BB	SO	ShO
1931	2	1	.667	4.39	5	2	26⅔	25	13	6	0
1932	8	6	.571	3.69	27	7	129⅓	124	62	49	0
1933	16	11	.593	3.76	36	15	220⅓	205	88	90	6
1934	11	9	.550	4.50	33	10	198	225	99	72	1
1935	9	8	.529	3.94	34	8	171⅓	171	63	49	0
1936	10	11	.476	4.90	36	9	174⅔	197	83	65	0
Career	83	78	.516	4.35	258	80	1,430	1,490	623	527	9

Hinton, Charles Edward

Indians: 1965–67, 1969–71
Outfielder, second baseman, first baseman, third baseman, catcher
Nickname: Chuck

Birthplace: Rocky Mount, North Carolina
B: May 3, 1934
Bats right, throws right
Ht. 6–1; **Wt.** 180

It could be said that Chuck Hinton was so coveted by the Indians they traded for him twice—and gave up two established players and one of their best prospects to get him in the two separate deals.

First, after Hinton had established himself with the Washington Senators as a dependable hitter who was versatile enough to play any position except pitcher, the Indians on December 1, 1964, acquired him for shortstop Woodie Held and rookie first baseman Bob Chance.

Then, after Hinton played three years in Cleveland, the Tribe sent him on November 29, 1967, to the California Angels for center fielder Jose Cardenal.

Oral Hildebrand

Chuck Hinton

One season later the Indians decided they wanted Hinton back and, to retrieve him, dealt outfielder Lou Johnson to the Angels on April 4, 1969.

Signed originally by Baltimore in 1956, Hinton won two minor league batting championships—he hit .358 in the Class C Northern League in 1959 and .369 in the Class C California League the following year—but never got a trial with the Orioles.

He was claimed by Washington in the expansion draft in December 1960 and was one of their best players the next three seasons, hitting .310 in 1962 and being named to the American League All-Star team in 1964.

With the Indians, Hinton played primarily in the outfield and was also employed at first, second, and third bases.

After returning to Cleveland, Hinton hit a career-high .318 in 1970 when he played five positions—including four games as the Indians' catcher—but he was released after batting .224 in 88 games in 1971.

Since retiring from professional baseball, Hinton has coached baseball at Howard University in Washington, D.C.

Hinton, Chuck

Indians	G	AB	H	BA	RBI	R	2B	3B	HR	SA	SB
1965	133	431	110	.255	54	59	17	6	18	.448	17
1966	123	348	89	.256	50	46	9	3	12	.402	10
1967	147	498	122	.245	37	55	19	3	10	.355	6
1969	94	121	31	.256	19	18	3	2	3	.388	2
1970	107	195	62	.318	29	24	4	0	9	.477	0
1971	88	147	33	.224	14	13	7	0	5	.374	0
Career	1,353	3,968	1,048	.264	443	518	152	47	113	.412	130

Hockett, Oris Leon

Indians: 1941–44
Outfielder
Birthplace: Amboy, Indiana
B: September 29, 1909

D: March 23, 1969
Batted left, threw right
Ht. 5–9; **Wt.** 182

Oris Hockett was one of the best of the wartime players, enjoying three respectable seasons with the Indians from 1942 to 1944, but he didn't last long once the servicemen returned to baseball.

After growing up in Norwalk, Ohio, Hockett hitchhiked to Norfolk, Nebraska, where he enrolled at Nebraska State College, intending to earn a degree that would lead to a career in medicine.

While a student at Nebraska State, Hockett signed—under the assumed name of "Jim Brown"—to play for the Norfolk team in the Class D Nebraska State League in 1932. Thus began an off-and-on minor league career as Brown (nee Hockett), quit and went home a couple of times before the Brooklyn Dodgers bought his contract and gave him a chance with them in 1938.

That season, despite batting .329 in 21 games for the Dodgers, Hockett was returned to the minors. He got another opportunity with the Dodgers in 1939, but this time played only nine games (hitting .231) and again was demoted.

Hockett wound up at Nashville of the Class A Southern Association where he hit .363 in 1940 and .359 in 1941, and his contract was purchased by the Tribe.

He played two games for the Indians in September 1941

and was a sensation the following spring training, becoming their regular right fielder as a 33-year-old rookie—though he claimed at the time to be only 29.

Hockett quit again in mid-June of 1943 and went home to Dayton, but returned a couple of days later because, as he said, his wife "wanted me to play baseball instead of being a machinist."

His best year with the Indians was 1944 when he hit .289 and was named to the American League All-Star team.

A line-drive hitter who did not have much power, Hockett was traded on December 12, 1944, to the Chicago White Sox for outfielder-pitcher Ed Carnett.

Though Hockett batted .293 in 106 games for the White Sox in 1945, it was his final season in the major leagues. Carnett, who hit .219 in 30 games for the Indians, also was gone when 1946 rolled around.

Hockett, Oris

Indians	G	AB	H	BA	RBI	R	2B	3B	HR	SA	SB
1941	2	6	2	.333	1	0	0	0	0	.333	0
1942	148	601	150	.250	48	85	22	7	7	.344	12
1943	141	601	166	.276	51	70	33	4	2	.354	13
1944	124	457	132	.289	50	47	29	5	1	.381	8
Career	551	2,165	598	.276	214	259	112	21	13	.365	43

Hodapp, Urban John

Indians: 1925–32
Second baseman,
  third baseman, first baseman
Nickname: Johnny
Birthplace: Cincinnati, Ohio

B: September 26, 1905
D: June 14, 1980
Batted right, threw right
Ht. 6–0; **Wt.** 185

Until he suffered a knee injury in 1931, Johnny Hodapp was one of the American League's best third basemen and then second basemen for four consecutive seasons when he batted over .300 from 1927 to 1930.

He was the Indians' third baseman (and also saw some action at first base) in 1927 and 1928, and he played second the next two years. In 1930, Hodapp led the league with 225 hits and 51 doubles, while driving in 121 runs, scoring 111, and batting .354. He also topped AL second baseman with 403 putouts in 1930.

Hodapp's knee injury kept him out of 32 games in 1931 and also affected both his range in the field and his offense. Though he still batted .295, his RBI production dropped to 56.

It led to his being traded on April 24, 1932, with outfielder Bob Seeds to the Chicago White Sox for better-fielding second baseman Bill Cissell and pitcher Jim Moore. The White Sox sent him to the Boston Red Sox as part of a six-player deal on December 15, 1932, and though he batted .312 in 115 games for Boston in 1933, that was his final season in the major leagues.

After his retirement, Hodapp talked about how close the Indians came to winning the pennant in 1926 when he was sidelined most of the season with an injury.

Hodapp had been purchased by the Indians on August 1, 1925, from Indianapolis of the American Association for $50,000 and three players. On April 5, 1926, with the Tribe in New Orleans for a spring training game, Hodapp stepped on a ball during batting and fielding practice and broke his

Johnny Hodapp

Horton, Anthony Darrin

Indians: 1967–1970
First baseman
Birthplace: Santa Monica, California

B: December 6, 1944
Bats right, throws right
Ht. 6–3; **Wt.** 210

Tony Horton was the principal in one of the Indians' greatest tragedies, though what happened to him could have been much worse.

Considered to have a future as one of baseball's great power hitters, Horton suffered a nervous breakdown on August 28, 1970, during a doubleheader in Cleveland against the California Angels. He was hospitalized after attempting suicide and never played again.

Acquired by the Indians from the Boston Red Sox on June 4, 1967, with outfielder Don Demeter for pitcher Gary Bell, Horton was an intense competitor and had difficulty coping with failure.

While Horton was in the process of smashing 27 homers and leading the Indians with 93 RBIs in 1969, they traded on April 19 for Ken Harrelson, who was basically a first baseman, though he played some in the outfield. Harrelson was one of manager Alvin Dark's favorite players.

During the winter of 1969–70, with Dark then negotiating all Tribe player contracts as well as managing the team on the field, Horton held out for $5,000 more than the $45,000 he was offered. The holdout continued into the first three weeks of spring training.

Dark's negotiating strategy was that, if Horton continued his holdout, the Indians would have Harrelson play first base.

Horton finally capitulated and reported to training camp in Tucson, Arizona, on March 18. The very next day Harrelson suffered a broken leg in an exhibition game against Oakland. Harrelson's injury-absence would have provided Horton the leverage he needed to get the raise he had been seeking.

Even before Harrelson was hurt, Horton was determined to prove that he deserved the raise he'd sought. Horton also was eager to disprove the manager's negative comments about his defensive ability.

And because of the holdout and things Dark had said

ankle in two places. As a result, he played only three games that season, on July 5, August 7, and September 7.

The Tribe finished second by three games to New York in 1926, and Hodapp said, "I'll always feel that a rainstorm beat us out of the championship.

"On the last western swing that fall the Yankees were only a game or two ahead of us when they came to Cleveland. George Uhle was our starting pitcher. He could always handle the Yankees, especially Babe Ruth.

"We got off to a 4–1 lead when a thundershower hit suddenly. Play was suspended for about 45 minutes, and during the delay, Uhle must have cooled off. He lost his stuff, and New York eventually won the game, 6–4.

"I'll always feel that if we had won that one it could have been different," said Hodapp.

Hodapp, Johnny

Indians	G	AB	H	BA	RBI	R	2B	3B	HR	SA	SB
1925	37	130	31	.238	14	12	5	1	0	.292	2
1926	3	5	1	.200	0	0	0	0	0	.200	0
1927	79	240	73	.304	40	25	15	3	5	.454	2
1928	116	449	145	.323	73	51	31	6	2	.432	2
1929	90	294	96	.327	51	30	12	7	4	.456	3
1930	154	635	225	.354	121	111	51	8	9	.502	6
1931	122	468	138	.295	56	71	19	4	2	.365	1
1932	7	16	2	.125	0	2	1	0	0	.188	0
Career	791	2,826	880	.311	429	378	169	34	28	.425	18

Tony Horton

about Horton, he often was booed by the fans, especially early in the season when he started slowly.

"I don't think I ever knew a more intense player than Tony," said Gabe Paul, then the president of the Indians. "He was so determined to prove that Dark was wrong, he drove himself to a breakdown."

Mike Paul, a teammate and close friend of Horton, said, "Tony even did eye exercises, something I never saw another player do, to help him see better and hit better."

Another teammate, third baseman Rich Rollins, said of Horton, "He never smiled. I mean never, not even after hitting a home run. And I don't think he ever relaxed, not even *after* he played a good game."

Though Horton had a great game on May 24, 1970, when he smashed three home runs in the nightcap of a doubleheader against New York, the pressure—and his intense determination to excel—became too much for Horton to handle.

After popping out and grounding out in the first and third innings of the second game of the August 28 doubleheader against the Angels, Horton cracked.

Horton went into the clubhouse when Dark sent Chuck Hinton in to pinch-hit for him in the bottom of the fifth, and the troubled—but tremendously talented—first baseman never played another game.

After being hospitalized for a brief period in Cleveland, Horton returned to his home in Santa Monica, California, and eventually went to work for a bank.

Three years after his breakdown, Horton said in a telephone interview, "I never think about playing baseball again. I started my life over and baseball is not part of it."

But until he was forced to give up the game, Horton was something special.

When Ted Williams, then a batting instructor for the Red Sox, first saw Horton in spring training in 1963, he said, "The kid is a natural. He has everything. Leave him alone. Don't fool with a swing like that."

Horton had been signed by the Red Sox for a $125,000 bonus in 1963 after he'd been a baseball star at University High in Los Angeles, where he also was a prep school All-America basketball player. He was granted an athletic scholarship to UCLA, but after a year chose to play professional baseball.

He got brief trials with the Red Sox in 1964, 1965, and 1966, then started the 1967 season as their first baseman before being traded to the Indians.

Horton, Tony

Indians	G	AB	H	BA	RBI	R	2B	3B	HR	SA	SB
1967	106	363	102	.281	44	35	13	4	10	.421	3
1968	133	477	119	.249	59	57	29	3	14	.411	3
1969	159	625	174	.278	93	77	25	4	27	.461	3
1970	115	413	111	.269	59	48	19	3	17	.453	3
Career	636	2,228	597	.268	297	251	102	15	76	.430	12

Houtteman, Arthur Joseph

Indians: 1953–57
Pitcher
Birthplace: Detroit, Michigan

B: August 7, 1927
Bats right, throws right
Ht. 6–2; **Wt.** 188

Art Houtteman overcame several major obstacles that threatened to end his major league pitching career prematurely, including a fractured skull in 1949, an entire year

(1951) away from baseball when he served in the army, and the tragic death of his infant daughter in an automobile accident during spring training in 1952.

Signed to his first professional contract off the Detroit sandlots by the Tigers in 1945, he made his first major league appearance that year at the age of 17, pitching in 13 games and compiling an 0–2 record.

He went 15–10 for the Tigers in 1949 and, after coming back from the fractured skull, had his biggest season, winning 19 games and losing 12 in 1950, and being named to the American League All-Star team.

It also was in 1950 that Houtteman led AL pitchers in shutouts with four. One of them was a one-hitter on August 19, a 6–0 victory over the St. Louis Browns. Jim Delsing singled in the second inning for the only hit.

On April 26, 1952, in Houtteman's third start after his return from army duty, he won his first game, a 13–0, one-hitter against the Indians. This time it was Harry Simpson who singled with two out in the ninth inning to ruin Houtteman's bid for a no-hitter.

But that was one of only eight victories Houtteman recorded in 1952, while losing 20, and when he lost six of his first eight decisions in 1953, the Tigers included him in an eight-player trade with the Indians on June 15. The Tribe also received pitcher Bill Wight, catcher Joe Ginsberg, and utility infielder Owen Friend for pitchers Steve Gromek, Al Aber, and Dick Weik and shortstop Ray Boone.

Houtteman went on to win seven and lose seven for the

Art Houtteman

Indians, and in 1954 he was their fifth starter as they won an American League–record 111 games and the pennant. Houtteman's record that year was 15–7 with a 3.35 earned run average.

But the next two seasons Houtteman won only 12 games while losing eight, and his earned run average was a bloated 6.56 in 1956. He complained that his troubles were caused by his not pitching regularly.

After three unimpressive appearances in 1957—and several confrontations with manager Kerby Farrell—Houtteman was sold on May 20 to Baltimore and retired at the end of the season.

Houtteman, Art

Indians	W	L	Pct	ERA	G	CG	IP	H	BB	SO	ShO
1953	7	7	.500	3.80	22	6	109	113	25	40	1
1954	15	7	.682	3.35	32	11	188	198	59	68	1
1955	10	6	.625	3.98	35	3	124⅓	126	44	53	1
1956	2	2	.500	6.56	22	0	46⅔	60	31	19	0
1957	0	0	—	6.75	3	0	4	6	3	3	0
Career	87	91	.489	4.14	325	78	1,555	1,646	516	639	14

Howser, Richard Dalton

Indians: 1963–66
Shortstop, second baseman
Birthplace: Miami, Florida
B: May 14, 1936

D: June 17, 1987
Batted right, threw right
Ht. 5–8; **Wt.** 155

The Indians never realized what a big man they had in little Dick Howser until it was too late.

They had a desperate need for a shortstop in 1963 when heralded rookie Tony Martinez failed to hit consistently, and on May 25 they acquired Howser from the Kansas City Athletics for catcher Doc Edwards and $75,000. Catcher Joe Azcue also came to Cleveland in the deal.

Howser had been the American League Rookie of the Year and was named to the All-Star team in 1961 when he hit .280, stole 37 bases, and scored 108 runs. He also led AL shortstops in putouts (299) and errors (38) that year.

However, shortly after his arrival in Cleveland, Howser suffered a severe hamstring injury and played only 49 games, hitting .247. He was the Tribe's regular shortstop in 1964, but was hurt again in 1965 and sidelined for 55 games.

He was replaced by Larry Brown, and, as it turned out, Howser never got his starting job back. He played some at both shortstop and second base in 1966, and that winter was traded on December 20 to the New York Yankees for minor league pitcher Gil Downs and cash.

It was Howser's latent leadership ability that the Indians could have utilized if he'd been given the chance to demonstrate it, as he was with the Yankees and Kansas City Royals.

After retiring as a player after the 1968 season, Howser served as a coach for the Yankees for the next 10 years, then coached the Florida State University baseball team in 1979.

Howser returned to manage the Yankees in 1980 and led them to the AL East championship with a 103–59 record, their best in 17 years. However, after the Yanks lost to Kansas City in the playoffs that year, New York owner George Steinbrenner wanted to fire third base coach Mike Ferraro, one of Howser's closest friends.

But Howser would have none of it. When Steinbrenner in-

Dick Howser

sisted, Howser resigned out of respect for Ferraro. But Howser didn't stay out of baseball long. In August 1981 he was hired to manage Kansas City, and it was under him that the Royals won the AL West in 1984 and the pennant and World Series in 1985.

It was a job Howser held until mid-1986, when he was diagnosed as having a brain tumor and was forced to retire. He underwent four operations and treatment, all the while vowing to return as the Royals manager in 1987—which he did.

But three days into spring training Howser had to retire, and he died three months later.

Howser, Dick

Indians	G	AB	H	BA	RBI	R	2B	3B	HR	SA	SB
1963	49	162	40	.247	10	25	5	0	1	.296	9
1964	162	637	163	.256	52	101	23	4	3	.319	20
1965	107	307	72	.235	6	47	8	2	1	.283	17
1966	67	140	32	.229	4	18	9	1	2	.350	2
Career	789	2,483	617	.248	165	398	90	17	16	.318	105

Hudlin, George Willis

Indians: 1926–40
Pitcher
Nickname: Ace
Birthplace: Wagoner, Oklahoma

B: May 23, 1906
Bats right, throws right
Ht. 6–0; **Wt.** 190

For 15 seasons between 1926 and 1940, Willis Hudlin was one of the Indians' most consistent pitchers, though he usually was overshadowed by others on the staff, in particular Mel Harder and Wesley Ferrell, and later Johnny Allen and Bob Feller.

Hudlin never was a 20-game winner, but went 18–12 in 1927, his first full season with the Tribe, and from 1927 to 1929 he registered 11 victories against the New York Yankees. Hudlin won in double figures nine times in his 16-year major league career, in which he also saw service with the Washington Senators, St. Louis Browns, and New York Giants.

On June 23, 1931, Hudlin beat the Boston Red Sox, 10–0, with a one-hitter in the second game of a doubleheader. Earl Webb's single in the second inning was Boston's only hit.

Hudlin is the seventh-winningest pitcher in Indians history, and ranks among team leaders in three other categories—most games, 475, third behind Harder and Feller; most innings, 2,558, fourth behind Feller, Harder, and Bob Lemon; and most losses, 151, third behind Harder and Feller.

It was off Hudlin that Babe Ruth socked his 500th career home run on August 11, 1929, a memory that remained vivid in the mind of the pitcher.

"I can still see the ball flying over that damned right field fence at League Park," he said in an interview 65 years after the fact. "My best pitch was a sinker and that's what the Babe hit, though I guess that sinker didn't sink the way it was supposed to sink."

It appeared that Hudlin's career was over in 1936 when he suffered most of the season with bone chips in his elbow and won only one game—and that one the day before the season ended—while losing five. He posted a 9.00 earned run average in 27 games.

"Everybody thought I was through that year, yet I think that's when I really learned how to pitch," Hudlin said later. "I found out I could no longer get by on just my fastball.

"Before that time I'd laugh at the fellows who were trying to learn how to throw a curve. That was sissy stuff to me. But I discovered in 1936 that there's nothing like a good hook when the fastball refuses to travel as it once did.

"So I asked Mel Harder to help me out. Mel worked with me for a while and I knew then that I'd be useful for years to come because my curveball not only broke, it dropped. There's no pitch like that downer, especially in a tough spot, and here I had it without even trying to master it."

Hudlin also credited catcher Rollie Hemsley for much of his success.

"Rollie catches me without using signs," he said. "That means that if I see a batter set himself for a fastball after I've started my windup, I whip my wrist and give him a curve. Rollie never is taken by surprise. He's always ready for anything."

After Hudlin won two and lost one of his first four starts in 1940, he was released by the Indians. He departed a few weeks before a contingent of players called on owner Alva Bradley demanding that manager Oscar Vitt be fired.

"I was gone by the time [the rebellion] happened, but I have to say I understood how the players felt," said Hudlin. "Unlike all my other managers in Cleveland, Vitt was not an easy man to play for. He had trouble everywhere, with everybody. He ripped players to cover up his own mistakes."

After being released by the Indians early in 1940 with a 2–1 record, Hudlin pitched for three other teams that season—the Senators, Giants, and Browns—compiling a combined record of 3–5 in 19 games.

Though he was let go by the Browns at the end of the season, Hudlin went back to the minor leagues as player-manager for Little Rock in the Class A1 Southern Association in 1941 and 1942, winning the pennant in the latter season.

Hudlin served as a flight instructor in the air force during World War II, and upon his discharge in late 1944 attempted a comeback with the Browns. But it didn't last long, only one game, a loss, and when the season ended, so did his major league pitching career.

He went back to the minor leagues again, serving as player-manager of Little Rock in 1945 and 1946, and Jackson of the Class B Southeastern League in 1947 and 1948, after which he retired as a pitcher. He continued to manage Jackson in 1949 and 1950, returned to manage Little Rock in 1952, and piloted Greenville of the Class C Cotton States League in 1954 and 1955.

Hudlin scouted for Detroit in 1956, was the Tigers' pitching coach from 1957 to 1959, and scouted for the New York Yankees from 1960 to 1974.

Hudlin, Willis

Indians	W	L	Pct	ERA	G	CG	IP	H	BB	SO	ShO
1926	1	3	.250	2.78	8	1	32⅓	25	13	6	0
1927	18	12	.600	4.01	43	18	264⅔	291	83	65	1
1928	14	14	.500	4.04	42	10	220⅓	231	90	62	0
1929	17	15	.531	3.34	40	22	280⅓	299	73	60	2
1930	13	16	.448	4.57	37	13	216⅔	255	76	60	1
1931	15	14	.517	4.60	44	15	254⅓	313	88	83	1
1932	12	8	.600	4.71	33	12	181⅓	204	59	65	0
1933	5	13	.278	3.97	34	6	147⅓	161	61	44	0
1934	15	10	.600	4.75	36	15	195	210	65	58	1
1935	15	11	.577	3.69	36	14	231⅓	252	61	45	3
1936	1	5	.167	9.00	27	1	64	112	31	20	0
1937	12	11	.522	4.10	35	10	175⅔	213	43	31	2
1938	8	8	.500	4.89	29	8	127	158	45	27	0
1939	9	10	.474	4.91	27	7	143	175	42	28	0
1940	2	1	.667	4.94	4	2	23⅔	31	2	8	0
Career	158	156	.503	4.41	491	155	2,613⅓	3,011	846	677	11

Jackson, Joseph Jefferson

Indians: 1910–15
Outfielder
Nickname: Shoeless Joe
Birthplace: Pickens County, South Carolina

B: July 16, 1889
D: December 5, 1951
Batted left, threw right
Ht. 6–1; **Wt.** 200

How different the story of *Eight Men Out*—a book by Eliot Asinof and a movie by John Sayles about the Black Sox Scandal of 1919—might have been if Shoeless Joe Jackson had remained in Cleveland and not been traded to the Chicago White Sox.

Probably the best of the eight players barred from baseball by Commissioner Kenesaw M. Landis, Jackson most certainly would be among the Indians who are now members of the Hall of Fame.

Jackson, who hit .408 for the Cleveland Naps in 1911 but finished second to Ty Cobb's .420, was traded to the White Sox on August 21, 1915, for pitcher Ed Klepfer, outfielders Bobby Roth and Larry Chappell, and an estimated $25,000.

It was a deal motivated in part by the failing financial status of Cleveland owner Charles W. Somers.

It was with the White Sox that Jackson and seven team-

"Shoeless Joe" Jackson

mates allegedly conspired to fix the outcome of the 1919 World Series against Cincinnati.

Though they were tried and acquitted in a Chicago court in the winter of 1920–21, Landis suspended all eight of them for life to "preserve the integrity of baseball."

Jackson was remarkably gifted in his ability to play baseball—but also was remarkably lacking in intellect and bereft of education, good judgment, and character.

He began in professional baseball in 1908 with the Greenville Spinners of the Class D Carolina Association and led the league in batting with a .346 average. Early that year Connie Mack signed Jackson and called him up to the Philadelphia Athletics for five games in September.

The following season Mack sent Jackson to Savannah of the Class C South Atlantic League, and once again he won the batting championship with a .358 mark that earned him another five games with the Athletics in September.

In 1910, Mack returned Jackson to the minor leagues, this time to New Orleans of the Class A Southern Association where, for the third consecutive year, he won a batting title, hitting .354.

It was said that Jackson's teammates turned him "sullen and ineffective" with their insensitive taunting of his illiteracy.

The Naps had expressed an interest in acquiring Jackson in spring training and, when they learned in midseason that Mack had made the hard-hitting outfielder available, they wasted no time going after him.

Finally, on July 30, 1910, it was announced that the Naps had purchased Jackson for a reported $6,000 and that he would report to Cleveland as soon as the Southern Association pennant race was decided.

After his first full year with the Naps, Jackson was being compared to Ty Cobb, Napoleon Lajoie, and Tris Speaker as the greatest hitters of that time. It even has been said that Babe Ruth patterned his batting stance after Jackson, who hit for power (though it was the era of the dead ball) as well as for average.

He also was a skillful defensive player with a powerful and accurate arm, and he was a smart base runner, stealing 41 bases in 1911.

Though Jackson was barred from baseball and is ineligible for the Hall of Fame, he holds four Cleveland franchise records: highest batting average, lifetime, .375; highest batting average, season, .408 (1911); most base hits, season, 233 (1911); and most triples, season, 26 (1912).

Jackson also is credited for having led the American League in hits in 1912 and 1913, doubles in 1913, and triples in 1912 (tied with Sam Crawford), 1916, and 1920. He also tied an American League record by hitting three triples in one game on June 30, 1912 (the second game of a doubleheader).

The nickname "Shoeless Joe" was hung on Jackson by a fan in Anderson, South Carolina, in 1908. Carter (Scoop) Latimer, veteran sports editor of the *Greenville News* (of South Carolina) once related the story as follows:

"Joe was called in from the outfield to pitch a game, and the shoe on his foot rubbed a blister on his heel. The next day the Greenville Spinners played in Anderson [in the Class D Carolina Association] and Joe was back in the outfield with a sore foot.

"Came his time at bat with a chance to win the game and he slipped off his shoe and went to the plate. He slammed a home run and as he rounded third, a bleacherite yelled, 'You shoeless so-and-so!'

"As a cub reporter, freelancing for a Greenville paper, I picked it up and tagged him 'Shoeless Joe,' and the nickname stuck."

Jackson, Joe

Indians	G	AB	H	BA	RBI	R	2B	3B	HR	SA	SB
1910	20	75	29	.387	11	15	2	5	1	.587	4
1911	147	571	233	.408	83	126	45	19	7	.590	41
1912	154	572	226	.395	90	121	44	26	3	.579	35
1913	148	528	197	.373	71	109	39	17	7	.551	26
1914	122	453	153	.338	53	61	22	13	3	.464	22
1915	83	303	99	.327	45	42	16	9	3	.469	10
Career	1,332	4,981	1,772	.356	785	873	307	168	54	.517	202

Jacoby, Brook Wallace

Indians: 1984–91, 1992
Third baseman, first baseman
Birthplace: Philadelphia, Pennsylvania

B: November 23, 1959
Bats right, throws right
Ht. 5–11; **Wt.** 175

Brook Jacoby couldn't get a break in five seasons as a member of the Atlanta Braves' organization, but he certainly did with the Indians. He was one of three players to be named after the Tribe traded pitcher Len Barker to the Braves on August 28, 1983.

Jacoby was assigned to the Indians on October 21, 1983, completing the deal in which they also received outfielder Brett Butler and pitcher Rick Behenna.

A seventh-round selection of the Braves in the amateur draft of 1979, Jacoby got a brief opportunity with Atlanta in 1981 when he played 11 games in September and batted .200. But with Bob Horner solidly entrenched at third base, Jacoby didn't get another chance with the Braves until 1983, when he played in four games, going 0-for-8.

It was a different story in Cleveland, however, as Jacoby es-

Brook Jacoby

| Jacoby, Brook | | | | | | | | | | | |
Indians	G	AB	H	BA	RBI	R	2B	3B	HR	SA	SB
1984	126	439	116	.264	40	64	19	3	7	.369	3
1985	161	606	166	.274	87	72	26	3	20	.426	2
1986	158	583	168	.288	80	83	30	4	17	.441	2
1987	155	540	162	.300	69	73	26	4	32	.541	2
1988	152	552	133	.241	49	59	25	0	9	.335	2
1989	147	519	141	.272	64	49	26	5	13	.416	2
1990	155	553	162	.293	75	77	24	4	14	.427	1
1991	66	231	54	.234	24	14	9	1	4	.333	0
1992	120	291	76	.261	36	30	7	0	4	.326	0
Career	1,311	4,520	1,220	.270	545	535	204	24	120	.405	16

Jamieson, Charles Devine

Indians: 1919–32   **D:** October 27, 1969
Outfielder   **Batted left, threw left**
Birthplace: Paterson, New Jersey   **Ht.** 5–8½; **Wt.** 165
B: February 7, 1893

When Charlie Jamieson was handed his unconditional release by the Indians on December 30, 1932, the story was written by Gordon Cobbledick in the *Cleveland Plain Dealer*:

"They come and they go in baseball, a racket wherein there's no place for either the aged or the incompetent, and you can't be mourning long for any of them.

"But still, without allowing yourself to grow too sentimental about it, you find yourself wishing old Jamie could have stuck around for another 14 years. He's that kind of a guy and that kind of ballplayer."

What kind of a ballplayer? Jamieson was called "the most popular player" in Tribe history, before Bob Feller, Lou Boudreau, and Rocky Colavito came along.

It also was said by many that Jamieson is the best player not in the Hall of Fame.

And, based on the statistics he compiled from 1915 to 1932—especially 1919–32 when he played in Cleveland—there's reason to believe he was *better* than many nonpitchers in the Hall of Fame.

At least Jamieson's lifetime batting average of .303 is higher than 44 Hall of Famers, and he played 1,779 games, more than 36 of the certified "immortals."

Jamieson started as a pitcher and, though he was switched to the outfield early in his career, he still made 13 appearances on the mound during his major league career.

Though he didn't hit with much power, Jamieson earned a reputation for being a sharp-eyed leadoff batter. He was one of the Indians' leaders in 1920 when they won their first pennant and the World Series, and he scored 130 runs in 1923, when he led the American League with 222 hits.

Jamieson batted .300 or better 10 times, including a career best .359 in 1924, and also was an excellent defensive player.

He is the only outfielder in major league history to start two triple plays in a season, and he did it in a period of just over two weeks in 1928—May 23 in the ninth inning of a 4–3, 10-inning loss to the White Sox in Chicago, and June 9 in the second inning of 7–3 loss to New York at League Park.

The acquisition of Jamieson represents one of the Indians' best deals. He came from the Philadelphia Athletics with third baseman Larry Gardner and minor league pitcher Elmer Myers on March 1, 1919, in exchange for outfielder Bobby Roth.

tablished himself as a solid major league hitter and third baseman, making the deal one of the best in Indians history—and one of the worst by the Braves.

He was named to the All-Star team in 1986 and 1990 and batted an even .300 with 32 homers in 1987, when he won the Man of the Year award. On July 3, 1987, Jacoby became the 16th Indians player to hit three home runs in one game, in a 14–9 loss to Chicago at the Stadium.

It was manager Pat Corrales who said of Jacoby in 1987: "There is no one on this club who is more respected for his work habits and the example he sets for others. What you will see is Brook Jacoby at the ballpark early and often working. What you won't see is a sulking, face-to-the-locker bad apple if he happened to have a bad game."

Confronted with the possibility of losing Jacoby to free agency, the Indians traded him on July 26, 1991, to Oakland for two minor leaguers, pitcher Apolinar Garcia and outfielder Lee Tinsley.

When the season ended and Jacoby became a free agent, he re-signed with the Indians on January 27, 1992. He batted .261, but his home run production fell off to four and he was released.

Jacoby played briefly in Japan in 1993, but retired before the season ended and is now coaching baseball at Ventura College in California.

Jamieson's major league career began in 1915 with the Washington Senators, who sold him to Philadelphia in mid-season 1917.

Jamieson loved the game and vowed during the prime of his career, "I'm going to play ball as long as they'll let me—major, minor, semipro, and sandlot."

In his testimony to Jamieson, Cobbledick also wrote: "He fell short of the stature of Napoleon Lajoie and Tris Speaker, but he has been accurately called the most popular ballplayer in Cleveland history. An incident in 1929 may explain why.

"It was 'Jamieson Day' at League Park, and fans had subscribed to a purse of $3,200 as a gift to their favorite.

"The Indians were playing the Athletics, and Lefty Grove was pitching. Jamie had made two hits and batted in one important run, but he came up in the ninth with the winning runs on base and bounced out to the third baseman.

"A few minutes later Indians owner Alva Bradley met the veteran at the door of the clubhouse. Jamie was nearly in tears. 'Mr. Bradley,' Jamieson said, 'I like money as well as the next guy, but I'd have given that whole $3,200 for one more hit off that big monkey [Grove].'"

Jamieson, Charlie

Indians	G	AB	H	BA	RBI	R	2B	3B	HR	SA	SB
1919	26	17	6	.353	2	3	2	1	0	.588	2
1920	108	370	118	.319	40	69	17	7	1	.411	2
1921	140	536	166	.310	46	94	33	10	1	.414	8
1922	145	567	183	.323	57	87	29	11	3	.429	15
1923	152	644	222	.345	51	130	36	12	2	.447	18
1924	143	594	213	.359	54	98	34	8	3	.458	21
1925	138	557	165	.296	42	109	24	5	4	.379	14
1926	143	555	166	.299	45	89	33	7	2	.395	9
1927	127	489	151	.309	36	73	23	6	0	.380	7
1928	112	433	133	.307	37	63	18	4	1	.374	3
1929	102	364	106	.291	26	56	22	1	0	.357	2
1930	103	366	110	.301	52	64	22	1	1	.374	5
1931	28	43	13	.302	4	7	2	1	0	.395	1
1932	16	16	1	.063	0	0	1	0	0	.125	0
Career	1,779	6,560	1,990	.303	552	1,062	322	80	18	.385	131

Johnston, Wheeler Roger

Indians: 1912–14, 1918–21
First baseman
Nickname: Doc
Birthplace: Cleveland, Tennessee
B: September 9, 1887
D: February 17, 1961
Batted left, threw left
Ht. 6–0; **Wt.** 170

D oc Johnston's primary claim to fame during his two tours of duty with the Indians was that he socked nine consecutive hits over a four-game series in 1919, the only time he batted over .300 (.305) in an 11-year major league career.

He did it with singles in the sixth and seventh innings against the White Sox in Chicago on June 1; three singles in the second, fourth, and fifth innings and a double in the eighth against the St. Louis Browns at League Park on June 2; singles in the fifth and eighth innings (after sacrificing in the second and third) in the opener of a doubleheader against the Browns; and a single in the fourth inning (after sacrificing in the second) of the nightcap on June 3. Johnston's streak was stopped in the sixth when he fouled to the catcher.

He was one of the Indians' leaders in 1920 when the Indians won the American League pennant, and in the World

Series he outhit his younger brother Jimmy, who then played for the Brooklyn Dodgers.

But it was Jimmy Johnston who wound up with the better career, playing 13 seasons with a .294 lifetime average compared to Doc's .263 with Cincinnati, Pittsburgh, and the Philadelphia Athletics, in addition to the Indians.

Johnston, Doc

Indians	G	AB	H	BA	RBI	R	2B	3B	HR	SA	SB
1912	43	164	46	.280	11	22	7	4	1	.390	8
1913	133	530	135	.255	39	74	19	12	2	.347	19
1914	103	340	83	.244	23	43	15	1	0	.294	14
1918	74	273	62	.227	25	30	12	2	0	.286	12
1919	102	331	101	.305	33	42	17	3	1	.384	21
1920	147	535	156	.292	71	68	24	10	2	.385	13
1921	118	384	114	.297	46	53	20	7	2	.401	2
Career	1,055	3,774	992	.263	381	478	154	68	14	.351	139

Jones, Douglas Reid

Indians: 1986–91
Pitcher
Birthplace: Covina, California
B: June 24, 1957
Bats right, throws right
Ht. 6–3; **Wt.** 195

D oug Jones went from limbo—he was all but finished in professional baseball after eight unimpressive seasons in the minor leagues—to become a major league rookie at age 30, and one of the best relief pitchers in the game three years later.

After being a third-round selection of Milwaukee in the 1978 amateur draft, Jones languished in the Brewers farm system as a starting pitcher from 1978 to 1984.

Jones was recovering from a sore shoulder in 1985 when

Doug Jones

the Indians signed him as a minor league free agent with their Waterbury club in the Class AA Eastern League, and it was then that he became a relief pitcher exclusively.

It was to be Jones' last chance, and he made the most of it, going 9–4 with seven saves in 39 games for Waterbury, earning a promotion to Maine of the Class AAA International League in 1986.

With a pitch that was a combination of a screwball and a change-up that he perfected at Waterbury, Jones made 43 relief appearances at Maine. Though his record was only 5–6 with nine saves, his 2.09 earned run average convinced the Indians to take another, longer look.

The following spring, as a nonroster invitee, Jones continued his progress and soon became the Indians' ace reliever. He saved a then club-record 37 victories in 1988, setting a major league record of 15 in a row, got 32 more in 1989, and broke his own mark with 43 in 1990 for a three-year total of 112.

He earned the Indians' Man of the Year award for both 1988 and 1990, as well as a place on the American League All-Star team three years in a row, 1988–90.

Jones slumped in 1991 and was demoted to Colorado Springs of the Class AAA Pacific Coast League in late July. He was recalled in September and was impressive as a starter in four games, but when the season ended, the Indians allowed Jones to become a free agent.

Their decision proved to be premature.

Jones signed with Houston and battled out of limbo again, posting 36 saves and an 11–8 record with a 1.85 earned run average in 80 games in 1992, and he was named to the National League All-Star team. In 71 games in 1993, Jones saved 26 victories, though his won-lost record fell to 4–10 and his ERA rose to 4.54, and he was traded to Philadelphia.

But Jones rebounded again with the Phillies, before the 1994 season was aborted on August 12 by the labor impasse between the players and management. Jones was credited with 27 saves, a 2–4 record, and 2.17 ERA while appearing in 47 of the Phillies' 115 games before the strike. He signed with Baltimore as a free agent in 1995.

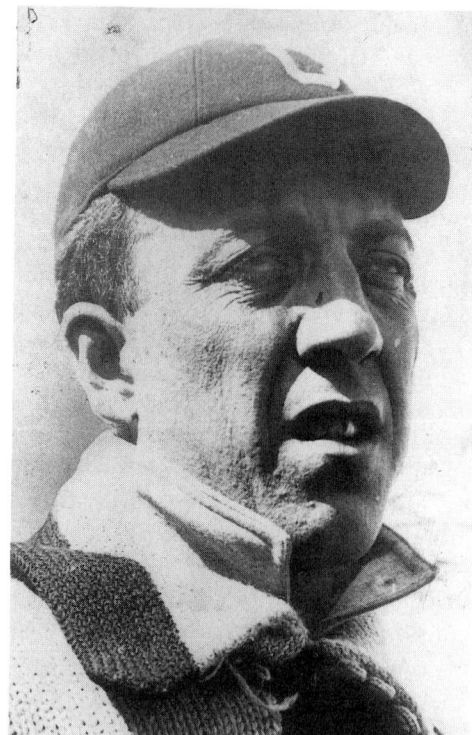

Addie Joss

Jones, Doug

Indians	W	L	Pct	ERA	G	CG	IP	H	BB	SO	ShO
1986	1	0	1.000	2.50	11	0	18	18	6	12	0
1987	6	5	.545	3.15	49	0	91⅓	101	24	87	0
1988	3	4	.429	2.27	51	0	83⅓	69	16	72	0
1989	7	10	.412	2.34	59	0	80⅔	76	13	65	0
1990	5	5	.500	2.56	66	0	84⅓	66	22	55	0
1991	4	8	.333	5.54	36	0	63⅓	87	17	48	0
Career	43	58	.426	3.12	526	0	721⅓	730	159	579	0

Joss, Adrian

Indians (Bronchos, Naps): 1902–10	**B:** April 12, 1880
Pitcher	**D:** April 14, 1911
Nickname: Addie	**Batted right, threw right**
Birthplace: Woodland, Wisconsin	**Ht. 6–3; Wt. 185**

Had he not died at the relatively young age of 31, after only nine seasons in the major leagues, Addie Joss might have gone on to become baseball's greatest pitcher.

As it was, Joss's record—which includes one of baseball's 13 perfect games in the modern era—established him as *one* of the all-time best, and certainly places him alongside Bob Feller, Mel Harder, Bob Lemon, Stan Coveleski, and Early Wynn as the most successful pitchers in the history of the Indians.

Joss won 160 games while losing 97 in a major league career that began with the Cleveland club (then called the Bronchos) in 1902, and was cut short when he died on April 14, 1911, of tubercular meningitis.

Not only was Joss considered an excellent pitcher, but he also was one of the best-liked players in baseball.

Cleveland's 1911 season opener was postponed so that players and fans could attend funeral services for Joss, and later that season American League players formed an all-star team to play the Naps for the benefit of his widow.

Though he did not play 10 seasons in the major leagues, as required for election to the Hall of Fame, the Veterans Committee waived the rule for Joss, and he was inducted in 1978.

There is little doubt that Joss belongs among baseball's immortals; he was a 20-game winner four consecutive seasons (1905–08), pitched 45 shutouts, tied for the league lead with 27 victories in 1907, five times recorded earned run averages of 1.83 or less, including a league-leading 1.59 in 1904 and 1.16 (eighth-lowest in history) in 1908, had a career 1.89 ERA that ranks second all-time, and, remarkably, completed 234 of his 260 starts.

In addition to the perfect game Joss pitched against Chicago on October 2, 1908, he also hurled a no-hitter against the White Sox on April 20, 1910, and five one-hitters, including one against the St. Louis Browns in his major league debut in 1902.

Joss's perfect game, won by the Naps, 1–0, and played at League Park, has been called one of baseball's all-time greatest by historians.

The Naps and White Sox were both fighting for the pennant, though they killed each other off in that final series and

Detroit won, beating Cleveland by four percentage points and Chicago by 1½ games.

Joss's opponent was Ed Walsh, who struck out 15 and allowed only four hits, one of them a bloop single by Joe Birmingham that resulted in the game's only run in the third inning. Birmingham stole second, went to third on an error, and scored on a wild pitch by Walsh, who later became an AL umpire.

The White Sox never came close to getting a hit off Joss, though the perfect game was in doubt until the last moment. With two out in the ninth John Anderson batted for Walsh and, with two strikes on him, topped a grounder to third baseman Bill Bradley.

Bradley grabbed the ball and fired it to first base. His throw was in the dirt, but George Stovall scooped it up, and umpire Silk O'Laughlin called Anderson out. (Walsh went on to win 40 games that season, with 15 losses.)

Though Joss suffered arm trouble and pitched only 13 games in 1910, when his record fell to 5–5, he pitched well the following spring training.

About two weeks before the season was to start, Joss became ill and fainted on the bench while the Naps were playing an exhibition game in Chattanooga, Tennessee.

Upon rejoining the team a few days later Joss apologized to his teammates for having "pulled a baby trick," but soon took sick again and returned to his home in Toledo, Ohio. His illness was diagnosed as tubercular meningitis, and within a week he was dead.

Joss had an overwhelming fastball that, opposing batters said, "came out of his hip pocket," and also had an exceptional curve.

He pitched for the University of Wisconsin prior to joining the Toledo, Ohio, team in the Inter-State League in 1900. The following season Joss won 25 games for Toledo, then in the Western Association, leading to his purchase by the Naps.

Willie Kamm

Joss, Addie

Indians	W	L	Pct	ERA	G	CG	IP	H	BB	SO	ShO
1902	17	13	.567	2.77	32	28	269⅓	225	75	106	5
1903	18	13	.581	2.19	32	31	283¾	232	37	120	3
1904	14	10	.583	1.59	25	20	192⅓	160	30	83	5
1905	20	12	.625	2.01	33	31	286	246	46	132	3
1906	21	9	.700	1.72	34	28	282	220	43	106	9
1907	27	11	.711	1.83	42	34	338¾	279	54	127	6
1908	24	11	.686	1.16	42	29	325	232	30	130	9
1909	14	13	.519	1.71	33	24	242⅔	198	31	67	4
1910	5	5	.500	2.26	13	9	107⅓	96	18	49	1
Career	160	97	.623	1.89	286	234	2,327	1,888	364	920	45

Kamm, William Edward

Indians: 1931–35
Third baseman
Nickname: Willie
Birthplace: San Francisco, California

B: February 2, 1900
D: December 21, 1988
Batted right, threw right
Ht. 5–10½; **Wt.** 170

Though his best years were behind him when he arrived in Cleveland, Willie Kamm quickly became a favorite of the fans—though obviously not with manager Walter Johnson in 1935.

Acquired from the Chicago White Sox on May 17, 1931,

in a trade for first baseman–second baseman Lew Fonseca, Kamm was an excellent fielder and consistent hitter who had a reputation for being extremely reserved, even shy.

That's what makes Kamm's problems with Johnson difficult to understand.

When the Indians were in Philadelphia early in the 1935 season, the manager told the media that he had discovered an "anti-Johnson" faction on the team and said that the two ringleaders were Kamm and catcher Glenn Myatt.

Taking action that he said was "for the good of the team," Johnson released Myatt and sent Kamm back to Cleveland under indefinite suspension.

Kamm went to Commissioner Kenesaw M. Landis and demanded a chance to clear his name. Landis held a hearing but ruled that he could do nothing about what he said was a personality clash between Kamm and Johnson.

Indians owner Alva Bradley also declined to take action in the matter other than to appoint the still-suspended Kamm a scout.

On August 4, 1935, with the Indians floundering in fifth place with a 46–48 record, Bradley fired Johnson, replacing him with Steve O'Neill—but did nothing to change the status of Kamm, who didn't play another game in the major leagues. He managed San Francisco in the Class AAA Pacific Coast League in 1936 and 1937.

Kamm had played for San Francisco when he was purchased by the White Sox in 1922 for $100,000—then the highest price ever paid for a minor leaguer player.

He hit .292 as a rookie in 1923 and a career-best .308 with 84 RBIs in 1928. Kamm led American League third baseman in fielding in eight of his 13 seasons, including 1932–34 with the Indians.

Kamm, Willie

Indians	G	AB	H	BA	RBI	R	2B	3B	HR	SA	SB
1931	114	410	121	.295	66	68	31	4	0	.390	13
1932	148	524	150	.286	83	76	34	9	3	.403	6
1933	133	447	126	.282	47	59	17	2	1	.336	6
1934	121	386	104	.269	42	52	23	3	0	.345	7
1935	6	18	6	.333	1	2	0	0	0	.333	0
Career	1,693	5,851	1,643	.281	826	802	348	85	29	.384	126

Keltner, Kenneth Frederick

Indians: 1937–44, 1946–49
Third baseman
Birthplace: Milwaukee, Wisconsin
B: October 31, 1916

D: December 12, 1991
Batted right, threw right
Ht. 6–0; **Wt.** 190

Ken Keltner always considered the highlight of his career to be the Indians' 8–3 victory over the Boston Red Sox in the 1948 playoff for the American League pennant—and with justifiable pride.

In the fourth inning of that pressureful game in Fenway Park, Keltner blasted a three-run homer that broke a 1–1 tie. He also singled and doubled in the playoff game. It got the Indians off and running into the World Series, which they also won in six games from the Boston Braves.

There was another game that Keltner well remembered—as do others, especially Joe DiMaggio.

It was played between the Indians and New York on July 17, 1941, in the Cleveland Stadium in front of a then record night-game crowd of 67,468 fans. The Yankees won, 4–3.

Keltner, considered to have been the best third baseman in Cleveland baseball history, made two sensational back-

Ken Keltner

handed plays on DiMaggio as the Indians ended the Yankee Clipper's consecutive-game hitting streak at 56.

Keltner fielded both behind the bag and retired DiMaggio with laser-beam throws to first base, the first in the first inning, the second in the seventh.

"I wasn't thinking about [DiMaggio's] streak when I made those plays," Keltner said. "All I was concerned about was winning the game because we still had a chance [in the pennant race]."

At the age of 19 in 1936, Keltner started in professional baseball with a bang for Fieldale of the Class D Bi-State League, smashing 33 homers, driving in 116 runs, and batting .360.

In 1937, Keltner continued to pound the ball for the Milwaukee Brewers of the Class AA American Association, connecting for 27 homers, 96 runs batted in, and a .310 average.

It was on August 28, 1937, that the Indians purchased Keltner for $25,000 and three players to be turned over to Milwaukee outright and three more to be optioned to the Brewers.

As a rookie in 1938, Keltner hit 26 homers and drove in 113 runs; in 1939 he hit a career-high .325; and in 1948 he had career highs with 31 homers and 119 RBIs. On May 25, 1939, he hit three home runs in a game at Fenway Park in Boston. He also led American League third basemen in fielding in 1939, 1941, and 1942, and was named to the AL All-Star team seven times (1940–44, 1946, and 1948).

Keltner enlisted in the navy on March 20, 1945, and served through March 15, 1946.

The Indians released Keltner on April 12, 1950, and he was signed by the Red Sox two days later. However, after playing only 13 games for Boston, he was released on June 6, ending his major league career.

Keltner, Ken

Indians	G	AB	H	BA	RBI	R	2B	3B	HR	SA	SB
1937	1	1	0	.000	1	0	0	0	0	.000	0
1938	149	576	159	.276	113	86	31	9	26	.497	4
1939	154	587	191	.325	97	84	35	11	13	.489	6
1940	149	543	138	.254	77	67	24	10	15	.418	10
1941	149	581	156	.269	84	83	31	13	23	.485	2
1942	152	624	179	.287	78	72	34	4	6	.383	4
1943	110	427	111	.260	39	47	31	3	4	.375	2
1944	149	573	169	.295	91	74	41	9	13	.466	4
1946	116	398	96	.241	45	47	17	1	13	.387	0
1947	151	541	139	.257	76	49	29	3	11	.383	5
1948	153	558	166	.297	119	91	24	4	31	.522	2
1949	80	246	57	.232	30	35	9	2	8	.382	0
Career	1,526	5,683	1,570	.276	852	737	308	69	163	.441	39

Kennedy, Robert Daniel

Indians: 1948–54
Outfielder
Birthplace: Chicago

B: August 18, 1920
Bats right, throws right
Ht. 6–2; **Wt.** 193

Bob Kennedy was renowned for having one of the strongest throwing arms in baseball, and he played a key role in helping the Indians win their second American League pennant and world championship in 1948.

That was the season Kennedy was acquired on June 2 from the Chicago White Sox for pitcher Al Gettel and outfielder Pat Seerey. He hit .301 in 66 games for the Tribe in 1948 when he often was inserted as a late-inning defensive replacement.

Bob Kennedy

Kern, James Lester

Indians: 1974–78, 1986	**B:** March 15, 1949
Pitcher	**Bats right, throws right**
Nicknames: Jim, Emu	**Ht.** 6–5; **Wt.** 185
Birthplace: Gladwin, Michigan	

Jim Kern had an overpowering fastball and a reputation for eccentricity, both of which served him well as a relief pitcher, though it was his performances as a starter that got him to the major leagues.

Signed as an undrafted amateur in 1967, Kern progressed through the Indians' farm system and was the winningest pitcher in the Class AAA American Association in 1974. He posted a 17–7 record and 2.52 earned run average in 25 games, all as a starter, earning a September 1 promotion to Cleveland.

Kern went back to Oklahoma City in 1975 and, though he struggled, was recalled by the Tribe in May and given a trial as a reliever. He made good and started only four games the rest of his career, which ended in 1986 after he'd returned to the Tribe.

In between, Kern pitched for Texas, the New York Mets, Cincinnati, Chicago White Sox, Philadelphia Phillies, and Milwaukee Brewers.

It was with the Indians from 1976 to 1978 and Texas in 1979 that Kern enjoyed his greatest success. In those four seasons, during which he averaged 8.6 strikeouts per nine innings, he won 41 games, saved 75, and was a member of the American League All-Star team in 1977 and 1979.

Nicknamed Emu because teammates thought he resembled an ostrichlike bird, Kern was traded with shortstop Larvell Blanks to the Rangers on October 3, 1978, for pitcher Len Barker and outfielder Bobby Bonds.

Kennedy had started his major league career with the White Sox in 1939 as a third baseman, but was switched to the outfield after joining Jim Tabor of Boston in committing the most errors, 33, by an AL third baseman in 1940. He missed three seasons (1943–45) while serving with the marines in World War II.

The continuation of the Korean conflict in 1952 resulted in Kennedy's being recalled to active duty by the U.S. Marine Air Corps. He reported for duty on May 29 but was discharged late in the year on dependency grounds.

Four days after the season opener in 1954, Kennedy was traded on April 17 to Baltimore for outfielder Jim Dyck.

He went back to the White Sox in 1955 and later played for Detroit, the White Sox for a third tour of duty, and the Brooklyn Dodgers, retiring as a player in 1957 after 16 seasons in the major leagues.

Kennedy managed the Chicago Cubs from 1963 until he was replaced after 58 games in 1965, scouted for the Cubs the remainder of 1965, coached for Atlanta in 1967, managed Oakland in 1968, and worked in the front offices of the St. Louis Cardinals, Cubs, Houston, and San Francisco.

His son, Terry Kennedy, who was born in Euclid, Ohio, in 1956 when Bob was playing for the Tigers, was a major league catcher (1978–91) with the St. Louis Cardinals, San Diego, Baltimore, and San Francisco.

Kennedy, Bob

Indians	G	AB	H	BA	RBI	R	2B	3B	HR	SA	SB
1948	66	73	22	.301	5	10	3	2	0	.397	0
1949	121	424	117	.276	57	49	23	5	9	.417	5
1950	146	540	157	.291	54	79	27	5	9	.409	3
1951	108	321	79	.246	29	30	15	4	7	.383	4
1952	22	40	12	.300	12	6	3	1	0	.425	1
1953	100	161	38	.236	22	22	5	0	3	.323	0
1954	1	0	0	—	0	0	0	0	0	—	0
Career	1,483	4,624	1,176	.254	514	514	196	41	63	.355	45

Jim Kern

With the Rangers in 1979, Kern was the cowinner (with Minnesota's Mike Marshall) of the AL Fireman of the Year award when his record was 13–5 with a career-high 29 saves and a 1.57 ERA.

Texas traded Kern to the Mets in December 1981, but two months later, before pitching a game for them, he was dealt to the Reds. Unhappy in Cincinnati, Kern forced a trade by growing a scraggly beard, which was against club rules, and in August 1982 he was sent to the White Sox, for whom he played in 1983.

Kern was with the Phillies and Brewers in 1984, then was released by Milwaukee after pitching only 11 innings in five games in 1985. The Indians re-signed Kern in 1986, but by then his fastball was only a memory, and he was let go at the end of the season.

Kern, Jim

Indians	W	L	Pct	ERA	G	CG	IP	H	BB	SO	ShO
1974	0	1	.000	4.70	4	1	15⅓	16	14	11	0
1975	1	2	.333	3.77	13	0	71⅔	60	45	55	0
1976	10	7	.588	2.37	50	0	117⅔	91	50	111	0
1977	8	10	.444	3.42	60	0	92	85	47	91	0
1978	10	10	.500	3.08	58	0	99⅓	77	58	95	0
1986	1	1	.500	7.90	16	0	27⅓	34	23	11	0
Career	53	57	.482	3.32	416	1	793⅓	670	444	651	0

Kirkland, Willie Charles

Indians: 1961–63
Outfielder
Birthplace: Siluria, Alabama

B: February 17, 1934
Bats left, throws right
Ht. 6–1; Wt. 206

Willie Kirkland could run and hit for average and power, but in three seasons with the Indians he never lived up to the great potential predicted for him.

"I guess I always concentrated too much on being a good outfielder," rationalized Kirkland, who was acquired with pitcher Johnny Antonelli in a trade with San Francisco on December 3, 1960, for outfielder Harvey Kuenn.

Though he never came close to the .272 career-high average he hit for the Giants in 1959, Kirkland enjoyed two days in the spotlight with the Indians in 1961 in back-to-back games—separated by four off days—against the Chicago White Sox and Minnesota.

Kirkland smashed three straight homers off Cal McLish in a 9–8 victory in the second game of a doubleheader on July 9 at the Stadium, then walked and sacrificed in his next (and last) two at bats. It was the final game before the All-Star break.

Then in the Indians' next game, on July 13 at the Stadium, Kirkland walked in his first trip to the plate, and in the third inning homered against Pedro Ramos in a 9–6 loss to the Twins, tying the major league record with four consecutive homers.

That was the season Kirkland led the Indians with 27 homers and 95 RBIs, and also tied for the American League lead in double plays (5) by an outfielder. He had led the National League (with 4) as a Giants rookie in 1958.

Kirkland also was famous for his superstition that he could shake himself out of a slump by showering in his full baseball uniform, including his hat, shoes, and glove—though the record would not substantiate his belief.

The Indians traded Kirkland on December 4, 1963, to Bal-

Willie Kirkland

timore for outfielder Al Smith and $25,000. He went on to play for the Washington Senators through 1966, and from 1968 to 1973 he played in Japan, where he married a Japanese woman.

Kirkland, Willie

Indians	G	AB	H	BA	RBI	R	2B	3B	HR	SA	SB
1961	146	525	136	.259	95	84	22	5	27	.474	7
1962	137	419	84	.200	72	56	9	1	21	.377	9
1963	127	427	98	.230	47	51	13	2	15	.375	8
Career	1,149	3,494	837	.240	509	443	134	29	148	.422	52

Klieman, Edward Frederick

Indians: 1943–48
Pitcher
Nickname: Ed
Birthplace: Norwood, Ohio

B: March 21, 1918
D: November 15, 1979
Batted right, threw right
Ht. 6–1; Wt. 170

Because his eyes were so bad, Ed Klieman became a pitcher and was a factor in helping the Indians win the American League pennant in 1948.

"I started in baseball as an outfielder, but I couldn't see well enough from out there and switched to pitching because I had a good strong arm," Klieman said after his eight-year major league career ended in 1950.

In addition to the Indians, Klieman also pitched for the Washington Senators, New York Yankees, Chicago White Sox, and Philadelphia Athletics.

Another factor in his success, he also explained, was how he learned to throw a sinker, which was his best pitch.

"I picked it up in 1942 when I was pitching for Cedar Rapids [in the Class B Three-I League]," he said. "An old fellow who came to all our games and always sat near the bull pen, asked me one night if I wanted to learn how to throw a sinker. I thought he was kidding, so I went along with him.

"He came down out of the stands, told me to hold the ball a certain way and how to snap my wrist when I threw it. And when I did, darned if the ball didn't do tricks. It was amazing. He kept coming around, helping me, and by the middle of the season I was going great with my new pitch."

So great that Klieman's won-lost record that season was 17–7. His contract was purchased by the Indians, who sent him in 1943 to their Class AAA International League farm club in Baltimore, where Klieman won 23 games and lost 11. This record earned him a September promotion to Cleveland, and he made the team in 1944.

Classified 4-F by the Selective Service because of his poor eyesight, Klieman was primarily a starter his first two seasons with the Tribe, but became strictly a relief pitcher in 1946. He led the American League with 58 appearances and was credited with 17 saves in 1947, and he posted a 3–2 won-lost record and 2.60 ERA in 44 games in 1948.

That winter Klieman was packaged with first baseman Eddie Robinson and pitcher Joe Haynes in a December 14, 1948, trade with Washington that brought pitcher Early Wynn and first baseman Mickey Vernon to the Tribe.

The Yankees purchased Klieman from the Senators for the waiver price on May 3, 1949, and 13 days later he was sold again, this time to the White Sox. When the season ended Klieman was traded to the Athletics, but he pitched only five games in 1950 and was released.

Klieman, Eddie

Indians	W	L	Pct	ERA	G	CG	IP	H	BB	SO	ShO
1943	0	1	.000	1.00	1	1	9	8	5	2	0
1944	11	13	.458	3.38	47	5	178⅓	185	70	44	1
1945	5	8	.385	3.85	38	4	126½	123	49	33	1
1946	0	0	—	6.60	9	0	15	18	10	2	0
1947	5	4	.556	3.03	58	0	92	78	39	21	0
1948	3	2	.600	2.60	44	0	79⅔	62	46	18	0
Career	26	28	.481	3.49	222	10	542	525	239	130	2

Knickerbocker, William Hart

Indians: 1933–36
Shortstop
Birthplace: Los Angeles
B: December 29, 1911

D: September 8, 1963
Batted right, threw right
Ht. 5–11; **Wt.** 170

There never was any doubt about Bill Knickerbocker's ability to hit, but his defensive shortcomings led to his being traded by the Indians in one of their biggest deals at that time.

On January 17, 1937, after he'd been the Tribe shortstop for three-plus seasons, Knickerbocker was packaged with outfielder Joe Vosmik and pitcher Oral Hildebrand and sent to the St. Louis Browns for shortstop Lyn Lary, outfielder Moose Solters, and pitcher Ivy Andrews.

The Indians had purchased Knickerbocker in 1931 from the Toledo (Ohio) Mud Hens of the Class AA American Association where he'd played for manager Casey Stengel.

Knickerbocker had been playing semipro baseball in Southern California and in 1930 hitchhiked to Toledo for a tryout with the Mud Hens. Stengel signed him, and Knickerbocker in 1932 set an American Association record for doubles with 69.

Knickerbocker played 80 games as a rookie for the Indians in 1933 and was a regular the next three seasons, hitting a career-high .317 in 1934. But he also committed 125 errors from 1933 to 1936, including 40 in 1936.

On August 19, 1935, the Indians were playing the Washington Senators at League Park. In the first inning Knickerbocker hit a high drive to right field, and the ball became wedged between the screen and wooden boards.

Knickerbocker thought it was a home run and circled the bases, but the umpire ordered him to return to second base, stating that the hit was a ground-rule double.

A noisy and prolonged argument ensued, but the umpire brought out the lineup cards and on the back was printed the ground rules, one of which stated: "Batted or thrown balls sticking in or going through the screen, two bases."

After one season with the Browns, Knickerbocker was traded to the New York Yankees. He later played for the Chicago White Sox and Philadelphia Athletics through 1942.

Ed Klieman

Knickerbocker, Bill

Indians	G	AB	H	BA	RBI	R	2B	3B	HR	SA	SB
1933	80	279	63	.226	32	20	16	3	2	.326	1
1934	146	593	188	.317	67	82	32	5	4	.408	6
1935	132	540	161	.298	55	77	34	5	0	.380	2
1936	155	618	182	.294	73	81	35	3	8	.400	5
Career	907	3,418	943	.276	368	423	198	27	28	.374	25

Kuenn, Harvey Edward

Indians: 1960
Outfielder
Birthplace: West Allis, Wisconsin
B: December 4, 1930

D: February 28, 1988
Batted right, threw right
Ht. 6–2; **Wt.** 187

Harvey Kuenn was under tremendous pressure upon joining the Indians in 1960, his only season in Cleveland, and often was booed unmercifully—and unfairly.

Fans blamed Kuenn for being traded to the Tribe by Detroit for popular Rocky Colavito on April 17, two days before the 1960 opener at the Stadium against the Tigers.

In his Cleveland debut Kuenn, playing center field, doubled and singled in seven at bats as the Tigers beat the Indians, 4–2, in 15 innings.

The American League Rookie of the Year in 1953 when he batted .308 and the batting champion in 1959 when his average soared to .353, Kuenn led the Indians with a .308 mark in 126 games in 1960, but never totally won over the fans.

Signed in 1952 as a shortstop out of the University of Wisconsin, Kuenn was promoted to the Tigers after playing only

Harvey Kuenn

63 games in the minor leagues. He was switched to the outfield full-time in 1958.

A line-drive hitter, Kuenn led the AL in hits four times and was an AL All-Star eight years in a row (1953–60).

Kuenn's only season with the Tribe was cut short by a broken left foot suffered August 26 when he was hit by his own foul ball in batting practice. He missed the next five games, but returned to play the next 13 in a row despite constant pain. Another X-ray examination disclosed the fracture, and Kuenn was sidelined for the rest of the season.

Two months later, on December 3, Kuenn was traded to San Francisco for pitcher Johnny Antonelli and outfielder Willie Kirkland. He was dealt to the Chicago Cubs in 1965, and then to the Philadelphia Phillies in 1966.

That would have been Kuenn's final season as a major league player, except for Frank Lane, who had made the Colavito-Kuenn trade in Cleveland. Lane had become the vice president and director of baseball operations for the Milwaukee Brewers and wanted to do a favor for Kuenn, who then lived in the Milwaukee area.

On September 1, 1971, when major league rosters could be expanded, Lane activated Kuenn, then going on 41, to enhance Harvey's retirement benefits.

The following year Kuenn became a coach for the Brewers and remained in that capacity until June 2, 1982, when he replaced Buck Rodgers as manager. The Brewers finished 72–43 under Kuenn, became known as Harvey's Wallbangers, and won the AL East Division championship.

They went on to beat California in the League Championship Series and came within one victory of winning the World Series, losing to St. Louis in seven games.

Kuenn was named AL Manager of the Year, but when the Brewers fell to fifth in 1983 he was replaced by Rene Lachemann.

Kuenn, Harvey

Indians	G	AB	H	BA	RBI	R	2B	3B	HR	SA	SB
1960	126	474	146	.308	54	65	24	0	9	.416	3
Career	1,833	6,913	2,092	.303	671	951	356	56	87	.408	68

Kuiper, Duane Eugene

Indians: 1974–81
Second baseman
Birthplace: Racine, Wisconsin

B: June 19, 1950
Bats left, throws right
Ht. 6–0; **Wt.** 175

The highlight of Duane Kuiper's career—he'll tell you with a straight face—was on August 29, 1977, when the second baseman hit the only home run of his major league career.

It came after 1,381 official trips to the plate for the Indians, and he failed to hit another homer—intentionally, he'll also tell you, still with a straight face—in 1,998 more at bats before retiring in 1985.

"One home run is better than none, but any more than one and people start expecting them," said Kuiper, one of the Indians' all-time most popular players.

Another offensive highlight of his career occurred on July 27, 1978, in the second game of a doubleheader in New York, won by the Indians, 17–5. Kuiper tied a major league record with two bases-loaded triples, a feat accomplished by only five others.

Though he batted a career-high .292 as a rookie in 1975

Duane Kuiper

and compiled a lifetime .271 average, Kuiper was better known for his outstanding defense. He twice led American League second basemen in fielding percentage before suffering a severe injury to his right knee on June 1, 1980.

There were fears that Kuiper's career might be over after he underwent reconstructive surgery, but he returned in 1981 and that winter was traded on November 14 to San Francisco for pitcher Ed Whitson.

He once said that deal represented the only regret he ever had in baseball. He pointed out, "It's not that I didn't want to go to San Francisco; I just didn't want to leave Cleveland."

Kuiper batted .280 in 1982, the only season he was a regular with the Giants, and retired on July 1, 1985, giving him exactly 10 full seasons in the major leagues.

In his seven-plus years with the Tribe, Kuiper spoiled potential no-hitters pitched by Andy Hassler, Nolan Ryan, and Ron Guidry. He won the Indians' Man of the Year award in 1977 and the Good Guy award in 1978.

That lone career home run by Kuiper was socked off Steve Stone in a 9–2 Indians victory over Baltimore at the Stadium.

After retiring as a player, Kuiper became a television and radio broadcaster for the Giants, for whom he still works, after a one-year stint with the Colorado Rockies in 1993.

Kuiper, Duane

Indians	G	AB	H	BA	RBI	R	2B	3B	HR	SA	SB
1974	10	22	11	.500	4	7	2	0	0	.591	1
1975	90	346	101	.292	25	42	11	1	0	.329	19
1976	135	506	133	.263	37	47	13	6	0	.312	10
1977	148	610	169	.277	50	62	15	8	1	.333	11
1978	149	547	155	.283	43	52	18	6	0	.338	4
1979	140	479	122	.255	39	46	9	5	0	.294	4
1980	42	149	42	.282	9	10	5	0	0	.315	0
1981	72	206	53	.257	14	15	6	0	0	.286	1
Career	1,057	3,379	917	.271	263	329	91	29	1	.316	52

Lajoie, Napoleon

Indians: 1902–14
Second baseman
Nicknames: Nap, Larry
Birthplace: Woonsocket, Rhode Island

B: September 5, 1874
D: February 7, 1959
Batted right, threw right
Ht. 6–1; **Wt.** 195

Napoleon Lajoie is considered by many to have been the best second baseman in the history of baseball and the most outstanding player to ever wear a Cleveland uniform.

He was elected to the Hall of Fame in 1937 as the sixth player to be enshrined, and also is often acknowledged as one of the first players to give the American League credibility.

Lajoie jumped from the Philadelphia Phillies of the established National League to the Philadelphia Athletics in 1901, the year the AL was founded, and in 1902 he was assigned to the Cleveland club (then called the Bronchos).

Cleveland got him, along with pitcher Bill Bernhard, in return for financial assistance that Bronchos owner Charles Somers had previously extended to Athletics owner Connie Mack.

Lajoie and Bernhard were available because of pending litigation against them by the Phillies, for whom they had played previously. Lajoie started with the Phillies in 1896, never hitting less than .324 for them in five seasons, and defected in a contract dispute, signing with the Athletics for a $2,400 salary in 1901.

When the Phillies obtained an injunction in June 1902 preventing Lajoie and Bernhard from playing with any other team in Pennsylvania, the "trade" with Cleveland was arranged, with the assistance of AL president Ban Johnson.

Lajoie won the first AL batting championship with either a .422 or .426 average in 1901, depending upon the research manual used. The *Macmillan Encyclopedia* and the *Sporting News Record Book* credit Lajoie with batting .422, while *Total Baseball* lists his average as .426.

So good—and so popular—was Lajoie that Cleveland fans in a contest sponsored by a newspaper voted overwhelmingly in 1903 to rename the Bronchos the Naps, in his honor.

Lajoie won a second batting championship when he hit

Napoleon Lajoie

.381 (according to the *Macmillan Encyclopedia* and the *Sporting News Record Book*) or .376 (according to *Total Baseball*) in 1904, the year he took over as player-manager of the team on September 10 (though William R. Armour continued to be listed as manager through the end of the season).

However, after the Naps finished as high as second only once (1908 when they lost the pennant to Detroit by one-half game) in the next four years, Lajoie resigned as manager in August 1909. The team was in sixth place with 57–57 record, and Lajoie cited the belief that handling both jobs was affecting his playing career.

Though he was injured and missed most of 1905 and 64 games in 1911, Lajoie continued as the Naps' second baseman through 1914, after which he was sold back to the Athletics.

After two seasons in Philadelphia, Lajoie returned to the minors in 1917 and, as player-manager for Toronto, won the batting championship of the International League with a .380 average in 151 games at the age of 43. His final season in baseball was 1918 when he played for Indianapolis of the American Association.

(The year after Lajoie left Cleveland, the nickname of the team was changed to Indians, reportedly in honor of Louis Sockalexis, who had played for the old National League Cleveland Spiders. He was a Penobscot Indian from Old Town, Maine, who in 1897 became the first American Indian to play major league baseball.)

After Lajoie won consecutive batting championships in 1903 and 1904, his principal rival for honors as the best player in baseball was Ty Cobb, who joined Detroit in 1905. They were completely different in temperament—Lajoie was quiet and unassuming, Cobb was fiery and cantankerous—and Lajoie also was much better liked than Cobb among fans as well as their peers.

In fact, it was Lajoie's popularity among AL players that reportedly helped him almost win the batting championship and a new Chalmers automobile in 1910.

With Cobb sitting out the last two games of the season to protect the slim lead he held in the race, Lajoie beat out seven bunts for hits and tripled to go 8-for-8 in a final-day doubleheader against the St. Louis Browns.

St. Louis manager Jack O'Connor—so great was his dislike for Cobb—had ordered his third baseman to play deep in both games, inviting—and allowing—Lajoie to beat out the bunts for hits. The tactic caused O'Connor to be fired.

Still, Lajoie's eight hits left his average one point behind Cobb's .385, though both men were presented with Chalmers automobiles anyway.

It later was learned in historical research by *The Sporting News*, however, that Cobb's average was inflated by two points because the hits he made in one of his games that season had been counted twice.

Lajoie's .384 mark should have won the title, though Commissioner Bowie Kuhn ruled in 1981 that the mistake would not be corrected.

Though playing in the dead-ball era, Lajoie led the AL in hits with 232 in 1901, 208 in 1904, 214 in 1906, and 227 in 1910, in home runs with 14 in 1901, and in runs batted in with 125 in 1901 and 102 in 1904.

He finished his major league career with 3,242 hits, 10th most in history, and 657 doubles, fifth most. He was renowned as a graceful, acrobatic second baseman with a strong arm, good hands, outstanding range, and excellent speed.

Lajoie, Nap

Indians	G	AB	H	BA	RBI	R	2B	3B	HR	SA	SB
1902	86	348	132	.379	64	81	35	5	7	.569	19
1903	125	485	167	.344	93	90	41	11	7	.518	21
1904	140	553	208	.376	102	92	49	15	6	.552	29
1905	65	249	82	.329	41	29	12	2	2	.418	11
1906	152	602	214	.355	91	88	48	9	0	.465	20
1907	137	509	152	.299	63	53	30	6	2	.393	24
1908	157	581	168	.289	74	77	32	6	2	.375	15
1909	128	469	152	.324	47	56	33	7	1	.431	13
1910	159	591	227	.384	76	94	51	7	4	.514	26
1911	90	315	115	.365	60	36	20	1	2	.454	13
1912	117	448	165	.368	90	66	34	4	0	.462	18
1913	137	465	156	.335	68	66	25	2	1	.404	17
1914	121	419	108	.258	50	37	14	3	0	.305	14
Career	2,480	9,589	3,242	.338	1,599	1,504	657	163	83	.467	380

LaRoche, David Eugene

Indians: 1975–77
Pitcher
Birthplace: Colorado Springs, Colorado

B: May 14, 1948
Bats left, throws left
Ht. 6–2; Wt. 200

His career with the Indians was brief, only two-plus years, but it was in Cleveland that Dave LaRoche established himself as one of the game's best relievers after five mediocre seasons with three other clubs—California, Minnesota, and the Chicago Cubs.

Dave LaRoche

Acquired by the Tribe from the Cubs on February 28, 1975, along with outfielder Brock Davis for pitcher Milt Wilcox, LaRoche saved 17 games that season to win the Man of the Year award, and was credited with a then-club-record 21 saves in 1976, appearing in 61 games each year with glittering earned run averages of 2.19 and 2.24. He was named to the American League All-Star team in 1976 and 1977.

The Indians' financial woes led to LaRoche's being traded with minor league pitcher Dave Schuler to the Angels, the team with which he began his professional career, on May 11, 1977, for first baseman Bruce Bochte, relief pitcher Sid Monge, and $250,000.

LaRoche, who was eligible to become a free agent at the end of the 1977 season, had been seeking a long-term contract at six figures that the Indians were unwilling to grant.

With California in 1978, LaRoche enjoyed his best season with 25 saves, a 10–9 won-lost record, and a 2.82 ERA in 59 games.

An outfielder when signed by the Angels in 1967, LaRoche became a pitcher in his second year in the minor leagues, and made it to the majors in 1970. He was dealt to the Twins in 1971 and to the Cubs in 1972. After leaving Cleveland, LaRoche was released by the Angels in 1981 and signed by the New York Yankees, for whom he pitched until released in 1983.

LaRoche appeared in 647 major league games, 632 as a reliever. His record in those 15 starts (nine in 1980) was 3–6.

Bob Lemon

LaRoche, Dave

Indians	W	L	Pct	ERA	G	CG	IP	H	BB	SO	ShO
1975	5	3	.625	2.19	61	0	82⅓	61	57	94	0
1976	1	4	.200	2.24	61	0	96⅓	57	49	104	0
1977	2	2	.500	5.30	13	0	18⅔	15	7	18	0
Career	65	58	.528	3.53	647	1	1,049½	919	459	819	0

Lemon, Robert Granville

Indians: 1941–42, 1946–58
Pitcher, third baseman, outfielder
Birthplace: San Bernardino, California

B: September 22, 1920
Bats left, throws right
Ht. 6–0; **Wt.** 180

Among the eager rookies trying to impress Indians manager Lou Boudreau in spring training 1946 was a strong-armed third baseman named Bob Lemon, who had compiled some impressive minor league statistics before serving three years (1943–45) in the navy in World War II.

Signed by the Tribe in 1938, Lemon batted .309 at New Orleans of the Class A1 Southern Association in 1939 and .301 at Wilkes-Barre of the Class A Eastern League in 1941. He hammered 21 homers with a .268 average at Baltimore of the Class AA International League in 1942.

Because the Indians had one of the best third basemen in baseball in Ken Keltner, Boudreau switched Lemon to center field where his instincts, speed, and throwing arm could best be utilized.

And in the 1946 season opener against Chicago, Lemon, playing center field, made a sensational game-saving catch to preserve Bob Feller's 1–0 victory.

But Lemon's bat fell silent. He batted .180 in 55 games in 1946, and by midseason was languishing on the bench—though he also threw some batting practice, which caught the eyes of Boudreau and Mel Harder, who was then a member of the Indians' pitching staff.

When the New York Yankees came to Cleveland in June, Boudreau went to their catcher, Bill Dickey, whose playing career was then winding down, and asked him about Lemon. They'd played together in the navy.

Dickey highly recommended Lemon—as a pitcher—and Boudreau and Harder began another conversion of the third baseman–turned–center fielder.

Lemon made 32 appearances on the mound, five as a starter the rest of the season, and though he won only four and lost five games, his earned run average was a sparkling 2.49. From then on there was no doubt about the position he'd play in the future.

"Once Lemon learned that he did not have to throw as hard as he could to get batters out, he became a good pitcher, a winning pitcher," said Harder.

He also became a Hall of Fame pitcher, elected in 1976, after being one of only four American Leaguers to win 20 games seven times, leading the league in victories in 1950 and tied for the most in 1954 and 1955, pitching a no-hitter on June 30, 1948 (2–0 over the Tigers in Detroit), making the AL All-Star team seven times from 1948 to 1954, and starting four World Series games—two victories against the Boston Braves in 1948 and two losses to the New York Giants in 1954.

Lemon also pitched two one-hitters, the first on May 29, 1951, in Detroit when his bid for a perfect game was ruined by Vic Wertz, who homered in the eighth inning of a 2–1 victory over the Tigers, and the second on opening day, April

14, 1953, at the Stadium, when Minnie Minoso's single with two out in the first inning was Chicago's only hit.

Lemon's 20 victories led the Indians to the pennant in 1948 when he topped the AL with 10 shutouts, 20 complete games, and 293⅔ innings pitched.

Five times he led the league in complete games, and four times in innings pitched, and he was the Indians' biggest winner with a 23–7 mark when they captured an AL-record 111 games in 1954.

Lemon won the Indians' Man of the Year award in 1949 and was cowinner in 1952 with Mike Garcia and Early Wynn.

Though he couldn't make it in the major leagues as a position player, Lemon often was used as a pinch hitter, totaling 31 hits in 109 opportunities (.284), and his 37 homers (including seven in 1949) were just one behind Wes Ferrell's record for pitchers.

After leaving the Indians in 1958, Lemon finished that season in the minors, winning two games for San Diego in the Class AAA Pacific Coast League.

He held various scouting, coaching, and managerial jobs the next eight years, and won the minor league Manager of the Year award by piloting Seattle in the PCL in 1966. Lemon applied for the vacant managerial job in Cleveland in 1967 but was turned down by Gabe Paul, who later called it "the biggest mistake I made in baseball."

Lemon managed the Kansas City Royals from 1970 to 1972, winning the AL Manager of the Year award in 1971. He won that award again in 1977 after taking over the Chicago White Sox, but was replaced after 74 games in 1978 by former Tribe teammate Larry Doby.

Before the 1978 season ended, however, Lemon took over the New York Yankees from Billy Martin, led them from third to a first-place tie with Boston, a one-game playoff for the pennant, and victory over Los Angeles in the World Series.

Lemon was replaced by Martin midway through 1979, but returned again to manage the Yankees in the second half of the strike-interrupted 1981 season. He led them to the division championship and a three-game sweep of Oakland for the pennant, but lost to the Dodgers in the World Series.

Lemon also managed the Yankees briefly in 1982 before retiring.

Lemon, Bob

Indians	W	L	Pct	ERA	G	CG	IP	H	BB	SO	ShO
1946	4	5	.444	2.49	32	1	94	77	68	39	0
1947	11	5	.688	3.44	37	6	167⅓	150	97	65	1
1948	20	14	.588	2.82	43	20	293⅔	231	129	147	10
1949	22	10	.688	2.99	37	22	279⅔	211	137	138	2
1950	23	11	.676	3.84	44	22	288	281	146	170	3
1951	17	14	.548	3.52	42	17	263⅓	244	124	132	1
1952	22	11	.667	2.50	42	28	309⅔	236	105	131	5
1953	21	15	.583	3.36	41	23	286⅔	283	110	98	5
1954	23	7	.767	2.72	36	21	258⅓	228	92	110	2
1955	18	10	.643	3.88	35	5	211⅓	218	74	100	0
1956	20	14	.588	3.03	39	21	255⅓	230	89	94	2
1957	6	11	.353	4.60	21	2	117⅓	129	64	45	0
1958	0	1	.000	5.33	11	0	25⅓	41	16	8	0
Career	207	128	.618	3.23	460	188	2,850	2,559	1,251	1,277	31

Levsen, Emil Henry

Indians: 1923–28	**B:** April 29, 1898
Pitcher	**D:** March 12, 1972
Nickname: Dutch	**Batted right, threw right**
Birthplace: Wyoming, Iowa	**Ht.** 6–0; **Wt.** 180

Though he was a pitcher who won just 21 games and lost 26 in a major league career that lasted but six years, Dutch Levsen probably will never be forgotten because he was the last to perform a feat that almost certainly will never be duplicated.

On August 28, 1926, Levsen started and pitched two complete games, winning both, 6–1 and 5–1, in a doubleheader against the Red Sox in Boston, allowing just four hits in each.

After the opener, Levsen was kidded by teammates about how easily he beat the Red Sox. Thus motivated, Levsen went to manager Tris Speaker and asked if he could also start the second game. Because the Indians pitching staff had been badly overworked, Speaker agreed, and Levsen practically duplicated his victory in the nightcap.

"Levsen's feat allowed Speaker to save George Uhle for the homecoming game with the [St. Louis] Browns at Dunn Field tomorrow," reported the *Cleveland Plain Dealer*.

Uhle went on to lead the American League with a 27–11 record that season, as the Indians almost won the pennant. They finished second, three games behind New York.

The *Plain Dealer* also reported the next day:

"To Emil Levsen goes the credit of performing the most unusual feat of modern pitching. In displaying wonderful skill and courage to successfully demonstrate that the iron men of the old days had nothing on him, Levsen worked his

"Dutch" Levsen

powerful right arm with such precision that the Red Sox gathered only eight hits off him in the two contests.

"Three of the hits of the first game were flukes, and happened to be bunched just right to allow Boston to escape a shutout, while one of the four in the second affair also was a scratch."

A graduate of Iowa State College, Levsen was purchased by the Indians from Cedar Rapids of the Class D Mississippi Valley League in 1923 where he compiled a won-lost record of 19–4.

He was farmed out to Terre Haute of the Class B Three-I League in 1924 where he was 14–8, and in 1925 the Indians sent him to Rochester of the Class AA International League where his record was 14–9, earning a promotion to Cleveland.

As proficient as Levsen was the day he started and won both ends of a doubleheader, he never was a winning pitcher after that season. The following spring he came up with arm trouble and went 3–7 in 1927 and, after going 0–3 in 1928, Levsen was sold to New Orleans of the Class AA Southern Association and retired from baseball shortly thereafter.

Levsen, Dutch

Indians	W	L	Pct	ERA	G	CG	IP	H	BB	SO	ShO
1923	0	0	—	0.00	3	0	4⅓	4	0	1	0
1924	1	1	.500	4.41	4	1	16⅓	22	4	3	0
1925	1	2	.333	5.55	4	2	24⅓	30	16	9	0
1926	16	13	.552	3.41	33	18	237⅓	235	85	53	2
1927	3	7	.300	5.49	25	2	80⅓	96	37	15	1
1928	0	3	.000	5.44	11	0	41⅓	39	31	7	0
Career	21	26	.447	4.17	80	23	404	426	173	88	3

Lowenstein, John Lee

Indians: 1970–77
Outfielder, designated hitter,
**   second baseman, third baseman,**
**   first baseman**
Nickname: Steiner

Birthplace: Wolf Point, Montana
B: January 27, 1947
Bats left, throws right
Ht. 6–0; **Wt.** 175

John Lowenstein was a model of consistency, and, though he spent most of his career with the Indians, his best years were in Baltimore, where he helped the Orioles reach the World Series in 1979 and 1983.

"You knew what you were going to get with me, most of the time, anyway," said Lowenstein after he batted exactly .242 in three of four seasons he played for the Tribe—1974, 1975, and 1977.

Though he was a fan favorite with the Orioles, Lowenstein was "famous" for something else during his eight seasons with the Indians.

When someone asked him if he'd like to see a banner hung in his honor at the Stadium, Lowenstein reacted as if he'd been shot.

"Basically, I am against all banners," he said. "If somebody puts up a sign about me, I'd immediately disqualify myself from the game. Signs have no ethereal value."

Still, when he was pressed on the subject, Lowenstein did offer a description of what he considered the perfect baseball banner about himself.

"It would be a huge white sign hung in the center-field bleachers at the Stadium where fans are not allowed to sit,"

John Lowenstein

he said. "There'd be no writing on the banner, and it would be displayed only when the Indians were on the road."

Yes, John Lowenstein was a little different—and thus was born the "Apathy Club" in honor of John Lowenstein.

A seventh-round selection in the 1968 amateur draft, Lowenstein was a shortstop in the minor leagues, but he played every position except pitcher and catcher in the major leagues.

Lowenstein departed the Indians on December 6, 1976—though they retrieved him three months later, on March 29, 1977.

These moves were part of an unusual chain of events that began with the loss of designated hitter–first baseman Rico Carty to Toronto in the American League expansion draft to stock the Blue Jays and Seattle Mariners franchises.

Wanting Carty back, Tribe general manager Phil Seghi sent Lowenstein and catcher Rick Cerone to the Blue Jays for Carty.

Then, obviously recognizing they'd made another mistake, they dealt shortstop Hector Torres to Toronto to return Lowenstein to Cleveland.

A year later, on February 28, 1978, Seghi traded Lowenstein again, this time to Texas with pitcher Tom Buskey for outfielder Willie Horton and pitcher David Clyde.

At the end of the season, after Lowenstein's average fell to .222, the Rangers traded him to Baltimore, which turned out to be a break for him and the Orioles.

Lowenstein played seven seasons for the Orioles, and, suddenly, whether he liked it or not, the unpretentious infielder-outfielder no longer was merely an average player with above-average quotes.

Though he was never a regular for the Orioles, Lowenstein filled in virtually everywhere and hit a career-high .320 in 122 games in 1982. He drove in 66 runs, scored 69 runs in 322 official at bats, and also walked 54 times.

"You could say I went from playing a lot, to playing a little, to being used sometimes, to playing on a platoon basis," said Lowenstein, who became a television broadcaster for the Orioles upon his retirement as a player in 1985.

Lowenstein, John

Indians	G	AB	H	BA	RBI	R	2B	3B	HR	SA	SB
1970	17	43	11	.256	6	5	3	1	1	.442	1
1971	58	140	26	.186	9	15	5	0	4	.307	1
1972	68	151	32	.212	21	16	8	1	6	.397	2
1973	98	305	89	.292	40	42	16	1	6	.410	5
1974	140	508	123	.242	48	65	14	2	8	.325	36
1975	91	265	64	.242	33	37	5	1	12	.404	15
1976	93	229	47	.205	14	33	8	2	2	.284	11
1977	81	149	36	.242	12	24	6	1	4	.376	1
Career	1,368	3,476	881	.253	441	510	137	18	116	.403	128

Mack (Mlckovsky), Raymond James

Indians: 1938–44, 1946
Second baseman
Birthplace: Cleveland
B: August 31, 1916

D: May 7, 1969
Batted right, threw right
Ht. 6–0; **Wt.** 200

When he teamed up with Lou Boudreau to form a sensational double-play combination at Buffalo of the Class AA International League in 1939, Ray Mack was expected to become one of the best-hitting second basemen in baseball.

Mack had batted .378 at Fargo-Moorhead (North Dakota) of the Class D Northern League in 1938, and was among the league leaders—as was Boudreau—when they were promoted as a tandem to Cleveland on August 7, 1939.

A native Clevelander who was signed off the sandlots, Mack also had been a local college football star fullback at Case School of Applied Science, nicknamed the Case Ace. His return home as the Tribe's new second baseman was eagerly anticipated.

Ray Mack

However, while Boudreau got off to a good start with the Indians in the final six weeks of their first season in Cleveland, Mack batted only .152 in 36 games.

There was improvement in 1940, beginning on opening day when Mack made a spectacular play with two outs in the ninth to save Bob Feller's no-hitter in Chicago. He went on to hit .283 with 12 homers and 69 RBIs, although everything that followed for Mack was downhill from there.

While he continued to field well, Mack's average declined into the .220s, and, after four seasons as a regular, he lost his job and alternated at second base with utility infielder Russ Peters.

With World War II still raging, Mack—whose family name was Mlckovsky—was drafted into the army and missed the 1945 season. When Mack returned he played behind new second baseman Dutch Meyer, hitting .205 in 61 games. That winter he was involved in what became for the Indians a very significant deal.

On December 20, 1946, they sent Mack and minor league catcher Sherman Lollar to the New York Yankees for outfielder Hal Peck and pitchers Al Gettel and Gene Bearden.

Mack played only one game for the Yankees in 1947, and then they sent him to Newark of the Class AAA International League. Later that season they sold him on waivers to the Chicago Cubs, for whom he batted .218 in 21 games. It was his final year in the major leagues.

After his retirement from baseball, Mack said, "I always believed I could hit, but the way it worked out, I let too many people try to tell me what to do, and I tried too many different things. I would have been better off if I'd gone on my own."

Mack, Ray

Indians	G	AB	H	BA	RBI	R	2B	3B	HR	SA	SB
1938	2	6	2	.333	2	2	0	1	0	.667	0
1939	36	112	17	.152	6	12	4	1	1	.232	0
1940	146	530	150	.283	69	60	21	5	12	.409	4
1941	145	500	114	.228	44	54	22	4	9	.342	8
1942	143	481	108	.225	45	43	14	6	2	.291	9
1943	153	545	120	.220	62	56	25	2	7	.312	8
1944	83	284	66	.232	29	24	15	3	0	.306	4
1946	61	171	35	.205	9	13	6	2	1	.281	2
Career	791	2,707	629	.232	278	273	113	24	34	.330	35

Mails, John Walter

Indians: 1920–22
Pitcher
Nicknames: Duster, The Great One
Birthplace: San Quentin, California

B: October 1, 1894
D: July 5, 1974
Batted left, threw left
Ht. 6–0; **Wt.** 195

The Indians would not have won the American League pennant in 1920, nor the World Series against Brooklyn that year, without Duster Mails, the often-eccentric pitcher who called himself The Great One.

Mails resented being called Duster because the nickname originated when he hit a batter with a pitch in 1915.

Mails was purchased by the Indians from Portland of the Class AA Pacific Coast League on August 21, 1920. He proceeded to win seven games without a loss while registering a

1.85 earned run average in nine appearances, eight of them starts.

Mails also pitched 15⅔ scoreless innings in the World Series against the Dodgers, the team with which he originally came to the major leagues.

He gave up three hits but blanked Brooklyn in 6⅔ innings in relief of Ray Caldwell in the third game, won by the Dodgers, 2–1, and was the starter and winner of Game 6 with a three-hit, 1–0 victory. The Indians won in seven games (when the Series was best-of-nine).

A big and boisterous man who laughed easily—and enjoyed the laughter of others—Mails was famous for his wisecracks and braggadocio, if not for his pitching after his first two seasons with the Indians.

Mails pitched for the Dodgers briefly in 1915 and 1916. He was sold to Pittsburgh in 1917 and sent to the minor leagues where he remained until purchased by the Indians.

Mails followed his 1920 season with a 14–8 record in 1921, but was bothered by arm problems and wildness in 1922 and sent back to the minor leagues. He attempted a comeback with the St. Louis Cardinals and went 7–7 for them in 1925, but was finished in the major leagues after one game in 1926.

Mails continued pitching in the minor leagues where he won a total of 226 games before he finally hung up his glove in 1936.

Rick Manning

Mails, Duster

Indians	W	L	Pct	ERA	G	CG	IP	H	BB	SO	ShO
1920	7	0	1.000	1.85	9	6	63⅓	54	18	25	2
1921	14	8	.636	3.94	34	10	194⅓	210	89	87	2
1922	4	7	.364	5.28	26	4	104	122	40	54	1
Career	32	25	.561	4.10	104	29	516	554	220	232	5

Manning, Richard Eugene

Indians: 1975–83
Center fielder
Nicknames: Rick, Archie
Birthplace: Niagara Falls, New York

B: September 2, 1954
Bats left, throws right
Ht. 6–1; Wt. 180

Originally a shortstop when the Indians made him their number-one selection in the 1972 amateur draft, Rick Manning became one of the best defensive center fielders in the game upon his promotion to Cleveland to stay in 1975.

Manning batted .285 as a rookie and .292 in 1976 when he won a Gold Glove, though that turned out to be his best of 13 seasons in the major leagues.

One of Manning's biggest thrills, he said, was catching the final out—a fly ball by Ernie Whitt—in Len Barker's perfect-game, 3–0, victory over Toronto on May 15, 1981.

Manning figured in one of the Indians' worst trades when he was sent with pitcher Rick Waits to the Milwaukee Brewers on June 6, 1983, for outfielder Gorman Thomas and pitchers Ernie Camacho and Jamie Easterly.

Manning retired after the 1987 season and has been a television broadcaster for the Indians since 1990.

Manning, Rick

Indians	G	AB	H	BA	RBI	R	2B	3B	HR	SA	SB
1975	120	480	137	.285	35	69	16	5	3	.358	19
1976	138	552	161	.292	43	73	24	7	6	.393	16
1977	68	252	57	.226	18	33	7	3	5	.337	9
1978	148	566	149	.263	50	65	27	3	3	.337	12
1979	144	560	145	.259	51	67	12	2	3	.304	30
1980	140	471	110	.234	52	55	17	4	3	.306	12
1981	103	360	88	.244	33	47	15	3	4	.336	25
1982	152	562	152	.270	44	71	18	2	8	.352	12
1983	50	194	54	.278	10	20	6	0	1	.325	7
Career	1,555	5,248	1,349	.257	458	664	189	43	56	.341	168

Maris, Roger Eugene

Indians: 1957–58
Outfielder
Birthplace: Hibbing, Minnesota
B: September 10, 1934

D: December 14, 1985
Batted left, threw right
Ht. 6–0; Wt. 197

Though he gained fame by breaking Babe Ruth's home run record in New York, it was with the Indians that Roger Maris began his baseball career before he became a key figure in one of the 51 trades involving 118 players made by general manager Frank Lane.

Maris was signed by the Tribe in 1953 for a $5,000 bonus when he disdained a college football scholarship to the University of Minnesota. He made it to Cleveland in 1957 when he batted .235 with 14 homers and 51 RBIs in 116 games. When he struggled with a .225 average in 51 games in 1958, Maris was packaged with pitcher Dick Tomanek and first baseman Preston Ward and traded to the Kansas City Athletics on June 15 for first baseman Vic Power and shortstop Woodie Held.

Roger Maris

Martin, Alfred Manuel

Indians: 1959	**B:** May 16, 1928
Second baseman, third baseman	**D:** December 25, 1989
Nicknames: The Kid, Billy	**Batted right, threw right**
Birthplace: Berkeley, California	**Ht.** 5–11½; **Wt.** 165

Though he became famous as, first, an aggressive and feisty second baseman for the New York Yankees, and then, an even more aggressive and feistier manager of the Yankees, Billy Martin played briefly for the Indians during the team's ill-fated Frank Lane era.

Looking for someone to spark the Tribe, Lane traded relief pitchers Don Mossi and Ray Narleski and minor league shortstop Ozzie Alvarez to Detroit on November 20, 1958, to get Martin and pitcher Al Cicotte.

"Billy is not a Mickey Mantle, but I want him because he will take charge on the field," is the way Lane explained his desire to acquire Martin.

"The Indians have needed a leader, and I don't mean simply a holler guy. What we've lacked is a hustling, scrappy player who will keep the others on their toes. That's the sort of player Martin is. It's the intangibles that make him so valuable."

But Martin, who'd been exiled by the Yankees in 1957 for his off-the-field shenanigans, did little to help the Indians in 1959, though they contended for the pennant most of the season.

Alternating at second base with Jim Baxes, and also filling in for four games at third, Martin batted .260 in 73 games and, after the season ended, was traded on December 15 to Cincinnati in another of Lane's deals that backfired on the Tribe.

Pitcher Cal McLish and minor league first baseman Gordy Coleman were sent with Martin to the Reds for another veteran second baseman, Johnny Temple, who didn't do much for the Indians. Coleman went on to play well for Cincinnati the next seven years.

The deal pleased Maris, who said at the time that he was "disgusted" with the Indians. "I wasn't Lane's or [manager Bobby] Bragan's type of player," he said. "They both made that very clear to me." Bragan was fired 12 days after Maris was traded.

Maris went on to hit .240 with 28 homers in 1958 and .273 with 16 homers in 1959, after which the Athletics—then sarcastically referred to as a "farm club of the Yankees"—sent him to New York in a seven-player deal.

Two years later Maris smashed 61 homers to break by one Ruth's 34-year-old single-season home run record. He was named the American League's Most Valuable Player in 1960 and 1961, and also was a member of the All-Star team from 1959 to 1962.

Maris, whose 12-year major league career ended in 1968, wound up with 275 homers and played in seven World Series, five with the Yankees and two with the St. Louis Cardinals.

Maris, Roger											
Indians	**G**	**AB**	**H**	**BA**	**RBI**	**R**	**2B**	**3B**	**HR**	**SA**	**SB**
1957	116	358	84	.235	51	61	9	5	14	.405	8
1958	51	182	41	.225	27	26	5	1	9	.412	4
Career	1,463	5,101	1,325	.260	851	826	195	42	275	.476	21

Billy Martin

Before joining the Indians, Martin was involved in a highly publicized brawl in a New York nightclub. He later battled St. Louis Browns catcher Clint Courtney, Boston Red Sox outfielder Jim Piersall, Chicago Cubs pitcher Jim Brewer, Minnesota pitcher Dave Boswell, and Twins traveling secretary Howard Fox. His fights with Boswell and Fox took place when he managed Minnesota in 1969.

In addition to playing for the Yankees and Tigers before joining the Indians, and the Reds after leaving Cleveland, Martin also played for the Kansas City Athletics, Milwaukee Braves, and Minnesota, retiring after the 1961 season.

He was a scout for Minnesota from 1962 to 1964, then a coach with the Twins from 1965 until May 1968 when he replaced Johnny Goryl as manager of the Denver Bears, the Twins' Class AAA affiliate in the Pacific Coast League. He became manager of the Twins in 1969 but was fired despite winning the American League West championship that year.

From 1971 to 1988, Martin managed the Tigers, Texas, Yankees (five times), and Oakland.

Martin, Billy

Indians	G	AB	H	BA	RBI	R	2B	3B	HR	SA	SB
1959	73	242	63	.260	24	37	7	0	9	.401	0
Career	1,021	3,419	877	.257	333	425	137	28	64	.369	34

McDowell, Samuel Edward

Indians: 1961–71
Pitcher
Nickname: Sudden Sam
Birthplace: Pittsburgh, Pennsylvania

B: September 21, 1942
Bats left, throws left
Ht. 6–5; **Wt.** 190

By his own admission, Sam McDowell was "the biggest, most hopeless and violent drunk in baseball," before he was kicked out of the game in 1975.

McDowell later became a highly successful alcohol and drug addiction counselor working for several major league teams, doing his best to help others avoid the demon that—most observers believe—prevented him from making it into the Hall of Fame.

"There is absolutely no doubt in my mind that I would be in the Hall of Fame if I had not been a drunk, if I had not been kicked out of baseball because of my drinking," he said. Others share that opinion.

Signed for a then-whopping bonus of $75,000 in 1960, McDowell got his first taste of the major leagues in 1961, though it wasn't until 1964 that he made it to Cleveland to stay—until the Tribe finally gave up and traded him on November 29, 1971, to San Francisco.

It was a good deal for the Indians as they received Gaylord Perry, who would go on to win 70 games over the next three and a half seasons, and Frank Duffy, who would be their regular shortstop for the next six years.

But it's also possible that McDowell, had he become sober sooner, would have gone on to be one of the game's greatest pitchers, as had been expected with his blazing fastball and a curve that, batters said, "was like a ball falling off a table."

As it was, despite his drinking problems, McDowell led American League pitchers in strikeouts five times between 1965 and 1970, twice fanning over 300 batters (which only Rube Waddell, Sandy Koufax, Walter Johnson, Nolan Ryan, and J. R. Richard had been able to do as many times).

Sam McDowell

Though wildness was a problem, especially early in McDowell's career, he also led the AL in 1965 with a 2.18 earned run average, despite walking a league high 132 batters, and 325 strikeouts in 273 innings, fourth-best total in baseball's modern era until then. His 10.71 strikeouts per nine innings was a major league record until Dwight Gooden broke it 19 years later.

McDowell pitched four one-hitters, including two back to back in 1966, against the Kansas City Athletics in a 2–0 victory on April 25, and when he beat Chicago, 1–0, on May 1. Jose Tartabull got the only hit for the Athletics, a sixth-inning single, and Don Buford blooped a double in the third for the White Sox.

He threw two more one-hitters against the Athletics, beating them, 8–1, in Kansas City on August 31, 1965, as Dick Green singled in the fourth inning, and after their move to Oakland, gaining a 3–0 victory on August 19, 1969, as Bert Campaneris singled in the fifth inning.

In 1968, McDowell led the AL with 283 strikeouts for the third of five times, and his 1.81 ERA was second best. He struck out 16 Athletics on May 1, and 15 Oakland batters on July 12.

He also struck out 15 batters in two games in 1970, against Chicago on May 6 and Washington on July 6.

Pitching for the Indians, who were never contenders during his tenure, McDowell became a 20-game winner for the only time in his career in 1970 when he struck out 304 in a league-high 305 innings and was named Pitcher of the Year by *The Sporting News*.

McDowell also won the Indians' Man of the Year award in 1969, shared it with battery mate Ray Fosse in 1970, and was named to the AL All-Star team six times (1965, 1966, 1968, 1969, 1970, and 1971).

The one game McDowell called his "best ever," which he said he'll always remember—with good reason—was in Detroit on September 18, 1966. That night he flirted with baseball's single-game strikeout record, which then was 18, by fanning 14 batters in six innings.

"I often wonder if I could have broken the record if I would have pitched the entire game," he said. "One thing I do know, I had everything going in that game. My fastball was as good as it ever was, and my control was nearly perfect.

"I got 14 strikeouts in only six innings. No matter what pitch I threw, I could put it anywhere I wanted. I was at my all-time best, and I don't think I was ever that good again.

"I went back to the dugout at the end of the sixth and told [interim manager] George Strickland my arm was beginning to tighten. I only said it because I wanted him to have somebody ready, just in case. We were winning (5–1) and I didn't want to take any chances.

"I remember telling George, 'I'm okay, and I want to stay in there. But maybe you should keep somebody ready just in case.' Just like that, he took me out. I was very disappointed, though I knew George did what he thought was best, for me and the team.

"I'd had some shoulder trouble early that season and Strick probably wanted to be sure I didn't hurt myself again.

"Nobody will ever know for sure what might have happened. Heck, I only needed four more strikeouts to tie the record and five to break it, and I had three innings to get them.

"That's why, of all the [425] games I pitched, it's the one I'll never forget."

As it turned out, McDowell didn't even get credit for a victory that night. Reliever John O'Donoghue blew the lead in the eighth inning, and the Indians had to rally for a run in the 11th to win, 6–5, behind Luis Tiant.

Interestingly, Tiant struck out five Tigers in 2⅔ innings, and O'Donoghue fanned two in 1⅓ innings to go with McDowell's 14, giving the Indians 21 for the game.

After being dealt to San Francisco, McDowell was 10–8 for the Giants in 1972. In 1973, he was 1–2 for San Francisco, and he went 5–8 after being traded to the New York Yankees on June 7.

Unable to stay sober and win in 1974, McDowell was released by the Yankees, but was granted one last trial with Pittsburgh, his hometown team, in 1975—with the condition that he stop drinking.

He did, but only temporarily, and at midseason in 1975 the Pirates also gave up on McDowell. It was the end of his pitching career.

McDowell said it took him four more years to hit bottom, which he did in 1979 in another drinking bout. That one lasted several days.

McDowell finally swore off the booze and turned his life around, and he is working now to help others avoid the demon that kept him out of the Hall of Fame.

McDowell, Sam

Indians	W	L	Pct	ERA	G	CG	IP	H	BB	SO	ShO
1961	0	0.	—	0.00	1	0	6¼	3	5	5	0
1962	3	7	.300	6.06	25	0	87⅔	81	70	70	0
1963	3	5	.375	4.85	14	3	65	63	44	63	1
1964	11	6	.647	2.70	31	6	173⅓	148	100	177	2
1965	17	11	.607	2.18	42	14	273	178	132	325	3
1966	9	8	.529	2.87	35	8	194⅓	130	102	225	5
1967	13	15	.464	3.85	37	10	236⅓	201	123	236	1
1968	15	14	.517	1.81	38	11	269	181	110	283	3
1969	18	14	.563	2.94	39	18	285	222	102	279	4
1970	20	12	.625	2.92	39	19	305	236	131	304	1
1971	13	17	.433	3.40	35	8	214⅔	160	153	192	2
Career	141	134	.513	3.17	425	103	2,492⅓	1,948	1,312	2,453	23

McLish, Calvin Coolidge Julius Caesar Tuskahoma

Indians: 1956–59
Pitcher
Nickname: Buster
Birthplace: Anadarko, Oklahoma

B: December 1, 1925
Bats both, throws right
Ht. 6–0; **Wt.** 179

The Indians' purchase of Cal McLish in October 1955 from the Chicago Cubs, for whom he was pitching at their Los Angeles farm club in the Pacific Coast League, turned out to be one of their best-ever deals.

But then, three years later, Frank Lane spoiled it with one of his worst-ever trades.

On December 15, 1959, less than three months after McLish won 19 games while losing eight to help keep the Tribe in contention for the pennant most of the season, he was traded by Lane to Cincinnati.

Lane sent McLish, along with first baseman Gordy Coleman and second baseman Billy Martin, to the Reds for second baseman Johnny Temple, who played little and without distinction for the Indians.

McLish went on to pitch four more years in the major leagues before arm trouble forced his retirement in 1964 from the Philadelphia Phillies. He then became a pitching coach—with Philadelphia in 1965 and 1966, Montreal from 1969 to 1975, and Milwaukee from 1976 to 1982.

McLish's career began early, at the tender age of 18 when he went right from American Legion baseball to the Brooklyn Dodgers in 1944, though he didn't spend a full season in the major leagues until 1951, with the Cubs.

Four seasons in the minors followed before McLish got his big break with the Indians in 1956 and, after making the team in spring training, appeared in 37 games, all but two in relief.

It was in 1957 that McLish experienced one of the worst days a pitcher could imagine. On May 22 in Boston, McLish tied a major league record by giving up four home runs in one inning. Gene Mauch opened the sixth with a homer, and Ted Williams followed with another. Jackie Jensen walked and then Dick Gernert and Frank Malzone hit two more homers, leading the Red Sox to an 11–0 victory.

McLish finally found success in 1958 when, employed strictly as a starter, he led the Indians' pitching staff with a

Cal McLish

McMahon, Donald John

Indians: 1964–66
Pitcher
Nickname: Don
Birthplace: Brooklyn, New York

B: January 4, 1930
D: July 22, 1987
Batted right, threw right
Ht. 6–2; **Wt.** 215

When they were together with the Milwaukee Braves, Don McMahon and manager Birdie Tebbetts had a falling out, and McMahon was sold to Houston on May 9, 1962.

Sixteen months later, after Tebbetts had become manager of the Indians, they were reunited in Cleveland when McMahon's contract was purchased from the Astros on September 30, 1963.

"We just didn't agree on some things," was the way McMahon sloughed off his differences with Tebbetts in Milwaukee.

The manager was even more vague on the subject. "I've forgotten whatever problems we had, but I never forgot the kind of pitcher McMahon was," Tebbetts explained after the durable and dependable reliever joined the Tribe.

The Indians' Man of the Year in 1964 when he appeared in 70 games, winning six and losing four with a 2.41 earned run average and 16 saves, McMahon didn't rely on gimmicks or trick pitches; his repertoire consisted of only a fastball and overhand curve.

McMahon pitched in 140 games for the Tribe before he was traded to Boston with pitcher Lee Stange for reliever Dick Radatz on June 2, 1966, and went on to play for the Chicago White Sox, Detroit, and San Francisco.

16–8 record and 2.99 earned run average. McLish was their best pitcher again in 1959, and was named to the American League All-Star team—and then was traded.

McLish often was asked the reason he has five given names, but never could fully explain how it happened. "All I know is that was my father who did it," he said.

"I don't know where the 'Calvin Coolidge' part of it came from because my dad wasn't even a Republican. I guess he just liked the name, the same as he probably liked 'Julius Caesar.'"

As for "Tuskahoma," McLish said it was the name of a town in the Indian territory of Oklahoma where his parents lived.

"Dad was one-quarter Chickasaw, mom was one-sixteenth Cherokee, which makes me one-eighth Chickasaw and one-thirty-second-Cherokee," said McLish, who also is part Scotch, English, Irish, and Dutch.

McLish, Cal

Indians	W	L	Pct	ERA	G	CG	IP	H	BB	SO	ShO
1956	2	4	.333	4.96	37	0	61⅔	67	32	27	0
1957	9	7	.563	2.74	42	2	144⅓	118	67	88	0
1958	16	8	.667	2.99	39	13	225⅔	214	70	97	0
1959	19	8	.704	3.63	35	13	235⅓	253	72	113	0
Career	92	92	.500	4.01	352	57	1,609	1,685	552	713	5

Don McMahon

When he retired in 1974 after 18 major league seasons, McMahon had appeared in 874 games, more than any pitcher in history except for Hoyt Wilhelm, Lindy McDaniel, and Cy Young. All but two of those appearances were in relief; he lost the only two games he ever started in the major leagues, for Houston in 1963.

It was in the minor leagues that he was converted to relief pitching by former star pitcher Whitlow Wyatt after McMahon had gone 2–13 with a 5.01 ERA as a starter in 1955 for Toledo of the American Association.

He reached the major leagues with Milwaukee in 1957, helping the Braves with the National League pennant that year and again in 1958, when he was a member of the NL All-Star team. McMahon also pitched in the World Series for Detroit in 1968 and in the NL Championship Series for the Giants in 1971.

After retiring as a player, McMahon coached for San Francisco in 1974–75, Minnesota in 1976–77, and the Giants again from 1980 to 1982. He was the Indians' pitching coach from 1983 to 1985.

McMahon, Don

Indians	W	L	Pct	ERA	G	CG	IP	H	BB	SO	ShO
1964	6	4	.600	2.41	70	0	101	67	52	92	0
1965	3	3	.500	3.28	58	0	85	79	37	60	0
1966	1	1	.500	2.92	12	0	12⅓	8	6	5	0
Career	90	68	.570	2.96	874	0	1,310⅔	1,054	579	1,003	0

Miller, Jacob Walter

Indians: 1924–31
Pitcher
Nickname: Jake
Birthplace: Wagram, Ohio

B: February 28, 1898
D: August 20, 1975
Batted left, threw left
Ht. 6–2; **Wt.** 170

Though he was inconsistent and injury prone, Jake Miller pitched seven-plus creditable seasons as both a starter and reliever for the Indians, three times winning in double figures.

A graduate of Ohio State University, Miller, in 1927, led the Tribe pitching staff with a 3.21 earned run average, and he posted 14 victories in 1929 when he was the number-three starter behind Willis Hudlin and Wes Ferrell.

Miller's total of 55 victories ties him with Al Milnar for sixth place among Cleveland's all-time left-handed pitchers.

Miller, Jake

Indians	W	L	Pct	ERA	G	CG	IP	H	BB	SO	ShO
1924	0	1	.000	3.00	2	1	12	13	5	4	0
1925	10	13	.435	3.31	32	13	190⅓	207	62	51	0
1926	7	4	.636	3.27	18	5	82⅔	99	18	24	3
1927	10	8	.556	3.21	34	11	185⅓	189	48	53	0
1928	8	9	.471	4.44	25	8	158	203	43	37	0
1929	14	12	.538	3.58	29	14	206	227	60	58	2
1930	4	4	.500	7.13	24	1	88⅓	147	38	31	0
1931	2	1	.667	4.35	10	1	41⅓	45	19	17	1
Career	60	58	.508	4.09	200	58	1,069⅔	1,260	340	305	8

Milnar (Mlinar), Albert Joseph

Indians: 1936, 1938–43
Pitcher
Nickname: Happy
Birthplace: Cleveland, Ohio

B: December 26, 1913
Bats left, throws left
Ht. 6–2; **Wt.** 195

Al Milnar was the third-winningest pitcher in the American League and tied Bob Feller and Ted Lyons for the most shutouts, four, in 1940 when the Indians lost the pennant by one game to Detroit.

That also was the year Milnar was named to the American League All-Star team.

A graduate of the Cleveland sandlots, Milnar won 18 games while losing 10 in 1940, and only Bob Feller, with 27, and the Tigers' Bobo Newsom, with 21, recorded more victories.

Milnar was signed by the Indians in 1933, but didn't make it to the major leagues full-time until 1938, despite compiling an outstanding minor league record, winning 46 games in 1934 and 1935 for New Orleans of the Class A Southern Association.

It was during Milnar's first season in professional baseball, on August 30, 1933, that the Indians stopped off in Zanesville, Ohio, to play a night exhibition game against their Class C Middle Atlantic League farm team. Milnar, then 19, pitched

Al Milnar

for Zanesville and struck out 18 Indians, gave up just three hits, and won, 7–2.

And in 1935 at New Orleans, Milnar set a league record by winning 17 consecutive games, from June 7 to August 11.

After he finally made it to the Indians, Milnar pitched and scored the winning run in a 2–1, 11-inning victory over Hall of Famer Lefty Gomez and the New York Yankees on May 5, 1939. He called it "my greatest thrill in baseball," and it earned him a $200 bonus from C. C. Slapnicka, vice president of the Indians.

Unfortunately for Milnar and the Indians, 1940 was his only great season in the major leagues. His record declined to 12–19 in 1941 and 6–8 in 1942.

One of Milnar's best performances took place on August 11, 1942, against Detroit in the opener of a twi-night doubleheader at the Stadium. The game was scoreless through eight innings, and Milnar had a no-hitter until the Tigers' Doc Cramer singled with two out in the ninth.

Milnar retired the next batter, but the Indians also were unable to score in the ninth, sending the game into extra innings. It remained scoreless through 14 innings when it was called because of darkness. Rudy York, who singled in the 13th inning, got the only other hit off Milnar.

At that time there was an American League rule that prohibited a game that started in daylight from being finished under the lights—so a few minutes after the game was called, the lights were turned on and the teams started the second game, which the Indians lost, 2–1.

The suspended first game was resumed the next day with the Tigers winning it, 2–0, against Indians reliever Joe Heving.

The following season, when his record was only 1–3, Milnar was sold to the St. Louis Browns on August 27. His total of 55 victories for the Indians ties him with Jake Miller for sixth place on Cleveland's all-time list of left-handed pitchers.

"If I had left well enough alone, my career probably would have been much better," Milnar said. "It was near the end of the 1940 season that I learned to throw a slider. [Former teammate] Johnny Allen taught it to me, but it was a pitch I should not have used."

Milnar hurt his shoulder throwing a slider early in the 1941 season, and he was never the same thereafter.

Milnar went only 1–2 for the Browns after joining them the final month of the 1943 season, and he spent the next two years in the army during World War II. He returned to the Browns in 1946, but his fastball was only a memory, and he retired after finishing the season with the Philadelphia Phillies.

Minoso, Saturnino Orestes Armas

Indians: 1949, 1951, 1958–59
Outfielder, third baseman, first baseman
Nickname: Minnie

Birthplace: Havana, Cuba
B: November 29, 1922
Bats right, throws right
Ht. 5–10; **Wt.** 175

Minnie Minoso came up through the Indians' farm system but spent most of his major league career—and had his best seasons—with the Chicago White Sox.

He was traded to the White Sox on April 30, 1951, in a three-team deal that also involved the Philadelphia Athletics and brought relief pitcher Lou Brissie to Cleveland. The Tribe also gave up pitcher Sam Zoldak and catcher Ray Murray.

An American League All-Star from 1951 to 1954 and again in 1957, 1959, and 1960, as well as a Gold Glove winner in 1957, 1959, and 1960, Minoso was reacquired by the Tribe on December 4, 1957.

It was Frank Lane, then the White Sox general manager, who got Minoso from the Indians in 1951, and it was Lane again, then the general manager of the Indians, who made the deal that returned him to Cleveland.

Though Minoso had two good seasons in 1958 and 1959—in each of which he batted .302—this deal proved to be another bad one for the Indians. To get Minoso back (along with utility infielder Fred Hatfield) they had to give up pitcher Early Wynn and outfielder Al Smith.

After those two seasons in Cleveland, during which he hit a career-high 24 homers in 1958, Minoso went back to the White Sox again. He was traded on December 6, 1959, along with catcher Dick Brown and pitchers Don Ferrarese and Jake Striker. Catcher John Romano, first baseman Norman Cash, and third baseman Bubba Phillips came to Cleveland.

Again Minoso proved he was far from finished. Though approaching 40, Minoso batted .311 and .280 for Chicago in 1960 and 1961, and went on to play for St. Louis in 1962 and

Minnie Minoso

Milnar, Al

Indians	W	L	Pct	ERA	G	CG	IP	H	BB	SO	ShO
1936	1	2	.333	7.36	4	1	22	26	18	9	0
1938	3	1	.750	5.00	23	2	68⅓	90	26	29	0
1939	14	12	.538	3.79	37	12	209	212	99	76	2
1940	18	10	.643	3.27	37	15	242⅓	242	99	99	4
1941	12	19	.387	4.36	35	9	229⅓	236	116	82	1
1942	6	8	.429	4.13	28	8	157	146	85	35	2
1943	1	3	.250	8.08	16	0	39	51	35	12	0
Career	57	58	.496	4.22	188	49	996⅓	1,043	495	350	10

Washington in 1963. He returned once more to the White Sox in 1964, retiring—but only temporarily—after that season.

As a White Sox coach in 1976, Minoso pinch-hit in three games, going 1-for-8, and went 0-for-2 in another brief comeback in 1980, giving him a major league record for having played in five decades, beginning in 1949 when he appeared in nine games for the Tribe.

Minoso, Minnie

Indians	G	AB	H	BA	RBI	R	2B	3B	HR	SA	SB
1949	9	16	3	.188	1	2	0	0	1	.375	0
1951	8	14	6	.429	2	3	2	0	0	.571	0
1958	149	556	168	.302	80	94	25	2	24	.484	14
1959	148	570	172	.302	92	92	32	0	21	.468	8
Career	1,835	6,579	1,963	.298	1,023	1,136	336	83	186	.459	205

Mitchell, Loren Dale

Indians: 1946–56
Outfielder
Birthplace: Colony, Oklahoma
B: August 23, 1921

D: January 5, 1987
Batted left, threw left
Ht. 6–1; **Wt.** 195

D ale Mitchell was strictly a contact hitter, but it was his only home run in 1954—and the final and 41st of his 11-year major league career—that won the game that clinched the 1954 pennant for the Indians.

Mitchell's homer gave the Tribe and Early Wynn a 3–2 victory over the Tigers in Detroit on September 18.

With a lifetime batting average of .312, Mitchell was a stalwart in left field for the Indians for seven seasons (1947–53) from the time he came up from the minor leagues in September 1946 and batted .432 in 11 games

During that time Mitchell hit .300 or better six times with a career-high .336 when the Indians won the pennant in

Dale Mitchell

1948. He led the American League with 203 hits and 23 triples in 1949. He was named to the AL All-Star team in 1949 and 1952.

It was after the 1949 season that Tribe manager Lou Boudreau said, "If anyone ever hits .400, Dale Mitchell will be the man."

On the other hand, Hank Greenberg, who was an Indians vice president during much of Mitchell's career in Cleveland, often chided the outfielder because of his unwillingness to swing for the fences.

"Singles hitters drive Fords, but home run hitters drive Cadillacs," Greenberg would tell Mitchell, who had decent power, but concentrated more on meeting the ball than driving it great distances.

After Mitchell was replaced by Al Smith as the Indians' regular left fielder in 1954, and slumped to .259 as a part-time player and pinch hitter in 1955, he was sold for $10,000 to the Brooklyn Dodgers on July 29, 1956.

It was with the Dodgers that Mitchell gained notoriety—unfairly so—in the fifth game of the World Series that year.

As a pinch hitter for Sal Maglie, Mitchell was the final batter retired by Don Larsen, completing a perfect game as the New York Yankees beat the Dodgers, 2–0. Mitchell was called out on strikes by umpire Babe Pinelli.

Mitchell, Dale

Indians	G	AB	H	BA	RBI	R	2B	3B	HR	SA	SB
1946	11	44	19	.432	5	7	3	0	0	.500	1
1947	123	493	156	.316	34	69	16	10	1	.396	2
1948	141	608	204	.336	56	82	30	8	4	.431	13
1949	149	640	203	.317	56	81	16	23	3	.428	10
1950	130	506	156	.308	49	81	27	5	3	.399	3
1951	134	510	148	.290	62	83	21	7	11	.424	7
1952	134	511	165	.323	58	61	26	3	5	.415	6
1953	134	500	150	.300	60	76	26	4	13	.446	3
1954	53	60	17	.283	6	6	1	0	1	.350	0
1955	61	58	15	.259	10	4	2	1	0	.328	0
1956	38	30	4	.133	6	2	0	0	0	.133	0
Career	1,127	3,984	1,244	.312	403	555	169	61	41	.416	45

Mitchell, William

Indians: 1909–16
Pitcher
Nickname: Willie
Birthplace: Pleasant Grove,
  Mississippi

B: December 1, 1889
D: November 23, 1973
Batted right, threw left
Ht. 6–0; **Wt.** 176

W illie Mitchell became one of the American League's best left-handed pitchers at the age of 20 when he won 12 games while losing eight for the Cleveland club (then called the Naps) in 1910. He improved to 14–8 with a 1.91 earned run average in 1913.

But Mitchell never got any better, and after his record fell below .500 in back-to-back seasons in 1914 and 1915 and he lost five of his first seven decisions in 1916, he was sold on June 20 to Detroit.

Still, his total of 64 victories for Cleveland ranks him fifth among the club's left-handed pitchers.

Mitchell started auspiciously in professional baseball in

1909 with San Antonio of the Texas League. His 13–9 record included a no-hitter on June 26 against Shreveport, and on August 21 he set a Texas League record by striking out 20 batters in one game against Galveston, all of which led to his contract being purchased by the Naps on August 26.

(That strikeout record of Mitchell's stood until July 16, 1976, when Dave Righetti of Tulsa struck out 21 Midland batters.)

After joining the Naps, Mitchell twice flirted with no-hitters: on September 11, 1910, in the first game of a doubleheader in St. Louis when he won, 3–0, as Roy Hartzell's single was the Browns' only hit, and on July 6, 1913, in the second game of a doubleheader at League Park when he beat Chicago, 7–0, as Buck Weaver's single was the only hit by the White Sox.

With the Tigers in 1917, Mitchell posted a 12–8 mark, but he won only one game the next two years, and his major league career ended in 1919.

Mitchell, Willie

Indians	W	L	Pct	ERA	G	CG	IP	H	BB	SO	ShO
1909	1	2	.333	1.57	3	3	23	18	10	8	0
1910	12	8	.600	2.60	35	11	183⅔	155	55	102	1
1911	7	14	.333	3.76	30	9	177⅓	190	60	78	0
1912	5	8	.385	2.80	29	8	163⅔	149	56	94	0
1913	14	8	.636	1.91	35	14	217	153	88	141	4
1914	12	17	.414	3.19	39	16	257	228	124	179	3
1915	11	14	.440	2.82	36	12	236	210	84	149	1
1916	2	5	.286	5.15	12	1	43⅔	55	19	24	0
Career	84	92	.477	2.88	276	93	1,632	1,464	605	921	16

Monge, Isidro Pedroza

Indians: 1977–81
Pitcher
Nickname: Sid
Birthplace: Agua Prieta, Mexico

B: April 11, 1951
Bats both, throws left
Ht. 6–2; **Wt.** 185

Sid Monge was acquired by the Indians in a deal of financial necessity on May 11, 1977. They traded reliever Dave LaRoche and minor league pitcher Dave Schuler to California for Monge and first baseman Bruce Bochte—and $250,000 to help meet the payroll.

Despite the money involved, it turned out to be an excellent deal for the Indians as Monge led the team in earned run average with 2.76 in 1978 and 2.40 in 1979. He set club records with 76 appearances and 12 relief victories, and also was credited with 19 saves in 1979, when he was named to the American League All-Star team.

But that was Monge's last good year for the Indians as he slumped to 3–5 records in both 1980 and 1981, when his ERA climbed to 3.53 and 4.34. He clashed several times with manager Dave Garcia and was traded on February 16, 1982, to the Philadelphia Phillies for outfielder Bake McBride.

Monge rebounded with a 7–1 record for the Phillies in 1982, and the following year, pitching for both the Phillies and San Diego, posted a 10–3 mark. He was traded to Detroit and was 3–1 in 1984, his final season in the major leagues.

Sid Monge

Monge, Sid

Indians	W	L	Pct	ERA	G	CG	IP	H	BB	SO	ShO
1977	1	2	.333	6.23	33	0	39	47	27	25	0
1978	4	3	.571	2.76	48	0	84⅔	71	51	54	0
1979	12	10	.545	2.40	76	0	131	96	64	108	0
1980	3	5	.375	3.53	67	0	94⅓	80	40	61	0
1981	3	5	.375	4.34	31	0	58	58	21	41	0
Career	49	40	.551	3.53	435	4	764	708	356	471	0

Moore, Earl Alonzo

Indians: 1901–07
Pitcher
Nickname: Steam Engine in Boots
Birthplace: Pickerington, Ohio

B: July 29, 1879
D: November 28, 1961
Batted right, threw right
Ht. 6–0; **Wt.** 195

A sidearmer with a blazing fastball that intimidated batters, Earl Moore pitched the American League's first no-hitter on May 9, 1901, but lost it and the game in the 10th inning when the Chicago White Sox scored twice for a 4–2 victory.

Until the 10th, Moore allowed only three base runners, all of them in the fourth inning when the White Sox scored twice on a walk, sacrifice bunt, stolen base, and two errors, one by Moore himself.

While the Cleveland team (then nicknamed the Blues) was being held to six hits by John Katoll, the White Sox scored in the 10th inning on singles by Sam Mertes and Fred Hartman, and two fielder's choices.

Moore came close to another no-hitter on August 12, 1901, in the first game of a doubleheader against the Chicago White Sox. The only hit he allowed was a single by Joe Sugden.

Ten years later he pitched another one-hitter on April 21, 1911. Moore, then with the Philadelphia Phillies, blanked the New York Giants, 3–0, allowing only a single by Fred Snodgrass.

Moore won in double figures each of his first five seasons in Cleveland, leading the AL with a 1.74 earned run average in 1903 when he won 19 games while losing nine.

He was a stubborn holdout and missed virtually all of the 1906 season when he pitched only five games with a 1–1 record, and was traded on May 16, 1907, to the New York Highlanders for pitcher Walter Clarkson.

A year later Moore was dealt to the Phillies and won a career-high 22 games in 1910, then he and Bill Steele of St. Louis led the National League with 19 losses in 1911. He went to the Chicago Cubs in 1913, then jumped to the newly formed Federal League, posting a 10–14 record for Buffalo in 1914, his final season in the major leagues.

Moore, Earl

Indians	W	L	Pct	ERA	G	CG	IP	H	BB	SO	ShO
1901	16	14	.533	2.90	31	28	251⅓	234	107	99	4
1902	17	17	.500	2.95	36	29	293	304	101	84	4
1903	19	9	.679	1.74	29	27	247⅔	196	62	148	3
1904	12	11	.522	2.25	26	22	227⅔	186	61	139	1
1905	15	15	.500	2.64	31	28	269	232	92	131	3
1906	1	1	.500	3.94	5	2	29⅔	27	18	8	0
1907	1	1	.500	4.66	3	1	19¼	18	8	7	0
Career	162	154	.513	2.78	388	230	2,776	2,474	1,108	1,403	34

Morgan, Edward Carre

Indians: 1928–33
First baseman, outfielder, third baseman
Birthplace: Cairo, Illinois

B: May 22, 1904
D: April 9, 1980
Batted right, threw right
Ht. 6–½; **Wt.** 180

Eddie Morgan's career with the Indians was brief, spanning only six seasons, but its impact was heavy as he set a home run record for right-handed batters that stood until the team moved out of League Park, with its vast left field, and into the Stadium.

He also played in an era when an outfielder or a first baseman who batted less than .330 was in danger of losing his job.

Regarded as one of the greatest all-around athletes developed at Tulane University, Morgan was a halfback, end, and tackle in football. After graduating from Tulane in 1927, Morgan began in professional baseball with New Orleans in the Southern Association, where he batted .354 and was purchased by the Indians.

Basically a first baseman, Morgan played the outfield part-time as a rookie in 1928 and full-time in 1929. It was in 1930 that he smashed 26 homers, a Tribe record for right-handed batters, and also hit 47 doubles while batting .349. That also was the season that he and Jimmie Foxx led the American League with 66 strikeouts.

Morgan hit a career-high .351 in 1931, when he also walked 83 times, but his power gradually declined. He hit only four homers in 1932, his last season as a regular for the

Eddie Morgan

Indians, and they let him go in 1933. He played for the Boston Red Sox in 1934, his last year in the major leagues.

Morgan's home run record for right-handed batters was tied by Ken Keltner in 1938 and Pat Seerey in 1946, and broken by Joe Gordon with 29 in 1947.

Morgan, Ed

Indians	G	AB	H	BA	RBI	R	2B	3B	HR	SA	SB
1928	76	265	83	.313	54	42	24	6	4	.494	5
1929	93	318	101	.318	37	60	19	10	3	.469	4
1930	150	584	204	.349	136	122	47	11	26	.601	8
1931	131	462	162	.351	86	87	33	4	11	.511	4
1932	144	532	156	.293	68	96	32	7	4	.402	7
1933	39	121	32	.264	13	10	3	3	1	.364	1
Career	771	2,810	879	.313	473	512	186	45	52	.467	36

Morton, Guy, Sr.

Indians: 1914–24
Pitcher
Nickname: Alabama Blossom
Birthplace: Vernon, Alabama

B: June 1, 1893
D: October 18, 1934
Batted right, threw right
Ht. 6–1; **Wt.** 175

Guy Morton had to be considered a very good prospect to survive his rookie season. He lost his first 13 games as a pitcher for the Indians in 1914.

That was the year the Tribe suffered 102 defeats, finishing last by 48½ games behind the Philadelphia Athletics.

Morton's consecutive losses as a rookie is still an American League record, though it was tied in 1982 by Terry Felton of Minnesota.

Morton started the 1914 season with Waterbury of the

Guy Morton

Morton, Guy

Indians	W	L	Pct	ERA	G	CG	IP	H	BB	SO	ShO
1914	1	13	.071	3.02	25	5	128	116	55	80	0
1915	16	15	.516	2.14	34	15	240	189	60	134	6
1916	12	8	.600	2.89	27	9	149⅔	139	42	88	0
1917	10	10	.500	2.74	35	6	161	158	59	62	1
1918	14	8	.636	2.64	30	13	214⅔	189	77	123	1
1919	9	9	.500	2.81	26	9	147⅓	128	47	64	3
1920	8	6	.571	4.47	29	6	137	140	57	72	1
1921	8	3	.727	2.76	30	3	107⅔	98	32	45	2
1922	14	9	.609	4.00	38	13	202⅔	218	85	102	3
1923	6	6	.500	4.24	33	3	129⅓	133	56	54	2
1924	0	1	.000	6.57	10	0	12⅓	12	13	6	0
Career	98	88	.527	3.13	317	82	1,629⅔	1,520	583	830	19

Mossi, Donald Louis

Indians: 1954–58
Pitcher
Nickname: The Sphinx
Birthplace: St. Helena, California

B: January 11, 1929
Bats left, throws left
Ht. 6–1; **Wt.** 195

Don Mossi's left arm was so crooked it kept him out of the service—but it didn't prevent him from being one of the best relief pitchers in baseball for most of his 12-year major league career.

"I don't know why, but I couldn't completely straighten my arm," said Mossi who, as a rookie, was a key factor in helping the Indians set an American League record by winning 111 games and the pennant in 1954.

"All I know is that, when I was examined for the [selective

Class B Eastern Association and compiled an 8–1 record that included a no-hitter against New Haven on June 16. Four days later he was in a Cleveland uniform making his major league debut—and starting his record losing streak.

Morton turned it around in 1915, winning 16 while losing 15, with a 2.14 earned run average. He went on to win in double figures for four consecutive seasons, and a total of five, in his 11-year career spent entirely with the Indians. His last season in the major leagues was 1924 when he went 0–1 in 10 games, all as a reliever.

Four times Morton came close to pitching a no-hitter: August 24, 1915, at League Park, 6–0 over New York, Ray Caldwell singled; June 1, 1917, at Boston, 3–0 over the Red Sox, Babe Ruth singled; May 23, 1918, at Boston, 1–0, over the Red Sox, Amos Strunk singled; and July 31, 1920, at League Park, 2–1 over Boston, Stuffy McInnis singled.

Morton also tied a major league record shared by many by striking out four batters in one inning against the Philadelphia Athletics on June 11, 1916.

His son, Guy, Jr., made a pinch-hitting appearance in his only major league game with the Red Sox on September 17, 1954. A former football and basketball player at the University of Alabama, Morton, Jr., went hitless in that only time at bat.

Don Mossi

service] draft, the doctor said I must have hurt my arm somehow, sometime, but I don't remember it.

"The first time I ever noticed that I couldn't straighten my arm was in high school. It bothered me some then, but not enough to stop me from pitching. It hurt me sometimes, but the more it hurt, the harder I threw."

Mossi pitched—often very well—for the Tribe from 1954 to 1958, and later with Detroit, the Chicago White Sox, and the Kansas City Athletics through 1965, his final year in the major leagues.

Mossi's crooked left arm might have been a reason his curveball was so effective. He was 6–1 with a 1.94 earned run average in 40 appearances in 1954.

That was the season Mossi retired 27 consecutive batters, the equivalent of a perfect game, before he yielded a home run to Joe Tipton of the Washington Senators with one out in the third inning on June 16.

The streak began when Mossi retired the last two batters to face him in the second inning on June 2, and followed by retiring two on June 4, one on June 6, three on June 8, three on June 10, nine on June 12, and seven on June 16 before he was touched for Tipton's homer.

Though Mossi started 22 games in 1957 (when his record was 11–10), he teamed up with bull pen partner Ray Narleski to give the Indians one of the most effective left-right relief tandems in baseball history. Mossi was named to the AL All-Star team in 1957.

"[Mossi and Narleski] were the best lefty-righty combination I've ever seen," said former teammate Herb Score, now a Tribe broadcaster.

Another former teammate, Al Rosen, said about Mossi's curveball: "It never stops breaking. I mean never."

Not only were Mossi and Narleski a tandem with the Tribe, but they also were traded as a pair, to Detroit on November 20, 1958, for second baseman Billy Martin and pitcher Al Cicotte. The Indians also sent shortstop Ossie Alvarez to the Tigers in the deal.

Mossi started for the Tigers most of his five years in Detroit, winning a career-high 17 games in 1959 and 15 in 1961. He went back to the bull pen in 1964 after being traded to the White Sox, and was a reliever for the Athletics in 1965.

Mossi, Don

Indians	W	L	Pct	ERA	G	CG	IP	H	BB	SO	ShO
1954	6	1	.857	1.94	40	2	93	56	39	55	0
1955	4	3	.571	2.42	57	0	81⅓	81	18	69	0
1956	6	5	.545	3.59	48	0	87⅔	79	33	59	0
1957	11	10	.524	4.13	36	6	159	165	57	97	1
1958	7	8	.467	3.90	43	0	101⅓	106	30	55	0
Career	101	80	.558	3.43	460	55	1,548	1,493	385	932	8

Myatt, Glenn Calvin

Indians: 1923–35
Catcher
Birthplace: Argenta, Arkansas
B: July 9, 1897

D: August 9, 1969
Batted left, threw right
Ht. 5–11; **Wt.** 165

Glenn Myatt was a central figure (along with third baseman Willie Kamm) in an incident that ripped the Indians apart in 1935, and he was a major factor in the firing of manager Walter Johnson.

Released after two seasons (1920, 1921) with the Philadelphia Athletics because owner-manager Connie Mack determined that he was not a good hitter, Myatt went back to the minor leagues.

Playing for Milwaukee in the American Association in 1922, Myatt batted .370 to lead the league and was purchased by the Indians, though he steadfastly maintained that "hitting is about the least important thing a catcher does."

The Indians' acquisition of Myatt proved to be a good move as he hit a career-high .342 in 105 games in 1924 and, from 1926 through 1932, served as a capable backup catcher to Luke Sewell, and then to Roy Spencer in 1933 and Frankie Pytlak in 1934.

It was in late May 1935, during Johnson's second season as manager of the Indians, that discontent and dissension erupted among the players, and Myatt and Kamm were accused of being the ringleaders.

With the team in Philadelphia, the manager told the media that he had discovered an "anti-Johnson" bloc among the Indians and said it was headed by Myatt and Kamm.

Johnson took immediate action, releasing Myatt and sending Kamm back to Cleveland under indefinite suspension for what he called "the good of the team."

Johnson's disciplinary action stood up as both Commissioner Kenesaw Mountain Landis and Indians owner Alva Bradley refused to intercede—though Bradley subsequently fired Johnson on August 4 and replaced him with coach Steve O'Neill.

Though Kamm never played again, becoming a scout for the Indians, Myatt signed with the New York Giants and finished the 1935 season with them after turning down offers from the Athletics and Chicago White Sox. He played for Detroit in 1936, ending a 16-year major league career with a .270 lifetime batting average.

Myatt, Glenn

Indians	G	AB	H	BA	RBI	R	2B	3B	HR	SA	SB
1923	92	220	63	.286	40	36	7	6	3	.414	0
1924	105	342	117	.342	73	55	22	7	8	.518	6
1925	106	358	97	.271	54	51	15	9	11	.455	3
1926	56	117	29	.248	13	14	5	2	0	.325	1
1927	55	94	23	.245	8	15	6	0	2	.372	1
1928	58	125	36	.288	15	9	7	2	1	.400	0
1929	59	129	30	.233	17	14	4	1	1	.302	0
1930	86	265	78	.294	37	30	23	2	2	.419	2
1931	65	195	48	.246	29	21	14	2	1	.354	2
1932	82	252	62	.246	46	45	12	1	8	.397	2
1933	40	77	18	.234	7	10	4	0	0	.286	0
1934	36	107	34	.318	12	18	6	1	0	.393	1
1935	10	36	3	.083	2	1	1	0	0	.111	0
Career	1,004	2,678	722	.270	387	346	137	37	38	.391	20

Naragon, Harold Richard

Indians: 1951, 1954–59
Catcher
Nickname: Hal
Birthplace: Zanesville, Ohio

B: October 1, 1928
Bats left, throws right
Ht. 6–0; **Wt.** 160

Only the presence of Jim Hegan kept Hal Naragon from establishing himself as one of baseball's best catchers in the 1950s.

Hal Naragon

When he came up as a rookie in 1954, in fact, he was called "a carbon copy of Hegan," though Naragon was never able to win a starting job.

An excellent receiver and handler of pitchers, Naragon played behind Hegan in Cleveland, and then backed up Earl Battey at Washington and Minnesota. He was traded by the Indians to Washington on May 25, 1959, with pitcher Hal Woodeshick for catcher Ed FitzGerald.

After retiring as a player in 1962, Naragon teamed up with Johnny Sain as pitching coaches for Minnesota from 1963 to '66 and Detroit from 1967 to '69.

Naragon, Hal

Indians	G	AB	H	BA	RBI	R	2B	3B	HR	SA	SB
1951	3	8	2	.250	0	0	0	0	0	.250	0
1954	46	101	24	.238	12	10	2	2	0	.297	0
1955	57	127	41	.323	14	12	9	2	1	.449	1
1956	53	122	35	.287	18	11	3	1	3	.402	0
1957	57	121	31	.256	8	12	1	1	0	.281	0
1958	9	9	3	.333	0	2	0	1	0	.556	0
1959	14	36	10	.278	5	6	4	1	0	.444	0
Career	424	985	262	.266	87	83	27	11	6	.334	1

Narleski, Raymond Edmond

Indians: 1954–58
Pitcher
Birthplace: Camden, New Jersey

B: November 25, 1928
Bats right, throws right
Ht. 6–1; **Wt.** 175

Though he was overshadowed by a starting pitching staff that was considered the best in the history of baseball, Ray Narleski was a key factor in the Indians' success in 1954, when they won an American League–record 111 games.

Narleski teamed with left-hander Don Mossi to give the Tribe outstanding relief pitching, not only in 1954—when they combined for a 9–4 won-lost mark and 20 saves—but also through 1958 before they were traded in tandem to Detroit.

With a fastball that was clocked in the mid to high 90s (mph), Narleski in 1955 led the American League with 60 appearances, as well as eight victories in relief and 19 saves, and in 1956 he posted a 1.52 earned run average in 32 games.

He was the Indians' all-time leader in saves, with 53 in five seasons, until that record was broken by Doug Jones in 1989.

Narleski always said he owed his success as a pitcher to his father, Bill Narleski, an infielder for the Boston Red Sox in 1929 and 1930.

"My dad worked out with me as a kid and always made me throw hard every day," said Ray. "I suppose that's how I developed into a reliever."

Something else the elder Narleski taught his son—and which Ray said he never forgot—was "Never give in to a hitter. Fight him all the way."

Despite his achievements as a reliever, it was as a starter that Narleski was picked on the American League All-Star team in 1958. That was the season he appeared in 44 games, 24 as a starter. He also started 15 games in 1957.

Narleski and Mossi, along with minor league shortstop Ossie Alvarez, were traded to Detroit on November 20, 1958, for second baseman Billy Martin.

With the Tigers, Narleski also was a spot starter-reliever in 1959, his final season in the major leagues, when his record was only 4–12 with a 5.78 ERA.

Narleski, Ray

Indians	W	L	Pct	ERA	G	CG	IP	H	BB	SO	ShO
1954	3	3	.500	2.22	42	1	89	59	44	52	0
1955	9	1	.900	3.71	60	1	111⅔	91	52	94	0
1956	3	2	.600	1.52	32	0	59⅓	36	19	42	0
1957	11	5	.688	3.09	46	7	154⅓	136	70	93	1
1958	13	10	.565	4.07	44	7	183⅓	179	91	102	0
Career	43	33	.566	3.60	266	17	702	606	335	454	1

Ray Narleski

Nettles, Graig

Indians: 1970–72
Third baseman
Birthplace: San Diego, California

B: August 20, 1944
Bats left, throws right
Ht. 6–0; **Wt.** 180

His best years were with the New York Yankees from 1973 to 1983, but it was in Cleveland that Graig Nettles established himself as one of the game's best third basemen and a home run hitter, though his lifetime batting average was only .248 for 22 major league seasons.

And, just as the acquisition of Nettles from Minnesota was a very good deal for the Indians, he figured in one of their worst trades three years later.

The Tribe got Nettles, along with outfielder Ted Uhlaender and pitchers Dean Chance and Bob Miller, on December 11, 1969, after he'd played only briefly, mostly in the outfield, for the Twins, in exchange for pitchers Luis Tiant and Stan Williams.

Though his batting average was nothing to rave about, Nettles hit 71 homers in his three seasons with the Indians.

Equally important was his defensive ability.

Nettles set two American League records for third basemen in 1971 with 412 assists and participating in 54 double plays. He also led the league that season with 159 putouts at third base. He was voted the Indians' Man of the Year for 1971.

Then, with Buddy Bell, also a third baseman, having come up from the minors and the financially strapped Indians needing help at several positions, they traded Nettles, along with catcher Gerry Moses, to the Yankees on November 27, 1972.

In exchange for Nettles and Moses, the Tribe received outfielders Charlie Spikes and Rusty Torres, catcher John Ellis, and second baseman Jerry Kenney, none of whom distinguished himself in Cleveland—though Nettles did in New York.

He led the league with 32 homers in 1976, hit a career-high 37 homers and drove in 107 runs in 1977, batted .276 in 1978, was named to the AL All-Star team in 1975 and 1977–80, made the NL team in 1985, and won Gold Glove awards in 1977 and 1978.

Graig Nettles

Nettles, who missed 67 games in 1987 when he was with Atlanta and had hepatitis, also played for San Diego from 1984 to 1986 and Montreal in 1988. He appeared in seven league championship series (one with the Twins, five with the Yankees, one with the Padres) and five World Series (four with the Yankees, one with the Padres).

Nettles holds the AL record for most homers by a third baseman, 319; and he tied a major league mark for the most home runs in the month of April with 11 in 1974. After his retirement, Nettles was a coach for the New York Yankees in 1991, scouted for them from 1992 to 1994, then joined the Padres as their third base coach. His brother Jim was an outfielder with Minnesota, Detroit, Kansas City, and Oakland between 1970 and 1981.

Nettles, Graig

Indians	G	AB	H	BA	RBI	R	2B	3B	HR	SA	SB
1970	157	549	129	.235	62	81	13	1	26	.404	3
1971	158	598	156	.261	86	78	18	1	28	.435	7
1972	150	557	141	.253	70	65	28	0	17	.395	2
Career	2,700	8,986	2,225	.248	1,314	1,193	328	28	390	.421	32

Newhouser, Harold

Indians: 1954–55
Pitcher
Nickname: Prince Hal
Birthplace: Detroit, Michigan

B: May 20, 1921
Bats left, throws left
Ht. 6–2; **Wt.** 180

Hal Newhouser didn't join the Indians until nearly the end of his career, but he played a key role as a long reliever when they set an American League record with 111 victories.

Ironically, Newhouser, who began in professional baseball with the Detroit Tigers in 1939 and made it to the major leagues to stay in 1940, almost signed with the Indians.

Newhouser didn't, he later said, only because a Tigers' scout showed up at his house in Detroit with a $500 bonus that he eagerly accepted—10 minutes before a representative of the Indians came calling with an even larger offer.

"That was during the Depression, and I was trying to earn money to go to a trade school by selling newspapers, setting pins in a bowling alley, and collecting pop bottles to get the deposit on them.

"In those days $500 seemed mighty big to me and my parents. I thought it was unbelievable to get that much money for playing baseball, until the Indians told me they were going to give my parents $15,000 and a new car worth $4,000," said Newhouser, who was elected to the Hall of Fame in 1992.

Kept out of the service during World War II because of a congenital heart ailment, Newhouser was the most dominant pitcher in baseball from 1944 to 1946 when he led the American League with 29, 25, and 26 victories. He is the only pitcher to win the Most Valuable Player award in two consecutive seasons (1944, 1945) and was a member of the AL All-Star team in the years 1942–44 and 1946–48.

Newhouser came close to pitching no-hitters twice: on May 6, 1945, when he beat St. Louis, 3–0, in the first game of a doubleheader in Detroit, as Vern Stephens singled; and on September 8, 1949, in a 10–0 victory over the Indians in Detroit, as Lou Boudreau's single was the only hit.

As a star pitcher for the Tigers, Newhouser engaged in many classic pitching duels with Bob Feller, who would have

Hal Newhouser

then the Indians' vice president and general manager, talked Newhouser into attempting a comeback.

The once-swift southpaw joined the Tribe and posted a 7–2 won-lost record with seven saves and a 2.51 earned run average in 26 games in 1954. Newhouser returned in 1955, but retired after the first month.

He later scouted for Baltimore from 1956 to 1961, signing Dean Chance in 1959, and for the Indians the next three years. In 1963, Newhouser became an executive for a bank in Pontiac, Michigan, rising to a vice presidency before retiring in 1984.

Newhouser, Hal

Indians	W	L	Pct	ERA	G	CG	IP	H	BB	SO	ShO
1954	7	2	.778	2.51	26	0	46⅔	34	18	25	0
1955	0	0	—	0.00	2	0	2⅓	1	4	1	0
Career	207	150	.580	3.06	488	212	2,993	2,674	1,249	1,796	33

Niekro, Philip Henry

Indians: 1986–87
Pitcher
Nickname: Knucksie
Birthplace: Blaine, Ohio

B: April 1, 1939
Bats right, throws right
Ht. 6–1; **Wt.** 180

P hil Niekro is one of many players who spent most of his career elsewhere, but achieved a major distinction during his brief career with the Indians.

Though he pitched only one season and four months of another in Cleveland, it was on June 1, 1987, that Niekro beat Detroit, 9–6, making him and Joe Niekro the winningest brother combination in major league history.

That victory was Phil's 314th, and with the 216 games won by Joe (for the Chicago Cubs, San Diego, Detroit, Atlanta, Houston, and New York Yankees), it gave the Niekros 530, one more than the total recorded by Gaylord and Jim Perry.

One of Phil's victories was against Joe on July 4, 1967, the first time brothers pitched against each other in a National League game. Phil, pitching for the Braves, beat Joe and the Cubs, 8–3. In later head-to-head confrontations, Joe won twice and Phil once, giving each a 2–2 record against the other.

been his teammate in Cleveland had the Indians' scout arrived earlier with their larger offer.

It was against Feller in 1948 that Newhouser beat the Indians, 7–1, on the final day of the regular season, October 3. It left the Tribe tied with Boston for first place, forcing a one-game playoff for the pennant.

That victory by Newhouser, working with one day's rest, was his 21st of the season, and it led to the shoulder problems that probably shortened his career with the Tigers. Newhouser's record declined to 18 victories in 1949 and 15 in 1950, and he won a total of only 15 games the next three years, retiring in 1953.

His former teammate with the Tigers, Hank Greenberg,

Phil Niekro

With a tantalizing knuckleball as his primary pitch, Phil went on to win 318 games, giving the Niekro brothers 539 victories.

It was with the Braves from 1964 to 1983 that Phil Niekro was most successful. He was named to the National League All-Star team in 1969, 1975, 1978, and 1982. Niekro also was chosen to be on the American League All-Star team in 1984, and his 300th victory was pitched for the New York Yankees. He did it on the final day of the 1985 season, beating Toronto, 8–0, on October 6, making him the 18th pitcher—and the oldest, at 46—to win 300 major league games.

Niekro also had the distinction of pitching a no-hitter, a 9–0 victory over San Diego in Atlanta on August 5, 1973.

He also flirted with no-hitters on two other occasions, both for the Braves in Cincinnati, on September 5, 1960, 11–2, the only hit being Tony Perez's first inning homer, and on October 2, 1976, when he beat the Reds, 3–0, with Cesar Geronimo getting a ninth-inning double.

After pitching for the Yankees in 1984 and 1985, winning 32 and losing 20, Niekro was purchased on April 3, 1986, by the Indians, for whom he went 11–11 and 7–11 the next two seasons.

Niekro was traded on August 9, 1987, to the Blue Jays for minor league outfielder Darryl Landrum and pitcher Don Gordon, and he finished the season—and ended his 24-year major league career—pitching one last game for the Braves, a no-decision against San Francisco, on September 27 in Atlanta.

Niekro started and had a 5–0 lead going into the fourth inning. He faced five batters in the fourth, all of whom scored to tie the game at 5–5, after which Niekro—then 48 years old—was removed. The Giants went on to win, 15–6, though Niekro was not charged with the loss.

Russ Nixon

Niekro, Phil

Indians	W	L	Pct	ERA	G	CG	IP	H	BB	SO	ShO
1986	11	11	.500	4.32	34	5	210⅓	241	95	81	0
1987	7	11	.389	5.89	22	2	123⅔	142	53	57	0
Career	318	274	.537	3.35	864	245	5,404⅓	5,044	1,809	3,342	45

Nixon, Russell Eugene

Indians: 1957–60
Catcher
Birthplace: Cleves, Ohio

B: February 19, 1935
Bats left, throws right
Ht. 6–1; **Wt.** 195

Russ Nixon and his twin brother Roy, a first baseman, were both signed by the Indians in 1953, but only Russ made it to the major leagues.

He did so on the wings of two minor league batting championships, winning the Class D Florida State League title with a .387 average for Jacksonville Beach in 1954 and the Class B Three-I League crown with a .385 average for Keokuk in 1955.

Promoted to the Indians in 1957, Nixon backed up Jim Hegan that first year. He took over as the starting catcher the following season after Hegan was traded to Detroit on February 18, 1958.

Nixon batted .301 in 113 games in 1958, but never hit or played that much again in a 12-year major league career that ended in 1968 with the Boston Red Sox.

In 1960, Nixon was twice traded by the Tribe, the first time on March 16 to the Red Sox for catcher Sammy White and first baseman–outfielder Jim Marshall. But when White refused to report to Cleveland and retired, the deal was called off.

Three months later, on June 13, the Indians again sent Nixon to the Red Sox, this time with outfielder Carroll Hardy for pitcher Ted Bowsfield and outfielder Marty Keough. Nixon went on to play for Minnesota in 1966, and in 1968 he went back to the Red Sox, with whom he ended his playing career.

Nixon managed in the Cincinnati farm system from 1970 to 1975, became a coach for the Reds in 1976, and replaced John McNamara as manager on July 21, 1982. When the Reds finished last in 1983, Nixon was dismissed. He served as a coach for Montreal in 1984 and 1985 and for Atlanta in 1986 and 1987.

Nixon began the 1988 season as manager of the Braves' Greenville club of the Class AA Southern League. On May 22 he replaced Chuck Tanner as manager of the Braves, a job he held until June 22, 1990, when he was fired and replaced by Bobby Cox. Nixon was out of baseball in 1991, but returned as a coach for Seattle in 1992. He retired from baseball the following year.

Nixon, Russ

Indians	G	AB	H	BA	RBI	R	2B	3B	HR	SA	SB
1957	62	185	52	.281	18	15	7	1	2	.362	0
1958	113	376	113	.301	46	42	17	4	9	.439	0
1959	82	258	62	.240	29	23	10	3	1	.314	0
1960	25	82	20	.244	6	6	5	0	1	.341	0
Career	906	2,504	670	.268	266	215	115	19	27	.361	0

O'Dea, Paul

Indians: 1944–45
Outfielder, first baseman
Nickname: Lefty
Birthplace: Cleveland

B: July 3, 1920
D: December 11, 1978
Batted left, threw left
Ht. 6–0; **Wt.** 200

Paul O'Dea was considered one of the best natural hitters in the Indians' farm system, and team officials had great expectations for the outfielder who had been a star on the Cleveland sandlots.

He batted .362 for Fargo-Moorhead of the Class D Northern League in 1938 and .342 for Springfield of the Class C Mid-Atlantic League in 1939.

Paul O'Dea

O'Dea, Paul

Indians	G	AB	H	BA	RBI	R	2B	3B	HR	SA	SB
1944	76	173	55	.318	13	25	9	0	0	.370	2
1945	87	221	52	.235	21	21	2	2	1	.276	3
Career	163	394	107	.272	34	46	11	2	1	.317	5

Olin, Steven Robert

Indians: 1989–92
Pitcher
Birthplace: Portland, Oregon
B: October 4, 1965

D: March 22, 1993
Batted right, threw right
Ht. 6–3; **Wt.** 185

Steve Olin was cut down in the prime of his life and career by a tragic boating accident that killed him and teammate Tim Crews and severely injured another Indians pitcher, Bob Ojeda, on March 22, 1993.

It happened on Little Lake Nellie in Clermont, Florida, as the three pitchers were enjoying a family outing during a day off from the rigors of spring training in Winter Haven, Florida.

Olin and Crews were killed when Crews' 18-foot, open-air fishing boat crashed into a dock. Ojeda, who suffered head and scalp injuries, recovered after a lengthy hospital stay, though he was left with psychological scars that took a long time to heal.

Ojeda didn't make it back to pitch for the Indians until August 7, appearing in nine games, seven as a starter, with a 2–1 won-lost record and 4.40 earned run average. When the season ended, Ojeda became a free agent and signed with the New York Yankees.

Crews, like Olin a reliever, was with the Indians as a spring training invitee after having signed as a minor league free agent.

Olin had become one of the best closers in the major leagues, saving 29 Tribe victories in 1992 while recording an 8–5 record and a 2.34 ERA in 72 games. His career total of 48 saves placed Olin third on the Indians' all-time list, behind Doug Jones (128) and Ray Narleski (53).

A submarine-style pitcher, Olin was a 16th-round selection of the Indians in the 1987 amateur draft. He made it to the major leagues to stay in 1992 after dividing parts of the three previous seasons between Cleveland and Colorado Springs of the Pacific Coast League.

Olin, Steve

Indians	W	L	Pct	ERA	G	CG	IP	H	BB	SO	ShO
1989	1	4	.200	3.75	25	0	36	35	14	24	0
1990	4	4	.500	3.41	50	0	92⅓	96	26	64	0
1991	3	6	.333	3.36	48	0	56¼	61	23	38	0
1992	8	5	.615	2.34	72	0	88⅓	80	27	47	0
Career	16	19	.457	3.10	195	0	273	272	90	173	0

O'Neill, Stephen Francis

Indians: 1911–23
Catcher
Nickname: Steve
Birthplace: Minooka, Pennsylvania

B: July 6, 1891
D: January 26, 1962
Batted right, threw right
Ht. 5–10; **Wt.** 165

One of four brothers who played in the major leagues, Steve O'Neill was the most successful—as a catcher for the In-

But that was before O'Dea was the victim of an accident that occurred during batting practice in spring training on March 21, 1940. In one cruel instant O'Dea's promising baseball career was all but shattered.

As O'Dea stood near the edge of the batting cage in the Tribe's training camp at Fort Myers, Florida, awaiting his turn to hit, he leaned around the protective screen to pick up a ball that had been fouled off.

In that moment the batter, a fellow rookie named Lou Kahn, swung at a pitch and lined it squarely into O'Dea's face.

Squarely into O'Dea's right eye, to be exact. The force of the blow destroyed O'Dea's vision in that eye and, for a man of lesser resolve, would have ended any hope of a baseball career.

But O'Dea refused to give up, though it took time and several operations before he could play again. Being a left-handed batter, O'Dea had to adjust his hitting style to utilize his good left eye. He launched a comeback on the Cleveland sandlots in 1942 and 1943.

He rejoined the Indians in 1944, becoming their regular right fielder, though he was never the same hitter as before the accident.

Still, O'Dea impressed everybody with his determination and ability. "It's simply remarkable the way that boy hits the ball," Connie Mack said after seeing O'Dea play against the Philadelphia Athletics.

Lou Boudreau, then the Indians manager, said, "The kid is a marvel," when O'Dea returned to the team and hit .318 in 76 games in 1944.

However, despite O'Dea's attempt to do with one eye what most men can't do with two, he struggled with a .235 average in 87 games in 1945. When the stars returned from World War II in 1946, O'Dea retired.

He took a front office job with the Indians and served as a scout until his death in 1978.

Steve O'Neill

dians for 13 seasons, and their manager from August 4, 1935, when he replaced Walter Johnson, through 1937.

O'Neill was one of the most popular men in baseball throughout his career, which continued through the mid-1950s.

He was behind the plate for the Indians in 1,335 games, second most in franchise history (to Jim Hegan's 1,491), caught 100 games or more in nine consecutive seasons (1915–23), and batted .300 or better three years in a row (1920–22), including a career-high .322 in 1921.

In 14 seasons as a major league manager, O'Neill never had a losing record, and his Detroit team won the American League pennant and World Series in 1945.

The primary complaint by critics of O'Neill as a manager was that he was too easygoing. After his team lost 11 of 13 games at one point in 1936, an open letter to O'Neill appeared in the *Cleveland News* under the headline "Get Mad, Steve! Get Mad!"

After being replaced by Oscar Vitt in 1938, O'Neill managed the Indians' farm team at Buffalo of the International League that season, and again in 1939 and 1940, where he was instrumental in the development of Lou Boudreau and other future major leaguers.

O'Neill took over as manager of the Tigers in 1943, a job he held through 1948, piloted the Boston Red Sox in 1950 and 1951, and led the Phillies from 1952 to 1954.

O'Neill's professional baseball career began in 1910 with Elmira of the Class B New York State League. The Philadelphia Athletics owned his contract but sold it to Worcester of the Class B New England League, where O'Neill batted .282 in 1911. On August 11, O'Neill was purchased by the Cleveland club (then called the Naps), and he played in nine games at the end of the 1911 season.

O'Neill alternated with Ted Easterly in 1912 and with Fred Carisch in 1913 and 1914. Then he was the Indians' regular catcher from 1915 until he was traded to the Red Sox in a seven-player deal on January 7, 1924.

In addition to O'Neill, the Tribe sent second baseman Bill Wambsganss, pitcher Danny Boone, and outfielder Joe Connolly to Boston for catcher Roxy Walters, first baseman George Burns, and second baseman–third baseman Chick Fewster.

After one season with the Red Sox, O'Neill went to the New York Yankees on waivers, December 15, 1924. He played in only 35 games with the Yankees in 1925 and after being released in late July, finished the season with Reading of the Class AAA International League. He switched over to Toronto, also of the International League, in 1926, but was back in the American League with the St. Louis Browns in 1927 and 1928.

O'Neill then coached and managed in the minor and major leagues until he retired from baseball in 1954.

O'Neill, Steve

Indians	G	AB	H	BA	RBI	R	2B	3B	HR	SA	SB
1911	9	27	4	.148	1	1	1	0	0	.185	2
1912	69	215	49	.228	14	17	4	0	0	.247	2
1913	80	234	69	.295	29	19	13	3	0	.376	5
1914	87	269	68	.253	20	28	12	2	0	.312	1
1915	121	386	91	.236	34	32	14	2	2	.298	2
1916	130	378	89	.235	29	30	23	0	0	.296	2
1917	129	370	68	.184	29	21	10	2	0	.222	2
1918	114	359	87	.242	35	34	8	7	1	.312	5
1919	125	398	115	.289	47	46	35	7	2	.427	4
1920	149	489	157	.321	55	63	39	5	3	.440	3
1921	106	335	108	.322	50	39	22	1	1	.403	0
1922	133	392	122	.311	65	33	27	4	2	.416	2
1923	113	330	82	.248	50	31	12	0	0	.285	0
Career	1,590	4,795	1,259	.263	537	448	248	34	13	.337	30

Paige, Leroy Robert

Indians: 1948–49
Pitcher
Nickname: Satchel
Birthplace: Mobile, Alabama

B: July 7, 1906
D: June 8, 1982
Batted right, threw right
Ht. 6–3½; **Wt.** 180

Unfortunately—and unfairly—it took Satchel Paige more than two decades to prove that he should be considered one of baseball's all-time greatest pitchers.

But once Paige joined the Indians, there was no doubt about his ability, even though he was then 40-something.

Tribe owner Bill Veeck signed the legendary black pitcher on July 7, 1948, after a brief "tryout" at the Stadium in which Paige threw for about 20 minutes to manager Lou Boudreau.

Boudreau's description of that workout: "Satch handed

Satchel Paige

me a folded-up handkerchief and told me to put it on the plate wherever I wanted him to pitch the ball, inside, outside, middle, wherever.

"First, I put it on the inside corner. He wound up and threw 10 pitches—fastballs and sliders, all with something on them—and nine of them were right over the handkerchief.

"Then he told me to move the handkerchief to the other side of the plate, and he threw 10 more pitches the same as before. His fastball had a hop to it, and his slider was tremendous. Seven or eight pitches were right over the handkerchief and those that missed, didn't miss by much.

"Next, Veeck wanted me to bat against Paige. I hit some line drives, but not many. I'd seen enough. He was tough, and I was satisfied that he could help us."

Which Paige did. He won six games and lost one with a 2.48 earned run average in 21 appearances, seven as a starter, that season as the Indians won the American League pennant and World Series.

Paige's performance made J. G. Taylor Spink, then the highly respected editor and publisher of *The Sporting News,* eat his words.

Spink blasted Veeck in an editorial at the time Paige was signed, saying it was nothing more than a blatant publicity stunt, and suggesting that if Paige were white, he would not have drawn a second thought from Veeck.

The editorial stated, "To bring in a pitching 'rookie' of Paige's age casts a reflection on the entire scheme of operations in the major leagues. To sign a hurler of Paige's age is to demean the standards of baseball in the big circuits."

Until then Paige had pitched in the Negro leagues for more than 20 years—how many more, nobody could be sure, because nobody knew his true birth date—not even Satchel himself, he insisted.

Paige made his first appearance for the Indians on July 9, pitching two scoreless innings in relief against the St. Louis Browns. He got his first major league victory in the second game of a doubleheader in Philadelphia on July 15 when he pitched three innings in relief of Bob Lemon.

On August 3, in front of a Cleveland Stadium crowd of 72,434 fans, Paige made his first start and pitched seven strong innings, allowing three runs on seven hits with six strikeouts in a 5–3 victory over Washington.

A couple of weeks later, after Paige had pitched a three-hit shutout against Chicago, Veeck sent Spink a telegram that read: "Paige pitching. No runs, three hits. He definitely is in line for Sporting News 'Rookie of the Year' award."

The confusion about his birth date, Paige explained, was due to the fact that he was one of 11 children and was born in Mobile, Alabama, when records were not always accurately kept.

While his achievements in the Negro League are legendary, so are stories about Paige's pitching performances on barnstorming tours, especially how he often called in his outfielders at the start of an inning and struck out the side.

Paige pitched in 31 games for the Indians in 1949, compiling a 4–7 won-lost record and 3.04 ERA, and was released after the season when Veeck sold the franchise.

Two years later, after Veeck had purchased the St. Louis Browns, he again signed Paige. Satchel pitched three more seasons, the best of which was 1952 when he went 12–10, including an AL-leading eight relief victories, with 10 saves. He was named to the American League All-Star team in 1952 and 1953.

Released by the Browns in 1954, Paige went back on the barnstorming circuit and also pitched for several Negro League and minor league teams the next 12 years. Paige returned for a final hurrah in the major leagues on September 25, 1965, when he pitched three innings as a starter for Charley Finley and his Kansas City Athletics.

This appearance ended an active career in which, according to one estimate, Paige pitched in 2,600 games and threw at least 300 shutouts, of which 55 were no-hitters.

After that brief appearance in Kansas City, Paige improved his pension by serving as a coach for Atlanta for two seasons. He was elected to the Hall of Fame in 1971.

Paige, Satchel											
Indians	W	L	Pct	ERA	G	CG	IP	H	BB	SO	ShO
1948	6	1	.857	2.48	21	3	72⅔	61	25	45	2
1949	4	1	.364	3.04	31	1	83	70	33	54	0
Career	28	31	.475	3.29	179		476	429	183	290	4

Perry, Gaylord Jackson

Indians: 1972–75
Pitcher
Birthplace: Williamston, North Carolina

B: September 15, 1938
Bats right, throws right
Ht. 6-4; **Wt.** 205

Did he or didn't he?

"That's for me to know and for you to worry about," is the way Gaylord Perry usually answered the question he was asked most often, to wit:

Did he throw an illegal pitch, in his case a "grease ball," as most batters charged, or was it really a forkball that looked like an illegal pitch, as he claimed?

Mainly, Perry was playing a game with the hitters' minds, although he admitted in his 1974 autobiography, *Me and the Spitter,* that, yes, sometimes he "loaded" his pitches.

Only once, however, did an umpire throw Perry out of a

Gaylord Perry

game for allegedly applying a foreign substance to a ball. That was in 1982 when Perry was pitching for Seattle against California. The umpire was Dave Phillips.

"He [Phillips] didn't find anything on me or the ball, but when he saw one of my pitches sink about two feet he came running out to the mound yelling, 'That's it, Gaylord, you're outta here!'"

When asked if he did indeed load up the pitch that sank two feet, Perry replied with a devilish glint in his eyes, "I was given a lie detector test by [famed attorney] F. Lee Bailey on television that winter, and they said I passed it with flying colors."

The fact is, Perry always wanted batters to think about the probability that he cheated. Those mind games were a factor in his 314 victories, 15th most in major league history. He became the 15th pitcher to win 300 games when he beat the New York Yankees, 7–3, for Seattle on May 6, 1982.

The only man to win the Cy Young award in both leagues—with the Indians in the American League in 1972 and with San Diego in the National League in 1978—Perry was one of the best acquisitions in the history of the Cleveland franchise.

The Indians got him on November 29, 1971, along with shortstop Frank Duffy, in a trade with San Francisco for Sam McDowell.

The following season Perry won 24 games—exactly one-third of the Indians' victories that year—and was elected Man of the Year, an award he again won with brother Jim in 1974.

The Perrys combined to win 529 games, second most (to Phil and Joe Niekro) in major league history.

When Gaylord and Jim, then with Detroit, started against each other on July 3, 1973, it was the first time in the AL that brothers had done so. The Tigers won, 5–4, and Gaylord was charged with the loss.

It was in 1974, between April 12 and July 3, that Gaylord won 15 consecutive games, tying the club record set by Johnny Allen in 1937. The streak ended on July 8 when Perry was beaten by Oakland, 4–3, in 11 innings.

Gaylord went on to win 70 games in three-plus seasons before he was traded to Texas on June 13, 1975, in what turned out to be another excellent deal for the Tribe.

The financially strapped Indians received pitchers Rick Waits, Jackie Brown, and Jim Bibby and $100,000 for Perry. The deal also cleared the air in the clubhouse, as Perry did not get along with manager Frank Robinson.

Their personality conflict dated back to the time both were in the NL, Perry with the Giants and Robinson with the Cincinnati Reds.

After leaving the Indians, Perry pitched for six teams—Texas, the New York Yankees, Atlanta, Seattle, San Diego, and the Kansas City Royals. He went 21–6 for the Padres to win the Cy Young award in 1978, and retired after going 7–14 for the Mariners and Royals in 1983.

One of only four pitchers to win 100 games in both leagues, Perry in his 22-year major league career that began in 1962, hurled a no-hitter for the Giants against St. Louis, 1–0, on September 17, 1968; one one-hitter; 13 two-hitters; and 53 shutouts. He struck out 3,534 batters and was a member of the All-Star team in the NL in 1966, 1970, and 1979 and in the AL in 1972 and 1974.

Perry, Gaylord

Indians	W	L	Pct	ERA	G	CG	IP	H	BB	SO	ShO
1972	24	16	.600	1.92	41	29	342⅔	253	82	234	5
1973	19	19	.500	3.38	41	29	344	315	115	238	7
1974	21	13	.618	2.51	37	28	322⅓	230	99	216	4
1975	6	9	.400	3.55	15	10	121⅓	120	34	85	1
Career	314	265	.542	3.11	777	303	5,350	4,938	1,379	3,534	53

Perry, James Evan

Indians: 1959–63, 1974–75
Pitcher
Birthplace: Williamston, North Carolina

B: October 30, 1936
Bats both, throws right
Ht. 6–4; Wt. 190

The Indians traded Jim Perry too soon and reacquired him too late, although the older but less famous brother of Gaylord was one of the best pitchers in baseball in 1970 when he won the American League Cy Young award while wearing a Minnesota uniform.

Jim started in the Tribe farm system in 1956 and made it to Cleveland in 1959 when he went 12–10 with a 2.65 earned run average in 44 games as a reliever–spot starter.

The following year Perry tied for the AL lead in victories, with 18, and starts, with 36, but slumped the next two seasons and was traded on May 2, 1963, to Minnesota for pitcher Jack Kralick.

Perry struggled for most of the next six seasons with the Twins, but became a big winner, going 20–6, in 1969 when Billy Martin took over as manager. Perry was even better in 1970 when he won the AL Cy Young award with a career-high 24 victories, while losing 12, which tied him with Baltimore's Dave McNally and Mike Cuellar as the league's winningest pitchers.

The Perrys were the only brothers to win Cy Young awards, as Gaylord did it twice, in the AL in 1972 and in the NL in 1978. Jim also was a member of the AL All-Star team in 1961, 1970, and 1971.

The Twins traded Jim to Detroit in 1973, and on July 3 that year he started for the Tigers against Gaylord and the Indians. It was the first time in the AL that brothers started

Jim Perry

against each other. Detroit won, 5–3, though neither brother was the pitcher of record.

The Indians reacquired Jim Perry from Detroit on March 19, 1974, in a three-way deal that also involved the New York Yankees. In addition to sending Perry to the Tribe, the Tigers also transferred pitcher Ed Farmer to Syracuse, an International League farm club of the Yankees, the Indians sent pitcher Rick Sawyer and outfielder Walter Williams to New York, and Detroit got catcher Gerry Moses from the Yankees.

After joining the Indians, Perry went 17–12 and was the cowinner with Gaylord of the Man of the Year award for 1974.

But eight starts into 1975, with Perry's record 1–6, he was traded with pitcher Dick Bosman on May 20 to Oakland for pitcher Blue Moon Odom and cash. Perry won only three games—one of them a one-hitter against Baltimore on June 10—and lost four for the Athletics, ending his 17-year major league career.

Perry, Jim

Indians	W	L	Pct	ERA	G	CG	IP	H	BB	SO	ShO
1959	12	10	.545	2.65	44	8	153	122	55	79	2
1960	18	10	.643	3.62	41	10	261⅓	257	91	120	4
1961	10	17	.370	4.71	35	6	223	238	87	90	1
1962	12	12	.500	4.14	35	7	193⅔	213	59	74	3
1963	0	0	—	5.23	5	0	10⅓	12	2	7	0
1974	17	12	.586	2.96	36	8	252	242	64	71	3
1975	1	6	.143	6.69	8	0	37⅔	46	18	11	0
Career	215	174	.553	3.45	630	109	3,285⅔	3,127	998	1,576	32

Piersall, James Anthony

Indians: 1959–61
Outfielder
Birthplace: Waterbury, Connecticut

B: November 14, 1929
Bats right, throws right
Ht. 6–0; **Wt.** 175

The 17-year major league career of Jim Piersall was marked by numerous zany stunts, including hiding behind the monuments in center field at Yankee Stadium while playing for the Indians in 1959.

Once, during another game the Indians played in Yankee Stadium that season, two fans jumped onto the field and ran toward Piersall. He saw them coming and charged at them. The two men quickly changed direction and scampered back to the stands, but didn't get there before Piersall landed a swift kick to the rear of one of them.

Four years later, with his career winding down, Piersall ran the bases backward after hitting his 100th career home run while playing for the New York Mets.

It all happened after Piersall suffered a nervous breakdown in 1952 when he played for the Boston Red Sox and was demoted to Birmingham in the Class AA Southern Association.

As chronicled in his book *Fear Strikes Out*, which was later made into a movie, the breakdown occurred when Piersall was switched from his natural center-field position to shortstop as a Red Sox rookie.

Piersall returned to play for Boston—and went back to center field—in 1953 and was a stalwart, being named to the American League All-Star team in 1954 and 1956, until his batting average slumped to .237 in 1958.

That winter, on December 2, the Indians traded first baseman Vic Wertz and outfielder Gary Geiger to the Red Sox for Piersall, a favorite of general manager Frank Lane—though he never was warmly admired by manager Joe Gordon.

When Gordon was traded on August 3, 1960, to the Detroit Tigers for their manager, Jimmy Dykes, Cleveland newspapers called Piersall the winner of a personality conflict with Gordon.

Nor was the tempestuous outfielder a favorite of Dykes, who said after he was fired at the end of the 1961 season, "I think I did as much with Piersall as anyone could have, but he can make it awful tough for any manager. You've got to pamper him and you've got to be tough with him. It's a problem."

It probably was not coincidental that Piersall, though he hit a career-high .322 in 1961, was traded away on October 5 that year, only three days after Mel McGaha was hired as the Tribe's new manager and six months after Gabe Paul replaced Lane as general manager.

It was a good deal for the Indians, who got pitcher Dick Donovan, outfielder-catcher Gene Green, infielder Jim Ma-

Jim Piersall

honey, and a minor league player from Washington for Piersall, who went on to play for the Mets in 1963 and the Los Angeles (and then California) Angels from 1963 to 1967.

After he retired as a player, Piersall worked in the front offices of several teams, managed briefly in the minor leagues, and later became a broadcaster with the Chicago White Sox, but was fired for being too outspoken and controversial.

Piersall, Jimmy

Indians	G	AB	H	BA	RBI	R	2B	3B	HR	SA	SB
1959	100	317	78	.246	30	42	13	2	4	.338	6
1960	138	486	137	.282	66	70	12	4	18	.434	18
1961	121	484	156	.322	40	81	26	7	6	.442	8
Career	1,734	5,890	1,604	.272	591	811	256	52	104	.386	115

Pinson, Vada Edward

Indians: 1970–71
Outfielder
Birthplace: Memphis, Tennessee
B: August 11, 1936

D: October 21, 1995
Batted left, threw left
Ht. 5–11; **Wt.** 170

Vada Pinson could do it all when he broke in with Cincinnati in 1958, and did it all most of his 18-year major league career, although he was slowing down when he joined the Indians in 1970 at the age of 34.

Still, Pinson had two good seasons in Cleveland, leading the Indians in 1970 with 164 hits, 28 doubles, six triples, and 82 runs batted in, and he also delivered 24 homers.

Vada Pinson

The Indians got Pinson from St. Louis on November 21, 1969, in a trade for Jose Cardenal. They unwisely traded him on October 5, 1971, with pitcher Alan Foster and outfielder Frank Baker, to California for outfielder Alex Johnson and catcher Gerry Moses. It was a deal Tribe officials lived to regret.

Pinson was a star at the same school, McClymonds High in Oakland, that produced Frank Robinson and Curt Flood and, after signing a $4,000 bonus contract with the Reds in 1956, became a teammate of Robinson in Cincinnati from 1958 to 1965.

Despite hitting .300 or better four times in 10 full seasons with the Reds—including a career-high .343 in 1961—Pinson usually was overshadowed by Robinson and, later, by Pete Rose and Tony Perez.

In his first full season with the Reds, Pinson led the National League with 131 runs and 47 doubles, hit 20 homers, and had a .316 average that was fourth best. But he lost the Rookie of the Year award to Willie McCovey, who played only 52 games for San Francisco.

NL president Warren Giles said of Pinson that year, "There's no telling how good he can become, maybe the best we've ever seen." Pinson made the NL All-Star team in 1959 and 1960, won a Gold Glove in 1961.

He hit 256 homers in his major league career, the first one a grand slam in his second game for the Reds. Another homer was his 1,000th hit in 1964, and his 2,000th hit was a homer for the Indians in 1970.

After leaving Cleveland, Pinson spent two seasons with the Angels, was traded to the Kansas City Royals, and ended his playing career in 1975. He served as a coach for Seattle from 1977 to 1980, the Chicago White Sox in 1981, the Mariners again in 1982 and 1983, and Detroit from 1985 to 1991.

Pinson, Vada

Indians	G	AB	H	BA	RBI	R	2B	3B	HR	SA	SB
1970	148	574	164	.286	82	74	28	6	24	.481	7
1971	146	566	149	.263	35	60	23	4	11	.376	25
Career	2,469	9,645	2,757	.286	1,170	1,366	485	127	256	.442	305

Porter, Richard Twilley

Indians: 1929–34
Outfielder
Nickname: Twitchy
Birthplace: Princess Anne, Maryland

B: December 30, 1901
D: September 24, 1974
Batted left, threw right
Ht. 5–10; **Wt.** 170

Though he was an outstanding hitter in the minor leagues—he batted .300 or better six consecutive seasons for Baltimore in the International League—Dick Porter didn't get to the major leagues with the Indians until 1929, at age 28.

He was acquired by the Tribe from Baltimore on November 17, 1928, for $30,000 and two players to be named later.

From 1930 to 1934, Porter was a member of the Indians' great outfield that included Earl Averill and Joe Vosmik. He hit over .300 every year from 1929 to 1932, including a career-high .350 in 1930, twice scoring more than 100 runs.

Porter was nicknamed Twitchy because of his wiggling and gyrating, and once said it "made me feel comfortable and relaxed" at the plate. "I tried to stop [wiggling], but when I did, I didn't hit very good."

"Twitchy Dick" Porter

Porter remained with the Indians until May 25, 1934, when they packaged him with pitcher Wes Ferrell and sent them to the Boston Red Sox for pitcher Bob Weiland, outfielder Bob Seeds, and $25,000.

Though the remainder of that season was Porter's last in the major leagues, it was a deal the Indians lived to regret as neither Weiland nor Seeds distinguished himself in Cleveland.

Porter, Dick

Indians	G	AB	H	BA	RBI	R	2B	3B	HR	SA	SB
1929	71	192	63	.328	24	26	16	5	1	.479	3
1930	119	480	168	.350	57	100	43	8	4	.498	3
1931	114	414	129	.312	38	82	24	3	1	.391	6
1932	146	621	191	.308	60	106	42	8	4	.420	2
1933	132	499	133	.267	41	73	19	6	0	.329	4
1934	13	44	10	.227	6	9	2	1	1	.386	0
Career	675	2,515	774	.308	282	426	159	37	11	.414	23

Powell, John Wesley

Indians: 1975–76
First baseman
Nickname: Boog
Birthplace: Lakeland, Florida

B: August 17, 1941
Bats left, throws right
Ht. 6–4½; **Wt.** 230

Boog Powell was near the end of his career when he rejoined former Baltimore teammate Frank Robinson in Cleveland in 1975, although the massive first baseman had one very good season for the Indians.

Powell batted .297 with 27 homers in 1975, but his numbers declined to .215 with nine homers the following season, and he was released, though he signed with the Los Angeles Dodgers in 1977 and played one more year.

The Indians got him with pitcher Don Hood on February 25, 1975, in a trade for catcher Dave Duncan and minor league outfielder Alvin McGrew.

It was with the Orioles that Powell enjoyed most success. As their regular first baseman from 1962 to 1974, he hit 303 homers, including a career-high 39 in 1964. He homered 37

Boog Powell

times in 1969 when he batted .304 and drove in 121 runs, both of which also were the best of his 17 years in the major leagues.

Powell also smashed three homers in one game three times, in 1963, 1964, and 1966, was voted the American League's Most Valuable Player in 1970 when he hit .297 with 35 homers and 114 RBIs, and was a member of the All-Star team every year from 1968 to 1971.

Powell, Boog

Indians	G	AB	H	BA	RBI	R	2B	3B	HR	SA	SB
1975	134	435	129	.297	86	64	18	0	27	.524	1
1976	95	293	63	.215	33	29	9	0	9	.338	1
Career	2,042	6,681	1,776	.266	1,187	889	270	11	339	.462	20

Power, Victor

Indians: 1958–61
First baseman, second baseman, third baseman, shortstop
Birthplace: Arecibo, Puerto Rico

B: November 1, 1931
Bats right, throws right
Ht. 6–0; **Wt.** 186

Flamboyant, stylish, and often controversial, Vic Power led American League first basemen in fielding percentage three times (1957, 1959, and 1960) during his 12 seasons in the major leagues with the Philadelphia–Kansas City Athletics, Indians, Minnesota, Los Angeles–California Angels, and Philadelphia Phillies.

Power started his professional career in the New York Yankees farm system and, in 1953, he and Elston Howard became the first black players on their 40-man roster.

However, before Power ever played a game for the Yankees, he was traded on December 16, 1953, to the Athletics

Vic Power

It also was in 1958 that Power attempted to charge into the stands behind the Indians dugout to retaliate against Ohio State football coach Woody Hayes, who was heckling Power for "showboating."

On another occasion in 1959, Power was involved in a confrontation with Chicago White Sox Manager Al Lopez, who also called the first baseman a "showboat." Power claimed that Lopez ordered his pitchers to throw at him.

The Indians traded Power on April 2, 1962, with pitcher Dick Stigman to the Twins for pitcher Pedro Ramos. Power played for Minnesota as well as the Angels and Phillies in 1964, then went back to California and ended his major league playing career in 1965.

Power, Vic

Indians	G	AB	H	BA	RBI	R	2B	3B	HR	SA	SB
1958	93	385	122	.317	53	63	24	6	12	.504	2
1959	147	595	172	.289	60	102	31	6	10	.412	9
1960	147	580	167	.288	84	69	26	3	10	.395	9
1961	147	563	151	.268	63	64	34	4	5	.369	4
Career	1,627	6,046	1,716	.284	658	765	290	49	126	.411	45

Pytlak, Frank Anthony

Indians: 1932–40
Catcher
Birthplace: Buffalo, New York
B: July 30, 1908

D: May 8, 1977
Batted right, threw right
Ht. 5–7½; **Wt.** 160

Frankie Pytlak never gained much notoriety for his performance behind the plate during his nine-year career with the Indians, though he batted over .300 four times, including a high of .321 in 75 games in 1936.

But Pytlak achieved a degree of fame on August 20, 1938, when he, along with the Tribe's third-string receiver, Hank Helf, broke what was then called the "altitude catching record" in front of an estimated 10,000 fans gathered on Cleveland's Public Square.

Both of them caught baseballs dropped from the top of the 708-foot-high Terminal Tower. Mathematicians estimated the balls were traveling 138 miles per hour when they landed in the gloves of Pytlak and Helf.

The two catchers were credited with breaking a record set 30 years earlier by Gabby Street and Billy Sullivan, who

in one of baseball's biggest deals. It involved 11 players, five of whom accompanied Power to Philadelphia (before that franchise relocated in Kansas City in 1955).

Power also was part of a major transaction between the Athletics and Indians on June 15, 1958. In one of Frank Lane's early trades (of the 51 involving 118 players he made in less than three full years in Cleveland), Power was acquired with shortstop Woodie Held for outfielder Roger Maris, first baseman Preston Ward, and pitcher Dick Tomanek.

He was a member of the American League All-Star team with the Athletics in 1955 and 1956 and with the Tribe in 1959 and 1960, and he won Gold Glove awards every year from 1958 to 1964.

With the Indians through 1961, Power also played a few games at shortstop and second and third bases, and he was a consistent, if not a great, hitter.

He was not a popular player with either Tribe manager Joe Gordon or Jimmy Dykes. Gordon often complained that Power tried to hit home runs instead of just making contact, and Dykes didn't appreciate Power's nonchalant style and called him "an incurably bad actor."

On August 14, 1958, Power tied a major league record by stealing home twice in the same game. He did it in the eighth and 10th innings against Detroit at the Stadium, giving the Indians a 10–9 victory.

Power also stole home in one other game that season, but those three thefts were his only stolen bases in 1958.

Frankie Pytlak

caught baseballs dropped from the top of the 550-foot-high Washington Monument in Washington, D.C.

Three other members of the 1938 Indians—regular catcher Rollie Hemsley and coaches Wally Schang and Johnny Bassler, both former catchers—tried but failed to match Pytlak's and Helf's feat.

"For a while I didn't know if the ball was going to hit me in the head or my glove," said Pytlak. "When I caught it, it stung more than Bob Feller's fastball."

Pytlak's lifetime batting average was a creditable .282, but he was injury prone and caught 100 or more games in only one season.

He came up with the Indians in 1932 and played for the Boston Red Sox in 1941, after which he went into the service for three and a half years during World War II.

The Indians received pitcher Jim Bagby, catcher Gene Desautels, and outfielder Gee Walker in the December 12, 1940, deal that sent Pytlak, third baseman Odell Hale, and pitcher Joe Dobson to Boston.

Pytlak returned to the Red Sox after the war, but played only nine games in 1945 and four in 1946, then retired.

Pytlak, Frankie

Indians	G	AB	H	BA	RBI	R	2B	3B	HR	SA	SB
1932	12	29	7	.241	4	5	1	1	0	.345	0
1933	80	248	77	.310	33	36	10	6	2	.423	3
1934	91	289	75	.260	35	46	12	4	0	.329	11
1935	55	149	44	.295	12	14	6	1	1	.369	3
1936	75	224	72	.321	31	35	15	4	0	.424	5
1937	125	397	125	.315	44	60	15	6	1	.390	16
1938	113	364	112	.308	43	46	14	7	1	.393	9
1939	63	183	49	.268	14	20	2	5	0	.333	4
1940	62	149	21	.141	16	16	2	1	0	.168	0
Career	795	2,399	677	.282	272	316	100	36	7	.363	56

Ramos, Pedro

Indians: 1962–64
Pitcher
Nickname: Pistol Pete
Birthplace: Pinar del Río, Cuba

B: April 28, 1935
Bats right, throws right
Ht. 6–0; **Wt.** 175

Though he had the dubious distinction of tying an American League record by losing the most games in four consecutive seasons—from 1958 to 1961 for the Washington Senators–Minnesota Twins—Pedro Ramos was still considered to have the potential for becoming one of the game's best pitchers.

Ramos was named to the American League All-Star team in 1959, and the Indians got him in a trade on April 2, 1962 (after the Washington franchise had relocated in Minnesota in 1961) for first baseman Vic Power and pitcher Dick Stigman.

Though he was a good hitter and one of the fastest runners in baseball, Ramos continued to be an erratic pitcher in Cleveland, and also became involved in some off-the-field escapades, including a marital problem, falling from favor with management.

Ramos smashed a grand slam off Baltimore's Chuck Estrada on May 30, 1962, and hit two homers in the second game of a twi-night doubleheader at the Stadium on July 31, 1963, against the Los Angeles Angels.

His second homer, in the sixth inning, was the second of

Pedro Ramos

four straight by the Indians, the first AL team to do so. Woodie Held homered ahead of Ramos, and Tito Francona and Larry Brown followed with homers. In addition to hammering two homers in that game, Ramos struck out 15 Los Angeles batters.

In his third consecutive so-so season with the Indians, and with the franchise experiencing severe financial problems, Ramos was traded on September 5, 1964, to the New York Yankees for pitchers Ralph Terry and Bud Daley and $75,000.

It was with the Yankees that Ramos finally blossomed. Used strictly in relief during the final four weeks of the season, Ramos went 1–0 with eight saves and a 1.25 earned run average to help the Yankees win the pennant.

He continued as their stopper the next two seasons, saving 19 victories in 1965 and 13 in 1966, but was traded to the Philadelphia Phillies. Ramos pitched for Pittsburgh and Cincinnati in 1969 and for the expansion Senators in 1970, with whom he ended his career.

Ramos, Pedro

Indians	W	L	Pct	ERA	G	CG	IP	H	BB	SO	ShO
1962	10	12	.455	3.71	37	7	201⅓	189	85	96	2
1963	9	8	.529	3.12	36	5	184⅔	156	41	169	0
1964	7	10	.412	5.14	36	3	133	144	26	98	1
Career	117	160	.422	4.08	582	73	2,355⅔	2,364	724	1,305	13

Reynolds, Allie Pierce

Indians: 1942–46
Pitcher
Nickname: Super Chief
Birthplace: Bethany, Oklahoma

B: February 10, 1915
D: December 26, 1994
Batted right, threw right
Ht. 6–0; **Wt.** 195

When the Indians sent Allie Reynolds to the New York Yankees on October 19, 1946, for second baseman Joe Gordon and third baseman Eddie Bockman, it was one of those few trades in major league history that truly benefited both teams.

The Indians would not have won the 1948 American League pennant without Gordon, and Reynolds helped the Yankees get to the World Series six times, in 1947 and 1949–53. His World Series won-lost record is 7–2.

Before the deal, Reynolds, who came up through the Cleveland farm system, always showed great promise but had trou-

Allie Reynolds

Association from 1969 to 1971, Reynolds said, "I still can remember every pitch I ever made. My wife would chart every game and I'd study each so hard that I couldn't forget. I was haunted by hitters I couldn't get out."

Reynolds, Allie

Indians	W	L	Pct	ERA	G	CG	IP	H	BB	SO	ShO
1942	0	0	—	0.00	2	0	5	5	4	2	0
1943	11	12	.478	2.99	34	11	198⅔	140	109	151	3
1944	11	8	.579	3.30	28	5	158	141	91	84	1
1945	18	12	.600	3.20	44	16	247⅓	227	130	112	2
1946	11	15	.423	3.88	31	9	183⅓	180	108	107	3
Career	182	107	.630	3.30	434	137	2,492⅓	2,193	1,261	1,423	36

Rhoads, Robert Barton

Indians: 1903–09
Pitcher
Nickname: Dusty
Birthplace: Wooster, Ohio

B: October 4, 1879
D: February 12, 1967
Batted right, threw right
Ht. 6–1; **Wt.** 215

Bob Rhoads, the first of many players nicknamed Dusty because of his surname, had a brief major league career, lasting only eight years, but was a very good pitcher for the Cleveland franchise (then known as the Naps) from 1904 to 1909.

He hurled a no-hitter, beating the Boston Red Sox, 2–1, on September 18, 1908, the year the Naps lost the pennant by half a game to Detroit.

In that no-hitter, the second in the history of the Cleveland franchise and 20th since the founding of the American League in 1901, Rhoads walked two (one intentionally), hit a batter, and threw a wild pitch. Boston's run was scored in the second inning on a walk, sacrifice, Napoleon Lajoie's error, and a wild pitch.

Previously, Rhoads had also come within one out of pitching a no-hitter against the Red Sox on September 27, 1904, at League Park. Boston's only hit was a single by center fielder Chick Stahl with two out in the ninth inning of the Indians' 3–1 victory.

Rhoads began his professional baseball career in 1901 with Memphis in the Southern Association and compiled a 22–12 record. He was purchased by the Chicago Cubs, pitched for them in 1902, and was traded to the St. Louis Cardinals in 1903. He was released in late August and picked up by Cleveland in early September.

He was a winning pitcher for the Naps in five consecutive seasons, posting a career-best 22–10 record in 1906, and retired after his record fell to 5–9 in 1909.

Rhoads, Bob

Indians	W	L	Pct	ERA	G	CG	IP	H	BB	SO	ShO
1903	2	3	.400	5.27	5	5	41	55	3	21	0
1904	10	9	.526	2.87	22	18	175⅓	175	48	72	0
1905	16	9	.640	2.83	28	24	235	219	55	61	4
1906	22	10	.688	1.80	38	31	315	259	92	89	7
1907	15	14	.517	2.29	35	23	275	258	84	76	5
1908	18	12	.600	1.77	37	20	270	229	73	62	1
1909	5	9	.357	2.90	20	9	133⅓	124	50	46	2
Career	97	82	.542	2.61	218	154	1,691⅓	1,604	494	522	21

ble harnessing his 90-plus-mph fastball and hard-breaking curve. He issued 109 bases on balls in 198⅔ innings in 1943 and led the American League with 130 walks in 247⅓ innings in 1945. He was nicknamed "Super Chief" because of his American Indian ancestry.

In four seasons with the Indians, Reynolds won more than 11 games only once, in 1945 when his record was 18–12, and he lost more games than he won in 1943 and 1946.

Actually, Bill Veeck, then the new owner of the Indians, offered another developing pitcher, Red Embree, to the Yankees for Gordon, whom he desperately wanted to plug a gaping hole at second base.

But Yankees general manager Larry MacPhail, after conferring with center fielder Joe DiMaggio, told Veeck they wanted Reynolds, even though their records were similar and Embree was two years younger.

Veeck reluctantly agreed and, as it turned out, MacPhail—because of DiMaggio's input—proved to be right. Reynolds went on to a much better career than did Embree.

(Ironically, Embree wound up with the Yankees in an October 10, 1947, trade for outfielder Allie Clark, compiling a 31–48 won-lost record in an eight-year major league career that ended in 1949.)

Reynolds pitched two no-hitters for the Yankees in 1951, the first a 1–0 victory over the Indians on July 12 and the second against Boston, 8–0, on September 28. It also was 1951 that he won the Hickock Belt as the top professional athlete of the year.

Reynolds led the American League with a 2.06 earned run average in 1952 when he was second in the AL Most Valuable Player voting and was a 20-game winner for the only time in his career. He was on the AL All Star team in 1949, 1950, 1952, 1953, and 1954.

Upon his retirement, when he became successful in the oil business in Oklahoma and was president of the American

Romano, John Anthony

Indians: 1960–64
Catcher
Nickname: Honey
Birthplace: Hoboken, New Jersey

B: August 23, 1934
Bats right, throws right
Ht. 5–11; **Wt.** 205

John Romano was one of the best power-hitting catchers in baseball until he suffered a broken finger in 1963 that cost him his position with the Indians and, ultimately his career.

He still holds three records for Tribe catchers: most homers in a career, 91; most homers in one season, 25 (1962); and most RBIs in one season, 81 (1962).

As a minor leaguer for the Chicago White Sox in 1955, Romano set a Three-I League record with 38 homers at Waterloo.

Romano made it to the White Sox to stay in 1959, backing up regular catcher Sherman Lollar. He batted .294 in 53 games, including going 8-for-13 as a pinch hitter to help Chicago win the American League pennant.

On December 6, 1959, Romano was traded to the Indians, along with third baseman Bubba Phillips and minor league first baseman Norm Cash, for outfielder Minnie Minoso, catcher Dick Brown, and pitchers Don Ferrarese and Jake Striker.

It was a great break for Romano, who became the Tribe's regular catcher in 1960, hitting 62 homers the next three seasons and making the All-Star team in 1961 and 1962.

John Romano

Then came the injury that shelved him—and that took several more years for Romano to overcome.

It was on May 26, 1963, at the Stadium that Romano suffered a broken little finger on his throwing hand when he tagged out Jackie Brandt at the plate in the eighth inning of the first game of a doubleheader against Baltimore.

"When it happened," Romano reminisced, "I was hitting about .340. I was supposed to be out for six weeks, but the Indians wanted me to get back sooner, so we took the cast off after two weeks and I played—but shouldn't have." He finished the season with a .216 average in 89 games.

"My hand didn't heal properly and bothered me for several years after that, especially in cold weather. It gave me trouble gripping the bat," he said.

It also was in 1963 that the Indians acquired Joe Azcue in a trade with the Kansas City Athletics. Given the chance to play because of Romano's injury, Azcue—as Romano said—"went crazy" at the plate, hitting .284 with 14 homers.

In 1964, though Romano played 106 games, he no longer was the Tribe's everyday catcher. Azcue caught 76 games, and his hot hitting led to Romano' being traded back to the White Sox a year later in a deal that the Indians lived to regret for a long time.

In his anxiety to reacquire fan favorite Rocky Colavito, Tribe general manager Gabe Paul, on January 20, 1965, packaged Romano with two young, very promising prospects, pitcher Tommy John and outfielder Tommie Agee, and sent them to Chicago.

The White Sox then got Colavito from the Kansas City Athletics for outfielders Jim Landis and Mike Hershberger and pitcher Fred Talbot, and sent Colavito to Cleveland with catcher Camilo Carreon.

"I liked it in Chicago, but I was happy in Cleveland," said Romano. "I've always wondered how my career might have been different if I had stayed with the Indians, if Gabe Paul hadn't felt it was so necessary to get Colavito back."

After two seasons with the White Sox, Romano was traded to the St. Louis Cardinals, for whom he hit only .121 in 24 games in 1967, backing up Tim McCarver, and was finished.

Romano, John

Indians	G	AB	H	BA	RBI	R	2B	3B	HR	SA	SB
1960	108	316	86	.272	52	40	12	2	16	.475	0
1961	142	509	152	.299	80	76	29	1	21	.483	0
1962	135	459	120	.261	81	71	19	3	25	.479	0
1963	89	255	55	.216	34	28	5	2	10	.369	4
1964	106	352	85	.241	47	46	18	1	19	.460	2
Career	905	2,767	706	.255	417	355	112	10	129	.443	7

Rosen, Albert Leonard

Indians: 1947–56
Third baseman, first baseman
Nickname: Flip
Birthplace: Spartanburg, South Carolina

B: February 29, 1924
Bats right, throws right
Ht. 5–10½; **Wt.** 180

Nobody played the game harder or was more intolerant of losing than Al Rosen, whose competitive spirit was best epitomized by an incident that occurred during the 1954 season.

With the Indians in the thick of the pennant race and in

Al Rosen

the process of winning an American League–record 111 games, Rosen fought a teammate who complained that his leg was too tight to play that night against the New York Yankees.

The teammate played—with a swollen left jaw as well as a strained thigh muscle—and so did Rosen, with a broken nose, and the Indians prevailed.

It was one of 11 times Rosen's nose was broken, and he also played most of that season with a broken right index finger, which offers more testimony as to his fierce determination to win.

Rosen had volunteered to move from third base, the position he'd always played, to first in order to make room in the lineup for Rudy Regalado, a rookie who'd had a phenomenal spring—but could only play third.

It was while he played first base that Rosen suffered the broken finger in June, but refused to let it keep him out of the game.

It also was in 1954 that Rosen hit .300 with 24 homers, drove in 102 runs, and was the hero of the American League's 11–9 victory in the All-Star Game played that year in Cleveland. Rosen hammered two homers and singled, driving in five runs, despite being unable to grip his bat properly because of his broken finger.

That was one of four times (1952–55) in Rosen's 10 seasons in the major leagues that he was selected on the AL All-Star team.

Rosen won the AL Most Valuable Player award in 1953 when he led the league with 43 homers and 145 RBIs, and came within .001 of capturing the Triple Crown.

"I don't think much about it anymore," Rosen said before he retired in 1992 as president and general manager of the San Francisco Giants, "though I admit, I was pretty disappointed at the time." With good reason, it could be said.

Rosen got three hits in five at bats in the final game of the season against Detroit for a .336 average (on 201-for-599), but Mickey Vernon went 2-for-4 for Washington to win the batting championship with a .337 mark (on 205-for-608).

In that final game against the Tigers, Rosen recalled, "Al Aber was pitching against us and he was kind of wild. In my last trip to the plate, figuring I needed one more hit to pass Vernon, I went to a 3-and-2 count and knew I had to swing at whatever Aber threw.

"I fouled off a couple of pitches that were outside the strike zone, and ended up hitting a high chopper to third base. It was a close play at first base, and I tried to jump into the bag like guys do to get that extra edge, but I wound up a few inches short.

"The umpire called me out—he was right, I was out—and that was it," said Rosen.

If he'd been able to get a hit in that last opportunity, Rosen would have finished at .3372, compared to Vernon's .3371.

Rosen also led the league with 37 homers in 1950 and with 105 RBIs in 1952. He came up through the Indians farm system, but didn't replace Ken Keltner as their starting third baseman until 1950.

After retiring in 1956 with a lifetime batting average of .285, 192 homers, and 717 RBIs, Rosen was in the investment business in Cleveland for 20 years.

In 1972, Rosen and George Steinbrenner made a bid to buy the Indians, but it was rejected by owner Vernon Stouffer, who sold the franchise to Nick Mileti and his partners.

But that didn't end Rosen's involvement in baseball. After the New York Yankees had been purchased by Steinbrenner, Rosen served as their president in 1978 and 1979. He also was president of the Houston Astros from 1981 to 1985 and the San Francisco Giants from 1986 to 1992.

It was during Rosen's presidency of the Yankees that they won the World Series in 1978, and he was president of the Giants when they won the NL pennant in 1989.

Rosen, Al

Indians	G	AB	H	BA	RBI	R	2B	3B	HR	SA	SB
1947	7	9	1	.111	0	1	0	0	0	.111	0
1948	5	5	1	.200	0	0	0	0	0	.200	0
1949	23	44	7	.159	5	3	2	0	0	.205	0
1950	155	554	159	.287	116	100	23	4	37	.543	5
1951	154	573	152	.265	102	82	30	1	24	.447	7
1952	148	567	171	.302	105	101	32	5	28	.524	8
1953	155	599	201	.336	145	115	27	5	43	.613	8
1954	137	466	140	.300	102	76	20	2	24	.506	6
1955	139	492	120	.244	81	61	13	1	21	.402	4
1956	121	416	111	.267	61	64	18	2	15	.428	1
Career	1,044	3,725	1,063	.285	717	603	165	20	192	.495	39

Salmon, Ruthford Eduardo

Indians: 1964–68
Second baseman, outfielder,
  first baseman, shortstop,
  third baseman
Nickname: Chico

Birthplace: Colón, Panama
B: December 3, 1940
Bats right, throws right
Ht. 5–10; **Wt.** 160

As the Indians' "supersub" for five seasons, Chico Salmon, a jack of all trades, always claimed his best position was "batting." It wasn't far from the truth, even though Salmon's lifetime average for nine seasons in the major leagues was only .249.

He was a good contact hitter and won the Class AAA Pacific Coast League batting championship with a .325 average for Denver in 1963, after which the Indians acquired him in a deal with the Milwaukee Braves.

Chico Salmon

It was initially announced on November 2, 1963, that the Indians purchased Salmon, and though the price was undisclosed, it was said to be "an appropriate amount of cash or a player of equal value to be named later."

On April 1, 1964, the Indians announced that Mike de la Hoz, who had been a utility infielder for the Tribe, was sent to the Braves as payment for Salmon, and that another player would be delivered to Milwaukee by October 1, 1964, to complete the deal.

Salmon was renowned throughout baseball for his belief in ghosts, and because of it, he always slept with the lights on in his bedroom.

Though Salmon played 100 games only twice in his major league career, which continued with Baltimore from 1969 to 1972, he was a valuable extra player. Indians Manager Birdie Tebbetts said in 1966 that Salmon belonged on the American League All-Star team, primarily because of his versatility.

Salmon filled in capably at shortstop following the collision of shortstop Larry Brown and left fielder Leon Wagner in New York on May 4, 1966, which sidelined Brown for six weeks.

When Tebbetts' praise was related to Salmon, he said, "What a thrill that would be! I'd be the biggest man in Panama! Everyone would want to talk to me. Imagine! The first boy from Panama to play in the All-Star Game! It would be wonderful."

Salmon wasn't selected, but he did play in two World Series with the Orioles in 1969 and 1970. After his retirement as a player, Salmon managed the national amateur team in Panama for several years.

Salmon, Chico											
Indians	G	AB	H	BA	RBI	R	2B	3B	HR	SA	SB
1964	86	283	87	.307	25	43	17	2	4	.424	10
1965	79	120	29	.242	12	20	8	0	3	.383	7
1966	126	422	108	.256	40	46	13	2	7	.346	10
1967	90	203	46	.227	19	19	13	1	2	.330	10
1968	103	276	59	.214	12	24	8	1	3	.283	7
Career	658	1,667	415	.249	149	202	70	6	31	.354	46

Score, Herbert Jude

Indians: 1955–59
Pitcher
Birthplace: Rosedale, New York

B: June 7, 1933
Bats left, throws left
Ht. 6–2; **Wt.** 185

Herb Score always said that he doesn't look back, that he doesn't think about what might have been.

But if Score doesn't, others do—especially concerning his career.

One of them was Bob Feller, the greatest pitcher in Indians history, and one of the best of all time. "If Herb hadn't gotten hurt, he would have been as good as Sandy Koufax," Feller has said of the misfortune that struck Score on May 7, 1957.

Then the most dominant young pitcher in baseball, Score fired a fastball at Gil McDougald, the second batter in a game against the New York Yankees at the Stadium.

McDougald's bat flashed, and the ball flew back at Score like a rocket.

It smashed with a sickening thud against Score's right cheekbone near his eye. He went down as though he'd been shot, and blood spurted from his eye, nose, and mouth.

Score was hospitalized for three weeks, and there were fears that he would lose the vision in his eye.

Fortunately, he didn't.

But, unfortunately, he was never the same pitcher when he returned in 1958.

Speculation persists that it was the eye injury that ruined Score's career—though he steadfastly has rejected that opinion.

"I came back as good as ever," he said. "What people forget is that I tore a tendon in my elbow early the next season [1958]. I kept pitching with an arm that hurt, and it just never came back."

Herb Score

"I could still throw hard, but the ball didn't move as it had before. I guess because of the earlier pain, I changed my motion and the ball straightened out."

The torn tendon—or the eye injury—made a prophet of Tris Speaker, a member of the Indians' front office when Score first came up from the minor leagues in 1955 to win the American League Rookie of the Year award.

"If nothing happens to Score, he has got to be the greatest," Speaker said, ironically only a week before the pitcher was hit in the eye.

Among the many who shared that opinion was Joe Cronin, general manager of the Boston Red Sox in 1957. During spring training that year Cronin called Indians general manager Hank Greenberg and offered to buy Score's contract for $1 million—then an unheard of price for a ballplayer.

Greenberg, who was part of the group that had recently purchased the Indians franchise for $3.9 million, told Cronin, "We wouldn't sell Score for two million dollars. He's not for sale at any price."

It was with sound reason that Cronin wanted Score—and that Greenberg refused to part with him.

After signing with the Indians for a $60,000 bonus in 1952, Score was 2–5 in 12 games for Indianapolis of the Class AAA American Association. He went 7–3 at Reading of the Class A Eastern League in 1953, and in 1954 at Indianapolis he blossomed into stardom with a 22–5 record, a 2.62 earned run average, and 330 strikeouts in 251 innings.

Score won 16 games and lost 10 in his 1955 debut with the Indians, and he struck out a league-leading, rookie-record 245 batters in 227⅓ innings. He came close to pitching a no-hitter against Baltimore on July 30. Jim Dyck spoiled it with a fourth-inning single in the Tribe's 7–0 victory.

Score was even better in 1956 when his record was 20–9 with a 2.53 ERA, and again he was the AL's strikeout king with 263 in 249⅓ innings, fanning 10 or more batters in a game 24 times, including a high of 16. Score also led the league with five shutouts while holding opposition batters to a .186 average.

Score was named to the All-Star team both seasons, and there seemed to be no limit to the heights of glory he'd reach.

And then, the following year with his record at 2–1 that fateful night in May, came the accident that scarred Score's career, if not ended it.

It also had a lasting, traumatic effect on McDougald. "I'll never forget the pitch he threw to me that night," said the former Yankees shortstop. "Most of the time he was up around the letters, but he threw this one low. I still don't know how I hit it.

"I don't know what I did then. I don't remember running to first base because as soon as the ball hit Herb, I saw blood fly.

"I really didn't feel like playing anymore. It took a few hitches out of me as a ballplayer, even though I know you can't control where the ball is going after you hit it. Everybody, including Herb's mother, tried to tell me it wasn't my fault."

Score pitched only 12 games, winning two and losing three, upon his return in 1958, and when his record was only 9–11 the following season, he was traded to the Chicago White Sox for pitcher Barry Latman.

The deal was made by general manager Frank Lane on April 18, 1960, one day before the season opener, and one day after Score's close friend, outfielder Rocky Colavito, was traded to Detroit for outfielder Harvey Kuenn.

In the next three seasons with the White Sox, Score won only six while losing 12 games, and then he retired, becoming a broadcaster for the Indians in 1964, a job he has held on television or radio continuously ever since.

Score, Herb

Indians	W	L	Pct	ERA	G	CG	IP	H	BB	SO	ShO
1955	16	10	.615	2.85	33	11	227⅓	158	154	245	2
1956	20	9	.690	2.53	35	16	249⅓	162	129	263	5
1957	2	1	.667	2.00	5	3	36	18	26	39	1
1958	2	3	.400	3.95	12	2	41	29	34	48	1
1959	9	11	.450	4.71	30	9	160⅔	123	115	147	1
Career	55	46	.545	3.36	150	47	858⅓	609	573	837	11

Seerey, James Patrick

Indians: 1943–48
Outfielder
Nickname: Fat Pat
Birthplace: Wilburton, Oklahoma

B: March 17, 1923
D: April 28, 1986
Batted right, threw right
Ht. 5–10; **Wt.** 200

Fans called him Fat Pat, but they did so with affection, not derision, because everybody loved Pat Seerey. Many thought he'd become baseball's home run king.

But it didn't happen. Seerey, who could indeed hit baseballs great distances, also had a penchant for striking out, which he did an average of every 3.7 at bats during his seven-year major league career.

As it was once said about Seerey in the *Cleveland News,* "He was one of the most frustrating—but also most fascinating—characters ever to wear a Cleveland uniform. He numbered his friends among the thousands and his critics by the tens of thousands.

"But even among the latter there was no real malice. They just couldn't stay mad at the guy.

"That big bat was the real secret of his appeal. Americans think in superlatives, and Pat could hit a baseball with more

Pat Seerey

sheer line drive force than anyone else in the history of the game."

Unfortunately for the Indians, the genial Irishman who was built like a fireplug never lived up to expectations, primarily because his bat didn't make contact with pitched baseballs often enough.

Seerey's greatest game as an Indian took place on July 13, 1945, in Yankee Stadium. He hit three homers and a triple, driving in eight runs in the Tribe's 16–4 victory over New York.

Though Seerey hit 26 homers in 1946, his batting average was never higher than the .237 he compiled in 1945.

Bill Veeck, who bought the Indians in 1946, tried virtually everything to make Seerey a more consistent hitter.

One year Veeck hired Hall of Famer Rogers Hornsby as a personal tutor for Seerey, but to no avail.

Another time Veeck even separated Seerey from his best friend and roommate, Jim Hegan, on the theory that the two players with hitting problems were discouraging each other.

But that didn't work either, and the Indians finally, reluctantly, gave up on Fat Pat.

They traded him, with pitcher Al Gettel, on June 2, 1948, to the Chicago White Sox for outfielder Bob Kennedy.

Six weeks later in Chicago, on July 18, Seerey blasted four home runs in the 11-inning opener of a doubleheader against Philadelphia, becoming only the third player at that time to do so in baseball's modern era.

They were among the 19 homers Seerey hit that season, and he was released after playing only four games in 1949.

Joe Sewell

Seerey, Pat

Indians	G	AB	H	BA	RBI	R	2B	3B	HR	SA	SB
1943	26	72	16	.222	5	8	3	0	1	.306	0
1944	101	342	80	.234	39	39	16	0	15	.412	0
1945	126	414	98	.237	56	56	22	2	14	.401	1
1946	117	404	91	.225	62	57	17	2	26	.470	2
1947	82	216	37	.171	29	24	4	1	11	.352	0
1948	10	23	6	.261	6	7	0	0	1	.391	0
Career	561	1,815	406	.224	261	236	73	5	86	.412	3

Sewell, Joseph Wheeler

Indians: 1920–30
Shortstop, third baseman
Birthplace: Titus, Alabama
B: October 9, 1898

D: March 6, 1990
Batted left, threw right
Ht. 5–6½; **Wt.** 155

Joey Sewell came along at precisely the right time for the Indians, replacing the injured Harry Lunte, who had taken over at shortstop when Ray Chapman died on August 17, 1920, after he was hit by a pitch from Carl Mays.

At the time Sewell was playing his first season in professional baseball at New Orleans of the Class A Southern Association. He had fewer than 100 at bats under his belt, but he hit .329 in the Tribe's final 22 games.

Sewell also was nearly flawless in the field, and the Indians probably would not have won their first pennant that year without him.

The slick-fielding shortstop went on to play 1,103 consecutive games between September 13, 1922, and April 30, 1930, still sixth longest of all time behind Cal Ripken, Jr., Lou Gehrig, Everett Scott, Steve Garvey, and Billy Williams.

More impressive are the major league records Sewell still

holds for the fewest strikeouts in one season, four, in 155 games in 1925 and in 152 games in 1929. He also holds the record for fewest strikeouts in 14 or more seasons (except pitchers) with 113 in 7,132 official appearances at the plate from 1920 to 1933.

It also is amazing that Sewell, while not a free swinger, wasn't a slap hitter either. He hit 49 homers in his career, including 11 for the New York Yankees in 1932, a year after he was released by the Indians.

Sewell's lifetime average was .312, and he led the Indians in runs batted in three times. Only once did he hit less than .299 while playing for Cleveland.

When Chapman was killed, the Indians immediately installed Lunte, a utility infielder, at shortstop, but he got hurt early in September. Then outfielder Doc Evans was tried at shortstop but was found wanting, and the team slumped.

Owner James Dunn recommended to manager Tris Speaker that Sewell be promoted, though Speaker initially resisted, thinking that Sewell was too inexperienced.

Finally Speaker relented. "Let's gamble on anything now," Speaker said. "We've got to have some help to win this race, and anyone is better than no shortstop at all."

It was a very costly deal—initially—because, based on the rules in effect at that time, the Indians had to pay the New Orleans club $6,000 and give up rights of option on all of the minor league team's players.

But Sewell made it pay dividends, becoming the catalyst, the unsung hero of 1920.

Sewell switched to third base in 1929, the position he played for the Yankees from 1930 until 1933, when he retired.

He coached for the Yankees in 1934–35, and he scouted for the Indians for 11 years and the New York Mets one season. He later coached baseball at the University of Alabama for six years, winning the Southeastern Conference championship and Coach of the Year award in 1968.

Elected to the Hall of Fame in 1977, Joey Sewell was one

of three brothers to play in the major leagues. The others were Luke, a catcher for the Indians, Washington, Chicago White Sox, and St. Louis Browns, and Thomas, an infielder, who had one at bat for the Chicago Cubs in 1927.

Sewell, Joe

Indians	G	AB	H	BA	RBI	R	2B	3B	HR	SA	SB
1920	22	70	23	.329	12	14	4	1	0	.414	1
1921	154	572	182	.318	93	101	36	12	4	.444	7
1922	153	558	167	.299	83	80	28	7	2	.385	10
1923	153	553	195	.353	109	98	41	10	3	.479	9
1924	153	594	188	.316	106	99	45	5	4	.429	3
1925	155	608	204	.336	98	78	37	7	1	.424	7
1926	154	578	187	.324	85	91	41	5	4	.433	17
1927	153	569	180	.316	92	83	48	5	1	.424	3
1928	155	588	190	.323	70	79	40	2	4	.418	7
1929	152	578	182	.315	73	90	38	3	7	.427	6
1930	109	353	102	.289	48	44	17	6	0	.371	1
Career	1,903	7,132	2,226	.312	1,055	1,141	436	68	49	.413	74

Sewell, James Luther

Indians: 1921–32, 1939
Catcher
Nickname: Luke
Birthplace: Titus, Alabama

B: January 5, 1901
D: May 14, 1987
Batted right, threw right
Ht. 5–9; **Wt.** 160

Luke Sewell was the backup catcher to Steve O'Neill his first two full seasons with the Indians in 1922–23 and alternated with Glenn Myatt in 1924–25, then took over as the regular behind the plate from 1926 to 1932.

He batted a career-high .294 in 1927 and always was considered one of the best receivers, throwers, and handlers of pitchers in the league while playing for the Indians through 1932, and then with Washington, the Chicago White Sox, and the St. Louis Browns.

Sewell caught three no-hitters: by Wes Ferrell, 9–0, over the Browns on April 29, 1931; by Vern Kennedy, 5–0, for the White Sox over the Indians on August 31, 1935; and by Bill Dietrich, 8–0, for the White Sox over the Browns on June 1, 1937.

Before returning to the Tribe as a player-coach in 1939, Sewell set a since-broken record by leading American League catchers in assists from 1926 to '28 and in 1936. He caught a total of 1,561 games and held the AL mark for logging 20 seasons as an active catcher until Carlton Fisk broke it with 24.

It's interesting to note that Sewell wasn't deemed good enough to play for his high school team in Titus, Alabama, and didn't play at the University of Alabama until his junior year. Prior to playing his first game for the Indians on June 30, 1921, Sewell appeared in only 17 minor league games, for Columbus of the American Association, from June 7 to 26, 1921.

It was following a contract argument with owner Alva Bradley that the Indians traded Sewell on January 7, 1933, to the Senators for catcher Roy Spencer.

Sewell's explanation of his problem with Bradley: "I had made a salary agreement with [general manager] Billy Evans, but Mr. Bradley wouldn't honor it and traded me."

After Sewell broke a finger in 1934 and it didn't heal quickly because it was not set properly, he was sold in 1935 to the White Sox for whom he played through 1938, then rejoined the Indians.

As a coach for them in 1940, Sewell was caught in the mid-

dle of the "Crybaby" Indians, when they petitioned Bradley to fire manager Oscar Vitt.

"Mr. Bradley and the board of directors came to me three times asking me to take over as manager," Sewell said before his death in 1987.

"I asked them what would happen to Vitt if I accepted, and they said, 'We're going to put him in a sanitarium.' I said, 'Oh, no! You couldn't think of doing a thing like that,' and Vitt remained as the manager through the end of the season."

Sewell was retained as a coach after Roger Peckinpaugh became manager of the Indians in 1941, but was hired on June 4, 1941, to manage the Browns. He won that franchise's only pennant in 1944 and was replaced in August 1946.

He managed Cincinnati for the final three games of 1949 and from 1950 to 1952, never finishing higher than sixth. He once called the Reds "the worst ball club I ever ran into."

Luke Sewell's older brother Joey was a shortstop–third baseman for the Indians from 1920 to 1930 and a third baseman for the New York Yankees from 1931 to 1933, and his younger brother Tommy was an infielder who got one at bat for the Chicago Cubs in 1927.

Sewell, Luke

Indians	G	AB	H	BA	RBI	R	2B	3B	HR	SA	SB
1921	3	6	0	.000	1	0	0	0	0	.000	0
1922	41	87	23	.264	10	14	5	0	0	.322	1
1923	10	10	2	.200	1	2	0	1	0	.400	0
1924	63	165	48	.291	17	27	9	1	0	.358	1
1925	74	220	51	.232	18	30	10	2	0	.295	6
1926	126	433	103	.238	46	41	16	4	0	.293	9
1927	128	470	138	.294	53	52	27	6	0	.377	4
1928	122	411	111	.270	52	52	16	9	3	.375	3
1929	124	406	96	.236	39	41	16	3	1	.298	6
1930	76	292	75	.257	43	40	21	2	1	.353	5
1931	108	375	103	.275	53	45	30	4	1	.384	1
1932	87	300	76	.253	52	36	20	2	2	.353	4
1939	16	20	3	.150	1	1	1	0	0	.200	0
Career	1,630	5,383	1,393	.259	696	653	272	56	20	.341	65

Shaute, Joseph Benjamin

Indians: 1922–30
Pitcher
Nickname: Lefty
Birthplace: Peckville, Pennsylvania

B: August 1, 1899
D: February 21, 1970
Batted left, threw left
Ht. 6–0; **Wt.** 190

The most impressive of Joe Shaute's claims to fame might be that he was reputed to have struck out Babe Ruth more times—33 in the pitcher's 13-year major league career—than anybody else.

It began, the pitcher once said, when Ruth was the first batter Shaute faced as a reliever for the Indians in the sixth inning of the second game of a doubleheader in New York on July 6, 1922. Shaute also fanned Ruth in the eighth inning of that game.

On the other hand, in 1927, when Ruth hit a then record 60 home runs, three of them were off Shaute.

Shaute's best season was 1924 when he was the Indians' winningest pitcher with a 20–17 record. He also tied for third-most victories in the American League—though his 17 losses also were the most in the AL that year. He won 10 or more games in four of his nine seasons in Cleveland.

Joe Shaute

Shaute's 78 victories for the Indians makes him the second-winningest left-hander in franchise history, behind Sam McDowell's 122.

After the Indians let Shaute go in 1930 when he appeared in four games without a decision, he joined the Brooklyn Dodgers, for whom he went 11–8 in 1931. He was a reliever–spot starter for them in 1932–33, then was sold to Cincinnati, ending his major league career with the Reds with an 0–2 record in 1934.

Shaute managed in the minor leagues in 1938, and later served as treasurer and sheriff of Lackawanna County, Pennsylvania.

Shaute, Joe

Indians	W	L	Pct	ERA	G	CG	IP	H	BB	SO	ShO
1922	0	0	—	19.64	2	0	3⅔	7	3	3	0
1923	10	8	.556	3.51	33	7	172	176	53	61	0
1924	20	17	.541	3.75	46	21	283	317	83	68	2
1925	4	12	.250	5.43	26	10	131	160	44	34	1
1926	14	10	.583	3.53	34	15	206⅔	215	65	47	1
1927	9	16	.360	4.22	45	14	230⅓	255	75	63	0
1928	13	17	.433	4.04	36	21	253⅔	295	68	81	1
1929	8	8	.500	4.28	26	8	162	211	52	43	0
1930	0	0	—	15.43	4	0	4⅔	8	4	2	0
Career	99	109	.476	4.15	360	103	1,818⅓	2,097	534	512	5

Siebert, Wilfred Charles

Indians: 1964–69
Pitcher
Nickname: Sonny
Birthplace: St. Mary's, Missouri

B: January 14, 1937
Bats right, throws right
Ht. 6–3; **Wt.** 190

Sonny Siebert was a hard-hitting first baseman–outfielder when he began in professional baseball in 1958. He didn't become a pitcher until he threatened to quit the Indians unless they let him take the mound.

They finally did, in 1960, and Siebert became one of the best pitchers in baseball in a 12-year major league career that began in 1964.

He hurled a no-hitter to beat the Washington Senators, 2–0, on June 10, 1966, the first of two consecutive seasons in which he posted career-best 16–8 records. He won the Indians' Man of the Year award in 1966 and was named to the American League All-Star team in 1966 and 1971.

Siebert came close to pitching two more no-hitters. Curt Blefary spoiled the first one with a seventh-inning double in the second game of a doubleheader in which the Tribe beat Baltimore, 2–0, at the Stadium on May 19, 1968. Jay Johnstone got the only hit, a single in the third inning as Boston beat California, 2–0, on July 31, 1970.

An All-American first baseman and basketball star at the University of Missouri, Siebert was drafted by the St. Louis Hawks of the National Basketball Association, but chose instead to sign a $35,000-bonus contract with the Indians.

They switched Siebert to the outfield because of his strong throwing arm, but he was going nowhere as a position player.

"They kept trying to change me . . . at that time the big theory in hitting was to pull the ball every pitch. But my stroke was pretty much what they later started to teach, to hit the ball where it's pitched," said Siebert.

It was in spring training that he rebelled. "I went back to the dormitory and started to pack up to go home," he said.

When Indians officials asked what it would take for him to stay, Siebert said he told them, "I didn't like playing the outfield, that I was bored out there, and that I felt my best tool was my throwing arm. I said I wanted to be a pitcher, not an outfielder, and if they wouldn't let me try it [pitching], I was going home."

The Indians acquiesced, and after four seasons in the minor leagues, Siebert made it to the major leagues in 1964 and pitched there through 1975.

It was on April 19, 1969, that the Indians let Siebert get away, trading him with catcher Joe Azcue and reliever Vicente Romo to the Red Sox for first baseman–outfielder Ken Harrelson and pitchers Dick Ellsworth and Juan Pizarro.

Sonny Siebert

It was not a good deal for the Indians, but it helped the Red Sox as Siebert led their starting pitchers in winning percentage in 1970 and 1971, going 15–8 and 16–10.

Siebert went on to pitch for Texas, the St. Louis Cardinals, San Diego, and Oakland. On September 11, 1974, while with the Cardinals, Siebert beat the New York Mets, 4–3, in the second-longest game by innings, 25, in National League history.

After his retirement as a player, Siebert became a minor league pitching coach for the Padres in 1984. He climbed through the ranks as a scout and instructor at every level of their farm system for 10 years, prior to joining them as a coach at the major league level in 1994.

Siebert, Sonny

Indians	W	L	Pct	ERA	G	CG	IP	H	BB	SO	ShO
1964	7	9	.438	3.23	41	3	156	142	57	144	1
1965	16	8	.667	2.43	39	4	188⅔	139	46	191	1
1966	16	8	.667	2.80	34	11	241	193	62	163	1
1967	10	12	.455	2.38	34	7	185⅓	136	54	136	1
1968	12	10	.545	2.97	31	8	206	145	88	146	4
1969	0	1	.000	3.21	2	0	14	10	8	6	0
Career	140	114	.551	3.21	399	67	2,152	1,919	692	1,512	21

Sims, Duane B

Indians: 1964–70
Catcher, first baseman, outfielder
Nickname: Duke
Birthplace: Salt Lake City, Utah

B: June 5, 1941
Bats left, throws right
Ht. 6–2; **Wt.** 197

Duke Sims was up and down with the Indians from 1964 to 1966, and was their regular catcher in 1968 when he blossomed into a strong power hitter.

In desperate need of pitching, the Indians traded Sims on December 11, 1970, to Los Angeles for pitchers Ray Lamb and Alan Foster, and in 1971 he batted .274 for the Dodgers.

After he was sold to Detroit on August 4, 1972, Sims batted .316 down the stretch, helping the Tigers win the Amer-

Duke Sims

ican League East division championship. He went to the New York Yankees in 1973 and ended his major league career with Texas in 1974.

Sims, Duke

Indians	G	AB	H	BA	RBI	R	2B	3B	HR	SA	SB
1964	2	6	0	.000	0	0	0	0	0	.000	0
1965	48	118	21	.178	15	9	0	0	6	.331	0
1966	52	133	35	.263	19	12	2	2	6	.444	0
1967	88	272	55	.202	37	25	8	2	12	.379	3
1968	122	361	90	.249	44	48	21	0	11	.399	1
1969	114	326	77	.236	45	40	8	0	18	.426	1
1970	110	345	91	.264	56	46	12	0	23	.499	0
Career	843	2,422	580	.239	310	263	80	6	100	.401	6

Smith, Alfred John

Indians: 1940–45
Pitcher
Birthplace: Belleville, Illinois
B: October 12, 1907

D: April 28, 1977
Batted left, threw left
Ht. 5–11; **Wt.** 180

Al Smith was most famous for being one of the two pitchers (Jim Bagby, Jr., was the other) who stopped Joe DiMaggio's consecutive-game hitting streak at 56 on July 17, 1941.

But before joining the Indians in 1940, when they purchased him from Buffalo of the Class AA International League, Smith was a 14-game winner, while losing 13, for the New York Giants when they won the National League pennant in 1936.

He went 5–4 for the Giants the following season when they repeated for the championship, but developed arm trouble and was sold to the Philadelphia Phillies on December 29, 1937.

The Phillies also gave up on Smith after he won only one game and lost four in 1938 and was 0–0 in five appearances in 1939.

Smith went back to the minors and became a finesse pitcher, perfecting a screwball, and was picked up by the Indians on January 25, 1940.

The laconic left-hander made no promises when he was granted another chance in the major leagues. "I just keep trying my best," he said. "Sometimes I get 'em out, sometimes they pin my ears back. Sometimes I feel good, sometimes I feel bad, and I don't know why in either case.

"If I knew as much about pitching as I do about fishing, I'd lead the league."

Given a new lease on his career at the age of 32, Smith came through with 15 victories. It was the first of four consecutive seasons in which he won 10 or more games, including 1943 when he went 17–7 and was named to the American League All-Star team.

Smith flirted with no-hitters twice during his career with the Indians. On August 14, 1940, he allowed only a third-inning single by Skeeter Webb in a 4–0 victory over the Chicago White Sox, and on June 20, 1942, DiMaggio got the Yankees' only hit, a second-inning double, as the Tribe beat New York, 1–0.

Smith was the starter in the game in which DiMaggio was held hitless in three at bats (with a walk) for the first time since his record-setting streak began on May 15, 1941.

Al (Alfred) Smith

He retired DiMaggio in the first inning on a good play by third baseman Ken Keltner, walked the Yankees slugger in the fourth inning, and got him to ground out to Keltner again in the seventh.

Bagby replaced Smith with one out in the eighth and induced DiMaggio to hit into a double play, ending the inning and the streak.

Interestingly, the only time Smith faced DiMaggio earlier in the streak was on June 15 in New York. DiMaggio also went 0-for-2 against Smith that time, though he had extended his streak to 28 in that game with a first-inning homer off Bagby, the starter.

Smith's record fell off to 7–13 in 1944 and to 5–12 in 1945, his last two seasons in the major leagues.

Smith, Al (Alfred)

Indians	W	L	Pct	ERA	G	CG	IP	H	BB	SO	ShO
1940	15	7	.682	3.44	31	11	183	187	55	46	1
1941	12	13	.480	3.83	29	13	206⅔	204	75	76	2
1942	10	15	.400	3.96	30	7	168⅓	163	71	66	1
1943	17	7	.708	2.55	29	14	208⅓	186	72	72	3
1944	7	13	.350	3.42	28	7	181⅔	197	69	44	1
1945	5	12	.294	3.84	21	8	133⅔	141	48	34	3
Career	99	101	.495	3.72	356	75	1,662⅓	1,707	587	587	16

Smith, Alphonse Eugene

Indians: 1953–57, 1964
Outfielder, third baseman
Nickname: Fuzzy
Birthplace: Kirkwood, Missouri

B: February 7, 1928
Bats right, throws right
Ht. 6–½; **Wt.** 189

A versatile player who was equally adept at third base and in the outfield, Al Smith was the regular left fielder when the

Indians won the pennant in 1954, as well as for the Chicago White Sox when they were the American League champion in 1959.

His first big year was 1954, when he batted .281 in 131 games, after which Tribe manager Al Lopez said, "Smith could turn out to be as good as Larry Doby, and maybe better."

Smith didn't, but he was named to the AL All-Star team and elected the Indians' Man of the Year in 1955, when he hit .306 and led the league with 123 runs. Two years later he was sent to the White Sox in the first trade made by Frank Lane, who became general manager of the Indians in November 1957.

Determined to make a headline deal to launch his stewardship of the Tribe, Lane reacquired one of his all-time favorite players, Minnie Minoso, who had been traded to the White Sox in 1951 by Hank Greenberg, then the Cleveland general manager.

Unfortunately for the Indians, to get Minoso back, Lane gave Smith and pitcher Early Wynn to the White Sox, also receiving utility infielder Fred Hatfield in the December 4, 1957, transaction.

By then, Minoso was nearly finished—but not Smith or Wynn.

Smith hit a career-high .315 in 1960, when he again made the AL All-Star team. He played five seasons for the White Sox, who traded him to Baltimore on January 14, 1963. Eleven months later he was sent, along with $25,000, to the financially strapped Indians on December 4, 1963, in exchange for outfielder Willie Kirkland.

But—again, unfortunately for the Tribe—by then Smith was all but finished.

He batted .162 in 61 games for the Indians in 1964 and was released on August 5. Smith was picked up by the Boston Red Sox for whom he played 29 games, batting .216 for a final season average of .176, and retired.

Al (Alphonse) Smith

Smith, Al (Alphonse)

Indians	G	AB	H	BA	RBI	R	2B	3B	HR	SA	SB
1953	47	150	36	.240	14	28	9	0	3	.360	2
1954	131	481	135	.281	50	101	29	6	11	.435	2
1955	154	607	186	.306	77	123	27	4	22	.473	11
1956	141	526	144	.274	71	87	26	5	16	.433	6
1957	135	507	125	.247	49	78	23	5	11	.377	12
1964	61	136	22	.162	9	15	1	1	4	.272	0
Career	1,517	5,357	1,458	.272	676	843	258	46	164	.429	67

Smith, Elmer

Indians	G	AB	H	BA	RBI	R	2B	3B	HR	SA	SB
1914	13	53	17	.321	8	5	3	0	0	.377	1
1915	144	476	118	.248	67	37	23	12	3	.366	10
1916	79	213	59	.277	40	25	15	3	3	.418	3
1917	64	161	42	.261	22	21	5	1	3	.360	6
1919	114	395	110	.278	54	60	24	6	9	.438	15
1920	129	456	144	.316	103	82	37	10	12	.520	5
1921	129	431	125	.290	85	98	28	9	16	.508	0
Career	1,012	3,195	881	.276	541	469	181	62	70	.437	54

Smith, Elmer John

Indians: 1914–16, 1917, 1919–21
Outfielder
Birthplace: Sandusky, Ohio
B: September 21, 1892

D: August 3, 1984
Batted left, threw right
Ht. 5–10; **Wt.** 165

Elmer Smith was one of three Cleveland players who distinguished themselves in Game 5 of the 1920 World Series, in which the Indians beat the Brooklyn Dodgers in seven games (it was a best-of-nine series then).

Smith, who also played for the Washington Senators, Boston Red Sox, New York Yankees, and Cincinnati, hit a grand slam homer off Hall of Famer Burleigh Grimes in the first inning of what became an 8–1 Indians victory at League Park on October 10.

It came after Charlie Jamieson led off with a single to right, Bill Wambsganss singled to center, and Tris Speaker was credited with a bases-loading single when Grimes fell down trying to field his bunt. Smith followed with his blast over the right-field fence.

It was the first grand slam ever hit in a World Series game. Fifteen have been hit since then.

In the fourth inning, Tribe pitcher Jim Bagby, Sr., became the first pitcher to hit a home run in the World Series, a three-run shot into the center-field stands, and a half inning later Wambsganss, the Indians' second baseman, pulled off the only unassisted triple play in the World Series.

Smith, who broke in with the Tribe in 1914, was traded on August 18, 1916, with infielder Joe Leonard to the Senators for pitcher Joe Boehling and outfielder Danny Moeller.

The Indians got him back from Washington in a $4,000 purchase on June 13, 1917, and Smith had his best year in 1920, hitting .316 with 12 homers and 103 runs batted in. But one year later the Tribe sent him away again.

On December 24, 1921, Smith was traded again, this time with first baseman George Burns and outfielder Joe Harris to the Red Sox for first baseman Stuffy McInnis.

But Smith didn't stay long in Boston, either. Seven months later he was part of a six-player deal that sent him to the Yankees, who released him in 1923.

In 1924, Smith played for Louisville in the Class AA American Association where he batted .334, scored 132 runs, and had 28 homers, 17 triples, and 45 doubles among his 216 hits. He was back in the major leagues with the Reds for a final season in 1925 when he hit .271 in 96 games, ending his career with a lifetime average of .276 in 10 seasons.

Smith and Tris Speaker still share the major league record for the most career unassisted double plays, four, by an outfielder.

Snyder, James Cory

Indians: 1986–90
Outfielder, shortstop,
  third baseman, designated hitter
Birthplace: Inglewood, California

B: November 11, 1962
Bats right, throws right
Ht. 6–4; **Wt.** 175

Cory Snyder was the Indians' number-one selection (fourth overall) in the 1984 amateur draft, the year he'd been a first-team All-American third baseman at Brigham Young University and a star on the U.S. Olympic team.

Snyder, switched to right field because of his strong throwing arm, played less than two seasons in the minors, earning a promotion to the Indians in early 1986 after batting .302 in 49 games at Maine of the Class AAA International League.

Immediately taking over as the Indians' regular right fielder, Snyder smashed 24 homers and hit .272 as a Tribe rookie in 103 games the rest of the 1986 season.

His average declined to .236 in 157 games in 1987, though his home runs increased to 33, including three in a game on May 21 against Minnesota, won by the Indians, 6–3, at the Stadium. It also was in 1987 that Snyder set the Indians' record for striking out 166 times in one season.

He bounced back to .272 with 26 homers in 1988, but that was Snyder's last good year for the Tribe. On December 4,

Cory Snyder

1990, he was traded with minor league infielder Lindsay Foster to the Chicago White Sox for pitchers Eric King and Shawn Hillegas.

Snyder subsequently was traded to Toronto on July 14, 1991, and when the decline in his play continued, the Blue Jays released him at the end of the season. He signed as a free agent with San Francisco on January 13, 1992, and then with Los Angeles on December 5, 1992. He played for the Dodgers through 1994. He was signed by the Boston Red Sox in 1995 and played with Pawtucket in the International League.

Snyder, Cory

Indians	G	AB	H	BA	RBI	R	2B	3B	HR	SA	SB
1986	103	416	113	.272	69	58	21	1	24	.500	2
1987	157	577	136	.236	82	74	24	2	33	.456	5
1988	142	511	139	.272	75	71	24	3	26	.483	5
1989	132	489	105	.215	59	49	17	0	18	.360	6
1990	123	438	102	.233	55	46	27	3	14	.404	1
Career	1,068	3,656	902	.247	488	439	178	13	149	.425	28

Speaker, Tristram E.

Indians: 1916–26
Outfielder
Nicknames: Tris, The Gray Eagle, Spoke
Birthplace: Hubbard, Texas

B: April 4, 1888
D: December 8, 1958
Batted left, threw left
Ht. 5–11½; **Wt.** 193

On September 12, 1907, a stocky, 19-year-old rookie outfielder named Tris Speaker was introduced to major league pitching as a sixth-inning replacement for Boston right fielder Bunk Congalton. He went hitless in two at bats.

It was the beginning of a career that would span 22 major league seasons—but also would wind up under a cloud of suspicion, though not enough to deny Speaker induction into the Hall of Fame.

Two days after his inauspicious debut Speaker was unsuccessful again, this time as a pinch hitter for pitcher Cy Morgan.

Tris Speaker

Then, on September 17, 1907, in Washington, Speaker singled off the Senators' Tom Hughes. He went on to register 3,514 hits, fifth most in baseball history, and score 1,882 runs, eighth most, establishing him as one of the greatest players of all time.

Hall of Fame voters agreed with that assessment as Speaker became in 1937 the seventh player elected to the shrine. He was preceded by Ty Cobb, Babe Ruth, Honus Wagner, Christy Mathewson, Walter Johnson, and Napoleon Lajoie.

Though his major league career began with the Red Sox, it was in Cleveland that Speaker gained most of his fame.

It also was with the Indians that Speaker almost fell from grace, upon allegedly being involved in a 1919 conspiracy with teammate "Smoky Joe" Wood and two members of the Detroit Tigers, Ty Cobb and Hubert "Dutch" Leonard, to fix and bet on a game.

The allegation wasn't raised until seven years later, in 1926. All four players subsequently were cleared by Commissioner Kenesaw Mountain Landis, but not until significant potentially damaging revelations had come to light.

Speaker was acquired by the Indians on April 8, 1916, in a trade that turned out to be one of the best in the club's history and, interestingly, was motivated by a Cleveland sportswriter named Ed Bang.

The Indians got Speaker for pitcher Sad Sam Jones, infielder Fred Thomas, and $55,000—though several complications developed before the deal was consummated.

Speaker had batted .322 in 1915 to lead the Red Sox to the American League pennant and victory in five games over the Philadelphia Phillies in the World Series, and he was anticipating a nice raise for 1916.

But when his contract arrived in the mail that winter, Speaker was outraged when he was offered the same salary—$9,000—he had been paid in 1915.

Boston owner Joe Lannin justified the proposed contract by citing the fact that Speaker's batting average had declined every year since he hit .383 in 1912. But Speaker would have none of it and refused to sign.

When the Red Sox opened spring training in Hot Springs, Arkansas, in 1916, Speaker was still outraged, and still sitting at home, demanding a raise to $15,000.

Lannin was equally adamant and vowed to trade Speaker, which is when Bang, then sports editor of the *Cleveland News,* came into the picture.

After reading about the impasse between Speaker and Lannin, Bang called Bob McRoy, then general manager of the Indians. "I know Lannin," Bang told McRoy, "and I know he'll sell any player if he's offered enough money."

Thus motivated, McRoy called Lannin and made the deal, clinching it with the $55,000 payment.

Then McRoy called Speaker, who said he wouldn't consider playing in Cleveland.

"You've got a bad ball club, for one thing," he said. "And Cleveland isn't a good baseball town either. I don't want to go to Cleveland and wind up in the second division."

When told the deal already had been made, Speaker relented—but only on one condition.

"All right, I'll go to Cleveland, but I want $10,000 of the purchase price, and I want it from the Red Sox," Speaker told McRoy.

Lannin objected, but American League president Ban Johnson interceded. He ordered Lannin to meet Speaker's demand, and the deal finally was consummated.

Speaker thrived in Cleveland and quickly became the team's favorite player. He led the American League in 1916 with a .386 batting average, 211 hits, 41 doubles, and eight triples, and went on to hit .300 or better in 10 of his 11 seasons with the Tribe.

Less than four years after joining the Indians, Speaker became their manager, as well as their star center fielder, replacing Lee Fohl on July 18, 1919. He led the Tribe to the pennant and world's championship in 1920.

Speaker continued as player-manager of the Indians through 1926, when he resigned both jobs in the wake of the allegations raised by Leonard that he had participated in the fixed game between Cleveland and Detroit.

After leaving the Tribe, Speaker continued his playing career with Washington in 1927 and with the Philadelphia Athletics in 1928.

The gambling scandal surfaced during the 1926 season, after Wood and Leonard already had been retired.

Apparently resentful of the way he'd been treated by Cobb, Leonard charged that the Indians, with second place locked up in 1919, deliberately lost a game to the Tigers late in the season. He claimed that all four players had made and won large bets on the fixed game.

Leonard even produced letters from Cobb and Wood that supported his allegations and implicated all four players.

However, after a lengthy investigation, Speaker and Cobb were cleared by Commissioner Kenesaw Mountain Landis, though both were required by AL president Johnson to resign as player-managers of their teams.

Cobb spent the next two seasons playing for the Athletics and was Speaker's teammate in Philadelphia in 1928, after which both retired.

Speaker ended his 22 years in the major leagues with the fifth-best lifetime batting average, .345, in baseball history, and his 792 doubles are more than any other player ever hit.

His determination to excel was evident at an early age when he was a right-handed schoolboy pitcher in the early 1900s. When he broke his pitching arm, Speaker learned to throw left-handed and became an outfielder—and eventually one of the best center fielders to play the game.

Speaker's first year in professional baseball was 1906 when he played for Cleburne in the Class D Texas League. When Cleburne did not field a club in 1907, Speaker joined Houston of the Texas League (Class C in 1907). The Red Sox liked what they saw of Speaker, who led the league in batting, and purchased his contract for $750.

But he didn't hit and the following spring was left at Little Rock, then in the Class A Southern Association, as payment for the training camp expenses incurred by the Red Sox.

Before the 1908 season was over, however, Speaker was hitting well and led the Southern Association with a .350 average, and the Red Sox reacquired him for $500. He joined them in Boston and never returned to the minor leagues, except as manager of Newark in the Class AA International League in 1929 and until June 26, 1930.

In 1912, Speaker won the Chalmers Award—in the form of a $1,950 automobile—the predecessor of the Most Valuable Player award. In addition to his batting feats, Speaker is the all-time major league leader in outfield assists (448) and double plays (139) and the AL leader in outfield putouts (6,787). He and Elmer Smith share the major league record for most career unassisted double plays, four, by an outfielder.

Speaker did some broadcasting for NBC in the early 1930s. He rejoined the Indians in 1947 to coach their outfielders, primarily Larry Doby, the AL's first black player, who previously had been an infielder in the Negro League.

Speaker, Tris

Indians	G	AB	H	BA	RBI	R	2B	3B	HR	SA	SB
1916	151	546	211	.386	79	102	41	8	2	.502	35
1917	142	523	184	.352	60	90	42	11	2	.486	30
1918	127	471	150	.318	61	73	33	11	0	.435	27
1919	134	494	146	.296	63	83	38	12	2	.433	15
1920	150	552	214	.388	107	137	50	11	8	.562	10
1921	132	506	183	.362	75	107	52	14	3	.538	2
1922	131	426	161	.378	71	85	48	8	11	.606	8
1923	150	574	218	.380	130	133	59	11	17	.610	8
1924	135	486	167	.344	65	94	36	9	9	.510	5
1925	117	429	167	.389	87	79	35	5	12	.578	5
1926	150	539	164	.304	86	96	52	8	7	.469	6
Career	2,789	10,195	3,514	.345	1,529	1,882	792	222	117	.500	432

Spikes, Leslie Charles

Indians: 1973–77
Outfielder
Nickname: Charlie
Birthplace: Bogalusa, Louisiana

B: January 23, 1951
Bats right, throws right
Ht. 6–3; Wt. 215

Charlie Spikes joined the Indians with big—make that *very big*—credentials and expectations as the key man in a November 27, 1972, six-player trade between the Indians and New York Yankees.

Cleveland also received catcher John Ellis, outfielder Rusty Torres, and second baseman Jerry Kenney in the deal for third baseman Graig Nettles and catcher Gerry Moses, but Spikes was the guy the Indians wanted.

"Charlie is capable of hitting .275–.280 with 40 to 50 homers a year for a lot of years," said Tribe general manager Phil Seghi at the time the trade was made.

All of which proves again how inexact the "science" of baseball scouting can be.

Spikes was New York's number-one selection in the 1969 amateur draft, and his minor league credentials gave every indication that the Yankees were right. Seghi, too.

Unfortunately, the deal turned sour for the Indians, despite the fact that Spikes showed signs of delivering as advertised during his first two seasons in Cleveland.

He hammered 23 homers (though his batting average was only .237) in 1973, and 22 (with a .271 mark) in 1974. But then something happened to the "Bogalusa Bomber," as Spikes was nicknamed because of his—at least initially—awesome power.

"I don't know what it was . . . my stroke just seemed to leave me," said Spikes, whose career went downhill after those first two seasons in Cleveland.

One theory was that all the advance publicity and great expectations put more pressure on Spikes than he could han-

Charlie Spikes

in the 1970 amateur draft, was traded to the Indians for pitcher Dennis Kinney on June 14, 1978. He continued his success as a reliever until late in the next season.

But then began a series of switches back and forth from the bull pen to the starting rotation and back to relief again, which Spillner handled well most of the time.

He was the Indians' second leading winner with a 16–11 record as a starter in 1980, after which *The Sporting News* said Spillner had "one of the five best arms in baseball," meaning he could start or pitch short or long relief.

One of his victories was a one-hitter, a 3–0 victory over the Chicago White Sox on August 20. Leo Sutherland got Chicago's only hit, a single in the ninth inning with one out.

It was the second one-hitter of Spillner's career. On June 19, 1974, while pitching for the Padres, he beat the Chicago Cubs, 1–0. The only hit off Spillner was Rick Monday's third-inning single.

"It doesn't make any difference to me what they want me to do, start or relieve," he said. "I'm not a finesse pitcher; I just throw the ball as hard as I can for as long as I can. I guess you can say I have a strong arm and a strong back."

Spillner returned to the bull pen exclusively in 1982 and 1983 and was the Tribe's busiest pitcher, appearing in a total of 125 games. He set a club record (since broken) with 21 saves in 1982.

When the Indians embarked upon a financial austerity program in 1984, unloading many of their high-priced players, Spillner—whose salary was $350,000 that year and the next—was traded to the Chicago White Sox for minor league pitcher Jim Siwy on June 21, 1984.

That was the season the Indians also divested themselves of pitchers Rick Sutcliffe, who was making $900,000, and George Frazier, $425,000, catcher Ron Hassey, $500,000, and second baseman Alan Bannister, $350,000.

Spillner ended his major league career in 1985 with a 4–3 record in 53 games for the White Sox, all as a reliever.

dle, to which he said again, "I don't know if that was it or not. I can't explain it."

Nobody could. His average fell to .229 with only 11 homers in 111 games in 1975, and, after two more unproductive seasons, during which he hit a total of only six homers, Spikes was traded to the highest bidder. It was Detroit.

On December 9, 1977, the Tigers sent shortstop Tom Veryzer to the Indians for Spikes, who played only 10 games in Detroit in 1978.

Spikes then was picked up by Atlanta, but his stroke was still AWOL, and he was out of the major leagues after playing 41 games without hitting even one homer in 1980.

Spikes, Charlie

Indians	G	AB	H	BA	RBI	R	2B	3B	HR	SA	SB
1973	140	506	120	.237	73	68	12	3	23	.409	5
1974	155	568	154	.271	80	63	23	1	22	.431	10
1975	111	345	79	.229	33	41	13	3	11	.380	7
1976	101	334	79	.237	31	34	11	5	3	.326	5
1977	32	95	22	.232	11	13	2	0	3	.347	0
Career	670	2,039	502	.246	256	240	72	12	65	.389	27

Spillner, Daniel Ray

Indians: 1978–84
Pitcher
Birthplace: Casper, Wyoming

B: November 27, 1951
Bats right, throws right
Ht. 6–1; **Wt.** 190

Dan Spillner was a mediocre starting pitcher at best the first three years of his career (1974–76) in San Diego when he compiled an 16–35 won-lost record.

But, switched to the bull pen in 1977, Spillner became one of the most dependable relievers in baseball as a setup pitcher for Rollie Fingers, appearing in 76 games.

Spillner, who had been the Padres' number-two selection

Dan Spillner

Spillner, Dan

Indians	W	L	Pct	ERA	G	CG	IP	H	BB	SO	ShO
1978	3	1	.750	3.67	36	0	56⅓	54	21	48	0
1979	9	5	.643	4.62	49	3	157⅔	153	64	97	0
1980	16	11	.593	5.28	34	7	194⅓	225	74	100	1
1981	4	4	.500	3.14	32	1	97⅓	86	39	59	0
1982	12	10	.545	2.49	65	0	133⅔	117	45	90	0
1983	2	9	.182	5.07	60	0	92⅓	117	38	48	0
1984	0	5	.000	5.65	14	0	51	70	22	23	0
Career	75	89	.457	4.21	556	19	1,492⅔	1,585	605	878	3

Stephenson, Jackson Riggs

Indians: 1921–25
Second baseman, third baseman, outfielder
Nicknames: Old Hoss, Riggs
Birthplace: Akron, Alabama

B: January 5, 1898
D: November 15, 1985
Batted right, threw right
Ht. 5–10; **Wt.** 185

He was a very good hitter, but the Indians couldn't find a place for Riggs Stephenson to play in the field. As a result, he didn't become a regular until after he had left Cleveland and joined the Chicago Cubs.

Originally tried at second base where he filled in on occasion for Bill Wambsganss, Stephenson batted .330 in 65 games in 1921, then went on to hit .319 or better in 12 of his 14 seasons in the major leagues, the final nine with the Cubs. His .336 lifetime batting average is 18th on the all-time list.

Stephenson's primary problem was that he had a weak arm, the result of an injury suffered when he played football at the University of Alabama. It was difficult for him to make the pivot at second base and throw to first on double plays.

His troubles in the field notwithstanding, Stephenson had few weaknesses at the plate. He batted a career-high .371 in 71 games in 1924, but only .296 in 19 games in 1925. On June 2 he was optioned to Kansas City of the Class AA American Association.

There, Stephenson was switched to the outfield and returned to the major leagues with the Cubs in 1926. He was a regular from 1927 to 1929, and the latter two seasons played alongside Hall of Fame outfielders Hack Wilson and Kiki Cuyler.

Injuries forced Stephenson to leave the Cubs after 38 games in 1934, but he played and managed in the minor leagues from 1936 to 1939.

Stephenson, Riggs

Indians	G	AB	H	BA	RBI	R	2B	3B	HR	SA	SB
1921	65	206	68	.330	34	45	17	2	2	.461	4
1922	86	233	79	.339	32	47	24	5	2	.511	3
1923	91	301	96	.319	65	48	20	6	5	.475	5
1924	71	240	89	.371	44	33	20	0	4	.504	1
1925	19	54	16	.296	9	8	3	1	1	.444	1
Career	1,310	4,508	1,515	.336	773	714	321	54	63	.473	53

Stovall, George Thomas

Indians: 1904–11
First baseman, second baseman, third baseman, outfielder
Nickname: Firebrand
Birthplace: Independence, Missouri

B: November 23, 1878
D: November 5, 1951
Batted right, threw right
Ht. 6–2; **Wt.** 180

George Stovall had a stormy career with the Cleveland club (then called the Naps), which he managed briefly in 1911. Later he became the first star player to jump to the outlaw Federal League in 1914.

A slick-fielding first baseman, Stovall's hot temper and angry outbursts at other players and umpires was the reason he was nicknamed Firebrand.

Early in his career, in fact, Stovall even reportedly smashed a chair over the head of Napoleon Lajoie, the manager of the Naps.

Still, Stovall was very popular among his teammates. It was Stovall who organized a "strike" on opening day, April 16, 1911, forcing postponement of the game so that the Naps could attend the funeral of Addie Joss in Toledo.

Though he never batted .300 in his 12-year major league career, Stovall was a slick-fielding first baseman and played more games (801) at that position in his eight seasons with the Cleveland club than anybody except Hal Trosky (1,111).

Stovall became manager of the Naps on May 3, 1911, replacing James McGuire, under whom the team had lost 11 of its first 17 games, falling into seventh place.

With Stovall at the helm the rest of the season, the Naps won 74 games and lost 62, finishing in third place with an overall 80–73 record, though they were 22 games behind the pennant-winning Philadelphia Athletics.

Prior to Stovall's promotion as manager, however, Naps owner Charles Somers made a secret deal with Athletics owner Connie Mack. It was to hire Philadelphia first baseman Harry Davis to manage the Cleveland team in 1912.

Davis was signed on October 27, 1911—to howls of protest by Naps players—and Stovall was traded to the St. Louis Browns for pitcher Thomas "Lefty" George the following February 17.

Stovall played two seasons for the Browns, and also was their manager for 115 games in 1912, when he took over for Bobby Wallace in June, and for 134 games in 1913, before being replaced by Jimmy Austin in September.

He was fired by the Browns reportedly after a series of incidents, including his refusal to give tryouts to college players and spitting tobacco juice in the eyes of umpires.

Not only did Stovall jump to the Federal League to be player-manager of the Kansas City club in 1914, but he also induced other established American and National league players to follow.

When the Federal League folded after the 1915 season, during which Stovall hit .231 in 130 games, he retired. He later became president of the Association of Professional Ball Players of America.

Stovall's older brother Jesse pitched six games for the Naps in 1903, and also pitched for Detroit in 1904.

Stovall, George

Indians	G	AB	H	BA	RBI	R	2B	3B	HR	SA	SB
1904	52	181	54	.298	31	18	10	1	1	.381	3
1905	112	423	115	.272	47	41	31	1	1	.357	13
1906	116	443	121	.273	37	54	19	5	0	.339	15
1907	124	466	110	.236	36	38	17	6	1	.305	13
1908	138	534	156	.292	45	71	29	6	2	.380	14
1909	145	565	139	.246	49	60	17	10	2	.322	25
1910	142	521	136	.261	52	49	19	4	0	.313	16
1911	126	458	124	.271	79	48	17	7	0	.338	11
Career	1,414	5,222	1,382	.265	564	547	231	56	15	.339	142

Strickland, George Bevan

Indians: 1952–57, 1959–60
Shortstop, third baseman,
   second baseman
Nickname: Bo

Birthplace: New Orleans, Louisiana
B: January 10, 1926
Bats right, throws right
Ht. 6–1; Wt. 175

It wasn't George Strickland's bat the Indians wanted when they traded for him in 1952. It was his glove and leadership—which they got, and both of which paid big dividends.

Strickland was acquired with pitcher Ted Wilks from Pittsburgh on August 18, in exchange for shortstop–second baseman Johnny Berardino, minor league pitcher Charley Sipple, and $50,000.

The Indians thought they had a chance to win the American League pennant but were concerned because their shortstop, Ray Boone, whose range was limited even when he was sound, was playing on a pair of sore knees.

It was a good deal for the Tribe, though not immediately. Strickland batted only .216 in 31 games the rest of 1952, and the Indians again finished second to the New York Yankees.

Strickland boosted his average to a career high .284 in 1953, but his value to the Indians was even greater in 1954 because of his defense. Though he hit only .213, Strickland solidified the infield, and the Indians won an American League–record 111 games and the pennant.

In a game against the Yankees in New York on July 23, Strickland suffered a fractured left jaw when he was hit by a thrown ball while sliding into third base.

After it happened, manager Al Lopez said of Strickland, "He was as close to being an indispensable player as we have on this team."

Less than two weeks later, Strickland was back at shortstop, playing with his jaw wired shut—and playing every bit as well.

And though Strickland never came close to hitting as much as he did in 1953, his value to the team was indisputable.

He led AL shortstops in double plays in 1953 with 103, and in fielding percentage (.976) in 1955, and he still shares the major league record for shortstops with five double plays in one game (September 27, 1952).

Strickland retired and went home to New Orleans after the 1957 season, and in 1958 the Indians employed five different shortstops in an attempt to fill his shoes.

That winter Tribe coach Red Kress, en route to managing a winter league team in Venezuela, ran into Strickland and encouraged him to make a comeback.

Strickland did, and, though his batting average, .238, was nothing to rave about, he was outstanding in the field again, and the Indians almost beat the Chicago White Sox for the pennant.

Strickland hung up his spikes after playing 32 games in 1960—but he still wasn't finished in baseball. He remained with the Indians in 1961 as a scout and joined the Minnesota Twins as their third base coach in 1962.

And when Birdie Tebbetts became the Tribe manager in 1963, the first man he hired as a coach was Strickland.

When Tebbetts was felled with a heart attack on April 1, 1964, Strickland was named interim manager of the Indians. Their record was 33–39 under Strickland before Tebbetts returned on July 3.

Strickland again took over as manager of the Indians when Tebbetts was fired on August 19, 1966. They went 15–24 the rest of the season under Strickland, and he returned to the coaching ranks, remaining with the Indians through 1969.

He coached for the Kansas City Royals from 1970 to 1972 as an assistant to manager Joe Gordon, who had been the Indians' pilot during Strickland's last season as a player in Cleveland.

George Strickland

Strickland, George

Indians	G	AB	H	BA	RBI	R	2B	3B	HR	SA	SB
1952	31	88	19	.216	8	8	4	0	1	.295	0
1953	123	419	119	.284	47	43	17	4	5	.379	0
1954	112	361	77	.213	37	42	12	3	6	.313	2
1955	130	388	81	.209	34	34	9	5	2	.273	1
1956	85	171	36	.211	17	22	1	2	3	.292	0
1957	89	201	47	.234	19	21	8	2	1	.308	0
1959	132	441	105	.238	48	55	15	2	3	.302	1
1960	32	42	7	.167	3	4	0	0	1	.238	0
Career	971	2,824	633	.224	284	305	84	27	36	.311	12

Summa, Homer Wayne

Indians: 1922–28
Outfielder
Birthplace: Gentry, Missouri
B: November 3, 1898

D: January 29, 1966
Batted left, threw right
Ht. 5–10½; **Wt.** 170

Though he was never highly publicized, Homer Summa was one of the most consistent hitters in Indians history, compiling a .302 average in 10 major league seasons.

He was purchased by the Tribe from Wichita Falls of the Class A Texas League after winning his second minor league batting championship in 1922 with a .362 average. Summa also led the Class B Virginia League in 1920 and as a result got a brief trial with Pittsburgh.

Summa batted .328 in his first full season (1923) with the Indians. He was their regular right fielder through 1928, though he missed 79 games because of injuries in 1925.

On May 31, 1927, in a game against Detroit, Summa smacked a line drive to first baseman Johnny Neun, who turned it into an unassisted triple play.

Summa's career with the Indians ended on January 5, 1929, when he was sold to the Philadelphia Athletics, for

Homer Summa

whom he batted .278 in 25 games in 1930, his final season in the major leagues.

Summa, Homer

Indians	G	AB	H	BA	RBI	R	2B	3B	HR	SA	SB
1922	12	46	16	.348	6	9	3	3	1	.609	1
1923	137	525	172	.328	69	92	27	6	3	.419	9
1924	111	390	113	.290	38	55	21	6	2	.390	4
1925	75	224	74	.330	25	28	10	1	0	.384	3
1926	154	581	179	.308	76	74	31	6	4	.403	15
1927	145	574	164	.286	74	73	41	7	4	.402	6
1928	134	504	143	.284	57	60	26	3	3	.365	4
Career	840	3,001	905	.302	361	414	166	34	18	.398	44

Sutcliffe, Richard Lee

Indians: 1982–84
Pitcher
Nickname: Rick
Birthplace: Independence, Missouri

B: June 21, 1956
Bats left, throws right
Ht. 6–7; **Wt.** 215

Rick Sutcliffe had two good seasons in Cleveland, leading the American League with a 2.96 earned run average in 1982 and winning the Indian's Man of the Year award in 1983. In 1984 his $850,000 salary made him the highest-paid player in the history of the franchise until then.

But it wasn't enough to keep Sutcliffe happy, and several times he expressed a desire to be traded. He finally was, on June 13, 1984, to the Chicago Cubs with catcher Ron Hassey and pitcher George Frazier.

Though the Indians were not eager to let Sutcliffe go, the deal turned out to be a good one as it brought outfielders Joe Carter and Mel Hall and pitchers Don Schulze and Darryl Banks.

Neither Schulze nor Banks was productive for the Tribe, and Hall didn't contribute much either. But Carter had five-plus good seasons in Cleveland, and when he was traded to San Diego in December 1989, the Indians got catcher Sandy Alomar, Jr., and second baseman Carlos Baerga, as well as outfielder Chris James.

Sutcliffe, who'd been up and down with Los Angeles in 1976 and 1978–81, went 17–10 for the Dodgers in 1979, when he won the National League Rookie of the Year award. But he couldn't get along with manager Tommy Lasorda.

The Indians acquired Sutcliffe on December 9, 1981, with second baseman Jack Perconte for outfielder Jorge Orta and two minor leaguers, pitcher Larry White and catcher Jack Fimple.

Sutcliffe won 31 games while losing 19 in 1982 and 1983, but when he started slowly in 1984, going 4–5 in his first 15 starts, he was sent to the Cubs.

With a new lease on his career in Chicago, Sutcliffe finished the season at 16–1—including the last 14 in a row—and was the unanimous winner of the NL Cy Young Award. It was the first time a pitcher won it after starting the season in the other major league.

He was a member of the AL All-Star team in 1983 and the NL team in 1987 and 1989.

Sutcliffe's unhappiness in Cleveland and his subsequent demand to be traded were based, he said, on the fact that the Indians were a noncontender. He also cited a "lack of com-

Rick Sutcliffe

Swindell, Forest Gregory

Indians: 1986–91

Pitcher

Nickname: Greg

Birthplace: Houston, Texas

B: January 2, 1965

Bats right, throws left

Ht. 6–2; Wt. 225

Greg Swindell's major league debut with the Indians was horrendous—he was mercifully replaced in the fourth inning of a 24–5 loss to Boston on August 21, 1986, his first season in professional baseball.

As a star pitcher at the University of Texas and the youngest member of the 1984 U.S. Olympic team, Swindell was the Indians' first pick (second overall) in the 1986 amateur draft. He started that season at Waterloo of the Class A Midwest League, and was promoted to the Indians after just three games, with a 2–1 record.

Swindell recovered from that inauspicious initiation to the major leagues to go 5–2 in 1986. On May 10, 1987, Swindell struck out 15 batters in a 4–2 victory over Kansas City to become the first Tribe pitcher to fan that many in one game since Sam McDowell did it in 1970.

But shortly thereafter Swindell suffered a torn ligament in his elbow and on June 30 was placed on the disabled list, where he remained the rest of the season. He had elbow problems several times later in his career.

Swindell was named to the American League All-Star team in 1989. His record was 11–2 at the break, but he won only two games and lost four the rest of the season, which was interrupted by another 15-day stay on the disabled list.

The Indians traded Swindell to Cincinnati on November 15, 1991, for pitchers Jack Armstrong, Scott Scudder, and minor leaguer Joe Turek. It was a deal forced by Swindell, who announced his intention of becoming a free agent at the end of the 1992 season.

Swindell went 12–8 with the Reds in 1992, and on December 4, 1992, signed with Houston, where he struggled with

munication" between club officials and players. At the time, the Indians were up for sale following the death of owner F. J. "Steve" O'Neill.

"You can't run a successful business unless you communicate with the employees, no matter if it is a baseball team or a liquor store," Sutcliffe said then. "The Indians have not talked about anything with me. Not money and not the number of years on the contract. They sort of let everything ride, and I think it's time for me to go."

After his big season with the Cubs, Sutcliffe struggled, partly because of injuries in 1985 and 1986. He bounced back to lead the NL with 18 victories (while losing 10 games) in 1987, but he was troubled with more arm and back problems in 1988 and 1990–91.

Sutcliffe returned to the AL in 1992, signing as a free agent with Baltimore, and won 26 games while losing 25 the next two seasons. He also spent more time on the disabled list in 1993.

Sutcliffe became a free agent again and in 1994 went back to the NL with St. Louis, where he was 6–4 before the Players Association went on strike, ending the season.

Sutcliffe, Rick

Indians	W	L	Pct	ERA	G	CG	IP	H	BB	SO	ShO
1982	14	8	.636	2.96	34	6	216	174	98	142	1
1983	17	11	.607	4.29	36	10	243⅓	251	102	160	2
1984	4	5	.444	5.15	15	2	94⅓	111	46	58	0
Career	171	139	.552	4.08	457	72	2,697⅔	2,662	1,081	1,679	18

Greg Swindell

more physical problems. His record was 12–13 in 1993, then 8–5 in 1994 before the season was cut short by the players strike.

Swindell, Greg

Indians	W	L	Pct	ERA	G	CG	IP	H	BB	SO	ShO
1986	5	2	.714	4.23	9	1	61⅔	57	15	46	0
1987	3	8	.273	5.10	16	4	102⅓	112	37	97	1
1988	18	14	.563	3.20	33	12	242	234	45	180	4
1989	13	6	.684	3.37	28	5	184⅓	170	51	129	2
1990	12	9	.571	4.40	34	3	214⅔	245	47	135	0
1991	9	16	.360	3.48	33	7	238	241	31	169	0
Career	102	94	.520	3.80	272	40	1,748⅓	1,839	372	1,188	12

Tabler, Patrick Sean

Indians: 1983–88
First baseman, designated hitter, outfielder, third baseman
Birthplace: Hamilton, Ohio

B: February 2, 1958
Bats right, throws right
Ht. 6–3; Wt. 175

Though he wound up as the Indians' first baseman after being tried at third base, second base, and the outfield, Pat Tabler was best suited as a designated hitter.

Tabler did not hit with much power but was very good in the clutch, especially with the bases loaded. He went 29-for-55 (.527) with the sacks full in his five-plus seasons with the Indians.

Originally the property of the New York Yankees, who drafted Tabler in the first round (16th overall) of the 1976 amateur draft, Tabler was acquired by the Indians on April 1, 1983, in a trade with the Chicago White Sox for shortstop Jerry Dybzynski.

Pat Tabler

Tabler's best season in Cleveland was 1986 when he batted .326, and he was named to the American League All-Star team in 1987 when he hit .307.

The Indians traded him to Kansas City on June 3, 1988, for pitcher Bud Black; the Royals traded him to the New York Mets on August 30, 1990; and Tabler signed as a free agent with Toronto on December 5, 1990. He played two seasons for the Blue Jays and retired.

Tabler, Pat

Indians	G	AB	H	BA	RBI	R	2B	3B	HR	SA	SB
1983	124	430	125	.291	65	56	23	5	6	.409	2
1984	144	473	137	.290	68	66	21	3	10	.410	3
1985	117	404	111	.275	59	47	18	3	5	.371	0
1986	130	473	154	.326	48	61	29	2	6	.433	3
1987	151	553	170	.307	86	66	34	3	11	.439	5
1988	41	143	32	.224	17	16	5	1	1	.294	1
Career	1,202	3,911	1,101	.282	512	454	190	25	47	.379	16

Thornton, Andre

Indians: 1977–79, 1981–87
Designated hitter, first baseman
Birthplace: Tuskegee, Alabama

B: August 13, 1949
Bats right, throws right
Ht. 6–3; Wt. 200

If not for injuries, Andre Thornton undoubtedly would have become the Indians' all-time leader in home runs during his career in Cleveland, which began with one of the team's best ever trades.

Thornton was acquired on December 10, 1976, from Montreal in a deal for pitcher Jackie Brown. The slugging first baseman–designated hitter smashed 214 homers while wearing a Tribe uniform, only 12 fewer than Earl Averill's franchise-record 226.

A quiet, dignified, and distinguished man whose wife and daughter were killed in a tragic automobile accident on October 17, 1977 (Thornton and his son were injured but survived), he was the consummate professional and led the Indians by example during an era when they were not very successful.

In addition to Averill, Hal Trosky, with 216, and Larry Doby, with 215, hit more homers than Thornton, who played less than 10 full seasons for the Indians. In other Tribe all-time batting lists, Thornton is eighth with 749 runs batted in, ninth with 419 extra-base hits, 10th with 1,954 total bases, and 10th with a .453 slugging percentage.

Averill, who played 11 seasons for the Indians, leads in RBIs with 1,084, extra-base hits with 724, and total bases with 3,200, and Hal Trosky, who played nine seasons in Cleveland, is number one with a .551 slugging percentage.

Thornton walked 109 times in 1982 when he became only the second Indian with 100 bases on balls and 100 RBIs in the same season. (Only Mike Hargrove, with 111, walked more times in one season than Thornton.) He was elected the Indians' Man of the Year in 1978 and 1982, when he shared the award with Toby Harrah, and was named to the American League All-Star team in 1982 and 1984.

Unfortunately, seldom during Thornton's career with the Indians did he have the luxury of being surrounded by many other good hitters, a team weakness that pitchers usually tried to exploit, as Jim Palmer admitted before both players retired.

"Whenever I face the Indians, I only worry about one

Andre Thornton

Tiant, Luis Clemente

Indians: 1964–69
Pitcher
Nickname: Looie
Birthplace: Marianao, Cuba

B: November 23, 1940
Bats right, throws right
Ht. 6–0; **Wt.** 180

When Luis Tiant was promoted in 1964 by the Indians from their Portland farm club in the Class AAA Pacific Coast League, outfielder Al Smith said, "If the kid is half as good as his old man was, we've got a helluva pitcher."

Smith knew Tiant's father, Luis, Sr., because he had played against him in the Negro League in 1946 and 1947.

Suffice to say, Luis, Jr., was more than "half as good" as his father, and the Indians did indeed have a "helluva pitcher" for six seasons, until they traded him to Minnesota on December 11, 1969.

Tiant was packaged with pitcher Stan Williams and sent to the Twins for pitchers Dean Chance and Bob Miller, third baseman Graig Nettles, and outfielder Ted Uhlaender.

Tiant made his major league debut on July 19, 1964, in the second game of a doubleheader in New York, and fired a four-hit, 3–0 victory, striking out 11.

It was the first of 229 major league victories (with 172 losses), of which 75 were registered for the Indians (with 64 losses) for Tiant, who was discovered in Cuba by Bobby Avila in 1959.

Avila, the Tribe's second baseman from 1949 to 1958 and American League batting champion in 1954, owned the Mexico City Tigres and signed Tiant to pitch for his team. The Indians purchased Tiant after the 1961 season.

thing," said Palmer. "I don't want to face Andre Thornton in the late innings. If I do, I'll walk him. He can change a 1–0 win into a 2–1 loss with one swing of his bat."

Other problems that limited Thornton's contributions to the Indians included two knee operations (one of which caused him to miss the entire 1980 season) and a dislocated shoulder that also required surgery. He also was out for much of 1981, as well as parts of 1985 and 1986.

And though he had another year on his contract at a guaranteed salary of $1.1 million, Thornton wasn't invited back by the Indians in 1988.

Despite his disappointment, Thornton accepted the decision with grace, which always was his style.

He said then, "We can part company feeling very good about the fact that I certainly tried to uphold my end of the bargain. I gave the Indians the best I could for as long as I could."

Thornton, Andre

Indians	G	AB	H	BA	RBI	R	2B	3B	HR	SA	SB
1977	131	433	114	.263	70	77	20	5	28	.527	3
1978	145	508	133	.262	105	97	22	4	33	.516	4
1979	143	515	120	.233	93	89	31	1	26	.449	5
1981	69	226	54	.239	30	22	12	0	6	.372	3
1982	161	589	161	.273	116	90	26	1	32	.484	6
1983	141	508	143	.281	77	78	27	1	17	.439	4
1984	155	587	159	.271	99	91	26	0	33	.484	6
1985	124	461	109	.236	88	49	13	0	22	.408	3
1986	120	401	92	.229	66	49	14	0	17	.392	4
1987	36	85	10	.118	5	8	2	0	0	.141	1
Career	1,565	5,291	1,342	.254	895	792	244	22	253	.452	48

Luis Tiant

So, while Tiant was called a rookie when he reported to the Tribe in 1964, he was far from inexperienced.

And he also was aware of one of baseball's most-used axioms.

"If you have luck, you win. If you do not have luck, you lose," he said.

Tiant might have had luck, but he also pitched very well. He went 10–4 with a 2.83 earned run average as a rookie, and he led the AL with a 1.60 ERA in 1968 when he won 21 games, lost nine, pitched nine shutouts, and allowed an average of only 5.3 hits per nine-inning game.

That was the year the Indians asked Tiant not to pitch winter ball. He complied with their request, but in 1969 his won-lost record was virtually reversed, 9–20, after which he was traded to Minnesota.

The Twins released Tiant on March 31, 1971; the Atlanta Braves signed him as a free agent and then released him May 15. Two days later Boston signed him, and, after an injury-plagued 1971 season, Tiant's career took a big swing upward again.

Before he was finished in 1982 with California, Tiant logged three more 20-victory seasons while pitching for the Red Sox, Yankees, and Pittsburgh, in addition to the Angels.

He was an AL All-Star with the Indians in 1968 and with Boston in 1974 and 1976, and three times came close to pitching no-hitters: on June 16, 1965, Woodie Held singled in the seventh inning for Washington's only hit as the Indians beat the Senators, 5–0, at the Stadium; on September 25, 1968, Mickey Mantle singled in the first inning for the Yankees' only hit in a 3–0 Tribe victory in New York; and on July 8, 1979, Rickey Henderson singled in the third inning for the Athletics' only hit in Tiant's 2–0 victory for the Yankees in Oakland.

Tiant's father was a left-hander who pitched in the Negro League from 1930 to 1947 for the Cuban Stars and New York Cubans.

Hal Trosky

Tiant, Luis

Indians	W	L	Pct	ERA	G	CG	IP	H	BB	SO	ShO
1964	10	4	.714	2.83	19	9	127	94	47	105	3
1965	11	11	.500	3.53	41	10	196⅓	166	66	152	2
1966	12	11	.522	2.79	46	7	155	121	50	145	5
1967	12	9	.571	2.74	33	9	213⅔	177	67	219	1
1968	21	9	.700	1.60	34	19	258⅓	152	73	264	9
1969	9	20	.310	3.71	38	9	249⅔	229	129	156	1
Career	229	172	.571	3.30	573	187	3,486⅓	3,075	1,104	2,416	49

Trosky (Troyavesky), Harold Arthur, Sr.

Indians: 1933–41
First baseman
Birthplace: Norway, Iowa
B: November 11, 1912

D: June 18, 1979
Batted left, threw right
Ht. 6–2; **Wt.** 207

If he had not been afflicted with migraine headaches most of his career, Hal Trosky might have established himself as one of baseball's greatest hitters and first basemen.

As it was, Trosky, who missed all of the 1942, 1943, and 1945 seasons because of the illness, is the Indians' all-time slugging leader with a .551 percentage, and also is included among the top 10 offensive players in eight other categories:

He is second with 216 home runs (10 behind Earl Averill), third with 911 runs batted in, third with 556 extra-base hits, fifth with 2,406 total bases, eighth with 758 runs, eighth with 287 doubles, ninth with a .313 batting average, and ninth with 1,365 hits.

Trosky's best year was 1936 when he led the American League with 162 RBIs, fashioned a 28-game hitting streak, and batted .343, one of four seasons he hit .300 or better. He hit 30 or more doubles eight times, 25 or more homers six years, and drove in 100 or more runs six consecutive seasons.

Trosky also smashed three homers in one game twice—in the nightcap of a doubleheader on May 30, 1934 (consecutively), against Chicago at League Park as the Indians won, 5–4, and in the opener of a doubleheader on July 5, 1937, against the Browns in St. Louis in a 14–4 victory.

In 1940, when the "Crybaby" Indians demanded that owner Alva Bradley fire manager Oscar Vitt, Trosky, then one of the senior players on the team, was believed to be one of the ring-leaders in the rebellion. It tarnished Trosky's otherwise honorable reputation.

"For what I've done, I offer no apologies . . . but I've been blasted for something I haven't done," is the way Trosky denied being the leader of the effort to get Vitt replaced.

After the 1941 season, when Trosky played only 89 games because of migraine headaches, he announced his retirement because of the illness.

Two years later, after being classified 4-F in the Selective Service draft during World War II, and making it known he would consider a comeback, Trosky was sold to the White Sox on November 6, 1943.

He hit .241 with 10 homers and 70 RBIs for Chicago in 1944, laid off for another season, and returned to the White Sox in 1946, batting .254 in 88 games, then retired for good.

Trosky scouted briefly for the White Sox, the team for which his son, Hal, Jr., made two appearances as a pitcher in 1958.

Trosky, Hal

Indians	G	AB	H	BA	RBI	R	2B	3B	HR	SA	SB
1933	11	44	13	.295	8	6	1	2	1	.477	0
1934	154	625	206	.330	142	117	45	9	35	.598	2
1935	154	632	171	.271	113	84	33	7	26	.468	1
1936	151	629	216	.343	162	124	45	9	42	.644	6
1937	153	601	179	.298	128	104	36	9	32	.547	3
1938	150	554	185	.334	110	106	40	9	19	.542	5
1939	122	448	150	.335	104	89	31	4	25	.589	2
1940	140	522	154	.295	93	85	39	4	25	.529	1
1941	89	310	91	.294	51	43	17	0	11	.455	1
Career	1,347	5,161	1,561	.302	1,012	835	331	58	228	.522	28

Turner, Terrence Lamont

Indians: 1904–18
Shortstop, third baseman,
   second baseman, outfielder
Nicknames: Cotton, Terry
Birthplace: Sandy Lake, Pennsylvania

B: February 28, 1881
D: July 18, 1960
Batted right, threw right
Ht. 5–8; Wt. 149

The all-time leader in games played for the Cleveland baseball franchise is an otherwise seldom recognized shortstop, Terry Turner. He broke in with the team in 1904 when it was known as the Naps and finished in 1918 after the nickname had been changed to Indians.

Turner, who appeared in two games for Pittsburgh in 1901, three years before going to the Naps, played 1,619 games in Cleveland, five more than runner-up Napoleon Lajoie.

Turner also batted the third-most times, 5,787 (to Lajoie's 6,034 and Earl Averill's 5,909), is seventh in triples with 77, and made 1,472 hits, eighth most in franchise history.

Though not noted for his hitting, Turner batted a career-high .308 in 1912. He was exclusively a shortstop through 1907, then played third base, shortstop, second base, and the outfield the next 11 seasons in Cleveland.

Turner also was well known for his head-first slides, which he believed he introduced to the major leagues.

"I discovered that sliding feet first wasn't for me," he once observed. "I caught my spikes too often and hurt my ankles. I suppose head-first slides were dangerous, too, for I still have scars on my hands where I was stepped on. But for me, head-first was better."

In January 1919, after Ray Chapman, Larry Gardner, and Bill Wambsganss were established as the regulars at third, shortstop, and second, the Indians sold Turner to the Philadelphia Athletics.

Turner, Terry

Indians	G	AB	H	BA	RBI	R	2B	3B	HR	SA	SB
1904	111	404	95	.235	45	41	9	6	1	.295	5
1905	155	586	155	.265	72	49	16	14	4	.360	17
1906	147	584	170	.291	62	85	27	7	2	.372	27
1907	140	524	127	.242	46	57	20	7	0	.307	27
1908	60	201	48	.239	19	21	11	1	0	.303	18
1909	53	208	52	.250	16	25	7	4	0	.322	14
1910	150	574	132	.230	33	71	14	6	0	.275	31
1911	117	417	105	.252	28	59	16	9	0	.333	29
1912	103	370	114	.308	33	54	14	4	0	.368	19
1913	120	388	96	.247	44	60	13	4	0	.302	13
1914	121	428	105	.245	33	43	14	9	1	.327	17
1915	75	262	66	.252	14	35	14	1	0	.313	12
1916	124	428	112	.262	38	52	15	3	0	.311	15
1917	69	180	37	.206	15	16	7	0	0	.244	4
1918	74	233	58	.249	23	24	7	2	0	.296	6
Career	1,659	5,921	1,499	.253	528	699	207	77	8	.318	256

Uhle, George Ernest

Indians: 1919–28, 1936
Pitcher
Nickname: The Bull
Birthplace: Cleveland, Ohio

B: September 18, 1898
D: February 26, 1985
Batted right, threw right
Ht. 6–0; Wt. 190

They called George Uhle the "smartest pitcher in baseball" during his 17-year major league career that began in 1919, directly off the Cleveland sandlots.

Uhle, who'd pitched the Cleveland Standard Parts team to the world amateur baseball championship in 1918, also earned several other distinctions while compiling a 200–166 career record (147–119 for the Indians).

George Uhle

As one of the first pitchers in baseball to throw the slider, Uhle is acknowledged as having named the pitch by describing its motion.

Uhle was the American League's winningest pitcher twice, with 26 victories in 1923 and 27 in 1926, when his winning percentage of .711 was the best. Three times he was the leader in games started, twice in complete games, and twice in innings pitched—all of which led to his being nicknamed The Bull.

On May 13, 1928, in a game at League Park, Uhle shut out the Philadelphia Athletics on one hit, a double by Mickey Cochrane in the second inning.

And a year later, on May 24, 1929, pitching for Detroit in a game in Chicago, Uhle pitched the first 20 shutout innings of the Tigers' 21-inning 6–5 victory.

The only Cleveland pitcher ever to win more games in a single season than Uhle did in 1926 was Jim Bagby, Sr., whose record was 31–12 in 1920, though Addie Joss (in 1907) and Bob Feller (in 1940) also were 27-game winners.

Uhle also was the all-time best hitting pitcher (500 or more at bats) with a lifetime average of .289 (393-for-1,360) in 722 games. In 1923, when he hit .361 in 144 plate appearances, he set the record for most hits, 52, by a pitcher in one season, though it was tied by Wes Ferrell in 1935.

And to further establish his credentials as an excellent hitter, Uhle was the only player ever to pinch-hit for Hall of Fame center fielder Tris Speaker, whose lifetime average was .345, seventh best of all time.

Uhle also was called by Babe Ruth the best pitcher he ever faced, with good reason.

As Uhle recalled before his death in 1985, "Early in the Babe's career he hit a pop-fly home run off me in the [New York] Polo Grounds, but he never got another off me until after I was traded to Detroit.

"The way I pitched to Ruth, I'd give him a lot of slow breaking stuff, then try to blow the fastball by him. None of the great hitters like slow stuff because it throws their timing off. They all want to hit fastballs."

On the other hand, Uhle freely admitted having trouble pitching to two relatively unknown players, Fatty Fothergill of the Tigers, and Bib Falk of the Chicago White Sox. "They both hit me like they owned me," he said.

The Yankees and White Sox also were interested in Uhle when he signed with the Indians, but he wanted to pitch for the team he watched growing up.

Though Uhle never spent a day in the minor leagues at the start of his career, he pitched for Toledo of the Class AA American Association in 1934.

The Indians traded Uhle on December 11, 1928, to the Tigers for pitcher Ken Holloway and shortstop Jackie Tavener.

After four seasons in Detroit, Uhle was sold on April 24, 1933 to the New York Giants, who released him less than three months later, on July 8, after he went 1–1 for them in six games. Sixteen days later, on July 24, Uhle was signed by the New York Yankees, for whom he won six and lost one in 12 appearances the rest of the 1933 season. Uhle was 2–4 for the Yankees in 1934, but he finished the season pitching for Toledo, and he was out of baseball in 1935.

Uhle rejoined the Indians in 1936, but by then his fastball and slider were only memories. He pitched in seven games without a decision, was released, and returned as a coach in

1937. Uhle also coached in the minor leagues in 1938 and 1939, and again in the major leagues for the Chicago Cubs in 1940 and Washington Senators in 1944. He also served as a scout for the Brooklyn Dodgers in 1941 and 1942.

Uhle, George

Indians	W	L	Pct	ERA	G	CG	IP	H	BB	SO	ShO
1919	10	5	.667	2.91	26	7	127	129	43	50	1
1920	4	5	.444	5.21	27	2	84⅔	98	29	27	0
1921	16	13	.552	4.01	41	13	238	288	63	63	2
1922	22	16	.579	4.07	50	23	287⅓	328	89	82	5
1923	26	16	.619	3.77	54	29	357⅔	378	102	109	1
1924	9	15	.375	4.77	28	15	196⅓	238	75	57	0
1925	13	11	.542	4.10	29	17	210⅔	218	78	68	1
1926	27	11	.711	2.83	39	32	318⅓	300	118	159	3
1927	8	9	.471	4.34	25	10	153⅓	187	59	69	1
1928	12	17	.414	4.07	31	18	214⅓	252	48	74	2
1936	0	1	.000	8.53	7	0	12⅔	26	5	5	0
Career	200	166	.546	3.99	513	232	3,119⅔	3,417	966	1,135	21

Vernon, James Barton

Indians: 1949–50, 1958
First baseman
Nickname: Mickey
Birthplace: Marcus Hook, Pennsylvania

B: April 22, 1918
Bats left, throws left
Ht. 6–2; **Wt.** 170

Mickey Vernon served two brief tours of duty with the Indians, and both times he was traded away rank among their worst-ever deals.

Vernon was a major leaguer for four decades and appeared in 2,237 games at first base, second by 175 to baseball's all-time leader at that position, Eddie Murray, a first baseman in 2,412 games in a career that began in 1977 and continued through 1995.

A seven-time member of the American League All-Star team (in 1946, 1948, 1953, 1954, 1955, 1956, and 1958), Vernon twice won the AL batting championship while playing for Washington, in 1946 with a .353 average and in 1953

Mickey Vernon

when he hit .337—and went 2-for-4 on the final day of the season to clinch the title by a margin of .001 over the Tribe's Al Rosen.

In that last game in 1953 against the Philadelphia Athletics, Vernon lined out in his final at bat, leaving him with a .337 average. By then the Senators had received word that Rosen had gone 3-for-5 against Detroit and finished with a .336 mark.

Vernon could have left the game at that point, but didn't—though he didn't go to the plate again. In Washington's last at bat, two of his teammates were retired in baserunning blunders, which some thought were intentional to protect Vernon's average.

The Indians got Vernon on December 14, 1948, with pitcher Early Wynn for pitchers Joe Haynes and Ed Klieman and first baseman Eddie Robinson. It was a good deal for the Tribe that was made because Senators owner Clark Griffith was eager to acquire Haynes, his son-in-law.

Vernon hit .291 in 153 games in 1949, but the following season the Indians wanted to make room for Luke Easter's arrival through the minor league system. First, Easter was tried in the outfield but was found wanting. So, the Tribe traded Vernon back to Washington for relief pitcher Dick Weik in what proved to be a disastrous deal.

The Senators subsequently traded Vernon to the Boston Red Sox on November 8, 1955. The Indians reacquired Vernon in a cash purchase on January 29, 1958, and he batted .293 in 119 games that season.

Then they let him go again on April 11, 1959, in a trade with the Milwaukee Braves for minor league pitcher Humberto Robinson, in another deal that turned out badly.

Vernon went to Pittsburgh as a player-coach in 1960, appearing in nine games, replaced Cookie Lavagetto in 1961 as manager of the Senators, a job he held until May 22, 1963, coached for the Pirates in 1964 and St. Louis Cardinals in 1965, and also managed and coached in the minor leagues.

| Vernon, Mickey | | | | | | | | | | | |
Indians	G	AB	H	BA	RBI	R	2B	3B	HR	SA	SB
1949	153	584	170	.291	83	72	27	4	18	.443	9
1950	28	90	17	.189	10	8	0	0	0	.189	2
1958	119	355	104	.293	55	49	22	3	8	.439	0
Career	2,409	8,731	2,495	.286	1,311	1,196	490	120	172	.428	137

Vosmik, Joseph Franklin

Indians: 1930–36
Outfielder
Birthplace: Cleveland
B: April 4, 1910

D: January 27, 1962
Batted right, threw right
Ht. 6–0; **Wt.** 185

It was Joe Vosmik's blond hair and classic good looks that got him a contract with the Indians in 1929, and it was a rash decision—compounded by darkness-shortened game—that prevented him from winning the American League batting championship in 1935.

A native Clevelander, Vosmik played in an all-star amateur game at League Park that was witnessed by Indians general manager Billy Evans and his wife.

Evans, according to reports, was not greatly impressed by

Joe Vosmik

any of the sandlot players in the game, though one of them caught the eye of Mrs. Evans.

"Which of the players do you like?" Evans reportedly asked his wife. She answered, "That good-looking blond Viking over there," and pointed to Vosmik.

Evans, as a public relations gesture as much as anything, took his wife's advice and signed Vosmik to a contract with Frederick (Maryland) of the Class D Blue Ridge League.

Vosmik proceeded to hit .381 in 112 games for Frederick, had a .397 average the next season at Terre Haute of the Class B Three-I League, and was promoted to the Indians in September 1930—undoubtedly, thanks to Mrs. Evans.

As it turned out, the Indians also had to be grateful that she liked the looks of the "blond Viking," as Vosmik blossomed into one of the AL's best hitters. He batted .320 as a rookie in 1931 and was part of what many have considered to be the best outfield in the history of the franchise.

Vosmik played left field with Earl Averill in center and Dick Porter in right.

As for the batting championship that Vosmik narrowly missed winning, he went into the final day of the 1935 season, a doubleheader against the St. Louis Browns, with a three-percentage-point lead—.348 to .345—over his nearest competitor, Buddy Myer.

Because the Indians were safely lodged in third place with neither a chance to move up to second nor any danger of falling to fourth, Vosmik asked manager Steve O'Neill if he could sit out the doubleheader to protect his lead over Myer.

O'Neill consented, though Vosmik pinch-hit in the ninth inning of the opener and made an out.

Between games, however, the Indians received word that Myer, playing for the Washington Senators in their final game against the Philadelphia Athletics, went 4-for-5. It boosted his average to .349, one point ahead of Vosmik.

So, when the second game started, Vosmik went back to left field knowing he needed to go at least 2-for-4 to overtake Myer.

Vosmik singled once and was retired twice in his first three trips to the plate, climbing to less than one point behind Myer.

But he never got any closer.

Before Vosmik could bat again the game was called after six innings because of darkness. In those days baseball under lights was only a far-fetched dream.

Thus, Myer finished with a .349026 average (215-for-616), while Vosmik's final mark was .348387 (216-for-620), meaning the Tribe outfielder lost the batting title by .000639. One more hit would have given Vosmik a .350 average.

As it was, Vosmik led the AL in hits, doubles (47), and triples (20) in 1935, and he was picked on the AL All-Star team.

A longtime favorite of the Cleveland fans, Vosmik batted .300 or better in four of his five full seasons with the Indians, but after his average fell to .287 in 1936, he was traded to the Browns.

The deal, made on January 17, 1937, sent Vosmik, shortstop Bill Knickerbocker, and pitcher Oral Hildebrand to St. Louis for shortstop Lyn Lary, pitcher Ivy Andrews, and outfielder Moose Solters.

Vosmik came back strong with a .325 average for the Browns in 1937, then was traded to the Boston Red Sox, for whom he hit .324 and again led the AL in hits with 201 in 1938. The Red Sox sold him to Brooklyn on February 12, 1940, and he played for the Dodgers in 1940 and 1941. He was a part-time outfielder for the Washington Senators in 1944, ending his major league career with a .307 lifetime average.

Vosmik managed Indians' teams in the minor leagues from 1947 to 1951 and scouted for them in 1951 to 1952.

Vosmik, Joe

Indians	G	AB	H	BA	RBI	R	2B	3B	HR	SA	SB
1930	9	26	6	.231	4	1	2	0	0	.308	0
1931	149	591	189	.320	117	80	36	14	7	.464	7
1932	153	621	194	.312	97	106	39	12	10	.462	2
1933	119	438	115	.263	56	53	20	10	4	.381	0
1934	104	405	138	.341	78	71	33	2	6	.477	1
1935	152	620	216	.348	110	93	47	20	10	.537	2
1936	138	506	145	.287	94	76	29	7	7	.413	5
Career	1,414	5,472	1,682	.307	874	818	335	92	65	.438	23

Wagner, Leon Lamar

Indians: 1964–68
Outfielder
Nickname: Daddy Wags
Birthplace: Chattanooga, Tennessee

B: May 13, 1934
Bats left, throws right
Ht. 6–1; **Wt.** 195

Leon Wagner was the Indians' "Good Humor Man" and one of their best hitters the first three seasons he played in Cleveland, but his disposition changed drastically in 1967, and he demanded to be traded—and was—a year later.

The reason for Wagner's unhappiness was that manager Joe Adcock platooned him in left field with Rocky Colavito (who also was displeased by the strategy).

Wagner was outspoken in his criticism of the manager, and it was reflected in his batting average. It fell to .242 in 1967 after three productive seasons—31 homers and 100 RBIs in 1964, .294 with 28 homers in 1965, and .279 with 23 homers in 1966.

Ironically, the Indians acquired Wagner in a trade that involved Adcock. Wagner came to Cleveland from the Los Angeles Angels in exchange for Adcock and pitcher Barry Latman on December 2, 1963. Adcock became manager of the Indians in 1967, but he was fired before that season ended.

Wagner broke in with San Francisco in 1958, played briefly for the St. Louis Cardinals in 1960, and was the Angels' biggest gun from 1961 to '63, hitting 91 homers, including 37—third most in the American League—in 1962. He was named to the AL All-Star team that season and again in 1963.

The Indians traded Wagner to the Chicago White Sox for outfielder Russ Snyder on June 13, 1968. Six months later he was sold to Cincinnati, but the deal subsequently was nullified, and Wagner returned to the White Sox in 1969.

The White Sox released Wagner on April 5, 1969, after which he wound up with Phoenix, an affiliate of the San Francisco Giants in the Class AAA Pacific Coast League. He hit .295 in 78 games, and the Giants called him up to San Francisco on September 1. Wagner batted .333 (4-for-12) in 11 games with the Giants and was released at the end of the season.

After retiring from baseball Wagner appeared in several movies, including *The Bingo Long Traveling All-Stars & Motor Kings,* and also owned a clothing store in Los Angeles whose advertising logo was "Buy Your Rags at Daddy Wags."

Wagner, Leon

Indians	G	AB	H	BA	RBI	R	2B	3B	HR	SA	SB
1964	163	641	162	.253	100	94	19	2	31	.434	14
1965	144	517	152	.294	79	91	18	1	28	.495	12
1966	150	549	153	.279	66	70	20	0	23	.441	5
1967	135	433	105	.242	54	56	15	1	15	.386	3
1968	38	49	9	.184	6	5	4	0	0	.265	0
Career	1,352	4,426	1,202	.272	669	636	150	15	211	.455	54

Leon Wagner

Waits, Michael Richard

Indians: 1975–83
Pitcher
Nickname: Rick
Birthplace: Atlanta, Georgia

B: May 15, 1952
Bats left, throws left
Ht. 6-3; **Wt.** 194

Rick Waits figured in one of the Indians' biggest trades, came to be hated (if only briefly) by the New York Yankees, and was the team's biggest winner in 1979.

With 74 victories for the Indians, Waits became the third-winningest left-hander in franchise history (behind Sam McDowell's 122 and Joe Shaute's 78).

But Waits' career in Cleveland didn't last long after he suffered a knee injury in 1981 that affected him for several seasons thereafter, and he was traded away in a deal that quickly turned sour.

Waits began his professional career in the Texas farm system in 1970. He appeared in one game for the Rangers, earning a one-inning save in 1973, but otherwise never pitched in the major leagues until he was acquired by the Tribe on June 13, 1975.

In addition to Waits, the Indians also received pitchers Jim Bibby and Jackie Brown and $100,000, for pitcher Gaylord Perry.

After three mediocre seasons, Waits won in double figures for the first time in 1978, going 13–15, with his final victory being a 9–2 decision over New York. The loss dropped the Yankees into a first-place tie with Boston, forcing a one-game playoff that New York won, 5–4, for the American League East championship.

A curveball specialist, Waits enjoyed his best season in 1979, winning nine of his first 13 decisions, beginning with a one-hit, 3–0 victory over the Red Sox in the Tribe's home opener on April 7. Jerry Remy singled in the sixth inning to spoil Waits' bid for a no-hitter. He also hurled a pair of two-hitters. beating Toronto, 1–0, on May 14, and Minnesota, 2–0, on July 25, and won seven of his last 11 decisions to finish with a career-best and team-leading 16–13 record.

Waits' record declined to 13–14 in 1980 and to 8–10 in the strike-interrupted season of 1981, when he suffered tendinitis in his knee that hampered him for several years.

After winning only two games while losing 13 in 1982 and going 0–1 in his first eight games in 1983, Waits was traded on June 6, with outfielder Rick Manning, to the Milwaukee Brewers for outfielder Gorman Thomas and pitchers Jamie Easterly and Ernie Camacho.

Waits was never able to recapture his winning form and was finished in the major leagues after going 0–3 in 1983, 2–4 in 1984, and 3–2 in 1985 for the Brewers.

Waits, Rick

Indians	W	L	Pct	ERA	G	CG	IP	H	BB	SO	ShO
1975	6	2	.750	2.94	16	3	70⅓	57	25	34	0
1976	7	9	.438	4.00	26	4	123⅔	143	54	65	2
1977	9	7	.563	3.99	37	1	135⅓	132	64	62	0
1978	13	15	.464	3.20	34	15	230⅓	206	86	97	2
1979	16	13	.552	4.44	34	8	231	230	91	91	3
1980	13	14	.481	4.45	33	9	224⅓	231	82	109	2
1981	8	10	.444	4.92	22	5	126⅓	173	44	51	1
1982	2	13	.133	5.40	25	2	115	128	57	44	0
1983	0	1	.000	4.58	8	0	19⅔	23	9	13	0
Career	79	92	.462	4.25	317	47	1,427	1,514	568	659	10

Wambsganss (Wamby), William Adolph

Indians: 1914–23
Second baseman, shortstop, third baseman
Birthplace: Cleveland

B: March 19, 1894
D: December 8, 1985
Batted right, threw right
Ht. 5-11; **Wt.** 175

Bill Wambsganss, whose name was shortened to "Wamby" by a printer setting type for the box score of an Indians game, always said he "just happened to be in the right place at the right time."

And because he was, Wambsganss gained lasting fame for making the only unassisted triple play in World Series history.

The right place at the right time for Wambsganss was three strides to the right of second base at League Park on October 10, 1920, when the Indians beat Brooklyn, 8–1, in the fifth game.

Until then the Series was tied, 2–2, and in the top of the fifth inning the Dodgers were threatening to cut the Indians' 7–0 lead. Pete Kilduff led off with a single and stopped at second as Otto Miller also hit safely. It brought relief pitcher Clarence Mitchell to the plate against Jim Bagby, Sr.

What happened next is what provided a lasting niche in baseball's all-time record book for Wambsganss, who was the Indians' second baseman most of the time from 1914 to 1923. He played for the Boston Red Sox in 1924 and 1925 and Philadelphia Athletics in 1926, finishing with a lifetime .259 average.

Mitchell hit a line drive. Wambsganss leaped and caught it. In three strides he stepped on second base to double Kilduff, who had broken for third at the crack of the bat. Then

Rick Waits

Bill Wambsganss

Wambsganss, Bill											
Indians	G	AB	H	BA	RBI	R	2B	3B	HR	SA	SB
1914	43	143	31	.217	12	12	6	2	0	.287	2
1915	121	375	73	.195	21	30	4	4	0	.227	8
1916	136	475	117	.246	45	57	14	4	0	.293	13
1917	141	499	127	.255	43	52	17	6	0	.313	16
1918	87	315	93	.295	40	34	15	2	0	.356	16
1919	139	526	146	.278	60	60	17	6	2	.344	18
1920	153	565	138	.244	55	83	16	11	1	.317	9
1921	107	410	117	.285	47	80	28	5	2	.393	13
1922	142	538	141	.262	47	89	22	6	0	.325	17
1923	101	345	100	.290	59	59	20	4	1	.380	10
Career	1,491	5,237	1,359	.259	520	710	215	59	7	.327	140

Weatherly, Cyril Roy

Indians: 1936–42
Center fielder
Nicknames: Stormy, Little Thunder
Birthplace: Warren, Texas

B: February 25, 1915
D: January 19, 1991
Batted left, threw right
Ht. 5–6½; **Wt.** 170

Roy Weatherly was called Stormy and Little Thunder for a couple of reasons. First, the nicknames were a play on his surname and stature.

But they also aptly described his temperament.

Weatherly was indeed stormy, and probably was the first—and perhaps is still the only—major league ballplayer to be granted a bonus for not being ejected from a game. Or at least *another* game.

That was in 1940 after Weatherly had been banished by umpire Bill McGowan and allegedly "blacklisted" by other arbiters in the American League.

Indians owner Alva Bradley promised Weatherly $500 at the end of the season if he stayed out of further trouble.

Wambsganss turned toward first base. To his surprise, there was Miller a few feet away, trying to stop.

As Wambsganss described it, "I intended to throw the ball to first to nail Miller, but when I saw him so near, I instinctively tagged him [for the third out]. It was no big thing."

Not at the time, anyway.

"After the game I had one newspaper interview. A guy from Brooklyn talked to me. He asked how it felt to make an unassisted triple play. I said it was the chance of a lifetime, which it was."

But later, and until his death in 1985, as Wambsganss said, "You'd have thought I was born the day before [the triple play] and died the day after. The only credit I deserve is that I just happened to be in the right place at the right time."

The unassisted triple play wasn't even the highlight of his career, the Cleveland portion of which ended on January 7, 1924, when he was traded with catcher Steve O'Neill, pitcher Danny Boone, and outfielder Joe Connolly to the Red Sox for first baseman George Burns, catcher Roxy Walters, and infielder Chick Fewster.

"The biggest thing for me was winning the world's championship," Wambsganss said of the Indians' seven-game victory over Brooklyn in what was then a best-of-nine World Series.

Roy Weatherly

There was little doubt where Weatherly's temper came from, according to the newspaper account of a game played at League Park in 1936.

When Weatherly was called out on a close play at first base, his white-haired father hopped out of a field-level box to register his protest with the startled umpire. No punches were thrown, as the elder Weatherly was restrained by several players before he could reach the umpire.

But it wasn't just his often-angry disposition that made Weatherly famous. He also was a very good center fielder, and a pretty good hitter, especially in 1940, his first season as a regular, when he batted .303—and wasn't ejected from a game.

It also was in 1940, the year of the infamous "Crybaby Indians," that Weatherly incurred the wrath of many of his teammates. They were angered because of Weatherly's reluctance to sign a petition demanding that manager Oscar Vitt be fired.

When Weatherly said he wanted time to consider the merits of the rebellion, he was told by one of the players, "You're either with us or against us."

Weatherly replied, "If you feel that way about it, the hell with it," and didn't participate in the revolt that, in the end, failed to get Vitt replaced. According to most of the participants, it also cost the Indians the pennant.

They finished one game behind Detroit when they were unable to sweep a final series from the Tigers, winning only two of the last three games.

After hitting .300 or better in three of his seven seasons in Cleveland, Weatherly was traded with infielder Oscar Grimes on December 17, 1942. They went to the New York Yankees for catcher Buddy Rosar and outfielder Roy Cullenbine.

Weatherly batted .264 in 77 games for the Yankees in 1943, then entered the army for three years. Upon his return from World War II in 1946, Weatherly played only two games for New York and broke his leg, effectively ending his major league career.

But, true to his nature, Weatherly wouldn't quit. He went back to the minors, earning another chance with the New York Giants, for whom he hit .261 in 52 games in 1950, and ended his major league career with a lifetime .286 average.

Weatherly, Roy

Indians	G	AB	H	BA	RBI	R	2B	3B	HR	SA	SB
1936	84	349	117	.335	53	64	28	6	8	.519	3
1937	53	134	27	.201	13	19	4	0	5	.343	1
1938	83	210	55	.262	18	32	14	3	2	.386	8
1939	95	323	100	.310	32	43	16	6	1	.406	7
1940	135	578	175	.303	59	90	35	11	12	.464	9
1941	102	363	105	.289	37	59	21	5	3	.399	2
1942	128	473	122	.258	39	61	23	7	5	.368	8
Career	811	2,781	794	.286	290	415	152	44	43	.418	42

Wertz, Victor Woodrow

Indians: 1954–58
First baseman, outfielder
Birthplace: York, Pennsylvania
B: February 9, 1925

D: July 7, 1983
Batted left, threw right
Ht. 6–0; **Wt.** 186

As long as baseball is played and highlight films are shown, Vic Wertz will be remembered as the victim of Willie Mays'

Vic Wertz

spectacular catch in the first game of the 1954 World Series, when the Indians were swept by the New York Giants.

Longtime Cleveland fans also will never forget the message scrawled in lipstick on the top of Wertz's bald head after the Indians clinched the American League pennant that year on September 18.

It said, "We're In," and a photograph of it was published in newspapers across the country.

There was much more, however, to recall about Wertz, a hard-hitting outfielder who was converted to first base upon his acquisition by the Tribe on June 1, 1954.

Without Wertz's potent bat and surprisingly good defensive play at an unfamiliar position, the Indians might not have won the pennant that season—at least not as easily, with an AL-record 111 victories, as they did.

Wertz was acquired from Baltimore in a deal for pitcher Bob Chakales; he hit .275 with 14 homers and 48 RBIs in 94 games for the Indians.

Prior to joining the Indians, Wertz had played only in the outfield for Detroit, from 1947 until mid-1952, and then for the St. Louis Browns until they moved to Baltimore in 1954 and he was traded to Cleveland.

But with Bill Glynn struggling as the Tribe's first baseman, manager Al Lopez asked Wertz to switch to that position. It proved to be a masterstroke.

Near-disaster struck the following season, however, as Wertz contracted polio on August 28 and was hospitalized for 20 days.

Without Wertz the Indians floundered and finished in second place, three games behind the pennant-winning New York Yankees.

Though it was initially feared that Wertz would not play again, he made a remarkable comeback in 1956, hitting .264 with a career-high 32 homers and 106 RBIs, and he was voted the Indians' Man of the Year.

Wertz also missed most of the 1958 season with a severe leg injury, and then was traded on December 2 with outfielder Gary Geiger to the Boston Red Sox for outfielder Jim Piersall.

In that World Series of 1954, Wertz smashed a 460-foot drive to center field at the Polo Grounds in the eighth inning of the opening game with two on and the Indians and Giants tied, 2–2. It would have been a three-run homer in any other major league park.

Mays turned at the crack of the bat and ran—and ran and ran—finally catching the ball over his shoulder with his back to the plate. It choked off a Tribe rally, maintained the tie, and enabled the Giants to win, 5–2, on Dusty Rhodes' 10th-inning pinch homer that popped over the 260-foot right-field fence, and New York went on to sweep the Series.

A member of the AL All-Star team in 1949, 1950, 1952, and 1957, Wertz went back to the Tigers in a waiver purchase from the Red Sox on September 8, 1961, playing in Detroit until he was released on May 10, 1963. Minnesota then signed Wertz on June 18, 1963, and released him after the season, ending his career.

Wertz, Vic

Indians	G	AB	H	BA	RBI	R	2B	3B	HR	SA	SB
1954	94	295	81	.275	48	33	14	2	14	.478	0
1955	74	257	65	.253	55	30	11	2	14	.475	1
1956	136	481	127	.264	106	65	22	0	32	.509	0
1957	144	515	145	.282	105	84	21	0	28	.485	2
1958	25	43	12	.279	12	5	1	0	3	.512	0
Career	1,862	6,099	1,692	.277	1,178	867	289	42	266	.469	9

Westlake, Waldon Thomas

Indians: 1952–55
Outfielder
Nickname: Wally
Birthplace: Gridley, California

B: November 8, 1920
Bats right, throws right
Ht. 6–0; **Wt.** 186

Wally Westlake spent most of his career in the National League where, in his first four years (1947–50) with Pittsburgh he smashed 81 homers, consistently batted .280, and twice hit for the cycle.

After going to the St. Louis Cardinals in 1951 and then to Cincinnati, Westlake was purchased on August 7, 1952, by the Indians, hoping he could help them win the pennant. He didn't, nor could he make a difference in 1953 even though he hit a career-high .330.

Wally Westlake

But Westlake was a positive factor as a role player and pinch hitter in 1954, when the Indians won an American League–record 111 games and their third pennant.

He delivered a key hit, a fifth-inning, two-out double off New York Yankees southpaw Tommy Byrne that drove in two runs, giving the Indians a 3–2 victory in the nightcap of a doubleheader at the Stadium on September 12.

Some called Westlake's hit the "most dramatic" of the season because it enabled the Indians to sweep the doubleheader and increase their first-place margin to 8½ games and all but mathematically eliminate the Yankees.

Westlake's double was somewhat tainted, he admitted after the game, in describing the hit. "[Byrne] hung a curveball, and I hit it off the left-center-field fence," he said.

"As I swung out to make my turn [at first base], Red Kress, the coach, yelled several times, 'You can't make it!' But I looked up and the ball's bouncing off the fence, so I kept going and got down there to second base."

It was then, as he stood on second with 86,563 fans—the largest crowd in baseball history at that time—cheering for him, that Westlake realized he had missed first base.

"I'm out there on second and I'm dying," he said. "I'm saying Hail Marys, saying, 'Please Lord, make Byrne throw a pitch' [so the Yankees could not appeal that he had failed to tag first base]." Which Byrne did.

After the next batter, Hank Majeski, was retired, ending the inning, Westlake went to the dugout, got his glove, and trotted to the outfield where he was playing in place of injured Larry Doby.

"As I ran past [first base] umpire Jim Honochick, he says, 'Hey, pal, next time you come by, you better touch that thing [the base],'" related a much-relieved Westlake.

Westlake was traded with outfielder Dave Pope to Baltimore on June 15, 1955, for outfielder Gene Woodling and third baseman Billy Cox (though Cox subsequently retired, and the Orioles made a cash payment to the Tribe to complete the deal).

A member of the NL All-Star team in 1951, Westlake went back to that league in 1956 but played only five games for the Philadelphia Phillies, ending his major league career.

Westlake, Wally

Indians	G	AB	H	BA	RBI	R	2B	3B	HR	SA	SB
1952	29	69	16	.232	9	11	4	1	1	.362	1
1953	82	218	72	.330	46	42	7	1	9	.495	2
1954	85	240	63	.262	42	36	9	2	11	.454	0
1955	16	20	5	.250	1	2	1	0	0	.300	0
Career	958	3,117	848	.272	539	474	107	33	127	.450	19

Whitfield, Fred Dwight

Indians: 1963–67
First baseman
Nickname: Wingy
Birthplace: Vandiver, Alabama

B: January 7, 1938
Bats left, throws left
Ht. 6–1; **Wt.** 190

When the Indians traded for Tony Horton early in 1967, it marked the end of Fred Whitfield's days in Cleveland and, essentially, his major league career as well, which was unfortunate, the way things turned out.

Fred Whitfield

Because he hit so well against New York pitchers, Whitfield was tagged a "Yankee killer." He was one of the Tribe's best offensive players from 1963, upon his acquisition from the St. Louis Cardinals, through 1966.

The Indians got him in a December 15, 1962, trade for pitcher Ron Taylor and shortstop Jack Kubiszyn.

In his four seasons as a regular for the Indians, Whitfield smashed 84 homers, including a career-high 27 in 1966. That was the reason for his bewilderment and subsequent discontent when the Indians replaced him at first base with Horton.

"I'm not mad at anybody, certainly not Tony, but I don't understand why they don't seem to want me in the lineup," said Whitfield, whose only position was first base because of a weak throwing arm.

"Every year since I came here I've hit pretty good, but they've always been trying to find someone to take my job. It's probably best if they trade me."

The Indians did, on November 21, 1967, with pitcher George Culver to Cincinnati for outfielder Tommy Harper. (In the deal the Reds also received pitcher Bob Raudman from the Cubs, who owed the Indians a player from an earlier trade.)

With the Reds, Whitfield played little the next two years, and wound up in Montreal in 1970. He appeared in only four games for the Expos and retired.

Wood, Howard Ellsworth

Indians: 1917–22
Outfielder
Nickname: Smoky Joe
Birthplace: Kansas City, Missouri

B: October 25, 1889
D: July 27, 1985
Batted right, threw right
Ht. 5–11; **Wt.** 180

It was Walter Johnson who once said, "There's no man alive can throw harder than Smoky Joe Wood." That was in 1912 when Wood led American League pitchers with a 34–5 won-lost record.

Unfortunately for the Indians, they didn't get Wood until five years later, when on February 24, 1917, they purchased his contract for $15,000 from the Boston Red Sox, for whom he won a total of 116 games and lost only 56 in eight seasons with that team.

He pitched a no-hitter against the St. Louis Browns in Boston in the first game of a doubleheader on July 29, 1911, and two years later slipped on wet grass and broke the thumb on his pitching hand.

Wood returned to action too quickly and subsequently injured his arm. The injury eventually forced him to give up pitching after going 15–5 for the Red Sox in 1915, leading the American League with a .750 winning percentage.

Wood didn't play in 1916, but persuaded the Indians to give him another chance. They did and made the deal with the Red Sox. He appeared in 10 games for the Tribe in 1917, five as a pitcher, five as a pinch hitter, and pitched in one game in 1919 and one in 1920.

In 1918, Wood batted .296 in 119 games—95 in the outfield, 19 at second base, and four at first base. He hit .366 as a part-time outfielder in 1921 and .297 in 142 games in 1922. In 1923 he became the head baseball coach at Yale University, a job he held until 1942.

It was in 1919—though the charge wasn't made until December 1926—that Wood allegedly participated with Indians player-manager Tris Speaker and two Detroit players, Ty Cobb and Hubert "Dutch" Leonard, in a conspiracy to fix the outcome of a game between Cleveland and the Tigers.

It was Leonard who alleged that the four players had gambled on the game, and he even produced letters from Cobb and Wood that supported his claim and implicated all four players. Wood admitted in his letter that he bet and won on the game.

Commissioner Kenesaw Mountain Landis and AL president Ban Johnson conducted intensive investigations. The four players subsequently were cleared of any wrongdoing by Landis, though Johnson remained unconvinced of their innocence.

Whitfield, Fred

Indians	G	AB	H	BA	RBI	R	2B	3B	HR	SA	SB
1963	109	346	87	.251	54	44	17	3	21	.500	0
1964	101	293	79	.270	29	29	13	1	10	.423	0
1965	132	468	137	.293	90	49	23	1	26	.513	2
1966	137	502	121	.241	78	59	15	2	27	.440	1
1967	100	257	56	.218	31	24	10	0	9	.362	3
Career	817	2,284	578	.253	356	242	93	8	108	.443	7

Wood, Smoky Joe

Indians	G	AB	H	BA	RBI	R	2B	3B	HR	SA	SB
1917	10	6	0	.000	0	1	0	0	0	.000	0
1918	119	422	125	.296	66	41	22	4	5	.403	8
1919	72	192	49	.255	27	30	10	6	0	.370	3
1920	61	137	37	.270	30	25	11	2	1	.401	1
1921	66	194	71	.366	60	32	16	5	4	.562	2
1922	142	505	150	.297	92	74	33	8	8	.442	5
Career	696	1,952	553	.283	325	266	118	31	23	.411	23

Woodling, Eugene Richard

Indians: 1943, 1946, 1955–57   **B:** August 16, 1922
Outfielder   **Bats left, throws right**
Birthplace: Akron, Ohio   **Ht.** 5–9½; **Wt.** 195

Gene Woodling stubbornly insisted that all the so-called experts were wrong when they said he couldn't hit, even that he didn't fit into their teams' plans.

And eventually, Woodling proved to be right, going on to play—and play well—for six major league teams in a 17-year career that began in the Indians' farm system in 1940 and didn't end until 1962.

Most of Woodling's success was in New York where he played a large role in helping the Yankees win five consecutive World Championships from 1949 to 1953.

In that respect, Woodling represents one of the few personnel mistakes committed by Bill Veeck, who owned the Indians from June 21, 1946, through the 1949 season.

Woodling signed with the Indians in 1940 and proceeded to win three minor league batting championships, earning a September promotion to Cleveland in 1943. Then Uncle Sam beckoned, and Woodling spent the next two years in the army during World War II.

When he returned to the Indians in 1946, Woodling played 61 games and, still rusty from his time away from the game, hit only .188. "I sat more than I played," said Woodling. "I spent most of the season keeping track of Bob Feller's strikeouts."

By then Veeck also was aboard as the Indians' chief, and his desire to acquire Al Lopez as a backup catcher and veteran leader led to Woodling's departure to Pittsburgh on December 7, 1946.

Gene Woodling

Things didn't get much better for Woodling in 1947 with the Pirates; in fact, he was demoted to Newark of the Class AAA International League where he batted .289, but everything brightened for the underrated outfielder in 1948.

Woodling went to San Francisco and won the batting championship of the Class AAA Pacific Coast League with a .385 average, prompting his purchase by the Yankees. After five good seasons, often platooned with Hank Bauer, Woodling slumped to .250 in 1954 and was traded to Baltimore.

It turned out to be a great deal for the Yankees, who got pitchers Bob Turley and Don Larsen and shortstop Billy Hunter for Woodling and five other players.

Seven months later, on June 15, 1955, Woodling wound up where he had started, at "home" in Cleveland with third baseman Billy Cox, in exchange for outfielders Dave Pope and Wally Westlake. (Cox subsequently retired, and the Orioles made a cash payment to the Indians to complete the deal.)

After two seasons in Cleveland, in which he batted a major-league-high .321 in 1957 and won the Indians' Man of the Year award, he was sent back to the Orioles. He was traded on April 1, 1958, along with pitcher Bud Daley and utility man Dick Williams, for outfielder Larry Doby and pitcher Don Ferrarese.

Claimed by Washington in the 1961 expansion draft, Woodling hit .313 for the Senators. The following midseason he was sold to the New York Mets, for whom he batted .274 in 81 games, ending his career with a lifetime .284 average.

Woodling, Gene

Indians	G	AB	H	BA	RBI	R	2B	3B	HR	SA	SB
1943	8	25	8	.320	5	5	2	1	1	.600	0
1946	61	133	25	.188	9	8	1	4	0	.256	1
1955	79	259	72	.278	35	33	15	1	5	.402	2
1956	100	317	83	.262	38	56	17	0	8	.391	2
1957	133	430	138	.321	78	74	25	2	19	.521	0
Career	1,796	5,587	1,585	.284	830	830	257	63	147	.431	29

Wynn, Early

Indians: 1949–57, 1963   **B:** January 6, 1920
Pitcher   **Bats both, throws right**
Nickname: Gus   **Ht.** 6–0; **Wt.** 190
Birthplace: Hartford, Alabama

It was always said about Early Wynn that he'd knock down his own grandmother if she dug in at the plate against him, an accusation which the burly, hard-nosed pitcher usually denied.

"Aw, I wouldn't do a thing like that—unless it meant winning the game," Wynn would drawl in rebuttal.

Whether he really would knock down his own grandmother or not, there was no doubting Wynn's competitiveness from the beginning to the end of his 23-year major league career, which culminated in his winning a 300th game in 1963.

Wynn pitched 10 seasons in two tours of duty with the Indians, was elected to the Hall of Fame in 1972, won the American League Cy Young Award in 1959, was a member of the AL All-Star team six consecutive seasons, 1955–60,

Early Wynn

and was cowinner of the Indians' Man of the Year award with Bob Lemon and Mike Garcia in 1952 when his record was 23–12.

He flirted with no-hitters twice. On May 22, 1955, with the Indians, Wynn beat the Tigers in Detroit, 4–0, with Fred Hatfield getting the only hit, a single in the fourth inning. On May 1, 1959, with Chicago, Wynn allowed only a first-inning single to Pete Runnels in a 1–0 victory over Boston.

It all began for Wynn in the farm system of the original Washington Senators in 1937. Except for three appearances (0–2, 5.75 ERA) with Washington in 1939, and five games (3–1, 1.57 ERA) in 1941, he spent five years in the minor leagues.

With a blazing fastball—but not much else except his fierce competitive spirit—Wynn made it to the Senators to stay in 1942. He was their best pitcher with an 18–12 record and 2.91 ERA in 1943, and after spending 1945 in the military service, went 17–15 in 1947. All the while the Senators were among the losingest teams in baseball.

The Indians got Wynn in one of their best-ever trades, on December 14, 1948, and later gave him away in one of their worst-ever deals.

He was acquired with first baseman Mickey Vernon for pitchers Joe Haynes (the son-in-law of Senators owner Clark Griffith) and Ed Klieman and first baseman Eddie Robinson.

Under the tutelage of pitching coach Mel Harder in Cleveland, Wynn developed a curveball, slider, and change-up and perfected the knuckleball he'd toyed with in Washington.

Wynn's record was only 11–7 with an uncharacteristic 4.15 ERA that first year with the Indians, but he was a big winner the next eight seasons, especially in 1954.

That was the year Wynn and Lemon each won 23 games for the most victories in the AL, and the two of them teamed with Garcia, Art Houtteman, and Bob Feller to form what many consider the greatest starting pitching staff in baseball history. With the additional help of relievers Ray Narleski

and Don Mossi, the Indians won an AL-record 111 games and the pennant.

When Wynn suffered his first losing record, 14–17, with the Indians in 1957, general manager Frank Lane, on December 4, packaged him with outfielder Al Smith and sent them to the Chicago White Sox for aging outfielder Minnie Minoso and utility infielder Fred Hatfield.

It was a disastrous deal for the Tribe but a great one for Chicago. After going 14–16 in 1958, Wynn pitched the White Sox to the pennant in 1959 at the age of 39, again leading the AL in victories with 22 (while losing 10), and won the Cy Young Award.

Wynn's ability began to decline in 1960, and when his won-lost record fell to 7–15 in 1962—and 299–242 lifetime—the White Sox released him.

Signed by the Indians in the spring of 1963, Wynn made five starts, two of them resulting in losses, before winning the elusive 300th game on July 13.

"Some people called it tainted, but I didn't care," Wynn said of his 7–4 victory over the Kansas City Athletics.

Those who demeaned it were critical because Wynn pitched only five innings and turned the lead over to reliever Jerry Walker to protect, which he did.

"I had absolutely the worst stuff in that game than in any of the other 299 victories, and a lot of the losses, too," he said.

It was one of the two games that Wynn called the "most memorable" of his career. The other was one he pitched for Washington in the nightcap of a doubleheader in New York on September 26, 1941.

"I'll always remember it because that little shortstop for the Yankees, Phil Rizzuto, ruined it for me," he said. "Imagine, there I was getting out guys like Joe DiMaggio, King Kong Keller, Bill Dickey, Joe Gordon, Red Rolfe, and Tommy Henrich, but I lose the game, 1–0, because that little pipsqueak Rizzuto hit a home run."

It was one of only 38 Rizzuto hit in his 13-year major league career.

"From that game on I always thought bad things about anybody who hit a home run off me.

"And if I had not let Rizzuto beat me in that [1941] game, I would have won my 300th a helluva lot sooner."

Wynn retired the day after his 300th victory and was a coach for the Indians from 1964 to 1966 and for Minnesota from 1967 to 1969. He later was a broadcaster for the Toronto Blue Jays.

Wynn, Early											
Indians	**W**	**L**	**Pct**	**ERA**	**G**	**CG**	**IP**	**H**	**BB**	**SO**	**ShO**
1949	11	7	.611	4.15	26	6	164⅔	186	57	62	0
1950	18	8	.692	3.20	32	14	213⅔	166	101	143	2
1951	20	13	.606	3.02	37	21	274⅓	227	107	133	3
1952	23	12	.657	2.90	42	19	285⅔	239	132	153	4
1953	17	12	.586	3.93	36	16	251⅓	234	107	138	1
1954	23	11	.676	2.73	40	20	270⅔	225	83	155	3
1955	17	11	.607	2.82	32	16	230	207	80	122	6
1956	20	9	.690	2.72	38	18	277⅔	233	91	158	4
1957	14	17	.452	4.31	40	13	263	270	104	184	1
1963	1	2	.333	2.28	20	1	55⅓	50	15	29	0
Career	300	244	.551	3.54	691	290	4,564	4,291	1,775	2,334	49

Young, Denton True

Spiders: 1890–98; **Indians:** 1909–11
Pitcher
Nicknames: Cy, Foxy Grandpa
Birthplace: Gilmore, Ohio

B: March 29, 1867
D: November 4, 1955
Batted right, threw right
Ht. 6–2; **Wt.** 210

The man who is generally acknowledged to have been the greatest pitcher in baseball history, Cy Young, got his start in the major leagues in Cleveland, with the Spiders, who represented the city in the National League from 1889 to 1899.

Nicknamed Cy because his fastball was "like a cyclone," according to his first catcher, Young joined the Spiders in July 1890 after they purchased his contract from the Canton club of the minor Tri-State League.

The price the Spiders paid for the pitcher who would be credited with winning 511 games in the major leagues (with 316 losses) and would have the most prestigious pitching award named in his honor, was $250, with a salary of $75 a month.

Young didn't pitch for the team that came to be known as the Indians until very late in his career, 1909, when his record already was 478–282, two and a half seasons before he hung up his spikes.

With the forerunner of the Indians, then called the Naps, Young was 19–15 in 1909, 7–10 in 1910, and 3–4 before he was released on August 15, 1911. Four days later he was signed by the Boston Braves, for whom he won four and lost five, then retired.

Young's complete record, including his first nine years with the Spiders, includes three no-hitters: a 6–0 victory against Cincinnati on September 18, 1897, in the first game of a doubleheader in Cleveland; a perfect-game, 3–0 victory for the Red Sox against the Philadelphia Athletics on May 5, 1904; and an 8–0 victory for the Red Sox over the New York Yankees on June 30, 1908.

In 1937, Young became the eighth player to be elected to the Hall of Fame (following Ty Cobb, Babe Ruth, Honus Wagner, Christy Mathewson, Walter Johnson, Napoleon Lajoie, and Tris Speaker).

Young won 20 or more games 15 times, including 30 or more in five seasons, struck out 2,800 batters, won two complete games in one day on October 4, 1890, pitched 24 consecutive hitless innings, from the seventh inning on April 25 through the sixth inning on May 11, 1904, for the Red Sox, and pitched more innings (7,354⅔) and complete games (749) than anyone else in baseball history.

It is unfortunate that his initial tour of duty in Cleveland didn't continue beyond 1898. At that time the club was owned by Frank DeHaas Robison, who also had purchased the St. Louis franchise in the National League.

It was Robison's opinion that St. Louis was a better baseball town than Cleveland. And because he held this view, Robison transferred Young and several of his best teammates to St. Louis.

The Cleveland team was left in shambles, and in 1899 the Spiders compiled the worst won-lost record in the history of major league baseball, 20–134.

When the season ended the NL, in effect, kicked Cleveland out of the league, paving the way for the city to get a

Cy Young

franchise in the American League when it was founded by Ban Johnson in 1900 and started play in 1901.

Young, meanwhile, won big in St. Louis in 1899 and 1900, then pitched for the Red Sox from 1901 to 1908, when he was purchased by Cleveland.

Young, Cy

Indians	W	L	Pct	ERA	G	CG	IP	H	BB	SO	ShO
1909	19	15	.559	2.26	35	30	295	267	59	109	3
1910	7	10	.412	2.53	21	14	163⅓	149	27	58	1
1911	3	4	.429	3.88	7	4	46⅓	54	13	20	0
Career	511	316	.618	2.63	906	749	7,356⅔	7,092	1,217	2,803	76

Zoldak, Samuel Walter

Indians: 1948–50
Pitcher
Nickname: Sad Sam
Birthplace: Brooklyn, New York

B: December 8, 1918
D: August 25, 1966
Batted left, threw left
Ht. 5–11½; **Wt.** 185

Sam Zoldak's record isn't glossy, and he never was a big winner. But he pitched for two pennant-winning teams, the St. Louis Browns in 1944 and the Indians in 1948.

He was fond of making the humorous claim that he pitched in 12 straight World Series games.

"You won't find it in the box scores," he would say. "I did my work in the bull pen. Both series with the Browns and Indians went six games and I pitched every one of them, went the whole nine innings in most, and never got called on. That's how I got the nickname 'Sad Sam.' Who wouldn't be sad after all that wasted labor?"

Zoldak was acquired by the Tribe from the Browns on June 15, 1948, in exchange for pitcher Bill Kennedy and $100,000.

Bill Veeck, then the Indians owner, admitted that the price he paid for Zoldak was exorbitant, but said at the time, "If he helps us win [the pennant], he's worth three times what we gave up to get him."

Zoldak certainly did help, with nine victories and six losses in 23 games as a spot starter and reliever, though his overall record that year, 11–10, was the only time he won in double figures.

After two lackluster seasons in 1949 and 1950, when Zoldak won a total of five games with four saves, he was involved in a three-team deal, April 30, 1951, that included the Chicago White Sox and Philadelphia Athletics. Zoldak and catcher Ray Murray went to Philadelphia, outfielder Minnie Minoso wound up in Chicago, and the Indians received relief pitcher Lou Brissie.

Two and a half months after joining the Athletics, Zoldak pitched the best game of his career. On July 15, 1951, in the second game of a doubleheader in Chicago, Zoldak beat the White Sox, 5–0, with Chico Carrasquel getting the only hit, a third-inning single.

Zoldak, Sam

Indians	W	L	Pct	ERA	G	CG	IP	H	BB	SO	ShO
1948	9	6	.600	2.81	23	4	105⅔	104	24	17	1
1949	1	2	.333	4.25	27	0	53	60	18	11	0
1950	4	2	.667	3.96	33	0	63⅔	64	21	15	0
Career	43	53	.448	3.54	250	30	929⅓	956	301	207	5

All the Team's Men

The following list of more than 1,400 men comprises all the players who have performed for the Cleveland Indians between 1901 and 1995 (including their years as the Blues, Bronchos, and Naps).

Figures in parentheses indicate years played with the Indians. All statistics refer only to the players' careers with the Indians and do not account for service with other major league teams.

A

Abbott, Fred (1903–04) catcher–first baseman: 82-for-385, .213, in 118 games.

Abbott, Paul (1993) pitcher: 0–1 with 6.38 ERA in 5 games.

Aber, Al (1950, 53) pitcher: 2–1 with 4.20 ERA in 7 games.

Abernathie, Bill (1952) pitcher: 0–0 with 13.50 ERA in 1 game.

Abernathy, Ted (1963–64) pitcher: 9–8 with 3.68 ERA in 96 games.

Ables, Harry (1909) pitcher: 1–1 with 2.12 ERA in 5 games.

Adams, Bert (1910–12) catcher: 15-for-72, .208, in 27 games.

Adcock, Joe (1963) first baseman: 71-for-283, .251, in 97 games.

Agee, Tommie (1962–64) outfielder: 9-for-53, .170, in 31 games.

Aguayo, Luis (1989) third baseman–shortstop–second baseman: 17-for-97, .175, in 47 games.

Aguirre, Hank (1955–57) pitcher: 6–6 with 3.84 ERA in 30 games.

Akerfelds, Darrel (1987) pitcher: 2–6 with 6.75 ERA in 16 games.

Aldrete, Mike (1991) first baseman–outfielder: 48-for-183, .262, in 85 games.

Alexander, Bob (1957) pitcher: 0–1 with 9.00 ERA in 5 games.

Alexander, Gary (1978–80) catcher–designated hitter: 198-for-860, .230, in 276 games.

Alexander, Hugh (1937) outfielder: 1-for-11, .091, in 7 games.

Allanson, Andy (1986–89) catcher: 296-for-1,204, .246, in 395 games.

Allen, Bob (1961–63, 66–67) pitcher: 7–12 with 4.11 ERA in 204 games.

Allen, Johnny (1936–40) pitcher: 67–34 with 3.65 ERA in 150 games.

Allen, Neil (1989) pitcher: 0–1 with 15.00 ERA in 3 games.

Allen, Rod (1988) designated hitter: 1-for-11, .091, in 5 games.

Allison, Milo (1916–17) outfielder: 10-for-53, .189, in 46 games.

Allred, Beau (1989–91) outfielder: 38-for-165, .230, in 65 games.

Alomar, Sandy, Jr. (1990–95) catcher: 447-for-1,638, .273, in 482 games.

Alston, Dell (1979–80) outfielder–designated hitter: 30-for-116, .259, in 106 games.

Altizer, Dave (1908) outfielder: 19-for-89, .213, in 29 games.

Altobelli, Joe (1955, 57) first baseman: 33-for-162, .204, in 125 games.

Alvarado, Luis (1974) second baseman: 25-for-114, .219, in 61 games.

Alvis, Max (1962–69) third baseman: 874-for-3,514, .249, in 951 games.

Amaro, Ruben (1994–95) outfielder: 17-for-83, .205, in 54 games.

Hank Aguirre

Andersen, Larry (1975, 77, 79) pitcher: 0–1 with 5.40 ERA in 22 games.

Anderson, Bud (1982–83) pitcher: 4–10 with 3.68 ERA in 64 games.

Anderson, Dwain (1974) second baseman: 1-for-3, .333, in 2 games.

Andrews, Ivy (1937) pitcher: 3–4 with 4.37 ERA in 20 games.

Andrews, Nate (1940–41) pitcher: 0–1 with 6.91 ERA in 8 games.

Antonelli, Johnny (1961) pitcher: 0–4 with 6.56 ERA in 11 games.

Aponte, Luis (1984) pitcher: 1–0 with 4.11 ERA in 25 games.

Arlin, Steve (1974) pitcher: 2–5 with 6.60 ERA in 11 games.

Armstrong, Jack (1992) pitcher: 6–15 with 4.64 ERA in 35 games.

Armstrong, Mike (1987) pitcher: 1–0 with 8.68 ERA in 14 games.

Ted Abernathy

A rare photograph of Indians outfielder Jack Graney in the uniform of Cleveland's Class A sandlot team, named for its sponsor—a men's clothing store.

Earl Averill, Sr.

Arnsberg, Brad (1992) pitcher: 0–0 with 11.81 ERA in 8 games.

Ashby, Alan (1973–76) catcher: 122-for-537, .227, in 200 games.

Aspromonte, Ken (1960–62) second baseman–third baseman: 153-for-557, .275, in 159 games.

Assenmacher, Paul (1995) pitcher: 6–2 with 2.82 ERA in 47 games.

Atherton, Keith (1989) pitcher: 0–3 with 4.15 ERA in 32 games.

Austin, Rick (1970–71) pitcher: 2–5 with 4.86 ERA in 54 games.

Autry, Martin (1926–28) catcher: 30-for-110, .273, in 41 games.

Averill, Earl, Sr. (1929–39) outfielder: 1,903-for-5,909, .322, in 1,509 games.

Averill, Earl, Jr. (1956, 58) catcher–third baseman: 32-for-148, .216, in 59 games.

Bobby Avila

Joe Azcue

Avila, Bobby (1949–58) second baseman–third baseman: 1,236-for-4,356, .284, in 1,207 games.

Ayala, Benny (1985) outfielder: 19-for-76, .250, in 46 games.

Aylward, Dick (1953) catcher: 0-for-3, .000, in 4 games.

Azcue, Joe (1963–69) catcher: 506-for-1,904, .266, in 594 games.

B

Baerga, Carlos (1990–95) second baseman–third baseman–shortstop: 971-for-3,185, .305, in 819 games.

Bagby, Jim, Sr. (1916–22) pitcher: 122–85 with 3.10 ERA in 290 games.

Bagby, Jim, Jr. (1941–45) pitcher: 55–54 with 3.45 ERA in 145 games.

Bailes, Scott (1986–89) pitcher: 31–41 with 4.70 ERA in 172 games.

Bailey, Steve (1967–68) pitcher: 2–6 with 3.88 ERA in 34 games.

Baker, Bock (1901) pitcher: 0–1 with 5.63 ERA in 1 game.

Baker, Frank (1969, 71) outfielder: 82-for-353, .232, in 125 games.

Baker, Howard (1912) third baseman: 5-for-30, .167, in 11 games.

Ball, Neal (1909–12) second baseman–shortstop–third baseman: 260-for-987, .263, in 305 games.

Ballinger, Mark (1971) pitcher: 1–2 with 4.67 ERA in 18 games.

Bando, Chris (1981–88) catcher: 291-for-1,282, .227, in 496 games.

Banks, George (1964–66) outfielder–third baseman: 7-for-26, .269, in 17 games.

Bannister, Alan (1980–83) outfielder–second baseman: 340-for-1,219, .279, in 367 games.

Barbare, Walter (1914–16) third base-

man: 74-for-346, .214, in 105 games.

Barbeau, Jap (1905–06) third baseman–second baseman: 35-for-166, .211, in 53 games.

Barker, Len (1979–83) pitcher: 56–49 with 4.31 ERA in 144 games.

Barker, Ray (1965) first baseman: 0-for-6, .000, in 11 games.

Barkley, Jeff (1984–85) pitcher: 0–3 with 5.40 ERA in 24 games.

Barnes, Brian (1994) pitcher: 0–1 with 5.40 ERA in 6 games.

Barnes, Rich (1983) pitcher: 1–1 with 6.94 ERA in 4 games.

Barnhart, Les (1928, 30) pitcher: 1–1 with 6.75 ERA in 3 games.

Baskette, Jim (1911–13) pitcher: 9–6 with 3.30 ERA in 35 games.

Bassler, Johnny (1913–14) catcher: 14-for-79, .177, in 44 games.

Bates, Ray (1913) third baseman: 5-for-30, .167, in 27 games.

Baxes, Jim (1959) second baseman–third baseman: 59-for-247, .239, in 77 games.

Bay, Harry (1902–08) outfielder: 683-for-2,467, .277, in 628 games.

Bayne, Bill (1928) pitcher: 2–5 with 5.13 ERA in 37 games.

Beall, Johnny (1913) outfielder: 1-for-6, .167, in 6 games.

Bean, Belve (1930–31, 33–35) pitcher: 9–7 with 5.03 ERA in 76 games.

Bearden, Gene (1947–50) pitcher: 29–18 with 3.76 ERA in 84 games.

Bearse, Kevin (1990) pitcher: 0–2 with 12.91 ERA in 3 games.

Beck, Erve (1901) second baseman: 156-for-539, .289, in 135 games.

Beck, George (1914) pitcher: 0–0 with 0.00 ERA in 1 game.

Jim Bagby Jr.

Buddy Bell

Becker, Heinz (1946–47) first baseman: 44-for-149, .295, in 52 games.

Becker, Joe (1936–37) catcher: 20-for-
83, .241, in 40 games.

Bedford, Gene (1925) second baseman: 0-for-3, .000, in 2 games.

Bedgood, Phil (1922–23) pitcher: 1–2
with 4.88 ERA in 10 games.

Beebe, Fred (1916) pitcher: 5–3 with
2.41 ERA in 20 games.

Beene, Fred (1974–75) pitcher: 5–4
with 5.72 ERA in 51 games.

Behenna, Rick (1983–85) pitcher: 0–7
with 7.16 ERA in 12 games.

Bell, Beau (1940–41) outfielder–first
baseman: 144-for-548, .263, in 168
games.

Bell, Buddy (1972–78) third baseman–outfielder: 1,016-for-3,712,
.274, in 987 games.

Bell, David (1995) third baseman: 0-
for-2, .000, in 2 games.

Gary Bell

Bell, Eric (1991–92) pitcher: 4–2 with
3.78 ERA in 17 games.

Bell, Gary (1958–67) pitcher: 96–92
with 3.71 ERA in 419 games.

Bell, Jay (1986–88) shortstop: 78-for-
350, .223, in 116 games.

Belle, Albert (1989–95)
outfielder–designated hitter: 827-
for-2,839, .291, in 755 games.

Bemis, Harry (1902–10) catcher–first
baseman: 569-for-2,229, .255, in
704 games.

Benge, Ray (1925–26) pitcher: 2–0
with 2.70 ERA in 10 games.

Benjamin, Stan (1945) outfielder: 7-
for-21, .333, in 14 games.

Benn, Henry (1914) pitcher: 0–0 with
0.00 ERA in 1 game.

Benton, Al (1949–50) pitcher: 13–8
with 2.58 ERA in 76 games.

Benton, Butch (1985) catcher: 12-for-
67, .179, in 31 games.

Berardino, Johnny (1948–50, 52) second baseman–third
baseman–shortstop–first baseman:
56-for-300, .187, in 155 games.

Berg, Moe (1931, 34) catcher: 26-for-
110, .236, in 39 games.

Berger, Boze (1932, 35–36) second
baseman–first baeman: 128-for-514,
.249, in 153 games.

Berger, Heinie (1907–10) pitcher:
32–29 with 2.60 ERA in 90 games.

Bergman, Al (1916) second baseman:
3-for-14, .214, in 8 games.

Bernazard, Tony (1984–87) second
baseman: 473-for-1,794, .264, in
518 games.

Bernhard, Bill (1902–07) pitcher:
77–56 with 2.45 ERA in 146
games.

Berry, Joe (1946) pitcher: 3–6 with
3.38 ERA in 21 games.

Berry, Ken (1975) outfielder: 8-for-40,
.200, in 25 games.

Johnny Berardino

Bescher, Bob (1918) outfielder: 20-
for-60, .333, in 25 games.

Bevacqua, Kurt (1971–72) second
baseman–outfielder: 32-for-172,
.186, in 74 games.

Bibby, Jim (1975–77) pitcher: 30–29
with 3.36 ERA in 95 games.

Bielecki, Mike (1993) pitcher: 4–5
with 5.90 ERA in 13 games.

Billings, Josh (1913–18) catcher: 35-
for-195, .179, in 110 games.

Biras, Steve (1944) second baseman:
2-for-2, 1.000, in 2 games.

Birmingham, Joe (1906–14) outfielder–third baseman: 669-for-
2,634, .254, in 770 games.

Bishop, Lloyd (1914) pitcher: 0–1
with 5.63 ERA in 3 games.

Beau Bell

Jim Bibby

Bisland, Rivington (1914) shortstop: 6-for-57, .105, in 18 games.

Black, Bud (1988–90, 95) pitcher: 29–26 with 3.93 ERA in 89 games.

Black, Don (1946–48) pitcher: 13–16 with 4.27 ERA in 66 games.

Blaeholder, George (1936) pitcher: 8–4 with 5.09 ERA in 35 games.

Blair, Willie (1991) pitcher: 2–3 with 6.75 ERA in 11 games.

Blanco, Ossie (1974) first baseman: 7-for-36, .194, in 18 games.

Blanding, Fred (1910–14) pitcher: 45–46 with 3.13 ERA in 144 games.

Blanks, Larvell (1976–78) shortstop–second baseman–third baseman: 233-for-843, .276, in 279 games.

Blyleven, Bert (1981–85) pitcher: 48–37 with 3.23 ERA in 104 games.

Bochte, Bruce (1977) outfielder–first baseman: 119-for-392, .304, in 112 games.

Bockman, Eddie (1947) third baseman: 17-for-66, .258, in 46 games.

Boehling, Joe (1916–17, 20) pitcher: 3–11 with 3.68 ERA in 27 games.

Bohnet, John (1982) pitcher: 0–0 with 6.94 ERA in 3 games.

Boley, Joe (1932) shortstop: 1-for-4, .250, in 1 game.

Bolger, Jim (1959) pinch hitter: 0-for-7, .000, in 8 games.

Bolton, Cecil (1928) first baseman: 2-for-13, .154, in 4 games.

Bond, Walt (1960–62) outfielder: 57-for-233, .245, in 90 games.

Bonds, Bobby (1979) outfielder–designated hitter: 148-for-538, .275, in 146 games.

Bonner, Frank (1902) second baseman: 37-for-132, .280, in 34 games.

Bert Blyleven

Ray Boone

Bonness, Bill (1944) pitcher: 0–1 with 7.71 ERA in 2 games.

Booker, Buddy (1966) catcher: 6-for-28, .214, in 18 games.

Booles, Red (1909) pitcher: 0–1 with 1.99 ERA in 4 games.

Boone, Danny (1922–23) pitcher: 8–12 with 5.00 ERA in 38 games.

Boone, Ray (1948–53) shortstop: 414-for-1,600, .259, in 489 games.

Bosman, Dick (1973–75) pitcher: 8–15 with 4.91 ERA in 53 games.

Boss, Harley (1933) first baseman: 118-for-438, .269, in 112 games.

Boucher, Denis (1991–92) pitcher: 3–6 with 7.07 ERA in 13 games.

Boudreau, Lou (1938–50) shortstop–third baseman–first baseman: 1,706-for-5,754, .296, in 1,560 games.

Bowman, Abe (1914–15) pitcher: 2–8 with 4.74 ERA in 24 games.

Dick Bosman

Lou Boudreau

Bowsfield, Ted (1960) pitcher: 3–4 with 5.09 ERA in 11 games.

Boyd, Gary (1969) pitcher: 0–2 with 9.00 ERA in 8 games.

Bracken, Jack (1901) pitcher: 4–8 with 6.21 ERA in 12 games.

Bradford, Buddy (1970–71) outfielder: 38-for-201, .189, in 95 games.

Bradley, Bill (1901–10) third baseman–shortstop: 1,265-for-4,648, .272, in 1,231 games.

Bradley, Jack (1916) catcher: 0-for-3, .000, in 2 games.

Braggins, Dick (1901) pitcher: 1–2 with 4.78 ERA in 4 games.

Brennan, Ad (1918) pitcher: 0–0 with 3.00 ERA in 1 game.

Brennan, Tom (1981–83) pitcher: 8–6 with 3.89 ERA in 48 games.

Brenner, Bert (1912) pitcher: 1–0 with 2.77 ERA in 2 games.

Brenton, Lynn (1913, 15) pitcher: 2–3 with 3.57 ERA in 12 games.

Brenzel, Bill (1934–35) catcher: 42-for-193, .218, in 67 games.

Brewster, Charlie (1946) shortstop: 0-for-2, .000, in 3 games.

Bridges, Rocky (1960) shortstop–third baseman: 9-for-27, .333, in 10 games.

Briggs, Dan (1978) outfielder: 8-for-49, .163, in 15 games.

Briggs, Johnny (1959–60) pitcher: 4–3 with 3.86 ERA in 25 games.

Brissie, Lou (1951–53) pitcher: 7–5 with 3.59 ERA in 112 games.

Broaca, Johnny (1939) pitcher: 4–2 with 4.70 ERA in 22 games.

Jack Brohamer

Larry Brown

Tom Buskey

Brodowski, Dick (1958–59) pitcher: 3–2 with 1.35 ERA in 23 games.

Brohamer, Jack (1972–75, 80) second baseman: 359-for-1,501, .239, in 461 games.

Bronkie, Herman (1910–12) third baseman: 3-for-31, .097, in 13 games.

Brookens, Tom (1990) third baseman–second baseman: 41-for-154, .266, in 64 games.

Brower, Frank (1923–24) first baseman: 143-for-504, .284, in 192 games.

Brown, Clint (1928–35, 41–42) pitcher: 60–65 with 4.36 ERA in 237 games.

Brown, Dick (1957–59) catcher: 102-for-428, .238, in 150 games.

Brown, Jackie (1975–76) pitcher: 10–13 with 4.26 ERA in 57 games.

Brown, Jumbo (1927–28) pitcher: 0–3 with 6.48 ERA in 13 games.

Brown, Larry (1963–71) shortstop–second baseman–third baseman: 718-for-3,014, .238, in 941 games.

Brown, Lloyd (1934–37) pitcher: 23–33 with 4.34 ERA in 135 games.

Browne, Jerry (1989–91) second baseman–outfielder–third baseman: 382-for-1,401, .273, in 400 games.

Buckeye, Garland (1925–28) pitcher: 30–39 with 3.79 ERA in 106 games.

Buelow, Fritz (1904–06) catcher: 76-for-444, .171, in 113 games.

Burchart, Larry (1969) pitcher: 0–2 with 4.25 ERA in 29 games.

Burnett, Johnny (1927–34) shortstop–third baseman–second baseman: 475-for-1,629, .292, in 488 games.

Burnitz, Jeromy (1995) outfielder: 4-for-7, .571, in 9 games.

Burns, George (1920–21, 24–28) first

baseman: 853-for-2,611, .327, for 757 games.

Burton, Ellis (1963) outfielder: 6-for-31, .194, in 26 games.

Busby, Jim (1956–57) outfielder: 130-for-568, .229, in 165 games.

Buskey, Tom (1974–77) pitcher: 12–13 with 3.41 ERA in 161 games.

Butcher, Hank (1911–12) outfielder: 48-for-215, .223, in 64 games.

Butcher, John (1986) pitcher: 1–5 with 6.93 ERA in 13 games.

Butler, Bill (1972) pitcher: 0–0 with 1.54 ERA in 6 games.

Butler, Brett (1984–87) outfielder: 663-for-2,302, .288, in 609 games.

C

Caffie, Joe (1956–57) outfielder: 37-for-127, .291, in 44 games.

Clint Brown

Johnny Burnett

Brett Butler

Ernie Camacho

Caffyn, Ben (1906) outfielder: 20-for-103, .194, in 30 games.

Cage, Wayne (1978–79) designated hitter–first baseman: 37-for-154, .240, in 65 games.

Caldwell, Bruce (1928) outfielder: 6-for-27, .222, in 18 games.

Caldwell, Ray (1919–21) pitcher: 31–17 with 3.95 ERA in 77 games.

Callahan, Dave (1910–11) outfielder: 12-for-60, .200, in 19 games.

Calvert, Paul (1942–45) pitcher: 1–3 with 4.57 ERA in 42 games.

Camacho, Ernie (1983–87) pitcher: 7–16 with 3.66 ERA in 141 games.

Camilli, Lou (1969–72) shortstop–second baseman–third baseman: 22-for-151, .146, in 107 games.

Campbell, Bruce (1935–39) out-

Bruce Campbell

Tom Candiotti

fielder: 576-for-1,889, .305, in 553 games.

Campbell, Soup (1940–41) outfielder: 96-for-390, .246, in 139 games.

Camper, Card (1977) pitcher: 1–0 with 3.86 ERA in 3 games.

Candiotti, Tom (1986–91) pitcher: 72–65 with 3.53 ERA in 176 games.

Carbo, Bernie (1978) designated hitter: 50-for-174, .287, in 60 games.

Cardenal, Jose (1968–69) outfielder: 293-for-1,149, .257, in 303 games.

Cardenas, Leo (1973) shortstop: 42-for-195, .215, in 72 games.

Carisch, Fred (1912–14) catcher: 89-for-394, .226, in 147 games.

Carlton, Steve (1987) pitcher: 5–9 with 5.37 ERA in 23 games.

Carnett, Eddie (1945) outfielder: 16-for-73, .219, in 30 games.

Carr, Charlie (1904–05) first baseman: 99-for-426, .232, in 121 games.

Carrasquel, Chico (1956–58) shortstop–third baseman: 263-for-1,022, .257, in 315 games.

Carreon, Camilo (1965) catcher: 12-for-52, .231, in 19 games.

Carson, Kit (1934–35) outfielder: 10-for-40, .250, in 21 games.

Jose Cardenal

Carter, Joe (1984–89) outfielder–first baseman–designated hitter: 876-for-3,256, .269, in 773 games.

Carter, Paul (1914–15) pitcher: 2–4 with 3.10 ERA in 16 games.

Carty, Rico (1974–77) designated hitter–first baseman–outfielder: 451-for-1,487, .303, in 430 games.

Case, George (1946) outfielder: 109-for-484, .225, in 118 games.

Casian, Larry (1994) pitcher: 0–2 with 8.64 ERA in 7 games.

Castillo, Carmen (1982–88) outfielder–designated hitter: 295-for-1,152, .256, in 464 games.

Center, Pete (1942–43, 45–46) pitcher: 7–7 with 4.10 ERA in 77 games.

Cermak, Ed (1901) outfielder: 0-for-4, .000, in 1 game.

Cerone, Rick (1975–76) catcher: 5-for-28, .179, in 14 games.

Chakales, Bob (1951–54) pitcher: 6–8 with 4.44 ERA in 32 games.

Chambliss, Chris (1971–74) first baseman: 428-for-1,520, .282, in 404 games.

Chance, Bob (1963–64) first baseman–outfielder: 124-for-442, .281, in 136 games.

Chance, Dean (1970) pitcher: 9–8 with 4.24 ERA in 45 games.

Chapman, Ben (1939–40) outfielder: 315-for-1,093, .288, in 292 games.

Chapman, Ray (1912–20) shortstop–second baseman–third baseman: 1,053-for-3,785, .278, in 1,051 games.

Chapman, Sam (1951) outfielder: 56-for-246, .228, in 94 games.

Chappell, Larry (1916) pinch hitter: 0-for-2, .000, in 3 games.

Charboneau, Joe (1980–82) outfielder–designated hitter: 172-for-647, .266, in 201 games.

George Case

Joe Charboneau

Chech, Charlie (1908) pitcher: 11–7 with 1.74 ERA in 27 games.

Cheeves, Virgil (1924) pitcher: 0–0 with 7.79 ERA in 8 games.

Christopher, Mike (1992–93) pitcher: 0–0 with 3.34 ERA in 19 games.

Christopher, Russ (1948) pitcher: 3–2 with 2.90 ERA in 45 games.

Churn, Chuck (1958) pitcher: 0–0 with 6.23 ERA in 6 games.

Cicotte, Al (1959) pitcher: 3–1 with 5.32 ERA in 26 games.

Cihocki, Al (1945) shortstop–third baseman–second baseman: 60-for-283, .212, in 92 games.

Cissell, Bill (1932–33) second baseman–shortstop: 267-for-950, .281, in 243 games.

Clanton, Uke (1922) first baseman: 0-for-1, .000, in 1 game.

Clark, Allie (1948–51) outfielder: 135-for-518, .261, in 178 games.

Clark, Bob (1920–21) pitcher: 1–2 with 5.44 ERA in 16 games.

Clark, Bryan (1985) pitcher: 3–4 with 6.32 ERA in 31 games.

Clark, Dave (1986–89) designated hitter–outfielder: 135-for-554, .244, in 212 games.

Clark, Ginger (1902) pitcher: 1–0 with 6.00 ERA in 1 game.

Clark, Jim (1971) outfielder: 3-for-18, .167, in 13 games.

Clark, Mark (1993–95) pitcher: 27–15 with 4.46 ERA in 68 games.

Clark, Watty (1924) pitcher: 1–3 with 7.01 ERA in 12 games.

Allie Clark

Clarke, Josh (1908–09) outfielder: 119-for-504, .236, in 135 games.

Clarke, Nig (1905–10) catcher: 317-for-1,204, .263, in 392 games.

Clarke, Sumpter (1923–24) outfielder: 24-for-107, .224, in 36 games.

Clarkson, Walter (1907–08) pitcher: 4–6 with 2.30 ERA in 19 games.

Cline, Ty (1960–62) outfielder: 110-for-444, .248, in 137 games.

Clingman, Billy (1903) second baseman: 18-for-64, .281, in 21 games.

Clinton, Lu (1965) outfielder: 6-for-34, .176, in 12 games.

Clyde, David (1978–79) pitcher: 11–15 with 4.66 ERA in 37 games.

Codiroli, Chris (1988) pitcher: 0–4 with 9.31 ERA in 14 games.

Colavito, Rocky (1955–59, 65–67) outfielder: 851-for-3,185, .267, in 913 games.

Colbert, Vince (1970–72) pitcher: 9–14 with 4.57 ERA in 95 games.

Cole, Alex (1990–92) outfielder–designated hitter: 202-for-711, .284, in 226 games.

Rocky Colavito

Cole, Bert (1925) pitcher: 1–1 with 6.14 ERA in 13 games.

Coleman, Bob (1916) catcher: 6-for-28, .214, in 19 games.

Coleman, Gordy (1959) first baseman: 8-for-15, .533, in 6 games.

Collamore, Allan (1914–15) pitcher: 5–12 with 2.92 ERA in 38 games.

Collard, Hap (1927–28) pitcher: 0–0 with 3.86 ERA in 5 games.

Collins, Don (1980) pitcher: 0–0 with 7.50 ERA in 4 games.

Collum, Jackie (1962) pitcher: 0–0 with 13.50 ERA in 1 game.

Combs, Merrill (1951–52) shortstop: 28-for-167, .168, in 71 games.

Comer, Steve (1984) pitcher: 4–8 with 5.68 ERA in 22 games.

Congalton, Bunk (1905–07) outfielder: 155-for-488, .318, in 138 games.

Connally, Sarge (1931–34) pitcher: 18–14 with 4.41 ERA in 98 games.

Connatser, Bruce (1931–32) first baseman: 28-for-109, .257, in 35 games.

Connolly, Ed (1967) pitcher: 2–1 with 7.48 ERA in 15 games.

Connolly, Joe (1922–23) outfielder: 44-for-154, .286, in 64 games.

Connor, Joe (1901) catcher: 17-for-121, .140, in 37 games.

Constable, Jim (1958) pitcher: 0–1 with 11.57 ERA in 6 games.

Conway, Jack (1941, 46–47) second baseman–shortstop: 68-for-310, .219, in 104 games.

Conyers, Herb (1950) first baseman: 3-for-9, .333, in 7 games.

Cook, Dennis (1992–93, 95) pitcher: 10–12 with 4.41 ERA in 68 games.

Coughtry, Marlan (1962) pinch hitter: 1-for-2, .500, in 3 games.

Coumbe, Fritz (1914–19) pitcher: 34–31 with 2.83 ERA in 145 games.

Coveleski, Stan (1916–24) pitcher: 172–123 with 3.02 ERA in 360 games.

Cox, Ted (1978–79) third baseman–outfielder–designated hitter: 93-for-416, .224, in 160 games.

Craghead, Howard (1931, 33) pitcher: 0–0 with 6.26 ERA in 15 games.

Craig, Rodney (1982) outfielder: 15-for-65, .231, in 49 games.

Crandall, Del (1966) catcher: 25-for-108, .231, in 50 games.

Creel, Keith (1985) pitcher: 2–5 with 4.79 ERA in 15 games.

Cristall, Bill (1901) pitcher: 1–5 with 4.84 ERA in 6 games.

Crosby, Ed (1974–76) shortstop–third baseman–second baseman: 49-for-216, .227, in 100 games.

Cross, Frank (1901) outfielder: 3-for-5, .600, in 1 game.

Cruz, Victor (1979–80) pitcher: 9–16 with 3.83 ERA in 116 games.

Cullenbine, Roy (1943–45) outfielder–first baseman: 304-for-1,072, .284, in 300 games.

Cullop, Nick (1913–14) pitcher: 3–8 with 4.37 ERA in 24 games.

Cullop, Nick (1927) outfielder: 16-for-68, .235, in 32 games.

Culmer, Wil (1983) outfielder: 2-for-19, .105, in 7 games.

Culver, George (1966–67) pitcher: 7–5 with 4.46 ERA in 58 games.

Curry, Tony (1966) pinch hitter: 2-for-16, .125, in 19 games.

Curtis, Jack (1963) pitcher: 0–0 with 18.00 ERA in 4 games.

Cypert, Al (1914) third baseman: 0-for-1, .000, in 1 game.

D

Dade, Paul (1977–79) outfielder–third baseman–designated hitter: 260-for-938, .277, in 271 games.

Dailey, Bill (1961–62) pitcher: 3–2 with 2.77 ERA in 39 games.

Dalena, Pete (1989) pinch hitter: 1-for-7, .143, in 5 games.

Daley, Bud (1955–57) pitcher: 3–9 with 4.87 ERA in 50 games.

Daly, Tom (1916) catcher: 16-for-73, .219, in 31 games.

Dashner, Lee (1913) pitcher: 0–0 with 5.40 ERA in 1 game.

Davalillo, Vic (1963–68) outfielder: 648-for-2,335, .278, in 693 games.

Davidson, Homer (1908) catcher: 0-for-4, .000, in 9 games.

Davis, Bill (1965–66) first baseman: 9-for-48, .188, in 33 games.

Davis, Harry (1912) first baseman: 0-for-5, .000, in 2 games.

Davis, Steve (1989) pitcher: 1–1 with 8.06 ERA in 12 games.

Dawson, Joe (1924) pitcher: 1–2 with 6.64 ERA in 4 games.

Dean, Chubby (1941–43) pitcher: 14–20 with 4.08 ERA in 52 games.

DeBerry, Hank (1916–17) catcher: 18-for-66, .273, in 40 games.

Dedmon, Jeff (1988) pitcher: 1–0 with 4.54 ERA in 21 games.

Delahanty, Frank (1907) outfielder: 9-for-52, .173, in 15 games.

de la Hoz, Mike (1960–63) shortstop–second baseman–third baseman: 127-for-495, .257, in 189 games.

Demeter, Don (1967) outfielder: 25-for-121, .207, in 51 games.

Demeter, Steve (1960) third baseman: 0-for-5, .000, in 4 games.

DeMott, Ben (1910–11) pitcher: 0–4 with 6.19 ERA in 7 games.

Dempsey, Rick (1987) catcher: 25-for-141, .177, in 60 games.

Denning, Otto (1942–43) catcher–first baseman: 76-for-343, .222, in 129 games.

Denny, John (1980–82) pitcher: 24–23 with 4.15 ERA in 56 games.

Dente, Sam (1954–55) shortstop–third baseman–second baseman: 72-for-274, .263, in 141 games.

Gene Desautels

Desautels, Gene (1941–43, 45) catcher: 117-for-545, .215, in 206 games.

DesJardien, Paul (1916) pitcher: 0–0 with 18.00 ERA in 1 game.

Detore, George (1930–31) third baseman–shortstop: 17-for-68, .250, in 33 games.

Devlin, Jim (1944) catcher: 0-for-1, .000, in 1 game.

Diaz, Bo (1978–81) catcher: 139-for-548, .254, in 198 games.

Dicken, Paul (1964, 66) pinch hitter: 0-for-13, .000, in 13 games.

Dickerson, George (1917) pitcher: 0–0 with 0.00 ERA in 1 game.

Dillard, Don (1959–62) outfielder: 85-for-338, .251, in 185 games.

Dillinger, Harley (1914) pitcher: 0–1 with 4.54 ERA in 11 games.

Dilone, Miguel (1980–83) outfielder–designated hitter: 360-for-1,244, .289, in 340 games.

Bud Daley

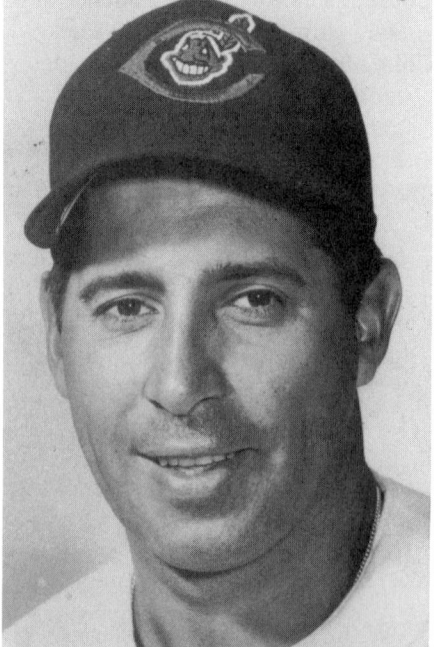

Sam Dente

Bo Diaz

Pat Dobson

Dick Donovan

Steve Dunning

DiPoto, Jerry (1993–94) pitcher: 4–4 with 3.63 ERA in 53 games.

Doane, Walt (1909–10) pitcher: 0–1 with 5.56 ERA in 7 games.

Dobson, Joe (1939–40) pitcher: 5–10 with 5.36 ERA in 75 games.

Dobson, Pat (1976–77) pitcher: 19–24 with 4.49 ERA in 68 games.

Doby, Larry (1947–55, 58) outfielder: 1,234-for-4,315, .286, in 1,235 games.

Doljack, Frank (1943) outfielder: 0-for-7, .000, in 3 games.

Donahue, Pat (1910) catcher: 1-for-6, .167, in 2 games.

Donahue, Red (1903–05) pitcher: 32–35 with 2.66 ERA in 71 games.

Donohue, Pete (1931) pitcher: 0–0 with 8.44 ERA in 2 games.

Donovan, Dick (1962–65) pitcher: 39–35 with 4.12 ERA in 106 games.

Donovan, Mike (1904) shortstop: 0-for-2, .000, in 2 games.

Donovan, Tom (1901) outfielder: 18-for-71, .254, in 18 games.

Doran, Bill (1922) third baseman: 1-for-2, .500, in 3 games.

Dorman, Red (1928) outfielder: 28-for-77, .364, in 25 games.

Dorner, Gus (1902–03) pitcher: 7–6 with 3.45 ERA in 16 games.

Dorsett, Brian (1987) catcher: 3-for-11, .273, in 5 games.

Dorsett, Cal (1940–41, 47) pitcher: 0–1 with 11.85 ERA in 8 games.

Dowling, Pete (1901) pitcher: 11–22 with 3.86 ERA in 33 games.

Drake, Logan (1922–24) pitcher: 0–1 with 7.71 ERA in 10 games.

Drake, Tom (1939) pitcher: 0–1 with 9.00 ERA in 8 games.

Duffy, Frank (1972–77) shortstop: 582-for-2,503, .233, in 805 games.

Duncan, Dave (1973–74) catcher-designated hitter: 165-for-769, .215, in 231 games.

Dunlop, George (1913–14) shortstop: 4-for-20, .200, in 8 games.

Dunning, Steve (1970–73) pitcher: 18–29 with 4.37 ERA in 70 games.

Dybzinski, Jerry (1980–82) shortstop–second baseman–third baseman: 123-for-517, .238, in 242 games.

Dyck, Jim (1954) pinch hitter: 1-for-1, 1.000, in 2 games.

E

Eagan, Truck (1901) second baseman: 3-for-18, .167, in 5 games.

Easter, Luke (1949–54) first baseman–outfielder: 472-for-1,725, .274, in 491 games.

Easterly, Jamie (1983–87) pitcher: 12–7 with 4.04 ERA in 146 games.

Easterly, Ted (1909–12) catcher–outfielder: 334-for-1,123, .297, in 372 games.

Larry Doby

Frank Duffy

Luke Easter

Eckersley, Dennis (1975–77) pitcher: 40–32 with 3.23 ERA in 103 games.

Edmondson, George (1922–24) pitcher: 0–0 with 9.64 ERA in 8 games.

Edmonson, Eddie (1913) outfielder–first baseman: 0-for-5, .000, in 2 games.

Edwards, Doc (1962–63) catcher: 47-for-174, .270, in 63 games.

Edwards, Hank (1941–43, 46–49) outfielder: 396-for-1,439, .275, in 413 games.

Edwards, Jim Joe (1922–25) pitcher: 17–24 with 4.22 ERA in 86 games.

Eells, Harry (1906) pitcher: 4–5 with 2.61 ERA in 14 games.

Egan, Ben (1914–15) catcher: 33-for-208, .159, in 71 games.

Egloff, Bruce (1991) pitcher: 0–0 with 4.76 ERA in 6 games.

Eibel, Hack (1912) outfielder: 0-for-3, .000, in 1 game.

Eichelberger, Juan (1983) pitcher: 4–11 with 4.90 ERA in 28 games.

Eichrodt, Fred (1925–27) outfielder: 96-for-399, .241, in 137 games.

Eisenstat, Harry (1939–42) pitcher: 10–13 with 3.22 ERA in 103 games.

Ellerbe, Frank (1924) third baseman: 31-for-120, .258, in 46 games.

Ellingsen, Bruce (1974) pitcher: 1–1 with 3.21 ERA in 16 games.

Ellis, John (1973–75) catcher–first baseman–designated hitter: 322-for-1,210, .266, in 347 games.

Ellison, George (1920) pitcher: 0–0 with 0.00 ERA in 1 game.

Ellsworth, Dick (1969–70) pitcher: 9–12 with 4.23 ERA in 63 games.

Embree, Alan (1992, 95) pitcher: 3–4 with 5.91 ERA in 27 games.

Embree, Red (1941–42, 44–47) pitcher: 23–32 with 3.29 ERA in 86 games.

Engel, Joe (1919) pitcher: 0–0 with 0.00 ERA in 1 game.

Engle, Clyde (1916) third baseman: 4-for-26, .154, in 11 games.

Enzmann, Johnny (1918–19) pitcher: 8–9 with 2.34 ERA in 44 games.

Eschen, Jim (1915) outfielder: 10-for-42, .238, in 15 games.

Escobar, Jose (1991) shortstop: 3-for-15, .200, in 10 games.

Espinoza, Alvaro (1993–95) third baseman–shortstop–second baseman: 164-for-637, .257, in 285 games.

Essegian, Chuck (1961–62) outfielder: 140-for-502, 279, in 166 games.

Essian, Jim (1983) catcher: 19-for-93, .204, in 48 games.

Eunick, Ferd (1917) third baseman: 0-for-2, .000, in 1 game.

Evans, Joe (1915–22) third baseman–outfielder–shortstop: 328-for-1,303, .251, in 495 games.

Evers, Hoot (1955–56) outfielder: 19-for-66, .288, in 42 games.

F

Faeth, Tony (1919–20) pitcher: 0–0 with 2.70 ERA in 19 games.

Fahr, Red (1951) pitcher: 0–0 with 4.76 ERA in 5 games.

Fain, Ferris (1955) first baseman: 30-for-118, .254, in 56 games.

Falk, Bibb (1929–31) outfielder: 244-for-778, .314, in 286 games.

Falkenberg, Cy (1908–11, 13) pitcher: 57–41 with 2.70 ERA in 123 games.

Fanwell, Harry (1910) pitcher: 2–9 with 3.62 ERA in 17 games.

Ed Farmer

Farmer, Ed (1971–73) pitcher: 7–11 with 4.40 ERA in 105 games.

Farmer, Jack (1918) third baseman: 2-for-9, .222, in 7 games.

Farr, Steve (1984, 94) pitcher: 4–12 with 4.66 ERA in 50 games.

Farrell, John (1987–90, 95) pitcher: 32–30 with 3.93 ERA in 90 games.

Feller, Bob (1936–41, 45–56) pitcher: 266–162 with 3.25 ERA in 570 games.

Fermin, Felix (1989–93) shortstop: 516-for-2,017, .256, in 652 games.

Ferrarese, Don (1958–59) pitcher: 8–7 with 3.48 ERA in 43 games.

Ferrell, Wes (1927–33) pitcher–outfielder: 102–62 with 3.67 ERA in 195 games.

Ferrick, Tom (1942, 46) pitcher: 3–2 with 2.54 ERA in 40 games.

Ferry, Cy (1905) pitcher: 0–0 with 13.50 ERA in 1 game.

Fewster, Chick (1924–25) second

John Ellis

Bibb Falk

Bob Feller

Wes Ferrell

Les Fleming

Ray Fosse

baseman–third baseman: 159-for-616, .258, in 194 games.

Firova, Dan (1988) catcher: 0-for-0, —, in 1 game.

Fischer, Carl (1937) pitcher: 0–1 with 27.00 ERA in 2 games.

Fischlin, Mike (1981–85) shortstop–second baseman–third baseman: 173-for-737, .235, in 387 games.

Fisher, Eddie (1968) pitcher: 4–2 with 2.85 ERA in 54 games.

Fisher, Gus (1911) catcher: 53-for-203, .261, in 70 games.

FitzGerald, Ed (1959) catcher: 35-for-129, .271, in 49 games.

Fitzke, Paul (1924) pitcher: 0–0 with 4.50 ERA in 1 game.

Fitzmorris, Al (1977–78) pitcher: 6–11 with 5.50 ERA in 36 games.

Flanigan, Ray (1946) pitcher: 0–1 with 11.00 ERA in 3 games.

Fleming, Les (1941–42, 45–47) first baseman–outfielder: 361-for-1,283, .281, in 402 games.

Flick, Elmer (1902–10) outfielder–second baseman: 1,058-for-3,537, .299, in 935 games.

Flores, Jesse (1950) pitcher: 3–3 with 3.74 ERA in 28 games.

Foiles, Hank (1953, 55–56, 60) catcher: 49-for-186, .263, in 94 games.

Fonseca, Lew (1927–31) first baseman–second baseman–third baseman: 504-for-1,494, .337, in 401 games.

Ford, Ted (1970–71, 73) outfielder: 55-for-282, .195, in 111 games.

Fosse, Ray (1967–72, 76–77) catcher–first baseman: 549-for-2,039, .269, in 600 games.

Foster, Alan (1971) pitcher: 8–12 with 4.16 ERA in 36 games.

Foster, Roy (1970–72) outfielder: 257-for-1,016, .253, in 337 games.

Foster, Slim (1908) pitcher: 1–0 with 2.14 ERA in 6 games.

Franco, Julio (1983–88) shortstop–second baseman–designated hitter: 1,051-for-3,561, .295, in 898 games.

Francona, Terry (1988) designated hitter: 66-for-212, .311, in 62 games.

Francona, Tito (1959–64) outfielder–first baseman: 832-for-2,926, .284, in 835 games.

Lew Fonseca

Frazier, George (1984) pitcher: 3–2 with 3.65 ERA in 22 games.

Frazier, Joe (1947) outfielder: 1-for-14, .071, in 9 games.

Freiburger, Vern (1941) first baseman: 1-for-8, .125, in 2 games.

Freisleben, Dave (1978) pitcher: 1–4 with 7.11 ERA in 12 games.

Fridley, Jim (1952) outfielder: 44-for-175, .251, in 62 games.

Friend, Owen (1953) second baseman: 16-for-68, .235, in 34 games.

Frierson, Buck (1941) outfielder: 3-for-11, .273, in 5 games.

Frobel, Doug (1987) outfielder: 4-for-40, .100, in 29 games.

Fry, Jay (1923) pitcher: 0–0 with 12.27 ERA in 1 game.

Fuller, Vern (1964, 66–70) second baseman–third baseman: 182-for-785, .232, in 325 games.

Tito Francona

Vern Fuller

Denny Galehouse

Mike Garcia

Funk, Frank (1960–62) pitcher: 17–14 with 3.08 ERA in 112 games.

G

Gaffke, Fabian (1941–42) outfielder: 12-for-71, .169, in 44 games.

Gagliano, Ralph (1965) pinch runner: 0-for-0, —, in 1 game.

Galatzer, Milt (1933–36) outfielder: 192-for 712, .270, in 248 games.

Galehouse, Denny (1934–38) pitcher: 25–29 with 4.75 ERA in 114 games.

Gallagher, Dave (1987) outfielder: 4-for-36, .111, in 15 games.

Gallagher, Jackie (1923) outfielder: 1-for-1, 1.000, in 1 game.

Gallagher, Shorty (1901) outfielder: 0-for-4, .000, in 2 games.

Gamble, Oscar (1973–75) designated hitter–outfielder: 327-for-1,192, .274, in 369 games.

Gandil, Chick (1916) first baseman: 138-for-533, .259, in 46 games.

Garbark, Bob (1934–35) catcher: 6-for-29, .207, in 11 games.

Garcia, Mike (1948–59) pitcher: 142–96 with 3.24 ERA in 397 games.

Gardner, Larry (1919–24) third baseman: 693-for-2,306, .301, in 673 games.

Gardner, Ray (1929–30) shortstop: 68-for-269, .253, in 115 games.

Gardner, Rob (1968) pitcher: 0–0 with 6.75 ERA in 5 games.

Garland, Wayne (1977–81) pitcher: 28–48 with 4.50 ERA in 99 games.

Garrett, Clarence (1915) pitcher: 2–2 with 2.31 ERA in 4 games.

Gassaway, Charlie (1946) pitcher: 1–1 with 3.91 ERA in 13 games.

Geiger, Gary (1958) outfielder: 45-for-195, .231, in 91 games.

Genins, Frank (1901) outfielder: 23-for-101, .228, in 26 games.

Gentile, Jim (1966) pinch hitter: 6-for-47, .128, in 33 games.

George, Greek (1935–36) catcher: 15-for-77, .195, in 25 games.

George, Lefty (1912) pitcher: 0–5 with 4.87 ERA in 11 games.

Gerken, George (1927–28) outfielder: 29-for-129, .225, in 44 games.

Gettel, Al (1947–48) pitcher: 11–11 with 3.91 ERA in 36 games.

Getz, Gus (1918) third baseman: 2-for-15, .133, in 6 games.

Gil, Gus (1967) second baseman: 11-for-96, .115, in 51 games.

Giles, Brian (1995) outfielder: 5-for-9, .556, in 6 games.

Frank Funk

Oscar Gamble

Wayne Garland

Gill, Johnny (1927–28) outfielder: 13-for-62, .210, in 23 games.

Ginn, Tinsley (1914) outfielder: 0-for-1, .000, in 2 games.

Ginsberg, Joe (1953–54) catcher: 32-for-111, .288, in 49 games.

Glavenich, Luke (1913) pitcher: 0–0 with 9.00 ERA in 1 game.

Gleeson, Jim (1936) outfielder: 36-for-139, .259, in 41 games.

Glendon, Martin (1903) pitcher: 1–2 with 0.98 ERA in 3 games.

Gliatto, Sal (1930) pitcher: 0–0 with 6.60 ERA in 8 games.

Glynn, Bill (1952–54) first baseman: 168-for-674, .249, in 302 games.

Glynn, Ed (1981–83) pitcher: 5–4 with 4.13 ERA in 62 games.

Gochnaur, John (1902–03) shortstop: 166-for-897, .185, in 261 games.

Gogolewski, Bill (1974) pitcher: 0–0 with 4.61 ERA in 5 games.

Goldman, Jonah (1928, 30–31) short-stop–third baseman: 87-for-389, .224, in 148 games.

Gomez, Ruben (1962) pitcher: 1–2 with 4.37 ERA in 15 games.

Gonzales, Rene (1994) third base-man: 8-for-23, .348, in 22 games.

Gonzalez, Denny (1989) designated hitter: 5-for-17, .294, in 8 games.

Gonzalez, Jose (1991) outfielder: 11-for-69, .159, in 33 games.

Gonzalez, Orlando (1976) first baseman: 17-for-68, .250, in 28 games.

Gonzalez, Pedro (1965–67) second baseman: 226-for-941, .240, in 306 games.

Gooch, Lee (1915) pinch hitter: 1-for-2, .500, in 2 games.

Good, Wilbur (1908–09) outfielder: 111-for-472, .235, in 140 games.

Gordon, Don (1987–88) pitcher: 3–7 with 4.27 ERA in 59 games.

Gordon, Joe (1947–50) second base-man: 530-for-2,021, .262, in 566 games.

Gould, Al (1916–17) pitcher: 9–11 with 3.05 ERA in 57 games.

Gozzo, Mauro (1990–91) pitcher: 0–0 with 11.73 ERA in 4 games.

Graber, Rod (1958) outfielder: 1-for-8, .125, in 4 games.

Graham, Peaches (1902) second base-man: 2-for-6, .333, in 2 games.

Gramly, Tommy (1968) pitcher: 0–1 with 2.70 ERA in 3 games.

Graney, Jack (1908, 10–22) outfielder: 1,178-for-4,705, .250, in 1,402 games.

Grant, Eddie (1905) second baseman: 3-for-8, .375, in 2 games.

Grant, George (1927–29) pitcher: 14–16 with 5.39 ERA in 65 games.

Grant, Jimmy (1943–44) second base-man: 30-for-121, .248, in 76 games.

Grant, Mudcat (1958–64) pitcher: 67–63 with 4.09 ERA in 227 games.

Grasso, Mickey (1954) catcher: 2-for-6, .333, in 4 games.

Gray, Gary (1980) designated hitter: 8-for-54, .148, in 28 games.

Gray, John (1957) pitcher: 1–3 with 5.85 ERA in 7 games.

Gray, Ted (1955) pitcher: 0–0 with 18.00 ERA in 2 games.

Green, Gene (1962–63) outfielder: 56-for-221, .253, in 109 games.

Jack Graney

Gregg, Dave (1913) pitcher: 0–0 with 18.00 ERA in 1 game.

Gregg, Vean (1911–14) pitcher: 72–36 with 2.31 ERA in 132 games.

Griffin, Alfredo (1976–78) shortstop: 9-for-49, .184, in 31 games.

Griggs, Art (1911–12) first baseman–second baseman: 100-for-341, .293, in 116 games.

Grim, Bob (1960) pitcher: 0–1 with 11.57 ERA in 3 games.

Grimes, Oscar (1938–42) first base-man–second baseman–shortstop–third baseman: 173-for-715, .242, in 262 games.

Grimsley, Jason (1993–95) pitcher: 8–6 with 5.09 ERA in 39 games.

Grimsley, Ross (1980) pitcher: 4–5 with 6.75 ERA in 14 games.

Gromek, Steve (1941–53) pitcher: 78–67 with 3.22 ERA in 309 games.

Groom, Bob (1918) pitcher: 2–2 with 7.06 ERA in 14 games.

Pedro Gonzalez

Joe Gordon

Mudcat Grant

Alfredo Griffin

Groth, Ernie (1947–48) pitcher: 0–0 with 3.37 ERA in 3 games.

Grubb, Harvey (1912) third baseman: 0-for-0, —, in 1 game.

Grubb, Johnny (1977–78) outfielder: 128-for-471, .272, in 147 games.

Guante, Cecilio (1990) pitcher: 2–3 with 5.01 ERA in 26 games.

Guisto, Lou (1916–17, 21–23) first baseman: 88-for-449, .196, in 156 games.

Gulley, Tom (1923–24) outfielder: 4-for-23, .174, in 10 games.

Gunkel, Red (1916) pitcher: 0–0 with 0.00 ERA in 1 game.

H

Hagerman, Rip (1914–16) pitcher: 15–29 with 3.37 ERA in 68 games.

Hale, Bob (1960–61) first baseman: 27-for-106, .255, in 112 games.

Hale, Odell (1931, 33–40) second baseman–third baseman: 1,046-for-3,575, .293, in 1,009 games.

Hall, Jimmie (1968–69) outfielder: 22-for-121, .182, in 57 games.

Hall, Mel (1984–88) outfielder–designated hitter: 498-for-1,765, .282, in 538 games.

Hall, Russ (1901) shortstop: 2-for-4, .500, in 1 game.

Halla, John (1905) pitcher: 0–0 with 2.84 ERA in 3 games.

Hallman, Bill (1901) shortstop: 4-for-19, .211, in 5 games.

Halt, Al (1918) third baseman: 12-for-69, .174, in 26 games.

Hamann, Doc (1922) pitcher: 0–0 with 0.00 ERA in 1 game.

Hamilton, Jack (1969) pitcher: 0–2 with 4.40 ERA in 20 games.

Hamilton, Steve (1961) pitcher: 0–0 with 3.00 ERA in 2 games.

Hammond, Jack (1915, 22) second baseman: 19-for-88, .216, in 36 games.

Hamner, Granny (1959) shortstop: 11-for-67, .164, in 27 games.

Hand, Rich (1970–71) pitcher: 8–19 with 4.37 ERA in 50 games.

Hansen, Doug (1951) pinch runner: 0-for-0, —, in 3 games.

Harder, Mel (1928–47) pitcher: 223–186 with 3.80 ERA in 582 games.

Hardy, Carroll (1958–60) outfielder: 23-for-120, .192, in 88 games.

Hardy, Jack (1903) outfielder: 3-for-19, .158, in 5 games.

Hargan, Steve (1965–72) pitcher: 56–74 with 3.78 ERA in 221 games.

Hargrove, Mike (1979–85) first baseman–outfielder–designated hitter: 860-for-2,945, .292, in 888 games.

Harkness, Specs (1910–11) pitcher: 12–9 with 3.37 ERA in 38 games.

Harper, Tommy (1968) outfielder: 51-for-235, .217, in 130 games.

Harrah, Toby (1979–83) third baseman–shortstop–designated hitter: 725-for-2,577, .281, in 712 games.

Harrell, Billy (1955, 57–58) shortstop–third baseman: 73-for-305, .239, in 136 games.

Harrelson, Ken (1969–71) outfielder–first baseman: 158-for-719, .220, in 218 games.

Harris, Billy (1968) second baseman–third baseman: 20-for-94, .213, in 38 games.

Harris, Charlie (1951) pitcher: 0–0 with 4.50 ERA in 2 games.

Harris, Joe (1917, 19) first baseman: 181-for-553, .327, in 174 games.

Harris, Mickey (1952) pitcher: 3–0 with 4.63 ERA in 29 games.

Harrison, Roric (1975) pitcher: 7–7 with 4.79 ERA in 19 games.

Harshman, Jack (1959–60) pitcher: 7–5 with 3.22 ERA in 28 games.

Harstad, Oscar (1915) pitcher: 3–5 with 3.40 ERA in 32 games.

Hart, Bill (1901) pitcher: 7–11 with 3.77 ERA in 20 games.

Hartford, Bruce (1914) shortstop: 4-for-22, .182, in 8 games.

Hartley, Grover (1929–30) catcher: 12-for-37, .324, in 25 games.

Hartman, Bob (1962) pitcher: 0–1 with 3.12 ERA in 8 games.

Harvel, Luther (1928) outfielder: 30-for-136, .221, in 40 games.

Oscar Grimes

Mel Harder

Ken Harrelson

Ron Hassey

Frank Hayes

Jeff Heath

Harvey, Ervin (1901–02) outfielder: 76-for-216, .352, in 57 games.

Hassey, Ron (1978–84) catcher–first baseman–designated hitter: 458-for-1,690, .271, in 569 games.

Hatfield, Fred (1958) third baseman: 1-for-8, .125, in 3 games.

Hauger, Art (1912) outfielder: 1-for-18, .056, in 15 games.

Hauser, Joe (1929) first baseman: 12-for-48, .250, in 37 games.

Havens, Brad (1988–89) pitcher: 2–3 with 3.14 ERA in 35 games.

Hawkins, Wynn (1960–62) pitcher: 12–13 with 4.17 ERA in 48 games.

Haworth, Howie (1915) catcher: 1-for-7, .143, in 7 games.

Hayes, Frankie (1945–46) catcher: 131-for-541, .242, in 170 games.

Hayes, Von (1981–82) outfielder–designated hitter–third baseman: 160-for-636, .252, in 193 games.

Heath, Jeff (1936–45) outfielder: 1,040-for-3,489, .298, in 957 games.

Heaton, Neal (1982–86) pitcher: 35–47 with 4.77 ERA in 133 games.

Hedlund, Mike (1965, 68) pitcher: 0–0 with 7.14 ERA in 9 games.

Heffner, Bob (1966) pitcher: 0–1 with 3.46 ERA in 5 games.

Hegan, Jim (1941–42, 46–57) catcher: 1,026-for-4,459, .230, in 1,526 games.

Heidemann, Jack (1969–72, 74) shortstop: 148-for-719, .206, in 239 games.

Held, Woodie (1958–64) shortstop–second baseman–outfielder–third baseman: 698-for-2,800, .249, in 855 games.

Helf, Hank (1938, 40) catcher: 1-for-14, .071, in 7 games.

Heman, Russ (1961) pitcher: 0–0 with 3.60 ERA in 6 games.

Hemphill, Charlie (1902) outfielder: 25-for-94, .266, in 25 games.

Hemsley, Rollie (1938–41) catcher: 344-for-1,302, .264, in 390 games.

Henderson, Bernie (1921) pitcher: 0–1 with 9.00 ERA in 2 games.

Hendrick, George (1973–76) outfielder: 547-for-2,047, .267, in 546 games.

Hendrick, Harvey (1925) first baseman: 8-for-28, .286, in 25 games.

Hendryx, Tim (1911–12) outfielder: 19-for-77, .247, in 27 games.

Hengel, Dave (1989) outfielder: 3-for-25, .120, in 12 games.

Hennigan, Phil (1969–72) pitcher: 17–10 with 3.91 ERA in 146 games.

Henry, Earl (1944–45) pitcher: 1–4 with 5.03 ERA in 17 games.

Hermoso, Angel (1974) second baseman: 27-for-122, .221, in 48 games.

Wynn Hawkins

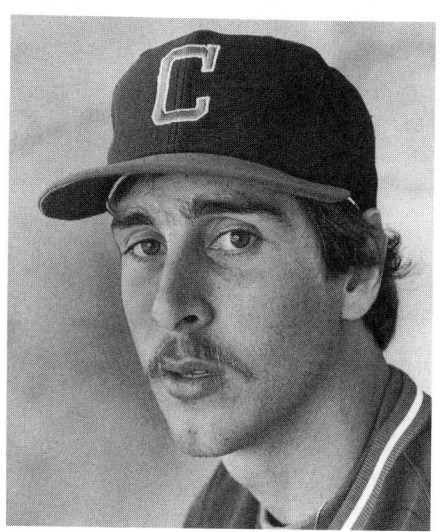

Von Hayes

Neal Heaton

Jim Hegan

Hernandez, Jeremy (1993) pitcher: 6–5 with 3.14 ERA in 49 games.

Hernandez, Jose (1992) shortstop: 0-for-4, .000, in 3 games.

Hernandez, Keith (1990) first baseman: 26-for-130, .200, in 43 games.

Hershiser, Orel (1995) pitcher: 16–6 with 3.87 ERA in 26 games.

Hess, Otto (1902, 04–08) pitcher–outfielder: 46–49 with 2.50 ERA in 118 games.

Heving, Joe (1937–38, 41–44) pitcher: 28–14 with 3.16 ERA in 190 games.

Hickey, John (1904) pitcher: 0–1 with 7.30 ERA in 2 games.

Hickman, Charlie (1902–04, 08) first baseman–second baseman–

Woodie Held

outfielder: 458-for-1,482, .309, in 384 games.

Higgins, Bob (1909) catcher: 2-for-23, .087, in 8 games.

Higgins, Dennis (1970) pitcher: 4–6 with 3.99 ERA in 58 games.

Higgins, Mark (1989) first baseman: 1-for-10, .100, in 6 games.

Hildebrand, Oral (1931–36) pitcher: 56–46 with 4.18 ERA in 171 games.

Hilgendorf, Tom (1972–74) pitcher: 12–7 with 3.46 ERA in 48 games.

Hill, Glenallen (1991–93) outfielder–designated hitter: 160-for-665, .241, in 205 games.

Hill, Herb (1915) pitcher: 0–0 with 0.00 ERA in 1 game.

Hill, Hugh (1903) pinch hitter: 0-for-1, .000, in 1 game.

Hill, Ken (1995) pitcher: 4–1 with 3.98 ERA in 12 games.

George Hendrick

Hillegas, Shawn (1991) pitcher: 3–4 with 4.34 ERA in 51 games.

Hinchman, Bill (1907–09) outfielder–shortstop: 342-for-1,435, .238, in 428 games.

Hinchman, Harry (1907) second baseman: 11-for-51, .216, in 15 games.

Hinton, Chuck (1965–67, 69–71) outfielder–first baseman–second baseman–third baseman: 447-for-1,740, .257, in 692 games.

Hinzo, Tommy (1987, 89) second baseman: 68-for-274, .248, in 85 games.

Hoag, Myril (1944–45) outfielder: 106-for-405, .262, in 107 games.

Hockett, Oris (1941–44) outfielder: 450-for-1,665, .270, in 415 games.

Hodapp, Johnny (1925–32) second baseman–third baseman–first baseman: 711-for-2,237, .318, in 608 games.

Hodge, Gomer (1971) first baseman–third baseman–second baseman: 17-for-83, .205, in 80 games.

Jack Heidemann

Rollie Hemsley

Chuck Hinton

Oris Hockett

Hoffer, Bill (1901) pitcher: 3–8 with 4.55 era in 16 games.

Hoffman, Tex (1915) third baseman: 2-for-13, .154, in 9 games.

Hogan, Harry (1901) outfielder: 0-for-4, .000, in 1 game.

Hogan, Ken (1923–24) pinch hitter: 0-for-1, .000, in 3 games.

Hohnhorst, Eddie (1910, 12) first baseman: 31-for-117, .265, in 33 games.

Holland, Dutch (1934) outfielder: 32-for-128, .250, in 50 games.

Holloway, Ken (1929–30) pitcher: 7–6 with 4.11 ERA in 37 games.

Hood, Don (1975–79) pitcher: 17–22 with 4.17 ERA in 152 games.

Hooper, Bob (1953–54) pitcher: 5–4 with 4.33 ERA in 60 games.

Horn, Sam (1993) designated hitter: 15-for-33, .455, in 12 games.

Horton, Tony (1967–70) first baseman: 506-for-1,878, .269, in 513 games.

Johnny Hodapp

Horton, Willie (1978) designated hitter: 42-for-169, .249, in 50 games.

Hoskins, Dave (1953–54) pitcher: 9–4 with 3.81 ERA in 40 games.

Houtteman, Art (1953–57) pitcher: 34–22 with 3.97 ERA in 114 games.

Howard, Doug (1976) first baseman: 19-for-90, .211, in 39 games.

Howard, Ivon (1916–17) second baseman: 50-for-285, .175, in 108 games.

Howard, Thomas (1992–93) outfielder: 141-for-536, .263, in 191 games.

Howell, Dixie (1940) pitcher: 0–0 with 1.80 ERA in 3 games.

Howell, Red (1941) pinch hitter: 2-for-7, .286, in 11 games.

Howser, Dick (1963–66) shortstop–second baseman: 307-for-1,246, .246, in 385 games.

Hudlin, Willis (1926–40) pitcher: 157–151 with 4.34 ERA in 475 games.

Huff, Mike (1991) outfielder: 35-for-146, .240, in 51 games.

Hughes, Roy (1935–37) second baseman–third baseman–shortstop: 362-for-1,250, .290, in 338 games.

Huismann, Mark (1987) pitcher: 2–3 with 5.09 ERA in 20 games.

Humphries, John (1938–40) pitcher: 11–14 with 6.37 ERA in 79 games.

Hunnefield, Bill (1931) shortstop: 17-for-71, .239, in 21 games.

Hunter, Bill (1912) outfielder: 9-for-55, .164, in 21 games.

Hunter, Billy (1958) shortstop: 37-for-190, .195, in 76 games.

I

Iott, Happy (1903) outfielder: 2-for-10, .200, in 3 games.

Irwin, Tommy (1938) shortstop: 1-for-9, .111, in 3 games.

Tony Horton

J

Jablonowski, Pete (1930–32) pitcher: 12–11 with 4.56 ERA in 72 games.

Jackson, Jim (1905–06) outfielder: 189-for-800, .236, in 214 games.

Jackson, Joe (1910–15) outfielder: 937-for-2,502, .375, in 674 games.

Jackson, Mike (1973) pitcher: 0–0 with 0.00 ERA in 1 game.

Jackson, Randy (1958–59) third baseman: 23-for-98, .235, in 32 games.

Jacobson, Baby Doll (1927) outfielder: 26-for-103, .252, in 32 games.

Jacoby, Brook (1984–91, 92) third baseman–first baseman: 1,180-for-4,332, .272, in 1,255 games.

James, Bill (1911–12) pitcher: 2–4 with 4.82 ERA in 11 games.

James, Chris (1990–91) designated hitter–outfielder–first baseman: 262-for-965, .272, in 255 games.

James, Dion (1989–90) outfielder–first baseman–designated hitter: 143-for-493, .290, in 158 games.

James, Lefty (1912–14) pitcher: 2–6 with 3.39 ERA in 31 games.

Jamieson, Charlie (1919–32) outfielder: 1,753-for-5,551, .316, in 1,483 games.

Jasper, Hi (1919) pitcher: 4–5 with 3.59 ERA in 12 games.

Jeanes, Tex (1921–22) outfielder: 2-for-4, .500, in 6 games.

Jeffcoat, Mike (1983–85) pitcher: 6–5 with 3.06 ERA in 83 games.

Jefferson, Reggie (1991–93) designated hitter–first baseman: 141-for-556, .254, in 163 games.

Jefferson, Stan (1990) outfielder: 27-for-98, .276, in 49 games.

Jessee, Dan (1929) pinch runner: 0-for-0, —, in 1 game.

Jeter, John (1974) outfielder: 6-for-17, .353, in 6 games.

Jimenez, Houston (1988) second baseman: 1-for-21, .048, in 9 games.

John, Tommy (1963–64) pitcher: 2–11 with 3.61 ERA in 31 games.

Johnson, Alex (1972) outfielder: 85-for-356, .239, in 108 games.

Johnson, Bob (1974) pitcher: 3–4 wtih 4.38 ERA in 14 games.

Johnson, Cliff (1979–80) designated hitter: 105-for-414, .254, in 126 games.

Johnson, Jerry (1973) pitcher: 5–6 with 6.18 ERA in 39 games.

Johnson, Larry (1972, 74) catcher: 1-for-2, .500, in 2 games.

Johnson, Lou (1968) outfielder: 52-for-202, .257, in 65 games.

Johnson, Vic (1946) pitcher: 0–1 with 9.22 ERA in 9 games.

Alex Johnson

Johnston, Doc (1912–14, 18–21) first baseman: 697-for-2,557, .273, in 720 games.

Jones, Doug (1986–91) pitcher: 26–32 with 3.04 ERA in 272 games.

Jones, Hal (1961–62) first baseman: 11-for-51, .216, in 17 games.

Jones, Sad Sam (1914–15) pitcher: 4–9 with 3.62 ERA in 49 games.

Jones, Sam (1951–52) pitcher: 2–4 with 6.04 ERA in 16 games.

Jones, Willie (1959) third baseman: 4-for-18, .222, in 11 games.

Jordan, Scott (1988) outfielder: 1-for-9, .111, in 7 games.

Jordan, Tom (1946) catcher: 7-for-35, .200, in 14 games.

Joss, Addie (1902–10) pitcher: 160–97 with 1.89 ERA in 286 games.

Judnich, Walt (1948) outfielder–first baseman: 56-for-218, .257, in 79 games.

Jungels, Ken (1937–38, 40–41) pitcher: 1–0 with 6.88 ERA in 19 games.

K

Kahdot, Ike (1922) third baseman: 0-for-2, .000, in 4 games.

Kahl, Nick (1905) second baseman: 29-for-135, .215, in 40 games.

Kahler, George (1910–14) pitcher: 32–43 with 3.17 in 109 games.

Kaiser, Bob (1971) pitcher: 0–0 with 4.50 ERA in 5 games.

Kaiser, Jeff (1987–90) pitcher: 0–1 with 5.64 ERA in 16 games.

Kamm, Willie (1931–35) third baseman: 507-for-1,785, .284, in 522 games.

Kardow, Paul (1936) pitcher: 0–0 with 4.50 ERA in 2 games.

Karr, Benn (1925–27) pitcher: 19–21 with 4.90 ERA in 84 games.

Kavanagh, Marty (1916–18) first baseman: 19-for-96, .188, in 46 games.

Willie Kamm

Keedy, Pat (1989) outfielder: 3-for-14, .214, in 9 games.

Keefe, Dave (1922) pitcher: 0–0 with 6.19 ERA in 18 games.

Kekich, Mike (1973) pitcher: 1–4 with 7.02 ERA in 16 games.

Kelley, Tom (1964–67) pitcher: 6–9 with 3.97 ERA in 42 games.

Kelly, Bob (1958) pitcher: 0–2 with 5.20 ERA in 13 games.

Kelly, Pat (1981) designated hitter: 16-for-75, .213, in 48 games.

Keltner, Ken (1937–44, 46–49) third baseman: 1,561-for-5,655, .276, in 1,513 games.

Kendall, Fred (1977) catcher: 79-for-317, .249, in 103 games.

Kennedy, Bill (1948) pitcher: 1–0 with 11.12 ERA in 6 games.

Kennedy, Bob (1948–54) outfielder–third baseman: 425-for-1,559, .273, in 564 games.

Kennedy, Vern (1942–44) pitcher: 16–20 with 3.50 ERA in 68 games.

Kenney, Jerry (1973) second baseman: 4-for-16, .250, in 5 games.

Ken Keltner

Jim Kern

Keough, Marty (1960) outfielder: 37-for-149, .248, in 65 games.

Kern, Jim (1974–78, 86) pitcher: 30–31 with 3.44 ERA in 201 games.

Kibble, Jack (1912) third baseman: 0-for-8, .000, in 5 games.

Kilkenny, Mike (1972–73) pitcher: 4–1 with 4.05 ERA in 27 games.

Killian, Ed (1903) pitcher: 3–4 with 2.48 ERA in 9 games.

Kindall, Jerry (1962–64) second baseman–shortstop: 180-for-789, .228, in 263 games.

Kiner, Ralph (1955) outfielder: 78-for-321, .243, in 113 games.

King, Eric (1991) pitcher: 6–11 with 4.60 ERA in 25 games.

Ralph Kiner

King, Jim (1967) outfielder: 3-for-21, .143, in 19 games.

Kinney, Dennis (1978) pitcher: 0–2 with 4.42 ERA in 18 games.

Kirby, Wayne (1991–95) outfielder–designated hitter: 230-for-898, .256, in 352 games.

Kirke, Jay (1914–15) first baseman–outfielder: 171-for-581, .294, in 154 games.

Kirkland, Willie (1961–63) outfielder: 318-for-1,371, .232, in 410 games.

Kirsch, Harry (1910) pitcher: 0–0 with 6.00 ERA in 2 games.

Kiser, Garland (1991) pitcher: 0–0 with 9.64 ERA in 7 games.

Kittle, Ron (1988) designated hitter: 58-for-225, .258, in 75 games.

Kittridge, Malachi (1906) catcher: 1-for-10, .100, in 5 games.

Klein, Lou (1951) pinch hitter: 0-for-2, .000, in 2 games.

Kleine, Hal (1944–45) pitcher: 1–2 with 5.48 ERA in 14 games.

Klepfer, Ed (1915–17, 19) pitcher: 21–16 with 2.48 ERA in 85 games.

Klieman, Ed (1943–48) pitcher: 24–28 with 3.36 ERA in 197 games.

Klimchock, Lou (1968–70) third baseman–second baseman: 85-for-329, .258, in 142 games.

Kline, Steve (1974) pitcher: 3–8 with 5.07 ERA in 16 games.

Klippstein, Johnny (1960) pitcher: 5–5 with 2.19 ERA in 49 games.

Klugmann, Joe (1925) second baseman: 28-for-85, .329, in 38 games.

Knaupp, Cotton (1910–11) shortstop: 18-for-98, .184, in 31 games.

Knickerbocker, Bill (1933–36) shortstop: 594-for-2,030, .293, in 513 games.

Knode, Ray (1923–26) first baseman: 55-for-297, .266, in 109 games.

Koestner, Elmer (1910) pitcher: 5–10 with 3.04 ERA in 27 games.

Komminsk, Brad (1989) outfielder: 47-for-198, .237, in 71 games.

Kopf, Larry (1913) second baseman: 3-for-10, .300, in 6 games (played under name of Fred Brady).

Krakauskas, Joe (1941–42, 46) pitcher: 3–7 with 4.78 ERA in 44 games.

Kralick, Jack (1963–67) pitcher: 33–33 with 3.47 ERA in 117 games.

Kramer, Tom (1991, 93) pitcher: 7–3 with 4.51 ERA in 43 games.

Krapp, Gene (1911–12) pitcher: 15–14 with 3.66 ERA in 44 games.

Krause, Harry (1912) pitcher: 0–1 with 11.57 ERA in 2 games.

Kreuger, Rick (1978) pitcher: 0–0 with 3.86 ERA in 6 games.

Kroll, Gary (1969) pitcher: 0–0 with 4.13 ERA in 19 games.

Kroner, John (1937–38) second baseman–third baseman: 96-for-400, .240, in 137 games.

Krueger, Ernie (1913) catcher: 0-for-6, .000, in 5 games.

Kruger, Art (1910) outfielder: 38-for-223, .170, in 62 games.

Kubiszyn, Jack (1961–62) shortstop: 19-for-101, .188, in 50 games.

Kuenn, Harvey (1960) outfielder: 146-for-474, .308, in 126 games.

Kuhn, Bub (1924) pitcher: 0–1 with 27.00 ERA in 1 game.

Kuhn, Kenny (1955–57) shortstop–second baseman: 17-for-81, .210, in 71 games.

Kuiper, Duane (1974–81) second baseman: 786-for-2,865, .274, in 786 games.

Kurtz, Hal (1968) pitcher: 1–0 with 5.21 ERA in 28 games.

Kuzava, Bob (1946–47) pitcher: 2–1 wtih 3.74 ERA in 6 games.

L

Lacy, Bob (1981) pitcher: 0–0 with 7.59 ERA in 14 games.

LaChance, Candy (1901) first baseman: 166-for-548, .303, in 133 games.

Lacy, Guy (1926) second baseman: 4-for-24, .167, in 13 games.

Lajoie, Nap (1902–14) second baseman–first baseman–shortstop–third baseman: 2,046-for-6,034, .339, in 1,614 games.

Lamb, Ray (1971–73) pitcher: 14–21 with 3.58 ERA in 109 games.

Lambeth, Otis (1916–18) pitcher: 11–9 with 3.18 ERA in 43 games.

Lampkin, Tom (1988) catcher: 0-for-4, .000, in 4 games.

Land, Grover (1908–11, 13) catcher: 54-for-285, .189, in 95 games.

Landis, Jim (1966) outfielder: 35-for-158, .222, in 85 games.

Langford, Sam (1927–28) outfielder: 136-for-494, .275, in 130 games.

LaRoche, Dave (1975–77) pitcher: 8–9 with 2.51 ERA in 135 games.

Lary, Lyn (1937–39) shortstop: 339-for-1,214, .279, in 300 games.

Lasher, Fred (1970) pitcher: 1–7 with 4.06 ERA in 43 games.

Laskey, Bill (1988) pitcher: 1–0 with 5.18 ERA in 17 games.

Latman, Barry (1960–63) pitcher: 35–37 with 4.27 ERA in 159 games.

Lattimore, Bill (1908) pitcher: 1–2 with 4.50 ERA in 4 games.

Willie Kirkland

Jack Kralick

Napoleon Lajoie

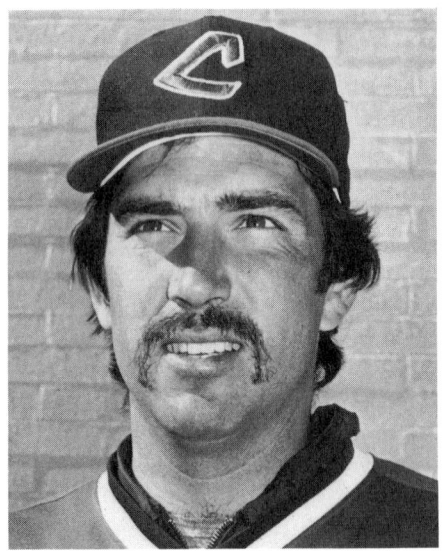

Dave LaRoche

Law, Ron (1969) pitcher: 3–4 with 4.99 ERA in 35 games.

Lawrence, Jim (1963) catcher: 0-for-0, —, in 2 games.

Lawson, Roxie (1930–31) pitcher: 1–4 with 7.05 ERA in 24 games.

Laxton, Bill (1977) pitcher: 0–0 with 5.40 ERA in 2 games.

Leber, Emil (1905) third baseman: 0-for-6, .000, in 2 games.

Lee, Cliff (1925–26) outfielder: 81-for-270, .300, in 98 games.

Lee, Leron (1974–75) outfielder: 57-for-255, .224, in 92 games.

Lee, Mike (1960) pitcher: 0–0 with 2.00 ERA in 7 games.

Lee, Thornton (1933–36) pitcher: 12–17 with 4.51 ERA in 102 games.

Leek, Gene (1959) third baseman: 8-for-36, .222, in 13 games.

Barry Latman

Lehner, Paul (1951) outfielder: 3-for-13, .231, in 12 games.

Lehr, Norm (1926) pitcher: 0–0 with 3.07 ERA in 4 games.

Leibold, Nemo (1913–15) outfielder: 233-for-895, .260, in 265 games.

Leitner, Dummy (1902) pitcher: 0–0 with 4.50 ERA in 1 game.

Lelivelt, Jack (1913–14) outfielder: 30-for-87, .345, in 57 games.

LeMaster, Johnnie (1985) shortstop: 3-for-20, .150, in 11 games.

Lemon, Bob (1941–42, 46–58) pitcher–outfielder: 207–128 with 3.23 ERA in 460 games.

Lemon, Jim (1950, 53) outfielder: 14-for-80, .175, in 28 games.

Leon, Eddie (1968–72) second baseman–shortstop: 344-for-1,417, .243, in 442 games.

Leonard, Joe (1916) second baseman: 0-for-2, .000, in 3 games.

Levis, Jesse (1992–95) catcher: 30-for-125, .240, in 72 games.

Levsen, Dutch (1923–28) pitcher: 21–26 with 4.17 ERA in 80 games.

Lewallyn, Dennis (1981–82) pitcher: 0–1 with 6.08 ERA in 11 games.

Lewis, Mark (1991–94) shortstop–second baseman: 220-for-852, .258, in 240 games.

Liebhardt, Glenn (1906–09) pitcher: 36–35 with 2.17 ERA in 90 games.

Lilliquist, Derek (1992–94) pitcher: 10–10 with 2.55 ERA in 163 games.

Lind, Carl (1927–30) second baseman–shortstop: 267-for-981, .272, in 256 games.

Linde, Lymie (1947–48) pitcher: 0–0 with 6.75 ERA in 4 games.

Lindsay, Bill (1911) third baseman: 16-for-66, .242, in 19 games.

Bob Lemon

Eddie Leon

Lindsey, Jim (1922, 24) pitcher: 4–5 wtih 6.54 ERA in 32 games.

Link, Fred (1910) pitcher: 5–6 with 3.17 ERA in 22 games.

Lintz, Larry (1978) pinch runner: 0-for-0, —, in 3 games.

Lipski, Bob (1963) catcher: 0-for-1, .000, in 2 games.

Lis, Joe (1974–76) first baseman: 42-for-173, .243, in 86 games.

Lister, Pete (1907) first baseman: 18-for-65, .277, in 22 games.

Littleton, Larry (1981) outfielder: 0-for-23, .000, in 26 games.

Livingston, Paddy (1901, 12) catcher: 11-for-49, .224, in 21 games.

Locke, Bobby (1959–61) pitcher: 10–11 with 3.68 ERA in 93 games.

Locklin, Stu (1955–56) outfielder: 4-for-24, .167, in 25 games.

Lofton, Kenny (1992–95) outfielder: 658-for-2,085, .316, in 526 games.

Lohr, Howard (1916) outfielder: 1-for-7, .143, in 3 games.

Lolich, Ron (1972–73) outfielder-designated hitter: 47-for-220, .214, in 85 games.

Lollar, Sherm (1946) catcher: 15-for-62, .242, in 28 games.

Lopez, Al (1947) catcher: 33-for-126, .262 in 61 games.

Lopez, Albie (1993–95) pitcher: 4–3 with 4.92 ERA in 19 games.

Lopez, Luis (1991) catcher–first baseman: 18-for-82, .220, in 35 games.

Lopez, Marcelino (1972) pitcher: 0–0 with 5.40 ERA in 4 games.

Lord, Bris (1909–10) outfielder: 113-for-459, .246, in 127 games.

Lowdermilk, Grover (1916) pitcher: 1–5 with 3.16 ERA in 10 games.

Lowenstein, John (1970–77) outfielder–designated hitter–second baseman–third baseman–first base-

John Lowenstein

Hank Majeski

Roger Maris

man: 428-for-1,790, .239, in 646 games.

Lund, Gordon (1967) shortstop: 2-for-8, .250, in 3 games.

Lundbom, Jack (1902) pitcher: 1–1 with 6.62 ERA in 8 games.

Lunte, Harry (1919–20) shortstop: 29-for-148, .196, in 49 games.

Luplow, Al (1961–65) outfielder: 166-for-694, .239, in 274 games.

Lush, Billy (1904) outfielder: 123-for-477, .258, in 138 games.

Lutzke, Rube (1923–27) third baseman–second baseman: 468-for-1,876, .249, in 572 games.

Lyon, Russ (1944) catcher: 2-for-11, .182, in 7 games.

M

Machemehl, Chuck (1971) pitcher: 0–2 with 6.38 ERA in 14 games.

Mack, Ray (1938–44, 46) second baseman: 612-for-2,629, .233, in 739 games.

Mackiewicz, Felix (1945–47) outfielder: 165-for-622, .265, in 200 games.

Maddern, Clarence (1951) outfielder: 2-for-12, .167, in 11 games.

Magallanes, Ever (1991) shortstop: 0-for-2, .000, in 3 games.

Maglie, Sal (1955–56) pitcher: 0–2 with 3.81 ERA in 12 games.

Magrann, Tom (1989) catcher: 0-for-10, .000, in 9 games.

Mahoney, Jim (1962) shortstop: 18-for-74, .243, in 41 games.

Mails, Walter (1920–22) pitcher: 25–15 with 3.96 ERA in 69 games.

Majeski, Hank (1952–55) second baseman–third baseman: 74-for-273, .266, in 179 games.

Maldonado, Candy (1990, 93–94) outfielder–designated hitter: 199-for-763, .261, in 225 games.

Manning, Rick (1975–83) outfielder: 1,053-for-3,997, .263, in 1,063 games.

Manto, Jeff (1990–91) first baseman–third baseman: 44-for-204, .216, in 77 games.

Maris, Roger (1957–58) outfielder: 125-for-540, .231, in 167 games.

Marsh, Freddie (1949) pinch runner: 0-for-0, —, in 1 game.

Martin, Billy (1959) second baseman: 63-for-242, .260, in 73 games.

Martin, Morrie (1958) pitcher: 2–0 with 2.41 ERA in 14 games.

Martinez, Carlos (1991–93) first baseman–designated hitter–third baseman: 197-for-747, .264, in 221 games.

Martinez, Dennis (1994–94) pitcher: 23–11 with 3.29 ERA in 52 games.

Martinez, Tony (1963–66) shortstop: 30-for-175, .171, in 73 games.

Mathias, Carl (1960) pitcher: 0–1 with 3.52 ERA in 7 games.

Maye, Lee (1967–69) outfielder: 188-for-704, .267, in 267 games.

McAleer, Jimmy (1901) outfielder: 1-for-7, .143, in 3 games.

McBride, Bake (1982–83) outfielder–designated hitter: 98-for-315, .311, in 97 games.

McCabe, Ralph (1946) pitcher: 0–1 with 11.25 ERA in 1 game.

McCarthy, Jack (1901–03) outfielder: 322-for-1,117, .288, in 289 games.

McCosky, Barney (1951–53) outfielder: 34-for-162, .210, in 107 games.

McCraw, Tom (1972, 74–75) first baseman–outfielder: 149-for-554, .269, in 197 games.

McCrea, Frank (1925) catcher: 1-for-5, .200, in 1 game.

McDonnell, Jim (1943–45) catcher: 20-for-95, .211, in 50 games.

Rick Manning

Billy Martin

Tom McCraw

McDowell, Oddibe (1989) outfielder: 53-for-239, .222, in 69 games.

McDowell, Sam (1961–71) pitcher: 122–109 with 2.99 ERA in 336 games.

McGuire, Deacon (1908, 10) catcher: 2-for-7, .286, in 2 games.

McGuire, Jim (1901) shortstop: 16-for-69, .232, in 18 games.

McHale, Marty (1916) pitcher: 0–0 with 5.56 ERA in 5 games.

McInnis, Stuffy (1922) first baseman: 164-for-537, .305, in 142 games.

McKain, Hal (1927) pitcher: 0–1 with 4.09 ERA in 2 games.

McLemore, Mark (1990) third baseman: 2-for-12, .167, in 8 games.

McLish, Cal (1956–59) pitcher: 46–27 with 3.35 ERA in 153 games.

McMahon, Don (1964–66) pitcher: 10–8 with 2.81 ERA in 140 games.

"Sudden Sam" McDowell

Don McMahon

McNeal, Harry (1901) pitcher: 5–5 with 4.43 ERA in 12 games.

McNulty, Pat (1922, 24–27) outfielder: 238-for-820, .290, in 308 games.

McQuillan, George (1918) pitcher: 0–1 with 2.35 ERA in 5 games.

Medina, Luis (1988–89, 91) designated hitter–first baseman: 31-for-150, .207, in 51 games.

Meixell, Moxie (1912) outfielder: 1-for-2, .500, in 3 games.

Mele, Sam (1956) outfielder: 29-for-114, .254, in 57 games.

Melton, Bill (1977) first baseman–designated hitter–third baseman: 32-for-133, .241, in 50 games.

Merullo, Matt (1994) catcher: 1-for-10, .100, in 4 games.

Mesa, Jose (1992–95) pitcher: 24–21 with 4.02 ERA in 162 games.

Messenger, Bud (1924) pitcher: 2–0 with 4.32 ERA in 5 games.

Metivier, Dewey (1922–24) pitcher: 7–7 with 5.74 ERA in 54 games.

Metkovich, Catfish (1947) outfielder: 120-for-473, .254, in 126 games.

Meyer, Dutch (1945–46) second baseman: 201-for-731, .275, in 202 games.

Middleton, John (1922) pitcher: 0–1 with 7.36 ERA in 2 games.

Milacki, Bob (1993) pitcher: 1–1 with 3.38 ERA in 5 games.

Milbourne, Larry (1982) second baseman–shortstop: 80-for-291, .275, in 82 games.

Miljus, Johnny (1928–29) pitcher: 9–12 with 4.47 ERA in 45 games.

Miller, Bob (1970) pitcher: 2–2 with 4.18 ERA in 15 games.

Miller, Ed (1918) first baseman: 22-for-96, .229, in 32 games.

Al Milnar

Miller, Jake (1924–31) pitcher: 55–52 with 3.92 ERA in 174 games.

Miller, Ray (1917) first baseman: 4-for-21, .190, in 19 games.

Milligan, Randy (1993) first baseman: 20-for-47, .426, in 19 games.

Mills, Buster (1942, 46) outfielder: 60-for-217, .276, in 89 games.

Mills, Frank (1914) catcher: 1-for-8, .125, in 4 games.

Mills, Jack (1911) third baseman: 5-for-17, .294, in 13 games.

Milnar, Al (1936, 38–43) pitcher: 55–55 with 4.19 ERA in 180 games.

Mingori, Steve (1970–73) pitcher: 2–8 with 2.97 ERA in 121 games.

Minoso, Minnie (1949, 51, 58–59) outfielder: 349-for-1,156, .302, in 314 games.

Mitchell, Dale (1946–56) outfielder: 1,237-for-3,960, .312, in 1,108 games.

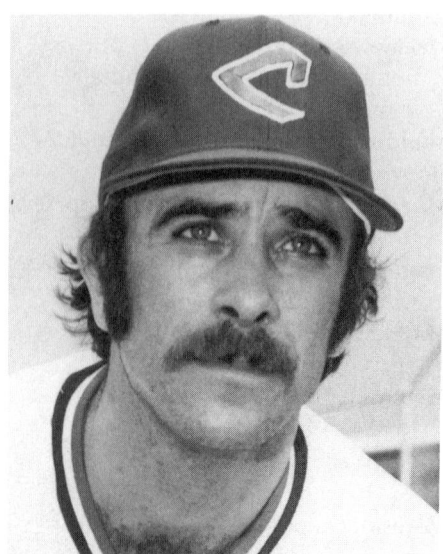

Steve Mingori

Minnie Minoso

Mitchell, Willie (1909–16) pitcher: 64–76 with 2.89 ERA in 219 games.

Mlicki, Dave (1992–93) pitcher: 0–2 with 4.37 ERA in 7 games.

Moeller, Danny (1916) outfielder: 2-for-30, .067, in 25 games.

Monaco, Blas (1937, 46) second baseman: 2-for-13, .154, in 17 games.

Monge, Sid (1977–81) pitcher: 23–25 with 3.38 ERA in 255 games.

Montague, Ed (1928, 30–32) shortstop–third baseman: 161-for-615, .262, in 220 games.

Moon, Leo (1932) pitcher: 0–0 with 11.12 ERA in 1 game.

Moore, Barry (1970) pitcher: 3–5 with 4.22 ERA in 13 games.

Moore, Earl (1901–07) pitcher: 81–68 with 2.58 ERA in 161 games.

Moore, Eddie (1934) second baseman: 10-for-65, .154, in 27 games.

Moore, Jim (1928–29) pitcher: 0–1 with 4.91 ERA in 3 games.

Mora, Andres (1980) outfielder: 2-for-18, .111, in 9 games.

Moran, Billy (1958–59, 64–65) second baseman–shortstop–third baseman: 97-for-449, .216, in 217 games.

Morgan, Eddie (1928–33) first baseman–outfielder–third baseman: 738-for-2,282, .323, in 633 games.

Morgan, Joe (1960–61) third baseman: 16-for-57, .281, in 26 games.

Moronko, Jeff (1984) third baseman: 3-for-19, .158, in 7 games.

Morris, Jack (1994) pitcher: 10–6 with 5.60 ERA in 23 games.

Morton, Guy (1914–24) pitcher: 98–88 with 3.13 ERA in 317 games.

Moses, Gerry (1972) catcher: 31-for-141, .220, in 52 games.

Moss, Howie (1946) third baseman: 2-for-32, .063, in 8 games.

Mossi, Don (1954–58) pitcher: 34–27 with 3.34 ERA in 224 games.

Mullins, Fran (1986) second baseman–shortstop: 7-for-40, .175, in 28 games.

Muncrief, Bob (1948) pitcher: 5–4 with 3.98 ERA in 21 games.

Murchison, Tim (1920) pitcher: 0–0 with 0.00 ERA in 2 games.

Murray, Eddie (1994–95) first baseman–designated hitter: 251-for-869, .289, in 221 games.

Murray, Ray (1948, 50–51) catcher: 39-for-140, .279, in 60 games.

Mutis, Jeff (1991–93) pitcher: 3–11 with 6.88 ERA in 23 games.

Myatt, Glenn (1923–35) catcher: 638-for-2,317, .275, in 850 games.

Myers, Elmer (1919–20) pitcher: 10–11 with 4.10 ERA in 39 games.

N

Nabholz, Chris (1994) pitcher: 0–1 with 11.45 ERA in 6 games.

Nagelsen, Lou (1912) catcher: 0-for-3, .000, in 2 games.

Nagelson, Russ (1968–70) outfielder: 10-for-44, .227, in 34 games.

Nagy, Charles (1990–95) pitcher: 57–49 with 3.97 ERA in 136 games.

Nahorodny, Bill (1982) catcher: 21-for-94, .223, in 39 games.

Naragon, Hal (1951, 54–59) catcher: 146-for-524, .279, in 239 games.

Narleski, Ray (1954–58) pitcher: 39–21 with 3.22 ERA in 224 games.

Nash, Ken (1912) shortstop: 4-for-23, .174, in 11 games (played one game under name of Costello).

Naymick, Mike (1939–40, 43–44) pitcher: 5–7 with 3.92 ERA in 51 games.

Neeman, Cal (1963) catcher: 0-for-9, .000, in 9 games.

Neher, Jim (1912) pitcher: 0–0 with 0.00 ERA in 1 game.

Neis, Bernie (1927) outfielder: 29-for-96, .302, in 32 games.

Nelson, Dave (1968–69) second baseman–shortstop: 69-for-312, .221, in 140 games.

Nelson, Rocky (1954) first baseman: 0-for-4, .000, in 4 games.

Nettles, Graig (1970–72) third baseman: 426-for-1,704, .250, in 465 games.

Netzel, Milo (1909) third baseman: 7-for-37, .189, in 10 games.

Newcombe, Don (1960) pitcher: 2–3 with 4.33 ERA in 20 games.

Newhouser, Hal (1954–55) pitcher: 7–2 with 2.39 ERA in 28 games.

Nicholls, Simon (1910) shortstop: 0-for-0, —, in 3 games.

Dale Mitchell

Don Mossi

Hal Naragon

Ray Narleski

Nichols, Rod (1988–92) pitcher: 11–30 with 4.39 ERA in 91 games.

Niehaus, Dick (1920) pitcher: 1–2 with 3.60 ERA in 19 games.

Niekro, Phil (1986–87) pitcher: 18–22 with 4.90 ERA in 56 games.

Nielsen, Milt (1949–51) outfielder: 1-for-15, .067, in 19 games.

Nieman, Bob (1961–62) outfielder: 23-for-66, .348, in 41 games.

Niles, Harry (1910) outfielder: 51-for-240, .213, in 70 games.

Nill, Rabbit (1907–08) shortstop: 17-for-66, .258, in 23 games.

Nipper, Al (1990) pitcher: 2–3 with 6.75 ERA in 9 games.

Nischwitz, Ron (1963) pitcher: 0–2 with 6.48 ERA in 14 games.

Nixon, Otis (1984–87) outfielder–designated hitter: 78-for-365, .214, in 277 games.

Nixon, Russ (1957–60) catcher: 247-for-901, .274, in 282 games.

Noboa, Junior (1984, 87) second baseman: 22-for-91, .242, in 62 games.

Noles, Dickie (1986) pitcher: 3–2 with 5.10 ERA in 32 games.

Norris, Jim (1977–79) outfielder–designated hitter: 295-for-1,108, .266, in 370 games.

Nunamaker, Les (1919–22) catcher: 92-for-284, .324, in 131 games.

O

O'Brien, Jack (1901) outfielder: 106-for-375, .283, in 92 games.

O'Brien, Pete (1907) second baseman–third baseman–shortstop: 33-for-145, .228, in 43 games.

O'Brien, Pete (1989) first baseman: 144-for 554, .260, in 155 games.

O'Dea, Paul (1944–45) outfielder: 107-for-394, .272, in 163 games.

Odenwald, Ted (1921–22) pitcher: 1–0 with 4.34 ERA in 11 games.

Odom, Blue Moon (1975) pitcher: 1–0 with 2.61 ERA in 3 games.

O'Donoghue, John (1966–67) pitcher: 14–17 with 3.51 ERA in 65 games.

Oelkers, Bryan (1986) pitcher: 3–3 with 4.70 ERA in 35 games.

Ogea, Chad (1994–95) pitcher: 8–4 with 3.45 ERA in 24 games.

O'Hagen, Hal (1902) first baseman: 5-for-13, .385, in 3 games.

Ojeda, Bob (1993) pitcher: 2–1 with 4.40 ERA in 9 games.

Olin, Steve (1989–92) pitcher: 16–19 with 3.10 ERA in 195 games.

Oliver, Dave (1977) second baseman: 7-for-22, .318, in 7 games.

Olson, Ivy (1911–14) shortstop–third baseman–second baseman–first baseman: 427-for-1,692, .252, in 458 games.

O'Neill, Steve (1911–23) catcher: 1,109-for-4,182, .265, in 1,365 games.

Onslow, Eddie (1918) outfielder: 1-for-6, .167, in 2 games.

Orosco, Jesse (1989–91) pitcher: 10–8 with 3.11 ERA in 171 games.

Orta, Jorge (1980–81) outfielder: 232-for-819, .283, in 217 games.

Ortiz, Junior (1992–93) catcher: 116-for-493, .235, in 181 games.

Ostdiek, Harry (1904) catcher: 3-for-18, .167, in 7 games.

Otis, Harry (1909) pitcher: 2–2 with 1.37 ERA in 5 games.

Otto, Dave (1991–92) pitcher: 7–17 with 5.49 ERA in 36 games.

Oulliber, Johnny (1933) outfielder: 20-for-75, .267, in 22 games.

Owchinko, Bob (1980) pitcher: 2–9 with 5.27 ERA in 29 games.

Steve O'Neill

P

Padgett, Ernie (1926–27) third baseman: 15-for-69, .217, in 43 games.

Pagel, Karl (1981–83) first baseman: 13-for-53, .245, in 45 games.

Paige, Pat (1911) pitcher: 1–0 with 4.50 ERA in 2 games.

Paige, Satchel (1948–49) pitcher: 10–8 with 2.78 ERA in 52 games.

Palmer, Lowell (1972) pitcher: 0–0 with 4.50 ERA in 1 game.

Papish, Frank (1949) pitcher: 1–0 with 3.19 ERA in 25 games.

Parker, Harry (1976) pitcher: 0–0 with 0.00 in 3 games.

Parrish, Lance (1993) catcher: 4-for-20, .200, in 10 games.

Parsons, Casey (1987) designated hitter: 4-for-25, .160, in 18 games.

Paschal, Ben (1915) pinch hitter: 1-for-9, .111, in 9 games.

Pascual, Camilo (1971) pitcher: 2–2 with 3.09 ERA in 9 games.

Paul, Mike (1968–71) pitcher: 14–33 with 4.39 ERA in 130 games.

Steve Olin

Jesse Orosco

Satchel Paige

Roger Peckinpaugh

Jim Perry

Pawloski, Stan (1955) second baseman: 1-for-8, .125, in 2 games.

Paxton, Mike (1978–80) pitcher: 20–19 with 4.97 ERA in 70 games.

Pearson, Alex (1903) pitcher: 1–2 with 3.56 ERA in 4 games.

Pearson, Monte (1932–35) pitcher: 36–31 with 4.21 ERA in 96 games.

Peck, Hal (1947–49) outfielder: 142-for 484, .293, in 192 games.

Peckinpaugh, Roger (1910, 12–13) shortstop: 59-for-281, .210, in 86 games.

Pena, Orlando (1967) pitcher: 0–3 with 3.36 ERA in 48 games.

Pena, Tony (1994–95) catcher: 102-for-375, .272, in 131 games.

Penner, Ken (1916) pitcher: 1–0 with 4.26 ERA in 4 games.

Perconte, Jack (1982–83) second baseman: 59-for-245, .241, in 107 games.

Perezchica, Tony (1991–92) third baseman–shortstop: 10-for-42, .238, in 35 games.

Perkins, Broderick (1983–84) designated hitter–first baseman–outfielder: 63-for-250, .252, in 137 games.

Perlman, Jon (1988) pitcher: 0–2 with 5.49 ERA in 10 games.

Perrin, Bill (1934) pitcher: 0–1 with 14.40 ERA in 1 game.

Perring, George (1908–10) third baseman–shortstop: 157-for-715, .220, in 216 games.

Perry, Gaylord (1972–75) pitcher: 70–57 with 2.71 ERA in 134 games.

Perry, Herb (1994–95) first baseman–designated hitter: 52-for-171, .304, in 56 games.

Perry, Jim (1959–63, 74–75) pitcher: 70–67 with 3.76 in 204 games.

Peters, John (1918) catcher: 0-for-1, .000, in 1 game.

Peters, Rusty (1940–44, 46) second baseman–shortstop–third baseman: 159-for-710, .224, in 269 games.

Peterson, Cap (1969) outfielder: 25-for-110, .227, in 76 games.

Peterson, Fritz (1974–76) pitcher: 23–25 with 4.34 ERA in 63 games.

Petty, Jesse (1921) pitcher: 0–0 with 2.00 ERA in 4 games.

Pezold, Larry (1914) third baseman: 16-for-71, .225, in 23 games.

Phelps, Ken (1990) first baseman: 7-for-61, .115, in 24 games.

Philley, Dave (1954–55) outfielder: 133-for-556, .239, in 176 games.

Phillips, Adolfo (1972) outfielder: 0-for-7, .000, in 12 games.

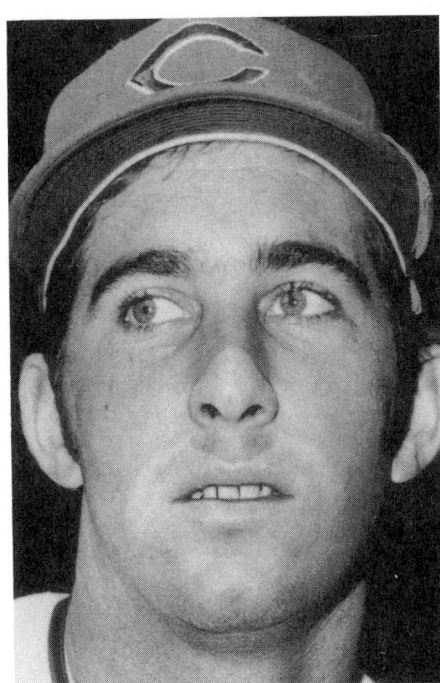

Mike Paul

Gaylord Perry

Fritz Peterson

Bubba Phillips

"Twitchy Dick" Porter

Vic Power

Phillips, Bubba (1960–62) third base-man–outfielder: 352-for-1,412, .249, in 404 games.

Phillips, Eddie (1935) catcher: 60-for-220, .273, in 70 games.

Phillips, Tom (1919) pitcher: 3–2 with 2.95 ERA in 22 games.

Pickering, Ollie (1901–02) outfielder: 244-for-840, .290, in 206 games.

Pieretti, Marino (1950) pitcher: 0–1 with 4.18 ERA in 29 games.

Piersall, Jimmy (1959–61) outfielder: 371-for-1,287, .288, in 359 games.

Pina, Horacio (1968–69) pitcher: 5–3 with 3.81 ERA in 43 games.

Piniella, Lou (1968) outfielder: 0-for-5, .000, in 6 games.

Pinson, Vada (1970–71) outfielder–first baseman: 313-for-1,140, .275, in 294 games.

Pitula, Stan (1957) pitcher: 2–2 with 4.98 ERA in 23 games.

Pizarro, Juan (1969) pitcher: 3–3 with 3.16 ERA in 48 games.

Plunk, Eric (1992–95) pitcher: 26–15 with 2.92 ERA in 225 games.

Poat, Ray (1942–44) pitcher: 7–16 with 4.94 ERA in 57 games.

Podbielan, Bud (1959) pitcher: 0–1 with 5.84 ERA in 6 games.

Podgajny, Johnny (1946) pitcher: 0–0 with 5.00 ERA in 6 games.

Polchow, Lou (1902) pitcher: 0–1 with 5.63 ERA in 1 game.

Poole, Jim (1995) pitcher: 3–3 with 3.75 ERA in 42 games.

Pope, Dave (1952, 54–56) outfielder: 88-for-310, .284, in 132 games.

Porter, Dick (1929–34) outfielder–second baseman: 694-for-2,250, .308, in 595 games.

Porter, Jay (1958) catcher: 17-for-85, .200, in 40 games.

Post, Wally (1964) outfielder: 0-for-8, .000, in 5 games.

Pott, Nellie (1922) pitcher: 0–0 with 31.50 in 2 games.

Pounds, Bill (1903) pitcher: 0–0 with 10.80 ERA in 1 game.

Powell, Boog (1975–76) first baseman: 192-for-728, .263, in 229 games.

Power, Ted (1992–93) pitcher: 3–5 with 3.32 ERA in 84 games.

Power, Vic (1958–61) first baseman–second baseman–third baseman: 612-for-2,123, .288, in 534 games.

Powers, Johnny (1960) outfielder: 2-for-12, .167, in 8 games.

Powers, Mike (1932–33) outfielder: 19-for-80, .237, in 38 games.

Price, Jackie (1946) shortstop: 3-for-13, .231, in 7 games.

Pruitt, Ron (1976–81) outfielder–catcher–third baseman: 188-for-703, .267, in 288 games.

Pytlak, Frankie (1932–40) catcher: 582-for-2,032, .286, in 676 games.

Q

Quirk, Jamie (1984) catcher: 1-for-1, 1.000, in 1 game.

Jim Piersall

Boog Powell

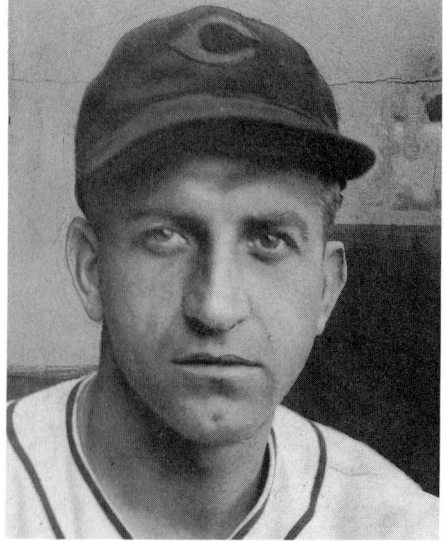

Frankie Pytlak

Dick Radatz

Pedro Ramos

Eddie Robinson

R

Rabbitt, Joe (1922) outfielder: 1-for-3, .333, in 2 games.

Radatz, Dick (1966–67) pitcher: 0–3 with 4.68 ERA in 42 games.

Raftery, Tom (1909) outfielder: 7-for-32, .219, in 8 games.

Ragland, Tom (1973) second baseman: 47-for-183, .257, in 67 games.

Raich, Eric (1975–76) pitcher: 7–8 with 5.85 ERA in 19 games.

Raines, Larry (1957–58) third baseman–shortstop–second baseman: 64-for-253, .253, in 103 games.

Ramirez, Manny (1993–95) outfielder: 236-for-827, .285, in 250 games.

Ramos, Domingo (1988) second baseman: 12-for-46, .261, in 22 games.

Ramos, Pedro (1962–64) pitcher: 26–30 with 3.87 ERA in 109 games.

Rath, Morrie (1910) third baseman: 13-for-67, .194, in 24 games.

Reed, Jerry (1982–83, 85) pitcher: 4–6 with 4.61 ERA in 46 games.

Regalado, Rudy (1954–56) third baseman: 63-for-253, .249, in 91 games.

Reich, Herm (1949) outfielder: 1-for-2, .500, in 1 game.

Reilley, Duke (1909) outfielder: 13-for-62, .210, in 20 games.

Reilly, Tom (1914) pinch hitter: 0-for-1, .000, in 1 game.

Reinholz, Art (1928) third baseman: 1-for-3, .333, in 2 games.

Reiser, Pete (1952) outfielder: 6-for-44, .136, in 34 games.

Reisigl, Bugs (1911) pitcher: 0–1 with 6.23 ERA in 2 games.

Reuschel, Paul (1978–79) pitcher: 4–5 with 4.73 ERA in 35 games.

Reynolds, Allie (1942–46) pitcher: 51–47 with 3.31 ERA in 139 games.

Reynolds, Bob (1975) pitcher: 0–2 with 4.66 ERA in 5 games.

Rhoads, Bob (1903–09) pitcher: 88–66 with 2.39 ERA in 185 games.

Rhomberg, Kevin (1982–84) outfielder: 18-for-47, .383, in 41 games.

Rice, Sam (1934) outfielder: 98-for-335, .293, in 97 games.

Riddleberger, Denny (1972) pitcher: 1–3 with 2.50 ERA in 38 games.

Ridzik, Steve (1958) pitcher: 0–2 with 2.08 ERA in 6 games.

Ripken, Billy (1995) second baseman: 7-for-17, .412, in 8 games.

Ritter, Reggie (1986–87) pitcher: 1–1 with 6.14 ERA in 19 games.

Rittwage, Jim (1970) pitcher: 1–1 with 4.15 ERA in 8 games.

Roa, Joe (1995) pitcher: 0–1 with 6.00 ERA in 1 game.

Robinson, Eddie (1942, 46–48, 57) first baseman: 222-for-876, .253, in 264 games.

Robinson, Frank (1974–76) designated hitter: 53-for-235, .226, in 100 games.

Eric Raich

Allie Reynolds

Frank Robinson

John Romano

Robinson, Humberto (1959) pitcher: 1–0 with 4.15 ERA in 5 games.

Rocco, Mickey (1943–46) first baseman: 444-for-1,721, .258, in 440 games.

Rodgers, Bill (1915) second baseman: 14-for-45, .311, in 16 games.

Rodriguez, Rick (1988) pitcher: 1–2 with 7.09 ERA in 10 games.

Rohde, Dave (1992) third baseman: 0-for-7, .000, in 5 games.

Rohn, Dan (1986) second baseman–third baseman: 2-for-10, .200, in 6 games.

Rohr, Billy (1968) pitcher: 1–0 with 6.87 ERA in 17 games.

Rollins, Rich (1970) third baseman: 10-for-43, .233, in 42 games.

Roman, Jose (1984–86) pitcher: 1–8 with 8.12 ERA in 14 games.

Vicente Romo

Romano, Johnny (1960–64) catcher: 498-for-1,891, .263, in 580 games.

Romero, Ramon (1984–85) pitcher: 2–3 with 6.28 ERA in 20 games.

Romo, Vicente (1968–69) pitcher: 6–4 with 1.68 ERA in 43 games.

Roof, Phil (1965) catcher: 9-for-52, .173, in 43 games.

Rosar, Buddy (1943–44) catcher: 195-for-713, .273, in 214 games.

Rosello, Dave (1979–81) second baseman–third baseman–shortstop: 75-for-308, .244, in 173 games.

Rosen, Al (1947–56) third baseman–first baseman: 1,063-for-3,725, .285, in 1,044 games.

Rosenthal, Larry (1941) outfielder: 14-for-75, .187, in 45 games.

Ross, Don (1945–46) third baseman: 136-for-516, .264, in 161 games.

Rossman, Claude (1904, 06) first baseman–outfielder: 135-for-458, .295, in 136 games.

Roth, Braggo (1915–18) outfielder: 407-for-1,423, .286, in 415 games.

Rothel, Bob (1945) third baseman: 2-for-10, .200, in 4 games.

Roy, Luther (1924–25) pitcher: 0–5 with 7.06 ERA in 22 games.

Rozek, Dick (1950–52) pitcher: 1–0 with 4.39 ERA in 29 games.

Rudolph, Don (1962) pitcher: 0–0 with 0.00 ERA in 1 game.

Ruhle, Vern (1985) pitcher: 2–10 with 4.32 ERA in 42 games.

Russell, Jack (1932) pitcher: 5–7 with 4.70 ERA in 18 games.

Russell, Jeff (1994) pitcher: 1–1 with 4.97 ERA in 13 games.

Russell, Lloyd (1938) pinch runner: 0-for-0, —, in 2 games.

Ruszkowski, Hank (1944–45, 47) catcher: 20-for-84, .238, in 40 games.

Rutherford, Jim (1910) outfielder: 1-for-2, .500, in 1 game.

Buddy Rosar

Al Rosen

Ryan, Buddy (1912–13) outfielder: 161-for-571, .282, in 166 games.

Ryan, Jack (1908) pitcher: 1–1 with 2.27 ERA in 8 games.

S

Salas, Mark (1989) designated hitter: 17-for-77, .221, in 30 games.

Salmon, Chico (1964–68) second baseman–outfielder–first baseman–shortstop–third baseman: 329-for-1,304, .252, in 484 games.

Salveson, Jack (1943, 45) pitcher: 5–3 with 3.46 ERA in 42 games.

Sanders, Ken (1973–74) pitcher: 5–2 with 3.99 ERA in 24 games.

Santana, Rafael, (1990) shortstop: 3-for-13, .231, in 7 games.

Santiago, Jose (1954–55) pitcher: 2–0 with 2.36 ERA in 17 games.

Schaefer, Germany (1918) second baseman: 0-for-5, .000, in 1 game.

Schaffernoth, Joe (1961) pitcher: 0–1 with 4.76 ERA in 15 games.

Schatzeder, Dan (1988) pitcher: 0–2 with 9.56 ERA in 15 games.

Scheibeck, Frank (1901) shortstop: 70-for-329, .213, in 93 games.

Scheinblum, Richie (1965, 67–69) outfielder: 70-for-321, .218, in 143 games.

Schlueter, Norm (1944) catcher: 15-for-122, .123, in 49 games.

Schreckengost, Ossee (1902) first baseman: 25-for-74, .338, in 18 games.

Schrom, Ken (1986–87) pitcher: 20–20 with 5.38 ERA in 66 games.

Schulze, Don (1984–86) pitcher: 11–20 with 5.30 ERA in 57 games.

Schwartz, Bill (1904) first baseman: 13-for-86, .151, in 24 games.

Score, Herb (1955–59) pitcher: 49–34 with 3.18 ERA in 115 games.

Scott, Ed (1901) pitcher: 8–6 with 4.40 ERA in 17 games.

Herb Score

Scudder, Scott (1992–93) pitcher: 6–11 with 5.42 ERA in 25 games.

Seanez, Rudy (1989–91) pitcher: 2–1 with 6.75 ERA in 34 games.

Seeds, Bob (1930–32, 34) outfielder: 166-for-601, .276, in 196 games.

Seerey, Pat (1943–48) outfielder: 328-for-1,471, .223, in 462 games.

Sepkowski, Ted (1942, 46–47) second baseman–third baseman: 6-for-26, .231, in 17 games.

Sewell, Joe (1920–30) shortstop–third baseman–second baseman: 1,800-for-5,621, .320, in 1,513 games.

Sewell, Luke (1921–32, 39) catcher: 820-for-3,195, .259, in 978 games.

Seyfried, Gordon (1963–64) pitcher: 0–1 with 0.93 ERA in 5 games.

Shaner, Wally (1923) outfielder: 1-for-4, .250, in 3 games.

Shaute, Joe (1922–30) pitcher: 78–88 with 4.11 ERA in 252 games.

Shaw, Jeff (1990–92) pitcher: 3–10 with 4.90 ERA in 43 games.

Joe Sewell

Shay, Danny (1901) shortstop: 17-for-75, .227, in 19 games.

Sheaffer, Danny (1989) designated hitter: 1-for-16, .063, in 7 games.

Shields, Pete (1915) first baseman: 15-for-72, .208, in 23 games.

Shilling, Jim (1939) second baseman: 27-for-98, .276, in 31 games.

Shinault, Ginger (1921–22) catcher: 13-for-44, .295, in 35 games.

Shipke, Bill (1906) second baseman: 0-for-6, .000, in 2 games.

Shoffner, Milt (1929–31) pitcher: 7–10 with 7.03 ERA in 47 games.

Shuey, Paul (1994–95) pitcher: 0–3 with 7.00 ERA in 21 games.

Siebert, Sonny (1964–69) pitcher: 61–48 with 2.76 ERA in 181 games.

Simpson, Harry (1951–53, 55) outfielder–first baseman: 276-for-1,120, .246, in 353 games.

Sims, Duke (1964–70) catcher–first baseman–outfielder: 369-for-1,561, .236, in 536 games.

Sitton, Carl (1909) pitcher: 3–2 with 2.88 ERA in 14 games.

Sonny Siebert

Skalski, Joe (1989) pitcher: 0–2 with 6.75 ERA in 2 games.

Skinner, Joel (1989–91) catcher: 145-for-601, .241, in 227 games.

Slattery, Jack (1903) first baseman: 0-for-11, .000, in 4 games.

Slocumb, Heathcliff (1993) pitcher: 3–1 with 4.28 ERA in 20 games.

Smith, Alfred (1940–45) pitcher: 66–67 with 3.47 ERA in 168 games.

Smith, Alphonse (1953–57, 64) outfielder–third baseman: 648-for-2,407, .269, in 669 games.

Smith, Charlie (1902) pitcher: 2–1 with 4.05 ERA in 3 games.

Smith, Clay (1938) pitcher: 0–0 with 6.55 ERA in 4 games.

Smith, Elmer (1914–16, 17, 19–21) outfielder: 615-for-2,185, .281, in 672 games.

Smith, Pop Boy (1916–17) pitcher: 1–3 with 4.98 ERA in 11 games.

Smith, Riverboat (1959) pitcher: 0–1 with 5.22 ERA in 12 games.

Pat Seerey

Luke Sewell

Duke Sims

Al (Alfred) Smith

Elmer Smith

Tris Speaker

Smith, Roy (1984–85) pitcher: 6–9 with 4.90 ERA in 34 games.

Smith, Sherry (1922–27) pitcher: 45–48 with 3.84 ERA in 140 games.

Smith, Syd (1910–11) catcher: 55-for-181, .304, in 67 games.

Smith, Tommy (1973–76) outfielder: 56-for-244, .230, in 100 games.

Smith, Willie (1967–68) first baseman–outfielder: 13-for-74, .176, in 54 games.

Snyder, Cory (1986–90) outfielder–shortstop–third baseman: 595-for-2,431, .248, in 657 games.

Snyder, Russ (1968–69) outfielder: 127-for-483, .263, in 190 games.

Sodd, Bill (1937) pinch hitter: 0-for-1, .000, in 1 game.

Solters, Moose (1937–39) outfielder: 258-for-890, .290, in 260 games.

Sorensen, Lary (1982–83) pitcher: 22–26 with 4.87 ERA in 68 games.

Sorrells, Chick (1922) shortstop: 0-for-1, .000, in 2 games.

Sorrento, Paul (1992–95) first baseman–designated hitter: 408-for-1,566, .261, in 487 games.

Sothoron, Allen (1921–22) pitcher: 13–7 with 3.71 ERA in 28 games.

Southworth, Billy (1913, 15) outfielder: 39-for-177, .220, in 61 games.

Speaker, Tris (1916–26) outfielder: 1,965-for-5,546, .354, in 1,519 games.

Speece, Byron (1925–26) pitcher: 3–5 with 4.15 ERA in 30 games.

Speed, Horace (1978–79) outfielder: 26-for-120, .217, in 96 games.

Spencer, Roy (1933–34) catcher: 47-for-234, .201, in 80 games.

Spikes, Charlie (1973–77) outfielder–designated hitter: 454-for-1,848, .246, in 539 games.

Spillner, Dan (1978–84) pitcher: 46–45 with 4.29 ERA in 290 games.

Spring, Jack (1965) pitcher: 1–2 with 3.74 ERA in 14 games.

Springer, Steve (1990) third baseman: 2-for-12, .167, in 4 games.

Sprinz, Joe (1930–31) catcher: 8-for-48, .167, in 18 games.

Spurgeon, Freddy (1924–27) second baseman–third baseman: 335-for-1,176, .285, in 316 games.

Stange, Lee (1964–66) pitcher: 13–12 with 3.60 ERA in 72 games.

Stanley, Fred (1971–72) shortstop: 31-for-141, .220, in 66 games.

Stanton, Mike (1980–81) pitcher: 4–6 with 5.02 ERA in 75 games.

Stark, Dolly (1909) shortstop: 12-for-60, .200, in 19 games.

Starnagle, George (1902) catcher: 0-for-3, .000, in 1 game.

Steen, Bill (1912–15) pitcher: 23–31 with 3.09 ERA in 88 games.

Steiner, Red (1945) catcher: 3-for-20, .150, in 12 games.

Al (Alphonse) Smith

Russ Snyder

Charlie Spikes

Stephens, Bryan (1947) pitcher: 5–10 with 4.01 ERA in 31 games.

Stephenson, Riggs (1921–25) second baseman–third baseman–outfielder: 348-for-1,034, .337, in 332 games.

Stewart, Lefty (1935) pitcher: 6–6 with 5.44 ERA in 24 games.

Stewart, Sammy (1987) pitcher: 4–2 with 5.67 ERA in 25 games.

Stigman, Dick (1960–61) pitcher: 7–16 with 4.55 ERA in 63 games.

Stirnweiss, Snuffy (1951–52) second baseman: 19-for-88, .216, in 51 games.

Stoddard, Tim (1989) pitcher: 0–0 with 2.95 ERA in 14 games.

Stovall, George (1904–11) first baseman–second baseman–third baseman–outfielder: 955-for-3,591, .266, in 955 games.

Stovall, Jesse (1903) pitcher: 5–1 with 2.05 ERA in 6 games.

Streit, Oscar (1902) pitcher: 0–7 with 5.23 ERA in 8 games.

Strickland, George (1952–57, 59–60) shortstop–third baseman–second baseman: 491-for-2,111, .233, in 734 games.

Strickland, Jim (1975) pitcher: 0–0 with 1.93 ERA in 4 games.

Striker, Jake (1959) pitcher: 1–0 with 2.70 ERA in 1 game.

Strom, Brent (1973) pitcher: 2–10 with 4.61 ERA in 27 games.

Stromme, Floyd (1939) pitcher: 0–1 with 4.85 ERA in 5 games.

Suarez, Ken (1968–69, 71) catcher: 51-for-218, .234, in 103 games.

Suche, Charley (1938) pitcher: 0–0 with 27.00 ERA in 1 game.

Billy Sullivan

Sudakis, Bill (1975) first baseman: 9-for-46, .196, in 20 games.

Sullivan, Billy (1936–37) catcher: 160-for-487, .329, in 165 games.

Sullivan, Denny (1908–09) outfielder: 1-for-8, .125, in 7 games.

Sullivan, Jim (1923) pitcher: 0–1 with 14.40 ERA in 3 games.

Sullivan, Lefty (1939) pitcher: 0–1 with 4.26 ERA in 7 games.

Summa, Homer (1922–28) outfielder: 861-for-2,844, .303, in 768 games.

Susce, George (1941–44) catcher: 15-for-63, .238, in 35 games.

Sutcliffe, Rick (1982–84) pitcher: 35–24 with 3.92 ERA in 85 games.

Sutherland, Darrell (1968) pitcher: 0–0 with 8.10 ERA in 3 games.

Swan, Russ (1994) pitcher: 0–1 with 11.25 ERA in 12 games.

Swindell, Greg (1986–91) pitcher: 60–55 with 3.79 ERA in 153 games.

Swindell, Josh (1911) pitcher: 0–1 with 2.08 ERA in 4 games.

George Strickland

Homer Summa

T

Tabler, Pat (1983–88) first baseman–outfielder–designated hitter–third baseman: 729-for-2,476, .294, in 707 games.

Tanner, Chuck (1959–60) outfielder: 19-for-73, .260, in 35 games.

Tasby, Willie (1962–63) outfielder: 74-for-315, .235, in 127 games.

Taubensee, Eddie (1991) catcher: 16-for-66, .242, in 26 games.

Tavarez, Julian (1993–95) pitcher: 12–5 with 3.93 ERA in 66 games.

Tavener, Jackie (1929) shortstop: 53-for-250, .212, in 92 games.

Taylor, Dummy (1902) pitcher: 1–3 with 1.59 ERA in 4 games.

Taylor, Ron (1962) pitcher: 2–2 with 5.94 ERA in 8 games.

Taylor, Sammy (1963) catcher: 3-for-10, .300, in 4 games.

Tebbetts, Birdie (1951–52) catcher: 61-for-238, .256, in 97 games.

Tedrow, Al (1914) pitcher: 1–2 with 1.21 ERA in 4 games.

Temple, Johnny (1960–61) second baseman–third baseman: 245-for-899, .273, in 227 games.

Terry, Ralph (1965) pitcher: 11–6 with 3.69 ERA in 30 games.

Thielman, Jake (1907–08) pitcher: 15–11 with 2.69 ERA in 31 games.

Thomas, Carl (1960) pitcher: 1–0 with 7.45 ERA in 4 games.

Thomas, Fay (1931) pitcher: 2–4 with 5.18 ERA in 16 games.

Thomas, Gorman (1983) outfielder: 82-for-371, .221, in 106 games.

Thomas, Pinch (1918–21) catcher: 35-for-163, .215, in 96 games.

Thomas, Stan (1976) pitcher: 4–4 with 2.30 ERA in 37 games.

Thomas, Valmy (1961) catcher: 18-for-86, .209, in 27 games.

Thomason, Art (1910) outfielder: 12-for-70, .171, in 20 games.

Thome, Jim (1991–95) third baseman: 318-for-1,142, .278, in 349 games.

Thompson, Rich (1985) pitcher: 3–8 with 6.30 ERA in 57 games.

Thoney, Jack (1902–03) outfielder–second baseman–shortstop: 55-for-227, .242, in 60 games.

Thornton, Andre (1977–79, 81–87) designated hitter–first baseman: 1,095-for-4,313, .254, in 1,225 games.

Tiant, Luis (1964–69) pitcher: 75–64 with 2.84 ERA in 211 games.

Tidrow, Dick (1972–74) pitcher: 29–34 with 3.78 ERA in 85 games.

Andre Thornton

Dick Tidrow

Del Unser

Tiefenauer, Bobby (1960, 65, 67) pitcher: 0–7 with 3.16 ERA in 26 games.

Timmerman, Tom (1973–74) pitcher: 9–8 with 4.96 ERA in 33 games.

Tingley, Ron (1988) catcher: 4-for-24, .167, in 9 games.

Tipton, Joe (1948, 52–53) catcher: 77-for-304, .253, in 137 games.

Tolson, Chick (1925) first baseman: 3-for-12, .250, in 3 games.

Tomanek, Dick (1953–54, 57–58) pitcher: 5–4 with 5.41 ERA in 54 games.

Torkelson, Red (1917) pitcher: 2–1 with 7.66 ERA in 4 games.

Torres, Rusty (1973–74) outfielder: 92-for-462, .199, in 230 games.

Townsend, Jack (1906) pitcher: 3–7 with 2.91 ERA in 17 games.

Treadway, Jeff (1993) third base-man–second baseman: 67-for-221, .303, in 97 games.

Tresh, Mike (1949) catcher: 8-for-37, .216, in 38 games.

Trillo, Manny (1983) second base-man: 87-for-320, .272, in 88 games.

Trosky, Hal (1933–41) first baseman: 1,365-for-4,365, .313, in 1,124 games.

Trouppe, Quincy (1952) catcher: 1-for-10, .100, in 6 games.

Tucker, Ollie (1928) outfielder: 6-for-47, .128, in 14 games.

Tucker, Scooter (1995) catcher: 0-for-20, .000, in 17 games.

Tucker, Thurman (1948–51) outfielder: 129-for-541, .238, in 221 games.

Turchin, Eddie (1943) third baseman: 3-for-13, .231, in 11 games.

Turner, Matt (1994) pitcher: 1–0 with 2.13 ERA in 9 games.

Turner, Terry (1904–18) shortstop–third baseman–second baseman–outfielder: 1,472-for-5,787, .254, in 1,619 games.

Tyriver, Dave (1962) pitcher: 0–0 with 4.22 ERA in 4 games.

U

Uhlaender, Ted (1970–71) outfielder: 271-for-973, .279, in 282 games.

Uhle, George (1919–28, 36) pitcher: 147–119 with 3.92 ERA in 357 games.

Ujdur, Jerry (1984) pitcher: 1–2 with 6.91 ERA in 4 games.

Underhill, Willie (1927–28) pitcher: 1–4 with 5.70 ERA in 15 games.

Unser, Del (1972) outfielder: 91-for-383, .238, in 132 games.

Upp, Jerry (1909) pitcher: 2–1 with 1.69 ERA in 7 games.

Upshaw, Cecil (1974) pitcher: 0–1 with 3.38 ERA in 7 games.

Upshaw, Willie (1988) first base-man: 121-for-493, .245, in 149 games.

Usher, Bob (1957) outfielder: 1-for-8, .125, in 10 games.

Ussat, Dutch (1925, 27) third base-man: 3-for-17, .176, in 5 games.

V

Vail, Mike (1978) outfielder: 8-for-34, .235, in 14 games.

Valdez, Efrain (1990–91) pitcher: 1–1 with 2.73 ERA in 20 games.

Valdez, Sergio (1990–91) pitcher: 7–6 with 4.85 ERA in 30 games.

Valentinetti, Vito (1957) pitcher: 2–2 with 4.94 ERA in 11 games.

Valo, Elmer (1959) outfielder: 7-for-24, .292, in 34 games.

Van Camp, Al (1928) first baseman: 4-for-17, .235, in 5 games.

Vande Berg, Ed (1987) pitcher: 1–0 with 5.10 ERA in 55 games.

Vander Meer, Johnny (1951) pitcher: 0–1 with 18.00 ERA in 1 game.

Varney, Dike (1902) pitcher: 1–1 with 6.14 ERA in 3 games.

Vasbinder, Moses (1902) pitcher: 0–0 with 9.00 ERA in 2 games.

Velez, Otto (1983) designated hitter: 2-for-25, .080, in 10 games.

Luis Tiant

Hal Trosky

Joe Vosmik

Vernon, Mickey (1949–50, 58) first baseman: 291-for-1,029, .283, in 300 games.

Versalles, Zoilo (1969) second baseman–third baseman: 49-for-217, .226, in 72 games.

Veryzer, Tom (1978–81) shortstop: 364-for-1,449, .251, in 463 games.

Vidal, Jose (1966–68) outfielder: 19-for-120, .158, in 70 games.

Vinson, Rube (1904–05) outfielder: 41-for-183, .224, in 54 games.

Vizquel, Omar (1994–95) shortstop: 222-for-828, .268, in 205 games.

Von Ohlen, Dave (1985) pitcher: 3–2 with 2.91 ERA in 26 games.

Vosmik, Joe (1930–36) outfielder: 1,003-for-3,207, .313, in 824 games.

Vukovich, George (1983–85) outfielder: 316-for-1,183, .267, in 407 games.

W

Waddell, Tom (1984–85, 87) pitcher: 15–11 with 4.30 ERA in 113 games.

Wagner, Leon (1964–68) outfielder: 581-for-2,189, .265, in 630 games.

Waits, Rick (1975–83) pitcher: 74–84 with 4.18 ERA in 235 games.

Wakefield, Howard (1905, 07) catcher: 9-for-63, .143, in 36 games.

Walker, Ed (1902–03) pitcher: 0–1 with 4.50 ERA in 4 games.

Walker, Gee (1941) outfielder: 126-for-445, .283, in 121 games.

Walker, Jerry (1963–64) pitcher: 6–7 with 4.88 ERA in 45 games.

Walker, Mike (1988, 90–91) pitcher: 2–8 with 4.97 ERA in 26 games.

Walker, Mysterious (1912) pitcher: 0–0 with 0.00 ERA in 1 game.

Walker, Roy (1912, 15) pitcher: 4–9 with 3.92 ERA in 26 games.

Walters, Roxy (1924–25) catcher: 23-for-94, .245, in 37 games.

Wambsganss, Bill (1914–23) second baseman–shortstop–third baseman: 1,083-for-4,191, .258, in 1,170 games.

Ward, Aaron (1928) third baseman: 1-for-9, .111, in 6 games.

Ward, Colby (1990) pitcher: 1–3 with 4.25 ERA in 22 games.

Ward, Preston (1956–58) first baseman–third baseman–outfielder: 90-for-309, .291, in 145 games.

Ward, Turner (1990–91) outfielder: 39-for-146, .267, in 54 games.

Wardle, Curt (1985) pitcher: 7–6 with 6.88 ERA in 15 games.

Wasdell, Jimmy (1946–47) first baseman: 11-for-42, .262, in 33 games.

Washington, Ron (1988) shortstop: 57-for-223, .256, in 69 games.

Wayenberg, Frank (1924) pitcher: 0–0 with 5.40 ERA in 2 games.

Weatherly, Roy (1936–42) outfielder: 701-for-2,430, .288, in 680 games.

Bill Wambsganss

Weaver, Floyd (1962, 65) pitcher: 3–2 with 5.16 ERA in 33 games.

Webb, Skeeter (1938–39) shortstop: 87-for-327, .266, in 101 games.

Webber, Les (1946, 48) pitcher: 1–1 with 25.50 ERA in 5 games.

Webster, Mitch (1990–91) outfielder: 114-for-469, .243, in 141 games.

Webster, Ray (1959) second baseman: 15-for-74, .203, in 40 games.

Weigel, Ralph (1946) catcher: 2-for-12, .167, in 6 games.

Weik, Dick (1950, 53) pitcher: 1–3 with 3.81 ERA in 11 games.

Weiland, Bob (1934) pitcher: 1–5 with 4.11 ERA in 16 games.

Weingartner, Elmer (1945) shortstop: 9-for-39, .231, in 20 games.

Welf, Ollie (1916) pinch runner: 0-for-0, —, in 1 game.

Wensloff, Butch (1948) pitcher: 0–1 with 10.80 ERA in 1 game.

Wertz, Bill (1993–94) pitcher: 2–3 with 4.08 ERA in 35 games.

Wertz, Vic (1954–58) first baseman–outfielder: 430-for-1,591, .270, in 473 games.

Leon Wagner

Jerry Walker

Roy Weatherly

Vic Wertz

West, Hi (1905, 11) pitcher: 5–6 with 3.87 ERA in 19 games.

Westlake, Wally (1952–55) outfielder: 156-for-547, .285, in 212 games.

Weyhing, Gus (1901) pitcher: 0–0 with 7.94 ERA in 2 games.

Wheeler, Ed (1945) third baseman–shortstop: 14-for-72, .194, in 46 games.

Whisenant, Pete (1960) outfielder: 1-for-6, .167, in 7 games.

Whitehill, Earl (1937–38) pitcher: 17–16 with 6.00 ERA in 59 games.

Whiten, Mark (1991–92) outfielder: 195-for-766, .255, in 218 games.

Whitfield, Fred (1963–67) first baseman: 480-for-1,866, .257, in 579 games.

Whitson, Ed (1982) pitcher: 4–2 with 3.26 ERA in 40 games.

Wickander, Kevin (1989–90, 92–93) pitcher: 2–1 with 3.34 ERA in 67 games.

Wight, Bill (1953, 55) pitcher: 2–1 with 3.20 ERA in 37 games.

Fred Whitfield

Wihtol, Sandy (1979–80, 82) pitcher: 1–0 with 3.75 ERA in 28 games.

Wilcox, Milt (1972–74) pitcher: 17–26 with 4.55 ERA in 99 games.

Wilhelm, Hoyt (1957–58) pitcher: 3–7 with 2.49 ERA in 32 games.

Wilie, Denney (1915) outfielder: 33-for-131, .252, in 45 games.

Wilkins, Eric (1979) pitcher: 2–4 with 4.39 ERA in 16 games.

Wilkinson, Roy (1918) pitcher: 0–0 with 0.00 ERA in 1 game.

Wilks, Ted (1952–53) pitcher: 0–0 with 4.70 ERA in 11 games.

Willard, Jerry (1984–85) catcher: 136-for-546, .249, in 191 games.

Williams, Rip (1918) first baseman: 17-for-71, .239, in 28 games.

Williams, Dick (1957) outfielder–third baseman: 58-for-205, .283, in 67 games.

Williams, Eddie (1986–88) third baseman: 16-for-92, .174, in 37 games.

Williams, Pap (1945) first baseman: 4-for-19, .211, in 16 games.

Williams, Reggie (1988) outfielder: 7-for-31, .226, in 11 games.

Williams, Stan (1965, 67–69) pitcher: 25–29 with 3.12 ERA in 124 games.

Williams, Walt (1973) outfielder–designated hitter: 101-for-350, .289, in 104 games.

Willis, Les (1947) pitcher: 0–2 with 3.48 ERA in 22 games.

Wills, Frank (1986–87) pitcher: 4–5 with 4.93 ERA in 32 games.

Wilson, Art (1921) catcher: 0-for-1, .000, in 2 games.

Stan Williams

Walter "No Neck" Williams

Wilson, Frank (1928) pinch hitter: 0-for-1, .000, in 2 games.

Wilson, Jim (1985) first baseman–designated hitter: 5-for-14, .357, in 4 games.

Wilson, Red (1960) catcher: 19-for-88, .216, in 32 games.

Winchell, Fred (1909) pitcher: 0–3 with 6.28 ERA in 4 games.

Winegarner, Ralph (1930, 32, 34–36) pitcher: 8–6 with 5.12 ERA in 61 games.

Winfield, Dave (1995) designated hitter: 22-for-115, .191, in 46 games.

Winn, George (1922–23) pitcher: 1–2 with 4.29 ERA in 9 games.

Wise, Rick (1978–79) pitcher: 24–29 with 4.02 ERA in 67 games.

Wojna, Ed (1989) pitcher: 0–1 with 4.09 ERA in 9 games.

Wolf, Ernie (1912) pitcher: 0–0 with 6.35 ERA in 1 game.

Wolff, Roger (1947) pitcher: 0–0 with 3.94 ERA in 7 games.

Wood, Bob (1901–02) catcher–first baseman: 177-for-604, 2.93, in 179 games.

Wood, Roy (1914–15) outfielder–first baseman: 67-for-298, .225, in 105 games.

Wood, Smoky Joe (1917–22) outfielder–second baseman: 432-for-1,456, .297, in 470 games.

Woodeshick, Hal (1958) pitcher: 6–6 with 3.64 ERA in 14 games.

Woodling, Gene (1943, 46, 55–57) outfielder: 326-for-1,164, .280, in 381 games.

Workman, Chuck (1938, 41) outfielder: 2-for-9, .222, in 11 games.

Worthington, Craig (1992) third baseman: 4-for-24, .167, in 9 games.

Wright, Ab (1935) outfielder: 38-for-160, .238, in 67 games.

Early Wynn

Wright, Clarence (1902–03) pitcher: 10–20 with 4.69 ERA in 36 games.

Wright, Lucky (1909) pitcher: 0–4 with 3.21 ERA in 5 games.

Wyatt, Joe (1924) outfielder: 2-for-12, .167, in 4 games.

Wyatt, Whit (1937) pitcher: 2–3 with 4.44 ERA in 29 games.

Wynn, Early (1949–57, 63) pitcher: 164–102 with 3.24 ERA in 343 games.

Y

Yeager, George (1901) catcher: 31-for-139, .223, in 39 games.

Yett, Rich (1986–89) pitcher: 22–24 with 4.99 ERA in 131 games.

Yingling, Earl (1911) pitcher: 1–0 with 4.43 ERA in 4 games.

York, Mike (1991) pitcher: 1–4 with 6.75 ERA in 14 games.

Yoter, Elmer (1924) third baseman: 18-for-66, .273, in 19 games.

Young, Bobby (1955–56) second baseman: 14-for-45, .311, in 19 games.

Young, Cliff (1993) pitcher: 3–3 with 4.62 ERA in 21 games.

Young, Cy (1909–11) pitcher: 29–29 with 2.50 ERA in 63 games.

Young, George (1913) pinch hitter: 0-for-2, .000, in 2 games.

Cy Young

Young, Matt (1993) pitcher: 1–6 with 5.21 ERA in 22 games.

Young, Mike (1989) designated hitter: 11-for-59, .186, in 32 games.

Yowell, Carl (1924–25) pitcher: 3–4 with 5.40 ERA in 16 games.

Z

Zinn, Jimmy (1929) pitcher: 4–6 with 5.04 ERA in 18 games.

Zoldak, Sam (1948–50) pitcher: 14–10 with 3.48 ERA in 83 games.

Zuber, Bill (1936, 38–40) pitcher: 4–5 with 5.69 ERA in 50 games.

Zuvella, Paul (1988–89) shortstop: 46-for-188, .245, in 75 games.

Zuverink, George (1951–52) pitcher: 0–0 with 5.06 ERA in 17 games.

Sam Zoldak

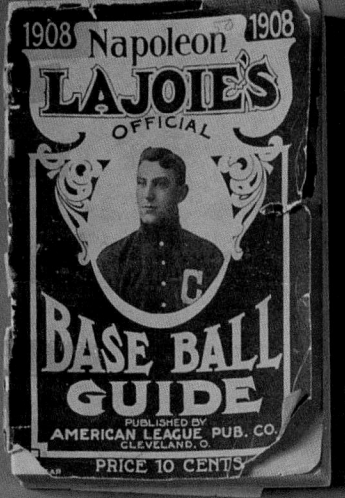

League Park

AND THEN

IT ALL BEGAN on June 2, 1869, when the first game of professional baseball in Cleveland was played on the Case Commons, a park area located on Putnam Avenue (now E. 38th Street) between Scovill and Central Avenues. Admission to the grounds was twenty-five cents for pedestrians and fifty cents for rigs, which ringed the field. A crowd of 2,000 attended.

The Cleveland Forest Citys had forsaken the ranks of amateurs to meet the celebrated Cincinnati Red Stockings, who themselves had just turned professional and embarked on a nation-wide tour.

The Red Stockings won the game, 25 to 6, but the Forest Citys "conducted themselves in a worthy manner" and professional baseball took hold in Cleveland. Twenty years later, the city entered a team in the National League and, in 1901, became a charter member of the American League.

Cleveland's first baseball hero was catcher Jim White (seated, second from left) and the first pitcher was Art Pratt (standing, third from left). The identity of other members of the 1869 Forest Citys have long since faded into obscurity.

5

On June 2, 1869 the first game of professional baseball in Cleveland was played on the Case Commons. The team (see photograph above) was called the Cleveland Forest Citys. They played against the Cincinnati Red Stockings who won the game 25-6.

Cleveland
INDIANS

VS.

Boston
BRAVES

1948

WORLD SERIES

Cleveland
INDIANS
Sketch Book of 1948

WORLD SERIES
CLEVELAND OHIO 1948

CLEVELAND INDIANS
WORLD SERIES
1948

107TH YEAR—NO. 286   CLEVELAND, TUESDAY MORNING, OCTOBER 12, 1948   36 PAGES   FIVE CENTS

INDIANS WIN WORLD TITLE

BEARDEN HALTS RALLY TO SAVE LEMON'S 4-3 VICTORY OVER BRAVES

Tribe Southpaw Enters Game With Bases Full in Eighth Inning; Double Play Checks Boston in Ninth; Cleveland Tags Two Hurlers for 10 Hits; Gordon Raps Voiselle for Home Run

BY HARRY JONES

The 1954 "Big Four" with manager Al Lopez taken at a 1989 reunion. From left to right: Early Wynn, Al Lopez, Bob Feller, Mike Garcia, and Bob Lemon.

1954 American League Champs

First Row: (Left to Right) Al Smith, Dave Hoskins, Bill Glynn, Bob Avila, Dave Pope, Sam Dente, Harold Klug, batboy.
Second Row: Ray Narleski, Hal Naragon, Tony Cuccinello, Al Lopez, Red Kress, Bill Lobe, Mel Harder.
Third Row: Spud Goldstein, traveling secretary, Don Mossi, Bob Feller, Dave Philley, Hank Majeski, Al Rosen, Vic Wertz, Dale Mitchell, Jim Hegan, Wally Bock, trainer.
Fourth Row: Larry Doby, Early Wynn, Mike Garcia, Mickey Grasso, Hal Newhouser, Wally Westlake, Bob Hooper, Art Houtteman, George Strickland, Bob Lemon, Rudy Regalado.

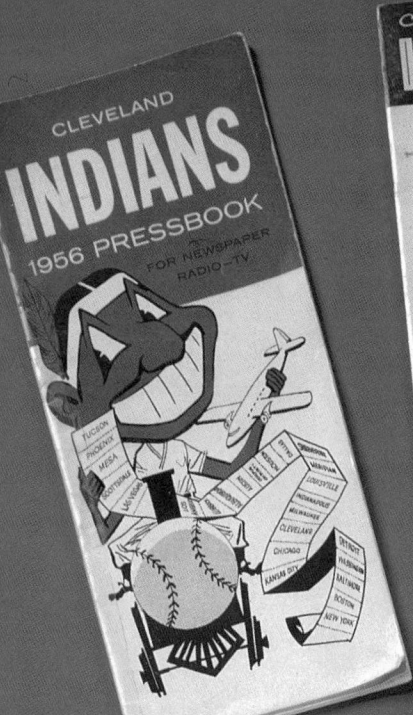

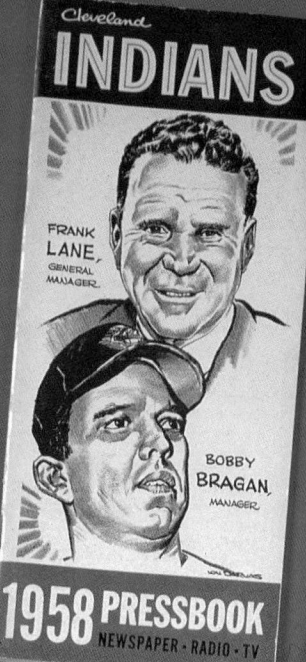

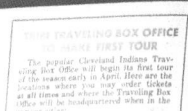

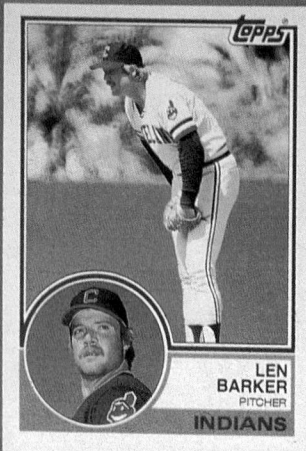

LEN BARKER
PITCHER
INDIANS

SAM McDOWELL   pitcher

LEE STANGE   pitcher

BOB ALLEN PITCHER
INDIANS

DON McMAHON   pitcher

JOHN O'DONOGHUE   pitcher

STEVE HARGAN   pitcher

BOB HEFFNER   pitcher

SCOTT BAILES

DUKE SIMS CATCHER
INDIANS

BOB HALE
First Base   Cleveland Indians

CHICO SALMON 2B-OF
INDIANS

DAVE CLARK

VIC DAVALILLO OUTFIELD
INDIANS

CHUCK HINTON   outfield

BAKE McBRIDE
INDIANS

THE TRIBE

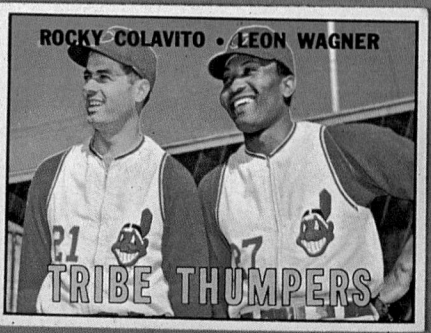

ROCKY COLAVITO • LEON WAGNER
TRIBE THUMPERS

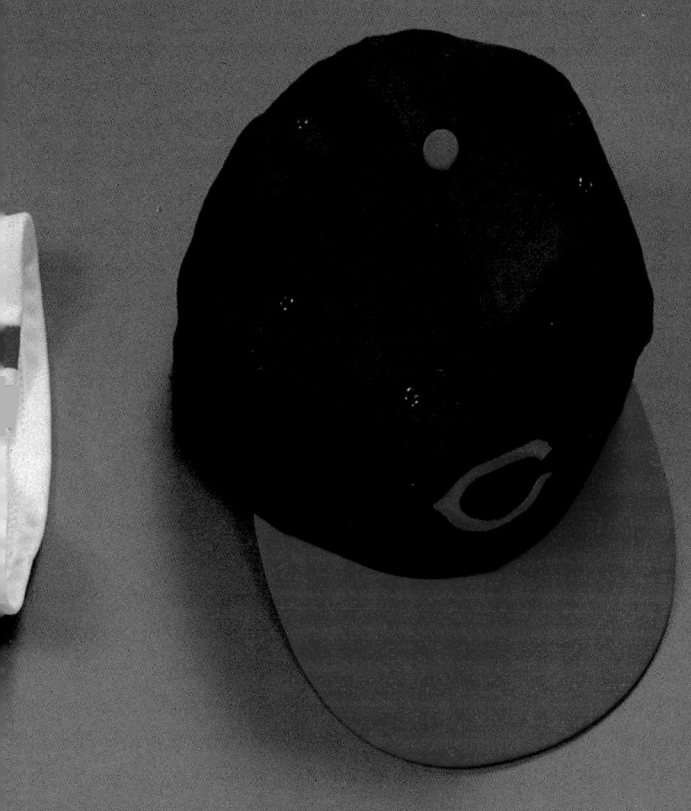

CLEVELAND PLAIN DEALER — 7 O'CLOCK FINAL

CLEVELAND WINS WORLD'S SERIES

Plain Dealer Photographer Snaps High Lights in Yesterday's Final Victory — DEFEATS BROOKLYN IN SEVENTH GAME

CLEVELAND PLAIN DEALER — FINAL

INDIANS WIN FIRST PENNANT IN 28 YEARS; BEARDEN VICTOR, 8-3

BOUDREAU'S 2 HOMERS LEAD 13-HIT ASSAULT THAT REPELS RED SOX

CLEVELAND PLAIN DEALER — FINAL

INDIANS WIN WORLD TITLE

TRUMAN AIMS TO BUILD AMPLIFIED NEW DEAL; DEWEY BACKS T-H ACT

BEARDEN HALTS RALLY TO SAVE LEMON'S 4-3 VICTORY OVER BRAVES

CLEVELAND PLAIN DEALER

INDIANS CLINCH PENNANT

DULLES ABANDONS HOPE FOR FRANCE ON EUROPE TEAM

HOMERS BEAT DETROIT, END YANKS' REIGN

Best OF THEM ALL...

JESSE BURKETT — STANLEY COVELESKIE — CY YOUNG — NAPOLEON LAJOIE

ELMER FLICK — ADDIE JOSS — LOU BOUDREAU — SATCHEL PAIGE — EARL AVERILL

TRIS SPEAKER — SAM RICE — JOE SEWELL

BOB FELLER — BOB LEMON — EARLY WYNN — FRANK ROBINSON — AL LOPEZ

17 Indians in the HALL OF FAME

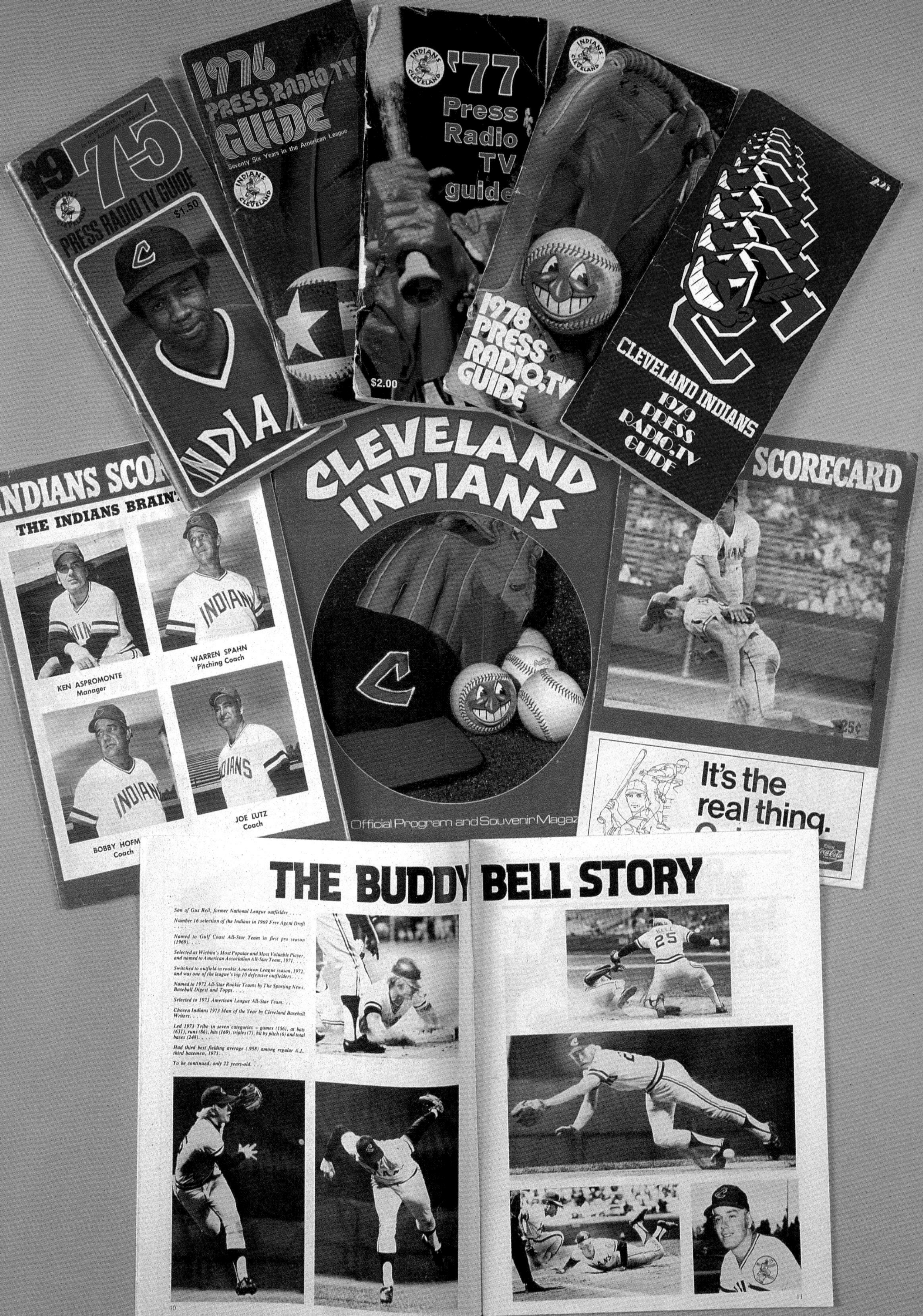
1975
Seventy-Five Years in the American League
PRESS RADIO TV GUIDE
$1.50
INDIANS CLEVELAND
1976 PRESS, RADIO, TV GUIDE
Seventy Six Years in the American League
'77 Press Radio TV guide
$2.00
1978 PRESS RADIO, TV GUIDE
CLEVELAND INDIANS 1979 PRESS RADIO, TV GUIDE
INDIANS SCOR
THE INDIANS BRAIN
KEN ASPROMONTE
Manager
WARREN SPAHN
Pitching Coach
BOBBY HOFM
Coach
JOE LUTZ
Coach
CLEVELAND INDIANS
Official Program and Souvenir Magaz
SCORECARD
25¢
It's the real thing.
THE BUDDY BELL STORY
Son of Gus Bell, former National League outfielder . . . .
Number 16 selection of the Indians in 1969 Free Agent Draft . . . .
Named to Gulf Coast All-Star Team in first pro season (1969). . . .
Selected as Wichita's Most Popular and Most Valuable Player, and named to American Association All-Star Team, 1971. . . .
Switched to outfield in rookie American League season, 1972, and was one of the league's top 10 defensive outfielders. . . .
Named to 1972 All-Star Rookie Teams by The Sporting News, Baseball Digest and Topps. . . .
Selected to 1973 American League All-Star Team. . . .
Chosen Indians 1973 Man of the Year by Cleveland Baseball Writers. . . .
Led 1973 Tribe in seven categories – games (156), at bats (631), runs (86), hits (169), triples (7), hit by pitch (6) and total bases (248). . . .
Had third best fielding average (.958) among regular A.L. third basemen, 1973. . . .
To be continued, only 22 years-old. . . .
BELL 25
10
11

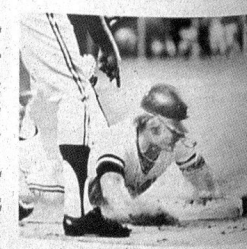

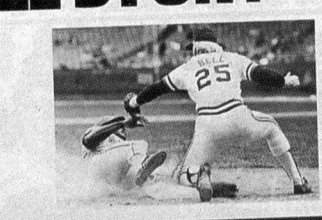

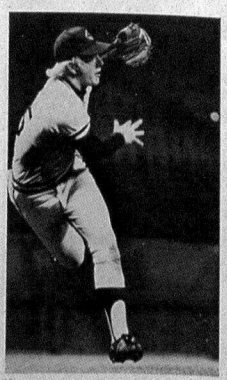

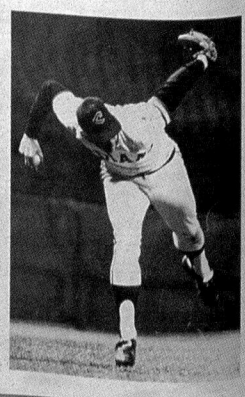

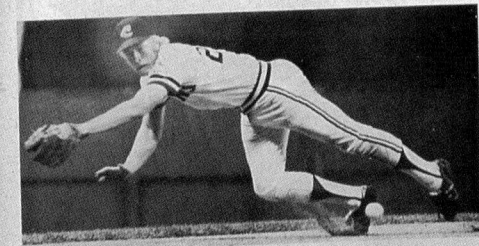

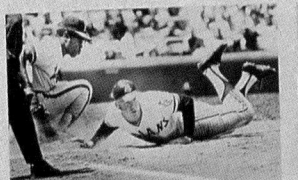

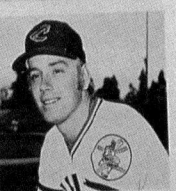

1980 MEDIA GUIDE
2.50
CLEVELAND INDIANS

$2.75
1981 MEDIA GUIDE CLEVELAND INDIANS

1982 INDIANS media guide
$3

'84 MEDIA GUIDE CLEVELAND INDIANS
$3
CLEVELAND INDIANS
AMERICAN LEAGUE CHAMPIONS

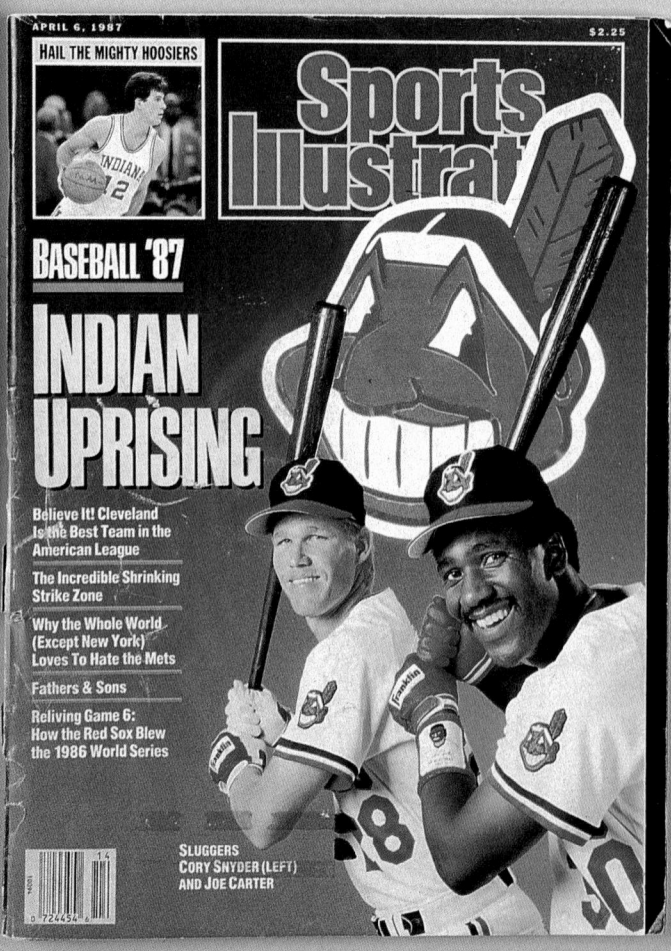

APRIL 6, 1987
HAIL THE MIGHTY HOOSIERS
Sports Illustrated
$2.25
BASEBALL '87
INDIAN UPRISING
Believe It! Cleveland Is the Best Team in the American League
The Incredible Shrinking Strike Zone
Why the Whole World (Except New York) Loves To Hate the Mets
Fathers & Sons
Reliving Game 6: How the Red Sox Blew the 1986 World Series
SLUGGERS CORY SNYDER (LEFT) AND JOE CARTER

$3
media guide
CLEVELAND INDIANS
'83

TRIBE '85
this is my team!

CLEVELAND INDIANS
media guide

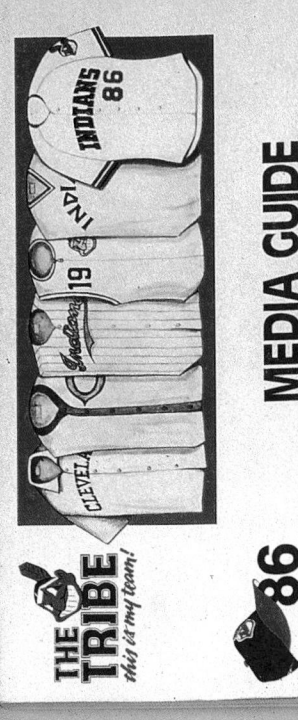

THE TRIBE
this is my team!

MEDIA GUIDE
86

CLEVELAND INDIANS
MEDIA GUIDE '87

CARTER
30

BASEBALL 1987

Pow! Wow!

The lost Tribe is back, thanks to the bats of
young sluggers Joe Carter and Cory Snyder
By Ron Fimrite

OFFICIAL
PROGRAM
$3.00

1981 ALL-STAR GAME

CLEVELAND 1981

1988
CLEVELAND INDIANS

INDIANS
88

MEDIA GUIDE
$5.00

CLEVELAND
INDIANS

1989
MEDIA
GUIDE
$5

INDIANS PARK

CLEVELAND INDIANS CHARITIES

Cleveland Indians Charities was established in 1989. Its mission is to make a positive contribution to the quality of life for Northeast Ohio youth by providing educational and recreational opportunities.

Through various fundraising events that include the Cleveland Indians Charities Golf Classic; The Stop-n-Shop Wahoo Winterfest; and the popular Speedy Muffler Speed Pitch machine, Cleveland Indians Charities has donated nearly $300,000 to numerous organizations in Northeast Ohio over the last five years.

Just a few of the organizations that have received donations from Cleveland Indians Charities include: The Boys and Girls Clubs of Cleveland, Luke Easter Park, the Community Fund for Area Missing Youth (A.M.Y.), Shoes for Kids, Andre Thornton Summer Camp Program, United Negro College Fund, Cleveland Baseball Federation and Esperanza.

1993 Roberto Clemente Award recipient demonstrates the Indians' commitment to the Cleveland

**OTHER HOMES OF THE
CLEVELAND INDIANS**

LEAGUE PARK

DATE OPENED: May 1, 1891; Cleveland Spiders vs. Cincinnati Redlegs. Spiders won 12-3 in front of 9,000.

WP: Cy Young

DATE CLOSED: September 21, 1946; Cleveland Indians vs. Detroit Tigers. Tigers won 5-3 in front of 2,472.

WP: Paul Trout

LP: Jonas Berry

CAPACITY: 9,000 (1891-1910)
21,000 (1911-1938)
22,500 (1939-1946) (.566)

RECORD 1901-1946: Four 1920 World Series games, including Bill Wambsganss' unassisted triple play and Elmer Smith's 1st grand slam in world series history, all in game 5... Addie Joss' perfect game on October 2, 1908... Babe Ruth's 500th homer on August 11, 1929... Joe DiMaggio hits in his 56th and final game in a row on July 16, 1941...4 no-hitters.

CLEVELAND STADIUM

DATE OPENED: July 31, 1932; Cleveland Indians vs. Philadelphia Athletics. The A's won 1-0 in front of 76,979.

WP: Lefty Grove

LP: Mel Harder

DATE CLOSED: October 3, 1993; Cleveland Indians vs. Chicago White Sox. The White Sox were 4-0 winners in front of 72,390. (Cleveland Stadium will still be used for football.)

WP: Jason Bere

LP: Charles Nagy

CAPACITY: 74,483

RECORD 1932-1993: 2234-1951 (.534)

HISTORICAL EVENTS: Hosted four (4) All-Star games and five (5) World Series contests... Len Barker's perfect game vs. Toronto on May 15, 1981... Bob Feller's 3rd no-hitter on July 1, 1951... First night game played on June 27, 1939 vs. the Tigers... Nolan Ryan's 324th and final win on June 27, 1993... Ted Williams 500th home run on July 17, 1960... Joe DiMaggio's 56-game hitting streak is stopped on July 17, 1941... Frank Robinson's opening day home run on April 8, 1975; his first game as player/manager... nine (9) no-hitters.

Jacobs Field

○ Field Box .... SOLD OUT
○ Lower Box $14.00
● Lower Reserved $12.00
● Mezzanine Seating $12.00
● Club Seating .... SOLD OUT
○ Upper Box $12.00
○ Upper Reserved $10.00
○ Reserve Gen. Admission $6.00
○ Bleachers $6.00
▨ Angled Seating (stripes)

Cleveland Municipal Stadium

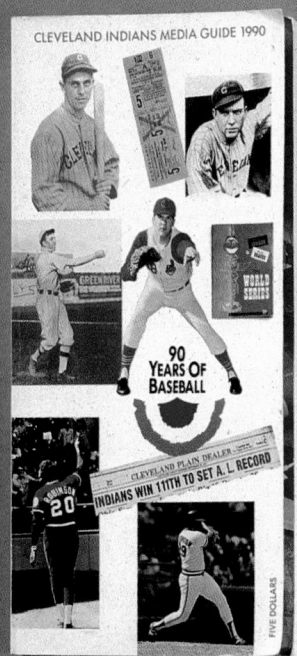

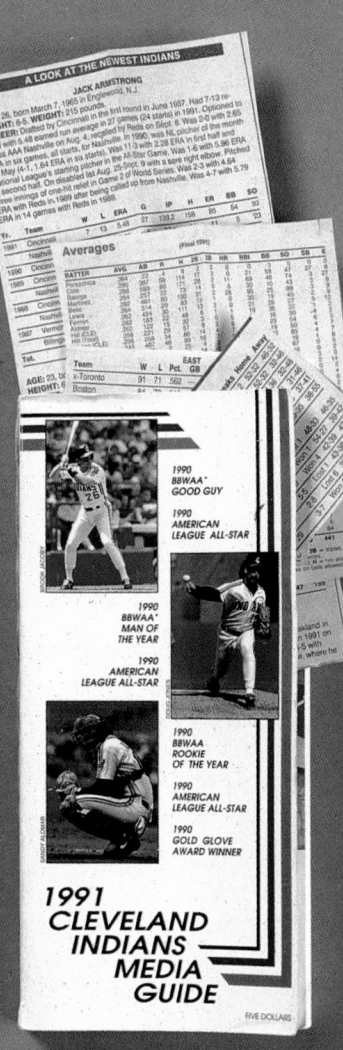

JACOBS FIELD

The Strategists

Forty men have served as managers of the Cleveland Indians (and their predecessors, the Blues, Bronchos, and Naps), including Roger Peckinpaugh, who had two tours of duty at the helm, and six who filled in on an interim basis—Bill Bradley, Bibb Falk, Jo Jo White, Mel Harder (twice), George Strickland (twice), and John Hart.

Ten also played during their tenure as Cleveland's manager, though only Napoleon Lajoie, Joe Birminghman, Tris Speaker, Lou Boudreau, and Frank Robinson were hired to perform both jobs.

The others who played, though only briefly, while also serving as manager were James McAleer, in 1901; Bill Bradley, 1905; James McGuire, 1910; George Stovall, 1911; and Harry Davis, 1912.

Manager Profiles

1901

McAleer, Jimmy

Record: 55–82 (.401)
Birthplace: Youngstown, Ohio
B: July 10, 1864; **D:** April 29, 1931

Jimmy McAleer was a veteran outfielder who played for the Cleveland Spiders in the National League before becoming the first manager of the Cleveland Blues—the forerunner of the Indians—upon the inception of the American League in 1901.

But he didn't remain in Cleveland long after piloting the Blues to a seventh-place finish, 28½ games behind the Chicago White Sox, who won the first AL pennant.

McAleer's departure, however, didn't end his managerial career. After the 1901 season McAleer joined the St. Louis Browns, who replaced Milwaukee in the AL.

Not only did McAleer serve as the Browns' manager for the next eight years, but he also helped build them. He raided the NL St. Louis Cardinals for players, including future Hall of Famers Jesse Burkett and Bobby Wallace, who'd been McAleer's teammates with the Spiders.

McAleer began his major league career as an outfielder for the Spiders in 1889, when he hit .235 in 110 games. The following season he jumped to the Cleveland club in the newly formed Players League and batted .267. When the league folded after one year, McAleer returned to the Spiders and played for them through 1898.

Though he retired as a player and, thus, wasn't a member of the woeful Spiders in 1899—the team that posted the worst record, 20–134, in the history of major league baseball—McAleer returned to Cleveland at the behest of the Blues' new owners, Charles W. Somers and Jack Kilfoyl.

The Blues under McAleer lost 18 of their first 25 games,

James R. McAleer

including the first no-hitter in the new league. Earl Moore held Chicago hitless for nine innings on May 9, though the White Sox scored two unearned runs in the fourth on a walk and two errors, and won the game, 4–2, in the 10th on two singles and two fielders' choices.

The highlight of the season for McAleer and the Blues was

Former Indians managers at a 1938 reunion at League Park (left to right, with years they managed in parenthesis): Joe Birmingham (1912–15), Lee Fohl (1915–19), and Tris Speaker (1919–26).

289

on May 13 when they rallied for nine runs with two out in the last of the ninth inning to beat Washington, 14–13.

The Blues climbed to within 10 games of .500 (16–26) in mid-June, but their record never got any better, and they never made it higher than sixth place, finishing the season with 19 losses in their last 29 games.

McAleer played in three games for the Blues in 1901, and in two each in 1902 and 1907 for St. Louis. After leaving the Browns in 1909, he managed the Washington Senators in 1910 and 1911, then was a part owner of the Boston Red Sox in 1912 and 1913.

McAleer, Jimmy

	W	L	T	Pct.
1901	55	82	1	.401
Blues	55	82	1	.401
Career	736	889	33	.453

1902–04

Armour, Bill

Record: 232–195 (.543)
Birthplace: Homestead, Pennsylvania
B: September 3, 1869; **D:** December 2, 1922

The Cleveland club, whose nickname was changed to "Bronchos" in 1902, and then to "Naps" in 1903, fared better—but not much—after Bill Armour replaced Jimmy McAleer as manager in 1902, a position he held through 1904.

In their first season under Armour the Bronchos got off to another poor start, losing 24 of their first 35 games, before second baseman Napoleon Lajoie, the most famous player of that time, was acquired along with pitcher Bill Bernhard from the Philadelphia Athletics.

With Lajoie and Bernhard, the Bronchos went 46–33, and by September 1 reached the .500 mark with a 57–57 record. They vaulted into fifth place, but their early-season deficit was too great to make up.

Despite injuries to their three best pitchers, Bernhard, Addie Joss, and Earl Moore, the Bronchos climbed into third place under Armour in 1903, and were in the thick of the pennant race in 1904 until the final month.

Then more injuries knocked the Naps out of contention, and with the team torn by disorganization and dissension, Armour announced on September 9 that he was resigning.

However, Armour continued as the manager through the end of the season, though Lajoie, as team captain, was in charge on the field.

When the race ended, with the Naps fourth by 7½ games behind Boston, Lajoie was named manager.

Armour took over as manager of Detroit, a position he held in 1905 and 1906, during which he was credited with finding Ty Cobb and buying his contract for $500 to play for the Tigers. (Interestingly, Armour in 1906 used pinch hitters for Cobb on three occasions—Sam Crawford on April 23, Fred Payne on May 30, and George Mullin on September 17—and each of them came through with a hit. These were the only times in Cobb's career that he was replaced by a pinch hitter.)

After leaving the Tigers in 1907, Armour became a part

owner of the Toledo club in the American Association, later scouted for the St. Louis Cardinals, and was business manager of the minor league Milwaukee and Kansas City teams in 1914 and 1915.

Armour, Bill

	W	L	T	Pct.
1902	69	67	1	.507
1903	77	63	0	.550
1904	86	65	3	.570
Bronchos, Naps	232	195	4	.543
Career	382	347	7	.524

1905–09

Lajoie, Napoleon

Record: 377–309 (.550)
Birthplace: Woonsocket, Rhode Island
B: September 5, 1874; **D:** February 7, 1959

Napoleon Lajoie was one of the greatest players—perhaps *the* greatest—in baseball in the early 1900s, but he was far from being successful as a manager his first couple of seasons at the helm of the team nicknamed in his honor.

A great part of Lajoie's trouble in 1905, his first season as the Naps' manager, was that he himself was injured and unable to play for nearly three months. Lajoie was spiked in a play at second base in early July, but remained in the game. The wound became infected, and blood poisoning set in.

It idled Lajoie until late August when he played five games and received another injury, this one putting him out of action for the rest of the season.

During Lajoie's midseason absence, third baseman Bill Bradley served as manager of the team. Later, Bradley also was injured, and so were outfielders Elmer Flick and Harry Bay. The Naps, who'd started the season fast and held first place for a brief time, wound up fifth.

The 1906 season was a virtual replay for Lajoie and the Naps. They again got off to a good start and were in or near first place until August when illness and injuries to key players cost them the pennant, which was won by Chicago.

When Lajoie's average dropped below .300 (to .299) in 1907 for the first time in his major league career, some people speculated that his managerial duties were interfering with his playing ability. However, the Naps again were in the pennant race until the final month.

The Naps did even better in 1908 when they lost the pennant by a margin of .004 and a half game to Detroit. The difference was that the Tigers lost one less game, perhaps a game that was canceled because of rain and not made up (which would be required under today's rules).

But the Naps never played that well under their namesake again, and Lajoie's final season as manager was 1909.

The Naps had been favored to win the Cleveland franchise's first pennant, but struggled from the onset of the season. With the team hopelessly out of contention on August 17, Lajoie offered to resign. Five days later James "Deacon" McGuire replaced Lajoie, though he continued as the Naps' second baseman through 1914, serving under three different managers.

After his retirement Lajoie once commented on an incident that he said was more vivid to him than any other. It happened during his managerial career and involved one of his players, George Stovall, who later also managed the Cleveland club.

Lajoie said he encountered Stovall in a hotel lobby, and Stovall hit him over the head with a heavy chair. Asked by the interviewer what he did to Stovall, Lajoie replied, "Nothing at all. George didn't mean anything by it."

Lajoie, Napoleon

	W	L	T	Pct.
1905	56	57	1	.496
1906	89	64	4	.582
1907	85	67	6	.559
1908	90	64	3	.584
1909	57	57	0	.500
Naps	377	309	14	.550
Career	377	309	14	.550

1905

Bradley, Bill

Record: 20–21 (.488)
Birthplace: Cleveland
B: February 13, 1878; **D:** March 11, 1954

Because an injury forced Napoleon Lajoie out of action—and out of uniform—third baseman Bill Bradley took over as manager of the Naps for 41 games at midseason in 1905.

The Naps held their own under Bradley, going 20–21, but were unable to get back into contention.

Bradley played for the Naps through 1910, his last season as a player. He returned to baseball in 1914 to manage Brooklyn in the newly organized Federal League, but lasted only one season as the Tip Tops went 77–77 and finished in fifth place.

Bradley, Bill

	W	L	T	Pct.
1905	20	21	0	.488
Naps	20	21	0	.488
Career	97	98	3	.497

1909–11

McGuire, Deacon

Record: 91–117 (.438)
Birthplace: Youngstown, Ohio
B: November 18, 1863; **D:** October 31, 1936

James "Deacon" McGuire was another longtime professional baseball player before becoming a major league manager for Washington in the National League in 1898, Boston in the American League in 1907 and 1908, and the Cleveland Naps (forerunners of the Indians), when he came out of retirement on August 22, 1909, to replace Napoleon

Jim McGuire

Lajoie for the final 41 games of that season, and continued through 17 games in 1911.

Only in 1910 did McGuire manage for an entire season, when he piloted the Naps to a 71–81 record (with nine ties) and a fifth-place finish, 32 games behind the Philadelphia Athletics. None of his teams ever had a winning record.

The 1910 season began with great expectation as the Naps started fast and moved into first place by early May. But then, beset by injuries and illness, they soon fell out of contention, never recovered, and were scorned by the media and fans who ridiculed them with the nickname "Molly McGuires."

When the Naps won only six of their first 17 games in 1911, falling into seventh place, McGuire resigned on May 3 and was replaced by first baseman George Stovall. He never managed in the major leagues again.

Before becoming a manager at the age of 34, McGuire was a catcher in the American Association in 1884, the National League from 1885 to 1888 (and 26 games for Cleveland in the AA in 1888), the International League in 1889, the AA again in 1890 and 1891, the NL again from 1892 to 1901, the American League in 1902 when he played for Detroit through 1903, the New York Highlanders from 1904 to 1907, Boston in the latter part of 1907 and 1908, and Cleveland for one game each in 1908 and 1910, and one for Detroit in 1912.

McGuire still holds the record for appearing in more major league seasons, 26, than any other catcher in baseball history. He was behind the plate for 1,611 games, most of them prior to the formation of the AL in 1901.

McGuire, Deacon

	W	L	T	Pct.
1909	14	25	2	.359
1910	71	81	9	.467
1911	6	11	0	.353
Naps	91	117	11	.438
Career	210	287	19	.423

1911

Stovall, George

Record: 74–62 (.544)
Birthplace: Independence, Missouri
B: November 23, 1878; **D:** November 5, 1951

A longtime member of the Naps as their first baseman from 1904 to 1911, George Stovall was one of their most popular players among fans and teammates, though not among umpires and club officials because of his renowned hot temper.

Though he did a good job reversing the Naps' losing ways—their record was 6–11 when he took over, and they went on to win 74 and lose 62 to finish third under Stovall—he was not retained by owner Charles W. Somers.

Reportedly, the reason Stovall didn't keep his job was that Somers had made a secret deal with Philadelphia Athletics owner Connie Mack to hire his first baseman, Harry Davis, to manage the Naps in 1912.

After Davis was appointed, Stovall was traded to the St. Louis Browns on February 17, 1912, much to the resentment of the fans.

Stovall opened the 1912 season as the Browns' first baseman and became their player-manager after 40 games, replacing Bobby Wallace in June. Stovall remained in those dual positions until September 6, 1913, when he was fired from both jobs after a series of controversial incidents involving the owner of the team and several American League umpires.

He then jumped to the Federal League to become player-manager of the Kansas City Packers and actively recruited other major league players to join him in the newly organized league. He lured so many players to the outlaw league that he was called by *The Sporting News* "the Jesse James of the loop."

After two years with the Packers, when baseball peace was declared, Stovall was assigned to Toledo of the American Association in 1916 and managed Vernon in the Pacific Coast League in 1917. He worked in the shipyards during World War I and returned to the game in 1922 as manager of Jacksonville in the Florida State League.

Later Stovall went to the California oil fields where he managed semipro baseball teams. In 1933 and 1934 he coached baseball at Loyola University in Los Angeles, and from 1935 to 1940 he scouted for Pittsburgh. He returned to the shipyards in 1941 and worked until 1946 when he retired.

Stovall, George

	W	L	T	Pct.
1911	74	62	3	.544
Naps	74	62	3	.544
Career	313	376	9	.454

1912

Davis, Harry

Record: 54–71 (.432)
Birthplace: Philadelphia, Pennsylvania
B: July 19, 1873; **D:** August 11, 1947

Harry Davis had a long and illustrious career as a major league first baseman, outfielder, and third baseman from 1895 to 1917, but his tenure as a manager was brief and unsuccessful in Cleveland in 1912.

After a secret agreement with Philadelphia Athletics owner Connie Mack, Cleveland owner Charles W. Somers hired Davis on October 27, 1911, to replace the popular George Stovall.

The appointment did not meet with great approval among either the Cleveland players or the fans, and Davis's status never improved. He was a very strict disciplinarian, and team morale suffered as a result. The Naps played poorly most of the season; they were never in contention for the pennant.

Finally, on September 2, with the Naps lodged in sixth place with a 54–71 record, Davis resigned and was replaced by Joe Birmingham, an outfielder on the team. Davis returned to the Athletics as a player-coach in 1913, though he played only a few games each season through 1917, then served strictly as a coach through 1919.

Davis, Harry

	W	L	T	Pct.
1912	54	71	2	.432
Naps	54	71	2	.432
Career	54	71	2	.432

1912–15

Birmingham, Joe

Record: 170–191 (.471)
Birthplace: Elmira, New York
B: August 6, 1884; **D:** April 24, 1946

The first thing Joe Birmingham did upon replacing Harry Davis and becoming the third (of six) full-time player-managers of the Cleveland club was to lighten many of the strict disciplinary rules that had been in place.

He also made several lineup and roster changes, and the Naps responded by winning 21 of their final 28 games, though they still finished well out of contention, in fifth place, 30½ games behind pennant-winning Boston.

The appointment of Birmingham was a popular move, except in the opinion of Napoleon Lajoie, who did not get along well with the new manager. They had been teammates from the time Birmingham joined the Naps in 1906, and Birmingham, of course, played under Lajoie, who managed the team through August 21, 1909.

Birmingham, an outstanding defensive center fielder, benched Lajoie on several occasions in 1913, after one of which Lajoie openly cursed the manager to his face and in the newspapers.

Despite the animosity between the two men, Lajoie and the team played well, and the Naps finished third under Birmingham in 1913, only 9½ games behind Philadelphia.

The following season, however, was a disaster as the Naps fell into the basement with the Cleveland franchise's first 100-loss season, and Birmingham's popularity quickly eroded.

Lajoie, who continued to be regularly at odds with Birmingham, slumped to .258 and, at his request, was sold to the Philadelphia Athletics after the season ended.

In 1915, with the nickname of the team changed from "Naps" to "Indians" because of the departure of Lajoie, Birmingham couldn't reverse the losing trend. He was fired after only 28 games, with a record of 12–16, and replaced by Lee Fohl.

Somers said he fired Birmingham because, "I felt Cleveland demanded a change."

Not only was it the end of Birmingham's managerial career, but he also was finished as a major league player.

Birmingham, Joe

	W	L	T	Pct.
1912	21	7	0	.750
1913	86	66	3	.566
1914	51	102	4	.333
1915	12	16	0	.429
Naps, Indians	170	191	7	.471
Career	170	191	7	.471

1915–19

Fohl, Lee

Record: 327–310 (.513)
Birthplace: Pittsburgh, Pennsylvania
B: November 28, 1870; **D:** October 30, 1965

Lee Fohl was not much of a player. He appeared in only five major league games as a catcher, one for Pittsburgh in 1902 and four for Cincinnati in 1903, and was a coach for the Indians when he was hired to manage the team in 1915.

The previous season Fohl was the player-manager of Cleveland's farm team, Waterbury, in the Class B Eastern Association. When that league disbanded prior to the 1915 season, Fohl was invited by the Indians to spring training as pitching coach.

Fohl replaced Joe Birmingham on May 21, 1915, with the Indians languishing in sixth place with a 12–16 record. They were even worse under Fohl the rest of the season, going 45–79, and wound up in seventh place.

It was a year of travail for the franchise. Owner Charles W. Somers lost a great deal of money in several real estate ventures, and attendance at Tribe games had fallen off badly because the team was playing so poorly.

To ease the financial strain, Somers traded the team's best young player, outfielder Joe Jackson, to the Chicago White Sox for three players, none of whom made any long-term contributions to the Indians. Most important, the Tribe also received $31,500, a large sum of money then.

The deal helped Somers' cash flow, but not the Indians—or Fohl—though there soon appeared what seemed to be a light at the end of the long, dark tunnel.

The following winter, on February 21, 1916, Somers sold the franchise to a syndicate headed by James C. "Sunny Jim" Dunn, who vowed he'd spare no effort to build the Indians into a first-rate pennant contender.

Two months later, on April 12, Dunn lived up to his promise by obtaining Tris Speaker from the Boston Red Sox in a trade that cost the Indians two players and $55,000. It was the biggest deal in baseball up until that time.

Dunn also issued a vote of confidence in Fohl, and it was his quiet and patient leadership, along with the contributions of Speaker, that enabled the Indians to play .500 ball in 1916.

Speaker became Fohl's first lieutenant, the Indians' captain on the field. Fohl had utmost confidence in his center fielder and always—except once in 1919—relied completely on Speaker's counsel.

And that one time in 1919 when the manager ignored Speaker's advice, it cost Fohl his job.

But first, Fohl got even more out of the Indians in 1917. Despite the loss of nine players to military service because of World War I, they rose to third place. They were even better in 1918, finishing second, 2½ games behind Boston, which won its third pennant in four seasons.

In fact, had the 1918 season not been shortened because of the war, the Indians might have caught Boston. The Red Sox played three fewer games than the Indians' 129 (two finished in ties), and lost three fewer.

The Indians got off to a good start in 1919, though their 44–33 record the morning of July 18 had them in third place, 4½ games behind Chicago and .004 percentage points behind New York.

That day the Red Sox were in town for a game at League Park, and the Indians were leading, 7–3, going into the ninth inning. The Red Sox scored a run and loaded the bases with two out, bringing Babe Ruth to the plate against right-hander Elmer Myers, working in relief of starter Hi Jasper.

Fohl looked out to Speaker for advice, and the center fielder signaled for the manager to put in one of two right-handers warming up in the bull pen.

But Fohl, this time, ignored—or possibly misread—Speaker's wigwag and replaced Myers with southpaw Fritz Coumbe.

Ruth hit Coumbe's second pitch over the right-field wall for a grand slam homer and an 8–7 lead that held up as the final score.

Dunn was apoplectic after the game and, in effect, fired Fohl, though he didn't tell the manager until after he'd summoned Speaker to his office. The owner said that Fohl had resigned and wanted Speaker to take the job of managing the Indians. Speaker wanted to hear it from Fohl himself.

Fohl, who blamed himself for losing the game, was told of Dunn's decision and immediately encouraged Speaker to take the job—which Speaker did.

It ended Fohl's managerial career in Cleveland, but not in baseball.

He remained out of baseball in 1920, but managed the St. Louis Browns from 1921 until late in 1923, coming within one game of winning the pennant in 1922, and the Red Sox from 1924 to 1926.

Fohl, Lee

	W	L	T	Pct.
1915	45	79	2	.363
1916	77	77	3	.500
1917	88	66	2	.571
1918	73	54	2	.575
1919	44	34	0	.564
Indians	327	310	9	.513
Career	713	792	14	.474

1919–26

Speaker, Tris

Record: 617–520 (.543)
Birthplace: Hubbard, Texas
B: April 4, 1888; **D:** December 8, 1958

Tris Speaker

He was one of the greatest players in the game, certainly one of the Indians' all-time best, and brought them the franchise's first pennant and world championship.

But Tris Speaker's managerial reputation was tainted by an ugly allegation that he conspired with Ty Cobb and two other players to fix the outcome of a game involving the Indians late in 1919. That was the season in which Speaker became the team's fourth full-time player-manager on July 19, succeeding the fired Lee Fohl.

The charge that Speaker's Indians deliberately lost a late-season, meaningless game to Cobb's Detroit Tigers as neither team's place in the standings would be affected, was leveled by Hubert "Dutch" Leonard, who claimed he was part of the conspiracy. The fourth player named was Tribe outfielder Smoky Joe Wood.

Leonard didn't allege the wrongdoing until seven years later, during the 1926 season, after he and Wood had retired, though Speaker and Cobb were still managing and playing for the Indians and Tigers, respectively.

Leonard even produced letters written to him by Cobb and Wood that incriminated all four men. Wood's letter included a certified check for $1,630 which, he said, was Leonard's share of the money that was won on the game.

The case developed into a full-fledged controversy between Commissioner Kenesaw Mountain Landis and American League president Byron "Ban" Johnson, who were at odds with each other even before Leonard's charges were raised.

Johnson wanted to bar all four players permanently from baseball and, in fact, did insist that Speaker and Cobb give up their managerial positions and leave their teams at the end of the 1926 season.

Landis, however, claimed to be unconvinced of the guilt of Speaker, Cobb, Wood, and Leonard.

After a long period of deliberation, Landis cleared them on January 27, 1927, more than a month after the scandal had first been made public and two months after Speaker's resignation had really started the rumors flying.

And, following Landis's exoneration of the four, Johnson backed off from his original indictment. He issued an official report stating that Speaker was forced out as manager of the Indians because he "had been too fond of horse races and too tolerant of similar proclivities among his players," and

that he made Cobb resign as manager of the Tigers because he "had been too violent to be a good manager."

If Speaker had been less than honorable as manager of the Indians from 1919 to 1926, it certainly wasn't evident.

After replacing Fohl in 1919 he led the Indians to a second-place finish, 3½ games behind the Chicago White Sox, and then to the pennant in 1920 in a torrid race with the White Sox and New York Yankees.

The Indians prevailed in the final week after the White Sox eliminated the Yankees. They had a one-game lead over Chicago with five left to play when seven members of the White Sox were suspended following indictment by a Cook County (Illinois) Grand Jury on charges they conspired to fix the 1919 World Series.

While the White Sox, with a makeshift lineup, were losing two of three to St. Louis, the Indians won three of their last five to capture the pennant by two lengths.

It was a great personal triumph for Speaker, who batted .388 (second in the AL only to George Sisler's .407) after his average had declined to .296 the previous season.

The Indians also won the World Series, beating Brooklyn five games to two in what was then a best-of-nine tournament.

Speaker, who in 1937 became the seventh player elected to the Hall of Fame, had another good year in 1921—until he suffered torn ligaments in his right knee on September 11 and was unable to play the rest of the season.

Until then the Indians had either led the AL or were close to the top, but Speaker getting hurt was the last—and most important—of a series of injuries to key players. They faltered in the final three weeks and were finished after losing three of four to the Yankees in New York, September 23–26, and wound up second by 4½ games.

It was the closest the Indians came to repeating their 1920 championship for the next four seasons under Speaker, as they fell to fourth place in 1922, to third by 16½ games in 1923, and to sixth in both 1924 and 1925.

They made another run at the pennant in 1926, despite a horrendous midseason letdown that saw them fall into fifth place. They recovered, however, and nearly caught New York in the final 10 days of the season.

The Yankees were leading by 5½ games at the September 15 start of a six-game series at League Park. The Indians needed a sweep to take over first place, but won only four games and finished second by three lengths.

Two months later, on November 29, Speaker announced his resignation as manager of the Indians and his intended retirement as a player. It wasn't learned until later that he was doing so at the order of Johnson, the AL president. A month earlier, Cobb also had announced his resignation as manager of the Tigers and intended retirement as a player.

Commissioner Landis's subsequent ruling cleared Speaker and Cobb (as well as Wood and Leonard), and overruled Johnson's edict requiring the two managers to leave the American League.

Landis said, "These players have not been, nor are they now found guilty of fixing a ball game. By no decent system of justice could such a finding be made."

Consequently, Speaker joined the Washington Senators and Cobb the Philadelphia Athletics in 1927, and both played for the Athletics in 1928, their final season as active players.

Speaker, Tris

	W	L	T	Pct.
1919	40	21	0	.656
1920	98	56	0	.636
1921	94	60	0	.610
1922	78	76	1	.506
1923	82	71	0	.536
1924	67	86	0	.438
1925	70	84	1	.455
1926	88	66	0	.571
Indians	617	520	2	.543
Career	617	520	2	.543

1927

McCallister, Jack

Record: 66–87 (.431)
Birthplace: Marietta, Ohio
B: January 19, 1879; **D:** October 18, 1946

A severe injury to his right knee suffered while participating in a benefit baseball game in 1902 cut short what appeared to be a promising playing career for Jack McCallister, though it wasn't enough to cause him to quit baseball.

Idled for the next two years, McCallister became an umpire in 1905, and though he tried again in 1906 and 1907 to play in the minor leagues, he finally returned to Ohio to work in the front office of the Portsmouth and then the Akron clubs in the Ohio State League the next five years.

It was McCallister's work at Akron that caught the attention of Cleveland Naps owner Charles W. Somers, and in 1913 he was hired as a coach and scout.

McCallister became the chief assistant to Tris Speaker in 1919 when Speaker became manager of the Cleveland team, by then nicknamed Indians. It was a position McCallister held until through 1926, and when Speaker resigned at the end of that season, McCallister replaced him as manager.

The Indians, who'd been a pennant contender the previous season, did not fare well under McCallister, finishing sixth. When the club was sold in November 1927 to a syndicate headed by Alva Bradley, McCallister was released.

Jack McCallister

He called it one of his greatest disappointments in baseball, and when asked why the Indians didn't do better in 1927, McCallister replied, "I guess it is that I just can't play center field."

His comment was a reference, of course, to the fact that he could replace Speaker as manager, but not Speaker the player, who was the Tribe's center fielder and one of the greatest at that position, as well as a lifetime .345 hitter.

After leaving the Indians, McCallister joined Detroit as a coach and scout in 1928, then scouted for Boston from 1929 to 1933, Cincinnati in 1934, and the Boston Braves from 1936 to 1946.

McCallister, Jack

	W	L	T	Pct.
1927	66	87	0	.431
Career	66	87	0	.431

1928–33, 1941

Peckinpaugh, Roger

Record: 490–481 (.505)
Birthplace: Wooster, Ohio
B: February 5, 1891; **D:** November 17, 1977

At 23 years of age, Roger Peckinpaugh became the youngest man to manage a major league baseball team when he was placed in charge of the New York Highlanders (predecessors of the Yankees) for the final 20 games of the 1914 season, replacing Frank Chance.

Under Peckinpaugh the Highlanders won 10 and lost 10 games.

Then the American League's premier shortstop, Peckinpaugh returned to the ranks of the players in 1915 when "Wild Bill" Donovan was hired to manage the Yankees.

Roger Peckinpaugh

Peckinpaugh played on the Cleveland sandlots and was signed by the Naps, who later were nicknamed the Indians. He played briefly for the Naps in 1910 and 1912, then was traded to the Yankees on May 20, 1913, for infielder Bill Stumpf and outfielder Jack Lelivelt.

It was in New York that Peckinpaugh blossomed, playing eight seasons, putting together a 29-game hitting streak and batting a career-high .305 in 1919. He hit .288 in 1921, the season before he was traded to Washington.

Peckinpaugh ended his playing career with the Chicago White Sox in 1927, and that winter he was hired by the Indians' new general manager, Billy Evans, to replace Jack McCallister as the Cleveland manager.

Instead of an improvement, however, the Tribe's fortunes worsened under Peckinpaugh in 1928. Despite winning 12 of their first 18 games the Indians fell into seventh place, losing 30 more games than they won.

Thereafter, with the addition in 1929 of outfielders Earl Averill, Dick Porter, and Bibb Falk and first baseman Lew Fonseca (who won the batting championship), as well as the promotion of pitcher Wesley Ferrell from the minor leagues, the Indians became respectable under Peckinpaugh the next four seasons, though they were unable to catch Philadelphia, which won the American League pennant in 1929, 1930, and 1931, or New York in 1932.

When the Indians floundered in 1933, losing seven of eight games on an eastern trip to Washington, Philadelphia, and New York from May 15 to 23, and then five straight to Detroit and St. Louis at home, Peckinpaugh was fired on June 9.

He was replaced by Walter Johnson, the former great pitcher who had managed Washington from 1929 to 1932 (though Falk managed the Indians on June 10, prior to the arrival of Johnson in Cleveland).

It was not a popular move as Peckinpaugh was a favorite of Cleveland fans and the media, while Johnson had developed a reputation for impatience while managing Washington, which finished second once, third twice, and fifth once in his four seasons there.

It was then that Bradley first made an announcement for which he would become famous, and which he would repeat on other occasions in the future.

"We only hire the manager; the public fires him," Bradley said of his and Evans' decision to replace Peckinpaugh with Johnson. Bradley claimed the Indians "lacked pep" and "played loosely" under Peckinpaugh.

After leaving the Indians, Peckinpaugh managed Kansas City in the American Association in 1934, worked for the AL promotional bureau from 1935 to 1938, was vice president and manager of New Orleans in the Southern Association in 1939, returned to the AL promotional bureau in 1940, rejoined the Indians as their manager in 1941, served as the Tribe's vice president and general manager from 1942 to 1946, and retired after being general manager of Buffalo in the Class AAA International League in 1947.

Peckinpaugh replaced beleaguered manager Oscar Vitt on November 12, 1940, after the Indians lost the pennant in the final three days of that season.

Peckinpaugh immediately announced, "We should win the [pennant] race . . . we've got the best team in the league."

Despite a fast start, in which the Indians vaulted into first place on April 29 with 11 victories in their first 15 games and remained at the top of the AL for two months, they didn't come close to winning the pennant.

After a midseason collapse, they plummeted out of contention, finished in a fourth-place tie with Detroit, and Peckinpaugh was kicked upstairs. He replaced front office chief C. C. "Cy" Slapnicka, who had resigned, citing health problems.

Peckinpaugh, Roger				
	W	L	T	Pct.
1928	62	92	1	.403
1929	81	71	0	.533
1930	81	73	0	.526
1931	78	76	1	.506
1932	87	65	1	.572
1933	26	25	0	.510
1941	75	79	1	.487
Indians	490	481	4	.505
Career	500	491	4	.505

1933

Falk, Bibb

Record: 1–0 (1.000)
Birthplace: Austin, Texas
B: January 27, 1899; **D:** June 8, 1989

Bibb Falk, a veteran outfielder acquired by the Indians on February 28, 1929, in a trade with the Chicago White Sox for catcher Chick Autry, managed the Indians for only one game, on June 10, 1933, while the team awaited the arrival of the newly hired Walter Johnson.

In Falk's debut—which also was his finale as a manager—the Indians defeated the St. Louis Browns, 5–2, at the Stadium, behind the pitching of Wes Ferrell.

Falk, who'd played for the White Sox from 1920 to 1928, spent three .300-plus seasons (1929–31) with the Indians, the last two as the American League's most productive pinch hitter, then retired with a lifetime .314 batting average.

Falk was the baseball coach at the University of Texas from 1940 to 1967 (except for three years during World War II). His teams compiled a 468–176 record and won two national titles and 20 Southwest Conference championships.

Falk, Bibb

	W	L	T	Pct.
1933	1	0	0	1.000
Indians	1	0	0	1.000
Career	1	0	0	1.000

1933–35

Johnson, Walter

Record: 179–168 (.516)
Birthplace: Humboldt, Kansas
B: November 6, 1887; **D:** December 10, 1946

He was a great pitcher, the second winningest—to only Cy Young—in the history of baseball.

But Walter Johnson had problems as a major league manager, first with the Washington Senators from 1929 to 1932, and then with the Indians, after he replaced Roger Peckinpaugh on June 9, 1933.

Johnson also had managed Newark in the International League in 1928, the year after he retired as a pitcher.

Renowned as a quiet, unassuming, and gentle man during his 21-year pitching career with the Senators, Johnson became impatient and often contentious as manager of the Indians.

His taking over for Peckinpaugh did not produce positive results. The Indians went 48–51 under Johnson in 1933, though they climbed one place in the standings to fourth.

It was in 1934 that Johnson came under severe criticism by the Cleveland media for his handling—*mis*handling, it was alleged—of the Indians' pitching staff, the result primarily of several publicized disputes he had with Oral Hildebrand. Johnson also was blamed for the trading of Wes Ferrell to Boston, where he became a big winner.

Johnson was ripped in the newspapers, especially by Ed Bang, sports editor of the *Cleveland News*, who wrote in a column on July 17, 1934, that "Johnson showed anything but mental alertness and managerial ability," and that "he fell so far short of what a wide-awake manager should do that the fans who were wont to cheer him . . . as a great pitcher, groaned in despair and booed him."

By the end of July, Johnson and beat reporters covering the team quit speaking except when it was absolutely necessary.

Still, it wasn't so bad that the Indians didn't improve under Johnson. They did, finishing third, 16 games over .500, though the situation between Johnson and his players—who were supported by the media and fans—worsened early in 1935. It led to the managerial demise of the Hall of Fame pitcher.

Walter Johnson

While the Indians were in Philadelphia for a three-game series, Johnson announced on May 23 that catcher Glenn Myatt was being released and third baseman Willie Kamm had been instructed to return to Cleveland for a future-deciding conference with team president Alva Bradley.

Johnson said the action was taken "for the good of the team," that he had discovered an "anti-Johnson" bloc headed by Myatt and Kamm.

The two players, supported by most of their teammates, proclaimed their innocence. Kamm demanded and received a hearing before Commissioner Kenesaw Mountain Landis in an effort to clear his name.

Owner Alva Bradley said he could do nothing to change Johnson's disciplinary action, and neither Kamm nor Myatt played another game for Cleveland.

Kamm subsequently was appointed a scout for the Indians, while Myatt signed and played with the New York Giants the remainder of that season, then ended his major league career in Detroit in 1936.

Trouble between Johnson and the players—as well as between Johnson and the media—continued until August 4, when Bradley took action with the team in fifth place and going nowhere with a 46–48 record.

Stating, as he did two years earlier in dismissing Roger Peckinpaugh, that "we only hire the manager; the public fires him," Bradley replaced Johnson with coach Steve O'Neill the next day.

Ironically, it also was in 1935 that Johnson was elected in the initial class of former players to the Hall of Fame, along with Ty Cobb, Babe Ruth, Honus Wagner, and Christy Mathewson.

His firing by the Indians ended the managerial career of Johnson, who returned to Washington as a color commentator for Senators' games on radio in 1936, and later made an unsuccessful bid for election to the U.S. Congress from Maryland.

Johnson, Walter

	W	L	T	Pct.
1933	48	51	0	.485
1934	85	69	0	.552
1935	46	48	2	.489
Indians	179	168	2	.516
Career	529	432	5	.550

1935–37

O'Neill, Steve

Record: 199–168 (.542)
Birthplace: Minooka, Pennsylvania
B: July 6, 1891; **D:** January 26, 1962

His predecessor, Walter Johnson, often was blamed for being too impatient and critical of his players, but the perception was just the opposite with Steve O'Neill, who took over as manager of the Indians on August 5, 1935.

A headline in the *Cleveland News* one afternoon in 1936 blared out, "Get Mad, Steve! Get Mad!"

It was atop an open letter to O'Neill in which he was criticized for being too easygoing, too lenient on the Indians, suggesting they'd play better if he were tougher on them.

But anger and agitation were not traits of O'Neill, often called "the genial Irishman," and it's doubtful that he could have gotten any more out of his players had he been any different.

Upon replacing Johnson for the final 60 games in 1935, O'Neill led the Indians to a 36–23 record (with one tie), which lifted them out of fifth place and into third.

One of the Indians' best and most popular players as a catcher from 1911 to 1923, O'Neill, as their manager in 1936, "inherited" a 17-year-old, flame-throwing rookie pitcher named Bob Feller, who would go on to set major league strikeout records and be elected to the Hall of Fame.

O'Neill, in fact, was Feller's first catcher, in an exhibition game on July 6 against the St. Louis Cardinals. Feller struck out eight batters in the three innings he pitched, and O'Neill continued as his tutor.

Aside from Feller's arrival, 1936 was only a mediocre season for the Indians and their manager after great things had been predicted based on the team's strong finish the year before. The Indians fell back to fifth place and, though they finished six games over .500, didn't win as many as they did in 1935.

The following season also was a disappointment as Feller suffered a sore arm in spring training and couldn't pitch regularly until midseason, and Earl Averill, the team's best hitter, slumped 79 points.

The Indians fell out of contention early as they lost 10 of 12 games between June 15 and 27, and when the season ended, O'Neill was fired.

But the dismissal certainly didn't end O'Neill's long managerial and coaching career, which had begun in the minor leagues the season after he retired as a major league player.

O'Neill's managerial career started as player-manager with Toronto of the Class AA International League in 1929. He held the post until he joined the Toledo Mud Hens of the Class AA American Association as player-coach in 1932, and took over as Toledo's player-manager in 1933 and 1934. O'Neill served the Indians as a coach in 1935 (until he replaced Johnson as manager) and was fired after the close of the 1937 season.

He managed Buffalo in the Class AA International League from 1938 to 1940, and it was during his tenure there in 1939 that he helped develop Lou Boudreau.

O'Neill coached for Detroit in 1941, and in 1942 he managed Beaumont, the Tigers' farm club in the Class A1 Texas League. He succeeded Del Baker as Detroit's manager in 1943 and remained in that position through 1948. His 1945 Tigers won the American League pennant and beat the Chicago Cubs in seven games in the World Series.

He returned to the Indians as a coach in 1949 and went to the Boston Red Sox in a similar role in 1950. He succeeded Joe McCarthy as the Red Sox manager on June 23, 1950, and held the post until he was replaced by Boudreau for the 1952 season.

The Red Sox then made O'Neill a scout, a position he held just before succeeding Eddie Sawyer as manager of the Philadelphia Phillies on June 27, 1952. He continued at the helm of the Phillies until he was fired July 15, 1954.

In 14 seasons as a major league manager, O'Neill's teams never had a losing record.

O'Neill, Steve

	W	L	T	Pct.
1935	36	23	1	.610
1936	80	74	3	.519
1937	83	71	1	.539
Indians	199	168	5	.542
Career	1,040	821	17	.559

Steve O'Neill

1938–40

Vitt, Oscar

Record: 262–198 (.570)
Birthplace: San Francisco, California
B: January 4, 1890; **D:** January 31, 1963

Oscar Vitt presided over the Indians during what probably was the stormiest period of their existence.

He was hired by owner Alva Bradley to instill a fighting spirit among the players in the wake of the easygoing approach by Steve O'Neill—but the combativeness the players developed under Vitt definitely was not what Bradley had in mind.

A former good-fielding but light-hitting third baseman for Detroit from 1912 to 1918 and the Boston Red Sox from 1919 to 1921, Vitt gained fame as a smart and feisty minor league manager, leading the Newark Bears to the International League pennant in 1937.

The Bears were considered by experts to be as good as most major league teams, and Vitt appeared to be exactly what Bradley was seeking as a replacement for O'Neill.

Upon his appointment on October 20, 1937, Vitt said, "I don't know much about this team, but I can tell you one thing. We'll have the damnedest fighting team you ever had here. There'll be no loafing, Ol' Os will see to that."

Vitt's first season started well enough as the Indians took over first place in early May and held it, or were close to the top, for nearly two months. But once the New York Yankees got hot, there was no stopping them. They dislodged the Indians on July 13 and never relinquished the lead.

The Indians won 20 more games than they lost, but finished third, 13 lengths behind the Yankees in Vitt's first year.

It was during the roller-coaster, up-and-down 1939 season, in which the Indians wound up third again, that trouble began to brew. Vitt, frustrated by the Yankees' domination, often criticized his players behind their backs, in front of teammates, and in the media.

Vitt had major problems with ace pitcher Johnny Allen, and even got into several arguments with Indians front office chief C. C. "Cy" Slapnicka. Once, in fact, he told Slapnicka, "You run the front office, and I'll run the ball club," which was duly reported in the newspapers.

The 1940 season began in a blaze of glory for the Indians—especially Bob Feller, who pitched the only opening-day no-hitter in baseball history, against the White Sox in Chicago—but soon disintegrated in a torrent of complaints against Vitt.

The crisis came in the wake of three consecutive losses in New York and Boston, June 9–12, that dropped the Indians' record to 28–21 and left them in third place, two games out of first.

A contingent of 12 players, with Mel Harder as the spokesman, called on Bradley the morning of June 13. They presented Bradley with a petition asking that Vitt be fired and said they were sure they could win the pennant under another manager.

Bradley promised only that he'd "look into the matter, investigate it thoroughly, and determine if any action should be taken."

None was—until the end of the season, after the Indians had lost the pennant to Detroit by one game.

Then, on October 28, Bradley fired Vitt, ending the most tumultuous season in Indians history.

Oscar Vitt

Vitt, Oscar				
	W	**L**	**T**	**Pct.**
1938	86	66	1	.566
1939	87	67	0	.565
1940	89	65	1	.578
Indians	262	198	2	.570

1942–50

Boudreau, Lou

Record: 728–649 (.529)
Birthplace: Harvey, Illinois
B: July 17, 1917

After the Indians embarked on what owner Alva Bradley called a "strengthening, not rebuilding" program with the reappointment in 1941 of Roger Peckinpaugh to replace fired manager Oscar Vitt (see p. 296), another major change took place in 1942.

Though Peckinpaugh established a more stable atmosphere than had prevailed during Vitt's stormy regime, the Indians' record worsened instead of improved. When the 1941 season ended, Peckinpaugh was promoted to vice president, replacing C. C. "Cy" Slapnicka, who resigned citing health problems.

Lou Boudreau

Peckinpaugh's departure paved the way for the hiring of Lou Boudreau, to the great surprise of virtually everybody in baseball.

Boudreau was only 24 years old with less than three seasons of major league playing experience and immediately was dubbed—derisively by some—the "Boy Manager."

"I applied for the job because I thought I could handle it, although, in retrospect, if I had it to do all over again, I probably wouldn't," Boudreau said. "In fact, no sooner did I drop my letter of application in the mailbox than I wanted to get it back."

It was too late, of course, and three days later, on November 23—to Boudreau's great surprise—he received a telephone call from Bradley inviting him to report to Cleveland to be interviewed by the Indians' directors.

Boudreau met with them, as did another candidate, the venerable Burt Shotton, who was virtually the exact opposite in terms of age and experience. Shotton, 57, had managed the Philadelphia Phillies from 1928 to 1933 and Cincinnati in 1934. He also had managed in the minor leagues and been a major league coach with several other teams.

But the Indians' directors, tired of the team's failure to win and hoping to instill new enthusiasm among the fans, chose Boudreau. He was hired on November 25.

"I believe they wanted a middle-of-the-road type manager, someone who was neither as jovial and outgoing as Steve O'Neill had been [1935–37], nor as introverted and tough as Vitt [1938–40], or as outgoing and pleasant as Peckinpaugh [in 1941]," Boudreau said of his appointment.

One stipulation was ordered by Bradley and the directors. It was that Boudreau surround himself with experienced coaches because of his youth. Boudreau readily agreed, immediately hiring Shotton, and later Oscar Melillo, George Susce, Del Baker, and Bill McKechnie.

It was the beginning of a new baseball era in Cleveland that would coincide with the arrival of master promoter Bill Veeck in 1946 and culminate in what would become known as the Indians' Golden Years.

But not immediately.

World War II intervened less than two weeks after Boudreau became the fifth (of six) player-manager in Tribe history. Bob Feller, then baseball's premier pitcher, immediately enlisted in the navy and was gone for 44 months, along with many other major league stars.

Still, Boudreau's debut was auspicious—though his success was only temporary that first year. The Indians won a club-record 13 consecutive games from April 18 to May 2, 1942, though they didn't come close to maintaining that pace and finished the season in fourth place.

They climbed to third in 1943, regressed in 1944, improved slightly in 1945, but dropped back again in 1946, during which Veeck purchased the franchise from Bradley on June 22. His immediate plan was to replace Boudreau with Jimmy Dykes as manager.

However, Boudreau, who had become one of the most popular Indians in franchise history, was under contract through 1947. If Veeck fired Boudreau the manager, he also would be losing the American League's premier shortstop, something he didn't want to do.

Thus, Boudreau—the manager as well as the shortstop—remained in Cleveland, and the Indians climbed over the .500 mark and into fourth place in 1947.

When the season ended, Veeck again set out to change managers. This time his intention was to trade Boudreau to the St. Louis Browns in a deal for shortstop Vernon Stephens, and name Al Lopez, then the Indians' backup catcher, the team's new manager.

But now the fans interceded and saved Boudreau's job.

When news leaked out of the plan to trade Boudreau for Stephens, Veeck was overwhelmed with complaints.

The *Cleveland News* printed a "Boudreau Ballot" on page one and asked readers to vote to keep Boudreau or trade him. Of the more than 100,000 responses, 90 percent wanted Veeck to call off the deal.

In a grandiose public relations move, Veeck said he was bowing to the will of the fans and re-signed Boudreau to a new two-year contract.

But by then the proposed trade that would have sent Boudreau and cash to the Browns for Stephens and several other players already had been killed by Veeck. It died because St. Louis owner Bill DeWitt demanded more money than Veeck was willing to include with the package of players.

And when the Indians won the pennant in 1948 in a dramatic, unprecedented one-game playoff with the Boston Red Sox, Veeck gave credit to Boudreau.

"Lou was determined to prove I was a jerk . . . and he did," said Veeck, who added, "We didn't win the pennant in 1948, we won it on November 24, 1947, the day I rehired Lou Boudreau."

And with that, Veeck gave Boudreau another new contract, through 1950.

But the Indians couldn't duplicate their success and ended up eight games behind the New York Yankees, who won the pennant in 1949. The third-place finish devastated Veeck, but instead of making another attempt to replace Boudreau, he sold the franchise on November 22 and left town.

The buyer was a syndicate headed by Cleveland insurance executive Ellis Ryan. One of his first moves was to sign Hank Greenberg to a three-year contract as vice president and general manager.

Greenberg, who'd been Veeck's right-hand man, shared

many of the former owner's opinions, including his less-than-complete confidence in Boudreau as a manager.

After Greenberg almost totally rebuilt the Indians in 1950 but they still failed to dethrone the Yankees despite improving their won-lost record by three games, Boudreau was fired on November 10.

By then getting rid of the one-time Boy Manager was no problem. Boudreau no longer was the AL's premier shortstop; in fact, he wasn't even a regular on his own team.

But it wasn't the end of Boudreau's managerial career.

In 1951 he signed with Boston as a utility infielder, appearing in 82 games at shortstop, third base, and first base. The following year Boudreau replaced his former mentor, Steve O'Neill, as Red Sox manager, a position he held through 1954. And from 1955 through August 5, 1957, he managed the Kansas City Athletics.

Boudreau then began in 1958 a broadcasting career doing color commentary of Chicago Cubs games—but, as it turned out, he still wasn't finished as a manager.

In 1960, after the Cubs got off to a 6–11 start under Charlie Grimm, owner Phil Wrigley asked Boudreau to leave the radio booth and take over as manager of the team. He did, and the Cubs went 54–83 under Boudreau, after which he returned to the microphone. He was elected to the Hall of Fame in 1970 and remained on the air until he retired in 1988.

Boudreau, Lou

	W	L	T	Pct.
1942	75	79	2	.487
1943	82	71	0	.536
1944	72	82	1	.468
1945	73	72	2	.503
1946	68	86	2	.442
1947	80	74	3	.519
1948	97	58	1	.626
1949	89	65	0	.578
1950	92	62	1	.597
Indians	728	649	12	.529
Career	1,162	1,224	18	.487

1951–56

Lopez, Al

Record: 570–354 (.617)
Birthplace: Tampa, Florida
B: August 20, 1908

Though Bill Veeck was stymied by the fans in his efforts in 1947 to hire Al Lopez to manage the Indians, there was nothing to block Hank Greenberg, then the team's vice president and general manager.

In announcing the hiring of Lopez on November 10, 1950, Greenberg diplomatically paid tribute to Lou Boudreau.

"We knew we had a man as manager who was probably the most popular player in the history of the Cleveland Baseball Club. We also knew we had a fine outstanding gentleman everybody loved," Greenberg said.

"For one month we have been working diligently to get Lou a manager's job somewhere else. Today we learned of one club that was interested, and I think he will have a job in the major leagues."

Al Lopez

And with that, Greenberg introduced Lopez, expressing confidence that the former catcher would lead the Indians back to prominence.

Lopez did—though they won only one pennant under his direction the next five years, setting an American League record with 111 victories in 1954, and then were ignominiously swept by the New York Giants in the World Series.

Still, Lopez's .617 winning percentage as a Tribe manager is the best in franchise history, and his 570 victories are third most (behind only Boudreau's 728 and Tris Speaker's 616).

Though his popularity did not match Boudreau's—none did—Lopez was highly respected as an excellent manager and fine person, refuting the Leo Durocher axiom that claimed "nice guys finish last."

In his book, *Veeck as in Wreck*, Veeck stated, "If Al Lopez has a weakness as a manager—and I said *if*—it is that he is too decent."

A master handler of pitchers during his 19-year major league playing career, Lopez was the architect of what many believe was the greatest pitching staff in baseball history in 1954. It included starters Bob Lemon, Early Wynn, Mike Garcia, Art Houtteman, and Bob Feller and relievers Ray Narleski, Don Mossi, and Hal Newhouser.

"I don't know if it was the best pitching staff ever, but it was by far the best I saw in all my years in the game," said Lopez.

The five seasons the Indians didn't win the pennant under Lopez they finished second to New York, the dominant team of that era. Lopez's Tribe was runner-up to the Yankees by five games in 1951, two in 1952, 8½ in 1953, three in 1955, and nine in 1956, after which Lopez resigned.

"I was disappointed and depressed, my nerves were shot, and my stomach was bothering me," Lopez said, explaining his decision to leave the Indians. "I wasn't mad at anybody, I just needed a change of scenery."

Shortly thereafter, on October 29, 1956, Lopez signed to manage the Chicago White Sox, a job he held for nine seasons. After another brief retirement in 1967, Lopez returned to manage the White Sox on an interim basis for 47 games in 1968, and again for 17 games in 1969.

Lopez led the White Sox to the pennant in 1959 and was the only manager to finish ahead of the Yankees in the 1950s. Except for 1954 and 1959 his teams finished second that entire decade, and 10 times overall in his 15 full seasons as a manager.

His career won-lost record was 1,410–1,004 for a .584 percentage, ninth on the all-time list.

Lopez was elected to the Hall of Fame in 1977, and in a poll of retired major league players conducted in the mid-1980s he was rated the seventh-best manager of all time, as well as the seventh-best defensive catcher.

Lopez's playing career began in 1925 with Tampa of the Class D Florida State League. After a late-season trial with Brooklyn in 1928, he returned to the major leagues in 1930 to play for the Dodgers through 1935, the Boston Bees (Braves) from 1936 to 1940, and Pittsburgh from 1940 to 1946. He was traded to the Indians on December 7, 1946, for outfielder Gene Woodling.

He batted .262 in 61 games for the Tribe in 1947, and until Bob Boone passed him in 1987, Lopez had caught more games (1,918) than any other player in baseball history.

When the story broke in October 1947 that Veeck wanted to replace Boudreau as manager by trading him to the St. Louis Browns, Lopez said he already had made it clear he didn't want the job.

"I told [Veeck] that I'd refuse it," Lopez recalled the episode. "I said I didn't think it would be right for me to take the job of a man I'd worked for, although I also told him that maybe two or three years down the road, after I'd quit playing, I would be interested."

And it was three years down the road that Greenberg was interested in Lopez.

First, Lopez returned to the minor leagues to manage Indianapolis of the American Association. His team won the AA pennant in 1948, finished second but won the playoffs and the Junior World Series in 1949, and was second again in 1950, after which Greenberg offered him the job of managing the Indians.

"I told Hank that I'd take it only if he'd already made the decision to fire Boudreau," said Lopez. When he was assured Greenberg had done so, Lopez accepted.

"I'd always wanted to manage in the big leagues, but I wanted to do it [get the job] the right way," he said.

In his first season with the Indians they equaled a club record by winning 13 games in a row from August 2 to 15. By August 23 they were in first place with a 78–43 record and a three-game lead over the Yankees. But then they lost 13 of their next 25, relinquished first place on September 17, and never recovered.

It got better in 1952, but not enough, as five teams—Chicago, Boston, and Washington, as well as the Yankees and Indians—were in contention at the All-Star break. The Tribe took over first place by .001 on August 22 after winning 18 of 25, but couldn't hold it, and dropped into second place to stay on September 12.

In 1953, except for the first week of the season, New York led the league and became the first major league team to win five consecutive pennants.

The Yankees' domination was stopped in 1954, though only temporarily.

The Indians started the season only 3–6, but won 11 straight and took over first place on May 16. They were displaced by the White Sox for four days in early June, but after the All-Star break went 55–16. No other team has ever done so well in the second half of a season, and the Tribe clinched

the pennant on September 18 with a 3–2 victory over Detroit. Seven days later the Indians recorded their AL-record-setting 111th victory, 11–1, also against the Tigers.

But what followed in the World Series was a disaster for Lopez, the Indians, and their fans, beginning with an 11th-inning, three-run pinch-hit homer by Dusty Rhodes that won the opener, 5–2, for the Giants. Three more consecutive losses followed, 3–1, 6–2, and 7–4—and many believe the Indians have been jinxed ever since.

The Yankees regained the pennant in 1955 in another roller-coaster race that saw the Indians in and out of first place until the final 11 days of the season. They lost six of their last nine games in the midst of a 15–4 streak by the Yankees, after which Lopez announced his intention to resign as manager but was talked out of it by Greenberg.

There was no changing Lopez's mind in the wake of the 1956 season. It turned into a pennant runaway by the Yankees after the Indians fell out of first place on May 16. From July 15 to the end of the season the Indians were never closer than seven games behind the Yankees.

On the morning of the final day of the season, September 30, Lopez again announced his intention to resign. Greenberg again attempted to dissuade him; he couldn't.

In the years since Lopez left, the Indians have appeared in the World Series only once, in 1995, when they lost to Atlanta in six games.

In 1959 they were beaten out of the pennant in the final three weeks of the season by, ironically, Lopez's White Sox. And in 1994 they were denied what appeared to be a certain place in the AL Championship Series when a 50-day strike by the Players Association prematurely ended the season on August 12.

Lopez, Al

	W	L	T	Pct.
1951	93	61	1	.604
1952	93	61	1	.604
1953	92	62	1	.597
1954	111	43	2	.721
1955	93	61	0	.604
1956	88	66	1	.571
Indians	570	354	6	.617
Career	1,410	1,004	11	.584

1957

Farrell, Kerby

Record: 76–77 (.497)
Birthplace: Leapwood, Tennessee
B: September 3, 1913; **D:** December 17, 1975

Hank Greenberg's first choice to replace Al Lopez in 1957 was Leo Durocher, who had managed Brooklyn (1939–46 and 1948) and the New York Giants (1948–55).

At the time he was approached by Greenberg, Durocher was working for NBC-TV as color commentator on the network's baseball telecasts.

But Durocher's price tag was too high, and on November 28, 1956, Greenberg instead promoted Kerby Farrell, who'd been a successful minor league manager in the Indians' farm system. He had led their top affiliate, Indianapolis of the American Association, into the Junior World Series in 1956.

Kerby Farrell

The choice of Farrell proved to be a disaster for the Indians, who fell from contention into the second division with a losing record, their worst in 11 years.

The Tribe started poorly and fell into last place on April 21. More trouble followed when Herb Score, the best young pitcher in baseball, was lost for the rest of the season on May 7 when he was hit in the eye by a line drive off the bat of Gil McDougald.

But Farrell rallied the Indians and, by May 21, they'd climbed eight games over .500 and into second place. However, they never got any better, only worse.

When the season ended, September 29, Farrell was fired and Bobby Bragan hired by Greenberg—who then, on October 16, was himself fired, effective December 31.

It was a disheartening turn of events for Farrell, who, despite his limited experience as a major league first baseman, had been successful virtually everywhere he'd played and managed in the minor leagues.

Farrell played briefly for the Boston Braves in 1943 and batted .268 in 85 games, and for the Chicago White Sox for whom he hit .258 in 103 games in 1945.

Before those opportunities came along, Farrell's minor league record reads like a bus schedule: Jackson, Mississippi; Beckley, West Virginia; Tyler, Texas; Memphis, Tennessee; Greenville, South Carolina; Canton, Ohio; Erie, Pennsylvania; Indianapolis, Indiana; Little Rock, Arkansas; Spartanburg, South Carolina; and Cedar Rapids, Iowa. He was a player-manager at Erie in 1941 and 1942, Spartanburg from 1947 to 1950, and Cedar Rapids in 1951.

After being fired by the Indians, Farrell returned to the minor leagues and managed Miami of the International League in 1958, Buffalo of the International League from 1959 to 1963, Salinas of the California League in 1964, and Williamsport of the Eastern League, and Buffalo again in 1965.

He coached for the Chicago White Sox from 1966 to 1969 and the Indians in 1970 and 1971, then went back to the mi-

nor leagues to manage Lynchburg in the Carolina League in 1972 and Tacoma in the Pacific Coast League in 1973. He ended his baseball career as a scout for Minnesota in 1974.

Farrell, Kerby

	W	L	T	Pct.
1957	76	77	0	.497
Indians	76	77	0	.497
Career	76	77	0	.497

1958

Bragan, Bobby

Record: 31–36 (.463)
Birthplace: Birmingham, Alabama
B: October 30, 1917

Frank Lane and Bobby Bragan took over the Indians in 1958, but it was not a lasting relationship.

First, Bragan was named manager on September 29, 1957; then, Lane was hired as Hank Greenberg's replacement on November 13, 1957.

Bragan's term ended quickly, after only 67 games and 73 days into the season, to be exact.

On June 26, after a 2–1 loss to Boston in which Ted Williams hit a game-winning, ninth-inning homer, there was a message in Bragan's office for him to go upstairs to see Lane.

"I knew what he wanted . . . I was no virgin," said Bragan, who'd previously managed and been fired by Pittsburgh, and later would manage and be fired by the Milwaukee-Atlanta Braves.

On that June day in 1958, with the Indians in sixth place, 12 games behind the New York Yankees, Bragan's intuition proved correct.

"Bobby," Lane said to the soon-to-be-former Tribe manager, "I don't know how we're going to get along without you, but starting tomorrow we're going to try."

Bobby Bragan

With his 31–36 record, Bragan's tenure was the shortest of any manager in Tribe history (excluding all the interim pilots).

Selected by Lane to replace Bragan was Joe Gordon, the Tribe's star second baseman from 1947 to 1950.

Shortly after Bragan left Cleveland a story circulated that seemed to make great sense, especially in later years. It was that Bragan, angry about being fired by Lane, hired a witch to put a curse on the Indians.

"If people in Cleveland want to believe that, let 'em," Bragan said at one point during the Tribe's lack of success between 1959 to 1994.

"The whole thing was a figment of some disc jockey's imagination. The guy asked me how I felt after I was fired, and I told him I felt like putting a curse on the entire organization. I was only joking, but [the disc jockey] thought I was serious, or knew it would make a good story."

A month after he was fired by Lane, Bragan took a minor league managing job with Spokane in the Pacific Coast League and held it through 1959, coached for the Los Angeles Dodgers in 1960, scouted for Houston in 1961, coached for that team in 1962, and resurfaced as manager of the Braves from 1963 until August 9, 1966, when he was fired again.

Bragan played in the major leagues as a shortstop for the Philadelphia Phillies from 1940 to '42, then switched positions and was a part-time catcher for Brooklyn in 1943 and 1944. After serving in the Army in 1945 and 1946, Bragan returned to play for the Dodgers in 1947 and briefly in 1948. He went back in the minor leagues as a player-manager for Fort Worth in the Texas League from 1948 to '52, and for Hollywood in the Pacific Coast League from 1953 to '55.

Noted for his umpire baiting as a player, coach, and manager, Bragan was president of the Texas League from 1969 to 1975, during which time he was in charge of the league's umpires.

In 1976 he succeeded Hank Peters as president of the National Association (minor leagues) and served until 1979 when he resigned so he could move back to Fort Worth where he had lived for many years.

But Bragan didn't sever his ties with baseball. He joined Commissioner Bowie Kuhn's staff as an executive adviser in field services for both the commissioner's office and the National Association. In addition, he joined the Texas Rangers in a public relations capacity.

Bragan, Bobby

	W	L	T	Pct.
1958	31	36	0	.463
Indians	31	36	0	.463
Career	443	478	6	.481

1958–60

Gordon, Joe

Record: 184–151 (.549)
Birthplace: Los Angeles
B: February 18, 1915; **D:** April 14, 1978

Cursed by Bobby Bragan or not, the Indians under Joe Gordon the rest of 1958 were respectable if not spectacular, posting a 46–40 record, and wound up in fourth place, one game over .500 (77–76).

Joe Gordon

Upon joining the Indians, Gordon described his method of managing: "I'm as gentle as a kitten, but I scratch sometimes," both of which proved to be true.

Under Gordon the following year the Indians' record was even better, though it turned into a tempestuous season. He had ongoing problems with two of Frank Lane's favorite players, Jim Piersall and Billy Martin, which, of course, created trouble between the manager and general manager.

The difficulties reached the point where Gordon decided he'd had enough and announced on September 18—10 days before the end of the season—that he was resigning, effective after the final game, no matter where the Indians finished.

At the time, the Tribe was in second place with an 84–62 record, four games behind the Chicago White Sox with eight games left.

Lane, angered by Gordon's declaration, retaliated with one of his own. He said that Gordon would be relieved of his managerial duties after the game in which the Tribe was mathematically eliminated.

Lane also immediately contacted Leo Durocher in an attempt to hire him as the Indians' next manager. But again, as he had done when offered the job by Hank Greenberg in 1957, Durocher priced himself out of the market.

After the Indians lost to Chicago, 4–2, on September 22, clinching the pennant for the White Sox, Lane announced that Gordon was out "as of now" as Tribe manager. Coach Mel Harder was placed in charge of the team for the final four games.

The next day Lane called another press conference. "Gentlemen, I want you to meet the man who will manage the Indians next year," Lane told the assembled reporters.

The door opened, and Gordon, smiling broadly, walked into the room.

Though conjecture was that the Indians were unwilling to meet Durocher's salary demands, Lane calmly stated that he'd "made a mistake" in his decision to let Gordon go and that he "decided I didn't have to live with it, so I tried to correct it."

Not only was the order firing Gordon rescinded, but Lane also gave him a two-year contract through 1961, at a raise in pay. It was a popular move by the controversial general manager.

Gordon, one of the Indians' heroes on the 1948 pennant-winning and world championship team, had been a player-manager for Sacramento in the Pacific Coast League in 1951 and 1952, a scout for Detroit from 1953 to '55, and a coach with the Tigers from April 17 to June 28, 1956. He managed San Francisco in the PCL from July 9, 1956, through 1957. Gordon was out of baseball in 1958, until taking over for Bobby Bragan on June 26.

Lane's change of heart regarding Gordon, together with the fact that the Indians battled the White Sox nearly to the wire, made for an interesting season. It also provided hope for even better results in 1960—though such was not the case, beginning two days before the opener.

Lane shocked and angered most Cleveland fans by sending their idol, outfielder Rocky Colavito, to Detroit for outfielder Harvey Kuenn on April 17.

And the very next day, April 18, Lane traded pitcher Herb Score to the Chicago White Sox for pitcher Barry Latman.

As it turned out, those deals were only the beginning of Lane's feverish wheeling and dealing in 1960.

After a slow start that season, a resurgence was followed by another slump—13 losses in 17 games—that left the Indians in fourth place with a 49–46 record, and Lane swung into action again.

On August 3, in a deal that stunned everybody, he sent Gordon to Detroit for Tigers manager Jimmy Dykes.

It was the first time major league managers were traded for each other—and hasn't happened since.

That night, before the two men could report to their new teams, coach Jo Jo White managed the Indians to a 7–4 victory over Washington. Five days later White was released by the Indians and rejoined Gordon in Detroit. Luke Appling, who'd worked for Dykes with the Tigers, also was let go and was reunited with his boss in Cleveland.

After Gordon took over the Tigers, they won 26 and lost 31 games, finishing sixth, the same position they were in under Dykes.

Gordon resigned as manager of the Tigers after the 1960 season and three days later, on October 5, signed to manage the Kansas City Athletics, a job he held through June 6, 1961.

Gordon served as a batting instructor and scout for the Los Angeles Angels from 1962 to 1968. He managed the Kansas City Royals in 1969, after which his contract was not renewed though he remained with the club as coordinator of instruction in 1970 and 1971.

Gordon, Joe

	W	L	T	Pct.
1958	46	40	0	.535
1959	89	65	0	.578
1960	49	46	0	.516
Indians	184	151	0	.549
Career	305	308	2	.498

1960

White, Jo Jo

Record: 1–0 (1.000)
Birthplace: Red Oak, Georgia
B: June 1, 1909; **D:** October 9, 1986

Jo Jo White was a major league outfielder for Detroit from 1932 to 1938, the Philadelphia Athletics in 1943 and 1944, and Cincinnati in 1944, compiling a .256 lifetime batting average.

He managed in the minor leagues for 10 years and joined the Indians as a coach in 1958 when Joe Gordon was appointed manager.

On August 8, 1960, five days after Gordon was traded to Detroit for Tigers manager Jimmy Dykes, White was released by the Indians and immediately rejoined Gordon.

The day of the Gordon-Dykes deal, August 3, White managed the Indians in a 7–4 victory over the Senators in Washington. It was the only time he managed a major league team.

White coached for the Kansas City Athletics in 1961 and 1962 and the Milwaukee/Atlanta Braves from 1963 to 1966, managed Dallas–Fort Worth in the Texas League in 1967, and rejoined Gordon as a coach for the Kansas City Royals in 1969.

White, Jo Jo

	W	L	T	Pct
1960	1	0	0	1.000
Indians	1	0	0	1.000
Career	1	0	0	1.000

1960–61

Dykes, Jimmy

Record: 103–115 (.472)
Birthplace: Philadelphia, Pennsylvania
B: November 10, 1896; **D:** June 15, 1976

It could be classified as a deal that didn't help either team, after Jimmy Dykes came to Cleveland and Joe Gordon went to Detroit on August 3, 1960.

They were the only major league managers to be traded for each other, though Dykes saw it differently.

"Let's face it," he said upon reporting to Cleveland. "This was not a trade. It was a case of a couple of guys being fired and getting fielded on the first bounce by a couple of other guys."

Those "other guys" were Frank Lane, general manager of the Indians, and Bill DeWitt, his counterpart with the Tigers, and Dykes probably was right that he and Gordon actually had been fired, not merely traded.

Whatever, under Dykes, the Indians won 26 and lost 32 of the final 58 games that season. Under Gordon, their record had been three over .500 (49–46), and they were fourth, seven games out of first place. They were still fourth when the season ended.

The Tigers improved slightly after Dykes departed. With Gordon, they went from eight under .500 to five under and finished in sixth place, though he was fired at the end of the 1960 season.

Jimmy Dykes

Dykes survived 1960 in Cleveland—he'd been re-signed for another season by Lane—but the controversial general manager himself was let go at year's end when his contract expired on December 31, 1960, and was not renewed.

Two former Tribe players, Hoot Evers and Bob Kennedy, shared the player personnel duties in the front office on an interim basis until Gabe Paul was hired as general manager on April 27, 1961.

That season, in the midst of a 10-game winning streak in early June, Dykes piloted the Indians into first place, but stayed there only nine days, from June 6 to 14, when their record was 38–22. But from there they went 40–61 the rest of the season and dropped into fifth place to stay.

With one game left and the Indians with a 77–83 record on October 1, Dykes was fired, ending his 21-year major league managerial career.

The firing should not have come as any great surprise, after the arrival of Paul, who had been the longtime general manager of Cincinnati and previously fired Dykes as manager of the Reds in 1958.

Coach Mel Harder was placed in charge of the team for its final game, an 8–5 victory over the California Angels in Los Angeles.

It couldn't have been a lack of experience that was the cause of Dykes' failure to rejuvenate the Indians. He previously managed the Chicago White Sox from 1934 to 1946, the Philadelphia Athletics from 1951 to 1953, Baltimore in 1954, Cincinnati the final six weeks of 1958, and Detroit for 137 games in 1959, before being traded for Gordon.

Dykes also deserves mention for longevity without having achieved much success.

He held the major league record for managing the most years, 21, without winning a pennant, until it was broken by Gene Mauch (who wound up a 26-year career in 1987 without winning a pennant). The highest a Dykes team finished was third (Chicago in 1936, 1937, and 1941).

The 1,541 games his teams lost in those 21 years are the 10th most by a manager in major league baseball history.

Dykes also managed Hollywood in the Pacific Coast League the last two months of 1946 and in 1947 and 1948, and was a coach for the Athletics in 1949 and 1950, for Cincinnati from 1955 until he took over for Birdie Tebbetts as manager on August 14, 1958, and for Pittsburgh at the start of the 1959 season, then replaced Bill Norman as manager of the Tigers on May 3.

After leaving the Indians, Dykes joined the Milwaukee Braves as a coach in 1962 and finished his baseball career as a coach for the Kansas City Athletics in 1963 and 1964.

Though he saw action at every position except catcher—he even pitched two innings in 1927, allowing two hits, a walk, and a run—Dykes was primarily an infielder and played mostly at third base. He was with the Athletics from 1918 to 1932 and the White Sox from 1933 to 1939, compiling a lifetime batting average of .280 in 22 seasons. He was a player-manager for Chicago from 1934 to 1939.

It was in 1929, when Dykes hit a career-high .327, that Athletics owner and manager Connie Mack said, "Having one Dykes is like having five or six players and only one to feed, clothe, and pay."

Dykes reputedly had the ability to throw harder than any nonpitcher in baseball, batted .300 or better five times between 1924 and 1930, and helped the Athletics win three American League pennants in 1929 through 1931.

His playing career continued until he was 43 years old because, he said, "I ran all the time. I kept my legs in shape. There's nothing better, not calisthenics, nothing. Just running."

Dykes also was renowned as a bench jockey, and he took great delight in riding the Indians in 1940 when they were called "Crybabies" because of their rebellion against manager Oscar Vitt.

What's more, Dykes—in his opinion—was an "expert" on how reporters should cover sports. "Print only nice things," he said while managing the Indians. "Don't go looking for trouble. People want to read about how well the team is doing. You should overlook the bad things."

Dykes, Jimmy

	W	L	T	Pct.
1960	26	32	0	.448
1961	77	83	0	.481
Indians	103	115	0	.472
Career	1,406	1,541	13	.477

1961, 1962

Harder, Mel

Record: 3–0 (1.000)
Birthplace: Beemer, Nebraska
B: October 15, 1909

A coach for the Indians for 16 seasons, Mel Harder served as interim manager of the Indians on two different occasions. He led them to an 8–5 victory over the Los Angeles Angels on October 1, 1961, after Jimmy Dykes was fired, and to a sweep of a doubleheader over the Angels on September 30, 1962, after taking over for Mel McGaha.

Harder, Mel

	W	L	T	Pct.
1961	1	0	0	1.000
1962	2	0	0	1.000
Indians	3	0	0	1.000
Career	3	0	0	1.000

1962

McGaha, Mel

Record: 78–82 (.488)
Birthplace: Bastrop, Louisiana
B: September 26, 1926

After firing Jimmy Dykes, the next move by Gabe Paul was to promote Indians first base coach Mel McGaha to manage the team in 1962. At 35, McGaha was at that time the youngest manager in the major leagues (though El Tappe, then a member of the Chicago Cubs' board of coaches, was 16 months younger than McGaha).

McGaha's primary task, it was said, would "consist of trying to cut out the cancer that caused the [1961] Tribe to fall apart—the bickering and whining by a small core of players."

As Paul said, "We know we have a personality problem on this club. It has hurt us. That's the reason McGaha was brought in. He's seen the clubhouse lawyers in action. He knows the situation, and it's up to him to handle it."

Dykes acknowledged the problem when he was fired. "This job is murder," he said then. "The troublemakers make it a suicide position."

McGaha's comment: "It doesn't scare me a bit," though it should have.

"I have one philosophy," added McGaha, "and that is to win. I play to win, and I'll do anything to achieve that purpose."

Mel McGaha

Prior to joining the Tribe to work under Dykes in 1961, McGaha managed seven years in the minor leagues, the first five as a player-manager for Shreveport in the Texas League from 1954 to 1957 and Mobile in the Southern Association in 1958. McGaha also managed Mobile in 1959 and Toronto in the International League in 1960, winning pennants his first season at Shreveport and at Toronto.

But his minor league success didn't carry over into the major leagues, and the Indians fell into sixth place, though their won-lost record improved slightly under McGaha.

It wasn't enough to save McGaha's job, and he, too, was fired by Paul on September 29 with two games left in the season.

And, when he left Cleveland, McGaha could only blame the lack of talent on the team. "We just didn't have enough good players, and nobody can win without good players," he said.

Pitching coach Mel Harder again was placed in charge of the Indians, and under his direction they defeated the Los Angeles Angels, 4–1 and 6–1.

McGaha was an outstanding, three-sport athlete at the University of Arkansas, though he never made it to the major leagues after 11 seasons in the minors as a catcher–first baseman–outfielder, mostly in the St. Louis Cardinals organization.

Playing for Duluth in the Northern League in 1948, McGaha and his teammates figured in a serious accident in which the team bus was wrecked. Four players, the manager, and driver were killed, and McGaha suffered a dislocation of his right shoulder that hampered him the rest of his baseball playing career.

In addition to baseball at Arkansas, McGaha also played football and basketball and was a member of the New York Knickerbockers in the National Basketball Association in the 1948–49 season.

After his dismissal by the Indians, McGaha joined the Kansas City Athletics as a coach in 1963. In 1964, after 52 games, he replaced Ed Lopat as manager.

Under McGaha the rest of that season the Athletics' record was 40–70, and they finished last in the American League. In 1965, after Kansas City won only five of its first 26 games under McGaha, he was fired and replaced by Haywood Sullivan.

McGaha managed the Oklahoma City 89ers, then Houston's top farm club, in the Class AAA Pacific Coast League in 1966 and 1967, then was a coach for the Astros from 1968 to 1971.

McGaha, Mel

	W	L	T	Pct.
1962	78	82	0	.488
Indians	78	82	0	.488
Career	123	173	1	.416

1963–66

Tebbetts, Birdie

Record: 278–259 (.518)
Birthplace: Burlington, Vermont
B: November 10, 1912

Birdie Tebbetts, another who had felt the ax at the hands of Gabe Paul at Cincinnati, was given a second chance to please the man who had become the Indians' president–trea-

Birdie Tebbetts

surer–general manager and who was promising Cleveland fans a new era of success.

"I know Birdie Tebbetts, and I know he is the best man to do the job here that needs to be done," is the way Paul introduced his new manager.

It was an obvious reference to the problem that Mel McGaha had inherited the previous season and was unable to solve.

"I think the talent is here . . . we just have to bring it out," is the way Tebbetts addressed the "problem."

It also was a homecoming of sorts for Tebbetts, an Indians catcher in 1951 and 1952 and manager of their Indianapolis farm club in the American Association in 1953.

Paul originally hired Tebbetts to manage the Reds in 1954, a job Birdie held until he was replaced on August 14, 1958, by Jimmy Dykes. Under Tebbetts the Reds finished fifth his first two years, climbed to third in 1956—when he was named Manager of the Year in the National League—but fell back to fourth in 1957 and 1958, after which he was fired by Paul.

"Birdie and I had a turbulent coexistence in Cincinnati . . . he certainly wasn't a yes man, but that was one of the reasons I thought so highly of him," Paul also said upon his introduction of Tebbetts as the Tribe's 22nd manager since 1901.

After leaving the Reds, Tebbetts became executive vice president of the Milwaukee Braves in 1958, but he returned to uniform in the final month of 1961, replacing Chuck Dressen, and managed the team to a 12–13 record.

He continued as the Braves manager through 1962, then resigned to rejoin Paul in Cleveland, where the Indians were touting three rookies—center fielder Vic Davalillo, third baseman Max Alvis, and shortstop Tony Martinez—as the cornerstone of their anticipated resurgence.

But it wasn't that easy; the best they could do was tie Detroit for fifth place, and when the 1964 season started, Tebbetts was hospitalized with a heart attack he suffered April 1 in spring training.

Third base coach George Strickland was put in charge of the team until Tebbetts returned to uniform on July 5. By then the Indians had dropped into sixth place.

There was a difference in Tebbetts' managerial style after his heart attack, according to Paul, who said, "Birdie became

overly cautious . . . he seemed to lose much of the feistiness, the boldness that I thought had made him such a good manager."

Still, the Indians climbed over .500 in 1965 for the first time in six years, and opened the 1966 season with an American League record–setting 10 consecutive victories. They held first place or were close to it through the first two weeks of June.

But all that followed was disastrous, and the Indians began a free fall into fifth place (where they finished the season with a .500 record), and Tebbetts agreed to resign on August 19 with the Indians' record 66–57.

Tebbetts' decision to leave the Tribe—and Paul's willingness to let him go—was finalized the previous day, according to the ex-manager.

He said, "I told Gabe, 'Look, we're getting on each other's nerves . . . I think you are a so-and-so and you think the same of me. I don't want to take the team on the road again [three days hence], so why don't you let George [Strickland] take over?'"

Paul agreed, and Tebbetts went down to the clubhouse. "I told Gabe to let you handle the club," Tebbetts told Strickland. "I know. He already called me," responded Strickland.

"That's when I knew Gabe had already made up his mind to fire me," added Tebbetts.

His departure ended Tebbetts' uniformed career, which included 14 seasons as a player in the major leagues for Detroit and Boston, as well as Cleveland, during which he caught 1,108 games and compiled a .270 lifetime batting average.

He was a member of the Tigers who beat the Indians for the pennant in 1940, and also played for the Red Sox when they lost the pennant to the Indians in an unprecedented one-game playoff in 1948. Tebbetts, in fact, made the final out in that game.

As for his decision to resign as manager of the Indians, Tebbetts said, "I did what I thought was best for baseball in Cleveland. I came here happy and I'm leaving the same way. I have no complaints and no gripes. It's just that I sincerely believe a fresh start would be the best thing for everybody."

After leaving the Indians in 1966, Tebbetts never managed again, though he continued in baseball as a scout for the New York Mets, the Orioles, and the New York Yankees.

Tebbetts, Birdie

	W	L	T	Pct.
1963	79	83	0	.488
1964	46	44	1	.511
1965	87	75	0	.537
1966	66	57	0	.537
Indians	278	259	1	.518
Career	748	705	2	.515

1964, 1966

Strickland, George

Record: 48–63 (.432)
Birthplace: New Orleans, Louisiana
B: January 10, 1926

George Strickland took over as interim manager of the Indians twice, the first time on April 2, 1964, when Birdie Tebbetts suffered a heart attack, and again on August 20, 1966, after Tebbetts complied with Gabe Paul's request that he resign.

George Strickland

Neither time did the Tribe respond well in the won-lost column to Strickland's leadership, and the former shortstop never managed again, though he remained in baseball as a coach through 1972.

He continued with the Indians as a coach under Joe Adcock in 1967 and Alvin Dark in 1968 and 1969, then joined the Kansas City Royals where he worked under former teammate Bob Lemon from June 10, 1970, through 1972.

Under Strickland in his first stint as interim manager the Indians won 33 and lost 39 until Tebbetts returned on July 3. They finished the 1964 season in a tie with Minnesota for sixth place with a 79–83 record.

Two years later when Strickland again replaced Tebbetts on August 20 the Tribe was third with a 66–57 record and still had a chance to catch the streaking Baltimore Orioles.

Instead, the Indians faltered badly the rest of the way, losing 24 of their final 39 games, ending what earlier had appeared to be a chance for a return to glory.

The poor showing also ended whatever hope Strickland had for being named manager of the Indians.

Strickland, George				
	W	L	T	Pct.
1964	33	39	1	.458
1966	15	24	0	.385
Indians	48	63	1	.432
Career	48	63	1	.432

1967

Adcock, Joe

Record: 75–87 (.463)
Birthplace: Coushatta, Louisiana
B: October 30, 1927

When Gabe Paul asked for Birdie Tebbetts' resignation as manager of the Indians and didn't let George Strickland keep the job when the team wound up in fifth place in 1966, both were blamed for failing to stress discipline and fundamentals.

It's also what motivated Paul to hire Joe Adcock and give him a two-year contract to manage the Tribe through 1968.

"After listening to Joe for just half an hour, I knew he was the man I wanted, the man we needed," Paul said in his introduction of Adcock.

Paul previously had contacted Walter Alston, who had been working on a year-to-year basis as manager of the Los Angeles Dodgers. But Alston chose to remain with the Dodgers when they re-signed him for 1967, reportedly with a $10,000 raise in pay.

Another applicant for the job was Bob Lemon, who'd managed Seattle in the Pacific Coast League the previous season. But Paul rejected Lemon because he thought the former pitcher would be too easygoing as a manager.

Adcock had been a hard-nosed, slugging first baseman for Paul's Cincinnati Reds from 1950 to '52 and with the Milwaukee Braves from 1953 to '62, the Tribe in 1963, and the Los Angeles/California Angeles from 1964 to '66. He also played briefly in left field for the Reds (1950–52) and the Braves in (1958–59).

In his 17-year major league career Adcock hit .277 with 336 homers, including four in one game on July 31, 1954, in Brooklyn while playing for the Braves. Adcock also doubled in that game, and his 18 total bases are still a major league record for one game.

Vowing to "run a tight ship," Adcock said, "If I don't succeed, it won't be because somebody else caused me to fail. We'll work on fundamentals from the first day of spring training until the last day of the season."

He also promised, "Things are going to be different around here. There'll be no hanky-panky, and if I see things I don't like, the players are going to think that hell was turned loose backwards."

An example of Adcock's strict rules was that Latin players were forbidden to speak Spanish to each other while on the field.

Joe Adcock

As it turned out, the Indians—though they might have been better disciplined under Adcock—were even bigger losers on the field, dropping into eighth place. Their 75–87 record and .463 winning percentage were the worst by a Cleveland team in 21 years.

Adcock also was heavily criticized for platooning the Tribe's top sluggers, Leon Wagner and Rocky Colavito, in left field.

The day the season ended, October 1, Adcock was fired, after which Paul said that not hiring Lemon was the biggest mistake he'd made in more than half a century in baseball.

His dismissal ended Adcock's career in baseball, and he returned to his farm in Coushatta, Louisiana, where he raises thoroughbred horses.

Adcock, Joe

	W	L	T	Pct.
1967	75	87	0	.463
Indians	75	87	0	.463
Career	75	87	0	.463

1968–71

Dark, Alvin

Record: 266–321 (.453)
Birthplace: Comanche, Oklahoma
B: January 7, 1922

They started out as partners and friends, Gabe Paul and Alvin Dark, dedicated to returning the Indians to glory.

That was in 1968 after Paul again had switched gears, deciding that the Indians needed an experienced leader who'd known success.

He gave a two-year contract to Dark, who had managed the San Francisco Giants from 1961 to 1964, and then the Kansas City Athletics in 1966 and for 121 games in 1967. His Giants won the National League pennant in 1962. Later Dark's contract was extended through 1973 at a salary of $50,000 a year.

Initially, Dark proved to be an excellent choice, though Paul would live to regret his choice of the new manager, never mind his first year's success.

A former star shortstop who played 14 years in the NL for the Boston Braves, New York Giants, St. Louis Cardinals, Chicago Cubs, Milwaukee Braves, and Philadelphia Phillies, Dark compiled a .289 lifetime average and was known as a fierce competitor.

Once, while managing the Giants in 1963, Dark was angered by a sloppily played loss and, in a clubhouse tirade, hurled a metal stool across the room. The tip of the little finger on his right hand was torn off because it got caught under the seat of the stool.

In Cleveland in 1968, with Dark calling the shots on the field and Paul in charge of the front office, the Indians rebounded from the disaster of 1967 under Joe Adcock and climbed back to respectability.

They won 86 games and lost 75 to finish third, their highest place in the standings in nine years, since they came in second to Al Lopez's White Sox in 1959.

But Paul soon regretted hiring Dark. A behind-the-scenes power struggle developed between them during the winter of 1968–69. The conservative Paul moved too slowly to satisfy Dark, who thought the Indians should be more aggressive,

Alvin Dark

and made his opinion known—albeit secretly—to owner Vernon Stouffer.

Stouffer, who had built a lunch counter business into Stouffer Foods Corporation, one of the nation's largest and best known restaurant and food chains, was a willing listener. Soon, without the knowledge of Paul, he gave Dark more authority.

Paul learned of it when Dark got the approval of Stouffer for the Indians to acquire Ken Harrelson from the Boston Red Sox.

Though it was Paul who announced the April 19, 1969, trade for Harrelson, a longtime favorite of Dark's, it was in fact the manager who set it up and saw to it—with the full support of Stouffer—that it was consummated.

The deal was not a good one for the Indians. To get Harrelson they gave up their best reliever, Vicente Romo, one of their best starting pitchers, Sonny Siebert, and their regular catcher, Joe Azcue.

Two journeymen pitchers, Dick Ellsworth and Juan Pizarro, neither of whom subsequently distinguished himself for the Tribe, came to Cleveland with Harrelson.

Paul strongly opposed the deal, he admitted later, because the Indians already had Tony Horton to play first base, and neither he nor Harrelson was an accomplished outfielder.

Though an official announcement was never issued by the Indians, Stouffer acknowledged in a newspaper story on July 8 that he had in fact placed Dark in charge of all player personnel matters, as well as having the authority to call the shots on the field.

Paul retained the title of president and general manager, but was responsible only for the financial, marketing, and promotional affairs of the Indians.

Ostensibly, the club was run by a "committee"—Stouffer's characterization of the operation—which included Dark, Paul, Stouffer's son Jim, and vice president/farm director Hank Peters.

But it was not effective. The Indians plummeted back to less than mediocrity in 1969, losing their first five games and 15 of 16, and were last in the American League East from wire to wire, finishing with a 62–99 record. A rainout in New York on the final day enabled the Tribe to avert what might have been the franchise's second 100-loss season in 69 years.

The Indians started poorly again in 1970, were out of contention with a 38–48 record at the All-Star break, lost Tony Horton for the final four and a half weeks to a nervous break-down on August 28, and finished 76–86 in fifth place. It was their highest position all season.

It was another devastating and sobering experience for Stouffer who, that winter—again without issuing a public an-nouncement—restored Paul to power in the front office, leaving Dark in charge on the field only.

The two men, with Dark clearly subservient to Paul, main-tained a cool relationship on the surface, but there was no doubt about their true feelings toward each other. Paul no longer trusted Dark, and Dark feared Paul.

It was an awkward situation for everybody, including the players.

As Paul later explained, team unity was destroyed, and the Indians were fined $5,000 by Commissioner Bowie Kuhn (and suffered considerable embarrassment as well) because Dark had signed four players to illegal performance-bonus contracts—Sam McDowell, Harrelson, Vada Pinson, and Graig Nettles.

And with the Indians floundering on the field for a third straight season in 1971, Paul took action, this time with the full support of Stouffer.

On the morning of July 30, in the wake of a distressing, 7–2, loss to the California Angels that left the Indians in sixth place with a 42–61 record, 22 games out of first place, Paul instructed traveling secretary Charlie Morris to summon Dark to the Stadium.

Morris called the manager on the telephone and said, "Alvin, Mr. Paul wants to see you in his office as soon as pos-sible."

Dark asked Morris, "Is it a formal meeting, or just Gabe and me . . . and how should I dress?"

As Morris related the story, he replied, "It's just you and Mr. Paul . . . and I think something dark would be most ap-propriate."

It was. Dark reported to Paul's office and was fired, though it didn't end his managerial career.

Three years later Dark rejoined Charlie Finley to manage the Oakland Athletics in 1974 and 1975. They won the Amer-ican League West championship both years; in 1974 they went on to win the pennant, then beat Los Angeles in the World Series in five games.

Fired by Finley when the Athletics failed to win the pen-nant in 1975, Dark remained out of baseball for a year, then returned as manager of San Diego in 1977, though he didn't last the season. He was dismissed in early August with the Padres in fifth place with a 48–65 record, and never managed again.

Dark, Alvin

	W	L	T	Pct.
1968	86	75	1	.534
1969	62	99	0	.385
1970	76	86	0	.469
1971	42	61	0	.408
Indians	266	321	1	.453
Career	994	954	2	.510

1971

Lipon, Johnny

Record: 18–41 (.305)
Birthplace: Martin's Ferry, Ohio
B: November 10, 1922

Johnny Lipon always wanted to be a manager, as evidenced by the fact that he was still managing minor league teams into his 70s, but he only got one brief chance in the major leagues.

That opportunity came on July 30, 1971, when he was ap-pointed interim manager of the Indians after Alvin Dark was fired.

Lipon, who'd been a Tribe coach since 1968, said upon re-placing Dark, "There is no doubt in my mind that I'll be the manager of this club for several years to come."

But it didn't happen that way, even though Gabe Paul said, "Nobody expects John to be a miracle man, and his fu-ture won't be decided by how many games he wins or loses.

"More important to us is whether Lipon can restore the feeling of unity that every solid club must have."

The fact is, the Indians won only 18 of the Tribe's remain-ing 59 games in 1971, and on October 14 it was announced that Lipon would not be retained as the team was left in com-plete disarray by the problems that existed between Dark and Paul.

Instead, the Indians chose Ken Aspromonte to manage the team in 1972. He was hired on November 9.

Lipon, who'd managed in the Indians' farm system from 1959 to 1967, winning three pennants, returned to the minor leagues where he managed at every level for the Detroit Tigers in 1972, 1973, and 1986 through 1992, and for Pitts-burgh from 1974 to 1985.

Lipon was a slick-fielding shortstop for the Tigers in 1942 and, after three and a half years in the navy during World

Johnny Lipon

War II, again from 1946 to 1952. He later played for the Boston Red Sox, St. Louis Browns, and briefly with Cincinnati, compiling a lifetime batting average of .259.

Lipon, Johnny

	W	L	T	Pct.
1971	18	41	0	.305
Indians	18	41	0	.305
Career	18	41	0	.305

1972–74

Aspromonte, Ken

Record: 220–260 (.458)
Birthplace: Brooklyn, New York
B: September 22, 1931

Ken Aspromonte, another who'd always aspired to be a major league manager, won out in competition with Johnny Lipon to lead the Indians in 1972, but it was still a period of travail, heightened by the sale of the franchise and then by baseball's first player strike.

Aspromonte was hired by Gabe Paul on November 9, 1971, four months before Vernon Stouffer sold the Indians to a group of investors headed by Nick Mileti. The new manager took over with high hopes, only to be "devastated" by the work stoppage that began on April 1, seven days prior to the season opener.

"It was very discouraging," Aspromonte reflected on that first year. "I was devastated. After all the hard work we'd put in spring training, and then [the strike] happened."

The players returned after 13 days, and the season started April 15, but it didn't mark the end of Aspromonte's troubles, the primary cause of which was Alex Johnson.

Johnson, an outfielder who'd won the American League batting championship while playing for the California Angels in 1970, was acquired by Paul on October 5, 1971, five weeks before Aspromonte was hired.

Though he was a great hitter, Johnson was not a good influence on the team, complicating Aspromonte's job.

On the other hand, three weeks after Aspromonte was signed, the Indians traded Sam McDowell to the San Francisco Giants for Gaylord Perry and shortstop Frank Duffy. It proved to be one of the franchise's all-time best deals as Perry and Duffy were positive influences on the team.

But not enough to provide the dramatic improvement the Indians needed. Despite an 18–10 start that vaulted them into first place by May 23, the Indians finished fifth with a 72–84 record in Aspromonte's first season.

Then his job became even more difficult.

First, Paul resigned as president/treasurer/general manager of the Indians and was named, on January 10, 1973, president of the New York Yankees. He also was a limited partner under George Steinbrenner, who had become principal owner of the team.

Paul's departure led to the promotion of vice president Phil Seghi to general manager of the Tribe.

Seghi got rid of Johnson in a trade with the Texas Rangers on March 8, but then swung a deal with Oakland on March 24 to acquire George Hendrick, another enigmatic outfielder with whom Aspromonte had trouble coexisting.

Ken Aspromonte

"I'd fine George for not hustling, and the front office—yes, Seghi—would rescind it, the same as had been done with Johnson," said Aspromonte. "When I complained, I was told, 'That's the way it goes,' or something like that. It was very difficult."

Especially for a manager of Aspromonte's temperament. He was a hot-headed second baseman who came up through the minor leagues with the Boston Red Sox. After winning the Pacific Coast League batting championship with a .334 average for San Francisco in 1957, he was called up by the Red Sox for the final month of that season.

Aspromonte went on to play for the Washington Senators, Indians, Los Angeles/California Angels, Milwaukee Braves, and Chicago Cubs through 1963.

His service with the Indians included two tours of duty—they got him from the Senators on May 15, 1960, in a trade for outfielder Pete Whisenant, lost him to the Angels in the expansion draft of 1961, and repurchased him on July 3, 1961. Aspromonte stayed with the Tribe until June 24, 1962, when he was traded to the Braves for pitcher Bob Hartman.

Aspromonte wound up his playing career with the Taiyo Whales of the Japanese Central League from 1964 to 1966, remained out of the game in 1967, and took his first job as a manager of the Indians' Sarasota rookie team in the Gulf Coast League in 1968.

"I know my temper hurt me throughout my baseball career," said Aspromonte. "It kept me on the bench a lot and probably was a factor in my being traded so much. I took everything too personal, though I had better control of myself after I became a manager."

He went on to manage Reno in the California League in 1969 and Wichita, the Tribe's top affiliate in the Class AAA American Association, in 1970 and 1971.

While Wichita's won-lost records under Aspromonte were nothing to rave about—67–73 in 1970 and 66–74 in 1971—it was under his tutelage there that a crop of the Indians' best prospects honed their skills and graduated to the major leagues.

Among them were Buddy Bell, Chris Chambliss, Jack Brohamer, Ed Farmer, Jack Heidemann, John Lowenstein, Steve Mingori, and Dick Tidrow. These successes certainly helped Aspromonte get the job as manager of the Indians in 1972.

After that first season under Aspromonte, the Indians fell to 71–91 and into sixth (and last) place in 1973, but as he said, "We were still developing and I felt we were making progress."

They were, and in 1974 the Indians—with Gaylord Perry leading the way, and despite Aspromonte's problems with Hendrick—showed signs of challenging for the pennant. As late in the season as September 6 they were within 4½ games of first place, and excitement was building.

Six days later, with the Indians' record 71–71, Seghi—unbeknownst to Aspromonte—claimed Frank Robinson on waivers from the Angels.

"[Seghi] did it on his own . . . I never knew a thing about it until Robinson showed up in the clubhouse."

When asked about it, Seghi shrugged and said, "We need another right-handed bat, and Robinson gives us a good one."

Naturally, Robinson's presence set off speculation that he would be in line to replace Aspromonte as manager of the Indians if they did not win in 1974—and they didn't.

With Robinson hitting only .200 (10-for-50) with two homers and five RBIs in 15 of the final 20 games, the Indians won only six and lost 14, winding up in fourth place, 14 lengths behind Baltimore.

The day after the season ended, October 3, the speculation came true. Aspromonte's contract was not renewed, and Robinson was signed to a one-year contract to manage the Indians.

"The way things have turned out, I have no regrets, not any longer," said Aspromonte.

But he did when he was fired from the job he'd always wanted. "Things were bad with the Indians in those days," said Aspromonte. "They needed a fall guy for all the bad things that had happened, and I was it.

"I didn't feel I deserved the treatment I got. My problem with Seghi wasn't only because of Robinson. It also involved George Hendrick. Phil wouldn't back me with George. I guess it was because Seghi felt a kinship with Hendrick from the time they were both with Oakland.

"So, yes, I was bitter. But not anymore. Everything has worked out well for me and my brother Bob."

After leaving Cleveland, Ken Aspromonte worked in public relations for Caesar's Palace in Las Vegas, a job which led to a connection with Coors Brewery. As a result, Ken and his brother Bob got a Coors distributorship in Houston in December 1975, which is now one of the largest in the United States.

Aspromonte, Ken

	W	L	T	Pct.
1972	72	84	0	.462
1973	71	91	0	.438
1974	77	85	0	.475
Indians	220	260	0	.458
Career	220	260	0	.458

1975–77

Robinson, Frank

Record: 186–189 (.496)
Birthplace: Beaumont, Texas
B: August 31, 1935

The Indians didn't wait long to confirm month-long speculation that Frank Robinson would be the sixth player-manager in the 75-year history of the Cleveland franchise.

The appointment—some called it the "anointing"—of Robinson as baseball's first black manager was formally announced October 3, 1975, the day after the Indians ended the managerial career of Ken Aspromonte.

"The impact of Frank Robinson being named manager of the Indians, the first black manager in major league history, is second in importance only to Jackie Robinson's entry into baseball," solemnly intoned American League president Lee MacPhail, who attended the press conference.

Commissioner Bowie Kuhn was more subdued in his comments, though obviously equally pleased that the so-called "managerial color line" finally was broken.

"Now that it has happened," said Kuhn, "I'm not going to get up and shout that this is something for baseball to be exceptionally proud of, because it is so long overdue."

Any credit—if, indeed, credit should be bestowed on anybody—belonged to Alva T. "Ted" Bonda, the Indians' executive vice president and chief operating officer, as well as general manager Phil Seghi, who were running the club at that time.

It was Bonda who encouraged Seghi to hire the best-qualified African-American for the job. Also considered was former Tribe outfielder Larry Doby, the American League's first black player in 1947 and a Cleveland coach in 1974.

A factor in the ultimate choice of Robinson was that he had been acquired as a player in September 1974 and, it was assumed, would continue to be at least a designated hitter as well as manager of the Indians.

So it was that in his very first game at the helm of the Indians, Robinson—as their designated hitter and second batter in the lineup—put on a show that even a Hollywood script writer would consider too implausible to invent.

The date was April 8, and 56,715 opening-day fans in the Stadium roared mightily when Robinson went to the plate for the first time with one out in the first inning and Doc Medich on the mound for the visiting New York Yankees.

Frank Robinson

Medich's first two pitches were strikes, one called, one swinging. Robinson fouled off the next two, two more were wide of the plate, and he fouled off another.

Then, on Medich's eighth offering, a slider that broke over the plate thigh high, Robinson swung, and the ball arched high and far to left-center field. The fans stood as one, roaring their approval—although some, to be sure, gasped in disbelief—as the ball flew over the fence.

It was one of the most dramatic moments in baseball history, and certainly in the history of the Cleveland franchise, as well as in the storied career of Robinson.

The home run led to a 5–3 victory for the Indians, though the euphoria it created didn't last long.

Even before that historic season Robinson had problems with the Indians' best pitcher, Gaylord Perry. Their less than friendly relationship began on a sour note the very night that Robinson joined the Indians in 1974.

They quarreled and almost came to blows because Robinson resented comments attributed to Perry in a newspaper article that day. The story reported that Robinson, in 1975, would be paid the same salary—$173,500—he was getting in 1974, to which Perry was quoted as saying that he would demand one dollar more.

The two headstrong athletes also bickered in spring training, and naturally it was speculated that Perry's problems with Robinson were racially motivated—that Perry, born and raised in the South, resented being managed by a black man.

On one occasion in spring training Perry defiantly retorted, "I'm nobody's slave," in protest to the conditioning regimen put in place by Robinson.

Perry also objected to Robinson's requirement that pitchers do a prescribed amount of running backward to strengthen their legs. "I've never run backwards in my life. Not for anyone, and I am not going to start now," he said.

Gaylord's complaints often were echoed by his older brother Jim, who also was a pitcher on the team, though he did not express them as vociferously.

As a result, both Perrys were gone before the halfway point of Robinson's first season. First, Jim Perry was traded to Oakland on May 20. Then, Gaylord Perry was sent to Texas on June 13, when the Indians' record was nine games below .500 (23–32), and they were lodged in last place in the AL East.

Their departure underscored Robinson's authority, and, although there was not an immediate improvement after the Perrys were traded, the Indians went 55–41 from June 21 through the end of the season.

It gave them a final 79–80 record that came closest to .500 by an Indians team in seven years. (Three rained-out games against Minnesota were not made up.)

It was even better for Robinson and the Indians in 1976. As late as July 1 they were second with a 36–33 record, until they lost three out of four to the first-place New York Yankees, and then five of their next six on a West Coast trip.

Still, it was an improvement as the Indians went over .500 (81–78) for the first time since 1968—and only the fourth since 1959.

That season also marked the end of Robinson's remarkable playing career, though he made his decision against the wishes of Seghi.

Robinson had suffered an injury to his right shoulder in 1975. It was surgically repaired that winter, though Robinson never regained full strength in his shoulder. The weakened joint hampered his throwing, even swinging a bat.

In his final plate appearance on September 18 at the Stadium, Robinson hit a run-scoring pinch single off Baltimore's Rudy May in a 2–1 loss to the Orioles.

His only disappointment, Robinson admitted later, was that his playing career ended 57 hits short of 3,000, and 14 homers fewer than 600, while compiling a 21-year major league batting average of .294 with 1,812 RBIs.

Robinson's 586 homers were fourth-most in baseball history, while his 2,808 games were eighth on the all-time list, and his 1,829 runs were ninth. When he batted for the last time it was his 10,006th official plate appearance, establishing him as the 11th player to exceed 10,000.

The only man to win the Most Valuable Player award in both leagues—the National in 1961 and the American in 1966—Robinson played for Cincinnati from 1956 (when he won the Rookie of the Year award) through 1965, Baltimore from 1966 to 1971, the Los Angeles Dodgers in 1972, and California from 1973 until he joined the Indians in September 1974.

He won the Triple Crown in 1966, was a member of the NL and AL All-Star teams 11 times, and was elected to the Hall of Fame in 1982, his first year of eligibility.

It was after the Indians did so well in 1976 that Robinson was re-signed to manage the team in 1977—but it also marked the beginning of several new problems for the man who would soon become major league baseball's first black *ex*-manager.

Rico Carty, who had won the Indians' Man of the Year award for 1976, got Robinson's season of new travail under way at a fan club luncheon on April 25.

Everybody was shocked—Bonda, Seghi, and, most notably, Robinson himself—when Carty publicly criticized the manager for what he called Robinson's "lack of leadership."

Carty subsequently was suspended for 15 days and fined $1,000 for "insubordination"—which probably inflamed the situation, rather than helped it—and virtually everything that followed for Robinson and the Indians was downhill.

At least until June 19.

That was the day Robinson was fired with the Indians lodged in fifth place and struggling with a 26–31 record.

Seghi had wanted to dismiss Robinson earlier; in mid-May he had spoken to former Tribe coach Dave Garcia about taking over as manager. Not only did Bonda reject Seghi's suggestion, but Garcia also said he would decline the job if it was offered.

After speculation surfaced that he would be fired, Robinson said, "I know [Seghi] believes the team is better than it is. He put it together. When it doesn't perform, he's going to point a finger at someone else.

"I'm not surprised. Phil has to give people an answer when they ask him about his team. Besides, I think it was common knowledge that Seghi didn't want me back."

Bonda eventually relented. "Phil was convinced that we had to make a change, that things would only get worse under Robinson, so I finally told him to go ahead.

"I wanted to keep Frank, but I caved in to too many pressures, from the media and the fans, as well as from . . . well, my associates," he said, meaning Seghi in particular.

Some of the "pressure" mentioned by Bonda came from

Joe Tait, then the Indians' play-by-play announcer. He was quoted early in the season as saying, "I don't believe Frank [Robinson] has the mental and emotional capability to manage well. He is not a good instructor or leader, and I don't think he brings out the players' ability."

When the end came, Robinson bit his tongue, chose his words carefully, and never let his emotions betray his true feelings.

Asked if he was resentful toward Seghi, Robinson replied, "No, I'm not upset; disappointed is a better way to say it. It's almost like they're telling me I failed, and I don't believe I failed in anything."

Jeff Torborg, then a Tribe coach, took over as manager, and the team under him the rest of the season was 45–59, a winning percentage of .433 compared to Robinson's .456 through the team's first 57 games. The Indians finished in fifth place.

Robinson returned to the Angels as a coach the rest of the 1977 season, coached for the Orioles and managed their Rochester farm club in the Class AAA International league through 1980, then managed the San Francisco Giants from 1981 to August 4, 1984, almost winning the NL pennant in 1982.

Robinson returned to the Orioles as a coach in 1985 and on April 12, 1988, replaced Cal Ripken, Sr., as manager, a position he held through May 22, 1991. He then moved into the front office as assistant to the general manager.

Robinson, Frank

	W	L	T	Pct.
1975	79	80	0	.497
1976	81	78	0	.509
1977	26	31	0	.456
Indians	186	189	0	.496
Career	680	751	0	.475

1977–1979

Torborg, Jeff

Record: 157–201 (.439)
Birthplace: Plainfield, New Jersey
B: November 26, 1941

Initially Jeff Torborg said no. "I won't take it unless Frank says it's okay," Torborg told Indians general manager Phil Seghi.

"Frank" was Frank Robinson, whom Seghi fired on June 19, 1977, as Tribe manager. Torborg was offered the job despite his limited experience.

Then only 35, Torborg, a former catcher for the Los Angeles Dodgers and California Angels from 1964 to 1973, was out of professional baseball in 1974 until he was hired by Robinson as a coach in 1975.

"My first loyalty is to Frank," Torborg said to Seghi. "He's the guy who hired me, gave me my first job [as a coach]. I don't want to take his job, no way."

But Robinson assured Torborg that he understood, that if Torborg wouldn't be the man to replace him, somebody else would.

"That's when I finally agreed . . . but reluctantly, because of my great respect for Frank Robinson," said Torborg.

Conjecture was that Torborg—a milk shake drinker who regularly read the Bible, didn't smoke or chew tobacco, seldom cursed, smiled a lot, and looked young enough to be playing, not managing or even coaching in the major leagues—wasn't "tough" enough for the job he was undertaking.

But that wasn't the problem. More important was the fact that the Indians simply didn't have enough good players.

Torborg had gained the respect of Robinson when they were teammates in 1973 with the Angels.

As a catcher for the Dodgers and Angels, Torborg was behind the plate for three no-hitters, by Sandy Koufax in 1965, Bill Singer in 1970, and Nolan Ryan in 1973, and compiled a lifetime .214 batting average in 10 major league seasons.

When he was released in spring training of 1974, after being traded to the St. Louis Cardinals, Torborg went home and took a job as athletic director at a New Jersey prep school, hoping to become the baseball coach at Princeton University.

The Indians' record under Robinson was 26–31 (.456) when he was fired. It was worse under Torborg; they went 45–59 (.433), but afterward he was given a two-year contract through 1979.

The Tribe played no better in 1978, finishing sixth in the American League East, and still was sixth with a 43–52 (.453) record in 1979 when Torborg was replaced by Dave Garcia.

Garcia had been a coach under Robinson in 1975 and 1976, but left to accept a similar position with the Angels in 1977. He became their manager on July 11, 1977, but lasted less than a year, being fired on May 31, 1978, after which he rejoined the Indians during the winter of 1978–79.

By then F. J. "Steve" O'Neill and Gabe Paul also had returned to Cleveland after five years in New York, O'Neill as a limited partner under George Steinbrenner, the principal owner of the Yankees, and Paul as president of the team.

Jeff Torborg

O'Neill, who'd been a major investor in the ownership of the Indians in the 1960s, came back to purchase control of the franchise in February 1978 from the group headed by Alva T. "Ted" Bonda.

Paul was installed by O'Neill as president and chief executive officer of the Indians.

Phil Seghi, who'd handled all player personnel matters while Paul was with the Yankees, retained his title, vice president and general manager, under O'Neill and Paul, but his authority was curtailed.

Paul, who was in complete control of the franchise, tried to hire Bob Lemon to replace Torborg—the same Bob Lemon whose application to manage the Indians was rejected by Paul in the winter of 1966–67.

This time, however, Lemon rejected Paul, and Torborg remained manager of the Indians in 1978.

But not for long. He was fired on July 22, 1979, and was succeeded by Garcia.

Also, by then Garcia did not have the same reluctance to manage the Indians that he'd had in 1977, when he declined Seghi's request for him to replace Robinson.

At the time Torborg was fired, the Tribe was struggling— and Torborg himself was frustrated to the extent that he was ready to depart.

Paul's earlier attempt to hire Lemon was preying on Torborg's mind, and, on July 2 in Detroit, after a 10–2 loss to the Tigers the night before, the manager's emotions got the better of him.

With the Indians in sixth place, already 19 games behind the leader and their record only 34–42, Torborg said he planned to resign at the end of the season.

When the team went on to lose 10 of its next 19 games, Paul decided not to wait and instructed Seghi to replace Torborg with Garcia.

But Torborg was not out of work for long. Only four days later, in fact, Torborg was hired as a coach by the Yankees. He remained with them under Billy Martin, Dick Howser, Gene Michael, Lemon, Michael again, Clyde King, Martin again, Yogi Berra, Martin for a third time, Lou Piniella, Martin for a fourth time, and Piniella again, through 1988.

Torborg managed the Chicago White Sox from 1989 to 1991, leading them to second-place finishes in the AL West in 1990 and 1991. He was named Manager of the Year by *The Sporting News* in 1990. After he was replaced by Gene Lamont as manager of the White Sox in 1992, Torborg managed the New York Mets from 1992 through May 19, 1993, when he was replaced by Dallas Green. He did not manage in 1994 and instead entered the field of broadcasting.

Torborg, Jeff

	W	L	T	Pct.
1977	45	59	0	.433
1978	69	90	0	.434
1979	43	52	0	.453
Indians	157	201	0	.439
Career	479	526	0	.477

1979–82

Garcia, Dave

Record: 247–244 (.503)
Birthplace: East St. Louis, Illinois
B: September 15, 1920

The Indians finished strong in 1979, after Dave Garcia replaced Jeff Torborg, winning 38 and losing 28, but couldn't climb out of sixth place, and never fared much better the next three seasons.

Only in the second half of 1981, which was interrupted by a 50-day strike by the players, did the Indians get out of the basement of the American League East, and then into fifth place.

A 20-year minor league infielder who never played a game in the major leagues, Garcia managed for 17 seasons in the minors, the first nine, from 1948 to 1957, as a player-manager, winning four pennants, two while he was a player-manager and two as a bench manager.

A longtime friend of general manager Phil Seghi, Garcia served as a Cleveland coach under Frank Robinson in 1975 and 1976.

Prior to joining the Indians, Garcia also scouted for San Francisco, coached for San Diego from 1970 to 1973, and managed El Paso of the Class AA Texas League in 1974.

Garcia resigned his job with the Tribe to take a similar position with the California Angels in 1977 and was offered the job of managing the Indians when Robinson was fired on June 19, 1977, but declined. A month later, on July 11, 1977, Garcia replaced Norm Sherry as the Angels manager, but was himself replaced on May 31, 1978, by Jim Fregosi.

Garcia rejoined the Indians that winter as a coach under Jeff Torborg and, with the team floundering with a 45–59 record, was named manager on July 22, 1979. His contract only ran through the end of the season because the Indians still were hoping Bob Lemon would reconsider his previous rejection and be willing to manage the team in 1981. (He didn't.)

"The first thing I told the players was that I have the advantage of not being afraid to lose my job because I've been

Dave Garcia

fired before," Garcia said upon his promotion. "And if I get fired, I'll get fired for making my own decisions."

The Tribe immediately embarked upon a 10-game winning streak under Garcia and went on to win 38 of 66. He was named the Indians' Man of the Year for 1979 and signed to a new contract for 1980.

But Garcia's success didn't continue. The following season the Indians lost eight of their first 10 games and, though they climbed three games over .500 (30–27) in June, collapsed and fell back into sixth place.

Their lackluster performance apparently didn't hurt Garcia's standing, however, as he was rehired for 1981, which was marred by the first midseason player strike in the history of professional sports in the United States and Canada.

When the strike began on June 12, the Indians' record was 26–24. When the season resumed on July 31, the Indians went on to win 26 and lose 27, and Garcia was rehired for another year.

But matters worsened in 1982. Garcia called it "the toughest season of my baseball career," though he vowed in late August that he wouldn't quit. "If they want to fire me, they know where to find me," he said.

"Considering what I have had to work with, I think I have done my best job ever as a manager."

His comment was a reference to a series of injuries to key players, all of which came in the wake of Gabe Paul's preseason prediction that the Indians would win 90 games and battle for the AL pennant.

They didn't, instead finishing with a 78–84 record—again in sixth place—and Garcia wasn't rehired.

"I think this is the right thing for the club and me . . . the best for the club, the fans, and for me that I don't come back as manager," he said after the last game.

"I don't think a manager can turn a team around on his own. At least, I don't think I was capable of doing it. Besides, too long in one place is not good for a manager."

He also expressed disappointment in some of the players. "I don't want to leave a bitter taste in anyone's mouth, so I won't name names," said Garcia. "But there have been some times I felt some players should have been playing and they weren't. Sometimes you wonder about their attitudes."

Garcia departed as the Tribe's winningest manager since Birdie Tebbetts' teams won 278 games and lost 259 for a .518 winning percentage from 1963 through August 19, 1966.

Upon leaving the Indians, Garcia was a coach for the Milwaukee Brewers in 1983 and 1984, scouted for them from 1985 to 1991, and was a scout for California in 1993 and 1994.

Garcia, Dave

	W	L	T	Pct.
1979	38	28	0	.576
1980	79	81	0	.494
1981	52	51	0	.505
1982	78	84	0	.481
Indians	247	244	0	.503
Career	307	310	0	.498

1983

Ferraro, Mike

Record: 40–60 (.400)
Birthplace: Kingston, New York
B: August 14, 1944

Gabe Paul knew Mike Ferraro and had become a great fan of him when they were together with the New York Yankees, Paul as president and Ferraro as a manager in their farm system (1974–78).

"I hired Mike [as a minor league manager] and watched him come up through the ranks—New York–Penn League, Florida State League, Eastern League, and Pacific Coast League. I was impressed by his hard work and dedication," Paul said of Ferraro, whose teams had won three minor league pennants.

Paul left the Yankees to return to Cleveland in 1978, and Ferraro became a Yankee coach in 1979. When Dave Garcia's contract as manager of the Indians was not renewed at the end of 1982, Paul thought he knew the man who could restore the franchise to prominence.

It was Ferraro, despite his having had only a brief and inauspicious playing career in the major leagues. A longtime minor league third baseman, Ferraro played parts of two seasons (1966 and 1968) with the Yankees, went to the Seattle Pilots in the expansion draft and played five games for them in 1969, and was Milwaukee's regular third baseman in 1972.

Ferraro was given a two-year contract to manage the Indians through 1984, but shortly thereafter a health problem developed that had to have a negative impact on his frame of mind, and probably performance.

On February 9, two weeks prior to the start of spring training, Ferraro underwent surgery for the removal of a cancerous kidney. He returned to duty, ostensibly in good condition, though there were whispers that his ordeal had caused a change in Ferraro's personality, that it had robbed him of some tenacity.

When the Indians floundered at the onset of the season, Ferraro did not last long as manager.

By the end of May the Indians had plummeted into last place in the American League East with a 21–25 record. They won only 19 of their next 54 games, and on July 30, Ferraro's major league managerial career was ended.

Ferraro was fired and replaced by Pat Corrales, who only 12 days earlier had been fired himself as manager of the Philadelphia Phillies.

"We felt a change was advisable," was Paul's brief explanation for firing Ferraro. "I don't want to discuss it further. Mike is a fine young gentleman, and this was a very hard decision for me."

The following season Ferraro was hired as a coach by Dick Howser, then manager of the Kansas City Royals. They had worked together with the Yankees in 1980. When Howser was forced to step down in 1986 because of a brain tumor that eventually took his life, Ferraro served as interim manager of the Royals, leading them to a 36–38 record.

Ferraro returned to the Yankees as a coach in 1987 and remained with them through 1991.

Mike Ferraro (left) and Indians president Gabe Paul

Ferraro, Mike

	W	L	T	Pct.
1983	40	60	0	.400
Indians	40	60	0	.400
Career	76	98	0	.437

1983–87

Corrales, Pat

Record: 280–355 (.441)
Birthplace: Los Angeles
B: March 20, 1941

The Indians said they wanted a manager who would be "much more aggressive" when they hired Pat Corrales to take over on July 31, 1983, for Mike Ferraro, and there was no doubt that Corrales was just that—much more aggressive.

"Pat is a good manager, a very aggressive manager, the best we could get at this point. We are excited about him and what he can do with our ball club," said Paul, who, before hiring Corrales, had offered the job to Billy Martin, but was rejected.

"I don't tolerate sloppy baseball. Losing head-to-head is one thing. Giving the game away is another," said Corrales.

Despite his notices, Corrales didn't make much of a difference.

The Indians finished 1983 with an improved record under Corrales, winning 30 of their final 62 games, though many of the problems he had been expected to solve persisted in subsequent seasons.

Prior to joining the Indians, Corrales had become the only major league manager to be fired—on July 18, 1983—with his team in first place. He had piloted the Philadelphia Phillies to a 43–42 record and the lead in the National League East.

"I got fired," he said, "because they weren't happy with my discipline. I treated everyone the same, from the superstar to the 25th player."

Upon his arrival in Cleveland, Corrales also became the fourth man to manage a team in both major leagues the same season. The others were John McGraw (Baltimore and New York) 1902, Rogers Hornsby (St. Louis Browns and Cincinnati) 1952, and Bill Virdon (New York Yankees and Houston) 1975.

A backup catcher to Johnny Bench with the Reds during most of his playing career, Corrales also managed the Texas Rangers for the final game in 1978 and in 1979 and 1980, before taking over the Phillies in 1982.

In 1984, Corrales' first full season at the helm of the Indians, they improved slightly to 75–87.

The following year, however, they were even worse—much worse—after the death of principal owner F. J. "Steve" O'Neill, the retirement of Gabe Paul as president/chief executive officer, and the demotion of vice president/general manager Phil Seghi.

Patrick O'Neill, a nephew of the late principal owner, became chairman of the board and hired veteran front office executives Peter Bavasi as president/chief operating officer, Dan

Pat Corrales

O'Brien as assistant to the president (and later senior vice president), and Joe Klein as vice president of baseball operations.

When they lost 102 games in 1985, only the third time in franchise history the Indians exceeded 100 losses, their lack of success didn't seem to hurt Corrales' status.

On October 1, four days before the season ended, Bavasi rewarded Corrales with what the organization called a "perpetual contract."

"It's like a marriage contract," said Bavasi. "If things aren't going right, it can be terminated. But we are committed to a long-term program here, and we expect Pat to be part of it."

Perhaps it was the organization's avowed confidence in Corrales that turned the Indians' fortunes around in 1986. After a 7–8 start, and with four regulars going on to hit .300, the Indians improved their record by 24 games, though they climbed only as high as fifth in the standings.

They finished 84–78, and their winning percentage of .519 was the best in 18 years.

But the euphoria faded quickly in 1987. So did Corrales, despite his "perpetual contract."

After a 1–10 start, another 100-loss season ensued. Before it was over—on July 16, after 87 games, only 31 of which were victories—Corrales was fired and replaced by coach Doc Edwards.

By then, Richard E. and David H. Jacobs had purchased the franchise from the O'Neill estate, Bavasi was gone, and O'Brien and Klein tried to explain the decision to fire Corrales.

O'Brien claimed the new owners had nothing to do with it. "It was our call," he said, speaking for himself and Klein.

"We just didn't win enough games. The won-lost record at the major leagues is the most visible thing," said Klein.

Under the terms of the perpetual contract, Corrales received the remainder of his 1987 salary and an additional year's pay in 1988.

Corrales managed Toledo in the International League in 1988, was out of baseball in 1989, and since 1990 has been a coach for the Atlanta Braves.

Corrales, Pat

	W	L	T	Pct.
1983	30	32	0	.484
1984	75	87	1	.463
1985	60	102	0	.370
1986	84	78	1	.519
1987	31	56	0	.356
Indians	280	355	1	.441
Career	572	634	5	.474

1987–89

Edwards, Doc

Record: 173–207 (.455)
Birthplace: Red Jacket, West Virginia
B: December 10, 1936

Doc Edwards said his primary objective was "to put some electricity back in the clubhouse and on the field" when he was named manager of the Indians on November 18, 1987, replacing the fired Pat Corrales.

"I want the players to be loosey-goosey, to have some fun. We didn't have the kind of life in the clubhouse that we did last year [1986]. If you can get life back in there, maybe it will carry out into the field.

"What I really want for the players is for them to get their respect back. This team earned a lot of respect [in 1986], but lost it [earlier in 1987]," said Edwards, whose ambition it always had been to manage in the major leagues.

Signed to his first professional player contract by the Indians in 1958, Edwards made it to Cleveland in 1962, but the following year was traded to the Kansas City Athletics. He went on to play for the New York Yankees and Philadelphia Phillies in the major leagues, mainly as a backup catcher, through 1970.

Edwards then managed in the minor leagues for 13 years, the last four (1982–85) for the Indians, and was appointed their bull pen coach on September 13, 1985. He remained in that position until replacing Corrales.

"Doc was the only man we considered," said Dan O'Brien, then the club's senior vice president in charge of baseball operations. "[Edwards] has been in our system, knows the organization, has managed successfully, and has gotten to know our big league talent.

"We expect him to do well, and to be our manager for a long time," added O'Brien, though Edwards was signed only through the remainder of the 1987 season.

The Indians won 30 of their final 75 games under Edwards, and his contract was renewed through 1988, when they continued to play well, especially in the first half of the season. They were only a game out of first place with a plus-13 (36–23) won-lost record as late as June 10.

But they fell back the latter half of the season—though Edwards was given another one-year extension—and the regression continued in 1989. The relapse, as well as ongoing problems with several players who Edwards thought were not giving their best effort, cost him the job he had coveted for so long.

After three losses in four games with Toronto, Edwards was fired on September 12. His replacement was John Hart, a former minor league manager for the Baltimore Orioles who was then a special assignment scout for the Indians.

Edwards was a coach for the New York Mets in 1990 and 1991, and he managed Buffalo of the Class AAA American Association in 1993 and 1994.

Doc Edwards

Edwards, Doc

	W	L	T	Pct.
1987	30	45	0	.400
1988	78	84	0	.481
1989	65	78	0	.455
Indians	173	207	0	.455
Career	173	207	0	.455

1989

Hart, John

Record: 8–11 (.421)
Birthplace: Tampa, Florida
B: July 21, 1948

When John Hart took over as interim manager of the Indians on September 12, 1989, the date marked the beginning of his meteoric rise in the team's hierarchy.

Then a special assignment scout for the Tribe, Hart replaced the fired Doc Edwards and managed the team to an 8–11 record in its final 19 games.

Shortly thereafter, following the hiring of John McNamara as manager of the Indians, Hart was named assistant to president Hank Peters, later became director of baseball operations, and on September 18, 1991, replaced the retired Peters.

Hart was given the additional title of vice president, as well as general manager, in 1992, and a year later was promoted to executive vice president and general manager, second in command only to owner Richard E. Jacobs.

Prior to joining the Indians as a special assignment scout in 1989, Hart was Baltimore's third base coach in 1988, managed in the Orioles' farm system for six years, and was a minor league catcher in the Baltimore and Montreal organizations for seven years.

Hart, John

	W	L	T	Pct.
1989	8	11	0	.421
Indians	8	11	0	.421
Career	8	11	0	.421

1990–91

McNamara, John

Record: 102–137 (.427)
Birthplace: Sacramento, California
B: June 4, 1932

John McNamara tied a major league record when he signed a two-year contract on November 3, 1989, to manage the Indians.

It was his sixth managerial assignment, equaling the record held by Jimmy Dykes and Dick Williams, dating back to 1901. McNamara previously managed Oakland, San Diego, Cincinnati, California, and Boston in a professional baseball career that began in 1951.

"All I wanted when I signed with the Indians was one more chance," he said. "Managing in the major leagues is a tough life, but I still have a burning desire to get back there again."

John McNamara

"Back there" was the World Series. Unfortunately for McNamara—and the Indians—he never made it.

Widely recognized as a good organization man and excellent handler of pitchers, McNamara's only fault, some believed, was that he sometimes was "too nice." It was a reputation he disputed without completely denying it.

"I treat my players with respect, the same as I expect them to treat me, and I want them to be happy. But I can be a nasty s.o.b. when I think it's necessary," he argued.

While McNamara's first season in Cleveland was a good one, the Indians wound up in fourth place, their highest finish in 14 years. But they plummeted to the basement in 1991 with 105 losses, most in franchise history. It also was the fifth time they lost more than 100 games. McNamara wasn't around at the end.

In fact, McNamara wasn't even around at the middle of the season. He was fired on July 6 with the Indians floundering with a 25–52 record, 20 games out of first place. He was replaced by first base coach Mike Hargrove.

McNamara had no excuses when it happened. "We didn't get the job done, and nobody feels worse about it than I do . . . what more can I say?" he said upon departing Cleveland.

The disappointing season capped a major league managerial career in which McNamara's teams won 1,150 games and lost 1,215 in 18 seasons, with two first-place finishes—Cincinnati in the National League in 1979 and Boston in the American League in 1986.

A light-hitting catcher, McNamara signed his first professional contract in 1951 with the Kansas City Athletics and played 14 years in the minor leagues, the last nine, 1959–67, as a player-manager.

He managed the Athletics the final two weeks of 1969 and in 1970, after they'd moved to Oakland; the Padres, 1974–77; the Reds, 1979–82; the Angels, 1983 and 1984; and the Red Sox, from 1985 until mid-1988.

McNamara was a special assignment scout for Seattle in 1989. He returned to that job with the Angels after being fired by the Indians in 1991.

McNamara, John

	W	L	T	Pct.
1990	77	85	0	.475
1991	25	52	0	.325
Indians	102	137	0	.427
Career	1,150	1,215	2	.486

1991–

Hargrove, Mike

Record: 350–316 (.526)
Birthplace: Perryton, Texas
B: October 26, 1949

Mike Hargrove

Nobody paid his managerial dues more diligently or worked harder to get back to the major leagues than Mike Hargrove, who became the Indians' 36th field leader on July 6, 1991, replacing John McNamara.

The Tribe's first base coach since 1990, Hargrove completed a 12-year major league playing career when he was released in spring training in 1986 by Oakland.

But he refused to give up the game.

Hargrove returned to the minor leagues as a hitting instructor for Batavia in the New York–Penn League for rookies in 1986, then managed Kinston in the Class A Carolina League in 1987, Williamsport in the Class AA Eastern League in 1988, and Colorado Springs in the Class AAA Pacific Coast League in 1989. He won Manager of the Year honors at both Kinston and Colorado Springs.

"I never thought about being a manager until the last year of my playing career, and then I decided it was what I really wanted to do," said the former first baseman whose lifetime batting average was a commendable if unspectacular .290.

"Once I started managing, the day I first stepped on the field at Kinston, I knew it was the job for me. Don't ask me why. It just felt good. And when something feels good, it's usually right."

Hargrove's managerial career in Cleveland did not take off quickly; in fact, it almost died, not just once, but several times before he received assurance that he was leading the Indians in the right direction.

They struggled to a 76–86 record that tied New York for fourth place in 1992, and Hargrove's contract wasn't renewed until June 30.

The same thing happened in 1993 as the Indians were duplicating their won-lost record of the year before, but wound up sixth instead of fourth.

Finally, with less than two months left in the season the Indians picked up the option on Hargrove's contract on August 6, and he was assured of another season in the job that he had come to love.

And in 1994, when it all came together for the Indians—when they became a pennant contender for the first time since 1959—Hargrove got the recognition he deserved.

It came on July 25 in the form of a new two-year contract with a club option intended to keep Hargrove in Cleveland at least through 1997.

"This means that the Indians believe in me," he said. "It means that [vice president] John Hart, [owner] Dick Jacobs, and [assistant general manager] Dan O'Dowd feel I'm doing a good job. It is very gratifying."

Jacobs's and Hart's belief in Hargrove paid handsome dividends in 1995. Hargrove led the Indians to their first pennant in 41 years, winning the AL Central Division by 30 games—the second largest championship margin since 1902—and beating Seattle in six games for the pennant, before losing to Atlanta in six games in the World Series.

Hart praised Hargrove for his diligence and dedication.

"Mike has been through the difficult times with us," he said. "He's helped in developing our young players. He's gone into seasons when we knew we couldn't win. But our objective this year was to break through. We promised no pennants. We put no pressure on Mike. But I certainly think we've broken through."

Jacobs said Hargrove's new contract was "richly deserved" and expressed confidence that "Mike will grow and grow and grow because he's still a young man as a manager."

Jacobs also explained why—in the opinion of some observers—it took the Indians so long to give Hargrove the security of a long-term contract. "I've always believed you hire slowly and you fire slowly. That way you get the best people," he said.

When the Indians first got Hargrove as their manager in 1991, it ended an odyssey that had begun 20 years earlier, when he began his professional baseball career in Geneva, New York. That was the same league, New York–Penn, in which he began his career as a coach and manager.

In those 20 years Hargrove, his wife Sharon, and their family, which had grown to include five children, made 64 moves between 19 cities in 11 states.

Hargrove, Mike

	W	L	T	Pct.
1991	32	53	0	.376
1992	76	86	0	.469
1993	76	86	0	.469
1994	66	47	0	.584
1995	100	44	0	.694
Indians	350	316	0	.526
Career	350	316	0	.526

The Front Office

Byron Bancroft "Ban" Johnson is recognized as the founder—the "father," if you will—of the American League of Professional Baseball Clubs, but much credit for its survival belongs to Charles W. Somers, who was co-owner of the first Cleveland franchise.

It was Somers, then a wealthy young Clevelander, whose financial support of several other franchises kept the new league alive to have a chance of becoming what Johnson bragged it would: "The greatest baseball league in America."

Perhaps as a portent of the future of baseball in Cleveland, Somers ran out of money 16 years later and, to avoid bankruptcy, was forced to sell the franchise.

Since Johnson—and Somers—got the American League started in 1901, there have been 12 changes in the ownership of the Cleveland team that began as the Blues, then became the Bronchos, the Naps, and finally the Indians in 1915.

Times were particularly difficult in the 1960s and 1970s, during the ownership of Gabe Paul, Vernon Stouffer, Nick Mileti, and Alva T. "Ted" Bonda, as the Indians were beset with severe financial problems and were on the brink of bankruptcy several times.

There also were occasions at that time, and even in the 1980s, when the franchise came close to being moved because of attendance problems and a constant shortage of operating capital.

Solvency and financial stability returned in 1986 when the club was purchased by Richard E. and David H. Jacobs. Eight seasons later the team moved into a new ballpark, Jacobs Field, that revitalized not only the franchise but downtown Cleveland as well.

Getting to that point was not easy, and certainly would not have happened—nor might there even be an American League of Professional Baseball Clubs today—had it not been for Charles W. Somers.

The Owners/Presidents

1901–16

John F. Kilfoyl and Charles W. Somers

John F. Kilfoyl was the president of the first Cleveland professional baseball team to play in the American League, founded by Byron Bancroft "Ban" Johnson in 1900.

When Johnson wanted to include Cleveland in his new league—though it was only a revamping of the Western Baseball League, a minor league of which Johnson was president that was to be designated "major" in 1901—he called on Davis Hawley, one of the city's leading businessmen.

Hawley, a banker, previously had been associated with the Cleveland Spiders when that team played in the National League from 1889 to 1899.

Hawley, however, wasn't interested in Johnson's proposition and recommended Kilfoyl and Charles W. Somers, another young and wealthy Clevelander.

Kilfoyl owned a men's clothing store and also was involved in his family's real estate business, and Somers was in the coal business with his father.

The two men, then in their thirties, accepted and formed a partnership. Kilfoyl was installed as president and treasurer, and Somers as vice president.

It was Somers, however, who played the larger role in the birth of the Cleveland team and who also was, with his family's money, a major financier of the Boston Puritans (also known as the Somersets, later the Puritans, and finally the Red Sox), Philadelphia Athletics, and St. Louis Browns in the new league.

Part ownership of more than one club, called syndicate baseball, was permitted then, though it has since been banned.

Somers, in fact, is still listed as having been the owner of the Boston club in 1901 and 1902, at the same time that he was the co-owner of the Cleveland Blues.

It was Somers' support of the Athletics that led to owner Connie Mack's decision to send two of his stars, second baseman Napoleon Lajoie and pitcher Bill Bernhard, to Cleveland in 1902.

It was a move to protect the two players against prosecution because they had jumped from their National League team, the Philadelphia Phillies, to Mack's Athletics.

Mrs. James C. Dunn, who became the owner of the Indians upon the death of her husband, is shown here in a 1922 photograph with manager Tris Speaker.

Somers also loaned Charles Comiskey, owner of the Chicago White Sox, enough money to finish construction of Comiskey Park on Chicago's South Side.

While both Kilfoyl and Somers were rabid fans of their team, Kilfoyl was much more intense. In 1908 when the Cleveland team failed to win the pennant, Kilfoyl took the loss so hard that his health suffered, forcing him to retire. Somers then became president.

It was Somers who made Lajoie the team's player-manager in 1904 and, in 1908, rejected an opportunity to acquire a young Ty Cobb in a deal for an aging Elmer Flick.

It also was Somers who built one of the first concrete grandstands in baseball at League Park in 1909.

By 1916, Somers was nearly $2 million in debt because of several imprudent investments. A committee of bankers took over the management of his various enterprises, other than the team, by then nicknamed the Indians.

Somers was told to sell the Indians. Without them he could save his coal mines and other business ventures; otherwise, he stood a good chance of losing everything.

With the help of Johnson and Comiskey, Somers sold the team on February 21, 1916, to a group headed by James C. "Sunny Jim" Dunn. The price was $500,000, of which Johnson, on behalf of the American League, and Comiskey each pledged $100,000.

Somers reluctantly stepped down. Though he retained ownership of the New Orleans Pelicans of the Class A Southern Association, he returned to the business world and recouped the fortune he'd nearly lost with the Indians.

He died June 29, 1934, at the age of 65, leaving an estate valued at $3 million.

Included in his legacy, it most certainly can be said, is the American League, which probably would not have survived without his contributions.

1916–27

James C. "Sunny Jim" Dunn

It was during a social meeting of American League president Byron Bancroft "Ban" Johnson, Chicago White Sox owner Charles Comiskey, and others in Chicago in early 1916 that the subject of Charles W. Somers' financial problems entered into the discussion.

Among those at the table was James Christopher "Sunny Jim" Dunn, a partner in a railroad construction firm. Johnson turned to Dunn and said, "Jim, you are going to own the Cleveland ball club." Dunn gulped and said to Johnson, "Me? Why me?"

Instead of answering Dunn, Johnson asked another question. "How much money can you get together in a hurry?" Dunn replied, "Probably $15,000 this minute, but I might be able to get more if I had some time."

With that, Pat McCarthy, one of Dunn's business partners, said, "I'll put up $10,000," and others also volunteered, among them being fellow Chicagoans John Burns, a bartender, and Thomas Walsh, a former catcher for the Chicago Cubs.

When Johnson and Comiskey pledged $100,000 each, Dunn rounded up other investors and closed the deal. The purchase price was $500,000. Dunn became president.

However, knowing little about the game and even less about the operation of a major league franchise, Dunn leaned on Johnson for advice.

Johnson recommended his former secretary in the AL office, a man named Bob McRoy, who worked for the Boston club. Not only was McRoy willing to join Dunn as general manager of the Indians, but he also invested $5,000 in the partnership.

But Johnson's endorsement of McRoy wasn't without a hidden motive. Dunn's appointment of McRoy as general manager, placing him second in command of the franchise, left Ernest Sargent "Barney" Barnard, who had been vice president and general manager, without a position.

It was Johnson's way of putting down Barnard, whom Johnson considered a threat to his position as president of the league.

A former college football coach who had become a highly respected Columbus, Ohio, sportswriter, Barnard joined the Cleveland club as its traveling secretary—the first in baseball history—in 1904. Four years later, upon the illness and retirement of Jack Kilfoyl, Somers promoted Barnard to vice president, giving him almost unlimited authority.

When Dunn announced the appointment of McRoy as general manager, the media immediately asked what position the popular Barnard would have in the new organization.

"Barnard goes," Dunn responded, immediately setting off a wave of anguish and resentment among the media. Ed Bang and Henry Edwards, the sports editors of the *Cleveland News* and *Cleveland Plain Dealer*, respectively, were particularly vocal in support of Barnard, and finally Dunn relented.

Dunn agreed to let Barnard stay on as an employee in the front office, but it was McRoy who was second in command and essentially ran the club. When he became ill and also was forced into retirement in 1918, Barnard was elevated back to his previous position.

Before McRoy retired he played a large role in the acquisition of Tris Speaker in a controversial trade with the Boston Red Sox in 1916, and it was under Dunn's ownership that the Indians did well both at the gate and on the field. They won the franchise's first pennant in 1920, a year after Speaker became the Indians' manager.

It also was under Dunn's ownership that in 1920 the name of League Park was changed to Dunn Field, though it reverted back to its former name in 1927, after the ownership of the franchise changed hands again.

After the Indians won the World Series that season, Dunn was so happy that he gave bonuses equal to 10 days' pay to all the players—all of whom then signed their 1921 contracts even before leaving Dunn Field after the final game.

And in return, the players presented the owner with a set of diamond-studded cuff links.

Things did not go so well for Sunny Jim and his Indians the following year, and prior to the start of the 1922 season, Dunn's health failed. He died on June 9, at the age of 57.

Ownership of the franchise was left to Dunn's widow, Edith (Forney) Dunn. Barnard took over as president, despite the presence of Tom Walsh, one of the men who invested in the club when it was purchased by Dunn, and who held the title of vice president.

The next five years were chaotic for the Indians under Mrs. Dunn and Barnard. Speaker, charged in 1926 of having conspired with Ty Cobb and two other players to fix the outcome of a game between Cleveland and Detroit seven years earlier, resigned as manager.

Jack McCallister, a coach under Speaker, was promoted to manager of the Indians, who fell into sixth place in 1927, and on November 17 the franchise was sold for $1 million to a syndicate headed by Alva Bradley.

Barnard resigned as president and the following year was elected president of the American League, replacing Byron "Ban" Johnson, who had stepped down on October 17, 1927, as head of the league he founded in 1901. Barnard held the AL presidency until his death on March 27, 1931.

1927–46

Alva Bradley

Baseball history in Cleveland certainly would have been different—and undoubtedly much better—if Alva Bradley had been successful in the acquisition of two players for whom he made major bids after becoming the principal owner and president of the Indians in 1927.

They were Lou Gehrig and Rogers Hornsby, both of whom are in the Hall of Fame. They would have improved the fortunes of the Indians during the Bradley era.

Shortly after Bradley and his partners purchased the franchise for the then outrageous price of $1 million from the estate of James C. Dunn on November 17, 1927, he attempted to buy and then trade for Gehrig, at the time a budding young star of the New York Yankees.

On December 29, 1927, exactly six weeks after taking over the Indians, Bradley wrote to Yankees owner Ed Barrow:

"From time to time during the last week there have been articles in the Cleveland newspapers referring to your inability to sign Lou Gehrig.

"The thought has occurred to me that if you are having real trouble with him, that you might want to sell him. I am authorized to make an offer [for Gehrig] of $150,000."

After it was rejected, Bradley made another proposal to

Alva Bradley (left) with Oscar Vitt, who managed the Indians from 1938 to 1940.

the Yankees for Gehrig, this one $175,000 plus first baseman George Burns, who was no slouch himself. He'd batted .319 in 1927 and .358 the year before that.

But Barrow was every bit as adamant as Bradley was persistent.

When he was rejected again, Bradley raised his offer to $250,000 and Burns, but Barrow still said no, shortly after which he signed Gehrig.

Bradley followed with another letter to Barrow on January 11, 1928, this time saying, "I was selfish enough to hope you would have more trouble [signing Gehrig]. My sole effort is to build up an organization that will put Cleveland back on the baseball map."

A week later, in a letter dated January 18, 1928, Bradley made a pitch for Hornsby, then playing for the Boston Braves.

He wrote to Emil Fuchs, president of the Braves:

"Some of the sportswriters are riding the new owners of the Cleveland club because we have not been able to purchase any new material. My associates and myself have gone into baseball for the sport in it, rather than with the idea that we are ever going to become rich in its operation.

"We are desirous of building up a real organization, and the thought occurred to me that it just might be possible, on account of the number of angles I hear expressed, that the Boston club might want to sell Rogers Hornsby, and the National League might have a happier situation if he were waived out. If so, we are interested."

Fuchs wasn't—but Bradley's efforts to acquire Gehrig and Hornsby spoke well of his interest in building a winning team in Cleveland.

Unfortunately, Bradley was not successful. The Indians in 19 years under his ownership never won a pennant. They finished as high as second only once, in 1940, the chaotic and tumultuous season that was marred by a players' rebellion against manager Oscar Vitt.

A wealthy native Clevelander whose family fortune was built in real estate, Bradley was a gracious, handsome man who had maintained a lifelong interest in sports, dating from his days as a prep quarterback at Cleveland's exclusive University School. He managed the family's extensive properties in downtown Cleveland.

Bradley was suave, even-tempered, and usually inclined to adopt a conciliatory attitude in disputes. He had been elected president of the Cleveland Chamber of Commerce at the age of 37.

Bradley's syndicate included seven other local businessmen-industrialists: his brother Charles L. Bradley, John Sherwin, Sr., brothers O. P. and M. J. Van Sweringen, Newton D. Baker, Joseph C. Hostetler, and Percy Morgan.

In his memoirs, Bradley admitted he had no knowledge of the business of baseball and only the average layman's understanding of the playing side of the game. But he and his partners all believed strongly that the Indians should be owned and operated by Clevelanders.

In addition to his attempts to acquire Gehrig and Hornsby, another of Bradley's moves upon taking control of the franchise was to hire Billy Evans, a former sportswriter and umpire, as general manager. He also installed Roger Peckinpaugh as the Indians' new field manager, replacing Jack McCallister, who was released.

It also was Bradley, early in his ownership of the franchise, who was influential in helping to provide the initial impetus for the construction of Cleveland's Municipal Stadium.

In only the second month of his first season as president of the Indians, Bradley wrote, in a letter dated May 22, 1928, to Cleveland city manager William R. Hopkins:

"So far this year we have had three capacity crowds [at League Park]. At those games, I would safely estimate, we could have shown to fifty and perhaps one hundred thousand more people, if we'd had the capacity to take care of them.

"I have found in my short experience in baseball that it is necessary to have a park large enough to take care of your capacity crowds in order to have the necessary income to build up a pennant contender. The expense incurred in developing a ballplayer is great, and things have changed in the major leagues to the extent that it is almost impossible for a team that is within striking distance of the top to purchase material.

"I am, of course, anxious within the next two or three years to be able to bring a pennant to Cleveland, but in so doing we must have the necessary facilities to take care of the crowds. I hope that some definite action will soon be taken on the stadium."

It was, though it took another four years before the Stadium was constructed at a cost of $2,986,685—and then, ironically, Bradley soon decided it was too large.

After the Stadium was opened on July 31, 1932, the Indians played 32 games in the new facility that season, and all their home games in the 80,000-plus-capacity park in 1933.

However, when attendance declined in 1933 to 387,936—an average of less than 6,000 per date—Bradley reconsidered his earlier sentiments and canceled the Indians' lease with the Stadium.

In a letter to Cleveland mayor Ray T. Miller dated October 13, 1933, Bradley wrote, "We have to date played 91 games in the Stadium (in 1932 and 1933). Figures show that in these 91 games we played to 529,340 people for a total gross revenue . . . $338,228.94, an average of 5,817 (people) per game and $3,716.80 per game.

"At League Park the last 91 games we played to 663,407 people; revenue $487,853.89, average per game, 6,960 people and $5,361.03. Only on two days were crowds at the Stadium larger than we could have taken care of at League Park.

"After studying these figures and comparing our extra expense at the stadium, we are convinced that the Cleveland Baseball company cannot afford to be tenants any longer. I think we have given the Stadium a thorough trial, and in accordance with our lease, we are notifying you of our desire to cancel."

Bradley's decision resulted in the Stadium being called a white elephant as the Indians returned to League Park to play their home games from 1934 through 1936 (though they did play in the Stadium once in 1936).

Thereafter, through the 1946 end of the ownership of the franchise by the Bradley syndicate, the Indians played a limited number of games on selected dates at the Stadium—15 in 1937, 18 in 1938, 30 in 1939, 49 in 1940, 32 in 1941, 46 in 1942, 48 in 1943, 44 in 1944, 46 in 1945, and 41 in 1946, the year that Bill Veeck purchased the club.

It was in the wake of the disastrous 1933 season that Bradley banned play-by-play broadcasts of Tribe games on the radio because, he believed, they hurt attendance, a position from which he veered after one year.

It also was in 1933 that Bradley coined the expression, "We only hire the manager; the public fires him," when he replaced Roger Peckinpaugh with Walter Johnson, though he was reluctant to dismiss Oscar Vitt when the players petitioned that he do so in 1940.

That was during the infamous "Vitt rebellion," and, in his memoirs, Bradley again admitted that he was wrong and the players were right on that issue.

In a statement to club directors on October 8, 1940, Bradley said, "We should have won the pennant. I have no alibis to offer for not winning it, but circumstances and developments during the year were such that I am very happy they [the players] did as well as they did in the race.

"Our real trouble started June 13th when a group of 10 of the players came to my office. They made four distinct charges against their manager and asked for his dismissal.

"The problem that faced me . . . was not only a Cleveland problem, but affected baseball in general. Consequently, I felt that I should do everything in my power to protect the game of baseball.

"[But the fact is] the four charges made against Vitt, on investigation I have made, were 100 percent correct."

It was at that meeting of club directors that Bradley announced his decision to fire Vitt, saying, "My experience with Oscar Vitt has not been a pleasant one. While I think that he was, personally, a very affable fellow, I am convinced that he is not a leader of young men."

Bradley also was the president of the Indians when, a year after Vitt was fired and replaced by Peckinpaugh, Lou Boudreau became the youngest manager in major league baseball history. He was hired on November 25, 1941, shortly after Peckinpaugh had been named general manager.

Hiring Boudreau proved to be a good move, though it was one that Bradley initially opposed. His choice to manage the Indians in 1942 was the veteran Burt Shotton, Bradley admitted later.

"I told Lou," Bradley said before his death on March 29, 1953, "that I'd consider his application along with many others, but that offhand the idea [of Boudreau's being a player-manager] didn't appeal to me.

"I pointed out that nothing Lou could do as manager would be as valuable as what he was doing at shortstop. I didn't feel inclined to take a chance on reducing his efficiency as a player by giving him the responsibility of management."

Bradley's opinion notwithstanding, Boudreau was invited to appear before the directors to state his qualifications and, if hired, his plans for managing the Indians.

After the interview Bradley took a vote of the directors, and only one of the 12, George A. Martin, favored hiring Boudreau.

However, as Bradley said, Martin was so taken by Boudreau, he convinced the other 11 directors—including Bradley—that it was time to try something else.

Boudreau managed the Indians the next nine seasons, through 1950, leading them to the pennant in 1948, only the second in franchise history—though by then, Bradley was gone.

Bradley's syndicate sold the Indians to Bill Veeck on June 22, 1946—though it almost did not come to pass. Selling to Veeck was another decision that Bradley initially opposed.

"I just thought that the Cleveland Baseball Club should be owned by Cleveland people," said Bradley, who had been approached by a local group that wanted to buy the franchise.

By then, however, Bradley was told by his attorney that negotiations with Veeck had proceeded too far. "If Veeck could meet the financial requirements, the club would be sold to him," Bradley said.

Veeck did. And to seal the deal, he offered to make $200,000 worth of stock available to any one or more of the previous owners. None accepted.

"I wasn't interested in a partnership with Veeck," said Bradley. "There was nothing personal in my attitude—I never knew the man well enough to have any personal feelings about him.

"I just didn't like his way of running a ball club, and I felt that way when he still was in the minor leagues. High-pressure promotion, in the long run, will hurt baseball more than it will help it."

On the day the sale closed, June 22, 1946, Bradley went to League Park for the final time and saw the Indians—Veeck's Indians—beat Boston, 4–3.

"I sat in my usual place near our dugout," he said. "Veeck came in late and made no move to join me. On the contrary, he traveled all around the park, sitting first with one group of fans, then another. About the seventh inning I left. I didn't see another game until the World Series of 1948."

So ended the Bradley era in Cleveland baseball. It wasn't the most successful period, but the ownership and presidency of the Indians by Alva Bradley was the longest in the history of the franchise.

1946–49

Bill Veeck

Bill Veeck arrived like a whirlwind, and his stewardship of the Indians, while brief, created one of the most interesting and exciting of times in baseball anywhere, not only in Cleveland.

Called the Barnum of baseball, Veeck was the game's most imaginative promoter, and only the fans had more fun than Veeck himself.

He purchased the franchise for $2 million on June 22, 1946, and kept it until December 18, 1949, making a near-perfect prophet of previous owner Alva Bradley.

"I predicted that Veeck would not stay in Cleveland more than three years," Bradley said before his death in 1953. "[Veeck] stayed about three and a half years, so I was close to being right."

Ah, but those three and a half years certainly were different from anything that preceded Veeck's arrival.

The Indians won their second pennant and World Series in 1948, the season that is generally considered the most exciting and dramatic in franchise history, and set what was then an all-time attendance record of 2,620,627.

Not all the action took place between the white lines, however.

It was during the winter of 1947–48 that Veeck created an uproar among Tribe fans by his avowed intention to trade player-manager Lou Boudreau, then—and still—one of Cleveland's most popular athletes.

He also set the baseball establishment on its collective ear with one unique promotion after another, including monstrous postgame fireworks displays; vaudeville acts; a "night" for what Veeck called a "typical fan" in which he was showered with

Bill Veeck

gifts valued at $15,000; funeral and burial services for the 1948 pennant after the Indians were mathematically eliminated in 1949; giveaways of beer, cases of food, orchids, cigarettes, perfume, nylon stockings, and even live pigs; and special appearances by baseball clowns Max Patkin and Jackie Price.

Veeck's ownership marked the beginning of what Bradley later lamented as the "intensive commercialization" of the game in which, he said, "The big question has become, 'How many people are in the park?' Get them in somehow. Give them souvenirs, give them all sorts of sideshows. Just get them in the park."

As Boudreau said of Veeck's promotional efforts, "We weren't very good when Bill bought the club, so he used diversionary tactics to get fans to come to the games until he was able to put together a good team."

Which Veeck did with his near-incessant wheeling and dealing. "It seemed we always had three teams in those early days [of Veeck's ownership], one on the field, one coming, one going," added Boudreau.

An ex-marine who suffered a crushed right foot during the firing of an artillery weapon in the South Pacific during World War II, ex-owner of the minor league Milwaukee Brewers of the American Association, ex-treasurer of the Chicago Cubs of the National League, and ex-peanut vendor at Wrigley Field when his father was president of the Cubs, Bill Veeck generated more excitement than Cleveland sports fans had before his arrival—and probably more than they've experienced since his departure.

Three years before buying the Indians, Veeck in 1943 attempted to purchase the Philadelphia Phillies with the intention of stocking the franchise with African-American players, but backed out—a move he later said he regretted. At that time there were no black players in the major leagues.

Veeck's right-hand man when he bought the Indians was Harry Grabiner, a native Chicagoan who had worked in the front office of the White Sox for 40 years.

Two other clubs reportedly were on the market at the time, Pittsburgh and the St. Louis Browns, and though Bradley was not anxious to sell, Veeck and Grabiner believed the Indians also were available. Their reasoning was based on the fact that five major stockholders had died in the previous year and their widows were participating in the affairs of the Indians.

Though he owned only 30 percent of the stock in the new corporation with an initial investment of less than $700,000, Veeck was in firm control of the Indians. None of the other 20 stockholders, about 10 of whom were Clevelanders, held more than 6 percent of the total, including Grabiner.

Among them was movie star and comedian Bob Hope, who was raised in Cleveland and, he said, had spent many afternoons at League Park as a youth watching the Indians play.

Though nobody in the front office was fired, Veeck, upon his arrival, made an announcement that he, as president, also would serve as the Indians' general manager, which led to the voluntary resignation of Roger Peckinpaugh.

Eighteen months after Veeck's arrival, he brought in former Detroit Tigers slugger Hank Greenberg, who had been released by the Pittsburgh Pirates after playing for them in 1947. Greenberg was appointed farm director of the Indians, and later purchased stock in the club. Owning stock solidified his role in the hierarchy and also set the stage for him to eventually replace Veeck as chief executive officer.

Another of Veeck's early decisions was that, beginning in 1947, the Indians would play all their home games in the Stadium, and that an internal outfield fence, five feet high, would be erected to make the field "fair" for both hitters and pitchers.

Initially the fence was "portable," enabling the groundskeepers—on Veeck's orders—to move it closer to or farther from the plate, depending upon the opponent. That option, however, was outlawed the following season with the implementation of a rule that required fences at all ballparks to remain where positioned on opening day.

Before the installation of the internal fence, the distances from home plate had been 320 feet down the left- and right-field foul lines and 470 feet to dead center.

It also was Veeck who, on July 3, 1947, purchased the contract of Larry Doby from the Newark Eagles of the Negro National League, making him the American League's first black player and the second (to Jackie Robinson) in major league history.

A year later, on July 7, 1948, to the great dismay of many baseball purists, including J. G. Taylor Spink, editor-publisher of *The Sporting News*, Veeck signed Satchel Paige, who was believed at that time to be 42 years old. Spink accused Veeck of making a mockery of the game and said that his signing of Paige was nothing but a "cheap publicity stunt."

The fact is, however, the Indians probably would not have won the 1948 pennant and World Series without Paige.

When the Indians failed to repeat as AL champion in 1949, though season attendance still surpassed the 2 million mark (2,233,771), Veeck looked for new challenges. On November 21, 1949, he sold the Indians for $2.2 million to a group headed by Cleveland insurance executive Ellis Ryan.

Veeck purchased the St. Louis Browns in 1951 and sold

that franchise in 1953 when the AL rejected his attempt to move the team to Baltimore (which new owners were allowed to do in 1954).

Involved in numerous endeavors outside of baseball the next six years, Veeck bought the White Sox in 1959, during which time they won the AL pennant, and sold them in 1961. He returned to baseball as the owner of the White Sox again from 1975 to 1980.

Veeck, who died of lung cancer on January 2, 1986, came close to returning to the Indians in 1958, when news surfaced that owner William R. Daley might move the franchise to Minneapolis–St. Paul.

Veeck's reason: it would be impossible, he said then, to "recapture the rapture" the Indians had known—that he had brought to Cleveland—a decade earlier.

1949–52

Ellis W. Ryan

Ellis W. Ryan was an insurance executive and sportsman, though he had a greater interest in hockey than in baseball when he headed a group of investors that bought the Indians from Bill Veeck for $2.2 million on November 21, 1949.

"I hope to be connected with the Indians for the rest of my life, and I will do my utmost to give the fans a winning team," said the 45-year-old Ryan. "But that does not mean I will attempt to follow in Bill Veeck's footsteps. That is an impossibility as everybody knows.

"Let me put it this way; I hope to be able to strike a happy medium between Alva Bradley and Bill Veeck."

In order to finance the deal, it was reported that Ryan's group placed 3,000 shares of common stock on sale at $100 a share, as well as $900,000 in debenture bonds, and obtained a bank loan of $1 million.

The ascension of Ryan as president also resulted in greater authority for Hank Greenberg, though he was given a lesser title in the new corporation.

When Greenberg joined the Indians in 1948 as vice president and farm director, it was Veeck who had the final word on all player personnel decisions at the major league level.

Under Ryan, who admittedly was not professionally knowledgeable in baseball nor well versed in its operations, Greenberg was given a new three-year contract and the title of general manager, and became essentially the Indians' chief operating officer.

"Hank will have a free hand in all player matters," said Ryan. "He and I will work as a team, but I don't want him to think that his hands will be tied."

Ryan said nothing about the future of manager Lou Boudreau, other than, "I understand he has another year on his contract."

Ryan was described as being "completely the opposite" of Veeck in personality and demeanor in newspaper articles that called him "tall, lean and urbane . . . a perfect candidate for a 'man of distinction' advertisement."

It also was said of Ryan, "His clothes and manners are meticulous," and, "He will never be barred from a place because he refuses to wear a coat or tie."

The latter was an obvious reference to Veeck, who had a

Ellis W. Ryan (seated) with members of the Indians front office (left to right): Harry Small, treasurer; Don Hornbeck, attorney; Hank Greenberg, general manager; and George Medinger, vice president.

deep contempt for conventions, both social and business—and steadfastly refused to ever wear a tie.

A former lieutenant colonel in the U.S. Army Air Corps and then the Office of Strategic Services during World War II, Ryan commanded a unit that trained personnel in espionage and commando tactics against the Japanese in the China-Burma-India theater of war. He was awarded the Legion of Merit and decorated by the king of Thailand (Siam) for his services.

Prior to his involvement with the Indians, Ryan had been a vice president of the Cleveland Browns of the National Football League and Cleveland Barons of the American Hockey League. He also built and was part owner of the Toledo Ice House, home of the Toledo Mercurys minor league hockey team.

Ryan's six associates in the purchase of the Indians were Donald W. Hornbeck, George A. Medinger, Guy W. Waters, Harry E. Small, Jack B. John, and Nate Dolin.

They were sometimes called the Big Seven, although, as Ryan quipped, "Maybe that should be the Silly Seven."

Named directors of the club were Ryan, Hornbeck, Medinger, Small, Waters, B. F. Bernet, and Mathew A. Baxter.

Prominent among other stockholders were Myron H. "Mike" Wilson, Jr., Judge Frank J. Merrick, and Gordon A. Stouffer, as well as several who had owned shares in the previous corporation under Veeck and retained an interest in the club—Hollywood actor and comedian Bob Hope, who was raised in Cleveland, and David R. Jones.

The Indians failed to win another pennant during Ryan's stewardship of the franchise—and Greenberg's leadership of the team. Failure on the field cost Boudreau his job as manager and led to another shake-up in the hierarchy.

After the Indians fell into fourth place in 1950, Greenberg

fired Boudreau, replaced him with Al Lopez, and embarked upon a rebuilding program. "We may lose the flag again in 1951, but not with this team," he vowed.

Under Lopez the Indians finished second in 1951 and 1952, but discontent continued to fester in the front office and among the stockholders.

Ryan, by then, had become more involved in the day-to-day operations of the franchise, as well as the team on the field, and several times indicated his intention to oust Greenberg as vice president and general manager.

His involvement divided the board of directors and created a chasm between Greenberg's supporters and those who were loyal to Ryan.

In one newspaper account a director was quoted anonymously as saying, "The big thing wrong with Ellis [Ryan] is that he can't make up his mind as to what he wants."

The rift broke into the open during the major-minor league meetings at Phoenix, Arizona, December 4, 1952.

Ryan left abruptly for Cleveland that day, and a meeting of stockholders was called for December 18. In the showdown, Ryan was unable to muster a majority of the 3,000 voting shares, receiving the support of only 1,464, compared to 1,526 in opposition to him.

Among those opponents were Hornbeck, Small, Dolin, Medinger, and Baxter, and the showdown served to strengthen the position of Greenberg.

Having failed to gain a vote of confidence, Ryan resigned as president and sold his stock to the opposition group, as did the five directors loyal to him—Waters, Bernet, Broderick, Johns, and Jones.

Each received $600 per share for their stock. Since Ryan had purchased his 551 shares at $100 apiece three years earlier, the transaction netted him a profit of more than $250,000.

A compromise candidate, Myron H. "Mike" Wilson, Jr., was elected to succeed Ryan.

1952–56

Myron H. "Mike" Wilson, Jr.

Myron H. "Mike" Wilson was not a major stockholder in the ownership of the Indians, even when he first joined the group headed by his longtime friend, Ellis W. Ryan, that bought out Bill Veeck in 1949.

Describing himself as "just an average fan," Wilson was a Yale graduate and an insurance executive. He owned only 100 shares of stock in the Indians, slightly more than 3 percent of the total, which he said he purchased as a "civic responsibility."

Wilson accepted the presidency of the Indians, he said, "to restore unity and management" to the club. In that respect Wilson was eminently successful.

"I have always been interested in baseball," said Wilson, 65 at the time he became president of the Indians. "Tris Speaker, Nap Lajoie, and Addie Joss were my first favorites. Tris and I have since become very good friends."

From the time he joined Ryan's group three years earlier until the overthrow of Ryan, Wilson had not taken an active part in the management of the club's affairs.

He indicated he would simply act as chief administrator, leaving the officials in charge of their respective duties.

Early in Wilson's tenure as president, it was reported that general manager Hank Greenberg asked him about a proposed deal.

Wilson responded, "Hank, you could talk to me about this for a long time and I wouldn't know any more about it than I do now. If you think it is a good deal, go ahead and make it. That's your job." This response epitomized Wilson's mode of operation.

When the fight for control of the franchise developed, Wilson, as a director who had considerable influence over other members of the board, took sides against his friend Ryan. The issue involved Ryan's attempt to oust Hank Greenberg and take over the duties of general manager himself.

In his belief that Greenberg was a baseball man, and that Ryan wasn't, Wilson cast the deciding vote that led to Ryan's resignation as president and his decision to sell out.

Before doing so, however, Ryan stipulated that Wilson should be named president, to which both sides agreed.

Although the restructuring enabled Greenberg to retain his authority in matters of player personnel, another controversy among members of the hierarchy developed later. It also revolved around Greenberg.

Near the end of the 1953 season, with the Indians about to finish second for a third straight year, it was reported that Al Lopez was planning to resign as manager of the team.

Wilson led a pilgrimage of directors to Lopez's office, asking him to sign a new contract that had been offered by Greenberg. Lopez initially resisted, but finally agreed, and the Indians went on to win the pennant the following season.

Later Lopez admitted that the only reason he returned was that Wilson and the directors had convinced him to change his mind about quitting.

1956–62

William R. Daley

William R. Daley bought the Indians on February 29, 1956, as part of a three-man syndicate that included Ignatius A. O'Shaughnessy and Hank Greenberg.

The purchase price was $3,961,800, which was believed to be the most money ever paid for a major league franchise.

Daley, a 63-year-old Cleveland industrialist and financial wizard; O'Shaughnessy, a St. Paul, Minnesota, businessman; and Greenberg paid $1,550 for each of the 2,556 shares of stock, including $800 in cash and a note for $750.

As part of the transaction the new owners issued a total of

Myron H. "Mike" Wilson (right) with Indians General Manager Frank Lane.

William R. Daley

6,000 shares at $100 each. They also permitted the former stockholders to buy one share in the new organization for each one they owned in the old corporation.

Thus, the Daley group had to pay only about $1,750,000—or less than half of the announced purchase price—to obtain controlling interest of slightly more than 55 percent.

Though Daley was named chairman of the board, Myron "Mike" Wilson, Jr., remained as president of the new corporation.

And in Greenberg's new role as a minority owner, his stature as general manager and, essentially, chief operating officer, was further strengthened.

But not for long.

In a startling development less than 20 months after Daley's group purchased control of the Indians, directors on October 16, 1957, voted 10–2 to fire Greenberg as of December 31, with a year remaining on his contract. Greenberg, who owned 19 percent of the stock in the corporation and was himself a director, abstained in the voting.

When asked the reason for Greenberg's dismissal, Wilson's only explanation was, "Fan reaction. The fans insisted on it."

Not only had the Indians finished in sixth place, their worst position in 11 years, but attendance also had declined to 722,256, second lowest in the American League and the poorest in Cleveland since 1945.

Another factor in the firing of Greenberg was that he and several unnamed stockholders had begun a behind-the-scenes campaign to relocate the franchise in Minneapolis–St. Paul.

Wilson strongly objected to a move and publicly stated that he would "do everything I can to keep the team here."

However, being only a minor shareholder, Wilson could do little except tell Daley and the directors of his personal feelings, which resulted in the decision to fire Greenberg, though he continued to be a shareholder and remained on the board.

Later, during an August 1959 directors meeting, Greenberg was quoted as saying that "baseball is dead in Cleveland."

Following the decision to fire Greenberg, Tribe directors met twice with William O. DeWitt, former AL club official, with a view toward hiring him as general manager.

However, on November 9, 1957, Frank Lane put in a bid for the job, although he had just completed the second year of a three-year contract as general manager of the St. Louis Cardinals.

Three days later, after Cardinals owner August A. Busch, Jr., gave the Indians permission to negotiate with Lane, he was given a three-year contract. It called for a base salary of $50,000 annually and a bonus of five cents for each admission over 800,000.

Lane was eager to get the job because he'd been given an ultimatum by Busch that he'd be fired if the Cardinals failed to win the National League pennant in 1958.

Despite the departure of Greenberg and the arrival of Lane, other cities continued to bid for the Indians, including Houston, which in 1958 attempted to buy the team for $6 million and move it to that city.

Daley finally and firmly rejected all offers, saying, "We think the [Indians] baseball club is a good thing for Cleveland, and we think we can restore Cleveland to where it was, a leading baseball city."

Lane's tenure in Cleveland lasted slightly more than three years, until January 3, 1961. His three-year contract was not renewed, and shortly thereafter he was hired as general manager of the Kansas City Athletics. Lane was replaced on April 27 by Gabe Paul, who'd left the Houston Colt 45s and joined the Indians as general manager.

The death of Wilson on August 19, 1962, preceded another reorganization of the Indians. Daley became president of the Indians in September 1962, but two months later Paul became the largest stockholder in the franchise.

1963–72

Gabe Paul

In a $6 million deal completed November 20, 1962, Ignatius A. O'Shaughnessy (a leading stockholder in the Indians), vice presidents Nate Dolin and George Medinger, and treasurer Harry Small sold their interests in the club.

The old corporation—with William R. Daley as chairman of the board and president—was liquidated and a new one set up.

Gabe Paul became the largest individual stockholder in the new organization, owning 20 percent of the 6,000 shares.

Two of Paul's associates, Grayle Howlett, the club's director of ticket sales, and A. Ray Smith, owner of the Tulsa club of the Class AA Texas League, acquired approximately 10 percent interest together.

The remaining 70 percent, and control, was held by Daley and a group of Clevelanders.

It was reported that the cost of the stock in the new cor-

Gabe Paul (left) with Indians Manager Birdie Tebbetts.

poration was $100 per share, with each stockholder being required to buy a $400 debenture bond with each share of common stock. Exactly half of the purchase price was raised by the sale of stock and debentures. The other $3 million was acquired in a bank loan.

In setting up the new organization Paul was elected president and treasurer, as well as general manager, and Daley continued as chairman of the board with 19 directors named, including Paul, Howlett, Smith, and Thomas A. Burke, a former mayor of Cleveland and U.S. senator.

Paul had been general manager of the Cincinnati Reds from 1951 to 1960, and even before taking over the expansion Houston Colt 45s (later renicknamed the Astros) in 1961, he had what he called "a standing offer" to head the Indians.

"I took the job in Houston because it was an exciting challenge, but as soon as I realized I'd made a mistake, I jumped at the chance to go to Cleveland," he said. A falling-out with Judge Roy Hofheinz, owner of the Colt 45s, hastened Paul's departure from Houston.

Paul also jumped at the chance to become the largest stockholder in the Indians, although his ownership of the franchise was a near financial disaster as attendance continued to plummet to 562,507 in 1963.

There were reports that the club lost upwards of $1.2 million, and, presumably as a means of covering some of the deficit, the Indians sold a stock issue of $300,000 to the men who were then the club's owners.

The club's fortune's were also bad in 1964 when Paul admitted that losses would approximate $1.2 million again. He further revealed that, in order for the club to have an operating fund, each stockholder had been called upon to contribute cash over and above his original investment. In his own case, Paul said, it amounted to $60,000.

All of which, of course, rekindled rumors that the Indians would move, and speculation was rife that the franchise would go to Seattle, Oakland, or Dallas.

Later, in a meeting of the board on October 5, 1964, Paul admitted that the directors had virtually made up their minds to move the franchise.

Not only was the Indians' cash flow very bad again, but the directors also were angered because they were having a problem with Mayor Ralph S. Locher in negotiating a new lease for the Stadium.

"If a vote had been taken, I'm sure it would have been to get out, to sell to the highest bidder," said Paul.

The only reason a vote wasn't taken was because of a motion by one of the directors, Maurice Saltzman, a wealthy and longtime Cleveland businessman.

According to Paul, Saltzman moved to send Paul and Daley on a fact-finding mission to the three cities—Seattle, Oakland, and Dallas—that wanted the Indians.

"It was approved, and we were commissioned by the board to investigate and evaluate those cities, and report back in 10 days," said Paul.

"More importantly, what it did was buy time . . . time for everybody to cool off and for us to get together with the city to hammer out a better lease."

Paul and Daley made the trip, then reported back to the directors that, if a satisfactory lease could be worked out, it would be best for all concerned for the Indians to stay in Cleveland.

Which, of course, they did.

Later Paul said that Cleveland had come even closer to losing the Indians in 1958. "That's when Hank Greenberg wanted to take them to Minneapolis. I was with the Reds at the time, and I thought it [moving the Indians] would be a big mistake.

"I absolutely always thought Cleveland was a good baseball town, that all the fans ever needed was a winning team."

Despite the ongoing financial problems, Paul made a bold attempt in 1965 to restore fan interest by reacquiring Rocky Colavito, the popular slugger who had been traded by Frank Lane in 1960.

Though it proved to be an unwise deal for the Tribe, the reappearance of Colavito helped boost attendance by nearly 300,000 to 934,786.

It also was in July 1965, during the annual summer meetings, that Paul was favored by some to be a candidate to replace the retiring commissioner of baseball, Ford Frick, though he made it clear he would not take the job if it were offered.

"I'm not finished yet in Cleveland," he said. "I want to build a winner."

The following year Paul gave up trying to make ends meet.

On August 13, 1966, Vernon Stouffer became the ninth owner of the Indians, though his ascendancy didn't end Paul's time in Cleveland or his efforts to build the team into a winner.

1966–72

Vernon Stouffer

Controlling interest in the Indians passed into new hands on August 13, 1966, when Vernon Stouffer, a 65-year-old restaurant and frozen foods magnate, purchased the stock held by William R. Daley and his associates for a reported $8 million.

Stouffer took over as chairman and announced plans to revamp the board of directors to include only Clevelanders "to make sure the club stays [in Cleveland]."

Vernon Stouffer

It was the fifth change of ownership since 1946 when Bill Veeck bought the franchise for $2 million.

Stouffer, who had been a minor stockholder and director since 1962, also announced that Gabe Paul would continue as president and general manager—although, three years later, Stouffer demoted Paul, albeit unofficially and only temporarily.

On July 8, 1969, at the height of a power struggle between Paul and manager Alvin Dark, Stouffer sided with Dark, placing him in charge of player personnel matters and making him, in essence, the general manager without title.

Paul was relegated to handling the Indians' financial, marketing, and promotional duties.

However, two years later, after the Indians flopped in 1969 under Dark to a 62–99 record—second worst in the history of the franchise—Paul was restored to power and, on July 30, 1971, fired Dark.

Prior to gaining control of the club, Stouffer owned only 150 of the 9,000 shares outstanding. He bought out all of the stockholders, paying each nearly $300 per share, which was almost $200 more than the original cost of each. Stouffer also purchased all of the stockholders' debentures at a cost of $2.5 million.

All told, in his purchase of the Indians it was estimated that he put up about $5.5 million of his own money, along with a bank loan of more than $2.5 million.

Paul, who had been the largest individual shareholder during the Daley regime, was permitted to buy 100 shares of the stock in Stouffer's new corporation and was given a stock-option plan to buy more.

Paul also was signed through 1976 as president and general manager, though he did not fulfill the term of the contract. He resigned on January 10, 1973, to become president of the New York Yankees.

Unfortunately for Stouffer—and the Indians—he suffered a massive financial setback when the stock market plunged in 1970. A severe austerity program was instituted, including drastic budget cuts in player development and the scouting department.

At midseason in 1971, with the Indians in a particularly difficult financial bind, Stouffer went to Henry J. "Hank" Peters, then vice president of player development, and asked how much it would hurt to reduce the farm system budget by one-third.

Peters later recalled his response to the owner. "First, I asked Mr. Stouffer if he was going to sell the team. I told him, 'If you intend to sell, don't look back. But if you intend to keep the club, you just committed suicide.'"

Peters resigned shortly thereafter, amid great criticism of Stouffer by fans who accused the owner of being cheap.

It also was shortly thereafter that Stouffer began receiving bids from out-of-town interests to buy the Indians and move them.

As Paul acknowledged in a speech at the time, "Vernon Stouffer has been criticized for everything. But did you know he had the opportunity to go to Dallas at a great profit? And he turned it down. Did you know he had the opportunity to go to Washington at a great profit? And he turned it down."

Then Paul promised, "The people of Cleveland are hungry for winning baseball, and you're going to get it."

But instead of winning baseball, less than two months later they got another change in ownership of the Indians.

The buyer was a group headed by Nick Mileti. In selling to Mileti, Stouffer on December 6, 1971, rejected a bid to buy the franchise by Cleveland businessman George Steinbrenner III and former Indians star third baseman Al Rosen.

In retrospect, the bid by Steinbrenner and Rosen for $8.6 million, which included the assumption of a $300,000 debt owed by the club to a local television station, probably was better than Mileti's offer of $9.75 million, according to Paul.

That's because "Mileti's [offer] consisted of green stamps and promises," Paul said.

Whatever the case may have been, Steinbrenner and Rosen were "shocked" when they were rejected in favor of Mileti, because they thought they had a verbal agreement to buy the Indians.

"We were excited because we had a great group put together," said Steinbrenner. "We'd been dealing with Stouffer's son Jim, and it was our understanding that we had a deal, though it wasn't finalized.

"Unbeknownst to us, Mileti also was working to get the Indians. He went in one night, got together with Vernon and ... bought the club right out from under us.

"It came as a complete shock to Al [Rosen] and me when we found out that the deal [between Stouffer and Mileti] was done," said Steinbrenner. A year later, with a group comprised primarily of Clevelanders, Steinbrenner purchased the New York Yankees for $10 million.

"I've often thought about what might have been if we had bought the Indians," added Steinbrenner. "I am sure we could have been successful in Cleveland, just as successful as we were in New York, maybe even more successful."

1972–77

Nick J. Mileti

Prior to selling the franchise to Nick Mileti for a reported $9.75 million on March 22, 1972, Vernon Stouffer made a tentative agreement with New Orleans interests for the Indians to play a minimum of 30 "home" games annually in the Louisiana Superdome.

Stouffer was concerned with declining attendance in Cleveland, but he was opposed to selling the franchise and having it moved.

Nick Mileti

But the "twin-city concept," as the New Orleans plan was called, became a source of great concern among civic leaders in Cleveland. They feared that, if Cleveland shared the Indians with New Orleans for 30 games, the team would eventually play full-time in the Superdome unless attendance at the Stadium improved dramatically.

Mileti, a 41-year-old lawyer/entrepreneur, pledged to keep the Indians in Cleveland "forever" and quickly canceled Stouffer's tentative agreement with the Superdome.

When he headed the syndicate that purchased the Indians, Mileti also owned the Cleveland Cavaliers of the National Basketball Association, the Cleveland Barons of the American Hockey League, and the Cleveland Arena. He later purchased the Cleveland Crusaders of the World Hockey Association and two Cleveland radio stations, and built the Richfield Coliseum.

Mileti's personal investment in the Indians amounted to only about $500,000, though he steadfastly refused to reveal the precise percentages of either his or any of the partners' financial interest. He said only that he personally owned or controlled more than 50 percent.

Soon after taking over as president, Mileti issued a widely disseminated statement that claimed the Indians were "the best financed club in the major leagues because there are people in our town who care."

However, it quickly became evident that, not only were the Indians not the best financed club in baseball, they actually were among the worst.

Prominent among Mileti's partners were Alva T. "Ted" Bonda, who took over as chief operating officer in 1973, though Mileti continued as president; Howard M. Metzenbaum, who became a U.S. senator; Armond D. Arnson; C. Bingham and Dudley S. Blossom III; C. C. Tippit; Bruce and Marshall Fine; Bob Hope; and Ted Stepien.

Metzenbaum said there were three reasons that he invested in Mileti's group. "First is Nick's leadership. Second is our concern for the community, and for keeping the Indians here. And third, we hope to have some fun out of this."

Initially, Vernon and Jim Stouffer, F. J. "Steve" O'Neill, and Paul retained financial interests in Mileti's partnership. Eventually the Stouffers were bought out, and O'Neill and Paul sold their holdings when, on January 10, 1973, they

joined George Steinbrenner who then owned the New York Yankees.

With Paul's departure, Phil Seghi was promoted to general manager. He had been a vice president in charge of player development.

Seven months after Paul and O'Neill left the Indians, Mileti was forced by the partnership to resign as chief operating officer, though he retained the title of president.

Mileti announced that he "stepped aside" because of the press of other business commitments. However, the change was made because his fellow shareholders were upset as a result of a two-year deficit of almost $2 million incurred under Mileti's leadership.

Several months prior to Mileti's resignation as chief operating officer, the ownership of the Indians was restructured from a corporation to a limited partnership, primarily for the purpose of tax savings, and also in the hope of attracting new investors.

Approval of the restructuring was required by at least nine of the 12 American League club owners, but was denied in a mail vote. It was later granted at a league meeting in Chicago on May 10, after what was described as a "lot of cantankerous wrangling and accusations that the Indians were undercapitalized," which they were.

Replacing Mileti on August 29, 1973, in the daily operation of the club was Bonda, 56, a prominent Cleveland businessman. He assumed the title of executive vice president.

Differences between Bonda and Mileti continued to worsen after Bonda hired Frank Robinson as baseball's first black manager on October 3, 1974. Five months later, on March 20, 1975, Bonda was named president of the Indians.

Mileti stepped down, but not out of the corporate structure, continuing as general partner of the organization, which by then was composed of 41 limited partners.

Bonda remained in charge of day-to-day operations of the club and, on March 31, 1977, formed IBC Corporation (Indians Baseball Corporation), which served as the new general partner of the club.

In effect, Bonda was established as the principal owner, as well as president, of the Indians.

1975–78

Alva T. "Ted" Bonda

There is little doubt that, without Ted Bonda's expertise, the Indians would have either gone bankrupt and out of business, or been sold and moved out of Cleveland.

Although he did not become the general partner and, essentially, owner of the Indians until April 12, 1977, it was Bonda who steered the Indians through one crisis after another from the time he joined Nick Mileti's original partnership of eight in 1972.

The financially floundering franchise reportedly suffered losses of $500,000 in 1972, $1.4 million in 1973, $500,000 in 1974, $1,075,000 in 1975, $680,000 in 1976, and $1 million in 1977, for a total of more than $5.1 million.

"The man is a miracle worker" is the way Bonda was praised in a speech in 1978 by Cleveland Browns owner Art Modell, who as president of the Cleveland Stadium Corporation also was the Indians landlord.

Alva T. "Ted" Bonda

"The Indians were totally insolvent when Bonda took over the club [as chief operating officer in 1973]. But he was able to successfully employ his talents to keep the banks and other creditors from closing in. He was able to sell small pieces of the partnership interests to new people, to keep pumping the club with an infusion of capital.

"When a franchise—any kind of a sports franchise whether it be baseball, football, basketball, hockey, or what have you—is in trouble as the Indians were for so long, the quickest way to cure the trouble is to move it.

"History is full of franchises moving to greener pastures, and as long as there is a New Orleans or a Washington—any major city that has an empty stadium—there's always the prospect that somebody will come along and lift your franchise, move it away.

"But Ted Bonda never let that happen. No matter how dire the straits were—and they were very dire—he was able to keep the sheriff from the door, to keep juggling all the balls until something could be done.

"Above all, Bonda did an outstanding job of keeping the Indians franchise in a condition that would allow a new group to come in and take over."

Which is what happened on February 3, 1978, when F. J. "Steve" O'Neill and Gabe Paul returned to the Indians.

The Indians were purchased by O'Neill, who headed a group of seven investors, two of whom were Bonda himself and Modell.

Bonda joined the group and reinvested in the O'Neill partnership after his corporation, IBC, sold out as general partner.

As for Modell, it was he who generated O'Neill's interest in returning to Cleveland and helped put together the partnership that also included C. C. Tippit, who became chairman of the board, Dudley S. Blossom III, Maurice Stonehill, and Paul, who was named president and chief executive officer.

The financial investment by the O'Neill partnership was $6 million, plus the assumption of more than $5 million in debts.

Prior to the return of O'Neill, and through the last few years of Bonda's stewardship of the franchise, he actively sought a buyer for the Indians, one who would assure that the club stayed in Cleveland.

Bonda dealt extensively with Youngstown, Ohio, businessman and developer Edward J. DeBartolo, who had a genuine interest in buying the Indians. However, DeBartolo was fearful that his ownership application would be rejected, as it had been a few years earlier when he attempted to buy the Chicago White Sox.

Another who wanted to buy the Indians was Donald Trump. But Bonda steadfastly refused to negotiate with him unless Trump was willing to give assurance that he would not move the club out of Cleveland.

1978–86

F. J. "Steve" O'Neill, Gabe Paul, and Patrick O'Neill

Gabe Paul well remembered his and F. J. "Steve" O'Neill's return to the Indians on February 3, 1978.

"The club was practically bankrupt . . . they [the Indians] would have gone under if we had not stepped in," Paul said, speaking for O'Neill and the partnership that invested a reported $11 million to take over the franchise. Included was the base purchase price of $6 million and the assumption of more than $5 million in debts.

Paul said that, with the financial reorganization, the Indians for the first time in two decades would have "unlimited funds" to return the franchise to the success it enjoyed in the 1950s when it was among the best in the major leagues.

O'Neill, 78, explained his reason for returning to the Indians. "I'm a Clevelander, always have been," he said. "I love baseball as a fan, and when I saw the sad situation with the team here, I wanted to help. When Gabe agreed to come back to Cleveland, I was anxious to be a part of it."

In another statement by Paul that was widely disseminated—and also oft repeated, usually with derision, during most of the next 16 years—he called the Cleveland sports community "a sleeping giant."

The phrase was a reference to attendance problems suffered by the Indians through most of the previous 18 seasons, dating back to 1959.

"It [the sleeping giant] only needs to be reawakened. That won't come with words, only action. But give the fans what they want, a winning team, and they will react like no other city has.

"And if we don't succeed, we can't blame it on the people, only ourselves," added Paul as he began his second term at the helm of the Indians.

The "giant," however, continued to slumber under the new ownership, as well as through subsequent seasons, until the Indians made what turned out to be an aborted return to glory in 1994.

Paul initially came to Cleveland as the Indians general manager in 1961 and remained in either a top-management or ownership position for 12 years. On January 10, 1973, it was announced that Paul and O'Neill had sold their interests in the Indians and were joining George Steinbrenner's partnership that purchased the New York Yankees.

Though it was O'Neill who put up most of the money to purchase the Indians, he remained out of the limelight: his only position in the hierarchy was as a member of the seven-man board of directors, along with Paul, C. C. Tippit, Dudley S. Blossom III, Alva T. "Ted" Bonda, Art Modell, and Maurice Stonehill.

Bonda joined the group as an investor after selling his IBC Corporation, which had been the general partner in the previous ownership of the Indians.

Modell, as the majority owner of the Browns, was prohibited by National Football League rules from having a financial interest in the Indians, but he was appointed to the board because of his involvement in organizing the new group.

"I see this as a start of a new era for the Indians," said Modell. "Football is my activity, but as a member of this [Indians] board, I'll be available for consultation as needed."

Stonehill said of his involvement, "It's a good investment in Cleveland, and that's what counts with me."

Paul was named president and chief executive officer, and C. C. Tippit chairman of the board.

For Paul, 68, it turned out to be the culmination—without the great satisfaction he'd sought—of a long career in baseball.

It began in 1928 when Paul was a sportswriter in Rochester, New York. That job led to his being hired as publicity director and ticket manager of the Rochester Red Wings of the International League. He became publicity director of the Cincinnati Reds in 1937, and that team's traveling secretary in 1938.

During World War II, Paul served in the army from 1943 to 1945, then returned as assistant to the president of the Reds in 1948, was promoted to vice president in 1949, and was their general manager from 1951 to 1960.

He left the Reds in 1960 to become general manager of the expansion Houston Colt 45s, a decision he called "one of my biggest mistakes in baseball."

It was a mistake Paul quickly corrected when he accepted what he said had been "a standing offer" to be general manager of the Indians on April 27, 1961.

Upon leaving the Indians in 1973 after 12 years, during which he was on various occasions owner, president, general manager, and treasurer, Paul served as president of the Yankees when they won the pennant in 1976 and the World Series in 1977.

Despite Paul's promise of "unlimited funds" and his determination to rebuild the Indians into a winning team, the "sleeping giant" continued to slumber, and in 1978 attendance declined for the fourth consecutive year.

It improved slightly, edging over the million mark in 1979 and 1980, though two more sixth-place finishes gave them three in a row, and the franchise was back on the market.

Two out-of-town buyers surfaced—New York theater tycoon James Neiderlander and Los Angeles attorney Neil Papiano—and on October 30, 1980, it was announced that the Indians were being sold again. Both gave assurance of their intention to keep the Indians in Cleveland.

The financial arrangements, according to Neiderlander, were that he and Papiano were acquiring 58 percent of the franchise for $8.7 million, which set the total value at about $15 million.

O'Neill was to retain 10 percent of his original 60 percent ownership of the Indians, and Paul would keep 7 percent and continue as club president.

O'Neill, Paul, and Neiderlander had been partners in the ownership of the Yankees, and it was Paul who worked out the foundation of Neiderlander's and Papiano's proposal to buy the Indians.

Neiderlander and Papiano were required to put up only 10 percent of the purchase price, or $3.5 million, immediately, with the remainder to be paid over five years.

Additionally, the new owners were supposed to take over a long-term bank debt of the Indians of $2.75 million, of which $1 million was due at that time. They also were to assume responsibility for the 1980 operating loss of $2.1 million.

A letter of agreement "in principle" was signed on October 22, and the deal was to be finalized after January 1, 1981.

However, on January 6, 1981, instead of being ratified, the transaction was called off by the Indians.

Neither side would offer a detailed explanation as to why the deal collapsed.

O'Neill said only that "it was a purely financial thing that could not be resolved."

Paul said, "It is one thing to shake hands, but you don't have a deal until the final papers are signed. Things like this happen all the time."

Papiano, speaking for Neiderlander and himself, said first that he was "absolutely shocked," then "unbelieving" and "heartsick."

"We were not sure what the exact problem was. All we know is that we were very happy with the way things stood and we were not given a chance to iron out the differences. We were just informed the deal was off," he said.

After the shock dissipated—and the ridicule subsided—Paul pronounced, "We have no plans to find any other investors, and we are not talking to anyone. Things will stay as they are, with Mr. O'Neill owning the club."

It also was in 1981 that O'Neill, until then only a director despite being the principal owner of the Indians, became chairman replacing Tippit, who remained on the board, though no announcement or explanation was provided for the change.

Though Paul didn't mean that the Indians would continue to lose on the field and at the gate when he said, "Things will stay as they are," the fact is, the team finished sixth again in 1981 and 1982.

Operating deficits also continued to pile up, including a reported $10.7 million from 1981 to 1983, including $5 million in 1982, and renewed speculation arose that multimillionaire Youngstown developer and sportsman Edward J. DeBartolo was interested in buying the club.

However, it became evident again that, should DeBartolo attempt to purchase the Indians, he would be rejected by American League club owners, though nobody in the baseball hierarchy would give a reason for refusing to let him join the fraternity.

Then, with the Indians still floundering in 1983 and doomed to wind up in seventh place with 92 losses, their most in 12 years (since finishing with a 60–102 record in 1971), O'Neill died on August 29 at age 84.

Principal ownership of the Indians reverted to O'Neill's estate, and the franchise was immediately put up for sale by the executor of the will, Patrick J. O'Neill, a nephew of the late owner.

Patrick O'Neill became chairman of the board, with Paul continuing as president, and for the next three years the Indians were up for sale on the open market.

Early on, O'Neill made clear a condition that had to be met by any buyer: the Indians had to be kept in Cleveland "not for any specified period of time, but a long-term commitment."

Another condition, though not publicly stated, was that Patrick O'Neill was to be retained by the new owner as a "consultant" at a fee of $4,000 per month for 10 years.

Several prospective buyers surfaced, most notably Walter Laich, a Cleveland businessman who had been a minor investor in the club and a member of the board, and David E. LeFevre, a New York attorney who was the grandson of Cleveland millionaire industrialist Cyrus Eaton.

Laich's bid was rejected, but negotiations between LeFevre and O'Neill went on for more than eight months in late 1983 and 1984. Finally they reached what was termed a "tentative agreement" on June 21 for LeFevre to purchase controlling interest for $16.48 million.

But that deal was blocked by a lawsuit by Laich, then restructured for LeFevre to buy the total assets of the Indians for $31.5 million, plus the assumption of approximately $11 million in liabilities.

However, that proposal also was halted when three of the 54 limited partners in the ownership of the franchise refused to consent to the sale. One hundred percent agreement was necessary.

Finally, on November 14, 1984, LeFevre withdrew his bid. "To continue negotiations," he said, "would be detrimental to the Indians, the city of Cleveland, and all parties in the transaction."

Nothing further developed for more than a year—although, on November 29, 1984, Peter Bavasi was hired as president, replacing Paul, who was nudged into retirement as of December 31.

1984–86

Peter Bavasi

Prior to joining the Indians as president on November 29, 1984, Peter Bavasi was a paid consultant for Tampa–St. Petersburg and Indianapolis interests in their efforts to obtain major league franchises.

Because of his company, Peter Bavasi Sports, Inc., and his previous association with Tampa–St. Petersburg and Indianapolis, Bavasi was suspected by the Cleveland media and fans of being a "double agent." As president of the Indians he would be in position to see them sold to out-of-town investors and moved.

Bavasi, who had been executive vice president and then president of the Toronto Blue Jays from 1977 to 1981, after serving as an executive of the San Diego Padres from 1968 to 1977, breezed into Cleveland at O'Neill's behest and cleaned house in the Indians front office.

First to go was Gabe Paul, who was convinced to retire, though he remained on the board and continued as a paid "consultant" working out of his home in Tampa.

Two months later, on February 18, 1985, vice president and general manager Phil Seghi was "reassigned," though in actuality he was demoted to "senior personnel adviser" and sent home to Thousand Oaks, California, where he was to serve as a scout.

Patrick J. O'Neill

Peter Bavasi

Bavasi also announced the "resignation" of Bob Quinn, though Quinn said he'd been fired as vice president and director of player development and scouting, after being in that position since 1973.

Then Bavasi, who was being paid $160,000 a year, hired two assistants—though "partners" is what he called them—Dan O'Brien, a veteran baseball executive who initially was given the title "assistant to the president" and later "senior vice president/baseball administration/player relations," and Joe Klein, "vice president/baseball operations" and then "general manager."

It was a tumultuous time as Bavasi raised the cost of tickets, banned what he deemed were "derogatory" banners at the Stadium, closed the popular and modestly priced bleachers for night games, and authorized new Tribe uniforms that were bereft of any mention of Cleveland, giving rise to new speculation that the team would be moved.

Bavasi also commissioned a study that, he said, "debunked" the popular "sleeping giant" theory that claimed Cleveland fans would support a winning team as they did in large numbers in the late 1940s and early 1950s.

The study proved that blame for the Indians' attendance problems was because the "environment is not supportive," he said.

"And who creates the environment? The media. Nothing is good, everything is bad. And if the study is right, we've got trouble in River City because there is no sleeping giant."

Bavasi even blamed the media for the "negative attitude" of players. "Why do they not want to play in Cleveland? Because of the Stadium? No. Ticket prices? No. Promotions? No. It's the environment. And it's the media that creates the environment," he said again.

But those weren't the only reasons Patrick O'Neill had trouble finding a buyer for the franchise. The Indians reportedly had $11.5 million in debts as of October 15, 1985, and also were contracted to between $4 million and $13.5 million in guaranteed deferred salaries through the year 2016.

However, early in 1986 real estate developers Richard E. and David H. Jacobs of Westlake, Ohio—perhaps impressed by a resurgence of the Indians on the field—inquired into the possibility of buying the franchise. Their interest was welcomed with open arms.

On July 1, O'Neill gave the Jacobs brothers an option good for 45 days to buy the total assets of the Indians for $35.5 million, plus the assumption of approximately $12 million in debts.

This time the agreement in principle stood.

The following day, in confirming the impending sale, O'Neill said, "For three years I have been looking for the right buyer. I had to put up with a lot of crap while I was working—yes, working—to sell this team. In the Jacobs family, I've not only found the right buyer but also the right family to keep the Indians in Cleveland.

"I've talked to at least 25 people who had a reasonable chance of buying the team. At least five of them, and I'm talking about local people, were offering more money. They were beautiful people, but in the Jacobs, we have people with the desire, dedication, and means to build this thing up."

On November 13, 1986, O'Neill and the Jacobses finalized their agreement. The sale of the franchise was approved by

AL club owners during baseball's winter meetings on December 11.

Exactly five weeks later, on January 23, 1987, Bavasi announced his resignation as president of the Indians. The position wasn't immediately filled, though Richard E. Jacobs became chairman of the board and chief executive officer, and his older brother David H. Jacobs became vice chairman of the board.

1986–

Richard E. Jacobs, David H. Jacobs, and Henry J. "Hank" Peters

After their purchase of the Indians for $35.5 million (and the assumption of approximately $12 million in debts) was approved by the American League on December 11, 1986, Richard E. and David H. Jacobs set out to hire a president.

Though he was not immediately available, longtime baseball administrator and executive Henry J. "Hank" Peters agreed on November 2, 1987, to join the Indians as president and chief operating officer. Essentially, he also was general manager.

Purchase of the franchise by the Jacobs brothers included a commitment by them to keep the franchise in Cleveland for a minimum of five years.

The $35.5 million price included $18 million put up by the Jacobses, $12 million in borrowed capital, and $2.5 million in subordinated debentures. The remaining $3 million was in the form of a loan from the estate of the late F. J. "Steve" O'Neill.

Their takeover marked the beginning of a new period of stability for a team that had been unsuccessful at both the gate and on the field for more than three decades.

Peters, a veteran of 42 years in professional baseball dating back to 1946 when he worked in the minor league department

Richard E. Jacobs

of the St. Louis Browns, was accompanied to the Indians by Tom Giordano, whose title was assistant to the president.

They had been together in Baltimore, where Peters was the executive vice president/general manager of the Orioles for 12 years and Giordano was his assistant.

Another aide who rejoined Peters in Cleveland in 1989 was a former minor league player and manager, and the Orioles' third base coach, John Hart.

Initially a special assignment scout and later director of baseball operations, then vice president and general manager in 1991, Hart became executive vice president of the Indians in 1993 shortly after the retirement of Peters.

The arrival of Peters and his front office team led to the departure of general manager Joe Klein after the 1987 season. Senior vice president/baseball operations/player relations Dan O'Brien left near the end of 1988, and Peter Bavasi exited the Wigwam early in January 1988.

While Klein and O'Brien were highly respected by the Cleveland media and most of the Tribe's fans, no tears were shed upon the departure of Bavasi.

Rick Bay, who'd been the athletic director at Ohio State and the University of Minnesota, joined the Indians as executive vice president on November 18, 1991, and was appointed president and chief operating officer of the Indians on January 1, 1992, upon the retirement of Peters. Bay didn't stay long, less than a year, resigning the following November 20 "to pursue other interests," he said.

The Indians have not had a president since Bay, though Richard Jacobs, as chairman of the board and chief executive officer, has taken an active role in the operation of the club. The older Jacobs brother, David, died September 17, 1992, at age 71.

Peters previously was an Indians vice president and director of player personnel during Gabe Paul's and Vernon Stouffer's ownerships from 1966 to 1971. He was president of the National Association of Professional Baseball Clubs (minor leagues) from 1971 to 1975. He also was general manager of the Kansas City Athletics in 1965.

Under the leadership of Peters the Orioles won American League pennants in 1979 and 1983 and the World Series in 1983.

Though there was no great improvement in the Indians on the field during Peters' first three years, and they hit rock bottom with a franchise-record 105 losses in 1991, attendance climbed over a million each season.

But it also was in 1991 that Cuyahoga County voters approved a tax on alcohol and cigarettes to finance a new downtown ballpark for the Indians and arena for the NBA Cavaliers. Ground was broken in 1992, and Jacobs Field and Gund Arena were completed in 1994.

In 1992 the Indians under Hart instituted a new program of signing their best young players to multiyear contracts—a program that proved to be so successful that, within a year, it was adopted by other clubs as a means to prevent their best players from declaring free agency.

And in 1994, after two more seasons of play that was mediocre at best, the Indians, in their jewel of a new ballpark, became a bona fide pennant contender for the first time in 35 seasons.

"The only thing that stopped us," said Hart, "was the strike." He was right.

The strike by the players began on August 12. It was the eighth work stoppage in 22 years, and it forced cancellation of the rest of the season, as well as—for only the second time in 92 years—the World Series.

But in 1995, only the Atlanta Braves managed to stop the Indians, and only after they'd won the franchise's fourth pennant, and their first in 41 years.

The General Managers

1903–27

Ernest S. "Barney" Barnard

In the beginning, from the time Byron "Ban" Johnson founded the American League in 1901 and the Cleveland franchise was established by John F. Kilfoyl and Charles W. Somers, player matters were handled by the owners themselves.

In those early days Sunday games were not allowed in Cleveland. So Kilfoyl and Somers took their team to Dayton or Columbus to play that day, and it was because of that practice that Ernest S. "Barney" Barnard was able to begin what proved to be a long and distinguished career in baseball.

A one-time football coach at Otterbein College in Westerville, Ohio, when he was still an undergraduate—his team beat Ohio State, 16–14, in 1894—Barnard wound up as the second president of the American League from November 2, 1927, until his death on March 27, 1931.

In 1903, Barnard was sports editor of the *Columbus Dispatch,* and it was in that position that he covered Naps' Sunday games in Columbus and Dayton. He also was involved in operations of the American Association and was a director of the Columbus club in that league.

After joining the club in Cleveland in early March 1903, Barnard's title with the Naps was business manager and secretary. (Previously an office employee had accompanied the team on the road.) One of Barnard's first duties was to arrange for the Naps to hold spring training in New Orleans in 1903.

Unfortunately for the Naps—and baseball in Cleveland—Somers continued to handle all player matters, including his rejection of Ty Cobb when the then young but already cantankerous outfielder was offered in trade to Cleveland in 1908.

Somers said no to a deal for Cobb proposed by Detroit manager Hughie Jennings, who wanted veteran outfielder Elmer Flick. When told by Jennings that Cobb "can't get along with our players," that "he's had two fights already this spring," Somers said thanks but no thanks.

"We'll keep Flick," he told Jennings. "Maybe [Flick] is not as good a batter as Cobb, but he's much nicer to have on the team."

By the end of that 1908 season Somers took over as president of the club, replacing Kilfoyl, whose health was failing. Barnard was promoted to vice president and set about establishing one of baseball's first farm systems.

Soon the Naps controlled teams located in Toledo and

Ironton, Ohio; Portland, Oregon; New Orleans; and Waterbury, Connecticut.

It was the beginning of Barnard's tenure in a position now considered "general manager," though he wasn't given that title until later.

First, Barnard was fired, albeit temporarily, by James C. Dunn when he purchased the Cleveland franchise from Somers in 1916.

Upon taking control of the franchise, Dunn announced that Bob McRoy would be the team's new "executive" manager, as the position was then called. When sportswriters asked the status of Barnard, Dunn replied, "Barnard goes."

Dunn's intention to let Barnard go so angered the sportswriters that Dunn reconsidered and kept him, though in a subordinate position to McRoy.

However, when McRoy became ill and retired in 1917, Barnard, who by then had gained Dunn's confidence, was elevated back to his previous position and given the title—general manager—that he did not have previously.

Barnard served as general manager of the Indians the next four years, until Dunn's health also failed and he died on June 9, 1922. It left the ownership of the franchise in the hands of Dunn's widow, who immediately put Barnard in charge as president, and subsequently authorized him to find a buyer.

He did, and quickly. It was Alva Bradley, who headed a syndicate that purchased the franchise for $1 million on November 17, 1927.

Barnard was anxious to sell the club for Mrs. Dunn and to step down as president because he'd been offered the presidency of the American League.

Two weeks before Bradley's group closed the deal for the Indians, Barnard was formally elected the AL's second president, replacing Johnson, who had resigned on October 17, 1927.

Before leaving the Indians, however, Barnard laid the groundwork with Cleveland's civic leaders for the construction of a new ballpark—the Municipal Stadium.

It took another year before a stadium bond issue was passed, and the Stadium wasn't completed until 1932, more than a year after Barnard had died.

But it was Barnard's vision of the future of baseball in Cleveland that was the genesis of what was then called "the ultimate athletic facility in the United States."

When Barnard was elected president of the AL, it was said by Tom Shibe, president of the Philadelphia Athletics: "We have figured on Barnard for the last two years as the ultimate successor to Ban Johnson. In fact, there never has been anyone else."

Colonel Jacob J. Ruppert, owner of the New York Yankees, said of Barnard: "We have a president of whom we can be proud. We have a president who knows baseball, a man upon whom we can rely, and one who will be a credit to the office."

And when Barnard died less than four years after taking office, Henry P. Edwards, former sports editor of the *Cleveland Plain Dealer,* wrote, "The grand old game needed him, for Barney was a great builder, one who looked far into the future and appreciated the needs of the minor as well as the major leagues. He was the best friend the game ever had."

1916–17

Bob McRoy

When James C. "Sunny Jim" Dunn purchased the Indians on February 21, 1916, he turned to American League president Byron "Ban" Johnson for advice in assembling an administrative staff.

"I know nothing about this business of baseball. I've got to have some help," Dunn said to Johnson.

"I've got just the man for you," Johnson responded to Dunn. "Bob McRoy. He used to be my secretary [1901–11] until he went to the Boston club. He'll buy $5,000 worth of stock and be your executive manager. He knows baseball and how to run a club."

There also was an ulterior motive, however, in Johnson's eagerness for Dunn to hire McRoy.

Johnson was aware of growing sentiment against his leadership of the American League, and he knew that several of the club owners were lobbying for Ernest S. "Barney" Barnard to replace him as president. Strongly recommending McRoy to Dunn was Johnson's way of putting down Barnard, who was then a vice president of the Indians.

When Dunn took Johnson's advice and hired McRoy, he initially announced that the popular Barnard would be dismissed, raising a howl of protest by the Cleveland media. Dunn relented and allowed Barnard to keep his job, but in a subservient position to McRoy.

As it was, McRoy did well for Dunn, though he remained with the Indians for only two years. Having been an employee and then part owner of the Boston Red Sox from 1911 to 1916, McRoy was in a position to help the Indians acquire Tris Speaker.

It was during the winter of 1915–16 that Speaker became embroiled in a contract dispute with Red Sox owner Joseph Lannin, who wanted to cut the outfielder's salary from $11,000 to $9,000. Speaker steadfastly refused to sign.

McRoy stepped in and negotiated a trade with Lannin on April 8, 1916, that brought Speaker to the Indians in exchange for pitcher Sad Sam Jones, rookie infielder Fred Thomas, and $55,000.

Before Speaker would consent to join the Indians, however, he insisted upon getting $10,000 of the $55,000 that Dunn was paying the Red Sox. Lannin disagreed, and the deal was held up.

Finally Johnson, eager to make McRoy look good, interceded and convinced Lannin to go along with Speaker's demand.

It proved to be one of the best trades the Indians ever made.

Two years later illness forced McRoy to retire, and he died December 2, 1917.

By then Dunn had become aware of Barnard's expertise and efficiency and placed him in charge of all operations. Barnard became president of the Indians upon Dunn's death in 1922. It was a position he held until the club was sold to Alva Bradley and shortly thereafter Barnard was elected president of the AL.

1927–35

Billy Evans

Billy Evans also started his career as a sportswriter, for the *Youngstown Vindicator*, but in 1905, at the age of 21, he substituted for an umpire in a game he was covering in the Class C Ohio-Pennsylvania League. Evans liked it so much that he continued to umpire in his spare time.

Soon, Evans gave up his newspaper job and became an umpire full-time. It proved to be a good move, as in 1906 he became the first (and still the only) umpire promoted directly from Class C to the major leagues, and the youngest umpire in the history of the American League.

Evans was an AL umpire for 22 seasons, during which he continued to write articles and author books. When the Indians were purchased by Alva Bradley in 1927, Evans was hired as general manager, replacing Ernest S. "Barney" Barnard, who had been elected president of the AL.

Under Evans' leadership the Indians acquired or developed Earl Averill, Dick Porter, Joe Vosmik, Hal Trosky, Roy Hughes, Odell Hale, and Monte Pearson.

An extremely principled man, Evans quit in 1935 when Bradley refused to support him following a dispute with Walter Johnson, the manager of the Indians, and also after differences over money with the club's directors.

Evans disagreed when Johnson demanded that catcher Glenn Myatt be released and third baseman Willie Kamm be suspended "for the good of the team." When Johnson accused the general manager of "disloyalty," Evans countered that he refused to be a "yes man for anybody."

He resigned when directors voted to slash his salary from $17,500, including a $5,000 bonus, to $7,500 because it was the height of the Great Depression and money was so tight.

Evans was not unemployed for long. The Boston Red Sox hired him as farm director, but he left that job after seven years, again as a matter of protest, after one of the players he'd developed, Pee Wee Reese, was sold to Brooklyn without his approval.

From there Evans became general manager of the Cleve-

Billy Evans

land Rams of the National Football League, but only for a year. Baseball was in Evans' blood, and in 1942 he was appointed president of the Southern Association.

It was a position Evans held until 1946 when he returned to the major leagues as vice president and general manager of Detroit and stayed with the Tigers until he retired in 1951.

Once during his umpiring career Evans got into a postgame fight with Ty Cobb after two close calls at the plate went against the player-manager of the Tigers. They met under the stands after the game and, according to witnesses, Cobb wound up with his knee on Evans' chest and was holding the umpire by the throat when the fight was broken up.

Evans continued to write during his umpiring career, authoring the book *Umpiring from the Inside*. From 1920 to 1927 he wrote a syndicated column, "Billy Evans Says" for the Newspaper Enterprise Association that was published in more than 100 newspapers.

Evans died January 23, 1956, and was elected to the Hall of Fame in 1973.

1935–41

C. C. "Cy" Slapnicka

He was an undistinguished minor league pitcher for 18 seasons, appeared in 10 major league games—winning one and losing six—for the Chicago Cubs in 1911 and Pittsburgh in 1918, and he was general manager of the Indians from 1935 to 1941.

But it was as a scout that C. C. "Cy" Slapnicka became famous.

He discovered and signed for the Indians more than 30 major leaguers, including Hall of Famers Bob Feller, Earl Averill, and Lou Boudreau, as well as Mel Harder, Hal Trosky, Odell Hale, Jeff Heath, Ken Keltner, Bobby Avila, Jim Hegan, and Herb Score, among others.

It was in 1935, shortly before his November 19 promotion to the front office upon the resignation of general manager Billy Evans, that Slapnicka found Feller.

His recollection: "It was in the outskirts of Des Moines [Iowa], not far from my home in Cedar Rapids, and I'd heard about this kid pitcher [Feller].

"I watched a couple of pitches from the first base line, and I got the funny feeling that this was something extra. So I moved over behind the backstop and sat down on an automobile bumper and perched there for six innings. It must have been uncomfortable, but I never noticed.

"All I knew was that this was a kid pitcher I had to get. I knew he was something special. His fastball was fast and fuzzy; it didn't go in a straight line; it wiggled and shot around.

"I didn't know then that he was smart and that he had the heart of a lion, but I knew I was looking at an arm the likes of which you see only once in a lifetime."

Back in Cleveland, Slapnicka raved about Feller during a meeting of Indians directors.

"Gentlemen, I've found the greatest young pitcher I ever saw," he said. "I suppose this sounds like the same old stuff, but this boy will be one of the greatest pitchers the world has ever known."

Slapnicka's term as the Indians' general manager was a

C. C. Slapnicka

turbulent time. He was twice called on the carpet by Commissioner Kenesaw M. Landis, and also was thrust in the middle of the players' 1940 rebellion against manager Oscar Vitt.

Landis conducted investigations into Slapnicka's dealings and subsequent signing of Feller and outfielder Tommy Henrich, another of the scout's prized discoveries.

Landis established that Slapnicka had broken rules then in effect in both cases, and Feller and Henrich were given the opportunity to become free agents.

Feller declined, saying he preferred to stay with the Indians, though Henrich took his freedom and signed with the New York Yankees.

In the Vitt case, Slapnicka advised owner Alva Bradley to keep the manager despite the players' demand that he be replaced. Bradley heeded Slapnicka's advice, but the Indians lost the pennant by one game.

Calling scouting "my first love," Slapnicka resigned his job with the Indians on September 27, 1941.

"Since taking over the post of general manager I have tried hard to develop a pennant winner for Cleveland, and my only disappointment is that the Indians have not reached that goal," he said then.

"I was greatly disappointed when we failed to win in 1940, and felt reasonably certain the past spring that we would come through this year."

A month later Slapnicka was hired as a scout by the St. Louis Browns. He worked in that capacity for the Cubs from 1943 to 1945, then rejoined the Indians as a scout in 1946 after Bill Veeck bought the franchise. Slapnicka retired in 1970 and died October 20, 1979, at the age of 93.

1941–46

Roger Peckinpaugh

It was the resignation of C. C. "Cy" Slapnicka on September 27, 1941, as general manager that indirectly led to the hiring of Lou Boudreau as the Indians' player-manager in 1941.

Two months later, on November 25, Indians owner Alva Bradley announced the "promotion," as he called it, of Roger Peckinpaugh, and the appointment of Boudreau.

It ended Peckinpaugh's second term as manager of the Indians; he led them to a tie for fourth place with a 75–79 record in 1941, and previously was at the helm of the team from 1928 until he was fired on June 9, 1933, and replaced by Walter Johnson.

A favorite of the fans because he grew up on the Cleveland sandlots, Peckinpaugh had an undistinguished career in the front office, though World War II was a factor in the Indians' lack of success at that time. They finished fourth in 1942, third in 1943, and fourth again in 1944 and 1945.

Good wartime players were hard to come by because most of those who were available were either too old to serve in the armed forces, or were classified 4-F in the Selective Service. Many players even declined to stay in professional baseball, instead taking jobs in shipyards and war plants to stay out of the service.

Because of the manpower shortage, outfielder Roy Cullenbine was the Indians' backup third baseman, pitcher Jim Bagby, Jr., would have filled in at second base if necessary, pitchers Al Milnar, Al Smith, and Allie Reynolds practiced daily in the outfield and served as pinch hitters, catcher Otto Denning played first base, and Paul O'Dea, who was blind in one eye, played the outfield.

The only significant deals Peckinpaugh was able to make from the time he replaced Slapnicka through early 1946 were to send aging center fielder Roy Weatherly and utility infielder Oscar Grimes to the New York Yankees for Cullenbine and catcher Buddy Rosar and to trade outfielder Jeff Heath to Washington for outfielder George Case.

Thus, in his efforts to build the Indians into a pennant contender, Peckinpaugh had little to choose from, until 1946 when the soldiers and sailors came home from the war.

So did an ex-marine named Bill Veeck, who limped into Cleveland on a leg that had been wounded at Bougainvillea in the South Pacific. On June 22, 1946—when the Indians were in a fifth-place tie with a 26–33 record—Veeck purchased the franchise from Alva Bradley's syndicate.

Veeck immediately made it clear that he intended to be his own general manager, and Peckinpaugh resigned.

After leaving the Indians, Peckinpaugh served as general manager of the Buffalo Bisons of the Class AAA International League through the 1947 season. Then he retired, ending 37 years in professional baseball as a player, manager, and front office executive. He died November 17, 1977.

1946–49

Bill Veeck

Bill Veeck was what he called himself—a "playing owner"—in the truest sense, as he not only controlled the business side of the franchise, but also was in charge of all player personnel matters.

His two most famous acquisitions probably were Larry Doby, the American League's first black player and the second in the major leagues (to Jackie Robinson), and the legendary black pitcher Satchel Paige.

Doby was purchased for $10,000 from the Newark Eagles of the Negro National League on July 3, 1947, and Paige was signed on July 7, 1948, after a long career in the Negro League. Both made major contributions as the Indians won the American League pennant and World Series in 1948.

But they weren't the only key players brought to Cleveland by Veeck—he also traded for or purchased second baseman Joe Gordon, pitchers Gene Bearden, Early Wynn, Russ Christopher, and Sam Zoldak, outfielder Bob Kennedy, catcher Al Lopez, and first baseman Mickey Vernon, among others who played significant roles in the fortunes of the Indians in that era.

During the World Series of 1947, between the New York Yankees and Brooklyn Dodgers, Veeck met with Hank Greenberg, the former Detroit slugger who had just retired after one season with Pittsburgh.

First, Veeck tried to talk Greenberg into making a comeback with the Indians, but the 36-year-old future Hall of Famer declined. When Greenberg made it clear that he wanted to get into the business side of baseball, Veeck was a willing listener. He offered to let Greenberg buy into the franchise in exchange for his services as a consultant and hitting instructor.

Greenberg agreed and, on March 27, 1948, it was announced that he had made a financial investment in the Indians and would be in charge of their farm system. It was a position he held through November 21, 1949, when Veeck sold the club to the group headed by Ellis W. Ryan.

Hank Greenberg

1950-57

Hank Greenberg

Hank Greenberg was general manager of the Indians for eight years, during which the club won one pennant and finished second five times, fourth once, and sixth once.

In no other eight-year period in the franchise's long history did the Indians win so many games and lose so few: 738–493.

But in that same eight-year span attendance declined steadily, from 2,233,771 in 1949, the last season of Bill Veeck's ownership, to 722,256 in 1957.

Most fans blamed Greenberg, while Greenberg blamed a "hostile" press.

In his autobiography, *The Story of My Life,* published posthumously in 1989, Greenberg admitted that he tried to get the Indians moved from Cleveland to Minneapolis–St. Paul and complained that the media were the cause of most of the Indians' attendance and financial problems.

His failed attempt to relocate the franchise was a factor in Greenberg's 1957 demise as vice president and general manager, though he remained a stockholder and director until 1959.

Greenberg's term in Cleveland began on a deceptive note, which didn't enhance his image in the eyes of the media and

fans. It had been announced by Veeck on March 27, 1948, that Greenberg had become a "major stockholder" in the club, but it later became known that he had not invested one dime.

The official explanation was that the stock Greenberg had expected to acquire was made unavailable by the refusal of its holder to sell. Thus the former home run hitter and future Hall of Famer was only a salaried employee, the farm director of the Indians.

When Veeck sold the club to the group headed by Ellis W. Ryan on November 21, 1949, Greenberg was elevated to vice president and general manager—essentially, the chief operating officer of the Indians—because of Ryan's lack of expertise in baseball.

Within a year Greenberg fired popular manager Lou Boudreau after the Indians fell into fourth place in 1950.

Their problems began even before Veeck sold out. Boudreau wrote in his autobiography, *Covering All the Bases,* that he often was "second-guessed" by Greenberg.

Al Lopez succeeded Boudreau and, despite leading the Indians back into pennant contention, also had differences with Greenberg. Several times during his six seasons as manager Lopez reportedly was determined to resign, but he was talked out of it on each occasion except the last, after the 1956 season.

Greenberg then brought up Kerby Farrell from the minor leagues to manage the Indians in 1957, but the Indians only got worse. Shortly thereafter not only was Farrell fired, so was Greenberg.

On October 16, 1957, directors of the Indians voted 10–2 to dismiss Greenberg with a year remaining on his contract, even though, at that time, he owned 19 percent of the stock in the corporation and was himself a director.

When asked the reason for Greenberg's dismissal, Indians president Myron "Mike" Wilson, Jr., replied, "Fan reaction. The fans insisted on it."

Ironically, Wilson had become president of the Indians as an indirect result of a power struggle between Ryan and Greenberg.

It led to a showdown between the two executives, and when Ryan failed to win a vote of confidence from the club's directors on December 18, 1952, he resigned as president. Ownership of the franchise was restructured, and Wilson became president.

Ryan's departure enhanced Greenberg's position essentially as chief operating officer of the Indians, and he became even stronger when the franchise changed hands again 38 months later.

Greenberg joined William R. Daley and Ignatius A. O'Shaughnessy as a major investor in the Indians on February 29, 1956. Though Wilson remained as president, Daley became chairman of the board, and Greenberg, as the third-largest investor in the club, was for all practical purposes in charge of all operations.

Greenberg was a staunch advocate of interleague baseball, though his efforts to get it passed always were rejected. He also was the first to lobby rule makers in the early 1950s to ban the practice of players leaving their gloves on the field when their team was batting.

But Greenberg's animosity toward Cleveland, its fans, and the media never changed, nor did his opinion that the city would not support a major league team.

During an August 1959 directors meeting, when Greenberg was still on the board though no longer employed by the Indians, he was quoted as saying that "baseball is dead in Cleveland," even though attendance that season was rebounding from a 13-year low of 663,805 in 1958 to 1,497,976.

In his book Greenberg claimed, "The press [in Cleveland] was on me constantly. Minneapolis–St. Paul was a great baseball town and was begging us to come there. I had been pleading with our board of directors to make the move because of the constant pressure from the press.

"Our players needed some encouragement. It is very difficult for players to pick up the papers every morning, particularly after losing, and have the press lecture on what the team is doing wrong."

Of his failed effort to relocate the franchise, Greenberg wrote, "Our management was composed primarily of native Clevelanders and they were afraid to make the move. Instead, they got rid of me."

In a newspaper interview in 1984, Greenberg said, when asked if he ever had any inclination to return to Cleveland, "The closest I ever want to get to Cleveland is 30,000 feet away—while I'm in an airplane flying over the city on my way to New York."

But he also wanted fans to remember that it was he who put the 1954 Indians together. "If a New York team had won 111 games as we did that season, we'd never hear the end of it," he said.

"But in Cleveland, we didn't get the recognition we deserved because the writers at that time were so negative."

Upon leaving the Indians, Greenberg rejoined Veeck as a part owner and vice president of the Chicago White Sox from 1959 until he retired in 1963. Veeck mounted a campaign in 1962 for Greenberg to be elected commissioner of baseball when Ford Frick retired, but General William D. Eckert got the job in 1965.

Greenberg died September 4, 1986, at the age of 75.

1957–61

Frank Lane

A few weeks after Hank Greenberg was fired, Indians president Myron "Mike" Wilson, Jr., received a call from St. Louis.

It was Frank Lane, then general manager of the St. Louis Cardinals, applying for the general manager's job vacated by Greenberg.

The Indians at the time were interested in William O. De-Witt, who'd been owner, president, and general manager of the St. Louis Browns and would become president of the Detroit Tigers—and as such, be involved with Lane in one of baseball's wackiest deals.

When Lane expressed interest, Indians directors jumped at what they thought was a golden opportunity to hire an executive with a reputation for making things happen—one whose reputation was virtually opposite from that shared by the conservative and even stodgy Greenberg and DeWitt.

They were hoping, of course, that the man who would be aptly nicknamed "Frantic Frank" and "Trader Lane" would rekindle baseball excitement in Cleveland.

What they didn't know, however, was that Lane was under the gun with the Cardinals. Though he was under contract for another year, he'd been given an ultimatum by St. Louis owner August A. Busch, Jr., that if the Cardinals didn't win the National League pennant in 1958 he'd be fired.

Lane also was under fire in St. Louis because he had traded longtime Cardinals favorite Red Schoendienst the previous season, and because he had been rumored to be lining up a deal for Stan Musial.

Thus Busch had no qualms about giving the Indians permission to interview Lane, and they hired him on November 12, 1957, three days after he had called Wilson.

Frank Lane

Lane was signed to a three-year contract with a base salary of $50,000 annually—and a bonus of five cents for each admission over 800,000.

And although Lane didn't lead—or trade—the Indians to a pennant, he certainly generated excitement, as advertised.

Between November 12, his first day on the job in Cleveland, and January 3, 1961, his last day as the Indians' general manager, Lane made 59 transactions involving 120 players.

As did Bill Veeck a decade earlier, Lane always seemed to have a team coming, one going, and another on the field.

He also sent Tribe manager Joe Gordon to Detroit, then operated by DeWitt, for Tigers manager Jimmy Dykes, the first—and still the only—time in major league baseball history that managers have been traded for each other.

Among the players Lane sent packing in those 59 deals were Early Wynn, Al Smith, Jim Hegan, Gene Woodling, Dick Williams, Chico Carrasquel, Roger Maris, Ray Narleski, Don Mossi, Bobby Avila, Vic Wertz, Hoyt Wilhelm, Larry Doby, Mickey Vernon, Minnie Minoso, Cal McLish, Billy Martin, Norm Cash, Rocky Colavito, Herb Score, and Harvey Kuenn.

Among the players Lane acquired were Minoso, Fred Hatfield, Vernon, Doby, Billy Hunter, Vic Power, Woodie Held, Martin, Jim Piersall, Tito Francona, Granny Hamner, John Romano, Cash, Bubba Phillips, Johnny Temple, Bob Grim, Kuenn, Barry Latman, Ken Aspromonte, Rocky Bridges, Don Newcombe, Johnny Antonelli, and Willie Kirkland.

The deal for which Lane always will be remembered—and for which he'll never be forgiven by most Tribe fans—was another one he made with DeWitt, on April 17, 1960, two days before the opener, in which Colavito was sent to the Tigers for Kuenn.

Shortly after joining the Indians, Lane fired manager Bobby Bragan on June 26, 1958, only 67 games into his first season, hired Gordon, fired Gordon on September 18, 1959, rehired Gordon the next day, and the following season traded Gordon for Dykes.

Through it all Lane tried a couple of times to hire Leo Durocher to manage the Indians, but they could never agree on contract terms. Durocher always priced himself out of the job.

The Indians didn't win the pennant during Lane's three seasons in Cleveland, though they came close in 1959, failing in the final week. And except for 1959, neither was there a dramatic increase in attendance, though Lane collected on his nickel-a-head bonus agreement in two of those three seasons.

The turnstile count fell to 663,805 in 1958, but climbed to 1,497,976 in 1959, and leveled off at 950,985 in 1960, meaning that Lane made an additional $34,898.80 the second year and $7,549.25 the third.

When the 1960 season ended, so did Lane's three-year contract, and he was not rehired. The general manager's position was filled on an interim basis by farm director Walter "Hoot" Evers and his assistant, Bob Kennedy, until April 27, 1961, when Gabe Paul arrived.

During Lane's always tumultuous career, he also was general manager of Cincinnati and the Chicago White Sox, in addition to the Cardinals, the Indians, and the Kansas City Athletics after leaving Cleveland.

Before his death March 19, 1981, at the age of 85, Lane estimated that he made more than 400 deals and said, "The only deals that irked me are the ones I didn't make."

Despite his penchant for wheeling and dealing that often resulted in turmoil, Lane was considered a good judge of talent and turned several losing teams into winners, though he couldn't get the Indians to go all the way while he was in Cleveland.

Lane never admitted to having made a mistake in the Colavito-for-Kuenn trade that so outraged most Tribe fans. At a banquet a few years later he further enraged the Colavito loyalists when he said, "If I had it to do all over again, I'd still trade that Dago fruit peddler [Colavito] for Kuenn."

1961–73, 1978–84

Gabe Paul

The Indians again almost hired veteran baseball executive William O. DeWitt as general manager in 1961, after the departure of Frank Lane.

Instead, on April 27, two and a half weeks after the 1961 season had started, principal owner William R. Daley ended negotiations with DeWitt and chose Gabe Paul to rebuild the Indians and, essentially, undo the perceived damage to the franchise wreaked by Lane.

It was an unexpected decision as, only six months earlier, Paul had joined the embryo Houston Colt 45s, a National League expansion team that was to begin operation in 1962.

Paul's "champion," the man who was primarily instrumental in convincing Daley to hire Paul, was Indians vice president and part owner Nate Dolin.

Prior to taking the job of building the Colt 45s (who subsequently were renicknamed Astros), Paul had served the Cincinnati Reds for 25 years, the last 10 as general manager.

"I left [Houston] for personal reasons," was Paul's only explanation at that time, though he later called the decision to take the Houston job "one of the biggest mistakes of my baseball career."

It was a falling out with Judge Roy Hofheinz, owner of the Colt 45s, that hastened Paul's departure from Houston.

Nineteen months after joining the Indians, on November 20, 1962, Paul became a part owner of the club, buying stock put up for sale by Dolin, and was elected president and treasurer of the new corporation.

Paul also continued as general manager of the Indians for 12 years, through the ownership of Vernon Stouffer, though his authority as general manager was temporarily and unofficially usurped by Alvin Dark in 1969.

Paul regained command of the club in 1970 and continued in charge until January 10, 1973, when he resigned, sold his stock, and invested in the New York Yankees, then became their president.

Ironically, in coming to Cleveland, Paul was reunited with Jimmy Dykes, the manager he previously had fired in Cincinnati, who had been acquired by Lane in a managerial trade the previous season.

Two years later Paul hired another manager he'd fired in Cincinnati, Birdie Tebbetts.

Between those two, Mel McGaha was brought up from the Tribe farm system to manage the team in 1962.

Paul's initial term at the helm of the Indians as both general manager and owner was fraught with failure on the field and doused in red ink in the counting room.

The highest they finished in the standings was third in 1968, but otherwise they were fifth six times, sixth four times, and eighth once. Financial losses were recorded virtually every year as attendance never climbed higher than 934,786 in 1965 and was much lower most of the time, plummeting to 562,507 in 1963.

It could be said that Paul's greatest achievement as the Indians' chief was simply keeping the franchise in Cleveland despite numerous offers by out-of-town buyers, as well as efforts by some of the directors to move the franchise. Among the cities most often mentioned as wanting or about to get the Indians were Seattle, Oakland, and Dallas–Fort Worth before they were granted expansion teams, as well as Washington and New Orleans.

Many of Paul's trades during his first 12-year term at the helm of the Indians were dictated by financial factors—that is, unloading high-salaried players or players whose sale would bring large amounts of money in order to meet semi-monthly payrolls.

Among the latter were trades in which Paul in 1964 sent two of the Tribe's best pitchers, Jim "Mudcat" Grant and Pedro Ramos to Minnesota and the Yankees, respectively.

Another of Paul's biggest trades, which brought Rocky Colavito back to his adoring fans in Cleveland in 1965, was well-intended but turned out to be a disaster.

The Indians gave up pitcher Tommy John, who went on to win 288 major league games, outfielder Tommie Agee, who became a star for the New York Mets and played in the National and American leagues for 12 years, and John Romano, a better-than-average catcher, for Colavito and catcher Camilo Carreon.

Colavito played less than three seasons in Cleveland, then was literally given away on July 29, 1967, because he was unhappy being platooned by manager Joe Adcock, and Carreon played only 19 games for the Tribe in 1965 and was back in the minor leagues in 1966.

On the credit side for Paul during his first 12 years as the Indians' chief were the trades he made to acquire Joe Azcue and Dick Howser, and Leon Wagner in separate deals in 1963, and Gaylord Perry and Frank Duffy in a package during the winter of 1971–72.

Paul returned to the Indians an investor in a group headed by F. J. "Steve" O'Neill on February 3, 1978, and again became president and chief executive officer.

Phil Seghi, who was general manager of the Indians during the five years that Paul was gone, retained that title in the O'Neill regime. However, he was in a subordinate position to Paul in all matters regarding player personnel.

Though O'Neill brought fresh money to the franchise, losses continued to mount, reportedly to more than $10.7 million from 1981 to 1983 alone, keeping the franchise in nearly as precarious a financial situation as had been the case under the Nick Mileti–Alva T. "Ted" Bonda ownerships from 1973 to 1978.

What's more, the team also continued to flounder on the field, falling into sixth place for five consecutive seasons, 1978–82.

O'Neill died August 29, 1983, and ownership of the franchise reverted to his estate. O'Neill's nephew, Patrick J. O'Neill became chairman of the board, and Paul retired at the end of the 1984 season, though he continued as a director of the club for the next two years.

Phil Seghi was promoted to vice president and took over the duties of general manager that had been handled primarily by Paul.

1973–85

Phil Seghi

It wasn't long after Phil Seghi took over as general manager of the Indians on January 10, 1973, replacing Gabe Paul, that he was given a nickname by an enterprising reporter.

It was "Seghi the Swapper," an obvious play on the nickname—"Trader Lane"—that Frank Lane had been called, with good reason.

Seghi, who first joined the Tribe on November 11, 1971, as vice president and director of player personnel, immediately set about rebuilding the team that finished sixth with a 60–102 record, the second-most losses in the 71-year history of the franchise.

By the end of the 1973 season only four players remained from the Tribe's final roster of 1971.

At the time of his promotion to general manager Seghi said, "This is the moment of fruition. I'm elated and confident. I've been a copilot long enough. I think I've served my apprenticeship, and I'm ready for this job."

However, all of Seghi's "swapping" had little effect on the Indians' fortunes. They returned to sixth place in 1973 (after finishing fifth the previous season), were fourth the next three years, and finished fifth in 1977.

Gabe Paul returned to the Indians in 1978 as president and chief executive officer. As such, he was in charge of player personnel matters once again, though Seghi retained the title of vice president and general manager.

A former minor league player and manager for 26 years—and previously a Northwestern University three-sport star

Phil Seghi

and then a sportswriter—Seghi began his administrative career in professional baseball working with and then for Paul in Cincinnati.

He started as a scout for the Reds in 1956, became their farm director two years later, and went to the Oakland Athletics as farm director in 1968, before rejoining Paul, who was then general manager of the Indians. At that time Paul called his protege "the finest evaluator of baseball talent in the game."

When Paul resigned to become a part owner and president of the New York Yankees, Seghi was a natural successor.

Fifteen months later Seghi and Paul made a trade that in the final analysis hurt the Tribe and was very good for the Yankees, one in which Seghi's critics complained that he'd been swindled by Paul, his former boss.

Seghi swapped first baseman Chris Chambliss and relief pitchers Dick Tidrow and Cecil Upshaw to the Yankees for pitchers Fritz Peterson, Steve Kline, Fred Beene, and Tom Buskey—none of whom distinguished himself for the Indians, while Chambliss and Tidrow became stars in New York.

There were other trades that Seghi made that didn't work out, including Pedro Guerrero for Bruce Ellingsen and Alfredo Griffin for Victor Cruz.

Among Seghi's better deals were the acquisition of Andre Thornton for Jackie Brown; Rick Sutcliffe for Jorge Orta; Mike Hargrove for Paul Dade; Len Barker and Bobby Bonds for Jim Kern and Larvell Blanks; Bert Blyleven for Cruz, Bob Owchinko, and Gary Alexander; John Denny for Bonds; Julio Franco, Jerry Willard, and George Vukovich for Von Hayes; Brett Butler, Brook Jacoby, Rick Behenna, and $150,000 for Barker; Pat Tabler for Jerry Dybzynski; and George Hendrick for Ray Fosse.

Another that should be included among the good deals was the one that brought Joe Carter, Mel Hall, and Don Schulze to Cleveland for Sutcliffe, even though Sutcliffe went on to be a big winner for the Chicago Cubs. The Indians subsequently traded Carter for Sandy Alomar, Jr., Carlos Baerga, and Chris James.

And, like Paul before him, Seghi also was hampered by an almost constant lack of money, which necessitated his trading of Dave LaRoche for Sid Monge and Bruce Bochte and $250,000—which, Seghi admitted, "helped us on our payroll."

Money also was a major consideration when Seghi sent away Sutcliffe and Denny, both of whom won Cy Young Awards. "You can't build a skyscraper with an erector set," he said.

Lack of ready cash also cost the Indians the services of Jim Bibby, which was unfairly blamed on Seghi. Because the team was late in paying Bibby a $10,000 incentive bonus he'd won in 1977, he was declared a free agent and was lost to the Tribe.

That same winter Seghi was spared considerable embarrassment when he miscalculated pay cuts in contracts offered to Rick Manning, Don Hood, and Buskey. Intending to cut them the maximum allowable 20 percent, Seghi inadvertently divided by four (25 percent) instead of five (20 percent).

Agents for the players took it to arbitration, and the players, had they chosen to do so, could have been declared free agents. Instead, all re-signed—without having to take any cut in pay—though Buskey was traded a few months later.

It also was Seghi, under the direction of Indians president

and owner Alva T. "Ted" Bonda, who hired Frank Robinson as major league baseball's first black manager on October 3, 1974.

And, of course, it was Seghi who made Robinson major league baseball's first ex-manager when he fired him on June 19, 1977.

Seghi slipped back into a subordinate position, though he retained the title of vice president and general manager, when Paul returned to the Indians in 1978.

Peter Bavasi was named president and chief operating officer on November 29, 1984, and immediately nudged Paul into retirement.

On February 18, 1985, Bavasi demoted Seghi, gave him a fancy title—"senior player personnel adviser"—and assigned him to perform routine scouting duties in California.

Always the professional, Seghi took it gracefully when relieved of his duties as general manager. "I've enjoyed every minute of my stay in Cleveland," he said. "There aren't many people who can do what they want for a lifetime, as I did."

As for his performance as general manager, the "Swapper" said, "I'm not going to defend myself. It isn't necessary to my friends, and it would make no difference to my enemies."

Less than two years later, on January 8, 1987, Seghi died.

1985-87

Joe Klein

Joe Klein was part of the triumvirate of front office executives in charge of operating the Indians during the ill-fated and brief tenure of Peter Bavasi.

A former Washington Senators minor league player and manager, Klein worked eight years in the Texas Rangers organization, serving as general manager from 1982 to 1984. He joined the Indians on March 8, 1985, four weeks after general manager Phil Seghi was demoted.

Initially, Klein was vice president/baseball operations for the Indians, though he handled the duties of general manager and eventually was given that title.

In Klein's nearly three years in that position the Indians failed to make any appreciable headway. Twice, in fact, they regressed, losing 102 and then 101 games before and after raising hopes of the fans with an 84–78 record in 1986.

That winter the Indians were expected to contend for the pennant in 1987. They were called the "Erie sensation" in *Sport* magazine and appeared on the cover of *Sports Illustrated.*

But instead of winning—or even coming close—the Indians collapsed and fell back into their familiar position in the basement of the American League East.

With the franchise up for sale and operating under even tighter budget constraints than usual, as imposed by the estate of the late F. J. "Steve" O'Neill, there was little Klein could do but exchange mediocre players in the trade mart, and hope to keep the best.

It was one of the worst periods in Indians history, especially the 1987 season, which was the first under the ownership of Richard E. and David H. Jacobs.

By then Bavasi was gone, though Hank Peters had not yet arrived to take command of the franchise, and Dan O'Brien and Klein were calling all the shots regarding player personnel.

When the season ended, Brett Butler, one of the Tribe's

best players, opted for free agency, and veteran slugger Andre Thornton retired.

The 1987 season also ended Klein's term as general manager; he was fired on December 18, shortly after Henry J. "Hank" Peters was hired as president and chief operating officer of the Indians.

Since then Klein has been a scout for Detroit in 1988 and 1989, vice president/director of player personnel for Kansas City in 1990 and 1991, and general manager of the Tigers from 1992 to 1995.

1987–91

Henry J. "Hank" Peters

Stepping into a difficult situation upon joining the Indians on November 2, 1987, Henry J. "Hank" Peters set out initially to stabilize the franchise, restructure the player development program, and rebuild the farm system, which was woefully lacking in talent as a result of the rigidly enforced frugality of previous ownerships.

Peters' title was president and chief operating officer, and, as such, he also served as general manager.

Peters inherited manager Doc Edwards and was able to make only cosmetic changes in the roster in 1988. The Indians wound up in sixth place, which was an improvement—but only slightly—over their 101 losses of the previous season.

That winter Peters made the first of two major trades for which he long will be remembered and, certainly, criticized.

But they truly were deals of necessity.

On December 6, 1988, Peters sent shortstop–second baseman Julio Franco to Texas for three players, none of whom played well or lasted long with the Indians—second baseman Jerry Browne, first baseman Pete O'Brien, and outfielder Oddibe McDowell.

Henry J. "Hank" Peters

On March 25, 1989, Peters exchanged shortstop Jay Bell for Pittsburgh shortstop Felix Fermin.

In the case of Franco, the Indians were motivated by the old "addition by subtraction" theory espoused by Branch Rickey. Peters and his aides were convinced the team would be better without Franco and settled for the best offer they received for him.

Franco, who resisted being switched from shortstop to second base in Cleveland, became a fine second baseman for Texas. He also won the 1991 American League batting championship with a .341 average and went on to be a solid designated hitter for the Chicago White Sox.

The decision to trade Bell was prompted by two factors: first, despite Bell's offensive ability, his range in the field was limited; and second, Fermin would greatly improve the Indians' infield defense until Mark Lewis, the expected shortstop of the future, would be ready to claim the position.

Lewis, the Indians number-one pick (second overall) in the 1988 amateur draft, failed to develop as expected and, while Fermin was more than adequate, Bell was the National League's All-Star shortstop in 1993 and Gold Glove winner in 1994.

There was yet another faux pas committed by Peters and his staff that will not soon be forgotten by Indians fans. Again, their intentions were sound, though the result left much to be desired.

In an effort to provide a proven veteran leader that Peters felt the team desperately needed, on December 7, 1989, he signed 36-year-old first baseman Keith Hernandez to a guaranteed two-year contract worth $3.5 million. It was at that time the highest salary ever paid a member of the Indians.

But Hernandez, instead of being a proven veteran leader, proved to be an absolute, abysmal bust. He was disabled three times in 1990 with a torn left calf muscle and was able to play just 43 games, in which he batted .200 (26-for-130) with eight RBIs.

Then, to make matters worse, that winter Hernandez said he injured his back moving furniture, underwent surgery, and in 1991 never even donned an Indians uniform, but still collected his $1.75 million salary.

The unpleasant experience with Hernandez undoubtedly—and understandably—turned off owner Richard Jacobs.

It was a factor in the Indians' unwillingness to get into a bidding contest to retain the services of their best pitcher, Tom Candiotti, who was due to become a free agent at the end of the 1991 season. Instead, Peters traded Candiotti to Toronto on June 27.

On the other hand, several of Peters' trades proved beneficial to the Tribe in the long run. One in particular was the deal with San Diego for Joe Carter on December 6, 1989.

For Carter, who'd been the Indians' best all-around player, the Padres sent catcher Sandy Alomar, Jr., third baseman–second baseman Carlos Baerga, and outfielder Chris James to Cleveland. Alomar and Baerga, then only prospects, became key players in the Indians' resurgence in 1994.

Peters' high regard for Hart also became evident early and was quickly substantiated.

On September 12, 1989, with the Indians in the throes of another losing season, Peters fired Edwards and appointed Hart interim manager of the team. The reason for putting Hart in charge with only 19 games remaining, Peters said, was to give him an opportunity to better evaluate the personnel.

John McNamara was hired to manage the Indians in 1990, with minor league manager Mike Hargrove brought up to become first base coach, and Hart received his first promotion, to director of baseball operations.

A year and a half later, as the Indians were falling back into the basement of the AL East with a franchise-worst 57–105 record, Hargrove replaced McNamara on July 6, 1991.

When the season mercifully ended, Peters retired on December 31, 1991, and Rick Bay was named president. He had joined the organization as executive vice president on September 18, 1991, and left the Indians on November 20, 1992, saying he was resigning to pursue other opportunities.

1991–

John Hart

There was no doubt about the identity of the man who would assume the duties of general manager of the Indians even before the December 31, 1991, retirement of Henry J. "Hank" Peters.

It was his protege, John Hart.

A former minor league player, manager, and third base coach of the Baltimore Orioles, Hart rejoined Peters in Cleveland in 1989 as a special assignment scout, then assistant to the president, then director of baseball operations, before being named vice president and general manager on September 18, 1991.

At the time he was promoted to director of baseball operations Hart admitted he'd always aspired to be a major league manager.

"I think anybody who has been brought up and trained in baseball will tell you that being a manager—winning a late-inning game and the day-to-day routine of running a ball club—is a gratifying experience," he said.

John Hart

"I am not going to forget how to manage, but I will let the future take care of itself. What develops will develop."

Hart's first deal as general manager, made November 15, 1991, was not a good one, though it was forced by the fact that Greg Swindell, one of the Indians' best pitchers, would be eligible for free agency the following season. Swindell was sent to Cincinnati for pitchers Jack Armstrong, Scott Scudder, and minor leaguer Joe Turek.

However, a month later, on December 10, Hart acquired Kenny Lofton in a deal with Houston that will rank as one of the Indians' all-time best. To acquire Lofton and minor league infielder Dave Rohde, Hart traded catcher Ed Taubensee and pitcher Willie Blair, neither of whom figured in the Tribe's plans.

Later that winter of 1991–92, Hart, with owner Richard Jacobs, designed and implemented a plan to protect themselves against the loss of the Indians' best young players, those who were considered the "core" of the club.

It was, Hart said, "[A plan] to build a competitive club within a fiscally responsible program, and still present a growing, stable club to the fans, which is what really counts."

It also was a plan that subsequently was endorsed by other major league clubs and became a standard for the industry.

Initially, 12 players were signed to extended contracts that included club options: Sandy Alomar, Jr., Carlos Baerga, Charles Nagy, Mark Whiten, Armstrong, Scudder, Glenallen Hill, Dennis Cook, Steve Olin, Dave Otto, Rod Nichols, and Alex Cole.

A year later Hart did the same with Albert Belle, Lofton, Paul Sorrento, Carlos Martinez, Felix Fermin, and Thomas Howard.

Hart admitted they'd made some mistakes in their evaluation of Scudder, Cook, Otto, Nichols, Cole, and Martinez, but they assured themselves of keeping the players they wanted before their salaries would escalate out of sight in the open market.

Having players locked into reasonable contracts also enhanced their trade value, as was the case with Whiten, Hill, Fermin, and Howard, and it certainly made Armstrong more attractive to Florida, which selected him in the National League expansion draft of 1992.

Though he was part of the decision making under Peters, Hart inherited Mike Hargrove, who had replaced John McNamara as manager of the Indians on July 6, 1991, and, beginning in 1992, was working under a year-to-year contract.

The option on Hargrove's contract was exercised on June 30, 1992, as the Indians were in the process of improving to a still-disappointing 76–86 record. When the record was duplicated in 1993 (though the Indians fell from fourth to sixth place), it wasn't until August 6 that Hart made the decision to keep Hargrove for another year.

The decision proved to be a good one as the Indians, for the first time since 1959, legitimately contended for the pennant, though their hopes to win the newly formed American League Central Division were snuffed out on August 12.

That's when, with the Indians only one game behind Chicago and owning the third-best won-lost record, 66–47, in the entire AL, the Major League Baseball Players Association went out on strike, ending the season and forcing cancellation of the League Championship Series and World Series.

Before the walkout, Hart had signed Hargrove to a new two-year contract to manage the Indians through 1996.

And after the season was aborted by the strike, on October 20, Hart was granted a five-year contract with two options that could keep him at the helm of the Indians through the year 2001.

Five days later *The Sporting News* named Hart the major leagues' Executive of the Year, an award that hadn't been presented to an Indians chief since Bill Veeck got it in 1948, the last time Cleveland won the World Series.

The Support Staff

Baseball's first traveling secretary was Ernest S. "Barney" Barnard, who began his career as a sportswriter in Columbus, Ohio, and wound up as the second president of the American League, succeeding Byron Bancroft "Ban" Johnson in December 1927.

Barnard, who was described in the 1930 Reach Official Baseball Guide as having "executive ability, poise, tact and untiring energy," served as president of the AL only three and a half years before his death on March 27, 1931, at the age of 56.

Until he was hired by the Indians in 1903 by co-owners John F. Kilfoyl and Charles W. Somers, Barnard was sports editor of the *Columbus Dispatch*. The duties of traveling secretary—as well as most other positions filled by full-time employees today—were handled by the owners of the teams or part-time workers.

Barnard, who also had the distinction of being the first football coach at Otterbein (Ohio) College—whose team beat Ohio State, 16–14, in 1894—continued to handle the Cleveland club's travel arrangements until he became vice president in 1908.

Bill Blackwood replaced Barnard as road secretary, and was succeeded in that position by Frank Kohlbecker in 1937, and then by Lewis Mumaw, who held the job from 1939 to 1943, before Kohlbecker returned for three years, 1944–46.

Spud Goldstein, who was Bill Veeck's right-hand man, was the Indians' traveling secretary from 1947 to 1961. Charlie Morris, who came to Cleveland with Gabe Paul in 1961, held the job from 1962 to 1966, then stepped aside while Dan Zerbey made the travel arrangements in 1967. Morris took over again from 1968 until his sudden death during spring training in 1969.

Morris was replaced by former Indians pitcher Wynn Hawkins, who made the travel plans in 1970. Coach Bobby Hofman doubled as traveling secretary in a cost-cutting measure in 1971. Then came Bob Gill, whose employment with the Indians began in the mid-1920s in the concession stands at League Park and continued for more than 50 years.

Gill operated several minor league clubs for the Indians in the 1930s, until becoming "confidential secretary" to general manager C. C. "Cy" Slapnicka in 1935. When Slapnicka left the Indians in 1941, Gill worked for Alva Bradley, Hank Greenberg, Frank Lane, and Gabe Paul before returning to the road as traveling secretary from 1972 until he retired in 1974.

That's when Mike Seghi, the son of the late general manager Phil Seghi, took over the transporting of the team. He has been traveling secretary since 1975.

The first trainer of the Indians, then a part-time job, was James Payne, who committed suicide at age 35 on September 28, 1919.

Payne was succeeded by Percy Smallwood, though it was Max "Lefty" Weisman who became the first full-time trainer, holding the job from 1921 to 1949.

Weisman was a newsboy around Fenway Park in Boston, and his idol was Tris Speaker, who played for the Red Sox from 1907 to 1915. Weisman was heartbroken when Speaker was traded to the Indians in 1916.

After Speaker became manager of the Indians in 1919, Weisman saved his money and took a trip to Cleveland. He helped the trainer, Percy Smallwood, then a part-time worker, doing odd jobs around the clubhouse. The experience motivated Weisman to take courses in treating athletic injuries.

When Smallwood was forced by poor health to retire in 1921, Speaker got owner James C. "Sunny Jim" Dunn to give the trainer's job to Weisman.

As colorful as he was popular, Weisman named his first son in honor of the Indians' "million dollar outfield" of 1931–33. He took the first letter of each player's first name—Joe Vosmik, Earl Averill, and Dick Porter—and named the boy Jed.

In 1946, in observance of Weisman's 25th year with the Indians, club owner Bill Veeck honored the trainer with a "night" and gave him a wheelbarrow full of an estimated 50,000 silver dollars. The fans loved it even more than Weisman, who didn't have the education, knowledge, or skills of trainers who came along later but was respected by all the players for his treatment of their injuries and ailments.

Upon Weisman's death at age 54 in 1949 he was succeeded by Wally Bock, who held the job for the next 21 years.

Traveling secretary Bob Gill

Trainer Wally Bock

When Bock retired, he was replaced in 1971 by Jim Warfield, who still tends to the Indians' aches and pains.

Dr. Don Kelly was the Indians' physician from 1954 to 1961, then the team had no regular doctor until Vic Ippolito took over and held the job from 1964 to 1970. Dr. William Wilder has been the team physician since 1971. He was assisted by Dr. Earl Brightman in 1981 and 1982 and by Dr. William Bohl in 1983.

The duties of publicity director were filled by any front office executive who wasn't busy until Veeck came to the Indians in 1946 and put Bob Fishel in charge of media relations. When Veeck bought the St. Louis Browns in 1950, Fishel went with him—and it was Fishel who signed the midget Eddie Gaedel to a contract.

Fishel later served as public relations director of the New York Yankees for 20 years. He was the American League's vice president for public relations at the time of his death at 74 in 1988. An award for the outstanding baseball publicist each year is named in his honor.

Marsh Samuel followed Fishel as the Indians' public relations chief from 1947 to 1952 and was the first to publish a media guide that contained more than just a roster of players. Samuel went on to work for Veeck with the White Sox in Chicago, and later joined George Steinbrenner with the New York Yankees.

Nate Wallack handled media relations for the Indians during the years 1953–61, preceding Eddie Uhas, 1964–71; Bob Walczak, 1972; Bob Brown, 1973; Dino Lucarelli, 1974; Randy Adamack, 1975–78; Harry Jones, 1979; Joe Bick, 1980; Bob DiBiasio, 1981–86; Rick Minch, 1987; and DiBiasio, who returned in 1988 and is now vice president for public relations.

When Veeck took over the club on June 22, 1946, he inherited from the Bradley regime an office staff of six, including Bradley's assistant and general manager, Roger Peckinpaugh; Kohlbecker; Mark Wanstall, an auditor who started to work for Somers in 1920; Edna Jameson, who was in charge of tickets and had joined the staff in 1913; Byron Smith, a ticket seller; and switchboard operator Ada Ireland.

On hand, too, was Emil Bossard, the famous groundskeeper who started working for the Indians in 1935, and his two sons who assisted him, Harold and Marshall Bossard.

Emil Bossard was affectionately known as "the evil genius of groundskeepers" because of the way he tailored—not illegally—the League Park and Stadium infields to benefit the Indians or hinder the team they were playing.

He slanted the foul lines one way or another to keep bunts fair or help them roll foul; cut the grass short to speed up ground balls or left it long to slow them down; soaked the ground in front of the plate or hardened it, depending on whether a sinkerball pitcher was on the mound for the Indians or their opponents; and if the other team's runners were particularly fast, he watered the base paths to nullify some of their speed.

"This is a game of inches," Bossard said before his death at age 88 in 1981. "An inch is often the difference between a base hit and an out. We try to have the inches go our way." With him, they usually did.

It also was on the recommendation of Emil Bossard that the Indians for years kept two infield tarpaulins. One could be put in place in a matter of about two minutes during a rain delay, if the Indians were behind and wanted the game to be resumed.

But if they were ahead and would win if the game was rained out, a "spare" tarpaulin was hauled out. It was heavy and unwieldy and took the grounds crew much longer to put in place, usually allowing the infield to get thoroughly soaked.

When Emil Bossard retired in the mid-1970s he was succeeded by Harold, assisted by Marshall. And when Harold retired in 1978, Marshall took over until he retired in 1985.

Another of Emil's sons, Gene, was the groundskeeper at Comiskey Park in Chicago in the 1960s and 1970s, and two grandsons of the "evil genius," Brian and Roger Bossard, later worked for the Indians and White Sox in the 1980s.

The two women employees Veeck inherited from the Bradley regime, Edna Jameson and Ada Ireland, continued to work for the Indians through the 1950s before they also retired.

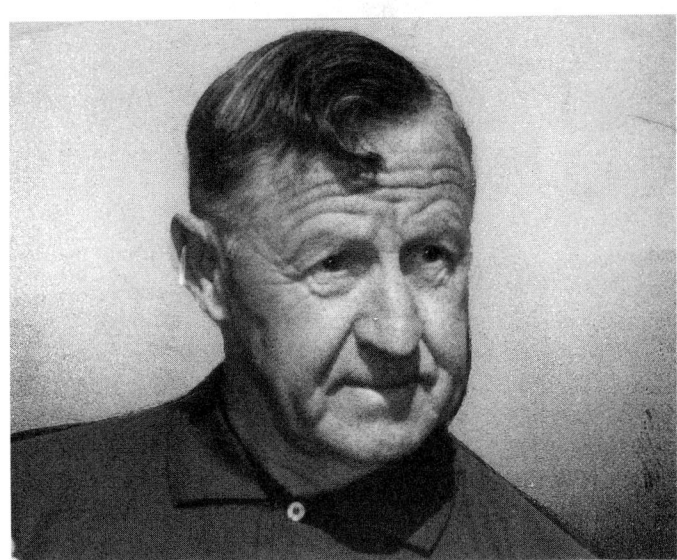

Groundskeeper Emil Bossard

The Ballparks

In the earliest days of baseball in Cleveland the hometown team, then called the Forest Citys, played its first game on June 2, 1869, on a field called Case Commons. It was located at what is now East 38th Street between Scovill and Community College avenues.

Case Commons was the first of eight fields and parks that Cleveland's professional teams called home, though only the last three—League Park, Municipal Stadium, and Jacobs Field—would be considered "major league" by today's standards.

The Forest Citys used Case Commons for two years, then in 1871 and 1872 played at National Association Grounds, at what is now Central Avenue and East 55th Street.

The price of admission then was 25 cents, though neither Case Commons nor National Association Grounds had seats; spectators either stood or sat on the ground or in their carriages surrounding the field.

In 1871 fans were given the opportunity to buy season tickets, which were advertised as follows:

"If only for yourself, the cost will be six dollars for the season. But if you wish to bring a lady, there is a special deal available, only ten dollars for yourself, your lady and your carriage."

The advertisement further stated that "the carriage or rig could be pulled up to a specified location behind first or third base and there would be no necessity of stepping down on the turf at any time."

There was no professional baseball in Cleveland from 1873 through 1878, until a new team, again called the Forest Citys, was formed. It joined the National League and played in a new park, this one called National League Park, located at what is now Cedar Avenue and East 46th Street.

There were trees in the outfield the first year the park was open, and left field was so short in 1880 and 1881 that balls hit over the fence were only doubles. The Forest Citys played there through 1884, when they dropped out of the league and disbanded.

Three years later, in 1887, the Forest Citys were reorganized by Cleveland businessman Frank DeHaas Robison and entered the American Association, which was then considered a second major league.

The Forest Citys played in spacious Brookside Park, constructed by Robison for his new team. Located at what is now Payne Avenue and East 39th Street, the park's outfield fences were more than 400 feet from the plate. It was renamed Spider Park when the team's nickname was changed to Spiders in 1889. That also was the year the team left the American Association and rejoined the National League.

In June 1890 a severe thunderstorm struck the park, causing considerable damage. The team played the rest of the season at Spider Park but moved into brand-new League Park in 1891.

Built by Robison at the corner of Lexington Avenue and East 66th Street, League Park was the focal point for two streetcar lines owned by him and his brother, M. Stanley Robison.

It also was in 1890 that a team was formed to represent Cleveland in the outlaw Players League, which was organized by players who were dissatisfied with salaries paid by the National League and American Association.

The team, which lasted only one year, was known as the Cleveland Infants and played its games at Brotherhood Park, which was located in an area bounded by East 55th Street, Kinsman Road, Diamond Avenue, and the current Rapid Transit tracks.

It also is interesting to note that two Cleveland teams once played major league games on fields that later became well-known amusement parks.

In 1888, to get around the municipal blue law, the Spiders of the American Association played their Sunday games at Beyerle's Park, which today is Geauga Lake amusement park (in the far southeastern section of Greater Cleveland).

Jacobs Field, home of the Cleveland Indians.

In 1898, three years after Euclid Beach Park (then in the Cleveland suburb of Euclid) was built, Cleveland played two Sunday games there.

The first, on June 12, was interrupted by a severe thunderstorm after five innings. The second was stopped in the eighth inning by police in the Collinwood neighborhood and all the Cleveland players were arrested just after the Spiders had taken a 4–3 lead.

League Park

The Spiders' first game at League Park on May 1, 1891, was called "a magical opening" by the *Cleveland Plain Dealer.* "There never was one like it and there never may be another."

The legendary Cy Young pitched for the Spiders, who beat Cincinnati, 12–3, in front of a capacity crowd of 9,000 spectators.

The headline over the story read:

"A Tremendous Crowd at the New League Game—Cleveland's Good Baseball Club Wins From the Cincinnati Redlegs—Music, Flowers and Handsome Women."

The story reported:

"At eight minutes past 4 o'clock . . . Denton Young, ex–rail splitter, wet a brand new Spalding base ball with his fingers, smiled grimly and then propelled his arm through space, releasing the ball as he did it.

"It sailed gently toward a rubber plate firmly fastened in the ground some fifty-five feet in front of him and passed directly over the center of that plate.

"Standing on one side of that plate of rubber was a young man dressed in a baggy blue flannel uniform with a great big bat in his hand. This man was 'Bid' McPhee. He made not a move when that ball passed over the plate and umpire Phil Powers gently announced 'one strike.'

"The base ball season of 1891 was open in Cleveland and the heart of the lover of the game was glad."

The facility—officially given the name "National League Park," which was shortened to "League Park" almost immediately—was adorned with flags and bunting for that opener. The Spiders were transported to the game aboard one of Robison's decorated trolley cars in a parade that included circus animals and a 16-piece marching band.

It was quite a start.

At that time, before League Park was renovated and enlarged in 1909, there was very little foul territory. Fans in the stands, sitting on wooden benches, were so close to the field they could hear the players curse and virtually smell their sweat.

And after the renovation, and for the 37 seasons League Park was used for major league baseball, there was hardly any perceptible change. It eventually became the smallest park in the American League, and when it was phased out by Bill Veeck in 1947, it was one of only three in the majors without lights.

The dimensions made League Park cozy and intimate—and greatly favored left-handed batters. A 40-foot-high right-field fence was only 290 feet from the plate from the time League Park opened until the Indians moved out at the end of the 1946 season.

It was built with such a short right field and long left and center fields because, according to historians, the owners of a saloon and two adjacent houses in the neighborhood refused to sell their properties when Robison constructed the park.

He was determined to build at that particular location because of his streetcar lines and, consequently, laid out the field to fit the available area.

When League Park was constructed, the grandstands were all wood and consisted of a single deck behind the plate, a covered pavilion behind first base, and a small bleacher section. A second deck from foul pole to foul pole was added in 1909.

The right-field wall, originally a 20-foot wooden base (later replaced by concrete) topped by a 20-foot wire screen, turned

League Park.

routine fly balls into home runs, and sharply hit line drives (homers almost everywhere else) into singles and doubles.

It was difficult to play right field because balls came off the wall in bizarre ways. When it was obvious that a ball would hit the fence, the right fielder, center fielder, and often the second baseman converged. They'd wait for the carom, which could go in any direction, depending upon whether the ball came off the screen, one of the vertical steel support poles, or the wooden (later concrete) base. Sometimes a ball would hit the screen and stick there for a ground-rule double.

There was no such thing as a routine fly to right field at League Park.

Many right-handed batters even adjusted their swing to punch the ball to right field in the hope of either clearing the fence or getting a wild bounce off the base.

Lexington Avenue, outside the right-field wall, was a favorite place for youngsters to congregate during batting practice and games. They'd get free admission to a game by retrieving and returning balls hit over the fence.

Just as League Park was a favorite place for left-handed batters, it was a nightmare for those who swung from the other side of the plate.

But left field was not an easy position to play either, especially late in the afternoon when the sun was setting over the first base stands. (In this park, home plate lay at the northwest corner of the diamond.) The distance to the left-field bleachers was 375 feet, and to dead center it was 460 feet, though center field subsequently was shortened to 420 feet.

The Spiders played their home games at League Park into the 1899 season when, upon compiling the worst record in baseball history—20–134, finishing last, 84 games out of first place!—they were booted out of the National League.

Only once that season did the Spiders win two games in a row, and after early June when their total attendance was only 3,179 in 27 home games, they played the rest of their games on the road.

After a one-year hiatus, baseball returned to League Park in 1901 in the form of the newly founded American League. Cleveland's team, now owned by John F. Kilfoyl and Charles W. Somers, was called the Blues.

Initially, Robison was reluctant to sell or rent League Park to the team. But when he learned that the two new club owners were considering building their own park—which would not be located near Robison's streetcar lines—Robison changed his mind and sold League Park to Kilfoyl and Somers.

And when the AL got under way with its first game in Cleveland—the Blues beat Milwaukee, 4–3, on April 29, 1901—League Park became the centerpiece of major league baseball in the city for the next 46 years.

It never lost its intimacy, and old-timers insist there wasn't a bad seat in the house.

As former pitcher Mel Harder remembered from his career with the Indians that began in 1928, "Fans in the stands could hear the players cussing, and we [players on the field] could hear just about every word the fans were saying, especially their criticism."

Because of Cleveland's blue law then in effect that prohibited the playing of baseball on Sunday, the team played some of its home Sunday games in other cities in 1902 and 1903, as follows: June 8, 1902, at Fairview Park, Dayton, Ohio; June 15, 1902, at Mahaffey Park, Canton, Ohio; June 22,

1902, at Jailhouse Flats, Fort Wayne, Indiana; August 3, 1902, at Neil Park, Columbus, Ohio; August 31, at Jailhouse Flats; May 10, 1903, at Mahaffey Park; May 17, 1903, at Neil Park; and June 23, 1903, at Mahaffey Park.

Attendance at League Park climbed to a franchise record 422,242 in 1908, and, after the 1909 season, when attendance was 354,627, League Park was renovated and the seating capacity increased from 9,000 to about 21,000, plus approximately 2,000 seats in the bleachers, the size of which often changed from one season to the next.

The wooden grandstands and pavilion were replaced by steel and concrete, and box seats were installed, though the newly built left-field bleachers consisted of wooden benches. The double-decked grandstand went from foul pole to foul pole, and a single deck of stands ran from 10 feet outside the left-field foul pole to left-center.

The scoreboard was in dead center, a little shorter than the right-field screen. It gave an inning-by-inning line score of each American League game being played, but none in the National League.

The bullpens were located in the left- and right-field corners, tucked in between the foul lines and grandstands. The Indians' dugout was behind first base, the visitors' was behind third base, and the club offices were under the stands from home plate to first base.

The press box, directly behind home plate, was called the most dangerous in baseball because it was windowless and very close to the field.

Some of the Indians' greatest games were played at League Park, beginning with Addie Joss's perfect game, only the second in American League history, on October 2, 1908, a 1–0 victory over Chicago in front of 10,598 fans.

On July 24, 1911, three months after Joss died of tubercular meningitis at the age of 31, League Park was the site of major league baseball's first all-star game—though it was neither recognized nor recorded as such.

It was a benefit game that raised $13,000 for Joss's family, and the *Cleveland Plain Dealer* called it "the greatest array of players ever seen on one field." The all-star team, which featured Ty Cobb, Tris Speaker, Eddie Collins, Frank "Home Run" Baker, and Walter Johnson, beat the Cleveland team, then called the Naps, 5–3.

Four years later, in 1915, the Naps were renamed Indians, and they won the franchise's first pennant and world championship in 1920.

That also was the year League Park was renamed Dunn Field by owner James C. "Sunny Jim" Dunn. However, after Dunn died in 1922 and the franchise was sold to a syndicate headed by Alva Bradley in 1927, the name reverted to League Park.

It was during the World Series of 1920 that one of baseball's most memorable games was played at League Park. It was the fifth game of the Series against Brooklyn and took place on October 10 in front of a standing-room crowd of 26,884 fans. Three Indians distinguished themselves.

In the first inning outfielder Elmer Smith hit the first grand slam home run in postseason history; three innings later Jim Bagby, Sr., became the first pitcher to hit a home run in a World Series game; and in the fifth inning second baseman Bill Wambsganss pulled off what is still the only unassisted triple play in a World Series game.

The Indians won, 8–1, and went on to beat the Dodgers,

five games to two (it was a best-of-nine-game series then), with a 3–0 victory at League Park in the finale on October 12.

League Park also was the scene of many other memorable games—and plays—including the time in 1930 that Smead Jolley, a hefty and slow-footed right fielder for the Chicago White Sox, committed two errors on the same play, and should have been charged with three, according to former Tribe pitcher Mel Harder.

Here's how it happened:

The Indians' Glenn Myatt hit a sinking liner to right that landed a few feet in front of Jolley and bounced through his legs for error number one.

The ball caromed off the concrete base of the wall and, after Jolley turned and bent down to field it, it skipped past him for what could have been error number two.

Finally, with Myatt racing around first and second, Jolley retrieved the ball and fired it to third base—except that his throw was about 15 feet over the head of third baseman Willie Kamm for another charged error.

Other memories of the old ballpark are more pleasant, though not necessarily for Cleveland teams:

- On May 9, 1901, Earl Moore pitched a nine-inning no-hitter for the Blues but lost to the Chicago White Sox, 4–2, in the 10th inning.

- On May 23, 1901, the Blues fashioned the greatest comeback in baseball history by scoring nine runs with two out in the last of the ninth to beat the Washington Senators, 14–13.

- On June 9, 1908, a major league record was set when every player in the Naps' lineup batted safely and scored a run in the fifth inning of a 15–6 victory over Boston.

- On July 19, 1909, Naps shortstop Neal Ball made the first unassisted triple play in modern major league history, against Boston. Only nine have been made since then, including the one by Wambsganss in the 1920 World Series.

- On September 17, 1914, Naps player-manager Napoleon Lajoie made his 3,000th hit in an 8–1 loss to Boston.

- On September 24, 1916, the Indians' Martin Kavanagh delivered baseball's first pinch-hit grand slam home run to beat Boston, 5–3, when the ball he hit rolled under the screen in front of the left-field pavilion.

- On May 17, 1925, Indians player-manager Tris Speaker made his 3,000th hit in a 2–1 victory over the Senators.

- On July 29, 1928, the Indians set a major league record with 24 singles (since broken) as they beat the Yankees, 24–6.

- On August 11, 1929, the Yankees' Babe Ruth hit his 500th career home run over the right-field fence off the Indians' Willis Hudlin.

- On May 11, 1930, the Indians Bibb Falk went 5-for-5 and scored in five straight innings in a 25–7 victory over the Philadelphia Athletics.

- On April 29, 1931, Indians right-hander Wes Ferrell pitched a no-hitter to beat the St. Louis Brown, 9–0.

- On July 10, 1932, Indians shortstop Johnny Burnett set a major league record with nine hits in an 18-inning, 18–17 loss to the Athletics.

- On July 6, 1936, Bob Feller struck out eight batters in three innings in his first major league appearance as the Indians beat the St. Louis Cardinals, 7–6, in an exhibition game.

- On August 23, 1936, Feller struck out 15 batters and won his first major league start, 4–1, against the Athletics.

- On September 13, 1936, Feller set an American League record by striking out 17 batters in a 5–2 victory over the Athletics.

- On September 9, 1938, rookie Lou Boudreau made his major league debut at third base, replacing Ken Keltner in the seventh inning. In two plate appearances against Tommy Bridges, Boudreau walked in the seventh inning and grounded out in the ninth.

- On July 16, 1941, Joe DiMaggio extended his hitting streak to a final 56th consecutive game with two singles off Al Milnar and a double off Joe Krakauskas as the Yankees beat the Indians, 10–3.

- On September 13, 1946, Ted Williams hit an inside-the-park homer to beat the Indians, 1–0, and clinch the pennant for Boston.

- On September 21, 1946, Dizzy Trout pitched Detroit to a 5–3, 11-inning victory over the Indians in the final major league baseball game at League Park, witnessed by 2,772 fans.

League Park also was the scene for one of the ugliest and most violent player-umpire brawls in baseball history. It occurred on Memorial Day, 1932, after a doubleheader between the Indians and Chicago.

Umpire George Moriarty's ball-and-strike decisions in the ninth inning of the second game enraged the White Sox, who became even angrier after Earl Averill's triple drove in the winning run for a 12–11 Indians victory.

In the runway after the game, Moriarty challenged the White Sox players and in the ensuing fight suffered a broken hand, spike wound, and numerous bruises. Three Chicago players and manager Lew Fonseca were suspended and fined a total of $1,350 by American League president William Harridge. Moriarty received a reprimand.

League Park also was the home field for the Cleveland Buckeyes of the Negro American League from 1942 to 1947, and they won the Negro World Series there in 1945.

The Cleveland Rams of the National Football League played their regular season home games at League Park from 1936 to 1945 (with the exception of 1943 when they suspended operations because of World War II).

During a game on November 11, 1945, between the Rams and Green Bay Packers, witnessed by 28,686 spectators at League Park, a section of temporary bleachers collapsed causing more than 700 fans to fall to the ground, though nobody was seriously injured.

The city of Cleveland purchased League Park from the Indians in 1951, tore down all but the East 66th Street (first base) side of the facility, and turned it into a playground.

Municipal Stadium

It was the winter of 1926–27 when Indians president Ernest S. "Barney" Barnard, who would become president of the American League a year later, first proposed the construction of a larger ballpark for the team.

Barnard believed that the 21,414-capacity League Park, then called Dunn Field, was inadequate because on special occasions an additional 6,000 or 7,000 fans would be squeezed into the facility in roped-off, standing-room sections in left and center fields.

Barnard dreamed of a 50,000- to 60,000-seat stadium, comparable to New York's Polo Grounds, which he had helped plan previously. A former Cleveland mayor, Clayton Townes, also had talked about a municipal stadium several years earlier, when Barnard started thinking about a larger facility.

But Barnard's interest in a new ballpark wasn't solely for the benefit of the Indians. They were up for sale because of the death of owner James C. "Sunny Jim" Dunn several years earlier. Barnard was running the club for Dunn's widow, but he knew he was going to soon become president of the AL.

If he could get plans under way for a larger and more modern facility, not only would it enhance the Indians' sale value, but Barnard knew it also would strengthen the entire league that he would soon be heading.

It also was at that point in time that a syndicate headed by Alva Bradley was making inquiries about purchasing the franchise.

In a meeting with Peter P. Evans, then president of the Osborn Engineering Company of Cleveland, and city manager William R. Hopkins, Barnard developed preliminary plans for the stadium he had in mind.

The project was set aside when Barnard left the Indians but was subsequently picked up by Bradley, whose purchase of the franchise closed on November 17, 1927.

In a letter to Hopkins on May 22, 1928, Bradley pointed out that the Indians, in only their first two months of that season, had played to three capacity crowds at League Park. He estimated they could have "shown to fifty and perhaps one hundred thousand more people, if we'd had the capacity to take care of them."

Bradley concluded by telling Hopkins, "I hope that some definite action will soon be taken on the stadium."

It was, less than six months later.

On November 6, 1928, a $2.5 million bond issue was approved by voters, 112,448 to 76,975, to finance construction of the Cleveland Municipal Stadium. The site was filled-in land on the lakefront about three city blocks north of Public Square where it would not be bounded by city streets, houses, or buildings, nor would it be subject to zoning laws.

The stadium was designed for a multitude of events, not just sports, which is the reason for its circular construction. At the time it was built, backers were hopeful of attracting the 1932 Olympic Games to Cleveland, though the Olympics ultimately were awarded to the Los Angeles Coliseum.

To convince voters to support the bond issue, some 60 possible uses for the facility were listed, according to published accounts at the time, including "pageants, dramatic offerings, musical entertainment, civic gatherings and business expositions, as well as athletic contests."

It was claimed that "in athletics alone . . . the new facility could be used for boxing and wrestling matches, gymnastics, track and field events, skating, hockey, tennis, soccer and even cricket, in addition to football and baseball."

Several obstacles, including a lawsuit filed by a taxpayer, delayed the start of the project until June 24, 1930, and despite an accident that claimed the lives of two steelworkers, the Stadium was completed in 370 working days, on July 1, 1931, at a cost of $3,035,245.

It was a massive park with the most expansive playing area in the major leagues. Initially the distances to the base of the walls surrounding the field were 322 feet at the foul lines, 463 feet in the power alleys, and 470 feet to center field.

When Babe Ruth entered the Stadium for the first time he exclaimed, "You'd have to have a horse to play outfield here."

The first player to hit a home run in the new park was Indians shortstop Johnny Burnett, who did so against Alphonse

Cleveland Municipal Stadium in 1933, one year after its completion.

Thomas of the Washington Senators in the first game of a doubleheader on August 7, 1932.

It came in the seventh game played in the Stadium, and Burnett's homer was socked into the lower right-field stands in the sixth inning of the Indians' 7–4 victory. Earl Averill hit the Stadium's second homer in the nightcap of the doubleheader, also won by the Indians, 6–2.

The first upper-deck homer at the Stadium wasn't hit until May 25, 1941, when Indians outfielder Jeff Heath blasted one into the right-field stands off former teammate Johnny Allen in a 6–0 victory over the St. Louis Browns.

Indians first baseman Luke Easter was credited with the longest home run at the Stadium, a 477-foot blast into the upper deck in right field on June 23, 1950, off Joe Haynes as the Indians beat Washington, 13–4.

But in all the years that major league baseball was played in the Stadium—4,196 games, including five in the World Series, and four All-Star Games in 47 full seasons and parts of 13 others—nobody ever reached the center-field bleachers with a batted ball, although Jose Canseco of the Oakland Athletics came close.

Canseco drove a pitch from Tom Candiotti against the facing of the bleachers in left-center field, the ball hitting about three feet from the top, on July 8, 1990, in Oakland's 8–3 victory over the Indians.

In 1947, after Bill Veeck purchased the Indians, an eight-foot-high inner fence was installed that cut the distances to 365 feet in left-center and right-center fields, to 385 in the power alleys, and to 400 in dead center.

Initially, the fence was portable and was moved in and out, depending upon the Indians' opponent. However, the following year the AL ruled that the fence had to remain in whatever position it was placed in on opening day.

Until then, naturally, pitchers loved the Stadium.

"Back in my day you had to hit a ball pretty good to even get one over an outfielder's head," said Mel Harder, who pitched for the Indians from 1928 to 1947 and was their starter in the very first game played at the Stadium.

"Guys would hit a ball real hard and it would go deep, but usually it was just an out. And if an outfielder tried to cut off a ball hit to the outfield and it got past him, it was a triple, maybe even an inside-the-park home run."

The first municipally owned major league baseball stadium, it was built with two decks and 78,189 permanent seats—37,896 in the main or lower deck, 29,320 upstairs, 60 in the press box, and 10,913 in uncovered bleachers in center field.

"We'll fill the place often, every Sunday," was Bradley's enthusiastic reaction to the new facility.

Two days after its completion, the Stadium housed its first event—a heavyweight boxing match between champion Max Schmeling and Young Stribling. A crowd of 36,936 saw Schmeling successfully defend his title with a 15-round technical knockout.

But it wasn't until more than a year later, on July 31, 1932, that the Stadium became even the part-time home of the Indians.

It was called "a magnificent structure" and, even better, the "ultimate athletic facility in the country," as a reporter described the Stadium in the *Cleveland Plain Dealer*.

Daniel Morgan, then Cleveland's city manager, proclaimed, "The Stadium will be an enduring monument to the spirit and aspirations of our people."

The Philadelphia Athletics, behind pitcher Lefty Grove, beat the Indians and Harder, 1–0, in that inaugural game.

Five future Hall of Famers were on the field that day: Grove, Jimmie Foxx, Mickey Cochrane, and Al Simmons for Philadelphia and Earl Averill for the Indians. Connie Mack, then the Athletics' owner and manager, also is in the Hall of Fame.

Here's how the *Plain Dealer* reported that first game:

"The Cleveland Indians came home to the $3,000,000 stadium yesterday and found 80,184 (76,979 paid) friends and relations standing on the figurative steps to cry them welcome to set a new world's record for baseball crowds and to toss the depression, yelping feebly, over the wall into Lake Erie.

"You who said the Cleveland Stadium would never be filled can paste the figures in your hats, eat them in alphabet soup and stencil them on the bed room ceiling so you'll dream about them at night.

"The authority for the new world's record is William Harridge, president of the American League, who sat in a field box to watch . . . the tightest game you'll see this year."

The *Cleveland Press* also was lavish in its commendation of the opening game, which was called "a milestone in middle western sports."

In pregame ceremonies, "Connie Mack [owner and manager of the Athletics] took the public address microphone and thanked Alva Bradley and [Indians general manager] Billy Evans for their roles in providing the Indians, and all of baseball with such a magnificent structure."

But the novelty of the magnificent structure soon wore off.

The Indians played 32 of their remaining 53 games of the 1932 season, and all of the next in the Stadium. But when attendance declined to only 387,936 in 1933—almost 100,000 less than it was in 1931, Bradley lost his enthusiasm for the "magnificent structure."

He pulled the Indians out of the Stadium in 1934, moving them back to League Park where the next three seasons they played all their home games (except for one in 1936), a decision that angered city officials.

During those three years the Stadium, devoid of baseball and, most of the time, other major events as well, was referred to as a white elephant.

Bradley yielded to public pressure in 1937, agreeing to play a "limited number" of games at the Stadium, and the Indians were again the only major league team to use two home parks.

They played selected games at the Stadium, usually on weekends and at night, whenever a large crowd was expected. A typical schedule in those days would have the Indians playing Sunday games and doubleheaders at the Stadium and all the other games at League Park.

The Indians continued to travel back and forth between the Stadium and League Park until 1947, the first full year of Bill Veeck's ownership.

The final game at League Park was played September 21, 1946, a 5–3 loss to Dizzy Trout and the Detroit Tigers in front of only 2,772 fans. The next day's papers reported simply that Veeck had announced—without fanfare—that from then on all home games would be played at the Stadium.

Lights were installed at the Stadium in 1939, and the first night game in Cleveland was played that season on June 27. It was an appropriate inaugural as Bob Feller pitched a one-hitter to beat Detroit, 5–0, before 53,305 fans.

The Indians' won-lost record in their 60 seasons at the Stadium was 2,224–1,951 with 12 ties. Boston was the winningest visiting team in the Stadium with 256 victories (and 219 losses), and Detroit was close behind with a 254–220 record. The losingest visiting team was New York with a 222–254–3 record.

Five World Series games were played in the Stadium, three in 1948 and two in 1954. In 1948, when the Indians beat the Boston Braves, they won Game 3, 2–0, and Game 4, 2–1, and lost Game 5, 11–5. In 1954, when they were swept by the New York Giants, the Indians lost Game 3, 6–2, and Game 4, 7–4.

It was during the pennant-winning and world championship season of 1948 that the Indians set a major league season attendance record (since broken) of 2,620,627. They also went over the 2 million mark in 1949, with 2,233,771, and in 1993, with 2,177,908.

However, the largest crowd ever assembled in the Stadium was not to see a sporting event, but when 125,000 attended religious services of the Eucharistic Congress in 1935.

Cleveland also hosted the All-Star Game four times, more than any other city. In 1935 the score was AL 4, NL 1; in 1954, AL 11, NL 9; in 1963, NL 5, AL 3; and in 1981, NL 5, AL 4.

Nine no-hitters were pitched at the Stadium, six by Indians Don Black, Bob Feller, Sonny Siebert, Dick Bosman, Dennis Eckersley, and Len Barker, the others by Allie Reynolds of New York, Dean Chance of Minnesota, and Dave Stieb of Toronto.

And seven Indians hit three home runs in one game at the Stadium: Larry Doby, Willie Kirkland, Tony Horton, George Hendrick, Cory Snyder, Brook Jacoby, and Albert Belle.

The Stadium, which was refurbished in 1967 and again in 1974, also was the site of four still-standing attendance records: 84,587 for a doubleheader against New York, September 12, 1954; 78,382 for a night game against Chicago on August 20, 1948; 74,420 for a single day game against Detroit, April 7, 1973; and 65,934 for a twi-night doubleheader against New York, August 1, 1986.

Among the memorable games played in the Stadium:

- On July 31, 1932, Lefty Grove and the Philadelphia Athletics beat Mel Harder and the Indians, 1–0.

- On August 7, 1932, Johnny Burnett hit the first home run in the Stadium to lead the Indians to a 7–4 victory over Washington.

- On July 8, 1935, the AL won the All-Star Game, 4–1, on a home run by Jimmie Foxx.

- On October 3, 1938, Bob Feller set a major league record by striking out 18 batters, but lost to Detroit, 4–1.

- On September 27, 1940, the Indians lost the pennant as

Aerial view of Cleveland Stadium in 1948.

Detroit rookie pitcher Floyd Giebell beat Bob Feller, 2–0, on Rudy York's home run.

- On May 25, 1941, Jeff Heath hit the first upper-deck home run in the Stadium to lead the Indians to a 6–0 victory over St. Louis.

- On July 17, 1941, third baseman Ken Keltner made two sensational plays as Al Smith and Jim Bagby stopped Joe DiMaggio's consecutive-game hitting streak at 56 in a 4–3 loss to New York.

- On July 7, 1942, an AL all-star team beat Bob Feller's team of U.S. servicemen, 6–0, in a War Relief benefit game.

- On August 24, 1945, Bob Feller returned from 44 months duty in the navy during World War II and beat Detroit, 4–2, in his first start.

- On July 10, 1947, Don Black pitched the first no-hitter at the Stadium to beat Philadelphia, 2–0.

- On June 20, 1948, a record crowd of 82,781 saw Bob Feller and Bob Lemon sweep Philadelphia in a doubleheader, 4–3 and 10–0.

- On July 9, 1948, Satchel Paige made his major league debut as a reliever in a 5–3 loss to St. Louis.

- On August 3, 1948, a record night-game crowd of 72,434 saw Satchel Paige make his first major league start in a 5–3 victory over Washington.

- On August 8, 1948, injured player-manager Lou Boudreau limped off the bench to deliver a key pinch hit that led the Indians to a doubleheader sweep of New York, 8–6 and 2–1.

- On August 20, 1948, a night-game record crowd of 78,382 saw Satchel Paige pitch a three-hitter to beat Chicago, 1–0.

- On September 13, 1948, Don Black was stricken with an aneurysm while batting in a game against St. Louis, won by the Browns, 3–2.

- On October 3, 1948, the Indians lost to Detroit, 7–1, to finish the season in a tie with Boston, forcing a one-game playoff.

- On June 23, 1950, Luke Easter hit a Stadium-record 477-foot home run in a 13–4 victory over Washington.

- On July 2, 1950, Bob Feller beat Detroit, 5–3, for his 200th career victory.

- On July 1, 1951, Bob Feller pitched his third career no-hitter to beat Detroit, 2–1.

- On July 12, 1951, Allie Reynolds pitched a no-hitter as New York beat the Indians, 1–0.

- On May 23, 1954, Bob Feller beat Baltimore, 14–3, for his 250th career victory.

- On July 13, 1954, the AL won the All-Star Game, 11–9.

- On September 2, 1954, another record crowd of 86,563 (84,587 paid) saw the Indians sweep a doubleheader from New York, 4–1 and 3–2.

- On September 25, 1954, the Indians set a season victory record of 111 as Early Wynn pitched a two-hitter to beat Detroit, 11–1.

- On May 1, 1955, Bob Feller pitched his 12th one-hitter and Herb Score fanned 16 as the Indians swept a doubleheader from Boston, 2–0 and 2–1.

- On September 11, 1956, Bob Lemon beat Baltimore, 3–1, for his 200th career victory.

- On May 7, 1957, Herb Score was hit in the eye by a line drive off the bat of Gil McDougald in the Indians' 2–1 victory over New York.

- On August 13, 1958, Rocky Colavito made his first appearance as a relief pitcher in a 3–2 loss to Detroit.

- On June 17, 1960, Wynn Hawkins gave up Ted Williams' 500th career homer as Boston beat the Indians, 3–1.

- On July 9, 1963, the NL won the All-Star Game, 5–3.

- On July 31, 1963, Woodie Held, Pedro Ramos, Tito Francona, and Larry Brown hit consecutive homers in the sixth inning of the second game of a twi-night doubleheader in a 9–5 victory over California.

- On April 25 and May 1, 1966, Sam McDowell pitched back-to-back one-hitters to beat Kansas City, 2–0, and Chicago, 1–0.

- On June 10, 1966, Sonny Siebert pitched a no-hitter to beat Washington, 2–0.

- On August 25, 1967, Dean Chance pitched a no-hitter as Minnesota beat the Indians, 2–1, in the second game of a twi-night doubleheader.

- On July 3, 1968, Luis Tiant struck out 19 in a 1–0, 10-inning victory over Minnesota.

- On July 30, 1968, Ron Hansen made an unassisted triple play against the Indians, but they beat Washington, 10–1.

- On April 7, 1973, a record opening-day crowd of 74,420 saw the Indians beat Detroit, 2–1.

- On July 3, 1973, brothers Gaylord and Jim Perry were the opposing starting pitchers and, though neither was able to finish, Gaylord was the loser and a Detroit reliever was credited with the victory as the Tigers beat the Indians, 5–4.

- On June 4, 1974, a "Beer Night" riot caused the Indians to forfeit to Texas.

- On July 19, 1974, Dick Bosman pitched a no-hitter to beat Oakland, 4–0.

- On April 8, 1975, Frank Robinson homered in his first at bat as baseball's first black manager in a 5–3 victory over New York.

- On May 30, 1977, Dennis Eckersley pitched a no-hitter to beat California, 1–0.

- On May 15, 1981, Len Barker pitched baseball's 10th perfect game in a 3–0 victory over Toronto.

- On August 9, 1981, the NL won the All-Star Game, 5–4.

- On June 14, 1985, Bert Blyleven beat Oakland, 6–1, for his 200th career victory.

A near-capacity crowd in Cleveland Stadium in 1981.

• On August 1, 1990, Alex Cole stole five bases in a 4–1 victory over Kansas City.

• On September 2, 1990, Dave Stieb pitched a no-hitter as Toronto beat the Indians, 3–0.

• On May 3, 1992, Alex Cole stole five bases in a 6–3 loss to California.

• On April 8, 1993, Carlos Baerga set a major league record by hitting two homers in one inning from both sides of the plate in a 15–5 victory over New York.

• On May 24, 1993, Julio Franco's homer deprived Tommy Kramer of a perfect game in a 4–1 victory over Texas.

• On May 26, 1993, Carlos Martinez was credited with a home run when his fly ball bounced off Jose Canseco's head and went over the fence in a 7–6 victory over Texas.

One other game at the Stadium also is memorable because it featured an "Oscar-winning" performance by Earl Weaver, who managed the Baltimore Orioles during the years 1968–82 and 1985–86.

On June 18, 1979, in front of 21,506 fans, Weaver violently disagreed with a decision by plate umpire Ted Hendry concerning an obstruction call that Weaver thought Hendry should have made.

After arguing with Hendry for several minutes, Weaver spun around and dashed into the Orioles dugout. He emerged a few minutes later with a rule book that he shoved in Hendry's face while screaming in protest.

But still to no avail.

Finally, when it became obvious that his tirade was falling on deaf ears—as well as what he considered Hendry's blind eyes—Weaver methodically tore the pages out of the rule book and threw them in the air.

By then crew chief Larry Barnett had more than enough, and Weaver, described by one poet in the press box as a "flanneled Barrymore," stomped off the field in disgust.

And though he didn't win the argument, Weaver's histrionics will long be remembered as one of the all-time great performances in the history of the Stadium.

The Indians closed out their last season at the Stadium in a three-game series against the Chicago White Sox on October 1, 2, and 3, 1993.

The White Sox won all three games, 4–2, 4–2, and 4–0, in front of sold-out crowds of 72,454, 72,060, and 72,390 fans, giving the Indians a season attendance total of 2,177,908, third most in franchise history.

For the record: Harder's first pitch in that 1932 opener at the Stadium was hit foul into the left-field stands by Philadelphia second baseman Max Bishop, his second pitch was a ball, and Bishop hit the third for a single to right. The final pitch at the Stadium was swung at and missed by Indians shortstop Mark Lewis, who fanned on a 2-and-2 count at the hands of White Sox reliever Jose DeLeon.

After the Indians' last game at the Stadium, it became the exclusive home of the National Football League Cleveland Browns, who came into existence in 1946.

The Cleveland Rams represented the city in the NFL prior to the formation of the Browns. They played most of their home games at League Park, but beat Washington, 15–14, at the Stadium on December 16, 1945. It gave them their only NFL championship and also was their final game in Cleveland. They became the Los Angeles Rams in 1946. After 49 seasons in Los Angeles (1946–1994), the Rams relocated to St. Louis in 1995.

Jacobs Field

The cavernous and mammoth Municipal Stadium, which made it difficult to sell season tickets, and periodic disputes between the Indians and their landlord, Cleveland Stadium Corporation, were factors that led to the construction of Jacobs Field.

But it didn't come easily.

Proposals for a new baseball facility surfaced as far back as the mid-1960s when there also was speculation that the Indians would move out of Cleveland because of declining attendance and dissatisfaction with terms of their Stadium lease.

They had trouble initially with the city, which owns and, at that time, operated Municipal Stadium, and which had allowed the once "magnificent" building to fall into disrepair because of financial problems.

"We were constantly fighting with the city to get things done, and when we thought it couldn't get any worse, it did," Gabe Paul, the former longtime Indians chief said after his retirement in 1985.

The reason it got worse, in Paul's opinion, was that, in 1974, Cleveland Stadium Corporation was formed by Arthur B. Modell, owner of the National Football League Cleveland Browns, and took over operation of the Stadium.

The facility, then 42 years old, was leased by the city to Modell's company for 25 years. Rent for the first five years was $150,000 annually, then escalated to $375,000 a year through 1998. The agreement also called for Stadium Corporation to make $10 million worth of improvements in the building.

Thus, Stadium Corporation (which subsequently became a subsidiary of the Browns) was the Indians' landlord, a relationship which led to numerous disagreements between the two entities.

Among them was the Indians' lease, which Paul called "the worst in baseball," an allegation that was angrily denied by Modell.

By 1983 their relationship further deteriorated to the extent that the Indians filed a lawsuit against Modell, who promptly countersued.

After considerable posturing by both sides and much negative publicity, their dispute eventually was settled out of court, though the rift remained.

It intensified the Indians' determination to get out of the Stadium and into a new facility of their own, raising speculation that the franchise would be moved to another city.

In that respect the hostility between the Indians and Browns (and Stadium Corporation) produced a positive result. It alerted community leaders that Cleveland was in jeopardy of losing its major league baseball franchise.

The situation worsened before it improved. On May 8, 1984, Cuyahoga County voters rejected by a 2-to-1 margin an issue that would have increased property taxes to build a publicly funded, $150 million, 72,000-seat domed stadium in downtown Cleveland.

The defeat at the polls, however, didn't stop efforts by community leaders to placate the Indians. If anything, in fact, it accelerated a move to provide a new home for the baseball team.

Within 18 months another method of funding was developed, and new plans were on the drawing board. This time it was decided that an open-air, baseball-only facility should be constructed. Despite the previous voter rejection, and even before the issue went back on the ballot, the project proceeded.

Design objectives were agreed upon, property was acquired, and, by June 1987, demolition of existing buildings at the site, in the heart of downtown Cleveland, got under way.

Total cost of the project would be $375 million to be funded by a "sin tax" (on alcohol and cigarettes) in Cuyahoga County.

Adjacent to a ballpark—and please don't call it a "stadium," its backers pleaded—costing $161 million, was to be an arena for basketball, hockey, and other indoor events.

The help of Fay Vincent, who was then baseball commissioner, and AL president Dr. Bobby Brown was enlisted. Both indicated that unless a new ballpark was built, Cleveland could lose the Indians to another city.

There was no mistaking Vincent's message: "Should this facility not be available in Cleveland, should the vote [on the sin tax] be a negative one, we may find ourselves confronting a subject that we want to avoid."

The issue was placed on the ballot on May 8, 1990, and passed, though just barely, by a 1.2 percent margin: 197,044 in favor, 185,209 opposed.

The Gateway Economic Development Corporation was then created, and work on the project began immediately. The first concrete was poured in April 1992, and two years later Jacobs Field was completed and ready for baseball.

Naming rights were purchased for $13.9 million for 20 years by Richard E. Jacobs, who had bought the Indians in 1986 with his brother David H. Jacobs (since deceased). Richard Jacobs signed a 20-year lease for the team to play in the new park.

Six months after Jacobs Field was opened for business, Gund Arena, next to the ballpark at Gateway, was completed for the Cavaliers, Cleveland's team in the National Basketball Association. Owners Gordon and George Gund also paid a reported $13.9 million for 20 years for the naming rights to that building.

Jacobs Field is, as its planners wanted it to be, a "new, old park . . . cozy and intimate," with real grass, triple decked with a seating capacity of 42,400. Asymmetrical in design, the dimensions of the playing field are fair: 325 feet to the left- and right-field foul lines, 370 to left-center, 405 to center, and 375 to right-center.

A state-of-the-art, 26-by-37-foot, four-color scoreboard/information board featuring a Sony Jumbotron for replays towers over and behind the bleachers in left field and a field-level, out-of-town scoreboard.

Included are 119 luxury loges, 10 at field level behind home plate (and closer to the batter than the pitcher) between the two dugouts. High-tech lights, set vertically (said to resemble giant toothbrushes), help keep fly balls from being lost in the glare.

The Indians and visitors clubhouses are plush and spacious (the Tribe's storage area, in fact, is bigger than the old locker room at Municipal Stadium), and the press area also is large and well-appointed, capable of accommodating the crush of national media that covered the Indians during the 1995 division series against Boston, the AL championship series against Seattle, and the World Series against Atlanta.

It has been said that Gateway in its entirety is symbolic of the rejuvenation that has taken place in downtown Cleveland.

As Jacobs said, "It's more than just a sports complex, it's an icon for all of northeastern Ohio. It's something that everyone should be proud of."

If the first game played at League Park 103 years earlier was "a magical opening . . . there never was one like it and there never may be another," as stated in 1891, and if the Stadium was "a magnificent structure . . . the ultimate athletic facility in the country" and "an enduring monument to the spirit and aspirations of [Cleveland's] people," as it was called at its inaugural game in 1932, wordsmiths had to find it difficult to describe the April 4, 1994, dedication of Jacobs Field.

President Bill Clinton headed the list of dignitaries, which also included Ohio Governor George V. Voinovich, Cleveland Mayor Michael R. White, and Hall of Fame pitcher Bob Feller. Indians outfielder Wayne Kirby delivered a game-winning hit to score Eddie Murray and cap an 11th-inning rally that beat Seattle, 4–3.

Though the Indians won the game, it had shaped up as less than thrilling for Cleveland fans as Seattle's Randy John-son flirted with a no-hitter for seven innings. Catcher Sandy Alomar, Jr., spoiled it with a single in the eighth when the Indians scored twice to tie the game.

The honor of making the first pitch at Jacobs Field went to Dennis Martinez (it was called a strike by umpire Larry Barnett) to the first batter, Mariners second baseman Rich Amaral; the first run was scored by Mariners third baseman Edgar Martinez in the first inning after he was hit by a pitch, moved around to third on two walks, and went home on a sacrifice fly by left fielder Eric Anthony; and the first hit (and home run) also was made by Anthony, a drive into the lower-right field stands in the third inning.

The first winning pitcher was reliever Eric Plunk, and Kevin King was the first loser.

The Indians went on to win 35 of 51 games in their new ballpark before the season was cut short by a players' strike on August 12. With their 31–31 road record added to their success at home, the Indians in their inaugural season at Jacobs Field became a pennant contender for the first time in 34 years.

The final standings placed them second in the AL Central Division, one game behind Chicago. They had the third-best record (66–47 .584) in the league and the fifth-best in both leagues.

That first winning record in eight years and the amenities of Jacobs Field produced a season attendance total of 1,995,174, an average of 39,121 for each of the Tribe's 51 home dates. If 30 openings had not been canceled, season attendance certainly would have exceeded 3 million—largest in franchise history.

Indians Home Records at Each Ballpark

Park	Years	W	L	T	Pct.
League Park	1901–46	1,696	1,317	30	.563
Municipal Stadium	1932–33, 1936–93	2,224	1,951	12	.533
Jacobs Field	1994–95	89	34	0	.724

The first game played at Jacobs Field, April 4, 1994, between the Indians and Seattle Mariners.

7

The Hall of Famers

Twenty-six men who wore Cleveland uniforms and three former club executives are enshrined in the Hall of Fame at Cooperstown, New York, well establishing the fact that the Indians—as well as their predecessors, the Spiders, Blues, Bronchos, and Naps—have had their share of the game's greatest players.

Though several gained much of their fame playing for other teams, they all made contributions to the Cleveland franchise, which proudly claims them among those who spent most or all of their careers playing at League Park and Municipal Stadium.

Twelve of the 26 players made their way into the Hall of Fame primarily by their achievements on the field while wearing a Cleveland uniform—Earl Averill, Lou Boudreau, Stan Coveleski, Bob Feller, Elmer Flick, Addie Joss, Napoleon Lajoie, Bob Lemon, Al Lopez (as an Indians manager), Joey Sewell, Tris Speaker, and Early Wynn.

The immortal Cy Young started in professional baseball in Cleveland long before the American League was established and returned to his roots for a brief fling near the end of his career, but won most of his games elsewhere.

Another, the legendary Satchel Paige, earned his way into the Hall of Fame pitching in the Negro League, but joined the Indians late in his career and proved that he was of major league caliber.

And Gaylord Perry had only three outstanding seasons in Cleveland, though the credentials he established elsewhere during his brilliant 22-year career certainly qualify him for the Hall of Fame.

Seven others—Steve Carlton, Walter Johnson, Ralph Kiner, Hal Newhouser, Sam Rice, Frank Robinson, and Hoyt Wilhelm—staked their claims to baseball immortality elsewhere, but spent brief portions of their careers in Cleveland.

Also in the hallowed Hall are four men who, though they didn't play for the Indians, served as coaches for the team—Luke Appling, Bill McKechnie, Al Simmons, and Warren Spahn.

The former club executives who are enshrined are Billy Evans, who gained fame as an umpire before he served as general manager of the Indians from 1927 to 1935; Hank Greenberg, the legendary Detroit Tigers slugger who was a part owner, vice president, and general manager of the Cleveland franchise from 1948 to 1957; and Bill Veeck, who owned the club from 1946 to 1949.

Five other Hall of Famers played for Cleveland teams prior to the formation of the American League in 1901—Jesse Burkett, John Clarkson, Ed Delahanty, Buck Ewing, and Bobby Wallace.

Tris Speaker, Napoleon Lajoie, and Cy Young at the July 31, 1932 opening of Cleveland Municipal Stadium. All would later be inducted into the Hall of Fame.

Lucius Benjamin Appling

Coach
Indians: 1960–61
Major leagues: 1930–43, 1945–50
(player), 1967 (manager)
Elected: 1964
Birthplace: High Point, North Carolina
B: April 2, 1907
D: January 3, 1991
Batted right, threw right

	G	AB	H	BA	RBI	R	2B	3B	HR	SA	SB
Career	2,422	8,856	2,749	.310	1,116	1,319	440	102	45	.398	179

H is nickname was "Old Aches and Pains," but if Luke Appling was hurting, it never showed in the way he played shortstop for 20 years for the Chicago White Sox. Appling had the remarkable ability to foul off pitches he didn't like. Appling apparently never lost his ability to hit. At the Crackerjack Old-Timers Classic in 1982, Appling, then 75 years old, delighted a national television audience by hitting a home run off Warren Spahn over the left-field fence at Robert F. Kennedy Memorial Stadium in Washington, to highlight the American Leaguers' 7–2 victory. Appling joined the Indians as a coach on August 9, 1960, accompanying his boss, Jimmy Dykes, who had been sent to Cleveland by Detroit for Joe Gordon, the only time in baseball history that two managers were traded for each other. Appling remained with the Indians in 1961, but was dismissed with Dykes at the end of that season.

Howard Earl Averill

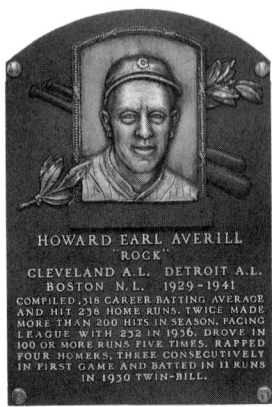

Center fielder
Indians: 1929–39
Major leagues: 1929–41
Elected: 1975
Birthplace: Snohomish, Washington
B: May 21, 1902
D: August 16, 1983
Batted left, threw right

	G	AB	H	BA	RBI	R	2B	3B	HR	SA	SB
Indians	1,509	5,909	1,903	.322	1,084	1,154	377	121	226	.542	66
Career	1,668	6,353	2,019	.318	1,164	1,224	401	128	238	.534	70

A s the *Hall of Fame Yearbook* reports, "Earl Averill had amazing power for his size—5 9½ and 170 pounds." He still holds the Indians career record for most homers with 226, thanks in part to the short right-field fence at League Park, and also is the franchise leader in RBIs with 1,084. Averill became the first American League player to homer in his first at bat in the major leagues against Earl Whitehill of Detroit in 1929, and he went on to hit 18, then a Cleveland season record. Averill also was the first major leaguer to hit four homers in a doubleheader, on September 17, 1930, against Washington, three in the first game (he missed a fourth by two feet in his fourth at bat) and one in his first at bat in the second game. Averill's season high was 32 homers each in 1931 and 1932, and he batted .300 or better in eight of his first 10 seasons, including a career-best .378 in 1936 when he led the AL with 232 hits and 15 triples.

Louis Boudreau

Shortstop-manager
Indians: 1938–50
Major leagues: 1938–50 (player),
1942–50, 1952–57, 1960
(manager)
Elected: 1970
Birthplace: Harvey, Illinois
B: July 17, 1917
Bats right, throws right

	G	AB	H	BA	RBI	R	2B	3B	HR	SA	SB
Indians	1,560	5,754	1,706	.296	740	823	367	65	63	.416	50
Career	1,646	6,029	1,779	.295	789	861	385	66	68	.415	51

T hough he was elected to the Hall of Fame as a slick-fielding shortstop and consistent hitter, Lou Boudreau also was one of the game's best managers in 1948, the year the Indians won their second pennant and World Series. Not only was he an inspirational leader on the field, but the innovative Boudreau also made what some called "hunch decisions" that paid off remarkably well. One of the most important was his unexpected choice of Gene Bearden to pitch the playoff game against Boston that won the pennant for the Indians. That was in 1948, and Boudreau was voted the American League's Most Valuable Player. He won the AL batting championship in 1944 when he batted .327. Boudreau also deserves much of the credit for the transformation of Bob Lemon from a light-hitting third baseman–outfielder to a Hall of Fame pitcher, and he also was the manager who designed the "Williams shift," which was subsequently adopted by other teams.

Steven Norman Carlton

STEVEN NORMAN CARLTON
"LEFTY"
ST. LOUIS, N.L., 1965-1971
PHILADELPHIA, N.L., 1972-1986
SAN FRANCISCO, N.L., 1986
CHICAGO, A.L., 1986
CLEVELAND, A.L., 1987
MINNESOTA, A.L., 1987-1988
EXTREMELY FOCUSED COMPETITOR WITH COMPLETE DEDICATION
TO EXCELLENCE. THRIVED ON MOUND BY PHYSICALLY AND MENTALLY
CHALLENGING HIMSELF OFF THE FIELD. OUT PITCH WAS HARD,
BITING SLIDER. 329 VICTORIES SECOND ONLY TO SPAHN AMONG
LEFTIES AND 4,136 STRIKEOUTS EXCEEDED ONLY BY RYAN. SHARES
N.L. RECORD WITH 19 STRIKEOUTS IN GAME. SIX 20 WIN SEASONS.
ONLY HURLER TO WIN 4 CY YOUNG AWARDS.

Pitcher
Indians: 1987
Major leagues: 1965–88
Elected: 1994
Birthplace: Miami, Florida
B: December 22, 1944
Bats left, throws left

	W	L	Pct.	ERA	G	CG	IP	H	BB	SO	ShO
Indians	5	9	.357	5.37	23	3	109	111	63	71	0
Career	329	244	.574	3.22	741	254	5,217⅓	4,672	1,833	4,136	55

Though he played less than one full season for the Indians and joined them near the end of his career, Steve Carlton picked up a pitching staff that was badly depleted in 1987. Signed as a free agent on April 3, Carlton appeared in 23 games, 14 as a starter, posting a 5–9 record for a team that went on to win only 61 games while losing 101. He was traded to the Minnesota Twins on July 31 for a minor league player. Before joining the Indians, Carlton was one of the greatest pitchers in the game. His 329 career victories are second most by a left-handed pitcher only to Warren Spahn, his 4,136 strikeouts were exceeded only by Nolan Ryan, he shares the National League single-game strikeout record of 19, and he was a 20-game winner six times and won four Cy Young Awards while pitching for the St. Louis Cardinals (1965–71), Philadelphia Phillies (1972–86), San Francisco Giants (1986), and Chicago White Sox (1986) before joining the Indians, and for the Twins through 1988.

Stanley Anthony Coveleski

STANLEY ANTHONY COVELESKI
PHILADELPHIA A.L.   1912
CLEVELAND A.L. 1916-1924
WASHINGTON A.L. 1925-1927
NEW YORK A.L.   1928
STAR PITCHER WITH A RECORD OF 214 WINS,
141 LOSSES, AVERAGE .603, E.R.A. 2.88,
WON 20 OR MORE GAMES IN 5 SEASONS. WON
15 STRAIGHT GAMES IN 1925, PITCHED AND
WON 3 GAMES FOR CLEVELAND IN 1920
WORLD SERIES WITH E.R.A. 0.67.

Pitcher
Indians: 1916–24
Major leagues: 1912, 1916–28
Elected: 1969
Birthplace: Shamokin, Pennsylvania
B: July 13, 1889
D: March 20, 1984
Batted right, threw right

	W	L	Pct.	ERA	G	CG	IP	H	BB	SO	ShO
Indians	172	123	.583	2.80	360	194	2,502⅓	2,450	616	856	31
Career	215	142	.602	2.89	450	224	3,082	3,055	802	981	38

One of the Indians' heroes of 1920 when he won three games in the World Series, a feat equaled by only 11 other pitchers in baseball history, Stan Coveleski also was one of the 17 who were allowed to continue throwing spitballs when it was outlawed—but the new rule was "grandfathered"—in 1920. Coveleski also had a good fastball and curve, averaged less than three walks per game over 14 seasons, and always said he learned control by throwing rocks at tin cans as a youngster. Coveleski was a 20-game winner four times with the Indians and once with Washington in 1925 after being traded to the Senators. He is still among the Indians' career pitching leaders in eight categories: victories, fourth, 172; shutouts, third, 31; earned run average, sixth, 2.80; winning percentage, eighth, .583; games, seventh, 360; innings, fifth, 2,502⅓; strikeouts, tenth, 856; and losses, fifth, 123.

William George Evans

WILLIAM GEORGE EVANS
UMPIRE AND EXECUTIVE
EMPLOYED BY AMERICAN LEAGUE IN
1906 AT AGE 22, MAKING HIM YOUNGEST
UMPIRE EVER IN MAJORS. SERVED ON A.L.
STAFF THROUGH 1927. OFFICIATED IN
SIX WORLD SERIES. GENERAL MANAGER
OF CLEVELAND INDIANS, 1927-1935. FARM
DIRECTOR OF BOSTON RED SOX 1936-1940
PRESIDENT OF SOUTHERN ASSOCIATION,
1942-1946. GENERAL MANAGER OF
DETROIT TIGERS, 1947-1951.

General manager
Indians: 1927–35
Major leagues: 1906–27 (umpire),
    1927–35, 1946–51 (general
    manager)
Elected: 1973
Birthplace: Chicago
B: February 10, 1884
D: January 23, 1956

Billy Evans began his career as a sportswriter for the *Youngstown* (Ohio) *Vindicator* in 1903, quit to become a minor league umpire in 1905, and was promoted to the American League the following year when he was only 22. Evans remained an umpire—and always was rated one of the best—for 22 years, during which he also wrote a syndicated column for the Newspaper Enterprise Association (NEA). Evans took over as general manager of the Indians when the franchise was purchased by Alva Bradley in 1927. He left in 1935 and later worked for the Boston Red Sox, the Detroit Tigers, and the Cleveland Rams of the National Football League. He served as president of the Southern Association from 1942 to 1946. In 1954, after Evans' retirement, Ed Bang, sports editor of the *Cleveland News,* wrote of him: "Baseball and Billy Evans were and are synonymous. The sport never had a better booster. He wrote it, umpired it, and administered it. Most important, he loved the game and sold it everywhere he went."

Robert William Andrew Feller

Pitcher
Indians: 1936–41, 1945–56
Major leagues: 1936–41, 1945–56
Elected: 1962
Birthplace: Van Meter, Iowa
B: November 3, 1918
Bats right, throws right

	W	L	Pct.	ERA	G	CG	IP	H	BB	SO	ShO
Indians	266	162	.621	3.25	570	279	3,827	3,271	1,764	2,581	44
Career	266	162	.621	3.25	570	279	3,827	3,271	1,764	2,581	44

There always will be conjecture as to how many games Bob Feller would have won if his career had not been interrupted by World War II. Two days after the Japanese bombed Pearl Harbor on December 7, 1941, Feller, then the best pitcher in baseball, enlisted in the navy. He spent 44 months aboard the U.S.S. *Alabama* earning eight battle stars, and didn't return to the Indians until late 1945, beating Detroit, 4–2, on August 24. The winningest pitcher in Indians history with 266 victories, Feller was elected to the Hall of Fame in his first year of eligibility, and his uniform number 19 is one of five permanently retired by the team (along with Earl Averill's number 3, Lou Boudreau's 5, Larry Doby's 14, and Mel Harder's 18). A 20-game winner six times, Feller fired three no-hitters and 12 one-hitters. He set a single-game strikeout record of 18 (since broken) on October 2, 1938, against Detroit, and a season strikeout record of 348 (also since broken) in 1946.

Elmer Harrison Flick

Right fielder
Indians (Bronchos, Naps): 1902–10
Major leagues: 1898–1910
Elected: 1963
Birthplace: Bedford, Ohio
B: January 11, 1876
D: January 9, 1971
Batted left, threw right

	G	AB	H	BA	RBI	R	2B	3B	HR	SA	SB
Indians	935	3,537	1,058	.299	376	533	164	106	19	.422	207
Career	1,483	5,597	1,752	.313	756	948	268	164	48	.445	330

Elmer Flick hit .367 for the Philadelphia Phillies in 1900, though his average was only second best in the National League batting race. Five years later while playing for Cleveland his average was 59 points lower but won the 1905 American League title. His .308 mark for the Naps that season was the lowest to win the title in major league history until 1968, "the year of the pitcher," when Carl Yastrzemski did so with a .301 mark. Flick was one of the Phillies (Napoleon Lajoie and Bill Bernhard were two others) who jumped to the Philadelphia Athletics after the AL was formed in 1901. He was sent to Cleveland to avoid prosecution in Pennsylvania. Flick's career went downhill in 1908 after he suffered a mysterious stomach ailment. He played only nine games in 1908, and only 99 in his final three seasons.

Henry Benjamin Greenberg

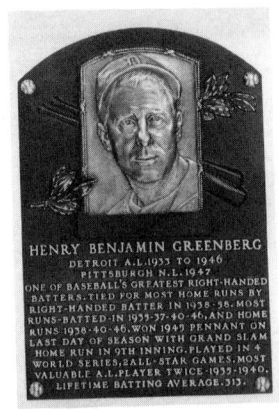

Part owner, vice president, general manager
Indians: 1948–57
Major leagues: 1930, 1933–41, 1945–47 (player), 1948–57, 1959–61
Elected: 1956
Birthplace: New York City
B: January 1, 1911
D: September 4, 1986
Batted right, threw right

	G	AB	H	BA	RBI	R	2B	3B	HR	SA	SB
Career	1,394	5,193	1,628	.313	1,276	1,051	379	71	331	.605	58

Following his outstanding playing career in 1947, after 12 seasons with Detroit and one with Pittsburgh, Hank Greenberg joined the Indians as farm director under Bill Veeck. He later became a part owner, vice president, and general manager of the club, and remained with the Indians until August 1959 when he left to rejoin Veeck with the Chicago White Sox. As a player, Greenberg was noted for his power hitting and, despite losing four prime seasons to World War II and another to a fractured wrist in 1936, he hit 331 homers and drove in 1,276 runs while compiling a .313 average as both an outfielder and first baseman. Twice elected the American League's Most Valuable Player, Greenberg's peak years were 1938 when he slugged 58 homers and 1937 when he led the AL with 183 RBIs.

Walter Perry Johnson

Manager
Indians: 1933–35
Major leagues: 1907–27 (player),
　　　　　　　1929–35 (manager)
Elected: 1936
Birthplace: Humboldt, Kansas
B: November 6, 1887
D: December 10, 1946
Batted right, threw right

	W	L	Pct.	ERA	G	CG	IP	H	BB	SO	ShO
Career	417	279	.599	2.16	802	666	5,923⅔	4,914	1,363	3,509	110

Walter Johnson never pitched for the Indians, but he took over for Roger Peckinpaugh as their manager in 1933, then was replaced during the 1935 season by Steve O'Neill. His managerial record was not nearly as outstanding as his pitching career; under Johnson's tutelage the Indians' record was 48–51 in 1933, 85–69 in 1934 when they finished third, and 46–48 in 1935. It was during the 1935 season that Johnson had problems with two popular Tribe players, Willie Kamm and Glenn Myatt, that led to his dismissal by owner Alva Bradley. He managed the Washington Senators from 1929 to 1932, but his firing by the Indians ended Johnson's baseball career. It included 21 seasons as a pitcher for the Senators, for whom he won 417 games, second most (to Cy Young) in baseball history, and hurled 110 shutouts, more than any other major league pitcher.

Adrian Joss

Pitcher
Indians (Bronchos, Naps): 1902–10
Major leagues: 1902–10
Elected: 1978
Birthplace: Woodland, Wisconsin
B: April 12, 1880
D: April 14, 1911
Batted right, threw right

	W	L	Pct.	ERA	G	CG	IP	H	BB	SO	ShO
Indians	160	97	.623	1.89	286	234	2,327	1,888	364	920	45
Career	160	97	.623	1.89	286	234	2,327	1,888	364	920	45

An exception to the Hall of Fame eligibility rules was made in the case of Addie Joss, who pitched only nine seasons (instead of the required 10) because he contracted tubercular meningitis and died on the eve of the 1911 season. There could be no doubt, however, that Joss was among the greatest pitchers of his era and would have established himself as one of the best of all time. On October 2, 1908, Joss hurled the second perfect game in American League history—only 11 have been pitched since then—in a memorable duel against Ed Walsh, 40-game winner of the Chicago White Sox. Joss prevailed, 1–0, as Walsh pitched a four-hitter and struck out 15. That was the season the Naps lost the pennant to Detroit by one-half game and Joss registered a 1.16 earned run average, eighth lowest of all time. Two years later Joss pitched another no-hitter against the White Sox. Perhaps the most remarkable of Joss's achievements was that he completed 234 of his 260 starts.

Ralph McPherran Kiner

Left fielder
Indians: 1955
Major leagues: 1946–55
Elected: 1975
Birthplace: Santa Rita, New Mexico
B: October 27, 1922
Bats right, throws right

	G	AB	H	BA	RBI	R	2B	3B	HR	SA	SB
Indians	113	321	78	.243	54	56	13	0	18	.452	0
Career	1,472	5,205	1,451	.279	1,015	971	216	39	369	.548	22

One of baseball's great sluggers, Ralph Kiner played the final year of his career in Cleveland after being acquired by the Indians on November 16, 1954, from the Chicago Cubs for two players and $60,000. Kiner hit 369 homers in a relatively brief, 10-year career that was cut short by back trouble. Eighteen of his homers were hit for the Indians in 1955. Kiner won or shared the National League home run title in each of his first seven seasons in Pittsburgh, with his top output being 54 in 1949. Kiner's ratio of 7.1 home runs per 100 at bats is second only to Babe Ruth. He averaged better than 100 RBIs a season in leading the National League in slugging percentage three times.

Napoleon Lajoie

Second baseman–manager
Indians (Bronchos, Naps): 1902–14
Major leagues: 1896–1916 (player),
1905–09 (manager)
Elected: 1937
Birthplace: Woonsocket, Rhode Island
B: September 5, 1874
D: February 7, 1959
Batted right, threw right

	G	AB	H	BA	RBI	R	2B	3B	HR	SA	SB
Indians	1,614	6,034	2,046	.339	919	865	424	78	34	.452	240
Career	2,480	9,589	3,242	.338	1,599	1,504	657	163	83	.467	380

The sixth player elected to the Hall of Fame, Napoleon Lajoie was a graceful, sure-handed, strong-armed second baseman and an outstanding hitter. He is regarded by many as having been the greatest player in Cleveland baseball history. Lajoie batted .426 in 1901, the year he jumped from the Philadelphia Phillies of the National League to the Philadelphia Athletics of the newly founded American League. The following season he was sent to Cleveland to avoid prosecution in Pennsylvania. The first of six Cleveland player-managers, Lajoie batted .300 or better in 16 of his 21 major league seasons, nine times topping .350. He went to the plate more times, 6,034, than anybody who played for Cleveland, his 2,046 hits are the most, his 1,614 games played are five fewer than the all-time leader (Terry Turner, 1904–18), his .339 Cleveland career batting average is third best, and only Earl Averill (with 1,084) had more RBIs than Lajoie's 919.

Robert Granville Lemon

Pitcher
Indians: 1941–42, 1946–58
Major leagues: 1941–42, 1946–58
(player), 1970–72, 1977–79,
1981–82 (manager)
Elected: 1976
Birthplace: San Bernardino, California
B: September 22, 1920
Bats left, throws right

	W	L	Pct.	ERA	G	CG	IP	H	BB	SO	ShO
Indians	207	128	.618	3.23	460	188	2,850	2,559	1,251	1,277	31
Career	207	128	.618	3.23	460	188	2,850	2,559	1,251	1,277	31

Eight years after his debut in professional baseball as a third baseman and later an outfielder, Bob Lemon turned to pitching and became one of the best in Indians history. He took the mound for the first time during a three-year (1943–45) stint in the navy. One of his teammates was future Hall of Fame catcher Bill Dickey, who recommended to the Indians that Lemon be given a trial as a pitcher. That was in 1946, after Lemon had opened the season in center field and made a sensational game-saving catch to preserve Bob Feller's 1–0 victory over Chicago. Lemon went on to win 20 or more games seven times in nine years, 1948–56, hurled a no-hitter against Detroit in 1948, and became the third-winningest pitcher in franchise history. Lemon is fourth with a .618 winning percentage, tied for third with 31 shutouts, fourth with 460 games pitched, third with 2,850 innings, and third with 1,277 strikeouts.

Alfonso Raymond Lopez

Catcher, manager
Indians: 1947, 1951–56
Major leagues: 1928, 1930–47
(player), 1951–65, 1968–69
(manager)
Elected: 1977
Birthplace: Tampa, Florida
B: August 20, 1908
Bats right, throws right

	G	W	L	Pct.
Indians	930	570	354	.617
Career	2,425	1,410	1,004	.584

It was as a manager that Al Lopez was elected to the Hall of Fame, though he also was an outstanding and durable catcher during a 19-year major league playing career that ended in 1947 with the Indians. For many years he held the major league record for the most games caught (1,918) and was tied with Gabby Hartnett for the National League record for the most seasons (12) catching 100 or more games. Both records have since been broken. After taking over as manager of the Indians in 1951, he led them to the pennant in 1954 when they set an American League record with 111 victories, as well as five second-place finishes in six seasons. Lopez then managed the Chicago White Sox, 1957–65 and 1968–69, winning another pennant in 1959 and finishing second five more times. It was Lopez who developed what many believe was the greatest pitching staff in baseball history on the Indians' 1954 team: starters Bob Lemon, Early Wynn, Mike Garcia, Art Houtteman, and Bob Feller and relievers Don Mossi, Ray Narleski, and Hal Newhouser.

William Boyd McKechnie

Coach

Indians: 1947–49

Major leagues: 1907, 1910–18, 1920 (player), 1915, 1922–26, 1928–46 (manager)

Elected: 1962

Birthplace: Wilkinsburg, Pennsylvania

B: August 7, 1887

D: October 29, 1965

Batted left and right, threw right

	G	W	L	Pct.
Career	3,647	1,896	1,723	.524

Nicknamed Deacon because of his scholarly demeanor and approach to the game, Bill McKechnie joined Lou Boudreau's staff as a coach in 1947 after a 24-year managerial career with Pittsburgh, the St. Louis Cardinals, the Boston Braves, and Cincinnati. He is the only National League manager to have won pennants with three different clubs—the Pirates in 1925, Cardinals in 1928, and Reds in 1939 and 1940. A former major league infielder who batted .251 in his 11-year playing career, McKechnie's 1925 and 1940 teams won the World Series, and he was named Manager of the Year twice. He came to Cleveland at the request of Bill Veeck, who wanted to provide Boudreau with a more experienced staff, was instrumental in helping the Indians win the world championship in 1948, and remained with the club until his retirement after the 1949 season. McKechnie came out of retirement to coach once again under Boudreau with the Boston Red Sox in 1952 and 1953.

Harold Newhouser

Pitcher

Indians: 1954–55

Major leagues: 1939–55

Elected: 1992

Birthplace: Detroit, Michigan

B: May 20, 1921

Bats left, throws left

	W	L	Pct.	ERA	G	CG	IP	H	BB	SO	ShO
Indians	7	2	.778	2.39	28	0	49	35	22	26	0
Career	207	150	.580	3.06	488	212	2,993	2,674	1,249	1,796	33

A longtime nemesis of the Indians when he pitched for Detroit, Hal Newhouser's duels against Bob Feller were legendary. Newhouser entered the major leagues with the Tigers in 1939 and signed with the Indians as a free agent after being released by Detroit at the end of the 1953 season, bolstering the staff as a long reliever in 1954. He started 1955 with the Indians, but retired with a sore arm before the season was a month old. He'd been able to pitch only 2⅓ innings in two games without a record. With the Tigers in the first 15 years of his career, Newhouser became the only pitcher in major league history to win back-to-back Most Valuable Player awards, in 1944 and 1945, winning 54 games those two seasons. He also led the American League in victories four times, with 29 in 1944, 25 in 1945, 26 in 1946, and 21 in 1948.

Leroy Robert Paige

Pitcher

Indians: 1948–49

Major leagues: 1948–49, 1951–53, 1965

Elected: 1971

Birthplace: Mobile, Alabama

B: July 7, 1906

D: June 8, 1982

Batted right, threw right

	W	L	Pct.	ERA	G	CG	IP	H	BB	SO	ShO
Indians	10	8	.556	2.78	52	4	155⅔	131	58	99	2
Career	28	31	.475	3.29	179	7	476	429	183	290	4

It took Satchel Paige 22 years to make it to the major leagues because black players weren't signed until 1946, but upon his arrival in 1948 there was no doubt that he belonged. A legend in the Negro Leagues, Paige also was outstanding in his annual off-season barnstorming tours in which he played on even terms against major league stars. He was signed by Bill Veeck on his 42nd birthday, July 7, 1948, after a 20-minute tryout at the Stadium in which he threw his "two-hump blooper" change-up, "Little Tom" medium fastball, "Long Tom" hard fastball, and "hesitation pitch," in which he momentarily stopped his delivery to upset the batter's timing. Paige made his major league debut in relief two days after signing and started his first major league game on August 3, a 5–3 victory over Washington. He went on to post a 6–1 record and 2.48 earned run average that season, without which the Indians probably would not have won the pennant.

Gaylord Jackson Perry

Pitcher
Indians: 1972–75
Major leagues: 1962–83
Elected: 1991
Birthplace: Williamston,
   North Carolina
B: September 25, 1938
Bats right, throws right

	W	L	Pct.	ERA	G	CG	IP	H	BB	SO	ShO
Indians	70	57	.551	2.71	134	96	1,130⅔	918	330	773	17
Career	314	265	.542	3.11	777	303	5,350½	4,938	1,379	3,534	53

He didn't join the Indians until late in his career, but Gaylord Perry was one of their brightest stars for three seasons, and in 1978 he became the only pitcher to win the Cy Young Award in both leagues. Perry first captured the award in 1972, his first season in Cleveland, when he went 24–16 with a remarkable 1.92 earned run average for a team that had a total of only 72 victories and finished in fifth place. He pitched a no-hitter for San Francisco in 1968, and in 1974, when Perry's record was 21–13, he won 15 consecutive games for the Indians, tying the club mark set by Johnny Allen in 1937. After being traded by the Indians on June 13, 1975, Perry went on to win the Cy Young Award in the National League in 1978 with San Diego. He won 314 games and struck out 3,534 batters, sixth most in baseball history, for the eight teams for which he pitched: San Francisco, Cleveland, Texas, San Diego, New York Yankees, Atlanta, Seattle, and Kansas City.

Edgar Charles Rice

Outfielder
Indians: 1934
Major leagues: 1915–34
Elected: 1963
Birthplace: Morocco, Indiana
B: February 20, 1890
D: October 13, 1974
Batted left, threw right

	G	AB	H	BA	RBI	R	2B	3B	HR	SA	SB
Indians	97	335	98	.293	33	48	19	1	1	.364	5
Career	2,404	9,269	2,987	.322	1,078	1,514	498	184	34	.427	351

The Indians didn't get Sam Rice until the last season of his 20-year major league career, but his accomplishments for the Washington Senators from 1915 to 1933 were remark-

able. Despite his small stature (5–9, 150 pounds) Rice batted over .300 in 13 seasons, including a career-high .350 in 1925, and led the American League with 216 hits in both 1924, when the Senators won the American League pennant and World Series, and 1926. Rice, who started in professional baseball as a pitcher, was primarily a contact hitter and averaged only one strikeout every 34 at bats. He also led the AL with 63 stolen bases in 1920, had 351 for his career, and batted .302 in 15 World Series games in 1924, 1925, and 1933. Rice hit 34 career home runs, 21 of which were inside the park, and was able to make only 98 hits in 335 trips to the plate (for a .293 average) in 97 games in the final season of his career in Cleveland, finishing just 13 hits shy of 3,000.

Frank Robinson

Designated hitter–manager
Indians: 1974–77
Major leagues: 1956–76 (player),
   1975–77, 1981–84, 1988–91
   (manager)
Elected: 1982
Birthplace: Beaumont, Texas
B: August 31, 1935
Bats right, throws right

	G	AB	H	BA	RBI	R	2B	3B	HR	SA	SB
Indians	100	235	53	.226	39	30	6	1	14	.438	0
Career	2,808	10,006	2,943	.294	1,812	1,829	528	72	586	.537	204

As the Indians' sixth player-manager, Frank Robinson saw action in only 100 games during his tenure in Cleveland after arriving on September 12, 1974, but his previous service with Cincinnati, Baltimore, the Los Angeles Dodgers, and the California Angels was outstanding. He was the National League Rookie of the Year in 1956 and won the Most Valuable Player Award in the National League in 1961 and the American League in 1966, becoming the first player to win it in both leagues. Robinson also won the Triple Crown with the Orioles in 1966 when they won the pennant and World Series. Primarily a designated hitter with the Indians, Robinson became major league baseball's first black manager in 1975, until he was replaced on June 19, 1977. The Indians' record under him was 186–189. A shoulder injury in 1975 necessitated surgery, cutting short his playing career with 586 homers, fourth most in baseball history, and leaving him 57 hits shy of 3,000.

Joseph Wheeler Sewell

Shortstop
Indians: 1920–30
Major leagues: 1920–33
Elected: 1977
Birthplace: Titus, Alabama
B: October 9,1898
D: March 6, 1990
Batted left, threw right

	G	AB	H	BA	RBI	R	2B	3B	HR	SA	SB
Indians	1,513	5,621	1,800	.320	869	857	375	63	30	.425	71
Career	1,903	7,132	2,226	.312	1,055	1,141	436	68	49	.422	74

One of the all-time great contact hitters, Joey Sewell holds the major league record for having struck out only 114 times in 1,903 games over 14 years, only three times in 353 at bats in 1930, and three in 503 trips to the plate for the New York Yankees in 1932. Equally remarkable was that Sewell led the Indians in RBIs three times, with 106 in 1924, 98 in 1925, and 92 in 1927, and in his 11 seasons in Cleveland failed to bat .300 only twice, with a high of .353 in 1923. Sewell also was one of the best defensive infielders of his era, leading American League shortstops in putouts four straight seasons (1924–27), in assists four times, and in fielding percentage twice. Sewell joined the Indians in 1920 under the most difficult of circumstances. After shortstop Ray Chapman was killed when hit by a pitch from Carl Mays of the Yankees on August 16, Sewell was called up from the minor leagues and stayed for 14 years, 11 with the Indians and three with the Yankees.

Aloysius Harry Simmons

Coach
Indians: 1950
Major leagues: 1924–41, 1943–44 (player), 1940–42, 1945–50 (coach)
Elected: 1953
Birthplace: Milwaukee, Wisconsin
B: May 22, 1902
D: May 26, 1956
Batted right, threw right

	G	AB	H	BA	RBI	R	2B	3B	HR	SA	SB
Career	2,215	8,759	2,927	.334	1,827	1,507	539	149	307	.535	87

Al Simmons joined the Indians in 1950 as a coach in Lou Boudreau's final season as manager and retired because of illness during spring training in 1951. As a left fielder for the Philadelphia Athletics, Chicago White Sox, Detroit, Washington, Boston Braves, Cincinnati, and Boston Red Sox for 20 seasons, Simmons compiled more hits than any other right-handed American League batter until Al Kaline. A deadly clutch hitter who was renowned for his "foot in the bucket" style, Simmons was the AL's Most Valuable Player in 1929 when he hit .365, batted .300 a total of 13 times, won the AL batting championship in 1930 (.381) and 1931 (.390), led the league with 157 RBIs in 1929, drove in 100 or more runs 12 times, and was a member of the All-Star team from 1933 to 1935. Simmons was a player-coach for the Athletics from 1940 to 1942, then a coach only with the A's from 1945 to 1949, before joining the Indians.

Warren Edward Spahn

Coach
Indians: 1972–73
Major leagues: 1942, 1946–65 (player), 1965, 1972–73 (coach)
Elected: 1973
Birthplace: Buffalo, New York
B: April 23, 1921
Bats left, throws left

	W	L	Pct.	ERA	G	CG	IP	H	BB	SO	ShO
Career	363	245	.597	3.09	750	382	5,243⅔	4,830	1,434	2,583	63

Warren Spahn never played for the Indians and, in fact, beat them to prolong the World Series in 1948, but tutored their pitchers in 1972 and 1973 under manager Ken Aspromonte. Spahn's outstanding career, during which he recorded the most victories, 363, of any left-handed pitcher in the history of baseball, was spent entirely in the National League. All but seven of the games he won were for the Boston-Milwaukee Braves, before winding up his career with the New York Mets and San Francisco Giants in 1965. Spahn pitched two no-hitters, and he won the Cy Young Award in 1957. He was a 20-game winner 13 times, six years in a row, and he led the NL in victories eight times and in complete games nine times.

Tristram E Speaker

Center fielder–manager
Indians: 1916–26
Major leagues: 1907–28 (player),
1919–26 (manager)
Elected: 1937
Birthplace: Hubbard, Texas
B: April 4, 1888
D: December 8, 1958
Batted left, threw left

	G	AB	H	BA	RBI	R	2B	3B	HR	SA	SB
Indians	1,519	5,546	1,965	.354	884	1,079	486	108	73	.520	153
Career	2,789	10,195	3,514	.345	1,529	1,882	792	222	117	.500	434

Perhaps the best center fielder to play the game, Tris Speaker also was a great hitter, as attested by his lifetime batting average of .345, which is fifth highest in baseball history. He was the Indians' player-manager in 1920 when they won the franchise's first American League pennant and World Series. The seventh player elected to the Hall of Fame, Speaker recorded more assists, 450, than any other outfielder; won the AL batting championship with a .386 average in 1916, his first season in Cleveland after breaking in with Boston in 1907; has a career total of 3,514 hits, fifth most of all time; is the leader with 792 doubles; is sixth with 222 triples; and is eighth with 1,882 runs. In 11 seasons with the Indians, Speaker's batting average of .354 is second only to Joe Jackson's (a .375 mark compiled from 1910 to 1915). His 1,965 hits for Cleveland are topped only by Napoleon Lajoie's 2,046.

William Louis Veeck Jr.

Owner
Indians: 1946–49
Major leagues: 1946–49, 1951–53,
1959–61, 1976–80
Elected: 1991
Birthplace: Chicago
B: February 9, 1914
D: January 2, 1986

Baseball's all-time most ingenious and aggressive promoter, Bill Veeck purchased the Indians in 1946 and built them into a pennant winner in 1948 when they set a season attendance record of 2,620,627. Veeck probably had more fun than anybody that year. He sold the franchise in 1949, bought the lowly and bedraggled St. Louis Browns in 1951, and in 1953 tried to move the team to Baltimore but was blocked by other American League owners. The experience convinced Veeck to sell, and the following season the Browns were allowed to become the Baltimore Orioles. In 1959, Veeck purchased the Chicago White Sox, building them into another championship team that season, when they also set a franchise attendance record. He sold the White Sox in 1961, wrote a couple of books, and operated Suffolk Downs race track, then bought the White Sox again in 1976, owning them through 1980.

James Hoyt Wilhelm

Pitcher
Indians: 1957–58
Major leagues: 1952–72
Elected: 1985
Birthplace: Huntersville,
North Carolina
B: July 26, 1923
Bats right, throws right

	W	L	Pct.	ERA	CG	IP	H	BB	SO	ShO
Indians	3	7	.300	2.49	1	94	72	36	57	0
Career	143	122	.540	2.52	20	2,254	1,757	778	1,610	5

Hoyt Wilhelm pitched only briefly for the Indians during his 21-year major league career, after being purchased from the St. Louis Cardinals on September 21, 1957. His departure—he was sold to Baltimore for the waiver price on August 23, 1958—obviously represents one of Frank Lane's worst deals. After leaving Cleveland, Wilhelm went on to record 97 of his 143 major league victories, pitching 14 more seasons for the Chicago White Sox, California, Atlanta, Chicago Cubs, and Los Angeles, in addition to Baltimore (and the New York Giants and Cardinals before the Indians). As the game's premier reliever of his era, Wilhelm was a knuckleball pitcher who, in one of his infrequent starts, pitched a no-hitter for the Orioles against the New York Yankees on September 20, 1958, less than a month after the Indians gave him up. Wilhelm appeared in 1,070 games, more than any other pitcher, and his 124 victories in relief also are the most in baseball history.

Early Wynn

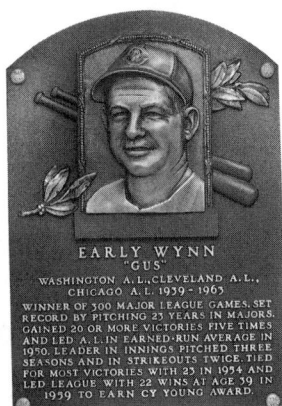

Pitcher
Indians: 1949–57, 1963
Major leagues: 1939, 1941–44, 1946–63
Elected: 1972
Birthplace: Hartford, Alabama
B: January 6, 1920
Bats both, throws right

	W	L	Pct.	ERA	G	CG	IP	H	BB	SO	ShO
Indians	164	102	.617	3.24	343	144	2,286⅔	2,037	877	1,277	24
Career	300	244	.551	3.54	691	290	4,564	4,291	1,755	2,334	49

Early Wynn was noted for his tenacity, which was a factor in his setting the American League record for pitching 23 seasons, as well as his ability to win 300 games, 164 of them for the Indians after he was acquired in one of the franchise's best trades. Bill Veeck got Wynn and Mickey Vernon from Washington in a deal for Joe Haynes, Ed Klieman, and Eddie Robinson. Wynn led the American League with 23 victories in 1954 when the Indians starting staff also included Bob Lemon, Mike Garcia, Art Houtteman, and Bob Feller. He also won 23 in 1952 and was a 20-game winner in 1951 and 1956. After joining the Chicago White Sox, Wynn won the AL Cy Young Award in 1959 when his record was 22–10 and they won the pennant. Wynn pitched for the White Sox for five seasons and rejoined the Indians in 1963, needing one more victory for a career total of 300. He got it, 7–4, against Kansas City on July 13.

Denton True Young

Pitcher
Spiders: 1890–98
Indians (Naps): 1909–11
Major leagues: 1890–1911
Elected: 1937
Birthplace: Gilmore, Ohio
B: March 29, 1867
D: November 4, 1955
Batted right, threw right

	W	L	Pct.	ERA	G	CG	IP	H	BB	SO	ShO
Indians	29	29	.500	2.50	63	48	504⅔	470	99	187	4
Career	511	316	.618	2.63	906	749	7,354⅔	7,092	1,219	2,800	76

Though he played only 11 seasons in baseball's modern era (since 1901), Cy Young was the game's most prolific winner with 511 victories. Young, who grew up on a farm in Tuscarawas County in southern Ohio, was the eighth player elected to the Hall of Fame (following Ty Cobb, Babe Ruth, Honus Wagner, Christy Mathewson, Walter Johnson, Napoleon Lajoie, and Tris Speaker). Young began his career in the midst of the 1890 season with the Cleveland Spiders of the National League, and in each of the next eight years he won 21 or more games, including 36 in 1892, 35 in 1895, and 34 in 1893. He was assigned in 1899 to the St. Louis Cardinals, jumped in 1901 to Boston of the new American League, and won 33 that season and 32 in 1902. Young was traded back to Cleveland, then the "Naps," in 1909. Though he won 19 games that season, he was only a shadow of his old self. He retired after being sold to the Boston Braves in 1911.

8

Great Moments

Despite their inability to win more than four pennants and two World Series, Cleveland teams have had many great moments, memorable games, and brilliant individual performances, perhaps the most thrilling of which was their victory in the playoff game for the American League championship in 1948.

The moments of high drama described in this chapter include, among others, perfect games by Addie Joss and Len Barker, two of only 13 in baseball since 1901; Cy Young's 500th and Early Wynn's 300th victories; Bob Feller's opening-day no-hitter in 1940, the only one in history; the game in which Feller set a major league strikeout record of 18 that stood for 31 years; the games in which Napoleon Lajoie and Tris Speaker got their 3,000th hits; the debuts of Larry Doby as the American League's first black player and Frank Robinson as baseball's first black manager; and, most recently, the first game played at Jacobs Field in 1994.

Gene Bearden's 1948 Victory over Boston— The Biggest in Cleveland Baseball History

It was the most important—crucial, significant, memorable, unforgettable, take your choice—game in Indians history.

Except to Gene Bearden.

"I had a job to do, and when Lou [manager Lou Boudreau] gave me the ball, I went out and did my best," Bearden said.

His best resulted in an 8–3 victory over the Boston Red Sox on October 4, 1948, in an unprecedented one-game playoff in Fenway Park that won the American League pennant for the Indians.

In fact, retrospectively in Bearden's mind, winning that key game wasn't even the biggest thrill of his seven-year major league career—though it certainly was the highlight of what is universally considered to have been the Indians' greatest season.

The Indians went on to beat the Boston Braves in six games in the World Series for their second world championship.

"Don't get me wrong," said Bearden, a 28-year-old rookie southpaw when, to the great surprise of everybody, he was handed the ball by Boudreau and then held the Red Sox to five hits in a ballpark that is supposed to be difficult for left-handers.

"I think of that game quite often, but I have wonderful memories of that entire season. It was great from beginning to end."

It certainly was for Bearden, who won 20 games while losing seven, then picked up another victory in the third game of the World Series and saved Bob Lemon's 4–3 triumph in the deciding sixth game.

But it was the playoff for the pennant that took precedence.

After a season-long battle with the Red Sox, Philadelphia Athletics, and New York Yankees, the Indians in the second-to-last game clinched at least a tie for the pennant as Bearden hurled his sixth shutout to beat Detroit, 8–0, on October 2.

They lost to the Tigers the next day, 7–1, while Boston was beating New York, 10–5, ending the race deadlocked with Cleveland, forcing the playoff, the first time it ever happened in American League history.

Because he'd been working with only two days rest—and also based on the fact that Fenway Park's short left-field wall makes it difficult for left-handers to pitch there—Bearden was not thought to be a candidate to start what had become the most important game of the season for the Indians.

Speculation was that Boudreau would give the ball to Lemon or even Bob Feller, who had pitched 2⅓ innings in the loss to the Tigers in the regular-season finale.

Boudreau's only comment when asked the night before the playoff game was "It could be anybody, but no one's going to know our pitcher until he walks out to take his warm-up pitches."

No one, that is, except those most directly involved—the Indians themselves.

"Lou asked me if I could do it, and I told him I'd try," said Bearden. "He said that was good enough for him, and told the rest of the guys that I would pitch, but he wanted to keep it a secret until just before the game.

"I wasn't nervous . . . there wasn't time to be nervous," Bearden answered the obvious question. "None of us had time to be nervous. After we lost to Detroit we had to jump on a train and go to Boston.

"Besides, how could we be nervous after going through a season like we did?"

Indeed, it had been a summer of crises, one after another, for the Indians as well as the other three teams that were in the thick of the race until the final three weeks.

In fact, on the morning of Labor Day, September 6, with only 23 games left to play, the Indians were in third place, 4½ lengths behind Boston and three in arrears of New York.

But they went on to win 18 while losing only five to dead-

Gene Bearden is carried off the field by his jubilant teammates after he beat the Red Sox, 8–3, in Boston in a one game playoff for the pennant on October 4, 1948.

377

lock the Red Sox, who had eliminated the Yankees by beating them on the second-to-last day of the season. Philadelphia finished fourth but was in the race until the first week of September.

"Nobody was what you'd call tight," continued Bearden. "Maybe, because we were tired, we just went out and played. We knew it was win another game or go home.

"Heck, Boudreau put Allie Clark [an outfielder] on first base because he wanted his right-handed bat in the lineup, even though Clark had never ever played a game at first base.

"One thing I'll never forget is Clark saying to me before the game, 'Don't you dare throw over here and try to pick anybody off. Remember, I never played here before.'"

The Red Sox sprung a surprise starter, too, veteran right-hander Denny Galehouse, whose record was 8–8, fifth best on the staff.

Manager Joe McCarthy chose Galehouse over Mel Parnell (15–8) and Ellis Kinder (10–7), either of whom was expected to get the assignment, because Galehouse had pitched well in relief against the Indians a couple of weeks earlier.

The Indians got a run in the first inning when Boudreau hit a solo homer, but the Red Sox got it back in their first opportunity when Johnny Pesky doubled with one out and scored on a two-out single by Vernon Stephens.

The score remained tied until the fourth when Boudreau again ignited an uprising with a leadoff single, Joe Gordon followed with another single and, as Bearden picked up the story, "Benny hit one into the screen [atop Fenway Park's left-field wall], and I knew we would win . . . it gave everybody a lift," he said.

"Benny," Bearden explained, "was my roommate Kenny Keltner. I always called him Benny the Beltner."

Keltner's homer knocked Galehouse out of the game, and his successor, Kinder, was greeted by Larry Doby's double that caromed two feet off the top of the wall—a.k.a. the

Indians owner Bill Veeck (left) confers with Manager Lou Boudreau prior to the pennant playoff game against the Red Sox in Boston on October 4, 1948.

"Green Monster"—in left-center field. He was sacrificed to third and scored on an infield grounder for a 5–1 lead.

Boudreau hit another home run, his second of the game and 18th of the season, with the bases bare and two out in the fifth to put the Indians ahead, 6–1.

The Red Sox retaliated with two runs in the sixth after an error by Gordon and Bobby Doerr's two-out homer, but the Indians got one of them back in the eighth, and the other in the ninth (on Boudreau's fourth hit of the game).

It was more than enough for Bearden, who allowed only a single by Ted Williams through the final three innings and completed a five-hitter for the victory and the pennant, only the second in franchise history.

Gene Bearden (center) celebrates with teammates Bob Lemon (left) and Jim Hegan after Bearden's relief pitching saved Lemon's 4–3 victory in the sixth game of the 1948 World Series, clinching the world championship for the Indians.

Still shunning the spotlight, Bearden said, "There were a lot of guys who did a lot of good things in that game; give everybody credit, especially Lou."

"Lou," of course, was Boudreau. "He was a great player, and, in my book, he also was a great manager. He was always thinking a couple of innings ahead of everybody else," said Bearden. "I liked playing with him and for him."

As for Bearden's biggest thrill in baseball, if it wasn't winning that historic playoff game, "It was putting on a big league uniform and pitching my first game," he said.

"I'll never forget it. It was in Washington, in old Griffith Stadium, in 1948. The date was May 8. You work all your life to get there, and there I was, in the big leagues. I pitched against Sid Hudson, and we won, 6–1. Larry Doby hit a home run that must have traveled 550 feet, clear out of the park. I doubt that anybody ever hit a ball harder or farther."

It's also doubtful that anybody ever pitched a game with more meaning or under greater pressure than Bearden did on October 4, 1948.

Certainly, it was the most important—crucial, significant, memorable, unforgettable, take your choice—game in Indians history.

October 4, 1948

Indians	AB	R	H	RBI
Mitchell, lf	5	0	1	0
Clark, 1b	2	0	0	0
Robinson, 1b	2	1	1	0
Boudreau, ss	4	3	4	2
Gordon, 2b	4	1	1	0
Keltner, 3b	5	1	3	3
Doby, cf	5	1	2	0
Kennedy, rf	2	0	0	0
Hegan, c	3	1	0	1
Bearden, p	3	0	1	0
Totals	**35**	**8**	**13**	**6**

Boston	AB	R	H	RBI
DiMaggio, cf	4	0	0	0
Pesky, 3b	4	1	1	0
Williams, lf	4	1	1	0
Stephens, ss	4	0	1	1
Doerr, 2b	4	1	1	2
Spence, rf	1	0	0	0
Goodman, 1b	3	0	0	0
Tebbetts, c	4	0	1	0
Galehouse, p	0	0	0	0
Kinder, p	2	0	0	0
a-Hitchcock, ph	0	0	0	0
b-Wright, pr	0	0	0	0
Totals	**30**	**3**	**5**	**3**

Indians	1	0	0	4	1	0	0	1	1—8
Boston	1	0	0	0	0	2	0	0	0—3

a-Walked for Spence in ninth
b-Ran for Hitchcock in ninth

Errors: Gordon, Williams; Two-base hits: Pesky, Doby 2, Keltner; Home runs: Doerr, Boudreau 2, Keltner; Sacrifices: Kennedy 2, Robinson; Double plays: Hegan and Boudreau; Gordon, Boudreau, and Robinson; Bearden, Gordon, and Robinson; Stephens, Doerr, and Goodman 2; Left on base: Cleveland 7, Boston 5; Bases on balls: Galehouse 1, Kinder 3, Bearden 5; Strikeouts: Galehouse 1, Kinder 2, Bearden 6; Hits off Galehouse, 5 in 3 innings (none out in fourth); Wild pitches: Kinder 1; Losing pitcher: Galehouse; Time: 2:24; Attendance: 33,957; Umpires: McGowan, Summers, Rommel, Berry.

Addie Joss's Perfect Game against Chicago in 1908

It was called "the most remarkable game of ball ever witnessed in Cleveland" when, on October 2, 1908, Addie Joss of the Naps hurled a perfect game, and his opponent, Big Ed Walsh of Chicago, allowed only four hits and struck out 15.

Cleveland beat the White Sox, 1–0. It kept the Naps in second place, a half game behind Detroit, preserving their pennant hopes with four games remaining.

Joss had to be perfect to win the game and raise his record to 24–11 as Walsh, with the exception of the third inning, was nearly flawless himself.

The Naps registered the game's only run on a wild pitch by Walsh that allowed Joe Birmingham to score after he'd led off the inning with a single.

When Walsh tried to pick him off first, Birmingham raced to second and was safe when he was hit in the head by first baseman Frank Isbell's throw; he took third when the ball caromed into right-center field.

Birmingham held third as George Perring grounded out and Joss struck out. But with two strikes on Wilbur Good, Walsh crossed up catcher Ossie Schreckengost and flung a wild pitch, enabling Birmingham to score.

Otherwise, Walsh was never in trouble. He struck out one batter in the first inning, and two or more in six of the subsequent seven innings, including Good four times and player-manager Napoleon Lajoie twice.

Birmingham singled again in the eighth inning, and the other two Cleveland hits were made by Lajoie in the fourth inning and Perring in the eighth.

While Joss was in command all the way, he required an outstanding play by first baseman George Stovall and the benefit of a controversial call by umpire Silk O'Loughlin to preserve the perfect game.

After Joss retired the first two of three pinch hitters in the ninth, "Honest John" Anderson batted for Walsh and lined a drive to left field that landed foul by inches. Then, with two strikes on him, Anderson scorched a grounder to third baseman Bill Bradley.

Bradley fielded the ball behind third base—it was his first chance of the game—and threw low to Stovall at first. The ball bounced in the dirt but was scooped up by Stovall, and O'Loughlin called Anderson out amid howls of protest by the White Sox.

They charged that, first, Anderson had beaten the throw and, second, that Stovall juggled the ball after he dug it out of the dirt, but to no avail. O'Loughlin's decision stood—and so did Joss's perfect game, the second in the eight-year history of the American League.

However, while the Naps' victory kept their pennant hopes alive, they failed to overtake Detroit. The Tigers prevailed by half a game because they were not required to make up a game that had been rained out.

October 2, 1908

Chicago	AB	R	H	RBI
Hahn, rf	3	0	0	0
Jones, cf	3	0	0	0
Isbell, 1b	3	0	0	0
Dougherty, lf	3	0	0	0
Davis, 2b	3	0	0	0
Parent, ss	3	0	0	0
Schreckengost, c	2	0	0	0
Shaw, c	0	0	0	0
a-White, ph	1	0	0	0
Tannehill, 3b	2	0	0	0
b-Donahue, ph	1	0	0	0
Walsh, p	2	0	0	0
c-Anderson, ph	1	0	0	0
Totals	**27**	**0**	**0**	**0**

Naps	AB	R	H	RBI
Good, rf	4	0	0	0
Bradley, 3b	4	0	0	0
Hinchman, lf	3	0	0	0
Lajoie, 2b	3	0	1	0
Stovall, 1b	3	0	0	0
Clarke, c	3	0	0	0
Birmingham, rf	3	1	2	0
Perring, ss	2	0	1	0
Joss, p	3	0	0	0
Totals	**28**	**1**	**4**	**0**

Chicago	0	0	0	0	0	0	0	0	0—0
Cleveland	0	0	1	0	0	0	0	0	x—1

a-Grounded out for Shaw in ninth
b-Struck out for Tannehill in ninth
c-Grounded out for Walsh in ninth

Errors: Isbell; Stolen bases: Birmingham 2, Lajoie, Perring; Left on base: Cleveland 4; Bases on balls: Walsh 1; Strikeouts: by Walsh 15, by Joss 3; Wild pitch: by Walsh 1; Umpires: Connolly, O'Loughlin; Time: 1:40; Attendance: 10,598.

Len Barker's Perfect Game against Toronto in 1981

Len Barker said he knew right away that it would be a special night for him and the Indians.

The date was May 15, 1981, in Cleveland's Municipal Stadium, and the 6-4, 215-pound right-hander nicknamed "Large Lenny" was seeking only his third victory and attempting to keep the Indians in first place against Toronto.

"I knew that I had good stuff, maybe awesome stuff, but I didn't start thinking about it until the last inning," Barker said in the wake of his perfect game against the Blue Jays, giving the Indians a 16-8 record and a one-game lead over Baltimore.

"I was so confident, it was weird. Even though it was a tight game, it felt so easy."

It was the first perfect game in the Stadium, the second by an Indians pitcher, and only the eighth in modern baseball history (since 1901) and 10th of all-time (since 1880).

"I've always had a good curveball, but tonight it was the best I ever had. My control was excellent, too. I had total command. I could throw anything, anywhere I wanted," added Barker, whose fastball was clocked at 96 miles per hour.

"Wherever [catcher] Ron Hassey put his glove, I could hit it. He called a great game. Everybody was great."

Barker was right about that, although he didn't require any exceptional plays to retire every one of the 27 Blue Jays he faced on a misty and cold—48 degrees Fahrenheit—night in front of a slim turnout of 7,290 fans.

Hassey concurred with his battery mate. "Lenny always has a good curve, but tonight it was something special," said the catcher (who, 10 years later, was behind the plate for Dennis Martinez when he pitched baseball's 11th perfect game (since 1901) for Montreal on July 28, 1991, beating Los Angeles, 2–0).

Though he had no strikeouts through the first three innings, the 25-year-old Barker fanned 11 from the fourth through the ninth.

Only two Blue Jays connected squarely with the ball—Damaso Garcia lashed a line drive into the left-center field alley that Rick Manning caught to end the second inning, and Rick Bosetti led off the sixth with a sizzling one-hopper to Duane Kuiper, who backhanded the ball behind second base and threw to Mike Hargrove for the out.

The only other difficult defensive plays were made by third baseman Toby Harrah in the fifth inning and by Kuiper in the seventh. Willie Upshaw hit a twisting pop foul near the

Len Barker drinks champagne after pitching a perfect game, only the eighth in modern major league baseball history, beating the Toronto Blue Jays, 3–0, on May 15, 1981.

third base dugout that Harrah dived into the stands to catch. A slow bounder by Alfredo Griffin was fielded by Kuiper, whose throw to first was barely in time.

With the fans on their feet in the ninth, Barker disposed of the Blue Jays routinely. Bosetti popped to Harrah, Al Woods batted for Danny Ainge and struck out on three pitches, and Ernie Whitt, pinch-hitting for Buck Martinez, went to a 1-and-2 count and lofted an easy fly to Manning.

All 11 of Barker's strikeouts were swinging. There were four ground outs to second, three to shortstop; four fly outs to center, one to left; two pop-fly outs to third, one to second, and one to first.

Barker needed to be very good to win the game as the Indians did not provide him with much offensive support against Luis Leal.

Their first two runs came in the first inning after Manning opened with a single, went to third when John Mayberry committed an error on Hargrove's one-out grounder, and scored on Andre Thornton's sacrifice fly, then Hargrove came home on a single by Hassey. Jorge Orta solo homered in the eighth.

May 15, 1981

Toronto	AB	R	H	RBI
Griffin, ss	3	0	0	0
Moseby, rf	3	0	0	0
Bell, lf	3	0	0	0
Mayberry, 1b	3	0	0	0
Upshaw, dh	3	0	0	0
Garcia, 2b	3	0	0	0
Bosetti, cf	3	0	0	0
Ainge, 3b	2	0	0	0
a-Woods, ph	1	0	0	0
B. Martinez, c	2	0	0	0
b-Whitt, ph	1	0	0	0
Totals	27	0	0	0

Indians	AB	R	H	RBI
Manning, cf	4	1	1	0
Orta, rf	4	1	3	1
Hargrove, 1b	4	1	1	0
Thornton, dh	3	0	0	1
Hassey, c	4	0	1	1
Harrah, 3b	4	0	1	0
Charboneau, lf	3	0	0	0
Kuiper, 2b	3	0	0	0
Veryzer, ss	3	0	0	0
Totals	32	3	7	3

Toronto	0	0	0	0	0	0	0	0	0—0
Cleveland	2	0	0	0	0	0	0	1	x—3

a-Struck out for Ainge in ninth
b-Flied out for Martinez in ninth

Errors: Mayberry, Garcia, Griffin; Left on base: Cleveland 6. Home run: Orta; SF: Thornton.

Toronto	IP	H	R	ER	BB	SO
Leal (L)	8	7	3	1	0	5

Indians	IP	H	R	ER	BB	SO
Barker (W)	9	0	0	0	0	11

Time: 2:09; Attendance: 7,290; Umpires: Garcia, Kosc, Denkinger, McKean.

Bob Feller's Opening-Day No-Hitter against Chicago in 1940

There's always something special about opening day, but the Indians' first game on April 16, 1940, at Comiskey Park in Chicago was extra special, especially to their ace pitcher Bob Feller.

Feller hurled and won the only opening-day no-hitter in baseball history, beating the White Sox, 1–0, in front of 14,000 spectators on a windy and cold day against a pitcher, Edgar Smith, who was almost as good. Smith allowed only six hits in eight innings, and struck out five.

A nine-inning opening-day no-hitter was pitched in the National League on April 15, 1909, by Red Ames of the New York Giants against Brooklyn, but he yielded a hit in the 10th inning and lost, 3–0, in the 13th.

Feller had trouble getting loose in the 47-degree temperature, walking three while striking out five White Sox batters in the first two innings, which consumed 48 minutes.

Chicago threatened in the second when Taft Wright reached with one out when his fly ball to center was misjudged, misplayed, and then dropped by Roy Weatherly for a two-base error. Feller struck out Eric McNair, but walked the next two, Mike Tresh and Smith, loading the bases.

With his parents and sister in the stands, Feller struck out rookie Bob Kennedy to end the threat and the inning.

Thereafter Feller relied solely on his fastball and, thanks to several good defensive plays behind him, stopped the White Sox cold, though he walked two more batters, including Luke Appling with two out in the last of the ninth.

The base on balls brought Wright to the plate, and he smashed a hot grounder toward right field. Second baseman Ray Mack dashed to his left, knocked down the ball, and, while on his knees, threw to first baseman Hal Trosky to nip the runner by half a step.

Feller, who had pitched three one-hitters earlier in his career, got the only run he needed in the fourth inning, which began with Trosky being retired on a drive to right field that Wright caught against the fence.

Jeff Heath singled and, after Ken Keltner was retired, Rollie Hemsley slashed a liner to right. The drive sliced away from Wright for a triple, scoring Heath with the game's only run.

In addition to his fielding gem for the final out, Mack had also made an outstanding play an inning earlier when he charged a slow roller by Larry Rosenthal and made a quick throw to Trosky for the putout.

"I had some pretty fancy support out there," Feller acknowledged after the game. "Ben Chapman saved my bacon twice, and Kenny [Keltner] and Ray [Mack] each made a couple of swell plays. Sure, I had pretty good stuff, but I was lucky, too.

"I knew I had a chance for a no-hitter in the ninth, but I tried to put the thought out of my mind by reminding myself you never have a no-hitter until the last man is out. I wasn't sure I had it until Ray made that last play. It was the hardest ball hit off me all day. It really was tagged."

Two other defensive gems were turned in by Chapman and one by Keltner.

In the third inning Appling sent a hard shot that Chapman caught in short right, and Chapman made a similar catch of Wright's sinking liner in the fourth. And Keltner made a bare-handed grab and good throw to Trosky on a slow grounder by Bob Kennedy in the sixth.

April 16, 1940

Indians	AB	R	H	RBI
Boudreau, ss	3	0	0	0
Weatherly, cf	4	0	1	0
Chapman, rf	3	0	0	0
Trosky, 1b	4	0	0	0
Heath, lf	4	1	1	0
Keltner, 3b	4	0	1	0
Hemsley, c	4	0	2	1
Mack, 2b	4	0	1	0
Feller, p	3	0	0	0
Totals	**33**	**1**	**6**	**1**

Chicago	AB	R	H	RBI
Kennedy, 3b	4	0	0	0
Kuhel, 1b	3	0	0	0
Kreevich, cf	3	0	0	0
Solters, lf	4	0	0	0
Appling, ss	3	0	0	0
Wright, rf	4	0	0	0
McNair, 2b	3	0	0	0
Tresh, c	2	0	0	0
Smith, p	1	0	0	0
a-Rosenthal, ph	1	0	0	0
Brown, p	0	0	0	0
Totals	**28**	**0**	**0**	**0**

Cleveland	0	0	0	1	0	0	0	0	0—1
Chicago	0	0	0	0	0	0	0	0	0—0

a-Grounded out for Smith in eighth

Errors: Weatherly, McNair; Two-base hits: Mack; Three-base hits: Hemsley; Stolen bases: Kuhel; Double plays: Kuhel unassisted; Left on base: Cleveland 7, Chicago 6; Bases on balls: Feller 5, Smith 2; Strikeouts: Feller 8, Smith 5; Hits off Smith 6 in 8, Brown 0 in 1; Umpires: Geisel, McGowan, Kolls; Time: 2:24; Attendance: 14,000.

Bill Wambsganss' Unassisted Triple Play in the 1920 World Series

There had never been anything like it in any previous World Series game, and there hasn't been anything like it since.

It was Game 5, played at League Park on October 10, 1920, won by the Indians, 8–1, over the Brooklyn Dodgers. It gave the Indians a 3–2 lead, and they went on to capture the next two games and the world championship in what was then a best-of-nine series.

Dodgers manager Wilbert Robinson said, "I have been in baseball 40 years, and I never saw one like this."

Not only did Wambsganss pull off the only unassisted triple play ever made in a World Series game, but two of his teammates also made history.

Right fielder Elmer Smith hit the first grand slam home run in a World Series game, and Jim Bagby, Sr., smashed the first home run hit by a pitcher.

Wambsganss, whose name was shortened to "Wamby" by a printer setting type for the box scores of Indians games, didn't think his unassisted triple play was such a great achievement until later. Obviously, neither did the sportswriters who covered the game.

"I just happened to be in the right place at the right time," Wambsganss often said.

After the game he was interviewed by exactly one reporter. "A guy from Brooklyn talked to me," recalled Wambsganss.

"He asked me how it felt to make an unassisted triple play. I told him it was the chance of a lifetime, which it was."

It happened in the fifth inning with the Indians ahead, 7–0. The Dodgers had Pete Kilduff on second and Otto Miller on first with Clarence Mitchell at the plate. A pitcher, Mitchell was a left-handed batter who also filled in at first base and the outfield. He had a 6-for-18 record as a pinch hitter that season.

Mitchell cracked Bagby's pitch on a line toward right-center. Wambsganss turned to his right and reached up for the ball with a backhand grab for one out. He continued to second base where he easily doubled Kilduff off the bag for the second out. Then, turning to throw to first, Wambsganss was confronted by Miller, who was frozen on the base path, several feet from second, where he was easily tagged for the third out.

The crowd of 26,884 was momentarily silent, not immediately realizing what had transpired. Then the fans broke into thunderous applause for Wambsganss.

As a footnote to Wambsganss' sensational play, Mitchell, in his very next at bat, grounded into a double play, making him responsible for five outs in two trips to the plate.

Wambsganss also played a role in the drama that produced Smith's grand slam. It began in the first inning when the Indians' leadoff batter, Charlie Jamieson, singled off future Hall of Fame spitball pitcher Burleigh Grimes. Wambs-

Indians second baseman Bill Wambsganss (left) and the three victims of his unassisted triple play on October 10, 1920, the only one in World Series history. Beside Wambsganss are (left to right) Pete Kilduff, Otto Miller, and Clarence Mitchell.

ganss followed with another single, and Tris Speaker, attempting to lay down a sacrifice bunt, reached when Grimes fell down fielding the ball, loading the bases.

Smith, a .316 batter who'd hit 12 home runs in 1920, swung at Grimes' 1-and-2 pitch and drove the ball over the temporary bleachers in right field and the screen atop the wall, giving the Indians a 4–0 lead.

The Indians increased their margin to 7–0 in the fourth after Doc Johnston singled and took second on a passed ball, and Steve O'Neill was intentionally walked. Bagby, a 31-game winner (with 12 losses) in 1920—who hit only two homers in his entire nine-year regular-season major league career—drove a Grimes pitch into the temporary bleachers in right-center field.

Little wonder that Robinson said he'd never seen anything like what happened that day. Nobody had.

October 10, 1920

Brooklyn	AB	R	H	RBI
Olson, ss	4	0	2	0
Sheehan, 3b	3	0	1	0
Griffith, rf	4	0	0	0
Wheat, lf	4	1	2	0
Myers, cf	4	0	2	0
Konetchy, 1b	4	0	2	1
Kilduff, 2b	4	0	1	0
Miller, c	2	0	2	0
Krueger, c	2	0	1	0
Grimes, p	1	0	0	0
Mitchell, p	2	0	0	0
Totals	**34**	**1**	**13**	**1**

Indians	AB	R	H	RBI
Jamieson, lf	4	1	2	0
a-Graney, lf	1	0	0	0
Wambsganss, 2b	5	1	1	0
Speaker, cf	3	2	1	0
Smith, rf	4	1	3	4
Gardner, 3b	4	0	1	1
Johnston, 1b	3	1	2	0
Sewell, ss	3	0	0	0
O'Neill, c	2	1	0	0
Thomas, c	0	0	0	0
Bagby, p	4	1	2	3
Totals	**33**	**8**	**12**	**8**

Brooklyn	0	0	0	0	0	0	0	0	1—1
Cleveland	4	0	0	3	1	0	0	0	x—8

a-Struck out for Jamieson in eighth

Errors: Sheehan, Gardner, O'Neill; Three-base hits: Konetchy, Smith; HR: Bagby, Smith; Sacrifices: Sheehan, Johnston; Double plays: Olson, Kilduff, and Konetchy; Jamieson and O'Neill, Gardner, Wambsganss, and Johnston; Johnston, Sewell, and Johnston; Triple play: Wambsganss (unassisted); Left on base: Brooklyn 7, Indians 6; Bases on balls: Grimes 1, Mitchell 3; Strikeouts: Mitchell 1, Bagby 3; Hits: off Grimes 9 in 3⅓ innings, off Mitchell 3 in 4⅔ innings; Wild pitch: Bagby; Passed ball: Miller; Losing pitcher: Grimes; Umpires: Klem, Connolly, O'Day, Dineen. Time: 1:49; Attendance: 26,884.

Frank Robinson's 1975 Debut as Baseball's First Black Manager

The morning of Frank Robinson's first game as player-manager of the Indians and major league baseball's first black manager, general manager Phil Seghi made a suggestion.

"Hey, slugger," Seghi said to Robinson, "why don't you hit a homer the first time you go to the plate?"

Afterward Seghi said, "I never dared dream he'd do it, though I should have. Knowing Frank Robinson, I shouldn't be surprised by anything about the man's ability to rise to the occasion. Frank Robinson doing the unusual is only usual for him."

Which it was on April 8, 1975, in front of 56,715 fans in Cleveland's Municipal Stadium.

As the Indians' second batter in the first inning, Robinson went to the plate against New York Yankees right-hander George "Doc" Medich and did, indeed, hit a home run, establishing Seghi as something of a prophet.

It was the 575th homer of Robinson's Hall of Fame career, led the Indians to a 5–3 victory, and will forever rank as one of the most dramatic moments in baseball history.

Later Seghi was right again when he said, "It was the kind of a day, the kind of a game you only dream about, like Alice in Wonderland."

For the record, Robinson delivered with the count 2-and-2, on the eighth pitch by Medich. The first two were quick strikes. Robinson fouled off the next two, two more were wide of the plate, then another foul, and finally the home run that arched high and deep into the left-field stands.

"Any home run is a thrill, but I've got to say this one was a bigger thrill," confessed Robinson. It also was "the single most satisfying thing that happened, other than winning," he said in the wake of the victory.

"Right now I feel better than I have after anything I've done in baseball. Take all the pennants, the personal awards, the World Series, the All-Star games, and this moment is the greatest."

One of the first to congratulate Robinson after his trip around the bases was Gaylord Perry, who had feuded with Robinson ever since he'd joined the team as a player seven months earlier.

And after the game Robinson was the first to congratulate Perry, who survived a second-inning, three-run uprising by the Yankees to gain credit for the victory.

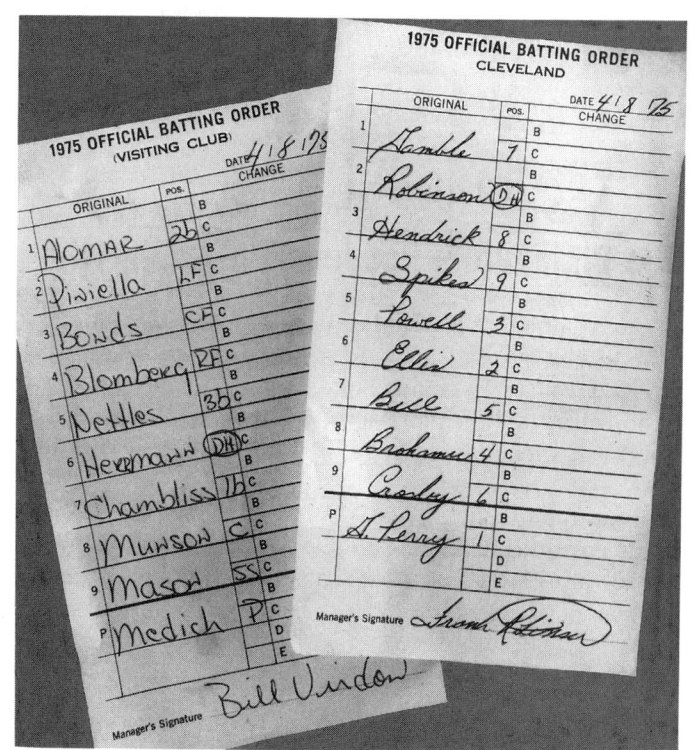

The first lineup card filled out by Frank Robinson for the Indians 1975 opening day game against the New York Yankees in the Cleveland Stadium. Robinson smashed a home run in his first at-bat in the first inning, and the Indians won the game, 5–3.

Indians General Manager Phil Seghi (left) introduces Frank Robinson as major league baseball's first black manager on October 3, 1974.

The Indians cut their deficit to 3–2 in their half of the second on singles by Boog Powell and John Ellis, and Jack Brohamer's sacrifice fly, and tied the score in the fourth on Powell's solo homer.

A walk and Powell's double provided the Indians' go-ahead run, and then Powell scored on Brohamer's single for an insurance run in the sixth.

April 8, 1975

New York	AB	R	H	RBI
Alomar, 2b	2	0	0	0
a-A. Johnson, ph	1	0	0	0
Stanley, 2b	0	0	0	0
Piniella, lf	4	0	0	0
Bonds, cf	4	0	0	0
Blomberg, rf	4	1	2	0
Nettles, 3b	4	1	1	0
Herrmann, dh	4	0	1	0
1-White, pr	0	0	0	0
Chambliss, 1b	4	1	3	2
Munson, c	4	0	2	1
Mason, ss	3	0	0	0
Medich, p	0	0	0	0
May, p	0	0	0	0
Lyle, p	0	0	0	0
Totals	34	3	9	3

Indians	AB	R	H	RBI
Gamble, lf	5	0	1	0
Robinson, dh	3	1	1	1
Hendrick, cf	3	1	0	0
Spikes, rf	4	0	0	0
Powell, 1b	3	3	3	2
Ellis, c	3	0	2	0
Bell, 3b	4	0	0	0
Brohamer, 2b	3	0	2	2
Crosby, ss	4	0	1	0
Perry, p	0	0	0	0
Totals	32	5	10	5

New York	0	3	0	0	0	0	0	0	0—3
Cleveland	1	1	0	1	0	2	0	0	x—5

a-Struck out for Alomar in seventh
1-Ran for Herrman in ninth

Errors: Lyle; Two-base hits: Chambliss, Powell; Home runs: Robinson, Powell; Stolen base: Hendrick; SF: Brohamer; Left on base: New York 5, Cleveland 8; DP: Cleveland 1.

New York	IP	H	R	ER	BB	SO
Medich, L	6	8	5	5	2	2
May	1	0	0	0	1	1
Lyle	1	2	0	0	1	0

Cleveland	IP	H	R	ER	BB	SO
Perry, W	9	9	3	3	1	4

PB: Munson. Time: 2:43. Attendance: 56,715. Umpires: Chylak, McCoy, Brinkman, Cooney.

Joe DiMaggio's Record 56-Game Hitting Streak Stopped in 1941

It was a game that Joe DiMaggio can't forget, and one that the 67,468 fans in Cleveland's Municipal Stadium on July 17, 1941, will always remember.

So will Al Smith, Jim Bagby, Jr., Ken Keltner, and Lou Boudreau, even though the Indians lost to the New York Yankees, 4–3.

It was the first time since May 15 that DiMaggio failed to get at least one hit, after he doubled and singled twice in four at bats off Al Milnar and Joe Krakauskas the previous day at League Park, extending his consecutive-game hitting streak to a record 56.

Fifteen days earlier, on July 2, DiMaggio had broken the major league record of 44 consecutive games logged by "Wee Willie" Keeler in the National League in 1897. He had also eclipsed George Sisler's American League record of 41 set in 1922.

Smith and Bagby were the Indians pitchers who were credited with retiring DiMaggio three times (he also walked once),

Keltner made two outstanding plays to rob the famed "Yankee Clipper" of hits in the first and seventh innings, and Boudreau turned DiMaggio's eighth-inning, bad-hop grounder into a double play.

DiMaggio handled it with class. "I'm not happy that I failed to get a hit," he said after the game, "but I guess it's accurate to say I am relieved. Although I haven't been under much strain since I broke [Keeler's] record, there always was a little pressure in every game until I got a hit."

He also had praise for Keltner. "Smith pitched a good game, but he didn't break my streak. And neither did Bagby. The guy who turned the trick was Keltner. He was a little rough on me," said DiMaggio.

"Keltner was playing so damned deep that he was almost on the outfield grass, and he couldn't have been more than three feet off the line," observed Yankees first baseman Johnny Sturm. "He could play that way because he has a real good arm, and he knew Joe would not bunt.

"The first ball Joe hit would normally go for a stand-up double. But Keltner made a good stab and threw Joe out by half a step, and the second was almost a carbon copy of the first."

Later, DiMaggio offered another theory. "It's true, Keltner played me halfway out to left field and right on the line, but you've got to take into account the fact that it had rained the night before," he said. "I believe I would have beaten out both of those grounders to Keltner if the ground had not been so wet and slow."

As for Boudreau's play on DiMaggio with the bases loaded and one out in the eighth, Indians coach Dutch Zwilling said, "Not another shortstop in baseball would have correctly judged that false hop. I've been in the game for 33 years and spent most of my spare time singing the praise of Honus Wagner, but Boudreau has him topped."

Ironically, except for a baserunning blunder by the Indians' Larry Rosenthal, DiMaggio might have gotten one more chance to keep the streak alive in extra innings.

With the Indians trailing, 4–1, in the bottom of the ninth, Gee Walker, who had legged out an inside-the-park home run in the fourth inning, led off with a single, and Oscar Grimes followed with another, chasing Lefty Gomez in favor of Johnny Murphy, the Yankees' ace reliever.

Rosenthal greeted Murphy with a triple to right center, narrowing the Indians' deficit to one run. Hal Trosky, another pinch hitter, followed with a grounder to Sturm at first base. Rosenthal could have gone home and tied the score, but didn't, holding third as Sturm fielded the ball and stepped on first to retire Trosky.

Then Clarence "Soup" Campbell, batting for Rollie Hemsley, slapped a ball back at Murphy; this time, Rosenthal tried to score but was an easy out at the plate.

The game ended—instead of being tied and going into extra innings, which would have given DiMaggio another time at bat—when the next batter, Roy Weatherly, grounded out.

July 17, 1941

New York	AB	R	H	RBI
Sturm, 1b	4	0	1	0
Rolfe, 3b	4	1	2	1
Henrich, rf	3	0	1	1
DiMaggio, cf	3	0	0	0
Gordon, 2b	4	1	2	1
Rosar, c	4	0	0	0
Keller, lf	3	1	1	0
Rizzuto, ss	4	0	0	0
Gomez, p	4	1	1	1
Murphy, p	0	0	0	0
Totals	33	4	8	4

Indians	AB	R	H	RBI
Weatherly, cf	5	0	1	0
Keltner, 3b	3	0	1	0
Boudreau, ss	3	0	0	0
Heath, rf	4	0	0	0
Walker, lf	3	2	2	1
Grimes, 1b	3	1	1	0
Mack, 2b	3	0	0	0
a-Rosenthal, ph	1	0	1	2
Hemsley, c	3	0	1	0
b-Trosky, ph	1	0	0	0
Smith, p	3	0	0	0
Bagby, p	0	0	0	0
c-Campbell, ph	1	0	0	0
Totals	33	3	7	3

New York	1	0	0	0	0	0	1	2	0—4	
Indians	0	0	0	1	0	0	0	0	2—3	

a-Tripled for Mack in ninth
b-Grounded out for Hemsley in ninth
c-Grounded out for Bagby in ninth

Two-base hits: Henrich, Rolfe; Three-base hits: Keller, Rosenthal; Home runs: Walker, Gordon; Double play: Boudreau, Mack, and Grimes; SH: Boudreau; LOB: New York 5, Cleveland 7; Bases on balls: Smith 2, Bagby 1, Gomez 3; Strikeouts Gomez 5, Smith 4, Bagby 1; Hits off Smith 7 in 7⅓ innings, off Gomez 6 in 8 innings (none out in ninth). PB: Hemsley; Winning pitcher: Gomez; Losing pitcher: Smith; T: 2:05; A: 67,468; Umpires: Summers, Rue, Stewart.

Cy Young's 500th Career Pitching Victory against Washington in 1910

He was near the end of his career, and nobody knew it better than Cy Young in 1910.

But the venerable pitcher, then 43 years old, still was good enough to pitch 11 strong innings and record his 500th victory on July 19, in the second game of a doubleheader in Washington.

Young, whose career began in 1890 with the Cleveland Spiders in the National League, beat the Senators, 5–2, in front of what was reported as a "capacity crowd" in Griffith Stadium (which was later reported by *Sporting Life* to have been 7,380).

It was the 21st season of a 22-year career for Young, who pitched for the Spiders from 1890 to 1898, the St. Louis Cardinals in 1899 and 1900, and the Boston Red Sox from 1901 to 1908.

He was returned to Cleveland on February 18, 1909, in a trade for pitchers Charlie Chech and Jack Ryan, and $12,500. Young went 19–15 with a 2.26 earned run average for the Naps in 1909, but it was his last winning record.

Still, there is no doubt that Young will forever remain the winningest pitcher in the history of baseball.

It took two big rallies by the Naps for Young to win that 500th game in 1910.

They'd lost the opener, 7–0, and were trailing, 1–0, against Washington's Doc Reisling going into the ninth inning of the nightcap. Jack Graney led off with a walk, and Terry Turner bunted and was safe on a fielder's choice.

Player-manager Napoleon Lajoie also bunted and was safe when first baseman John Henry fielded the ball but nobody covered first base.

The tying run scored as Ted Easterly hit a long fly to center, and the Naps went ahead, 2–1, when George Stovall lofted another fly to deep right.

The Senators tied the game again in their half of the ninth when Clyde Milan walked and scored on successive singles by Jack Lelivelt and Wid Conroy before Young retired the side.

Both teams were blanked in the 10th, but the Naps got to reliever Bob Groom in the 11th. Harry Niles and Graney led off with walks, Turner beat out an infield hit, and Easterly also walked, forcing in a tie-breaking run. When Stovall singled to left, two more runs scampered across the plate.

Young faltered momentarily in the bottom of the 11th as Milan singled to start the inning. But the next three batters were retired, and Young had his 500th victory.

He won four more games that season for a 7–10 record—only the first time since his first season in 1890 that he failed to win in double figures.

And in 1911, after seven games and a 3–4 record in July, Young was sold to the Braves, for whom he finished his career with four victories and five losses in 10 appearances.

July 19, 1910

Naps	AB	R	H	RBI
Niles, rf	4	1	0	0
Graney, lf	2	2	1	0
Turner, ss	4	2	2	0
Lajoie, 2b	5	0	2	0
Easterly, c	3	0	0	2
Stovall, 1b	4	0	2	3
Birmingham, cf	3	0	0	0
Perring, 3b	5	0	0	0
Young, p	4	0	0	0
Totals	**34**	**5**	**7**	**5**

Washington	AB	R	H	RBI
Milan, cf	3	2	1	0
Lelivelt, lf	5	0	1	0
Conroy, 2b	5	0	1	1
Gessler, rf	4	0	0	0
McBride, ss	4	0	0	0
Killefer, 2b	4	0	0	0
Henry, 1b	3	0	0	0
b-Elberfeld, ph	1	0	0	0
Unglaub, 1b	0	0	0	0
Street, c	1	0	0	0
Beckendorf, c	3	0	1	0
Reisling, p	1	0	0	0
a-Schaefer, ph	1	0	0	0
Groom, p	1	0	0	0
Totals	**36**	**2**	**4**	**1**

```
Cleveland    0 0 0 0 0 0 0 0 2 0 3—5
Washington   1 0 0 0 0 0 0 0 1 0 0—2
```

a-Batted for Reisling in ninth
b-Batted for Henry in tenth

Errors: Turner, Young, Street, Reisling; Stolen base: Lajoie; Sacrifices: Turner, Birmingham, Reisling; Sacrifice flies: Easterly, Stovall; DP: Killefer, Henry, and Street; Left on base: Cleveland 6, Washington 5; Bases on balls: off Reisling 2, off Groom 3, off Young 3; Strikeouts: Reisling 3, Young 3; Hits: off Reisling 5 in 9 innings, off Groom 2 in 2 innings; Hit by pitcher: Birmingham (by Reisling); Losing pitcher: Groom; Umpire: Perrine; Time: 2:10.

Johnny Allen's 15 Consecutive Victories in 1937

It took a one-hitter by Jake Wade to deprive Johnny Allen of what would have tied an American League record for the most consecutive victories in one season.

Until October 3, 1937, Allen had won 15 games in a row—17 straight including his final two victories in 1936—but Wade, aided by Pete Fox and Hank Greenberg, outdueled the Indian ace, who pitched the final game of the season with only two days' rest.

In Allen's mind, Wade also was helped by Indians third baseman Odell Hale, and it was that opinion by the fiery and temperamental pitcher that almost resulted in a clubhouse brawl between the two players.

Allen thought Hale should have fielded a grounder to left field off the bat of Greenberg in the first inning. The ball got through Hale, was scored a single, and drove in Fox, who had doubled with one out.

It gave Greenberg the remarkable total of 183 runs batted in for the season which, even more remarkably, was one short of the major league record held by Lou Gehrig.

Hale did not appreciate Allen's criticism, and the two players had to be separated by teammates after the game.

Hale later was quoted as saying, "Johnny Allen never lost a game . . . someone else lost it for him."

Despite the defeat, which gave Allen a final won-lost record of 15–1, he wound up the season with a major-league-record winning percentage of .938 (still an American League mark but topped in the National League by Elroy Face's .947, 18–1, in 1959). Allen's earned run average also was a commendable 2.55 in 1937.

His statistics for the season are outstanding considering that he underwent an emergency appendectomy on June 20, when his record was 4–0, and was expected to be sidelined the rest of the season.

But Allen came back to win his fifth consecutive game on August 14, exactly 55 days later. His 15th consecutive victory was by a 6–4 score over the White Sox in Chicago in the opener of a doubleheader on September 30, which was his 32nd birthday.

In beating the White Sox, Allen allowed seven hits and was staked to a 2–0 lead in the first inning, 5–1 in the third, and 6–1 in the fifth. The White Sox got a run in the sixth and cut their deficit to two in the seventh, the rally being launched on an error by Tribe shortstop Lyn Lary that also infuriated Allen.

With a chance to tie the record set by Walter Johnson in 1912 and equaled by Smoky Joe Wood later that season, by Lefty Grove in 1931, and by Schoolboy Rowe in 1934, Allen was given the opportunity by manager Steve O'Neill to pitch the Indians' finale in Detroit three days later.

Unfortunately for Allen, he drew Wade for an opponent.

The Indians' only chance to win for Allen came in the seventh inning when Lary walked and Hal Trosky got the only hit allowed by Wade, a ground single over second base. With two out, Julius Solters was hit by a pitch, loading the bases, but Bruce Campbell lined to Gee Walker in left field to end the uprising.

Allen's record-tying streak began with a 9–2 victory over the St. Louis Browns on April 23, and after a couple of no-decision appearances and being sidelined several weeks with stomach pains (which later were diagnosed as appendicitis) he went on to beat Chicago, 15–3, May 29; New York, 5–3, June 4; Philadelphia, 2–0, June 13; Chicago, 4–3, August 14; St. Louis, 9–1, August 19; Boston, 4–3, August 24; Washington, 11–4, August 29; St. Louis, 15–3, September 3; Detroit, 6–1, September 8; St. Louis, 6–1, September 12; Boston, 4–1, September 17; Washington, 6–3, September 21; and Detroit, 9–3, September 26; before recording that 15th victory against the White Sox.

Allen's two victories at the end of the 1936 season were 5–4 over New York on September 10, and 13–2 over Boston on September 15.

By winning 17 straight over two seasons, Allen set an AL record that was tied by Baltimore's Dave McNally in 1968–69.

October 3, 1937

Indians	AB	R	H	RBI
Lary, ss	2	0	0	0
Kroner, 2b	2	0	0	0
Averill, cf	4	0	0	0
Trosky, 1b	4	0	1	0
Solters, lf	2	0	0	0
Campbell, rf	3	0	0	0
Hale, 3b	3	0	0	0
Pytlak, c	2	0	0	0
Allen, p	3	0	0	0
Totals	**25**	**0**	**1**	**0**

Detroit	AB	R	H	RBI
White, cf	4	0	0	0
Fox, rf	3	1	2	0
Gehringer, 2b	4	0	0	0
Greenberg, 1b	3	0	1	1
York, c	3	0	1	0
Walker, lf	3	0	1	0
Owen, 3b	3	0	0	0
Rogell, ss	1	0	0	0
Wade, p	3	0	0	0
Totals	**27**	**1**	**5**	**1**

Cleveland	0	0	0	0	0	0	0	0	0—0
Detroit	1	0	0	0	0	0	0	0	x—1

Two-base hits: Fox 2; Sacrifice hit: Kroner; Double plays: Lary, Kroner, and Trosky; Trosky and Lary; Left on base: Cleveland 4, Detroit 6; Bases on balls: off Allen 4, off Wade 4; Strikeouts: Allen 4, Wade 7; Hit by pitcher: Solters (by Wade); Umpires: Hubbard, Ormsby, Johnston; Time: 1:35; Attendance: 21,500.

Gaylord Perry's 15 Consecutive Victories in 1974

It began for Gaylord Perry on April 12, 1974, and continued for 15 straight games, through July 3, when he beat the Milwaukee Brewers, 4–2, tying Johnny Allen's club record.

But Perry's bid to equal the American League mark of 16 straight victories in one season ended under the cruelest of circumstances on July 8, when he lost to the Athletics in Oakland, 4–3, in 10 innings in front of 47,582 rain-dampened fans.

Stung by a ninth-inning run that sent the game into extra innings, Perry faltered in the 10th by walking leadoff batter Pat Bourque. "Blue Moon" Odom ran for Borque and was sacrificed to second by Tim Hosley. Bert Campaneris was retired on a grounder, with Odom taking third, and rookie Claudell Washington lined Perry's first pitch for a single to left that scored the winning run.

Indians catcher Dave Duncan smashed a two-run homer in the seventh inning off former battery mate Vida Blue that provided Perry with a 3–2 margin, but it was nullified in the ninth, when the Athletics tied the score on Joe Rudi's triple and Gene Tenace's sacrifice fly.

Despite the loss, which left Perry with a 15–2 record, his performance was remarkable considering that he pitched—again—with an ankle injury that would have put most players on the disabled list.

Though he refused to tell anybody but Indians trainer Jim Warfield, Perry suffered a severe sprain on April 28 during a 10–2 victory over California, his third straight in the streak.

"It was a very bad injury," confirmed Warfield. "Gaylord should have taken some time off to rest and let it get better, but he wouldn't. It was particularly bad because it was his right ankle, the leg that he uses to push off the mound, and every time he pitched, he aggravated it, made it worse.

"There was considerable swelling, along with the pain, and I knew it was bad because Gaylord complained, which he almost never does when he's hurting. But he wouldn't let me tell anybody.

"The man is amazing, absolutely amazing," added Warfield.

In order to continue pitching, Perry had Warfield tape his right ankle so tightly that it was almost as though he was wearing a cast.

"I didn't want anybody to know because if the story got out, I was afraid if teams found out, they'd start bunting on me, or take advantage of my bad ankle, knowing that I couldn't move very well," said Perry.

The injury bothered Perry the rest of the season—though he steadfastly refused to give in to it—and he finished with a 21–13 record and 2.51 earned run average.

Perry lost the season opener, 6–1, to the Yankees in New York on April 6. He came back six days later to beat them, 9–1, at the Stadium and launched the streak that came within two pitches—the one that Rudi smacked for a triple and the one that Washington hit for a game-winning single—of tying the AL record for the most consecutive victories.

He went on to beat Oakland, 2–1, on April 23; California, 10–2, April 28; Oakland again, 8–2, May 4; Boston, 6–2, May 14; Detroit, 2–1, May 19; Baltimore, 2–0, May 23; Texas, 8–0, May 28; Kansas City, 5–2, June 2; Kansas City again, 3–1, June 7; Chicago, 10–1, June 12; Chicago again, 4–3, June 17; Boston, 11–0, June 22; and Boston again, 2–1, June 28; before beating the Brewers five days later to tie Allen's club record, but leaving him one short of the mark set by Walter Johnson in 1912, which was equaled later that season by Smoky Joe Wood, by Lefty Grove in 1931, and by Schoolboy Rowe in 1934.

In that record-tying, 4–2 victory over Milwaukee, John Lowenstein drove in all the Indians' runs as Perry scattered seven hits. He trailed, 1–0, before Lowenstein cracked a three-run homer in the fifth. After Bobby Coluccio solo-homered for the Brewers in their half of the fifth, Lowenstein's sacrifice fly in the seventh scored Buddy Bell with an insurance run that Perry didn't need.

July 8, 1974

Indians	AB	R	H	RBI
Lowenstein, lf	4	0	0	1
Brohamer, 2b	4	0	0	0
Ellis, 1b	4	0	0	0
Spikes, rf	4	0	0	0
Hendrick, cf	4	1	1	0
Bell, 3b	3	0	1	0
Gamble, dh	4	1	1	0
Duncan, c	4	1	1	2
Duffy, ss	3	0	0	0
Perry, p	0	0	0	0
Totals	34	3	4	3

Oakland	AB	R	H	RBI
Campaneris, ss	4	0	0	0
C. Washington, dh	5	0	2	1
Bando, 3b	4	0	0	0
R. Jackson, rf	4	0	0	0
Rudi, lf	3	1	1	0
H. Washington, pr	0	1	0	0
North, cf	0	0	0	0
Tenace, 1b	3	1	2	3
Mangual, cf	4	0	0	0
Kubiak, 2b	3	0	0	0
b-Borque, ph	0	0	0	0
1-Odom, pr	0	1	0	0
Haney, c	2	0	1	0
a-Alou, ph	1	0	0	0
Hosley, c	0	0	0	0
Blue, p	0	0	0	0
Totals	33	4	6	4

```
Cleveland   0 0 0 0 1 0 2 0 0  0—3
Oakland     0 2 0 0 0 0 0 0 1  1—4
```

a-Lined out for Haney in eighth
b-Walked for Kubiak in tenth
1-Ran for Borque in tenth

Left on base: Cleveland 4, Oakland 5; Three-base hit: Rudi, C. Washington; Home run: Duncan, Tenace; Sacrifice: Hosley; Sacrifice fly: Tenace.

Cleveland	IP	H	R	ER	BB	SO
Perry, L	9⅔	6	4	4	2	13

Oakland	IP	H	R	ER	BB	SO
Blue, W	10	4	3	3	3	7

HBP: Rudi (by Perry). Time: 2:34. Attendance 47,582. Umpires: Bremigan, Chylak, McCoy, Brinkman.

Napoleon Lajoie's 3,000th Career Hit in 1914

Baseball statisticians were not as alert in Napoleon Lajoie's day as they were later, or are today; otherwise the Indians star second baseman would not have been ignored on the day, September 17, 1914, when he became only the third player in history to make 3,000 hits.

He went 1-for-4 against Boston pitcher Rube Foster at League Park in an 8–1 victory by the Red Sox, but Henry Edwards, the *Cleveland Plain Dealer* sportswriter who covered the game, never even mentioned Lajoie's name in his report, which stated:

"All that Boston did was to show superiority at the bat, in the field, on the bases, in the box, and behind the bat."

But absolutely nothing about Lajoie—with good reason.

At the time, it was believed Lajoie's hit, a single, was his 2,991st. Lajoie had been credited with only 220 hits in 1901, when he played for the Philadelphia Athletics, a year before he joined the Cleveland club, then called the Bronchos.

Thus what was thought to be hit number 3,000 was reported to have been made 10 days later, on September 27, 1914, when Lajoie doubled for a second time in the first game of a doubleheader against New York, won by Cleveland, then renicknamed the Naps.

Lajoie was heralded then for reaching that level, achieved previously only by Cap Anson and Honus Wagner. (Since then 16 players have made 3,000 hits in their careers, most recently by Eddie Murray in 1995, and topped by Pete Rose's 4,256.)

However, it was subsequently discovered by baseball historians that somehow Lajoie "lost" nine hits in that 1901 season and, when credited for them, it turned out that his 3,000th was made on September 17th instead of the 27th.

When Lajoie ended his career in 1916 he had 3,242 hits, 10th most in baseball history, behind Rose, Ty Cobb, 4,189; Hank Aaron, 3,771; Stan Musial, 3,630; Tris Speaker, 3,514; Carl Yastrzemski, 3,419; Wagner, 3,415; Eddie Collins, 3,312; and Willie Mays, 3,283.

September 17, 1914

Boston	AB	R	H	RBI
Hooper, rf, cf	5	2	2	n/a
Scott, ss	3	1	2	n/a
Speaker, cf	0	1	0	n/a
Rehg, rf	1	0	0	n/a
Lewis, lf	4	1	1	n/a
Hoblitzel, 1b	4	1	1	n/a
Gainer, 1b	0	0	0	n/a
Janvrin, 2b	4	1	0	n/a
Gardner, 3b	5	1	2	n/a
Carrigan, c	2	0	2	n/a
Thomas, c	0	0	0	n/a
Foster, p	4	0	1	n/a
Totals	33	8	11	n/a

Naps	AB	R	H	RBI
Leibold, cf	4	0	2	n/a
Chapman, 2b	4	0	0	n/a
Jackson, rf	4	0	0	n/a
Lajoie, 1b	4	0	1	n/a
Graney, lf	4	1	1	n/a
Turner, 3b	4	0	1	n/a
Barbare, ss	4	0	1	n/a
Bassler, c	3	0	0	n/a
Mitchell, p	2	0	0	n/a
a-Kirke, ph	1	0	0	n/a
Dillinger, p	0	0	0	n/a
Totals	34	1	6	n/a

```
Boston      2 0 1 1 0 0 4 0 0—8
Cleveland   0 0 0 0 0 0 1 0 0—1
```

a-Batted for Mitchell in seventh

Errors: Janvrin, Leibold, Chapman, Barbare, Bassler, Mitchell; Two-base hits: Leibold, Lewis, Carrigan, Hooper; Three-base hits: Barbare, Gardner; Sacrifice hits: Scott, Janvrin; Sacrifice fly: Speaker; Stolen bases: Gardner, Carrigan; Double plays: Chapman, Lajoie, and Bassler; Chapman, Barbare, and Lajoie; Lajoie and Turner; Hits: off Mitchell 10 in 7 innings; off Dillinger 1 in 2 innings; Bases on balls: off Mitchell 5, off Dillinger 1; HBP: Lewis (by Mitchell); Struck out: by Mitchell 5; Left on base: Cleveland 6, Boston 8. Time: 2:00. Umpires: Cahill, Connolly.

Early Wynn's 300th Career Pitching Victory in 1963

It was a long time coming, but Early Wynn, as tenacious a pitcher as any who ever wore a toeplate, finally achieved the goal that automatically reserved his place in the Hall of Fame:

His 300th major league victory.

Wynn got it on July 13, 1963, in Kansas City, at the age of 43, after failing six times—three earlier in the season and three at the end of 1962 before he was released by the Chicago White Sox with a 7–15 record.

"I feel I had this one coming after pitching well and losing so many tough ones," Wynn said in the wake of the Indians' 7–4 decision over the Athletics in the nightcap of a double-header witnessed by 13,565 fans in Kansas City.

It was achieved with relief help from Jerry Walker, who took over in the sixth inning with the Indians clinging to a precarious 5–4 lead. They got two more runs, one in the seventh and another in the ninth, while Walker was blanking the Athletics on three hits.

Wynn thus became the 14th pitcher in the history of baseball to win 300 games, and the first to do so while wearing an Indians uniform. (Cy Young registered his 500th victory while pitching for Cleveland in 1910, but won most of his games in the modern era for the Boston Red Sox.)

Young, who finished with a 511–315 lifetime record, was followed by Walter Johnson, 417; Christy Mathewson and Grover Alexander, each with 373; Kid Nichols, 361; Pud Galvin, 360; Tim Keefe, 342; Warren Spahn, 339 (he went on to win 363); John Clarkson, 328; Eddie Plank, 326; Old Hoss Radbourn, 309; Mickey Welch, 307; Lefty Grove, 300; and Wynn.

(Since 1963, six more pitchers have won 300 games: Steve Carlton, 329; Don Sutton and Nolan Ryan, 324; Phil Niekro, 318; Gaylord Perry, 314; and Tom Seaver, 311.)

Only 164 of Wynn's victories were for Cleveland, including 20 or more in 1951, 1952, 1954, and 1956, and he also had several outstanding seasons for the White Sox from 1958 to 1962, including 1959 when he won the American League Cy Young Award.

In his 300th victory game Wynn staggered but, typically, fought the Athletics all the way.

"I was pooped," he said after his five-inning stint. "I had good stuff, but I couldn't get it over the plate. Every pitch got to be a great effort. I tried to make every one of them perfect. [Manager] Birdie Tebbetts had to get me out of there when he did or I might have fallen on my face. I was exhausted."

Tebbetts said there was no doubt that Wynn deserved all the accolades a 300-game winner gets. "He made three good starts for us before today, and pitched two scoreless relief innings last week. "With any luck he could have—probably should have—won three or even four of those games," said Tebbetts.

The critical point in Wynn's victory came in the fifth inning when the Indians scored four runs to break a 1–1 tie against losing pitcher Moe Drabowsky.

It was Wynn himself who started the rally with a single to left. After Tito Francona flied out, Dick Howser beat out a roller 30 feet down the third base line. Willie Kirkland fouled out, but Max Alvis coaxed a walk to load the bases.

Joe Adcock singled for two runs and, after John Romano walked to reload the bases, Al Luplow singled against reliever Dale Willis for two more. The rally was halted when Romano was retired when he also tried to score.

But it didn't matter, though Wynn barely survived the bottom of the fifth, which was necessary to gain credit for the victory.

Ken Harrelson and Gino Cimoli singled to start the inning, and Jose Tartabull beat out a bunt to load the bases with nobody out. Wynn got Wayne Causey on a pop fly, but Jerry Lumpe lined a double to right that cleared the bases and cut the Indians' margin to one run.

However, before the dust cleared, Lumpe was out trying to stretch his hit into a triple, and Wynn got George Alusik, who had homered in the fourth inning, to fly out.

That inning finished Wynn's work for the night, and Walker preserved the coveted victory.

Though Wynn didn't win again, he made 15 more appearances during the season, all but one in relief, and finished with a 1–2 record and an outstanding 2.28 earned run average.

He retired as a player, became the Indians' pitching coach in 1964, and was inducted into the Hall of Fame in 1972.

Brett Butler showers Phil Niekro with champagne after Niekro registered his 314th career victory, beating the Detroit Tigers, 9–6, on June 1, 1987. It gave the Niekro brothers, Phil and Joe (then pitching for the New York Yankees), a total of 530 victories, the most by a brother combination in major league history.

July 13, 1963

Indians	AB	R	H	RBI
Francona, lf	5	0	1	0
Tasby, lf	0	0	0	0
Howser, ss	5	1	2	0
Kirkland, cf	5	2	1	0
Alvis, 3b	4	1	0	0
Adcock, 1b	4	1	1	3
Romano, c	3	1	2	1
Luplow, rf	2	0	2	2
Brown, 2b	4	0	1	1
Wynn, p	2	1	1	0
c-Held, ph	1	0	1	0
Walker, p	0	0	0	0
Totals	**35**	**7**	**12**	**7**

Kansas City	AB	R	H	RBI
Tartabull, cf	5	1	1	0
Causey, ss	5	0	0	0
Lumpe, 2b	4	0	1	3
Alusik, rf	3	1	1	1
Lau, c	3	0	1	0
Charles, 3b	2	0	1	0
Essegian, lf	4	0	0	0
Harrelson, 1b	3	1	2	0
Drabowsky, p	1	0	1	0
Willis, p	0	0	0	0
a-Cimoli, ph	1	0	1	0
b-LaRussa, pr	0	1	0	0
Fischer, p	0	0	0	0
d-Siebern, ph	1	0	0	0
Lovrich, p	0	0	0	0
e-Edwards, ph	1	0	0	0
Totals	**33**	**4**	**9**	**4**

Indians	0	1	0	0	4	0	1	0	1—7
Kansas City	0	0	0	1	3	0	0	0	0—4

a-Singled for Willis in fifth
b-Ran for Cimoli in fifth
c-Doubled for Wynn in sixth
d-Struck out for Fischer in sixth
e-Fouled out for Lovrich in ninth

Error: Harrelson; Two-base hits: Lumpe, Held, Lau; Three-base hit: Kirkland; Home run: Alusik; Stolen base: Kirkland; Sacrifice fly: Adcock; Double play: Lumpe, Causey, and Harrelson; Left on base: Indians 8, Kansas City 7.

Cleveland	IP	H	R	ER	BB	SO
Wynn, W	5	6	4	4	3	3
Walker	4	3	0	0	2	2

Kansas City	IP	H	R	ER	BB	SO
Drabowsky, L	4⅔	6	5	5	5	5
Willis	⅓	1	0	0	0	0
Fischer	1	2	0	0	0	0
Lavrich	3	3	2	1	1	1

Time: 2:42. Attendance: 13,565. Umpires: Napp, Kinnamon, Umont, Stevens.

Bob Feller Strikes Out a Major-League-Record 18 Batters

More than 27,000 fans crowded into Cleveland's Municipal Stadium on October 2, 1938, the final day of the season, to see if Hank Greenberg would break Babe Ruth's home run record.

Instead, they witnessed a record-setting pitching performance by Bob Feller, while Greenberg swung in vain and finished with 58 homers, two shy of Ruth's season mark.

Feller, only two years out of high school, struck out 18 batters—including Greenberg twice—though the Indians lost to Harry Eisenstat and the Detroit Tigers, 4–1, in the opener of a doubleheader. Detroit also won the nightcap, 10–8.

Feller's performance broke the record of 17 strikeouts in one game that he had shared with Dizzy Dean of the St. Louis Cardinals.

It became apparent early in the game that the record was being threatened. Feller, a month shy of his 20th birthday,

On October 2, 1938, Bob Feller is carried off the field on the shoulders of Indians batboy Joe Maxse after striking out 18 batters to break the major league single game record. To Maxse's right is Al Milnar, and to Maxse's left are (left to right) Jeff Heath, Bruce Campbell, and Frankie Pytlak.

struck out Benny McCoy, the Tigers' leadoff batter, on three pitches in the first inning. He fanned three each in the second, third, and fourth innings, and added two in the fifth and again in the sixth, giving him 14 going into the seventh.

Eisenstat, the left-hander who held the Indians to four hits to win his ninth game in 15 decisions, struck out as Detroit's first batter in the seventh, and McCoy and Pete Fox were retired on grounders to end that inning.

Feller walked Roy Cullenbine and Greenberg to start the eighth, and Birdie Tebbetts, who already had made two hits and walked once, sacrificed. Chet Laabs then struck out for a fourth time, raising the total to 16.

A walk to Tony Piet loaded the bases, and Mark Christman, who had fanned in his three previous at bats, singled for two runs, boosting the Tigers' lead to 4–0.

Eisenstat, who also had struck out three times, drew a walk, and McCoy lined out to end the inning, leaving Feller in need of two strikeouts in the final inning to break the record.

He fanned Fox on three pitches to start the ninth, and Cullenbine singled to right. The ball probably would have been caught by Bruce Campbell, except that he was among those rooting for Feller to set the record and allowed the ball to fall in front of him.

Greenberg flied to Roy Weatherly for the second out. It brought to the plate Birdie Tebbetts, who had been tough on Feller throughout the game, to be followed by Chet Laabs, who fanned in his first four times at bat—a fact which Feller undoubtedly had in mind.

He proceeded to walk Tebbetts and, after going to a 2-and-1 count against Laabs, fired two called strikes against the Detroit center fielder to break the record and end the game.

When umpire Cal Hubbard jerked his right hand in the air to signal the third strike against Laabs, Feller dashed for the Indians' dugout accompanied by a tremendous roar from the crowd and was greeted with a rousing welcome by his teammates.

Though it was Feller's 11th loss instead of his 18th victory, the 18 strikeouts gave him 240 in 277⅔ innings, and the American League strikeout championship, 14 more than runner-up Bobo Newsom of the St. Louis Browns.

October 2, 1938

Detroit	AB	R	H	RBI
McCoy, 2b	5	0	0	0
Fox, rf	5	0	0	0
Cullenbine, lf	4	2	3	0
Greenberg, 1b	4	2	1	0
Tebbetts, c	2	0	2	2
Laabs, cf	5	0	0	0
Piet, 3b	1	0	0	0
Christman, ss	4	0	1	2
Eisenstat, p	3	0	0	0
Totals	33	4	7	4

Indians	AB	R	H	RBI
Irwin, ss	3	0	0	0
Weatherly, cf	4	0	1	0
Campbell, rf	4	1	1	0
Heath, lf	4	0	1	0
Trosky, 1b	3	0	0	1
Pytlak, c	4	0	1	0
Keltner, 3b	3	0	0	0
Grimes, 2b	2	0	0	0
Feller, p	3	0	0	0
Totals	30	1	4	1

Errors: McCoy; Two-base hits: Greenberg, Tebbetts; Stolen bases: Cullenbine, Piet; Sacrifice: Tebbetts; Double play: McCoy, Christman, and Greenberg; Left on base: Detroit 11, Cleveland 5; Bases on balls: off Feller 7, off Eisenstat 3; Strikeouts: by Feller 18, by Eisenstat 3; Hit by pitcher: Piet (by Feller); Umpires: Hubbard, Grieve, Moriarty; Time: 2:07; Attendance: 27,000 (est.).

Detroit	0	0	0	0	0	2	0	2	0—4
Indians	0	0	0	0	0	0	0	0	1—1

Indians Lose Opener at Cleveland Municipal Stadium, 1–0, in 1932

"Do I remember it? How could I ever forget?" Mel Harder replied with questions of his own when he was asked his recollection of the first game the Indians played in the Cleveland Municipal Stadium on July 31, 1932, in front of 80,154 fans.

Then a young pitcher of 22 in only his third full major league season, Harder was given the starting assignment by manager Roger Peckinpaugh against the reigning American League champion Philadelphia Athletics.

Harder's opponent was future Hall of Famer Lefty Grove, who won 31 games and lost only four in 1931, and was in the process of fashioning a 25–10 record in 1932.

"Pitching that game was the biggest thrill of my career," said Harder, despite losing, 1–0, to the Athletics.

"I was disappointed, of course, that we got beat, but I enjoyed every minute of the game. It was a wonderful experience for all of us.

"Actually, I got the assignment by accident. Wes Ferrell was supposed to pitch that game, and I was scheduled to start the next day.

"But when Ferrell reported to the Stadium, he told Peckinpaugh that his arm was a little stiff, and he didn't know if he could work or not.

"Peck didn't hesitate. He came over, handed me the ball, and said, 'Mel, you're pitching today.' That was it. It was no big thing. There was no hoopla or anything like that."

Harder recalled that he also was told that the ball he would throw for the first pitch was to be saved and presented to Ohio Governor George White.

"Unfortunately, nobody told Max Bishop . . . or else they told him and he ignored it," said Harder.

"I wound up and just laid the first pitch in there, expecting that Bishop would take it, the umpire would make his call, toss the ball out of play, and we'd start all over again.

"But Bishop took a helluva cut and hit a line drive into the left field stands. We were lucky it went foul.

"After that, everything was forgotten. As far as I know, the governor never got a ball."

A couple of pitches later Bishop got the first hit of the game—and, of course, the honor of making the first hit in the Stadium—though Harder pitched himself out of trouble. He struck out Mule Haas, walked Mickey Cochrane, struck out Al Simmons, and retired Jimmy Foxx on a routine fly to center.

Bishop's single was one of only five hits allowed by Harder, who went on to strike out seven in eight innings. Oral Hildebrand pitched the ninth and gave up one hit.

Later in the game Harder struck out three of baseball's greatest hitters in order—Cochrane, Simmons, and Foxx.

Cochrane was called out on strikes to end the fifth inning with Grove on third and Haas on first, the result of singles. Then Harder fanned Simmons and Foxx, the first two batters in the sixth.

Unfortunately for Harder and his teammates, Grove was even better. He hurled a four-hitter, striking out six and walking two. He allowed only one runner to advance as far as third base.

The break in Harder's duel with Grove came as Bishop, whose nickname was "Camera Eye," walked to lead off the eighth inning.

As reported in the *Cleveland Plain Dealer* the next morning: "[The winning rally] was started by the eagle-eyed Bishop, the game's foremost practitioner of the fine art of coaxing bases on balls out of unwilling pitchers."

Haas, the next batter, sacrifice bunted Bishop to second, and Cochrane followed with a single to score the game's only run.

"Cochrane hit a fastball inside," said Harder. "It was a pretty good pitch, but Cochrane hit it for a single, so it must not have been good enough." The ball bounced up the middle, barely eluding Harder and out of the reach of second baseman Bill Cissell, and Haas scored easily.

The Indians had two legitimate chances to score, but each time Grove prevailed.

Cissell got the first hit off Grove, a single to start the third, took second on Willie Kamm's sacrifice bunt, and went to third on Harder's grounder to Bishop. But Dick Porter flied out to end the threat.

An even better opportunity occurred in the seventh when Earl Averill led off with a single and Joe Vosmik beat out a bunt for another hit.

Eddie Morgan went to the plate with orders to sacrifice the runners along, but his bunt was pounced upon by Grove, who threw to Jimmy Dykes to force Averill at third. It was described in the *Plain Dealer* as "a remarkably expert play, one that couldn't have been made by any but a left-handed pitcher."

Grove then fanned Luke Sewell for the second out, and his first pitch to Cissell was lashed on a line to right field.

"We thought it was a hit for sure, and that two runs would score," said Harder.

So did the fans, 80,154 of them (76,979 paid), who jumped to their feet with a jubilant, deafening roar that quickly died as the liner sliced foul and landed about a foot outside the right-field line.

Then Grove retired Cissell on an easy grounder to Bishop, and the Indians never threatened again.

Averill, Vosmik, and Morgan went out in order in the ninth, though not without one last hurrah—and one last second guess for the fans.

The final putout was Morgan's long fly to right fielder Bing Miller, who caught the ball in front of the stands.

Had the game been played at League Park, Morgan's drive probably would have cleared the 40-foot-high right-field wall that was only 290 feet from the plate.

At the Stadium, prior to the 1947 installation of an interior outfield fence, Morgan's long fly was, the *Plain Dealer* reported, "only a lazy out."

And so, the result of Harder's biggest thrill in a 20-year major league pitching career went into the record book as a heartbreaking loss.

However, despite the defeat, that first game in the Stadium was, as reported at the time, "a milestone event in middle western sports," and the Stadium itself was described as "a magnificent structure" and "the ultimate athletic facility in the country."

July 31, 1932

Philadelphia	AB	R	H	RBI
Bishop, 2b	3	1	1	0
Haas, cf	3	0	1	0
Cochrane, c	3	0	1	0
Simmons, lf	4	0	1	1
Foxx, 1b	4	0	1	0
McNair, ss	3	0	0	0
Miller, rf	4	0	0	0
Dykes, 3b	4	0	0	0
Grove, p	3	0	1	0
Totals	31	1	6	1

Indians	AB	R	H	RBI
Porter, rf	3	0	0	0
Burnett, ss	4	0	1	0
Averill, cf	4	0	1	0
Vosmik, lf	4	0	1	0
Morgan, 1b	4	0	0	0
Sewell, c	3	0	0	0
Cissell, 2b	2	0	1	0
Kamm, 3b	2	0	0	0
Harder, p	2	0	0	0
a-Ferrell, ph	1	0	0	0
Hildebrand, p	0	0	0	0
Totals	29	0	4	0

Philadelphia	0	0	0	0	0	0	0	1	0—1
Indians	0	0	0	0	0	0	0	0	0—0

a-Batted for Harder in eighth

Error: Morgan; Two-base hit: Foxx; DP: Burnett, Cissell, and Morgan; Left on base: Philadelphia 7, Cleveland 5; Sacrifice: Kamm, Haas, McNair; Caught stealing: Burnett.

Philadelphia	IP	H	R	ER	BB	SO
Grove, W	9	4	0	0	2	6

Cleveland	IP	H	R	ER	BB	SO
Harder, L	8	5	1	1	2	7
Hildebrand	1	1	0	0	0	0

Time: 1:50; Attendance: 80,154; Umpires: Guthrie, Ormsby, Geisel, Connolly.

Cleveland's First American League Victory in 1901

Cleveland's first-ever victory in the newly founded American League was achieved by a well-traveled pitcher named Billy Hart, though he probably would not have prevailed without the help of five errors by the opposition, two of which provided six runs.

The Blues (then the Cleveland team's nickname), beat the White Sox in Chicago, 10–4, after losing the first two games. Chicago won the 1901 opener, 8–2, and the second game, 7–3, despite Erv Beck's home run for the Blues, the first in the American League.

In their third game, the Blues, though outhit, 10–9, scored four runs for a 4–2 lead in the third inning, after Chicago second baseman Dave Brain committed an error, and got three more in the third thanks to a miscue by center fielder William "Dummy" Hoy.

Hoy also blundered on the bases in the sixth inning when he slid into third while Blues third baseman Bill Bradley was trying to retrieve catcher Bob Wood's wild throw. Bradley finally got the ball, and Hoy was tagged out when he overslid the bag.

The White Sox wound up making five errors, including two more by Brain for three in the game, and one by third baseman Fred Hartman, in addition to the fly ball dropped by Hoy.

Hart, who'd pitched in the American Association and the National League before joining the Blues for their first season, went on to post a 7–11 record in 1901, but he didn't pitch in the major leagues again.

April 27, 1901

Blues	AB	R	H	RBI
Pickering, rf	5	2	1	n/a
McCarthy, lf	2	1	0	n/a
Genins, cf	5	1	2	n/a
LaChance, 1b	5	0	1	n/a
Bradley, 3b	5	0	0	n/a
Beck, 2b	5	0	1	n/a
Hallman, ss	4	1	0	n/a
Wood, c	5	2	2	n/a
Hart, p	4	3	2	n/a
Totals	40	10	9	n/a

Chicago	AB	R	H	RBI
Hoy, cf	4	0	1	n/a
Jones, rf	4	0	1	n/a
Mertes, lf	5	1	3	n/a
Shugart, ss	5	0	0	n/a
Isbell, 1b	5	2	1	n/a
Hartman, 3b	3	1	2	n/a
Brain, 2b	4	0	2	n/a
Sullivan, c	4	0	0	n/a
Katoll, p	4	0	0	n/a
Totals	38	4	10	n/a

Cleveland	0	0	4	3	0	0	0	3	0—10
Chicago	0	2	0	0	2	0	0	0	0—4

Errors: Bradley, Hallman, Hoy, Hartman, Brain 3; Two-base hits: Hartman, Pickering; Left on base: Cleveland 7, Chicago 10; Stolen bases: Hoy, Mertes 2; Strikeouts: by Hart 6, Katoll 1; Bases on balls: off Hart 3, Katoll 4; Wild pitch: Hart; Passed ball: Sullivan; Time: 1:45; Umpire: Connolly.

Lou Boudreau's Pinch Hit Leads Indians to Sweep over New York

Lou Boudreau called it the biggest thrill of his career, and Bill Veeck said it was the most courageous thing he'd seen in baseball.

It happened on August 8, 1948, in Municipal Stadium during a doubleheader between the Indians and New York Yankees, in the thick of the pennant race.

Boudreau, who had been sidelined with a sprained ankle, strained left knee, and bruised right shoulder, injuries he'd sustained three days earlier in a collision at second base, sent himself to the plate as a pinch hitter against the Yankees' ace reliever, Joe Page.

The situation was critical; when the day began the Indians, New York, and Philadelphia were in a virtual tie for first place (though Cleveland's winning percentage was .598, New York's was .596, and Philadelphia's was .592), with Boston (.578) in fourth place, 1½ games behind.

The Indians were trailing, 6–4, in the seventh inning of the opener of the doubleheader against the Yankees, with the bases loaded, two out, and left-handed hitting Thurman Tucker due to bat against Page.

Boudreau, the inspirational player-manager, who had been soaking his ankle in a bucket of ice until then, quickly put on his sock and shoe, grabbed a bat, and limped to the plate to the cheers of 73,484 fans.

"I was sure that [New York manager] Bucky Harris figured I couldn't hit because I was hurt, and knew the only other right-handed batters we had on the bench were Joe Tipton and Bob Kennedy," Boudreau said of his decision to put himself in to bat for Tucker.

"I felt it would be our last shot [to win] and also, however immodest it sounds, I knew I was the best [hitter] we had available."

The count on Boudreau went to 2-and-2, and he swung at Page's next pitch, a fastball, lining it to the right of second base into center field. "It might have been a double, but I barely made it to first base, my ankle hurt so much," Boudreau said.

It scored two runs, tying the game, and when Boudreau hobbled off the field upon being replaced by a pinch runner, the fans gave him a five-minute standing ovation.

Page retired the next batter to maintain the 6–6 deadlock, but the Indians, buoyed by Boudreau's key hit, rallied for two more runs in the eighth.

It happened again with two out as Johnny Berardino walked and Eddie Robinson smashed his second home run of the game over the right-field fence. It gave the Tribe a two-run lead that relievers Satchel Paige and Russ Christopher protected in the ninth for the victory.

The Indians went on to win the second game, 2–1, boosting them into first place, six percentage points ahead of the Athletics, two games over the Yankees, and 2½ atop the Red Sox.

August 8, 1948, First game

New York	AB	R	H	RBI
Stirnweiss, 2b	5	2	2	1
Henrich, rf	5	1	3	1
Lindell, lf	3	1	3	1
e-Keller, ph, lf	3	0	0	0
DiMaggio, cf	4	0	0	1
Johnson, 3b	4	0	1	1
Souchock, 1b	3	0	0	0
McQuinn, 1b	1	0	0	0
Niarhos, c	3	0	0	0
Berra, c	1	0	0	0
Rizzuto, ss	4	2	3	0
Shea, p	2	0	0	0
Page, p	0	0	0	0
d-Brown, ph	1	0	0	0
Totals	37	6	12	5

Indians	AB	R	H	RBI
Mitchell, lf	4	1	3	0
Tucker, cf	3	0	0	0
a-Boudreau, ph	1	0	1	2
1-Kennedy, rf	0	0	0	0
Doby, rf, cf	4	0	0	1
Keltner, 3b	3	1	0	0
Gordon, 2b	3	0	1	0
Berardino, ss	3	2	1	2
Robinson, 1b	4	2	2	3
Hegan, c	4	1	1	0
Zoldak, p	2	0	0	0
Klieman, p	0	0	0	0
b-Peck, ph	0	0	0	0
c-Clark, ph	0	0	0	0
2-Lemon, pr	0	1	0	0
Paige, p	0	0	0	0
Christopher, p	0	0	0	0
Totals	31	8	9	8

New York	1	0	0	1	2	0	2	0	0—6
Cleveland	1	0	0	0	0	0	5	2	x—8

a-Singled for Tucker in seventh
1-Ran for Boundreau in seventh
b-Announced as pinch hitter for Klieman in seventh
c-Walked for Peck in seventh
2-Ran for Clark in seventh
d-Fouled out for Page in ninth
e-Grounded out for Lindell in ninth

Errors: Robinson, Berardino; Two-base hits: Henrich 2, Lindell, Mitchell; Home runs: Berardino, Robinson 2; Sacrifice: Shea; Double play: Zoldak, Gordon, Berardino, and Robinson; Left on base: New York 6, Cleveland 3; Bases on balls: Zoldak 1, Shea 1, Page 3; Strikeouts: Shea 1, Zoldak 2, Page 2; Hits: off Shea 6 in 6⅔, Page 3 in 1⅓, Zoldak 10 in 6⅓; Klieman 0 in ⅓; Paige 2 in 1⅓; Christopher 0 in ⅓; Balk: Paige; Winner: Paige; Loser: Page; Time: 2:30; Attendance: 73,484; Umpires: Passarella, Rommel, Boyer.

Baseball's Largest Crowd Sees Indians Lose Game 5 of the 1948 World Series

A crowd of 86,288, largest ever to see a baseball game, jammed Cleveland's Municipal Stadium on October 10, 1948, expecting to see the Indians crowned world champions, but went home disappointed for a couple of reasons.

For one thing, the Indians were beaten—overwhelmed, really—by the Boston Braves, 11–5, forcing a sixth game the next day in Boston.

What's more, Bob Feller, one of the greatest pitchers to wear a Cleveland uniform, and one of the best of all time, was the loser, shelled by the Braves and ignominiously chased to the showers in the seventh inning.

It was the second defeat in the Series for Feller, who failed to win the opener despite hurling a two-hitter, as he sought one of the few objectives he failed to achieve in an outstanding major league career that began in 1936.

Feller was charged with seven runs, four of them coming on a pair of homers by Braves third baseman Bob Elliott, the first with two aboard in the first inning, the second with the bases bare in the third.

The Indians rallied for a 5–4 lead in the fourth, but Feller couldn't hold it, surrendering a tying run in the sixth, and was the primary victim as the Braves exploded for six more runs in the seventh.

That six-run lead was more than enough for Warren Spahn, who took over in the fourth inning in relief of Nelson Potter when Indians catcher Jim Hegan smashed a three-run homer.

Feller, who had waited 12 years for the chance every pitcher dreams of—to pitch and win a World Series game—had no alibi for his unusually poor performance. "I don't have any excuses," he said. "I couldn't seem to loosen up, and I didn't have any control. All I can say is that I just didn't have it."

The defeat left him with the dubious distinction of having lost the only two games his team failed to win.

The record crowd surpassed the previous all-time mark of 82,781 also set by the Indians four months earlier, on June 20, when the Indians swept a doubleheader from the Philadelphia Athletics, 4–3 and 10–0.

Not only was it the largest to see a baseball game, but it also was part of the 117,475 Cleveland fans who paid their way into the Stadium on that date.

After the Braves beat the Indians in the afternoon, another turnout of 31,187 saw the Cleveland Browns beat Brooklyn, 30–17, in an All-America Football Conference game at the Stadium that night.

(Since then, the single-baseball-game attendance record was broken on October 6, 1959, when 92,706 fans attended the fifth game of the World Series in the Los Angeles Coliseum between the Dodgers and Chicago White Sox.)

October 10, 1948

Boston	AB	R	H	RBI
Holmes, rf	5	2	2	0
Dark, ss	4	1	1	0
Torgeson, 1b	5	1	2	1
Elliott, 3b	4	3	2	4
Rickert, lf	5	1	1	1
Salkeld, c	4	2	1	1
McCormick, cf	5	1	1	1
Stanky, 2b	3	0	1	1
Potter, p	2	0	1	0
Spahn, p	2	0	0	1
Totals	39	11	12	10

Indians	AB	R	H	RBI
Mitchell, lf	3	1	1	1
Doby, cf	4	0	0	0
Boudreau, ss	4	0	2	0
Gordon, 2b	3	1	1	0
Keltner, 3b	3	1	0	0
Judnich, rf	3	1	1	1
b-Boone, ph	1	0	0	0
Peck, rf	0	0	0	0
Robinson, 1b	4	0	0	0
Hegan, c	4	1	1	3
Feller, p	2	0	0	0
Klieman, p	0	0	0	0
Christopher, p	0	0	0	0
Paige, p	0	0	0	0
a-Rosen, ph	1	0	0	0
Muncrief, p	0	0	0	0
c-Tipton, ph	1	0	0	0
Totals	33	5	6	5

Boston	3	0	1	0	0	1	6	0	0—11
Cleveland	1	0	0	4	0	0	0	0	0—5

a-Popped out for Paige in seventh
b-Struck out for Judnich in eighth
c-Struck out for Muncrief in ninth

Errors: Doby, Keltner; Two-base hits: Boudreau; Home runs: Elliott 2, Mitchell, Hegan, Salkeld; Sacrifice: Dark; Left on base: Boston 6, Cleveland 4; Earned runs: Boston 11, Cleveland 5; Bases on balls: Potter 2, Spahn 1, Feller 2, Klieman 2; Strikeouts: Feller 5, Spahn 7; Hits: off Potter 5 in 3⅓ innings, Spahn 1 in 5⅔ innings, Feller 8 in 6¾ innings, Klieman 1 in 0 (pitched to 3 batters), Christopher 2 in 0 (pitched to 2 batters), Paige 0 in ⅔, Muncrief 1 in 2; Runs–Earned Runs: off Potter 5–5, Feller 7–7, Klieman 3–3, Christopher 1–1; Balk: Paige. Winner: Spahn; Loser: Feller. Time: 2:39; Attendance: 86,288; Umpires; Barr, Summers, Stewart, Grieve, Paparella, Pinelli.

Rocky Colavito's Four Homers against Baltimore in 1959

Rocky Colavito entered his name in the record book alongside those of seven of baseball's all-time great sluggers on June 10, 1959, when he smashed four home runs in one game, an 11–8 victory over the Orioles in Baltimore.

All of the homers came in consecutive times at bat, establishing Colavito as one of only three players to achieve that feat, along with Lou Gehrig of the New York Yankees in 1932 and Bobby Lowe of the Boston Braves in 1894.

Others who hit four in one game were Joe Adcock, Milwaukee Braves, 1954; Gil Hodges, Brooklyn, 1950; Pat Seerey, Chicago White Sox, 1948; Chuck Klein, Philadelphia Phillies, 1936; and Ed Delahanty, Phillies, 1896.

(Since then four more players have joined the select group: Willie Mays, San Francisco, 1961; Mike Schmidt, Phillies, 1976; Bob Horner, Atlanta, 1986; and Mark Whiten, St. Louis, 1993, though only Schmidt's homers were hit consecutively.)

Making Colavito's achievement even more noteworthy is that such renowned sluggers as Babe Ruth, Mel Ott, Jimmy Foxx, Hank Greenberg, Hack Wilson, Joe DiMaggio, and Ted Williams never hit as many as four home runs in one game.

A crowd of 15,883 in Baltimore's Memorial Stadium witnessed Colavito's assault on three Oriole pitchers—Jerry Walker, Arnold Portocarrero, and Ernie Johnson. Upon reaching home after the fourth circuit blow, Colavito, unable to conceal his jubilation, jumped on the plate with both feet while smiling broadly.

"Each time I was just swinging for base hits," Colavito said after the game, "Honest, I was just trying to meet the ball, even when I batted the fourth time. I thought I already had a pretty good night, hitting three [homers]."

Home run No. 1 was hammered in the third inning off Walker. "It was a slider, right down the middle of the plate," Colavito said.

No. 2, in the fifth inning, off Portocarrero, was "either a slider or a curve, I'm not sure."

No. 3, in the sixth inning, also off Portocarrero, was "a fastball, away, on the outside half of the plate."

And No. 4, in the ninth inning, off Johnson, was hit off "a fastball up and in on me," said Colavito.

They gave Colavito six RBIs for the night and 31 for the season, and raised his home run total to 18 in the Tribe's 51 games.

Minnie Minoso and Billy Martin also homered for the Indians in that game, making it easy for Gary Bell to even his record at 5–5, though he needed relief help from Mike Garcia in the seventh.

June 10, 1959

Indians	AB	R	H	RBI
Held, ss	5	1	1	0
Power, 1b	4	1	0	0
Francona, cf	5	2	2	1
Colavito, rf	4	5	4	6
Minoso, lf	5	1	3	3
Jones, 3b	3	0	0	0
Strickland, 3b	2	0	1	0
Brown, c	4	0	1	0
Martin, 2b	3	1	1	1
a-Webster, 2b	1	0	0	0
Bell, p	3	0	0	0
Garcia, p	1	0	0	0
Totals	40	11	13	11

Baltimore	AB	R	H	RBI
Pearson, cf	3	1	2	0
Pilarcik, rf	5	1	1	2
Woodling, lf	5	1	3	1
Triandos, c	2	0	1	1
Ginsberg, c	1	1	0	0
Hale, 1b	3	0	0	0
Zuverink, p	0	0	0	0
b-Boyd, ph	1	0	0	0
Johnson, p	0	0	0	0
c-Nieman, ph	1	1	1	0
Klaus, 3b	5	0	2	4
Carrasquel, ss	5	0	0	0
Gardner, 2b	4	1	1	0
Walker, p	1	1	1	0
Portocarrero, p	1	0	0	0
Lockman, 1b	1	1	0	0
Totals	38	8	12	8

Cleveland	3	1	2	0	1	3	0	0	1—11
Baltimore	1	2	0	0	0	0	4	0	1— 8

a-Popped out for Martin in seventh
b-Flied out for Zuverink in seventh
c-Doubled for Johnson in ninth

Two-base hits: Brown, Held, Francona, Klaus, Nieman; Home runs: Colavito 4, Minoso, Martin; Left on base: Cleveland 5, Baltimore 8; Stolen base: Minoso; Sacrifice fly: Triandos.

Cleveland	IP	H	R	ER	BB	SO
Bell, W	6⅓	8	7	7	4	3
Garcia	2⅔	4	1	1	0	3

Baltimore	IP	H	R	ER	BB	SO
Walker, L	2⅓	4	6	6	2	1
Portocarrero	3⅓	7	4	4	1	3
Zuverink	1⅓	0	0	0	0	0
Johnson	2	2	1	1	0	0

Time: 2:54; Attendance: 15,883; Umpires: Summers, McKinley, Soar, Chylak.

Tris Speaker Becomes Fifth Player to Get 3,000 Career Hits

After 18 major league baseball seasons Tris Speaker's legs, by his own admission, were "wearing out."

But they still were strong enough on May 17, 1925, for the Indians' player-manager to get a double and two singles, the last his 3,000th hit in the ninth inning of a 2–1 loss to the Washington Senators at League Park.

All three of Speaker's hits were socked off Tom Zachary, who allowed the Indians a total of nine, but never more than one an inning except the ninth.

That's when the Indians got their only run as, after Speaker led off with his single, Luke Sewell doubled with one out sending Ray Knode, running for Speaker, to third. Knode then scored on a sacrifice fly by Cliff Lee, but George Burns popped out, ending the game.

Speaker, nearing 40, almost didn't play the game because his legs were bothering him, but put himself in the lineup because the Indians were battling the defending American League champions.

A few days earlier Speaker had suffered a dislocated fibula in his leg and, though it was put back in place by Dr. Harry Knight, a specialist from Rochester, New York, inflammation resulted, causing pain and soreness.

Dr. Knight gave Speaker approval to play, but warned the center fielder that he would not be free of the inflammation for two or three more days.

Speaker became the fifth player to make 3,000 hits in their major league careers. Preceding Speaker to that level were Ty Cobb, Honus Wagner, Napoleon Lajoie, and Eddie Collins.

(Since then 13 more players have made 3,000 hits, including the all-time leader, Pete Rose, Hank Aaron, Stan Musial, Carl Yastrzemski, Willie Mays, Paul Waner, Rod Carew, Lou Brock, Al Kaline, Roberto Clemente, Robin Yount, George Brett, Dave Winfield, and Eddie Murray.)

May 17, 1925

Washington	AB	R	H	RBI
Rice, rf	4	2	2	n/a
B. Harris, 2b	3	0	1	n/a
J. Harris, lf, 1b	4	0	1	n/a
Goslin, cf, lf	4	0	1	n/a
Shirley, 1b	3	0	0	n/a
McNeely, cf	1	0	0	n/a
Bluege, 3b	3	0	1	n/a
Peckinpaugh, ss	4	0	1	n/a
Ruel, c	4	0	1	n/a
Zachary, p	2	0	0	n/a
Totals	32	2	8	n/a

Indians	AB	R	H	RBI
Jamieson, lf	4	0	0	0
Lutzke, 3b	4	0	1	0
Speaker, cf	4	0	3	0
J. Sewell, ss	3	0	0	0
L. Sewell, c	4	0	2	0
Lee, rf	3	0	1	1
Burns, 1b	4	0	1	0
Fewster, 2b	2	0	0	0
Klugman, 3b	1	0	0	0
Uhle, p	3	0	1	0
1-Knode, pr	0	1	0	0
Totals	32	1	9	1

Washington	0	0	1	0	0	0	0	1	0—2
Cleveland	0	0	0	0	0	0	0	0	1—1

1-Ran for Speaker in ninth

Errors: Jamieson, J. Sewell, Fewster; Two-base hits: Rice, Goslin, Lutzke, Speaker, Burns, L. Sewell; Sacrifices: Zachary, B. Harris, Lee; Double plays: Peckinpaugh and B. Harris; B. Harris and Shirley; Bluege, B. Harris, and Shirley; Fewster, J. Sewell, and Burns; Left on base: Washington 6, Cleveland 6; Bases on balls: off Uhle 1; Strikeouts: by Zachary 1, Uhle 6; Hit by pitcher: J. Sewell (by Zachary); Time: 1:45; Umpires: Geisel, Moriarty, Rowland.

Larry Doby's Debut as American League's First Black Player

Larry Doby's arrival as the American League's first black player and the second—by four months to Jackie Robinson—in the major leagues, belongs among the Indians' "Great Moments," except for the greeting he received from some of his new teammates.

It was July 5, 1947, and Doby had just joined the Tribe in Chicago prior to a game that day against the White Sox in Comiskey Park.

"[Indians manager] Lou Boudreau had all the players lined up in front of their lockers for me to meet," recalled Doby. "I can laugh now, looking back at what happened, but it wasn't funny at the time.

"I was a scared kid then, and Boudreau said as we got to the first player, 'Larry, this is Ken Keltner,' I stuck out my hand and Keltner shook it. Then Boudreau introduced me to Joe Gordon, and he shook my hand.

"When we got to the next player and Boudreau introduced me, I put out my hand but he just stood there. He didn't shake my hand . . . he didn't say anything. There were four guys who wouldn't shake hands with me that day," said Doby, who never publicly identified them.

Though that day and several that followed are not among Doby's favorite memories, and understandably so, what transpired in his first game must be included as a memorable event in the history of the Cleveland baseball franchise.

Doby went to the plate as a pinch hitter for pitcher Bryan Stephens in the seventh inning, his first at bat in the major leagues, and struck out against reliever Earl Harrist. He hit a foul to left on a 2-and-2 count, but otherwise didn't touch the ball, for an inauspicious debut.

That was it—except for an anecdote subsequently related by Indians owner Bill Veeck, as reported by the Associated Press:

"[Doby] swung at three pitches and missed each by at least a foot. He was so discouraged . . . he returned to the dugout and sat in the corner, all alone, with his head in his hands.

"Joe Gordon was up next . . . and missed each of three pitches by at least two feet, returned to the dugout, sat down next to Doby, and put his head in his hands, too."

Veeck called it a "remarkable gesture," which it was—or would have been.

Doby denied the validity of that report, but said, "It was something that a guy like Joe Gordon would have done. He was a good man. I'll always be grateful to him for making it easier for me."

The Indians lost the game, 6–5, and the opener of a doubleheader the next day, 3–2, but won the nightcap, 5–1, as Doby was in the starting lineup for the first time as the Indians' first baseman. He went 1-for-4, driving in his first run with a single off Orval Grove in the third inning.

July 5, 1947

Indians	AB	R	H	RBI
Metkovich, cf	5	0	2	2
Mitchell, lf	5	0	3	2
Seerey, rf	3	0	0	1
Boudreau, ss	4	0	0	0
Robinson, 1b	4	0	1	0
Gordon, 2b	3	1	0	0
Keltner, 3b	3	0	0	0
Lopez, c	2	0	0	0
a-Edwards, ph	1	1	0	0
Ruszkowski, c	0	1	0	0
Harder, p	2	1	1	0
Stephens, p	0	0	0	0
b-Doby, ph	1	0	0	0
Lemon, p	0	0	0	0
c-Fleming, ph	0	1	0	0
Totals	33	5	7	5

Chicago	AB	R	H	RBI
Baker, 3b	3	2	1	1
Appling, ss	5	1	4	1
Wright, rf	5	0	2	1
Wallaesa, lf	5	1	0	1
York, 1b	4	0	1	0
Philley, cf	2	2	1	1
Dickey, c	3	0	1	1
Michaels, 2b	3	0	1	0
Smith, p	3	0	0	0
Harrist, p	1	0	0	0
Maltzberger, p	0	0	0	0
Totals	34	6	11	6

Cleveland	0	0	1	0	0	0	2	0	2—5
Chicago	2	0	0	1	2	0	0	1	x—6

a-Grounded into force for Lopez in seventh
b-Struck out for Stephens in seventh
c-Walked for Lemon in ninth

Two-base hits: Appling 3, Harder, Michaels; Three-base hits: Metkovich, Philley; Stolen bases: Philley 2; Double plays: Appling, Michaels, and York; Boudreau, Gordon, and Robinson; Left on base: Cleveland 8, Chicago 10; Bases on balls: Harder 3, Lemon 2, Smith 4, Harrist 2; Strikeouts: Harder 2, Lemon 1, Smith 3, Harrist 3; Hits: off Harder 9 in 4⅔ innings, Stephens 1 in 1⅓, Lemon 1 in 2, Smith 3 in 6 (none out in seventh), Harrist 3 in 2 (none out in ninth), Maltzberger 1 in 1; Hit by pitcher: Philley (by Lemon); Wild pitch: Smith; Winner: Smith; Loser: Harder; Time: 2:28; Attendance: 14,655; Umpires: McKinley, Summers, Rue, Paparella.

Bob Feller Strikes Out 17 in 1936 to Set a New American League Record

With his father seeing him pitch in the major leagues for the first time, Bob Feller, the Indians' 17-year-old rookie, set an American League record by striking out 17 batters in a 5–2 victory over the Philadelphia Athletics in the opener of a doubleheader on September 13, 1936.

Exactly three weeks after winning his first game, Feller hurled a two-hitter to raise his won-lost mark to 3–2.

Feller's 17 strikeouts also tied the National League record set by the St. Louis Cardinals' Dizzy Dean on July 30, 1933, against the Chicago Cubs.

Denny Galehouse won the nightcap, 5–4, after Feller fanned George Puccinelli for the final out in the opener to break the previous AL record of 16 set 28 years earlier by Rube Waddell of the St. Louis Browns against Philadelphia on July 29, 1908.

Feller's victims included Wally Moses, Chubby Dean, and Bob Johnson in the first inning; Hugh Luby and Frank Hayes in the second; Johnson and Pinky Higgins in the third; Randy Gumpert and Lou Finney in the fifth; Luby, Russ Peters, and Hayes in the sixth; Gumpert and Puccinelli in the seventh; and Higgins and Luby in the eighth, before he struck out Puccinelli with two out in the ninth.

When Luby went down swinging in the eighth, it broke Feller's personal high of 15 strikeouts set in his first major league start, and victory, 4–1, over the St. Louis Browns on August 23.

Feller's performance was far from being a masterpiece, however, as he walked nine batters, hit one, and uncorked a wild pitch, and also allowed the Athletics to steal seven bases.

Both of Philadelphia's runs came in the third inning. Finney walked with one out and stole second. After Moses also walked, Dean singled for one run, and Moses scored on a double steal with Johnson at bat. The uprising ended when Feller struck out Johnson and Higgins.

September 13, 1936

Philadelphia	AB	R	H	RBI
Finney, cf	1	1	0	0
Puccinelli, rf	2	0	0	0
Moses, rf, cf	2	1	1	0
Dean, 1b	3	0	1	1
Johnson, lf	4	0	0	0
Higgins, 3b	2	0	0	0
Luby, 2b	4	0	0	0
Peters, ss	4	0	0	0
Hayes, c	4	0	0	0
Gumpert, p	3	0	0	0
a-Moss, ph	0	0	0	0
Totals	29	2	2	1

Indians	AB	R	H	RBI
Hughes, 2b	3	2	1	0
Knickerbocker, ss	2	2	1	0
Averill, cf	2	1	1	2
Trosky, 1b	4	0	2	0
Weatherly, rf	4	0	0	1
Hale, 3b	4	0	0	0
Heath, lf	3	0	1	0
George, c	4	0	1	0
Feller, p	4	0	0	0
Totals	30	5	7	3

Philadelphia	0	0	2	0	0	0	0	0	0—2
Cleveland	2	0	2	0	0	0	1	0	x—5

a-Walked for Gumpert in ninth

Error: Peters; Two-base hits: Hughes, Averill; Stolen bases: Finney 2, Higgins 2, Dean, Moses, Moss; Sacrifice: Knickerbocker; Double play: Luby, Peters, and Dean; Left on bases: Philadelphia 10, Cleveland 7; Bases on balls: off Gumpert 5, Feller 9; Strikeouts: Feller 17, Gumpert 2; Hit by pitcher: Moses (by Feller); Wild pitch: Feller; Balk: Gumpert; Time: 2:03; Attendance: 6,500; Umpires: Kolls, Johnston, Owens.

Carlos Baerga Sets Record With Left- and Right-Handed Homers in Same Inning in 1993

Of the thousands of switch-hitters in the history of major league baseball, Carlos Baerga became the first to hit two home runs in the same inning while batting left-handed and right-handed.

It happened in the seventh inning of the Indians' 15–5 victory over the New York Yankees in Cleveland's Municipal Stadium on April 8, 1993.

Baerga's first homer was hit from the right side of the plate on a 3-and-2 pitch, a two-run shot over the left-field fence off southpaw Steve Howe. It gave the Indians an 8–5 lead.

Then, after the Indians had scored six more runs, Baerga batted again, this time left-handed against right-hander Steve Farr with the bases empty and two out. He hit a 2-and-0 pitch over the fence in right field, completing the feat that had never previously been done in major league baseball.

"When I got back to the dugout [after the second homer] the guys told me it was a record, but I didn't believe them," said Baerga. "Then, when I got to the clubhouse after the game and was told that nobody had ever done it before, I figured it was true—but it's still hard to believe."

Immediately before Baerga's second homer, Indians pinch hitter Alvaro Espinoza cracked a three-run homer.

Then, immediately after yielding Baerga's second homer, Farr was ejected from the game by umpire Al Clark for throwing his next pitch too close to the Tribe's next batter, Albert Belle.

It was the 92nd time a player hit home runs from both sides of the plate in the same game, but never in the same inning.

The two homers gave Baerga four hits in five at bats. They were among the 17 collected by the Indians against five New York pitchers who worked in that game. The Indians also employed five pitchers, with the victory credited to starter Mike Bielecki.

April 8, 1993

New York	AB	R	H	RBI
B. Williams, cf	5	1	2	0
Boggs, 3b	5	0	1	0
Mattingly, 1b	5	1	2	0
Tartabull, rf	4	0	1	1
Humphreys, cf	1	0	0	0
O'Neill, lf	3	1	2	2
a-Leyritz, ph, c	1	0	1	2
Nokes, c	3	0	0	0
b-Stanley, ph	0	0	0	0
c-James, ph, lf	1	0	0	0
Maas, dh	3	0	0	0
Owen, ss	4	1	2	0
Kelly, 2b	3	1	1	0
e-Gallego, ph, 2b	1	0	0	0
Totals	39	5	12	5

Indians	AB	R	H	RBI
Lofton, cf	5	1	1	1
Treadway, 3b	3	1	2	0
d-Espinoza, 3b	2	2	2	3
Baerga, 2b	5	4	4	3
Belle, lf	4	2	1	1
Sorrento, 1b	5	2	2	2
Jefferson, dh	3	1	1	1
Hill, rf	5	2	3	3
Alomar, c	3	0	1	0
Ortiz, c	0	0	0	0
Fermin, ss	3	0	0	1
Totals	38	15	17	15

New York	0	0	0	1	0	1	3	0	0— 5
Cleveland	2	0	3	0	0	1	9	0	x—15

a-Singled for O'Neill in seventh
b-Announced for Nokes in seventh
c-Grounded out for Stanley in seventh
d-Homered for Treadway in seventh
e-Grounded out for Kelly in eighth

Errors: Kelly, Alomar; Left on base: New York 8, Cleveland 4; Two-base hits: B. Williams, Boggs, Mattingly, Baerga 2, Sorrento, Hill; Three-base hit: Hill; Home runs: Baerga 2, Espinoza, O'Neill; Sacrifice: Fermin; Double play: Owen, Gallego, and Mattingly.

New York	IP	H	R	ER	BB	SO
Militello, L	2⅔	6	5	4	2	0
Monteleone	3⅓	3	1	1	0	2
Howe	0	5	6	6	0	0
Farr	⅔	3	3	3	0	0
Heaton	1⅓	0	0	0	0	1

Indians	IP	H	R	ER	BB	SO
Bielecki, W	6	6	2	2	1	5
Power	0	3	3	3	0	0
Wickander	⅔	2	0	0	0	1
Plunk	⅓	0	0	0	0	0
Christopher	2	1	0	0	0	1

Hit by pitcher: Belle (by Howe); Time: 3:04; Attendance: 13,834; Umpires: Clark, Morrison, Barnett, Kosc.

Cleveland Plays Major League Baseball's Most Bizarre Game in 1901

It was a game for the record book, even though it did not involve the kind of individual performance that usually is historic.

It took place in the American League's first season, on May 23, 1901, at League Park between the Cleveland team then nicknamed the Blues and the Washington Senators.

"Never . . . has there been a more sensational finish," is the way the *Cleveland Plain Dealer* reported the Blues' 14–13 victory, after they'd scored nine runs after two were out in the last of the ninth.

"It was a game of hopeless defeat turned into glorious victory, and never before did an audience show as much inclination to go totally insane or give a better oral demonstration."

As the paper reported, Cleveland went into the ninth trailing, 13–5, and facing what seemed to be the inevitable. "The people had left the stands by scores, disgusted with such a one-sided game. The few who remained did so to scoff, but some stayed on to cheer."

Then, sounding much like a rendition of "Casey at the Bat," the story went on to say that the first two Cleveland batters were retired in the ninth as "Hoffer struck out and Pickering was thrown out at first."

But, "McCarthy sent a clean single to right field and the spectators were offended. It seemed like a useless delay. Bradley hit another one safe and the opinion was that the players were only trying to help their batting averages.

"But LaChance, after going after two bad ones, pounded a single to center and McCarthy crossed the plate.

"Wood was hit by a pitched ball and the bags were full, but no one had the slightest hope of pulling the game out of the fire.

"Scheibeck, however, hit the ball square on the nose for a double. Genins cracked out a single, and [opposing pitcher] Patton was taken out of the box and Lee substituted.

"Egan took four bad ones, and Beck, who batted for Hoffer, sent the ball so close to the left-field fence that Foster could not handle it and the runner took two bases.

"In the meantime seven runs had been scored in the inning and one more would tie the game.

"Then Pickering singled and Beck went home.

"By this time the audience gave a life-sized picture of pandemonium let out for recess. A crowd of Indians on a red hot warpath could not have been more demonstrative.

"They roared, they jumped, they shouted. They threw everything within reach in the air. Hats, umbrellas, canes, cushions went up as if a cyclone had struck that part of the landscape. They rushed on the field and came close to losing the game for Cleveland by forfeit.

"McCarthy was the man who was given the opportunity of batting in the winning run, and he accepted it. A single to left sent Pickering across the plate, he having gone to second on a passed ball.

"The demonstration that followed may be imagined—it cannot be described."

And wasn't, except for this last statement:

"Cleveland's ninth inning will be remembered until the last person who saw it can remember no more."

May 23, 1901

Washington	AB	R	H	RBI
Farrell, cf	6	1	1	n/a
Dungan, rf	4	0	1	n/a
Quinn, 2b	5	1	2	n/a
Foster, lf	5	1	2	n/a
Everett, 1b	3	1	0	n/a
Grady, c	4	2	2	n/a
Clingman, ss	4	3	2	n/a
Coughlin, 3b	3	2	2	n/a
Patton, p	4	2	2	n/a
Lee, p	0	0	0	n/a
Totals	40	13	14	n/a

Blues	AB	R	H	RBI
Pickering, rf	6	1	1	n/a
McCarthy, lf	5	2	2	n/a
Bradley, 3b	5	2	4	n/a
LaChance, 1b	5	1	3	n/a
Wood, c	4	1	1	n/a
Scheibeck, ss	5	2	4	n/a
Genins, cf	4	1	1	n/a
Eagan, 2b	4	2	1	n/a
Hoffer, p	4	1	1	n/a
a-Beck, ph	1	1	1	n/a
Totals	43	14	19	n/a

Washington	0	5	0	1	3	0	2	0	2—13
Cleveland	0	0	0	4	0	0	1	9—14

a-Doubled for Hoffer in ninth

Errors: Foster, Grady, Bradley 2, Wood, Scheibeck; Double play: Clingman, Quinn, and Everett; Two-base hits: Scheibeck, Beck, Coughlin; Three-base hit: Dungan; Sacrifice hits: Patton, Everett, Clingman, Coughlin; Stolen bases: Grady, Clingman; Left on base: Washington 7, Cleveland 7; Hits: off Patton 16 in 8⅔ innings, Lee 3 in 0; Bases on balls: Patton 2, Lee 1, Hoffer 3; Strikeouts: Patton 2; Hit by pitcher: Wood (by Patton); Losing pitcher: Lee; Passed ball: Grady; Time: 2:00; Attendance: 1,250; Umpire: Cantillon.

Indians Win Wildest Opener in Major League History in 1925

If there ever was a wilder opening-day game in major league history than the one the Indians won on April 14, 1925, nobody has yet pointed it out.

After blowing leads of 4–1, 7–1, 8–4, and 9–6, the Indians rallied from a seventh-inning, 13–9 deficit with 12 runs in the eighth to beat the Browns, 21–14, in St. Louis.

Stuart M. Bell, the sports editor of the *Cleveland Plain Dealer,* reported that "the teams opened the season with a loud detonation," and went on to say, "Without the assistance of any lightning calculators, your correspondent can only report the score as being 21 to 14."

Bell then wrote that he "cannot be held accountable for the accuracy" of his account of the game, calling it a "travesty on the well known national pastime." He said that it was "even a burlesque on spring training exhibitions, the climax of some terrible pitching and worse fielding coming in the eighth inning," when the Indians scored 12 runs on six hits and five errors by the Browns.

"It was not like a major league opening which Clevelanders have been accustomed to. Hundreds of bleachers were empty when the two circuses took the ring, and thousands of bleacher and grandstand seats were vacant when Joe Shaute, the fifth thrower used by Manager Tris Speaker of the Tribe, retired the last man in the ninth.

"There was a band, which could not be heard above the din of the crashing balls and the crescendo of jeers for Herschel Bennett and Marty McManus, who made seven errors between them."

April 14, 1925

Indians	AB	R	H	RBI
Jamieson, lf	7	4	4	n/a
Spurgeon, 3b	6	2	2	n/a
Speaker, cf	5	2	2	n/a
J. Sewell, ss	4	1	1	n/a
Myatt, c	3	2	2	n/a
a-Lee, ph	1	0	0	n/a
L. Sewell, c	3	0	0	n/a
Stephenson, rf	5	2	0	n/a
Knode, 1b	4	1	2	n/a
Burns, 1b	1	2	0	n/a
Fewster, 2b	4	2	3	n/a
S. Smith, p	3	1	1	n/a
Speece, p	1	0	0	n/a
Edwards, p	0	0	0	n/a
Buckeye, p	0	0	0	n/a
b-Uhle, ph	1	0	1	n/a
c-McNulty, pr	1	2	1	n/a
Shaute, p	0	0	0	n/a
Totals	**49**	**21**	**19**	**n/a**

St. Louis	AB	R	H	RBI
Tobin, rf	6	1	3	n/a
Robertson, 3b	5	2	1	n/a
Sisler, 1b	6	2	3	n/a
Williams, lf	6	2	3	n/a
McManus, 2b	4	2	2	n/a
Evans, cf	1	0	0	n/a
Bennett, cf	4	0	2	n/a
Severeid, c	5	1	3	n/a
Gerber, ss	3	2	1	n/a
Bush, p	1	0	0	n/a
Grant, p	1	0	0	n/a
Wingard, p	2	2	2	n/a
Davis, p	0	0	0	n/a
d-Dixon, ph	0	0	0	n/a
Stauffer, p	0	0	0	n/a
e-Rice, ph	1	0	0	n/a
Totals	**45**	**14**	**20**	**n/a**

Cleveland	4	1	2	1	1	0	0	(12)	0—21
St. Louis	1	0	3	3	2	4	0	0	1—14

a-Batted for Myatt in fifth
b-Batted for Buckeye in eighth
c-Ran for Uhle in eighth
d-Batted for Davis in eighth
e-Batted for Stauffer in ninth

Errors: Sisler 4, McManus 3, Bennett 3, J. Sewell, Fewster; Two-base hits: Williams 2, Severeid 2, Tobin, McManus 2, J. Sewell, Spurgeon, Bennett; Home runs: Jamieson, Myatt, Williams, Speaker, McNulty; Stolen bases: Knode, Speaker, Jamieson, Fewster; Sacrifices: Spurgeon, Speaker, Fewster, Robertson, Bennett; Double plays: Grant, Robertson, and Sisler; J. Sewell (unassisted); J. Sewell, Fewster, and Burns; Left on bases: Cleveland 11, St. Louis 13; Bases on balls: off Smith 1, Bush 2, Grant 1, Davis 2, Wingard 2, Edwards 1, Speece 1, Shaute 4; Strikeouts: Grant 1, Davis 1, Wingard 2, Stauffer 1, Shaute 1; Hits: off Smith 9 in 3⅔ innings, Speece 4 in 1⅓, Edwards 3 in ⅓, Buckeye 2 in 1⅓, Shaute 2 in 2, Bush 9 in 2⅔, Grant 3 in 2, Wingard 4 in 2⅔, Davis 3 in ⅔, Stauffer 0 in 1; Wild pitches: Bush, Speece; Passed balls: L. Sewell 2; Winning pitcher: Buckeye; Losing pitcher: Wingard; Time: 2:46; Umpires: Owen, Rowland.

Indians Open Jacobs Field with a 4–3 Victory over Seattle

They were held hitless for seven innings after President Bill Clinton threw out the traditional first pitch, but the Indians prevailed in the 11th to perfectly inaugurate brand-new Jacobs Field in front of a sellout crowd of 41,459 on April 4, 1994.

Wayne Kirby singled to drive in Eddie Murray with the deciding run in the second extra inning to provide the Tribe and fourth reliever Eric Plunk a 4–3 victory over the Seattle Mariners.

"I can't think of a better way to open this jewel of a ballpark," said Tribe manager Mike Hargrove. "It was scary for awhile, but it ended perfectly."

Hargrove was correct on both counts.

Mariners southpaw Randy Johnson had the fans, as well as the Indians, thinking about the only no-hitter ever pitched on an opening day—by Bob Feller 54 years earlier—until catcher Sandy Alomar, Jr., spoiled it in the eighth.

Even Feller, who was in attendance, admitted he was concerned about Johnson matching his 1940 achievement, though he did so without complaint. "Hey, every time a pitcher flirts with a no-hitter on opening day, I get my name in the paper," he quipped.

Alomar ended the suspense when he lined a 1-and-2 pitch into right field for a single after Candy Maldonado led off with a walk.

Apparently shaken by the turn of events, Johnson heaved a wild pitch to the next batter, Manny Ramirez, who then doubled to left for two runs, tying the score. The uprising ended when Ramirez was picked off second and Johnson retired the next two batters.

Though the Mariners got a run in the 10th, the Indians fought back to tie it again in their half of the inning, and again Ramirez was a key figure in the rally, as he walked with one out.

Kirby ran for Ramirez, took third on Jim Thome's double to right, waited as Kenny Lofton was intentionally walked, and scored when the Mariners were unable to turn a double play on Omar Vizquel's ground out, before Carlos Baerga flied out.

The Indians won it in the 11th when Eddie Murray doubled with one out, went to third as Paul Sorrento flied out, held as Alomar was intentionally walked, and scored on Kirby's single to left.

April 4, 1994

Seattle	AB	R	H	RBI
Amaral, 2b	5	0	1	0
E. Martinez, 3b	0	1	0	0
Blowers, 3b	5	0	1	0
Griffey, Jr., cf	4	1	1	0
Buhner, rf	3	0	0	0
Anthony, lf	4	1	1	2
T. Martinez, 1b	4	0	1	0
Jefferson, dh	3	0	1	0
b-Mitchell, ph, dh	1	0	1	1
D. Wilson, c	4	0	0	0
Fermin, ss	5	0	0	0
Totals	**38**	**3**	**7**	**3**

Indians	AB	R	H	RBI
Lofton, cf	3	0	0	0
Vizquel, ss	4	0	0	1
Baerga, 2b	5	0	0	0
Belle, lf	5	0	1	0
Murray, 1b	5	1	2	0
Maldonado, dh	2	1	0	0
a-Sorrento, ph, dh	2	0	0	0
S. Alomar, c	3	1	1	0
Ramirez, rf	3	0	1	2
1-Kirby, pr, rf	1	1	1	1
Lewis, 3b	2	0	0	0
c-Thome, ph, 3b	1	0	1	0
Totals	**36**	**4**	**7**	**4**

```
Seattle      1 0 1 0 0 0 0 0 0 1  0—3
Cleveland    0 0 0 0 0 0 0 2 0 1  1—4
```

a-Struck out for Maldonado in ninth
b-Singled for Jefferson in 10th
c-Doubled for Lewis in 10th
1-Ran for Ramirez in 10th

Errors: T. Martinez, Murray; Double plays: Fermin and T. Martinez (2); Left on base: Seattle 11, Cleveland 8; Two-base hits: Amaral, Belle, Murray, Ramirez, Thome; Home run: Anthony; Caught stealing: Lofton; Sacrifice: Buhner, D. Wilson; Sacrifice fly: Anthony; HBP: E. Martinez (by D. Martinez); WP: R. Johnson; Time: 3:29; Attendance: 41,459; Umpires: Barnett, Kosc, Clark, Morrison.

Seattle	IP	H	R	ER	BB	SO
R. Johnson	8	2	2	2	5	2
Davis	⅔	2	0	0	0	0
Ayala	⅔	0	1	1	1	2
King, L	1⅓	3	1	1	2	0

Indians	IP	H	R	ER	BB	SO
D. Martinez	7	3	2	2	4	4
Swan	1	1	0	0	0	1
Mesa	1⅓	2	1	1	0	1
Lilliquist	⅓	1	0	0	1	0
Plunk, W	1⅓	0	0	0	0	1

Box Scores of Other Noteworthy Games

Cleveland's First American League Game

April 24, 1901
Chicago 7, Blues 2

Cleveland	AB	R	H
Pickering, rf	4	0	1
McCarthy, lf	4	0	2
Genins, cf	4	0	0
LaChance, 1b	4	1	1
Bradley, 3b	4	0	0
Beck, 2b	3	0	2
Hallman, ss	3	1	0
Wood, c	4	0	1
Hoffer, p	4	0	0
Totals	**34**	**2**	**7**

Chicago	AB	R	H
Hoy, cf	5	0	1
Jones, rf	2	2	1
Mertes, lf	3	2	1
Shugart, ss	2	2	0
Isbell, 1b	3	1	1
Hartman, 3b	4	0	1
Brain, 2b	4	0	0
Sullivan, c	4	1	2
Patterson, p	4	0	0
Totals	**31**	**8**	**7**

```
Cleveland   0 0 0 1 0 0 1 0  0—2
Chicago     2 5 0 0 0 0 1 0  x—8
```

Errors: LaChance, Hallman, Hartman; LOB: Cleveland 3, Chicago 5; 2B: Beck; DP: Brain, Shugart, and Isbell; Hoffer, Hallman, and LaChance; Strikeouts: by Hoffer 1; Bases on balls: by Hoffer 6, Patterson 2; Time: 1:30; Attendance: 14,500; Umpire: Connolly.

Cleveland's First American League Home Game

April 29, 1901
Blues 4, Milwaukee 3

Milwaukee	AB	R	H
Waldron, rf	5	0	1
Gilbert, 2b	4	0	0
Hallman, lf	3	1	1
Anderson, 1b	4	0	1
Conroy, ss	4	1	0
Duffy, cf	3	0	1
Burke, 3b	4	1	2
Leahy, c	3	0	1
Hawley, p	4	0	1
Totals	**34**	**3**	**8**

Cleveland	AB	R	H
Pickering, rf	4	1	1
McCarthy, lf	4	1	1
Genins, cf	4	1	1
LaChance, 1b	4	1	3
Bradley, 3b	3	0	1
Beck, 2b	4	0	0
Hallman, ss	4	0	1
Yeager, c	3	0	1
Hoffer, p	3	0	0
Totals	**33**	**4**	**9**

```
Milwaukee   0 1 1 1 0 0 0 0  0—3
Cleveland   0 0 0 1 0 0 0 3  x—4
```

Errors: Gilbert, Burke 2, Pickering, McCarthy 2, Hallman 2; 2B: Bradley, Pickering, Hallman, Hawley; 3B: McCarthy; SH: Duffy, Leahy; SB: LaChance, Yeager, Conroy; DP: Conroy and Leahy; Hallman and Burke; LOB: Milwaukee 7, Cleveland 6; ER: Milwaukee 1, Cleveland 2; Bases on balls: by Hoffer 1; Strikeouts: by Hawley 3; HBP: Bradley (by Hawley 1); T: 1:47; A: 8,000; Umpires: Mannassau, Sheridan.

Addie Joss Pitches One-Hitter in Major League Debut

April 26, 1902
Bronchos 3, St. Louis 0

Cleveland	AB	R	H
Pickering, cf	3	0	1
McCarthy, lf	3	0	2
Harvey, rf	3	0	0
Schreckengost, 1b	4	1	2
Bonner, 2b	2	0	0
Thoney, 2b	2	0	0
Bradley, 3b	4	1	0
Gochnaur, ss	3	1	2
Bemis, c	3	0	0
Joss, p	4	0	1
Totals	**31**	**3**	**8**

St. Louis	AB	R	H
Burkett, lf	4	0	1
Heidrick, cf	4	0	0
Jones, rf	2	0	0
Anderson, 1b	4	0	0
Wallace, ss	4	0	0
Padden, 2b	3	0	0
McCormick, 3b	2	0	0
Donahue, c	2	0	0
Sudhoff, p	2	0	0
Totals	**27**	**0**	**1**

```
Cleveland    0 0 0 0 0 0 3 0  0—3
St. Louis    0 0 0 0 0 0 0 0  0—0
```

Errors: Gochnaur, Baurkett, Wallace, McCormick; 2B: Joss; SH: Donahue, McCarthy, Harvey, SB: Jones; DP: Gochnaur and Schreckengost; Donahue, McCormick, and Anderson; LOB: Cleveland 5, St. Louis 5; ER: Cleveland 1; Bases on balls: by Joss 4, Sudhoff 2; Strikeouts: by Joss 5, Sudhoff 6; PB: Donahue, Bemis; T: 1:50; A: 3,500; Umpire: Caruthers.

Napoleon Lajoie's Cleveland Debut

June 4, 1902
Bronchos 4, Boston 3

Boston	AB	R	H
Dougherty, lf	5	1	1
Collins, 3b	4	1	0
Stahl, cf	3	0	1
Freeman, rf	3	0	2
Parent, ss	4	0	1
LaChance, 1b	3	1	1
Ferris, 2b	4	0	0
Warner, c	4	0	2
Prentiss, p	3	0	0
a-Gleason, ph	1	0	0
Totals	**34**	**3**	**8**

Cleveland	AB	R	H
Pickering, cf	4	0	0
McCarthy, lf	4	2	2
Flick, rf	3	0	0
Lajoie, 2b	3	1	1
Hickman, 1b	4	0	0
Bradley, 3b	3	0	2
Gochnaur, ss	3	0	0
Wood, c	3	1	1
Moore, p	3	0	0
Totals	30	4	6

Boston	2	0	0	1	0	0	0	0	0—3
Cleveland	0	0	0	2	0	1	1	0	x—4

a-Batted for Prentiss in ninth

Errors: Parent, Ferris, Hickman, Bradley 2, Gochnaur 2; 2B: Bradley, McCarthy 2, Lajoie, Wood, Freeman, LaChance; SH: Lajoie, Stahl; SB: Pickering, Freeman; DP: Bradley, Lajoie, and Hickman; Gochnaur, Lajoie, and Hickman; LOB: Boston 4, Cleveland 8; ER: Cleveland 2; Bases on balls: by Prentiss 1, Moore 3; Strikeouts: by Prentiss 1, Moore 5; T: 1:40; A: 9,827; Umpire: Johnstone.

Nap Lajoie Goes 8-For-8 in Doubleheader to Win Title

October 9, 1910 (First Game)
St. Louis 5, Naps 4

Cleveland	AB	R	H
Bronkie, 3b	3	1	1
Graney, lf	4	1	1
Jackson, cf	4	1	2
Lajoie, 2b	4	1	4
Easterly, rf	4	0	0
Stovall, 1b	4	0	2
Smith, c	4	0	0
Peckinpaugh, ss	4	0	0
Blanding, p	4	0	0
Totals	35	4	10

St. Louis	AB	R	H
Truesdale, 2b	5	0	0
Corriden, 3b	5	2	3
Stone, lf	5	0	2
Griggs, 1b	5	1	3
Wallace, ss	3	0	1
Northen, cf	4	0	0
Hartzell, rf	3	2	1
Stephens, c	3	0	2
Nelson, p	3	0	1
*Totals	36	5	13

Cleveland	3	1	0	0	0	0	0	0	0—4
St. Louis	1	1	1	0	0	1	0	0	1—5

*None out when winning run scored

Errors: Truesdale, Wallace, Bronkie; 2B: Griggs, Jackson, Corriden, Graney, Stephens; 3B: Griggs, Lajoie; LOB: St. Louis 12, Cleveland 5; SH: Stephens; SB: Bronkie, Stovall, Griggs; Bases on balls: off Nelson 1, Blanding 4; Strikeouts: by Nelson 4, Blanding 4; WP: Blanding; T: 1:42; Umpire: Evans.

October 9, 1910 (Second Game)
Naps 3, St. Louis 0

Cleveland	AB	R	H
Birmingham, 3b	4	1	2
Graney, lf	5	2	0
Jackson, cf	4	0	2
Lajoie, 2b	4	0	4
Easterly, rf	4	0	0
Hohnhorst, 1b	3	0	1
McGuire, c	3	0	0
Peckinpaugh, ss	4	0	1
Falkenberg, p	3	0	0
Totals	34	3	10

St. Louis	AB	R	H
Truesdale, 2b	4	0	0
Corriden, 3b	4	0	2
Stone, lf	4	0	1
Griggs, 1b	4	0	1
Wallace, ss	3	0	1
Northen, cf	3	0	0
Hartzell, rf	3	0	1
O'Connor, c	0	0	0
Killefer, c	3	0	0
Malloy, p	3	0	0
Totals	31	0	5

Cleveland	1	0	2	0	0	0	0	0	0—3
St. Louis	0	0	0	0	0	0	0	0	0—0

Errors: Truesdale, Corriden, Malloy, Graney 2; 2B: Birmingham, Corriden; SH: Lajoie; LOB: St. Louis 4, Cleveland 10; DP: Malloy, Truesdale, and Griggs; Lajoie, Peckinpaugh, and Hohnhorst; SB: Stone; HBP: McGuire (by Malloy); Bases on balls: off Malloy 4; Strikeouts: by Falkenberg 1, Malloy 6; WP: Malloy; PB: McGuire, Killefer; T: 1:15; Umpire: Evans.

AL Stars Beat Cleveland in Benefit for Joss Family

July 24, 1911
AL Stars 5, Naps 3

All-Stars	AB	R	H
Speaker, cf	2	1	2
Milan, cf	3	1	2
Collins, 2b	5	1	2
Cobb, rf	4	0	2
Baker, 3b	4	1	1
Crawford, lf	4	0	1
Chase, 1b	3	1	3
Wallace, ss	3	0	0
Street, c	2	0	1
Livingston, c	2	0	1
Wood, p	0	0	0
Johnson, p	1	0	0
Ford, p	2	0	0
Totals	35	5	15

Cleveland	AB	R	H
Graney, lf	4	0	1
Olson, ss	4	1	2
Jackson, rf	2	0	0
Butcher, rf	2	0	1
Stovall, 1b	2	1	1
Lajoie, 1b	2	0	0
Birmingham, cf	4	0	1
Ball, 2b	4	0	0
Turner, 3b	3	0	1
Smith, c	1	0	0
Easterly, c	3	0	0
Young, p	0	0	0
a-Griggs, ph	1	0	0
Kahler, p	1	0	0
Blanding, p	1	1	1
Totals	34	3	8

All-Stars	2	1	0	1	0	0	1	0	0—5
Cleveland	0	1	0	0	0	0	0	2	0—3

a-Batted for Young in third

Errors: Olson, Birmingham; 2B: Birmingham, Speaker, Milan, Blanding; 3B: Collins, Olson; LOB: All-Stars 6, Cleveland 5; SF: Wood, Chase; SB: Speaker, Graney, Milan, Livingston; DP: Olson, Ball, and Stovall; Hits–Runs: off Wood 2–1 in 2 innings, Johnson 1–0 in 3, Ford 5–2 in 4, Young 6–3 in 3, Kahler 4–1 in 3, Blanding 5–1 in 3; Bases on balls: Ford 1, Kahler 1; Strikeouts: by Johnson 1, Ford 1, Blanding 2; T: 1:32; A: 15,272; Umpires: Egan, Connolly.

Kavanagh Gets Baseball's First Pinch-Hit Grand Slam

September 24, 1916
Indians 5, Boston 3

Boston	AB	R	H
Hooper, rf	4	0	2
Janvrin, 2b	5	0	0
Walker, cf	3	0	0
Shorten, cf	0	0	0
Gainer, 1b	2	0	0
Hoblitzel, 1b	1	0	0
Lewis, lf	3	1	1
Gardner, 3b	2	1	1
Scott, ss	3	0	1
Carrigan, c	2	0	1
Thomas, c	1	0	0
Leonard	3	0	0
b-Henriksen, ph	0	0	0
1-McNally, pr	0	1	0
c-Ruth, ph	1	0	0
2-Walsh, pr	0	0	0
Totals	30	3	6

Cleveland	AB	R	H
Graney, lf	4	0	0
Barbare, 3b	4	0	0
Speaker, cf	4	0	1
Roth, rf	3	0	0
Wambsganss, ss	3	0	1
Gandill, 1b	3	1	1
Turner, 2b	2	1	0
O'Neill, c	2	1	0
Boehling, p	1	0	0
a-Kavanagh, ph	1	1	1
Bagby, p	1	1	0
Totals	28	5	4

Boston	0	0	0	2	0	0	0	0	1—3
Cleveland	0	0	0	0	4	0	0	0	1—5

a-Batted for Boehling in fifth
b-Batted for Scott in ninth
1-Ran for Gardner in ninth
c-Batted for Leonard in ninth
2-Ran for Thomas in ninth

Errors: Turner, Scott, Thomas; 2B: Wambsganss, Gandil, Speaker; HR: Kavanagh; LOB: Boston 8, Cleveland 1; SH: Gardner; SF: Hooper; Base on balls: off Boehling 3, Bagby 2, Leonard 1; Hits and earned runs: off Boehling 5–2 in 5 innings, Bagby 1–1 in 4, Leonard 4–4 in 8; Strikeouts: Boehling 3, Bagby 2, Leonard 7; HBP: O'Neill (by Leonard), Thomas (by Bagby); T: 1:50; A: 11,786; Umpires: O'Loughlin, Nallin.

Ray Chapman Dies After Being Hit by a Pitch

August 16, 1920
Indians 4, New York 3

Cleveland	AB	R	H
Jamieson, lf	5	0	2
Chapman, ss	1	0	0
Lunte, ss	1	0	0
Speaker, cf	4	1	0
Smith, rf	4	0	0
Gardner, 3b	3	1	1
O'Neill, c	4	2	3
Johnston, 1b	4	0	1
Wambsganss, 2b	4	0	0
Coveleski, p	3	0	0
Totals	33	4	7

New York	AB	R	H
Ward, 3b	4	0	0
Peckinpaugh, ss	4	0	0
Ruth, rf	4	1	1
Pratt, 2b	3	1	1
Lewis, lf	4	0	0
Pipp, 1b	3	0	1
Bodie, cf	4	1	2
Ruel, c	3	0	2
Mays, p	2	0	0
a-Vick, ph	1	0	1
Thormahlen, p	0	0	0
b-O'Doul, ph	1	0	0
Totals	33	3	7

Cleveland	0	1	0	2	1	0	0	0	0—4
New York	0	0	0	0	0	0	0	0	3—3

a-Batted for Mays in eighth
b-Batted for Thormahlen in ninth

Errors: Ward, Ruel; 2B: Bodie; HR: O'Neill; SH: Chapman, Ruel, Coveleski; DP: Pipp (unassisted); LOB: Cleveland 6, New York 6; Bases on balls: off Mays 1, Coveleski 2; Hits: off Mays 7 in 8 innings, Strikeouts: by Mays 3, Coveleski 4; HBP: Chapman (by Mays); Losing pitcher: Mays; Time: 1:56; Umpires: Connolly, Nallin.

Dutch Levsen Pitches and Wins Doubleheader

August 28, 1926 (First Game)
Indians 6, Boston 1

Cleveland	AB	R	H
Jamieson, lf	5	0	0
Spurgeon, 2b	5	0	2
Speaker, cf	4	1	1
Burns, 1b	4	2	3
J. Sewell, ss	3	1	1
Summa, rf	3	0	1
L. Sewell, c	4	1	0
Lutzke, 3b	4	1	1
Levsen, p	3	0	1
Totals	35	6	10

Boston	AB	R	H
Tobin, rf	4	0	0
Rigney, ss	4	0	0
Jacobson, cf	4	0	0
Rosenthal, lf	3	1	2
Regan, 2b	3	0	1
Todt, 1b	2	0	1
Herrera, 3b	2	0	0
Gaston, c	2	0	0
Wiltse, p	1	0	0
Russell, p	1	0	0
a-Bratschi, ph	1	0	0
Lundgren, p	0	0	0
Totals	27	1	4

Cleveland	0	0	0	5	0	0	0	1	0—6
Boston	0	1	0	0	0	0	0	0	0—1

a-Batted for Russell in eighth

Errors: J. Sewell, Tobin, Regan, Herrera; LOB: Cleveland 6, Boston 1; 2B: J. Sewell, Burns. SB: Summa; SH: Summa, Gaston, J. Sewell; DP: Lutzke, Spurgeon, and Burns; Jamieson and Burns; Levsen, Spurgeon, and Burns; Bases on balls: off Levsen 1, Wiltse 1, Russell 1; Strikeouts: by Wiltse 1; Hits: off Wiltse 5 in 3⅓ innings, Russell 3 in 4⅔; Losing pitcher: Wiltse; Umpires: Evans, Owens.

August 28, 1926 (Second Game)
Indians 5, Boston 1

Cleveland	AB	R	H
Jamieson, lf	4	2	3
Spurgeon, 2b	4	0	0
Speaker, cf	4	0	1
Burns, 1b	5	0	0
J. Sewell, ss	3	1	2
Summa, rf	4	2	2
L. Sewell, c	4	0	1
Lutzke, 3b	4	0	0
Levsen, p	4	0	1
Totals	36	5	10

Boston	AB	R	H
Tobin, rf	4	0	1
Rigney, ss	4	0	1
Jacobson, cf	4	0	0
Rosenthal, lf	3	1	1
Regan, 2b	4	0	1
Todt, 1b	4	0	0
Haney, 3b	1	0	0
Bischoff, c	3	0	0
Harriss, p	1	0	0
MacFayden, p	0	0	0
a-Bratschi, ph	1	0	0
b-Shaner, ph	1	0	0
Lundgren, p	0	0	0
Totals	30	1	4

Cleveland	1	0	1	2	0	0	0	1	0—5
Boston	0	0	0	0	0	0	1	0	0—1

a-Batted for Harriss in fifth
b-Batted for MacFayden in eighth

Errors: Regan, Todt 2; LOB: Cleveland 7, Boston 4; 2B: Jamieson, Speaker, Summa, Regan; SB: Tobin, J. Sewell, Summa; SH: Spurgeon; DP: Regan, Rigney, and Todt; Rigney, Regan, and Todt; Bases on balls: off Harriss 2, Levsen 2, MacFayden 1; Strikeouts: by Harriss 2; Hits: off Harriss 8 in 5 innings, MacFayden 1 in 3, Lundgren 1 in 1; HBP: Haney (by Levsen); Losing pitcher: Harriss; Umpires: Ormsby, Evans.

Johnny Burnett Gets Nine Hits in One Game

July 10, 1932
Philadelphia 18, Indians 17 (18 innings)

Philadelphia	AB	R	H	RBI
Haas, rf	9	3	2	0
Cramer, cf	8	2	2	1
Dykes, 3b	10	2	3	4
Simmons, lf	9	4	5	2
Foxx, 1b	9	4	6	8
McNair, ss	10	0	2	1
Heving, c	4	0	0	0
Madjeski, c	5	0	0	0
Williams, 2b	8	1	2	0
Krausse, p	1	0	0	0
Rommel, p	7	2	3	1
Totals	80	18	25	17

Cleveland	AB	R	H	RBI
Porter, rf	10	3	3	2
Burnett, ss	11	4	9	2
Averill, cf	9	3	5	4
Vosmik, lf	10	2	2	1
Morgan, 1b	11	1	5	4
Myatt, c	7	2	1	0
Cissell, 2b	9	1	4	3
Kamm, 3b	7	1	2	0
C. Brown, p	4	0	2	0
Hudlin, p	0	0	0	0
Ferrell, p	5	0	0	0
Totals	83	17	33	16

Philadelphia	201	201	702	000	000	201—18
Cleveland	303	011	601	000	000	200—17

E: Rommel, Burnett, Cissell 2, Morgan, C. Brown; 2B: Burnett 2, Myatt, Cissell, Vosmik, Morgan 2, Haas, Dykes, Kamm, Porter, McNair, Foxx; 3B: Williams; HR: Foxx 3, Averill; SB: Cissell; SH: Kamm, Ferrell; DP: Williams, McNair, and Foxx; Burnett, Cissell, and Morgan; Kamm, Cissell, and Morgan; Williams, Madjeski, and Foxx; LOB: Philadelphia 15, Cleveland 24; WP: Rommel 2; T: 4:05; A: 10,000; Umpires: Hildebrand, Owens.

Philadelphia	IP	H	R	BB	SO
Krausse	1	4	2	1	0
Rommel, W	17	29	15	9	7

Cleveland	IP	H	R	BB	SO
C. Brown	6⅔	13	8	1	3
Hudlin	0	0	2	2	0
Ferrell, L	11⅓	12	8	4	7

Bob Feller's Major League Debut

July 19, 1936 (Second Game)
Washington 9, Indians 5

Cleveland	AB	R	H	RBI
Hughes, 2b	5	1	2	2
Hale, 3b	5	1	3	1
Averill, cf	4	0	1	1
Trosky, 1b	4	0	2	0
Weatherly, rf	4	0	1	0
Sullivan, c	4	1	1	0
Vosmik, lf	4	1	1	1
Knickerbocker, ss	4	0	1	0
Blaeholder, p	2	0	0	0
a-Campbell, ph	0	0	0	0
Allen, p	0	0	0	0
Feller, p	0	0	0	0
b-Pytlak, ph	1	1	0	0
Totals	37	5	12	5

Washington	AB	R	H	RBI
Chapman, cf	5	2	2	1
Lewis, 3b	5	0	0	0
Kuhel, 1b	5	0	0	1
Stone, lf	4	2	2	2
Travis, rf	4	2	1	0
Myer, 2b	3	1	2	1
Bluege, 2b	1	1	1	0
Bolton, c	4	1	2	2
Kress, ss	3	0	1	1
Weaver, p	3	0	0	0
Totals	37	9	11	8

Cleveland	0	0	1	0	0	1	0	0	3—5
Washington	0	1	0	0	1	3	1	3	x—9

a-Batted for Blaeholder in seventh
b-Batted for Feller in ninth

Errors: Hughes, Hale, Lewis; 2B: Hale, Myer, Chapman, Sullivan; 3B: Hale 2, Knickerbocker; HR: Stone; DP: Kuhel and Kress; Bluege, Kress, and Kuhel. LOB: Cleveland 6, Washington 6; WP: Allen; HBP: Kress (by Feller); T: 2:11; A: 18,000; Umpires: Geisel, Ormsby.

Cleveland	IP	H	R	BB	SO
Blaeholder, L	6	8	5	0	1
Allen	1	3	4	0	1
Feller	1	0	0	1	1

Washington	IP	H	R	BB	SO
Weaver, W	9	12	5	1	1

Indians Win American League's First Night Game

May 16, 1939
Indians 8, Philadelphia 3 (10 innings)

Cleveland	AB	R	H	RBI
Weatherly, cf	5	2	1	1
Hemsley, c	3	0	0	0
b-Hale, ph	1	0	1	1
Pytlak, c	0	1	0	0
Trosky, 1b	4	2	2	1
Solters, lf	2	0	0	0
Heath, lf	3	1	2	2
B. Chapman, rf	2	0	0	0
Campbell, rf	3	1	0	1
Keltner, 3b	4	0	1	1
Shilling, 2b	5	0	0	1
Grimes, ss	3	1	1	0
Milnar, p	2	0	0	0
a-Averill, ph	1	0	0	0
Humphries, p	1	0	0	0
Totals	39	8	8	8

Philadelphia	AB	R	H	RBI
Miles, rf	5	1	1	0
Gantenbein, 2b	2	1	0	0
S. Chapman, cf	4	0	1	1
Johnson, lf	3	0	1	0
Etten, 1b	5	0	0	1
Nagel, 3b	5	0	2	0
Hayes, c	4	1	1	1
Newsome, ss	3	0	1	0
c-Brucker, ph	1	0	0	0
Ambler, ss	0	0	0	0
Nelson, p	3	0	1	0
Parmelee, p	1	0	0	0
Totals	36	3	8	3

Cleveland	0	0	0	1	0	0	0	2	0	5—8
Philadelphia	1	1	0	0	0	0	1	0	0	0—3

a-Batted for Milnar in eighth
b-Batted for Hemsley in eighth
c-Batted for Newsome in eighth

Errors: Hemsley, Shilling, Gantenbein; LOB: Cleveland 7, Philadelphia 9; 2B: Heath 2, Weatherly, Nagel 2; HR: Hayes, Trosky; SB: Gantenbein, Campbell; SH: S. Chapman, Keltner; DP: Milnar and Grimes; Bases on balls: off Nelson 1, off Milnar 4, off Parmelee 4, off Humphries 1; Strikeouts: by Nelson 4, Milnar 6, Parmelee 1, Humphries 2; Hits: off Milnar 7 in 7 innings, Nelson 6 in 7⅔, Humphries 1 in 3, Parmelee 2 in 2⅓; Winning pitcher: Humphries; Losing pitcher: Parmelee; T: 2:41; A: 15,109; Umpires: Summers, Basil, Ormsby, Pipgras.

Indians Win First Night Game in Cleveland

June 27, 1939
Indians 5, Detroit 0

Detroit	AB	R	H	RBI
McCosky, cf	4	0	0	0
Fox, rf	4	0	0	0
Averill, lf	3	0	1	0
Higgins, 3b	3	0	0	0
Kress, 2b	3	0	0	0
Greenberg, 1b	3	0	0	0
Rogell, ss	3	0	0	0
b-York, ph	0	0	0	0
Tebbetts, c	4	0	0	0
Newsom, p	0	0	0	0
a-Bell, ph	1	0	0	0
Coffman, p	1	0	0	0
Totals	29	0	1	0

Cleveland	AB	R	H	RBI
Hemsley, c	2	1	1	1
Campbell, rf	3	1	3	2
Chapman, cf	3	0	1	1
Trosky, 1b	3	0	0	1
Heath, lf	4	0	1	0
Keltner, 3b	4	0	1	0
Grimes, 2b	4	1	2	0
Webb, ss	4	1	1	0
Feller, p	3	1	0	0
Totals	30	5	10	5

Detroit	0	0	0	0	0	0	0	0	0—0
Cleveland	2	2	0	1	0	0	0	x—5

a-Batted for Newsom in second
b-Batted for Rogell in ninth

Errors: Grimes, Kress, Tebbetts; 3B: Hemsley; SB: Grimes; SH: Trosky, Hemsley 2; DP: Kress, Rogell, and Greenberg; LOB: Detroit 8, Cleveland 7; Bases on balls: off Newsom 1, Coffman 1, Feller 6; Strikeouts: Newsom 1, Coffman 2, Feller 13; Hits: off Newsom 5 in 1 inning, Coffman 4 in 8; Losing pitcher: Newsom; T: 2:03; A: 55,305; Umpires: Rue, Geisel, Basil, Ormsby.

Indians Lose the Pennant in Loss to Floyd Giebell

September 27, 1940
Detroit 2, Indians 0

Detroit	AB	R	H	RBI
Bartell, ss	2	0	0	0
McCosky, cf	3	0	0	0
Gehringer, 2b	3	1	0	0
Greenberg, lf	3	0	1	0
York, 1b	4	1	1	2
Campbell, rf	2	0	0	0
Higgins, 3b	2	0	0	0
Sullivan, c	3	0	1	0
Giebell, p	3	0	0	0
Totals	25	2	3	2

Cleveland	AB	R	H	RBI
Chapman, lf	3	0	0	0
Weatherly, cf	4	0	0	0
Boudreau, ss	4	0	0	0
Trosky, 1b	4	0	0	0
Bell, rf	4	0	2	0
Keltner, 3b	4	0	1	0
Mack, 2b	4	0	1	0
Hemsley, c	4	0	2	0
Feller, p	1	0	0	0
a-Heath, ph	1	0	0	0
Totals	33	0	6	0

Detroit	0	0	0	2	0	0	0	0	0—2
Cleveland	0	0	0	0	0	0	0	0	0—0

a-Batted for Feller in ninth

E: Bartell, Gehringer, Boudreau; 2B Greenberg; HR: York; SB: Bartell; DP: Mack, Boudreau, and Trosky; Boudreau, Mack, and Trosky; York (unassisted); Boudreau and Trosky; LOB: Detroit 4, Cleveland 9; WP: Giebell; T: 2:39; A: 48,533; Umpires: Summers, Geisel, Basil, Pipgras.

Detroit	IP	H	R	ER	BB	SO
Giebell, W	9	6	0	0	2	6

Cleveland	IP	H	R	ER	BB	SO
Feller, L	9	3	2	2	8	4

Jeff Heath Hits First Upper-Deck Homer in the Stadium

May 25, 1941
Indians 6, St. Louis 0

St. Louis	AB	R	H	RBI
Strange, ss	4	0	0	0
Grace, rf	4	0	2	0
McQuinn, 1b	3	0	1	0
Cullenbine, cf	4	0	2	0
Lucadello, lf	4	0	0	0
Clift, 3b	4	0	0	0
Ferrell, c	2	0	0	0
Niggeling, p	0	0	0	0
b-Judnich, ph	1	0	0	0
Heffner, 2b	4	0	1	0
Allen, p	2	0	0	0
a-Estalella, ph	1	0	1	0
Grube, c	1	0	0	0
Totals	34	0	7	0

Cleveland	AB	R	H	RBI
Boudreau, ss	4	1	1	0
Weatherly, cf	3	1	1	0
Walker, lf	4	1	1	1
Trosky, 1b	3	1	1	1
Heath, rf	4	2	3	3
Keltner, 3b	3	0	1	0
Mack, 2b	4	0	1	0
Desautels, c	4	0	0	1
Feller, p	4	0	0	0
Totals	33	6	9	6

St. Louis	0	0	0	0	0	0	0	0	0—0
Cleveland	0	2	0	1	2	0	1	0	x—6

a-Batted for Allen in seventh
b-Batted for Niggeling in ninth

E: McQuinn, Trosky, Strange, Grube; 2B: Weatherly, Walker, Mack; 3B: Heath; HR: Heath; SH: Weatherly; SB: Walker; DP: Strange, Heffner, and McQuinn; Mack, Boudreau, and Trosky; LOB: St. Louis 9, Cleveland 7; Bases on balls: Feller 2, Allen 2; Strikeouts: Feller 13, Allen 4; Hits: off Allen 7 in 6 innings, Niggeling 2 in 2; PB: Grube; T: 2:03; A: 20,888; Umpires: Grieve, McGowan.

Feller Returns from World War II and Wins First Game

August 24, 1945
Indians 4, Detroit 2

Detroit	AB	R	H	RBI
Outlaw, 3b	4	1	0	0
Borom, 2b	4	0	1	1
Cramer, cf	4	0	2	1
Greenberg, lf	4	0	0	0
Cullenbine, rf	3	0	0	0
York, 1b	4	0	0	0
Webb, ss	3	0	0	0
a-Hostetler, ph	1	0	0	0
Richards, c	2	1	1	0
b-Mayo, ph	1	0	0	0
Newhouser, p	2	0	0	0
c-Maier, ph	0	0	0	0
Totals	32	2	4	2

Cleveland	AB	R	H	RBI
Cihocki, ss	4	0	0	0
Rocco, 1b	4	2	2	0
Seerey, rf	4	1	1	2
Heath, lf	3	1	1	0
Meyer, 2b	3	0	0	1
Ross, 3b	4	0	2	1
Mackiewicz, cf	3	0	0	0
Hayes, c	4	0	1	0
Feller, p	2	0	0	0
Totals	31	4	7	4

Detroit	0	0	2	0	0	0	0	0	0—2
Cleveland	2	0	1	0	1	0	0	0	x—4

a-Batted for Webb in ninth
b-Batted for Richards in ninth
c-Batted for Newhouser in ninth

Error: Cihocki; 2B: Ross, Richards, Rocco, Heath; 3B: Cramer; HR: Seerey; LOB: Detroit 8, Cleveland 7; WP: Newhouser; T: 2:17; A: 46,477; Umpires: Rommel, Passarella, McGowan.

Detroit	IP	H	R	BB	SO
Newhouser, L	8	7	4	4	6

Cleveland	IP	H	R	BB	SO
Feller, W	9	4	2	5	12

Lou Boudreau Unveils "Williams Shift"

July 14, 1946 (Second Game)
Boston 6, Indians 4

Cleveland	AB	R	H	RBI
Case, lf	5	2	2	1
Conway, 2b	1	1	0	0
Seerey, cf	4	0	1	0
Edwards, rf	5	1	2	1
Boudreau, ss	4	0	1	1
Keltner, 3b	4	0	0	0
Wasdell, 1b	3	0	1	0
Lollar, c	3	0	0	0
Jordan, c	1	0	1	1
Embree, p	2	0	0	0
a-Woodling, ph	1	0	0	0
Lemon, p	0	0	0	0
b-Meyer, ph	1	0	0	0
Gassaway, p	0	0	0	0
Totals	34	4	8	4

Boston	AB	R	H	RBI
Culberson, rf	3	0	1	0
McBride, cf	0	0	0	0
Pesky, ss	4	0	2	0
DiMaggio, cf	4	0	1	1
Williams, lf	2	2	1	0
Doerr, 2b	3	2	1	0
York, 1b	3	1	2	2
Russell, 3b	4	0	1	1
Wagner, c	4	0	0	1
Zuber, p	2	1	0	0
Ferriss, p	0	0	0	0
Totals	29	6	9	5

Cleveland	0	0	1	0	0	0	1	1	1—4
Boston	0	3	0	0	0	2	1	0	x—6

a-Batted for Embree in seventh
b-Batted for Lemon in eighth

2B: Edwards, Russell, Williams; HR: Case; SB: Case, Conway; SH: McBride; DP: Conway, Boudreau, and Wasdell; Keltner, Conway, and Wasdell; Russell, Doerr, and York; LOB: Cleveland 11, Boston 5; Bases on balls: Embree 3, Lemon 2, Zuber 7, Ferriss 1; Strikeouts: Embree 1, Zuber 5, Ferris 3; Hits: off Embree 7 in 6 innings, Lemon 2 in 1, Gassaway none in 1, Zuber 8 in 7⅔, Ferriss 3 in 1⅓; Winning pitcher: Zuber; Losing pitcher: Embree; T: 2:12; A: 31,508; Umpires: Boyer, Grieve, Rommel.

Indians Lose Final Game at League Park

September 21, 1946
Detroit 5, Indians 3 (11 innings)

Detroit	AB	R	H	RBI
Lake, ss	5	1	1	0
Kell, 3b	6	2	2	0
Evers, cf	6	0	1	1
Greenberg, 1b	3	1	1	1
Wakefield, lf	5	1	1	1
Cullenbine, rf	4	0	1	0
Bloodworth, 2b	4	0	0	0
Tebbetts, c	5	0	0	0
Trout, p	4	0	2	0
Totals	42	5	9	3

Cleveland	AB	R	H	RBI
Moss, 3b	6	0	1	0
Conway, ss	5	0	1	0
Robinson, 1b	4	0	2	0
Edwards, rf	3	1	1	0
Mitchell, cf	5	1	2	1
Seerey, lf	3	0	0	0
Mack, 2b	2	0	1	0
a-Fleming, ph	1	0	1	0
Meyer, 2b	2	0	0	0
Weigel, c	2	0	0	0
b-Wasdell, ph	1	0	0	1
Jordan, c	2	1	1	0
Kuzava, p	3	0	0	0
c-Becker, ph	1	0	1	1
1-Gromek, pr	0	0	0	0
Berry, p	0	0	0	0
Lemon, p	0	0	0	0
d-Woodling, ph	1	0	1	0
Totals	41	3	12	3

Detroit	0	1	1	0	1	0	0	0	0	0	2—5
Cleveland	0	0	0	0	0	2	0	1	0	0	0—3

a-Singled for Mack in sixth
b-Batted for Weigel in sixth
c-Singled for Kuzava in eighth
1-Ran for Becker in eighth
d-Singled for Lemon in 11th

E: Moss 2, Kuzava; 2B: Edwards, Mitchell; 3B: Mack, Kell; SB: Jordan; SH: Robinson, Bloodworth; DP: Bloodworth, Lake, and Greenberg; Meyer and Robinson; Bloodworth and Greenberg; LOB: Detroit 13, Cleveland 11; T: 2:40; A: 2,772; Umpires: Rue, Passarella, Berry

Detroit	IP	H	R	BB	SO
Trout, W	11	12	3	5	6

Cleveland	IP	H	R	BB	SO
Kuzava	8	4	3	7	3
Berry, L	2⅔	5	2	1	0
Lemon	⅓	0	0	0	0

Indians Draw Record 18 Walks Against Boston

May 20, 1948
Indians 13, Boston 4

Boston	AB	R	H	RBI
DiMaggio, cf	5	0	1	2
Moses, rf	4	0	1	0
Williams, lf	5	0	1	2
Stephens, ss	5	0	1	0
Doerr, 2b	2	0	0	0
Goodman, 3b	4	0	2	0
Jones, 1b	4	0	0	0
Tebbetts, c	2	2	0	0
Harris, p	0	0	0	0
McDermott, p	4	2	2	0
Totals	35	4	8	4

Cleveland	AB	R	H	RBI
Tucker, cf	4	2	2	0
Clark, lf	3	1	2	3
Boudreau, ss	4	2	1	1
Robinson, 1b	3	1	1	2
Gordon, 2b	3	2	1	1
Keltner, 3b	3	1	0	2
Seerey, rf	2	1	1	2
Hegan, c	4	1	0	1
Lemon, p	3	2	0	1
Totals	29	13	8	13

Boston	0	0	2	2	0	0	0	0	0— 4
Cleveland	2	5	0	2	1	1	0	2	x—13

E: Moses, Goodman; 2B: Robinson, McDermott, DiMaggio, Goodman; HR: Boudreau; SH: Clark; DP: Goodman, Doerr, and Jones; Doerr, Stephens, and Jones; LOB: Boston 9, Cleveland 11; Bases on balls: Harris 7, McDermott 11, Lemon 5; Strikeouts: Harris 1, McDermott 6, Lemon 6; Hits: off Harris 4 in 1⅓ innings, McDermott 4 in 6⅔; WP: McDermott; Losing pitcher: Harris; T: 2:33; A: 43,158; Umpires: Hurley, Grieve, Berry.

Satchel Paige's Major League Debut

July 9, 1948
St. Louis 5, Indians 3

St. Louis	AB	R	H	RBI
Dillinger, 3b	4	0	1	0
Stevens, 1b	4	0	2	0
Priddy, 2b	2	1	1	0
Platt, lf	3	1	1	1
Zarilla, cf, rf	4	1	0	0
Kokos, rf	2	0	1	1
Lehner, cf	0	0	0	0
Partee, c	4	0	1	2
Pellagrini, ss	4	0	0	0
Sanford, p	3	2	2	1
Garver, p	1	0	0	0
Totals	31	5	9	5

Cleveland	AB	R	H	RBI
Mitchell, lf	5	1	1	0
Berardino, 1b	5	0	0	0
Edwards, rf	5	0	1	0
Boudreau, ss	5	0	1	1
Gordon, 2b	3	1	3	0
Keltner, 3b	4	0	1	1
Judnich, cf	4	1	3	0
Hegan, c	4	0	1	0
Lemon, p	1	0	0	0
a-Peck, ph	0	0	0	0
Paige, p	0	0	0	0
b-Doby, ph	1	0	1	1
1-Kennedy, pr	0	0	0	0
Klieman, p	0	0	0	0
c-Tucker, ph	1	0	0	0
Gromek, p	0	0	0	0
Totals	38	3	12	3

St. Louis	3	1	0	0	0	0	1	0	0—5
Cleveland	1	0	0	0	0	1	1	0	0—3

a-Batted for Lemon in fourth
b-Batted for Paige in sixth
1-Ran for Doby in sixth
c-Batted for Klieman in eighth

E: Sanford, Judnich; 2B: Hegan, Judnich, Keltner; 3B: Judnich; HR: Sanford; SB: Dillinger; SH: Priddy, Dillinger, Stevens; DP: Pellagrini, Priddy, and Stevens; Gordon and Boudreau; Gordon, Boudreau, and Berardino; LOB: St. Louis 7, Cleveland 10; Bases on balls: Lemon 2, Klieman 2, Gromek 1; Strikeouts: Paige 1, Gromek 1, Lemon 2, Garver 2; Hits: off Lemon 5 in 4 innings, Paige 2 in 2, Klieman 1 in 2, Gromek 1 in 1, Sanford 12 in 6⅔, Garver 0 in 2⅓; PB: Partee; Winning pitcher: Sanford; Losing pitcher: Lemon; T: 2:22; A: 34,780; Umpires: McGowan, Hubbard, Paparella.

Satchel Paige's First Major League Start

August 3, 1948
Indians 5, Washington 3

Washington	AB	R	H	RBI
Yost, 3b	4	0	0	0
Kozar, 2b	2	1	2	0
Coan, lf	3	1	0	1
Stewart, cf	3	0	2	2
Vernon, 1b	4	0	1	0
McBride, rf	4	0	0	0
Christman, ss	3	0	1	0
Early, c	4	0	0	0
Wynn, p	2	1	1	0
Thompson, p	0	0	0	0
a-Robertson, ph	1	0	0	0
Masterson, p	0	0	0	0
c-Gillenwater, ph	1	0	0	0
Totals	31	3	7	3

Cleveland	AB	R	H	RBI
Mitchell, lf	5	0	2	0
Clark, rf	4	1	2	0
Kennedy, rf	2	0	0	0
Doby, cf	4	2	1	1
Keltner, 3b	5	0	3	1
Gordon, 2b	3	1	0	0
Boudreau, ss	3	0	1	1
Robinson, 1b	3	0	0	0
Hegan, c	3	1	1	1
Paige, p	3	0	1	0
b-Peck, ph	1	0	0	1
Klieman, p	0	0	0	0
Totals	33	5	11	5

Washington	2	0	0	0	1	0	0	0	0—3
Cleveland	0	0	0	1	2	1	1	0	x—5

a-Batted for Thompson in seventh
b-Batted for Paige in seventh
c-Batted for Masterson in ninth

2B: Mitchell, Keltner 2, Wynn, Doby; 3B: Stewart; HR: Hegan; SH: Boudreau; DP: Christman, Kozar, and Vernon; Gordon, Boudreau, and Robinson; LOB: Washington 6, Cleveland 12; Bases on balls: off Wynn 4, Masterson 3, Paige 4, Klieman 1; Strikeouts: Wynn 1, Paige 6; Hits: off Wynn 5 in 4⅓ innings, Thompson 5 in 1⅔, Masterson 1 in 2, Paige 7 in 7, Klieman 0 in 2; PB: Early; Winning pitcher: Paige; Losing pitcher: Thompson; T: 2:29; A: 72,434; Umpires: Boyer, Passarella, Rommel.

Don Black Suffers Aneurysm While Batting

September 13, 1948
St. Louis 3, Indians 2

St. Louis	AB	R	H	RBI
Dillinger, 3b	5	1	1	0
Zarilla, lf	5	0	2	0
Priddy, 2b	4	1	2	0
Kokos, rf	4	0	1	2
Arft, 1b	4	0	1	0
Lehner, cf	4	1	3	0
Moss, c	3	0	0	0
1-Garver, pr	0	0	0	0
Partee, c	0	0	0	0
Pellagrini, ss	2	0	0	0
b-Lund, ph	0	0	0	0
Dente, ss	1	0	0	0
W. Kennedy, p	2	0	1	0
c-Platt, ph	1	0	0	0
Drews, p	0	0	0	0
d-Schultz, ph	1	0	1	1
2-Fannin, pr	0	0	0	0
Sanford, p	0	0	0	0
Totals	36	3	12	3

Cleveland	AB	R	H	RBI
Mitchell, lf	4	0	2	0
Clark, rf	4	0	0	0
Zoldak, p	0	0	0	0
Christopher, p	0	0	0	0
Bearden, p	0	0	0	0
Boudreau, ss	4	0	1	0
Gordon, 2b	2	1	1	1
Keltner, 3b	3	0	0	0
Tucker, cf	4	1	1	0
Judnich, 1b	3	0	0	1
Hegan, c	3	0	0	0
e-Robinson, ph	1	0	0	0
Black, p	0	0	0	0
a-Lemon, ph	1	0	0	0
Muncrief, p	1	0	0	0
Gromek, p	1	0	1	0
R. Kennedy, rf	0	0	0	0
Totals	31	2	6	2

St. Louis	0	0	0	0	0	0	0	2	1—3
Cleveland	0	1	0	1	0	0	0	0	0—2

a-Batted for Black in second
b-Walked for Pellagrini in seventh
c-Struck out for W. Kennedy in seventh
1-Ran for Moss in ninth
d-Singled for Drews in ninth
2-Ran for Schultz in ninth
e-Struck out for Hegan in ninth

E: Kokos, Zoldak, Boudreau, Hegan; 2B: Boudreau, Tucker, Mitchell, Priddy; HR: Gordon; SH: Moss; DP: Dillinger, Priddy, and Arft; Keltner, Gordon, and Judnich 2; Keltner, Hegan, and Judnich; LOB: St. Louis 8, Cleveland 6; Bases on balls: W. Kennedy 4, Gromek 1; Strikeouts: W. Kennedy 1, Sanford 1, Black 3, Gromek 1; Hits: off W. Kennedy 5 in 6 innings, Drews 1 in 2, Sanford 0 in 1, Black 2 in 2, Muncrief 5 in 4 (none out in seventh), Gromek 2 in 1⅓, Zoldak 2 in ⅔, Christopher 1 in ⅔, Bearden 0 in ⅓; Winning pitcher: Drews; Losing pitcher: Zoldak; T: 2:27; A: 7,008; Umpires: Summers, Jones, Stevens.

Indians Lose to Detroit to Finish Tied with Boston

October 3, 1948
Detroit 7, Indians 1

Detroit	AB	R	H	RBI
Lipon, ss	4	2	3	1
Berry, 2b	4	2	2	0
Wertz, rf	4	1	3	3
Mullin, cf	3	1	1	0
Wakefield, lf	5	0	1	2
Mayo, 3b	5	0	2	1
Vico, 1b	3	1	2	0
Swift, c	3	0	1	0
Newhouser, p	5	0	0	0
Totals	36	7	15	7

Cleveland	AB	R	H	RBI
Mitchell, lf	4	0	0	0
Clark, rf	4	1	2	0
Boudreau, ss	3	0	0	0
Gordon, 2b	4	0	1	1
Keltner, 3b	3	0	0	0
Doby, cf	3	0	0	0
Robinson, 1b	3	0	1	0
Hegan, c	3	0	0	0
Feller, p	0	0	0	0
Zoldak, p	0	0	0	0
Klieman, p	0	0	0	0
a-Rosen, ph	1	0	0	0
Gromek, p	0	0	0	0
b-Berardino, ph	1	0	1	0
Garcia, p	0	0	0	0
c-Murray, ph	1	0	0	0
Groth, p	0	0	0	0
Totals	**30**	**1**	**5**	**1**

Detroit	0	0	4	2	0	0	0	0	1—7
Cleveland	0	0	0	0	0	0	0	0	1—1

a-Batted for Klieman in third
b-Batted for Gromek in sixth
c-Batted for Garcia in eighth

2B: Wertz 3, Wakefield, Mayo, Berry, Lipon; SH: Swift, Berry; DP: Swift and Lipon; Lipon, Berry, and Vico; Gromek, Boudreau, and Robinson; LOB: Detroit 12, Cleveland 4; Bases on balls: Newhouser 2, Feller 3, Zoldak 1, Gromek 2, Groth 2; Strikeouts: Newhouser 3, Gromek 1, Garcia 1; Hits: off Feller 3 in 2⅓ innings, Zoldak 1 in 0, Klieman 0 in ⅔, Gromek 5 in 3, Garcia 3 in 2, Groth 1 in 1; Losing pitcher: Feller; T: 2:29; A: 74,181; Umpires: Summers, Berry, Grieve, McKinley.

Indians Get 14 Runs in First to Tie Major League Record

June 18, 1950 (Second Game)
Indians 21, Philadelphia 2

Philadelphia	AB	R	H	RBI
Dillinger, 3b	5	0	1	1
McCosky, lf	1	0	0	0
Lehner, lf	3	0	0	0
Valo, rf	4	1	2	0
Chapman, cf	4	0	2	0
Fain, 1b	4	0	1	0
Joost, ss	4	0	1	0
Suder, 2b	4	0	2	1
Astroth, c	4	0	0	0
Brissie, p	0	0	0	0
Scheib, p	1	0	0	0
Burtschy, p	0	1	0	0
a-Guerra	1	0	0	0
Totals	**35**	**2**	**9**	**2**

Cleveland	AB	R	H	RBI
Mitchell, lf	5	3	4	0
Kennedy, rf	4	2	1	1
Easter, 1b	3	3	1	2
Doby, cf	3	3	1	1
Rosen, 3b	4	2	0	1
Gordon, 2b	3	2	1	1
Avila, 2b	0	0	0	0
Boone, ss	4	3	2	5
Hegan, c	3	2	2	6
Murray, c	3	0	0	0
Garcia, p	5	1	2	1
Totals	**37**	**21**	**14**	**18**

Philadelphia	0	0	0	1	0	0	1	0	0—2
Cleveland	(14)	0	4	0	0	0	0	3	x—21

a-Flied out for Burtschy in ninth

E: Lehner, Joost, Suder, Rosen; 2B: Mitchell, Fain; 3B: Dillinger; HR: Boone, Hegan; DP: Suder, Joost, and Fain 2; Joost and Suder; LOB: Philadelphia 7, Cleveland 8; Bases on balls: Brissie 6, Scheib 3, Burtschy 7, Garcia 1; Strikeouts: by Burtschy 4; Hits: off Brissie 3 in ⅓ inning, Scheib 9 in 2⅔, Burtschy 2 in 5; Winning pitcher: Garcia; Losing pitcher: Brissie; T: 2:18; A: 35,521; Umpires: Paparella, Hubbard, Rommel.

Luke Easter's 477-Foot Homer Is Longest in the Stadium

June 23, 1950
Indians 13, Washington 4

Washington	AB	R	H	RBI
Yost, 3b	3	0	0	1
1-Nagy, pr	0	1	0	0
Pearce, p	0	0	0	0
b-Ortiz, ph	1	0	0	0
Noren, cf	3	0	1	0
Vernon, 1b	4	0	1	1
Mele, rf	4	0	0	1
Stewart, lf	2	0	0	0
Dente, 2b	3	1	0	0
Combs, ss	3	1	1	0
Evans, c	3	0	1	0
Okrie, c	0	0	0	0
Ross, p	1	0	0	0
Haynes, p	1	0	0	0
a-Robertson, ph, 3b	2	1	1	0
Totals	**30**	**4**	**5**	**3**

Cleveland	AB	R	H	RBI
Mitchell, lf	4	2	1	1
Kennedy, rf	3	1	2	0
Easter, 1b	4	3	2	6
Doby, cf	4	2	1	1
Tucker, cf	0	0	0	0
Rosen, 3b	3	1	3	3
Boone, ss	5	0	3	2
Avila, 2b	4	1	1	0
Hegan, c	3	1	0	0
Murray, c	1	0	0	0
Lemon, p	3	2	1	0
Totals	**34**	**13**	**14**	**13**

Washington	0	0	1	0	0	0	0	3	0—4
Cleveland	0	1	3	2	0	3	4	0	x—13

1-Ran for Yost in eighth
a-Singled for Haynes in eighth
b-Struck out for Pearce in ninth

E: Easter; 2B: Rosen, Evans, Lemon; 3B: Rosen; HR: Easter 2; SB: Boone; SH: Kennedy, Lemon; DP: Boone and Easter; Vernon and Combs; Yost, Dente, and Vernon; Avila, Boone, and Easter; Boone, Avila, and Easter; Combs, Dente, and Vernon; LOB: Cleveland 8, Washington 6; Bases on balls: Lemon 7, Ross 5, Haynes 3; Strikeouts: Ross 1, Lemon 4, Haynes 1; Hits: off Ross 4 in 3⅓ innings, Haynes 9 in 3⅔, Pearce 1 in 1; HBP: Rosen (by Haynes); Winning pitcher: Lemon; Losing pitcher: Ross; T: 2:48; A: 25,629; Umpires: McGowan, Hurley, McKinley.

Bob Feller and Bob Cain Pitch One-Hitters

April 23, 1952
St. Louis 1, Indians 0

Cleveland	AB	R	H	RBI
Simpson, rf	4	0	0	0
Berardino, 2b	2	0	0	0
Reiser, cf	3	0	0	0
Easter, 1b	3	0	1	0
Rosen, 3b	2	0	0	0
Fridley, lf	3	0	0	0
Boone, ss	2	0	0	0
Tebbetts, c	3	0	0	0
Feller, p	2	0	0	0
a-Avila, ph	1	0	0	0
Totals	**25**	**0**	**1**	**0**

St. Louis	AB	R	H	RBI
Young, 2b	4	1	1	0
Marion, ss	2	0	0	1
Rivera, cf	2	0	0	0
Wright, lf	3	0	0	0
Hopp, rf	3	0	0	0
Delsing, rf	0	0	0	0
Goldsberry, 1b	3	0	0	0
Thomas, 3b	3	0	0	0
Courtney, c	3	0	0	0
Cain, p	3	0	0	0
Totals	**26**	**1**	**1**	**1**

Cleveland	0	0	0	0	0	0	0	0	0—0
St. Louis	1	0	0	0	0	0	0	0	x—1

a-Flied out for Feller in ninth

E: Rosen; 3B: Young; DP: Courtney and Young; Young and Goldsberry; Marion, Young, and Goldsberry; LOB: Cleveland 1, St. Louis 3; Bases on balls: Feller 2, Cain 3; Strikeouts: Feller 5, Cain 7; R-ER: off Feller 1-1; T: 1:58; A: 7,110; Umpires: Honochick, Rommel, Berry.

Bob Feller Wins 250th Major League Game

May 23, 1954 (First Game)
Indians 14, Baltimore 3

Baltimore	AB	R	H	RBI
Coan, cf	3	1	1	0
Kryhoski, 1b	4	1	1	0
Young, 2b	3	0	0	1
Mele, lf	4	1	1	2
Wertz, rf	4	0	0	0
Stephens, 3b	4	0	1	0
Courtney, c	4	0	2	0
Hunter, ss	3	0	1	0
Kretlow, p	1	0	1	0
Littlefield, p	1	0	0	0
a-Kennedy, ph	1	0	0	0
Koslo, p	0	0	0	0
Totals	**32**	**3**	**8**	**3**

Cleveland	AB	R	H	RBI
Smith, lf	3	4	2	1
Avila, 2b	5	1	3	1
Majeski, 2b	0	0	0	0
Philley, rf	4	3	2	4
Rosen, 1b	4	1	2	3
Glynn, 1b	0	0	0	0
Doby, cf	4	2	1	1
Pope, c	0	0	0	0
Regalado, 3b	5	0	2	4
Strickland, ss	5	0	1	0
Dente, ss	0	0	0	0
Hegan, c	4	1	1	0
Feller, p	2	2	2	0
Totals	**36**	**14**	**16**	**14**

Baltimore	0	0	0	0	0	3	0	0	0—3
Cleveland	3	0	0	4	0	2	0	5	x—14

a-Struck out for Littlefield in seventh

E: Hunter, Coan; 2B: Regalado, Smith, Kryhoski; HR: Philley, Mele; SH: Feller; SF: Rosen, Young; DP: Feller, Strickland, and Rosen; Avila, Strickland, and Rosen; Stephens, Young, and Kryhoski; LOB: Baltimore 4, Cleveland 6; Bases on balls: Kretlow 5, Littlefield 1, Feller 1; Strikeouts: Feller 2, Kretlow 5, Littlefield 1; Hits: off Kretlow 6 in 4 innings, Littlefield 3 in 2, Koslo 7 in 2; R-ER: Kretlow 7-7, Littlefield 2-2, Feller 3-3, Koslo 5-3; Losing pitcher: Kretlow; T: 2:14; A: 24,301; Umpires: Paparella, Honochick, Chylak.

Indians Win American League Record 111th Game

September 25, 1954
Indians 11, Detroit 1

Detroit	AB	R	H	RBI
Kuenn, ss	3	0	0	0
Herbert, p	0	0	0	0
d-Nieman, ph	1	0	0	0
Marlowe, p	0	0	0	0
Hatfield, 2b	3	1	1	0
Delsing, lf	3	0	0	0
Boone, 3b	2	0	0	0
Souchock, 3b	2	0	1	1
Belardi, 1b	4	0	0	0
Kaline, rf	4	0	0	0
Tuttle, cf	3	0	0	0
Wilson, c	1	0	0	0
Streuli, c	0	0	0	0
Zuverink, p	1	0	0	0
Lary, p	0	0	0	0
c-King, ph	1	0	0	0
Bullard, ss	1	0	0	0
Totals	**29**	**1**	**2**	**1**

Cleveland	AB	R	H	RBI
Smith, lf, rf	4	3	3	1
Avila, 2b	4	3	3	0
Doby, cf	3	1	2	1
Rosen, 3b	1	0	1	0
a-Regalado, pr, 3b	1	0	1	2
b-Mitchell, ph	1	1	1	2
Majeski, 3b	2	0	0	0
Glynn, 1b	5	1	1	0
Philley, rf, lf	5	1	1	2
Strickland, ss	2	1	1	1
Hegan, c	4	0	0	0
Wynn, p	4	0	0	1
Totals	**36**	**11**	**14**	**10**

Detroit	0	0	0	0	0	0	0	0	1— 1
Cleveland	1	0	2	0	4	0	4	0	x—11

a-Ran for Rosen in first
b-Doubled for Regalado in fifth
c-Flied out for Lary in sixth
d-Grounded out for Herbert in eighth

E: Kaline, Bullard; 2B: Doby, Avila, Mitchell, Philley; 3B: Souchock; DP: Wilson and Hatfield; LOB: Detroit 5, Cleveland 7; Bases on balls: off Zuverink 3, Lary 1, Herbert 2, Wynn 4; Strikeouts: Zuverink 2, Marlowe 1, Wynn 4; R–ER: off Zuverink 6–5, Lary 1–1, Herbert 4–0, Marlowe 0–0, Wynn 1–1; Hits: off Zuverink 7 in 4⅓, Lary 2 in ⅔, Herbert 5 in 2, Marlowe 0 in 1; WP: Wynn; Losing pitcher: Zuverink; T: 2:28; A: 8,647; Umpires: Runge, Summers, McKinley, Hurley.

Herb Score is Hit in Right Eye by Batted Ball

May 7, 1957
Indians 2, New York 1

New York	AB	R	H	RBI
Bauer, rf	3	0	1	1
McDougald, ss	4	0	0	0
Mantle, cf	4	0	0	0
Berra, c	4	0	1	0
Skowron, 1b	4	0	1	0
Martin, 2b	4	0	0	0
Howard, lf	3	1	1	0
c-Slaughter, ph	1	0	0	0
Carey, 3b	2	0	1	0
d-Collins, ph	1	0	0	0
Sturdivant, p	2	0	1	0
Totals	**32**	**1**	**6**	**1**

Cleveland	AB	R	H	RBI
Strickland, 2b	4	0	0	0
Woodling, lf	4	1	2	0
Smith, 3b	4	0	1	0
Wertz, 1b	3	1	2	0
Raines, ss	0	0	0	0
Maris, cf	3	0	1	0
Colavito, rf	2	0	0	1
Carrasquel, ss	3	0	0	0
b-Altobelli, 1b	1	0	0	0
Hegan, c	2	0	0	0
a-Ward, ph	1	0	0	0
Nixon, c	0	0	0	0
Score, p	0	0	0	0
Lemon, p	3	0	0	0
Totals	**30**	**2**	**6**	**1**

New York	0	0	0	0	0	0	1	0	0—1
Cleveland	0	0	0	0	0	0	1	1	x—2

a-Struck out for Hegan in seventh
b-Flied out for Carrasquel in eighth
c-Flied out for Howard in ninth
d-Struck out for Carey in ninth

E: Bauer, Martin, Smith 2; 2B: Skowron, SH: Sturdivant, Carey, Colavito; DP: Carrasquel, Strickland, and Wertz; Berra and Martin; LOB: New York 7, Cleveland 8; Bases on balls: Sturdivant 2, Lemon 1; Strikeouts: Sturdivant 9, Lemon 2; R–ER: Sturdivant 2–0, Lemon 1–1; Hits: off Score 0 in ⅔ inning, HBP: Maris (by Sturdivant); Winning pitcher: Lemon; T: 2:29; A: 18,386; Umpires: Rice, Rommel, Stevens, Napp.

Four Indians Hit Consecutive Homers

July 31, 1963 (Second Game)
Indians 9, California 5

California	AB	R	H	RBI
Pearson, cf	4	1	3	0
Fregosi, ss	5	1	1	1
Thomas, 1b	5	1	1	2
Wagner, lf	4	1	2	2
Moran, 2b	4	0	1	0
Rodgers, c	2	0	1	0
Foiles, c	1	0	0	0
Torres, 3b	4	0	1	0
Hunt, rf	4	1	1	0
Grba, p	1	0	0	0
Lee, p	0	0	0	0
a-Kostro, ph	1	0	0	0
Foytack, p	0	0	0	0
Spring, p	0	0	0	0
b-Sadowski, ph	1	0	0	0
Navarro, p	0	0	0	0
c-Koppe, ph	1	0	0	0
Totals	**37**	**5**	**11**	**5**

Cleveland	AB	R	H	RBI
Francona, lf	4	2	3	1
Brown, ss	5	2	2	1
Kirkland, cf	4	1	1	0
Alvis, 3b	2	0	0	0
Kindall, 2b	2	0	2	0
Whitfield, 1b	4	1	1	4
Azcue, c	4	0	1	0
Luplow, rf	4	0	0	0
Held, 2b, 3b	4	1	1	1
Ramos, p	4	2	2	2
Bell, p	0	0	0	0
Totals	**37**	**9**	**13**	**9**

California	1	0	0	0	0	0	4	0	0—5
Cleveland	0	0	5	0	0	4	0	0	x—9

a-Struck out for Lee in fifth
b-Popped out for Spring in seventh
c-Struck out for Navarro in ninth

E: Fregosi, Moran, Held; 2B: Azcue, Fregosi; HR: Thomas, Ramos 2, Whitfield, Held, Francona, Brown, Wagner; DP: Fregosi, Moran, and Thomas; Kindall, Brown, and Whitfield; LOB: California 7, Cleveland 6; T: 2:42; A: 7,288; Umpires: Soar, Stewart Salerno, Runge.

California	IP	H	R	ER	BB	SO
Grba, L	2⅓	4	4	4	1	1
Lee	1⅔	2	1	1	0	1
Foytack	1⅔	5	4	4	0	1
Spring	⅓	2	0	0	0	0
Navarro	2	0	0	0	1	2

Cleveland	IP	H	R	ER	BB	SO
Ramos, W	8⅓	11	5	5	2	15
Bell	⅔	0	0	0	0	0

Indians Win 10th Consecutive Game at Start of Season

April 28, 1966
Indians 2, California 1

California	AB	R	H	RBI
Cardenal, cf	4	0	0	0
Fregosi, ss	4	0	1	0
Knoop, 2b	4	0	1	0
Siebern, 1b	3	0	1	0
b-Adcock, ph	1	0	0	0
Rodgers, c	4	0	0	0
Warner, rf	3	0	0	0
Reichardt, lf	2	1	1	1
Schaal, 3b	3	0	1	0
Lopez, p	1	0	0	0
Lee, p	1	0	0	0
Totals	**30**	**1**	**5**	**1**

Cleveland	AB	R	H	RBI
Davalillo, cf	4	0	1	0
Alvis, 3b	4	0	1	0
Landis, lf	2	1	1	0
Colavito, rf	4	0	2	1
Whitfield, 1b	4	0	0	0
Gonzalez, 2b	4	1	1	0
Brown, ss	1	0	0	0
Howser, ss	3	0	2	0
Azcue, c	3	0	3	0
a-Wagner, ph	0	0	0	1
Sims, c	0	0	0	0
Siebert, p	4	0	1	0
Allen, p	0	0	0	0
Totals	**33**	**2**	**12**	**2**

California	0	0	0	0	0	0	1	0—1
Cleveland	1	0	0	0	0	0	1	x—2

a-Hit sacrifice fly for Azcue in eighth
b-Flied out for Siebern in eighth

E: Fregosi; 2B: Colavito, Alvis; HR: Reichardt; SH: Lopez; SF: Wagner; LOB: California 4, Cleveland 10; HBP: Reichardt (by Siebert); T: 2:33; A: 5,057; Umpires: Stevens, Stewart, Haller, Ashford.

California	IP	H	R	ER	BB	SO
Lopez	6⅔	10	1	1	1	8
Lee, L	1⅓	2	1	0	1	0

Cleveland	IP	H	R	ER	BB	SO
Siebert, W	8⅓	5	1	1	0	7
Allen	⅔	0	0	0	0	0

Luis Tiant Strikes Out 19 in 10-Inning Game

July 3, 1968
Indians 1, Minnesota 0 (10 innings)

Minnesota	AB	R	H	RBI
Tovar, 3b, ss	4	0	1	0
Holt, lf	3	0	1	0
a-Killebrew, ph	1	0	0	0
Allison, lf	0	0	0	0
Uhlaender, cf	4	0	1	0
Oliva, rf	4	0	0	0
Reese, 1b	4	0	1	0
Quilici, 2b	3	0	1	0
Roseboro, c	4	0	1	0
Hernandez, ss	3	0	0	0
b-Rollins, ph	1	0	0	0
Clark, 3b	0	0	0	0
Merritt, p	4	0	0	0
Totals	**35**	**0**	**6**	**0**

Cleveland	AB	R	H	RBI
Alvis, 3b	4	0	0	0
Brown, ss	3	0	0	0
Johnson, lf	4	1	1	0
Azcue, c	4	0	2	1
Cardenal, cf	3	0	0	0
Sims, 1b	3	0	1	0
Harper, rf	3	0	0	0
Fuller, 2b	3	0	0	0
Tiant, p	3	0	0	0
Totals	**30**	**1**	**4**	**1**

Minnesota	0	0	0	0	0	0	0	0	0	0—0
Cleveland	0	0	0	0	0	0	0	0	0	1—1

a-Struck out for Holt in ninth
b-Struck out for Hernandez in 10th

E: Tovar; 2B: Tovar, Reese; SH: Quilici; LOB: Minnesota 6, Cleveland 3; T: 2:15; A: 21,135; Umpires: Runge, Rice, Drummond, Odom.

Minnesota	IP	H	R	ER	BB	SO
Merritt	*9	4	1	0	1	7

Cleveland	IP	H	R	ER	BB	SO
Tiant	10	6	0	0	0	19

*Pitched to 2 batters in 10th
None out when winning run scored

Gaylord, Jim Perry Start against Each Other

July 3, 1973
Detroit 5, Indians 4

Detroit	AB	R	H	RBI
Stanley, cf	4	0	0	0
G. Brown, dh	4	1	1	0
Sims, c	3	0	0	0
Cash, 1b	4	2	2	3
McAuliffe, 2b	4	0	0	0
Northrup, rf	4	1	2	0
Reese, lf	3	1	1	1
Sharon, rf	1	0	0	0
Rodriguez, 3b	4	0	0	0
Brinkman, ss	3	0	2	1
Totals	34	5	8	5

Cleveland	AB	R	H	RBI
Bell, 3b	5	0	0	0
Lowenstein, 2b	4	1	1	0
Gamble, lf	4	1	1	1
Ellis, c	2	1	0	0
1-Ragland, 2b	0	0	0	0
Spikes, dh	2	1	1	3
2-R. Lolich, pr	0	0	0	0
Chambliss, 1b	3	0	0	0
a-Williams, ph	1	0	0	0
Ashby, c	0	0	0	0
Hendrick, cf	4	0	1	0
Torres, rf	3	0	0	0
Cardenas, ss	4	0	2	0
Totals	32	4	6	4

Detroit	2	0	0	0	0	0	3	0	0—5
Cleveland	0	0	0	3	0	1	0	0	0—4

1-Ran for Ellis in eighth
2-Ran for Spikes in eighth
a-Flied out for Chambliss in eighth

2B: Hendrick; HR: Cash 2, Spikes, Gamble; DP: Sims and Rodriguez; Cardenas, Lowenstein, and Chambliss; LOB: Detroit 3, Cleveland 6; HBP: Spikes (by J. Perry); WP: G. Perry; PB: Ellis; T: 2:35; A: 9,064; Umpires: Denkinger, Anthony, Deegan, Umont.

Detroit	IP	H	R	ER	BB	SO
J. Perry	5⅔	6	4	4	2	3
Farmer, W	1⅔	0	0	0	2	1
Hiller	1⅔	0	0	0	0	2

Cleveland	IP	H	R	ER	BB	SO
G. Perry, L	6⅔	7	5	4	0	6
Johnson	2⅓	1	0	0	1	2

"Beer Night" Riot Causes Indians to Forfeit

June 4, 1974
Texas 9, Indians 0

Texas	AB	R	H	RBI
Tovar, cf	4	0	1	1
Randle, 2b	4	0	0	0
Johnson, lf	5	0	0	0
Lovitto, cf	0	0	0	0
Burroughs, rf	3	0	0	0
Grieve, dh	4	3	3	2
Fregosi, 1b	3	1	1	0
Brown, 3b	1	0	1	0
Harrah, ss	4	0	2	2
Cardenas, 3b	2	0	0	0
Hargrove, 1b	1	0	0	0
Sundberg, c	3	1	1	0
Totals	34	5	9	5

Cleveland	AB	R	H	RBI
Lowenstein, 3b	4	0	0	1
Brohamer, 2b	4	1	1	0
Lee, lf	4	2	3	0
Spikes, rf	4	0	1	0
Gamble, dh	4	0	1	1
Hendrick, cf	4	1	2	1
Blanco, 1b	3	0	1	0
a-Crosby, ph	1	1	1	1
Duncan, c	3	0	0	0
b-Torres, ph	1	0	1	0
Duffy, ss	3	0	0	0
c-Ashby, c	1	0	1	0
Totals	36	5	12	4

Texas	0	1	1	1	0	2	0	0	0—5
Cleveland	0	0	0	1	0	2	0	0	2—5

a-Singled for Blanco in ninth
b-Singled for Duncan in ninth
c-Singled for Duffy in ninth

E: Hargrove; 2B: Sundberg, Tovar, Harrah, Brohamer; 3B: Harrah; HR: Grieve 2; SF: Lowenstein; DP: Brohamer, Duffy, and Blanco; Randle, Harrah, and Fregosi; Cardenas, Randle, and Fregosi; LOB: Texas 7, Cleveland 6; T: n/a; A: 25,134; Umpires: McCoy, Brinkman, Bremigan, Chylak.

Texas	IP	H	R	ER	BB	SO
Jenkins	5⅔	6	3	1	0	2
Foucault	3	6	2	2	0	4

Cleveland	IP	H	R	ER	BB	SO
Peterson	3	3	2	2	1	2
Bosman	2⅔	5	3	3	0	1
Buskey	1	0	0	0	3	0
Wilcox	2⅓	1	0	0	1	1

(Indians were at bat with two outs in ninth when game was declared a forfeit.)

Andre Thornton Walks Six Times to Tie AL Record

May 2, 1984
Indians 9, Baltimore 7 (16 innings)

Cleveland	AB	R	H	RBI
Butler, cf	4	0	0	0
Bernazard, 2b	5	0	0	1
Fischlin, 2b	0	1	0	0
Franco, ss	8	2	2	0
Thornton, dh	2	1	0	0
Tabler, 1b	4	2	1	0
Hargrove, 1b	1	0	0	0
Jacoby, 3b	7	2	2	4
Hassey, c	8	0	3	1
Vukovich, rf	7	0	0	1
Nixon, lf	2	0	0	0
a-Castillo, lf	5	1	2	0
Totals	53	9	10	7

Baltimore	AB	R	H	RBI
Bumbry, cf	3	1	2	1
Shelby, cf	5	0	1	0
Dwyer, rf	2	0	0	0
G. Roenicke, rf	4	0	0	0
Ripken, ss	4	0	0	0
Murray, 1b	7	1	3	3
Lowenstein, lf	3	0	1	0
Ayala, lf	2	0	0	0
Singleton, dh	7	0	1	0
Gross, 3b	3	3	2	1
Cruz, 3b	3	0	0	0
Rayford, c	7	1	1	2
Dauer, 2b	4	1	2	0
Sakata, 2b	2	0	0	0
Totals	56	7	13	7

Cleveland	000	200	131	000	000	2—9
Baltimore	004	110	010	000	000	0—7

a-Fouled out for Nixon in seventh

E: Gross 2, Sutcliffe, Murray; 2B: Murray, Tabler, Castillo, Franco; 3B: Gross; HR: Rayford, Murray, Jacoby, Gross; SB: Bumbry; LOB: Cleveland 14, Baltimore 6; DP: Cleveland 2, Baltimore 1; SH: Dwyer, Butler, Bernazard 2, Hargrove; SF: Jacoby; Balks: Jeffcoat, Underwood; T: 5:02; A: 12,958.

Cleveland	IP	H	R	ER	BB	SO
Sutcliffe	4	8	6	5	2	4
Jeffcoat	3	2	0	0	0	1
Aponte	1	1	1	1	1	0
Waddell	2	0	0	0	0	2
Camacho	3	1	0	0	1	1
Frazier, W	3	1	0	0	0	2

Baltimore	IP	H	R	ER	BB	SO
McGregor	7⅓	3	5	2	5	0
Stewart	0	1	1	1	0	0
T. Martinez	1⅔	2	1	1	1	1
Underwood	4	2	0	0	2	3
Palmer, L	3	2	2	2	5	0

Niekros Become Winningest Brothers in Baseball

June 1, 1987
Indians 9, Detroit 6

Detroit	AB	R	H	RBI
Bergman, 1b	3	2	2	0
d-Herndon, ph	1	0	0	0
Hernandez, p	0	0	0	0
Henneman, p	0	0	0	0
Evans, dh, 1b	5	0	1	3
Gibson, lf	4	1	1	1
Trammell, ss	3	0	1	0
Nokes, c	5	1	2	1
Sheridan, cf	3	0	0	0
a-Lemon, cf	1	0	0	0
Grubb, rf	3	0	1	1
b-Harper, rf	0	0	0	0
Brookens, 3b, 2b	4	1	1	0
Walewander, 2b	3	1	1	0
c-Heath, 3b	1	0	0	0
Totals	36	6	10	6

Cleveland	AB	R	H	RBI
Butler, cf	3	1	1	1
Franco, ss	5	0	2	2
Tabler, dh	4	1	1	0
Carter, 1b	5	0	2	1
Hall, lf	3	1	1	1
b-Thornton, ph	1	0	0	0
Frobel, lf	0	0	0	0
Jacoby, 3b	4	1	1	2
Snyder, rf	3	1	0	0
Bernazard, 2b	3	3	2	1
Bando, c	4	1	2	1
Totals	35	9	12	9

Detroit	1	0	0	0	1	4	0	0	0—6
Cleveland	1	1	5	0	0	0	0	2	x—9

a-Lined out for Sheridan in seventh
b-Walked for Grubb in eighth
c-Grounded out for Walewander in eighth
d-Struck out for Bergman in eighth

E: Carter, Hall, Heath; 2B: Gibson, Carter 2, Tabler, Bergman, Nokes, Evans, Bernazard; HR: Bernazard, Jacoby; SB: Gibson, Hall; SF: Gibson; DP: Bando and Franco; Trammell, Brookens, and Evans; LOB: Detroit 8, Cleveland 7; WP: Petry, Huismann; PB: Nokes; T: 3:15; A: 6,509; Umpires: Brinkman, Cooney, Reilly, Welke.

Detroit	IP	H	R	ER	BB	SO
Petry, L	2⅔	6	7	7	3	2
Snell	2⅓	3	0	0	0	1
Hernandez	2⅓	2	2	1	1	3
Henneman	⅔	0	0	0	1	0

Cleveland	IP	H	R	ER	BB	SO
P. Niekro, W	5⅔	9	6	5	3	1
Vande Berg	1⅓	0	0	0	1	1
Huismann	⅔	0	0	0	0	0
Bailes, S	1⅓	1	0	0	0	1

Indians' Longest Game

August 31, 1993
Minnesota 5, Indians 4 (22 innings)

Cleveland	AB	R	H	RBI
Lofton, cf	9	0	1	0
Kirby, rf	10	2	3	0
Baerga, 2b	9	1	4	1
Belle, lf	9	1	2	2
Sorrento, 1b	7	0	1	0
b-Milligan, ph, 1b	1	0	0	0
Treadway, dh	5	0	2	0
c-Maldonado, ph, dh	2	0	0	0
Thome, 3b	3	0	2	1
Espinoza, 3b	4	0	0	0
Fermin, ss	9	0	1	0
Alomar, c	8	0	0	0
Totals	76	4	16	4

Minnesota	AB	R	H	RBI
Mack, cf	10	0	1	0
Knoblauch, 2b	7	0	1	1
Puckett, rf	9	1	2	0
Hrbek, 1b	7	0	2	0
d-Munoz, ph, lf	2	1	1	1
Winfield, dh	9	0	1	0
Harper, c	8	0	4	1
McCarty, rf, 1b	9	1	1	0
Jorgensen, 3b	4	1	2	1
1-Reboulet, pr, ss, 3b	5	0	1	0
Meares, ss	2	0	0	0
a-Hale, 2b, 3b, ss	6	1	1	1
Totals	78	5	17	5

```
Cleveland   001 000 030 000 000 000 000 0—4
Minnesota   000 000 121 000 000 000 000 1—5
```

a-Singled for Meares in eighth
b-Walked for Sorrento in 18th
c-Popped out for Treadway in 18th
d-Grounded out for Hrbek in 20th
1-Ran for Jorgensen in ninth

E: Fermin, Knoblauch; LOB: Cleveland 15, Minnesota 17; 2B: Kirby, Baerga, Belle 2, Sorrento, Thome, Fermin, Puckett, Winfield, Marty, Jorgensen; HR: Munoz; SB: Lofton, Knoblauch; SH: Espinoza, Alomar; WP: Plunk, Banks; T: 6:17; A: 17,968; Umpires: Garcia, Ford, Young, Meriwether.

Cleveland	IP	H	R	ER	BB	SO
Mesa	7	6	3	2	1	7
Plunk	1	0	0	0	1	0
DiPoto	2	2	1	1	0	0
J. Hernandez	4	2	0	0	0	3
Wertz	5	5	0	0	3	6
Mutis	1	1	0	0	1	0
Grimsley, L	*1	1	1	1	1	1

Minnesota	IP	H	R	ER	BB	SO
Banks	7	10	4	2	1	3
Casian	⅔	1	0	0	0	1
Willis	2⅔	2	0	0	1	1
Aguilera	2⅔	1	0	0	1	1
Hartley	4	1	0	0	1	2
Tsamis	2	0	0	0	2	0
Merriman, W	3	1	0	0	1	0

*Nobody out when winning run scored

Indians Lost Their Final Game in the Stadium

October 3, 1993
Chicago 4, Indians 0

Chicago	AB	R	H	RBI
Burks, rf	1	2	0	0
a-Newson, rf	2	0	1	0
Cora, 2b, 3b	5	1	1	1
Thomas, dh	4	0	2	2
Ventura, 3b	2	0	1	1
Grebeck, 3b, ss	1	0	0	0
Pasqua, 1b	3	0	1	0
c-Denson, 1b	1	0	1	0
Jackson, lf	3	0	1	0
Sax, lf	2	0	1	0
Johnson, cf	3	0	1	0
Huff, cf	1	0	0	0
Karkovice, c	3	1	1	0
b-Calderon, ph	1	0	0	0
LaValliere, c	1	0	0	0
Guillen, ss	1	0	0	0
Martin, 2b	2	0	0	0
Totals	36	4	11	4

Cleveland	AB	R	H	RBI
Lofton, cf	4	0	2	0
Kirby, rf	4	0	1	0
Thome, 3b	4	0	0	0
Belle, lf	4	0	0	0
Sorrento, 1b	2	0	0	0
Horn, dh	3	0	2	0
1-Ramirez, pr	0	0	0	0
Treadway, 2b	4	0	0	0
Fermin, ss	2	0	0	0
Lewis, ss	2	0	0	0
Ortiz, c	3	0	1	0
Totals	32	0	6	0

```
Chicago    1 2 0 0 0 1 0 0 0—4
Cleveland  0 0 0 0 0 0 0 0 0—0
```

a-Singled for Burks in sixth
b-Grounded out for Karkovice in seventh
c-Singled for Pasqua in eighth
1-Ran for Horn in ninth

E: Treadway; LOB: Chicago 14, Cleveland 8; 2B: Thomas, Karkovice, Kirby; SB: Cora; SH: Guillen; HBP: Horn (by DeLeon); WP: Nagy; PB: Ortiz; T: 2:53; A: 72,390; Umpires: Barnett, Clark, Kosc, Morrison.

Chicago	IP	H	R	ER	BB	SO
Bere, W	7	6	0	0	2	2
Belcher	1	0	0	0	0	1
DeLeon	1	0	0	0	0	1

Cleveland	IP	H	R	ER	BB	SO
Nagy, L	3	4	3	2	3	2
Milacki	1⅔	1	0	0	0	0
Christopher	1⅓	2	1	1	1	0
DiPoto	2	4	0	0	1	2
Slocumb	1	0	0	0	0	2

Pennant-Clinching Games

October 2, 1920
Indians 10, Detroit 1

Cleveland	AB	R	H
Evans, lf	6	0	1
Wambsganss, 2b	6	2	3
Speaker, cf	6	2	3
Burns, 1b	6	1	2
Gardner, 3b	5	0	1
Wood, rf	2	2	2
Sewell, ss	5	1	1
O'Neill, c	1	1	0
Nunamaker, c	1	0	0
Bagby, p	5	1	1
Totals	43	10	14

Detroit	AB	R	H
Young, 2b	4	0	0
Bush, ss	4	0	2
Cobb, cf	4	0	1
Veach, lf	4	0	1
Heilmann, 1b	4	1	3
Flagstead, rf	4	0	2
Jones, 3b	4	0	1
Manion, c	4	0	0
Oldham, p	2	0	0
a-Hale, ph	1	0	1
Baumgartner, p	0	0	0
Totals	35	1	11

```
Cleveland  0 0 3 0 0 2 4 1 0—10
Detroit    0 0 0 0 0 0 0 0 1— 1
```

a-Doubled for Oldham in eighth

E: Young, Cobb, Heilmann, Jones; 2B: Burns, Cobb, Hale; 3B: Bagby, Wood; SB: Heilmann, Flagstead; DP: Wambsganss, Sewell, and Burns 2; Young and Heilmann; Sewell and Burns; LOB: Cleveland 12, Detroit 7; Bases on balls: off Oldham 5; Hits: off Oldham 13 in 8 innings; off Baumgartner 1 in 1; HBP: O'Neill (by Oldham); Strikeouts: Bagby 1; Losing pitcher: Oldham; T: 1:28; A: 10,000; Umpires: Chill, Owens.

October 4, 1948
Indians 8, Boston 3

(For box score see page 379.)

September 18, 1954
Indians 3, Detroit 2

Cleveland	AB	R	H	RBI
Smith, lf	4	0	3	0
Avila, 2b	4	0	1	0
Doby, cf	4	0	1	0
Rosen, 3b	4	0	0	0
Wertz, 1b	3	0	1	0
Glynn, 1b	1	0	0	0
Philley, rf	3	1	1	0
Strickland, ss	2	0	0	0
a-Mitchell, ph	1	1	1	1
Dente, ss	1	0	1	0
Hegan, c	4	1	2	2
Wynn, p	2	0	0	0
Narleski, p	0	0	0	0
Totals	33	3	11	3

Detroit	AB	R	H	RBI
Kuenn, ss	5	1	3	0
Hatfield, 2b	4	0	1	0
Delsing, lf	3	0	1	1
Boone, 3b	3	0	1	1
Belardi, 1b	4	0	0	0
Kaline, rf	4	0	0	0
Tuttle, cf	4	1	2	0
House, c	4	0	0	0
Gromek, p	2	0	0	0
b-Nieman, ph	1	0	1	0
c-Bertoia, pr	0	0	0	0
Herbert, p	0	0	0	0
d-Dropo, ph	1	0	0	0
Totals	36	2	9	2

```
Cleveland  0 0 0 0 0 0 3 0 0—3
Detroit    0 0 1 0 0 0 1 0 0—2
```

a-Homered for Strickland in seventh
b-Singled for Gromek in seventh
c-Ran for Nieman in seventh
d-Struck out for Herbert in ninth

2B: Delsing; 3B: Tuttle; HR: Mitchell, Hegan; SH: Wynn; SF: Boone; DP: Boone, Hatfield, and Belardi; Belardi and Kuenn; LOB: Cleveland 5, Detroit 9; Bases on balls: Wynn 2, Gromek 1; Strikeouts: Wynn 6, Narleski 2, Gromek 2, Herbert 1; Hits: off Wynn 8 in 6⅔ innings, Narleski 1, in 2⅓, Gromek 9 in 7, Herbert 2 in 2; R–ER: off Wynn 2–2, Gromek 3–3; Winning pitcher: Wynn; Losing pitcher: Gromek; T: 2:10; A: 6,913; Umpires: McKinley, Napp, Chylak, Grieve.

No-Hit Games by Cleveland Pitchers

Earl Moore

May 9, 1901
Chicago 4, Blues 2 (10 innings)

Chicago	AB	R	H
Hoy, cf	3	0	0
Jones, rf	4	1	0
Mertes, 2b	3	1	1
Isbell, 1b	4	1	0
Hartman, 3b	4	1	1
Shugart, ss	4	0	0
McFarland, lf	4	0	0
Sullivan, c	4	0	0
Katoll, p	3	0	0
Totals	33	4	2

Cleveland	AB	R	H
Pickering, rf	4	1	2
McCarthy, lf	3	0	0
Genins, cf	4	0	1
LaChance, 1b	4	0	1
Bradley, 3b	4	0	0
Beck, 2b	3	0	0
Shay, ss	4	0	0
Wood, c	4	1	2
Moore, p	3	0	0
a-Yeager, ph	1	0	0
Totals	34	2	6

Chicago	0	0	0	2	0	0	0	0	2—4
Cleveland	0	0	2	0	0	0	0	0	0—2

a-Flied out for Moore in 10th

E: Beck, Moore; LOB: Chicago 1, Cleveland 6; 2B: Pickering; SH: McCarthy, Mertes; SB: Isbell; Bases on balls: Katoll 3, Moore 1; T: 2:00; A: 400; Umpires: Sheridan, Mannassau.

Robert B. Rhoads

September 18, 1908
Naps 2, Boston 1

Boston	AB	R	H
Niles, 2b	4	0	0
Lord, 3b	4	0	0
Speaker, cf	3	0	0
Gessler, rf	1	1	0
Thoney, cf	2	0	0
Wagner, ss	3	0	0
Stahl, 1b	3	0	0
Donahue, c	3	0	0
Arellanes, p	3	0	0
Totals	26	1	0

Cleveland	AB	R	H
Good, rf	4	1	1
Bradley, 3b	4	0	0
Hinchman, lf	4	0	0
Lajoie, 2b	4	1	1
Stovall, 1b	3	0	1
Bemis, c	3	0	1
Birmingham, cf	3	0	0
Perring, ss	3	0	0
Rhoads, p	3	0	1
Totals	31	2	5

Boston	0	1	0	0	0	0	0	0	0—1
Cleveland	0	0	0	1	0	0	0	1	x—2

E: Gessler, Wagner, Donahue, Bradley, Lajoie; 3B: Rhoads, Lajoie; SH: Thoney 2, Gessler 2; Bases on balls: Rhoads 2, Arellanes 5; WP: Rhoads1, Arellanes 2; HBP: Speaker (by Rhoads); LOB: Cleveland 5, Boston 5; T: 1:39; A: 6,950; Umpire: Connolly.

Addie Joss

October 2, 1908
Naps 1, Chicago 0 (perfect game)

(For box score see page 380.)

Addie Joss

April 20, 1910
Naps 1, Chicago 0

Cleveland	AB	R	H
Kruger, lf	4	1	2
Bradley, 3b	4	0	1
Turner, 2b	4	0	2
Lajoie, 1b	3	0	0
Lord, rf	4	0	1
Clarke, c	3	0	1
Birmingham, cf	3	0	0
Ball, ss	3	0	0
Joss, p	3	0	0
Totals	31	1	7

Chicago	AB	R	H
Hahn, rf	4	0	0
Zeider, 2b	4	0	0
Gandil, 1b	3	0	0
Barrows, lf	3	0	0
Parent, cf	2	0	0
Purtell, 3b	2	0	0
Blackburne, ss	3	0	0
Payne, c	3	0	0
White, p	2	0	0
Totals	26	0	0

Cleveland	0	0	0	0	0	1	0	0	0—1
Chicago	0	0	0	0	0	0	0	0	0—0

E: Bradley; 2B: Kruger; SH: Purtell; SB: Bradley, Turner; Double play: Payne and Gandil; LOB: Chicago 2, Cleveland 6; Bases on balls: White 2, Joss 2; Strikeouts: White 4, Joss 2; HBP: Birmingham (by White); T: 1:40; A: 5,000; Umpires: Perrine, O'Loughlin.

Ray Caldwell

September 10, 1919 (First Game)
Indians 3, New York 0

Cleveland	AB	R	H
Graney, lf	3	1	0
Chapman, ss	2	1	1
Speaker, cf	3	0	1
Harris, 1b	3	1	2
Gardner, 1b	4	0	1
Wambsganss, 2b	4	0	0
Smith, rf	4	0	0
O'Neill, c	3	0	0
Caldwell, p	4	0	1
Totals	30	3	6

New York	AB	R	H
Fewster, rf	4	0	0
Peckinpaugh, ss	4	0	0
Baker, 3b	3	0	0
Pipp, 1b	3	0	0
Pratt, 2b	3	0	0
Lewis, lf	3	0	0
Bodie, cf	3	0	0
Hannah, c	2	0	0
Mays, p	2	0	0
a-Vick, ph	1	0	0
Totals	28	0	0

Cleveland	2	0	0	0	0	1	0	0	0—3
New York	0	0	0	0	0	0	0	0	0—0

a-Batted for Mays in ninth

E: Wambsganss; 2B: Harris, Caldwell, HR: Harris; SH: Speaker, Chapman, Harris; LOB: New York 2, Cleveland 7; Bases on balls: Mays 3, Caldwell 1; Strikeouts: Mays 2, Caldwell 5; Earned runs: off Mays 3; HBP: Graney (by Mays); T: 1:40; A: 25,000; Umpires: Evans, Moriarty.

Wes Ferrell

April 29, 1931
Indians 9, St. Louis 0

St. Louis	AB	R	H	RBI
Levey, ss	2	0	0	0
Burns, 2b	4	0	0	0
Goslin, lf	3	0	0	0
Kress, rf	4	0	0	0
Schulte, cf	4	0	0	0
Storti, 3b	3	0	0	0
Melillo, 2b	3	0	0	0
R. Ferrell, c	3	0	0	0
Gray, p	2	0	0	0
Stiles, p	0	0	0	0
a-Waddey, ph	1	0	0	0
Totals	29	0	0	0

Cleveland	AB	R	H	RBI
Burnett, 3b	4	2	2	0
Fonseca, 1b	4	0	1	1
Averill, cf	5	1	2	2
Hodapp, 2b	4	0	1	1
Vosmik, lf	4	0	1	0
Falk, rf	4	0	0	0
Hunnefield, ss	4	2	2	0
Sewell, c	3	2	2	0
W. Ferrell, p	4	2	2	4
Totals	36	9	13	8

St. Louis	0	0	0	0	0	0	0	0—0
Cleveland	0	1	1	2	0	0	2	3	x—9

a-Batted for Gray in eighth

Errors: Hunnefield 3; 2B: Hunnefield, Vosmik, W. Ferrell; HR: W. Ferrell, Averill; SH: Fonseca; DP: Burnett and Fonseca; LOB: St. Louis 5, Cleveland 6; Bases on balls: Ferrell 3, Stiles 2; Strikeouts: Ferrell 8, Gray 1; Hits: off Gray 10 in 7 innings; Stiles 3 in 1; Losing pitcher: Gray; T: 1:41; A: 4,000; Umpires: Geisel, Moriarty, Hildebrand.

Bob Feller

April 16, 1940
Indians 1, Chicago 0

(For box score see page 382.)

Bob Feller

April 30, 1946
Indians 1, New York 0

Cleveland	AB	R	H	RBI
Case, lf	4	0	2	0
Lemon, cf	4	0	1	0
Edwards, rf	2	0	0	0
Fleming, 1b	3	0	1	0
Keltner, 3b	1	0	0	0
Boudreau, ss	3	0	0	0
Hayes, c	4	1	2	1
Mack, 2b	3	0	1	0
Feller, p	4	0	0	0
Totals	28	1	7	1

New York	AB	R	H	RBI
Rizzuto, ss	3	0	0	0
Stirnweiss, 3b	3	0	0	0
Henrich, rf	1	0	0	0
DiMaggio, cf	4	0	0	0
Keller, lf	3	0	0	0
Etten, 1b	3	0	0	0
Gordon, 2b	3	0	0	0
Dickey, c	2	0	0	0
Bevens, p	3	0	0	0
Totals	25	0	0	0

Cleveland	0	0	0	0	0	0	0	0	1—1
New York	0	0	0	0	0	0	0	0	0—0

E: Rizzuto, Bevens, Keltner, Fleming; HR: Hayes; SB: Case, Henrich; SH: Boudreau, Keltner, Stirnweiss, Edwards, Henrich; DP: Gordon, Rizzuto, and Etten; Stirnweiss, Rizzuto, and Etten; Dickey and Rizzuto; LOB: Cleveland 8, New York 5; Bases on balls: Bevens 5, Feller 5; Strikeouts: Bevens 5, Feller 11; T: 2:14; A: 37,144; Umpires: Rommel, Boyer, Jones.

Don Black

July 10, 1947 (First Game); Indians 3, Philadelphia 0

Philadelphia	AB	R	H	RBI
Joost, ss	3	0	0	0
McCosky, lf	2	0	0	0
Valo, rf	2	0	0	0
Binks, rf	2	0	0	0
Fain, 1b	2	0	0	0
Chapman, cf	4	0	0	0
Rosar, c	2	0	0	0
Suder, 2b	3	0	0	0
Majeski, 3b	3	0	0	0
McCahan, p	3	0	0	0
Totals	26	0	0	0

Cleveland	AB	R	H	RBI
Metkovich, cf	4	0	1	1
Mitchell, lf	4	0	2	0
Edwards, rf	3	0	0	0
Boudreau, ss	4	0	2	0
Robinson, 1b	4	1	1	0
Gordon, 2b	4	1	1	0
Keltner, 3b	3	0	0	0
Hegan, c	3	1	1	1
Black, p	2	0	2	1
Totals	31	3	10	3

Philadelphia	0	0	0	0	0	0	0	0	0—0
Cleveland	0	3	0	0	0	0	0	0	x—3

SH: Black; DP: Boudreau, Gordon, and Robinson; McCahan, Joost, and Fain; LOB: Philadelphia 5, Cleveland 6; Bases on balls: Black 6, McCahan 1; Strikeouts: Black 5, McCahan 2; T: 1:43; A: 47,371; Umpires: Rommel, Passarella, McKinley.

Bob Lemon

June 30, 1948 Indians 2, Detroit 0

Cleveland	AB	R	H	RBI
Mitchell, lf	4	1	2	0
Berardino, 1b	4	0	1	0
Boudreau, ss	4	1	1	1
Edwards, rf	4	0	0	1
Kennedy, rf	0	0	0	0
Judnich, cf	4	0	1	0
Gordon, 2b	4	0	0	0
Keltner, 3b	2	0	0	0
Hegan, c	3	0	0	0
Lemon, p	3	0	0	0
Totals	32	2	5	2

Detroit	AB	R	H	RBI
Lipon, ss	3	0	0	0
b-Wertz, ph	1	0	0	0
Mayo, 2b	4	0	0	0
Kell, 3b	3	0	0	0
Wakefield, lf	2	0	0	0
Evers, cf	3	0	0	0
Mullin, rf	3	0	0	0
Vico, 1b	2	0	0	0
Swift, c	2	0	0	0
a-Hutchinson, ph	1	0	0	0
Houtteman, p	3	0	0	0
Wagner, c	0	0	0	0
Totals	27	0	0	0

Cleveland	2	0	0	0	0	0	0	0	0—2
Detroit	0	0	0	0	0	0	0	0	0—0

a-Flied out for Swift in eighth
b-Grounded out for Lipon in ninth

E: Lipon, Kell; 2B: Boudreau; SB: Mitchell; LOB: Cleveland 4, Detroit 3; Bases on balls: Lemon 3, Houtteman 1; Strikeouts: Lemon 4, Houtteman 1; T: 1:33; A: 49,628; Umpires: Hubbard, Paparella, McGowan.

Bob Feller

July 1, 1951 (First Game); Indians 2, Detroit 1

Detroit	AB	R	H	RBI
Lipon, ss	3	1	0	0
a-Hutchinson, ph	1	0	0	0
Berry, ss	0	0	0	0
Priddy, 2b	3	0	0	0
b-Keller, ph	1	0	0	0
Kell, 3b	4	0	0	1
Wertz, rf	3	0	0	0
Evers, lf	3	0	0	0
Kryhoski, 1b	3	0	0	0
Ginsberg, c	3	0	0	0
Groth, cf	2	0	0	0
Cain, p	2	0	0	0
Totals	28	1	0	1

Cleveland	AB	R	H	RBI
Mitchell, lf	3	1	1	0
Avila, 2b	4	0	1	0
Chapman, cf	4	0	1	0
1-Nielsen	0	1	0	0
Doby, cf	0	0	0	0
Easter, 1b	4	0	1	2
Simpson, 1b	0	0	0	0
Rosen, 3b	4	0	0	0
Kennedy, rf	4	0	0	0
Boone, ss	2	0	0	0
Hegan, c	3	0	2	0
Feller, p	2	0	0	0
Totals	30	2	6	2

Detroit	0	0	0	1	0	0	0	0	0—1
Cleveland	1	0	0	0	0	0	0	1	x—2

a-Flied out for Lipon in eighth
b-Flied out for Priddy in ninth
1-Ran for Chapman in eighth

E: Boone, Feller; 3B: Chapman; SB: Lipon; LOB: Detroit 3, Cleveland 7; Bases on balls: Cain 3, Feller 3; Strikeouts: Cain 3, Feller 5; T: 2:05; A: 42,891; Umpires: Berry, Napp, Hurley, Passarella.

Sonny Siebert

June 10, 1966 Indians 2, Washington 0

Washington	AB	R	H	RBI
Blasingame, 2b	4	0	0	0
Saverine, 3b, ss	4	0	0	0
King, rf	3	0	0	0
Howard, lf	3	0	0	0
Nen, 1b	2	0	0	0
Lock, cf	3	0	0	0
Casanova, c	3	0	0	0
Brinkman, ss	2	0	0	0
a-Chance, ph	1	0	0	0
McMullen, 3b	0	0	0	0
Ortega, p	2	0	0	0
b-Valentine, ph	1	0	0	0
Totals	28	0	0	0

Cleveland	AB	R	H	RBI
Davalillo, cf	3	1	0	0
Salmon, ss	4	0	2	1
Wagner, lf	4	1	1	1
Landis, rf	0	0	0	0
Alvis, 3b	3	0	1	0
Whitfield, 1b	3	0	1	0
Colavito, rf	3	0	0	0
Hinton, lf	0	0	0	0
Howser, 2b	3	0	0	0
Azcue, c	3	0	0	0
Siebert, p	3	0	0	0
Totals	29	2	5	2

Washington	0	0	0	0	0	0	0	0	0—0
Cleveland	1	0	1	0	0	0	0	0	x—2

a-Batted for Brinkman in ninth
b-Batted for Ortega in ninth

E: Brinkman, Salmon; LOB: Washington 2, Cleveland 5; HR: Wagner; SB: Davalillo; T: 2:13; A: 10,469; Umpires: Honochick, Neudecker, Kinnamon, Umont.

Washington	IP	H	R	ER	BB	SO
Ortega	8	5	2	2	2	5

Cleveland	IP	H	R	ER	BB	SO
Siebert	9	0	0	0	1	7

Dick Bosman

July 19, 1974 Indians 4, Oakland 0

Oakland	AB	R	H	RBI
North, cf	4	0	0	0
Campaneris, ss	3	0	0	0
Bando, 3b	3	0	0	0
Jackson, rf	3	0	0	0
Rudi, lf	3	0	0	0
Washington, dh	3	0	0	0
Bourque, 1b	3	0	0	0
Green, 2b	3	0	0	0
Haney, c	2	0	0	0
a-J. Alou, ph	1	0	0	0
Totals	28	0	0	0

Cleveland	AB	R	H	RBI
Lowenstein, lf	3	0	0	0
Torres, lf	0	0	0	0
Duffy, ss	4	0	0	0
Hendrick, cf	3	0	1	0
Spikes, rf	3	0	0	0
Ellis, c	3	1	1	0
Bell, 3b	3	1	2	1
McCraw, 1b	3	1	1	1
Lis, dh	2	1	1	2
Gamble, dh	1	0	0	0
Brohamer, 2b	2	0	1	0
Totals	27	4	7	4

Oakland	0	0	0	0	0	0	0	0	0—0
Cleveland	0	0	2	2	0	0	0	0	x—4

a-Batted for Haney in ninth

E: Bosman; 2B: Bell; HR: Lis; DP: Oakland 2; LOB: Oakland 1; Cleveland 1; HBP: Brohamer (by Hamilton); T: 1:56; A: 24,302; Umpires: Springstead, Goetz, Denkinger, Morgenweck.

Oakland	IP	H	R	ER	BB	SO
Hamilton, L	3⅓	5	4	4	0	4
Odom	3⅔	1	0	0	1	1
Knowles	1	1	0	0	0	0

Cleveland	IP	H	R	ER	BB	SO
Bosman	9	0	0	0	0	4

Dennis Eckersley

May 30, 1977
Indians 1, California 0

California	AB	R	H	RBI
Flores, cf	4	0	0	0
Remy, 2b	3	0	0	0
Solaita, 1b	2	0	0	0
Rudi, lf	3	0	0	0
Bonds, rf	3	0	0	0
Baylor, dh	3	0	0	0
Chalk, 3b	3	0	0	0
Grich, ss	3	0	0	0
Humphrey, c	2	0	0	0
a-Aikens, ph	1	0	0	0
Totals	**27**	**0**	**0**	**0**

Cleveland	AB	R	H	RBI
Manning, cf	3	0	0	0
Kuiper, 2b	3	1	1	0
Norris, rf	2	0	0	1
Carty, dh	3	0	2	0
Bochte, 1b	3	0	1	0
Blanks, ss	3	0	0	0
Duffy, ss	0	0	0	0
Bell, 3b	2	0	0	0
Dade, lf	3	0	1	0
Fosse, c	3	0	0	0
Totals	**25**	**1**	**5**	**1**

California	0	0	0	0	0	0	0	0	0—0
Cleveland	1	0	0	0	0	0	0	0	x—1

a-Batted for Humphrey in ninth

2B: Carty; 3B: Kuiper; SF: Norris; DP: California 1, Cleveland 2; LOB: California 1, Cleveland 2; WP: Eckersley; T: 2:02; A: 13,400; Umpires: Deegan, McKean, Ford, DiMuro.

California	IP	H	R	ER	BB	SO
Tanana	8	5	1	1	1	6

Cleveland	IP	H	R	ER	BB	SO
Eckersley	9	0	0	0	1	12

Len Barker

May 15, 1981
Indians 3, Toronto 0 (perfect game)

(For box score see page 381.)

The Postseason

Indians versus Brooklyn Dodgers World Series

1920

It took the Cleveland baseball franchise 20 years to win an American League championship, though the Naps came close in 1908, and again in 1918 and 1919.

The 1908 Naps finished second by half a game and four percentage points to Detroit. The Tigers (90–63 .588) were rained out of a late-season game against Washington and lost one less game than Cleveland (90–64 .584).

A few years later the rules were changed, requiring postponed games to be made up at the end of the season if they would possibly have a bearing on the outcome of the pennant race.

The Indians finished second to Boston in 1918 by 2½ games, and to Chicago in 1919 by 3½ lengths. In both years the seasons were cut short, in 1918 by 25 games because of World War I, and in 1919 by 14 games for what were called economic reasons; otherwise, the Indians might have overtaken the Red Sox or White Sox.

As it was, they clinched the pennant in 1920 in the final week of the season after seven players on the defending champion White Sox team were among eight suspended by Chicago White Sox president Charles Comiskey after they were indicted for conspiring to fix the 1919 World Series.

Some called it a "tainted" championship because, when the Chicago players were suspended, the Indians were ahead by only one game. They went on to win three of their last five, while the White Sox, forced to use a makeshift lineup, lost two of their final three. The Indians finished first by two games.

It had been a difficult season for the Indians as, with seven and a half weeks remaining, they lost shortstop, Ray Chapman, one of their best hitters, with a .303 average, and a key defensive player.

Chapman was hit in the head by a pitch from Carl Mays of the New York Yankees on August 16, and died the next day, the only man in major league baseball history to be killed playing the game.

Fortunately, the Indians were able to bring up Joey Sewell from the minor leagues in September. Only a year earlier Sewell was playing football for the University of Alabama, but he batted .329 in the final 22 games of the season helping the Indians win the pennant.

The call-up launched Sewell's splendid 14-year major league career (including 11 seasons in Cleveland), which culminated in his election to the Hall of Fame in 1977.

For more than six seasons, beginning in 1914, the Indians double play combination of shortstop Ray Chapman (left) and second baseman Bill Wambsganss was one of the best in the American League. It was broken up on August 16, 1920, when Chapman was hit in the head by a pitch thrown by Carl Mays of the New York Yankees and died the next day, the only player in major league baseball history to be killed on the field.

Pitcher Satchel Paige is congratulated by player-manager Lou Boudreau after one of Paige's six victories in 1948 that helped the Indians win the pennant and World Series.

The Dodgers—who also were called the Robins by some in reference to the name of their manager, Wilbert Robinson—prevailed in a six-team race until the final month in the National League.

In addition to Brooklyn, Cincinnati, Chicago, Pittsburgh, Boston, and Philadelphia all held first place at one time or another, and the Dodgers didn't lock up the pennant until the final week and a half. They finished seven lengths ahead of the Giants.

Cleveland went into the Series as a slight favorite, although some thought the Dodgers had an edge because they'd had the opportunity to rest for nearly a week, while the Indians had to battle nearly to the end of the season to clinch their first title.

"All my players are in good physical condition and well rested," said Brooklyn manager Robinson. "They are full of confidence and expect to win the Series from Cleveland, and I feel the same way about it."

Brooklyn was led by spitball pitcher Burleigh Grimes, who'd won 23 games while losing 11, left fielder Zack Wheat (.328), and first baseman Ed Konetchy (.308). Grimes and Wheat also would be elected to the Hall of Fame.

Manager Tris Speaker was equally sure his team would win when the Indians embarked by train for Ebbets Field in Brooklyn, for the opener of what was then a best-of-nine World Series.

"The series against [the Dodgers] will be no harder than our long struggle during the American League season, and we won there," said Speaker. "My team is in the best of physical condition and filled with determination to defeat the National League champion."

Speaker's confidence was well founded. He was one of six regulars in the Indians' lineup who batted .300, and their pitching staff featured three 20-game winners.

Tris Speaker, the player-manager of the Indians from 1919 to 1926, batted .388 in 1920 to lead the team to its first American League pennant and world championship.

Speaker's average was .388, second best in the American League to George Sisler's .407, while the Indians' other .300 hitters were catcher Steve O'Neill (.321), left fielder Charlie Jamieson (.319), right fielder Elmer Smith (.316), and third baseman Larry Gardner (.310), as well as Chapman.

Jim Bagby was the major leagues' winningest pitcher with a 31–12 record, while Stan Coveleski was 24–14, and Ray Caldwell 20–10.

Game One

The Indians jumped off to a 2–0 lead in the second inning and scored again in the fourth, and Coveleski, pitching a five-hitter, was in command all the way as he blanked the Dodgers except for a run in the seventh.

"Cleveland was the victor because of the wonderfully effective hurling of Stanley Coveleski, the excellent support accorded him, and the timely batting of Steve O'Neill. There it is in a nutshell," is the way the game was reported in the *Cleveland Plain Dealer* on October 6.

Rube Marquard, who started for the Dodgers, also pitched a five-hitter, though the first hit—and run—by Cleveland's George Burns was tainted.

Burns' pop fly leading off the second inning fell behind first baseman Ed Konetchy for a single, and when Konetchy threw the ball wildly into left field, Burns raced all the way around the bases for the game's first run.

Smoky Joe Wood, who'd been an outstanding pitcher for the Boston Red Sox before an arm injury forced him to switch to the outfield, reached on a walk by Marquard, who apparently was shaken by Konetchy's error.

Joey Sewell followed with a single, and O'Neill doubled to score Wood for a 2–0 lead. Coveleski grounded to Konetchy

for the second out, and it was turned into a double play as Sewell was retired after rounding third base too far.

The Indians scored again in the fourth when, with one out, Wood sent a long drive to left-center for a double, the ball hitting the bleacher fence about six inches short of being a home run. After Sewell flied out, O'Neill came through again with another double for another run.

Coveleski didn't yield a hit until Ivy Olson and Tommy Griffith singled in the fourth, but died on base. Olson singled again in the sixth, and the Dodgers broke the shutout in the seventh when Zack Wheat led off with a double and came around on two infield outs.

It was in the eighth that the Dodgers mounted one last threat, but Speaker made his second outstanding play of the game to preserve the victory. Ernie Krueger led off with a liner to left center that, had it fallen in, would have been a triple. Speaker had also made a sensational catch to rob Wheat of a hit in the second inning.

After Speaker's catch of Krueger's liner, Clarence Mitchell singled and Olson walked, but Coveleski got the next two batters.

The Dodgers went down in order in the ninth as Speaker

made another exceptional catch of a ball hit by Hy Myers for the second out.

Afterward, the *Plain Dealer* extolled Speaker's ability, calling him "the greatest outfielder in baseball and, perhaps, the greatest outfielder that has ever lived."

And Wheat claimed the Indians won "because they got all the breaks." He also second-guessed manager Wilbert Robinson for "not walking O'Neill when he came up for the second time [in the fourth] and got his second double."

As for the play of Speaker, Wheat said, "He was all over the lot. His eighth inning catch [of the ball hit by Krueger] told our fate."

Game Two

Burleigh Grimes was as dominating for Brooklyn in the second game as Stan Coveleski was for the Indians in the first, and the Dodgers won, 3–0, tying the Series at one victory each.

With his spitball giving the Cleveland batters fits—as Coveleski's did to the Dodgers in the opener—Grimes did not permit a runner past second base until the eighth inning when he temporarily lost control and walked the first two batters, Charlie Jamieson and George Burns.

The back-to-back walks brought Tris Speaker to the plate, to the great concern of the 22,559 fans who jammed Ebbets Field, but this time the Indians' peerless player-manager couldn't deliver.

Speaker grounded out, sending Burns to second and Jamieson to third, and after Elmer Smith fouled out, Larry Gardner also walked, loading the bases. But Grimes was equal to the threat, forcing Doc Johnston to ground out, and again in the ninth he halted the Indians after pinch hitter Les Nunamaker singled with two out in the ninth.

As for Jim Bagby's performance, the *Plain Dealer* reported that "his actual hurling was not so much to blame as his fielding and the inexperience of Joe Sewell, who did not shine with any undue amount of brilliance."

The Dodgers got a run in the first inning when Jimmy Johnston beat out a hit to Sewell, stole second as Bagby failed to hold him on base, and scored on Zack Wheat's two-out double.

After Grimes singled to start the third, Bagby committed an error as Ivy Olson bunted back to the mound trying to sacrifice, and after the next batter was retired, Tommy Griffith doubled for a 2–0 lead.

The Dodgers scored again in the fifth, and again it was "undeserved," according to the *Plain Dealer*. Olson singled with one out, took second as Jimmy Johnston was retired by his brother, Indians first baseman Doc Johnston, and scored when Griffith's grounder got away from Sewell, but was ruled a hit.

"It was just a matter of superior pitching," Speaker said after the loss. "Sarge [Bagby] pitched pretty well, but Grimes was better."

And Wheat called it "a typical game for us. We've always been able to come back after a run of bad luck."

Game Three

It took Brooklyn only 10 minutes to score all the runs needed by Sherry Smith, who pitched a three-hitter to beat the Indians, 2–1, giving the Dodgers a two-games-to-one lead and sending the World Series to League Park for the first time in baseball history.

Again it was Zack Wheat who played a dominant role in the Dodgers' success, and again it was rookie Joey Sewell's erratic defense behind starting pitcher Ray Caldwell that hurt the Indians.

Ivy Olson, the Dodgers' first batter in the first inning, walked, was sacrificed to second, and took third when Sewell fumbled Tommy Griffith's grounder. Wheat singled for one run and Hy Myers singled for another before reliever Walter "Duster" Mails replaced Caldwell and retired the next two batters to end the rally.

Thereafter the Dodgers were blanked on four hits by Mails and George Uhle, who pitched the eighth, but the Indians were virtually helpless against Smith.

Several reportedly "phenomenal" defensive plays by right fielder Griffith, shortstop Olson, second baseman Pete Kilduff, and first baseman Ed Konetchy enabled Smith to shut out the Indians in every inning except the fourth.

Especially Olson, Kilduff, and Konetchy. As reported by the *Plain Dealer*: "The Indians simply could not hit the ball past them. They scooped up bad hoppers and ugly grounders like wizards. They threw from any old position and they never failed to get their man."

It was Olson's fielding gem to retire Bill Wambsganss leading off the fourth inning that prevented the Indians from tying the score. Tris Speaker, the Tribe's next batter, doubled to left field and raced around the bases to score when the ball got past Zack Wheat. If Olson had not made the play on Wambsganss, the game would have been tied.

Instead, Smith preserved the one-run lead, allowing only two more hits, both by catcher Steve O'Neill, singles in the fifth and eighth innings.

The loss did not lessen Speaker's optimism. "We have just begun to fight," he said. "You know [American League teams] had us down a few times during the season, but they could not keep us down.

"Brooklyn has us down now, but it cannot keep us down. We will win the Series," he said of the next four games to be played in Cleveland.

Speaker also gave a vote of confidence to Sewell, despite the shortstop's defensive lapses. "Some day that boy is going to be one of the best," the manager said.

Game Four

Just as he did in the opener, Stan Coveleski completely checked the Dodgers, this time on five hits, and just as Brooklyn jumped off to a two-run lead in the first 10 minutes of Game 3, so did the Indians in Game 4, winning, 5–1, to even the Series at two-all.

Joey Sewell was charged with another error, but this time it didn't hurt as the Dodgers were unable to solve Coveleski's spitball, except in the fourth inning when they scored their only run on Jimmy Johnston's single and Tommy Griffith's double.

The Indians' two runs in the first off Brooklyn right-hander Leon Cadore came on a walk to Bill Wambsganss, one-out singles by Tris Speaker and Elmer Smith, and Larry Gardner's deep fly to center, which in those days was recorded in the box score simply as a sacrifice.

Three consecutive singles by Wambsganss, Speaker, and George Burns starting the third produced two more runs for the Indians. They added an insurance run in the sixth as Coveleski himself started the rally with a two-out single, and Joe Evans and Wambsganss followed with hits.

"We're back on the right track now," said Speaker.

But Zack Wheat, the Dodgers' spokesman, also exuded confidence. "I figure we are going to get [win] this Series, and I'll tell you why," he said. "Both teams are practically equal in the infield and outfield. Where we have the edge is in the pitching staff, and there we certainly are a little to the good.

"Coveleski is the Cleveland ace, and he has won twice. Now he can't pitch for three days, but where we have the advantage is that we have [Burleigh] Grimes and [Sherrod] Smith to come back. I am confident we will win."

Obviously, Wheat didn't have great respect for Jim Bagby, even though he'd won 31 games, more than any other pitcher in baseball in 1920.

Game Five

In one of the most famous games in World Series history, the Indians took a 3–2 lead over the Dodgers with an 8–1 victory behind Jim Bagby's pitching, the sensational hitting of Elmer Smith, and the outstanding fielding of second baseman Bill Wambsganss.

Though he yielded 13 hits, one more than the Tribe got off Burleigh Grimes and Clarence Mitchell, Bagby became the first pitcher to hit a home run in the 18-year history of the World Series.

Bagby was able to coast after Smith smashed a first-inning grand slam homer that also was a World Series first.

And then Wambsganss, who later minimized his deed by saying, "I was just in the right place at the right time," pulled

Right fielder Elmer Smith made baseball history by being the first player to hit a grand slam in a World Series game. Smith's homer was a highlight of the Indians 8–1 victory over the Brooklyn Dodgers in the fifth game played at League Park on October 10, 1920.

off the first—and, to date, only—unassisted triple play in a World Series game. It occurred in the fifth inning and stymied the Dodgers who, by then, were losing, 7–0.

The unprecedented play was set up when Pete Kilduff and Otto Miller opened with singles off Bagby, putting runners on first and second. Mitchell followed with a line drive toward center field.

The runners were off with the crack of the bat, and so was Wambsganss, who made a leaping catch about three strides from second. His momentum carried him to the base where he easily doubled off Kilduff, then turned to throw to first, only to find Miller stopped in his tracks near him. Instead of throwing to first, Wambsganss merely trotted over to Miller and tagged him for the third out.

The Dodgers were stunned, and so was the crowd of 26,884 fans in League Park, who initially did not comprehend what had transpired, or that it was a triple play, the first—unassisted or otherwise—in Series history.

Initially, too, it obviously wasn't considered such an outstanding feat as, according to Wambsganss, he was interviewed by only one reporter, a sportswriter from Brooklyn, after the game.

Wambsganss told the Brooklyn reporter, "It was the chance of a lifetime, and I can't think of words to express how happy I am. I must have been born lucky, for it takes luck to have everything set for an unassisted triple play. Lots of players have made more wonderful catches than I made, but the stage was not set right for them to do what I did."

The stage for Smith's grand slam was set when Charlie Jamieson and Wambsganss singled, and Tris Speaker was credited with a hit when he beat out a sacrifice bunt, as Grimes fell down attempting to field the ball, loading the bases.

Smith, with a 2-and-1 count on him, drilled Grimes' fourth pitch over the right-field fence, which then was only 290 feet down the line, a 20-foot-high concrete base topped by a 20-foot-high wire screen.

Bagby, who batted .252 (33-for-131 in 1920), hit his homer in the fourth off Grimes after Doc Johnston singled and took second on a passed ball; Steve O'Neill was then intentionally walked with one out. Bagby, who hit only two regular-season home runs in his nine-year major league career, lined Grimes' second pitch into the temporary stands set up in front of the bleachers, where the home run distance normally was 420 feet from the plate.

Bagby's homer finished Grimes, and the Indians scored another run in the fifth off Mitchell when Speaker reached on an error and came around on singles by Smith and Larry Gardner.

The homers by Bagby and Smith, and Wambsganss' triple play, were described by Henry P. Edwards, then sports editor of the *Plain Dealer* and later publicity director of the American League, in prophetic terms:

"The Indians established records that probably never will be excelled even though world's series go on to the end of time. It was a history-making day in baseball, and the 26,884 fans who were present could well congratulate themselves on their good fortune in having witnessed the three most notable achievements ever displayed in a single ball game."

But Zack Wheat said the Indians were lucky and insisted the Dodgers still would win. "We are still there [with a chance to win], and we are due for some breaks," he said.

"Everything was against us [in Game 5]. Jim Bagby had horseshoes in every pocket and, despite 13 hits, we could score only one run."

Wheat also called Bagby's homer "a bit of luck [because] in the regular season that ball could easily have been handled by [Hy] Myers in center."

Speaker, on the other hand, praised his players—and again predicted the Indians would prevail in the World Series.

"We gave future teams playing in the World Series something to shoot at," he said. "It was one of the most remarkable games I ever took part in, and must have been a great game to watch. It surely was one of which I could feel proud to have participated in.

"As a manager, I am proud of every Indian who took part in the contest. Everyone performed notably. I don't think I ever saw a bunch of players act with more inspiration. No play was too hard for them to attempt and, for that matter, to carry through. They played with remarkable dash, and I can imagine that the Robins [Dodgers] were carried off their feet by the spectacular feats they were up against.

"The series is not over, but I am confident that we will win."

Game Six

W alter "Duster" Mails pitched briefly for Brooklyn in 1915 and 1916, but spent most of his career in the minors until the Indians purchased his contract from Portland of the Class AA Pacific Coast League on August 21, 1920.

And without his contributions as a rookie that season—a 7–0 won-lost record and 1.85 ERA in nine games—the Indians would not have won the pennant.

Mails, who was nicknamed Duster because of his penchant for throwing close to batters in the minors, also made a major contribution in the World Series, hurling a five-hitter to beat the Dodgers, 1–0, in the sixth game, giving the Indians a 4–2 lead. (It was then a best-of-nine series.)

Mails had also pitched 6⅔ innings of shutout ball, yielding only three hits, in relief of Ray Caldwell in Game 3, won by the Dodgers, 2–1.

Opposed by Sherrod Smith, the left-hander who'd beaten the Indians on a three-hitter in that third game, Mails survived several threats.

The Dodgers loaded the bases with two out in the second inning on a single by Ed Konetchy and errors by Joey Sewell and Larry Gardner. Hy Myers singled and Ed Konetchy walked with one out in the fourth, Bernie Neis walked to start the sixth, and Ivy Olson doubled with one out in the eighth, but each time Mails was equal to the task.

Sewell, who had several defensive problems in the first five games, made two sensational plays in the sixth inning to keep Mails out of more trouble. First, he went deep in the hole to field Zack Wheat's grounder and throw him out at first, then chased behind second to snare Hy Myers' grounder and retire him by half a step at first.

The Indians, held to seven hits by Smith, got the only run Mails needed in the sixth when Speaker singled with two out and scored on a double by George Burns.

Later—for the first time in the Series—Wheat had nothing positive to say about the Dodgers' chances. "It is going to be hard to catch 'em now, especially with [Stan] Coveleski ready to pitch [the seventh game]," he said. "[The Indians'] pitching is better than we expected."

Speaker also was low-key on the eve of what would be the final game. "I've been proud of my boys all the way through, and I know I will be prouder of them when this is all over, whenever that may be," said the player-manager.

Game Seven

S tan Coveleski tied a major league record held at that time by seven other pitchers when he won his third game of the World Series by firing a five-hitter to defeat the Dodgers, 3–0, and give the Indians their first world's championship.

As Henry Edwards, sports editor of the *Plain Dealer,* wrote in his page one story:

"The better the day, the better the deed.

"On October 12, 1492. Christopher Columbus discovered America, and thus paved the way for the organization of the American Baseball League.

"On October 12, 1920, the Cleveland Indians—no relation to those discovered by Columbus 428 years ago—won the world's baseball championship.

"It was a long time to wait, but the prize was worth waiting for."

All of which probably was stretching a point, but as Edwards also explained, "for 42 years or more Cleveland has been striving to win a major league pennant. Year after year it was doomed to disappointment.

"Yesterday, Columbus Day, its ambitions were realized."

When the game ended as Coveleski retired the last batter,

Ed Konetchy on a grounder to Joey Sewell, 15,000 fans swarmed onto the field at League Park and surrounded owner James C. Dunn's box.

"I am the happiest man in the whole world today," he told the crowd. "I know you are happy, too. After all, it is your team; it is Cleveland's team more than it is mine."

Coveleski, whose three-game earned run average was a minuscule 0.67, tied the feat first achieved in 1903 by Bill Dineen of the Boston Red Sox and Deacon Phillippe of Pittsburgh, and equaled by Christy Mathewson, New York Giants, 1905; Babe Adams, Pittsburgh, 1909; Jack Coombs, Philadelphia Athletics, 1910; Smoky Joe Wood, Boston Red Sox, 1912; and Red Faber, Chicago White Sox, 1917.

(Since then four more pitchers have won three games in a World Series: Harry Breecheen, St. Louis Cardinals, 1946; Lew Burdette, Milwaukee Braves, 1957; Bob Gibson, St. Louis Cardinals, 1967; and Mickey Lolich, Detroit, 1968.)

Burleigh Grimes, working with only two days' rest after losing Game 5 on October 10, allowed seven hits as the Indians scored single runs in the fourth, fifth, and seventh innings.

Their first run came home on a throwing error by Grimes with two out after Larry Gardner and Doc Johnston singled and attempted a delayed double steal. When Grimes' throw to second was wild, Gardner trotted home.

Player-manager Tris Speaker, who batted .320 in the seven-game series, tripled for the Indians' second run with two out in the fifth after Charlie Jamieson singled and stole second.

Steve O'Neill, who with Charlie Jamieson were the Indians' best hitters in the Series with .333 averages, led off the seventh with a double. Coveleski tried to sacrifice him to third, but on the bunt O'Neill was run down between second and third and tagged out. Coveleski managed to reach second on the play. Jamieson then doubled to score Coveleski with the last run of the Series.

"I knew we could do it," Speaker said during the postgame celebration. "From the start, I never had any doubt of our being able to win the championship of the world.

"The fact that we had to fight it right out to the finish [of the American League race] helped us against Brooklyn. We were playing at top speed when the regular season ended and kept going the same gait until we won the world's title.

"I presume some thought I was overconfident when I predicted four straight. Nothing of the kind. I knew our boys and they came through just as I expected."

Coming through as they did resulted in a World Series payoff of approximately $4,200 for each of the Indians and $2,400 for the Dodgers. (The *Reach Guide* in 1921 reported that each Indians' share was $4,204, and $2,387 for the Dodgers, while the *Spalding Guide* said the Indians received $4,168 each, and the Dodgers $2,419.)

Game 1
Tuesday, October 5, at Brooklyn

Indians	AB	R	H	RBI	PO	A
Evans, lf	2	0	0	0	1	0
b-Jamieson, lf	1	0	0	0	0	0
Wambsganss, 2b	3	0	0	0	0	2
Speaker, cf	4	0	0	0	4	0
Burns, 1b	3	1	1	0	9	1
e-E. Smith, rf	1	0	0	0	0	0
Gardner, 3b	4	0	0	0	1	3
Wood, rf	2	2	1	0	4	0
f-D. Johnston,1b	1	0	0	0	0	1
Sewell, ss	3	0	1	0	3	4
O'Neill, c	3	0	2	2	3	0
Coveleski, p	3	0	0	0	2	2
Totals	30	3	5	2	27	13

Brooklyn	AB	R	H	RBI	PO	A
Olson, ss	3	0	2	0	0	3
J. Johnston, 3b	3	0	0	0	1	3
Griffith, rf	4	0	1	0	1	0
Wheat, lf	4	1	1	0	4	0
Myers, cf	4	0	0	0	1	0
Konetchy, 1b	4	0	0	1	12	1
Kilduff, 2b	3	0	0	0	1	3
Krueger, c	3	0	0	0	7	1
Marquard, p	1	0	0	0	0	0
a-Lamar	1	0	0	0	0	0
Mamaux, p	0	0	0	0	0	1
c-Mitchell	1	0	1	0	0	0
d-Neis	0	0	0	0	0	0
Cadore, p	0	0	0	0	0	1
Totals	31	1	5	1	27	13

Cleveland	0	2	0	1	0	0	0	0	0—3
Brooklyn	0	0	0	0	0	1	0	0	0—1

a-Popped out for Marquard in sixth
b-Grounded out for Evans in eighth
c-Singled for Mamaux in eighth
d-Ran for Mitchell in eighth
e-Grounded out for Burns in ninth
f-Grounded out for Wood in ninth

Error: Konetchy; Two-base hits: O'Neill 2, Wheat, Wood; Sacrifice Hits: J. Johnston, Wambsganss; Double Play: Konetchy, Krueger, to J. Johnston; Left on Base: Cleveland 3, Brooklyn 5; Umpires: Klem (NL), Connolly (AL), O'Day (NL), Dineen (AL); Time: 1:41; Attendance: 23,573.

Indians	IP	H	R	ER	BB	SO
Coveleski, W	9	5	1	1	1	3

Brooklyn	IP	H	R	ER	BB	SO
Marquard, L	6	5	3	1	2	4
Mamaux	2	0	0	0	0	3
Cadore	1	0	0	0	0	0

Game 2
Wednesday, October 6, at Brooklyn

Indians	AB	R	H	RBI	PO	A
Jamieson, lf	4	0	1	0	2	0
Wambsganss, 2b	3	0	0	0	3	0
b-Burns	0	0	0	0	0	0
Lunte, 2b	0	0	0	0	0	0
Speaker, cf	3	0	2	0	2	0
E. Smith, rf	4	0	0	0	3	0
Gardner, 3b	3	0	2	0	1	2
D. Johnston, 1b	4	0	0	0	3	3
Sewell, ss	4	0	0	0	1	1
O'Neill, c	4	0	1	0	7	2
Bagby, p	2	0	0	0	2	1
a-Graney	1	0	0	0	0	0
Uhle, p	0	0	0	0	0	0
c-Nunamaker	1	0	1	0	0	1
Totals	33	0	7	0	24	10

Brooklyn	AB	R	H	RBI	PO	A
Olson, ss	4	1	1	0	3	2
J. Johnston, 3b	4	1	1	0	0	1
Griffith, rf	4	0	2	2	3	0
Wheat, lf	3	0	1	1	3	0
Myers, cf	3	0	1	0	2	0
Konetchy, 1b	3	0	0	0	10	1
Kilduff, 2b	3	0	0	0	2	3
Miller, c	3	0	0	0	3	1
Grimes, p	3	1	1	0	1	4
Totals	30	3	7	3	27	12

Cleveland	0	0	0	0	0	0	0	0	0—0
Brooklyn	0	1	0	1	0	0	0	1	x—3

a-Struck out for Bagby in seventh
b-Walked for Wambsganss in eighth
c-Singled for Uhle in ninth

Error: Bagby; Two-base hits: Gardner, Wheat, Griffith, Speaker; Stolen Bases: J. Johnston; Double Play: Gardner to O'Neill to D. Johnston to O'Neill; Left on Base: Cleveland 10, Brooklyn 4; Umpires: Connolly (AL), O'Day (NL), Dineen (AL), Klem (NL); Time: 1:55; Attendance: 22,559.

Indians	IP	H	R	ER	BB	SO
Bagby, L	6	7	3	2	1	0
Uhle	2	0	0	0	0	3

Brooklyn	IP	H	R	ER	BB	SO
Grimes, W	9	7	0	0	4	2

Game 3
Thursday, October 7, at Brooklyn

Indians	AB	R	H	RBI	PO	A
Evans, lf	4	0	0	0	2	0
Wambsganss, 2b	3	0	0	0	2	2
Speaker, cf	4	1	1	0	2	0
Burns, 1b	3	0	0	0	12	0
Gardner, 3b	3	0	0	0	0	0
Wood, rf	3	0	0	0	1	0
Sewell, ss	2	0	0	0	2	3
O'Neill, c	3	0	2	0	2	2
b-Jamieson	0	0	0	0	0	0
Uhle, p	0	0	0	0	0	1
Caldwell, p	0	0	0	0	0	0
Mails, p	2	0	0	0	1	3
c-Nunamaker, c	1	0	0	0	0	0
Totals	28	1	3	0	24	11

Brooklyn	AB	R	H	RBI	PO	A
Olson, ss	2	1	1	0	0	6
J. Johnston, 3b	3	0	0	0	0	4
Griffith, rf	1	1	0	0	2	0
a-Neis, rf	3	0	0	0	0	0
Wheat, lf	4	0	3	1	1	0
Myers, cf	4	0	2	1	1	0
Konetchy, 1b	3	0	0	0	17	2
Kilduff, 2b	1	0	0	0	2	6
Miller, c	1	0	0	0	2	0
S. Smith, p	3	0	0	0	2	2
Totals	25	2	6	2	27	20

Cleveland	0	0	0	1	0	0	0	0	0—1
Brooklyn	2	0	0	0	0	0	0	0	x—2

a-Grounded out for Griffith in third
b-Ran for O'Neill in eighth
c-Hit into double play for Mails in eighth

Errors: Sewell, Wheat; Two-base hit: Speaker; Sacrifice Hits: J. Johnston, Kilduff, Miller; Double Plays: Mails to Burns, Olson to Kilduff to Konetchy, Wambsganss to Sewell to Burns, J. Johnston to Kilduff to Konetchy; Left on Base: Cleveland 2, Brooklyn 7; Umpires: O'Day (NL), Dineen (AL), Klem (NL), Connolly (AL); Time: 1:47; Attendance: 25,088.

Indians	IP	H	R	ER	BB	SO
Caldwell, L	⅓	2	2	1	1	0
Mails	6⅔	3	0	0	4	2
Uhle	1	1	0	0	0	0

Brooklyn	IP	H	R	ER	BB	SO
S. Smith, W	9	3	1	0	2	2

Game 4
Saturday, October 9, at Cleveland

Brooklyn	AB	R	H	RBI	PO	A
Olson, ss	4	0	1	0	1	2
J. Johnston, 3b	4	1	2	0	1	0
f-Neis	0	0	0	0	0	0
Griffith, rf	4	0	1	1	1	0
Wheat, lf	4	0	0	0	0	0
Myers, cf	3	0	0	0	6	1
Konetchy, 1b	2	0	0	0	5	0
Kilduff, 2b	3	0	1	0	2	4
Miller, c	3	0	0	0	7	0
Cadore, p	0	0	0	0	1	0
Mamaux, p	1	0	0	0	0	0
Marquard, p	0	0	0	0	0	1
d-Lamar	1	0	0	0	0	0
Pfeffer, p	1	0	0	0	0	0
Totals	**30**	**1**	**5**	**1**	**24**	**8**

Indians	AB	R	H	RBI	PO	A
Jamieson, lf	2	0	0	0	1	0
c-Evans, lf	3	0	1	0	0	0
Wambsganss, 2b	4	2	2	1	4	6
Speaker, cf	5	2	2	0	3	0
E. Smith, rf	1	0	1	1	1	0
a-Burns, 1b	2	0	1	1	7	0
Gardner, 3b	3	0	1	1	2	3
D. Johnston, 1b	1	0	0	0	4	0
b-Wood, rf	2	0	0	0	0	0
e-Graney, rf	1	0	0	0	0	0
Sewell, ss	4	0	2	0	1	7
O'Neill, c	2	0	1	0	4	0
Coveleski, p	4	1	1	0	0	2
Totals	**34**	**5**	**12**	**4**	**27**	**18**

Brooklyn	0	0	0	1	0	0	0	0	0—1
Cleveland	2	0	2	0	0	1	0	0	x—5

a-Singled for E. Smith in third
b-Flied out for D. Johnston in third
c-Flied out for Jamieson in fourth
d-Grounded out for Marquard in sixth
e-Hit into force play for Wood in seventh
f-Ran for J. Johnston in ninth

Errors: Wheat, Burns, Sewell; Two-base hits: Griffith; Sacrifice Hit: Gardner; Double Plays: Myers to Olson to Kilduff, Sewell to Wambsganss to Burns, Gardner to Wambsganss to Burns; Passed Ball: Miller; Wild Pitch: Pfeffer; Left on Base: Brooklyn 3, Cleveland 10; Umpires: Dineen (AL), Klem (NL), Connolly (AL), O'Day (NL); Time: 1:54; Attendance: 25,734.

Brooklyn	IP	H	R	ER	BB	SO
Cadore, L	*1	4	2	2	1	1
Mamaux	†1	2	2	2	0	1
Marquard	3	2	0	0	1	2
Pfeffer	3	4	1	1	2	1

Indians	IP	H	R	ER	BB	SO
Coveleski, W	9	5	1	1	1	4

*Pitched to two batters in second
†Pitched to two batters in third

Game 5
Sunday, October 10, at Cleveland

Brooklyn	AB	R	H	RBI	PO	A
Olson, ss	4	0	2	0	3	5
Sheehan, 3b	3	0	1	0	1	1
Griffith, rf	4	0	0	0	0	0
Wheat, lf	4	1	2	0	3	0
Myers, cf	4	0	2	0	0	0
Konetchy, 1b	4	0	2	1	9	2
Kilduff, 2b	4	0	1	0	5	6
Miller, c	2	0	2	0	0	1
Krueger, c	2	0	1	0	2	1
Grimes, p	1	0	0	0	0	1
Mitchell, p	2	0	0	0	1	0
Totals	**34**	**1**	**13**	**1**	**24**	**17**

Indians	AB	R	H	RBI	PO	A
Jamieson, lf	4	1	2	0	2	1
a-Graney, lf	1	0	0	0	0	0
Wambsganss, 2b	5	1	1	0	7	2
Speaker, cf	3	2	1	0	1	0
E. Smith, rf	4	1	3	4	0	0
Gardner, 3b	4	0	1	1	2	2
D. Johnston, 1b	3	1	2	0	9	1
Sewell, ss	3	0	0	0	2	4
O'Neill, c	2	1	0	0	3	1
Thomas, c	0	0	0	0	1	0
Bagby, p	4	1	2	3	0	2
Totals	**33**	**8**	**12**	**8**	**27**	**13**

Brooklyn	0	0	0	0	0	0	0	0	1—1
Cleveland	4	0	0	3	1	0	0	0	x—8

a-Struck out for Jamieson in eighth

Errors: Sheehan, Gardner, O'Neill; Three-base hits: Konetchy, E. Smith; Home Runs: Bagby, E. Smith; Sacrifice Hits: D. Johnston, Sheehan; Double Plays: Olson to Kilduff to Konetchy, Jamieson to O'Neill, Gardner to Wambsganss to D. Johnston, D. Johnston to Sewell to D. Johnston; Triple Play: Wambsganss (unassisted); Passed Ball: Miller; Wild Pitch: Bagby; Left on Base: Brooklyn 7, Cleveland 6; Umpires: Klem (NL), Connolly (AL), O'Day (NL), Dineen (AL); Time: 1:49; Attendance: 26,884.

Brooklyn	IP	H	R	ER	BB	SO
Grimes, L	3⅓	9	7	7	1	0
Mitchell	4⅔	3	1	0	3	1

Indians	IP	H	R	ER	BB	SO
Bagby, W	9	13	1	1	0	3

Game 6
Monday, October 11, at Cleveland

Brooklyn	AB	R	H	RBI	PO	A
Olson, ss	4	0	1	0	4	1
Sheehan, 3b	4	0	0	0	0	3
Neis, rf	2	0	0	0	3	0
a-Krueger	1	0	0	0	0	0
Griffith, rf	0	0	0	0	0	0
Wheat, lf	4	0	0	0	2	0
Myers, cf	4	0	1	0	1	0
Konetchy, 1b	3	0	1	0	9	1
b-McCabe	0	0	0	0	0	0
Kilduff, 2b	4	0	0	0	2	2
Miller, c	3	0	0	0	3	3
S. Smith, p	3	0	0	0	0	3
Totals	**32**	**0**	**3**	**0**	**24**	**13**

Indians	AB	R	H	RBI	PO	A
Evans, lf	4	0	3	0	4	0
Wambsganss, 2b	4	0	0	0	1	2
Speaker, cf	3	1	1	0	3	0
Burns, 1b	2	0	1	1	10	0
Gardner, 3b	3	0	0	0	2	2
Wood, rf	3	0	1	0	2	0
Sewell, ss	3	0	1	0	2	3
O'Neill, c	3	0	0	0	3	2
Mails, p	3	0	0	0	0	1
Totals	**28**	**1**	**7**	**1**	**27**	**10**

Brooklyn	0	0	0	0	0	0	0	0	0—0
Cleveland	0	0	0	0	0	1	0	0	x—1

a-Hit into force play for Neis in eighth
b-Ran for Konetchy in ninth

Errors: Gardner, Sewell 2; Two-base hits: Burns, Olson; Left on Base: Brooklyn 7, Cleveland 4; Umpires: Connolly (AL), O'Day (NL), Dineen (AL), Klem (NL); Time: 1:34; Attendance: 27,194.

Brooklyn	IP	H	R	ER	BB	SO
S. Smith, L	8	7	1	1	1	1

Indians	IP	H	R	ER	BB	SO
Mails, W	9	3	0	0	2	4

Game 7
Tuesday, October 12, at Cleveland

Brooklyn	AB	R	H	RBI	PO	A
Olson, ss	4	0	0	0	1	1
Sheehan, 3b	4	0	1	0	1	1
Griffith, rf	4	0	0	0	3	0
Wheat, lf	4	0	2	0	2	0
Myers, cf	4	0	0	0	4	0
Konetchy, 1b	4	0	1	0	8	0
Kilduff, 2b	3	0	0	0	1	4
Miller, c	2	0	0	0	2	1
b-Lamar	1	0	0	0	0	0
Krueger, c	0	0	0	0	1	0
Grimes, p	2	0	1	0	0	2
c-Schmandt	1	0	0	0	0	0
Mamaux, p	0	0	0	0	0	0
Totals	**33**	**0**	**5**	**0**	**24**	**9**

Indians	AB	R	H	RBI	PO	A
Jamieson, lf	4	1	2	1	3	0
Wambsganss, 2b	4	0	1	0	4	3
Speaker, cf	3	0	1	1	3	0
E. Smith, rf	3	0	0	0	3	1
Gardner, 3b	4	1	1	0	1	3
D. Johnston, 1b	2	0	1	0	11	1
Sewell, ss	4	0	0	0	0	6
O'Neill, c	4	0	1	0	1	0
Coveleski, p	3	1	0	0	1	1
Totals	**31**	**3**	**7**	**2**	**26**	**15**

Brooklyn	0	0	0	0	0	0	0	0	0—0
Cleveland	0	0	0	1	1	0	1	0	x—3

a-Olson hit by batted ball in third
b-Grounded out for Miller in seventh
c-Grounded out for Grimes in eighth

Errors: Sheehan, Grimes, Sewell 2, Coveleski; Two-base hits: Jamieson, O'Neill; Three-base hit: Speaker; Stolen Bases: Jamieson, D. Johnston; Left on Base: Brooklyn 6, Cleveland 8; Umpires: O'Day (NL), Dineen (AL), Klem (NL), Connolly (AL); Time: 1:55; Attendance: 27,525.

Brooklyn	IP	H	R	ER	BB	SO
Grimes, L	7	7	3	2	4	2
Mamaux	1	0	0	0	0	1

Indians	IP	H	R	ER	BB	SO
Coveleski, W	9	5	0	0	0	1

COMPOSITE BATTING AVERAGES

Brooklyn Dodgers

Player-Position	G	AB	R	H	2B	3B	HR	RBI	BA
Konetchy, 1b	7	23	0	4	0	1	0	2	.174
Kilduff, 2b	7	21	0	2	0	0	0	0	.095
Olson, ss	7	25	2	8	1	0	0	0	.320
J. Johnston, 3b	4	14	2	3	0	0	0	0	.214
Griffith, rf	7	21	1	4	2	0	0	3	.190
Myers, cf	7	26	0	6	0	0	0	1	.231
Wheat, cf	7	27	2	9	2	0	0	2	.333
Miller, c	6	14	0	2	0	0	0	0	.143
Sheehan, 3b	3	11	0	2	0	0	0	0	.182
Krueger, c, ph	4	6	0	1	0	0	0	0	.167
Neis, pr, rf	4	5	0	0	0	0	0	0	.000
Lamar, ph	3	3	0	0	0	0	0	0	.000
Schmandt, ph	1	1	0	0	0	0	0	0	.000
McCabe, pr	1	0	0	0	0	0	0	0	—
Elliott	Did not play								
Ward	Did not play								
Taylor	Did not play								
Grimes, p	3	6	1	2	0	0	0	0	.333
S. Smith, p	2	6	0	0	0	0	0	0	.000
Mitchell, p, ph	2	3	0	1	0	0	0	0	.333
Marquard, p	2	1	0	0	0	0	0	0	.000
Mamaux, p	3	1	0	0	0	0	0	0	.000
Pfeffer, p	1	1	0	0	0	0	0	0	.000
Cadore, p	2	0	0	0	0	0	0	0	—
Mohart	Did not play								
Miljus	Did not play								
Totals	7	215	8	44	5	1	0	8	.205

Cleveland Indians

Player-Position	G	AB	R	H	2B	3B	HR	RBI	BA
D. Johnston, ph, 1b	5	11	1	3	0	0	0	0	.273
Wambsganss, 2b	7	26	3	4	0	0	0	1	.154
Sewell, ss	7	23	0	4	0	0	0	0	.174
Gardner, 3b	7	24	1	5	1	0	0	2	.208
E. Smith, ph, rf	5	13	1	4	0	1	1	5	.308
Speaker, cf	7	25	6	8	2	1	0	1	.320
Jamieson, pr, lf	6	15	2	5	1	0	0	1	.333
O'Neill, c	7	21	1	7	3	0	0	2	.333
Evans, lf, ph	5	13	0	4	0	0	0	0	.308
Burns, 1b, ph	4	10	1	3	1	0	0	2	.300
Wood, rf, ph	4	10	2	2	1	0	0	0	.200
Graney, ph, rf, lf	3	3	0	0	0	0	0	0	.000
Nunamaker, ph, c	2	2	0	1	0	0	0	0	.500
Lunte, 2b	1	0	0	0	0	0	0	0	—
Thomas, c	1	0	0	0	0	0	0	0	—
Coveleski, p	3	10	2	1	0	0	0	0	.100
Bagby, p	2	6	1	2	0	0	1	3	.333
Mails, p	2	5	0	0	0	0	0	0	.000
Uhle, p	2	0	0	0	0	0	0	0	—
Caldwell, p	1	0	0	0	0	0	0	0	—
Morton	Did not play								
Clark	Did not play								
Ellison	Did not play								
Totals	7	217	21	53	9	2	2	17	.244

COMPOSITE PITCHING AVERAGES

Brooklyn Dodgers

Pitcher	G	IP	H	R	ER	BB	SO	W	L	ERA
Grimes	3	19⅓	23	10	9	9	4	1	2	4.19
S. Smith	2	17	10	2	1	3	3	1	1	0.53
Marquard	2	9	7	3	1	3	6	0	1	1.00
Mitchell	1	4⅔	3	1	0	3	1	0	0	0.00
Mamaux	3	4	2	2	2	0	5	0	0	4.50
Pfeffer	1	3	4	1	1	2	1	0	0	3.00
Cadore	2	2	4	2	2	1	1	0	1	9.00
Mohart	Did not play									
Miljus	Did not play									
Totals	7	59	53	21	16	21	21	2	5	2.44

Cleveland Indians

Pitcher	G	IP	H	R	ER	BB	SO	W	L	ERA
Coveleski	3	27	15	2	2	2	8	3	0	0.67
Mails	2	15⅔	6	0	0	6	6	1	0	0.00
Bagby	2	15	20	4	3	1	3	1	1	1.80
Uhle	2	3	1	0	0	0	3	0	0	0.00
Caldwell	1	⅓	2	2	1	1	0	0	1	27.00
Morton	Did not play									
Clark	Did not play									
Ellison	Did not play									
Totals	7	61	44	8	6	10	20	5	2	0.89

Indians versus Boston Braves World Series

1948

Only three times from 1921 through 1947 did the Indians came close to winning another American League championship:

In 1921 they ended up in second place, 4½ games behind the New York Yankees.

In 1926 they finished second by three games to the Yankees.

In 1940 they lost the pennant by one game to Detroit in the last series of the season.

They nearly blew it again in 1948, also in a loss to the Tigers in the final game of the season, though that one dropped the Indians into a tie with Boston. It forced an unprecedented one-game playoff in which the Tribe prevailed, 8–3.

The 1948 AL race was hectic from the beginning and one of the tightest in history. The Yankees and Philadelphia Athletics were in contention with the Indians and Red Sox most of the way.

The four clubs were in a virtual tie for the lead in early August. Only six percentage points separated them on August 3. One month later the Indians faltered while the Red Sox and Yankees moved up, with Boston taking over first place.

On the morning after the Labor Day doubleheaders the

Indians were 4½ games behind, in third place, and were being counted out by most of the experts.

However, they staged a remarkable comeback in that final month, winning 18 of their last 23 games to climb back into a share of first place. As late as nine days before the season's close, there was a three-way tie for the lead among Cleveland, New York, and Boston.

The Yankees were eliminated from contention at Boston on the next-to-last day of the season, leaving the Indians one game in front of the Red Sox entering that final day. But the Tribe was beaten by Detroit, 7–1, in the closing game, while the Red Sox were beating the Yankees, 10–5, to give the American League its first dead heat in 48 years.

The next day, October 4, at Fenway Park in Boston, the Indians beat the Red Sox, 8–3, as rookie Gene Bearden won his 20th game and Lou Boudreau hit two home runs to become the second player-manager in franchise history to lead the team to a pennant.

The National League champion Boston Braves had an easier time reaching the World Series, also for only the second time it their history, winning by 6½ lengths over the St. Louis Cardinals.

The Braves had five .300 hitters: outfielders Tommy Holmes (.325), Mike McCormick (.303), and Jeff Heath (.319), shortstop Alvin Dark (.322), and second baseman Eddie Stanky

Player-manager Lou Boudreau's second homer of the game, in the fifth inning, led the Indians to an 8–3 victory over the Boston Red Sox on October 4, 1948, in the American League's first pennant playoff. Greeting Boudreau as he crossed the plate is second baseman Joe Gordon.

(.320). (Heath, a former member of the Indians, was injured and couldn't play in the World Series.)

Boston manager Billy Southworth also had a potent one-two pitching punch of Johnny Sain (24–15), the NL's biggest winner, and Warren Spahn (15–12), about whom the phrase, "Spahn and Sain and pray for rain," had been coined during the Braves' season.

Despite the Indians' difficulty winning the AL pennant, they were installed as favorites to beat the Braves and win the World Series.

Game One

It began in the worst possible manner, especially for Bob Feller, the longtime ace of the Indians whose avowed goal throughout his career was to win a World Series game.

But he failed in his first opportunity and, though years later a principal in the Braves' 1–0 victory would admit that Feller was wrongly thwarted, the admission only heightened the frustration that tormented the Hall of Fame pitcher.

The controversial play came in the eighth inning. After Feller had allowed only one hit, a fifth-inning single by Marv Rickert, he walked Bill Salkeld leading off the eighth. Phil Masi, a pinch runner, was sacrificed to second, and Eddie Stanky was intentionally walked, setting up a potential double play.

Then came the play—and the decision—that Feller can't forget.

He and shortstop Lou Boudreau had practiced and perfected a pickoff play earlier in the season, but kept it under wraps until the time was precisely right.

Now it was.

Feller took his stretch and looked back at Masi. At that time, Boudreau flashed a signal, positioning his glove a certain way on his left knee. Feller counted to himself, "one-thousand-one, one-thousand-two, one-thousand-three," then whirled and threw to second base, where Boudreau was in the process of sneaking behind Masi.

Boudreau caught Feller's throw and tagged Masi, as he dived head first back to the bag. Everyone in Braves Field saw that Masi was out.

Everyone, that is, except National League umpire Bill Stewart, working at second base.

Stewart called Masi safe, saying that the shortstop's tag was applied "too high," that Masi, in diving back to the bag, had reached it with his hands before Boudreau slapped him on the shoulder with his glove holding the ball.

Though photographs clearly showed that Stewart was wrong, that Boudreau had tagged Masi before the runner reached the base, the umpire's call stood, of course.

Feller tried to shrug off the controversial call and retired Sain on a fly to right.

But he couldn't get past Holmes, who lashed a single to left that scored Masi.

Feller retired Dark to end the inning, but Johnny Sain, pitching a four-hitter for the Braves, didn't allow a Cleveland runner past second base, and the Braves prevailed, 1–0.

Several years later, after Stewart died, Masi met Feller at a banquet and told him not only that he was indeed tagged out by Boudreau, but also that the umpire had admitted privately to Masi that he blew the call.

Game Two

It might have been the Indians' failed pickoff play—or umpire Bill Stewart's controversial call—in the first game that saved Bob Lemon in the second game, as he recovered from a shaky start to beat the Braves, 4–1, the next day.

Alvin Dark, the second batter to face Lemon in the first inning, reached on an error by Joe Gordon, went to third on Earl Torgeson's single to right, and scored on Bob Elliott's single, which also advanced Torgeson to second.

Then, with Marv Rickert at bat, Lemon and shortstop Lou Boudreau attempted the same pickoff play that umpire Bill Stewart disallowed in the first game. This time it worked as American League umpire Bill Grieve called Torgeson out.

"I don't know for sure, but it's my opinion that, because Stewart was caught napping in the first game, all the umpires were more alert to our pickoff play thereafter," said Boudreau, who was the Indians' offensive leader in the game, as he'd been all season.

Boudreau—who'd batted .355 and driven in 106 runs in 1948, and who was elected the AL's Most Valuable Player, practically by acclamation—doubled to lead off the fourth inning and scored on Gordon's single. After Warren Spahn retired Ken Keltner, Larry Doby followed with another single for another run, and the Indians were never headed.

In the fifth, Dale Mitchell singled, was sacrificed to second, and scored on another hit by Boudreau. Jim Hegan reached on an error and Bob Kennedy singled for another run in the ninth.

Lemon admitted, "I had all kinds of butterflies in my stomach when I went out for the first inning, and maybe that's why I had a little trouble. But getting [picking off] Torgeson helped settle me down."

"Lem's fastball doesn't sink if he's too strong, and once he got it zeroed in, he was fine," Boudreau said of Lemon, who gave up a single and a walk each in the second, fourth, and sixth innings, as well as a single in the eighth and a double in the ninth, but not another run.

Indians catcher Jim Hegan (left) congratulates Bob Lemon after Lemon scattered eight hits in beating the Boston Braves, 4–1, on October 7, 1948, in the second game of the World Series.

More congratulations for Bob Lemon (right), this time by player-manager Lou Boudreau, after the Indians defeated the Boston Braves, 4–1, on October 7, 1948, in the second game of the World Series.

Game Three

With the Series tied at one apiece, it shifted to Cleveland where a crowd of 70,306 in the Stadium saw their first World Series game in 28 years, and watched Gene Bearden continue the pitching excellence he'd displayed all season.

With remarkable control of his celebrated knuckleball, the rookie southpaw didn't walk a batter and blanked the Braves on a five-hitter. It was the first time in 37 games, 29 as a starter, that Bearden did not issue a base on balls.

What's more, Bearden also ignited a third-inning uprising that provided the Indians' first run. With one out he doubled off Vern Bickford, waited as Dale Mitchell walked, and scored when Alvin Dark threw wildly to first base when Larry Doby grounded into a force at second base.

The Indians went ahead, 2–0, in the fourth when Ken Keltner walked and scored as Eddie Robinson and Jim Hegan singled. Bearden, who started his professional career as a first baseman, also singled, loading the bases and knocking Bickford out of the game, though Bill Voiselle came on and ended the rally.

Though the Indians didn't threaten again, Bearden didn't need any more help. He allowed only two hits the rest of the way and retired the last eight batters in order.

Within the space of a single week, Bearden had (1) won the game that clinched at least a tie for the pennant, (2) won the game that gave the Indians the pennant, and (3) won the game that put the Tribe ahead, 2–1, in the World Series.

"I'll be ready to pitch again, whenever Lou [Boudreau] wants me, but to tell you the truth, I don't think I'll be needed," said Bearden. "I think we're on our way . . . I think we'll win this [World Series] in the next two games."

Game Four

Larry Doby homered and Steve Gromek scattered seven hits as the Indians took a commanding three-to-one lead in the World Series in front of a single-game record crowd of 81,897 in the Stadium.

And after the Tribe's 2–1 victory was finalized, Gromek, the son of Polish immigrants who was born and raised in Hamtramck, Michigan, was photographed hugging Doby, the American League's first black player and second in major league baseball.

"It is something I'll never forget," said Doby. "I will always cherish it because it showed that emotions can be put into a form that's something other than skin color. We—Steve and I—were just so happy to have won the game, we just grabbed each other and hugged. It was a wonderful moment."

The photograph was published in newspapers across the country.

It also was a wonderful game for the Indians to win.

"We're not planning to go back to Boston [for a sixth game]," said Tribe player-manager Lou Boudreau, meaning he expected to beat the Braves a fourth straight time in Game 6.

Boudreau got the Indians started early in this victory against Boston ace Johnny Sain, who had won the Braves' only game, 1–0, in the opener of the Series.

After Dale Mitchell led off the first inning with a single, Boudreau doubled with one out for a 1–0 lead. Doby homered over the right-field fence with two out in the third, and Gromek made it stand up.

The Braves didn't get on the scoreboard until the seventh, when Marv Rickert led off with a homer over the right-field fence on a 3-and-0 pitch. "I was just trying to get it in there for a strike," said Gromek. "I thought he'd be taking, not swinging."

Mike McCormick followed with a single, but Gromek went on to retire the next five batters in order and nine of 10, the last two on strikeouts, in his best performance all season.

Game Five

Bob Feller got another chance to win a World Series game, but failed again—and this time he had only himself to blame, not an umpire for making a bad call.

Before another record crowd of 86,288 fans in the Stadium, Feller was bombed, and the Indians were blasted, 11–5, by the Braves, who kept their hopes alive and sent the Series back to Boston.

Bob Elliott, the Braves' third baseman, who until this game had only two singles in the first four, clubbed two homers off Feller, driving in Boston's first four runs, igniting the rout with a three-run shot in the first inning. He homered again in the third, as did Bill Salkeld in the sixth.

"I haven't any excuses," said Feller, who was replaced in the seventh when the Braves rallied for six runs to break a 5–5 deadlock. "I couldn't seem to loosen up, and I didn't have any control. All I can say is that I just didn't have it."

Dale Mitchell solo homered for the Indians in the bottom of the first, and Jim Hegan hit a three-run shot in the fourth when the Indians rebounded for four runs to take a 5–4 lead.

But Feller couldn't hold it as Salkeld hammered a bases-empty homer in the sixth, tying the score. It set the stage for the Braves' seventh-inning explosion, which continued against relievers Ed Klieman, Russ Christopher, and Satchel Paige after Feller was sent to the showers.

The Braves' Warren Spahn, who replaced Nelson Potter in the fourth when the Indians rallied for four runs and a short-lived, 5–4, lead, was the winning pitcher. He struck out seven and blanked the Tribe on one hit in 5⅔ innings.

The victory bolstered the Braves' hopes. "What a relief to get some runs and some good pitching, too," said manager Billy Southworth. "Now we're on our way."

"They outslugged us and they got relief pitching that we didn't get," said Boudreau. "I had hoped we'd end it here, but we beat them in Boston [in Game 2], and we'll just have to do it again."

Game Six

Gene Bearden, who was the Indians' go-to guy all season, did it again—and because he did, the world's championship of baseball returned to Cleveland after a 28-year absence.

The Indians beat the Braves, 4–3, in the sixth game of the World Series and, while Bearden wasn't the winning pitcher, he saved the victory that concluded the franchise's most dramatic and colorful season since the formation of the American League in 1901.

Bearden, a 20-game winner who halted the Braves, 2–0, in the third game of the Series, replaced Bob Lemon on the mound in the eighth inning under the most difficult of conditions.

The Braves, trying to overcome a 4–1 deficit, loaded the bases with one out in the eighth as Tommy Holmes singled, Earl Torgeson doubled, and Bob Elliott walked.

Player-manager Lou Boudreau signaled for Bearden to rescue Lemon, who had given up Boston's only run in the fourth on Elliott's single, a walk, and another single by Mike McCormick with two out.

Bearden retired the first batter he faced, Clint Conatser, on a fly to center that scored Holmes, but yielded a double to Phil Masi that got Torgeson home and Elliott to third base with the potential tying run.

With the crowd of 40,103 in Braves Field pleading for a hit that would score Elliott, Mike McCormick bounced out to Bearden, ending the inning.

But it wasn't yet the end of the Braves.

The Indians scored a run in the third on doubles by Dale Mitchell and Boudreau, two more in the sixth on a solo homer by Joe Gordon and a walk, Eddie Robinson's single, and an infield out, and another in the eighth on singles by Ken Keltner, Thurman Tucker, and Robinson.

Cleveland Mayor Thomas Burke (right) greets player-manager Lou Boudreau at the celebration following the Indians' victory over the Boston Braves in the 1948 World Series.

After they went down in order in the top of the ninth, Eddie Stanky walked to start the Braves' last stand. Connie Ryan ran for Stanky, and in his anxiety to get into scoring position, Ryan committed one of baseball's cardinal sins.

With pinch hitter Sibby Sisti trying to lay down a sacrifice bunt, Ryan took off from first base too soon, instead of waiting to see the ball on the ground. It popped into the air, catcher Jim Hegan snared it, and his throw to first doubled Ryan.

Holmes, the final batter, was easy. He lofted a routine fly to left. Bob Kennedy camped under it, and the Series was over. Bearden was carried off the field on the shoulders of his teammates.

"No doubt about it, it was Bearden's series all the way, all his," chortled Boudreau—who could have called it Bearden's year, all the way, all his.

By winning, the Indians earned individual World Series shares of $6,772.07, while the losing Braves each received $4,570.73.

Game 1
Wednesday, October 6, at Boston

Indians	AB	R	H	RBI	PO	A
Mitchell, lf	4	0	0	0	2	0
Doby, cf	4	0	1	0	3	0
Boudreau, ss	4	0	0	0	2	1
Gordon, 2b	4	0	1	0	1	1
Keltner, 3b	4	0	1	0	1	1
Judnich, rf	4	0	0	0	2	0
Robinson, 1b	3	0	0	0	10	1
Hegan, c	3	0	1	0	2	1
Feller, p	2	0	0	0	1	4
Totals	32	0	4	0	24	9

Boston	AB	R	H	RBI	PO	A
Holmes, rf	4	0	1	1	5	0
Dark, ss	4	0	0	0	1	1
Torgeson, 1b	2	0	0	0	4	0
Elliott, 3b	3	0	0	0	1	0
Rickert, lf	3	0	1	0	5	0
Salkeld, c	1	0	0	0	5	1
a-Masi, c	0	1	0	0	1	0
M. McCormick, cf	2	0	0	0	5	0
Stanky, 2b	2	0	0	0	0	1
b-Sisti, 2b	0	0	0	0	0	0
Sain, p	3	0	0	0	0	0
Totals	24	1	2	1	27	3

Cleveland	0	0	0	0	0	0	0	0	0—0
Boston	0	0	0	0	0	0	0	1	x—1

a-Ran for Salkeld in eighth
b-Ran for Stanky in eighth

Errors: Elliott 2; Sacrifice Hits: Feller, M. McCormick, Salkeld; Stolen Base: Gordon, Hegan, Torgeson; Left on Bases: Cleveland 6, Boston 4; Umpires: Barr (NL), Summers (AL), Stewart (NL), Grieve (AL), Paparella (AL), Pinelli (NL); Time: 1:42; Attendance: 40,135.

Indians	IP	H	R	ER	BB	SO
Feller, L	8	2	1	1	3	2

Boston	IP	H	R	ER	BB	SO
Sain, W	9	4	0	0	0	6

Game 2
Thursday, October 7, at Boston

Indians	AB	R	H	RBI	PO	A
Mitchell, lf	5	1	1	0	1	0
Clark, rf	3	0	0	0	2	0
Kennedy, rf	1	0	1	1	0	0
Boudreau, ss	5	1	2	1	4	2
Gordon, 2b	4	1	1	1	2	3
Keltner, 3b	4	0	0	0	0	0
Doby, cf	4	0	2	1	0	0
Robinson, 1b	3	0	1	0	8	3
Hegan, c	3	1	0	0	7	0
Lemon, p	4	0	0	0	3	6
Totals	36	4	8	4	27	14

Boston	AB	R	H	RBI	PO	A
Holmes, rf	4	0	0	0	2	1
Dark, ss	4	1	1	0	0	2
Torgeson, 1b	4	0	2	0	14	1
Elliott, 3b	4	0	1	1	1	5
Rickert, lf	4	0	0	0	5	0
Salkeld, c	1	0	1	0	2	0
a-Masi, c	1	0	0	0	1	0
M. McCormick, cf	4	0	2	0	1	0
Stanky, 2b	2	0	1	0	1	3
Spahn, p	2	0	0	0	0	1
Barrett, p	0	0	0	0	0	0
b-F. McCormick	1	0	0	0	0	0
Potter, p	0	0	0	0	0	0
c-Sanders	1	0	0	0	0	0
Totals	32	1	8	1	27	13

Cleveland	0	0	0	2	1	0	0	0	1—4
Boston	1	0	0	0	0	0	0	0	0—1

a-Ran for Salkeld in sixth
b-Struck out for Barrett in seventh
c-Grounded out for Potter in ninth

Errors: Gordon, Dark 2, Elliott; Two-base hits: Boudreau, Doby, Stanky; Sacrifice Hits: Clark, Stanky; Double Plays: Holmes to Torgeson, Boudreau to Gordon to Robinson, Gordon to Boudreau to Robinson; Left on Base: Cleveland 8, Boston 8; Umpires: Summers (AL), Stewart (NL), Grieve (AL), Barr (NL), Pinelli (NL), Paparella (AL); Time: 2:14; Attendance: 39,633.

Indians	IP	H	R	ER	BB	SO
Lemon, W	9	8	1	0	3	5

Boston	IP	H	R	ER	BB	SO
Spahn, L	4⅓	6	3	3	2	1
Barrett	2⅔	1	0	0	0	1
Potter	2	1	1	0	0	1

Game 3
Friday, October 8, at Cleveland

Boston	AB	R	H	RBI	PO	A
Holmes, rf	4	0	0	0	2	0
Dark, ss	4	0	1	0	3	2
M. McCormick, lf	4	0	1	0	6	0
Elliott, 3b	3	0	1	0	2	1
F. McCormick, 1b	3	0	1	0	5	1
Conatser, cf	3	0	0	0	1	0
Masi, c	3	0	0	0	2	0
Stanky, 2b	3	0	1	0	2	3
Bickford, p	0	0	0	0	0	0
Voiselle, p	1	0	0	0	1	0
a-Ryan	1	0	0	0	0	0
Barrett, p	0	0	0	0	0	0
Totals	29	0	5	0	24	7

Indians	AB	R	H	RBI	PO	A
Mitchell, lf	3	0	0	0	2	0
Doby, cf	3	0	1	0	1	0
Boudreau, ss	3	0	0	0	1	2
Gordon, 2b	4	0	0	0	3	4
Keltner, 3b	3	1	0	0	0	4
Judnich, rf	3	0	0	0	1	0
Robinson, 1b	3	0	1	0	14	0
Hegan, c	3	0	1	1	5	0
Bearden, p	3	1	2	0	0	6
Totals	28	2	5	1	27	16

Boston	0	0	0	0	0	0	0	0	0—0
Cleveland	0	0	1	1	0	0	0	0	x—2

a-Struck out for Voiselle in eighth

Error: Dark; Two-base hits: Bearden, Dark; Sacrifice Hit: Bickford; Double Plays: Dark to Stanky to F. McCormick, Bearden to Gordon to Robinson, Keltner to Gordon to Robinson; Left on Base: Boston 3, Cleveland 7; Umpires: Stewart (NL), Grieve (AL), Barr (NL), Summers (AL), Paparella (AL), Pinelli (NL); Time: 1:36; Attendance: 70,306.

Boston	IP	H	R	ER	BB	SO
Bickford, L	3⅓	4	2	1	5	1
Voiselle	3⅔	1	0	0	0	0
Barrett	1	0	0	0	0	0

Indians	IP	H	R	ER	BB	SO
Bearden, W	9	5	0	0	0	4

Game 4
Saturday, October 9, at Cleveland

Boston	AB	R	H	RBI	PO	A
Holmes, rf	4	0	0	0	0	1
Dark, ss	4	0	0	0	2	5
Torgeson, 1b	3	0	2	0	11	2
Elliott, 3b	4	0	0	0	2	2
Rickert, lf	4	1	2	1	2	0
M. McCormick, cf	4	0	1	0	1	0
Masi, c	3	0	0	0	3	1
a-Salkeld	1	0	0	0	0	0
Stanky, 2b	3	0	1	0	1	1
Sain, p	2	0	1	0	2	2
Totals	32	1	7	1	24	14

Indians	AB	R	H	RBI	PO	A
Mitchell, lf	4	1	1	0	2	0
Doby, cf	3	1	1	1	2	0
Boudreau, ss	3	0	1	1	2	4
Gordon, 2b	3	0	0	0	4	1
Keltner, 3b	3	0	0	0	1	2
Judnich, rf	3	0	0	0	1	0
Kennedy, rf	0	0	0	0	1	0
Robinson, 1b	3	0	2	0	8	1
Hegan, c	2	0	0	0	5	1
Gromek, p	3	0	0	0	1	1
Totals	27	2	5	2	27	10

```
Boston      0  0  0  0  0  0  1  0  0—1
Cleveland   1  0  1  0  0  0  0  0  x—2
```

a-Flied out for Masi in ninth

Two-base hits: Boudreau, Torgeson 2; Home Runs: Doby, Rickert; Sacrifice Hits: Hegan, Sain; Double Play: Boudreau to Gordon to Robinson; Left on Base: Boston 6, Cleveland 2; Umpires: Grieve (AL), Barr (NL), Summers (AL), Stewart (NL), Pinelli (NL), Paparella (AL); Time: 1:31; Attendance: 81,897.

Boston	IP	H	R	ER	BB	SO
Sain, L	8	5	2	2	0	3

Indians	IP	H	R	ER	BB	SO
Gromek, W	9	7	1	1	1	2

Game 5
Sunday, October 10, at Cleveland

Boston	AB	R	H	RBI	PO	A
Holmes, rf	5	2	2	0	0	0
Dark, ss	4	1	1	0	1	1
Torgeson, 1b	5	1	2	1	10	1
Elliott, 3b	4	3	2	4	1	3
Rickert, lf	5	1	1	1	3	0
Salkeld, c	4	2	1	1	8	0
M. McCormick, cf	5	1	1	0	2	0
Stanky, 2b	3	0	1	1	1	2
Potter, p	2	0	1	0	1	0
Spahn, p	2	0	0	1	0	1
Totals	39	11	12	10	27	8

Indians	AB	R	H	RBI	PO	A
Mitchell, lf	3	1	1	1	3	0
Doby, cf	4	0	0	0	4	0
Boudreau, ss	4	0	2	0	0	3
Gordon, 2b	3	1	1	0	2	1
Keltner, 3b	3	1	0	0	1	1
Judnich, rf	3	1	1	1	3	0
b-Boone	1	0	0	0	0	0
Peck, rf	0	0	0	0	0	0
Robinson, 1b	4	0	0	0	8	2
Hegan, c	4	1	1	3	4	1
Feller, p	2	0	0	0	1	0
Klieman, p	0	0	0	0	0	0
Christopher, p	0	0	0	0	0	0
Paige, p	0	0	0	0	0	0
a-Rosen	1	0	0	0	0	0
Muncrief, p	0	0	0	0	1	0
c-Tipton	1	0	0	0	0	0
Totals	33	5	6	5	27	8

```
Boston      3  0  1  0  0  1  6  0  0—11
Cleveland   1  0  0  4  0  0  0  0  0— 5
```

a-Popped out for Paige in seventh
b-Struck out for Judnich in eighth
c-Struck out for Muncrief in ninth

Errors: Doby, Keltner; Two-base hit: Boudreau; Home Runs: Elliott 2, Hegan, Mitchell, Salkeld; Sacrifice Hit: Dark; Balk: Paige; Left on Base: Boston 6, Cleveland 4; Umpires: Barr (NL), Summers (AL), Stewart (NL), Grieve (AL), Paparella (AL), Pinelli (NL); Time: 2:39; Attendance: 86,288.

Boston	IP	H	R	ER	BB	SO
Potter	3⅓	5	5	5	2	0
Spahn, W	5⅔	1	0	0	1	7

Indians	IP	H	R	ER	BB	SO
Feller, L	6⅓	8	7	7	2	5
Klieman	*0	1	3	3	2	0
Christopher	†0	2	1	1	0	0
Paige	⅔	0	0	0	0	0
Muncrief	2	1	0	0	0	0

*Pitched to three batters in seventh
†Pitched to two batters in seventh

Game 6
Monday, October 11, at Boston

Indians	AB	R	H	RBI	PO	A
Mitchell, lf	4	1	1	0	3	0
Kennedy, lf	1	0	0	0	1	0
Doby, rf	4	0	2	0	1	0
Boudreau, ss	3	0	1	1	2	2
Gordon, 2b	4	1	1	1	3	3
Keltner, 3b	4	1	1	0	0	3
Tucker, cf	3	1	1	0	3	1
Robinson, 1b	4	0	2	1	12	0
Hegan, c	4	0	1	1	2	2
Lemon, p	3	0	0	0	0	3
Bearden, p	1	0	0	0	0	1
Totals	35	4	10	4	27	15

Boston	AB	R	H	RBI	PO	A
Holmes, rf	5	1	2	0	1	0
Dark, ss	4	0	1	0	1	0
Torgeson, 1b	4	1	1	0	5	1
Elliott, 3b	3	1	3	0	4	3
Rickert, lf	3	0	0	0	5	0
b-Conatser, cf	1	0	0	1	0	0
Salkeld, c	2	0	0	0	4	1
c-Masi, c	1	0	1	1	3	0
M. McCormick, cf, lf	4	0	1	1	2	0
Stanky, 2b	1	0	0	0	3	2
d-Ryan	0	0	0	0	0	0
Voiselle, p	1	0	0	0	0	0
a-F. McCormick	1	0	0	0	0	0
Spahn, p	0	0	0	0	0	1
e-Sisti	1	0	0	0	0	1
Totals	31	3	9	3	27	9

```
Cleveland   0  0  1  0  0  2  0  1  0—4   10  0
Boston      0  0  0  1  0  0  0  2  0—3    9  0
```

a-Grounded out for Voiselle in seventh
b-Flied out for Rickert in eighth
c-Doubled for Salkeld in eighth
d-Ran for Stanky in ninth
e-Hit into double play for Spahn in ninth

Two-base hits: Boudreau, Masi, Mitchell, Torgeson; Home Run: Gordon; Sacrifice Hit: Voiselle; Double Plays: Tucker to Robinson, Lemon to Boudreau to Robinson, Gordon to Boudreau to Robinson, Elliott to Stanky to Torgeson, Hegan to Gordon; Hit by Pitcher: Boudreau (by Voiselle); Balk: Lemon; Left on Base: Cleveland 7, Boston 7; Umpires: Summers (AL), Stewart (NL), Grieve (AL), Barr (NL), Pinelli (NL), Paparella (AL); Time: 2:16; Attendance: 40,103.

Indians	IP	H	R	ER	BB	SO
Lemon, W	7⅓	8	3	3	4	1
Bearden, S	1⅔	1	0	0	1	0

Boston	IP	H	R	ER	BB	SO
Voiselle, L	7	7	3	3	2	2
Spahn	2	3	1	1	0	4

COMPOSITE BATTING AVERAGES

Cleveland Indians Player-Position	G	AB	R	H	2B	3B	HR	RBI	BA
Robinson, 1b	6	20	0	6	0	0	0	1	.300
Gordon, 2b	6	22	3	4	0	0	1	2	.182
Boudreau, ss	6	22	1	6	4	0	0	3	.273
Keltner, 3b	6	21	3	2	0	0	0	1	.095
Judnich, rf	4	13	1	1	0	0	0	1	.077
Doby, cf, rf	6	22	1	7	1	0	1	2	.318
Mitchell, lf	6	23	4	4	1	0	1	1	.174
Hegan, c	6	19	2	4	0	0	2	5	.211
Tucker, cf	1	3	1	1	0	0	0	0	.333
Clark, rf	1	3	0	0	0	0	0	0	.000
Kennedy, rf, lf	3	2	0	1	0	0	0	1	.500
Peck, rf	1	0	0	0	0	0	0	0	—
Boone, ph	1	1	0	0	0	0	0	0	.000
Rosen, ph	1	1	0	0	0	0	0	0	.000
Tipton, ph	1	1	0	0	0	0	0	0	.000
Berardino		Did not play							
Edwards		Did not play							
Lemon, p	2	7	0	0	0	0	0	0	.000
Bearden, p	2	4	1	2	1	0	0	0	.500
Feller, p	2	4	0	0	0	0	0	0	.000
Gromek, p	1	3	0	0	0	0	0	0	.000
Christopher, p	1	0	0	0	0	0	0	0	—
Klieman, p	1	0	0	0	0	0	0	0	—
Muncrief, p	1	0	0	0	0	0	0	0	—
Paige, p	1	0	0	0	0	0	0	0	—
Zoldak		Did not play							
Black		Did not play (injured)							
Totals	6	191	17	38	7	0	4	16	.199

Boston Braves Player-Position	G	AB	R	H	2B	3B	HR	RBI	BA
Torgeson, 1b	5	18	2	7	3	0	0	1	.389
Stanky, 2b	6	14	0	4	1	0	0	1	.286
Dark, ss	6	24	2	4	1	0	0	0	.167
Elliott, 3b	6	21	4	7	0	0	2	5	.333
Holmes, rf	6	26	3	5	0	0	0	1	.192
M. McCormick, cf, lf	6	23	1	6	0	0	0	2	.261
Rickert, lf	5	19	2	4	0	0	1	2	.211
Salkeld, c, ph	5	9	2	2	0	0	1	1	.222
Masi, pr, c, ph	5	8	1	1	1	0	0	1	.125
F. McCormick, ph, 1b	3	5	0	1	0	0	0	0	.200
Conatser, cf, ph	2	4	0	0	0	0	0	1	.000
Sisti, pr, 2b, ph	2	1	0	0	0	0	0	0	.000
Ryan, ph, pr	2	1	0	0	0	0	0	0	.000
Sanders, ph	1	1	0	0	0	0	0	0	.000
Heath		Did not play (injured)							
Russell		Did not play (illness)							
Sturgeon		Did not play							
Sain, p	2	5	0	1	0	0	0	0	.200
Spahn, p	3	4	0	0	0	0	0	1	.000
Potter, p	2	2	0	1	0	0	0	0	.500
Voiselle, p	2	2	0	0	0	0	0	0	.000
Barrett, p	2	0	0	0	0	0	0	0	—
Bickford, p	1	0	0	0	0	0	0	0	—
Hogue		Did not play							
Shoun		Did not play							
Lyons		Did not play							
White		Did not play							
Totals	6	187	17	43	6	0	4	16	.230

COMPOSITE PITCHING AVERAGES

Cleveland Indians

Pitcher	G	IP	H	R	ER	BB	SO	W	L	ERA
Lemon	2	16⅓	16	4	3	7	6	2	0	1.65
Feller	2	14⅓	10	8	8	5	7	0	2	5.02
Bearden	2	10¾	6	0	0	1	4	1	0	0.00
Gromek	1	9	7	1	1	1	2	1	0	1.00
Muncrief	1	2	1	0	0	0	0	0	0	0.00
Paige	1	⅔	0	0	0	0	0	0	0	0.00
Christopher	1	0	2	1	1	0	0	0	0	inf.
Klieman	1	0	1	3	3	2	0	0	0	inf.
Zoldak	Did not play									
Black	Did not play (injured)									
Totals	7	53	43	17	16	16	19	4	2	2.72

Boston Braves

Pitcher	G	IP	H	R	ER	BB	SO	W	L	ERA
Sain	2	17	9	2	2	0	9	1	1	1.06
Spahn	3	12	10	4	4	3	12	1	1	3.00
Voiselle	2	10⅔	8	3	3	2	2	0	1	2.53
Potter	2	5⅓	6	6	5	2	1	0	0	8.44
Barrett	2	3⅔	1	0	0	0	1	0	0	0.00
Bickford	1	3⅓	4	2	1	5	1	0	1	2.70
Hogue	Did not play									
Shoun	Did not play									
Lyons	Did not play									
White	Did not play									
Totals	7	52	38	17	15	12	26	2	4	2.60

Indians versus New York Giants World Series

1954

It was expected to be a lopsided runaway, a rout by the team that was considered one of the best in the history of baseball.

As it turned out, the 1954 World Series was indeed a lopsided runaway, a rout—except that the wrong team won, not the one that was being compared to the greatest of all time.

The Indians had run roughshod through the American League, winning 111 games, the most in the major leagues since the National League Chicago Cubs captured 116 in 1906.

Bob Lemon (23–7), Early Wynn (23–11), Mike Garcia (19–8), Art Houtteman (15–7), and Bob Feller (13–3) comprised what is still thought to be the greatest starting pitching staff ever assembled, complemented by the remarkable righty-lefty relief tandem of Ray Narleski and Don Mossi.

The AL's batting champion, Bobby Avila (.341), was the Indians' second baseman; their center fielder was Larry Doby, who led the AL with 32 homers and 126 RBIs, and third baseman Al Rosen was another .300 hitter, who smashed 24 homers and drove in 102 runs.

They also had Vic Wertz, a midseason acquisition from Baltimore who went on to hit .275 with 14 homers for the Tribe.

And Al Lopez, one of the smartest men in the game, was the manager of the Indians who dethroned the New York Yankees after they'd won the pennant five consecutive seasons, 1949–53.

The Indians took over first place on May 16 and, except for four days in June, stayed there through the end of the season. They clinched the pennant on September 18, during an 11-game winning streak, with a 107th victory that gave them an eight-game lead over the New York Yankees.

The Giants, on the other hand, didn't even win 100 games—their record in the NL was 97–57—and a late-season slump almost cost them the pennant, though they finally won it by five games over Brooklyn.

The Giants started slowly, too, and didn't climb over .500 to stay until May 22, when their record was 17–16.

It was the franchise's 15th pennant since 1900, most in the NL, and climaxed a remarkable comeback for Leo Durocher's team, which had finished fifth in 1953, 35 games behind Brooklyn.

NL batting champion Willie Mays, in his first year out of the service, was the Giants' offensive leader with a .345 average, 41 homers, and 110 RBIs. Close behind at .342 was right fielder Don Mueller.

As for pitching, the Giants' staff couldn't compare with the Indians—or so the experts thought—as Johnny Antonelli (21–7), acquired from the Milwaukee Braves the previous winter, was their only 20-game winner.

But the Giants upset everybody, especially the Indians, and their biggest hero turned out to be little-known Dusty Rhodes, a part-time outfielder who was used primarily as a pinch hitter. The Giants won in four games to become only the second NL team since the 1914 Boston Braves to sweep the World Series.

Baseball Commissioner Ford Frick (center) meets with Indians manager Al Lopez (right) and Leo Durocher, manager of the New York Giants, prior to the 1954 World Series.

Game One

The Indians got off to a fast start with two runs in the first inning as Vic Wertz tripled with two out, driving in Al Smith, who'd been hit by a pitch from Sal Maglie, and Bobby Avila, who singled.

But the Giants quickly retaliated against Bob Lemon, tying the score in the third on hits by Whitey Lockman and Alvin Dark, a walk to Willie Mays, and Hank Thompson's one-out single.

It stayed that way until the eighth when, as many observers still believe, the turning point of the game—and the Series—occurred upon the arrival of relief pitcher Don Liddle. Liddle replaced Maglie, who had walked Larry Doby to start the inning, then relinquished a single by Al Rosen.

Vic Wertz smashed a long drive to center field. It would have been a home run anywhere else—including Cleveland's Municipal Stadium where the distance to the fence was then 400 feet from the plate—but not in the Polo Grounds.

Especially not in the Polo Grounds with Mays playing center field.

He raced back, back, back and, still running, reached up with his gloved hand and caught the ball over his left shoulder, an estimated 460 feet from the plate. It was a remarkable catch, and, while some say he made many that were more difficult, it's unlikely that any was more important.

Doby and Rosen, understandably thinking the ball would go over Mays' head for at least a double, broke from their bases. Though Doby retraced his steps, tagged up, and

reached third after the catch, Rosen was barely able to return safely to first as Mays, who had fallen, got up and threw the ball back to the infield.

Marv Grissom replaced Liddle to pitch to pinch hitter Dale Mitchell, who walked. The next two batters, Dave Pope and Jim Hegan, were retired without the Indians scoring.

Heightening the Tribe's frustration was that Hegan went out on a liner to left field that also would have been a home run in Cleveland. Instead, it was caught by Monte Irvin near the 280-foot left-field foul pole.

According to Indians manager Al Lopez, "Monte told me after the game that he thought [Hegan's ball] was a grand slam homer until the wind brought it back."

But the worst for the Tribe was yet to come.

Neither team scored in the ninth, and the Indians were blanked by Grissom in the 10th. Lemon struck out Don Mueller leading the Giants' half of the extra inning, but then walked Mays, who promptly stole second.

Standard strategy dictated that Hank Thompson be intentionally walked, setting up a double play, with Irvin due to bat next.

Instead, Giants manager Leo Durocher sent Dusty Rhodes to the plate as a pinch hitter, and he belted Lemon's first pitch to right field, near the foul pole where the distance to the stands was only 258 feet.

Right fielder Dave Pope raced back to the wall, but the ball was out of his reach. It fell into the stands, one of the short-

Dusty Rhodes, who ruined the Indians' bid to win a third World Championship in 1954, is shown delivering a pinch-hit home run in the tenth inning, giving the New York Giants a 5–2 victory in the opener of the World Series on September 29 in the Polo Grounds.

est home runs in World Series history, and the Giants had a 5–2 victory that seemed to set the stage for everything that followed in the Series.

"If we'd opened in Cleveland, not only would Wertz's hit be a homer, so would the ball that Hegan hit, and Rhodes' homer would have been only a routine fly," lamented Lopez.

Durocher joked that he had saved his "secret weapon," Rhodes, "until just the right time," with which nobody could disagree.

As for Mays, he minimized the degree of difficulty, if not the impact of his catch of Wertz's bid for a home run.

"I'd gotten the good jump and I had running room, and the ball stayed up for me. I didn't have to pick it off the grass, I didn't have to avoid another fielder, I didn't have to crash the wall, I didn't have to jump in the air, I didn't have to gauge the wind or some eccentric thing the ball itself did," he was quoted as saying later.

Wertz said in an interview before his death in 1983, "I'm very proud that I'm remembered in connection with [Mays' catch]. I look at it this way. If it had been a home run or a triple, would people have remembered it? Not very likely."

Game Two

If the Indians were able to put Dusty Rhodes out of mind after losing the opener, they were reminded of him soon enough in Game 2 of the World Series, which the Giants also won, 3–1.

But first, Al Smith stepped into the spotlight, if only briefly.

Smith hit the first pitch of the game by Johnny Antonelli for a home run, staking the Indians and Early Wynn to a 1–0 lead, though they failed to capitalize on a couple of subsequent opportunities that—again—might have changed the course of the Series.

After Smith's first-inning homer the Indians loaded the bases with two out as Al Rosen and Vic Wertz walked and Wally Westlake singled to center, but to no avail as George Strickland popped out.

Jim Hegan led off the second with a double and was sacrificed to third, but died there, and Wertz singled and Westlake walked with two out in the third, but couldn't score.

Meanwhile, Wynn was in absolute command, retiring the first 12 batters in order, until he walked Willie Mays leading off the fifth. Hank Thompson followed with a single, paving the way for Giants manager Leo Durocher to summon once again his "secret weapon."

Yes, it was Rhodes. He batted for Monte Irvin and looped a single to center scoring Mays and tying the game at 1–1. Two batters later another run came home as Antonelli grounded out, putting the Giants ahead, 2–1.

But that still wasn't the last the Indians saw of Rhodes.

Durocher left him in the game to play left field, and the next time Rhodes came to the plate leading the Giants' seventh, he hit another homer.

And, yes, it was another cheap homer into the cozy right-field stands that would have been only a routine out in Cleveland. It provided an insurance run that Antonelli didn't really need, and the Indians were down, two games to none, and almost out.

"We have too good a club for this to be happening to us," said Lopez. "We've just got to get out of this park. We'll be all right when we get home."

The New York Giants' Dusty Rhodes, whose tenth-inning pinch homer won game one of the 1954 World Series, delivered again in the second game, hitting another homer and a single, driving in two runs as the Indians lost, 3–1, on September 30.

Game Three

The locale changed, but not the Indians' fortunes, and the third game of the World Series was over almost as soon as it started.

With Mike "Big Bear" Garcia, the number-three member of the vaunted Big Four, on the mound against Ruben Gomez, the Indians fell behind early and lost, 6–2, though it wasn't even that close, to the dismay of 71,555 disenchanted Cleveland fans.

The Giants got a run in the first inning on Whitey Lockman's single, George Strickland's throwing error, and Willie Mays' two-out single, and boosted their margin to 4–0 in the third when they knocked Garcia out of the box.

And, yes, that man—Leo Durocher's "secret weapon"—was a factor again.

The Giants loaded the bases with one out on singles by Alvin Dark and Don Mueller and an intentional walk to Hank Thompson.

It brought Rhodes to the plate as a pinch hitter for Monte Irvin, and he singled for two runs and a 3–0 lead. A suicide squeeze bunt by Davey Williams caught the Indians off guard and got the Giants' fourth run home.

They added single runs in the fifth and sixth before the Indians could break the shutout, and Hoyt Wilhelm, who took over for Gomez in the eighth, locked up the victory that all but officially locked up the Series for the Giants.

Rhodes, whose three pinch hits in the three games tied a World Series record, insisted he was concerned only about winning one more game.

"I ain't thinking about no records; all I care about is seein' the Giants win," said the Giants secret weapon—or miracle man, take your choice.

"I got enough to worry about just tryin' to hit the ball, let alone botherin' about records. But I sure would like to win this thing for Leo [Durocher], and I think we will."

Vic Wertz disagreed, though he did not sound too convincing in the wake of the Indians' third consecutive defeat.

"So nobody's won the Series after losing the first three?" he said. "Well, nobody in the American League ever won 111 games either. Maybe we're due for another first."

Al Lopez tried to reassure the fans and his players, too. "We're still a good ball club, but we can't win without hitting, and we're not getting it," he said. "Maybe we'll snap out of it."

Then, with a trace of despair in his voice, Lopez added, "We have to."

Game Four

It was an act of desperation, not intended as a slight for the pitcher who was the greatest of his era, Bob Feller, when Indians manager Al Lopez started Bob Lemon with two days' rest in the fourth game of the World Series.

"I think Lem gives us our best chance to stay alive," said Lopez. "He pitched before with only two days between starts, and I think he can be successful doing it again. And if he is, Feller will get his chance tomorrow."

But tomorrow never came for Feller or the Indians as Lemon was knocked out of the box in the fifth inning and the Giants completed their sweep of the 1954 World Series, winning the fourth game, 7–4.

For a change, for the first time in the Series, Dusty Rhodes did not contribute to the victory—but also for a change, for the first time in the Series, he wasn't needed.

The Giants scored twice in the second inning when Hank Thompson walked, Monte Irvin doubled, and the obviously uptight Indians committed back-to-back errors by Vic Wertz and Wally Westlake.

New York added a run in the third on one-out singles by Alvin Dark and Monte Irvin, and Willie Mays' double, then erupted for four more in the fifth when Hal Newhouser replaced Lemon as the first of four relievers rushed to the mound by Lopez.

The normally sure-handed Giants committed two errors after the first two Indians were retired in the bottom of the fifth, and pinch hitter Hank Majeski followed with a three-run homer. But all it did was make the game a little closer.

The Indians scored again in the seventh, but Hoyt Wilhelm and then Johnny Antonelli came on in relief of Don Liddle to nail down the victory that gave the Giants their fifth world's championship since 1903, and first since 1933.

It also gave the Giants a winners' share of $11,147.90, while each of the Indians received $6,712.50.

"Everything we did seemed to be just right, and everything they did seemed to go against them," said Giants manager Leo Durocher.

Nobody could argue with Durocher's assessment.

Dark, the Giants' captain who had been a member of the Boston Braves who lost to Cleveland in the 1948 World Series, was kind in his comments about the Indians.

"Don't be too hard on them," said Dark. "They are a fine ball club. It's just that we had a club that simply wouldn't be beaten. I doubt if there ever was a club that could have beaten us in this series."

He also was correct.

Among the vanquished Indians, only Feller was more disappointed than Lopez—though Feller said he understood the choice of Lemon to start the fourth game.

"Sure, I wanted to pitch and, of course, I am disappointed that I didn't, and that we didn't win," acknowledged Feller.

"But I understand. We lost the first three games, and that forced Al to go along with his top pitchers all the way. It was a desperation deal. He had to go with his aces. If we had won today, I probably would have pitched tomorrow."

Lopez said of the Giants, "They played championship baseball. They were good offensively and defensively, and their pitching was terrific. My hat is off to them."

Later, Lopez offered this explanation for the humiliating defeat:

"What happened to us is what happens to every club at one time or another during a season. We went into a rut, a slump, the only one we had all year, and the Giants got hot at just the right time. I don't remember us losing more than two games in a row all season until we got into the Series. It's hard to explain, but, to me, it's not hard to understand.

"What happened to us is what happens to every team over the course of a season," he said again.

Game 1
Wednesday, September 29, at New York

Indians	AB	R	H	RBI	PO	A
Smith, lf	4	1	1	0	1	0
Avila, 2b	5	1	1	0	2	3
Doby, cf	3	0	1	0	3	0
Rosen, 3b	5	0	1	0	1	3
Wertz, 1b	5	0	4	2	11	1
d-Regalado	0	0	0	0	0	0
Grasso, c	0	0	0	0	1	0
Philley, rf	3	0	0	0	0	0
a-Majeski	0	0	0	0	0	0
b-Mitchell	0	0	0	0	0	0
Dente, ss	0	0	0	0	0	0
Strickland, ss	3	0	0	0	2	3
c-Pope, rf	1	0	0	0	0	0
Hegan, c	4	0	0	0	6	1
e-Glynn, 1b	1	0	0	0	0	0
Lemon, p	4	0	0	0	1	1
Totals	**38**	**2**	**8**	**2**	***28**	**12**

New York	AB	R	H	RBI	PO	A
Lockman, 1b	5	1	1	0	9	0
Dark, ss	4	0	2	0	3	2
Mueller, rf	5	1	2	1	2	0
Mays, cf	3	1	0	0	2	0
Thompson, 3b	3	1	1	1	3	3
Irvin, lf	3	0	0	0	5	0
f-Rhodes	1	1	1	3	0	0
Williams, 2b	4	0	0	0	1	1
Westrum, c	4	0	2	0	5	0
Maglie, p	3	0	0	0	0	2
Liddle, p	0	0	0	0	0	0
Grissom, p	1	0	0	0	0	0
Totals	**36**	**5**	**9**	**5**	**30**	**8**

Cleveland	2	0	0	0	0	0	0	0	0	0—2
New York	0	0	2	0	0	0	0	0	0	3—5

*One out when winning run scored

a-Announced for Philley in eighth
b-Walked for Majeski in eighth
c-Struck out for Strickland in eighth
d-Ran for Wertz in 10th
e-Struck out for Hegan in 10th
f-Homered for Irvin in 10th

Errors: Mueller 2, Irvin; Two-base hit: Wertz; Three-base hit: Wertz; Home Run: Rhodes; Stolen Base: Mays; Sacrifice Hits: Dente, Irvin; Hit by Pitch: Smith (by Maglie); Wild Pitch: Lemon; Left on Base: Cleveland 13, New York 9; Umpires: Barlick (NL), Berry (AL), Conlan (NL), Stevens (AL), Warneke (NL), Napp (AL); Time: 3:11; Attendance: 52,751.

Indians	IP	H	R	ER	BB	SO
Lemon, L	9⅓	9	5	5	5	6

New York	IP	H	R	ER	BB	SO
Maglie	†7	7	2	2	2	2
Liddle	⅓	0	0	0	0	0
Grissom, W	2⅔	1	0	0	3	2

†Pitched to two batters in eighth

Game 2
Thursday, September 30, at New York

Indians	AB	R	H	RBI	PO	A
Smith, lf	4	1	2	1	3	0
Avila, 2b	4	0	1	0	2	2
Doby, cf	5	0	0	0	2	0
Rosen, 3b	3	0	1	0	0	0
b-Regalado, 3b	1	0	0	0	0	0
Wertz, 1b	3	0	1	0	5	1
Westlake, rf	3	0	1	0	3	0
Strickland, ss	3	0	0	0	1	1
c-Philley	1	0	0	0	0	0
Dente, ss	0	0	0	0	0	0
Hegan, c	4	0	1	0	7	0
Wynn, p	2	0	1	0	1	1
d-Majeski	1	0	0	0	0	0
Mossi, p	0	0	0	0	0	1
Totals	**34**	**1**	**8**	**1**	**24**	**6**

New York	AB	R	H	RBI	PO	A
Lockman, 1b	4	0	0	0	8	0
Dark, ss	4	0	1	0	0	6
Mueller, rf	4	0	0	0	1	0
Mays, cf	2	1	0	0	1	0
Thompson, 3b	3	1	1	0	1	3
Irvin, lf	1	0	0	0	2	0
a-Rhodes, lf	2	1	2	2	1	0
Williams, 2b	3	0	0	0	4	0
Westrum, c	2	0	0	0	9	0
Antonelli, p	3	0	0	1	0	1
Totals	**28**	**3**	**4**	**3**	**27**	**10**

Cleveland	1	0	0	0	0	0	0	0	0	0—1
New York	0	0	0	0	2	0	1	0	x—3	

a-Singled for Irvin in fifth
b-Ran for Rosen in seventh
c-Struck out for Strickland in eighth
d-Grounded out for Wynn in eighth

Two-base hits: Hegan, Wynn; Home Runs: Rhodes, Smith; Sacrifice Hit: Wynn; Wild Pitch: Wynn; Left on Base: Cleveland 13, New York 3; Umpires: Berry (AL), Conlan (NL), Stevens (AL), Barlick (NL), Warneke (NL), Napp (AL); Time: 2:50; Attendance: 49,099.

Indians	IP	H	R	ER	BB	SO
Wynn, L	7	4	3	3	2	5
Mossi	1	0	0	0	0	0

New York	IP	H	R	ER	BB	SO
Antonelli, W	9	8	1	1	6	9

Game 3
Friday, October 1, at Cleveland

New York	AB	R	H	RBI	PO	A
Lockman, 1b	4	1	1	0	13	0
Dark, ss	4	0	1	0	2	2
Mueller, rf	5	2	2	0	0	0
Mays, cf	5	1	3	2	2	0
Thompson, 3b	3	2	1	0	0	3
Irvin, lf	1	0	0	0	0	0
a-Rhodes, lf	3	0	1	2	3	0
Williams, 2b	2	0	0	1	2	5
Westrum, c	4	0	1	1	4	0
Gomez, p	4	0	0	0	1	2
Wilhelm, p	0	0	0	0	0	0
Totals	**35**	**6**	**10**	**6**	**27**	**12**

Indians	AB	R	H	RBI	PO	A
Smith, lf	3	0	0	1	0	0
Avila, 2b	2	0	0	0	4	1
Doby, cf	4	0	1	0	2	0
Wertz, 1b	4	1	1	1	6	1
Majeski, 3b	4	0	0	0	2	1
Philley, rf	3	0	1	0	1	0
Strickland, ss	3	0	0	0	3	4
f-Pope	1	0	0	0	0	0
Hegan, c	2	0	0	0	8	1
d-Glynn	1	1	1	0	0	0
Naragon, c	0	0	0	0	1	0
Garcia, p	0	0	0	0	0	1
b-Lemon	1	0	0	0	0	0
Houtteman, p	0	0	0	0	0	0
c-Regalado	1	0	0	0	0	0
Narleski, p	0	0	0	0	0	1
e-Mitchell	1	0	0	0	0	0
Mossi, p	0	0	0	0	0	0
Totals	**30**	**2**	**4**	**2**	**27**	**10**

New York	1	0	3	0	1	1	0	0	0—6	
Cleveland	0	0	0	0	0	0	1	1	0—2	

a-Singled for Irvin in third
b-Struck out for Garcia in third
c-Grounded out for Houtteman in fifth
d-Doubled for Hegan in eighth
e-Grounded out for Narleski in eighth
f-Grounded out for Strickland in ninth

Errors: Dark, Strickland, Garcia; Two-base hits: Glynn, Thompson; Home Run: Wertz; Sacrifice Hits: Avila, Dark, Williams; Double Plays: Dark to Williams to Lockman, Strickland to Wertz; Wild Pitch: Garcia; Left on Base: New York 9, Cleveland 5; Umpires: Conlan (NL), Stevens (AL), Barlick (NL), Berry (AL), Napp (AL), Warneke (NL); Time: 2:28; Attendance: 71,555.

New York	IP	H	R	ER	BB	SO
Gomez, W	7⅓	4	2	2	3	2
Wilhelm	1⅔	0	0	0	0	2

Indians	IP	H	R	ER	BB	SO
Garcia, L	3	5	4	3	3	3
Houtteman	2	2	1	1	1	1
Narleski	3	1	1	1	1	2
Mossi	1	2	0	0	0	1

Game 4
Saturday, October 2, at Cleveland

New York	AB	R	H	RBI	PO	A
Lockman, 1b	5	0	0	0	10	0
Dark, ss	5	2	3	0	2	2
Mueller, rf	4	1	3	0	0	0
Mays, cf	4	1	1	1	5	0
Thompson, 3b	2	2	1	1	1	2
Irvin, lf	4	1	2	2	1	0
Williams, 2b	2	0	0	0	3	3
Westrum, c	1	0	0	2	5	0
Liddle, p	3	0	0	0	0	1
Wilhelm, p	1	0	0	0	0	1
Antonelli, p	0	0	0	0	0	0
Totals	**31**	**7**	**10**	**6**	**27**	**9**

Indians	AB	R	H	RBI	PO	A
Smith, lf	3	0	0	0	0	0
c-Pope, lf	1	0	0	0	0	0
e-Mitchell	1	0	0	0	0	0
Avila, 2b	4	0	0	0	4	4
Doby, cf	4	0	0	0	0	0
Rosen, 3b	4	0	1	0	1	0
Wertz, 1b	4	1	2	0	11	3
Westlake, rf	4	0	0	0	3	0
Dente, ss	3	1	0	0	1	1
Hegan, c	3	1	1	0	6	1
Lemon, p	1	0	0	0	1	1
Newhouser, p	0	0	0	0	0	0
Narleski, p	0	0	0	0	0	0
a-Majeski	1	1	1	3	0	0
Mossi, p	0	0	0	0	0	1
b-Regalado	1	0	1	1	0	0
Garcia, p	0	0	0	0	0	1
d-Philley	1	0	0	0	0	0
Totals	**35**	**4**	**6**	**4**	**27**	**12**

New York	0	2	1	0	4	0	0	0	0—7	
Cleveland	0	0	0	0	3	0	1	0	0—4	

a-Homered for Narleski in fifth
b-Singled for Mossi in seventh
c-Grounded out for Smith in seventh
d-Struck out for Garcia in ninth
e-Fouled out for Pope in ninth

Errors: Williams, Liddle, Wilhelm, Wertz, Westlake; Two-base hits: Irvin, Mays, Wertz; Home Run: Majeski; Sacrifice Hits: Mueller, Westrum, Williams; Sacrifice Flies: Westrum 2; Double Plays: Thompson to Williams to Lockman, Dente to Avila to Wertz; Wild Pitch: Liddle; Left on Base: New York 7, Cleveland 6; Umpires: Stevens (AL), Barlick (NL), Berry (AL), Conlan (NL), Warneke (NL), Napp (AL); Time: 2:52; Attendance: 78,102.

New York	IP	H	R	ER	BB	SO
Liddle, W	6⅔	5	4	1	1	2
Wilhelm	⅔	1	0	0	0	0
Antonelli, S	1⅔	0	0	0	1	3

Indians	IP	H	R	ER	BB	SO
Lemon, L	*4	7	6	5	3	5
Newhouser	†0	1	1	1	1	0
Narleski	1	0	0	0	0	0
Mossi	2	1	0	0	0	0
Garcia	2	1	0	0	1	1

*Pitched to three batters in fifth
†Pitched to two batters in fifth

COMPOSITE BATTING AVERAGES

New York Giants Player-Position	G	AB	R	H	2B	3B	HR	RBI	BA
Lockman, 1b	4	18	2	2	0	0	0	0	.111
Williams, 2b	4	11	0	0	0	0	0	1	.000
Dark, ss	4	17	2	7	0	0	0	0	.412
Thompson, 3b	4	11	6	4	1	0	0	2	.364
Mueller, rf	4	18	4	7	0	0	0	1	.389
Mays, cf	4	14	4	4	1	0	0	3	.286
Irvin, lf	4	9	1	2	1	0	0	2	.222
Westrum, c	4	11	0	3	0	0	0	3	.273
Rhodes, ph, lf	3	6	2	4	0	0	2	7	.667
Katt	Did not play								
Hofman	Did not play								
Gardner	Did not play								
Taylor	Did not play								
Castleman	Did not play								
Amalfitano	Did not play								
Gomez, p	1	4	0	0	0	0	0	0	.000
Maglie, p	1	3	0	0	0	0	0	0	.000
Antonelli, p	2	3	0	0	0	0	0	1	.000
Liddle, p	2	3	0	0	0	0	0	0	.000
Wilhelm, p	2	1	0	0	0	0	0	0	.000
Grissom, p	1	1	0	0	0	0	0	0	.000
Hearn	Did not play								
McCall	Did not play								
Corwin	Did not play								
Worthington	Did not play								
Konikowski	Did not play								
Giel	Did not play								
Totals	**4**	**130**	**21**	**33**	**3**	**0**	**2**	**20**	**.254**

Cleveland Indians Player-Position	G	AB	R	H	2B	3B	HR	RBI	BA
Wertz, 1b	4	16	2	8	2	1	1	3	.500
Avila, 2b	4	15	1	2	0	0	0	0	.133
Strickland, ss	3	9	0	0	0	0	0	0	.000
Rosen, 3b	3	12	0	3	0	0	0	0	.250
Philley, rf, ph	4	8	0	1	0	0	0	0	.125
Doby, cf	4	16	0	2	0	0	0	0	.125
Smith, lf	4	14	2	3	0	0	1	2	.214
Hegan, c	4	13	1	2	1	0	0	0	.154
Westlake, rf	2	7	0	1	0	0	0	0	.143
Majeski, ph, 3b	4	6	1	1	0	0	1	3	.167
Regalado, pr, 3b, ph	4	3	0	1	0	0	0	1	.333
Dente, ss	3	3	1	0	0	0	0	0	.000
Pope, ph, rf, lf	3	3	0	0	0	0	0	0	.000
Glynn, ph, 1b	2	2	1	1	1	0	0	0	.500
Mitchell, ph	3	2	0	0	0	0	0	0	.000
Grasso, c	1	0	0	0	0	0	0	0	—
Naragon, c	1	0	0	0	0	0	0	0	—
Lemon, p, ph	3	6	0	0	0	0	0	0	.000
Wynn, p	1	2	0	1	1	0	0	0	.500
Mossi, p	3	0	0	0	0	0	0	0	—
Garcia, p	2	0	0	0	0	0	0	0	—
Narleski, p	2	0	0	0	0	0	0	0	—
Houtteman, p	1	0	0	0	0	0	0	0	—
Newhouser, p	1	0	0	0	0	0	0	0	—
Feller	Did not play								
Hooper	Did not play								
Totals	**4**	**137**	**9**	**26**	**5**	**1**	**3**	**9**	**.190**

COMPOSITE PITCHING AVERAGES

New York Giants Pitcher	G	IP	H	R	ER	BB	SO	W	L	ERA
Antonelli	2	10⅔	8	1	1	7	12	1	0	0.84
Gomez	1	7⅓	4	2	2	3	2	1	0	2.45
Liddle	2	7	5	4	1	1	2	1	0	1.29
Maglie	1	7	7	2	2	2	2	0	0	2.57
Grissom	1	2⅔	1	0	0	3	2	1	0	0.00
Wilhelm	2	2⅓	1	0	0	0	3	0	0	0.00
Hearn	Did not play									
McCall	Did not play									
Corwin	Did not play									
Worthington	Did not play									
Konikowski	Did not play									
Giel	Did not play									
Totals	**4**	**37**	**26**	**9**	**6**	**16**	**23**	**4**	**0**	**1.46**

Cleveland Indians Pitcher	G	IP	H	R	ER	BB	SO	W	L	ERA
Lemon	2	13⅓	16	11	10	8	11	0	2	6.75
Wynn	1	7	4	3	3	2	5	0	1	3.86
Garcia	2	5	6	4	3	4	4	0	1	5.40
Mossi	3	4	3	0	0	1	1	0	0	0.00
Narleski	2	4	1	1	1	1	2	0	0	2.25
Houtteman	1	2	2	1	1	1	1	0	0	4.50
Newhouser	1	0	1	1	1	1	0	0	0	∞
Feller	Did not play									
Hooper	Did not play									
Totals	**4**	**35⅓**	**33**	**21**	**19**	**17**	**24**	**0**	**4**	**4.84**

10

The Golden Era

When a major league baseball franchise wins only three pennants in 95 years, it is difficult—in the case of the Indians, almost *impossible*—to zero in on a specific era and designate it "golden."

Sure, there were seasons that provided reason for hope, even great expectation. But more times than not when the future appeared promising, it was cruelly destroyed through incompetence, mismanagement, injury, or, as often was the case in Cleveland, financial problems.

From the early 1960s through the '70s and into the mid-'80s the Indians usually were badly undercapitalized, often to the extent that at times players had to be sold or traded, either to get out from under contracts that were considered too expensive for services rendered or simply to provide money to meet the next payroll.

Prime among the many examples of the latter were the deals that sent Mudcat Grant to Minnesota (for third baseman George Banks and pitcher Lee Stange) and Pedro Ramos to the New York Yankees (for pitchers Ralph Terry and Bud Daley and $75,000) in 1964, and Gary Bell to Boston in 1967 (for first baseman Tony Horton and outfielder Don Demeter).

In each case the former Indians helped their new teams win pennants (the Yankees in 1964, the Twins in 1965, and the Red Sox in 1967).

It also was unfortunate for Cleveland fans that, even when the Indians (or their predecessors) played very well, there often was another team that played better.

That certainly was the case in the early to mid-1950s, the period that came closest to being a "Golden Era" in Cleveland baseball history.

Again unfortunately, it coincided with the time period in baseball that was dominated by the New York Yankees.

The Indians won at least 90 games a year from 1951 through 1955—including an American League–record 111 in 1954—and 88 in 1956, but captured only one pennant. They finished second to New York from 1951 to 1953 and in 1955 and 1956, to the dismay of their frustrated fans.

In fact, despite those winning records—but presumably *because* of the Indians' inability to overtake the Yankees—attendance declined steadily in 1951, 1952, and 1953, again in 1955, and drastically in 1956 to 865,467, all of which very nearly caused the franchise to be moved out of Cleveland.

The reason: fans were tired of the Indians finishing second.

"I didn't blame them; we were, too," Al Rosen said in a 1995 interview.

But he also praised them. "There's no doubt in my mind that Cleveland baseball fans are the greatest in the world, and I've always felt that way."

The American League's Most Valuable Player in 1953 when he hit .336 and led the league with 43 home runs and 145 runs batted in, Rosen said he understood the fans' exasperation.

"We were frustrated, too. But I also think about how, at least until last year [1994], Indians fans would be delighted, not frustrated, for their team to finish second as we did so often in the 50s, instead of where they've finished so often since then."

Al Lopez, who was manager of the Indians from 1951 to 1956 and whose winning percentage of .617 (570–354) is the best in franchise history, endorsed Rosen's comments.

Lopez, who later managed the Chicago White Sox, readily acknowledged that Rosen was the inspirational as well as the physical leader of the Indians from the time he became the team's regular third baseman in 1950 until his retirement following the 1956 season.

"We had a lot of leaders, which was one of the reasons we did so well," said Lopez.

Indians manager Al Lopez was a big hero in Cleveland after the Indians won the pennant in 1954 with an American League record 111 victories. He is shown wearing an Indian headdress and receiving a congratulatory kiss from his wife Connie.

The Indians 1954 coaching staff with manager Al Lopez (center). Left to right, the coaches are Tony Cuccinello, Mel Harder, Red Kress, and Bill Lobe.

He named Bob Lemon, Early Wynn, and Mike Garcia in particular, though he added, "I've got to say that Rosen was the number-one guy. I had great respect for the way he played the game, and the way he demanded that others play the game."

To illustrate his admiration for the sometimes-maligned Rosen, Lopez recalled an incident that occurred "either in 1953 or 1954," in which he angrily—but incorrectly—chastised Cleveland fans.

"I called them 'bush' because I thought they had cheered when Rosen got hit in the face with a bad-hop grounder during a game against the Yankees," said Lopez.

"Here was a guy lying on the ground, blood pouring out of his nose, and the fans behind the third base dugout are standing up and cheering.

"The next day both of Al's eyes were black and swollen so bad that he could hardly see out of them, but he insisted on staying in the lineup. That's the kind of player he was, and as I recall, he even went 4-for-5 in the game.

"I ripped the fans in the newspapers, but it turned out that I shouldn't have. They were part of a large group that came from Buffalo to see the Yankees play. They were the ones who cheered when Rosen got hurt because, when the ball hit him in the face, it brought in a couple of runs for the Yankees.

"That was the way Al Rosen played the game, day in and day out, and I believe that it rubbed off on the other guys, which helped make us such a good team."

Another time, Lopez remembered, Rosen fought a teammate in the trainer's room because the other player claimed he was injured and couldn't play that night.

"They had a helluva battle, and both guys got hurt, but both of them played, and, as I recall, we won the game," said Lopez, declining to identify Rosen's adversary in the incident.

Some might consider that the Indians' "Golden Era" began in 1948, perhaps even as early as June 1946, with the arrival of Veeck and the blossoming into brilliance of Boudreau. From 1947 to 1950 the Indians won 358 games, an average of 89.5 per season.

But the departure of Veeck in 1949 left a void, and Hank Greenberg's 1950 firing of Boudreau, arguably the most popular player in franchise history, effectively ended that era, paving the way for a new one with the hiring of Al Lopez to manage the team.

Lopez, who'd had a long and illustrious playing career in the National League (1928, 1930–46), joined the Indians in 1947 as a backup catcher to Jim Hegan.

Veeck traded Gene Woodling to Pittsburgh (on December 7, 1946) to get Lopez. It was speculated that Veeck made the deal because he wanted to replace Boudreau as manager, though Lopez said he didn't know.

"I always wanted to manage when my playing career was finished, but if that was part of Veeck's plan when he got me, he never told me anything about it," Lopez said in a 1994 interview. "I heard later that [Veeck] had me in mind when he was planning to trade Boudreau [to the St. Louis Browns for Vernon Stephens] in the winter of 1947–48, but he never approached me about it.

"When I joined the Indians at the start of the 1947 season, I was 38 going on 39, and I told Veeck that when it ended, I

Indians President Ellis Ryan huddles over lunch with manager Al Lopez (left) and vice president and general manager Hank Greenberg (right).

planned to see if I could get a coaching or managing job someplace.

"I asked him, if I got a job I wanted, would he give me my release, and he said that I should consider myself released whenever I wanted it.

"But he never said anything about hiring me [as manager or a coach] himself," Lopez said again.

Lopez appeared in 61 games, all but four as a catcher, for the Indians in 1947, hitting .262. His 57 games behind the plate gave Lopez the record (since broken by Bob Boone) for catching the most games, 1,918, in major league history.

When the season ended, Lopez got his release, though he still didn't have a coaching or managing job—and, he said, Veeck didn't offer him one.

Lopez went to New York for the 1947 World Series between the Yankees and Brooklyn Dodgers and met with his old friend, former major league infielder Donie Bush, who was operating the Indianapolis club in the Class AAA American Association for Pittsburgh.

The Pirates offered Lopez the job of managing Indianapolis, which he took for the next three seasons. Under Lopez, Indianapolis won 100 games and the American Association pennant in 1948, but lost the playoffs. The team finished second in 1949, but won the playoffs and beat Montreal of the International League in the Little World Series. In 1950, Indianapolis was second by four games, but reached the championship finals of the playoffs, only to lose to Columbus in the 13th inning of the last game.

It's interesting to note that Lopez, looking back on his managerial career with the Indians (1951–56) and White Sox (1957–65, 1968–69), said, "We won the pennant in Cleveland in 1954 and in Chicago in 1959, but I think the best job I did as a manager was at Indianapolis my first year."

By the time Lopez took over as manager of the Indians in 1951, Veeck was gone from Cleveland, and Greenberg had become the chief operating officer of the club.

Greenberg was among the many who had a high regard for the former catcher and, initially, the two men had a congenial, mutually respectful relationship.

"Greenberg called me after the 1950 season and asked me to meet with him in Cleveland," said Lopez. "I had just signed a new two-year contract to go back to Indianapolis (in 1951 and 1952), but I was interested in what Greenberg had in mind.

"Boudreau had not been fired, though I figured the Indi-ans were going to make a change. I met with Greenberg, and we came to an agreement."

Lopez was hired on November 10, the same day that Greenberg announced that Boudreau would not be retained.

With Greenberg calling the shots in the front office, and Lopez, the patient "Senor," flashing the signs from the dugout, the Indians became one of the best teams in baseball.

"We worked well together," said Lopez. "Hank picked up some good players, guys who were especially important to us in 1954 when we had a lot of injuries.

"The club in those days didn't spend a lot of money, but Hank was able to do some things [acquire players] that didn't cost us a lot, which many people overlook because we did so well.

"We probably could not have won without guys like [shortstop] Sam Dente, [third-baseman–second baseman] Hank Majeski, Vic Wertz, who was an outfielder before we got him and became our regular first baseman, and [outfielder] Wally Westlake.

"Hank picked up all of those guys for very little, and all of them played a big role in our success. We had a lot of injuries that season, which makes what that team did all the more remarkable."

It's true. Strickland was out for more than a month with a broken jaw suffered when he was hit by a thrown ball while sliding into third base. Luke Easter had knee problems and was released in May. And Rosen was sidelined—though he refused to sit out for long—with a broken right index finger. Other regulars who were hampered by injuries that season were Bobby Avila and Larry Doby.

After Easter was released, Rosen switched to first base, but when he broke his finger, it led to the installation of Vic Wertz at that position. It proved to be a move that paid huge dividends.

"We were in Washington, and Rosen and Doby were hurt and couldn't play. The only guy I had who could give us the long ball was Westlake," said Lopez.

"I went to Wertz and asked if he'd ever played first base. He said only twice in spring training when he was with the St. Louis Browns, but that he dropped a pop fly and they put him back in the outfield.

"But we were desperate. I put him at first base and he was great. We kept him there the rest of the season."

Lopez also credited the compatibility of the Indians for much of their success during his years as manager.

"Everybody we got fitted in well with what we had. It was a very harmonious team, which to me is very important," he said. "I always tried to stay away from guys who didn't fit in, troublemakers, selfish players who put themselves above the welfare of the team.

"I don't want to mention any names, but we passed up [refused to accept] some pretty good players, guys that I felt would not follow my rules, who had their own agenda."

Still on the subject of Greenberg as he talked about the 1951–56 Indians, Lopez said, "Hank was an outspoken guy, and a lot of people didn't like him for that reason. But down inside he was a nice man, very considerate. He did a lot of things for a lot of people that weren't generally known.

"I think part of his handicap was that he was a former, very good player. He felt that anybody who had not been a player, who had never been on the field, wasn't qualified to say anything about the game, to be critical.

"One of his harshest critics was the editor of the *Cleveland Press* [Louis B. Seltzer], who personally did not like Greenberg. There also were a couple of veteran writers who disliked Hank because he was the one who fired Boudreau.

"I took over a pretty fair club," Lopez said of the 1951 Tribe. "I knew many of the players because I'd been with them in 1947. Being familiar with them and their abilities and habits helped, but I also knew that I couldn't let myself be too buddy-buddy with them, as I'd been previously."

It was Lopez's recollection of his first spring training as manager of the Indians that provided interesting insight into his laid-back style.

"I wasn't tough, but I think everybody respected me," he said. "As I recall our first team meeting, I said, 'Fellas, I have a curfew and I want you to be aware of it. But if you're out and know you won't make it back in time, call me or one of the coaches and let us know. That's all I ask.' "

Remarkably, in his five years as manager of the Indians, Lopez said he could remember fining only one player, Dave Hoskins, a pitcher who'd been a minor league outfielder but never hit enough and switched to the mound. He pitched for the Indians in 1953 and 1954, winning a total of nine games while losing four.

Lopez said he fined Hoskins—whom he called "one of the nicest guys you'd ever want to meet"—$200 for missing a train. "But I gave it back to him when the season ended because he never screwed up again," Lopez said.

"Maybe one of my former players who reads this will correct me, but I can't think of anybody else that I fined in Cleveland."

Lopez's first season with the Indians—the beginning of the "Golden Era"—was a good one for him and the team. They trailed the Yankees most of the way, but climbed into a one-game lead on September 15. The next day in New York in the opener of a two-game series, the Tribe lost, 5–1, falling into a tie with the Yankees, who also won, 2–1, on September 17.

The Indians never regained first place, dropping five of their last eight games while the Yankees were winning nine of 12. New York won the pennant by five lengths.

"We had a pretty good club, especially our pitching staff of Wynn, Lemon, Feller, and Garcia," said Lopez. Feller was the winningest pitcher in the AL with a 22–8 record, Garcia and Wynn each won 20 and lost 13, and Lemon was 17–14.

"New York was better, but if Luke Easter had come through the way we expected—Greenberg always thought Luke was go-

ing to be a superstar, another Babe Ruth, that he would make it to the Hall of Fame—we could have caught the Yankees.

"Our reports on Easter from Del Baker, who was then managing our Triple-A team at San Diego, also were outstanding. Everybody who'd seen him in the minor leagues thought he would be a world-beater for a long time. That's why Hank traded Mickey Vernon to Washington [on June 14, 1950], to make room for Easter on first base.

"Luke was a nice guy and a real character. You had to like him. But [putting him on first base] didn't work out because Luke was just too old by then; he had bad knees and was hurt a lot," said Lopez.

"Harry Simpson was another. We considered him to be a better prospect than Minnie Minoso, who also came up through our farm system. That's why we traded Minoso. But Simpson was another who never came through the way we expected.

"We also had a problem at shortstop. Ray Boone, who had taken over for Boudreau, was a pretty good hitter, but his range was too limited in the field. He finally became a good player when they moved him to third base in Detroit [in 1953].

"Looking back at it, I wish we had put Boone on third and moved Rosen to first, instead of going with Easter. But that's hindsight, and you know what they say; hindsight is 20–20.

"We didn't make a lot of changes in 1952, we just thought we'd play better, and in some ways we did. But our record (93–61) was the same, and though we picked up three games on the Yankees, we finished second again."

All season it was one of the tightest races in AL history. Five teams—Chicago, Washington, and Boston, as well as the Yankees and Indians—were bunched close together at the All-Star break.

The Indians went on to win 27 of 45 games through August 22, giving them a 69–51 record and a first-place lead of .001 over the Yankees. But it wasn't good enough. Despite going 24–10 down the stretch, the Indians couldn't maintain their lead, and the Yankees prevailed again, this time by two lengths.

Wynn (23–12), Lemon (22–11), and Garcia (22–11) were still pitching well and winning big, but Feller (9–13) was on the decline.

"It was frustrating, and I knew how the fans felt," acknowledged Lopez. "They were tired of seeing us finish second, losing to the Yankees, though the fact is, we were playing pretty good ball. The Yankees just kept playing better."

They did again in 1953 when the Indians' record, while still a commendable 92–62, left them 8½ games behind the Yankees.

"The big difference all along was that we didn't have the farm system they [the Yankees] did, nor the [financial] wherewithal to go out and buy somebody," said Lopez.

"When they needed a player down the stretch, they went out and bought him, guys like Enos Slaughter, Johnny Mize, Ewell Blackwell, and Johnny Hopp. But we couldn't do that, and we didn't have much at Triple A ready to help, either."

Lemon, with a 21–15 record, was the Tribe's only 20-game winner in 1953. Garcia, Wynn, and Feller combined for only 45 victories.

The offense also sagged, with the exception of Rosen. He almost won the Triple Crown and did become the first unanimous winner of the AL Most Valuable Player award since Ty

Cobb in 1911. Rosen hit .336, second by .001 to Mickey Vernon, with 43 homers and 145 runs batted in.

The race wasn't nearly as close in 1953 as the previous two seasons, as the Yankees under Casey Stengel won a record fifth straight pennant.

"I'd known Casey for a long time," said Lopez, who played for Stengel when he managed Brooklyn in 1934 and 1935 and the Boston Braves in 1938 and 1939.

"I assure you, Casey was no clown, though the media had a lot of fun with him, and he had a lot of fun with them. Stengel was a great guy and a fine manager. He loved to teach. He would get a young fellow and sit with him by the hour and talk about baseball.

"I learned a lot from Casey—but apparently not enough," Lopez quipped as he reflected on his five-year rivalry with Stengel.

At least not enough until 1954.

"A big factor in finally beating the Yankees was that we brought up [relievers] Ray Narleski and Don Mossi that spring," said Lopez. "They could throw hard, especially Narleski, who was as fast as anyone for a couple of innings, and Mossi was sneaky fast.

"Both were starters in the minors, and people give me a lot of credit for making them relief pitchers. But it's not that I was so smart, it was that we had so many good starters, we didn't need them in the rotation. I wanted them on the team."

Lopez rated the Indians' 1954 pitching staff the best in the history of baseball. Included were starters Lemon (23–7), Wynn (23–11), Garcia (19–8), Art Houtteman (15–7), and Feller (13–3), long reliever Hal Newhouser, and closers Narleski and Mossi.

Wynn, Lemon, Feller, and Newhouser are in the Hall of Fame.

"Everybody knows the story about how Lemon became a pitcher," said Lopez. "He was an outfielder–third baseman, a very good athlete, and had a strong arm, though he wasn't much of a hitter.

Two members of the Indians' dominating "Big Four" starting pitching staff in 1954: Mike Garcia (left) and Art Houtteman, who combined for 34 victories that season. Garcia's won-lost record was 19–8, and Houtteman's was 15–7.

"In fact, before he was switched to pitching, Veeck agreed to sell Lemon to the Washington Senators for the waiver price. But the next day he canceled it when [Senators owner] Clark Griffith prematurely announced the deal."

Shortly thereafter Lemon was given a chance to pitch and went on to win 20 games seven times, post a career record of 207–128, and be elected to the Hall of Fame in 1976.

"At times Lemon's arm was so strong and his fastball so live that it got away from him," said Lopez. "We pitched him with three days' rest because, when his arm was a little tired, he was at his best. Sometimes I even started him with only two days [rest].

"If he were pitching today, and getting four days between starts as most pitchers do, I'm convinced he'd be too wild to be a consistent winner."

For five seasons, from 1954 to 1958, Indians pitchers Don Mossi (left) and Ray Narleski formed one of the best—perhaps the best—left-right relief tandem in major league baseball history.

Left fielder Al Smith (left) hit a three-run homer, and center fielder Larry Doby (right) homered twice to make it easy for Early Wynn to beat the New York Yankees, 8–2, in a key game on July 23 during the Indians' pennant winning season of 1954.

Wynn was another pitcher who became a star during the Indians' "Golden Era."

"[Pitching coach] Mel Harder also had a lot to do with making a pitcher out of Wynn," said Lopez. "For one thing, Harder taught Wynn a curveball and gave him confidence in it. Wynn could take a batter to 3-and-2 and throw any pitch he wanted, including a curveball. It was only a small curve, but was sharp and quick.

"Early also fooled around with a knuckleball, which he'd learned when he was with Washington, before the Indians got him [in 1949]. But it was his fastball and curve—and the fact that he was such a fierce competitor—that made Wynn so successful.

"People have said that Early would throw at his own mother if she crowded the plate against him, but I don't think he ever tried to hit anybody—much," said Lopez, chuckling.

As for Garcia, another of the team leaders with Rosen, Lemon, and Wynn, Lopez said, "He threw such a 'heavy' ball, when you hit it, it felt like you were hitting a rock, not a baseball, even if you hit it on the good part of the bat.

"Houtteman came to us from Detroit [in the 1953 deal that sent Boone to the Tigers] and though he only had one real good year [1954], he was another of the good pickups by Greenberg."

Feller, the fifth starter in that 1954 pitching rotation, was nearing the end of his remarkable pitching career, but contributed 13 victories.

"I had great respect for Bob," said Lopez. "I liked him very much. How could you not appreciate a guy like that? He never gave me any trouble, he was always in shape, he was not a drinker, didn't carouse, and wasn't troublesome in any way.

"Bob Feller was a class guy in every respect. I know he was disappointed that I didn't give him a start in the [1954] World Series, but to his credit, he never ever said a word about it. He never complained once.

"Another thing about Feller. He was the easiest guy in the world to take out of a game. When I'd go out to get him, he'd say, 'Okay, meat'—which is what he called people he liked; it's short for meathead—'it looks like I didn't have much today,' and then he'd walk off the field.

"The toughest guy for me to take out of a game was Wynn. He growled and grumbled, but he always showed respect for me, as I did for all my pitchers."

Then Lopez corrected himself.

"I take that back. One time Early did not [show respect], but that's because he was having a bad time with the umpire. I went out to get him, and instead of handing me the ball, as I wanted all my pitchers to do, he tossed it to me, and it hit me right in the pit of my stomach.

"I said to him, 'Hand me the ball; don't ever throw it at me,' and after the game he came into my office and apologized."

Lopez gave much of the credit for the success of the pitching staff to catcher Jim Hegan. "He was a great receiver . . . he could do everything behind the plate. Pitchers loved to pitch to him, which is half the battle in being a great catcher.

"The only fault I found with Jim, and it wasn't really a complaint, was that I wish he had been more aggressive. If he had, he would have gone down as one of the all-time best. Being aggressive also is half the battle in being a great catcher."

In 1954 second baseman Bobby Avila won the batting championship with a .341 average, center fielder Larry Doby led the league with 32 homers and 126 RBIs, and, while Rosen did not match his 1953 numbers, he batted an even .300 with 24 homers and 102 RBIs.

It was a great season for the Indians, though they won only three of their first nine games, falling into the basement before the end of April.

But they rebounded quickly and, by May 16, roared into first place on the wings of an 11-game winning streak.

"Once we got there [first place] we stayed the rest of the season," Lopez said of the Indians' sprint to the pennant. Only on two occasions—April 15–18 and April 22–24—did the Indians lose as many as three games in a row that season.

Indians catcher Jim Hegan (left) gets some advice from manager Al Lopez, who had a career from 1928 to 1947 as a catcher for the Brooklyn Dodgers, Boston Braves, Pittsburgh Pirates, and Indians.

"We were 6½ games ahead of the Yankees when they came in for a doubleheader in September [the 12th] and I felt if we just split with them, we'd be in."

The Indians did even better. They won both games, 4–1 behind Lemon and 3–2 behind Wynn, in front of a record crowd of 84,587, and Lopez was right. They were "in."

The pennant-clincher came six days later, on September 18, in a 3–2 victory over Detroit. Even though the Yankees won 103 games, they finished eight games behind the Indians.

And then . . . well, as Lopez groaned, "I was afraid you'd ask, and I'd just as soon not talk about [being swept by the New York Giants in the World Series]."

But then he did. "What happened to us is something that happens to every ball club during the course of a season. The trouble is, it happened to us at the worst possible time. In the World Series.

"We went into a rut, a slump, the only one we had all year. Everything seemed to go wrong for us in the Series, including the Giants getting hot.

"Something else," continued Lopez. "If you check World Series records you'll see that one player almost always gets hot, and it's usually not the best player on the team. In this case it was Dusty Rhodes.

"But I still say, and I always will, if the Series had opened in Cleveland, we would have won it. At least, we would have won the first two games that we lost in the Polo Grounds.

"The ball that Vic Wertz hit [with two on in the eighth inning of the first game and the score tied, 2–2] would have gone into the bleachers at the Stadium."

Instead, Willie Mays made a remarkable catch of the ball running away from the plate in dead center field, the deepest part of the Polo Grounds.

Then Hegan smashed a drive to left that Lopez said also would have been a home run in Cleveland, but it was caught by Monte Irvin, maintaining the tie.

"And Rhodes' homers [which won the first and second games] would have been only routine fly balls in Cleveland," said Lopez.

The Giants stayed hot when the Series moved to Cleveland for the third and fourth games. They won both, obliterating the contention—at least in the minds of most—that the Indians, having won an AL-record 111 games, were a super team.

"There wasn't much we could say after that [losing the World Series]," said Lopez.

"That was the lowest point in my career because we'd had such a great season, especially after having enjoyed the highest point in my career, beating the Yankees and winning the [1954] pennant."

"I know a lot of people, including some of our own guys, think that we burned ourselves out because we went for the record (111 victories). That if we had not been concerned with breaking the record, we would have gone into the World Series fresh.

"But I don't buy that. I never did. What happened to us in the World Series was just as I said: we hit a slump, our only slump of the season, at the wrong time.

"And if we'd won it, even if we had lost but not been swept, that team [the 1954 Indians] would have received the credit it deserved."

"Lopez was right," said Strickland, the slick-fielding shortstop the Indians picked up from Pittsburgh in 1952. "It was a

After leading the Indians to the pennant in 1954, manager Al Lopez (right) is granted a new contract and a healthy raise by vice president Hank Greenberg.

short series, and we went bad at the wrong time," he said, referring to four straight losses (5–2, 3–1, 6–2, and 7–4) to the Giants in the World Series.

But he disagreed with Lopez and was one of those who thought the Indians burned themselves out.

"I always use the excuse that we were chasing the Yankees for so long, and when we finally caught them in 1954, it wasn't enough. Somebody came up with the idea that we should rub it in by going for the record.

"So we went for it, instead of resting and getting ready for the Series, and when we broke the record, everything that followed was almost anticlimactic. It shouldn't have been, but I think it was," said Strickland.

The Indians' 111th victory came in the second-to-last game of the season, 11–1, on a two-hitter by Wynn on September 25.

The next day the Tigers beat the Indians, 8–7, the first of what became five consecutive defeats that ended the season so ignominiously.

"It still bothers me," continued Strickland, "because, as Rosie [Rosen] was quoted in an article I read recently, losing the Series the way we did took away so much of what we accomplished all season.

"Even the team that everybody says was the greatest, the 1927 Yankees, didn't win as many games as we did.

"And if we'd been playing in New York instead of Cleveland, everybody would have written how great we were, that winning 111 games was the greatest thing since the invention of the wheel."

Another reason the Indians weren't accorded the credit they probably deserved was that they also failed to repeat as AL champion in 1955. They were beaten out of the pennant by the Yankees again in 1956.

Indians pitching and hitting heroes whoop it up after one of the team's 111 victories in 1954 (left to right): outfielders Al Smith and Larry Doby, relief pitcher Hal Newhouser, and second baseman Bobby Avila, who won the batting championship with a .341 average.

Herb Score was brought up in 1955 from Indianapolis, then a Tribe affiliate, and his addition should have made an already-strong pitching staff even stronger. Score posted a 16–10 record, led the league with 245 strikeouts in 227⅓ innings, and was named AL Rookie of the Year.

But none of the other starters did as well as Lopez had every reason to expect. Lemon's record slipped to 18–10, Wynn's to 17–11, Garcia's to 11–13, and Houtteman's to 10–6.

Feller was a nonentity for the first time since he joined the team as a precocious high school boy in 1936 (with the exception of his navy service from 1942 to 1945 during World War II). He was 4–4 in 25 games, 11 as a spot starter, including his 12th one-hitter on May 1, 2–0, against Boston.

Four months later Feller recorded the final victory of his career—No. 266—over the Yankees, 7–6, at the Stadium on August 27. It boosted the Indians into a tie with the Yankees for first place, each with 70–55 records.

The Indians were either in first place or tied for first until September 14.

Then, as Score recalled during a 1995 interview, "I think we had the best team, but the club that did us in was the worst in the league, Washington."

The Senators, who finished last by 43 games, won 13 of 22 against the Indians, who had a plus or .500 record against every other team in the AL that season.

Detroit's Billy Hoeft and Steve Gromek combined to shut out the Indians, 3–0, on September 16, which dropped them into second place, .002 behind the Yankees.

They remained second through the final eight games, only three of which were victories, while the Yankees were winning seven of nine to capture the pennant by three lengths.

The 1956 race was not nearly as hot as the previous five as the Yankees took over first place on May 16, when they beat the Indians, 4–1, and remained atop the AL the rest of the way, clinching the pennant on September 18.

Score, Wynn, and Lemon each won 20 games, and were second, third, and fourth (behind leader Whitey Ford) in ERA. But the Indians did not have a .300 hitter in their lineup, and while they finished nine lengths behind New York, led third-place Chicago by only three.

On the morning of the final game, an 8–4 loss to Detroit—which also was Feller's final appearance—Lopez announced his resignation.

"My stomach was giving me a lot of trouble because of nerves," he said. "Too many bases on balls and 3-and-2 counts. I was as frustrated and disappointed as the fans that we didn't do better."

Lopez also made sure that his reason for quitting was not as many had speculated.

Stars of the Indians in 1955 (left to right): shortstop George Strickland, pitcher Bob Lemon, reliever Ray Narleski, and center fielder Larry Doby.

"It wasn't that I had any problems with the front office or the owners, and certainly not with the players," he insisted. "I got along with Greenberg, and I was always appreciative that he gave me my chance to manage in the major leagues.

"It was just time for me to go."

And so ended the "Golden Era" of baseball in Cleveland.

Ah, but it was a good one, even though it produced only one pennant.

Rosen agreed. "No doubt about it. That string of seasons [1951–56] has to be the best the Indians ever put together," he said. "We had great teams; it's just that the Yankees always were a little better, except in 1954.

"I'll always believe that our team, for at least that one season, was one of the greatest, if not the greatest, ever put together. And the manager also was one of the greatest ever.

"I have been making excuses for what happened to us in the World Series ever since, and in my opinion, being swept is what hurt us the following season.

"We had basically the same club [in 1955], plus Herb Score, but somehow nothing went right. We couldn't put it back together again after it all came apart for us in the World Series.

"But, boy, it sure was a great time, everything else considered."

It sure was.

There were times, however, before and after the 1951–56 period that the Indians came close to achieving, if not a "Golden Era," then certainly a memorable season or two, only to fail for one reason or another.

Since 1956 (and until the strike-shortened season of 1994 when they were second in the AL's newly formed Central Division) the Indians finished as high as second only once, in

Rookie third baseman Rudy Regalado was a spring training sensation for the Indians in 1954, when he batted .447, hammered 11 homers, and drove in 21 runs.

1959 when they won 89 games, the most wins in any year from 1959 to 1994.

In fact, on only one other occasion, in 1968, did they even finish as high as third.

Rosen, who played briefly for the Indians from 1947 to 1949 and was their regular third baseman from 1950 to 1956, compiling a 10-year major league average of .285, was in partnership with Clevelander George Steinbrenner III and others when they tried to buy the Indians in December 1971.

Their offer of $8.6 million was rejected by owner Vernon Stouffer, who sold the franchise to a group headed by Nick Mileti, further weakening the club's financial stability.

When Steinbrenner purchased the Yankees the following year, Rosen joined him as president of the club. He later served as chief executive officer of the Houston Astros and San Francisco Giants before his retirement in December 1992.

Before that six-year period from 1951 to 1956 when the Indians' cumulative record was its winningest best—570–354, .617— the agony of defeat was attributed to a variety of factors. It included what could be considered an "act of God," and even World War I later getting in the way.

The franchise that John F. Kilfoyl and Charles W. Somers founded in 1901 made its first serious run at the AL pennant in 1906 as the Naps got off to a fast start and were in or near first place until August. Three starting pitchers—Addie Joss, Bob Rhoads, and Otto Hess—were 20-game winners, and second baseman–manager Napoleon Lajoie batted .355, second highest in the AL.

But injuries sidelined several key players, including Joss, third baseman Bill Bradley, and outfielder Harry Bay, and the team finished third, five games behind Chicago and two behind New York.

Two years later, when Joss registered 24 victories (three more than the great Cy Young), the Naps won as many games as Detroit. But they also lost one more than the Tigers, who captured the pennant with a 90–63 record (compared to Cleveland's 90–64).

This time it was a rainstorm—the aforementioned "act of God"—that forced the cancellation of a game between Detroit and Washington, preventing the Naps from possibly at least tying the Tigers for the 1908 pennant.

The Tigers and Senators were rained out on August 25 in Washington, and, because of the rules then in effect, the two teams were not required to make up the game. If they had, and if Washington had beaten Detroit, the Tigers' record would have been the same as the Naps'.

After the next 10 years of mediocrity, during which the Naps/Indians' best finish was third in 1911, 1913, and 1917, it was the United States' entry into World War I that conceivably cost the Cleveland franchise its first pennant.

That was 1918, and many of the best players in baseball complied with Secretary of War Newton D. Baker's July 19 "work-or-fight" rule and left their teams for jobs in factories that produced products for the war effort, or entered the service.

In the case of the Indians, who lost their share of players, they also were hurt probably even more by baseball's midseason decision to shorten the schedule in deference to the war. Play was suspended on Labor Day, September 2, wiping out 27 of the Indians' games.

Had the season been played to its scheduled 154-game conclusion, the Indians might have overtaken Boston as two of their pitchers, Stan Coveleski (22–13) and Jim Bagby (17–16), were among the five biggest winners in the AL. The Tribe's 73–54 record was only 2½ lengths behind the Red Sox (75–51) when the plug was pulled.

The Indians finished second again in 1919, this time 3½ lengths behind Chicago, and again their failure to catch the White Sox could be blamed on the fact that only 140 games were scheduled.

With the country recovering from World War I, "economic reasons" were cited for shortening the schedule by 14 games, and for the second year in a row the Indians lost the pennant in the final week of the season.

They finally won their first pennant in 1920, though some considered it "tainted," despite their having three 20-game winners in Bagby (whose 31–12 record was the best in baseball), Coveleski (24–14), and Ray Caldwell (20–10) and six .300 hitters among their eight regular position players—center fielder–manager Tris Speaker (.388), catcher Steve O'Neill (.321), left fielder Charlie Jamieson (.319), right fielder Elmer Smith (.316), third baseman Larry Gardner (.310), and shortstop Ray Chapman (.303), who died August 17 after being hit by a pitched ball.

The "tainted" tag was applied by some because the Indians prevailed in the final week of the season after seven members of the defending champion White Sox were indicted and suspended for conspiring to fix the 1919 World Series.

At the time the Chicago players—including four regulars and two starting pitchers—were forced out, the Indians were ahead of the White Sox by one game with five left to play. Chicago, which had three games remaining, lost two of them while the Indians were winning three. The wins gave Cleveland a 98–56 record, two games better than Chicago.

Again, injuries to several key players ruined the Indians' chances to repeat in 1921 when they won 94 games, at that time the second most in franchise history, but were beaten out for the pennant by the Yankees, who finished 4½ games ahead.

Sidelined for extended periods were second baseman Bill Wambsganss, O'Neill, and Speaker.

As it was, the Indians were in the thick of the race all the way and were in first place by a half game over New York (with a record of 90–53 to the Yankees' 89–53) on the morning of September 20.

After winning two of three games in Boston, while the Yankees were sweeping a rain-abbreviated two-game series from Detroit, the two teams were separated by only .002, with New York having a 91–53 (.632) record, while the Indians were 92–54 (.630).

The stage was set for a four-game showdown between the Indians and Yankees in the Polo Grounds that began September 23—but turned into a disaster for Cleveland. The Yankees all but mathematically clinched their first AL pennant by winning three of those games by scores of 4–2, 21–7, and 8–7.

It was in 1926, Speaker's last season in Cleveland, that the Indians came close again, this time recovering from a poor start to challenge New York in September, only to fail again in the final 10 days of the season.

The Yankees, holding a 5½-game lead over the Indians, vis-ited Cleveland September 15 for a crucial six-game series at League Park. They promptly won the opener, but the Indians came back to take four in a row and cut their deficit to 2½ lengths.

When the Yankees prevailed, 8–3, in the finale, it put them on top of the Tribe by 3½ games, a margin they maintained through the final week to capture their fourth pennant in six seasons.

It was 14 years before the Indians challenged again, and this time their failure was blamed on a rebellion they mounted against manager Oscar Vitt in 1940, earning them the sobriquet "Cleveland Crybabies."

With Feller leading the way with 27 victories, the Indians were in first place most of the season, before and after delivering a petition to owner Alva Bradley on June 13, demanding—unsuccessfully—that Vitt be fired.

But they slumped in September, losing six straight from September 2 to 7, eight of nine between September 2 and 11, and nine of 13 prior to September 15.

On September 19 the Indians and Tigers were tied for the lead prior to a three-game series between the two teams in Detroit. The Tigers won the first two, 6–5 and 5–0, and though the Indians won the finale, 10–5, they dropped into second place a game behind.

When the Indians split a subsequent two-game series against the St. Louis Browns, while the Tigers were beating Chicago twice, Detroit's lead was increased to two with three games left—in Cleveland, the weekend of September 27–29.

To win the pennant the Indians needed to sweep the Tigers—but didn't. Detroit rookie Floyd Giebell outpitched Feller to prevail in the series opener, 2–0. The Indians won the next two, 2–1 and 3–2, but finished one game behind.

Vitt was fired at the end of the season, but for the next seven years the Indians, under the helm of Roger Peckinpaugh in 1941, and then Lou Boudreau, didn't come close to being a contender, finishing as high as third only once (in 1943).

Bill Veeck bought the franchise in 1946, and two years later, with Boudreau leading the way, the Indians became the toast of baseball.

Not only did they win the 1948 AL pennant and defeat the Boston Braves in the World Series, but they also set a season attendance record of 2,620,627 (which stood until 1962 when the Los Angeles Dodgers broke it).

The Indians outlasted Boston, New York, and Philadelphia for the pennant, though a loss to Detroit in the final game dropped them into a tie with the Red Sox, whom they beat, 8–3, in an unprecedented, one-game playoff for the pennant.

With a pitching staff that featured Gene Bearden (20–7), Lemon (20–14), and Feller (19–15), the incomparable physical and emotional leadership of Boudreau, and heavy-hitting center fielder Larry Doby, second baseman Joe Gordon, and third baseman Ken Keltner, the 1948 team was expected to be the start of a dynasty for the Indians.

Instead, it was the Yankees who began a dynasty, and the Indians all but collapsed in 1949, despite the acquisition of Wynn and the arrival from the minor leagues of Garcia. They lost 17 of their first 29 games and never once reached first place; only a strong finish landed them as high as third. When the season ended, Veeck sold the team.

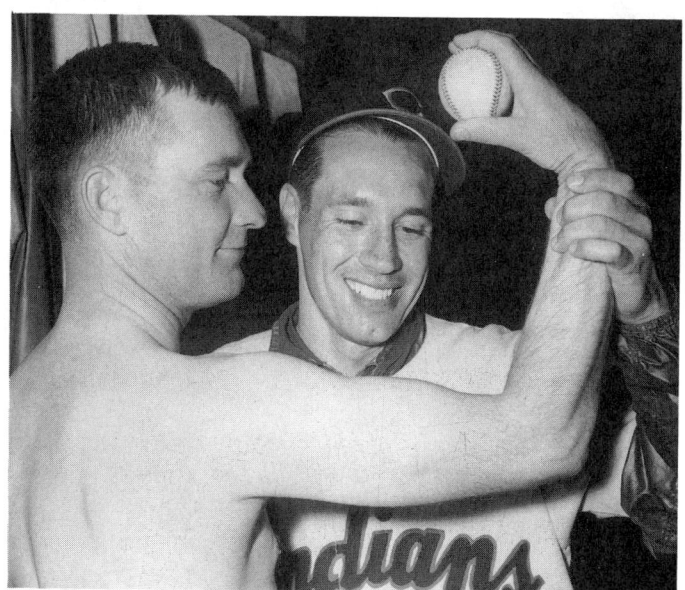

Bob Feller (right), who led the American League with 22 victories in 1951, checks the muscle in the right arm of Bob Lemon, who was a 17-game winner that season. Both pitchers are in the Hall of Fame.

A year later, even though they won 92 games, fourth most in franchise history, the Indians fell into fourth place as the Yankees won the second of what would be five consecutive pennants, and nine in 10 years.

Little wonder that in 1951, the year Lopez took over as manager of the Indians, an era of success began that was never previously enjoyed by a professional baseball team representing Cleveland.

And hasn't been equaled since his departure in 1956.

Off the Wall

In 95 years as a member of the American League the Indians (and their predecessors, the Blues, Bronchos, and Naps) managed to win more games than they lost only 49 times, while breaking even twice, and finishing under .500 in 44 seasons.

Despite their frequent ineptness, however, they've been interesting, to say the least. Following are 53 stories and anecdotes that, although they were not deemed significant enough to be reported fully elsewhere in this book, certainly are worthy of inclusion here.

Some probably will invoke a chuckle, others a groan, perhaps even a growl—or curse—or two.

But all are part of the legacy of the franchise, and this edition of *The Indians Encyclopedia* would be incomplete without them.

Rocky Colavito was a home-run-hitting outfielder for the Indians from 1955 to 1959 and from 1965 to 1967. He also made two appearances as a relief pitcher with a perfect 1–0 record and 0.00 earned run average. He pitched three innings in one game for the Indians in 1958 and was the winning pitcher in a two-inning stint for the New York Yankees in 1968.

Indians pitcher Mel Harder, who won the Most Valuable Player Award in the 1934 All-Star Game, receives the trophy from movie star and comedian Joe E. Brown prior to the Indians opener in 1935.

Slapnicka's Great Discovery

It was at a meeting in the spring of 1936 that Bob Feller's name was first mentioned in Cleveland.

"Gentlemen," said C. C. Slapnicka as he addressed the directors of the Cleveland Indians Baseball Company, "I've found the greatest young pitcher I ever saw."

Then the assistant to Indians owner Alva Bradley, Slapnicka went on to say, "I suppose this sounds like the same old stuff to you, but I want you to believe me. This boy that I found out in Iowa will be the greatest pitcher the world has ever known."

Though Slapnicka wasn't completely accurate in his prediction, he certainly came close—and also most certainly would have come closer if it had not been for World War II and the fact that Feller enlisted in the U.S. Navy two days after Pearl Harbor was bombed by the Japanese on December 7, 1941.

Feller served 44 months aboard a battleship in the Pacific, missing almost four full seasons of what would have been the prime of his career.

As testimony to Feller's character and integrity—and, of course, to the great relief of the Indians—he rejected an opportunity to become a free agent in 1936, which would have allowed him to sign with any team in baseball.

Commissioner Kenesaw M. Landis was prepared to make Feller a free agent because the Indians broke a rule then in effect that prohibited major league clubs from signing amateur players themselves.

That first contract Feller and his father signed was written on a scrap of paper and dated July 22, 1935. It purported to be with the Indians' farm club at Fargo, North Dakota.

It specified, "The Fargo club agrees to allow Robt. Feller to visit his folks at any time during the 1936 season, also to invite Robt. Feller's folks to visit him at Fargo during the summer of 1936 at the expense of the Fargo baseball club.

"The Fargo club has no objection to Robt. Feller playing basketball at any time."

It concluded, "For a consideration of one dollar paid to Robt. Feller this agreement is declared valid."

Not for Sale at Any Price

Bob Feller, whose credentials as a Hall of Fame pitcher certainly establish him as an expert judge of talent, left no doubt about his opinion of Herb Score, who was the American League Rookie of the Year in 1955.

"If Herb had not gotten hurt, he would have been as good as Sandy Koufax," Feller said of Score, who suffered a serious eye injury in 1957 and a torn tendon in his elbow the following year that led to his premature retirement in 1963.

Certainly the Boston Red Sox were among those who would agree with Feller's assessment of Score.

On March 19, 1957, Red Sox general manager Joe Cronin made a highly publicized call to his counterpart with the Indians, Hank Greenberg, and offered to purchase Score's contract for $1 million, then an exorbitant amount of money.

Greenberg, who'd been part of the group that, only three weeks earlier had bought the Indians for a reported $3.9 million, told Cronin, "We wouldn't sell Score for two million dollars. He's not for sale at any price."

Blame It on Bobby

All those years the Indians were among major league baseball's biggest losers—from 1960 through 1993—there was a reason.

Or at least a *rumored* reason.

It was that former Tribe manager Bobby Bragan, when he was fired by general manager Frank Lane in 1958, allegedly hired a witch to put a curse on the team.

"Aw, that's not true . . . but if folks in Cleveland want to believe it, let 'em," Bragan said in a 1992 interview. "I wasn't mad when Lane let me go. I was disappointed because I didn't think I'd had a chance to prove what I could do, but mad? Not me."

Bragan's firing, on June 26, 1958, ended the shortest tenure of any manager (other than "interim" pilots) in Cleveland baseball history.

Under Bragan's direction the Indians won 31 games and lost 36. They were in sixth place, 12 games out of first at the time.

Bragan was informed of his demise in the wake of a 2–1 loss to Boston at the Stadium. Lane told him, "Bobby, I don't know how we are going to get along without you, but starting tomorrow, we're going to try."

Hot-tempered catcher John Ellis in attack mode during a game at Cleveland Stadium in 1973. Attempting to restrain Ellis are (left to right) pitcher Ray Lamb, Indians manager Ken Aspromonte, and umpire Nestor Chylak.

Wertz's Remarkable Comeback

Vic Wertz probably is best remembered for having hit the 460-foot drive to center field that Willie Mays caught in the eighth inning of the first game of the 1954 World Series, which the Indians lost in four straight to the New York Giants.

It would have been a three-run homer in any other major league park, and Mays' catch was rated in a poll by *USA Today* as one of the 20 "greatest moments" in baseball history.

Wertz, a first baseman who helped the Tribe win the pennant in 1954 when he batted .275 in 94 games after being acquired on June 1 from Baltimore in one of Hank Greenberg's best trades, contracted polio the following season.

On August 26, 1955, Wertz was hospitalized for 20 days, and the future of his baseball career was in doubt.

But Wertz wouldn't give up and made a remarkable comeback from the disease in 1956 when he hit .264 with 32 homers and 106 RBIs, and was elected the Indians' Man of the Year.

Wertz went on to play eight more seasons for a total of 17 years in the major leagues, retiring in 1963 with a lifetime average of .277 and 266 homers.

Big Chief Oscar Vitt (left), the Indians manager from 1938 to 1940, receives good wishes from a real Indian on opening day at Cleveland Stadium in 1938.

Feller's Great Regret

It was a decision that broke Bob Feller's heart in the 1948 World Series, the memory of which still haunts the pitcher who probably was the best in Indians history and one of the greatest in the game.

It pains Feller so much because he failed in his only other chance to accomplish one of the few achievements that eluded him in an 18-year major league career.

"I've always been sorry that I never won a World Series game," Feller has said. He set single-game and season strike-out records, hurled three no-hitters and 12 one-hitters, won 20 games six times, and is enshrined in the Hall of Fame.

Feller might have won a World Series game in 1948, but lost instead, 1–0, to the Boston Braves in the opener. The Braves' only run came in the eighth inning as a result of a decision by National League umpire Bill Stewart.

Feller apparently picked off Phil Masi at second base—virtually everybody who saw it believed he did—except that Stewart called the runner safe. One out later Masi scored on a single by Tommy Holmes.

"Masi was out," former Braves shortstop Alvin Dark said during his tenure as manager of the Indians from 1968 to 1971. "All of us [on the Braves] knew . . . that Stewart called the play wrong."

Several years later, after Stewart died, Masi also admitted that he should have been called out by the umpire.

Of course, even if Masi had been called out, there's no way to be sure the Indians—and Feller—would have won, as they were held to four hits by Braves ace Johnny Sain.

Feller got another chance to achieve his goal when he started the fifth game of the 1948 World Series. He even was staked to a 5–4 lead, but was knocked out of the box in the seventh when the Braves erupted for six runs and an 11–5 victory.

And in 1954, when Feller's record was 13–3 and the Indians won their third pennant, he did not get the opportunity to pitch as the New York Giants swept the Series in four games, two of which were started by Bob Lemon, and one each by Early Wynn and Mike Garcia.

How Feller's Misfortune Helped Lemon

Bob Feller will always remember with anger and frustration the pickoff play at second base that National League umpire Bill Stewart blew in the opener of the 1948 World Series against the Boston Braves.

It led to the game's only run, which cost Feller and the Indians a 1–0 loss.

Bob Lemon remembers the play, too, but for a different reason—and with a different emotion.

"I know it hurt Feller, but it might have turned out good for me and the team," Lemon said a few years later. "If it hadn't happened, I might not have won the next day."

He explained. "I was in trouble, on the ropes in the first inning of the second game and [Manager] Lou Boudreau got the bull pen up. The Braves got a run in and had runners on first and second and only one out.

"I knew I was out of the game if I didn't get the next batter, and it was killing me. I was really struggling. No pitcher wants to come out of a game in the first inning, especially in the World Series.

"I don't remember the next batter, but before I made a pitch to him, we—Boudreau and I—decided to try the pickoff play again, the same one that Stewart blew for Feller the day before.

"This time the umpire at second base, Bill Grieve from the American League, called the runner, Earl Torgeson, out, and I got out of the inning."

It saved Lemon from being replaced, and the Indians went on to win, 4–1, and capture the Series in six games.

"The funny thing, the thing that makes it so ironic," continued Lemon, "is that Feller's pickoff play that wasn't called helped make mine good; I'm sure of it.

"All the hell that was raised because everybody thought Stewart blew the call for Feller made the umpires more alert, more aware that we might try it again.

"And because I got Torgeson at second, I got out of the inning instead of being knocked out of the game, and I stayed out of trouble the rest of the way."

Player-manager Lou Boudreau was one of the best shortstops in the history of baseball, but also went behind the plate on several occasions, including this one in 1943 when the Indians ran out of catchers.

Twelve Batters Who Frustrated Feller

Bob Feller pitched three no-hitters during his illustrious, 18-year major league career with the Indians, and came ever so close in 12 others, including two games in which he did not give up a hit until the seventh inning.

Perhaps the toughest to take was the no-hitter spoiled by Bobby Young of the St. Louis Browns on April 23, 1952. It probably should have been Feller's fourth no-hitter, because the Browns' only hit in that game, a night game in St. Louis, came on a routine fly by Young in the first inning.

Rookie left fielder Jim Fridley, playing in place of veterans Bob Kennedy and Dale Mitchell, broke the wrong way when Young's fly curved toward the line, apparently foul. Fridley tried to cut back but couldn't do so in time, and the ball sailed over his head for a triple.

Not only was it the sole hit allowed by Feller, but Young's triple also became the only run of the game. Young scored when the next batter, Marty Marion, grounded to third baseman Al Rosen, who muffed the ball for an error.

Left-hander Bob "Sugar" Cain, who pitched for the Browns, also fired a one-hitter—a single by Luke Easter in the fifth inning—but prevented the Indians from scoring. It was only the third double one-hitter in major league history and the second ever in the American League.

Another near no-hitter that was particularly frustrating for Feller occurred on July 12, 1940. Dick Siebert led off the eighth inning with a hard grounder that barely eluded sec-

ond baseman Ray Mack for a single, the Athletics' only hit of the game.

Two other potential no-hitters were broken up in the seventh inning: by outfielder Al Zarilla of St. Louis on April 22, 1947, and catcher Sammy White of Boston on May 1, 1955.

Bobby Doerr, a second baseman for Boston who was voted into the Hall of Fame in 1986, spoiled two of Feller's no-hitters with singles in the second inning, first on May 25, 1939, and again on July 31, 1946.

Former teammates of Feller were villains on three other occasions:

Infielder-catcher Billy Sullivan of St. Louis got the only hit in the sixth inning on April 20, 1938; outfielder (and future Hall of Famer) Earl Averill of Detroit ruined another no-hitter by Feller in the sixth inning on June 27, 1939; and catcher Frankie Hayes of Chicago singled in the second inning on August 8, 1946.

Yet another Hall of Famer, catcher Rick Ferrell of St. Louis, did it to Feller in the fifth inning of the second game of a doubleheader on September 26, 1941. Feller's other bids for no-hitters were spoiled by outfielder Jimmy Outlaw, Detroit, fifth inning, September 19, 1945, and shortstop Johnny Pesky, Boston, first inning, May 2, 1947.

Feller's three no-hitters, a major league record until Sandy Koufax pitched four, and then Nolan Ryan seven, were against Chicago 1–0, April 16, 1940; New York, 1–0, April 30, 1946; and Detroit, 2–1, in the first game of a doubleheader, July 1, 1951.

The Never-to-Be-Forgotten Harry Eisenstat

There is no plaque for Harry Eisenstat in the Hall of Fame, and there probably never will be. His entire major league career is summarized in 10 lines of agate type in the *Baseball Encyclopedia*.

But the left-handed pitcher whose career began with the Brooklyn Dodgers in 1935 and continued with Detroit and the Indians through 1942 is well remembered by many because of a record performance by somebody else.

Indians pitcher Johnny Allen (right), shown here with manager Oscar Vitt and the torn undershirt that led to his being fined $250. During a game in Boston on June 7, 1938, Red Sox players complained to umpire Bill McGowan that the torn sleeve was a distraction to the batters. McGowan ordered Allen to change the undershirt, or cut off the sleeve, but he refused, walking off the mound and out of the game.

"As long as baseball fans remember Bob Feller, my name probably will never be forgotten," Eisenstat once said.

That's because Eisenstat, then 23 years old, pitched—and won—the game on October 2, 1938, in which Feller set a major league record (since broken) by striking out 18 members of the Detroit Tigers, including outfielder Chet Laabs five times.

Eisenstat and the Tigers won the game, 4–1, in front of a Cleveland Stadium crowd of 27,000 fans, most of whom attended the season-ending doubleheader that day to see if Hank Greenberg could hit two homers and tie Babe Ruth's record of 60.

He didn't, as Feller struck out Greenberg twice, holding him to a double in four at bats. Greenberg also failed to hit a homer in the second game against Johnny Humphries and Clay Smith, though the Tigers also prevailed in that game, 10–8.

Eisenstat, primarily a reliever who pitched for the Indians from 1939 to 1942, had another memorable day earlier in that 1938 season. He was the winner in both games as the Tigers swept a doubleheader against the Philadelphia Athletics, thanks in part to three homers by Greenberg that day.

Rudy, the Red-Hot Rapper

It was the kind of spring training that players dream about. Especially rookies. It also was the kind of spring training that almost nobody ever has—rookie or veteran.

But Rudy Regalado did. It was in 1954 and Regalado himself could hardly believe what was happening. "It was amazing," he said. "I couldn't do anything wrong," though Regalado did once spring training ended and the season began.

Ironically, Regalado, then starting only his second year of professional baseball, wasn't even on the Indians' 40-man roster that spring. He was in Tucson, Arizona, for training camp only because he stopped off en route from his home in San Diego to Daytona Beach, Florida, where Tribe farmhands then trained.

When it came time for the Indians to play their first intrasquad game, they needed a second baseman because Bobby Avila was a holdout.

So, even though Regalado was a third baseman, manager Al Lopez played him at second. He hit the ball well in that intrasquad game—and never stopped all spring, during which he literally became a living legend. "Rudy the red-hot rapper," the media called him.

Regalado hit .447 with 11 homers in spring training and,

when it came time to break camp and open the 1954 American League season, he was signed to a major league contract. And to get Regalado's hot bat in the lineup, Lopez switched third baseman Al Rosen to first base.

But reality quickly arrived and, unfortunately for Regalado as well as the Indians, he turned out to be only a mirage in the Arizona desert.

Just as Regalado didn't know what caused him to hit so spectacularly well in spring training, nobody—including Regalado himself—could understand what caused him to not hit spectacularly well once the season started.

By midseason Regalado was struggling and soon was on the bench, with Rosen returned to third base and outfielder Vic Wertz, acquired on June 1, playing first base.

And, as mysteriously as Regalado found his batting eye in the spring of 1954, he—just as mysteriously—never found it again. He finished the 1954 season with a .250 average, two homers, and 24 RBIs in 65 games, and played only briefly for the Indians the next two seasons.

In 10 games in 1955 he hit .269 (7-for-26), and in 16 games in 1956 his average was .234 (11-for-47). He never played in the major leagues again.

Dr. Hardy at Second Base

Television soap opera fans knew him as "Dr. Hardy," but Cleveland baseball fans remember Johnny Berardino as a valuable utility infielder for the Indians when they won the pennant and World Series in 1948. He remained with the team into 1950, and returned for another season in 1952.

After his baseball-playing days ended, Berardino dropped the second *r* from his name and, to folks who knew him as Dr. Hardy on the ABC television show "General Hospital," he was simply John Beradino. He assumed the role in 1963.

The Indians acquired Berardino in the winter of 1947–48 in a trade with the St. Louis Browns. He was paid a then handsome salary of $80,000.

To get Berardino the Indians sent Catfish Metkovich and $50,000 to the Browns on December 9. Metkovich's contract subsequently was returned to the Indians because he had a

broken finger and couldn't play for the Browns, and they were compensated with an additional $15,000.

Berardino had played for St. Louis from 1939 to 1942 and in 1946 and 1947, during which his best batting average over a full season was .271 in 128 games in 1941. Though he hit only .190 in 66 games for the Indians in 1948, he was a valuable utility man with his ability to play every infield position.

On May 17, 1950, the Tribe optioned Berardino, a 10-year major league veteran, to San Diego of the Class AAA Pacific Coast League, with his consent. He played 17 games there, then was transferred to Sacramento, also of the PCL. After appearing in 40 games for Sacramento, Berardino was returned to Cleveland, given his free agency, and on August 12 was signed by Pittsburgh.

The Pirates released Berardino at the end of the 1950 season, during which he batted .213 in 44 games (40 for

Johnny Berardino, a utility infielder for the Indians from 1948 to 1950 and in 1952, became an actor when his baseball career ended in 1952, and played the role of Dr. Hardy in the television soap opera *General Hospital*.

Pittsburgh), and the following spring he was signed as a free agent by the St. Louis Browns. In mid-July 1951, Berardino was removed from their roster and named a coach, a job he held through the end of the season.

In February 1952, Berardino announced his intention to give up baseball for an acting career, but a month later he unretired and rejoined the Indians in spring training. He played 35 games for them and, on August 18, was traded back to Pittsburgh with minor league pitcher Charlie Sipple and $50,000 for shortstop George Strickland and relief pitcher Ted Wilks.

When the season ended, Berardino finally retired for good with a .249 average for 11 years in the major leagues, and shortly thereafter got his start in the movies and television.

In a 1988 interview promoting the 25th anniversary of the "General Hospital" program on television, Berardino said, "Most people don't realize that I was an actor long before I was a ballplayer. I was one of those brats in the 'Our Gang' comedies. I always loved acting."

The Indians' Most Bizarre Game

The Indians have been involved in many weird games, but it's unlikely that any was more bizarre than the one they played in their first season in the American League, on May 24, 1901, at League Park.

"Never in the history of the national game has there been a more sensational finish," is the way the *Cleveland Plain Dealer* reported Cleveland's 14–13 victory over Washington.

Not only was the game a gem, so was the newspaper's account of it.

"It was a case of hopeless defeat turned into glorious victory and never before did an audience show as much inclination to go totally insane or give a better oral demonstration," the story said.

Then called the Blues, the Cleveland team was losing, 13–5, going into the bottom of the ninth.

"Cleveland faced what seemed to be the inevitable . . . [and] the people had left the stands by scores, disgusted with such a one-sided game. The few who remained did so to scoff, but soon stayed on to cheer."

The story reported that the first two Cleveland batters were retired in the ninth this way: "Hoffer struck out and Pickering was thrown out at first."

Then, "McCarthy sent a clean single to right field and the spectators were offended. It seemed like a useless delay. Bradley hit another one safe and the opinion was that the players were only trying to help their batting averages.

Indians center fielder Russ Snyder (left) is introduced at a 1968 Wahoo Club luncheon by *Cleveland Plain Dealer* sportswriter Russ Schneider.

Indians manager Al Lopez is not kissing umpire John Rice in this 1956 photograph. He is disputing a called third strike Rice made against second baseman Bobby Avila.

"But LaChance, after going after two bad ones, pounded a single to center and McCarthy crossed the plate.

"Wood was hit by a pitched ball and the bags were full, but no one had the slightest hope of pulling the game out of the fire.

"Scheibeck, however, hit the ball square on the nose for a double. Genins cracked out a single, and [opposing pitcher] Patton was taken out of the box and Lee substituted.

"Egan took four bad ones and Beck, who batted for Hoffer, sent the ball so close to the left field fence that Foster could not handle it and the runner took two bases.

"In the meantime, seven runs had been scored in the inning and one more would tie the game.

"Then Pickering singled and Beck went home.

"By this time the audience gave a life-sized picture of pandemonium let out for recess. A crowd of Indians on a red hot warpath could not have been more demonstrative.

"They roared, they jumped, they shouted. They threw everything within reach in the air. Hats, umbrellas, canes, cushions went up as if a cyclone had struck that part of the landscape. They rushed on the field and came close to losing the game for Cleveland by forfeit.

"McCarthy was the man who was given the opportunity of batting in the winning run and he accepted it. A single to left sent Pickering across the plate, he having gone to second on a passed ball.

"The demonstration that followed may be imagined—it cannot be described.

"Cleveland's ninth inning will be remembered until the last person who saw it can remember no more."

A "Milestone" Event in Cleveland

The accolades were plentiful when Cleveland's Municipal Stadium first opened its doors to baseball on July 31, 1932.

The Indians' first game in the new facility, against the defending American League champion Philadelphia Athletics, was called "a milestone in middle western sports" by *Cleveland Press* sports editor Franklin Lewis.

"Cleveland strutted at the mere mention of the world's largest baseball plant," Lewis wrote. "Every seat in the new stadium had been sold for weeks as Cleveland put on its celebrating clothes and rushed to the lake front. The pregame ceremony was as impressive as the game itself.

"Baseball's brass shone beneath the omnipresent sun— [Baseball Commissioner] Judge Kenesaw Landis, [AL President] Will Harridge, A's President Tom Shibe, Ohio's Governor George White, who pitched the first ball, and the Mayor of Cleveland, Ray T. Miller, who caught it.

"Jack Graney, the old Naps' outfielder who became the Tribe's radio voice, introduced the stars of yesteryear: Cy Young, Tris Speaker, Bill Bradley, Lee Fohl, Elmer Flick, Elmer Smith, Bill Wambsganss, Chief Zimmer and the peerless Napoleon Lajoie.

"Connie Mack [owner and manager of the Athletics] took the public address microphone and thanked [Indians owner] Alva Bradley and [general manager] Billy Evans for their roles in providing the Indians and all of baseball with such a magnificent structure.

"There was naught but cheers that day, cheers sent up by a shirt-sleeved audience of 80,154, of whom 76,979 paid their

Two of Cleveland's greatest sports heroes of the 1940s and 50s ham it up for the photographer: former all-pro quarterback Otto Graham (left), who played for the Cleveland Browns in the All-America Football Conference and National Football League, and is in the Pro Football Hall of Fame, wears an Indians cap. Trading places with him is Bob Feller, who wears a Browns helmet and holds a football.

way in. These included the thousands in the center field bleachers who blocked the vision of batters so that the final score of 1–0, with the A's winning, was not unexpected."

The Tragic Loss of a Good Man

Luke Easter's career with the Indians got off to a late start because, until Jackie Robinson broke the so-called "color line" in baseball in 1946, African-Americans were not allowed to play in the major leagues.

There is little doubt, however, that Easter would have become one of the game's great sluggers if he had arrived in Cleveland sooner.

As it was, he broke in late in 1949, at the age of "about 35" (though his birth date was never confirmed), after he'd hit 25 homers in just two months for Class AAA San Diego of the Pacific Coast League.

But problems stemming from past knee injuries hampered Easter, and, though he displayed great power, he often was sidelined by his infirmities.

On June 23, 1950, in a game against Washington, Easter hit a pitch from Joe Haynes 477 feet into the upper deck of the right-field stands, the longest home run ever hit in the Stadium.

In three full seasons with the Indians, from 1950 to 1952, Easter hammered 86 homers.

Among those most impressed by Easter was teammate Bob Feller, who once said, "Luke had as much power as Mickey Mantle, maybe more, and I didn't play with or against anybody else who came close."

Easter played briefly for the Indians in 1953 and 1954, and returned to the minor leagues where he played for 10 more seasons—still hitting tape-measure home runs—though he had trouble running.

He finally retired in 1966 and returned to Cleveland, where he worked in a factory. Easter also was a union steward, and it was in that capacity that he lost his life on March 29, 1979. Easter was murdered by two thieves as he ran an errand to a bank for several of his coworkers.

A Bad Day for Birdie

It was the final series of the season, and the Indians had to sweep three games against Detroit at the Stadium to win the pennant in 1940.

The date was Friday, September 27, and Birdie Tebbetts, then a catcher for the Tigers, was seated in the visitors' bull pen as Detroit's Floyd Giebell pitched against the Tribe's ace, Bob Feller.

Cleveland fans were not in the best of mood as most were aware of the treatment their team had received in Detroit a week previously. Tigers fans had taunted the Indians, calling them "crybabies" because, earlier in the season, they had petitioned owner Alva Bradley to fire Manager Oscar Vitt.

It was Ladies Day, and 45,553 people were in the Stadium when one fan seated in an upstairs box directly over the Detroit bull pen dropped a basket of bottles and rotten fruit that landed on Tebbetts' head.

Tebbetts wasn't seriously injured—though he was very seriously angered.

As the fan was being escorted out of the Stadium by police, Tebbetts appeared and took a swing at the guy, hitting him in the jaw. "I would've killed him, if the cops had let me," Tebbetts said afterward.

The following season, when Tebbetts returned to Cleveland with the Tigers, a sheriff greeted him in the visitors' clubhouse with a warrant for his arrest.

The man Tebbetts hit—who had dropped the basket of bottles and rotten fruit on Birdie's head—wanted to press charges, claiming he was injured when he was punched in the jaw. The case was subsequently dismissed.

As for the game that day, Giebell outpitched Feller, the Tigers won, 2–0, and the Indians finished in second place.

Fritz, Mike, Susanne, and Marilyn

They kept following each other like traveling salesmen, from town to town. And what they had to sell far outweighed the talent in their left arms. They were an oddity, an almost sad curiosity.

They were Fritz Peterson and Mike Kekich, who will be remembered, not for their pitching, but as pitchers who traded wives, children, houses, and even family dogs while they were teammates with the New York Yankees in 1973.

Many believe their wife swapping led to Kekich's downfall. Once called "another Sandy Koufax" when he signed with the Los Angeles Dodgers in 1964, Kekich was 1–4 in 16 games for the Indians in 1973. His relationship with Marilyn Peterson and her two sons did not last, and they soon were divorced.

Kekich pitched in Japan in 1974 and briefly—but not very well—for Texas in 1975 and Seattle in 1977, after which his major league career ended.

It was different with Peterson, however, after he married Susanne Kekich. They had a daughter to go with Susanne's

two daughters from her marriage with Kekich, and they found religion.

Less than a year after they traded wives, Kekich was traded to the Tribe (on June 12, 1973, for minor league pitcher Lowell Palmer), though he did not stay long in Cleveland. Nor did he pitch well for the Indians, going 1–4 in 1973. He was released the following spring.

Shortly thereafter, on April 27, 1974, Peterson was acquired by the Indians (in a package with pitchers Steve Kline, Fred Beene, and Tom Buskey in exchange for first baseman Chris Chambliss and pitchers Cecil Upshaw and Dick Tidrow).

Peterson lasted slightly more than two seasons with the Tribe, going 9–14 in 1974 and 14–8 in 1975. After getting into a contract hassle with general manager Phil Seghi in the spring of 1976, Peterson, then with an 0–3 record, was traded to Texas on May 28 (for pitcher Stan Perzanowski).

Peterson won only one game while losing none for the Rangers that season, then suffered a shoulder injury that forced his retirement from baseball.

Indians center fielder Jim Piersall charges the mound against Jim Bunning of the Detroit Tigers in a game on June 25, 1961.

Joe Vosmik, "That Good-Looking Blond Viking"

It was Joe Vosmik's blond hair and classic good looks—in the opinion of Mrs. Billy Evans—that got him signed to an Indians contract in 1929. As it turned out, her advice proved to be very good.

Vosmik, who went on to hit .300 six times in his 13-year major league career, and who came within less than one percentage point of winning the American League batting championship in 1935, was first noticed by the Indians when he played in a sandlot all-star game at League Park.

Billy Evans, then general manager of the Indians, was invited to attend the game and look over the players to see if any of them were prospects for professional baseball. The date was August 26, 1928.

Evans took his wife to the game and, according to a story that appeared in the *Cleveland News* in 1937, asked Mrs. Evans, "Which of the players do you like?"

She reportedly replied, "That good-looking blond Viking over there."

It was Vosmik, then 18 years old, and the next day he was signed by the Tribe. He batted .381 in 112 games for Frederick (Maryland) of the Class D Blue Ridge League in 1929. The following season, after hitting .397 at Terre Haute (Indiana) of the Class B Three-I League, he was promoted to Cleveland in September, launching a 13-year major league career.

It was in 1935 that Vosmik nearly won the AL batting title. He went 1-for-3 in the final game of the season to finish with a .348387 average, but Washington second baseman Buddy Myer went 4-for-5 in the Senators' finale to bat .349026 to beat Vosmik by .0006.

Actually, Vosmik might have won the title except for a decision he made the morning of September 29, the final day of the season—a decision he lived to regret.

Vosmik had a three-point lead over Myer as the Indians went into a doubleheader against the St. Louis Browns, while the Senators were playing a single game against the Philadelphia Athletics.

To protect what he thought was a safe lead, Vosmik asked Manager Steve O'Neill if he could sit out the doubleheader. O'Neill consented as the Indians were lodged in third place with neither a chance to move up nor a possibility of falling down in the standings.

Vosmik pinch-hit in the ninth inning of the opener and made an out. Then, after receiving word that Myer had gone 4-for-5, Vosmik replaced Walter "Kit" Carson in the early innings of the nightcap of the doubleheader.

Knowing he had to go at least 2-for-4 to move ahead of Myer, Vosmik singled once in his first three trips to the plate, but never got another chance to bat. The game was called after six innings because of darkness, and Myer won the championship.

Vosmik was the left fielder for the Indians, with Earl Averill in center and Dick Porter in right, forming from 1931 to 1933 what many fans believe was the team's all-time best outfield.

The Vosmik-Averill-Porter triumvirate also provided the first name of the first son of Tribe trainer Lefty Weisman. He took the first initial of the first name of each of the outfielders—*J* for Joe, *E* for Earl, and *D* for Dick—and named the boy Jed.

Indians third-string catcher Hank Helf, who caught a ball dropped from the top of the 708-foot Terminal Tower in downtown Cleveland on August 20, 1938.

The House That George Burns Opened

Yankee Stadium long has been considered the "House That Ruth Built," because Babe Ruth hit so many of his career 714 homers into the cozy right-field stands.

But it was a former, and soon-to-be-again, member of the Indians who got the first hit in Yankee Stadium when it opened on April 18, 1923, in a game between New York and the Boston Red Sox.

George Burns, then Boston's first baseman, lined a single to left field in the second inning of that opener for the first hit in the new park, though Ruth homered later in the game.

But that first hit wasn't the only distinction attributed to Burns, who played for Detroit from 1914 to 1917, the Philadel-

phia Athletics from 1918 until May 29, 1920, when he was sold to the Indians, for whom he played through 1921, then with the Red Sox in 1922 and 1923, and back with Cleveland from 1924 until he went to the Yankees in 1928. He ended his major league career with the Athletics in 1929.

Burns appeared in 1,866 games for five clubs, compiling a 16-year major league average of .307. He hit .300 or better eight times, including a career-high .361 in 1921, and won the American League's Most Valuable Player award in 1926 when he batted .358 and drove in 114 runs. The runner-up for the award that year was Ruth, who hit .372 with 47 homers and 146 RBI.

Ninety-Nine Fans Wouldn't Know

Ask 100 baseball fans to identify Al Benton and 99 of them probably would be unable to do so.

It's true that Benton did little to distinguish himself during a 14-year major league career for four teams, including the Indians in 1949 and 1950, but he is the answer to one of baseball's best trivia questions.

Benton, primarily a relief pitcher when relievers were not glorified as they are today, was the only man to face both Babe Ruth and Mickey Mantle in championship games.

Benton pitched against Ruth in 1934, a year before the

Yankee slugger retired. At the time, Benton was a rookie with the Philadelphia Athletics, winning seven games and losing nine.

Then in 1952, when Benton pitched for the Boston Red Sox, his final year in the major leagues, he faced Mantle, who was playing his second season as the Yankees' brightest young star.

Between 1934 and 1952, Benton, a huge right-hander, appeared in 455 games for Detroit, as well as Cleveland, Boston, and Philadelphia, and posted a 98–88 career won-lost record with a 3.66 earned run average.

"Beer Night" Wasn't the Only Forfeit

It always will be remembered as one of the ugliest incidents in the history of the Cleveland baseball club.

It was a June 4, 1974, "Beer Night" promotion in which unlimited amounts of beer were sold for 10 cents a cup to the 25,135 fans who attended the game between the Tribe and Texas Rangers at the Stadium.

In the ninth inning, with the Indians fighting back from a 5–3 deficit, spectators—most of whom had too much to drink—swarmed onto the field, interrupting the game and fighting with several of the Texas players.

Umpire Nestor Chylak tried in vain to restore order, but couldn't and finally forfeited the game to the Rangers. Chylak later called the fans "uncontrolled beasts," and said, "I've never seen anything like it except in a zoo. It was frightening."

Texas manager Billy Martin said, "In the 25 years I've played, I've never seen an crowd act like that. It was ridiculous. That's probably the closest we'll come to seeing someone getting killed in the game of baseball."

It was one of six forfeited games in which a Cleveland team was involved (among 36 that have taken place since the American League was founded in 1901).

Cleveland was awarded victories over Washington on July 23, 1901, Philadelphia on July 20, 1918, and Chicago on April 26, 1925, and lost games by forfeit to Detroit on August 8, 1903, and to Chicago on September 9, 1917.

The strangest of the aforementioned six forfeits occurred in 1903 and 1917.

In the 1903 game, umpire Tom Connolly declared the game forfeited in the bottom of the 11th inning with Cleveland, then nicknamed Bronchos, trying to overcome the Tigers' 6–5 lead.

According to a report that appeared in *Sporting Life:* "[Catcher] Fritz Buelow of Detroit threw an old black ball into play. As soon as the Cleveland players detected it, they made a protest, but in vain. Thereupon, [second baseman Napoleon] Lajoie threw the ball over the grandstand and Umpire Connolly awarded the game to Detroit, 9 to 0."

It was a similar incident that caused the Indians to lose the game to Chicago in 1917.

Trouble between the Indians and umpire Brick Owens began in the top of the ninth inning when the Indians were trying to break a 3–3 tie.

Jack Graney, who would become the radio voice of the Indians in 1932, was called out in a close play at third base leading the inning. The call set off a violent argument that delayed the game for about 10 minutes.

According to a newspaper account, the Cleveland players "demonstrated their unhappiness by throwing their gloves in the air, and a couple of them [the players] rolled around the ground."

Order finally was restored, but trouble began again in the bottom of the 10th.

After Chicago pitcher Dave Danforth struck out, Indians catcher Steve O'Neill—another who would become manager of the team—"heaved the ball to the center fielder and Owens quickly forfeited the game to the White Sox."

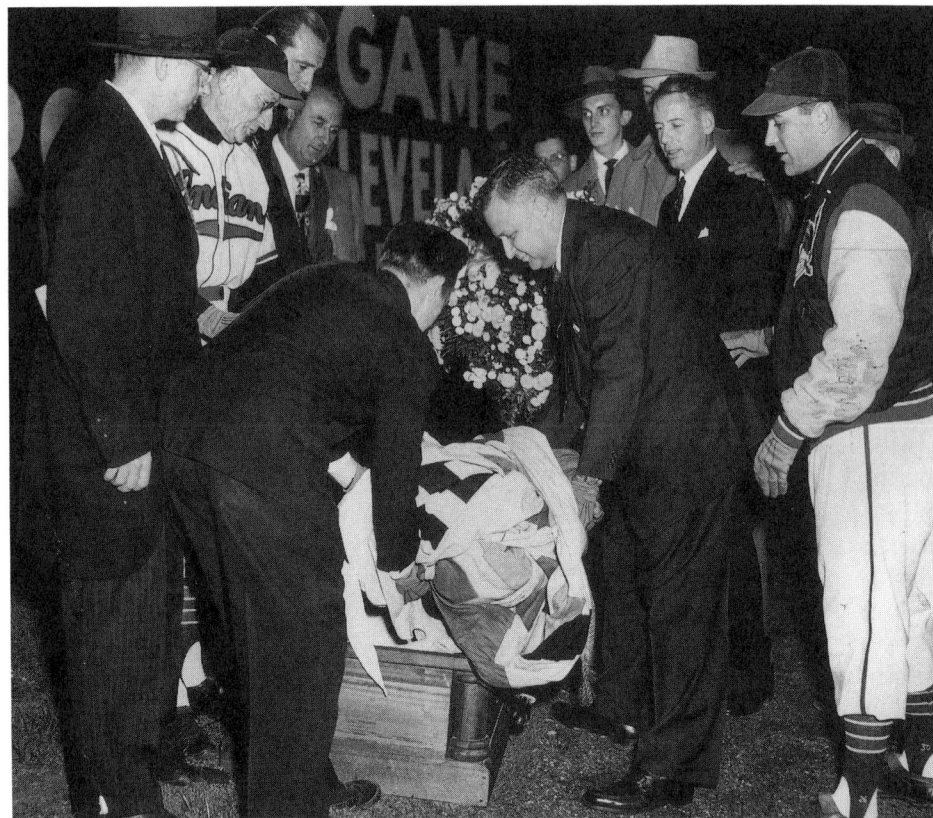

Mock funeral services were conducted at Cleveland Stadium in 1949 when the Indians were mathematically eliminated from the pennant race. Owner Bill Veeck ordered that the pennant the Indians won in 1948 be buried behind the center field fence. Shown in the photograph are (far left) business manager Rudie Schaffer, coach Bill McKechnie, Vice President Hank Greenberg (partially hidden by McKechnie), traveling secretary Spud Goldstein, an unidentified attendant (back to camera), publicity director Nate Wallack (bending over the casket), and Manager Lou Boudreau (far right).

Dudley and Neal: The Odd Couple

They were the odd couple of broadcasting: Jimmy Dudley and Bob Neal.

The two talented play-by-play announcers worked elbow-to-elbow on Indians games for eight years.

But they were antagonists, not partners.

Each blamed the other of letting professional jealousy cause their mutual problem. Dudley probably best summarized their relationship when he was quoted in a newspaper article in 1977: "Neal thought he should be number one, and I knew I was number one."

In many ways they were similar, which may have been the basis of their problem.

Whatever the reason, while they were an excellent team on the air, they had absolutely no relationship off the air.

Dudley started on the Indians' airwaves first. He initially teamed up with Jack Graney in 1948, the year Cleveland won its first pennant since 1920 (when Graney was the Tribe's left fielder).

When Graney retired after the 1953 season, he was replaced by Ed Edwards, who was Dudley's partner in 1954 and 1955. Tom Manning teamed with Dudley in 1956, after which Neal came along and shared the play-by-play microphone for the next five years (1957–61). Neal then switched to television for three seasons (1962–64), then returned to radio to work with Dudley for three years (1965–67).

When they were "partners" the two men often intentionally antagonized each other on the air, until Dudley's contract was not renewed in 1968.

Five years later Neal also was dismissed.

But neither mellowed in retirement.

Neal, who had health problems in his later years, died in 1983. During his illness, Dudley expressed sympathy for his former partner, but said nothing had changed in their relationship.

"No, I never hear from him," Dudley said about Neal—which would have been the same thing Neal would have said about Dudley.

No stunt was too big or too small for master showman and promoter Bill Veeck, who owned the Indians from 1946 to 1949.

The Day "Bad News" Hale Used His Head

His name was Arvel Odell Hale, so it's understandable why he was nicknamed "Sammy," even "Bad News."

Hale was a third baseman for the Indians in 1931 and again from 1933 to 1940, and for the Boston Red Sox and New York Giants in 1941, during which he compiled a .289 lifetime average.

But of all the plays "Bad News" made in the 1,062 games he played in the major leagues, probably none was stranger than the "three-ply slaying" he was said by a reporter for the *Cleveland Plain Dealer* to have started on September 7, 1935. It was in the ninth inning of the opener of the Indians' doubleheader at Fenway Park in Boston.

It has been recorded as the rarest triple play ever made, and Hale is given credit for it because he used his head—literally—to start it, enabling the Indians to sweep the Red Sox, 5–3 and 5–4.

Here's how the play was described in the paper the next morning:

"[The Indians] won the first game in spectacular fashion by pulling off one of the most unusual triple plays in all the annals of baseball, giving Mel Harder his 18th victory of the season.

"That three ply slaying came with stunning suddenness in the most dramatic possible situation that distinguished the afternoon from any other baseball day and gave 15,000 fans a memory to cherish.

"It had been a tight ball game most of the way, but Ab Wright had given Harder what looked like a safe lead of 5–1 by hammering a home run over the left field wall in the Indians half of the ninth. But it wasn't as safe as it looked as developments of the next few minutes showed.

"To start that spectacular last half inning [Indians second baseman] Roy Hughes lost Oscar Melillo's pop fly in the sun and it went for a hit. Bing Miller batted for Rube Walberg and singled. Dusty Cooke lined a single to center scoring Melillo, and Bill Werber plunked one to right, filling the bases.

"That finished Harder and brought Oral Hildebrand to the box to be greeted by Mel Almada's single, which drove in Miller and left the bases filled with the tying run on second, the winning run on first, nobody out and three of the best hitters in the Boston ensemble coming up.

"Then it happened.

"Joe Cronin slashed a whistling liner toward left. Hale

Don Rudolph was a relief pitcher for the Indians in 1962, and his wife was a burlesque queen whose stage name was "Patti Waggin, the Coed with the Educated Torso."

leaped in front of it and threw up his hands, but the ball tore through his glove, struck Hale squarely on the forehead and bounced high and to his left.

"The Boston runners, off with the crack of the bat, put on the brakes when they saw Hale grab for the ball, but were off and running again when it ripped through his hands. This set the play up perfectly.

"[Shortstop] Bill Knickerbocker was on the job to grab the ball as it caromed off Hale's head. He whirled and threw to Hughes at second, doubling Werber, and Roy's relay to Hal Trosky easily flagged Almada before he could scramble back to first, ending the inning and the game.

"It was a jubilant gang of Indians that went whooping off the field, and the broadest grin of the lot was the one that split Hale's features as he ruefully rubbed the bump on his head where the whole thing had started."

You Could Look It Up

The record book tells us that Cleveland Stadium was the site of the major league All-Star Game more times, four, than any other ballpark—in 1935, 1954, 1963, and 1981.

But that's only part of the story.

The city of Cleveland actually hosted the "Midsummer Classic," as the poets in the press box used to call it, seven times.

What's more, Cleveland—and Jacobs Field—will host the 1997 All-Star Game.

Overlooked were three other "all-star" games in Cleveland, two of which were staged before the present format was developed, and one that was played in 1942, during World

War II, between a team of servicemen and American League players.

In 1911, after the sudden death of Addie Joss, the best pitcher on the Cleveland club, a benefit game was played at League Park on July 24 between a team of American League all-stars—at that time called "the best baseball team ever assembled"—and the Naps.

The all-stars won, 5–3, in front of a crowd of 15,281, and a purse of $12,914 was raised for the Joss family.

Nine future Hall of Famers performed in that game, including seven for the all-stars: Tris Speaker, then the center fielder for Boston; Ty Cobb, right field, and Sam Crawford, left

Russell Schneider (center), author of this book and a former catcher, is signed to a minor league contract in 1949 by Indians vice president Hank Greenberg (right). Muddy Ruel, also a former catcher, was the Indians farm director.

field, Detroit; Bobby Wallace, shortstop, St. Louis Browns; Eddie Collins, second base, and Frank "Home Run" Baker, third base, Philadelphia; and Walter Johnson, pitcher, Washington.

Others on the team were Hal Chase, first base, New York; Gabby Street, catcher, Washington; and Smoky Joe Wood, pitcher, Boston.

Naps second baseman Napoleon Lajoie and pitcher Cy Young, both of whom also are in the Hall of Fame, played for Cleveland.

Young, who started and pitched the first three innings for the Naps, was charged with three runs and six hits, and the loss.

A second "all-star" game took place at League Park (though it was called Dunn Field at that time) on September 28, 1921, 12 years before the first official All-Star Game was played in Chicago on July 6, 1933.

That 1921 exhibition between the best players in the American and National leagues was organized, its sponsors said, in order "to stimulate interest in baseball, especially among youngsters," who were admitted free.

It was played in Cleveland because James Dunn, the owner of the Indians, offered to let the teams use Dunn Field without charge, and a total of 38 players were selected from the two leagues.

Speaker, then Cleveland's player-manager, was a coach for the AL team, but didn't play. Among the better known stars in the game were George Uhle, Jim Bagby, and Steve O'Neill of the Indians, Eddie Rommel, Dickie Kerr, Eppa Rixey, Edd Roush, Nick Altrock, and Al Schacht.

The AL won, 6–2, and more than 10,000 Cleveland youngsters were admitted free. Following the game, 1,000 baseballs, 500 bats, 250 gloves, and 50 catcher's masks were given away by a committee headed by Cleveland mayor William S. FitzGerald.

Plans were made to play the game again in 1922, but were canceled, as Judge Kenesaw M. Landis, who had just come to power as commissioner of baseball, wouldn't give his approval, reportedly because of his feud with AL president Ban Johnson.

Thus it wasn't until 1933 that the "official" All-Star Game came into existence. That first one was played at Comiskey Park in Chicago and won by the AL, 4–2. The AL also beat the NL in the second game, 9–7, at the Polo Grounds in New York, and then the stars came to Cleveland to play in the Stadium for the first time.

The AL also won that 1935 game, 4–1, and repeated with an 11–9 victory in 1954, though the NL prevailed, 5–3, in 1963, and again, 5–4, in 1981. The largest crowd in All-Star Game history, 72,086, attended the 1981 game. Paid attendance was 69,812 in 1935, 68,751 in 1954, and 44,160 in 1963.

The All-Star Game was played three times each in Comiskey Park, Chicago; Wrigley Field, Chicago; Yankee Stadium, New York; Sportsman's Park (no longer in existence), St. Louis; and Tiger Stadium, Detroit.

The 1942 game at the Stadium between major leaguers serving in the armed forces during World War II and AL stars was played on July 7, and $71,611 was raised for the Army-Navy Relief Fund.

A crowd of 62,094 saw the AL win, 5–0, as Bob Feller, then in the navy, started for the servicemen and was routed in the second inning and tagged with the loss.

Among the stars who played for the AL were Lou Boudreau, Phil Rizzuto, Ted Williams, Joe DiMaggio, Bobby Doerr, Ken Keltner, and Jim Bagby, Jr., while Cecil Travis, Pat Mullin, Frankie Pytlak, Sam Chapman, Johnny Rigney, and Johnny Sturm were in the servicemen's lineup, along with Feller.

Right Shoulder, Bats!

The Indians finished third—twice—in 1917, the year the United States was getting ready to enter World War I.

Because of the war, players who had not been drafted into the service prior to the season were ordered by the American and National League presidents to undergo military training.

Instructors were assigned to each team to conduct the drills, in which the players used bats instead of rifles. At the

end of the season each team was "graded," and the Indians were judged to be third best in the American League.

They also finished third in the standings, with an 88–66 won-lost record that left them 12 games behind pennant-winning Chicago.

The military drills were unveiled to fans on opening day, as reported in the *Cleveland Plain Dealer* on April 20:

When Hollywood produced a movie of the life and career of Hall of Fame pitcher Grover Cleveland Alexander—*The Winning Team*—in 1951, the lead role was given to Ronald Reagan (right). Signed as Reagan's "coach" and stand-in was Indians pitcher Bob Lemon, who had won 23 games the previous season.

"One feature of the afternoon [as the Indians defeated Detroit, 8–7, at League Park] which brought fans to their feet was the military drilling of the ball players.

"Directed by a uniformed soldier and carrying bats in place of rifles, the Detroit team seemed to have the edge on the home players so far as drill was concerned. Carrying something on their shoulders akin to a rifle made a tremendous amount of difference.

"But [the fans'] applause was not a marker to the roar of appreciation that went up when Drill Master Tris Speaker led his Indians through their formations.

"The Indians drilled well. You can't help but say that, but, without their shouldered bats they did not appear so military. President [James C.] Dunn of the Indians expects to get an officer here soon to drill his team regularly, and then watch 'em.

"The climax of the patriotic outbursts came when the players of the teams, headed by [a] band, marched around the field in military formation to the far corner of the field.

"Then, as the band played the Star Spangled Banner, 24,000 fans stood up, the men removing their hats, and Old Glory slowly and steadily slid up the flag pole behind the score board."

But the drills didn't end on opening day.

As reported in the 1918 edition of the *Reach Official American League Guide:*

"The players responded with good will and soon became so proficient by daily drills at home and abroad before each game that the officers were taken around the circuit and gave drills before each game.

"Near the close of the season army officers inspected the players during their drills and prizes were awarded to the most efficient. The St. Louis team won the $500 prize offered by [AL] President Ban Johnson as the best trained team in baseball. Second place was given to the Washington club and third place to Cleveland."

The Always Provocative Jim Piersall

It was quite an exhibition put on by Jim Piersall in a doubleheader between the Indians and Detroit at the Stadium on June 5, 1960.

Ironically, it happened less than two months before Tribe manager Joe Gordon was traded to the Tigers for their manager, Jimmy Dykes.

Detroit won the opener of that doubleheader, 7–2, but Piersall sparked the Indians to a 9–0 victory in the nightcap.

But that's not all Piersall sparked.

He socked a third-inning homer into the left-field stands off Pete Burnside. After hitting the ball, Piersall stood at the plate and made mocking gestures toward the Tigers' third base dugout as the ball soared over the head of left fielder Charley Maxwell.

Then Piersall raced full speed around the bases to third, where he stopped, again faced the Detroit bench, doffed his cap and bowed low before resuming his journey to the plate.

When Piersall batted again in the fifth, he wore an oversized Little League batting helmet and promptly got into an argument with Tigers catcher Red Wilson that nearly resulted in a fight.

Burnside's first two pitches were high and inside to Piersall, and he ran away from the plate when the third offering was aimed directly at him. Umpire John Flaherty jumped out in front of the plate, trotted to the mound, and warned Burnside, restoring order among the angry Tigers. (The warning cost the pitcher an automatic $50 fine.)

Piersall, who suffered a nervous breakdown and was institutionalized in 1952 when he played for the Boston Red Sox, was removed from the game in the seventh inning and was isolated in the trainer's room where he was seen crying. He refused to be interviewed.

Frank Lane, the Indians' general manager, urged reporters to leave Piersall alone. "Give him a break," Lane said. "You can't talk to him now. He's been trying to umpire, play center field, help the grounds crew, and do a lot of other things.

Dykes, who would "inherit" Piersall when he was traded

Bill Veeck served in the Marines in the South Pacific during World War II and suffered a leg injury in combat that led to partial amputation of the limb.

for Gordon, was angry at the emotional center fielder after the game.

"He invited trouble," Dykes said of Piersall's antics. "Any pitcher with red blood in his veins would do [what Burnside did]. What [Piersall] did was very bad for baseball. I have nothing against the kid, but I think he should be put in his place."

Ralph Kiner, a Most Unusual Player

He was called "one of the most unusual ballplayers in the history of the game" in a *Cleveland Press* article on December 15, 1954, and the description was accurate.

Ralph Kiner also was one of the greatest sluggers in the game, and it's a shame he didn't play for the Indians in his prime, prior to 1955, the last season of his productive 10-year career.

The reason Kiner was called "unusual" had to do with his integrity and humility.

When Kiner was acquired from the Chicago Cubs for two minor league players and $60,000 on November 16, 1954, he immediately entered into salary negotiations with Hank Greenberg, general manager of the Indians.

Kiner insisted upon a contract that called for a 40 percent cut—yes, 40 percent—from the $65,000 he made with the Cubs in 1954.

It was so unusual because, at that time, baseball's rules did not permit a major league club to cut a player more than 25 percent from one season to the next. (The limitation has since been changed to 20 percent.)

But Kiner, who acknowledged, "Maybe I should go to a psychiatrist," said he was only trying to be fair. He hit .285 with 22 homers and 73 RBIs for the Cubs in 1954.

"This is not a grandstand play," he said. "I simply want to begin a career with a new team in a new league on a fresh basis. I want my performance with the Indians to determine my future salary."

Kiner's contract "demand" was so unusual that Greenberg needed permission from American league President William Harridge, who said the 40 percent cut would be okay if it was okay with the player.

Which it was, and Kiner played for $39,000 in 1955, instead of $48,750.

As it turned out, Kiner wasn't worth much more than he received after the 40 percent cut. He hit .243 with 18 homers and 54 RBIs as the Indians failed to repeat as the AL champion, falling back into second place.

He retired when the season ended.

Second Baseman Sam McDowell

Sam McDowell was almost as good a second baseman as he was a pitcher on July 6, 1970, in a game against the Washington Senators at the Cleveland Stadium.

In the eighth inning, with McDowell holding a two-run lead and Frank Howard advancing to the plate with runners on first and third and two out, Indians manager Alvin Dark called time-out and strode out of the dugout toward the mound.

With the fans expecting Dark to remove McDowell, who always had trouble pitching to Howard, the manager shocked everybody—the 11,850 fans, his team, and the Senators as well.

Dark switched McDowell to second base, moved Eddie Leon from second to third, and took third baseman Graig Nettles out of the game.

Dark also brought right-hander Dean Chance in to walk Howard intentionally, loading the bases.

"I just didn't want Howard to beat us," the manager explained later. "By keeping McDowell in the game [at second base] I was able to counter any move the Senators made."

Rick Reichardt was the next batter, and he promptly whacked a pitch from Chance on the ground to Leon at third base. Though he had plenty of time to throw Reichardt out at first, or even run over to step on third for the final out of the inning, Leon fielded the grounder and threw to McDowell covering second.

With Howard bearing down on him, McDowell caught Leon's throw, falling to his knees on the base in the process, and the inning was over, the Indians' two-run lead protected.

"You're darned right I was shocked," said McDowell. "I was

Sam McDowell (right) shows his grip to Hall of Famer Sandy Koufax in 1967.

even more shocked when Leon threw the ball to me for a force at second base. But I guess that will put me in the record book as the only second baseman in baseball history with a 1.000 fielding percentage."

McDowell returned to the mound in the ninth inning and struck out the three Senators he faced to lock up a 6–4 victory, his 12th of the season.

Patti Waggin's Husband, the Pitcher

His wife was the famous one, but that didn't bother Don Rudolph.

Neither did the taunts directed his way from bench jockeys on the opposing team.

"She's good and I'm proud of her," Rudolph said of his wife when he reported for spring training with the Indians in 1962.

The Indians drafted Rudolph, a left-handed pitcher who, some said, reminded them of Whitey Ford.

However, Rudolph never approached Ford's degree of success as a pitcher—but then, Mrs. Ford never approached Mrs. Rudolph's degree of success, either.

Mrs. Rudolph, you see, was "Patti Waggin, the Coed with the Educated Torso."

She was a stripper.

With her 37–23–36 physical dimensions and dancing ability, Patti Waggin was in her husband's opinion "one of the

three top performers in burlesque, along with Lily St. Cyr and Tempest Storm."

Unfortunately for Rudolph and the Indians, he was never as good at pitching baseballs as his wife was at taking off her clothes on a burlesque stage.

Rudolph was up and down with the Chicago White Sox in 1957 and 1958, was traded to Cincinnati in May 1959, and was drafted by the Indians in December 1961.

However, a month into the 1962 season, during which Rudolph made only one appearance for the Tribe without a decision, he was traded to Washington for outfielder Willie Tasby.

Rudolph's major league career was finished at the end of 1964 with an 18–32 lifetime record—though Mrs. Rudolph continued to shed her clothes on the burlesque circuit for several more years.

Good Ol' Joe Earley

It was 1948, a truly Golden Year for baseball in Cleveland, for the Indians and their fans—especially one named Joe Earley.

Lou Boudreau and Bill Veeck were civic heroes. Household names were Ken Keltner, Joe Gordon, Dale Mitchell, Eddie Robinson, Larry Doby, Gene Bearden, Jim Hegan, and any of the 15 or 20 others who wore Tribe uniforms that season.

Children who were too young to stay up late got up early just to find out who won the Indians game the night before.

Housewives ironed and washed dishes and scrubbed floors to the accompaniment of Jack Graney and Jimmy Dudley doing the play-by-play of Tribe games on the radio.

Grandmothers who didn't know a strike from a double

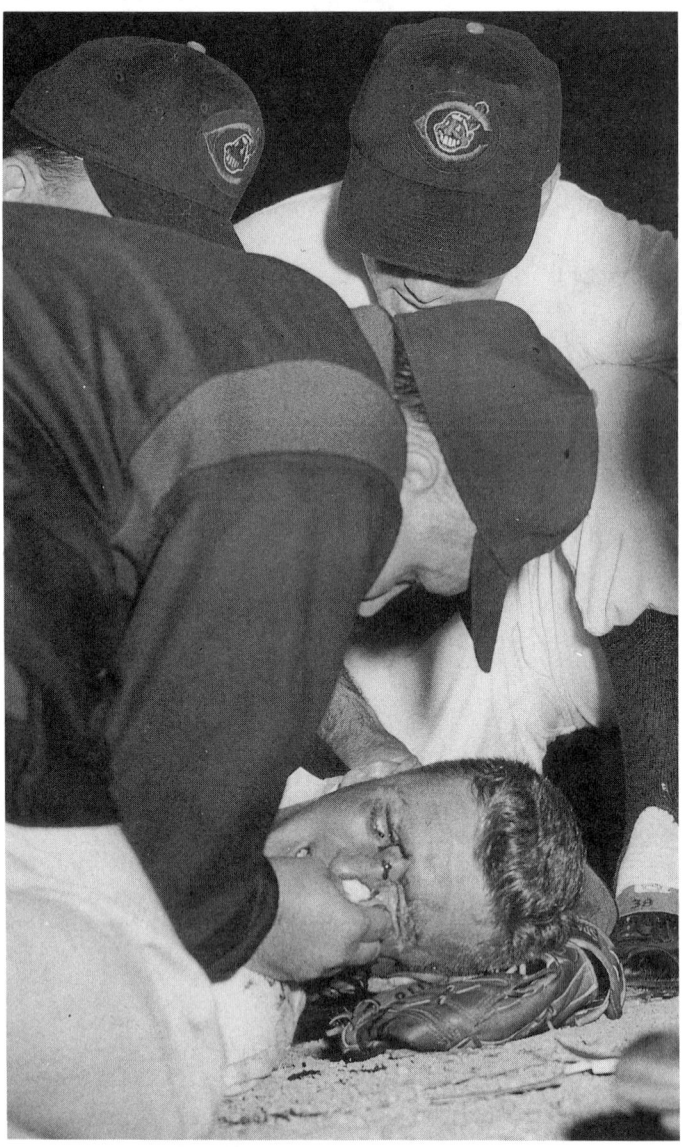

Indians southpaw Herb Score is seriously injured, but fortunately not blinded, after being hit in the eye by a line drive off the bat of Gil McDougald in a game against the New York Yankees at Cleveland Stadium on May 7, 1957.

play rejoiced when told that the Indians won, and were remorseful with the rest of the family when they lost. Some even cried.

And Veeck, called the "Barnum of baseball" with good reason as the Indians were in the process of winning the pennant in front of a record season attendance of 2,620,627 fans, came up with what might have been his best-ever promotion.

It developed after a fan named Joe Earley wrote a letter to the editor of the *Cleveland Press* suggesting that fans ought to get some recognition for supporting their team, the Indians, so well.

The letter was forwarded to Veeck, and he seized the opportunity to "honor" Earley as Cleveland's "Mr. Average Baseball Fan."

Earley was showered with more than $15,000 worth of gifts prior to a night game at the Stadium on September 28, and the promotion more than paid for itself by attracting a crowd of 60,405 customers.

In his book *Veeck as in Wreck,* the late owner of the Indians called the night for Earley "the gag that reaped us the most publicity."

He explained, "We started by announcing we were giving Earley a house, done in early American architecture. Out came an outhouse.

"We announced the presentation of an automobile, fully equipped. Out came one of those old Model T cars, filled to the scuppers with gorgeous women.

"After the fun was over, the real gifts came. A new Ford convertible, followed by a truck filled with gifts; refrigerator, washing machine, luggage, wristwatch, clothes, console, everything any quiz show subsequently thought of. Everything, to be frank, we could talk the local merchants into contributing to the cause."

Included among the $15,000 worth of nongag gifts was $5,400 in cash that Earley turned over to the Cancer Fund.

Everybody went home happy that night—especially Joe Earley.

"Charlie, Won't You Please Come Down?"

Of the thousands of rabid Indians fans who lived and died with their team in 1948, Charlie Lupica probably was the most faithful.

He displayed his trust in a most unique way—by living on a 4-foot-by-6-foot perch atop a 16-foot flagpole for 117 days.

It all began when Lupica, then a 38-year-old druggist, got into an argument with a couple of Yankee fans early in the 1949 season. At the time, the Indians were struggling to repeat the championship they'd won the year before.

Angry and frustrated, Lupica said he was so sure the Indians would soon regain first place and win the pennant again, he would "climb a flagpole" and stay aloft until they reached the top of the American League.

When his antagonists laughed, Lupica put his money where his mouth was, so to speak.

On May 31, with the 17–18 Indians lodged in seventh place in the eight-team AL race, Lupica climbed to the top of his flagpole and waited.

And waited and waited.

A tentlike canvas protected Lupica from the elements and hid him from view of curious spectators below, toilet facilities were installed, his meals were sent up by his wife, and for entertainment he had a television set and radio to enable him to keep up with the progress (and lack of same) by the Indians.

While "spies" often lurked below in an attempt to catch him cheating, Lupica remained aloft, even when his wife delivered their fourth child.

And through it all, the Indians continued to struggle.

They never did regain first place, and, on September 25, after a record 117 days on the flagpole, Lupica finally gave up on the Indians—but only because they were mathematically eliminated—and agreed to come down.

Indians catcher Jim Hegan in 1947 with his five-year-old son Mike, who later became a major league first baseman for four teams and is now one of the television voices of the Indians in Cleveland.

It paved the way to another of owner Bill Veeck's great stunts.

Veeck had Lupica's flagpole, with Charlie still at the top, loaded onto a flatbed truck and transported to the Stadium where 33,977 fans awaited his celebrated descent.

Veeck welcomed Lupica back to earth with a new Pontiac and gifts for his entire family—including a 50-foot flagpole to be installed outside Charlie's home.

Neal Ball's "Phenomenal" Play

It was the first ever in baseball history and was called "phenomenal," when shortstop Neal Ball pulled off an unassisted triple play for the Cleveland club, then called the Naps, in the first game of a doubleheader against Boston at League Park on July 19, 1909.

Only eight unassisted triple plays have been made since then, including the second in baseball history—and the only one in a World Series game—by Indians second baseman Bill Wambsganss against Brooklyn in 1920.

Ball's triple play occurred in the second inning of a 6–1 victory by the Naps and Cy Young over the Red Sox.

It came after Heinie Wagner led off with a single and Chick Stahl beat out a bunt, placing runners at first and second. Amby McConnell failed in two attempts to sacrifice, then hit a line drive toward center.

The runners were off with the crack of the bat, and so was Ball. He turned to his left, leaped in the air to catch McConnell's liner for one out, took two steps and stepped on second base, doubling Wagner, and tagged Stahl, who had no chance to return to first base.

The crowd was momentarily stunned, then broke into wild cheering upon the realization of Ball's achievement.

As the *Cleveland Plain Dealer* reported, "It was a play that had great bearing on the result of the game. Had McConnell's hit gone safe, Wagner would have scored and Boston still would have had men on first and third with no one out.

"Happening as it did to pull Cy Young out of the predicament in which he found himself involved, the veteran pitcher was able to keep the Red Sox tamed during the remainder of the contest.

"Ball did not stop with this record breaking play. In addition he accepted eight other chances, having nine put outs . . . three more than went to the credit of first baseman George Stovall of the Naps. This is thought to be a fielding record.

"And [Ball] was not content with carrying off the fielding honors either. When he came to bat in the second inning, after making his triple play, he was greeted with tremendous applause and responded to the cheers of the fans by hitting the ball over Tris Speaker's head in center field for a home run.

"In the fourth inning he made a two-bagger, while in the eighth inning he was safe at first on Doc Gessler's muff, but was caught trying to take two bases on the play.

"Surely that was glory enough for one player in one afternoon."

In a rare (for that era) postgame interview, it was reported, "Ball took his honors modestly. Never stopping to receive the congratulations of his teammates and the Boston players, he hustled to the bench to get out of sight.

"After the game he said, 'When McConnell hit to me, I was thinking that we were going to be lucky if the Bostons did not score a couple of runs before we retired them. I was wishing

Southpaw Joe Krakauskas, who gave up a single to Joe DiMaggio on July 16, 1941, the day before DiMaggio's 56-game hitting streak was stopped by the Indians.

that McConnell would hit a fast one to me on the ground that I might get a double play out of it.

"I never dreamed of making a triple play, though, until I had touched second base with my foot and saw Stahl charg-ing into me. He could not recover his balance in time to turn and chase back to first, so all I had to do was keep on going and touch him.

"That was all there was to it. It all happened in about two seconds. It was a play made to order to fit the situation, and I am mighty glad that I happened to be the one who was right in the right spot and able to pull it off.

"I don't suppose I will ever get the chance to make an-other such play, but I've got no kick coming. It's pretty fine to be able to make it once in a lifetime.

"Just think of the wonderful plays that [second baseman] Larry [Lajoie], [regular shortstop] Terry [Turner] and [third baseman] Bill Bradley have made since they have been in the big leagues, but yet they never had the chance to do what I, a utility man, a sub, did. It was just my good fortune to be in the game when such a chance was offered.

"Anyone could have made the play. In fact, I don't see how I could have done otherwise unless I had lost my head and tossed wide to Stovall instead of keeping on going until I touched Stahl."

It is ironic that, of the nine unassisted triple plays in the history of major league baseball, Cleveland players have been involved in five of them—in fact, every one of those made in the American League—though the Indians were the victims three times.

Eleven years after Ball made his fielding gem, Wambs-ganss did the same in Game 5 of the 1920 World Series against Brooklyn's Clarence Mitchell; Red Sox first baseman George Burns made the third unassisted triple play in major league history against Frank Brower of the Indians on Sep-tember 14, 1923, in Boston; Johnny Neun, a first baseman for the Tigers, retired three Indians by himself upon catching Homer Summa's liner on May 31, 1927 in Detroit; as did Washington shortstop Ron Hansen against Joe Azcue and the Indians on July 30, 1968 at the Stadium in Cleveland.

No Kidding, It Was "Ten Million"

With a name like his, it would have been much more ap-propriate for him to be playing in the current era, in-stead of the early 1900s.

Instead, Ten Million—honestly, that was his name—was a minor league outfielder whose contract was purchased by the Cleveland club, then called the Naps, in 1911. Unfortu-nately, he suffered a knee injury and never played a game in the major leagues.

According to Million's daughter, it was Ten's mother who had "a penchant for the unusual" and gave him the strange name when he was born in Mount Vernon, Washington, on October 14, 1889.

It was after he batted .276 in 160 games for Victoria of the Northwestern League that Cleveland bought Million. A base-ball card of his issued by OBAK Cigarettes that year said, "[Million] covers plenty of ground and is one of the leading throwers, is very fast and a good hitter."

Million, who grew up in Seattle, also played for Tacoma of the Northwestern League and Sioux City in the Western League in 1912, Spokane and Tacoma in the Northwestern League in 1913, and Tacoma and Moose Jaw in the Western Canada League in 1914, retiring with his bad knee after play-ing in 692 minor league games.

After his playing days ended, Million was a sporting goods salesman for Spalding, served in the army in World War I, and in the 1920s sold Ford automobiles. When the 10 mil-lionth Ford automobile rolled off the assembly line, it was taken on a tour of the United States, and a Seattle newspaper ran a photo of the car with Ten Million.

Ten Million later worked for the Corporation Counsel's office in Seattle, investigating injury claims, and for many years he umpired semipro baseball games and also was a foot-ball and basketball official.

Million's daughter also revealed that her grandmother—Ten's mother—paid her parents to name her Decillion Mil-lion, which they did—although they kindly nicknamed her Dixie. Her brother had a very ordinary name, "Barney," as did Ten's father, Elmer C. Million, a Seattle judge.

Ten Million died June 18, 1964, at Anacortes, Washington.

Indians pitcher Gaylord Perry going through his pre-pitch routine, which caused speculation that he threw illegal "grease ball' pitches.

The Time Sam Was Extra Sudden

"I'll never know what might have happened if I hadn't said anything to George Strickland that night, but I don't think I was ever throwing the ball better," Sam McDowell reminisced about the game in 1966 when he was at his sudden best.

The date was September 18, and the Indians were trying to climb into fifth place in what was then a 10-team American league race. Strickland was the interim manager after replacing Birdie Tebbetts, who'd resigned under fire a month earlier.

"I often wonder if I could have struck out 18 [and tied what was then the major league single game record] if I could have gone all the way," said McDowell.

"One thing I know. I had everything that night. My fastball was as good as it ever was, and my control was nearly perfect.

"I got 14 strikeouts in only six innings. No matter what pitch I threw, I could put it anywhere I wanted. I was at my all-time best, and I don't think I was ever that good after that night."

The late Emmett Ashford, the umpire working behind the plate that night, agreed. In a 1968 interview Ashford said, "I'd never seen any pitcher any better than Sam was that night, and I don't think I ever will again.

"Usually I get so immersed in a game I can't even tell you the score. But that night in Detroit, I guess because all the Tigers were talking about McDowell's stuff, I knew he had a chance for the record. He amazed me. He amazed everyone in that game, and I'll never forget it."

McDowell didn't break the record that night because he talked himself out of the game.

As Strickland testified in a recent interview, "It was after Sam came into the dugout from the sixth inning that he said to me, 'Strick, I can't pick my arm up anymore,' he said. I asked him, 'What's wrong?' And he tells me again, 'I can't pick up my arm. It's dead.' So I took him out of the game.

"The next day I read in the paper that McDowell told the writers he didn't know why I took him out. Can you beat that?

"But that was Sam. Who knows what was going through his head that night," added Strickland.

McDowell said, "All I told George was that my arm was beginning to tighten up. I only said it because I wanted him to keep somebody ready. But, just like that, he took me out. I know George did what he thought was best for me and the team, but I was very disappointed.

"Nobody will ever know what might have happened if I had been able to pitch those last three innings. Heck, I only needed four more strikeouts to tie the record.

"That's why, of all the games I pitched, that's the one I'll never forget."

As it turned out, McDowell didn't even get credit for a victory over the Tigers that night. Reliever John O'Donoghue, who replaced McDowell, blew the Indians' 5–1 lead in the eighth inning, and the Indians had to rally for a run in the 10th to win, 6–5 behind Luis Tiant.

"Uncle Hughie," Who Rejected Mantle

You'll not find his name among the stars of the Indians' past, and only one line in the *Baseball Encyclopedia* is devoted to Hugh Alexander.

It shows that Alexander, better known now as "Uncle Hughie" among his peers, played in seven games for the Tribe in 1937, and that he got one hit in 11 times at bat.

But there's more to be told about Hugh Alexander than meets the eye.

Now considered one of baseball's great talent scouts,

Farm director Bob Quinn (right) with utility infielder Gomer Hodge, who thought his batting average was 4.000 because he got four hits in his first four at-bats as a rookie pinch hitter in 1971.

Alexander was an 18-year-old power-hitting outfielder who was signed by C. C. Slapnicka in 1935—the same C. C. Slapnicka who found Bob Feller and a host of other players who became stars.

Alexander had two very productive seasons in the minor leagues and was called to Cleveland for the final month of the 1937 season. But then fate dealt him a cruel blow.

While he was working in the oil fields of Oklahoma during the winter of 1937–38, Alexander's left hand got caught in the gears of a derrick. He was alone when it happened, and the nearest doctor was 14 miles away. So Alexander drove all the way himself.

The minor league star hitter lost his hand, ending his playing career at age 20.

Shortly thereafter Slapnicka offered his once-prized prospect a job as a scout for the Indians, and Alexander embarked upon a new career in baseball. He worked for the Tribe for 14 years. One of his best discoveries was Allie Reynolds.

Alexander left the Indians in 1952 and has since worked for the Chicago White Sox, Los Angeles Dodgers, Philadelphia Phillies, and Chicago Cubs. Prominent among the other players he has signed were Don Sutton, Bill Russell, Frank Howard, and Davey Lopes.

But there also were some who got away, and in a 1990 interview he was big enough to admit it.

"The worst mistake of my career," he said, "was listening to a high school principal in Oklahoma when I was working for the Indians in 1948."

Alexander said he was told that a boy he wanted to see had osteomylitis, a bone disease in his leg. So Alexander canceled his plans to see the boy play.

That player was Mickey Mantle, whose Hall of Fame career might have been with the Indians instead of the New York Yankees if Alexander had not taken the advice of that school principal in 1948.

The Time Gomer Hodge Batted 4.000

No doubt about it, Gomer Hodge was a very good pinch hitter.

But he also was a terrible mathematician.

Gomer, whose given name was Harold, came up to the Indians as a 27-year-old rookie in 1971 after spending eight seasons in the minor leagues.

Hodge was nicknamed "Gomer" because of his uncanny resemblance in speech to actor-singer Jim Nabors, who starred in the popular television program "Gomer Pyle, U.S.M.C."

On opening day, against the Boston Red Sox, Hodge de-

livered an eighth-inning pinch single, then stayed in the game and stroked a game-winning hit in the last of the ninth as the Indians prevailed, 3–2.

A couple of games later Gomer got his third straight pinch single, and the next day did it again, making his record 4-for-4, after which he told a group of reporters interviewing him, "Gollee, Fellas, I'm hittin' four thousand! Ain't that somethin'?"

Unfortunately, Gomer's ability to hit turned as bad as his arithmetic. After that wonderful start, Hodge reverted to the form that had kept him in the minor leagues so long.

After those first four hits, Gomer went just 13-for-79 the rest of the season and finished with a .205 batting average, with one homer and nine RBIs in 80 games.

The following winter the Indians demoted Hodge to Class AAA Portland of the Pacific Coast League, and he never made it back to the major leagues.

The Indians' 1940 Price Tag: $1,848,000

In this day of multimillion dollar salaries and franchises being sold for more than $100 million, the price tag that owner Alva Bradley put on his Indians franchise in 1940 is interesting.

It came in the wake of what Bradley called the "melancholy mess" of the Tribe's inability to win the pennant that year, as several directors advocated selling the club.

They were disillusioned by the troubles that had surfaced in the players' rebellion against manager Oscar Vitt, earning them the nickname "Cleveland Crybabies."

Bradley, an unassuming man who later admitted he should have fired Vitt when the players demanded that he do so, established what he considered the "realistic value" of the franchise, but found nobody able to come up with the money.

Bradley's price tag was $1,848,000, which was a a huge sum in those days.

On September 9, 1940, Bradley wrote the following letter to Joseph C. Hostetler, then secretary of the Indians.

"Dear Joe: At the last meeting of the directors it was suggested that I write you a letter giving you what I thought would be the market price on the ball players we have on the Cleveland club, and I am enclosing the list which I think would be a fair value for our players.

"To this can be added $250,000 for all of the material we have in the minor leagues, which I would say would be about the price that they have cost us. I think, also, that to this figure you can add $600,000, which I think would cover the value of our park and the American League franchise."

Bradley's price tag on the 32 players then on the Indians' roster totaled $998,000—but only $598,000 if Bob Feller were not included. Feller, then an upcoming star, was the highest valued player at $400,000.

But after Feller there was a huge drop-off in the price tag Bradley put on his players—Lou Boudreau, Ken Keltner, and Ray Mack were valued at $75,000 each; Hal Trosky at $40,000; Roy Weatherly at $30,000; Mel Harder, Al Milnar, and Rollie Hemsley at $25,000 each; Jeff Heath and Clarence Campbell at $20,000 each; and Joe Dobson, Al Smith, and Russ Peters at $15,000 each.

Five players, including Johnny Allen, who already had won 117 games for the Indians, were considered by Bradley to be worth $10,000 each. The others were Mike Naymick, Roy Bell, Ben Chapman, and Del Jones.

Ten players were considered to be worth $7,500 each, including catcher Frankie Pytlak and pitcher Harry Eisenstat; and an outfielder named Murray Howell, whose major league career consisted of seven at bats with two hits in 11 games for the Indians in 1941, was valued by Bradley at $3,000.

Russell Schneider (center) interviews Indians president Gabe Paul (left) and manager Alvin Dark in 1968.

Brownie's "Record" Home Run

Larry Brown hit 47 home runs in his 12-year major league career, and the one he remembers best—though not for the obvious reason—was his first.

It came on July 31, 1963, in the second game of a doubleheader at the Stadium against the Los Angeles Angels, won by the Indians, 9–5.

The truth be told, it was a home run that Brown really didn't want to hit.

"There I was, just a rookie, and I knew he was going to knock me down," the former Indians infielder said about Angels pitcher Paul Foytack. "He had to throw at me . . . at least I thought he did."

The reason Brown expected to be knocked down was that the previous three batters—Woodie Held, Pedro Ramos, and Tito Francona—had whacked consecutive home runs off Foytack.

"I stepped into the batter's box, kind of loose, and jumped out on the first pitch. But it was right over the plate for strike one. I was really surprised," he said.

"I got back in the box and figured that, for sure, the next pitch was going to be right at my head.

"But that one came in right over the plate, too, for strike two.

"That made it 0-and-2, and I was positive Foytack was going to knock me down with his next pitch because he knew that I knew I had to stay in there.

"But again, Foytack comes right in with the ball. It was right over the plate. I swung, and there it went. Out of the park. My first big league homer and the fourth in a row off Foytack. It tied a major league record.

"As I ran around the bases [Los Angeles manager] Bill Rigney came out to take Foytack out of the game. I looked at them and Foytack kind of smiled at me, but didn't say any-

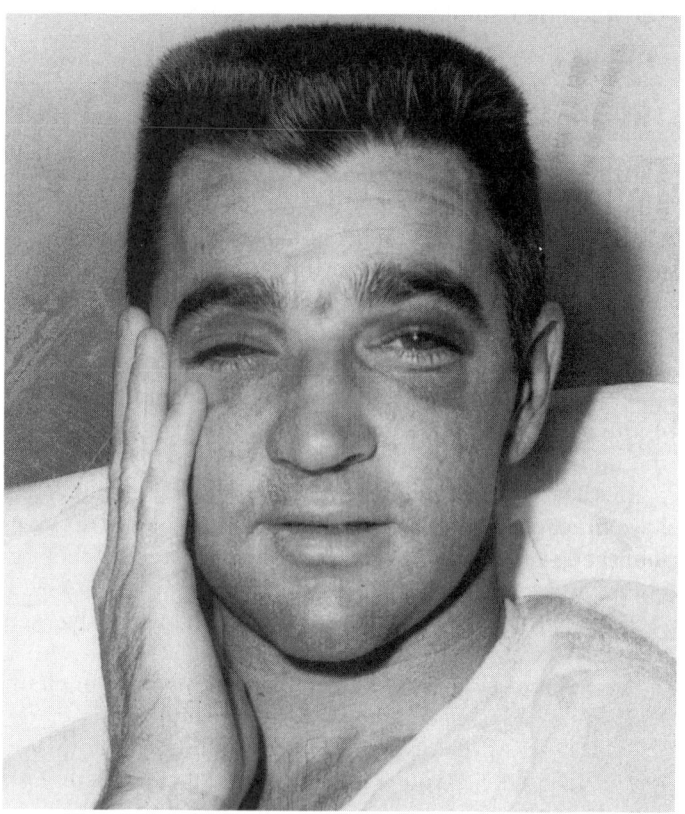

Shortstop Larry Brown suffered a fractured skull and other facial fractures in a frightening collision with left fielder Leon Wagner at Yankee Stadium on May 4, 1966. He was sidelined for six weeks.

thing—but I don't think he was very happy because I know Rigney was mad as hell."

A Unique "Run of the Mill" Game

It is one of baseball's most obscure records, and happened in one of the strangest games in history.

On June 9, 1908, the Cleveland club, then called the Naps, played the Boston Red Sox at League Park, and nothing like it has happened in the major leagues since then.

Here's how the *Cleveland Plain Dealer* described that game in which every player in the Naps lineup made a hit and scored a run in the same inning.

"It was a run of the mill game halfway through the contest. Boston enjoyed a 2–1 lead as the Naps went to bat in the fifth. But then it became a game that is unique in major league history.

"In that fifth inning each player in the Cleveland lineup made a hit and scored a run. (Nig Clarke actually scored two runs but he still had only one hit as he scored his second run of the inning after reaching base as the result of a Boston error.)

"Clarke started the Naps fifth with a single. In trying to advance Clarke with a sacrifice, Bill Hinchman popped to Amby McConnell. Piano Legs Hickman singled and so did Joe Birmingham. On Gavvy Cravath's wide throw to the plate, Clarke scored and Hickman and Birmingham reached second and third, respectively.

"Heinie Berger drove a single past Harry Lord and Hickman and Birmingham crossed the plate. Josh Clarke followed with another single and when Bill Bradley also hit safely, Berger scored."

At that point James "Deacon" McGuire, the Boston manager, decided he had seen enough of his pitcher, George Winter, and brought in Ralph Glaze.

George Stovall greeted the new pitcher with a base hit that registered Josh Clarke. Napoleon Lajoie, the Cleveland player-manager and second baseman, threw his bat at a wide one for a hit that filled the bases. Denny Sullivan in right muffed Nig Clarke's long fly and Bradley and Stovall were able to score.

"Hinchman got his hit for the inning. It was to center field for four bases [the only extra-base hit of the inning], driving in Lajoie and Nig Clarke ahead of him. Glaze then got Hickman and Birmingham to end the inning as a '10' was hung on the scoreboard. The fact that each team scored four more runs in the last three innings is of little importance."

As it turned out, however, those 10 runs Cleveland scored in the fifth inning were necessary as the Naps won the game, 15–6.

Gaylord Perry (left) and brother Jim (right), who pitched for the Minnesota Twins from 1963 to 1972, with their father, Evan Perry, in 1972. The Perry brothers were teammates with the Indians in 1974 and 1975.

The Pitch That Cost Sam $216

It happened during a game in Baltimore on September 14, 1969. The protagonists were Sam McDowell and American League senior umpire Larry Barnett, then a rookie working his first season.

McDowell was not pitching well and continually complained to Barnett. In the sixth inning, as the umpire recalled in a recent interview, "Sam said the magic words, called me a name I can't repeat, and I threw him out of the game."

The score was tied, 3–3, at the time, though the Indians lost, 7–3, after McDowell was succeeded by relievers Juan Pizarro, Gary Boyd, and Dick Ellsworth.

"On his way to the dugout McDowell took the ball and threw it up into the stands behind third base," said Barnett. "Naturally, I included that in my report.

"A few days later [American League President] Joe Cronin called me and asked where McDowell threw the ball, how far the ball went.

"I told him the best I could figure was that it landed about 10 feet from the top of the grandstand, about 205 rows up.

"So, as I later learned, Cronin fined McDowell $205. He based the amount on the number of feet the ball went, and charged McDowell a dollar a foot.

"But anybody who knew McDowell knows what Sam did next. He sent Cronin a check for $216 because, he said, the ball cleared the top of the stands and there were 216 rows in the stands."

When Averill's Career Almost Ended Early

The 13-year major league career of Earl Averill, which culminated in his 1975 election to the Hall of Fame, almost was ended in 1935 when the star center fielder nearly lost his right hand in an accident with a firecracker.

Averill, his wife, and their four sons were picnicking with three teammates and their families on June 26, when a firecracker exploded in his hand after he'd lighted it, dropped it, and then picked it up thinking the fuse had gone out.

According to newspaper accounts, the force of the explosion "seared the flesh off [Averill's] fingers and the palm of his right hand, and inflicted severe burns on his forehead and chest."

It was initially feared by Dr. Edward Castle, the Indians' club physician, that Averill's fingers might have to be amputated.

However, Averill's hand healed and, remarkably, he missed only 14 games, though the injuries he suffered obviously affected his play that year. Averill's batting average fell to .288, the first time he hit less than .300 since his arrival in Cleveland in 1929 upon his being purchased by the Indians from San Francisco of the Pacific Coast League.

Averill went on to play in the major leagues six more years, for Detroit as well as the Indians, and retired with a .318 lifetime average.

The accident occurred in the Cleveland suburb of Orange during an off-day in the Indians' schedule. Accompanying Averill, his wife, and his children were Tribe teammates Mel Harder, Odell Hale, and Joe Vosmik and their families.

The newspaper account stated: "After lunching, Averill and his sons [went] to shoot off some firecrackers. One of the firecrackers failed to explode and Averill, who had tossed it to the ground, picked it up again. The explosion occurred just as he was picking it up."

Indians manager Walter Johnson was quoted as being angered by the injury to Averill and said he had warned the players about fireworks.

"Strangely enough, I asked the fellows only a few days ago not to fool around with firecrackers. Averill and some of the other boys brought a bunch of them into the clubhouse and threw them at each other.

"It made me sore. There's not only the possibility of injury, but the aftereffect. That powder is poisonous. I don't know why ballplayers do it."

Lost in a Fog

Their critics would say they often played in a fog, but it wasn't until May 27, 1986, that the Indians actually were "fogged out."

Their game against Boston at the Stadium that night was called in the bottom of the sixth inning by umpire Larry Barnett because "baseball shouldn't be played under such conditions."

The Red Sox were 2–0 winners of the bizarre, abbreviated game that had been delayed twice for a total of 110 minutes before it was finally aborted.

The Indians, of course, were unhappy about Barnett's decision as they had runners on first and second with two out when the end was declared.

Barnett made his decision when Boston right fielder Dwight Evans jogged in to tell second base umpire Rocky Roe he couldn't see the batter.

Indians manager Pat Corrales was livid with anger when Barnett ended the game. "The umpires didn't call it, Evans did," charged Corrales. "He walked out of right field because he didn't want to play."

Corrales might have had a valid argument. Just prior to Evans' complaint, Boston center fielder Tony Armas made what was reported as "a miraculous catch" against the fence in right-center field. It robbed Mel Hall of an extra-base hit that probably would have tied the score, or possibly a homer."

Evans said he had to do something. "I'm standing up for the other outfielders, too. I'm not going to say I can see the ball when I can't. They had two runners on base, and what happens if they hit a high fly ball and it drops in? I'm not going to be a heel for the weather."

Earlier, during a delay in action, Indians coach Bobby Bonds hit a couple of fly balls with a fungo bat to test the visibility. Shortly thereafter the fog lifted slightly and the game was resumed. But only temporarily—until Evans' complaint convinced Barnett that enough was enough.

Emil "Dutch" Levsen started and pitched two complete games, allowing four hits in each and winning both, 6–1 and 5–1, in a doubleheader against the Red Sox in Boston on August 28, 1926. No pitcher has ever duplicated Levsen's feat—or even attempted it.

Moe Berg, a back-up catcher for the Indians in 1931 and 1934, and for several other teams during his major league career from 1923 to 1939, became a spy in Japan for the United States government prior to the start of World War II.

They Won't Let Max Forget

It was a game that Max Alvis has tried to forget ever since it was played on August 7, 1965, at Comiskey Park in Chicago.

"I remember like it happened yesterday because people are always kidding me, reminding me about it," said Alvis, the Indians' third baseman from 1963 to 1969. "I was never so embarrassed in all my life."

The incident that Alvis can't forget occurred in the bottom of the 10th inning with the Indians clinging to a 3–2 lead behind Luis Tiant. White Sox catcher J. C. Martin came to bat with one out, pinch runner Al Weis on first base, and lofted a pop fly that . . . well, let Alvis tell what happened.

"At first the ball started in foul territory, then began to drift fair, into the diamond. I broke quickly for the ball, but had to back up to stay with it because of the wind.

"As I was backpedaling the thought crossed my mind that I might be getting close to the base, but I said to myself, 'Oh, no, you've got plenty of room.'

"The next thing I know my head is bouncing off the ground and the ball landed right next to me for a hit.

"As I was backpedaling, I tripped over the bag. It was awful. I'll never live it down."

One of the reasons it was so embarrassing was that, after Martin reached base on the "hit," a subsequent single by Don Buford scored Weis with the tying run. Then Martin came home with the game winner on another single by Floyd Robinson for a 4–3 White Sox victory.

And the Band Played On

Even though the Indians sometimes fell flat and, in 1953, were making a habit of finishing second to the New York Yankees, the music was great.

That was the season an unusual mix of music and baseball was played at the Stadium. The Cleveland Orchestra scheduled about a dozen pregame concerts for the entertainment of the fans.

To accommodate the musicians, a stage was constructed in front of the bleachers and behind the center-field fence, and a special sound amplification system was installed.

The orchestra's inaugural performance was held on June 2, under the baton of conductor Louis Lane. The musical program consisted of standard pop tunes with a full orchestral rendition of "Take Me Out to the Ball Game" as the finale.

The performances were well received by music critics and baseball fans alike, but weren't resumed the following season.

Jim Bagby Sr., an Indians pitcher who won 31 games in 1920, became a minor league umpire after his major league career ended in 1923.

It Was a Very Bad Year

Three Indians pitchers lost their lives, and a fourth was so seriously injured that his career was in jeopardy, after two accidents marred the 1993 season.

The first occurred on March 22 in Clermont, Florida, near Winter Haven where the Indians were holding spring training. It was a day off from practice, and Steve Olin, Bob Ojeda, and Tim Crews and their families were picnicking at Crews' home on the shore of Little Lake Nellie in Clermont.

Olin and Crews were killed and Ojeda critically injured when the boat Crews was driving smashed into the dock jutting out from the shore of Little Lake Nellie. Ojeda was hospitalized for several months after suffering scalp and head injuries, but was able to return to the mound on August 7, to pitch two innings against the Orioles in Baltimore.

Then, a month after the season ended, Cliff Young was killed November 4 when he smashed his pickup truck into a tree near his home in Willis, Texas. He was dead at the scene of the accident.

Olin, 27, Crews, 31, and Ojeda, 35, were bass fishing in Crews' 18-foot, open-air boat. It was dusk, and apparently Crews did not see the dock. Olin was killed instantly, and Crews died a few hours later. Ojeda was hospitalized for nearly a month and didn't return to the Indians until late June.

Olin, who left wife Patti and three children, had become the year before one of the best relief pitchers in baseball, leading the Indians with 29 saves, eighth most in the American League, for a four-year major league total of 48.

Olin was up and down between Cleveland and Class AAA

Colorado Springs of the Pacific Coast League in 1989, 1990, and 1991, and in 1992 he appeared in 72 games, third most in the AL, with an 8–5 record and 2.34 earned run average.

Crews, who left wife Laurie and also had three children, was a nonroster player but was expected to be signed by the Indians to a major league contract. He previously pitched for Los Angeles from 1987 to 1992, compiling an 11–13 record, 3.44 ERA, and 15 saves.

Ojeda also had been signed as a free agent prior to the start of spring training in 1993; he was expected to be the Tribe's fifth starter. Ojeda started his career with Boston and pitched for the Red Sox from 1980 to 1985, New York Mets from 1986 to 1990, and Dodgers in 1991 and 1992,

compiling a major league career record of 113–97 with a 3.60 ERA.

After his return to the Indians, Ojeda appeared in nine games, seven as a starter, with a 2–1 record and 4.40 ERA. He became a free agent at the end of the season and signed a 1994 contract with the New York Yankees.

Young, 29, left wife Tamara and two sons. He pitched in 21 games, seven as a starter, for the Indians in 1993, with a 3–3 record and 4.62 ERA. He was signed as a minor league free agent prior to the season, after having pitched in the California Angels organization for 10 years.

Young spent parts of the 1990 and 1991 seasons with the Angels, for whom he appeared in 28 games, all in relief, with 2–1 record and 3.74 ERA.

It Was No April Fool's Joke

It was "April Fool's Day"—April 1, 1964—but what happened to Birdie Tebbetts was not a joke.

The 51-year-old manager of the Indians suffered a heart attack after practice that day in Tucson, Arizona, as spring training wound down and the season opener was less than two weeks away.

Tebbetts, who piloted the Tribe to a tie for fifth place, with a 79–83 record, in 1963, his first season at the helm, had high hopes for 1964, with a solid and deep pitching staff and several young players who were expected to blossom into stars.

The heart attack hit Tebbetts after he'd returned to the Indians' hotel following a workout that day, an open date in the Cactus League schedule.

He was initially attended by Regis McAuley, a *Cleveland Press* sportswriter covering the team, and then was rushed to St. Mary's Hospital, where he remained for several weeks. He

later went home to Anna Maria Island, Florida, to continue his recuperation.

George Strickland, then the Indians' third base coach, was named acting manager by general manager Gabe Paul, and Solly Hemus, a former National League manager and coach, was added to the staff, which also included Early Wynn and Elmer Valo.

Indians' hopes were high that spring with a pitching staff that included veteran starters Dick Donovan, Mudcat Grant, and Pedro Ramos, highly regarded youngster Sam McDowell, and rookies Sonny Siebert and Tommy John, as well as relievers Gary Bell, Don McMahon, Jerry Walker, and Ted Abernathy.

What's more, third baseman Max Alvis and center fielder Vic Davalillo were coming off impressive rookie seasons, catcher Joe Azcue had batted .284 with 14 homers after he'd

Indians pitcher Mel Harder was a member of the committee that met with major league club owners in New York in 1946 to form the Major League Baseball Players Association. Attending the meeting (clockwise from lower left) are Billy Herman, Dixie Walker, Marty Marion, Chicago Cubs owner William Wrigley, Boston Red Sox owner Tom Yawkey, New York Yankees owner Larry McPhail, Johnny Murphy, Joe Kuhel, Harder, unidentified participant, St. Louis Cardinals owner Sam Breadon, American League president William Harridge, and National League president Ford Frick.

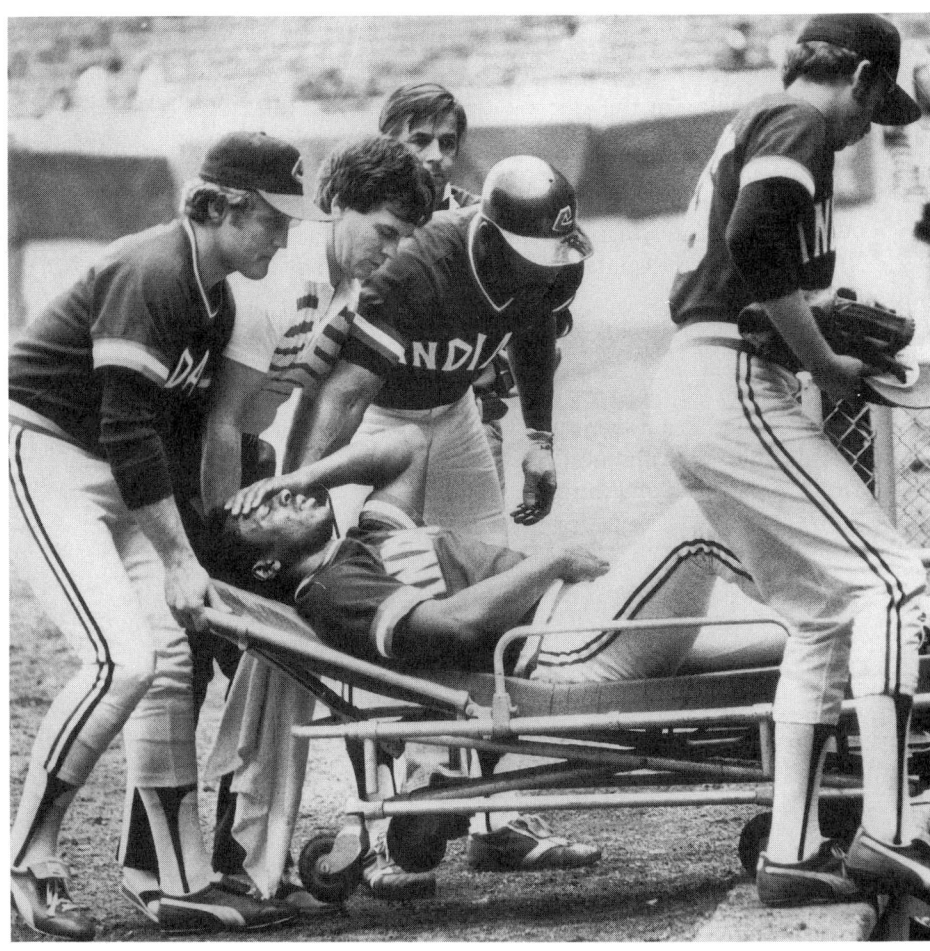

Indians outfielder Paul Dade is carried from the field on a stretcher after being hit by a pitched ball in 1977. Trainer Jim Warfield (second from the left) is assisted by outfielder Jim Norris (far left), an unidentified player, and pitcher Jim Kern (far right).

been acquired from the Kansas City Athletics in mid-1963, and the Indians also were looking for solid performances from outfielders Leon Wagner, Tito Francona, Al Smith, and rookie Tommie Agee, with Dick Howser, Woodie Held, Larry Brown, Jerry Kindall, and Fred Whitfield battling for infield positions.

As it turned out, the Indians, after getting off to an 11–5 start under Strickland, faltered in mid-May, fell below .500 (30–31) on June 23, and finished in sixth place with a 79–83 record, 20 games behind the New York Yankees.

Tebbetts made a full recovery from his heart attack and returned to the team on July 3, but didn't resume his full managerial duties until August 14, at which time the Indians were in seventh place with a 54–61 record.

He managed the Indians again in 1965 and into 1966, until he resigned under pressure on August 19 and again was replaced on an interim basis by Strickland. The Indians' record when Birdie left was 66–57, and they finished the season at 81–81, in fifth place.

A "Heady" Victory for the Tribe

It could be said that Texas right fielder Jose Canseco got the Indians "headed" in the right direction—literally and figuratively—in their 7–6 victory over the Rangers at the Stadium on May 26, 1993.

In the fourth inning, with the Rangers leading, 3–1, the Tribe's Carlos Martinez lofted a fly to right field that should have been caught by Canseco against the fence.

It wasn't. Instead, the ball went through Canseco's glove, hit him in the head, and bounced over the fence for a home run.

"I couldn't believe [Canseco] was still on his feet after he got conked," said Indians manager Mike Hargrove after Martinez's solo homer—however tainted anyone considered it to be—cut the Indians' deficit to 3–2.

The next two batters reached, Reggie Jefferson when he was hit by a pitch and Glenallen Hill on a walk, before Texas pitcher Kenny Rogers retired the next two batters. Then Thomas Howard also walked, and Felix Fermin singled for two runs and a 4–3 lead.

Thereafter the Indians were never headed, so to speak, taking a 7–3 lead in the sixth inning, which was enough to withstand Rangers' rallies that produced single runs in the seventh, eighth, and ninth innings.

Canseco insisted he wasn't upset by his gaffe. "I'll be on ESPN for a month . . . I'm sure it was very entertaining," he quipped. "But how can I be embarrassed? I've been through everything in baseball."

Satchel Paige's Rules for Longevity

He was still pitching at the ripe old age of 59, so maybe Satchel Paige was right in his adherence to what he called his "rules" for staying young.

They were

1. "Avoid fried meats which angry up the blood."

2. "If your stomach disputes you, lie down and pacify it with cool thoughts."

3. "Keep the juices flowing by jangling around gently as you move."

4. "Go very light on the vices, such as carrying on in society—the social ramble ain't restful."

5. "Avoid running at all times."

6. "Don't look back. Something might be gaining on you."

Former Indians pitcher Satchel Paige appeared as a cavalry sergeant in the movie *The Wonderful Country,* filmed in Durango, Mexico in 1959.

Schaefer's Unprecedented Stolen Base

Few will dispute that it was the most unusual play every performed against a Cleveland team—perhaps even by or against any team in major league baseball history.

It was executed by the legendary Germany Schaefer, who is reputed to have been one of baseball's all-time most eccentric players, and reportedly occurred in 1908 when Cleveland, then nicknamed the Naps, played Detroit at League Park.

Schaefer, who finished his career as a member of the Indians in 1918, was playing for the Tigers at the time. According to an account in Lawrence Ritter's *The Glory of Their Times,* Schaefer actually stole first base, and Detroit won the game, partly because of the unusual play.

The story, as told by Schaefer's teammate, Davy Jones:

"I saw Germany Schaefer steal first base. Yes, first base. They say it can't be done, but I saw him do it. In fact, I was standing right on third base, with my eyes popping out, when he did it.

"The score was tied in a late inning. I was on third base, Schaefer on first, and [Sam] Crawford was at bat. Before the pitcher wound up, Schaefer flashed me the sign for the double steal—meaning he'd take off for second on the next pitch, and when the catcher threw the ball to second, I'd take off for home.

"Well, the pitcher wound up and pitched, and sure enough Schaefer stole second. But I had to stay right where I was, on third, because Nig Clarke, the Cleveland catcher, just held on to the ball. He refused to throw to second, knowing I'd probably make it home if he did.

"So now we have men on second and third. Well, on the next pitch Schaefer yelled, 'Let's try it again!' And with a bloodcurdling shout he took off like a wild Indian back to first base, and dove in headfirst in a cloud of dust. He figured the catcher might throw to first—since he evidently wouldn't throw to second—and then I could come home same as before.

"But nothing happened. Nothing at all. Everybody just stood there and watched Schaefer, with their mouths open, not knowing what the devil was going on. Me, too. Even if the catcher had thrown to first, I was too stunned to move, I'll tell you that. But the catcher didn't throw. He just stared!

"In fact, George Stovall, the Cleveland first baseman, was playing way back and didn't even come in to cover the bag. He just watched this madman running the wrong way on the base path and didn't know what to do.

"The umpires were just as confused as everybody else. However, it turned out that at that time there wasn't any rule against a guy going from second back to first, if that's the way he wanted to play baseball, so they had to let it stand.

"So there we were, back where we started, with Schaefer on first and me on third. And on the next pitch darned if he didn't let out another war whoop and take off again for second base. By this time the Cleveland catcher evidently had enough, because he finally threw to second to get Schaefer,

Cleveland fans were so outraged in 1960 when Frank Lane traded Rocky Colavito to Detroit for Harvey Kuenn that they hanged the Indians general manager in effigy.

and when he did I took off for home and both of us were safe."

Jones never reported the score of the game, though the Tigers evidently won.

And a few years later the rule was changed, preventing a repeat of Schaefer's unprecedented steal of first base.

Pat Seerey's Brush with Fame

In the long history of major league baseball only 12 players have hit four home runs in one game. None of the 12 did it twice, though Pat Seerey, in his brief seven-year career, came the closest—and might have been successful in achieving the feat if he had been faster on his feet.

Seerey, playing for the Chicago White Sox in 1948, smashed four homers in an 11-inning, 12–11, victory over the Philadelphia Athletics in Shibe Park in the first game of a doubleheader on Sunday, July 18. It was Seerey's fourth homer in the final inning that gave the White Sox their one-run margin.

Just three years earlier, on Friday, July 13, 1945, when he was a member of the Indians, Seerey walloped three homers,

in the third, fourth, and seventh innings, as Cleveland beat New York, 14–6, in Yankee Stadium.

Seerey's homers followed a first-inning triple, a liner that skipped to the 457-foot sign in left-center field. A faster runner than the 5-10, 200-pound Seerey—whose nickname was "Fat Pat"—could have turned the drive into an inside-the-park homer, which, of course, would have given him four for the game.

Sportswriter Alex Zirin, in his report in the *Cleveland Plain Dealer* the next morning, wrote: "Everyone in the park, with the exception of the Yankees, was pulling for Pat when he batted in the ninth with a chance to tie [Lou] Gehrig's feat of four home runs in a game, but Pat lined out and the groans were loud indeed."

Trades, Acquisitions, and Sales

It was in the winter of 1915–16 that Tris Speaker waited not-so-patiently at his home in Hubbard, Texas, for his contract to arrive from the Boston Red Sox.

His eagerness was understandable. Speaker, then 28, was thought to be at the peak of his career, having put together seven outstanding seasons as the center fielder for the Red Sox. He batted .383 in 1912 and .363 in 1913, and he played a major role in winning American League pennants for Boston in 1912 and 1915.

Speaker also was the centerpiece, the catalyst of what was then called Boston's "dream outfield," playing between left fielder Duffy Lewis and right fielder Harry Hooper. He seemed to have every reason to expect a large raise over the $9,000 he was paid in 1915, when he hit .322.

However, when the contract arrived, instead of the $15,000 Speaker sought, he was chagrined to discover that Red Sox owner Joe Lannin was offering only the same salary he was paid the previous season.

Speaker, nicknamed the "Gray Eagle," was adamant in his refusal to sign the 1916 contract, which led to his being traded to the Indians in a deal that must be considered the best in the history of the Cleveland franchise (and one of the worst for Boston).

To get Speaker, the Indians gave up pitcher Sad Sam Jones, infielder Fred Thomas, and $55,000. The Gray Eagle went on to play 22 seasons in the major leagues, 11 in Cleveland, compiling a .345 career batting average, fifth best of all time, and was elected to the Hall of Fame in 1937.

What's more, Speaker became manager of the Indians in 1919, and the following season, when he batted .388 and drove in 107 runs, he led them to their first pennant and world championship.

All of which is not to say that the Indians did not pay dearly for Speaker.

Jones, whose major league record was only 4–9 in parts of two seasons (1914 and 1915) with the Indians, went on to have a very good career, though Thomas didn't stick with the Red Sox until 1918 and was back in the minors in 1921.

Jones won 225 games while losing 208 in 20 seasons with Boston (1916–21), the New York Yankees (1922–26), St. Louis Browns (1927), Washington Senators (1928–31), and Chicago White Sox (1932–35).

And the $55,000, along with Jones and Thomas, the Indians had to give the Red Sox for Speaker was the largest price paid for any player until then, making it the biggest deal in the history of the game at that time.

But without Speaker the Indians undoubtedly would not have won the pennant in 1920, nor have been a contender in 1918, 1919, 1921, and 1926.

Close behind the Speaker deal in importance to the franchise were two others, without which the Indians probably would not have won two other pennants, in 1948 and 1954.

They stole pitcher Early Wynn and first baseman Mickey Vernon from the Senators in the winter of 1948–49, three years after the acquisition of pitcher Gene Bearden in a five-player deal with the Yankees.

Wynn registered 23 victories in 1954, and Bearden was the American League Rookie of the Year when he won 20 games, including the pennant playoff against the Red Sox, in 1948. Bearden also was 1–0 and saved the deciding sixth-game victory against the Boston Braves in the World Series.

The foregoing, however, is not to suggest that the Indians' track record in the trade mart has been exemplary.

The franchise has been guilty of many mistakes, beginning as far back as 1915, ironically the year before the Indians obtained Speaker. On August 20, 1915, they dealt one of the game's potentially greatest hitters, Shoeless Joe Jackson, to the Chicago White Sox.

Center fielder Tris Speaker was acquired from the Boston Red Sox in 1916 for pitcher Sad Sam Jones, third baseman Fred Thomas, and $55,000. After eleven years with the Indians, he moved on to Washington in 1927 (hence the "W" on the cap) and ended his career with Philadelphia in 1928.

The career of Shoeless Joe Jackson probably would have been drastically different if he had not been traded by Cleveland in 1915 to the Chicago White Sox. In 1919, he was implicated in the conspiracy to fix the World Series and was banned from baseball.

It is fascinating to speculate what might have resulted for Jackson—as well as to the Indians and White Sox—if he'd not been traded.

If he had remained in Cleveland to play alongside the great Speaker, would the infamous "Black Sox" scandal—in which eight Chicago White Sox players, including Jackson, were barred for life from baseball for allegedly conspiring to fix the 1919 World Series—not have occurred?

And if Jackson had been a member of the Indians, would they and not the White Sox have won the pennant in 1919 when Cleveland finished second by 3½ games behind Chicago?

But trading away Jackson isn't even regarded as the worst in Tribe history. At least it's not to observers who were around in 1960, when general manager Frank Lane sent Rocky Colavito to Detroit for Harvey Kuenn.

It enraged most of the fans and resulted in absolute contempt for Lane—who is still held in contempt for that deal and others—and still is blamed for the Indians' decline from glory in 1960, the beginning of the franchise's three decades of noncontender status.

Rating the Indians' trades over the years is a subjective endeavor, of course, and certainly opinions will differ as to the degree of good and bad, and which deals were the best and worst.

The following lists were formulated based on contributions made by the players the Indians acquired, and not necessarily on the production of those who went elsewhere.

10 Best Trades

1. April 8, 1916

Pitcher Sad Sam Jones, third baseman Fred Thomas, and $55,000 to the Boston Red Sox for center fielder Tris Speaker.

Speaker performed brilliantly for the Indians, offensively and defensively, during his 11 years in Cleveland. He also was one of the franchise's most successful managers, serving in that capacity from 1919 to 1926, during which his teams won 616 games, second most in Tribe history, while losing 520, for a .542 won-lost percentage. Jones also went on to have a very good career, posting a 225–208 mark over 20 seasons (1916–35) for five teams (Boston Red Sox, New York Yankees, St. Louis Browns, Washington Senators, and Chicago White Sox). Thomas played in only 247 major league games over parts of three seasons for three teams after going to Boston.

2. December 20, 1946

Catcher Sherman Lollar and second baseman Ray Mack to the New York Yankees for pitchers Gene Bearden and Al Gettel and outfielder Hal Peck.

Bearden had only one good season with the Indians, but they couldn't have won the pennant and World Series in 1948 without him. Gettel was 11–10 in 1947, but was traded the following season. Peck batted .293 in 114 games in 1947 and was a consistent pinch hitter in 1948 and 1949. Lollar, a rookie when traded to the Yankees, would have played behind Jim Hegan had he remained with the Indians. He became a

Promising young catcher Sherman Lollar was traded with second baseman Ray Mack to the New York Yankees in December 1946 in the deal that brought pitchers Gene Bearden and Al Gettel, and outfielder Hal Peck to the Indians.

regular after joining the St. Louis Browns in 1949, and caught for the Chicago White Sox from 1952 to 1963. Mack played only one game for the Yankees and was traded to the Chicago Cubs in 1947, his last season in the major leagues.

3. December 14, 1948

Pitchers Joe Haynes and Eddie Klieman and first baseman Eddie Robinson to the Washington Senators for pitcher Early Wynn and first baseman Mickey Vernon.

Knowing that Washington owner Clark Griffith desperately wanted to acquire his son-in-law, Haynes, Bill Veeck got him from the White Sox (in an even-up deal for second-string catcher Joe Tipton). Twenty-two days later, before Haynes ever donned a Cleveland uniform, Veeck packaged him in the trade for Wynn and Vernon. Wynn went 163–100 the next nine seasons, though Vernon was traded back to the Senators in 1950. Haynes was 10–21 from 1949 to 1952 and was finished as a major league pitcher. Klieman pitched two games for Washington, was traded to the White Sox for whom he was 2–0 in 1949, and ended his career with the Philadelphia Athletics in 1950.

Greatness always was predicted for Sam McDowell, but he had a drinking problem and never lived up to expectations. On November 29, 1971 the Indians traded McDowell for pitcher Gaylord Perry and shortstop Frank Duffy in what proved to be one of the club's best deals.

4. November 29, 1971

Pitcher Sam McDowell to the San Francisco Giants for pitcher Gaylord Perry and shortstop Frank Duffy.

When the Indians solicited bids for the always-promising left-handed pitcher, the best offer came from San Francisco, then managed by Charlie Fox, who had been a scout for the Giants and tried to sign McDowell in 1960. At the time, the Giants also were concerned that the National League would crack down on Perry because of allegations that he threw illegal spitball pitches. The deal was made when they agreed to include rookie backup shortstop Frank Duffy. Perry went on to compile a 70–57 record for the Indians the next three and a half seasons, and Duffy anchored their infield for six seasons. McDowell won only 19 games and lost 25 the next four years, and his major league career ended in 1975.

5. October 19, 1946

Pitcher Allie Reynolds to the New York Yankees for second baseman Joe Gordon and third baseman Eddie Bockman.

Critics point out that Reynolds helped the Yankees win six pennants from 1947 to 1953, though only once (1945, when his record was 18–12) did he win more than 11 games in any of his four

Allie Reynolds helped the New York Yankees win six pennants in seven seasons after he was traded by the Indians on October 19, 1946, but the Indians would not have won the pennant in 1948 if not for second baseman Joe Gordon, whom they acquired (along with utility infielder Eddie Bockman) for Reynolds.

seasons with the Indians. But Gordon was indispensable to the Indians as he teamed with Lou Boudreau to provide them with the best double-play combination in the American League. Gordon also was a leader in 1948 when the Indians won their second pennant and world's championship. He hammered 32 homers and drove in 124 runs with a .280 batting average that year, and he was a mainstay of the infield through 1950. Bockman's contributions as a utility infielder were minor in 1947, and he was sold to Pittsburgh in 1948.

6. December 6, 1989

Outfielder Joe Carter to the San Diego Padres for catcher Sandy Alomar, Jr., third baseman Carlos Baerga, and outfielder Chris James.

Carter had several good seasons in Cleveland after he was acquired as a rookie in a seven-player deal with the Chicago Cubs in June 1984, and he went on to become one of the best players in the major leagues. But two of the players Cleveland got for Carter, Sandy Alomar, Jr., and Carlos Baerga, also are recognized as being among the best in baseball. Alomar was the American League's Rookie of the Year in 1990, and Baerga batted .312, .321, and .314 with 75 home runs and 389 RBIs from 1992 to 1995. James played two seasons with the Indians, batting .299 in 140 games in 1990, was released, and signed

as a free agent with San Francisco. He has since gone on to play for Houston, Texas, and Boston.

7. July 30, 1910

Outfielder Bris Lord to the Philadelphia Athletics for utility infielder Morris Rath and the opportunity to purchase minor league outfielder Joe Jackson.

Athletics owner Connie Mack wanted desperately to regain Lord, who had played for Philadelphia from 1905 to 1907 and for Cleveland in 1909. To make the deal, Mack gave Rath to Naps owner Charles Somers, along with the right to buy Jackson. Mack said, "I let [Somers] have Jackson because I was anxious to do him a good turn in appreciation for the way he had helped us out in Philadelphia." Jackson won the batting championships of the Class D Carolina Association in 1908, the Class C South Atlantic League in 1909, and the Class A Southern Association while playing for New Orleans in 1910, after being sold to the Naps. He was recalled by Cleveland in September 1910, hit .387 in 20 games, then batted .408 in 1911.

8. March 1, 1919

Outfielder Braggo Roth to the Philadelphia Athletics for third baseman Larry Gardner, outfielder Charlie Jamieson, and pitcher Elmer Myers.

Roth was a consistent hitter for Cleveland from 1916 to 1918 and was one of the stolen-base leaders each season. But two of the three players acquired for Roth played prominent roles in the Indians' success in 1920, when they won the pennant and World Series, and beyond. Gardner, Tris Speaker's teammate with the Boston Red Sox before Speaker became the Indians' player-manager in 1919, hit .310 in 1920 and a career-high .319 in 1921. Jamieson was one of the most popular players in franchise history while batting .300 or better in 10 of his subsequent 14 seasons in Cleveland. Myers compiled a 10–11 record in 1919 and part of 1920 before he was sold to the Red Sox.

9. December 10, 1991

Catcher Eddie Taubensee and pitcher Willie Blair to the Houston Astros for outfielder Kenny Lofton and second baseman Dave Rohde.

Lofton was best known as the sixth man on the nationally ranked University of Arizona basketball team that reached the NCAA Final Four in 1988. Though he did not play college baseball until his senior year, Lofton was an 18th-round selection by Houston in the 1988 draft. The Astros, in need of a left-handed-hitting catcher, traded Lofton and Rohde, a minor league infielder, for Taubensee, who had been acquired as a minor leaguer from Oakland in April 1991, and Blair, who also had spent most of his career in the minors. Taubensee played part-time for the As-

tros in 1992 and 1993 and for Cincinnati in 1994 and 1995, while Lofton became a star almost immediately upon joining the Indians in 1992.

10. October 3, 1978

Pitcher Jim Kern and shortstop Larvell Blanks to the Texas Rangers for pitcher Len Barker and outfielder Bobby Bonds.

After finishing fifth, 28½ games behind New York in the AL East in 1977, the Indians sought offensive and starting-pitching help. Figuring that Kern was

near the end as a premier reliever (though he had one more outstanding season in 1979) and that they no longer needed Blanks, a utility infielder, they sent them to Texas for Barker, who pitched well through 1982, including a perfect game in 1981, and Bonds, who batted .275 with 25 homers and 85 RBIs his only season in Cleveland. Enhancing the deal for the Indians was that they later dealt Bonds for pitcher John Denny and a minor league player, and Barker for Brett Butler, Brook Jacoby, a minor leaguer, and $150,000 in August 1983.

10 Worst Trades

1. April 17, 1960

Outfielder Rocky Colavito to the Detroit Tigers for outfielder Harvey Kuenn.

This was the deal that longtime Indians fans still lament and that many consider the beginning of the organization's 35-year decline. Colavito was not only one of baseball's premier sluggers (129 home runs in four seasons), but also one of the most popular players in franchise history. General manager Frank Lane called Colavito "selfish" because of his determination to hit home runs and considered Kuenn, the reigning AL batting champion, after compiling a .353 average in 1959, a complete player. As it turned out, Colavito went on to hit 173 homers the next five seasons, while Kuenn's average fell to .308 in 1960, after which he was traded to San Francisco.

2. April 12, 1960

First baseman Norm Cash to the Detroit Tigers for third baseman Steve Demeter.

Five days before Frank Lane traded fan favorite Rocky Colavito, he presented the Tigers with Cash, who would win the AL batting championship with a .361 average in 1961 when he hit 41 homers and drove in 132 runs. Cash was expendable because the Indians had Vic Power at first base, and Lane believed they needed a third baseman. Though Demeter had outstanding minor league statistics, he played only four games for the Indians, going 0-for-5. Cash, acquired in a seven-player deal with the Chicago White Sox in Decem-

Only five days before the Detroit Tigers acquired Rocky Colavito for Harvey Kuenn, they also stole first baseman Norm Cash from the Indians. General manager Frank Lane, determined to plug what he considered a hole at third base, traded Cash, then a minor league first baseman, for minor league hitting star Steve Demeter. Cash blossomed almost immediately, however, hitting .286 for the Tigers in 1960, and won the American League batting championship with a .361 average the following season. He played for the Tigers through 1974.

ber 1959, never appeared in a regular-season game for Cleveland, but played 17 years in the major leagues, with a career average of .271, 377 homers, and 1,103 RBIs.

3. December 4, 1957

Pitcher Early Wynn and outfielder Al Smith to the Chicago White Sox for outfielder Minnie Minoso and third baseman Fred Hatfield.

Early Wynn figured in two big deals for the Indians, one of which was good, the other very bad. The Indians got Wynn on December 14, 1948, with first baseman Mickey Vernon from Washington, in exchange for pitchers Joe Haynes and Ed Klieman, and first baseman Eddie Robinson. But nine years later, on December 4, 1957, Wynn was traded to the Chicago White Sox with outfielder Al Smith, for outfielder Minnie Minoso and utility infielder Fred Hatfield. Wynn was a 22 game winner for the White Sox in 1959, when they won the pennant, and he won the American League Cy Young Award.

While the acquisition of Early Wynn in December 1948 was the third-best deal in the history of the Indians, trading him with Smith nine years later was the third worst. (All three trades at the top of the "worst" list were made by Frank Lane.) Trading Wynn was Lane's first deal when he became general manager of the Indians on November 12, 1957. It was motivated by Lane's desire to re-acquire one of his favorites, Minoso, who had been traded away by Cleveland six years earlier (in a deal for reliever Lou Brissie). Al Lopez, who had managed Wynn and Smith in Cleveland, figured correctly that both veterans were still able to play, while Minoso was near the end of his career, and agreed to Hatfield as a "throw-in" at Lane's request.

4. April 3, 1974

Third baseman Pedro Guerrero to the Los Angeles Dodgers for pitcher Bruce Ellingsen.

When Phil Seghi traded Guerrero for Ellingsen, both were little-known minor leaguers. Guerrero had been signed by the Indians in January 1973 upon his arrival from Cuba, and Ellingsen had been drafted by the Dodgers in 1968. The Indians needed a left-handed reliever, and Ellingsen's minor league statistics were impressive. However, he failed to make the team in 1974 and was sent to Class AAA Oklahoma City until July 1. After rejoining the Indians, Ellingsen appeared in 16 games with a 1–1 record and 3.21 ERA. But that was Ellingsen's only season in the major leagues. Guerrero played 15 years for the Dodgers and St. Louis Cardinals, hitting .300 with 215 homers and 898 RBIs.

5. June 14, 1950

First baseman Mickey Vernon to the Washington Senators for pitcher Dick Weik.

This was another bad deal that negated one of the Indians' all-time best. They originally acquired Vernon in December 1948, but kept him only slightly more than one season, 1949, during which he batted .291 with 18 homers. With Luke Easter setting slugging records at Class AAA San Diego, general manager Hank Greenberg traded Vernon back to the Senators for Weik, who appeared in 11 games with a 1–3 record the rest of 1950. He was in the military service in 1951 and 1952 and was traded to Detroit in 1953. Vernon played 10 more seasons in the majors, winning the AL batting championship with a .337 average for the Senators in 1953.

Tommie Agee, who went on to become a star for the New York Mets after being included in the 1965 deal the brought Rocky Colavito back to Cleveland.

6. January 20, 1965

Pitcher Tommy John, catcher John Romano, and outfielder Tommie Agee to the Chicago White Sox (in a deal that also involved the Kansas City Athletics) for outfielder Rocky Colavito and catcher Camilo Carreon.

Cleveland fans still complain about the 1960 trade that sent Rocky Colavito to Detroit, but Gabe Paul's deal that returned the slugger was almost as bad. Colavito was nearing the end of his career and played only three more seasons, while Carreon caught only 19 games in 1965 and four for Baltimore in 1966, then never played in the major leagues again. John, whose record was 2–11 in less than two full seasons with Cleveland, went on to win 288 major league games through 1989; Agee became a star with the 1969 world champion New York Mets and played in the majors through 1973, compiling a career average of .255; and Romano played three more seasons for the White Sox and St. Louis Cardinals.

7. March 30, 1978

Pitcher Dennis Eckersley and catcher Fred Kendall to the Boston Red Sox for pitchers Rick Wise and Mike Paxton, catcher Bo Diaz, and third baseman–outfielder Ted Cox.

Eckersley, then young and erratic, and Kendall, a good receiver but weak hitter, were packaged for what Phil Seghi

Dennis Eckersley, one of major league baseball's greatest relievers, was traded by the Indians, with catcher Fred Kendall, to the Boston Red Sox on March 30, 1978, for pitchers Rick Wise and Mike Paxton, catcher Bo Diaz, and third baseman Ted Cox. None of them played well for Cleveland, while Eckersley continues—18 seasons later—to be one of the most dependable relief pitchers in the major leagues.

considered were three of Boston's best young players, along with Wise, a veteran. Seghi compared Diaz to Johnny Bench, though he played only 198 games over the next four years and was sent packing in a minor league deal; Paxton was 20–19 in three seasons and was never heard from again; Cox, who was expected to hit 30-plus homers a year, played two seasons and batted .233 and .212 with five homers; and though Wise was 24–29 in 1978 and 1979, he departed as a free agent. Though Kendall retired in 1981, Eckersley was still pitching in 1995 and had become one of the game's greatest relievers.

8. August 20, 1915

Outfielder Joe Jackson to the Chicago White Sox for outfielders Braggo Roth and Larry Chappell, pitcher Ed Klepfer, and a reported $31,500.

Fans always will wonder what might have been if Cleveland had not traded Jackson for Roth, Chappell, and Klepfer. It's possible that Jackson would have helped the Indians win the pennant in 1917, 1918, and 1919 and that the White Sox would not have thrown the 1919 World Series if he had not been on the team.

And if Jackson had remained with Cleveland, he probably would be in the Hall of Fame. As for the players the Indians got for Jackson, Chappell played three games in 1916, was dealt to Boston, and retired after four games in 1917; Roth played three seasons for the Indians, batting a high of .286, and was traded away; and Klepfer compiled a 21–16 record through 1919 and retired.

9. April 19, 1969

Pitchers Sonny Siebert and Vicente Romo and catcher Joe Azcue to the Boston Red Sox for outfielder–first baseman Ken Harrelson and pitchers Dick Ellsworth and Juan Pizarro.

General manager/manager Alvin Dark was so determined to get his buddy Harrelson with the Indians that he made a deal that hurt the club for several years. Though Azcue retired in 1973, Siebert won 79 games while losing 66 through 1975, and Romo registered 40 saves in the next seven seasons. Though Harrelson hit 27 homers for the Indians in 1969, he batted only .222 in 149 games and suffered a badly broken ankle in spring training of 1970 that all but ended his career. He played only 17 games that season, appeared in 52 in 1971, and retired. Ellsworth and Pizarro were nonentities. Ellsworth went 6–9 in 1969, had a 3–3 record in 1970, and was sold to Milwaukee; and Pizarro was 3–3 in 48 relief appearances for the Indians in 1969, then was sold to Oakland for the waiver price in late September.

10. December 6, 1988

Shortstop–second baseman Julio Franco to the Texas Rangers for first baseman Pete O'Brien, second baseman Jerry Browne, and outfielder Oddibe McDowell.

Branch Rickey would have called it "addition by subtraction," though it didn't turn out that way for the Indians after they got rid of Franco. They wanted Franco to switch to second base, a move he resisted (though he agreed to do so for the Rangers). Franco had four outstanding seasons in his five years with Texas, winning the batting title with a .341 average in 1991. He joined the Chicago White Sox as a free agent and hit .319 in 1994, then signed to play in Japan. Browne had two good seasons for the Indians in 1989 and 1990, but slumped in 1991 and became a free agent. O'Brien also became a free agent and left after one season, and McDowell was traded to Atlanta on July 2, 1989.

T hen, too, as Bill Veeck often said, "Some of the best deals are those that aren't made."

It's true, as was the case on at least two occasions in Veeck's ownership of the Indians.

Shortly after he purchased the club in June 1946, Veeck verbally agreed to sell to the Washington Senators, for the waiver price, the contract of Bob Lemon, who was at that time still a light-hitting outfielder–third baseman.

And a year later, after the Indians finished a distant fourth in the American League, Veeck wanted to trade player-manager Lou Boudreau to the St. Louis Browns.

The sale of Lemon was called off by Veeck because it had been "prematurely announced" by Clark Griffith, the owner of the Senators.

Veeck wanted to withhold the story until the following day in deference to the morning newspapers. Griffith, however, was eager to get the news out and leaked it to the media in Washington.

When Veeck heard what Griffith did, he angrily called off the deal, saying the papers hadn't been signed, even though Lemon was packed and ready to leave for Washington.

Shortly thereafter Lemon became a pitcher, won four games while losing five the remainder of that season, and wound up in the Hall of Fame with a 207–128 career record.

In the case of Veeck's desire to trade Boudreau, he planned to do so in order to hire Al Lopez to manage the team. Lopez had been the Indians' backup catcher in 1947 and was scheduled to manage Class AAA Indianapolis in 1948.

Veeck reportedly was ready to send Boudreau, outfielder George "Catfish" Metkovich, and $100,000 to the Browns for shortstop Vernon Stephens, outfielder Paul Lehner, and pitchers Jack Kramer and Ellis Kinder.

However, when that story leaked out during the 1947 World Series, fans in Cleveland were outraged and flooded Veeck with complaints.

As it turned out, the deal never materialized. Veeck, in a shrewd public relations gesture, claimed he called it off as a matter of "bowing to the will of the fans."

There was speculation, however, that the trade was killed by the Browns because they received a better offer for Stephens, sending him, along with Kramer, to the Boston Red Sox on November 17.

In exchange for Stephens and Kramer, the Browns received $310,000 and six players—catcher Roy Partee, shortstop Eddie Pellagrini, outfielder Pete Layden, and pitchers Al Widmar, Jim Wilson, and Joe Ostrowski.

On the other hand, there also were several proposed deals that, had they been made, probably would have benefited the Indians.

During spring training in 1908, Charles W. Somers, the owner of the Cleveland franchise then called the Naps, received a telephone call from Detroit Tigers manager Hughie

Gaylord Perry became the ace of the Indians staff after he was acquired, with shortstop Frank Duffy, in trade for Sam McDowell. Perry won 70 games for the Indians from 1972 until he was traded on June 13, 1975. Making the trade for McDowell look even better is the fact that Duffy took over as the Indians regular shortstop for six seasons, from 1972 to 1977.

Jennings. "I'd like to make a deal," said Jennings. "I'll give you Ty Cobb for Elmer Flick, even up."

Cobb, then only 21 and preparing for his second full season with the Tigers, had won the AL batting championship with a .350 average in 1907. Flick, 32, had batted .302 in his 10th season in the major leagues.

But Somers said no to the offer, because, it was reported, "Maybe [Flick] isn't quite as good a batter as Cobb, but he's much nicer to have on the team. We don't want any troublemakers either."

Nineteen years later, in November of 1927, shortly after Alva Bradley bought the franchise, he offered the New York Yankees $150,000—a tremendous amount of money at that time—for the contract of a young first baseman named Lou Gehrig.

When Ed Barrow, the owner of the Yankees, rejected the offer, Bradley raised his bid to $175,000, plus first baseman George Burns.

Rebuffed again, Bradley increased his bid to $250,000, but the answer was still no.

And in 1947, the year that Veeck purchased the contract of Larry Doby from the Newark Eagles, making Doby the first black player in the American League, the Indians owner rejected an opportunity to also purchase Monte Irvin.

Two years later Irvin joined the New York Giants and played in the major leagues through 1956, compiling a .293 career batting average.

Just as it is fascinating to speculate as to what might have been if Somers had said yes to the proposal for Cobb, or if the Yankees had agreed to sell Gehrig to the Indians, or if Veeck had signed Irvin as well as Doby, it also is interesting to speculate on the possible result of a bid the Red Sox made for Herb Score during spring training of 1957.

Joe Cronin, the general manager of the Red Sox, called his counterpart with the Indians, Hank Greenberg, and offered to buy Score's contract for $1 million.

To put the dollar amount into perspective, bear in mind that Greenberg was part of a new group of owners that had recently purchased the Indians franchise for $3.9 million.

Greenberg told Cronin, "We wouldn't sell Score for two million dollars. He's not for sale at any price."

But if Greenberg had said yes, and Score had been sold to the Red Sox, he probably would not have suffered the devastating eye injury that felled him on May 7, 1957, when he was struck by a liner off the bat of the New York Yankees' Gil McDougald.

And how might the fortunes of the Red Sox and Indians have been changed if Score had been sent to Boston?

Another left-handed pitcher, Sam McDowell, who came along a few years later, also was involved in a "what-if" scenario, this one during baseball's annual winter meetings in December 1970.

The Indians, unhappy with McDowell's off-the-field behavior and disappointed with his unrealized potential, offered him in trade to the Los Angeles Dodgers.

Alvin Dark, then calling the shots for the Indians, wanted four young players for McDowell—pitchers Don Sutton, Doyle Alexander, and Mike Strahler, and Bobby Valentine, who was then a minor league shortstop.

Al Campanis, the Dodgers' general manager, was willing to give up the three pitchers, but wouldn't part with Valentine, and offered minor league outfielder Bill Buckner instead.

But Dark refused. If Valentine was not included in the package, there'd be no deal.

Campanis held firm, and McDowell remained with the Indians for another season, during which he won 20 games for the first time, and was traded on November 29, 1971, to San Francisco for pitcher Gaylord Perry and shortstop Frank Duffy.

Would Sutton, Alexander, Strahler, and Buckner have done more for the Indians than did Perry and Duffy?

We'll never know . . . but the speculation is fascinating.

Finally, on the subject of trades, acquisitions, and sales, Cleveland was involved in three of the strangest deals in baseball history.

First, back in the days of the Cleveland Spiders, in the National League in 1898, team owner Frank DeHaas Robison traded pitcher Cy Young to himself. Indeed he did.

At the time, Robison owned the St. Louis Cardinals as well as the Spiders, and, wanting to strengthen the St. Louis team, he took Young and several of the other best players from Cleveland and transferred them to the Cardinals.

As a result, Young went 26–16 for the Cardinals in 1899, and the Spiders finished 12th and last with a 20–134 record, the worst in the history of major league baseball, and dropped out of the league the following season.

Another strange trade took place in 1960, swung by Indians general manager Frank Lane, who had a penchant for making deals—any and all kinds of deals.

After incurring the wrath of most Cleveland fans by trading their favorite player, Rocky Colavito, to Detroit on April 17, two days before the opener, Lane tried to justify the deal. He claimed it had been heartily endorsed by Indians manager Joe Gordon.

So, four months later, on August 3, Lane traded Gordon to the Tigers for Jimmy Dykes. It reunited Gordon with Colavito, and it was the first and only time in major league baseball history that two managers were traded for each other.

And finally, on November 27, 1972, newly appointed Indians general manager Phil Seghi traded all-star third baseman

Second baseman Joe Gordon teamed up with shortstop Lou Boudreau to give the Indians excellent defense up the middle, and his .280 batting average, 32 homers, and 124 RBIs were also key factors in winning the 1948 pennant. Gordon played for the Indians through the 1950 season.

Graig Nettles and catcher Gerry Moses to the New York Yankees for four young players—outfielders Charlie Spikes and Rusty Torres, catcher John Ellis, and infielder Jerry Kenney.

Making the trade for the Yankees was Gabe Paul who, less than six weeks earlier, had been Seghi's boss as general manager of the Indians.

Major Trades and Acquisitions

The preceding are the author's choices as the best and worst deals by the Indians since they became a charter member of the American League in 1901.

A complete list of all the significant trades, purchases, and sales follows.

1902, May 30
Outfielder Charlie Hemphill to St. Louis Browns for pitcher Red Donahue. Cleveland received Donahue in June 1903.

1902, June
Second baseman Frank Bonner and catcher Ossee Schreckengost to Philadelphia Athletics for pitcher Bill Bernhard.

1904, January
Pitchers Ed Killian and Jesse Stovall to Detroit Tigers for outfielder Billy Lush.

1904, August 7
First baseman Piano Legs Hickman to Detroit Tigers for catcher Fritz Buelow and first baseman Charlie Carr.

1906, December
Catcher Fritz Buelow to St. Louis Browns for second baseman Pete O'Brien.

Cy Young started in the major leagues in 1890 with the old National League Cleveland Spiders and was traded away at the height of his career in 1898. Young returned to Cleveland with the Naps in 1909, but by then he was well past his prime. He retired after the 1911 season.

1907, May 16
Pitcher Earl Moore to New York Highlanders for pitcher Walter Clarkson.

1907, August 11
Second baseman Pete O'Brien and catcher Howard Wakefield to Washington Senators for second baseman Rabbit Nill.

1909, February 18
Pitchers Charlie Chech and Jack Ryan to Boston Red Sox for pitcher Cy Young.

1910, July 23
Outfielder Bris Lord to Philadelphia Athletics for third baseman Morrie Rath.

1910, October
Catcher Nig Clarke to St. Louis Browns for first baseman Art Griggs.

1912, January
First baseman George Stovall to St. Louis Browns for pitcher Lefty George.

1913, May 20
Shortstop Roger Peckinpaugh to New York Yankees for outfielder Jack Lelivelt and shortstop Bill Stumpf.

1914, August 20
Pitcher Vean Gregg to Boston Red Sox for pitchers Fritz Coumbe and Adam Johnson and catcher Ben Egan.

1915, August 20
Outfielder Joe Jackson to Chicago White Sox for outfielders Larry Chappell and Braggo Roth, pitcher Ed Klepfer, and $31,500.

1916, April 8
Pitcher Sad Sam Jones, infielder Fred Thomas, and $55,000 to Boston Red Sox for outfielder Tris Speaker.

1916, August 18
Outfielder Elmer Smith and third baseman Joe Leonard to Washington Senators for pitcher Joe Boehling and outfielder Danny Moeller.

1919, March
Catcher Josh Billings to St. Louis Browns for catcher Les Nunamaker.

1919, March 1
Outfielder Braggo Roth to Philadelphia Athletics for third baseman Larry Gardner, outfielder Charlie Jamieson, and pitcher Elmer Myers.

1921, December 24
First basemen George Burns and Joe Harris and outfielder Elmer Smith to Boston Red Sox for first baseman Stuffy McInnis.

1923, January 8
Outfielder–third baseman Joe Evans to Washington Senators for first baseman Frank Brower.

1924, January 7
Pitcher Danny Boone, outfielder Joe Connolly, catcher Steve O'Neill, and second baseman Bill Wambsganss to Boston Red Sox for first baseman George Burns, second baseman Chick Fewster, and catcher Roxy Walters.

1924, December 12
Pitcher Stan Coveleski to Washington Senators for outfielder Carr Smith and pitcher Byron Speece.

1928, December 11
Pitcher George Uhle to Detroit Tigers for pitcher Ken Holloway and shortstop Jackie Tavener.

Ray Mack, nicknamed the "Case Ace" because he had been a football star at Case Institute of Technology in Cleveland, came to the Indians with excellent minor league credentials, but failed to hit consistently. He remained in the major leagues with the Yankees and Chicago Cubs only one season after being traded.

1929, February 28
Catcher Martin Autry to Chicago White Sox for outfielder Bibb Falk.

1931, May 17
First baseman Lew Fonseca to Chicago White Sox for third baseman Willie Kamm.

1932, April 24
Second baseman Johnny Hodapp and outfielder Bob Seeds to Chicago White Sox for second baseman Bill Cissell and pitcher Jim Moore.

1932, June 10
Pitcher Pete Jablonowski to Boston Red Sox for pitcher Jack Russell.

1932, December 15
First baseman Bruce Connatser and pitcher Jack Russell to Washington Senators for first baseman Harley Boss.

1933, January 7
Catcher Luke Sewell to Washington Senators for catcher Roy Spencer.

1933, October 12
Second baseman Bill Cissell to Boston Red Sox for pitcher Lloyd Brown.

1934, May 25
Pitcher Wes Ferrell and outfielder Dick Porter to Boston Red Sox for outfielder Bob Seeds, pitcher Bob Weiland, and $25,000.

1934, November 20
Infielder Johnny Burnett, pitcher Bob Weiland, and cash to St. Louis Browns for outfielder Bruce Campbell.

1935, May 14
Pitcher Belve Bean to Washington Senators for pitcher Lefty Stewart.

1935, December 11
Pitchers Monte Pearson and Steve Sundra to New York Yankees for pitcher Johnny Allen.

1936, December 10
In a three-team deal, Cleveland sent pitcher Thornton Lee to Chicago White Sox, Chicago sent pitcher Jack Salveson to Washington Senators, and Washington sent pitcher Earl Whitehill to Cleveland.

1937, January 17
Pitcher Oral Hildebrand, shortstop Bill Knickerbocker, and outfielder Joe Vosmik to St. Louis Browns for pitcher Ivy Andrews, shortstop Lyn Lary, and outfielder Moose Solters.

1938, February 10
Pitcher Ed Cole, second baseman Roy Hughes, and catcher Billy Sullivan to St. Louis Browns for catcher Rollie Hemsley.

1938, December 15
Pitcher Denny Galehouse and shortstop Tommy Irwin to Boston Red Sox for outfielder Ben Chapman.

1939, June 14
Outfielder Earl Averill to Detroit Tigers for pitcher Harry Eisenstat.

1940, January 20
Outfielder Bruce Campbell to Detroit Tigers for outfielder Beau Bell.

1940, December 12
Pitcher Joe Dobson, second baseman Odell Hale, and catcher Frankie Pytlak to Boston Red Sox for pitcher Jim Bagby, Jr., catcher Gene Desautels, and outfielder Gee Walker.

1940, December 21
Outfielder Ben Chapman to Washington Senators for pitcher Joe Krakauskas.

1941, February 7
Pitcher John Humphries to Chicago White Sox for pitcher Clint Brown.

1942, December 17
Infielder Oscar Grimes and outfielder Roy Weatherly to New York Yankees for outfielder Roy Cullenbine and catcher Buddy Rosar.

1944, December 12
Outfielder Oris Hockett to Chicago White Sox for outfielder Eddie Carnett.

Though Gene Bearden had only one good season with the Indians, he won 20 games, including the 1948 pennant playoff against the Boston Red Sox. He also won game three and saved Bob Lemon's victory in game six of the World Series.

1945, April 27
Outfielder Roy Cullenbine to Detroit Tigers for second baseman Dutch Meyer and third baseman Don Ross.

1945, May 29
Catcher Buddy Rosar to Philadelphia Athletics for catcher Frankie Hayes.

1945, December 12
Pitcher Jim Bagby, Jr., to Boston Red Sox for pitcher Vic Johnson and cash.

1945, December 14
Outfielder Jeff Heath to Washington Senators for outfielder George Case.

1946, May
First baseman Mickey Rocco to Chicago Cubs for first baseman Heinz Becker.

1946, June
Catcher Frankie Hayes to Chicago White Sox for catcher Tom Jordan.

1946, October 19
Pitcher Allie Reynolds to New York Yankees for third baseman Eddie Bockman and second baseman Joe Gordon.

1946, December 7
Outfielder Gene Woodling to Pittsburgh Pirates for catcher Al Lopez.

1946, December 20
Catcher Sherm Lollar and second baseman Ray Mack to New York Yankees for pitchers Gene Bearden and Al Gettel and outfielder Hal Peck.

1947, March 4
Outfielder George Case to Washington Senators for pitcher Roger Wolff.

1947, October 10
Pitcher Red Embree to New York Yankees for outfielder Allie Clark.

1947, November 20
Outfielders Joe Frazier and Dick Kokos, pitcher Bryan Stephens, and $25,000 to St. Louis Browns for outfielder Walt Judnich and pitcher Bob Muncrief.

1947, December 9
Outfielder Catfish Metkovich and $50,000 to St. Louis Browns for second baseman Johnny Berardino. Metkovich was returned to Cleveland because of a broken finger, and St. Louis Browns received another $15,000 to complete the trade.

1948, January 27
Catcher Ralph Weigel to Chicago White Sox for outfielder Thurman Tucker.

1948, June 2
Pitcher Al Gettel and outfielder Pat Seerey to Chicago White Sox for outfielder Bob Kennedy.

1948, June 15
Pitcher Bill Kennedy and $100,000 to St. Louis Browns for pitcher Sam Zoldak.

1948, November 22
Catcher Joe Tipton to Chicago White Sox for pitcher Joe Haynes.

1948, December 2
Pitchers Ernie Groth and Bob Kuzava to Chicago White Sox for pitcher Frank Papish.

1948, December 14
Pitchers Joe Haynes and Eddie Klieman and first baseman Eddie Robinson to Washington Senators for first baseman Mickey Vernon and pitcher Early Wynn.

1950, June 14
First baseman Mickey Vernon to Washington Senators for pitcher Dick Weik.

1951, April 1
Infielder Freddie Marsh and $35,000 to St. Louis Browns for shortstop Merrill Combs and second baseman Snuffy Stirnweiss.

1951, April 30
In a three-team deal, Cleveland obtains pitcher Lou Brissie from Philadelphia Athletics; Philadelphia gets catcher Ray Murray and pitcher Sam Zoldak from Cleveland and outfielders Dave Philley and Gus Zernial from Chicago White Sox; and Chicago gets outfielder Minnie Minoso from Cleveland and outfielder Paul Lehner from Philadelphia.

1951, May 10
Outfielder Allie Clark and second baseman Lou Klein to Philadelphia Athletics for outfielder Sam Chapman.

1952, August 18
Second baseman Johnny Berardino, pitcher Charlie Sipple, and $50,000 to Pittsburgh Pirates for shortstop George Strickland and pitcher Ted Wilks.

1952, December 19
Pitcher Dick Rozek and second baseman Bob Wilson to Philadelphia Athletics for pitcher Bob Hooper.

1953, June 15
Pitchers Al Aber, Steve Gromek, and Dick Weik and shortstop Ray Boone to Detroit Tigers for second baseman Owen Friend, catcher Joe Ginsberg, and pitchers Art Houtteman and Bill Wight.

1954, January 20
Catcher Joe Tipton to Washington Senators for catcher Mickey Grasso.

1954, February 19
Pitchers Bill Upton and Lee Wheat to

Minnie Minoso had his best years with the Chicago White Sox after he was traded by the Indians on April 30, 1951, and before he was reacquired by Cleveland on December 4, 1957.

Chicago White Sox for outfielder Dave Philley.

1954, April 17
Outfielder Bob Kennedy to Baltimore Orioles for outfielder Jim Dyck.

1954, June 1
Pitcher Bob Chakales to Baltimore Orioles for first baseman Vic Wertz.

1954, November 10
Pitcher Sam Jones, outfielder Gale Wade, and $60,000 to Chicago Cubs for outfielder Ralph Kiner.

1955, June 15
Outfielders Dave Pope and Wally Westlake to Baltimore Orioles for third baseman Billy Cox and outfielder Gene Woodling. Cox refused to report and announced retirement. Cleveland received $15,000 to complete trade.

1955, June 27
Third baseman Hank Majeski to Baltimore Orioles for second baseman Bobby Young.

1955, July 13
Pitcher Bill Wight to Baltimore Orioles for outfielder Hoot Evers.

1955, October 25
Outfielder Larry Doby to Chicago White Sox for outfielder Jim Busby and shortstop Chico Carrasquel.

1956, May 13
Outfielder Hoot Evers to Baltimore Orioles for outfielder Dave Pope.

1956, May 15
Catcher Hank Foiles to Pittsburgh Pirates for first baseman Preston Ward.

1957, June 13
Outfielder Jim Busby to Baltimore Orioles for outfielder Dick Williams.

1957, December 4
Outfielder Al Smith and pitcher Early Wynn to Chicago White Sox for third baseman Fred Hatfield and outfielder Minnie Minoso.

1958, February 18
Pitcher Hank Aguirre and catcher Jim Hegan to Detroit Tigers for catcher Jay Porter and pitcher Hal Woodeshick.

1958, February 25
Pitcher Pete Mesa to Washington Senators for second baseman Milt Bolling.

1958, March 27
Second baseman Milt Bolling and pitcher Vito Valentinetti to Detroit Tigers for pitcher Pete Wojey and $20,000.

1958, April 1
Pitcher Bud Daley and outfielders Dick Williams and Gene Woodling to Baltimore Orioles for outfielder Larry Doby and pitcher Don Ferrarese.

Pitcher Len Barker, who pitched a perfect game in 1981, figured in two of the Indians' best deals. He was acquired, along with outfielder Bobby Bonds, from the Texas Rangers in exchange for shortstop Larvell Blanks and relief pitcher Jim Kern on October 3, 1978. Five seasons later, on August 28, 1983, the Indians sent Barker to the Atlanta Braves for center fielder Brett Butler, third baseman Brook Jacoby, pitcher Rick Behenna, and $150,000.

1958, April 23
Third baseman Fred Hatfield to Cincinnati Reds for pitcher Bob Kelly.

1958, June 12
Shortstop Chico Carrasquel to Kansas City Athletics for shortstop Billy Hunter.

1958, June 15
Outfielder Roger Maris, pitcher Dick Tomanek, and first baseman Preston Ward to Kansas City Athletics for shortstop Woodie Held and first baseman Vic Power.

1958, October 27
Catcher Jay Porter to Washington Senators for shortstop Ossie Alvarez.

1958, November 20
Pitchers Don Mossi and Ray Narleski and shortstop Ossie Alvarez to Detroit Tigers for pitcher Al Cicotte and second baseman Billy Martin.

1958, December 2
Second baseman Bobby Avila to Baltimore Orioles for pitcher Russ Heman and $30,000.

1958, December 2
Outfielder Gary Geiger and first baseman Vic Wertz to Boston Red Sox for outfielder Jimmy Piersall.

1959, January 23
Catcher Earl Averill to Chicago Cubs for outfielder Jim Bolger and pitcher Johnny Briggs.

1959, March 21
Outfielder Larry Doby to Detroit Tigers for outfielder Tito Francona.

1959, April 11
First baseman Mickey Vernon to Milwaukee Braves for pitcher Humberto Robinson.

1959, May 4
Third baseman Randy Jackson to Chicago Cubs for pitcher Riverboat Smith.

1959, May 16
Pitcher Humberto Robinson to Philadelphia Phillies for shortstop Granny Hamner.

1959, May 25
Catcher Hal Naragon and pitcher Hal Woodeshick to Washington Senators for catcher Ed FitzGerald.

1959, June 6
Outfielder Jim Bolger and cash to Cincinnati Reds for third baseman Willie Jones.

1959, December 6
Outfielder Minnie Minoso, catcher Dick Brown, and pitchers Don Ferrarese and Jake Striker to Chicago White Sox for first baseman Norm Cash, third baseman Bubba Phillips, and catcher Johnny Romano.

1959, December 15
First baseman Gordy Coleman, second baseman Billy Martin, and pitcher Cal McLish to Cincinnati Reds for second baseman Johnny Temple.

1960, January 8
Second baseman Ray Webster to Boston Red Sox for pitcher Leo Kiely.

1960, March 16
Catcher Russ Nixon to Boston Red Sox for first baseman Jim Marshall and catcher Sammy White. Trade was canceled when White decided to retire.

1960, April 5
Pitcher Leo Kiely to Kansas City Athletics for pitcher Bob Grim.

1960, April 12
First baseman Norm Cash to Detroit Tigers for third baseman Steve Demeter.

1960, April 17
Outfielder Rocky Colavito to Detroit Tigers for outfielder Harvey Kuenn.

1960, April 18
Pitcher Herb Score to Chicago White Sox for pitcher Barry Latman.

1960, May 15
Outfielder Pete Whisenant to Washington Senators for second baseman Ken Aspromonte.

1960, May 31
Outfielder Johnny Powers to Pittsburgh Pirates for catcher Hank Foiles.

1960, June 13
Outfielder Carroll Hardy and catcher Russ Nixon to Boston Red Sox for pitcher Ted Bowsfield and outfielder Marty Keough.

1960, July 26
Catcher Hank Foiles to Detroit Tigers for shortstop Rocky Bridges and catcher Red Wilson.

1960, December 3
Outfielder Harvey Kuenn to San Francisco Giants for pitcher Johnny Antonelli and outfielder Willie Kirkland.

1961, May 10
Third baseman Joe Morgan, pitcher Mike Lee, and cash to St. Louis Cardinals

The acquisition of Harvey Kuenn, the defending American League batting champion, from Detroit on April 17, 1960, outraged Indians fans because general manager Frank Lane traded one of the franchise's all-time favorite players, Rocky Colavito. Kuenn remained with the Indians only one season and was traded on December 3, 1960, to San Francisco for pitcher Johnny Antonelli and outfielder Willie Kirkland.

for outfielder Bob Nieman (St. Louis received Lee on September 25, 1961).

1961, October 5
Outfielder Jimmy Piersall to Washington Senators for pitcher Dick Donovan, outfielder Gene Green, and shortstop Jim Mahoney.

1961, November 16
Second baseman Johnny Temple to Baltimore Orioles for first baseman Ray Barker, catcher Harry Chiti, and pitcher Art Kay.

1961, November 27
Pitcher Bobby Locke to Chicago Cubs for second baseman Jerry Kindall.

1962, March 20
Outfielder Mel Roach to Philadelphia Phillies for outfielder Tony Curry and pitcher Ken Lehman.

1962, April 2
First baseman Vic Power and pitcher Dick Stigman to Minnesota Twins for pitcher Pedro Ramos.

1962, May 3
Pitchers Steve Hamilton and Don Rudolph to Washington Senators for outfielder Willie Tasby.

1962, June 24
Second baseman Ken Aspromonte and cash to Milwaukee Braves for pitcher Bob Hartman.

1962, August 20
Pitcher Ruben Gomez to Minnesota Twins for pitchers Jackie Collum and Georges Maranda and cash.

1962, November 27
Third baseman Bubba Phillips to Detroit Tigers for pitchers Ron Nischwitz and Gordon Seyfried.

1962, November 27
Outfielders Ty Cline and Don Dillard and pitcher Frank Funk to Milwaukee Braves for first baseman Joe Adcock and pitcher Jack Curtis.

1962, December 15
Shortstop Jack Kubiszyn and pitcher Ron Taylor to St. Louis Cardinals for first baseman Fred Whitfield.

1963, February 27
Outfielder Chuck Essegian to Kansas City A's for pitcher Jerry Walker.

1963, May 2
Pitcher Jim Perry to Minnesota Twins for pitcher Jack Kralick.

1963, May 25
Catcher Doc Edwards and $100,000 to Kansas City A's for catcher Joe Azcue and shortstop Dick Howser.

1963, August 1
Outfielder Gene Green to Cincinnati Reds for catcher Sammy Taylor.

1963, December 2
First baseman Joe Adcock and pitcher Barry Latman to Los Angeles Angels for outfielder Leon Wagner.

1963, December 4
Outfielder Willie Kirkland to Baltimore Orioles for outfielder Al Smith and $25,000.

1964, April 1
Infielder Mike de la Hoz to Milwaukee Braves for infielder Chico Salmon.

1964, June 11
In a three-team deal, second baseman Jerry Kindall goes to Minnesota Twins, infielder Billy Moran comes to Cleveland from Los Angeles Angels, first baseman Vic Power and outfielder Lenny Green go to Los Angeles Angels from Minnesota Twins, and outfielder Frank Kostro goes to Minnesota from Los Angeles Angels.

1964, June 15
Pitcher Mudcat Grant to Minnesota Twins for third baseman George Banks and pitcher Lee Stange.

1964, September 5
Pitcher Pedro Ramos to New York Yankees for pitchers Bud Daley and Ralph Terry and $75,000.

1964, December 1
First baseman Bob Chance and short-stop Woodie Held to Washington Senators for outfielder Chuck Hinton.

1965, January 20
In a three-team deal, Cleveland sends outfielder Tommie Agee, pitcher Tommy John, and catcher Johnny Romano to Chicago White Sox; Kansas City A's send Rocky Colavito to Chicago, and he comes to Cleveland with catcher Camilo Carreon; Chicago sends outfielders Mike Hershberger and Jim Landis and pitcher Fred Talbot to Kansas City.

1965, May 10
First baseman Ray Barker to New York Yankees for second baseman Pedro Gonzalez.

1965, June 15
Outfielder Bubba Morton and cash to California Angels for catcher Phil Roof (California received Morton on September 15, 1965).

1965, December 1
Catcher Phil Roof and outfielder Joe Rudi to Kansas City A's for outfielder Jim Landis and pitcher Jim Rittwage.

1966, January 14
Outfielder Lu Clinton to New York Yankees for catcher Doc Edwards.

1966, April 6
Pitcher Ralph Terry and cash to Kansas City A's for pitcher John O'Donoghue.

The 1960 deal that cost the Indians the services of Rocky Colavito (left) was made even worse five seasons later when general manager Gabe Paul (right) determined to bring the popular outfielder back to Cleveland. To reacquire Colavito, then 31 years old, the Indians gave up pitcher Tommy John, outfielder Tommie Agee, and catcher John Romano. The Indians also received catcher Camilo Carreon with Colavito, but the deal proved to be disastrous.

1966, June 2
Pitchers Don McMahon and Lee Stange to Boston Red Sox for pitcher Dick Radatz.

1966, July 19
Outfielder Tony Curry to Houston Astros for first baseman Jim Gentile.

1966, December 20
Shortstop Dick Howser to New York Yankees for pitcher Gil Downs.

1967, January 4
Catcher Doc Edwards, outfielder Jim Landis, and pitcher Jim Weaver to Houston Astros for outfielder Lee Maye and catcher Ken Retzer.

1967, April 25
Pitcher Dick Radatz to Chicago Cubs for outfielder Bob Raudman and cash.

1967, June 4
Pitcher Gary Bell to Boston Red Sox for first baseman Tony Horton and outfielder Don Demeter.

1967, July 29
Outfielder Rocky Colavito to Chicago White Sox for outfielder Jim King and infielder Marv Staehle.

1967, November 21
Pitcher George Culver, outfielder Bob Raudman, and first baseman Fred Whitfield to Cincinnati Reds for outfielder Tommy Harper.

1967, November 28
Infielder Gordon Lund and pitcher John O'Donoghue to Baltimore Orioles for pitchers Eddie Fisher and Bob Scott and infielder John Scruggs.

1967, November 29
Outfielder Chuck Hinton to California Angels for outfielder Jose Cardenal.

1968, March 30
Pitcher Bobby Tiefenauer to Chicago Cubs for pitcher Rob Gardner.

1968, June 13
Outfielder Leon Wagner to Chicago White Sox for outfielder Russ Snyder.

1968, June 15
Outfielder Vic Davalillo to California Angels for outfielder Jimmie Hall.

1968, June 28
Outfielder Willie Smith to Chicago Cubs for outfielder Lou Johnson.

1968, October 8
Pitcher Eddie Fisher to California Angels for pitcher Jack Hamilton.

Catcher John Romano, lost by the Indians in the failed 1965 deal for Rocky Colavito.

1968, October 21
First baseman Bill Davis to San Diego Padres for shortstop Zoilo Versalles.

1969, March 31
Pitcher George Woodson to Washington Senators for outfielder Cap Peterson.

1969, April 4
Outfielder Lou Johnson to California Angels for outfielder Chuck Hinton.

1969, April 19
Pitchers Sonny Siebert and Vicente Romo and catcher Joe Azcue to Boston Red Sox for outfielder Ken Harrelson and pitchers Dick Ellsworth and Juan Pizarro.

1969, June 13
Pitcher Jack Hamilton to Chicago White Sox for pitcher Sammy Ellis.

1969, November 21
Outfielder Jose Cardenal to St. Louis Cardinals for outfielder Vada Pinson.

1969, December 5
Pitchers Ron Law and Horacio Pina and second baseman Dave Nelson to Washington Senators for pitchers Dennis Higgins and Barry Moore.

1969, December 10
Pitchers Luis Tiant and Stan Williams to Minnesota Twins for pitchers Dean Chance and Bob Miller, third baseman

Graig Nettles, and outfielder Ted Uhlaender.

1970, April 4
Third baseman Max Alvis and outfielder Russ Snyder to Milwaukee Brewers for outfielder Roy Foster, infielder Frank Coggins, and cash.

1970, May 22
Outfielder Russ Nagelson and pitcher Billy Rohr to Detroit Tigers for pitcher Fred Lasher.

1970, June 15
Pitchers Bob Miller and Barry Moore to Chicago White Sox for outfielder Buddy Bradford.

1970, December 11
Catcher Duke Sims to Los Angeles Dodgers for pitchers Alan Foster and Ray Lamb.

1971, May 8
Outfielder Buddy Bradford to Cincinnati Reds for infielder Kurt Bevacqua.

1971, October 5
Pitcher Alan Foster and outfielders Frank Baker and Vada Pinson to California Angels for outfielder Alex Johnson and catcher Gerry Moses.

1971, November 29
Pitcher Sam McDowell to San Francisco Giants for pitcher Gaylord Perry and shortstop Frank Duffy.

1971, December 2
Pitchers Rich Hand and Mike Paul, outfielder Roy Foster, and catcher Ken Suarez to Texas Rangers for pitchers Gary Jones, Terry Ley, and Denny Riddleberger and outfielder Del Unser.

1971, December 6
Outfielder Ted Uhlaender to Cincinnati Reds for pitcher Milt Wilcox.

1972, April 3
Outfielder Ted Ford to Texas Rangers for outfielders Roy Foster and Tom McCraw.

1972, June 11
Shortstop Fred Stanley to San Diego Padres for pitcher Mike Kilkenny.

1972, July 10
Outfielder Jim Clark to Kansas City Royals for pitcher Tom Hilgendorf.

1972, October 19
Infielder Eddie Leon to Chicago White Sox for outfielder Walt Williams.

1972, November 2
Infielder Kurt Bevacqua to Kansas City Royals for pitcher Mike Hedlund.

1972, November 27
Third baseman Graig Nettles and catcher Gerry Moses to New York Yankees for catcher John Ellis, infielder Jerry Kenney, and outfielders Charlie Spikes and Rusty Torres.

1972, November 27
Pitcher Phil Hennigan to New York Mets for pitchers Bob Rauch and Brent Strom.

1972, November 30
Pitcher Vince Colbert to Texas Rangers for infielder Tom Ragland.

1972, November 30
Outfielder Del Unser and infielder Terry Wedgewood to Philadelphia Phillies for outfielders Roger Freed and Oscar Gamble.

1973, March 8
Outfielder Alex Johnson to Texas Rangers for pitchers Vince Colbert and Rich Hinton.

1973, March 24
Catcher Ray Fosse and shortstop Jack Heidemann to Oakland A's for catcher Dave Duncan and outfielder George Hendrick.

1973, April 2
Outfielder Tom McCraw and second baseman Bob Marcano to California Angels for shortstop Leo Cardenas.

Tommy John, who went on to win 286 games after the Indians traded him away in the deal to re-acquire Rocky Colavito in 1965.

1973, May 10
Pitcher Steve Dunning to Texas Rangers for pitcher Dick Bosman and outfielder Ted Ford.

1973, June 12
Pitcher Lowell Palmer to New York Yankees for pitcher Mike Kekich.

1973, June 15
Pitcher Ed Farmer to Detroit Tigers for third baseman Kevin Collins and pitcher Tom Timmerman.

1973, December 3
Pitcher Jerry Johnson to Houston Astros for pitcher Cecil Upshaw.

1973, December 7
Outfielder Burnel Flowers to Pittsburgh Pirates for pitcher Bob Johnson.

1974, February 12
Shortstop Leo Cardenas to Texas Rangers for catcher Ken Suarez.

1974, March 19
In a three-team deal, Detroit sends pitcher Jim Perry to Cleveland and pitcher Ed Farmer to New York Yankees; Cleveland sends pitcher Rick Sawyer and outfielder Walt Williams to New York Yankees; and New York sends catcher Gerry Moses to Detroit.

1974, March 23
Pitcher Steve Hargan to Texas Rangers for pitcher Bill Gogolewski.

1974, April 3
Infielder Pedro Guerrero to Los Angeles Dodgers for pitcher Bruce Ellingsen.

1974, April 27
First baseman Chris Chambliss and pitchers Dick Tidrow and Cecil Upshaw to New York Yankees for pitchers Fred Beene, Tom Buskey, Steve Kline, and Fritz Peterson.

1974, June 1
Shortstop Jack Heidemann to St. Louis Cardinals for infielders Luis Alvarado and Ed Crosby.

1974, June 15
Pitchers Brent Strom and Jerry Lee to San Diego Padres for pitcher Steve Arlin.

1974, September 12
Catcher Ken Suarez, outfielder Rusty Torres, and cash to California Angels for outfielder Frank Robinson.

1975, February 25
Catcher Dave Duncan and outfielder Al McGrew to Baltimore Orioles for

pitcher Don Hood and first baseman Boog Powell.

1975, February 25
Pitcher Milt Wilcox to Chicago Cubs for outfielder Brock Davis and pitcher Dave LaRoche.

1975, March 6
Pitcher Tom Hilgendorf to Philadelphia Phillies for outfielder Nelson Garcia.

1975, May 20
Pitchers Dick Bosman and Jim Perry to Oakland A's for pitcher Blue Moon Odom and cash.

1975, June 7
Pitcher Blue Moon Odom and shortstop Bob Bailor to Atlanta Braves for pitcher Roric Harrison.

1975, June 13
Pitcher Gaylord Perry to Texas Rangers for pitchers Jim Bibby, Jackie Brown, and Rick Waits, and $100,000.

1975, September 30
Infielder Luis Alvarado to St. Louis Cardinals for first baseman Doug Howard.

1975, November 22
Outfielder Oscar Gamble to New York Yankees for pitcher Pat Dobson.

Steve Demeter was one of the best players in the minor leagues in 1959, but his acquisition by the Indians, in exchange for Norm Cash, proved to be one of the worst deals in club history. When Cash won the American League batting championship in 1961, Demeter was already finished in the major leagues. He played in just four games for the Indians in 1960, going 0 for 5, and never appeared in another major league game.

1975, December 9
Catcher John Ellis to Texas Rangers for catcher Ron Pruitt and pitcher Stan Thomas.

1975, December 12
Second baseman Jack Brohamer to Chicago White Sox for infielder Larvell Blanks.

1976, April 7
Pitcher Roric Harrison to St. Louis Cardinals for pitcher Harry Parker.

1976, May 28
Pitcher Fritz Peterson to Texas Rangers for pitcher Stan Perzanowski and cash.

1976, November 5
Catcher Alan Ashby and first baseman Doug Howard to Toronto Blue Jays for pitcher Al Fitzmorris.

1976, December 3
Pitcher Stan Perzanowski and cash to California Angels for third baseman Bill Melton.

1976, December 6
Outfielder John Lowenstein and catcher Rick Cerone to Toronto Blue Jays for designated hitter Rico Carty.

1976, December 8
Outfielder George Hendrick to San Diego Padres for outfielder Johnny Grubb, catcher Fred Kendall, and shortstop Hector Torres.

1976, December 10
Pitcher Jackie Brown to Montreal Expos for first baseman Andre Thornton.

1977, March 29
Shortstop Hector Torres to Toronto Blue Jays for outfielder John Lowenstein.

1977, May 11
Pitchers Dave LaRoche and Dave Schuler to California Angels for outfielder Bruce Bochte, pitcher Sid Monge, and $250,000.

1977, September 9
Catcher Ray Fosse to Seattle Mariners for pitcher Bill Laxton and cash.

1977, December 5
Pitcher Norm Churchill and outfielder Bruce Compton to Chicago Cubs for infielder Dave Rosello.

1977, December 9
Outfielder Charlie Spikes to Detroit Tigers for shortstop Tom Veryzer.

1977, December 9
Outfielder Garry Hancock to Boston Red Sox for first baseman Jack Baker.

1978, February 28
Pitcher Tom Buskey and outfielder John Lowenstein to Texas Rangers for pitcher David Clyde and outfielder Willie Horton.

1978, March 15
Designated hitter Rico Carty to Toronto Blue Jays for pitcher Denny DeBarr.

1978, March 24
Shortstop Frank Duffy to Boston Red Sox for pitcher Rick Kreuger.

1978, March 30
Pitcher Dennis Eckersley and catcher Fred Kendall to Boston Red Sox for catcher Bo Diaz, third baseman Ted Cox, and pitchers Rick Wise and Mike Paxton.

1978, June 14
Pitcher Dennis Kinney to San Diego Padres for pitcher Dan Spillner.

1978, June 15
Outfielder Mike Vail to Chicago Cubs for outfielder Joe Wallis.

1978, June 15
Outfielder Joe Wallis to Oakland A's for catcher Gary Alexander.

In 1974, the Indians were looking for a left-handed reliever, and they liked what they saw in Bruce Ellingsen, a minor league prospect in the Los Angeles Dodgers organization. They traded one of their minor league prospects, third baseman Pedro Guerrero for Ellingsen—and regretted the deal for a long time. Ellingsen spent one season in the majors leagues, winning one and losing one in 16 appearances for the Indians. He never pitched in another major league game. Guerrero went on to have a long and fruitful career in the National League.

1978, June 23
Pitcher Bill Laxton to San Diego Padres for pitcher Dave Freisleben.

1978, June 26
Pitcher Denny DeBarr to Chicago Cubs for pitcher Paul Reuschel.

1978, August 31
Outfielder Johnny Grubb to Texas Rangers for pitcher Bobby Cuellar and outfielder Dave Rivera.

1978, October 3
Pitcher Jim Kern and infielder Larvell Blanks to Texas Rangers for pitcher Len Barker and outfielder Bobby Bonds.

1978, December 5
Shortstop Alfredo Griffin and third baseman Phil Lansford to Toronto Blue Jays for pitcher Victor Cruz.

1978, December 8
Third baseman Buddy Bell to Texas Rangers for third baseman Toby Harrah.

1979, March 30
Outfielder Dan Briggs to San Diego Padres for second baseman Mike Champion.

1979, June 14
Outfielder Paul Dade to San Diego Padres for first baseman Mike Hargrove.

1979, June 15
Pitcher Don Hood to New York Yankees for designated hitter Cliff Johnson.

1979, December 6
Third baseman Ted Cox to Seattle Mariners for pitchers Bud Anderson, Bob Pietburgo, and Rafael Vasquez.

1979, December 7
Outfielder Bobby Bonds to St. Louis Cardinals for pitcher John Denny and outfielder Jerry Mumphrey.

1979, December 21
Pitcher Larry Andersen to Pittsburgh Pirates for pitcher John Burden and outfielder Larry Littleton.

1980, January 4
Pitcher David Clyde and outfielder Jim Norris to Texas Rangers for outfielder Mike Bucci, first baseman Gary Gray, and pitcher Larry McCall.

1980, February 15
Outfielder Jerry Mumphrey to San Diego Padres for pitcher Bob Owchinko and outfielder Jim Wilhelm.

1980, February 15
Pitcher Gary Melson to Atlanta Braves for pitcher Don Collins.

1980, June 13
Catcher Ron Pruitt to Chicago White Sox for outfielder Alan Bannister.

1980, June 23
Designated hitter Cliff Johnson to Chicago Cubs for outfielder Karl Pagel and cash.

1980, July 11
Infielder Dave Oliver to Montreal Expos for pitcher Ross Grimsley.

1980, December 9
Catcher Gary Alexander and pitchers Victor Cruz, Bob Owchinko, and Rafael Vasquez to Pittsburgh Pirates for pitcher Bert Blyleven and catcher Manny Sanguillen.

1981, March 26
First baseman Wayne Cage to Seattle Mariners for outfielder Rodney Craig.

1981, April 1
Second baseman Juan Bonilla to San Diego Padres for pitcher Bob Lacey.

1981, April 3
Outfielder Jim Lentine and cash to Houston Astros for shortstop Mike Fischlin.

1981, April 6
Pitcher Dominick Bullinger to New York Mets for pitcher Ed Glynn.

The Indians were looking for a gate attraction in 1969 and thought they got the player they needed in Ken "Hawk" Harrelson from the Boston Red Sox. It turned out, however, that the price they paid was much too high—pitcher Sonny Siebert (pictured here), catcher Joe Azcue, and reliever Vicente Romo—though they also received pitchers Dick Ellsworth and Juan Pizarro in the deal.

1981, November 14
Second baseman Duane Kuiper to San Francisco Giants for pitcher Ed Whitson.

1981, November 20
In a three-team deal, Cleveland traded catcher Bo Diaz to Philadelphia Phillies for outfielder Lonnie Smith and pitcher Scott Munninghoff; Cleveland then traded Smith to St. Louis Cardinals for pitchers Silvio Martinez and Lary Sorensen.

1981, December 9
Outfielder Jorge Orta, catcher Jack Fimple, and pitcher Larry White to Los Angeles Dodgers for pitcher Rick Sutcliffe and second baseman Jack Perconte.

1982, January 8
Shortstop Tom Veryzer to New York Mets for pitcher Ray Searage.

1982, February 16
Pitcher Sid Monge to Philadelphia Phillies for outfielder Bake McBride.

1982, July 3
Outfielder Larry Littleton to Minnesota Twins for infielder Larry Milbourne.

1982, September 12
Pitcher John Denny to Philadelphia Phillies for outfielder Wil Culmer and pitchers Jerry Reed and Roy Smith.

1982, November 18
Pitcher Ed Whitson to San Diego Padres for pitcher Juan Eichelberger and first baseman Broderick Perkins.

1982, December 9
Outfielder Von Hayes to Philadelphia Phillies for shortstop Julio Franco, second baseman Manny Trillo, pitcher Jay Baller, catcher Jerry Willard, and outfielder George Vukovich.

1983, April 1
Shortstop Jerry Dybzinski to Chicago White Sox for outfielder Pat Tabler.

1983, June 6
Outfielder Rick Manning and pitcher Rick Waits to Milwaukee Brewers for outfielder Gorman Thomas and pitchers Ernie Camacho and Jamie Easterly.

1983, June 8
Catcher John Malkin to Pittsburgh Pirates for pitcher Steve Farr.

1983, August 17
Second baseman Manny Trillo to Montreal Expos for outfielder Don Carter and $300,000.

1983, August 25
Outfielder Miguel Dilone to Chicago White Sox for pitcher Rich Barnes.

1983, August 28
Pitcher Len Barker to Atlanta Braves for pitcher Rick Behenna, outfielder Brett Butler, third baseman Brook Jacoby, and $150,000 (Butler and Jacoby were sent to Cleveland at the end of the season).

1983, December 6
Catcher Jim Essian to Oakland A's for shortstop Luis Quinones.

1983, December 7
Outfielder Gorman Thomas and second baseman Jack Perconte to Seattle Mariners for second baseman Tony Bernazard.

1984, January 21
Pitcher Tom Brennan to Chicago White Sox for infielder Craig Smajstrla (Cleveland received Smajstrla on July 8, 1985).

1984, February 4
Third baseman Toby Harrah and pitcher Rick Browne to New York Yankees for outfielder Otis Nixon and pitchers George Frazier and Guy Elston.

1984, March 24
Pitchers Paul Perry and Mike Poindexter to Boston Red Sox for pitcher Luis Aponte.

1984, June 13
Pitchers Rick Sutcliffe and George Frazier and catcher Ron Hassey to Chicago Cubs for outfielders Joe Carter and Mel Hall and pitchers Don Schulze and Darryl Banks.

1984, June 21
Pitcher Dan Spillner to Chicago White Sox for pitcher Jim Siwy.

1985, March 19
Outfielder Dwight Taylor to Kansas City Royals for pitcher Keith Creel (Kansas City received Taylor on October 3, 1985).

1985, April 1
Pitcher Jay Baller to Chicago Cubs for infielder Dan Rohn.

1985, April 4
Infielder Jeff Moronko to Texas Rangers for outfielder Kevin Buckley (Texas received Moronko on April 29, 1985).

1985, April 4
Kansas City Royals traded outfielder Mike Brewer to Cleveland for player to

Catcher Joe Azcue, who was packaged with pitcher Sonny Siebert and reliever Vicente Romo in the deal for Ken "Hawk" Harrelson.

be named later, but Brewer was returned to Kansas City on September 17, 1985.

1985, May 7
Pitcher Mike Jeffcoat and shortstop Luis Quinones to San Francisco Giants for shortstop Johnnie LeMaster.

1985, May 30
Shortstop Johnnie LeMaster to Pittsburgh Pirates for pitcher Scott Bailes (Cleveland received Bailes on July 3).

1985, July 26
Pitcher Dave Beard to Chicago Cubs for outfielder Tom Grant.

1985, August 1
Pitcher Bert Blyleven to Minnesota Twins for shortstop Jay Bell, outfielder Jim Weaver, and pitchers Curt Wardle and Rich Yett (Cleveland received Yett on September 17).

1985, December 15
Shortstop Mike Fischlin to New York Yankees for pitcher Kevin Trudeau (Cleveland received Trudeau on April 7, 1986).

1985, December 16
Pitcher Rich Thompson to Milwaukee Brewers for pitcher Scott Roberts.

1986, January 7
Pitchers Ramon Romero and Roy Smith to Minnesota Twins for pitchers Bryan Oelkers and Ken Schrom.

1986, June 20
Pitcher Neal Heaton to Minnesota Twins for pitcher John Butcher.

1987, February 23
Pitcher Curt Wardle to Oakland Athletics for pitcher Jeff Kaiser.

1987, May 5
Pitcher Jose Roman to New York Mets for outfielder Mike Westbrook.

1987, May 11
Pitcher Don Schulze to New York Mets for outfielder Ricky Nelson.

1987, May 12
Outfielder Dave Gallagher to Seattle Mariners for pitcher Mark Huismann.

1987, July 15
Second baseman Tony Bernazard to Oakland Athletics for pitcher Darrel Akerfelds and catcher Brian Dorsett.

1987, July 31
Pitcher Steve Carlton to Minnesota Twins for pitcher Jeff Perry (Cleveland acquired Perry on August 18).

1987, August 9
Pitcher Phil Niekro to Toronto Blue Jays for outfielder Darryl Landrum and pitcher Don Gordon.

1988, March 28
Pitcher Tommy Kurczewski to Atlanta Braves for pitcher Jeff Dedmon (Atlanta received Kurczewski on June 22).

1988, March 30
Infielder Junior Noboa to California Angels for outfielder Ted Milner.

1988, April 5
Pitcher Greg LaFever to Los Angeles Dodgers for outfielder Reggie Williams.

1988, June 3
First baseman Pat Tabler to Kansas City Royals for pitcher Bud Black.

1988, November 15
Pitcher John Githens and first baseman Don Lovell to Baltimore Orioles for catcher Tom Magrann and outfielder Gary Holtz.

1988, November 28
Pittsburgh Pirates traded infielder Denny Gonzalez to Cleveland for a player to be named later (which became part of the March 25, 1989 deal in which the Indians traded shortstop Jay Bell for shortstop Felix Fermin).

1988, December 6
Second baseman Julio Franco to Texas Rangers for first baseman Pete O'Brien, second baseman Jerry Browne, and outfielder Oddibe McDowell.

1989, January 23
Infielder Eddie Williams to Chicago White Sox for pitchers Joel Davis and Ed Wojna.

1989, March 19
Outfielder Mel Hall to New York Yankees for catcher Joel Skinner and outfielder Turner Ward.

1989, March 25
Shortstop Jay Bell to Pittsburgh Pirates for shortstop Felix Fermin.

1989, March 26
Outfielder Carmen Castillo to Minnesota Twins for pitcher Keith Atherton.

1989, April 2
Infielders Chuck Baldwin and Paul Noce to Seattle Mariners for outfielder Dave Hengel.

1989, July 2
Outfielder Oddibe McDowell to Atlanta Braves for outfielder Dion James.

1989, September 6
Catcher Ron Tingley to California Angels for infielder Mark McLemore (Cleveland received McLemore on August 17, 1990).

Ken "Hawk" Harrelson had been one of Manager Alvin Dark's favorites when they were together with the Kansas City Athletics in 1966, but the deal to get him for the Indians was one of the worst in club history. Harrelson initially refused to report to Cleveland unless he was given a huge raise in pay, and the following spring, Harrelson suffered a broken ankle that led to his premature retirement.

1989, November 20
Outfielder Dave Clark to Chicago Cubs for outfielder Mitch Webster.

1989, December 6
Outfielder Joe Carter to San Diego Padres for catcher Sandy Alomar, third baseman Carlos Baerga, and outfielder Chris James.

1989, December 12
Pitcher Steve Davis to Los Angeles Dodgers for infielder Manny Francois and outfielder Joe Kesselmark.

1990, January 9
Pitcher Scott Bailes to California Angels for pitcher Colin Charland and infielder Jeff Manto.

1990, March 18
Second baseman Tommy Hinzo to Atlanta Braves for outfielders Miguel Sabino and Jeff Wetherby.

1990, July 11
Catcher Tom Lampkin to San Diego Padres for outfielder Alex Cole.

1990, September 16
Pitcher Bud Black to Toronto Blue Jays for pitchers Steve Cummings, Mauro Gozzo, and Alex Sanchez.

1990, November 6
Pitcher Alex Sanchez to Toronto Blue Jays for pitcher Willie Blair.

1990, December 4
Outfielder Cory Snyder and infielder Lindsay Foster to Chicago White Sox for pitchers Shawn Hillegas and Eric King.

1991, May 16
Outfielder Mitch Webster to Pittsburgh Pirates for pitcher Mike York.

1991, May 21
Pitcher Steve Cummings to Detroit Tigers for pitcher Eric Stone (Cleveland received Stone on July 8).

1991, June 14
First baseman Tim Costo to Cincinnati Reds for first baseman Reggie Jefferson.

1991, June 27
Pitcher Tom Candiotti and outfielder Turner Ward to Toronto Blue Jays for pitcher Denis Boucher, outfielders Mark Whiten and Glenallen Hill, and cash.

1991, July 26
Third baseman Brook Jacoby to Oakland Athletics for pitcher Apolinar Garcia and outfielder Lee Tinsley.

1991, November 15
Pitcher Greg Swindell to Cincinnati Reds for pitchers Jack Armstrong, Scott Scudder, and Joe Turek.

1991, December 10
Pitcher Willie Blair and catcher Eddie Taubensee to Houston Astros for outfielder Kenny Lofton and infielder Dave Rohde.

1991, December 10
Pitcher Rudy Seanez to Los Angeles Dodgers for pitchers Mike Christopher and Dennis Cook.

1992, March 28
Pitchers Curt Leskanic and Oscar Munoz to Minnesota Twins for first baseman Paul Sorrento.

1992, April 15
Shortstop Jason Hardtke and pitcher Chris Maffett to San Diego Padres for outfielder Thomas Howard.

1992, July 3
Outfielder Alex Cole to Pittsburgh Pirates for pitcher John Carter and outfielder Tony Mitchell.

1992, July 14
Outfielder Kyle Washington to Baltimore Orioles for pitcher Jose Mesa.

1993, March 31
Outfielder Mark Whiten to St. Louis Cardinals for pitcher Mark Clark and shortstop Juan Andujar.

1993, May 7
Pitcher Kevin Wickander to Cincinnati Reds for pitcher Todd Ruyak.

1993, June 1
Shortstop Jose Hernandez to Chicago Cubs for pitcher Heathcliff Slocumb.

1993, June 1
Pitcher Fernando Hernandez and outfielder Tracy Sanders to San Diego Padres for pitcher Jeremy Hernandez.

1993, August 17
Outfielder Thomas Howard to Cincinnati Reds for first baseman Randy Milligan.

1993, August 19
Outfielder Glenallen Hill to Chicago Cubs for outfielder Candy Maldonado.

1993, November 2
Pitcher Heathcliff Slocumb to Philadelphia Phillies for outfielder Ruben Amaro, Jr.

1993, December 13
First baseman Randy Milligan to Montreal Expos for pitcher Brian Barnes.

1993, December 20
Shortstop Felix Fermin and first baseman Reggie Jefferson to Seattle Mariners for shortstop Omar Vizquel.

1994, February 14
First baseman Dave Duplessis and pitcher J. J. Thobe to Montreal Expos for pitcher Chris Nabholz.

1994, February 21
Pitcher Shawn Bryant to Minnesota Twins for shortstop Enrique Wilson.

1994, March 23
Catcher Junior Ortiz to Texas Rangers for pitcher Paul Lesch and player to be named later. Texas replaced Lesch with pitcher Igor Oropeza after Indians rejected Lesch because of shoulder injury. Indians got outfielder Andreaus Lewis on May 9 to complete deal.

1994, March 30
Outfielder Ken Ramos to Chicago Cubs for catcher Matt Merullo.

1994, April 3
Pitcher Jeremy Hernandez to Florida Marlins for pitcher Matt Turner.

1994, May 17
Pitcher Tom Kramer to Cincinnati Reds for pitcher John Hrusovsky.

1994, June 16
Pitcher Brian Barnes to Los Angeles Dodgers for infielder Eduardo Lantigua.

In the spring of 1957 the Indians turned down a $1 million cash offer for Herb Score from the Boston Red Sox, but three years later general manager Frank Lane traded the swift southpaw to the Chicago White Sox for Barry Latman.

1994, July 1
Pitchers Steve Farr and Chris Nabholz to Boston Red Sox for pitcher Jeff Russell.

1994, August 31
Minnesota Twins traded outfielder

Dave Winfield to Cleveland for player to be named later.

1994, November 18
Pitchers Paul Byrd, Jerry DiPoto, and Dave Mlicki and second baseman Jesus

Azuaje to New York Mets for outfielder Jeromy Burnitz and pitcher Joe Roa.

1994, December 14
Shortstop Mark Lewis to Cincinnati Reds for infielder Tim Costo.

Major Purchases and Other Acquisitions

1901, January
Pitcher Bill Hoffer from Pittsburgh Pirates.

1901, May
Outfielder Jack O'Brien from Washington Senators.

1901, May
Pitcher Pete Dowling from Milwaukee Brewers.

1901, June
Catcher Joe Connor from Milwaukee Brewers.

1901, August
Outfielder Ervin Harvey from Chicago White Sox.

1901, October
Catcher Ossee Schreckengost from Boston Somersets.

1902, May 16
Outfielder Elmer Flick from Philadelphia Athletics.

1902, May 30
Piano Legs Hickman from Boston Somersets.

1902, June
Second baseman Nap Lajoie from Philadelphia Athletics.

1905, August 11
Catcher Nig Clarke from Detroit Tigers.

1906, January
Pitcher Jack Townsend from Washington Senators.

1906, August 15
Catcher Mal Kittridge from Washington Senators.

1907, February
Catcher Howard Wakefield from Washington Senators.

1907, November
First baseman Piano Legs Hickman from Chicago White Sox.

1908, August
Shortstop Dave Altizer and Pitcher Cy Falkenberg from Washington Senators.

1908, August
Catcher Deacon McGuire from Boston Red Sox.

1908, September
Outfielder Denny Sullivan from Boston Red Sox.

1909, May
Shortstop Neal Ball from New York Yankees.

1910, May
Outfielder Harry Niles from Boston Red Sox.

1910, September
Catcher Pat Donahue from Philadelphia Athletics.

1911, August 20
Catcher Steve O'Neill from Philadelphia Athletics.

1911, December 6
Catcher Paddy Livingston from Philadelphia Athletics.

1912, July
Pitcher Harry Krause from Philadelphia Athletics.

1914, January
Outfielder Roy Wood from Pittsburgh Pirates.

1915, December
Catcher Tom Daly from Chicago White Sox.

1916, January
Second baseman Ivon Howard from St. Louis Browns.

1916, February 10
First baseman Chick Gandil from Washington Senators.

1916, April
Pitcher Grover Lowdermilk from Detroit Tigers.

1916, May
Pitcher Marty McHale from Boston Red Sox.

1916, May
Second baseman Marty Kavanagh from Detroit Tigers.

1917, February 24
Pitcher Smoky Joe Wood from Boston Red Sox.

1917, June 13
Outfielder Elmer Smith from Washington Senators.

1918, February 15
Pitcher Bob Groom from St. Louis Browns.

1918, June
Pitcher Ad Brennan from Washington Senators.

1918, June 1
Catcher Pinch Thomas from Boston Red Sox.

1920, May 29
First baseman George Burns from Philadelphia Athletics.

1921, April
Pitcher Allen Sothoron from Boston Red Sox.

1921, June 2
Pitcher Dave Keefe from Philadelphia Athletics.

1922, September 18
Pitcher Sherry Smith from Brooklyn Dodgers.

1924, June 3
Third baseman Frank Ellerbe from St. Louis Browns.

1925, July
Pitcher Bert Cole from Detroit Tigers.

1926, February
Third baseman Ernie Padgett from Boston Braves.

1927, June 12
Outfielder Baby Doll Jacobson from Boston Red Sox.

1927, December
Catcher Grover Hartley from Boston Red Sox.

1928, March 4
Second baseman Aaron Ward from Chicago White Sox.

When they were pitchers with the New York Yankees in 1973, Fritz Peterson (right) and Mike Kekich (second from left) traded wives and families. Later that season, on June 12, Kekich was acquired by the Indians in exchange for pitcher Lowell Palmer. The following season, on April 27, 1974, Peterson came to Cleveland, along with pitchers Fred Beene, Tom Buskey, and Steve Kline, in a deal for first baseman Chris Chambliss, and relievers Dick Tidrow and Cecil Upshaw.

1928, July 10
Pitcher Johnny Miljus from Pittsburgh Pirates.

1929, June 7
First baseman Joe Hauser from Philadelphia Athletics.

1930, November
Shortstop Bill Hunnefield from Chicago White Sox.

1931, April 2
Catcher Moe Berg from Chicago White Sox.

1932, June 6
Shortstop Joe Boley from Philadelphia Athletics.

1934, December
Catcher Eddie Phillips from Washington Senators.

1936, January 27
Pitcher George Blaeholder from Philadelphia Athletics.

1936, January 29
Catcher Billy Sullivan from Cincinnati Reds.

1936, December
Second baseman John Kroner from Boston Red Sox.

1938, November
Pitcher Johnny Broaca from New York Yankees.

1940, June 10
Pitcher Nate Andrews from St. Louis Browns.

1941, February 3
Pitcher Joe Heving from Boston Red Sox.

1941, May 29
Outfielder Larry Rosenthal from Chicago White Sox.

1941, August 9
Pitcher Chubby Dean from Philadelphia Athletics.

1941, September 22
Pitcher Tom Ferrick from Philadelphia Athletics.

1941, December 11
Pitcher Vern Kennedy from Washington Senators.

1943, August 11
Third baseman Jimmy Grant from Chicago White Sox.

1944, June 27
Outfielder Myril Hoag from Chicago White Sox.

1945, October 2
Pitcher Don Black from Philadelphia Athletics.

1946, May
Pitcher Joe Berry from Philadelphia Athletics.

1947, April 2
Outfielder Catfish Metkovich from Boston Red Sox.

1948, April 3
Pitcher Russ Christopher from Philadelphia Athletics.

1948, April 12
Pitcher Butch Wensloff from New York Yankees.

1949, January 12
Catcher Mike Tresh from Chicago White Sox.

1949, April 20
Pitcher Al Benton from Detroit Tigers.

1950, April 16
Pitcher Marino Pieretti from Chicago White Sox.

1950, December 13
Catcher Birdie Tebbetts from Boston Red Sox.

1951, May 2
Pitcher Charlie Harris from Philadelphia Athletics.

1951, May 10
Pitcher Johnny Vander Meer signed as a free agent.

1951, July 19
Outfielder Paul Lehner from St. Louis Browns.

1951, July 21
Outfielder Barney McCosky from Cincinnati Reds.

1952, April 22
Pitcher Mickey Harris from Washington Senators.

1952, June 10
Third baseman Hank Majeski from Philadelphia Athletics.

1952, June 23
Catcher Joe Tipton from Philadelphia Athletics.

1952, August 7
Outfielder Wally Westlake from Cincinnati Reds.

1953, May 3
Catcher Hank Foiles from Cincinnati Reds.

1955, June 15
Pitcher Ted Gray signed as a free agent.

1955, July 14
First baseman Ferris Fain signed as a free agent.

1955, July 31
Pitcher Sal Maglie from New York Giants.

1956, March 24
Outfielder Sam Mele signed as a free agent.

1957, May 20
First baseman Eddie Robinson signed as a free agent.

1957, August 24
Pitcher Vito Valentinetti from Chicago Cubs.

1957, September 21
Pitcher Hoyt Wilhelm from St. Louis Cardinals.

1958, January 29
First baseman Mickey Vernon from Boston Red Sox.

1958, March 26
Pitcher Chuck Churn from Boston Red Sox.

1958, June 7
Pitcher Jim Constable from San Francisco Giants.

1958, July 2
Pitcher Morrie Martin from St. Louis Cardinals.

1958, August 4
Third baseman Randy Jackson from Los Angeles Dodgers.

1959, July 30
Pitcher Jack Harshman from Boston Red Sox.

1960, April 11
Pitcher Johnny Klippstein from Los Angeles Dodgers for $25,000.

1960, April 29
Outfielder Pete Whisenant from Cincinnati Reds.

1960, May 12
Outfielder Johnny Powers from Baltimore Orioles.

1960, July 29
Pitcher Don Newcombe from Cincinnati Reds.

1960, August 9
Third baseman Joe Morgan from Philadelphia Phillies.

1961, May 3
Outfielder Chuck Essegian from Kansas City Athletics.

1961, July 3
Second baseman Ken Aspromonte from Los Angeles Angels.

1961, July 7
Pitcher Joe Schaffernoth from Chicago Cubs.

1962, July 2
Infielder Marlan Coughtry from Kansas City A's.

1963, April 2
Outfielder Ellis Burton from Houston Colt 45s.

1963, June 21
Pitcher Early Wynn signed as a free agent.

1963, September 30
Pitcher Don McMahon from Houston Colt 45s.

1963, November 18
Outfielder Wally Post signed as a free agent.

1965, March 30
Pitcher Stan Williams from New York Yankees.

1965, September 9
Outfielder Lu Clinton from California Angels (Clinton was claimed on waivers by Kansas City and played one game for them before Cleveland's claim was upheld).

1965, November 30
Catcher Del Crandall signed as a free agent.

1966, October 13
Outfielder Willie Smith from California Angels.

1966, October 15
Second baseman Gus Gil from Cincinnati Reds.

1967, May 6
Pitcher Orlando Pena from Detroit Tigers.

In the only trade involving two managers in the history of baseball, Indians general manager Frank Lane (right) sent Joe Gordon to the Detroit Tigers for Jimmy Dykes on August 3, 1960.

1967, July
Pitcher Gary Kroll from Houston Astros.

1970, May 13
Third baseman Rich Rollins signed as a free agent.

1971, March 26
Infielder Fred Stanley from Milwaukee Brewers.

1971, April 5
Pitcher Camilo Pascual signed as a free agent.

1972, March 29
Pitcher Marcelino Lopez from Milwaukee Brewers.

1972, July 11
Pitcher Bill Butler from Kansas City Royals.

1972, September 18
Pitcher Lowell Palmer from St. Louis Cardinals.

1973, March 6
Pitcher Jerry Johnson from San Francisco Giants.

1973, August 3
Pitcher Ken Sanders from Minnesota Twins.

1974, March 25
Infielder Jack Heidemann from Oakland A's.

1974, March 28
Outfielder Leron Lee from San Diego Padres.

1974, June 5
First baseman Joe Lis from Minnesota Twins.

1974, July 17
First baseman Tom McCraw from California Angels.

1975, February 13
Outfielder Ken Berry signed as a free agent.

1975, June 30
First baseman Bill Sudakis signed as a free agent.

1975, August 26
Pitcher Bob Reynolds from Detroit Tigers.

1975, December 9
Catcher Ray Fosse from Oakland A's.

1976, May 28
Pitcher Card Camper from St. Louis Cardinals.

1976, November 19
Pitcher Wayne Garland signed as a free agent.

1978, February 23
Shortstop Frank Duffy signed as a free agent.

1978, March 1
Outfielder Dan Briggs signed as a free agent.

1978, March 26
Outfielder Mike Vail from New York Mets.

1978, May 19
Infielder Larry Lintz signed as a free agent.

1978, June 15
Outfielder Bernie Carbo from Boston Red Sox.

1979, December 19
Outfielder Jorge Orta signed as a free agent.

1980, May 7
Outfielder Miguel Dilone from Chicago Cubs.

1980, June 20
Infielder Jack Brohamer from Boston Red Sox.

1980, December 8
Pitcher Dan Spillner signed as a free agent.

1980, December 29
Outfielder Pat Kelly signed as a free agent.

1981, April 17
Outfielder Ron Pruitt signed as a free agent.

1981, August 25
Pitcher Dennis Lewallyn from Texas Rangers.

1982, January 15
Pitcher Rick Waits signed as a free agent.

1982, January 20
Catcher Bill Nahorodny signed as a free agent.

1982, January 20
Pitcher Sid Monge signed as a free agent.

1982, February 8
Pitcher Mike Stanton from St. Louis Cardinals.

1982, February 13
Pitcher John Denny signed as a free agent.

1982, December 15
Outfielder Rick Manning signed as a free agent.

1983, January 21
Catcher Jim Essian from Seattle Mariners.

1983, February 1
Infielder Alan Bannister signed as a free agent.

1983, February 1
Outfielder Otto Velez signed as a free agent.

1983, February 9
Outfielder Miguel Dilone signed as a free agent.

1984, January 17
Pitcher Jamie Easterly signed as a free agent.

1984, January 19
Pitcher Steve Comer signed as a free agent.

1984, September 23
Catcher Jamie Quirk from Chicago White Sox.

1984, December 4
Designated hitter Andre Thornton signed as a free agent.

1984, December 20
Pitcher Vern Ruhle signed as a free agent.

1985, January 9
Pitcher Dave Von Ohlen signed as a free agent.

1985, April 15
Pitcher Bryan Clark signed as a free agent.

1985, April 19
Outfielder Benny Ayala signed as a free agent.

1985, December 12
Pitcher Tom Candiotti signed as a free agent.

1986, January 8
Pitcher Jamie Easterly signed as a free agent.

1986, January 8
Second baseman Tony Bernazard signed as a free agent.

1986, January 23
Infielder Fran Mullins from San Francisco Giants.

1986, February 8
Pitcher Dickie Noles signed as a free agent.

1986, February 25
Pitcher Jim Kern signed as a free agent.

1986, March 27
Pitcher Frank Wills signed as a free agent.

1986, April 3
Pitcher Phil Niekro signed as a free agent.

1987, January 27
Pitcher Ed VandeBerg signed as a free agent.

1987, February 3
Catcher Rick Dempsey signed as a free agent.

1987, April 4
Pitcher Steve Carlton signed as a free agent.

1987, April 24
Pitcher Mike Armstrong signed as a free agent.

1987, June 4
Pitcher Sammy Stewart signed as a free agent.

1987, December 7
Catcher Chris Bando signed as a free agent.

1988, January 1
Pitcher Bill Laskey signed as a free agent.

1988, January 8
Shortstop Paul Zuvella signed as a free agent.

1988, February 1
Shortstop Domingo Ramos signed as a free agent.

1988, February 9
Designated hitter Ron Kittle signed as a free agent.

1988, February 9
Pitcher Dan Schatzeder signed as a free agent.

1988, February 22
Pitcher Chris Codiroli signed as a free agent.

1988, February 28
Outfielder Terry Francona signed as a free agent.

1988, March 25
First baseman Willie Upshaw from Toronto Blue Jays.

1988, April 7
Pitcher Jon Perlman signed as a free agent.

1988, May 24
Pitcher Brad Havens signed as a free agent.

1988, June 2
Shortstop Houston Jimenez signed as a free agent.

1988, December 2
Infielder Luis Aguayo signed as a free agent.

1988, December 3
Pitcher Jesse Orosco signed as a free agent.

1988, December 5
Pitcher Bud Black signed as a free agent.

1989, January 18
Pitcher Tim Stoddard signed as a free agent.

1989, March 23
Pitcher Don Gordon signed as a free agent.

1989, April 1
Pitcher Neil Allen signed as a free agent.

1989, April 1
Catcher Mark Salas signed as a free agent.

1989, April 4
Outfielder Mike Young signed as a free agent.

1989, November 21
Pitcher Cecilio Guante signed as a free agent.

1989, November 28
Outfielder Candy Maldonado signed as a free agent.

1989, December 7
First baseman Keith Hernandez signed as a free agent.

1989, December 8
Infielder Tom Brookens signed as a free agent.

1990, January 10
Shortstop Rafael Santana signed as a free agent.

1990, February 20
Pitcher Al Nipper signed as a free agent.

1990, April 30
Pitcher Sergio Valdez from Atlanta Braves.

1990, May 7
Outfielder Stan Jefferson from Baltimore Orioles.

1990, June 17
Designated hitter Ken Phelps from Oakland Athletics.

1991, January 11
Infielder Luis Lopez signed as a free agent.

1991, January 16
Pitcher Dave Otto signed as a free agent.

1991, March 2
Infielder Carlos Martinez signed as a free agent.

1991, April 4
Catcher Eddie Taubensee from Oakland Athletics.

1991, August 6
Infielder Tony Perezchica from San Francisco Giants.

1991, August 15
Outfielder Jose Gonzalez from Pittsburgh Pirates.

1991, November 20
Pitcher Derek Lilliquist from San Diego Padres.

1991, December 16
Catcher Junior Ortiz signed as a free agent.

1992, February 25
Pitcher Brad Arnsberg signed as a free agent.

1992, April 3
Shortstop Jose Hernandez from Texas Rangers.

1992, April 5
Pitcher Ted Power signed as a free agent.

1992, April 9
Pitcher Eric Plunk signed as a free agent.

1992, April 18
Third baseman Craig Worthington signed as a free agent.

It was an awkward situation for Joe Gordon, (left) after he was traded on August 3, 1960 to Detroit in the first—and thus far only—deal involving two major league managers. With the Indians earlier that season, Gordon had advocated sending Rocky Colavito (right) to the Tigers for Harvey Kuenn. When Frank Lane swapped the two managers, Gordon was reunited with the player he didn't want in Cleveland.

1992, December 8
Pitcher Bob Ojeda signed as a free agent.

1992, December 14
Pitcher Mike Bielecki signed as a free agent.

1992, December 17
Infielder Jeff Treadway signed as a free agent.

1993, January 5
Pitcher Cliff Young signed as a free agent.

1993, March 27
Pitcher Paul Abbott signed as a free agent.

1993, April 6
Pitcher Bob Milacki signed as a free agent.

1993, April 6
Pitcher Matt Young signed as a free agent.

1993, April 7
Pitcher Jason Grimsley signed as a free agent.

1993, May 7
Catcher Lance Parrish signed as a free agent.

1993, December 2
Pitcher Dennis Martinez signed as a free agent.

1993, December 2
First baseman Eddie Murray signed as a free agent.

1994, January 21
Pitcher Russ Swan signed as a free agent.

1994, February 7
Catcher Tony Pena signed as a free agent.

1994, February 10
Pitcher Jack Morris signed as a free agent.

1994, February 10
Pitcher Steve Farr signed as a free agent.

1994, April 6
Infielder Rene Gonzales signed as a free agent.

1994, July 14
Pitcher Larry Casian from Minnesota Twins.

1994, October 17
Pitcher Dennis Cook from Chicago White Sox.

1994, December 13
Infielder Alvaro Espinoza signed as a free agent.

1995, April 25
Pitchers Bud Black and Jim Poole and catcher Tony Pena signed as free agents.

1995, May 15
Pitcher Matt Williams to Houston Astros for catcher Scooter Tucker.

1995, July 27
Infielder David Bell, pitcher Rick Heiserman, and catcher Pepe McNeal to St. Louis Cardinals for pitcher Ken Hill.

Major Sales

1901, April 28
Pitcher Bock Baker to Philadelphia Athletics.

1902, May
Pitcher Dummy Leitner to Chicago White Sox.

1902, September
Second baseman Jack Thoney to Baltimore Orioles.

1903, February
Outfielder Ollie Pickering to Philadelphia Athletics.

1903, April
Catcher Jack Slattery to Chicago White Sox.

1905, August 1
Catcher Nig Clarke to Detroit Tigers.

1905, December
Pitcher Red Donahue to Detroit Tigers.

1906, February
First baseman Charlie Carr to Cincinnati Reds.

1906, February
Outfielder Rube Vinson to Chicago White Sox.

1906, February
Catcher Howard Wakefield to Washington Senators.

1906, December
First baseman Claude Rossman to Detroit Tigers.

1907, May 20
Outfielder Bunk Congalton to Boston Red Sox.

1907, November
Outfielder Frank Delahanty to New York Highlanders.

1908, January
Third baseman Mike Donovan to New York Highlanders.

1910, September
Outfielder Art Kruger to Boston Doves.

1910, September
Pitcher Fred Link to St. Louis Browns.

1911, July
Pitcher Cy Young to Boston Rustlers.

1912, January
Catcher Ted Easterly to Chicago White Sox.

1912, March
Catcher Gus Fisher to New York Highlanders.

1912, May
Shortstop Neal Ball to Boston Red Sox.

1914, December 14
Shortstop Ivy Olson to Cincinnati Reds.

1915, January
Second baseman Nap Lajoie to Philadelphia Athletics.

1915, February
First baseman Doc Johnston to Pittsburgh Pirates.

1915, May
Second baseman Bill Rodgers to Boston Red Sox.

1915, June
Pitcher Bill Steen to Detroit Tigers.

1915, July 7
Outfielder Nemo Leibold to Chicago White Sox.

1916, May
Outfielder Larry Chappell to Boston Braves.

1916, June 20
Pitcher Willie Mitchell to Detroit Tigers.

1917, February 25
First baseman Chick Gandil to Chicago White Sox.

1917, September
Catcher Tom Daly to Chicago Cubs.

1917, October
Pitcher Grover Lowdermilk to St. Louis Browns.

1917, December
Pitcher Joe Boehling to Chicago Cubs.

1918, June
Third baseman Gus Getz to Pittsburgh Pirates.

1918, June
Second baseman Marty Kavanagh to St. Louis Cardinals.

1919, January
Shortstop Terry Turner to Philadelphia Athletics.

1919, December
Pitcher Johnny Enzmann to Philadelphia Phillies.

1920, June
Pitcher Elmer Myers to Boston Red Sox.

1922, February 16
First baseman Doc Johnston to Philadelphia Athletics.

1922, May 13
Second baseman Jack Hammond to Pittsburgh Pirates.

1922, June 21
Pitcher Dave Keefe to Philadelphia Athletics.

1922, November 5
Pitcher Jim Bagby, Sr., to Pittsburgh Pirates.

1923, January
First baseman Stuffy McInnis to Boston Braves.

1925, July
Pitcher Jim Joe Edwards to Chicago White Sox.

1926, January
Second baseman Chick Fewster to Brooklyn Robins.

1927, June 15
Outfielder Bernie Neis to Chicago White Sox.

1927, August 5
Outfielder Baby Doll Jacobson to Philadelphia Athletics.

1928, May 10
Outfielder Frank Wilson to St. Louis Browns.

1928, November 22
Pitcher Bill Bayne to Boston Red Sox.

1929, January 5
Outfielder Homer Summa to Philadelphia Athletics.

1930, June 30
Pitcher Ken Holloway to New York Yankees.

1931, May 28
Shortstop Bill Hunnefield to Boston Braves.

1935, January 11
Outfielder Bob Seeds to Detroit Tigers.

1936, April 11
Pitcher Clint Brown to Chicago White Sox.

1937, April
Second baseman Boze Berger to Chicago White Sox.

1937, May
Pitcher Carl Fischer to Washington Senators.

1937, August 14
Pitcher Ivy Andrews to New York Yankees.

1938, August
Pitcher Joe Heving to Boston Red Sox.

1939, May 3
Shortstop Lyn Lary to Brooklyn Dodgers.

1939, August 2
Outfielder Moose Solters to St. Louis Browns.

1940, December 24
Pitcher Johnny Allen to St. Louis Browns for $20,000.

1941, April 21
Pitcher Bill Zuber to Washington Senators.

1941, December 4
Catcher Rollie Hemsley to Cincinnati Reds.

1942, March 26
Outfielder Gee Walker to Cincinnati Reds.

1943, August 27
Pitcher Al Milnar to St. Louis Browns.

1943, November 6
First baseman Hal Trosky to Chicago White Sox.

1944, July 28
Pitcher Vern Kennedy to Philadelphia Phillies.

1945, September 17
Catcher Gene Desautels to Philadelphia Athletics.

1946, June 24
Pitcher Tom Ferrick to St. Louis Browns.

1946, December 7
Infielder Rusty Peters to St. Louis Browns.

1947, June 14
Pitcher Roger Wolff to Pittsburgh Pirates.

1947, December 4
First baseman Les Fleming to Pittsburgh Pirates.

1948, January 16
Third baseman Eddie Bockman to Pittsburgh Pirates.

1948, January 16
Infielder Jack Conway to New York Giants.

1948, November 20
Pitcher Bob Muncrief to Pittsburgh Pirates for $20,000.

1949, February 9
Outfielder Walt Judnich to Pittsburgh Pirates.

1949, April 30
First baseman Herm Reich to Washington Senators (Reich was returned to Cleveland on May 10).

1949, May 7
Outfielder Hank Edwards to Chicago Cubs.

1949, December 14
Pitcher Frank Papish to Pittsburgh Pirates.

1950, August 2
Pitcher Gene Bearden to Washington Senators.

1952, June 25
Outfielder Paul Lehner to Boston Red Sox.

1953, April 6
Outfielder Jim Fridley to St. Louis Browns.

1954, May 12
Outfielder Jim Lemon to Washington Senators.

1955, April 7
Second baseman Harry Malmberg to Detroit Tigers.

1955, April 13
Pitcher Bob Hooper to Cincinnati Reds.

1955, May 11
Outfielder Harry Simpson to Kansas City Athletics.

1955, July 2
Outfielder Dave Philley to Baltimore Orioles.

1955, July 16
Outfielder Jim Dyck to Baltimore Orioles.

1956, May 15
Pitcher Sal Maglie to Brooklyn Dodgers.

1956, May 16
Pitcher Jose Santiago to Kansas City Athletics.

1956, July 29
Outfielder Dale Mitchell to Brooklyn Dodgers.

1957, May 15
Outfielder Bob Usher to Washington Senators.

1957, May 20
Pitcher Art Houtteman to Baltimore Orioles.

1958, July 12
Pitcher Jim Constable to Washington Senators.

1958, August 23
Pitcher Hoyt Wilhelm to Baltimore Orioles.

1959, February 2
Infielder Billy Harrell to St. Louis Cardinals.

1959, July 1
Third baseman Willie Jones to Cincinnati Reds.

1960, May 18
Pitcher Bob Grim to Cincinnati Reds.

1960, July 30
Pitcher Johnny Briggs to Kansas City Athletics.

1960, September 2
Shortstop Rocky Bridges to St. Louis Cardinals.

1961, June 5
Pitcher Russ Heman to Los Angeles Dodgers.

1961, July 4
Pitcher Johnny Antonelli to Milwaukee Braves.

1961, July 26
First baseman Bob Hale to New York Yankees.

1961, October 14
Pitcher Joe Schaffernoth to Washington Senators.

1961, October 14
Pitcher Dave Tyriver to Washington Senators.

1962, April 26
Catcher Harry Chiti to New York Mets.

1962, April 29
Outfielder Bob Nieman to San Francisco Giants.

1962, November 27
Pitcher Wynn Hawkins to New York Mets.

1963, April 8
Pitcher Bill Dailey to Minnesota Twins.

1963, December 14
Pitcher Bob Allen to Pittsburgh Pirates.

1964, December 15
Outfielder Tito Francona to St. Louis Cardinals.

1965, April 9
Pitcher Bill Edgerton to Kansas City A's.

1965, April 14
Pitcher Bill Abernathy to Chicago Cubs.

1965, November 29
Outfielder Al Luplow to New York Mets.

1966, April 5
Pitcher Al Closter to Washington Senators.

1966, October 15
Pitcher Bob Heffner to New York Mets.

1967, May 1
Pitcher Jack Kralick to New York Yankees.

1969, April 14
Outfielder Jimmie Hall to New York Yankees.

1969, June 20
Outfielder Lee Maye to Washington Senators.

1969, July 26
Shortstop Zoilo Versalles to Washington Senators.

1969, September 21
Pitcher Juan Pizarro to Oakland A's.

1970, August 7
Pitcher Dick Ellsworth to Milwaukee Brewers.

1970, September 18
Pitcher Dean Chance to New York Mets.

1970, October 23
Outfielder Richie Scheinblum to Washington Senators.

1971, April 24
Shortstop Larry Brown to Oakland A's.

1971, May 22
Pitcher Camilo Pascual to San Diego Padres (Pascual was returned to Cleveland on May 26).

1971, July 15
Pitcher Dennis Higgins to St. Louis Cardinals.

1972, March 29
Pitcher Marcelino Lopez to Milwaukee Brewers.

1974, July 1
Pitcher Bob Johnson to Texas Rangers.

1976, December 13
Pitcher Steve Kline to Atlanta Braves.

1978, November 2
Pitcher Dave Freisleben to Toronto Blue Jays.

1981, September 8
Pitcher Bob Lacey to Texas Rangers.

1981, December 7
Pitcher Mike Stanton to St. Louis Cardinals.

1982, December 9
Infielder Larry Milbourne to Philadelphia Phillies.

1982, December 15
Pitcher Ray Searage to San Diego Padres (Searage was returned to Cleveland on March 28, 1983).

1983, February 15
Pitcher Sandy Wihtol to Chicago Cubs (Wihtol returned to Cleveland on March 27).

1984, March 25
Outfielder Alan Bannister to Houston Astros.

1985, December 10
Outfielder George Vukovich to Seibu Lions of Japanese Baseball League.

1988, June 7
Catcher Brian Dorsett to California Angels.

1989, November 8
Outfielder Mike Young to Hiroshima Toyo Carp of Japanese Baseball League.

1990, April 5
Outfielder Brad Komminsk to San Francisco Giants.

1990, September 4
Pitcher Kevin Bearse to Montreal Expos.

1991, July 3
Pitcher Efrain Valdez to Toronto Blue Jays.

1991, July 12
Outfielder Mike Huff to Chicago White Sox.

1991, December 6
Pitcher Jesse Orosco to Milwaukee Brewers.

1993, November 29
Pitcher Jeff Mutis to Florida Marlins.

1994, November 9
Pitcher Derek Lilliquist to Atlanta Braves.

1994, November 18
Pitcher Bill Wertz to Boston Red Sox.

1995, June 29
Catcher Scooter Tucker to Atlanta Braves.

Milestones, Honors, and Other Facts

No other sport utilizes, relies upon, even *cherishes* statistics and records as does baseball. It's the statistics and records that provide a measuring stick by which the great players of one era are compared to those of another time and place.

But for the figures—batting average, runs scored, runs batted in, assists, putouts, fielding percentage, and so on—how else could, say, Joe Gordon, the best second baseman of the 1940s, be compared to Napoleon Lajoie, the star second baseman and player-manager of Cleveland teams in the early 1900s who is considered by some to have been the greatest player in the history of the franchise?

Or home run hitters Hal Trosky, who played in the 1930s, and Rocky Colavito, his counterpart in the 1950s?

And because of the records he compiled in 18 seasons with the Indians, can there be any doubt that Bob Feller was the best pitcher the team ever had, based on his 266 victories and the strikeout records he began setting as a teenager in 1936?

Still, Addie Joss, whose career was tragically cut short when he died at age 31 in 1911, is the holder of the franchise career-earned-run record of 1.89, which is second best to Ed Walsh in major league history.

Following are lists of the most significant records and statistics compiled by Indians players, and milestones reached, honors received, and other facts collected—some major, some trivial—since the franchise came into being in 1901, when the American League was founded by Byron Bancroft "Ban" Johnson.

Addie Joss, who pitched the second perfect game in modern baseball history to beat the Chicago White Sox and Ed Walsh, 1–0, on October 2, 1908 at League Park in Cleveland, in what some have called the greatest baseball game ever played.

Indians in the Hall of Fame

Name	Years with Indians	Year Selected	Name	Years with Indians	Year Selected	Name	Years with Indians	Year Selected
Players			Bob Feller	1936–41, 45–56	1962	Al Lopez	1947, 51–56	1977
Earl Averill	1929–39	1975						
Lou Boudreau*	1938–50	1970	Addie Joss	1902–10	1978	**Owner**		
Elmer Flick	1902–10	1963	Bob Lemon	1941–42, 46–58	1976	Bill Veeck	1946–49	1991
Ralph Kiner	1955	1975						
Nap Lajoie*	1902–14	1937	Hal Newhouser	1954–55	1992	**General Managers**		
Sam Rice	1934	1963	Satchel Paige	1948–49	1971	Billy Evans	1927–35	1973
Frank Robinson*	1974–77	1982	Gaylord Perry	1972–75	1991	Hank Greenberg	1950–57	1956
Joe Sewell	1920–30	1977	Hoyt Wilhelm	1957–58	1985			
Tris Speaker*	1916–26	1937	Early Wynn	1949–57, 63	1972	**Coaches**		
			Cy Young	1909–11	1937	Luke Appling	1960–61	1964
Pitchers						Bill McKechnie	1947–49	1962
Steve Carlton	1987	1993	**Managers**			Al Simmons	1950	1953
Stan Coveleski	1916–24	1969	Walter Johnson	1933–35	1936	Warren Spahn	1972–73	1973

*Player-manager

An exultant Dick Bosman celebrates after his 4–0 no-hit victory over the Oakland Athletics at Cleveland Stadium on July 19, 1974.

Major Indians Award Winners

MOST VALUABLE PLAYER, AL
(League Award): George Burns
(1926); (Baseball Writers Association of America, *BBWAA*): Lou
Boudreau (1948), Al Rosen (1953)

CY YOUNG AWARD, AL (BBWAA):
Gaylord Perry (1972)

ROOKIE OF THE YEAR, AL
(*BBWAA*): Herb Score (1955),
Chris Chambliss (1971), Joe
Charboneau (1980), Sandy
Alomar, Jr. (1990); (*The Sporting News*): Herb Score (1955), Roy
Foster (1970), Chris Chambliss
(1971), Joe Charboneau (1980),
Sandy Alomar, Jr. (1990)

**ROOKIE PITCHER OF THE YEAR,
AL** (*The Sporting News*): Dick Tidrow
(1972), Dennis Eckersley (1975)

PLAYER OF THE YEAR, AL (*The
Sporting News*): Lou Boudreau
(1948), Luke Easter (1952), Al
Rosen (1953), Bobby Avila (1954)

PITCHER OF THE YEAR, AL (*The
Sporting News*): Bob Lemon (1948,
1950, 1954), Bob Feller (1951),
Dick Donovan (1962), Sam
McDowell (1970)

**MAJOR LEAGUE PLAYER OF THE
YEAR** (*The Sporting News*): Johnny
Allen (1937), Bob Feller (1940),
Lou Boudreau (1948), Al Rosen
(1953), Albert Belle (1995)

**MAJOR LEAGUE EXECUTIVE OF
THE YEAR** (*The Sporting News*): Bill
Veeck (1948), John Hart (1994,
1995)

GOLD GLOVE AWARDS (*The
Sporting News*): Vic Power, 1B
(1958, 1959, 1960, 1961), Minnie

Bob Lemon's no-hitter was a 2–0 victory over the Detroit Tigers in Detroit on June 30, 1948.

Minoso, OF (1959), Jimmy Piersall,
OF (1961), Vic Davalillo, OF
(1964), Ray Fosse, C (1970, 1971),
Rick Manning OF (1976), Sandy
Alomor, Jr., C (1990), Kenny
Lofton, OF (1993, 1994, 1995),
Omar Vizquel, SS (1994, 1995)

SILVER SLUGGER AWARDS (*The
Sporting News*): Andre Thornton,
DH (1984), Julio Franco, 2B
(1988), Carlos Baerga, 2B (1993,
1994), Albert Belle, OF (1993,1994)

COMEBACK PLAYER OF THE YEAR
(*The Sporting News*): Andre
Thornton (1982)

MANAGER OF THE YEAR, AL (*The
Sporting News*): Mike Hargrove
(1995)

FIREMAN OF THE YEAR, AL (*The
Sporting News*): Jose Mesa (1995)

ROLAIDS RELIEVER OF THE YEAR
Jose Mesa (1995)

First baseman Chris Chambliss, the Indians' first round draft selection in January 1970, was the American League rookie of the year in 1971.

Bob Feller, who authored three no-hitters and 12 one-hitters, is shown here with former teammate Allie Reynolds, who was traded to the New York Yankees in the deal that brought Joe Gordon to Cleveland in 1948.

All-Star Game Selections

1933	Earl Averill, of			Bob Feller, RHP		Lou Boudreau, ss*
	Wes Ferrell, RHP		1939	Bob Feller, RHP		Ken Keltner, 3b*
	Oral Hildebrand, RHP			Rollie Hemsley, c	1943	Jim Bagby, Jr., RHP
1934	Earl Averill, of		1940	Lou Boudreau, ss		Lou Boudreau, ss
	Mel Harder, RHP			Bob Feller, RHP		Jeff Heath, of
1935	Earl Averill, of[a]			Rollie Hemsley, c		Ken Keltner, 3b*
	Mel Harder, RHP			Ken Keltner, 3b		Buddy Rosar, c
	Joe Vosmik, of*			Ray Mack, 2b		Al Smith, LHP
1936	Earl Averill, of*			Al Milnar, LHP	1944	Lou Boudreau, ss
	Mel Harder, RHP		1941	Lou Boudreau, ss		Roy Cullenbine, of
1937	Earl Averill, of*			Bob Feller, RHP*		Oris Hockett, of
	Mel Harder, RHP			Jeff Heath, of*		Ken Keltner, 3b*
1938	Johnny Allen, RHP			Ken Keltner, 3b	1945	No game
	Earl Averill, of*		1942	Jim Bagby, Jr., RHP	1946	Bob Feller, RHP*

Frankie Hayes, c*
Ken Keltner, 3b*
1947 Lou Boudreau, ss*
Bob Feller, RHP[b]
Joe Gorrdon, 2b*
Jim Hegan, c
1948 Lou Boudreau, ss*
Bob Feller, RHP[c]
Joe Gordon, 2b*
Ken Keltner, 3b*
Bob Lemon, RHP
1949 Larry Doby, of
Joe Gordon, 2b
Jim Hegan, c
Bob Lemon, RHP
Dale Mitchell, of
1950 Larry Doby, of*
Bob Feller, RHP
Jim Hegan, c
Bob Lemon, p
1951 Larry Doby, of
Jim Hegan, c
Bob Lemon, RHP
1952 Bobby Avila, 2b*
Larry Doby, of
Mike Garcia, RHP
Jim Hegan, c
Bob Lemon, RHP
Dale Mitchell, of*
Al Rosen, 3b*
1953 Larry Doby, of
Mike Garcia, RHP
Bob Lemon, RHP
Al Rosen, 3b*
1954 Bobby Avila, 2b*
Larry Doby, of
Mike Garcia, RHP[d]
Bob Lemon, RHP
Al Rosen, 1b*
1955 Bobby Avila, 2b
Larry Doby, of
Al Rosen, 3b
Herb Score, LHP
Al Smith, of
Early Wynn, RHP
1956 Ray Narleski, RHP[e]
Herb Score, LHP
Early Wynn, RHP
1957 Don Mossi, LHP
Vic Wertz, 1b*
Early Wynn, RHP
1958 Ray Narleski RHP
Mickey Vernon, 1b
1959 Rocky Colavito, of*
Cal McLish, RHP
Minnie Minoso, of*
Vic Power, 1b
1960 Gary Bell, RHP
Harvey Kuenn, of
Vic Power, 1b
Dick Stigman, LHP

1961 Tito Francona, of
Barry Latman, RHP
Jim Perry, RHP
John Romano, c*
Johnny Temple, 2b*
1962 Dick Donovan, RHP
John Romano, c
1963 Mudcat Grant, RHP
1964 Jack Kralick, LHP
1965 Max Alvis, 3b
Rocky Colavito, of*
Vic Davalillo, of*
Sam McDowell, LHP
1966 Gary Bell, RHP
Rocky Colavito, of
Sam McDowell, LHP[f]
Sonny Siebert, RHP
1967 Max Alvis, 3b
Steve Hargan, RHP
1968 Joe Azcue, c
Sam McDowell, LHP
Luis Tiant, RHP*
1969 Sam McDowell, LHP
1970 Ray Fosse, c
Sam McDowell, LHP
1971 Ray Fosse, c[g]
Sam McDowell, LHP[h]
1972 Gaylord Perry, RHP
1973 Buddy Bell, 3b
1974 George Hendrick, of
Gaylord Perry, RHP*
1975 George Hendrick, of
1976 Dave LaRoche, LHP
1977 Dennis Eckersley, RHP
Jim Kern, RHP[i]
1978 Jim Kern, RHP
1979 Sid Monge, LHP
1980 Jorge Orta, of
1981 Len Barker, RHP
Bo Diaz, c

Dennis Eckersley, who has become one of the greatest relief pitchers in baseball history, pitched a no-hitter for the Indians on May 30, 1977, beating the California Angels, 1–0, at Cleveland Stadium.

1982 Toby Harrah, 3b
Andre Thornton, dh[j]
1983 Rick Sutcliffe, RHP
Manny Trillo, 2b*
1984 Andre Thornton, dh
1985 Bert Blyleven, RHP
1986 Brook Jacoby, 3b
Ken Schrom, p
1987 Pat Tabler, dh
1988 Doug Jones, RHP
1989 Doug Jones, RHP
Greg Swindell, LHP
1990 Sandy Alomar, Jr., c*
Brook Jacoby, 3b
Doug Jones, RHP

Sonny Siebert, a converted outfielder–first baseman, hurled a no-hitter on June 10, 1966, to beat the Washington Senators, 2–0, at Cleveland Stadium.

Len Barker pitched the eighth perfect game in modern baseball history to beat the Toronto Blue Jays, 3–0, on May 15, 1981.

Catcher Sandy Alomar Jr., who came to the Indians in one of the club's best-ever trades—Alomar, Carlos Baerga, and Chris James from San Diego for Joe Carter—won the rookie of the year award in 1990.

1991 Sandy Alomar, Jr., c*
1992 Sandy Alomar, Jr., c*
     Carlos Baerga, 2b
     Charles Nagy, RHP
1993 Carlos Baerga, 2b
     Albert Belle, of

1994 Albert Belle, of
     Kenny Lofton, of
1995 Carlos Baerga, 2b*
     Albert Belle, of*
     Kenny Lofton, of*k
     Dennis Martinez, RHP
     Jose Mesa, RHP
     Manny Ramirez, of

* Starters
aReplaced by Roger Cramer of Philadelphia
bReplaced by Early Wynn of Washington
cReplaced by Joe Dobson of Boston
dReplaced by Sandy Consuegra of Chicago
eReplaced by Herb Score
fReplaced by Sonny Siebert
gReplaced by Dave Duncan of Oakland
hReplaced by Wilbur Wood of Chicago
iReplaced Mark Fidrych of Detroit
jReplaced Rod Carew of California
kReplaced Ken Griffey Jr. of Seattle
Winning pitcher:
  Mel Harder (1934)
  Bob Feller (1946)
Home runs:
  1942: Lou Boudreau (Polo Grounds, New York)

Rocky Colavito became only the sixth player in modern baseball history to hit four homers in one game, and the second to do so in consecutive at bats, in an 11–8 victory over the Baltimore Orioles in Baltimore on June 10, 1959.

1954: Al Rosen (2) (Cleveland Stadium)
1954: Larry Doby (Cleveland Stadium)
1959: Rocky Colavito (Memorial Coliseum, Los Angeles)

Cleveland Baseball Writers Man of the Year Award

1946	Bill Veeck	1953	Al Rosen	1962	Dick Donovan
1947	Lou Boudreau	1954	Bobby Avila	1963	Max Alvis
1948	Gene Bearden	1955	Al Smith	1964	Don McMahon
1949	Bob Lemon	1956	Vic Wertz	1965	Rocky Colavito
1950	Larry Doby	1957	Gene Woodling	1966	Sonny Siebert
1951	Bob Feller	1958	Rocky Colavito	1967	Max Alvis
1952	Mike Garcia	1959	Tito Francona	1968	Luis Tiant
	Bob Lemon	1960	Jim Perry	1969	Sam McDowell
	Early Wynn	1961	Mel Harder	1970	Ray Fosse

Indians man of the year in 1947, Lou Boudreau, with wife Della.

Gene Bearden, the Indians man of the year in 1948.

Rico Carty, man of the year, 1976.

Co-men of the year, 1952 (left to right): Bob Lemon, Mike Garcia, and Early Wynn.

	Sam McDowell		Toby Harrah
1971	Graig Nettles	1983	Rick Sutcliffe
1972	Gaylord Perry	1984	Bert Blyleven
1973	Buddy Bell	1985	Brett Butler
1974	Gaylord Perry	1986	Joe Carter
	Jim Perry	1987	Brook Jacoby
1975	Dave LaRoche	1988	Doug Jones
1976	Rico Carty	1989	Jerry Browne
1977	Duane Kuiper	1990	Doug Jones
1978	Andre Thornton	1991	Carlos Baerga
1979	Dave Garcia	1992	Carlos Baerga
1980	Mike Hargrove	1993	Albert Belle
1981	Mike Hargrove	1994	no award
1982	Andre Thornton	1995	Jose Mesa

Duane Kuiper, man of the year, 1977.

All-Time Indians Greatest Team (Selected by Fans in 1969)

1B	Hal Trosky	C	Steve O'Neill	RHP	Bob Feller
2B	Nap Lajoie	LF	Charlie Jamieson	LHP	Vean Gregg
SS	Lou Boudreau	CF	Tris Speaker		
3B	Ken Keltner	RF	"Shoeless Joe" Jackson		

Indians Permanently Retired Numbers

	Number	Year Retired
Bob Feller	19	1957
Lou Boudreau	5	1970
Earl Averill	3	1965

	Number	Year Retired
Mel Harder	18	1990
Larry Doby	14	1994

Larry Doby, man of the year, 1950.

Gordon Cobbledick Golden Tomahawk Award Winners
(Selected by Indians Players)

1963	Jerry Kindall	1968	Stan Williams	
1964	Fred Whitfield	1969	Jose Cardenal	
1965	Dick Howser	1970	Sam McDowell	
1966	Larry Brown	1971	Ray Fosse	
1967	Joe Azcue	1972	Graig Nettles	

Rick Sutcliffe, man of the year, 1983.

Shortstop Jerry Dybzinski, Golden Tomahawk Award winner, 1982.

1973	Gaylord Perry
1974	John Ellis
1975	Frank Duffy
1976	Alan Ashby
1977	Buddy Bell
1978	Andre Thornton
	Duane Kuiper
1979	Andre Thornton
1980	Toby Harrah
1981	Mike Hargrove
1982	Jerry Dybzinski
1983	Andre Thornton
1984	Rick Sutcliffe
1985	Brett Butler
1986	Joe Carter
1987	Pat Tabler
1988	Joe Carter
1989	Jerry Browne
1990	Doug Jones
1991	Carlos Baerga
1992	Carlos Baerga
1993	Albert Belle
1994	no award

Cleveland Baseball Writers Frank Gibbons Good Guy Award Winners

1968	Alvin Dark	1977	Cy Buynak	1987	Andre Thornton
1969	Lou Klimchock	1978	Duane Kuiper	1988	Doc Edwards
1970	Larry Brown	1979	Sid Monge	1989	Tom Candiotti
1971	Hank Peters	1980	Rick Manning		Bud Black
1972	Dino Lucarelli	1981	Mike Seghi	1990	Brook Jacoby
1973	Bob Gill	1982	Dennis Sommers	1991	Mike Hargrove
1974	Harold Bossard	1983	Don McMahon	1992	Felix Ferrnin
	Marshall Bossard	1984	Andre Thornton	1993	Cy Buynak
1975	Boog Powell	1985	Mike Hargrove	1994	no award
1976	Jim Warfield	1986	Johnny Goryl	1995	Jim Thome

Oldest Living Indians Players
(As of November 1, 1995)

Player	Date of Birth	Player	Date of Birth	Player	Date of Birth
Joe Hauser	January 12, 1899	Ab Wright	November 16, 1905	Joe Becker	June 25, 1908
Ike Kahdot	October 22, 1901	Willis Hudlin	May 23, 1906	Al Lopez	August 20, 1908
Ray Benge	April 22, 1902	Thornton Lee	September 13, 1906	Mel Harder	October 15, 1909
Sal Gliatto	May 7, 1902	Whitlow Wyatt	September 27, 1907		

Nicknames of Indians Players

Abbott, Fred (Faithful Fred)
    1903–04
Ables, Harry (Hans) 1909
Allred, Dale (Beau) 1989–91
Altizer, Dave (Filipino) l908

Alvarado, Luis (Pimba) 1974
Anderson, Karl (Bud) 1982–83
Andrews, Ivy (Poison) 1937
Autry, Martin (Chick) 1926–28
Avila, Bobby (Beto) 1949–58

Azcue, Joe (The Immortal Cuban)
    1963–69

Bagby, Jim, Sr. (Sarge) 1916–22
Baker, Charles (Bock) 1901

Barbare, Walter (Dinty) 1914–16
Barbeau, William (Jap) 1905–06
Barker, Ray (Buddy) 1965
Bay, Harry (Deerfoot) 1902–08
Bayne, Bill (Beverly) 1928
Beck, Erve (Dutch) 1901
Beck, George (Eaglebeak) 1914
Becker, Heinz (Dutch) 1946–47
Bell, David (Buddy) 1972–78
Bell, Roy (Beau) 1940–41
Benge, Ray (Silent Cal) 1925–26
Benton, Alfred (Butch) 1985
Berg, Morris (Moe) 1931, 34
Berger, Louis (Boze) 1932, 35–36
Bergman, Alfred (Dutch) 1916
Berry, Joe (Jittery Joe) 1946
Billings, John (Josh) 1913–18
Birmingham, Joe (Dode) 1906–14
Black, Harry (Bud) 1988–90, 95
Blanks, Larvell (Sugar Bear) 1976–78
Bolger, Jim (Dutch) 1959
Bonner, Frank (The Human Flea)
    1902
Booker, Richard (Buddy) 1966
Booles, Seabron (Red) 1909
Boone, Ray (Ike) 1948–53
Bradford, Charles (Buddy) 1970–71
Brennan, Tom (The Gray Flamingo)
    1981–83
Brenner, Bert (Dutch) 1912
Brenton, Lynn (Buck) 1913, 15
Bridges, Everett (Rocky) 1960
Bronkie, Herman (Dutch) 1910–12
Brower, Frank (Turkeyfoot) 1923–24
Brown, Lloyd (Gimpy) 1934–37
Brown, Walter (Jumbo) 1927–28
Buckeye, Garland (Gob) 1925–28
Burns, George (Tioga George)
    1920–21, 24–28

Caffie, Joe (Rabbit) 1956–57
Caldwell, Ray (Slim) 1919–21
Campbell, Clarence (Soup) 1940–41
Cardenas, Leo (Chico) 1972
Carson, Walter (Kit) 1934–35
Chakales, Bob (Chick) 1951–54
Cheeves, Virgil (Chief) 1924
Cicotte, Al (Bozo) 1959
Clanton, Eucal (Cat) 1922
Clark, Harvey (Ginger) 1902
Clarke, Jay (Nig) 1905–10
Clarke, Josh (Pepper) 1908–09
Collard, Earl (Hap) 1927–28
Congalton, Bill (Bunk) 1905–07
Connally, George (Sarge) 1931–34
Connolly, Joe (Coaster Joe) 1922–23
Constable, Jim (Sheriff) 1958
Craghead, Howard (Judge) 1931, 33
Cullop, Nick (Tomato Face) 1927

Daley, Leo (Bud) 1955–57
Davidson, Homer (Divvy) 1908

Davis, Harry (Jasper) 1912
Dean, Alfred (Chubby) 1941–43
Delahanty, Frank (Pudgie) 1907
Denning, Otto (Dutch) 1942–43
Dente, Sam (Blackie) 1954–55
Desautels, Gene (Red) 1941–43, 45
DesJardien, Paul (Shorty) 1916
Diaz, Baudilio (Bo) 1978–81
Dillinger, Harley (Hoke) 1914
Dobson, Joe (Burrhead) 1939–40
Donahue, Francis (Red) 1903–05
Dorman, Dwight (Red) 1928
Dorsett, Calvin (Preacher) 1940–41, 47

Eagan, Charles (Truck) 1901
Edmonson, Eddie (Axel) 1913
Edwards, Howard (Doc) 1962–63
Edwards, James (Jim Joe) 1922–25
Eichrodt, Fred (Ike) 1925–27
Ellerbe, Frank (Governor) 1924
Ellingsen, Bruce (Little Pod) 1974
Embree, Charles (Red) 1941–42,
    44–47
Engle, Clyde (Hack) 1916
Enzmann, Johnny (Gentleman John)
    1918–19
Evans, Joe (Doc) 1915–22
Evers, Walter (Hoot) 1955–56

Fahr, Gerald (Red) 1951
Fain, Ferris (Burrhead) 1955
Falk, Bibb (Jockey) 1929–31
Falkenberg, Fred (Cy) 1908–11, 13
Feller, Bob (Rapid Robert) 1936–41,
    45–56
Ferry, Alfred (Cy) 1905
Fewster Wilson (Chick) 1924–25
Fleming, Les (Moe) 1941–42, 45–47
Foster, Eddy (Slim) 1908
Francona, John (Tito) 1959–64

Tito Francona, man of the year, 1959.

Frazier, Joe (Cobra Joe) 1947
Friend, Owen (Red) 1953

Gallagher, Charlie (Shorty) 1901
Gandil, Arnold (Chick) 1916
Garcia, Mike (The Big Bear)
    1948–59
Garrett, Clarence (Laz) 1915
Gassaway, Charlie (Sheriff) 1946
Genins, Frank (Frenchy) 1901
George, Charlie (Greek) 1935–36
Gerken, George (Pickles) 1927–28
Getz, Gus (Gee Gee) 1918
Gill, Johnny (Patcheye) 1927–28
Gleeson, Jim (Gee Gee) 1936
Glynn, Ed (The Flushing Flash)
    1981–83
Gordon, Joe (Flash) 1947–50
Gould, Al (Pudgy) 1916–17
Gozzo, Mauro (Goose) 1990–91
Graham, George (Peaches) 1902
Grant, Eddie (Harvard Eddie) 1905
Grant, Jim (Mudcat) 1958–64
Gregg, Dave (Highpockets) 1913
Gunkel, Woodward (Red) 1916

Hagerman, Zeriah (Rip) 1914–16
Hale, Odell (Bad News) 1931, 33–40
Hamann, Elmer (Doc) 1922
Hamilton, Jack (Hairbreadth Harry)
    1969
Hammond, Jack (Wobby) 1915, 22
Harder, Mel (Chief, Wimpy) 1928–47
Hardy, Jack (Do-Little) 1903
Hargrove, Mike (The Human Rain
    Delay) 1979–85
Harkness, Fred (Specs) 1910–11
Harrah, Colbert (Toby) 1979–83
Harrelson, Ken (Hawk) 1969–71
Harris, Joe (Moon) 1917, 19
Hart, Bill (Uncle Billy) 1901
Hartley, Grover (Slick) 1929–30
Harvel, Luther (Red) 1928
Harvey, Ervin (Zaza) 1901–02
Hauser, Joe (Unser Choe) 1929
Haworth, Homer (Cully) 1915
Hayes, Frankie (Blimp) 1945–46
Hedlund, Mike (Red) 1965, 68
Hemphill, Charlie (Eagle Eye) 1902
Henderson, Bernie (Barnyard) 1921
Hendrick, Harvey (Gink) 1925
Henry, Earl (Hook) 1944–45
Hernandez, Keith (Mex) 1990
Hickman, Charlie (Piano Legs)
    1902–04, 08
Hodge, Harold (Gomer) 1971
Hoffer, Bill (Wizard) 1901
Hoffman, Edward (Tex) 1915
Holland, Bob (Dutch) 1934
Howell, Millard (Dixie) 1940
Howell, Murray (Porky) 1941
Hudlin, Willis (Ace) 1926–40

Hughes, Roy (Jeep, Sage) 1935–37
Hunnefield, Bill (Wild Bill) 1931

Iott, Fred (Happy, Dimples) 1903

Jackson, Joe (Shoeless Joe) 1910–15
Jackson, Randy (Handsome Ransom)
 1958–59
Jacobson, Bill (Baby Doll) 1927
Jasper, Henry (Hi) 1919
Jeanes, Ernest (Tex) 1921–22
Jeter, John (The Jet) 1974
Jimenez, Alfonso (Houston) 1988
Johnson, Cliff (Heathcliff) 1979–80
Johnson, Lou (Slick) 1968
Johnston, Wheeler (Doc) 1912–14,
 18–21
Jones, Sam (Sad Sam) 1914–15
Jones, Sam (Toothpick Sam) 1951–52
Jungels, Ken (Curly) 1937–38,40–41

Kahdot, Ike (Chief) 1922
Kahler, George (Krum) 1910–14
Kardow, Paul (Tex) 1936
Karr, Benn (Baldy) 1925–27
Kibble, Jack (Happy) 1912
Killian, Ed (Twilight Ed) 1903
Kindall, Jerry (Slim) 1962–64
Kittle, Ron (Kitty) 1988
Klieman, Eddie (Babe) 1943–48
Knaupp, Henry (Cotton) 1910–11
Krapp, Gene (Rubber) 1911–12
Kuhn, Bernard (Bub) 1924
Kurtz, Hal (Bud) 1968
Kuzava, Bob (Sarge) 1946–47

LaChance, George (Candy) 1901
Lattimore, Bill (Slothful Bill) 1908
Lawson, Alfred (Roxie) 1930–31
Lehner, Paul (Gulliver) 1951
Lehr, Norm (King) 1926
Leibold, Harry (Nemo) 1913–15
Leitner, George (Dummy) 1902
Levsen, Emil (Dutch) 1923–28
Link, Fred (Laddie) 1910
Lord, Bris (The Human Eyeball)
 1909–10
Lowdermilk, Grover (Slim) 1916
Lutzke, Walter (Rube) 1923–27

Maglie, Sal (The Barber) 1955–56
Mahoney, Jim (Moe) 1962
Mails, Walter (Duster) 1920–22
Majeski, Hank (Heeney) 1952–55
Martin, Billy (The Kid) 1959
Mathias, Carl (Stubby) 1960
McBride, Arnold (Bake) 1982–83
McDowell, Sam (Sudden Sam)
 1961–71
McGuire, James (Deacon) 1908, 10
McInnis, John (Stuffy) 1922
McLish, Cal (Buster) 1956–59

Sudden Sam McDowell, who won the Man of
the Year Award in 1969, and shared it with his
catcher, Ray Fosse, in 1970.

McNeal, Harry (The Cleveland Kid)
 1901
Meixell, Merton (Moxie) 1912
Messenger, Andrew (Bud) 1924
Metkovich, George (Catfish) 1947
Meyer, Lambert (Dutch) 1945–46
Miljus, Johnny (Big Serb) 1928–29
Milnar, Al (Happy) 1936, 38–43
Morton, Guy (Alabama Blossom)
 1914–23
Mossi, Don (The Sphinx) 1954–58
Murray, Ray (Deacon) 1948, 50–51

Nagelson, Russ (Rusty) 1968–70
Nelson, Glenn (Rocky) 1954
Newhouser, Hal (Prince Hal) 1954–55
Niekro, Phil (Knucksie) 1986–87
Nill, George (Rabbit) 1907–08
Noboa, Milciades (Junior) 1984, 87

Odom, Johnny (Blue Moon) 1975
Ortiz, Adalberto (Junior) 1992–93
Otis, Harry (Cannonball) 1909

Padgett, Ernie (Red) 1926–27
Paige, Leroy (Satchel) 1948–49
Pascual, Camilo (Little Potato) 1971
Peters, John (Shotgun) 1918
Peters, Russ (Rusty) 1940–44, 46
Peterson, Charles (Cap) 1969
Petty, Jesse (The Silver Fox) 1921
Phillips, John (Bubba) 1960–62
Pieretti, Marino (Chick) 1950
Piniella, Lou (Sweet Lou) 1968
Podbielan, Clarence (Bud) 1959
Podgajny, John (Specs) 1946
Porter, Dick (Twitchy) 1929–34
Powell, John (Boog) 1975–76
Pruitt, Ron (Do-It) 1976–81

Radatz, Dick (The Monster) 1966–67
Reilley, Alexander (Duke, Midget)
 1909

Reiser, Harold (Pistol Pete) 1952
Reisigl, Jacob (Bugs) 1911
Reynolds, Allie (Superchief) 1942–46
Rhoads, Bob (Dusty) 1903–09
Rodgers, Bill (Raw Meat Bill) 1915
Rollins, Rich (Red) 1970
Romano, Johnny (Honey) 1960–64
Rosar, Warren (Buddy) 1943–44
Rosen, Al (Flip) 1947–56
Roth, Robert (Braggo) 1915–18
Russell, Lloyd (Tex) 1938
Ryan, Jack (Gulfport) 1908

Salmon, Ruthford (Chico) 1964–68
Sanders, Ken (Daffy) 1973–74
Santiago, Jose (Pants) 1954–55
Schaefer, Herman (Germany) 1918
Scheibeck, Frank (Archer) 1901
Schwartz, Bill (Blab) 1904
Seeds, Bob (Suitcase Bob) 1930–32, 34
Shaner, Wally (Skinny) 1923
Shinault, Enoch (Ginger) 1921–22
Shipke, Bill (Muskrat Bill) 1906
Siebert, Wilfred (Sonny) 1964–69
Simpson, Harry (Suitcase) 1951–53,
 55
Sims, Duane (Duke) 1964–70
Smith, Al (Fuzzy) 1953–57, 64
Smith, Clarence (Pop Boy) 1916–17
Smith, Robert (Riverboat) 1959
Smith, Willie (Wonderful Willie)
 1967–68
Solters, Julius (Moose) 1937–39
Sorrells, Raymond (Chick) 1922
Speaker, Tris (Spoke, The Gray
 Eagle) 1916–26
Sprinz, Joe (Mule) 1930–31
Stanley, Fred (Chicken) 1971–72
Stark, Monroe (Dolly) 1909
Steiner, James (Red) 1945
Stephenson, Riggs (Old Hoss)
 1921–25
Stirnweiss, George (Snuffy) 1951–52
Stovall, George (Firebrand) 1904–11
Stovall, Jesse (Scout) 1903
Strickland, George (Bo) 1952–57,
 59–60
Stromme, Floyd (Rock) 1939
Sudakis, Bill (Suds) 1975
Susce, George (Good Kid) 1941–44

Taylor, Luther (Dummy) 1902
Tebbetts, George (Birdie) 1951–52
Thomas, Chester (Pinch) 1918–21
Thomas, Fay (Scow) 1931
Thomason, Art (Sillie) 1910
Thoney, Jack (Bullet Jack) 1902–03
Tidrow, Dick (Dirt) 1972–74
Tolson, Charles (Chick, Slug) 1925
Tomanek, Dick (Bones) 1953–54,
 57–58
Torkelson, Chester (Red) 1917

Torres, Rosendo (Rusty) 1973–74
Townsend, John (Happy) 1906
Tucker, Eddie (Scooter) 1995
Tucker, Thurman (Joe E.) 1948–51
Turchin, Eddie (Smiley) 1943
Turner, Terrence (Cotton) 1904–18

Uhle, George (The Bull) 1919–28, 36
Ussat, William (Dutch) 1925, 27

Varney, Lawrence (Dike) 1902
Vidal, Jose (Papito) 1966–68
Vinson, Ernest (Rube) 1904–05

Wagner, Leon (Daddy Wags) 1964–68
Walker, Fred (Mysterious) 1912

Walker, Gerald (Gee) 1941
Walker, Roy (Dixie) 1912, 15
Walters, Alfred (Roxy) 1924–25
Weatherly, Roy (Stormy) 1936–42
Webb, James (Skeeter) 1938–39
Weigel, Ralph (Wig) 1946
Weik, Dick (Legs) 1950, 53
Weingartner, Elmer (Dutch) 1945
Wensloff, Charles (Butch) 1948
West, James (Hi) 1905, 11
Weyhing, Gus (Rubber-Winged Gus) 1901
Wihtol, Alexander (Sandy) 1979–80, 82
Wilks, Ted (Cork) 1952–53
Williams, Fred (Pap) 1945

Williams, Walt (No Neck) 1973
Willis, Les (Wimpy) 1947
Wilson, Art (Dutch) 1921
Wilson, Frank (Squash) 1928
Winn, George (Breezy) 1922–23
Wood, Joe (Smoky Joe) 1917–22
Wright, Albert (Ab) 1935
Wright, William (Lucky, Deacon) 1909

Yeager, George (Doc) 1901
Yingling, Earl (Chink) 1911
Young, Denton (Cy) 1909–11
Yowell, Carl (Sundown) 1924–25

Zoldak, Sam (Sad Sam) 1948–50
Zuber, Bill (Goober) 1936, 38–40

Local Boys Who Made Good (Indians Born in the Cleveland Area)

Al Aber, 1950, 53—Cleveland
Earl Averill, 1956, 58—Cleveland
Jim Bagby, Jr., 1941–45—Cleveland
Chris Bando, 1981–88—Cleveland
Bill Bonness, 1944—Cleveland
Jack Bracken, 1901—Cleveland
Bill Bradley, 1901–10—Cleveland
Ed Cermak, 1901—Cleveland
Frank Cross, 1901—Cleveland
Homer Davidson, 1908—Cleveland
Frank Delahanty, 1907—Cleveland
Frank Doljack, 1943—Cleveland
Jerry Dybzinski, 1980–82—Cleveland
Elmer Flick, 1902–10—Bedford
Jack Hardy, 1903—Cleveland
Ken Hogan, 1923–24—Cleveland
Larry Doby Johnson, 1972, 74—Cleveland
Bob Kelly, 1958—Cleveland

Emil Leber, 1905—Cleveland
Paddy Livingston, 1901, 12—Cleveland
Ray Mack, 1938–44, 46—Cleveland
Pat McNulty, 1922, 24–27—Cleveland
Al Milnar, 1936, 38–43—Cleveland
Dave Mlicki, 1992–93—Cleveland
Paul O'Dea, 1944–45—Cleveland
Jim Rittwage, 1970—Cleveland
Bob Rothel, 1945—Columbia Station
Hank Ruszkowski, 1944–45, 47—Cleveland
Bill Schwartz, 1904—Cleveland
Charlie Smith, 1902—Cleveland
Dick Tomanek, 1953–54, 57–58—Avon Lake
George Uhle, 1919–28, 36—Cleveland
Joe Vosmik, 1930–36—Cleveland
Bill Wambsganss, 1914–23—Cleveland

Pitcher Al Aber.

Jimmy Wasdell, 1946–47—Cleveland
Elmer Weingartner, 1945—Cleveland

Catcher Chris Bando (right) with brother Sal, who had a long playing career with the Kansas City/Oakland Athletics.

Ollie Welf, 1916—Cleveland
Bill Wertz, 1993–94—Cleveland
Gene Wright, 1902–03—Cleveland

Catcher Larry Doby Johnson.

Pitcher Bill Bonness.

Most Career Games With Indians

First Base

Hal Trosky	1933–41	1,111
George Stovall	1904–11	802
Mike Hargrove	1979–85	768
Doc Johnston	1912–14, 18–21	698
George Burns	1920–21, 24–28	681

Second Base

Nap Lajoie	1902–14	1,385
Bobby Avila	1949–58	1,098
Bill Wambsganss	1914–23	936
Duane Kuiper	1974–81	774
Ray Mack	1938–44, 46	767

Third Base

Ken Keltner	1937–44, 46–49	1,492

Bill Bradley	1901–10	1,193
Brook Jacoby	1984–92	1,109
Max Alvis	1962–69	935
Al Rosen	1947–56	932

Shortstop

Lou Boudreau	1938–50	1,486
Joe Sewell	1920–30	1,216
Ray Chapman	1912–20	957
Frank Duffy	1972–77	797
Terry Turner	1904–18	722

Outfield

Earl Averill	1929–39	1,483
Tris Speaker	1916–26	1,475
Charlie Jamieson	1919–32	1,386
Jack Graney	1908, 10–22	1,282
Larry Doby	1947–55, 58	1,165
Rick Manning	1975–83	1,051

Dale Mitchell	1946–56	929
Elmer Flick	1902–10	911
Jeff Heath	1936–45	892
Rocky Colavito	1955–59, 65–67	871
Joe Vosmik	1930–36	808
Homer Summa	1922–28	728
Joe Birmingham	1906–14	709
Joe Carter	1984–89	662
Vic Davalillo	1963–68	648

Catcher

Jim Hegan	1941–42, 46–57	1,491
Steve O'Neill	1911–23	1,339
Luke Sewell	1921–32, 39	944
Glenn Myatt	1923–35	654
Frankie Pytlak	1932–40	598

Most Years With Indians

20	Mel Harder	1928–47
18	Bob Feller	1936–41, 45–56
15	Terry Turner	1904–18
	Willis Hudlin	1926–40
	Bob Lemon	1941–42, 46–58
14	Jack Graney	1908, 10–22
	Charlie Jamieson	1919–32
	Jim Hegan	1941–42, 46–57
13	Nap Lajoie	1902–14
	Steve O'Neill	1911–23
	Luke Sewell	1921–32, 39
	Glenn Myatt	1923–35
	Lou Boudreau	1938–50
	Steve Gromek	1941–53
12	Ken Keltner	1937–44, 46–49
	Mike Garcia	1948–59
11	Guy Morton	1914–24

	Tris Speaker	1916–26
	George Uhle	1919–28, 36
	Joe Sewell	1920–30
	Earl Averill	1929–39
	Dale Mitchell	1946–56
	Sam McDowell	1961–71
10	Bill Bradley	1901–10
	Bill Wambsganss	1914–23
	Clint Brown	1928–35, 41–42
	Jeff Heath	1936–45
	Larry Doby	1947–55, 58
	Al Rosen	1947–56
	Bobby Avila	1949–58
	Early Wynn	1949–57, 63
	Gary Bell	1958–67
	Andre Thornton	1977–79, 81–87

Outfielder Jack Graney.

Players with Indians Two Times

Player	First Time	Second Time
Johnny Berardino	1948–50	1952
Moe Berg	1931	1934
Jack Brohamer	1972–75	1980
Clint Brown	1928–35	1941–42
George Burns	1920–21	1924–28
Rocky Colavito	1955–59	1965–67
Larry Doby	1947–55	1958
Steve Farr	1984	1994
Hank Foiles	1953, 55–56	1960
Ted Ford	1970–71	1973
Ray Fosse	1967–72	1976–77
Joe Heving	1937–38	1941–44
Piano Legs Hickman	1902–04	1908
Chuck Hinton	1965–67	1969–71
Doc Johnston	1912–14	1918–21
Jim Kern	1974–78	1986
Paddy Livingston	1901	1912

Player	First Time	Second Time
Tom McCraw	1972	1974–75
Minnie Minoso	1949, 51	1958–59
Billy Moran	1958–59	1964–65
Jim Perry	1959–63	1974–75
Dave Pope	1952, 54–55	1956
Eddie Robinson	1942, 46–48	1957
Bob Seeds	1930–32	1934
Luke Sewell	1921–32	1939
Al Smith	1953–57	1964
Elmer Smith	1914–16	1917, 19–21
Bobby Tiefenauer	1960	1965, 67
Joe Tipton	1948	1952–53
George Uhle	1919–28	1936
Mickey Vernon	1949–50	1958
Howard Wakefield	1905	1907
Gene Woodling	1943, 46	1955–57
Early Wynn	1949–57	1963

Brothers Who Played with the Indians

Dick (1957–59) and Larry (1963–71) Brown

Vean (1911–14) and Dave (1913) Gregg

Bill (1907–09) and Harry (1907) Hinchman

Gaylord (1972–75) and Jim (1959–63, 74–75) Perry

Joe (1920–30) and Luke (1921–32, 39) Sewell

George (1904–11) and Jesse (1903) Stovall

The Perry brothers, Gaylord (left) and Jim, with their dad, Evan. Jim won the Man of the Year Award in 1960, Gaylord in 1972, and they were co-winners in 1974.

Fathers and Sons Who Played with the Indians

Howard Earl (1929–39) and Earl Douglas (1956, 58) Averill

Jim Sr. (1916–22) and Jim Jr. (1941–45) Bagby

Tito (1959–64) and Terry (1988) Francona

Indians with Shortest Careers

Hitters	Position	Year	Average
1 game, 0 at bats			
Gagliano, Ralph	PR	1965	—
Grubb, Harvey	3B	1912	—
Jessee, Dan	PR	1929	—
Welf, Ollie	PR	1916	—
1 game, 1 at bat, 1 hit			
Gallagher, Jackie	OF	1923	1.000 (single)

Hitters	Position	Year	Average
1 game, 1 at bat, 0 hits			
Clanton, Uke	1B	1922	.000
Cypert, Al	3B	1914	.000
Devlin, Jim	C	1944	.000
Sodd, Bill	PH	1937	.000

Pitchers	L/R	Year	G	W–L	IP	H	BB	SO	ERA
Less than 1 inning									
Hamann, Doc	R	1922	1	0–0	0	3	0	0	∞
1 inning									
Beck, George	R	1914	1	0–0	1	1	0	0	0.00
Benn, Henry	R	1914	1	0–0	1	0	0	1	0.00
DesJardien, Paul	R	1916	1	0–0	1	1	1	0	18.00

Pitchers	L/R	Year	G	W–L	IP	H	BB	SO	ERA
Dickerson, George	R	1917	1	0–0	1	0	0	0	0.00
Ellison, George	R	1920	1	0–0	1	0	2	1	0.00
Glavenich, Luke	R	1913	1	0–0	1	3	3	1	9.00
Gregg, Dave	R	1913	1	0–0	1	2	0	0	18.00
Gunkel, Red	R	1916	1	0–0	1	0	1	1	0.00
Kuhn, Bub	R	1924	1	0–1	1	4	0	0	27.00
Neher, Jim	R	1912	1	0–0	1	0	0	0	0.00

Streaks

Hitting

29—Bill Bradley	1902	
28—Joe Jackson	1911	
28—Hal Trosky	1936	
27—Bruce Campbell	1938	
26—Harry Bay	1902	
23—Charlie Jamieson	1923	
23—Tris Speaker	1923	
23—Dale Mitchell	1951	
23—Ray Fosse	1970	
23—Mike Hargrove	1980	

22—Johnny Hodapp	1930
22—Dale Mitchell	1947
22—Al Smith	1956
22—Johnny Romano	1961
22—Julio Franco	1988
21—Nap Lajoie	1904
21—Odell Hale	1936
21—Dale Mitchell	1948
21—Larry Doby	1951
21—Dale Mitchell	1953
21—Joe Carter	1986
21—Julio Franco	1988
20—Nap Lajoie	1906
20—Earl Averill	1936
20—Roy Weatherly	1936
20—Joe Vosmik	1936
20—Al Rosen	1953
20—Vic Power	1960

Pitching, Wins

15—Johnny Allen	1937
15—Gaylord Perry	1974
13—Wes Ferrell	1930
12—Johnny Allen	1938
11—Bill Bernhard	1902
10—Addie Joss	1907
10—Cy Falkenberg	1913
10—Bob Lemon	1947
10—Fritz Peterson	1975

Pitching, Losses

13—Guy Morton	1914
8—Harry Fanwell	1910
8—Willie Mitchell	1911

Al Rosen, man of the year, 1953.

Ray Fosse, co-man of the year in 1970.

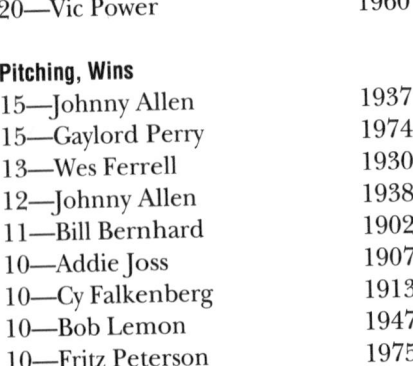

Indians in Pro Football

Carroll Hardy—San Francisco, NFL, 1955

Team Records

Composite Finishes (Over 95 Years)

Position	Number of Finishes	Position	Number of Finishes	Position	Number of Finishes
First	4	Fourth	19	Seventh	7
Second	13	Fifth	15	Eighth	2
Third	14	Sixth	21		

Year by Year

Year	Manager	Finish	Won	Lost	Pct.	Attendance	Year	Manager	Finish	Won	Lost	Pct.	Attendance
1901	Jimmy McAleer	7	55	82	.401	131,380	1932	Roger Peckinpaugh	4	87	65	.572	468,953
1902	Bill Armour	5	69	67	.507	275,395	1933	Roger Peckinpaugh, Bibb Falk, & Walter Johnson	4	75	76	.497	387,936
1903	Bill Armour	3	77	63	.550	311,280							
1904	Bill Armour	4	86	65	.570	264,749							
1905	Nap Lajoie & Bill Bradley	5	76	78	.494	316,306	1934	Walter Johnson	3	85	69	.552	391,338
1906	Nap Lajoie	3	89	64	.582	325,733	1935	Walter Johnson & Steve O'Neill	3	82	71	.536	397,615
1907	Nap Lajoie	4	85	67	.559	382,046							
1908	Nap Lajoie	2	90	64	.584	422,262	1936	Steve O'Neill	5	80	74	.519	500,391
1909	Nap Lajoie & Deacon McGuire	6	71	82	.464	354,627	1937	Steve O'Neill	4	83	71	.539	564,849
1910	Deacon McGuire	5	71	81	.467	293,456	1938	Oscar Vitt	3	86	66	.566	652,006
1911	Deacon McGuire & George Stovall	3	80	73	.523	406,296	1939	Oscar Vitt	3	87	67	.565	563,926
							1940	Oscar Vitt	2	89	65	.578	902,576
1912	Harry Davis & Joe Birmingham	5	75	78	.490	336,844	1941	Roger Peckinpaugh	4*	75	79	.487	745,948
1913	Joe Birmingham	3	86	66	.566	541,000	1942	Lou Boudreau	4	75	79	.487	459,447
1914	Joe Birmingham	8	51	102	.333	185,997	1943	Lou Boudreau	3	82	71	.536	438,894
1915	Joe Birmingham & Lee Fohl	7	57	95	.375	159,285	1944	Lou Boudreau	5*	72	82	.468	475,272
1916	Lee Fohl	6	77	77	.500	492,106	1945	Lou Boudreau	5	73	72	.503	558,182
1917	Lee Fohl	3	88	66	.571	477,298	1946	Lou Boudreau	6	68	86	.442	1,057,289
1918	Lee Fohl	2	73	54	.575	295,515	1947	Lou Boudreau	4	80	74	.519	1,521,978
1919	Lee Fohl & Tris Speaker	2	84	55	.604	538,135	1948	Lou Boudreau	1	97	58	.626	2,620,627
1920	Tris Speaker	1	98	56	.636	912,832	1949	Lou Boudreau	3	89	65	.578	2,233,771
1921	Tris Speaker	2	94	60	.610	748,705	1950	Lou Boudreau	4	92	62	.597	1,727,464
1922	Tris Speaker	4	78	76	.506	528,145	1951	Al Lopez	2	93	61	.604	1,704,984
1923	Tris Speaker	3	82	71	.536	558,856	1952	Al Lopez	2	93	61	.604	1,444,607
1924	Tris Speaker	6	67	86	.438	481,905	1953	Al Lopez	2	92	62	.597	1,069,176
1925	Tris Speaker	6	70	84	.455	419,005	1954	Al Lopez	1	111	43	.721	1,335,472
1926	Tris Speaker	2	88	66	.571	627,426	1955	Al Lopez	2	93	61	.604	1,221,780
1927	Jack McCallister	6	66	87	.431	373,138	1956	Al Lopez	2	88	66	.571	865,467
1928	Roger Peckinpaugh	7	62	92	.403	375,907	1957	Kerby Farrell	6	76	77	.497	722,256
1929	Roger Peckinpaugh	3	81	71	.533	536,210	1958	Bobby Bragan & Joe Gordon	4	77	76	.503	663,805
1930	Roger Peckinpaugh	4	81	73	.526	528,657	1959	Joe Gordon	2	89	65	.578	1,497,976
1931	Roger Peckinpaugh	4	78	76	.506	483,027	1960	Joe Gordon, Jo Jo White, & Jimmy Dykes	4	76	78	.494	960,985
							1961	Jimmy Dykes & Mel Harder	5	78	83	.484	725,547
							1962	Mel McGaha & Mel Harder	6	80	82	.494	716,076

Year	Manager	Finish	Won	Lost	Pct.	Attendance
1963	Birdie Tebbetts	5*	79	83	.488	562,507
1964	George Strickland & Birdie Tebbetts	6*	79	83	.488	653,293
1965	Birdie Tebbetts	5	87	75	.537	934,786
1966	Birdie Tebbetts & George Strickland	5	81	81	.500	903,359
1967	Joe Adcock	8	75	87	.463	662,980
1968	Alvin Dark	3	86	75	.534	857,994
1969	Alvin Dark	6	62	99	.385	619,970
1970	Alvin Dark	5	76	86	.469	729,752
1971	Alvin Dark & Johnny Lipon	6	60	102	.370	591,361
1972	Ken Aspromonte	5	72	84	.462	626,354
1973	Ken Aspromonte	6	71	91	.438	615,107
1974	Ken Aspromonte	4	77	85	.475	1,114,262
1975	Frank Robinson	4	79	80	.497	977,039
1976	Frank Robinson	4	81	78	.509	948,776
1977	Frank Robinson & Jeff Torborg	5	71	90	.441	900,365
1978	Jeff Torborg	6	69	90	.434	800,584
1979	Jeff Torborg & Dave Garcia	6	81	80	.503	1,011,644

Year	Manager	Finish	Won	Lost	Pct.	Attendance
1980	Dave Garcia	6	79	81	.494	1,033,827
1981	Dave Garcia	6	52	51	.505	661,395
1982	Dave Garcia	6	78	84	.481	1,044,021
1983	Mike Ferraro & Pat Corrales	7	70	92	.432	768,941
1984	Pat Corrales	6	75	87	.463	734,079
1985	Pat Corrales	7	60	102	.370	655,181
1986	Pat Corrales	5	84	78	.519	1,471,805
1987	Pat Corrales & Doc Edwards	7	61	101	.377	1,077,898
1988	Doc Edwards	6	78	84	.481	1,411,610
1989	Doc Edwards & John Hart	6	73	89	.451	1,285,542
1990	John McNamara	4	77	85	.475	1,225,240
1991	John McNamara & Mike Hargrove	7	57	105	.352	1,051,863
1992	Mike Hargrove	4*	76	86	.469	1,224,274
1993	Mike Hargrove	6	76	86	.469	2,177,908
1994	Mike Hargrove	2	66	47	.584	1,995,174
1995	Mike Hargrove	1	100	44	.694	2,842,725

*Tied

Biggest Innings

	Inning	Runs	Date	Opponent
By Indians	1	14	June 18, 1950(2)	vs. Philadelphia

	Inning	Runs	Date	Opponent
By opponents	8	13	June 15, 1925	at Philadelphia

Longest Extra-Inning Games

Innings	Date	Score	Site
22	August 31, 1993	Minnesota 5, Cleveland 4	at Minnesota
21	May 26, 1973 (Suspended game, completed May 28)	Chicago 6, Cleveland 3	at Chicago
20	September 14, 1971(2) (Suspended game, completed September 20)	Washington 8, Cleveland 6	at Cleveland

Best, Worst Season Starts

	Best		Worst	
Year	W–L	Year	W–L	
1948	6–0	1969	2–15	
1966	10–1	1945	2–7	
1935	9–1	1914	3–9	

	Best		Worst	
Year	W–L	Year	W–L	
1942	12–3	1971	6–14	
1923	10–3	1979	6–14	

Record against Opponents (1901–95)

Franchise	Years	W	L	Pct.
Baltimore Orioles	(1901–02)	19	20	.487
Baltimore Orioles	(1954–95)	344	336	.506

Franchise	Years	W	L	Pct.
Boston Red Sox	(1901–95)	956	882	.520
California Angels	(1961–95)	211	237	.471

Franchise	Years	W	L	Pct.
Chicago White Sox	(1901–95)	864	898	.490
Detroit Tigers	(1901–95)	883	944	.483
Kansas City Athletics	(1955–67)	151	106	.588
Kansas City Royals	(1969–95)	147	163	.474
Milwaukee Brewers	(1901)	11	9	.550
Milwaukee Brewers	(1970–95)	172	179	.490
Minnesota Twins	(1961–95)	230	224	.507
New York Yankees	(1903–95)	800	989	.447
Oakland Athletics	(1968–95)	143	177	.447

Franchise	Years	W	L	Pct.
Philadelphia Athletics	(1901–54)	642	529	.548
St. Louis Browns	(1902–53)	680	446	.604
Seattle Pilots	(1969)	7	5	.583
Seattle Mariners	(1977–95)	121	92	.568
Texas Rangers	(1972–95)	129	145	.471
Toronto Blue Jays	(1977–95)	110	129	.460
Washington Senators	(1901–60)	710	594	.544
Washington Senators	(1961–71)	106	91	.538
		7,436	7,195	.508

Indians' Longest Winning Streak—13 Games (1942)

Game	Date	Opponent	Score	Winning Pitcher
1	April 18	Chicago	1–0	Jim Bagby, Jr.
2	April 20	St. Louis	4–3	Al Smith
3	April 21	St. Louis	4–2	Al Milnar
4	April 22	St. Louis	3–2	Vern Kennedy
5	April 23	at St. Louis	9–2	Jim Bagby, Jr.
6	April 24	at St. Louis	2–0	Mel Harder
7	April 25	at Chicago	5–4	Chubby Dean

Game	Date	Opponent	Score	Winning Pitcher
8	April 26	at Chicago	3–2	Al Smith
9	April 28	at Philadelphia	6–4	Jim Bagby, Jr.
10	April 29	at Philadelphia	11–6	Joe Heving
11	April 30	at Philadelphia	6–1	Vern Kennedy
12	May 1	at Washington	12–6	Mel Harder
13	May 2	at Washington	12–3	Jim Bagby, Jr.

Indians' Longest Winning Streak—13 Games (1951)

Game	Date	Opponent	Score	Winning Pitcher
1	August 2	at Washington	5–2	Steve Gromek
2	August 3	at Philadelphia	3–2	Mike Garcia
3	August 4	at Philadelphia	4–2	Bob Feller
4	August 5(1)	at Philadelphia	6–3	Bob Lemon
5	August 5(2)	at Philadelphia	6–3(8)	Early Wynn
6	August 7	St. Louis	5–1	Mike Garcia
7	August 8	St. Louis	2–1	Bob Feller

Game	Date	Opponent	Score	Winning Pitcher
8	August 10	Chicago	6–4	Bob Lemon
9	August 11	Chicago	2–1	Early Wynn
10	August 12	Chicago	7–1	Mike Garcia
11	August 13	Detroit	2–1	Bob Feller
12	August 14	Detroit	6–5(10)	Lou Brissie
13	August 15	at St. Louis	9–4	Early Wynn

Indians' Longest Losing Streak—12 Games (1931)

Game	Date	Opponent	Score	Losing Pitcher
1	May 7	at St. Louis	10–4	Pete Jablonowski
2	May 8	Boston	8–4	Belve Bean
3	May 9	Boston	5–1	Willis Hudlin
4	May 10	Boston	9–4	Mel Harder
5	May 13	Washington	9–3	Wes Ferrell
6	May 14	Washington	5–4	Jake Miller

Game	Date	Opponent	Score	Losing Pitcher
7	May 15	Philadelphia	4–0	Clint Brown
8	May 16	Philadelphia	12–5	Fay Thomas
9	May 17	Philadelphia	15–10	Pete Jablonowski
10	May 18	Philadelphia	10–7	Willis Hudlin
11	May 19	New York	8–6	Clint Brown
12	May 21	New York	7–6	Willis Hudlin

Jacobs Field Firsts

First Game: April 4, 1994; Indians 4, Seattle 3; Attendance, 41,259.

First Pitch: By Dennis Martinez to Seattle second baseman Rich Amaral, called strike

First Game Time and Temperature: 1:21 P.M., 48 degrees

First Winning Pitcher: Eric Plunk, Indians

First Losing Pitcher: Kevin King, Seattle

First Save: Hipolito Pichardo, Kansas City, April 15, 1994

First Hit: Eric Anthony, Seattle, third inning home run, April 4, 1994

First Indians Hit: Sandy Alomar, single, eighth inning, April 4, 1994

First Run: Edgar Martinez, Seattle, first inning, April 4, 1994

First RBI: Eric Anthony, Seattle, first-inning sacrifice fly, April 4, 1994

First Indians Run: Candy Maldonado, eighth inning, April 4, 1994

First Indians RBI: Manny Ramirez, eighth-inning double, April 4, 1994

First Triple: Ken Griffey, Jr., Seattle, sixth inning, April 7, 1994

First Indians Home Run: Eddie Murray, seventh inning, April 7, 1994, off John Cummings, Seattle

First Grand Slam: None

First Putout: Eddie Murray on Rich Amaral's ground out, first inning, April 4, 1994

First Error: Eddie Murray, fourth inning, April 4, 1994

First Stolen Base: Omar Vizquel, third inning, April 7, 1994

First Caught Stealing: Kenny Lofton, first inning, April 4, 1994

First Strikeout: Ken Griffey, Jr., Seattle, third inning, April 4, 1994

First Walk: Ken Griffey, Jr., first inning, April 4, 1994

First Night Game: April 7, 1994, vs. Seattle

Largest Crowd: 42,023, August 1, 1995, Indians vs. Minnesota

Smallest Crowd: 24,477, April 25, 1994, Indians vs. Minnesota

Cleveland Stadium Lasts

Last Game: October 3, 1993, Chicago 4, Indians 0

Last Night Game: October 1, 1993, Chicago 4, Indians 2

Last Doubleheader: September 10, 1993, Indians 7, Boston 4; Boston 5, Indians 4 (11 innings)

Last-Game Attendance: 72,390

Last Victory: September 26, 1993, Indians 6, Milwaukee 4

Last Pitch: Chicago's Jose DeLeon, strike three, vs. Mark Lewis

Last Hit: Chicago's Drew Denson, single, eighth inning, off Jerry DiPoto, October 3, 1993

Last Indians Hit: Kenny Lofton, single, seventh inning, October 3, 1993

Last Run: Chicago's Joey Cora, sixth inning, October 3, 1993

Last Indians Run: Albert Belle, eighth-inning home run off Jose DeLeon, October 2, 1993

Last RBI: Chicago's Frank Thomas, sixth inning, October 3, 1993

Last Indians RBI: Albert Belle, eighth-inning home run, October 2, 1993

Last Home Run: Albert Belle, off Chicago's Jose DeLeon, October 2, 1993

Last Out: Mark Lewis, strikeout, ninth inning, October 3, 1993

Last Walk: Frank Thomas, eighth inning, October 3, 1993

Last Grand Slam: Carlos Baerga, July 20, 1993, off Oakland's Joe Boever

Last No-Hitter: Toronto's Dave Stieb, 3–0 victory over the Indians, September 2, 1990

Last No-Hitter by an Indians Pitcher: Lenny Barker, 3–0, over Toronto, May 15, 1981

Last All-Star Game: August 9, 1981, National League 5, American League 4

Spring Training Sites

1902–03	New Orleans, Louisiana	1913	Pensacola, Florida	1928–39	New Orleans, Louisiana
1904	San Antonio, Texas	1914	Athens, Georgia	1940–42	Fort Myers, Florida
1905–06	New Orleans, Louisiana	1915	San Antonio, Texas	1943–45	Lafayette, Indiana
1907–09	Macon, Georgia	1916–20	New Orleans, Louisiana	1946	Clearwater, Florida
1910–11	Alexandria, Louisiana	1921–22	Dallas, Texas	1947–92	Tucson, Arizona
1912	New Orleans, Louisiana	1923–27	Lakeland, Florida	1993–	Winter Haven, Florida

Indians Who Managed in the Major Leagues

	Games	Team (League)	Years		Games	Team (League)	Years
Joe Adcock	162	Cleveland (A)	1967	Bob Coleman	295	Boston (N)	1943–45
Joe Altobelli	844	San Francisco (N)	1977–79	Del Crandall	833	Milwaukee (A)	1972–75
		Baltimore (A)	1983–85			Seattle (A)	1983–84
		Chicago (N)	1991	Larry Doby	87	Chicago (A)	1978
Ken Aspromonte	480	Cleveland (A)	1972–74	Doc Edwards	380	Cleveland (A)	1987–89
Joe Birmingham	368	Cleveland (A)	1912–15	Jim Essian	122	Chicago (N)	1991
Lou Boudreau	2,404	Cleveland (A)	1942–50	Bibb Falk	1	Cleveland (A)	1933
		Boston (A)	1952–54	Lew Fonseca	318	Chicago (A)	1932–34
		Kansas City (A)	1955–57	Joe Frazier	207	New York (N)	1976–77
		Chicago (N)	1960	Joe Gordon	615	Cleveland (A)	1958–60
Bill Bradley	198	Cleveland (A)	1905			Detroit (A)	1960
		Brooklyn (F)	1914			Kansas City (A)	1961, 1969
Ben Chapman	474	Philadelphia (N)	1945–48	Bill Hallman	50	St. Louis (N)	1897

	Games	Team (League)	Years		Games	Team (League)	Years
Mel Harder	3	Cleveland (A)	1961–62	Steve O'Neill	1,879	Cleveland (A)	1935–37
Mike Hargrove	666	Cleveland (A)	1991–95			Detroit (A)	1943–48
Toby Harrah	76	Texas (A)	1992			Boston (A)	1950–51
Dick Howser	933	New York (A)	1978, 1980			Philadelphia (N)	1952–54
		Kansas City (A)	1981–86	Roger			
Billy Hunter	254	Texas (A)	1977–78	Peckinpaugh	995	New York (A)	1914
Bob Kennedy	545	Chicago (N)	1963–65			Cleveland (A)	1928–33,
		Oakland (A)	1968				1941
Mal Kittridge	18	Washington (A)	1904	Lou Piniella	1,322	New York (A)	1986–88
Lou Klein	147	Chicago (N)	1961–62,			Cincinnati (N)	1990–92
			1965			Seattle (A)	1993–95
Harvey Kuenn	279	Milwaukee (A)	1975,	Frank Robinson	1,431	Cleveland (A)	1975–77
			1982–83			San Francisco (N)	1981–84
Nap Lajoie	700	Cleveland (A)	1905–09			Baltimore (A)	1988–91
Bob Lemon	833	Kansas City (A)	1970–72	Luke Sewell	1,259	St. Louis (A)	1941–46
		Chicago (A)	1977–78			Cincinnati (N)	1949–52
		New York (A)	1978–79,	Jack Slattery	31	Boston (N)	1928
			1981–82	Allen Sothoron	8	St. Louis (A)	1933
Jim Lemon	161	Washington (A)	1968	Billy Southworth	1,770	St. Louis (N)	1929,
Al Lopez	2,425	Cleveland (A)	1951–56				1940–45
		Chicago (A)	1957–65,			Boston (N)	1946–51
			1968–69	Tris Speaker	1,139	Cleveland (A)	1919–26
Billy Martin	2,267	Minnesota (A)	1969	George Stovall	698	Cleveland (A)	1911
		Detroit (A)	1971–73			St. Louis (A)	1912–13
		Texas (A)	1973–75			Kansas City (F)	1914–15
		New York (A)	1975–79,	George Strickland	112	Cleveland (A)	1964, 1966
			1983,	Chuck Tanner	2,738	Chicago (A)	1970–75
			1985, 1988			Oakland (A)	1976
		Oakland (A)	1980–82			Pittsburgh (N)	1977–85
Jimmy McAleer	1,658	Cleveland (A)	1901			Atlanta (N)	1986–88
		St. Louis (A)	1902–09	Birdie Tebbetts	1,455	Cincinnati (N)	1954–58
		Washington (A)	1910–11			Milwaukee (N)	1961–62
Deacon McGuire	516	Washington (N)	1898			Cleveland (A)	1963–66
		Boston (A)	1907–08	Mickey Vernon	363	Washington (A)	1961–63
		Cleveland (A)	1909–11	Dick Williams	3,023	Boston (A)	1967–69
Stuffy McInnis	155	Philadelphia (N)	1927			Oakland (A)	1971–73
Sam Mele	963	Minnesota (A)	1961–67			California (A)	1974–76
Buster Mills	8	Cincinnati (N)	1953			Montreal (N)	1977–81
Joe Morgan	563	Boston (A)	1988–91			San Diego (N)	1982–85
Russ Nixon	578	Cincinnati (N)	1982–83			Seattle (A)	1986–88
		Atlanta (N)	1988–90	Cy Young	6	Boston (A)	1907

Indians Presidents

1901–10	John F. Kilfoyl	1950–52	Ellis W. Ryan	1985–86	Peter Bavasi
1910–15	Charles W. Somers	1953–62	Myron H. Wilson, Jr.	1986–87	Richard E. Jacobs
1916–22	James C. Dunn	1963–72	Gabe Paul	1988–91	Henry J. Peters
1922–27	Ernest S. Barnard	1972–75	Nick Mileti	1992	Rick Bay
1928–46	Alva Bradley	1975–77	Alva T. Bonda	1993–	Richard E. Jacobs
1946–49	Bill Veeck	1978–84	Gabe Paul		

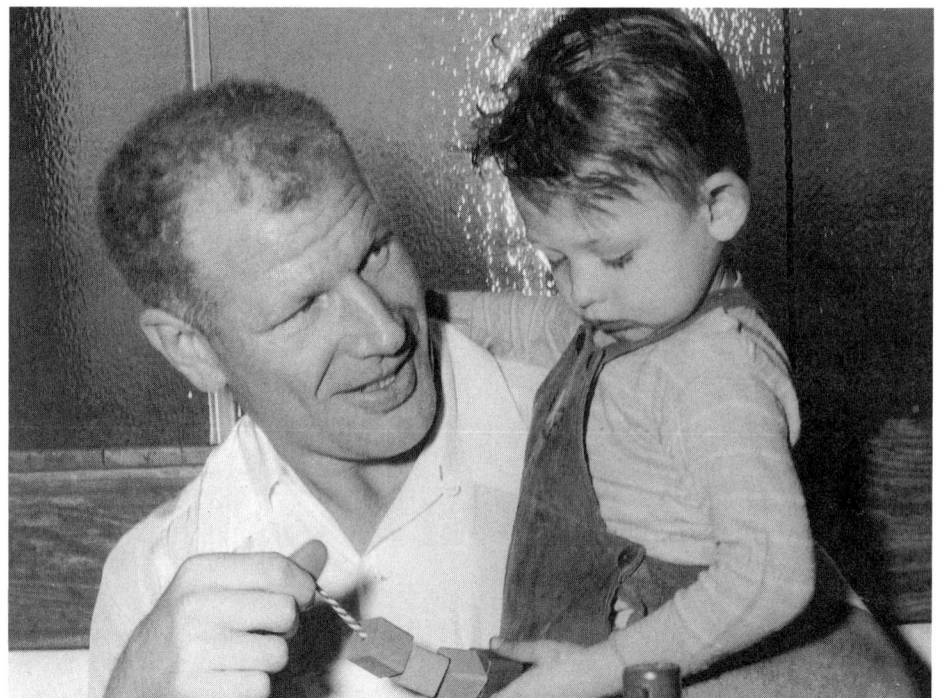

Bill Veeck was the Indians first man of the year in 1946.

Indians General Managers

1903–27	Ernest S. Barnard	1946–49	Bill Veeck	1985–87	Joe Klein
1916–17	Bob McRoy	1950–57	Hank Greenberg	1987–91	Hank Peters
1927–35	Billy Evans	1957–61	Frank Lane	1991–	John Hart
1935–41	C. C. Slapnicka	1961–73	Gabe Paul		
1941–46	Roger Peckinpaugh	1973–85	Phil Seghi		

Coaches (Since 1920)

Rick Adair	1992–93	Jake Flowers	1951–52
Jack Aker	1985–87	Dave Garcia	1975–76, 1979
Luke Appling	1960–61	Patsy Gharrity	1933–35
Del Baker	1943–44	Johnny Goryl	1982–88
Johnny Bassler	1938–40	Harvey Haddix	1975–78
Buddy Bell	1994–95	Mel Harder	1947, 1949–63
Ken Bolek	1992–93	Mike Hargrove	1990–91
Bobby Bonds	1984–87	Chuck Hartenstein	1979
Clay Bryant	1967, 1974	Grover Hartley	1928–30
Dom Chiti	1991–93	Solly Hemus	1964–65
Ron Clark	1992–93	Bobby Hofman	1971–72
Rocky Colavito	1973, 1976–78	Luis Isaac	1987–91, 1994–
Steve Comer	1987	Ray Katt	1962
Tony Cuccinello	1952–56	Fred Koenig	1985–86
Rich Dauer	1990–91	Red Kress	1953–60
Jim Davenport	1989	Bob Lemon	1960
Cot Deal	1970–71	Johnny Lipon	1968–71
Larry Doby	1974	Bill Lobe	1951–56
Dave Duncan	1978–81	Joe Lutz	1972–73
Luke Easter	1969	Gordy MacKenzie	1991
Doc Edwards	1985–87	Charlie Manuel	1988–89, 1994–
Chuck Estrada	1983	Harry Mathews	1926–27
Hoot Evers	1970	Jack McCallister	1920–26
Bibb Falk	1933	Tommy McCraw	1975, 1979–82
Kerby Farrell	1970–71	Mel McGaha	1961
Ed FitzGerald	1960	Bill McKechnie	1947–49

Pitching coach Mel Harder, shown here with Bob Feller (right), was elected man of the year in 1961.

Don McMahon (left), the man of the year in 1964, is shown here as pitching coach of the Indians in 1984, along with manager Pat Corrales.

Don McMahon	1983–85	Mel Queen	1982	George Strickland	1963–69
Oscar Melillo	1939–40, 1942, 1945–48, 1950	Phil Regan	1994	George Susce	1941–47, 1948–49
		Del Rice	1967		
Buster Mills	1946	Dave Roberts	1987	Jeff Torborg	1975–77
Joe Moeller	1978	Frank Roth	1923–25	George Uhle	1936–37
Jose Morales	1990–93	Muddy Ruel	1948–50	Elmer Valo	1963–64
Pat Mullin	1967	Jack Sanford	1968–69	Jo Jo White	1958–60
Ed Napoleon	1983–85	Wally Schang	1936–38	Earl Whitehill	1941
Dave Nelson	1992–	Luke Sewell	1939–41	Mark Wiley	1988–91, 95
Jeff Newman	1992–	Howie Shanks	1928–32	Ted Wilks	1960
Joe Nossek	1977–81	Burt Shotton	1942–45	Billy Williams	1990–91
Mickey O'Neil	1930	Al Simmons	1950–51	Earl Wolgamot	1931–33
Steve O'Neill	1935, 1949	Denny Sommers	1980–85	Early Wynn	1964–66
Regie Otero	1966	Warren Spahn	1972–73	Dutch Zwilling	1941
Tony Pacheco	1974	Tom Spencer	1988–89		
Salty Parker	1962	Eddie Stanky	1957–58		

Scouts (1942–95)

Hector Acevedo	1982–89	Jim Broderick	1968–69	Rick Colzie	1982–83
Rick Adair	1987–88	Mike Brumley	1973	Merrill Combs	1976–81
Hugh Alexander	1942, 47–49	John Burden	1988	Ramon Conde	1990–94
John Angel	1942, 44–47	Willis E. Butler	1944–48	Winston Conde	1989
Luis Aponte	1989–	Willie Calvino	1974–77		
Steve Avila	1990–	Brad Cameron	1994–		
Mark Baca	1992–94	Jack Card	1960, 62		
Delmar Baker	1953	Dan Carnevale	1973–86, 88–90, 92–		
Eddie Bane	1984–87				
Fred Barth	1962–64, 66	Jack Cassini	1976–85		
John C. Beckel	1948	Mike Catron	1948–52		
David (Gus) Bell	1967, 69	George Cecchetti	1991		
Bob Bennett	1963	Spurgeon (Spud) Chandler	1960–79		
Robert T. Berry	1954–55				
Ken Blackman	1961	Tom Chandler	1985–93		
Jack Bracken	1947–49	Dom Chiti	1994		
William J. Bradley	1942–45, 47–49, 51–54	Loyd E. Christopher	1967–74		
		Roy Clark	1988–89		
Jimmy Bragan	1978–80	Cogan, Paul	1995		
Ed Brawner	1949	Patrick Colgan	1960–62		

Pitcher Jim Rittwage.

Tom Couston	1983–	Don Jacoby	1994		
Chuck Cronin	1968–69	Hal Janvrin	1953		
Crist, Clark	1995	Henry Jefferis	1948–49		
Ed Crosby	1990–91	Len Johnston	1973		
Dan Crowley	1957	Gordon Jones	1949–50		
George Daddario	1957–58	Jerry Jordan	1994–		
Mark Danahey	1956–57	Mark Just	1979–81		
Al Daniels	1980–82	John E. Kall	1968–74		
Jeff Datz	1992–94	Buzzy Keller	1991–93		
Julio (Monchy)		Bob Kennedy	1958		
DeArcos	1955–66	Bill Killefer	1947–49		
Arthur Decatur	1942, 46	Jack Knight	1952–53		
Babe DelGreco	1974	Dave Koblentz	1987–91		
Joe DeLucca	1988–93	Don Kohler	1982		
Tony DeMacio	1991–94	Dave Kosher	1964		
Connie Dettling	1987–88	Jerome R. Krause	1967–70		
Mel Didier	1979–80	Gil Kubski	1994		
Roy Dissinger	1956–57	Jerry LaPenta	1991–93		
Abney Donahey	1952	Walter Laskowski	1946–54		
Harry Dorish	1974–76	George Lauzerique	1989–91		
Henry (Dutch)		Bill Lawlor	1989–92		
Dotterer	1962–74	Allan Lewis	1991–94		
Tom Downey	1951	Glenn A. (Gyp)			
Brian Doyle	1984–85	Lewis	1946–61		
Tom Dufour	1974	Joe Lewis	1987–88	Mel F. Nelson	1971–73
Ken Duzich	1991	Donald A.		Hal Newhouser	1962–65
Phil English	1982	Lindberg	1967–70, 73–74	Robert Nieman	1967–69, 73–75
Walter (Hoot)		George Lippe	1962–69	Jack O'Connor	1957
Evers	1957, 70	Winston Llenas	1990–	Paul O'Dea	1953–57, 60–78
Frank Fahey	1947–52	Bill Lobe	1963	Harry O'Donnell	1953–56
Jesse Flores	1993–	Dario Lodigiani	1959–60	Dave Oliver	1982
Red Gaskill	1974–87	Frank Lucchesi	1982–84	William (Yam)	
Rene Gayo	1994–	Gordon MacKenzie	1990, 92–93	Ornelas	1948, 52
Mark Germann	1991–	Guy Mader	1994–	Regie Otero	1967–73
Tom Giordano	1992–	Rick Magnante	1992–93	Art Parrack	1988
Roland Gladu	1953	Bobby Malkmus	1980–90	Floyd Patterson	1956
Robert Goff	1954–72	Cecil Mancuso	1968–70	Shawn Render	1992–93
Orlando Gomez	1986–87	Joseph Mancuso	1953–54, 58–69,	Henry J. Peters	1970
Eddie Goosetree	1958–60		74	Mike Piatnik	1988–90
Tony Governor	1948	Michael Marko	1965–70, 72–74	Frank Pietila	1973–74
Hank Gowdy	1949–52	C. A. (Runt) Marr	1960–61	Latimer Placek	1946–52, 58–61
Ivy Griffin	1947–49	Bobby Mattick	1964–66	Paul Pleasant	1948
James Gruzdis	1954–74	Bob Mayer	1992–	Dave Pope	1968
Leon Hamilton	1973–85	Carl W. Mays	1958–61	Bill Posedel	1961
Jay Hankins	1967–68	Arthur S.		George Powles	1964–66
Chuck Harmon	1963–65	Mazmanian	1967–70	Don Pries	1963
Earl Harrist	1964, 66–67	James McCabe	1946	George (Dutch)	
John Hart	1989	Edward McCarrick	1967–70, 72–74	Proechel	1963
Luther R. Harvel	1969–70	Tenny McDaniel	1947	Evo Pusich	1959–63
J. E. (Red) Haslett	1952–55	Kasey McKeon	1994–	Larry Quirico	1982
Wynn Hawkins	1967–69	Mark McKnight	1991–93	Horace L. (Red)	
Jeff Heath	1962	Michael J. McNally	1948–51, 60–65	Ralph	1946–48, 53–54
Bill Herring	1962–63	Oscar Melillo	1948	Joe Reardon	1955
Trey Hillman	1988	Buddy Mercado	1990–93	Hal Reason	1947–66
Pete Hodan	1967–69	William Meyer	1946, 84–87	Al Registro	1973–74
Bobby Hofman	1989	Jim Miller	1981–90	Kevin Rhomberg	1991
E. P. Holt	1946–54	Don Mitchell	1989–90	Jim Richardson	1990–
Clare Hoose	1951–52	Joseph D. Morlan	1962–74	Dave Roberts	1985–90
Charlie Hum	1963–69	J. C. Moss	1946	Jay Robertson	1991–93
Harold Irelan	1942, 44	Ray C. Mueller	1962–70	Jim Robinson	1963
Luis Isaac	1980–88	Pat Mullin	1968	William Rodgers	1954–57

Catcher Hank Ruszkowski.

Fernando (Cucho) Rodriguez	1967–70	Ted Simmons	1994–	Bill Veeck	1956
Raymond (Nap) Ross	1951–62	Cyril C. Slapnicka	1947–58, 60	Joseph Vosmik	1952
		Woody Smith	1982–87	Craig Wallenbrock	1994–
Ray Sanders	1967	Jim Stevenson	1994–	Mark Weidemaier	1991–
Jack Sanford	1956–57	William Stewart	1958–62	Phillip Weinert	1958
Frank M. Sansosti	1964–70	Anthony F. Stiel	1966–70	Bill Werle	1990, 92–
Larry Schmittou	1968–69	Chuck Stobbs	1983	H. B. (Buzz) Wetzel	1946–47, 50–60
Al Schoenberger	1988	George Strickland	1961	John (Poke) Whelan	1958–63
Fred Schulte	1957–61	Edward Stumpf	1947	Harold White	1958
John Schulte	1953–63	Dale Sutherland	1984–89	Joyner (Jo Jo) White	1953, 58
A. G. Schulz	1946	Gary Sutherland	1982–89	William Whitman	1948–52
Jose Seda	1963	Ray R. Swallow	1970	Carl Wiker	1973–74
Phil Seghi	1986	Doug Takaragawa	1990–93	Mark Wiley	1992–94
Semier, Max	1995	Joseph Taylor	1957	Ted Wilks	1961
Bill Serena	1963–67	Birdie Tebbetts	1983–88	Charlie Williams	1967–68
Joe Sewell	1953–62	Thompson, Gene	1995	Gene Woodling	1979–84
Walter Shannon	1963–65	Hollis Thurston	1948–50	Gil Yetter	1973–74
John (Jack) Sheehan	1954–55	Paul Tinnell	1990	Chester Ziemba	1962
		Gary Tuck	1994–	Ben Zientara	1962–70
Chick Shorten	1950–59	Albert B. Unser	1972–74, 82	William Zinser	1958, 62–66
Bob Shupala	1974, 76–80	Jack Vallely	1973–74, 80–85	Edward (Dutch) Zwilling	1942, 46–47
		Walter Van Uum	1952–54, 62–70		

Indians Minor League Teams (1947–95)

Team	Years	Classification	Team	Years	Classification
Ardmore, Okla.	1947–48	D	Grand Forks, N.D.	1963	A
Bakersfield, Calif.	1947–52	C	Green Bay, Wis.	1947–53	D
Baltimore, Md.	1947–48	AAA	Harrisburg, Pa.	1947–48, 50–51	B
Batavia, N.Y.	1947–51, 57–59	D	Indianapolis, Ind.	1952–56	AAA
Batavia, N.Y.	1976–86	A	Iola, Kan.	1949	D
Bloomingdale, N.J.	1948	D	Jacksonville, Fla.	1962–63	AAA
Buffalo, N.Y.	1983–84	AA	Jacksonville, Fla.	1971	AA
Buffalo, N.Y.	1987, 95	AAA	Jacksonville, Tex.	1947	C
Burlington, Iowa	1947–49	C	Jacksonville Beach, Fla.	1954	D
Burlington, N.C.	1958–62	B	Jersey City, N.J.	1977	AA
Burlington, N.C.	1963–64	A	Keokuk, Iowa	1954–57	B
Burlington, N.C.	1986–	Rookie	Kinston, N.C.	1987–	A
Canton-Akron, Ohio	1989–	AA	Knoxville, Tenn.	1956	A
Cedar Rapids, Iowa	1950–52	B	Lafayette, Ind.	1955	D
Charleston, W.Va.	1962	A	Lakeland, Fla.	1960	D
Charleston, W.Va.	1963–64	AA	Mattoon, Ill.	1948	D
Charleston, W.Va.	1981–83	AAA	Meridian, Miss.	1947–48	B
Charlotte, N.C.	1993–94	AAA	Minot, N.D.	1958–60	C
Chattanooga, Tenn.	1978–82	AA	Mobile, Ala.	1956–60	AA
Cocoa, Fla.	1957–58	D	Montgomery, Ala.	1956	A
Colorado Springs, Colo.	1988–92	AA	North Platte, Neb.	1957–59	D
Columbus, Ga.	1991–	A	Oklahoma City, Okla.	1947–50	AA
Cordele, Ga.	1947–49	D	Oklahoma City, Okla.	1973–75	AAA
Dallas, Tex.	1951–52	AA	Old Orchard Beach, Maine	1984–86	AAA
Dayton, Ohio	1947	D	Pawtucket, R.I.	1966–67	AA
Dayton, Ohio	1948–50	A	Peoria, Ill.	1953	B
Daytona Beach, Fla.	1950–53, 56	D	Pittsfield, Mass.	1947–50	C
Dubuque, Iowa	1961–62	D	Portland, Ore.	1964–69, 72, 78	AAA
Dubuque, Iowa	1963–66	A	Reading, Pa.	1952–61	A
Elmira, N.Y.	1972	AA	Reading, Pa.	1965	AA
Fargo-Moorhead, N.D.	1953–57	C	Reno, Nev.	1966–74, 91	A
Fayetteville, N.C.	1956	B	Rock Hill, S.C.	1967–68	A
Fort Smith, Ark.	1951–52	C	St. Petersburg, Fla.	1949	B

Team	Years	Classification	Team	Years	Classification
Salinas, Calif.	1965	A	Tifton, Ga.	1954	D
Salt Lake City, Utah	1961–62	AAA	Toledo, Ohio	1976–77	AAA
San Antonio, Tex.	1973–75	AA	Toronto, Ont.	1960	AAA
San Diego, Calif.	1949–51, 58–59	AAA	Tucson, Ariz.	1947–50	C
San Diego, Calif.	1957	Open	Tulsa, Okla.	1955	AA
San Jose, Calif.	1975–76	A	Union City, Tenn.	1947–49	D
Sarasota, Fla.	1968–75, 89	Rookie	Vidalia, Ga.	1955–56	D
Savannah, Ga.	1970	AA	Waterbury, Conn.	1968–69, 85–87	AA
Selma, Ala.	1955–62	D	Waterloo, Iowa	1977–88	A
Sherbrooke, Que.	1953, 55	C	Watertown, N.Y.	1989–94	A
Sherbrooke, Que.	1954	B	Wichita, Kan.	1951–52	A
Spartanburg, S.C.	1947–55	B	Wichita, Kan.	1970–71	AAA
Statesville, N.C.	1969	A	Wilkes-Barre, Pa.	1947–51	A
Stroudsburg, Pa.	1949	D	Williamsport, Pa.	1976, 88	AA
Sumter, S.C.	1970	A	Winter Haven, Fla.	1990	Rookie
Tacoma, Wash.	1950	B	Zanesville, Ohio	1949–50	D
Tacoma, Wash.	1979–80	AAA			

Indians Minor League Champions

Year	Team/League	Manager
1947	Spartanburg, Tri-State League—Class B	Kerby Farrell
1949	Dayton, Central League—Class A	Oscar Melillo
	Bakersfield, California League—Class C	Harry Griswold
	Burlington, Central Association—Class C	Lloyd Brown
	Stroudsburg, North Atlantic League—Class D	Frank Radler
1950	Wilkes-Barre, Eastern League—Class A	Bill Norman
1951	Wilkes-Barre, Eastern League—Class A	Bill Norman
1952	Dallas, Texas League—Class AA	Dutch Meyer
1953	Reading, Eastern League—Class A	Kerby Farrell
	Spartanburg, Tri-State League—Class B	James Bloodworth
	Fargo-Moorhead, Northern League—Class C	Zeke Bonura/ Santo Luberto
	Sherbrooke, Provincial League—Class C	Pinky May
	Daytona Beach, Florida State League—Class D	Edward Levy
	Green Bay, Wisconsin State League—Class D	Phil Seghi
1954	Indianapolis, American Association—Class AAA	Kerby Farrell
	Fargo-Moorhead, Northern League—Class C	Phil Seghi
1955	Reading, Eastern League—Class A	Jo Jo White
	Keokuk, Three-I League—Class B	Pinky May
	Spartanburg, Tri-State League—Class B	Spud Chandler

Year	Team/League	Manager
1956	Indianapolis, American Association—Class AAA	Kerby Farrell
1958	North Platte, Nebraska State League—Class D	Mark Wylie
1960	Toronto, International League—Class AAA	Mel McGaha
	Lakeland, Florida State League—Class D	John Lipon/ Charlie Gassaway
1961	Selma, Alabama-Florida League—Class D	Walter Novick/ Joe Morlan
1962	Jacksonville, International League—Class AAA	Ben Geraghty
1963	Charleston, Eastern League—Class AA	John Lipon
1980	Waterloo, Midwest League—Class A	Cal Emery
1986	Waterloo, Midwest League—Class A	Steve Swisher
1987	Burlington, Appalachian League—Class Rookie	Tom Chandler
1988	Kinston, Carolina League—Class A	Glenn Adams
1991	Kinston, Carolina League—Class A	Brian Graham
1992	Colorado Springs, Pacific Coast League—Class AAA	Charlie Manuel
1993	Charlotte, International League—Class AAA	Charlie Manuel
	Burlington, Appalachian League—Class Rookie	Jim Gabella
1995	Kinston, Carolina League—Class A	Gordie MacKenzie
	Watertown, New York, Penn League—Class A	Joel Skinner

Minor League Managers

Glenn Adams	1986–88	Brian Graham	1989–	Joe Morlan	1960–61
Jack Aker	1984–85	Harry Griswold	1947–52	Ray Mueller	1960–61, 68
Fred (Pat) Ankenman	1947–48	Jim Gruzdis	1957	Jim Napier	1986
Ken Aspromonte	1968–71	Bruno Haas	1948	Bob Nieman	1964
Joe Azcue	1974	Mike Hargrove	1987–89	Bill Norman	1947–51
Del Baker	1950–51	Bucky Harris	1949	Walter Novick	1960–64
Eddie Bane	1984–85	Mercer Harris	1947	Paul O'Dea	1947–48, 51,
Richard Bartel	1956	Edgar Hartness	1954–55		55, 58–60
John Beazley	1949	Gene Hasson	1948–49	Dave Oliver	1981–82
Les Bell	1947–48,	Ray Hathaway	1970–72	Tom Oliver	1956
	50–51	Charles Hawley	1948	John Orsino	1977–78
Ken Blackman	1957	Don Heffner	1956–57	Tony Pacheco	1973, 75
James Bloodworth	1952–54	Bill Herring	1961, 64	Shawn Pender	1992
Ken Bolek	1988–92	Myril Hoag	1949	J. Knowles Piercey	1950
Zeke Bonura	1953	Gomer Hodge	1976, 81–84	Dick Porter	1949
Jimmy Bragan	1987	Al Hollingsworth	1959–60	Dutch Prather	1947
Jack Brillheart	1950	Luis Isaac	1978	Wellington Quinn	1951
Lloyd Brown	1948–50	Jim Jeffries	1948	Frank Radler	1949
Mike Brown	1991–93	Winlow Johnson	1949	Thomas Reis	1950
Clay Bryant	1966, 68–69,	Len Johnston	1970–73	Tony Rensa	1947–49
	72	Bill Jurges	1950	Don Richmond	1957–58
Mike Bucci	1988–89	Dave Keller	1990–94	Red Ruffing	1950
Steve Bysco	1947	Bob Kennedy	1962	LeRoy Schalk	1947
Dolph Camilli	1950	Lou Klimchock	1972–73	Joe Schultz	1951
Dan Carnevale	1972	Eddie Kobesky	1949–51	Phil Seghi	1949–55
Jack Cassini	1976–77	Red Kress	1952	Skinner, Joel	1995
Phil Cavarretta	1965–68	Ted Kubiak	1994–	Donald Smith	1948
Spud Chandler	1954–55	Stephen Kuk	1948	Woody Smith	1974–75,
Tom Chandler	1986–87	Whitey Kurowski	1953–65		77–81
Patrick Colgan	1963	Ken Landenberger	1958–60	Joe Sparks	1976
Rick Colzie	1980	Walter Laskowski	1948	Spilman, Harry	1995
James Cooke	1948	Roxie Lawson	1947–48	Harry Sullivan	1949
Harold Cox	1951	Hal Lee	1948–49	George Susce	1948
Ray Dabek	1963	Henry Leiber	1950	Steve Swisher	1985–88
Jeff Datz	1994–	Edward Levy	1953, 55	Birdie Tebbetts	1953
Red Davis	1967–69,	Gene Lillard	1949, 52	Tommy Thomas	1947–48
	75–76	John Lipon	1959–60,	Jack Tighe	1947
Gene Desautels	1953		62–67	Frank Tornay	1957
Joseph Dotlich	1948	Santo Luberto	1953	Dean Treanor	1990
Brian Doyle	1983	Frank Lucchesi	1973, 81	Tom Trebelhorn	1979
Gene Dusan	1977–80	Joe Lutz	1969–70	Mike Tresh	1951
Doc Edwards	1982–85	MacKenzie, Gordie	1995	Gary Tuck	1991–92
Bob Elliott	1957	Joe Macko	1955	Elmer Valo	1965–66
Cal Emery	1979–81	Hank Majeski	1956–57	Joe Vosmik	1947–51
Kerby Farrell	1947–56	Charlie Manuel	1991–93	Gene Verble	1962
Mal Fichman	1991	Jack Maupin	1948	Lynnville Watkins	1947
Fred Fitzsimmons	1961	Pinky May	1952–62,	Earl Weaver	1956
Herman Franks	1961		67–72	JoJo White	1954–57
Jim Gabella	1989–90,	Clyde McCullough	1958	Ralph Winegarner	1952
	92–94	Mel McGaha	1958–60	Casey Wise	1963
Al Gallagher	1982–83	Pat McLaughlin	1949	Mark Wylie	1954–56,
Charlie Gassaway	1960	Oscar Melillo	1948–49		58–59
Ben Geraghty	1962–63	Minnie Mendoza	1992	Rudy York	1949, 57
Orlando Gomez	1986–87	George Metkovich	1957–59	Mike Young	1993–94
Ival Goodman	1947	Dutch Meyer	1951–52,	Del Youngblood	1974–75
Antone Governor	1947		55–56		
Hank Gowdy	1950	Bob Molinaro	1989–90		

Triple-A Farm Teams and Managers

Years	Team	League	Manager
1947–48	Baltimore	International League	Tommy Thomas
1949	San Diego	Pacific Coast League	Bucky Harris
1950–51	San Diego	Pacific Coast League	Del Baker
1952	Indianapolis	American Association	Gene Desautels
1953	Indianapolis	American Association	Birdie Tebbetts
1954–56	Indianapolis	American Association	Kerby Farrell
1957	San Diego	Pacific Coast League	Bob Elliott/George Metkovich
1958–59	San Diego	Pacific Coast League	George Metkovich
1960	Toronto	International League	Mel McGaha
1961	Salt Lake City	Pacific Coast League	Herman Franks/Fred Fitzsimmons
1962	Salt Lake City	Pacific Coast League	Bob Kennedy
	Jacksonville	International League	Ben Geraghty
1963	Jacksonville	International League	Ben Geraghty/Casey Wise
1964–67	Portland	Pacific Coast League	John Lipon
1968–69	Portland	Pacific Coast League	Red Davis
1970–71	Wichita	American Association	Ken Aspromonte
1972	Portland	Pacific Coast League	Ray Hathaway/Clay Bryant/Dan Carnevale
1973	Oklahoma City	American Association	Frank Lucchesi
1974–75	Oklahoma City	American Association	Red Davis
1976	Toledo	International League	Joe Sparks
1977	Toledo	International League	Jack Cassini
1978	Portland	Pacific Coast League	Gene Dusan
1979–80	Tacoma	Pacific Coast League	Gene Dusan
1981	Charleston	International League	Cal Emery/Frank Lucchesi
1982–83	Charleston	International League	Doc Edwards
1984–85	Old Orchard Beach	International League	Doc Edwards
1986	Old Orchard Beach	International League	Jim Napier
1987	Buffalo	American Association	Orlando Gomez/Steve Swisher
1988	Colorado Springs	Pacific Coast League	Steve Swisher
1989	Colorado Springs	Pacific Coast League	Mike Hargrove
1990	Colorado Springs	Pacific Coast League	Bob Molinaro/Charlie Manuel
1991–92	Colorado Springs	Pacific Coast League	Charlie Manuel
1993	Charlotte	International League	Charlie Manuel
1994	Charlotte	International League	Brian Graham
1995	Buffalo	American Association	Brian Graham

Team Hitting, Pitching, Fielding

Year	Hitting R	HR	BA/Rank	Year	Hitting R	HR	BA/Rank
1901	667	12	.271—6	1917	584	13	.245—6
1902	686	33	.289—1	1918	504*	9	.260—1
1903	639	31	.265—3	1919	636	25	.278—3
1904	647*	27	.260—1	1920	857*	35	.303—2
1905	567	18	.255—1	1921	925	42	.308—2
1906	663*	12	.279—1	1922	768	32	.292—3
1907	530	11	.241—6	1923	888*	59	.301—1
1908	568	18	.239—4	1924	755	41	.296—2
1909	493	10	.241—5	1925	782	52	.297—5
1910	548	9	.244—5	1926	738	27	.289—3
1911	691	20	.282—3	1927	668	26	.283—5
1912	677	12	.273—3	1928	674	34	.285—3
1913	633	16	.268—3	1929	717	62	.294—4
1914	538	10	.245—4	1930	890	72	.304—2
1915	539	20	.240—6	1931	885	71	.296—2
1916	630	16	.250—3	1932	845	78	.285—3

	Hitting					Hitting		
Year	R	HR	BA/Rank		Year	R	HR	BA/Rank
1933	654	50	.261—7		1966	574	155	.237—5
1934	814	100	.287—2		1967	559	131	.235—6
1935	776	93	.284—3		1968	516	75	.234—5
1936	921	123	.304—1		1969	573	119	.237—9
1937	817	103	.280—4		1970	649	183	.249—7
1938	847	113	.281—3		1971	543	109	.238—9
1939	797	85	.280—3		1972	472	91	.234—10
1940	710	101	.265—5		1973	680	158*	.256—7
1941	677	103	.256—7		1974	662	131	.255—8
1942	590	50	.253—5		1975	688	153*	.261—4
1943	600	55	.255—3		1976	615	85	.263—4
1944	643	70	.266—2		1977	676	100	.269—7
1945	557	65	.255—6		1978	639	106	.261—8
1946	537	79	.245—8		1979	760	138	.258—12
1947	687	112	.259—3		1980	738	89	.277—4
1948	840	155	.282—1		1981	431	39	.263—5
1949	675	112	.260—4		1982	683	109	.262—8
1950	806	164	.269—4		1983	704	86	.265—8
1951	696	140	.256—7		1984	761	123	.265—6
1952	763*	148*	.262—2		1985	729	116	.265—4
1953	770	160*	.270—2		1986	831*	157	.284—1
1954	746	156*	.262—4		1987	742	187	.263—7
1955	698	148	.257—6		1988	666	134	.261—6
1956	712	153	.244—7		1989	604	127	.245—13
1957	682	140	.252—5		1990	732	110	.267—2
1958	694	161	.258—3		1991	576	79	.254—11†
1959	745*	167*	.263—1		1992	674	127	.266—3
1960	667	127	.267—2		1993	790	141	.275—3
1961	737	150	.266—1		1994	679*	167*	.290—1
1962	682	180	.245—1		1995	840*	207*	.291—1
1963	635	169	.239—9					
1964	689	164	.247—6		*Led League			
1965	663	156	.250—3		†Tied			

	Pitching				Pitching	
Year	CG	ERA/Rank		Year	CG	ERA/Rank
1901	122	4.12—8		1922	76	4.59—7†
1902	116	3.28—2		1923	77	3.91—2
1903	125*	2.73—2		1924	87*	4.40—6
1904	141	2.22—2		1925	93*	4.49—5
1905	140*	2.85—6		1926	96*	3.40—2
1906	133†	2.09—1		1927	72	4.27—6
1907	127	2.26—2		1928	71	4.47—7
1908	108	2.02—1		1929	80	4.05—2
1909	110	2.40—4		1930	68	4.88—6†
1910	92	2.88—7		1931	76	4.63—6
1911	93	3.36—4		1932	94	4.12—2
1912	94	3.30—4		1933	74*	3.71—1
1913	93	2.54—2		1934	72	4.28—3
1914	69	3.21—8		1935	67	4.15—4
1915	62	3.13—7		1936	74	4.83—4
1916	65	2.90—6		1937	64	4.39—3
1917	73	2.52—3		1938	68	4.60—4
1918	78	2.64—3		1939	69	4.08—2
1919	80	2.94—2		1940	72	3.63—1
1920	94	3.41—2		1941	68	3.90—3
1921	81	3.90—2		1942	61	3.59—5†

Year	Pitching CG	ERA/Rank	Year	Pitching CG	ERA/Rank
1943	64	3.15—3	1970	34	3.91—9
1944	48	3.65—7	1971	21	4.28—12
1945	76	3.31—4	1972	47	2.92—4
1946	63	3.62—5	1973	55	4.58—11
1947	55	3.44—2	1974	45	3.80—9
1948	66	3.22—1	1975	37	3.84—5
1949	65	3.36—1	1976	30	3.47—7
1950	69	3.75—1	1977	45	4.10—7
1951	76	3.38—1	1978	36	3.97—11
1952	80	3.32—3	1979	28	4.57—11
1953	81	3.64—4	1980	35	4.68—14
1954	77	2.78—1	1981	33	3.88—11
1955	45	3.39—3	1982	31	4.11—11
1956	67	3.32—1	1983	34	4.43—13
1957	46	4.06—6	1984	21	4.26—12
1958	51	3.73—5	1985	24	4.91—14
1959	58	3.75—4	1986	31	4.58—12
1960	32	3.95—6	1987	24	5.28—14
1961	35	4.15—5	1988	35	4.16—11
1962	45	4.14—8	1989	23	3.65—5
1963	40	3.79—6	1990	12	4.26—13
1964	37	3.75—6	1991	22	4.23—9
1965	41	3.30—6	1992	13	4.11—11
1966	49	3.23—3	1993	7	4.58—11
1967	49	3.25—5	1994	17	4.36—5
1968	48	2.66—1†	1995	10	3.83—1
1969	35	3.94—10			

Year	Fielding E	DP	FA/Rank	Year	Fielding E	DP	FA/Rank
1901	329	99	.942—3	1929	198	162*	.968—5
1902	287	96	.950—5	1930	237	156	.962—7
1903	322	99*	.946—8	1931	232	143	.963—6
1904	255	86	.959—4	1932	191	129	.969—3
1905	229	84	.963—2	1933	156	127	.974—2
1906	216*	111*	.967—1	1934	172	164	.972—4
1907	264	137*	.960—2	1935	177	147	.972—4
1908	257	95	.962—3	1936	178	154	.971—5
1909	278	110*	.957—5	1937	159	153	.974—2
1910	247	112	.964—2	1938	151	145	.974—3
1911	302	108*	.954—3	1939	180	148	.970—3
1912	287	124	.954—4	1940	149*	164	.975—1
1913	242	124	.962—2	1941	142*	158	.976—1
1914	300	119*	.953—7	1942	163	175	.974—2
1915	280	82	.957—6	1943	157	183*	.975—2
1916	232	130	.965—5	1944	165	192*	.974—1
1917	242	136	.964—4	1945	126*	149	.977—1
1918	207	82	.962—5	1946	147	147	.975—2
1919	201	102	.965—4	1947	104*	178	.983—1
1920	184	124	.971—2	1948	114	183	.982—1
1921	204	124	.967—3	1949	103*	192	.983—1
1922	202	147	.968—5	1950	129	160	.978—4
1923	226	143	.964—7	1951	134*	151	.978—1
1924	205	130	.967—6	1952	155	141	.975—6
1925	210	146	.967—5	1953	127	197*	.979—2
1926	173	153	.972—2	1954	128	148	.979—2
1927	201	146	.968—5	1955	108*	152	.981—1
1928	221	187*	.965—7	1956	129	130	.978—2

Year	Fielding E	DP	FA/Rank
1957	153	154	.974—8
1958	152	171	.974—8
1959	127	138	.978—2
1960	128	165	.978—5
1961	139	142	.977—4
1962	139	168	.978—7
1963	143	129	.977—7
1964	118	149	.981—4
1965	114*	127	.981—1
1966	138	132	.978—4
1967	116	138	.981—2
1968	127	130	.979—3
1969	145	153	.976—9
1970	133	168	.979—6
1971	116	159	.981—2
1972	116	157	.981—3
1973	139	174	.978—4
1974	146	157	.977—3
1975	134	156	.978—2
1976	121	159	.980—2

Year	Fielding E	DP	FA/Rank
1977	130	145	.979—3
1978	123	142	.980—4
1979	134	149	.978—7
1980	105	143	.983—2
1981	87	91	.978—10
1982	123	129	.980—7
1983	122	174	.980—6
1984	146	163	.977—10
1985	141	161	.977—10
1986	157	148	.975—13
1987	153	128	.975—14
1988	124	131	.980—7
1989	118	126	.981—5
1990	117	146	.981—5
1991	149	150	.976—14
1992	141	176*	.978—12
1993	148	174*	.976—14
1994	90	119	.980—11
1995	101	142	.982—4†

League Leaders in Hitting

Average

1903	Lajoie	.344
1904	Lajoie	.376
1905	Flick	.308
1910	Lajoie	.384
1916	Speaker	.386
1929	Fonseca	.369
1944	Boudreau	.327
1954	Avila	.341

Runs

1906	Flick	98
1918	Chapman	84
1952	Doby	104
1953	Rosen	115
1955	Smith	123
1995	Belle	121

1954 American League batting champion and man of the year Bobby Avila.

Hits

1902	Hickman[a]	193
1904	Lajoie	208
1906	Lajoie	214
1910	Lajoie	227
1913	Jackson	197
1916	Speaker	211
1923	Jamieson	222
1926	Burns*	216
1930	Hodapp	225
1935	Vosmik	216
1936	Averill	232
1949	Mitchell	203
1994	Lofton	160

Doubles

1904	Lajoie	49
1906	Lajoie	48
1910	Lajoie	51
1913	Jackson	39
1916	Speaker*	41
	Graney*	41
1918	Speaker	33
1920	Speaker	50
1921	Speaker	52
1922	Speaker	48
1923	Speaker	59
1924	J. Sewell*	45
1926	Burns	64
1930	Hodapp	51
1935	Vosmik	47
1941	Boudreau	45
1944	Boudreau	45
1947	Boudreau	45
1960	Francona	36
1995	Belle*	52

Triples

1905	Flick	18
1906	Flick	22
1907	Flick	18
1912	Jackson	26
1935	Vosmik	20
1936	Averill*	15
1938	Heath	18
1941	Heath	20
1946	Edwards	16
1949	Mitchell	23
1952	Avila	11
1958	Power[b]	10
1986	Butler	14
1995	Lofton	13

Home Runs

1915	Roth[c]	7
1950	Rosen	37
1952	Doby	32
1953	Rosen	43
1954	Doby	32
1959	Colavito*	42
1995	Belle	50

Runs Batted In

1904	Lajoie	102
1936	Trosky	162
1952	Rosen	105
1953	Rosen	145
1954	Doby	126

1965	Colavito	108
1986	Carter	121
1993	Belle	129
1995	Belle	126

Stolen Bases

1903	Bay	45
1904	Bay*	38
	Flick*	38
1906	Flick	39
1946	Case	28
1992	Lofton	66
1993	Lofton	70
1994	Lofton	60
1995	Lofton	54

Total Bases

1902	Hickman[d]	288
1904	Lajoie	305
1910	Lajoie	304
1912	Jackson	331
1936	Trosky	405
1952	Rosen	297
1953	Rosen	367
1959	Colavito	301
1994	Belle	294
1995	Belle	377

Slugging Average

1903	Lajoie	.518
1904	Lajoie	.552
1905	Flick	.462
1913	Jackson	.551
1916	Speaker	.502
1952	Doby	.541
1953	Rosen	.613
1958	Colavito	.620
1995	Belle	.690

*Tied for league lead
[a]Began season with Boston
[b]Began season with Kansas City
[c]Began season with Chicago
[d]Began season with Boston

All-Time Hitting Leaders

Games

Turner	1,619
Lajoie	1,614
Boudreau	1,560
Hegan	1,526
Speaker	1,519
J. Sewell	1,513
Keltner	1,513
Averill	1,509
Jamieson	1,483
Graney	1,402

Runs

Averill	1,154
Speaker	1,079
Jamieson	942
Lajoie	865
J. Sewell	857
Boudreau	823
Doby	808
Trosky	758
Keltner	735
Graney	706

Total Bases

Averill	3,200
Speaker	2,886
Lajoie	2,728
Keltner	2,494
Trosky	2,406
Boudreau	2,392
J. Sewell	2,391
Jamieson	2,251
Doby	2,159
Thornton	1,954

At Bats

Lajoie	6,034
Averill	5,909

Turner	5,787
Boudreau	5,754
Keltner	5,655
J. Sewell	5,621
Jamieson	5,551
Speaker	5,546
Graney	4,705
Bradley	4,648

Hits

Lajoie	2,046
Speaker	1,965
Averill	1,903
J. Sewell	1,800
Jamieson	1,753
Boudreau	1,706
Keltner	1,561
Turner	1,472
Trosky	1,365
Bradley	1,265

Doubles

Speaker	486
Lajoie	424
Averill	377
J. Sewell	375
Boudreau	367
Keltner	306
Jamieson	296
Trosky	287
Bradley	238
Hale	235

Triples

Averill	121
Speaker	108
Flick	106
Jackson	89
Heath	83
Chapman	81
Graney	79

Lajoie	78
Turner	77
Bradley	74
Jamieson	74

Extra-Base Hits

Averill	724
Speaker	667
Trosky	556
Keltner	538
Lajoie	536
Boudreau	495
J. Sewell	468
Doby	450
Thornton	419
Heath	399

Stolen Bases

Turner	254
Lofton	250
Lajoie	240
Chapman	233
Flick	207
Bay	165
Butler	164
Bradley	157
Speaker	153
Graney	148

Home Runs

Averill	226
Trosky	216
Doby	215
Thornton	214
Belle	194
Rosen	192
Colavito	190
Keltner	163
Carter	151
Held	130

Runs Batted In

Averill	1,084
Lajoie	919
Trosky	911
Speaker	884
J. Sewell	869
Keltner	850
Doby	776
Thornton	749
Boudreau	740
Rosen	717

Batting Percent

Jackson	.375
Speaker	.354
Lajoie	.339
Burns	.327
Morgan	.323
Averill	.322
J. Sewell	.320
Hodapp	.318
Jamieson	.316
Lofton	.316
Vosmik	.313
Trosky	.313

Indians Triple Crown Leaders

Player	Year	Average	Home Runs	RBI
Nap Lajoie	1904	.376(1)	6*	102(1)
Nap Lajoie	1910	.384(1)	4	76
Joe Jackson	1911	.408(2)	7	83
Joe Jackson	1912	.395(2)	3	90*
Joe Jackson	1913	.373(2)	7	71
Joe Jackson	1914	.338(T2)	3	53
Tris Speaker	1923	.380(3)	17	130(2)
Earl Averill	1933	.301	11	92
Hal Trosky	1939	.335	25	104
Jeff Heath	1941	.340	24	123(2)
Les Fleming	1942	.292	14	82
Al Rosen	1953	.336(2)	43(1)	145(1)
Rocky Colavito	1958	.303	41(2)	113(2)
Max Alvis	1963	.274	22	67
Tony Horton	1969	.278	27*	93
Albert Belle	1994	.357(2)	36(3)	101(T3)

( ) = Ranking in league
*Tied for team lead

Man of the year in 1958 and 1965, Rocky Colavito.

Top 10 in Lifetime Slugging Percentage

Albert Belle	.571	Jeff Heath	.506
Hal Trosky	.551	Larry Doby	.500
Joe Jackson	.542	Rocky Colavito	.495
Earl Averill	.542	Al Rosen	.495
Tris Speaker	.520	Ed Morgan	.493

Albert Belle, man of the year, 1993.

Season Batting Leaders by Position

1b—Lew Fonseca	.369—1929		lf—Charlie Jamieson	.359—1924
2b—Nap Lajoie	.384—1910		cf—Tris Speaker	.389—1925
3b—Bill Bradley	.340—1902		rf—Joe Jackson	.408—1911
ss—Lou Boudreau	.355—1948		c—Steve O'Neill	.321—1920

.300 Hitters in Season

(Minimum 400 plate appearances)

Year	Player	AVG
1901	Ollie Pickering	.309
	Candy LaChance	.303
1902	Charlie Hickman	.378
	Bill Bradley	.340
1903	Nap Lajoie	.344
	Bill Bradley	.313
1904	Nap Lajoie	.376
	Elmer Flick	.306
	Bill Bradley	.300
1905	Elmer Flick	.308
	Harry Bay	.301
1906	Nap Lajoie	.355
	Bunk Congalton	.320
	Elmer Flick	.311
	Claude Rossman	.308
1907	Elmer Flick	.302
1909	Nap Lajoie	.324
1910	Nap Lajoie	.384
1911	Joe Jackson	.408
	Joe Birmingham	.304
1912	Joe Jackson	.395
	Nap Lajoie	.368
	Terry Turner	.308
1913	Joe Jackson	.373
	Nap Lajoie	.335
1914	Joe Jackson	.338
1916	Tris Speaker	.386
1917	Tris Speaker	.352
	Joe Harris	.304
	Ray Chapman	.302
1918	Tris Speaker	.318
1919	Ray Chapman	.300
	Larry Gardner	.300
1920	Tris Speaker	.388
	Steve O'Neill	.321
	Charlie Jamieson	.319
	Elmer Smith	.316
	Larry Gardner	.310
	Ray Chapman	.303
1921	Tris Speaker	.362
	Steve O'Neill	.322
	Larry Gardner	.319
	Joe Sewell	.318
	Charlie Jamieson	.310
1922	Tris Speaker	.378
	Charlie Jamieson	.323
	Steve O'Neill	.311
	Stuffy McInnis	.305
1923	Tris Speaker	.380
	Joe Sewell	.353
	Charlie Jamieson	.345
	Homer Summa	.328
1924	Charlie Jamieson	.359
	Tris Speaker	.344
	Joe Sewell	.316
	George Burns	.310
1925	Tris Speaker	.389
	George Burns	.336

Year	Player	AVG
	Joe Sewell	.336
	Pat McNulty	.314
1926	George Burns	.358
	Joe Sewell	.324
	Homer Summa	.308
	Tris Speaker	.304
1927	George Burns	.319
	Joe Sewell	.316
	Lew Fonseca	.311
	Charlie Jamieson	.309
1928	Johnny Hodapp	.323
	Joe Sewell	.323
	Charlie Jamieson	.307
1929	Lew Fonseca	.369
	Earl Averill	.332
	Joe Sewell	.315
	Bibb Falk	.312
1930	Johnny Hodapp	.354
	Dick Porter	.350
	Ed Morgan	.349
	Earl Averill	.339
	Charlie Jamieson	.301
1931	Ed Morgan	.351
	Earl Averill	.333
	Joe Vosmik	.320
	Dick Porter	.312
	Johnny Burnett	.300
1932	Bill Cissell	.320
	Earl Averill	.314
	Joe Vosmik	.312
	Dick Porter	.308
1933	Earl Averill	.301
1934	Joe Vosmik	.341
	Hal Trosky	.330
	Bill Knickerbocker	.317
	Earl Averill	.313
	Odell Hale	.302
1935	Joe Vosmik	.348
	Odell Hale	.304
1936	Earl Averill	.378
	Hal Trosky	.343
	Odell Hale	.316
1937	Moose Solters	.323
	Frankie Pytlak	.315
	Bruce Campbell	.301
1938	Jeff Heath	.343
	Hal Trosky	.334
	Earl Averill	.330
	Frankie Pytlak	.308
1939	Hal Trosky	.335
	Ken Keltner	.325
1940	Roy Weatherly	.303
1941	Jeff Heath	.340
1944	Lou Boudreau	.327
1945	Lou Boudreau	.307
	Jeff Heath	.305
1946	Hank Edwards	.301
1947	Dale Mitchell	.316
	Lou Boudreau	.307
1948	Lou Boudreau	.355

Year	Player	AVG
	Dale Mitchell	.336
	Larry Doby	.301
1949	Dale Mitchell	.317
1950	Larry Doby	.326
	Dale Mitchell	.308
	Ray Boone	.301
1951	Bobby Avila	.304
1952	Dale Mitchell	.323
	Al Rosen	.302
	Bobby Avila	.300
1953	Al Rosen	.336
	Dale Mitchell	.300
1954	Bobby Avila	.341
	Al Rosen	.300
1955	Al Smith	.306
1957	Gene Woodling	.321
1958	Vic Power	.317
	Rocky Colavito	.303
	Minnie Minoso	.302
1959	Tito Francona	.363
	Minnie Minoso	.302
1960	Harvey Kuenn	.308
1961	Jimmy Piersall	.322
	Tito Francona	.301
1965	Vic Davalillo	.301
1970	Ray Fosse	.307
1975	Rico Carty	.308
1976	Rico Carty	.310
1977	Bruce Bochte	.304
1979	Mike Hargrove	.325
1980	Miguel Dilone	.341
	Ron Hassey	.318
	Mike Hargrove	.304
1981	Mike Hargrove	.317*
1982	Toby Harrah	.304
1984	George Vukovich	.304
1985	Brett Butler	.311
1986	Pat Tabler	.326
	Julio Franco	.306
	Joe Carter	.302
	Tony Bernazard	.301

Mike Hargrove, the Indians man of the year in 1980 and 1981.

1987	Julio Franco	.319		1992	Carlos Baerga	.312		Kenny Lofton	.349
	Pat Tabler	.307		1993	Kenny Lofton	.325		Carlos Baerga	.314
	Brook Jacoby	.300			Carlos Baerga	.321			
1988	Julio Franco	.303		1994	Albert Belle	.357			

*Had 398 plate appearances in strike-shortened season

30 or More Home Runs in One Season

43	Al Rosen	1953		32	Hal Trosky	1937
42	Hal Trosky	1936		32	Joe Gordon	1948
42	Rocky Colavito	1959		32	Larry Doby	1952
41	Rocky Colavito	1958		32	Larry Doby	1954
38	Albert Belle	1993		32	Vic Wertz	1956
37	Al Rosen	1950		32	Andre Thornton	1982
36	Albert Belle	1994		32	Joe Carter	1987
35	Hal Trosky	1934		32	Brook Jacoby	1987
35	Joe Carter	1989		31	Earl Averill	1934
34	Albert Belle	1992		31	Ken Keltner	1948
33	Andre Thornton	1978		31	Luke Easter	1952
33	Andre Thornton	1984		31	Leon Wagner	1964
33	Cory Snyder	1987		31	Manny Ramirez	1995
32	Earl Averill	1931		30	Rocky Colavito	1966
32	Earl Averill	1932				

Andre Thornton, man of the year in 1978 and co-winner of the award with Toby Harrah in 1982, is congratulated after hitting a game-winning home run.

Grand Slam Home Runs in Career

9 Al Rosen
6 Rocky Colavito, Andre Thornton
5 Ken Keltner, Albert Belle
4 Earl Averill, Buddy Bell, Joe Carter, Larry Doby, Jim Hegan, Woodie Held, Cory Snyder, Tris Speaker, Hal Trosky
3 Ray Boone, Chico Carrasquel, Luke Easter, Rick Manning, Pat Seerey, Fred Whitfield, Paul Sorrento
2 Max Alvis, Bobby Avila, Bobby Bonds, Jim Busby, Ray Fosse, Julio Franco, Joe Gordon, Odell Hale, Toby Harrah, Tony Horton, Joe Jackson, Brook Jacoby, Bill Knickerbocker, Nap Lajoie, Minnie Minoso, Bubba Phillips, Pat Tabler, George Vukovich, Leon Wagner, Vic Wertz
1 Gary Alexander, Andy Allanson, Sandy Alomar, Alan Ashby, Carlos Baerga, Alan Bannister, Tony Bernazard, Walt Bond, Lou Boudreau, Buddy Bradford, Brett Butler, Bruce Campbell, Jose Cardenal, Carmen Castillo, Chris Chambliss, Ben Chapman, Joe Charboneau, Joe Connolly, Paul Dade, Mike de la Hoz, Bo Diaz, Don Dillard, Steve Dunning, Frank Ellerbe, John Ellis, Mike Fischlin, Roy Foster, Bill Glynn, Johnny Grubb, Mike Hargrove, Ken Harrelson, Jeff Heath, George Hendrick, Piano Legs Hickman, Chuck Hinton, Willie Horton, Reggie Jefferson, Cliff Johnson, Willie Kamm, Marty Kavanagh, Ralph Kiner, Leron Lee, Kenny Lofton, Ron Lolich, John Lowenstein, Ray Mack, Roger Maris, Carlos Martinez, Dale Mitchell, Graig Nettles, John O'Donoghue, Ivy Olson, Jorge Orta, Casey Parsons, Dave Philley, Vada Pinson, Dave Pope,

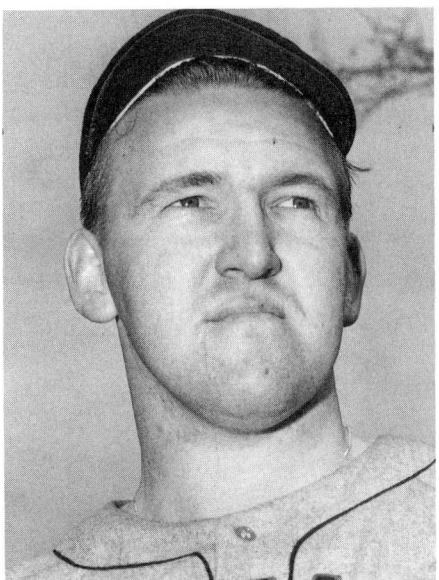

Pat Seerey, a member of the Indians from 1943 to 1948, when he was traded to the Chicago White Sox, hit four homers in an 11-inning game on July 18, 1948 at Shibe Park in Philadelphia.

Max Alvis, who won the Man of the Year Award in 1963 and again in 1967.

Dick Porter, Vic Power, Manny Ramirez, Pedro Ramos, Johnny Romano, Bud Ryan, Chico Salmon, Harry Simpson, Elmer Smith, Moose Solters, Charlie Spikes, George Strickland, Homer Summa, Joe Tipton, George Uhle, Mickey Vernon, Mitch Webster, Mark Whiten

Most Grand Slam Home Runs in One Season

4	Al Rosen	1951	2	Al Rosen	1950	2	Minnie Minoso	1959
3	Tris Speaker	1923	2	Luke Easter	1952	2	Bubba Phillips	1961
3	Andre Thornton	1979	2	Ray Boone	1953	2	Bobby Bonds	1979
2	Hal Trosky	1934	2	Al Rosen	1953	2	Joe Carter	1986
2	Ken Keltner	1940	2	Jim Busby	1956	2	Cory Snyder	1987
2	Ken Keltner	1944	2	Chico Carrasquel	1957	2	Albert Belle	1995
2	Pat Seerey	1945	2	Rocky Colavito	1958	2	Paul Sorrento	1995
2	Larry Doby	1950	2	Woodie Held	1959			

Three or More Home Runs in One Game

4	ROCKY COLAVITO	June 10, 1959, at Baltimore
3	EARL AVERILL	September 17, 1930, vs. Washington (first game)
	HAL TROSKY	May 30, 1934, vs. Chicago (second game)
	Hal Trosky	July 5, 1937, at St. Louis (first game)
	KEN KELTNER	May 25, 1939, at Boston
	Pat Seerey	July 13, 1945, at New York
	LARRY DOBY	August 2, 1950, vs. Washington
	Bobby Avila	June 20, 1951, at Boston
	Al Rosen	April 29, 1952, at Philadelphia
	BILL GLYNN	July 5, 1954, at Detroit (first game)
	WILLIE KIRKLAND	July 9, 1961, vs. Chicago
	Tony Horton	May 24, 1970, vs. New York (second game)
	GEORGE HENDRICK	June 19, 1973, vs. Detroit
	Joe Carter	August 29, 1986, at Boston
	Cory Snyder	May 21, 1987, vs. Minnesota
	Joe Carter	May 28, 1987, at Boston
	BROOK JACOBY	July 3, 1987, vs. Chicago
	JOE CARTER	June 24, 1989, at Texas
	Joe Carter	July 19, 1989, at Minnesota
	Albert Belle	September 6, 1992, vs. Seattle
	Carlos Baerga	June 17, 1993, at Detroit
	JIM THOME	July 22, 1994, vs. Chicago
	Albert Belle	September 19, 1995, at Chicago

(second game) — appears after ROCKY COLAVITO / Tony Horton

Caps denote consecutive homers

Hitting for the Cycle

Bill Bradley	September 24, 1903, at Washington
Earl Averill	August 17, 1933, vs. Philadelphia
Odell Hale	July 12, 1938, at Washington
Larry Doby	June 4, 1952, at Boston
Tony Horton	July 2, 1970, at Baltimore
Andre Thornton	April 22, 1978, at Boston

Indians Who Hit a Home Run in Their First Major League At Bat

Earl Averill	April 16, 1929, vs. Detroit, off Earl Whitehill
Jay Bell	September 29, 1986, at Minnesota, off Bert Blyleven

Indians 20–20 Club

Player	Year	HR	SB	Player	Year	HR	SB
Bobby Bonds	1979	25	34	Joe Carter	1987	32	31
Toby Harrah	1979	20	20	Joe Carter	1988	27	27
Joe Carter	1986	29	29	Albert Belle	1993	38	23

Most RBIs in One Season by Position

C	Johnny Romano	1962 (81)	SS	Joe Sewell	1923 (109)	CF	Earl Averill	1931 (143)
1B	Hal Trosky	1936 (162)	3B	Al Rosen	1953 (145)	RF	Rocky Colavito	1958 (113)
2B	Joe Gordon	1948 (124)	LF	Albert Belle	1993 (129)	DH	Andre Thornton	1982 (109)

Most RBIs in One Game

9	Chris James	May 4, 1991	8	Bill Glynn	July 5, 1954
8	Earl Averill	July 12, 1930			(first game)
8	Pat Seerey	July 13, 1945			

Three Triples in One Game

Elmer Flick	July 6, 1902	Joe Jackson	June 30, 1912
Bill Bradley	July 28, 1903		(second game)
Nap Lajoie	July 13, 1904	Ben Chapman	July 3, 1939

Four Doubles in One Game

Lou Boudreau   July 14, 1946 (first game)
Vic Wertz   September 26, 1956

200 or More Hits in One Season

1911	Joe Jackson	233	1936	Hal Trosky	216	1992	Carlos Baerga	205
1936	Earl Averill	232	1906	Nap Lajoie	214	1925	Joe Sewell	204
1910	Nap Lajoie	227	1920	Tris Speaker	214	1930	Ed Morgan	204
1912	Joe Jackson	226	1924	Charlie Jamieson	213	1948	Dale Mitchell	204
1930	Johnny Hodapp	225	1916	Tris Speaker	211	1949	Dale Mitchell	203
1923	Charlie Jamieson	222	1929	Lew Fonseca	209	1953	Al Rosen	201
1923	Tris Speaker	218	1931	Earl Averill	209	1986	Joe Carter	200
1926	George Burns	216	1904	Nap Lajoie	208	1993	Carlos Baerga	200
1935	Joe Vosmik	216	1934	Hal Trosky	206			

Six Hits in One Game

		1B	2B	3B				1B	2B	3B	
9	Johnny Burnett	7	2	0	July 10, 1932, vs. Philadelphia (18 innings)	Bruce Campbell	5	1	0	July 2, 1936, at St. Louis (first game)
6	Ervin Harvey	6	0	0	April 25, 1902, at St. Louis	Jim Fridley	6	0	0	April 29, 1952, at Philadelphia
	Frank Brower	5	1	0	August 7, 1923, at Washington	Jorge Orta	5	1	0	June 15, 1980, vs. Minnesota
	George Burns	2	3	1	June 19, 1924, at Detroit (first game)	Carlos Baerga	6	0	0	April 11, 1992, vs. Boston (19 innings)

100 or More RBIs in One Season

1936	Hal Trosky	162	1938	Jeff Heath	112
1953	Al Rosen	145	1992	Albert Belle	112
1931	Earl Averill	143	1959	Rocky Colavito	111
1934	Hal Trosky	142	1935	Joe Vosmik	110
1930	Ed Morgan	136	1938	Hal Trosky	110
1923	Tris Speaker	130	1923	Joe Sewell	109
1993	Albert Belle	129	1937	Moose Solters	109
1937	Hal Trosky	128	1965	Rocky Colavito	108
1936	Earl Averill	126	1920	Tris Speaker	107
1954	Larry Doby	126	1950	Luke Easter	107
1995	Albert Belle	126	1995	Manny Ramirez	107
1932	Earl Averill	124	1924	Joe Sewell	106
1948	Joe Gordon	124	1948	Lou Boudreau	106
1941	Jeff Heath	123	1956	Vic Wertz	106
1930	Johnny Hodapp	121	1987	Joe Carter	106
1986	Joe Carter	121	1952	Al Rosen	105
1921	Larry Gardner	120	1957	Vic Wertz	105
1930	Earl Averill	119	1978	Andre Thornton	105
1948	Ken Keltner	119	1989	Joe Carter	105
1920	Larry Gardner	118	1992	Carlos Baerga	105
1931	Joe Vosmik	117	1939	Hal Trosky	104
1950	Al Rosen	116	1952	Larry Doby	104
1982	Andre Thornton	116	1920	Elmer Smith	103
1926	George Burns	114	1929	Lew Fonseca	103
1993	Carlos Baerga	114	1951	Luke Easter	103
1934	Earl Averill	113	1904	Nap Lajoie	102
1935	Hal Trosky	113	1950	Larry Doby	102
1938	Ken Keltner	113	1951	Al Rosen	102
1958	Rocky Colavito	113	1953	Larry Doby	102

Joe Carter, man of the year, 1986.

1954	Al Rosen	102
1934	Odell Hale	101
1935	Odell Hale	101
1940	Lou Boudreau	101
1994	Albert Belle	101
1964	Leon Wagner	100

100 or More Runs Scored in One Season

1931	Earl Averill	140	1913	Joe Jackson	109	1921	Larry Gardner	101
1920	Tris Speaker	137	1925	Charlie Jamieson	109	1921	Joe Sewell	101
1936	Earl Averill	136	1935	Earl Averill	109	1926	Freddy Spurgeon	101
1923	Tris Speaker	133	1984	Brett Butler	108	1938	Earl Averill	101
1923	Charlie Jamieson	130	1986	Joe Carter	108			
1934	Earl Averill	128	1921	Tris Speaker	107			
1911	Joe Jackson	126	1916	Jack Graney	106			
1936	Odell Hale	126	1932	Dick Porter	106			
1936	Hal Trosky	124	1938	Hal Trosky	106			
1955	Al Smith	123	1949	Larry Doby	106			
1930	Ed Morgan	122	1985	Brett Butler	106			
1912	Joe Jackson	121	1993	Carlos Baerga	105			
1937	Earl Averill	121	1994	Kenny Lofton	105			
1995	Albert Belle	121	1902	Bill Bradley	104			
1934	Hal Trosky	117	1937	Hal Trosky	104			
1932	Earl Averill	116	1938	Jeff Heath	104			
1948	Lou Boudreau	116	1952	Larry Doby	104			
1993	Kenny Lofton	116	1901	Ollie Pickering	102			
1953	Al Rosen	115	1916	Tris Speaker	102			
1936	Roy Hughes	112	1928	Carl Lind	102			
1954	Bobby Avila	112	1930	Earl Averill	102			
1930	Johnny Hodapp	111	1952	Bobby Avila	102			
1929	Earl Averill	110	1959	Vic Power	102			
1937	Lyn Lary	110	1903	Bill Bradley	101			
1950	Larry Doby	110	1915	Ray Chapman	101			

Al Smith, man of the year, 1955.

1939	Ben Chapman	101	1930	Dick Porter	100
1952	Al Rosen	101	1950	Al Rosen	100
1954	Al Smith	101	1980	Toby Harrah	100
1964	Dick Howser	101	1982	Toby Harrah	100

Toby Harrah, co-man of the year, 1982.

300 or More Total Bases in One Season

1936	Hal Trosky	405	1934	Earl Averill	340	1904	Nap Lajoie	305
1936	Earl Averill	385	1911	Joe Jackson	337	1910	Nap Lajoie	304
1995	Albert Belle	377	1935	Joe Vosmik	333	1958	Rocky Colavito	303
1934	Hal Trosky	374	1912	Joe Jackson	331	1989	Joe Carter	303
1953	Al Rosen	367	1937	Hal Trosky	329	1993	Carlos Baerga	303
1931	Earl Averill	361	1993	Albert Belle	328	1938	Jeff Heath	302
1932	Earl Averill	359	1929	Earl Averill	322	1929	Lew Fonseca	301
1930	Ed Morgan	351	1930	Johnny Hodapp	319	1950	Al Rosen	301
1923	Tris Speaker	350	1936	Odell Hale	314	1959	Rocky Colavito	301
1941	Jeff Heath	343	1937	Moose Solters	314	1937	Earl Averill	300
1986	Joe Carter	341	1920	Tris Speaker	310	1938	Hal Trosky	300

10 or More Doubles, Triples, Home Runs, and Stolen Bases

Player	Year	2B	3B	HR	SB	Player	Year	2B	3B	HR	SB
Bill Bradley	1902	39	12	11	11	Odell Hale	1935	37	11	16	15
Piano Legs Hickman	1903	31	11	12	14	Bruce Campbell	1938	27	12	12	11
Tris Speaker	1923	59	11	17	10	Ken Keltner	1940	24	10	15	10
Earl Averill	1929	43	13	18	13	Jeff Heath	1941	32	20	24	18

75 or More Extra-Base Hits in One Season

103	Albert Belle	1995	84	Ed Morgan	1930	77	Odell Hale	1936
96	Hal Trosky	1936	83	Earl Averill	1932	77	Hal Trosky	1937
89	Hal Trosky	1934	82	Earl Averill	1936	77	Albert Belle	1993
87	Tris Speaker	1923	78	Earl Averill	1931	76	Jeff Heath	1941
85	Earl Averill	1934	77	Joe Vosmik	1935	75	Al Rosen	1953

150 or More Singles in One Season

172	Charlie Jamieson	1923	161	Dale Mitchell	1949	157	Nap Lajoie	1906
168	Charlie Jamieson	1924	160	Tris Speaker	1916	153	Joe Jackson	1912
165	Nap Lajoie	1910	159	Joe Sewell	1925	152	Carlos Baerga	1992
162	Joe Jackson	1911	158	Julio Franco	1984	150	Earl Averill	1936
162	Dale Mitchell	1948	157	Johnny Hodapp	1930			

40 or More Doubles in One Season

64	George Burns	1926	47	Joe Vosmik	1935	42	Carl Lind	1928
59	Tris Speaker	1923	46	Lyn Lary	1937	42	Dick Porter	1932
52	Tris Speaker	1921	46	Lou Boudreau	1940	42	Bruce Campbell	1937
52	Tris Speaker	1926	45	Joe Jackson	1911	42	Moose Solters	1937
52	Albert Belle	1995	45	Joe Sewell	1924	41	Nap Lajoie	1903
51	Nap Lajoie	1910	45	Hal Trosky	1934	41	Jack Graney	1916
51	George Burns	1927	45	Hal Trosky	1936	41	Tris Speaker	1916
51	Johnny Hodapp	1930	45	Lou Boudreau	1941	41	Joe Sewell	1923
50	Tris Speaker	1920	45	Lou Boudreau	1944	41	George Burns	1925
50	Odell Hale	1936	45	Lou Boudreau	1947	41	Joe Sewell	1926
49	Nap Lajoie	1904	44	Joe Jackson	1912	41	Homer Summa	1927
48	Nap Lajoie	1906	44	Lew Fonseca	1929	41	Ken Keltner	1944
48	Tris Speaker	1922	44	Odell Hale	1934	40	Joe Sewell	1928
48	Joe Sewell	1927	43	Earl Averill	1929	40	Hal Trosky	1938
48	Earl Averill	1934	43	Dick Porter	1930	40	Ben Chapman	1940
47	Ed Morgan	1930	42	Tris Speaker	1917			

15 or More Triples in One Season

26	Joe Jackson	1912	17	Elmer Flick	1904
23	Dale Mitchell	1949	17	Joe Jackson	1913
22	Bill Bradley	1903	17	Ray Chapman	1915
22	Elmer Flick	1906	16	Elmer Flick	1903
20	Joe Vosmik	1935	16	Earl Averill	1933
20	Jeff Heath	1941	16	Hank Edwards	1946
19	Joe Jackson	1911	15	Nap Lajoie	1904
18	Elmer Flick	1905	15	Lew Fonseca	1929
18	Elmer Flick	1907	15	Earl Averill	1936
18	Jeff Heath	1938	15	Earl Averill	1938

Outfielder Elmer Flick.

Most Pinch Hits in One Season

19	Bob Hale	1960	11	Hank Majeski	1953
16	Gomer Hodge	1971	11	Ralph Kiner	1955
15	Don Dillard	1961	11	Don Dillard	1962
14	Bibb Falk	1931	11	Chuck Hinton	1970
14	Dale Mitchell	1954	11	Carlos Baerga	1990
14	Richie Scheinblum	1969	11	Jerry Browne	1991
13	Bibb Falk	1930	10	Odell Hale	1939
13	Dale Mitchell	1955	10	Gene Green	1962
11	George Uhle	1924	10	Lee Maye	1967
11	Ralph Winegarner	1935	10	Chuck Hinton	1969

Jerry Browne, man of the year, 1989.

30 or More Stolen Bases in One Season

70	Kenny Lofton	1993	40	Alex Cole	1990	35	Braggo Roth	1918
66	Kenny Lofton	1992	39	Elmer Flick	1906	34	Bobby Bonds	1979
61	Miguel Dilone	1980	38	Harry Bay	1904	33	Miguel Dilone	1982
60	Kenny Lofton	1994	38	Elmer Flick	1904	33	Brett Butler	1987
54	Kenny Lofton	1995	37	Josh Clarke	1908	32	Von Hayes	1982
52	Ray Chapman	1917	36	Ollie Pickering	1901	32	Julio Franco	1983
52	Brett Butler	1984	36	Harry Bay	1905	32	Brett Butler	1986
51	Braggo Roth	1917	36	Ray Chapman	1915	32	Julio Franco	1987
47	Brett Butler	1985	36	Jose Cardenal	1969	31	Terry Turner	1910
45	Harry Bay	1903	36	John Lowenstein	1974	31	Joe Carter	1987
41	Elmer Flick	1907	35	Elmer Flick	1905	30	Tris Speaker	1917
41	Joe Jackson	1911	35	Joe Jackson	1912	30	Ray Chapman	1918
40	Jose Cardenal	1968	35	Tris Speaker	1916	30	Rick Manning	1979

Four or More Stolen Bases in One Game

5	Alex Cole	August 1, 1990, versus Kansas City	4	Willie Kamm	May 29, 1931, at St. Louis
5	Alex Cole	May 3, 1992, versus California	4	Kenny Lofton	April 12, 1992, versus Boston (first game)
4	Ray Chapman	May 14, 1917, versus Boston			
4	Ray Chapman	September 16, 1919, at Philadelphia			

100 or More Walks in One Season

1980	Mike Hargrove	111	1919	Jack Graney	105	1982	Mike Hargrove	101
1982	Andre Thornton	109	1916	Jack Graney	102	1950	Al Rosen	100
1942	Les Fleming	106	1951	Larry Doby	101			

Most Intentional Walks in One Season

18	Andre Thornton, 1982		Rocky Colavito, 1965	Alex Johnson, 1972

18	Andre Thornton, 1982	Rocky Colavito, 1965	Alex Johnson, 1972
17	Pete O'Brien, 1989	Duke Sims, 1968	Oscar Gamble, 1974
15	Ray Fosse, 1972	Rick Manning, 1980	Mike Hargrove, 1980
14	Andre Thornton, 1983	Andre Thornton, 1984	Jerry Browne, 1989
13	Albert Belle, 1993	Paul Sorrento, 1993	Carlos Baerga, 1992
12	Leon Wagner, 1964	10	Vic Wertz, 1956	Mark Whiten, 1992
	Mel Hall, 1988	Woodie Held, 1963	
11	Woodie Held, 1961	Larry Brown, 1968	

All-Time Pitching Leaders

Victories		Losses		Games	
Feller	266	Harder	186	Harder	582
Harder	223	Feller	162	Feller	570
Lemon	207	Hudlin	151	Hudlin	475
Coveleski	172	Lemon	128	Lemon	460
Wynn	164	Coveleski	123	G. Bell	419
Joss	160	Uhle	119	Garcia	397
Hudlin	157	McDowell	109	Coveleski	360
Uhle	147	Wynn	102	Uhle	357
Garcia	142	Joss	97	Wynn	343
Bagby, Sr.	122	Garcia	96	McDowell	336
McDowell	122				

Complete Games

Feller	279
Joss	234
Coveleski	194
Lemon	188
Harder	181
Uhle	166
Hudlin	154
Wynn	144
Moore	137
Bagby, Sr.	131

Shutouts

Joss	45
Feller	44
Coveleski	31
Lemon	31
Garcia	27
Harder	25
Wynn	24
McDowell	22
Tiant	21
Rhoads	19
Morton	19

Saves

D. Jones	128
Narleski	53
Mesa	48
Olin	48
Kern	46
Monge	46
G. Bell	45
Camacho	44
LaRoche	42
Spillner	41
Heving	32
Mossi	32

Innings Pitched

Feller	3,827
Harder	3,426⅓
Lemon	2,850
Hudlin	2,557⅔
Coveleski	2,502⅓
Joss	2,327
Wynn	2,286⅔
Uhle	2,200⅓
Garcia	2,138
McDowell	2,109⅔

Hits

Harder	3,706
Feller	3,271
Hudlin	2,930
Lemon	2,559
Coveleski	2,450
Uhle	2,442
Garcia	2,102
Wynn	2,037
Joss	1,888
Bagby, Sr.	1,772

Runs

Harder	1,714
Feller	1,557
Hudlin	1,434
Lemon	1,185
Uhle	1,137
Coveleski	972
Wynn	923
Garcia	865
Shaute	817
McDowell	805

Earned Runs

Harder	1,447
Feller	1,384
Hudlin	1,233
Lemon	1,024
Uhle	959
Wynn	824
Coveleski	779
Garcia	770
McDowell	702
Shaute	660

Walks

Feller	1,764
Lemon	1,251
Harder	1,118
McDowell	1,072
Wynn	877
Hudlin	832
Uhle	709
Garcia	696
G. Bell	670
Coveleski	616

Strikeouts

Feller	2,581
McDowell	2,159
Lemon	1,277
Wynn	1,277
Harder	1,160
G. Bell	1,104
Garcia	1,095
Tiant	1,041
Joss	920
Coveleski	856

League Leaders in Pitching

Victories

1907	Joss	27*
1920	Bagby	31
1923	Uhle	26
1926	Uhle	27
1939	Feller	24
1940	Feller	27
1941	Feller	25
1946	Feller	26*
1947	Feller	20
1950	Lemon	23
1951	Feller	22
1954	Lemon	23*
1954	Wynn	23*
1955	Lemon	18*
1960	J. Perry	18*
1972	G. Perry	24*

Games

1918	Bagby, Sr.	45*
1920	Bagby, Sr.	48
1938	Humphries	45
1940	Feller	43
1941	Feller	44
1944	Heving	63
1946	Feller	48
1947	Klieman	58
1955	Narleski	60

Complete Games

1920	Bagby, Sr.	30
1923	Uhle	29
1925	S. Smith	22*
1926	Uhle	32

1931	Ferrell	27*
1939	Feller	24*
1940	Feller	31
1946	Feller	36
1948	Lemon	20
1950	Lemon	22*
1952	Lemon	28
1954	Lemon	21*
1956	Lemon	21*
1972	G. Perry	29
1973	G. Perry	29
1986	Candiotti	17

Innings Pitched

1920	Bagby, Sr.	339⅔
1923	Uhle	357⅔
1926	Uhle	318⅓

1939	Feller	296⅔
1940	Feller	320⅓
1941	Feller	343
1943	Bagby, Jr.	273
1946	Feller	371⅓
1947	Feller	299
1948	Lemon	293⅔
1950	Lemon	288
1951	Wynn	274⅓
1952	Lemon	309⅔
1953	Lemon	286⅔
1954	Wynn	270⅔
1970	McDowell	305*

Earned Run Average

1903	Moore	1.74
1904	Joss	1.59
1908	Joss	1.16
1911	Gregg	1.80
1923	Coveleski	2.76
1933	Harder	2.95
1940	Feller	2.61
1948	Bearden	2.43
1949	Garcia	2.36
1950	Wynn	3.20
1954	Garcia	2.64
1965	McDowell	2.18
1968	Tiant	1.60
1982	Sutcliffe	2.96

Shutouts

1902	Joss	5
1917	Coveleski	9
1922	Uhle	5
1923	Coveleski	5
1930	C. Brown	3*
1933	Hildebrand	6
1934	Harder	6*
1940	Feller	4*
1940	Milnar	4*
1941	Feller	6
1946	Feller	10
1947	Feller	5*
1948	Lemon	10
1952	Garcia	6*
1954	Garcia	5*
1956	Score	5
1960	J. Perry	4*
1962	Donovan	5*
1966	Tiant	5*
1966	McDowell	5*
1967	Hargan	6*
1968	Tiant	9

Strikeouts

1920	Coveleski	133
1938	Feller	240
1939	Feller	246

1940	Feller	261
1941	Feller	260
1943	Reynolds	151
1946	Feller	348
1947	Feller	196
1948	Feller	164
1950	Lemon	170
1955	Score	245
1956	Score	263
1957	Wynn	184
1965	McDowell	325
1966	McDowell	225
1968	McDowell	283
1969	McDowell	279
1970	McDowell	304
1980	Barker	187
1981	Barker	127

Losses

1901	Dowling	26†
1924	Shaute	17*
1951	Lemon	14*
1969	Tiant	20
1977	Garland	19*
1978	Wise	19

*Tied for lead

†Four losses with Milwaukee, 22 with Cleveland

20-Game Winners

		Record						
1904	Bill Bernhard	23–13	1921	Stan Coveleski	23–13	1949	Bob Lemon	22–10
1905	Addie Joss	20–12	1922	George Uhle	22–16	1950	Bob Lemon	23–11
1906	Bob Rhoads	22–10	1923	George Uhle	26–16	1951	Bob Feller	22–8
	Addie Joss	21–9	1924	Joe Shaute	20–17		Mike Garcia	20–13
	Otto Hess	20–17	1926	George Uhle	27–11		Early Wynn	20–13
1907	Addie Joss	27–11	1929	Wes Ferrell	21–10	1952	Early Wynn	23–12
1908	Addie Joss	24–11	1930	Wes Ferrell	25–13		Mike Garcia	22–11
1911	Vean Gregg	23–7	1931	Wes Ferrell	22–12		Bob Lemon	22–11
1912	Vean Gregg	20–13	1932	Wes Ferrell	23–13	1953	Bob Lemon	21–15
1913	Cy Falkenberg	23–10	1934	Mel Harder	20–12	1954	Bob Lemon	23–7
	Vean Gregg	20–13	1935	Mel Harder	22–11		Early Wynn	23–11
1917	Jim Bagby, Sr.	23–13	1936	Johnny Allen	20–10	1956	Herb Score	20–9
1918	Stan Coveleski	22–13	1939	Bob Feller	24–9		Early Wynn	20–9
1919	Stan Coveleski	24–12	1940	Bob Feller	27–11		Bob Lemon	20–14
1920	Jim Bagby, Sr.	31–12	1941	Bob Feller	25–13	1962	Dick Donovan	20–10
	Stan Coveleski	24–14	1946	Bob Feller	26–15	1968	Luis Tiant	21–9
	Ray Caldwell	20–10	1947	Bob Feller	20–11	1970	Sam McDowell	20–12
			1948	Gene Bearden	20–7	1972	Gaylord Perry	24–16
				Bob Lemon	20–14	1974	Gaylord Perry	21–13

No-Hitters

By Indians

*May 9, 1901	Earl Moore, vs. Chicago	2–4
September 18, 1908	Bob Rhoads, vs. Boston	2–1

†October 2, 1908	Addie Joss, vs. Chicago	1–0
April 20, 1910	Addie Joss, at Chicago	1–0
September 10, 1919	Ray Caldwell, at New York	3–0
April 29, 1931	Wes Ferrell, vs. St. Louis	9–0

April 16, 1940	Bob Feller, at Chicago	1–0
April 30, 1946	Bob Feller, at New York	1–0
July 10, 1947(1)	Don Black, vs. Philadelphia	3–0
June 30, 1948	Bob Lemon, at Detroit	2–0
July 1, 1951(1)	Bob Feller, vs. Detroit	2–1
June 10, 1966	Sonny Siebert, vs. Washington	2–0
July 19, 1974	Dick Bosman, vs. Oakland	4–0
May 30, 1977	Dennis Eckersley, vs. California	1–0
†May 15, 1981	Len Barker, vs. Toronto	3–0

*Pitched nine hitless innings, lost on two hits in tenth inning
†Perfect game

Against Indians

May 12, 1910	Chief Bender, Philadelphia	4–0
*August 30, 1910	Tom Hughes, New York	0–5
May 31, 1914	Joe Benz, Chicago	6–1
August 26, 1916	Joe Bush, Philadelphia	5–0
August 31, 1935	Vern Kennedy, Chicago	5–0
August 27, 1938(2)	Monte Pearson, New York	13–0
†July 12, 1951	Allie Reynolds, New York	1–0
September 16, 1965	Dave Morehead, Boston	2–0
†August 25, 1967(2)	Dean Chance, Minnesota	2–1
†September 2, 1990	Dave Stieb, Toronto	3–0
September 4, 1993	Jim Abbott, New York	4–0

Don Black pitched a no-hitter against his former team, the Philadelphia Athletics, beating them, 3–0, in Cleveland on July 10, 1947. It was the first no-hitter pitched in Cleveland Stadium.

*Pitched 9⅓ hitless innings, lost on seven hits in 11 innings
†Game played in Cleveland

One-Hitters by Indians Pitchers

June 30, 1901	Pete Dowling	at Milwaukee	W 7–0
August 2, 1901	Pete Dowling	at Milwaukee	W 7–0
August 13, 1901(1)	Earl Moore	vs. Chicago	W 4–0
April 26, 1902	Addie Joss	at St. Louis	W 3–0
August 24, 1903	Addie Joss	vs. Philadelphia	W 3–0
September 27, 1904	Bob Rhoads	vs. Boston	W 3–1
September 25, 1906	Otto Hess	vs. Philadelphia	W 5–0
April 20, 1907	Addie Joss	vs. Detroit	W 4–1
September 5, 1907	Addie Joss	vs. Detroit	W 3–0
September 25, 1907	Addie Joss	at New York	W 3–1
September, 26 1907	Heinie Berger	at New York	W 6–0
September 1, 1908	Addie Joss	at Detroit	W 1–0
June 8, 1909	Addie Joss	at Philadelphia	W 2–0
September 11, 1910(1)	Willie Mitchell	at St. Louis	W 3–0
July 6, 1913(2)	Willie Mitchell	vs. Chicago	W 7–0
August 24, 1915	Guy Morton	vs. New York	W 6–0
May 20, 1917	Al Gould	vs. Philadelphia	W 3–1
June 1, 1917	Guy Morton	at Boston	W 3–0
September 19, 1917	Stan Coveleski	at New York	W 2–0
May 23, 1918	Guy Morton	at Boston	W 1–0
July 31, 1920	Guy Morton	vs. Boston	W 2–1
May 13, 1928	George Uhle	vs. Philadelphia	W 2–0
June 23, 1931(2)	Willis Hudlin	vs. Boston	W 10–0
August 6, 1932	Wes Ferrell	vs. Boston	W 3–0
April 26, 1933	Oral Hildebrand	vs. St. Louis	W 2–0
June 16, 1935	Mel Harder	vs. Boston	W 4–0
April 20, 1938	Bob Feller	vs. St. Louis	W 9–0
May 25, 1939	Bob Feller	at Boston	W 11–0
June 27, 1939	Bob Feller	vs. Detroit	W 5–0
July 12, 1940	Bob Feller	at Philadelphia	W 1–0
August 14, 1940	Al Smith	vs. Chicago	W 4–0
September 26, 1941(2)	Bob Feller	at St. Louis	W 3–2

June 20, 1942	Al Smith	vs. New York	W 1–0
September 19, 1945	Bob Feller	vs. Detroit	W 2–0
July 31, 1946	Bob Feller	vs. Boston	W 4–1
August 8, 1946(1)	Bob Feller	at Chicago	W 5–0
April 22, 1947	Bob Feller	vs. St. Louis	W 5–0
May 2, 1947	Bob Feller	vs. Boston	W 2–0
August 12, 1947(2)	Al Gettel	vs. Detroit	W 11–0
May 29, 1951	Bob Lemon	at Detroit	W 2–1
April 23, 1952	Bob Feller	at St. Louis	L 1–0
April 14, 1953	Bob Lemon	vs. Chicago	W 6–0
May 16, 1954(2)	Mike Garcia	vs. Philadelphia	W 6–0
July 4, 1954	Mike Garcia (1⅓), Ray Narleski (5⅔)(W), and Early Wynn (2)	vs. Chicago	W 2–1
May 1, 1955(1)	Bob Feller	vs. Boston	W 2–0
May 22, 1955	Early Wynn	at Detroit	W 4–0
July 30, 1955	Herb Score	at Baltimore	W 7–0
June 18, 1960	Dick Stigman (7) and Ted Bowsfield (2)(W)	vs. Boston	W 2–1
June 15, 1963	Pedro Ramos (7)(W) and Ted Abernathy (2)	vs. Washington	W 4–0
June 16, 1965	Luis Tiant	vs. Washington	W 5–0
August 31, 1965(1)	Sam McDowell	at Kansas City	W 8–1
April 25, 1966	Sam McDowell	vs. Kansas City	W 2–0
May 1, 1966	Sam McDowell	vs. Chicago	W 1–0
August 19, 1967	John O'Donoghue	at Detroit	W 5–0
April 24, 1968	Steve Hargan	vs. Detroit	W 2–0
May 19, 1968(2)	Sonny Siebert	vs. Baltimore	W 2–0
September 25, 1968	Luis Tiant	at New York	W 3–0
June 8, 1969(2)	Mike Paul (5)(L), Gary Kroll (2), Jack Hamilton (⅔), and Stan Williams (1⅓)	vs. California	L 3–2
August 19, 1969	Sam McDowell	at Oakland	W 3–0
August 28, 1970(2)	Rich Hand	vs. California	W 5–1
April 18, 1971(2)	Steve Dunning	vs. Washington	W 1–0
May 24, 1976	Dennis Eckersley (8)(W) and Stan Thomas (1)	at Baltimore	W 4–0
June 3, 1977	Dennis Eckersley (6)(W) and Jim Kern (3)	at Seattle	W 7–1
August 12, 1977(1)	Dennis Eckersley	vs. Milwaukee	W 2–0
April 7, 1979	Rick Waits	vs. Boston	W 3–0

Herb Score (right), now a radio voice of the Indians, was the team's first rookie of the year in 1955. Outfielder Joe Charboneau (left) won the award in 1980.

August 20, 1980	Dan Spillner	at Chicago	W 3–0
July 13, 1984	Bert Blyleven	at Texas	W 5–0
August 3, 1987	Tom Candiotti	vs. New York	W 2–0
May 4, 1989	John Farrell (8) (W) and Doug Jones (1)	vs. Kansas City	W 3–1
August 8, 1992	Charles Nagy	at Baltimore	W 6–0
May 24, 1993	Tom Kramer	vs. Texas	W 4–1

.650 Winning Percentage or Better in One Season

Year	Player	W	L	Pct.	Year	Player	W	L	Pct.
1937	Johnny Allen	15	1	.938	1913	Cy Falkenberg	23	10	.697
1995	Julian Tavarez	10	2	.833	1950	Early Wynn	18	8	.692
1954	Bob Feller	13	3	.813	1956	Herb Score	20	9	.690
1917	Ed Klepfer	14	4	.778	1956	Early Wynn	20	9	.690
1902	Bill Bernhard	17	5	.773	1906	Bob Rhoads	22	10	.688
1911	Vean Gregg	23	7	.767	1949	Bob Lemon	22	10	.688
1954	Bob Lemon	23	7	.767	1947	Bob Lemon	11	5	.688
1921	Allen Sothoron	12	4	.750	1957	Ray Narleski	11	5	.688
1948	Gene Bearden	20	7	.741	1908	Addie Joss	24	11	.686
1949	Mike Garcia	14	5	.737	1989	Greg Swindell	13	6	.684
1951	Bob Feller	22	8	.733	1940	Al Smith	15	7	.682
1984	Bert Blyleven	19	7	.731	1954	Art Houtteman	15	7	.682
1939	Bob Feller	24	9	.727	1903	Earl Moore	19	9	.679
1995	Orel Hershiser	16	6	.727	1945	Steve Gromek	19	9	.679
1995	Charles Nagy	16	6	.727	1929	Wes Ferrell	21	10	.677
1961	Barry Latman	13	5	.722	1950	Bob Lemon	23	11	.676
1920	Jim Bagby, Sr.	31	12	.721	1954	Early Wynn	23	11	.676
1907	Addie Joss	27	11	.711	1919	Stan Coveleski	24	12	.667
1926	George Uhle	27	11	.711	1935	Mel Harder	22	11	.667
1940	Bob Feller	27	11	.711	1952	Mike Garcia	22	11	.667
1943	Al Smith	17	7	.708	1952	Bob Lemon	22	11	.667
1995	Dennis Martinez	12	5	.706	1920	Ray Caldwell	20	10	.667
1954	Mike Garcia	19	8	.704	1936	Johnny Allen	20	10	.667
1959	Cal McLish	19	8	.704	1962	Dick Donovan	20	10	.667
1906	Addie Joss	21	9	.700	1953	Mike Garcia	18	9	.667
1968	Luis Tiant	21	9	.700	1958	Cal McLish	16	8	.667
1903	Bill Bernhard	14	6	.700	1965	Sonny Siebert	16	8	.667
					1966	Sonny Siebert	16	8	.667
					1986	Ken Schrom	14	7	.667
					1919	George Uhle	10	5	.667
					1933	Monte Pearson	10	5	.667

Bert Blyleven, man of the year, 1984.

Sonny Siebert, man of the year, 1966.

		W	L	Pct.
1930	Wes Ferrell	25	13	.658
1941	Bob Feller	25	13	.658
1952	Early Wynn	23	12	.657
1942	Jim Bagby, Jr.	17	9	.654
1918	Fritz Coumbe	13	7	.650
1975	Dennis Eckersley	13	7	.650
1976	Jim Bibby	13	7	.650

Dick Donovan, man of the year, 1962.

300 or More Innings Pitched in One Season

1946	Bob Feller	371⅓	1906	Addie Joss	333⅔	1906	Bob Rhoads	315
1923	George Uhle	357⅔	1908	Addie Joss	325	1920	Stan Coveleski	315
1973	Gaylord Perry	344	1974	Gaylord Perry	322⅓	1921	Stan Coveleski	315
1941	Bob Feller	343	1904	Bill Bernhard	320⅔	1918	Stan Coveleski	311
1972	Gaylord Perry	342⅔	1917	Jim Bagby, Sr.	320⅔	1952	Bob Lemon	309⅔
1920	Jim Bagby, Sr.	339⅔	1940	Bob Feller	320⅓	1970	Sam McDowell	305
1907	Addie Joss	338⅔	1926	George Uhle	318⅓			

200 or More Strikeouts in One Season

1946	Bob Feller	348	1955	Herb Score	245
1965	Sam McDowell	325	1938	Bob Feller	240
1970	Sam McDowell	304	1973	Gaylord Perry	238
1968	Sam McDowell	283	1967	Sam McDowell	236
1969	Sam McDowell	279	1972	Gaylord Perry	234
1968	Luis Tiant	264	1966	Sam McDowell	225
1956	Herb Score	263	1967	Luis Tiant	219
1940	Bob Feller	261	1974	Gaylord Perry	216
1941	Bob Feller	260	1976	Dennis Eckersley	200
1939	Bob Feller	246			

Luis Tiant, man of the year, 1968.

15 or More Strikeouts in One Game

19	Luis Tiant, July 3, 1968 (10 innings), vs. Minnesota
18	Bob Feller, October 2, 1938 (first game), vs. Detroit
17	Bob Feller, September 13, 1936 (first game), vs. Philadelphia
16	Bob Feller, August 25, 1937 (first game), vs. Boston
16	Herb Score, May 1, 1955 (second game), vs. Boston
16	Luis Tiant, August 22, 1967, vs. California
16	Sam McDowell, May 1, 1968, vs. Oakland
16	Luis Tiant, September 9, 1968, at Minnesota
15	Bob Feller, August 23, 1936, vs. St. Louis

15	Herb Score, May 19, 1956, vs. Washington
15	Sam McDowell, June 5, 1965 (10 innings), vs. Detroit
15	Sonny Siebert, June 17, 1965, vs. Washington
15	Pedro Ramos, July 31, 1963 (second game), vs. Los Angeles
15	Sam McDowell, July 12, 1968, at Oakland
15	Sam McDowell, May 6, 1970, at Chicago
15	Sam McDowell, July 6, 1970, vs. Washington
15	Greg Swindell, May 10, 1987, vs. Kansas City

10 or More Saves in One Season

1995	Jose Mesa	46	1974	Tom Buskey	17	1969	Stan Williams	12
1990	Doug Jones	43	1975	Dave LaRoche	17	1980	Victor Cruz	12
1988	Doug Jones	37	1991	Steve Olin	17	1956	Don Mossi	11
1989	Doug Jones	32	1957	Ray Narleski	16	1961	Frank Funk	11
1992	Steve Olin	29	1964	Don McMahon	16	1964	Ted Abernathy	11
1984	Ernie Camacho	23	1976	Jim Kern	15	1965	Don McMahon	11
1976	Dave LaRoche	21	1993	Eric Plunk	15	1970	Dennis Higgins	11
1982	Dan Spillner	21	1960	Johnny Klippstein	14	1993	Jerry DiPoto	11
1986	Ernie Camacho	20	1971	Phil Hennigan	14	1944	Joe Heving	10
1955	Ray Narleski	19	1980	Sid Monge	14	1949	Al Benton	10
1979	Sid Monge	19	1954	Ray Narleski	13	1966	Dick Radatz	10
1977	Jim Kern	18	1978	Jim Kern	13	1972	Steve Mingori	10
1947	Eddie Klieman	17	1962	Gary Bell	12	1979	Victor Cruz	10
1948	Russ Christopher	17	1963	Ted Abernathy	12	1993	Derek Lilliquist	10
1965	Gary Bell	17	1968	Vicente Romo	12			

Pitchers with .270 Batting Averages or Better in One Season
(40 At Bats or More)

Pitcher	Year	Average	Hits	At Bats	Pitcher	Year	Average	Hits	At Bats
Jimmy Zinn	1929	.381	16	42	Sherry Smith	1925	.304	28	92
George Uhle	1923	.361	52	144	Joe Shaute	1925	.302	16	53
Joe Shaute	1927	.325	27	83	George Uhle	1919	.302	13	43
Bob Lemon	1947	.321	18	56	Jim Perry	1959	.300	15	50
Wes Ferrell	1931	.319	37	116	Jack Russell	1932	.300	12	40
Joe Shaute	1924	.318	34	107	Wes Ferrell	1930	.297	35	118
Elmer Koestner	1910	.313	15	48	Al Gettel	1947	.294	15	51
Ralph Winegarner	1935	.310	26	84	Joe Shaute	1929	.293	17	58
George Uhle	1924	.308	33	107	Jim Bagby, Jr.	1945	.293	17	58
Al Smith	1940	.306	19	62	Al Smith	1945	.293	12	41

Jim Bagby, Jr., and Jim Bagby, Sr., both of whom pitched for the Indians.

Pitcher	Year	Average	Hits	At Bats	Pitcher	Year	Average	Hits	At Bats
George Uhle	1925	.287	29	101	Allen Sothoron	1921	.276	16	58
Bob Lemon	1948	.286	34	119	Early Wynn	1953	.275	25	91
George Uhle	1928	.286	28	98	Joe Shaute	1926	.274	20	73
Mudcat Grant	1960	.281	16	57	Bob Lemon	1950	.272	37	136
Willis Hudlin	1935	.279	24	86	Monte Pearson	1934	.272	25	92
Art Houtteman	1954	.277	18	65	Wes Ferrell	1933	.271	38	140

Pitchers Hitting Home Runs

37	Bob Lemon	
19	Wes Ferrell	
9	Early Wynn	
8	Bob Feller, Pedro Ramos	
6	Dick Donovan	
5	Garland Buckeye, Mudcat Grant, Willis Hudlin, Luis Tiant, George Uhle	
4	Steve Dunning, Mel Harder, Al Milnar, Sonny Siebert, Sherry Smith, Ralph Winegarner	
2	Jim Bagby, Sr., Jim Bagby, Jr., Gene Bearden, Clint Brown, Mike Garcia, Otto Hess, Barry Latman, Sam McDowell, Cal McLish, Jack Salveson	

1 Johnny Allen, Gary Bell, Fred Blanding, Lloyd Brown, Ray Caldwell, Bob Chakales, Sarge Connally, Stan Coveleski, Pete Dowling, Steve Hargan, Dave Hoskins, Art Houtteman, Addie Joss, Benn Karr, Eddie Klieman, Jack Kralick, Bobby Locke, Ray Narleski, John O'Donoghue, Monte Pearson, Gaylord Perry, Bob Rhoads, Herb Score, Ed Scott, Joe Shaute, Milt Shoffner, Al Smith, Ralph Terry, Dick Tomanek, Bob Weiland, Clarence Wright, Jimmy Zinn

Ray Caldwell pitched the fifth no-hitter in Cleveland baseball history, a 3–0 victory over the New York Yankees in New York on September 10, 1919.

Nonpitchers Who Pitched for the Indians

Player	Position	Year	W	L	ERA	G	GS	IP	H	BB	SO
Bill Bradley	3B	1901	0	0	0.00	1	0	1	4	0	0
Frank Brower	1B	1924	0	0	0.93	4	0	9⅔	7	4	0
Eddie Carnett	OF	1945	0	0	0.00	2	0	2	0	0	1
Rocky Colavito	OF	1958	0	0	0.00	1	0	3	0	3	1
Nick Cullop	OF	1927	0	0	9.00	1	0	1	3	0	0
Tom Donovan	OF	1901	0	0	5.14	1	0	7	16	3	0
Milt Galatzer	OF	1936	0	0	4.50	1	0	6	7	5	3
Gary Geiger	OF	1958	0	0	9.00	1	0	2	2	1	2
Piano Legs Hickman	1B-OF	1902	0	1	7.88	1	1	8	11	5	1
Myril Hoag	OF	1945	0	0	0.00	2	0	3	3	1	0
Charlie Jamieson	PH-OF	1919	0	0	5.54	4	1	13	12	8	0
Jimmy McAleer	OF	1901	0	0	0.00	1	0	⅓	2	3	0
Paul O'Dea	OF	1944	0	0	2.08	3	0	4⅓	5	6	0
Paul O'Dea	OF	1945	0	0	13.50	1	0	2	4	2	0
Willie Smith	OF	1968	0	0	0.00	2	0	5	2	1	1
Smoky Joe Wood	OF	1919	0	0	0.00	1	0	⅔	0	0	0
Smoky Joe Wood	OF	1920	0	0	22.50	1	0	2	4	2	1

Club Fielding Records

First Base

Percentage	.997 by Boog Powell, 1975
Putouts	1,567 by Hal Trosky, 1935
Assists	155 by Mickey Vernon, 1949
DPs	168 by Mickey Vernon, 1949

Second Base

Percentage	.988 by Duane Kuiper, 1979
Putouts	450 by Nap Lajoie, 1908
Assists	557 by Johnny Hodapp, 1930
DPs	138 by Carlos Baerga, 1992

Third Base

Percentage	.984 by Willie Kamm, 1933
Putouts	192 by Bill Bradley, 1901
Assists	412 by Graig Nettles, 1971
DPs	54 by Graig Nettles, 1971

Shortstop

Percentage	.986 by Frank Duffy, 1973
	.986 by Omar Vizquel, 1995
Putouts	378 by Ray Chapman, 1915
Assists	570 by Terry Turner, 1906
DPs	134 by Lou Boudreau, 1944

Catcher

Percentage	.997 by Jim Hegan, 1955
Putouts	854 by Ray Fosse, 1970
Assists	175 by Steve O'Neill, 1915
DPs	36 by Steve O'Neill, 1916

Outfield

Percentage	1.000 by Rocky Colavito, 1965
Putouts	448 by Brett Butler, 1984
Assists	32 by Joe Jackson, 1911
DPs	10 by Tris Speaker, 1916

Carlos Baerga, man of the year, 1991 and 1992.

Gold Glove Winners

1958	Vic Power, 1b		Jimmy Piersall, of	1990	Sandy Alomar, c
1959	Vic Power, 1b	1964	Vic Davalillo, of	1993	Kenny Lofton, of
	Minnie Minoso, of	1970	Ray Fosse, c	1994	Kenny Lofton, of
1960	Vic Power, 1b	1971	Ray Fosse, c		Omar Vizquel, ss
1961	Vic Power, 1b	1976	Rick Manning, of		

All-Time Fielding Team

Player		Year	Games	TC	E	Pct.
1b	Boog Powell	1975	121	1,069	3	.997
2b	Duane Kuiper	1979	140	734	9	.988
ss	Frank Duffy	1973	115	583	8	.986
3b	Willie Kamm	1933	131	380	6	.984
of	Rocky Colavito	1965	162	274	0	1.000

Player		Year	Games	TC	E	Pct.
	Brett Butler	1985	150	456	1	.998
	Cory Snyder	1989	125	309	1	.997
c	Jim Hegan	1955	111	619	2	.997
p	Clint Brown	1931	39	76	0	1.000

Triple Plays

Date	Opponent	Turned by Cleveland Fielders	Batter
August 21, 1906(1)	at Washington	Turner (ss) to Rossman (1b)	Lave Cross
July 19, 1909(1)	Boston	Ball (ss) unassisted	Amby McConnell
May 6, 1914	St. Louis	Turner (3b) to Lajoie (2b) to Johnston (1b) to Carisch (c)	Clarence Walker
September 14, 1914	Detroit	Leibold (cf) to O'Neill (c) to Chapman (2b) to Turner (3b) to Chapman to O'Neill	Bobby Veach
May 12, 1915	New York	Wood (1b) to Chapman (ss)	Fritz Maisel
July 24, 1915(2)	Philadelphia	Barbare (3b) to Wambsganss (2b) to Kirke (1b)	Nap Lajoie

Date	Opponent	Fielders	Batter
June 2, 1919	St. Louis	Wood (cf) to Chapman (ss) to Gardner (3b) to Wambsganss (2b) to Gardner to Wambsganss	Wally Gerber
April 30, 1922	at St. Louis	Wambsganss (2b) to McInnis (1b)	Wally Gerber
August 25, 1925	Philadelphia	Spurgeon (2b) to L. Sewell (c) to J. Sewell (ss)	Chick Galloway
June 5, 1926	New York	Buckeye (p) to Lutzke (3b) to Burns (1b)	Mark Koenig
September 11, 1926(1)	Washington	Uhle (p) to Burns (1b) to J. Sewell (ss) to L. Sewell (c)	Bennie Tate
May 23, 1928	at Chicago	Jamieson (lf) to L. Sewell (c) to J. Sewell (ss) to Hodapp (3b)	Bud Clancy
June 9, 1928	New York	Jamieson (lf) to Lind (2b) to Fonseca (1b) to L. Sewell (c)	Joe Dugan
September 7, 1935(1)	at Boston	Hale (3b) to Knickerbocker (ss) to Hughes (2b) to Trosky (1b)	Joe Cronin
August 7, 1936	Chicago	Trosky (1b) to Knickerbocker (ss) to Trosky	Tony Piet
September 19, 1939	at Washington	Keltner (3b) to Boudreau (ss) to Grimes (1b)	Early Wynn
May 13, 1946(2)	St. Louis	Krakauskas (p) to Boudreau (ss) to Rocco (1b)	Chuck Stevens
May 10, 1948	at Boston	Boudreau (ss) to Gordon (2b) to Robinson (1b)	Billy Goodman
August 15, 1950	Detroit	Kennedy (rf) to Boone (ss) to Easter (1b)	George Kell
August 22, 1952	at New York	Avila (2b) to Easter (1b)	Hank Bauer
August 21, 1954	at Baltimore	Lemon (p) to Avila (2b) to Wertz (1b)	Jim Fridley
July 31, 1955(2)	at Baltimore	Houtteman (p) to Strickland (ss) to Wertz (1b)	Dave Philley
September 15, 1957(1)	at Baltimore	Daley (p) to Carrasquel (ss) to Avila (2b)	George Zuverink
August 9, 1970(1)	at Washington	Nettles (3b) to Leon (2b) to Sims (1b)	Aurelio Rodriguez
September 3, 1973(2)	at Milwaukee	Brohamer (2b) to Chambliss (1b)	Don Money
June 7, 1976	Minnesota	Thomas (p) to Duffy (ss) to Howard (1b)	Butch Wynegar
May 23, 1981	at New York	Harrah (3b) to Bannister (2b) to Hargrove (1b)	Bucky Dent
August 7, 1992	at Baltimore	Lofton (cf) to Alomar (c) to Baerga (2b) to Thome (3b)	Brady Anderson

		Turned against Cleveland	
Date	**Opponent**	**Fielders**	**Batter**
September 26, 1901	at Baltimore	Williams (2b) to Keister (ss)	Harry McNeal
July 28, 1906	New York	Laporte (3b) to Moriarty (1b) to Elberfeld (ss)	Otto Hess
July 30, 1909	at Philadelphia	Collins (2b) to Baker (3b) to Davis (1b)	George Stovall
May 16, 1913	Philadelphia	Barry (ss) to Thomas (c) to Baker (3b) to Houck (p) to Baker to Barry to Collins (2b) to Baker to Oldring (lf)	Ivy Olson
June 17, 1913	at Washington	Gandil (1b) to McBride (ss)	Steve O'Neill
April 30, 1917	St. Louis	Austin (3b) to Kenworthy (2b) to Lavan (ss)	Terry Turner

Third baseman Rich Rollins (right) working out with fellow Clevelander, Gary Roggenburk, who went on to pitch for the Minnesota Twins, Boston Red Sox, and Seattle Pilots.

September 12, 1922	at Chicago	Collins (2b) to Johnson (ss) to Sheely (1b) to Yaryan (c)	Larry Gardner
August 22, 1923	Washington	Judge (1b) to Peckinpaugh (ss)	Tris Speaker
September 3, 1923(1)	St. Louis	Schliebner (1b) to Gerber (ss)	Charlie Jamieson
September 14, 1923	at Boston	Burns (1b) unassisted	Frank Brower
June 14, 1924	Boston	Shanks (1b) to Lee (ss)	Tris Speaker
May 29, 1927(2)	at St. Louis	Miller (3b) to Dixon (c) to Sisler (1b) to Dixon	Dutch Levsen
May 31, 1927	at Detroit	Neun (1b) unassisted	Homer Summa
April 30, 1929	at Chicago	Cissell (ss) to Clancy (1b) to Crouse (c) to Kamm (3b)	Carl Lind
June 6, 1931	at New York	Gehrig (1b) to Lary (ss)	Willie Kamm
August 12, 1934	at Detroit	Owen (3b) to Greenberg(1b)	Bill Knickerbocker
October 1, 1949	at Detroit	Kell (3b) to Berry (2b) to Kolloway (1b)	Joe Gordon
August 17, 1950	St. Louis	Friend (3b) to Stirnweiss (2b)	Dale Mitchell
May 13, 1951(1)	at Chicago	Rotblatt (p) to Carrasquel (ss) to Robinson (1b)	Jim Hegan
April 23, 1966	at Boston	Smith (2b) to Petrocelli (ss) to Scott (1b) to Tillman (c)	Max Alvis
July 30, 1968	Washington	Hansen (ss) unassisted	Joe Azcue
September 10, 1968	at Minnesota	Rollins (3b) to Carew (2b) to Allison (1b)	Tony Horton
September 7, 1979	Toronto	Howell (3b) to Gomez (2b) to Mayberry (1b)	Ted Cox
May 31, 1980	Seattle	Bochte (1b) to Anderson (ss) to Cruz (2b)	Toby Harrah
August 8, 1988	at Minnesota	Gladden (lf) to Lombardozzi (2b) to Larkin (1b)	Joe Carter

Top Indians Fielders (Career)

First Base	Pct.	PO	A	E	DP	Years Played
Paul Sorrento	.994	3,622	281	25	382	4
Mike Hargrove	.993	6,154	564	46	611	7
Hal Trosky	.990	10,085	662	105	961	9
Doc Johnston	.989	6,578	379	79	383	7
George Burns	.988	6,371	481	82	497	7

Second Base						
Duane Kuiper	.984	1,733	2,136	64	496	8
Bobby Avila	.979	2,708	2,985	121	762	10
Tony Bernazard	.977	1,079	1,438	59	305	4
Carlos Baerga	.975	1,368	1,959	87	482	6
Joe Gordon	.975	1,192	1,615	72	399	4

Third Base

Willie Kamm	.969	558	980	50	89	5
Ken Keltner	.965	1,568	3,060	170	306	12
Toby Harrah	.963	501	1,208	65	115	5
Al Rosen	.961	970	1,773	112	159	10
Buddy Bell	.960	752	1,918	112	182	7

Shortstop

Frank Duffy	.979	1,229	2,337	77	470	6
Lou Boudreau	.973	3,052	4,606	211	1,135	12
Felix Fermin	.971	949	1,786	83	362	5
George Strickland	.969	858	1,442	74	336	7
Larry Brown	.964	1,091	1,779	107	355	9

Outfield

Brett Butler	.993	1,712	45	12	13	4
George Hendrick	.987	1,273	33	17	10	4
Bob Kennedy	.986	808	38	12	10	7
Vic Davalillo	.986	1,407	41	21	8	6
Rick Manning	.986	2,892	62	43	11	9
Tito Francona	.985	983	15	15	1	5
Dale Mitchell	.985	1,903	41	30	8	11
Larry Doby	.983	2,947	79	52	22	9
Cory Snyder	.983	1,262	65	23	11	5
Kenny Lofton	.981	1,387	50	28	12	4
Joe Vosmik	.981	1,806	63	36	16	7
Rocky Colavito	.980	1,615	61	35	12	8
Joe Carter	.978	1,573	43	37	10	6
Dick Porter	.977	936	34	23	8	6
Albert Belle	.976	1,204	43	31	11	7
Tris Speaker	.976	3,837	222	100	69	11

Catcher

Ron Hassey	.994	2,599	230	18	30	7
Joe Azcue	.994	3,757	282	26	37	7
Frankie Pytlak	.991	2,497	347	25	57	9
Johnny Romano	.990	3,001	217	32	28	5
Jim Hegan	.990	6,959	642	79	126	14
Sandy Alomar	.990	2,635	193	30	28	6

Pitcher

Wes Ferrell	.978	75	287	8	15	7
Mike Garcia	.978	133	354	11	27	12
Stan Coveleski	.976	153	695	21	n/a	9
Greg Swindell	.976	32	129	4	6	6
Clint Brown	.975	57	299	9	17	10
Rick Waits	.975	81	233	8	10	9
Tom Candiotti	.975	120	194	8	12	6

Wes Ferrell hurled a 9–0 no-hitter against the St. Louis Browns at League Park on April 29, 1931.

League Leaders in Fielding*

First Basemen

Percentage

1908	George Stovall	.990
1909	George Stovall	.988
1910	George Stovall	.988
1911	George Stovall	.986
1916	Chick Gandil	.995
1922	Stuffy McInnis	.997
1942	Les Fleming	.993
1943	Mickey Rocco	.995
1945	Mickey Rocco	.992
1948	Eddie Robinson	.995
1953	Bill Glynn	.993
1960	Vic Power	.996
1975	Boog Powell	.997 (1)

Putouts

1909	George Stovall	1,478
1916	Chick Gandil	1,557
1932	Ed Morgan	1,430
1934	Hal Trosky	1,487
1935	Hal Trosky	1,567 (1)
1942	Les Fleming	1,503
1944	Mickey Rocco	1,467
1949	Mickey Vernon	1,438
1956	Vic Wertz	971
1980	Mike Hargrove	1,391

Assists

1909	George Stovall	109

1910	George Stovall	91
1911	George Stovall	87
1916	Chick Gandil	105
1929	Lew Fonseca	107
1934	Hal Trosky	86
1944	Mickey Rocco	138
1949	Mickey Vernon	155 (1)
1960	Vic Power	145
1961	Vic Power	142
1969	Tony Horton	100
1982	Mike Hargrove	123

Double Plays

1907	George Stovall	90
1908	George Stovall	79

*(1) club record; (2) league record

1909	George Stovall	80	1942	Les Fleming	152	1962	Tito Francona	157
1929	Lew Fonseca	141	1957	Vic Wertz	122	1969	Tony Horton	130
1934	Hal Trosky	145	1960	Vic Power	145			

Second Basemen

Percentage

1906	Nap Lajoie	.973
1907	Nap Lajoie	.969
1908	Nap Lajoie	.964
1913	Nap Lajoie	.970
1953	Bobby Avila	.986
1976	Duane Kuiper	.987
1979	Duane Kuiper	.988(1)

Putouts

1902	Nap Lajoie	272*
1906	Nap Lajoie	354
1908	Nap Lajoie	450(1)
1928	Carl Lind	390
1930	Johnny Hodapp	403
1936	Roy Hughes	421
1986	Tony Bernazard	351
1992	Carlos Baerga	400
1993	Carlos Baerga	347

Assists

1906	Nap Lajoie	415
1907	Nap Lajoie	461
1908	Nap Lajoie	538
1926	Freddy Spurgeon	479
1947	Joe Gordon	466
1953	Bobby Avila	445
1954	Bobby Avila	406
1962	Jerry Kindall	494
1992	Carlos Baerga	475
1993	Carlos Baerga	445

Double Plays

1902	Nap Lajoie	49
1906	Nap Lajoie	76
1907	Nap Lajoie	86
1908	Nap Lajoie	78
1909	Nap Lajoie	55
1917	Bill Wambsganss	70
1926	Freddy Spurgeon	93

1928	Carl Lind	116
1941	Ray Mack	109
1992	Carlos Baerga	138(1)

400 or More Putouts a Season

450	Nap Lajoie	1908
421	Roy Hughes	1936
414	Bill Wambsganss	1920
408	Odell Hale	1934
403	Johnny Hodapp	1930
400	Carlos Baerga	1992

500 or More Assists a Season

557	Johnny Hodapp	1930
538	Nap Lajoie	1908
505	Carl Lind	1928

*Lajoie's 272 putouts included 2 with Philadelphia, 270 with Cleveland.

Third Basemen

Percentage

1901	Bill Bradley	.930
1904	Bill Bradley	.955
1905	Bill Bradley	.945
1907	Bill Bradley	.938
1912	Terry Turner	.951
1914	Terry Turner	.963
1920	Larry Gardner	.976
1933	Willie Kamm	.984(1)
1934	Willie Kamm	.978
1939	Ken Keltner	.974
1941	Ken Keltner	.971
1942	Ken Keltner	.945
1970	Graig Nettles	.967
1983	Toby Harrah	.971

Putouts

1902	Bill Bradley	188
1905	Bill Bradley	188
1920	Larry Gardner	156
1923	Rube Lutzke	186
1931	Willie Kamm	158*
1939	Ken Keltner	187
1961	Bubba Phillips	188
1963	Max Alvis	170
1965	Max Alvis	169
1966	Max Alvis	180

1967	Max Alvis	169
1971	Graig Nettles	159
1973	Buddy Bell	144
1975	Buddy Bell	146
1987	Brook Jacoby	134

Assists

1903	Bill Bradley	299
1920	Larry Gardner	362
1921	Larry Gardner	335
1923	Rube Lutzke	358
1929	Joe Sewell	336
1931	Willie Kamm	240†
1935	Odell Hale	312
1936	Odell Hale	323
1941	Ken Keltner	346
1942	Ken Keltner	353
1944	Ken Keltner	369
1948	Ken Keltner	312
1950	Al Rosen	322
1953	Al Rosen	338
1971	Graig Nettles	412(1)
		(2)
1978	Buddy Bell	355

Double Plays

| 1901 | Bill Bradley | 25 |
| 1905 | Bill Bradley | 17 |

Graig Nettles, man of the year, 1971.

1907	Bill Bradley	18
1913	Terry Turner	27
1920	Larry Gardner	32
1922	Larry Gardner	24
1939	Ken Keltner	40
1941	Ken Keltner	36
1942	Ken Keltner	38
1944	Ken Keltner	37
1947	Ken Keltner	29
1953	Al Rosen	38

1971	Graig Nettles	54 (1) (2)
1973	Buddy Bell	44
1978	Buddy Bell	30

175 or More Putouts a Season

192	Bill Bradley	1901
188	Bill Bradley	1902
188	Bill Bradley	1905
188	Bubba Phillips	1961
187	Ken Keltner	1939
186	Rube Lutzke	1923
181	Ken Keltner	1941
180	Max Alvis	1966
179	Larry Gardner	1921
178	Bill Bradley	1904
175	Bubba Phillips	1962

350 or More Assists a Season

412	Graig Nettles	1971
369	Ken Keltner	1944
363	Buddy Bell	1973
362	Larry Gardner	1920
358	Rube Lutzke	1923
358	Graig Nettles	1970
355	Buddy Bell	1978
353	Ken Keltner	1942

*Kamm's 158 putouts included 29 with Chicago, 129 with Cleveland.
†Kamm's 240 assists included 32 with Chicago, 208 with Cleveland.

Buddy Bell, man of the year, 1973.

Shortstops

Percentage

1906	Terry Turner	.960
1907	Terry Turner	.950
1925	Joe Sewell	.967
1927	Joe Sewell	.962
1928	Joe Sewell	.963
1940	Lou Boudreau	.968
1941	Lou Boudreau	.966
1942	Lou Boudreau	.965
1943	Lou Boudreau	.970
1944	Lou Boudreau	.978
1946	Lou Boudreau	.970
1947	Lou Boudreau	.982
1948	Lou Boudreau	.975
1955	George Strickland	.976
1973	Frank Duffy	.986(1)
1976	Frank Duffy	.983

Putouts

1915	Ray Chapman	378(1)
1917	Ray Chapman	360
1918	Ray Chapman	321
1924	Joe Sewell	349

1925	Joe Sewell	314
1926	Joe Sewell	326
1927	Joe Sewell	361
1937	Lyn Lary	325
1941	Lou Boudreau	296
1943	Lou Boudreau	323
1944	Lou Boudreau	339
1946	Lou Boudreau	315

Assists

1906	Terry Turner	570(1)
1917	Ray Chapman	528
1924	Joe Sewell	514
1925	Joe Sewell	529
1927	Joe Sewell	480
1928	Joe Sewell	438
1940	Lou Boudreau	454
1944	Lou Boudreau	516

Double Plays

1906	Terry Turner	61
1907	Terry Turner	67
1928	Joe Sewell	103
1940	Lou Boudreau	116

1943	Lou Boudreau	122
1944	Lou Boudreau	134(1)
1947	Lou Boudreau	120
1948	Lou Boudreau	119
1953	George Strickland	103

325 or More Putouts a Season

378	Ray Chapman	1915
361	Joe Sewell	1927
360	Ray Chapman	1917
349	Joe Sewell	1924
339	Lou Boudreau	1944
328	Lou Boudreau	1943
326	Joe Sewell	1926
325	Lyn Lary	1937

500 or More Assists a Season

570	Terry Turner	1906
529	Joe Sewell	1925
528	Ray Chapman	1917
516	Lou Boudreau	1944
514	Joe Sewell	1924
512	Felix Fermin	1989

Outfielders

Percentage

1902	Harry Bay	.973
1904	Harry Bay	.987
1921	Tris Speaker	.984
1922	Tris Speaker	.983
1932	Joe Vosmik	.989
1933	Dick Porter	.996

1948	Dale Mitchell	.991
1949	Dale Mitchell	.994
1961	Jimmy Piersall	.991
1965	Rocky Colavito	1.000
		(1)(2)
1985	Brett Butler	.998
1989	Cory Snyder	.997

Putouts

1918	Tris Speaker	352
1919	Tris Speaker	375
1929	Earl Averill	384
1934	Earl Averill	410

Assists

1928	Charlie Jamieson	22
1988	Cory Snyder	16
1993	Wayne Kirby	19
1994	Kenny Lofton	13

Double Plays

1916	Tris Speaker	10(1)
1925	Tris Speaker	9
1930	Earl Averill	5
1954	Larry Doby	6
1958	Rocky Colavito	6
1961	Willie Kirkland	5

1964	Vic Davalillo	5
1976	George Hendrick	6
1993	Albert Belle	7
1994	Kenny Lofton	3

400 or More Putouts a Season

448	Brett Butler	1984
444	Joe Carter	1988
437	Brett Butler	1985
434	Brett Butler	1986
432	Joe Vosmik	1932
420	Kenny Lofton	1992
417	Rick Manning	1979
412	Earl Averill	1932
411	Larry Doby	1954
410	Earl Averill	1934
402	Kenny Lofton	1993

25 or More Assists a Season

32	Joe Jackson	1911
30	Joe Jackson	1912
28	Joe Birmingham	1907
28	Joe Jackson	1913
26	Tris Speaker	1923
25	Tris Speaker	1916
25	Tris Speaker	1919

Catchers

Percentage

1903	Harry Bemis	.988
1918	Steve O'Neill	.983
1940	Rollie Hemsley	.994
1944	Buddy Rosar	.989
1954	Jim Hegan	.994
1955	Jim Hegan	.997(1)
1967	Joe Azcue	.999
1968	Joe Azcue	.996

Putouts

1947	Jim Hegan	566
1948	Jim Hegan	637
1949	Jim Hegan	651
1970	Ray Fosse	854(1)
1988	Andy Allanson	691

Assists

1902	Harry Bemis	120
1915	Steve O'Neill	175(1)
1918	Steve O'Neill	154

1926	Luke Sewell	91
1927	Luke Sewell	119
1928	Luke Sewell	117
1937	Frankie Pytlak	80
1943	Buddy Rosar	91
1948	Jim Hegan	76
1949	Jim Hegan	73
1950	Jim Hegan	64
1971	Ray Fosse	73

Double Plays

1914	Steve O'Neill	22
1916	Steve O'Neill	36(1)(2)
1917	Steve O'Neill	19
1927	Luke Sewell	14
1928	Luke Sewell	13
1937	Frankie Pytlak	13
1944	Buddy Rosar	13
1945	Frankie Hayes	29*
1947	Jim Hegan	14
1948	Jim Hegan	17
1955	Jim Hegan	12
1971	Ray Fosse	16

1988	Andy Allanson	11
1993	Junior Ortiz	13

700 or More Putouts in Season

854	Ray Fosse	1970
752	Johnny Romano	1961
748	Ray Fosse	1971
714	Johnny Romano	1964
714	Joe Azcue	1965
713	Ray Fosse	1972

125 or More Assists in Season

175	Steve O'Neill	1915
154	Steve O'Neill	1916
154	Steve O'Neill	1918
145	Steve O'Neill	1917
134	Steve O'Neill	1914
128	Steve O'Neill	1920
125	Steve O'Neill	1919

*Hayes' 29 double plays included 6 with Philadelphia, 23 with Cleveland.

Media

Indians Broadcasters

Year	Radio	Announcers	TV	Announcers
June 28, 1946	WGAR	Jack Graney		
		Bob Neal		
	WJW	Earl Harper		
	WHK	Don Campbell		
	WTAM	Tom Manning		
1947	WGAR	Jack Graney		
		Van Patrick		
1948	WJW	Jack Graney	WEWS	Van Patrick
		Jimmy Dudley		
1949	WJW	Jack Graney	WEWS	Bob Neal
		Jimmy Dudley		Tris Speaker

One of the Indians earliest radio broadcasting teams—and the fans' favorite—Jimmy Dudley (left) and Jack Graney.

Year	Radio	Announcers	TV	Announcers
1950	WERE	Jack Graney Jimmy Dudley	WXEL	Jack Graney Jimmy Dudley
1951	WERE	Jack Graney Jimmy Dudley	WXEL	Hal Newell
1952	WERE	Jack Graney Jimmy Dudley	WXEL	Bob Neal Red Jones
1953	WERE	Jack Graney Jimmy Dudley	WXEL	Bob Neal Red Jones
1954	WERE	Jimmy Dudley Ed Edwards	WXEL	Ken Coleman Jim Britt
1955	WERE	Jimmy Dudley Ed Edwards	WXEL	Ken Coleman Jim Britt
1956	WERE	Jimmy Dudley Tom Manning	WEWS	Ken Coleman Jim Britt
1957	WERE	Jimmy Dudley Bob Neal	WEWS	Ken Coleman Jim Britt
1958	WERE	Jimmy Dudley Bob Neal	WEWS	Ken Coleman Bill McColgan
1959	WERE	Jimmy Dudley Bob Neal	WEWS	Ken Coleman Bill McColgan
1960	WERE	Jimmy Dudley Bob Neal	WEWS	Ken Coleman Bill McColgan
1961	WERE	Jimmy Dudley Bob Neal	WJW	Ken Coleman Harry Jones
1962	WERE	Jimmy Dudley Harry Jones	WJW	Ken Coleman Bob Neal
1963	WERE	Jimmy Dudley Harry Jones	WJW	Ken Coleman Bob Neal
1964	WERE	Jimmy Dudley Harry Jones	WJW	Bob Neal Herb Score
1965	WERE	Jimmy Dudley Bob Neal	WJW	Harry Jones Herb Score
1966	WERE	Jimmy Dudley Bob Neal	WJW	Harry Jones Herb Score
1967	WERE	Jimmy Dudley Bob Neal	WJW	Harry Jones Herb Score
1968	WERE	Bob Neal Herb Score	WJW	Harry Jones Mel Allen
1969	WERE	Bob Neal Herb Score	WJW	Harry Jones Dave Martin

Year	Radio	Announcers	TV	Announcers
1970	WERE	Bob Neal Herb Score	WJW	Harry Jones Dave Martin
1971	WERE	Bob Neal Herb Score	WJW	Harry Jones Dave Martin
1972	WERE	Bob Neal Herb Score	WJW	Harry Jones Rocky Colavito
1973	WWWE	Herb Score Joe Tait	WJW	Harry Jones Mudcat Grant
1974	WWWE	Herb Score Joe Tait	WJW	Harry Jones Mudcat Grant
1975	WWWE	Herb Score Joe Tait	WJW	Rocky Colavito Bob Brown
1976	WWWE	Herb Score Joe Tait	WJW	Rocky Colavito Bob Brown
1977	WWWE	Herb Score Joe Tait	WJW	Harry Jones Mudcat Grant
1978	WWWE	Herb Score Joe Tait	WJKW	Jim Mueller Eddie Doucette
1979	WWWE	Herb Score Joe Tait	WJKW	Joe Castiglione Fred McLeod
1980	WWWE	Herb Score Nev Chandler	WUAB	Joe Tait Bruce Drennan
1981	WWWE	Herb Score Nev Chandler	WUAB	Joe Tait Bruce Drennan
1982	WWWE	Herb Score Nev Chandler	WUAB Ten TV	Joe Tait Bruce Drennan Joe Castiglione Bob Feller
1983	WWWE	Herb Score Nev Chandler	WUAB Sports Extra	Joe Tait Reggie Rucker Bob Feller Jack Corrigan Denny Schreiner
1984	WWWE	Herb Score Nev Chandler	WUAB	Joe Tait Reggie Rucker
1985	WWWE	Herb Score Steve Lamar	WUAB	Joe Tait Jack Corrigan
1986	WWWE	Herb Score Steve Lamar	WUAB	Joe Tait Jack Corrigan
1987	WWWE	Herb Score Steve Lamar	WUAB	Joe Tait Jack Corrigan
1988	WWWE	Herb Score Paul Olden	WUAB	Jack Corrigan Steve Lamar
1989	WWWE	Herb Score Paul Olden	WUAB	Jack Corrigan Mike Hegan
1990	WWWE	Herb Score Tom Hamilton	WUAB	Jack Corrigan Mike Hegan
1991	WWWE	Herb Score Tom Hamilton	WUAB SportsChannel	Jack Corrigan Mike Hegan Rick Manning John Sanders
1992	WKNR	Herb Score Tom Hamilton	WUAB SportsChannel	Jack Corrigan Mike Hegan Rick Manning John Sanders
1993	WKNR	Herb Score Tom Hamilton	WUAB SportsChannel	Jack Corrigan Mike Hegan Rick Manning John Sanders
1994	WKNR	Herb Score	WUAB	Jack Corrigan

Year	Radio	Announcers	TV	Announcers
		Tom Hamilton	SportsChannel	Mike Hegan Rick Manning John Sanders
1995	WKNR	Herb Score Tom Hamilton	WUAB	Jack Corrigan Mike Hegan
			SportsChannel	Rick Manning John Sanders

Television broadcaster Mike Hegan, who grew up on the Cleveland sandlots and went on to play in the major leagues for the New York Yankees, Seattle Pilots, Milwaukee Brewers, and Oakland Athletics. He is the son of former Indians catcher Jim Hegan.

Cleveland Chapter, Baseball Writers Association of America

Bob Dolgan	*The Plain Dealer*
Dick Dugan	*The Plain Dealer*
Toni Grossi	*The Plain Dealer*
Steve Herrick	*Elyria Chronicle-Telegram*
Roy Hewitt	*The Plain Dealer*
Paul Hoynes	*The Plain Dealer*
Clyde Hughes	*Toledo Blade*
Jim Ingraham	*News Herald*
Hal Lebovitz	*News Herald*
Bill Livingston	*The Plain Dealer*
Chuck Melvin	Associated Press
Bob Nold	*Akron Beacon Journal*
Sheldon Ocker	*Akron Beacon Journal*
Mike Petica	*The Plain Dealer*
Terry Pluto	*Akron Beacon Journal*

Bud Shaw	*The Plain Dealer*
Mike Sullivan	*Columbus Dispatch*
Dick Svoboda	United Press International

Honorary

Hank Andrews	*The Cleveland Press*
Bob August	*The Cleveland Press*
Jack Darrow	*Warren Tribune*
Chuck Heaton	*The Plain Dealer*
Russell Schneider	*The Plain Dealer*
Hank Kozloski	*Lorain Journal*
Walter L. Johns, Sr.	Central Press Association
Bob Yonkers	*The Cleveland Press*

Almost Golden: The 1995 Season

When a pop foul off the bat of Baltimore's Jeff Huson landed in the glove of third baseman Jim Thome at precisely 11:02 P.M. on September 8, an elated Tom Hamilton, the radio play-by-play voice of the Indians, shouted into his microphone, "The season of dreams has become reality in Cleveland!"

Indeed it had.

Thome had made the final out in the Indians' 3–2 victory over the Orioles, which clinched the championship of the American League's Central Division.

But the truth is, Hamilton was only partly right. It was the moment of reality that Indians fans had awaited—and dreamed of—for *many* years. Forty-one, to be exact.

Not since 1954, when the Indians had last won the pennant by setting an American League record with 111 victories, only to be swept by the New York Giants in the World Series, had they even come close to repeating their championship. When it finally happened, when the Indians beat the Orioles to clinch the AL Central title in their 123rd game of 1995, it created yet another dream, a more ambitious one—to win the pennant and world championship.

"I thought we were on our way. . . . The way we'd played all season, I didn't think anybody could stop us," said catcher Sandy Alomar, Jr., who admitted he cried during an on-field celebration a few minutes after the clinching victory.

When the smoke cleared from a 10-minute fireworks display, Eddie Murray led his teammates to the flagpole in left-center field where the championship banner was hoisted. As the crowd cheered—and Alomar cried—the public address system played Garth Brooks' song "The Dance," which had special meaning to the Indians. It had been the favorite of Steve Olin, the Indians' former ace reliever who was killed with teammate Tim Crews in a tragic boating accident in spring training in 1993.

"I cried, thinking of Ollie and all we'd gone through to get where we are," said Alomar, one of only four players who were wearing Cleveland uniforms in 1991 when the Indians lost a franchise-record 105 games. The others: Albert Belle, Carlos Baerga, and Charles Nagy.

"It was a very happy time, but it also was a very sad time," said Alomar.

It got even happier, but then, also sadder—though nothing cooled off the fans' love affair for the Indians that began in 1994 and flourished before that season was cruelly aborted by the players' strike.

The Indians went on from their championship-clinching victory over the Orioles to go 14–7, winning 100 games for only the second time in franchise history. They swept Boston in the best-of-five Division Series, and beat Seattle, four games to two, for the pennant, their fourth since becoming a charter member of the American League in 1901.

But then the Tribe fell victim to Atlanta's outstanding pitching staff in the World Series, losing to the Braves in six games. That defeat did not, however, diminish the ardor of the fans. Two days after the final game, more than 50,000 people attended a rally in downtown Cleveland to honor their fallen—but still loved—baseball heroes.

The prevailing attitude was best stated by one fan who said, "Just because they're not World Series winners doesn't mean we can't show up and say, 'Thank you.'"

Manager Mike Hargrove told the crowd, "We can't guarantee we'll ever get to do this again, but if hard work, pride, and talent get you back and win the World Series, this bunch of guys will do it for you."

And, speaking for the players, 18 of whom attended the rally, Omar Vizquel flat-out promised, "We'll be back. We'll be in the World Series again."

The Indians didn't miss by much in 1995.

Third baseman Jim Thome snares the ball for the final out in a game against the Baltimore Orioles on September 8, 1995. The victory clinched the Tribe's AL Central Division title.

They beat the Red Sox three straight, the first two games at Jacobs field, the third in Fenway Park in Boston.

- Tony Pena's 13th-inning homer won the opener, 5–4.

- Orel Hershiser pitched a four-hitter to capture the second, 2–0.

- Then the Indians erupted for 11 hits, the biggest of which was a home run by Jim Thome, to complete the sweep with an 8–2 victory.

It was after that last game in Boston that the Indians, upon their return to Cleveland, were greeted at Hopkins International Airport by a crowd estimated at 2,000 to 3,000 fans at 3 A.M.—that's three o'clock in the morning!

Next came the Mariners, who had beaten the California Angels in a one-game playoff for the AL West championship. The Mariners were tougher than the Red Sox, but the Tribe prevailed again. The first two games were played in the Kingdome, the next three at Jacobs Field, and the sixth, which turned out to be the final, was back in Seattle.

In the ALCS the Indians

- lost the opener, 3–2, to rookie Bob Wolcott, a surprise starter for the weary Mariners,

- Won the second, 5–2, behind Hershiser's pitching and Manny Ramirez's two home runs,

- were stopped in the third game, 5–2, as Jay Buhner cracked two homers, the second a three-run shot in the 11th inning,

- tied the series in Game 4 as Ken Hill and three relievers combined on a six-hitter to win 7–0.

- went ahead, three games to two, beating the Mariners, 3–2, as Thome cracked a two-run homer in the sixth inning,

- and, upon returning to the Kingdome, refused to be intimidated by the overwhelming clamor and din of the Mariners fans to win the pennant as Dennis Martinez, relying mainly on guile and guts, outpitched Randy Johnson for a 4–0 victory.

The victory over the Mariners earned the Indians a rematch with the National League champion Braves, the most successful team of the 1990s, though they had lost the 1991 and 1992 World Series to Minnesota and Toronto, respectively.

The two teams had not played in 47 years, since the Indians beat the Braves, then located in Boston, in six games in the 1948 World Series.

The Indians couldn't do it again, however, as the Braves validated the old adage that states, "Good pitching always stops good hitting."

With the Series opening in Atlanta for the first two games, the Indians

- were beaten, 3–2, on a two-hitter by Greg Maddux,

- wasted numerous opportunities against Tom Glavine and three relievers, and lost the second game, 4–3,

- returned to the friendly confines of Jacobs Field and rallied for a 7–6 victory on Murray's 11th-inning single in a four hour, nine minute marathon in Game 3,

- put their backs against the wall by losing, 5–2, as the Braves' Ryan Klesko whacked two homers in the fourth game to overcome solo shots by Belle and Ramirez,

- fought back against Maddux in their 1995 Jacobs Field finale to stay alive as Belle and Thome homered, nullifying homers by Luis Polonia and Klesko, while Hershiser and Jose Mesa pitched well, and prevailed, 5–4,

- but finally capitulated, 1–0, when the Series returned to Atlanta and Glavine pitched a one-hitter, winning on David Justice's solo homer.

Five of the six games were decided by one run, three of them in favor of the Braves, who were acknowledged to have the best pitching staff in baseball and one of the best of all time.

"Naturally, I'm sorry we lost . . . disappointed as hell," said Hargrove. "But this was a good season. The only thing we didn't do was win this thing [the World Series]. But we played like champions. I really feel we did."

The Championship Season

Few would disagree with Mike Hargrove's claim that the Indians played like champions, certainly not anybody who witnessed the Indians all year. And many saw them in person, setting a franchise attendance record of 2,842,725, breaking the 1948 mark of 2,620,627. Included were 52 consecutive sellout crowds dating from June 12 through the final game. The largest turnout was on August 1 when 42,023 fans spun the turnstiles and saw the Indians lose to Minnesota, 6–5.

The Tribe won the AL Central Division by 30 lengths over Kansas City. It was the largest margin of victory of all time, beating the Pittsburgh Pirates, who finished 27½ games ahead of Brooklyn in the National League in 1902.

The Indians' won-lost record was 46–21 (.687) in the first half, and 54–23 (.701) after the All-Star break. They finished a mere .006 percentage points shy of being only the ninth team to post a winning percentage of .700, and their .694 was the 10th highest in modern baseball history (since 1901). It was the best in baseball since the 1954 Tribe played at a .721 clip (111–43).

After moving into a tie for the lead in the AL Central on May 10, the Indians took undisputed possession of first place in the division the next day, and stayed there through the end of the season for a total of 145 days.

They recorded 48 come-from-behind victories and won 27 games in their final at bat (17 at Jacobs Field) during the regular season, and their record stood at 89–34 (.724) for the two-year history of the facility.

At the other end of the scale the Indians scored eight runs before an out was made in the first inning of a game on May 9 against Kansas City, equaling a major league record. They also scored five or more runs in one inning 23 times, and their home record was a remarkable 54–18 (.750).

Seven regulars batted .300: Murray, whose .323 was fifth in the AL; Belle, .317; Thome, .314; Baerga, .314; Kenny Lofton, .310; Ramirez, .308; and Alomar, .300.

Belle, Baerga, Lofton, and Ramirez, along with pitchers Dennis Martinez and Mesa, made the All-Star team, the Indians largest representation since seven were picked to play in the 1952 midsummer classic.

The Indians led the AL in virtually every major offensive and pitching category during the regular season.

They were number one with a .291 average (first time since 1986 that they led the league, and their highest mark since 1936 when it was .304), 840 runs, 1,461 hits, 2,407 total bases, 207 home runs (a franchise record, 20 more than in 1987), 803 runs batted in, 132 stolen bases, .479 slugging average, and .361 on-base percentage. Their 766 strikeouts were fewest, and 279 doubles were third most in the league.

Tribe pitchers also dominated the statistics with the best team earned run average, 3.83 (the only one under 4.00 and the first time they led the league since 1968), 10 shutouts, and 50 saves. They also allowed the fewest walks, 445; runs, 607; and earned runs, 554. They were second in hits allowed, 1,261; home runs, 135; and opponents' batting average, .255; and were third with 926 strikeouts.

The Indians were the first American League team since Baltimore in 1971 to lead the league in batting average and ERA.

Defensively, they were tied for fourth with a .982 fielding percentage, committing 101 errors, seventh most, and making 142 double plays, seventh most.

Individually, Belle, Mesa, Hershiser, and Lofton were remarkable with their contributions to the Indians' success— especially Belle, the enigmatic outfielder, and Mesa, a starter his first 13 years in professional baseball and during his first four seasons and parts of two others in the major leagues with Baltimore, until coming to the Indians in mid-1992.

Belle hammered 31 homers in the last two months of the season, 14 in August and 17 in September, the latter tying Babe Ruth's major league record. With those 50 homers, Belle became the first member of the Indians to lead the major leagues in that department, and also was number one in the AL in total bases, 377; slugging percentage, .690; and extra base hits, 103. He finished in a tie for the lead in RBIs (with Boston's Mo Vaughn) with 126, doubles (with Seattle's Edgar Martinez) with 52; and runs (with Edgar Martinez) with 121.

Belle also became the first major leaguer to hit 50 homers and 50 (actually 52) doubles in the same season. "If someone had told me in spring training that I'd hit 50 (homers), I'd have laughed," said Belle. "I felt like I got into a groove during the home-run-hitting contest at the All-Star Game."

Belle also said he felt more pressure at home than on the road "because there always are so many more people to deal with" at Jacobs Field, and that the way he was treated away from Cleveland served to motivate him.

"I'd like to thank the fans in Chicago especially," he said facetiously. "After I hit those three home runs in a game at Comiskey Park [on September 19] everybody was yelling at [manager] Terry Bevington to have my bat checked.

"It was nice to get some revenge on them."

The last comment was a reference to what happened on July 19, 1994, when then White Sox manager Gene Lamont asked the umpires to examine Belle's bat. When they did, it was found to be corked, and Belle was suspended for 10 days by AL president Dr. Bobby Brown.

Mesa, who had only two major league saves prior to the 1995 season, was credited with 46 (in 48 opportunities) for a club record, breaking Doug Jones' mark of 43 set in 1990. Those 46 saves also were the most in the major leagues in 1995.

Mesa didn't even get an opportunity for his first save until May 5 in the Tribe's eighth game. He converted 38 in a row before blowing the first one against Detroit on August 25.

Hershiser, mainstay of the Los Angeles Dodgers pitching staff from 1984 until he suffered a shoulder injury that required reconstructive surgery in 1990, and the NL Cy Young Award winner in 1988 when his record was 23–8, made a complete comeback with the Indians.

Signed as a free agent in April after going only 6–6 with a 3.79 ERA for the Dodgers in 1994, Hershiser won 16 games, losing only six, tying Charles Nagy for the best record on the Cleveland staff. Hershiser won his last four starts, giving him 150 career victories. He also was outstanding in the postseason, shutting out the Red Sox in the Division Series, and beating the Mariners and Braves once each in the ALCS and World Series.

Though Lofton was hampered by injuries much of the season and able to play in only 118 games, he batted .300 (.310) for the third straight year.

Lofton stole 23 bases from September 1 through the final game, and 15 in the last 12, giving him 54 to win his fourth consecutive title in that department. The 1995 season also was the fourth since he came up from the minors in which Lofton stole 50 or more bases—66 in 1992, 70 in 1993, and 60 in 1994.

It would be difficult to pick a turning point in the Indians' glorious season, though several key victories quickly come to mind.

In sequential order, the first might have been on May 10, when they beat Kansas City, 3–2. The win boosted them into a tie for first place in the AL Central with Milwaukee, while the Brewers were splitting a doubleheader with Detroit.

Twenty-four hours later, almost as proof positive that 1995 would indeed be an Indian summer to savor, the Tribe assumed sole possession of the lead without even taking the field. By virtue of the Brewers' 8–0 loss to the Tigers, the Indians, who were not scheduled to play on May 11, moved a half game ahead of Milwaukee and never thereafter slipped out of first.

On May 16, in Yankee Stadium, Belle, Ramirez and Sorrento hit home runs as the Indians overwhelmed the Yankees, 10–5, strengthening both their hold on first place (to 2½ lengths) and a belief in themselves. It was the first meeting of the two teams since the Yankees beat the Indians nine times without retaliation in 1994.

Three games later the Indians' confidence level surged even higher in the wake of a 9–5 victory over another AL East power, the Red Sox, in Fenway Park. Trailing 5–3 in the ninth inning, the Indians erupted for six runs against Ken Ryan, Boston's ace reliever. The rally started with a solo homer by Ramirez, and three batters later, Belle put the Tribe on top, 7–5, with another homer. Before the inning ended, Ryan was gone and the Indians were coasting. It was the Indians' fourth victory in their last at bat, and their most impressive in the young season. It opened many eyes as to the volatility of the team's offense.

The Indians were even more impressive with victories over the Red Sox the next two nights, both times rallying from behind to win, 7–5 and 12–10, boosting their first-place margin to five.

Eight days later, on May 29, the Indians faced their first "crucial" test of the season in the opener of a four-game series against Chicago at Jacobs Field. In the 1994 strike-shortened season, the White Sox finished first, one game ahead of the Tribe, and were expected to provide the most competition again in 1995.

But the Indians won all four games, the first one, 7–6, after spotting the White Sox a 6–0 lead. The next three victories were by scores of 2–1, 6–3, and 7–4, and a day after the fourth loss, Lamont was fired by the White Sox, who were never a factor in the AL Central again.

By July 16 the Indians, with a 50–21 record, were comfortably ahead of Kansas City by 14½ games when Ramirez, four years out of high school and playing only his second full major league season, met up with Dennis Eckersley, one of baseball's all-time greatest relief pitchers.

The result was, "Wow!"

"Wow!" that is, on the part of Eckersley, who at that point had recorded 11 saves in the season for a career total of 305. He would go on to save 18 more games in 1995, giving him 323.

It happened in the 12th inning of the Athletics-Indians game at Jacobs Field, with Eckersley trying to protect Oakland's 4–3 lead. Baerga led off with a single, but Belle and Thome popped out, and some of the fans among the crowd of 41,767 started toward the exits. Eckersley got two quick strikes on Ramirez, who took the next two pitches for balls, evening the count at 2-and-2. The next pitch, one of the sidearm sliders for which Eckersley is famous, broke over the plate about thigh-high.

Ramirez swung viciously, met the pitch on the sweet spot of his bat, and the ball flew out faster than it came in. It was a rising, laserlike beam toward left field and landed deep in the bleachers for a two-run, game-winning homer, his 21st of the season.

As the fans roared their approval, a television camera caught Eckersley watching the flight of the ball, then turning and, as he headed for the dugout, viewers could read his lips as he exclaimed, "Wow!"

After the game Eckersley, who began his major league career in Cleveland in 1975 and pitched—as a starter—for the Indians through 1977, was among those most impressed. "It's phenomenal what's happening around here," said the 40-year-old right-hander. "It's almost like it's meant to be."

Ramirez shrugged off the praise, explaining, "I never faced Eckersley before, though I knew he was one of the best. I wasn't trying to hit a home run, I just wanted to stay back and try to hit the ball hard, the other way [to right field]."

It was the 13th game the Indians won in their final at bat, and it gave them 24 come-from-behind victories.

In the space of the next eight days the Indians further established their credibility, not only as a legitimate contender after years of mediocrity, but also as the dominant team in the American League.

On July 18, in a game against the California Angels, who at that time appeared to be running away with the championship of the AL West, Belle stepped into the limelight that had shone on Ramirez two days earlier. This time, instead of Eckersley, it was Lee Smith against whom the Indians fought back. Smith entered 1995 as baseball's all-time saves leader with 434, and he had boosted his total to 456 in the first three months of the season.

The Angels had beaten the Tribe, 8–3, the day before and appeared close to sweeping the two-game series, leading, 5–3, with Smith on the mound to start the ninth inning.

Pinch hitter Wayne Kirby led off with a single, stole second with one out, took third on a single by Vizquel, and waited as Baerga walked. But he didn't wait long. To be exact, for only three pitches to Belle by Smith. One was a strike, the other two balls. Smith's fourth offering, a slider over the heart of the plate, was drilled by Belle some 425 feet into the picnic area beyond the center-field fence. It was Belle's 16th homer and fourth career grand slam, giving the Indians a 7–5 victory.

Smith had nothing to say after the game. But Hargrove did.

"Nothing these guys do surprises me because they have never known when it's time to fold the tent and go home," he said, without fear of contradiction—certainly not by Smith.

On July 22, the Indians did it again to Eckersley, this time in Oakland on a two-out, two-run double by Thome in the ninth inning that overcame the Athletics' 4–3 lead. Paul Sorrento added insult to injury with another single, and Mesa came out of the bull pen to save the 6–4 victory.

"The feeling on this club right now is that we will not accept a loss," said Vizquel, who scored the tying run on Thome's hit, with Baerga going home with the tiebreaker.

And two days later, on July 24, the Tribe also did it again to Smith, who took over in the 10th inning of a 7–7 tie. Well aware of the damage they'd inflicted upon him six days earlier, Smith, pitching unusually (for him) defensively, walked Thome with one out. Ramirez followed with a double and Sorrento with a single for two runs and a 9–7 victory, and Smith's fourth loss instead of a 23rd save.

The victory gave the Tribe a seven-game winning streak, which included a ninth consecutive victory without a loss by Martinez. He beat the Athletics 6–1, reducing his ERA to 2.35 with a complete-game six-hitter, on July 21.

By August 20 the Indians had stretched their record to 71–34 and their lead over the Royals to a season-high 19 games, going 25–13 after the All-Star break as Mesa reached a significant milestone in his amazing season.

The 29-year-old right-hander, who wasn't thought to have the personality to be a closer when he was moved to the bull pen from the starting rotation in 1994, preserved an 8–5 victory over Milwaukee. It improved the Indians' record to 37 games over .500 (71–34) and their lead over Kansas City to 19 lengths.

It was the 37th consecutive save in 37 opportunities for Mesa, breaking the major league record held by Eckersley. "It's probably the most improbable thing anyone could imagine," is the way Hargrove marveled at Mesa's achievement. Mesa, who walked a batter upon entering the game in the ninth and then struck out two Brewers to end it, also was correct when he said, "People love me here."

After racking up save number 38 against Toronto in the Indians' 6–5 victory in the SkyDome on August 23, Mesa finally failed in his next outing on August 25. The blown save proved he is only human, not superhuman. The Indians prevailed anyway, beating Detroit, 6–5, thanks to Alomar's solo homer with one out in the last of the 11th inning.

It also was a big game for Belle, who celebrated his 29th birthday by clubbing his 30th and 31st homers and a single. It gave Hill and the Indians a 5–4 lead before Mesa took the mound in the ninth inning. He retired the first two batters, but couldn't get past Chad Curtis, who lofted Mesa's first pitch into the right-field stands, tying the game at 5–5.

After spoiling Mesa's perfect record, Curtis shrugged and said of the pitcher, "He throws hard enough that if the ball hits my bat it could go out . . . and it did." It was only the second home run allowed by Mesa in 1995, the first earned run against him since June 8, and it ended his streak of 18⅓ scoreless innings.

"I hated to see his streak come to an end, though we all knew it would end sometime," said Hargrove. "But if you had told me during spring training that, on August 25, Mesa would have 38 saves, I would have said that you are crazy."

Julian Tavarez blanked the Tigers in the 10th and 11th,

and was rewarded with his ninth victory in 11 decisions when Alomar unloaded his homer.

Belle's big day gave him 40-for-94 (.426) with 12 homers and 24 RBI in 25 games in August. He also became the first Tribesman to hit 30 or more homers in four consecutive seasons, and the 32nd player in baseball history to do it.

Belle won another game with another homer on August 30, his 32nd of the season and 14th in the month. He hit it in the 14th inning against Toronto's Tony Castillo after Baerga's sacrifice fly got the tying run home, and the Indians won, 4–3. It was their seventh in a row and they went on to stretch the winning streak to nine before losing again.

"Nothing Belle does surprises me . . . but you'll have to ask him if he goes to the plate trying to hit home runs," said Hargrove. Nobody bothered to ask Belle because this was one of the times he declined to talk to the media. But others did.

As Baerga remarked, "When Albert gets hot, he can do anything. And he is very hot right now."

By Labor Day, September 4, it was all but over—the Indians' "magic number" for clinching the division championship was down to 5—and they were riding a wave of success unprecedented for a Cleveland baseball team in four decades.

But Hargrove wouldn't let them relax. "We haven't won anything yet, and when we do, it'll only be the first step. We'll still have three more to go," he said, referring to, first, the Division Series, followed by the AL Championship Series, and then the World Series.

The end—though it really was, as Hargrove said, the beginning—came on September 8. That's when Thome caught Huson's pop foul and a dream became reality—and a city celebrated its first baseball championship since 1954, its first sports championship of any kind in 31 years since the Browns won the NFL in 1964.

"What we have to do now is keep our intensity," said Hargrove. "We can't afford a letdown because, if we do, we might not get started again."

It was the second-earliest clinching of a championship since Major League Baseball went to divisional play in 1969. Only the Cincinnati Reds, who won the National League West on September 7, 1975, did it faster. And prior to the advent of divisional play, the 1941 New York Yankees won the AL pennant on September 4, for the earliest clinching of all time.

Despite the Indians' success, Hargrove would not permit them to coast. To the manager's credit, he held pregame and open-date workouts in which the players practiced fundamentals. In fact, the day before the first game of the Division Series against Seattle, Hargrove had the pitchers fielding bunts, infielders covering bases and backing up throws, and outfielders hitting cutoff men while the catchers called out plays and took charge of all situations. It was reminiscent of the first day of spring training.

"We're doing these things because they're important," said Hargrove. "I'm not saying that I'm dissatisfied with what we've done so far. I just want to make sure we continue to do things the right way."

The Tribe did, through most of the final 21 games in the regular season, 14 of which were victories, including the last five in a row. They enabled the Indians to reach the century mark, though their winning percentage fell .006 percentage points short of .700.

"We don't care who we play. . . . The important thing is that we are going to play somebody for the right to win the pennant and go to the World Series," said Baerga.

Pitcher	W	L	G	GS	CG	IP	H	BB	SO	ERA
Paul Assenmacher	6	2	47	0	0	38⅓	32	12	40	2.82
Bud Black	4	2	11	10	0	47⅓	63	16	34	6.85
Mark Clark	9	7	22	21	2	124⅔	143	42	68	5.27
Dennis Cook	0	0	11	0	0	12⅔	16	10	13	6.39
Alan Embree	3	2	23	0	0	24⅔	23	16	23	5.11
John Farrell	0	0	1	0	0	4⅔	7	0	4	3.86
Jason Grimsley	0	0	15	2	0	34	37	32	25	6.09
Orel Hershiser	16	6	26	26	1	167⅓	151	51	111	3.87
Ken Hill	4	1	12	11	1	74⅓	77	32	48	3.98
Albie Lopez	0	0	6	2	0	23	17	7	22	3.13
Dennis Martinez	12	5	28	28	3	187	174	46	99	3.08
Jose Mesa	3	0	62	0	0	64	49	17	58	1.13
Charles Nagy	16	6	29	29	2	178	194	61	139	4.55
Chad Ogea	8	3	20	14	1	106⅓	95	29	57	3.05
Gregg Olson	0	0	3	0	0	2⅔	5	2	0	13.50
Eric Plunk	6	2	56	0	0	64	48	27	71	2.67
Jim Poole	3	3	42	0	0	50⅓	40	17	41	3.75
Joe Roa	0	1	1	1	0	6	9	2	0	6.00
Paul Shuey	0	2	7	0	0	6⅓	5	5	5	4.26
Julian Tavarez	10	2	57	0	0	85	76	21	68	2.44
Totals	(100)	44		144	10	(1,301)	1,261	445	926	(3.83)

Shutouts: Martinez (2), Hershiser, Nagy
Saves: Mesa (46), Plunk (2), Embree, Grimsley

Player	G	AB	R	H	2B	3B	HR	RBI	SB	AVG
Sandy Alomar	66	203	32	61	6	0	10	35	3	.300
Ruben Amaro	28	60	5	12	3	0	1	7	1	.200
Carlos Baerga (2B)	135	557	87	175	28	2	15	90	11	.314
David Bell	2	0	0	0	0	0	0	0	0	.000
Albert Belle (LF)	143	546	(121)	173	(52)	1	(50)	(126)	5	.317
Jeromy Burnitz	9	7	4	4	1	0	0	0	0	.571
Alvaro Espinoza	66	143	15	36	4	0	2	17	0	.252
Brian Giles	6	9	6	5	0	0	1	3	0	.556
Wayne Kirby	101	188	29	39	10	2	1	14	10	.207
Jesse Levis	12	18	1	6	2	0	0	3	0	.333
Kenny Lofton (CF)	118	481	93	149	22	(13)	7	53	(54)	.310
Eddie Murray (DH)	113	436	68	141	21	0	21	82	5	.323
Tony Pena (C)	91	263	25	69	15	0	5	28	1	.262
Herb Perry	52	162	23	51	13	1	3	23	1	.315
Manny Ramirez (RF)	137	484	85	149	26	1	31	107	6	.308
Billy Ripken	8	17	4	7	0	0	2	3	0	.412
Paul Sorrento (1B)	104	323	50	76	14	0	25	79	1	.235
Jim Thome (3B)	137	452	92	142	29	3	25	73	4	.314
Scooter Tucker	17	20	2	0	0	0	0	0	0	.000
Omar Vizquel (SS)	136	542	87	144	28	0	6	56	29	.266
Dave Winfield	46	115	11	22	5	0	2	4	1	.191
Totals		5,028	(840)	(1,461)	279	23	(207)	(803)	(132)	(.291)

Parentheses indicate league-leading statistics.

The Division Series

It turned out that the Indians' opponent in the division series would be the Red Sox, who won the AL East by seven games over New York, with an 86–58 (.597) record.

That matchup was finalized when the Yankees (79–65) won the wild-card berth to the Series, and played Seattle (79–66), which had beaten California in a one-game playoff for the AL West championship.

Though Baerga insisted that he and his teammates had no preference, everybody knew they usually had trouble beating Roger Clemens, Boston's ace, who would pitch the opener on October 3. Clemens was 18–6 lifetime against the Indians, but as Baerga said, "That was before we got good." Indeed it was. Slowed by arm injuries, Clemens was 0–2 with an 8.25 ERA against the Tribe dating back to 1994.

Martinez, 12–5 in 28 starts, but only 4–5 after the All-Star Game, and nursing an aching right elbow and sore left knee, pitched for the Indians but left after six innings. He gave up two runs on Mike Macfarlane's single and John Valentin's homer in the third.

Clemens departed in the seventh, trailing 3–2, after the Indians scored three times in the sixth on singles by Vizquel and Baerga, Belle's double, an error, and Murray's single, all after the first two batters in the inning were retired.

The Red Sox tied it in the eighth on Luis Alicea's solo homer off Tavarez, and it stayed that way until the 11th when each team scored a run. Boston's came on Tim Naehring's homer off Jim Poole, and the Indians' on Belle's homer off Rick Aguilera.

The score remained tied, 4–4, until Pena, who used to be Clemens' personal catcher, smashed a 3-and-0 pitch off Zane Smith for a homer into the left-field bleachers with two out in the 13th.

Hershiser and three relievers—Tavarez, Paul Assenmacher, and Mesa—made it look easy the next night, blanking the Red Sox, 4–0, on three hits. Two walks by Erik Hanson and Vizquel's double got two runs home for the Tribe in

the fifth, and another walk and Murray's homer added the final two runs in the eighth.

That sent the Series to Boston where the Indians completed a sweep with an 8–2 victory over the Red Sox and knuckleballer Tim Wakefield, who had been considered a Cy Young Award candidate in the first half, but wasn't the same after the All-Star break.

Thome started the barrage with a two-run homer in the second inning, then walked with the bases loaded in the third, when the Tribe went up 3–0, and it proved to be all the runs needed by Nagy, who pitched seven strong innings, and one each by Tavarez and Assenmacher.

"To jump out on them the way we did was very important," said Hargrove. "You come in here [to Fenway Park] with their fans, and it's very difficult to beat them."

Fenway also was a factor in Thome's mind. "The Red Sox were the team that scared us the most because of Fenway," said the third baseman who was only 1-for-10 in the first two games. "The home run was big, extra big because I was struggling. I think my first postseason is a learning experience, and the bottom line is to win and get big hits in big situations. I kept telling myself to be patient and keep fighting."

COMPOSITE BATTING STATISTICS
Boston Red Sox

Player	AB	R	H	2B	3B	HR	RBI	AVG
Alicea, 2b	10	1	6	1	0	1	1	.600
Macfarlane, c	9	0	3	0	0	0	1	.333
McGee, rf-ph	4	0	1	0	0	0	1	.333
Naehring, 3b	13	2	4	0	0	1	1	.308
J. Valentin, ss	12	1	3	1	0	1	2	.250
Jefferson, dh	4	1	1	0	0	0	0	.250
Greenwell, lf	15	0	3	0	0	0	0	.200
Canseco, dh	13	0	0	0	0	0	0	.000
Hosey, rf	12	1	0	0	0	0	0	.000
Haselman, c	2	0	0	0	0	0	0	.000
Stairs, ph	1	0	0	0	0	0	0	.000
Tinsley, cf	5	0	0	0	0	0	0	.000
M. Vaughn, 1b	14	0	0	0	0	0	0	.000
Totals	114	6	21	2	0	3	6	.184

Cleveland Indians

Player	AB	R	H	2B	3B	HR	RBI	AVG
Kirby, pr-rf	1	0	1	0	0	0	0	1.000
Pena, c	2	1	1	0	0	1	1	.500
Murray, dh	13	3	5	0	1	1	3	.385
Sorrento, 1b	10	2	3	0	0	0	1	.300
Baerga, 2b	14	2	4	1	0	0	1	.286
Belle, lf	11	3	3	1	0	1	3	.273
S. Alomar, c	11	1	2	1	0	0	1	.182
Vizquel, ss	12	2	2	1	0	0	4	.167
Lofton, cf	13	1	2	0	0	0	0	.154
Thome, 3b	13	1	2	0	0	1	3	.154
H. Perry, 1b	1	0	0	0	0	0	0	.000
M. Ramirez, rf	12	1	0	0	0	0	0	.000
Espinoza, 3b	1	0	0	0	0	0	0	.000
Totals	**114**	**17**	**25**	**4**	**1**	**4**	**17**	**.219**

COMPOSITE PITCHING STATISTICS
Boston Red Sox

Pitcher	G	IP	H	R	ER	BB	SO	ERA
Belinda	1	⅓	0	0	0	0	0	0.00
M. Maddux	2	3	2	0	0	1	1	0.00
Hudson	1	1	2	0	0	1	0	0.00
Stanton	1	2⅓	1	0	0	0	4	0.00
Clemens	1	7	5	3	3	1	5	3.86
Hanson, 0–1	1	8	4	4	4	4	5	4.50
Z. Smith, 0–1	1	1⅓	1	1	1	0	0	6.75
Wakefield, 0–1	1	5⅓	5	7	7	5	4	11.81
Cormier	2	⅔	2	1	1	1	2	13.49
Aguilera	1	⅔	3	1	1	0	1	13.50
Totals	**3**	**29⅔**	**25**	**17**	**17**	**13**	**22**	**5.16**

Cleveland Indians

Pitcher	G	IP	H	R	ER	BB	SO	ERA
Assenmacher	3	1⅓	0	0	0	0	3	0.00
Hershiser, 1–0	1	7⅓	3	0	0	2	7	0.00
K. Hill, 1–0	1	1⅓	1	0	0	0	2	0.00
Mesa	2	2	0	0	0	2	0	0.00
Plunk	1	1⅓	1	0	0	1	1	0.00
Nagy, 1–0	1	7	4	1	1	5	6	0.78
DeMartinez	1	6	5	2	2	0	2	3.00
Poole	1	1⅔	2	1	1	1	2	5.40
Tavarez	3	2⅔	5	2	2	0	3	6.75
Totals	**3**	**31**	**21**	**6**	**6**	**11**	**26**	**1.74**

SCORE BY INNINGS

Boston	0	0	2	1	0	0	0	2	0	0	1	0	0—6
Cleveland	0	2	1	0	2	8	0	2	0	0	1	0	1—17

E: Lofton (2), Baerga (1), Macfarlane (2). **DP:** Bos 0, Cle 1. **LOB:** Bos 28, Cle 27. **SB:** Alicea, Hosey, Vizquel. **CS:** Valentin. **S:** S. Alomar, Naehring, Vizquel. **SF:** Macfarlane. **IBB:** Off M. Maddux (Belle); off Poole (Jn. Valentin); off Plunk (Tinsley); off Hanson (Belle). **HBP:** by M. Maddux (Lofton); by Cormier (Baerga); by Hanson (Sorrento); by Wakefield (M. Ramirez). **WP:** Hershiser, Hudson. **PB:** Macfarlane 2. **Umps:** (Game 1 & 2) Welke, Hirschbeck, Brinkman, Roe, Denkinger, Morrison. (Game 3) McKean, McCoy, Garcia, Joyce, Reilly, Scott. **T:** Game 1 at Cleveland, 5:01. Game 2 at Cleveland, 2:33. Game 3 at Boston, 3:18. **A:** Game 1 at Cleveland, 44,218. Game 2 at Cleveland, 44,264. Game 3 at Boston, 34,211.

The American League Championship Series

After disposing of the Red Sox, the Indians returned to Cleveland to await the winner of the Seattle–New York series. Because of their dislike for the Kingdome, most of the players were hoping the Yankees would prevail, as it seemed they would, with victories in the first two games. But the Mariners fought back to win the next three, and the Indians repacked their bags and headed for Seattle for the best-of-seven series for the American League pennant that began October 10.

Game One

It seemed that the Indians were getting a break because Randy Johnson, arguably the best pitcher in the AL, had pitched three innings in relief two days earlier to save the Mariners' 6–5, 11-inning victory over the Yankees in the final game of their series. As it turned out, however, rookie Bob Wolcott, activated only a few hours before the game, did almost everything right and was the winning pitcher in the Mariners' 3–2 victory in the opener.

Obviously nervous at the onset, Wolcott walked the first three batters in the first inning on 13 pitches, and it seemed a rout was waiting to happen. But Belle, the fourth batter to face Wolcott, swung at the first pitch he saw and then struck out. Murray followed and, also after swinging at the first pitch, fouled out. Then Thome grounded out, and the Indians were blanked.

The futile effort proved to be a portent of things to come later that night, and the loss became the Indians' 20th in 26

games in the Kingdome since 1991. Martinez, still working with a sore elbow and knee, walked Jay Buhner with two out in the second, then served a home run to Mike Blowers. The Indians got a run in the third on singles by Baerga and Thome around a walk to Belle, and Belle solo homered to tie the game in the seventh. But in the home half of the seventh, Buhner's double, a throwing error by Thome allowing Blowers to reach, and Luis Sojo's double scored a go-ahead run. The Mariners made it stand up as Norm Charlton halted an Indians uprising in the eighth and blanked them in the ninth.

Hargrove said he knew the Indians were in trouble when they allowed Wolcott to escape the first inning unscathed after walking Lofton, Vizquel, and Baerga. "That probably was the tale of the game right there," said Hargrove. "That set the tone for everything that followed," as the Indians stranded 12 base runners.

Game Two

The loss left the Indians in a strange position—a *must-win* situation—for the first time all year, and Hershiser rose to the occasion again. He pitched eight strong innings, then turned the job over to Mesa, and the Indians prevailed, 5–2, tying the ALCS at 1–1. The former Dodger star allowed only four hits, one of them a solo homer by Ken Griffey, Jr., and

Mesa yielded Seattle's other run, another bases-empty homer by Buhner, but that's all the Mariners scored.

Meanwhile, Ramirez, who was 0-for-12 against the Red Sox, and 1-for-4 in the opener of the Seattle series, blasted a pair of homers off Tim Belcher and also singled twice in four at bats to lead the Tribe. Baerga's single with the bases loaded, after Ramirez led off with a single, put the Indians ahead 2–0 in the fifth. Two more runs came home in the sixth, one on Ramirez's first homer and one on Sorrento's single and Alomar's triple. Ramirez homered again in the eighth and, though the Mariners threatened in the ninth, Mesa squirmed out of trouble.

"As far as we were concerned, that was a game we absolutely had to win," acknowledged Hargrove, looking ahead to Game 3 in Cleveland when Johnson was scheduled to start for the Mariners.

"It was huge," agreed Hershiser, "especially coming after the opener. We didn't feel we got beat in that game, we felt we gave it away." It raised Hershiser's career postseason record to 6–0 with a 1.47 ERA, and was the second playoff game he won for the Indians.

Vizquel also deserved a large share of credit for the victory. The Gold Glove shortstop, who played five seasons for the Mariners before he was traded to the Tribe in 1994, made two sensational defensive plays to keep Hershiser out of serious trouble.

Game Three

J ohnson was every bit as difficult as the Indians thought he'd be, but it was Buhner and Charlton who made the difference for the Mariners in the third game on October 13 at Jacobs Field. Johnson held the Indians to two runs (one earned) on four hits in eight innings, and Nagy virtually duplicated that effort for the Indians, allowing two runs (one earned) on five hits also in eight innings. Each pitcher struck out six.

Buhner led off the second inning with a homer, and the Mariners made it 2–0 in the third on Griffey's two-out single and successive errors by Alomar and Alvaro Espinoza.

The Indians got their first run in the fourth on Lofton's leadoff triple and Vizquel's sacrifice fly, and tied the score in the eighth when Espinoza reached on Buhner's two-base error and Lofton again came through, this time with a single.

Mesa pitched a scoreless ninth, and Tavarez blanked the Mariners in the 10th, but ran into trouble in the 11th when Joey Cora singled. Assenmacher came out of the bull pen and retired Griffey, then turned the job over to Eric Plunk,

who got Edgar Martinez on a pop foul for the second out. But then, after Cora stole second and Tino Martinez was intentionally walked, Buhner smashed his second homer of the game for a 5–2 lead.

Meanwhile, the Indians were blanked by Charlton, who took over in the ninth for Johnson and held them hitless through the 11th to put Seattle ahead in the series, two games to one.

"I came out of this thing smelling like a rose," said Buhner, referring to his second home run that essentially nullified the eighth-inning error he committed that allowed the Indians to tie the score. "I was very upset and very frustrated after screwing up the way I did." Of his game-winning homer, Buhner said, "I was just trying to get a ball and juice it," which he did.

Hargrove was disappointed, of course, but not discouraged—at least not openly. "We've got a very resilient club," he said. "They come to play every day. They'll be back tomorrow."

Game Four

A nd the Indians were back—even without Belle and Alomar—in another must-win situation in Game 4. Belle couldn't play because of a badly bruised right ankle, and Alomar was out because of a pinched nerve in his neck.

But Ken Hill, the former National Leaguer whom the Indians acquired in July, and Jim Poole, Chad Ogea, and Alan Embree took matters into their own hands, combining on a six-hit, 7–0, victory. It was only the third time the Mariners were shut out in 1995.

"Anytime you get a guy who hit 50 home runs out of the lineup, you feel fortunate," said Seattle manager Lou Piniella. "But the story of this game was how well Ken Hill pitched."

It was Hill's first start in 16 days and second victory in the postseason. "We were in a situation where we needed a win,"

said Hill. "I made the pitches when I had to. They [the Indians] gave me a three-run lead and I relaxed."

That three-run lead was presented in the first inning. Lofton led off with a single, stole second, took third on a throwing error by catcher Dan Wilson, waited as Vizquel walked, and scored when Baerga grounded out. Then Murray smashed his second postseason homer.

An inning later Pena singled, then acting more like a high school kid than a 38-year-old veteran, hustled to third, reaching the base in a head-first dive as Kirby grounded out, then scored on Lofton's sacrifice fly.

Baerga singled and Thome homered for a 6–0 lead in the third, making it even easier for Hill to relax, and hits by Kirby and Vizquel scored a final run in the sixth. The victory tied the series at 2-all.

Game Five

H ershiser was the winning pitcher, thanks to Jim Thome's two-run homer, and Mesa earned his first save of the postseason as the Indians beat Seattle, 3–2, in Game 5, advancing to within one game of the World Series.

But an equally significant contribution to the victory was

made by Paul Assenmacher, the tall, mustachioed southpaw who appeared in 47 relief assignments for the Tribe in the regular season but seldom pitched to more than one or two batters—always left-handers—in each.

This time Assenmacher was called upon to face the dangerous Griffey with Mariners on first and third, one out in the seventh, and the Tribe clinging precariously to a one-run lead.

The inning began as Tavarez replaced Hershiser and Wilson reached on the first of back-to-back errors by Sorrento, the second on a grounder by Joey Cora that left the runners on first and second with nobody out. Tavarez got Edgar Martinez to force Cora at second, but Wilson, representing the tying run, made it to third, and the potential go-ahead run was at first with one out. That's when Assenmacher ambled in from the bull pen and, with the count 1-and-2 on Griffey, struck him out.

Normally, with Buhner, a tough right-handed power hitter who'd already belted three homers in the series, due to bat next, that would have been the end of Assenmacher's night's work. But not this time. Hargrove let him face Buhner, and Assenmacher struck him out, too.

The biggest reason Hargrove didn't turn the job over to Plunk, a right-hander, to pitch to Buhner, was that the manager remembered the last time those two met. It was in Game 3, and Buhner smashed a three-run homer off Plunk in the 11th inning to give the Mariners a 5–2 victory.

"Obviously, we did not get the results we were looking for the last time," Hargrove said of his unwillingness to replace Assenmacher with Plunk.

He did, however, employ Plunk the next inning, and it nearly resulted in another disaster. Assenmacher started the eighth by retiring Tino Martinez on a pop fly caught by Vizquel. Then, with switch-hitting Vince Coleman at the plate, Hargrove summoned Plunk, to the collective groan of the 43,607 fans in Jacobs Field. Their concern proved to be justified, as Coleman walked and stole second. Then Plunk also walked Alex Diaz, bringing Sojo to the plate and eliciting more groans and scattered boos from the crowd.

Plunk and Sojo dueled for nine pitches, the count going full. Then, finally, with the runners on the move with Plunk's next pitch, Sojo hit a line drive to the left of second base, toward center field. Vizquel darted to his left, leaped and made a one-handed catch of the ball, then trotted to second base, doubling off Coleman—it could have been a triple play if needed—ending the inning.

Mesa hurled the ninth and preserved the victory with just 14 pitches, though the last one was a drive to center field by Edgar Martinez that Lofton caught against the wall.

Hershiser, pitching on three days rest for the first time since July 5, 1993, won his second game of the series, allowing two runs (one earned) and five hits. He also survived two errors, these by Belle, limping on his injured right ankle, in the fifth inning when the Mariners scored their second run.

Thome supplied the power—and the two runs Hershiser needed—to overcome a 2–1 deficit with his second ALCS homer in the sixth. It was a 440-foot bomb into the right-field mezzanine off Chris Bosio, which followed a one-out double by Murray.

"That's one of the best feelings I've ever had," said the 25-year old Thome, playing only his second full season in the major leagues. "By far, that's the biggest hit of my career."

Game Six

Thome's game winner sent the series back to Seattle, where Johnson would try to keep the Mariners alive on October 17 in the raucous Kingdome, where another capacity crowd of more than 58,000 fans would implore their team to go on and win the franchise's first pennant since its inception in 1977.

But they couldn't. Dennis Martinez wouldn't let them. Starting in what would have been Nagy's regular turn (except for Nagy's distaste for domes and his lack of success under them), the sore-armed Martinez, with his personal catcher, Pena, again behind the plate, outpitched Johnson. Martinez blanked the Mariners on four hits through seven innings, then Tavarez and Mesa did the same in the eighth and ninth for a 4–0 victory, and the Indians' first pennant in four decades.

"Dennis Martinez wanted this game, and then he went out and showed why he is one of the best pitchers in baseball," said Baerga.

"After all I've been through in my career, this was the game I was looking for," said Martinez, who was beset by personal problems early in his career with Baltimore. "Finally, I did something we can all remember, that we'll all *want* to remember. The people of Cleveland have been waiting for this for such a long time, and so was I."

The victory didn't come easily, however, and was much closer than the score would indicate. Until the eighth, when the game turned in favor of the Indians because of Lofton—who'd triggered so many rallies in his four seasons in Cleveland—Martinez was clinging tenaciously to a 1–0 lead, which also was produced by Lofton, whose fifth-inning single with two out drove in Espinoza after he'd reached on Cora's error.

Pena led off the eighth with a double and took third when Lofton beat out an infield single. Then Lofton stole second, and moments later came the turning point on, of all things, a passed ball committed by Dan Wilson, the Mariners' catcher.

Ruben Amaro, running for Pena, scored easily, and—with surprising ease—Lofton raced home all the way from second, surprising Wilson in his pursuit of the ball and Johnson in his late coverage of the plate.

Johnson retired the next batter, but Baerga provided an insurance run with his first postseason homer. It finished Johnson and the Mariners as well, as Tavarez and Mesa assured the victory with hitless performances in the last two innings.

Hershiser was named the MVP of the series, though the award could have gone to several others, especially Lofton, who led the Indians with a .458 batting average (11-for-24) and stole five bases.

COMPOSITE BATTING STATISTICS
Cleveland Indians

Player	G	AB	R	H	2B	3B	HR	RBI	BB	SO	AVG	SB	CS	E
Lofton, cf	6	24	4	11	0	2	0	3	4	6	.458	5	0	0
Baerga, 2b	6	25	3	10	0	0	1	4	2	3	.400	0	0	0
Pena, c	4	6	1	2	1	0	0	0	1	0	.333	0	0	0
M. Ramirez, rf	6	21	2	6	0	0	2	2	2	5	.286	0	0	0
Alomar, c	5	15	0	4	1	1	0	1	1	1	.267	0	0	1
Thome, 3b	5	15	2	4	0	0	2	5	2	3	.267	0	0	1
Murray, dh	6	24	2	6	1	0	1	3	2	3	.250	0	0	0
Belle, lf	5	18	1	4	1	0	1	1	3	5	.222	0	0	2
Kirby, rf-lf	5	5	2	1	0	0	0	0	0	0	.200	1	0	0
Sorrento, 1b	4	13	2	2	1	0	0	0	2	3	.154	0	0	2
Espinoza, 3b	4	8	1	1	0	0	0	0	0	3	.125	0	0	1
Vizquel, ss	6	23	2	2	1	0	0	2	5	2	.087	3	0	0
Perry, 1b	3	8	0	0	0	0	0	0	1	3	.000	0	1	0
Amaro, pr	3	1	1	0	0	0	0	0	0	0	.000	0	0	0
Totals	6	206	23	53	6	3	7	21	25	37	.257	9	1	7

Seattle Mariners

Player	G	AB	R	H	2B	3B	HR	RBI	BB	SO	AVG	SB	CS	E
A. Diaz, ph-lf	4	7	0	3	1	0	0	0	1	1	.429	0	0	0
Griffey Jr, cf	6	21	2	7	2	0	1	2	4	4	.333	2	1	1
Buhner, rf	6	23	5	7	2	0	3	5	2	8	.304	0	0	1
Sojo, ss	6	20	2	5	2	0	0	1	0	2	.250	0	0	1
Cora, 2b	6	23	2	4	1	0	0	0	1	0	.174	2	0	1
Blowers, 3b	6	18	1	4	0	0	1	2	0	4	.222	0	0	0
T. Martinez, 1b	6	22	0	3	0	0	0	0	3	7	.136	0	0	1
Coleman, lf	6	20	0	2	0	0	0	0	2	6	.100	4	0	0
E. Martinez, dh	6	23	0	2	0	0	0	0	2	5	.087	1	1	0
D. Wilson, c	6	16	0	0	0	0	0	0	0	4	.000	0	0	1
Strange, ph-3b	4	4	0	0	0	0	0	0	0	2	.000	0	0	0
Amaral, ph	2	2	0	0	0	0	0	0	0	1	.000	0	0	0
Rodriguez, ph	1	1	0	0	0	0	0	0	0	1	.000	0	0	0
Widger, c	3	1	0	0	0	0	0	0	0	1	.000	0	0	0
Fermin, 2b-ss	1	0	0	0	0	0	0	0	0	0	—	0	0	0
Totals	6	201	12	37	8	0	5	10	15	46	.184	9	2	6

COMPOSITE PITCHING STATISTICS
Cleveland Indians

Pitcher	G	CG	IP	H	R	BB	SO	HB	WP	W	L	SV	ER	ERA
Hill	1	0	7	5	0	3	6	0	0	1	0	0	0	0.00
Assenmacher	3	0	1⅓	0	0	1	2	0	0	0	0	0	0	0.00
Poole	1	0	1	0	0	0	2	0	0	0	0	0	0	0.00
Ogea	1	0	⅔	1	0	0	2	0	1	0	0	0	0	0.00
Embree	1	0	⅓	0	0	0	1	0	0	0	0	0	0	0.00
Nagy	1	0	8	5	2	0	6	1	0	0	0	0	1	1.12
Hershiser	2	0	14	9	3	3	15	1	1	2	0	0	2	1.29
D. Martinez	2	0	13⅓	10	3	3	7	1	0	1	1	0	3	2.03
Mesa	4	0	4	3	1	1	1	0	0	0	0	1	1	2.25
Tavarez	4	0	3⅓	3	1	1	2	0	0	0	1	0	1	2.70
Plunk	3	0	2	1	2	3	2	0	0	0	0	0	2	9.00
Totals	6	0	55	37	12	15	46	3	2	4	2	1	10	1.64

Seattle Mariners

Pitcher	G	CG	IP	H	R	BB	SO	HB	WP	W	L	SV	ER	ERA
Charlton	3	0	6	1	0	1	5	1	1	1	0	1	0	0.00
Nelson	3	0	3	3	0	5	3	0	0	0	0	0	0	0.00
Risley	3	0	2⅔	2	0	1	2	0	0	0	0	0	0	0.00
Johnson	2	0	15⅓	12	6	2	13	0	0	0	1	0	4	2.35
Ayala	2	0	3⅔	3	1	3	3	0	0	0	0	0	1	2.45
Wolcott	1	0	7	8	2	5	2	0	0	1	0	0	2	2.57
Wells	1	0	3	2	1	2	2	0	0	0	0	0	1	3.00
Bosio	1	0	5⅓	7	3	2	3	0	0	0	1	0	2	3.38
Belcher	1	0	5⅔	9	4	2	1	0	0	0	1	0	4	6.35
Benes	1	0	2⅓	6	6	2	3	0	0	0	1	0	6	23.14
Totals	6	0	54	53	23	25	37	1	1	2	4	1	20	3.33

Scoring by Innings

Cleveland	4	1	3	1	3	5	1	5	0	0	0—23
Seattle	0	3	2	0	1	1	1	0	1	0	3—12

DP: Cle 4, Sea 7. **LOB:** Cle 44, Sea 49. **S:** Strange, Kirby. **SF:** Vizquel, Lofton. **IBB:** off Tavarez (E. Martinez); off Hershiser (E. Martinez); off Plunk (T. Martinez); off Nelson (Murray). **HBP:** by Hershiser (Cora); by Nagy (Cora); by Charlton (Belle); by D. Martinez (E. Martinez). **PB:** Wilson. **Umps:** Phillips, Cousins, Reed, Ford, McClelland, Coble. **T:** Game 1 at Seattle, 3:07. Game 2 at Seattle, 3.14. Game 3 at Cleveland, 3:18. Game 4 at Cleveland, 3:30. Game 5 at Cleveland, 3:37. Game 6 at Seattle, 2:54. **A:** Game 1 at Seattle, 57,065. Game 2 at Seattle, 58,144. Game 3 at Cleveland, 43,643. Game 4 at Cleveland, 43,686. Game 5 at Cleveland, 43,607. Game 6 at Seattle, 58,489.

The World Series

Meanwhile, the Braves were waiting for the Indians in Atlanta where the first game of the World Series would be played October 21. The Braves had won the National League pennant by disposing of the Colorado Rockies in four games in the Division Series, and then sweeping the Cincinnati Reds in the Championship Series.

Game One

Maddux, the only pitcher to win the Cy Young Award in four consecutive seasons (1992–95), was outstanding in besting Hershiser with a two-hitter for a 3–2 victory in Game 1. As Hargrove marveled afterward, "That was about as well-pitched a game as I've ever seen. We've been shut down before, but that was a masterful job of pitching."

Maddux got 19 of the 27 outs on ground balls. Thome and Lofton got the only hits, both singles, and the only other Tribesmen to get the ball into the outfield were Vizquel and Belle.

The Indians scored in the first and last innings. They took a 1–0 lead without a hit as Lofton reached on an error, stole second and third, and went home as Baerga grounded into the second out. Their second run also was unearned as Lofton singled with one out, then took second and also—unwisely—raced to third as Vizquel grounded out. Fortunately for Lofton, Braves first baseman Fred McGriff threw wildly to third, and the speedy Indians outfielder trotted home. It was, however, only the Tribe's second run, and a few moments later Baerga, who started the game on the bench with a sprained ankle, ended it as a pinch hitter by fouling out.

The Braves pulled even in the second on McGriff's solo homer, and went ahead, 3–1, in the seventh when Hershiser lost his control, walking the first two batters, McGriff and Justice. Assenmacher was summoned from the bull pen, but this time he wasn't equal to the challenge. He also walked pinch hitter Mike Devereaux and was sent to the showers, replaced by Tavarez. A tie-breaking run scored as pinch hitter Polonia forced Devereaux at second in what would have been a double play except that Vizquel couldn't control the ball. Then Rafael Belliard bunted to squeeze home Justice.

They were all the runs Maddux needed. "The guy pitched a great game," said Thome. "He has four quality pitches and he was throwing them all for strikes."

Game Two

It was more of the same—but even more frustrating for the Tribe—in Game 2, which the Braves won, 4–3, on another outstanding pitching performance, this one by Tom Glavine and reliever Mark Wohlers. A two-run, tie-breaking homer by Javy Lopez in the sixth inning made the difference.

Murray provided Martinez a 2–0 lead in the second with a home run, and Lofton singled, stole second, and scored on an error in the seventh, cutting the Braves' lead to one.

But in the eighth, with the Indians threatening to pull even, the rally was aborted when Ramirez, who had singled with one out, foolishly strayed too far off first base and was picked off by Lopez. It got worse for the Tribe as Thome then coaxed a walk, finishing Glavine in favor of Wohlers, but Sor-

rento flied deep to center, ending the inning. The eighth frame also finished the Indians, as it turned out, as Wohlers blanked them in the ninth after Vizquel singled with two out but was stranded at second.

Even before Lopez's homer, Martinez hurt himself by hitting Marquis Grissom with a pitch to open the third. After Mark Lemke singled, Grissom reached third when Martinez threw wildly on an attempted pickoff, then scored on Chipper Jones' sacrifice fly. Justice's two-out single got Lemke home with a tying run.

Justice's single leading off the sixth preceded Lopez's homer, and the Indians returned to Cleveland in another must-win situation.

Game Three

"This is as big a test as we've faced in a long time," acknowledged Hargrove before Murray's 11th-inning single gave the Tribe a 7–6 victory in Game 3 at Jacobs Field on October 24. Had the Indians lost, as it appeared they might, Hargrove himself would have been the goat, as he disdained the odds and stuck with Nagy too long, and the Braves overcame a 5–3 deficit with three runs in the eighth.

"I thought Charlie was still throwing the ball well. He'd made only 91 pitches going into the inning, which is a very low count for him," Hargrove said, defending his decision to stick with Nagy after Grissom led off the eighth with a double. When Polonia followed with a single to score Grissom, Hargrove called for Assenmacher, who issued a walk and re-

tired the next batter, but the tying run went home on an error by Baerga. Then Devereaux singled against Tavarez to put the Braves ahead.

In the Indians' half of the eighth Ramirez walked with one out, Sorrento singled, and Alomar doubled to tie the score again. The Tribe went on to load the bases, but Vizquel struck out and Baerga grounded out to end the rally.

Mesa took over in the ninth and, for the first time all season, pitched more than one inning. He held the Braves scoreless for three innings, and the Indians prevailed in the 11th when Baerga led off with a double, Belle was intentionally walked, and Murray singled.

"Thanks, we needed that," quipped a much-relieved Hargrove.

Game Four

But the Braves backed the Indians against the wall again, beating them, 5–2, in Game 4, as Steve Avery and three relievers combined to pitch a six-hitter. Two of the Tribe's hits were homers by Belle in the sixth and Ramirez in the ninth, but both came with the bases bare.

"I've faced more pleasing prospects, but the fact is, there are 26 clubs sitting at home that would like to have the chance to still be playing," said Hargrove, assessing the Indians' chances. They were not good, based on historical reference. Of the 39 teams that previously fell behind three games to one in the World Series, only six recovered to win the title. The last to do so were the Kansas City Royals who came back to beat St. Louis in 1985.

The verdict in this one was sealed in the seventh when Hill, starting for the first time in the postseason, walked Grissom with one out, and Polonia doubled for a run that broke the 1–1 tie. Hill was replaced by Assenmacher, who intentionally walked Jones and struck out McGriff, but couldn't get past Justice, who singled for two more runs. The Braves got another in the ninth on doubles by McGriff and Lopez.

"It's hard to beat anybody when you only get four or five hits," said Hargrove, referring to the Indians' .190 average (26-for-137) in the first four games of the World Series.

Game Five

Matters improved only slightly in Game 5, though the Indians solved Maddux for seven hits, one of which was Belle's second homer of the Series. The 5–4 victory was credited to Hershiser, aka "The Bulldog," although Mesa almost let it slip away in the ninth. Belle's homer was a two-run shot in the first inning, and Thome solo homered off reliever Brad Clontz in the eighth for a 5–2 lead. But the Braves in-

stilled a scare when McGriff doubled with one out, and Klesko homered with two out, before Lemke was called out on strikes to end the game.

"We're still alive, but we're still in a hole, a deep hole," said Hargrove, anticipating—but without much glee—a return to Atlanta on October 28.

Game Six

I t all came undone for the Indians in Game 6, although, as Hargrove intoned after the Braves won, 1–0, "We have nothing to be ashamed of or embarrassed about. Absolutely nothing."

He was right. Though the Indians fell one game short of their goal—actually, only one inning, even one pitch short—1995 was a glorious year for baseball in Cleveland. It was the season the Indians redeemed themselves after 41 years.

In that pressure-cooker finale, six Tribe pitchers almost did what Glavine accomplished by shutting out the Tribe on one hit, a broken-bat single by Pena in the sixth inning. The Braves got six hits, one of them Justice's sixth-inning homer off Poole, the first of five relievers to follow Martinez to the mound. Hill, Embree, Tavarez, and Assenmacher also saw action, and all of them kept the Braves off the scoreboard.

But so did Glavine, and the Indians' season of dreams came to an end.

"The only thing we didn't do was win this thing, the World Series," said Hargrove. "But we played like champions. I really feel we did." So did their legion of fans, more than 50,000 of whom made those sentiments clear two days later with their exultant outpouring of affection and respect—and anticipation of greater accomplishments to come.

COMPOSITE BATTING STATISTICS
Cleveland Indians

Player	G	AB	R	H	2B	3B	HR	RBI	BB	SO	AVG	SB	CS	PO	A	E
A. Espinoza, pr-3b	2	2	1	1	0	0	0	0	0	0	.500	0	1	1	0	0
Albert Belle, lf	6	17	4	4	0	0	2	4	7	5	.235	0	1	10	0	1
Manny Ramirez, rf	6	18	2	4	0	0	1	2	4	5	.222	1	0	8	0	0
Jim Thome, ph-3b	6	19	1	4	1	0	1	2	2	5	.211	0	0	3	5	1
Kenny Lofton, cf	6	25	6	5	1	0	0	0	3	1	.200	6	1	11	0	0
Sandy Alomar, c	5	15	0	3	2	0	0	1	0	2	.200	0	0	28	0	0
Carlos Baerga, 2b	6	26	1	5	2	0	0	4	1	1	.192	0	0	15	24	1
Paul Sorrento, ph-1b	5	11	0	2	1	0	0	0	0	4	.182	0	0	19	2	1
Omar Vizquel, ss	6	23	3	4	0	1	0	1	3	5	.174	1	0	12	22	0
Tony Pena, c	2	6	0	1	0	0	0	0	0	0	.167	0	0	7	1	0
Eddie Murray, 1b-dh	6	19	1	2	0	0	1	3	5	4	.105	0	0	27	0	0
Herbert Perry, 1b	3	5	0	0	0	0	0	0	0	2	.000	0	0	13	2	0
Dennis Martinez, p	2	3	0	0	0	0	0	0	0	1	.000	0	0	0	4	1
Ruben Amaro, ph-rf	2	2	0	0	0	0	0	0	0	1	.000	0	0	0	0	0
Orel Hershiser, p	2	2	0	0	0	0	0	0	0	0	.000	0	0	1	7	1
Wayne Kirby, ph-rf	3	1	0	0	0	0	0	0	0	1	.000	0	0	1	0	0
Jim Poole, p	2	1	0	0	0	0	0	0	0	0	.000	0	0	0	0	0
Paul Assenmacher, p	4	0	0	0	0	0	0	0	0	0	—	0	0	1	1	0
Alan Embree, p	4	0	0	0	0	0	0	0	0	0	—	0	0	0	3	0
Ken Hill, p	2	0	0	0	0	0	0	0	0	0	—	0	0	1	2	0
Jose Mesa, p	2	0	0	0	0	0	0	0	0	0	—	0	0	0	0	0
Charles Nagy, p	1	0	0	0	0	0	0	0	0	0	—	0	0	1	1	0
Julian Tavarez, p	5	0	0	0	0	0	0	0	0	0	—	0	0	0	2	0
Totals	**6**	**195**	**19**	**35**	**7**	**1**	**5**	**17**	**25**	**37**	**.179**	**8**	**3**	**159**	**76**	**6**

Atlanta Braves

Player	G	AB	R	H	2B	3B	HR	RBI	BB	SO	AVG	SB	CS	PO	A	E
Dwight Smith, ph	3	2	0	1	0	0	0	0	1	0	.500	0	0	0	0	0
Marquis Grissom, cf	6	25	3	9	1	0	0	1	1	3	.360	3	1	12	0	0
Mike Mordecai, ph-ss	3	3	0	1	0	0	0	0	0	1	.333	0	0	0	6	0
Ryan Klesko, ph-lf	6	16	4	5	0	0	3	4	3	4	.313	0	1	1	0	0
Chipper Jones, 3b	6	21	3	6	3	0	0	1	4	5	.286	0	0	6	13	1
Luis Polonia, ph-lf	6	14	3	4	1	0	1	4	1	3	.286	1	0	3	0	0
Mark Lemke, 2b	6	22	1	6	0	0	0	0	3	2	.273	0	1	10	23	1
Fred McGriff, 1b	6	23	5	6	2	0	2	3	3	5	.261	1	0	68	2	1
David Justice, rf	6	20	3	5	1	0	1	5	5	1	.250	0	0	16	0	0
Mike Devereaux, lf-rf	5	4	0	1	0	0	0	1	2	1	.250	0	0	1	0	1
Javier Lopez, ph-c	6	17	1	3	2	0	1	3	1	1	.176	0	0	32	4	0
Rafael Belliard, ss	6	16	0	0	0	0	0	1	0	4	.000	0	0	3	11	2
Tom Glavine, p	2	4	0	0	0	0	0	0	1	2	.000	0	0	1	3	0
Charlie O'Brien, c	2	3	0	0	0	0	0	0	0	1	.000	0	0	7	2	0
Greg Maddux, p	2	3	0	0	0	0	0	0	0	1	.000	0	0	2	4	0
Brad Clontz, p	2	0	0	0	0	0	0	0	0	0	—	0	0	0	0	0
Greg McMichael, p	2	0	0	0	0	0	0	0	0	0	—	0	0	0	1	0
Kent Mercker, p	1	0	0	0	0	0	0	0	0	0	—	0	0	0	0	0
Alejandro Pena, p	2	0	0	0	0	0	0	0	0	0	—	0	0	0	0	0
John Smoltz, p	1	0	0	0	0	0	0	0	0	0	—	0	0	0	0	0
Mark Wohlers, p	3	0	0	0	0	0	0	0	0	0	—	0	0	0	0	0
Totals	**6**	**193**	**23**	**47**	**10**	**0**	**8**	**23**	**25**	**34**	**.244**	**5**	**2**	**162**	**69**	**6**

COMPOSITE PITCHING STATISTICS
Cleveland Indians

Pitcher	G	CG	IP	H	R	BB	SO	HB	WP	W	L	SV	ER	ERA
Julian Tavarez	5	0	4⅓	3	0	2	1	1	0	0	0	0	0	0.00
Orel Hershiser	2	0	14	8	5	4	13	0	0	1	1	0	4	2.57
Alan Embree	4	0	3⅓	2	1	2	2	0	0	0	0	0	1	2.70
Dennis Martinez	2	0	10⅓	12	4	8	5	1	0	0	1	0	4	3.48
Jim Poole	2	0	2⅓	1	1	0	1	0	0	0	1	0	1	3.86
Ken Hill	2	0	6⅓	7	3	4	1	0	0	0	1	0	3	4.26
Jose Mesa	2	0	4	5	2	1	4	0	0	1	0	1	2	4.50
Charles Nagy	1	0	7	8	5	1	4	0	0	0	0	0	5	6.43
Paul Assenmacher	4	0	1⅓	1	2	3	3	0	0	0	0	0	1	6.75
Totals	**6**	**0**	**53**	**47**	**23**	**25**	**34**	**2**	**0**	**2**	**4**	**1**	**21**	**3.57**

Atlanta Braves

Pitcher	G	CG	IP	H	R	BB	SO	HB	WP	W	L	SV	ER	ERA
Pedro Borbon	1	0	1	0	0	0	2	0	0	0	0	1	0	0.00
Tom Glavine	2	0	14	4	2	6	11	0	1	2	0	0	2	1.29
Steve Avery	1	0	6	3	1	5	3	0	0	1	0	0	1	1.50
Mark Wohlers	4	0	5	4	1	3	3	0	0	0	0	2	1	1.80
Greg Maddux	2	1	16	9	6	3	8	0	0	1	1	0	4	2.25
Brad Clontz	2	0	3⅓	2	1	0	2	0	0	0	0	0	1	2.70
Greg McMichael	3	0	3⅓	3	2	2	2	0	1	0	0	0	1	2.70
Kent Mercker	1	0	2	1	1	2	2	0	0	0	0	0	1	4.50
Alejandro Pena	2	0	1	3	1	2	0	0	0	0	1	0	1	9.00
John Smoltz	1	0	2⅓	6	4	2	4	0	0	0	0	0	4	15.43
Totals	**6**	**1**	**54**	**35**	**19**	**25**	**37**	**0**	**2**	**4**	**2**	**3**	**16**	**2.67**

Scoring by Innings

Cleveland	5	2	2	0	0	3	2	2	2	0	1—19
Atlanta	1	1	2	1	1	5	6	3	3	0	0—23

DP: Atl 2, Cle 8. **LOB:** Cle 39, Atl 44. **S:** Belliard 2, Mordecai, O'Brien, Lemke. **SF:** Jones. Hershiser faced 2 batters in 7th (Game 1); Assenmacher faced 1 batter in 7th (Game 1); Nagy faced 2 batters in 8th (Game 3); A. Pena faced 3 batters in 11th (Game 3); Wohlers faced 2 batters in 9th (Game 4); Hill faced 1 batter in 7th (Game 6). **IBB:** off Wohlers 2 (Lofton 2), off A. Pena (Belle), off Avery (Ramirez), off Assenmacher (Jones), off Maddux (Belle), off Hershiser (Smith), off Embree (Jones), off Martinez (Klesko). **HBP:** by Martinez (Grissom), by Tavarez (Lopez). **PB:** Alomar. **Balk:** Avery. **Umps:** Wendelstedt, McKean, Froemming, Hirschbeck, Pulli, Brinkman. **T:** Game 1 at Atlanta, 2:37. Game 2 at Atlanta, 3:17. Game 3 at Cleveland, 4:09. Game 4 at Cleveland, 3:14. Game 5 at Cleveland, 2:33. Game 6 at Atlanta, 3:02. **A:** Game 1 at Atlanta, 51,876. Game 2 at Atlanta, 51,877. Game 3 at Cleveland, 43,584. Game 4 at Cleveland, 43,578. Game 5 at Cleveland, 43,595. Game 6 at Atlanta, 51,875.

Sources

Aaron to Zuverink by Rich Marazzi and Len Fiorito
American League Red Book
Ballparks of North America by Michael Benson
The Ballplayers edited by Mike Shatzkin
Baseball America
The Baseball Chronology edited by James Charlton
The Baseball Encyclopedia by Macmillan Publishing, Joseph L.
    Reichler, editor
Baseball Guides by *The Sporting News*
Baseball Registers by *The Sporting News*
The Baseball Trade Register by Joseph L. Reichler
Baseball Uniforms of the 20th Century by Mark Okkonen
Baseball Weekly
The Cleveland Indians Revisited (1954) by Bruce Dudley
The Cleveland Indians by Franklin Lewis
The Cleveland News
The (Cleveland) Plain Dealer
The Cleveland Press
The Complete Baseball Record Book by *The Sporting News*
Covering All The Bases: Lou Boudreau by Russell Schneider
Daguerreotypes by *The Sporting News*
Day by Day in Cleveland Indians History by Morris Eckhouse
The Encyclopedia of Minor League Baseball edited by Lloyd
    Johnson & Miles Wolff

Gonzalez, Raymond (SABR)
The Great All-Time Baseball Record Book by Joseph L. Reichler,
    revised by Ken Samelson
Green Cathedrals by Philip J. Lowry
Indians media guides
Indians yearbooks
National Baseball Hall of Fame and Museum Yearbook
The No-Hit Hall of Fame by Rich Coberly
Palmer, Pete (SABR)
Professional Baseball Franchises by Peter Filichia
Reach Official Baseball Guides
The (World) Series by *The Sporting News*
Spalding Official Baseball Guides
Spalding Official Baseball Record Books
The Sporting Life
The Sporting News
The Sports Encyclopedia: Baseball by David S. Neft and Richard
    M. Cohen
Streak: Joe DiMaggio and the Summer of '41 by Michael Seidel
Total Baseball edited by John Thorn and Pete Palmer
Trade Him! edited by Jim Enright
Tribe Memories I, II, III by Russell Schneider

Photo Credits

Photos courtesy of the Cleveland Indians, *The (Cleveland) Plain Dealer,* Gateway Economic Development Corporation, the Mel Harder Collection, *Indians Ink,* Ron Kuntz, the Collection of Ms. Effie Lydon (granddaughter of Bill Wambsganss), the Joseph P. Maxse Collection, MotoPhoto Studio in Parma, Ohio, and Bill Wamby, Jr.

Photographs of Hall of Fame plaques in chapter 7 are reproduced with permission of the National Baseball Library and Archive, Cooperstown, New York.

Acknowledgments

This encyclopedia would not have been completed without the counsel and special assistance of Joe Simenic, a dear friend, a valued colleague, a remarkable researcher, and one of the best baseball fans in the world. The author also wishes to thank Bob DiBiasio, Paul Hoynes, Jim Ingraham, Sheldon Ocker, Joe Maxse, Susie Gharrity, Bart Swain, Joel Gunderson, John Krepop, Russell Schneider, Jr., Catherine Schneider, Tom Hamilton, Herb Score, Joe Corrado, Angelo Murracco, Bob Feller, Mel Harder, Lou Boudreau, Al Lopez, and Rich Westcott.

About the Authors

Russell Schneider was a sportswriter and columnist for *The Plain Dealer* in Cleveland for 32 years, until leaving the newspaper on June 1, 1993. He has been a fan of the Cleveland Indians even longer, rejoicing with them through their (infrequent) best of times, and suffering with them through their (frequent) worst of times. After a two-year stint in the U.S. Marine Corps (1946–48), Schneider played minor league baseball in the Indians farm system—he was a good-fielding, light-hitting catcher—and then was recalled to active duty during the Korean War. He later played and managed semi-pro baseball teams in the Cleveland area. Schneider covered the Indians on a daily basis for fourteen years, from 1964 to 1977. He also was *The Plain Dealer* beat writer for the Cleveland Browns of the National Football League for six years, from 1978 to 1983, before concentrating on investigative reporting and special assignments and writing a sports column, "Plain Dealing," for *The Plain Dealer*. Schneider is the author of *Frank Robinson: The Making of a Manager* (1975), *Covering All the Bases*, the biography of Lou Boudreau (1993), and *The Glorious Indian Summer of 1995*. He has also published three editions of *Tribe Memories*, collections of profiles and stories about the Indians, and *Browns Memories*, a series of profiles of the men who have played on that NFL team. He and his wife Catherine have three children: Russell Jr., who played a major role in the writing, editing and production of *The Glorious Indian Summer of 1995*; Bryan; and Eileen, who is married to former Indians pitcher Eric Raich.

Joe Simenic, researcher *extraordinaire*, is also a former employee of *The Plain Dealer*. He served as a U.S. Army Air Force staff sergeant in England, France and Germany during World War II. Upon his discharge in 1946, he worked for the *Cleveland News* as a secretary to the general manager until that newspaper folded in 1960. He then joined *The Plain Dealer* as secretary to publisher and editor Thomas Vail, and stayed at the paper for 31 years until his retirement on January 1, 1992. A widower with two sons, Steve and Tom, and three grandchildren, Simenic is also a long-time, dedicated Indians fan and an indefatigable baseball researcher. He co-founded the Society for American Baseball Research (SABR) in 1971 and served the organization as vice president in 1974. His primary interest is the biographical research of players who were active in the major leagues prior to 1900.